International Business

International Business

An Emerging Vision

Edited by
Brian Toyne
and
Douglas Nigh

UNIVERSITY OF SOUTH CAROLINA PRESS

Copyright © 1997 Brian Toyne and Douglas Nigh
Published in Columbia, South Carolina, by the
University of South Carolina Press
01 00 99 98 97   5 4 3 2 1

Manufactured in the United States of America

Library of Congress Cataloging-in-Publication Data

International business: an emerging vision / Brian Toyne and Douglas Nigh, editors.
    p. cm.
  Papers presented at a conference held at the University of South Carolina, in May 1992.
  Includes bibliographical references.
  ISBN 1–57003–012–X (v. 1)
  1. International business enterprises—Congresses. 2. Export marketing—Congresses.
3. Competition, International—Congresses. I. Toyne, Brian. II. Nigh, Douglas, 1946– .
HD2755.5.I535   1997
658′.049—dc20   96-25393

To Zaida, who inspired me to seek more complete answers.
Brian Toyne

To my parents—the first of my great teachers.
Douglas Nigh

Contents

The impact of human uniqueness upon the world has been enormous because it has established a new kind of evolution to support the transmission across generations of learned knowledge and behavior. Human uniqueness resides primarily in our brains. It is expressed in the culture built upon our intelligence and the power it gives us to manipulate the world.

Stephen Jay Gould
The Mismeasure of Man, 1981

It is hardly possible to overrate the value, in the present low state of human improvement, of placing human beings in contact with persons dissimilar to themselves, and with modes of thought and action unlike those with which they are familiar . . . Such communication has always been and is peculiarly in the present age, one of the primary sources of progress.

John Stuart Mill
Principles of Political Economy, 1848

Preface

International business (IB) inquiry is evolving into an academic discipline that holds out considerable promise in the years ahead for the United States, its business community, and its people. Yet this potential has gone unrecognized by most of academia outside the IB area. Likewise, those responsible for IB's integration into institutions of higher learning have generally failed to appreciate the implications of the area's development for business research and the education of tomorrow's managers.

This does not mean that attempts have not been made to alert higher education to the international trend of the economic interdependence and interconnectedness of nation-states. To the contrary, many efforts have been made over the years to focus attention on the importance of and need for the "international" dimension of business research and education. For example, in the 1950s and 1960s, Indiana University held two widely-attended meetings that focused on IB education. In the 1950s, the participants gathered to discuss the proper development of an educational program that would offer rigorous academic work for young people interested in careers in "global corporations." In 1964, a second Indiana University meeting was held to share the experiences and plans of faculty members interested in the development (refinement) of international business programs.

These two meetings were subsequently followed by others. For example, four meetings during 1975 and 1976 were held by the Task Force on Business and International Education, Government/Academic Interface Committee, International Education Project, American Council on Education. The results of these meetings and the subsequent reflections of the Task Force were published in 1977 in a report, Business and International Education.

Also, the American Assembly of Collegiate Schools of Business (AACSB) has long recognized that IB needs to be an integral part of business programs. Unfortunately, no decisive attempt was made to make IB such a requirement using specific pedagogical approaches. Instead, the decision as to how the "international" dimension was to be incorporated into business programs was left in the hands of a largely uninterested and parochial business faculty.

Despite these limitations, the major reason for the failure of the field of IB to gain recognition can be traced to the field's hesitancy, if not unwillingness, to make clear what its purpose was in words understandable to the business disciplines and business schools. Other business disciplines, very early in their development, established clearly articulated statements concerning their domains of inquiry and their research priorities as first steps in making others aware of what was needed and to some extent what might be possible. In contrast, those interested in

IB as a topic of research and education felt no pressure to provide such a clarifying definition of IB, what it was, and where it could and should be going in terms of both teaching and research.

It was this failure to articulate such a statement that prompted us to initiate a multi-year research project involving the efforts of dozens of scholars. Although IB as a subject of research and education has made considerable progress in the last forty years, it has been thwarted to some extent by its lack of direction, coherence, legitimacy, and recognition. Thus, the primary purpose of the project was to establish the domain of IB and to establish its legitimacy as a distinct and creditable field of scientific inquiry and education. In addition, through this project we sought to identify the institutional arrangements that can best insure that IB scholars meet their full responsibilities in research and education.

At the core of the research project was a four-day conference in May 1992 at the University of South Carolina. About 150 scholars came from fifteen countries in North and South America, Europe, and Asia to engage in a lively conversation on issues critical to the future development of IB research and education. They came to discuss the ideas in papers prepared for and distributed in advance of the May meeting. This book and its companion volume, *International Business: Institutions and the Dissemination of Knowledge,* contain these papers that were prepared for, discussed at, and revised after the conference. The conference was designed to examine both the state of international business inquiry and the institutional status of international business. Its objectives were as follows:

1. To define the domain, phenomena, and relationships that constitute the field of IB inquiry, and to identify constructs that hold promise for integrating the field and for encouraging theory building and theory testing in the future.
2. To identify opportunities that exist for research in the field, to explore the limitations imposed by, and the benefits derived from, various research methodologies and their embedded paradigms, and to suggest directions that seem particularly fruitful for future research.
3. To help institutional administrators better understand the emerging importance of IB as a unified systematic body of knowledge, and to acquaint them with the unique research and educational issues and problems confronting the field.
4. To identify and explore the implications of current institutional arrangements and incentives as they relate to our ability to fulfill our responsibilities as scholars, researchers and educators, and to suggest ways that these institutional arrangements and incentives can be modified to encourage the field's advancement.

To achieve the four objectives, twelve topic sessions were organized that addressed issues related to domain, lines of inquiry, and education. In addition, three panels were assembled to address the following questions:

1. Can (should) IB develop into a viable and distinct field of inquiry given its lack of a unifying definition and its current and foreseeable dependency on the paradigms, theories and constructs of economics, political science, sociology, and the business disciplines?
2. How should the IB dimension be institutionally housed in order to simultaneously satisfy its theory building, research, and educational responsibilities?
3. What are the most effective teaching and learning forms for insuring that IB is adequately and properly covered in formal degree programs, in executive training programs, etc.?

The book in hand contains the papers presented at nine of the twelve sessions along with the panel assembled to discuss the need for a unifying definition. The nine topics included in this book are considered central to a better understanding of the scope, content, and intricacies of IB. In our judgment, they constitute the foundation on which future IB research and education will be based. Three internationally renowned scholars were asked to research and write original papers for each topic. Two additional and equally well-known scholars were asked to critique these papers for theoretical and empirical content, rigor, and logic. This was done to insure that the theoretical and research dimensions of each topic were adequately and comprehensively covered. In these nine sessions, the perspectives of both the major business disciplines (e.g., finance, marketing, organization theory, organization behavior, and strategic management) and the social sciences (e.g., economics and political science) were brought to bear on the field of international business.

At the time of the conference, a panel consisting of four distinguished scholars contributed papers "for the record" and jointly addressed the controversial issue of whether a unifying conceptual framework is required to insure that the body of knowledge related to IB is systematically and scientifically accumulated. The papers prepared for this session are likewise include in this book.

The remaining three topics addressed issues that are of direct and immediate concern to institutions and organizations associated with higher education, including accreditation organizations, educational consortia, and universities and colleges offering business education programs at the undergraduate, masters, and doctoral levels. The three topics collectively explore the historical and current institutional attempts that have been made and are being made to encourage IB research and education. Also explored are the advantages and disadvantages of these attempts as they relate to the

encouragement of IB theory building, research, and educational activities. The papers for these three sessions and those prepared by the panelists for the other two panels appear in a second volume, *International Business: Institutions and the Dissemination of Knowledge.*

For all fifteen sessions over the four days of the conference, we sought maximum engagement and discussion among all participants. Since most papers were distributed in advance and available for a complete review by the participants prior to the session, the authors of the papers generally took only a short time to reiterate their major points. Consequently, a substantial portion of the formal sessions consisted of a lively conversation among all in attendance. In addition, the discussion and debates carried over into the coffee breaks and lunches and beyond into the evening.

At any one time, only one session was scheduled. There were no concurrent sessions—again, to promote maximum engagement of IB issues among the participants. Although the participants had in common a strong interest in some aspect of international business, they came from quite disparate academic backgrounds. During the conference those with a finance background, for example, listened, thought about, and commented on the issues and perspectives presented by those with an organizational behavior background, and vice versa. Like John Stuart Mill, we believed that such contact and communication held out the promise of real progress for the field of international business.

This book and its companion volume reflect the intellectual energy of the conference in a number of ways. First, the authors had the opportunity to revise their papers to reflect and update their thinking as a result of the happenings at the conference. Second, some authors drafted replies to the critiques of their papers, thus bringing into print some of the back-and-forth debate occurring during the conference. Third, the two of us have made our own sense of what went on at the conference and used this as one component in our synthesis of the issues addressed in the entire research project.

At the conference, people who cared about the future of international business got together, wrestled with some tough issues usually left unexamined, agreed about some things, and disagreed sharply about others. The conversation continues and we invite the reader to take part.

In concluding this preface, we would like to express our most sincere appreciation to the many individuals and organizations that made possible the conference and consequently this book and its companion volume. First we thank the authors whose work appears in the books. They were not given the easiest of specifications or deadlines within which to work. Our special thanks for their patience, tolerance, and willingness to share their experience and expertise. To the participants of the conference who made substantial contributions to the discussions and subsequent development of everyone's thought must also go our gratitude, for the conference results exceeded our highest expectations. We thank the conference session chairs, who managed to keep the sessions focused on the major topics and yet reflective of all the participants' ideas.

The highest compliment we can pay those involved with the accommodations and arrangements for the conference is to state that we all had a great time and the two of us never had to worry about them. We thank Colette Gauthier, then Administrative Assistant of USC's Center for International Business Education and Research (CIBER), for doing her usual excellent job of handling all the administrative tasks before, during, and after the conference. We also thank Michael Shealy, current CIBER Managing Director for carrying through this project to the publication of the two conference books. To Christine Carson and the rest of the staff of the Daniel Management Center, we say thanks for providing an atmosphere in which such a fruitful exchange could take place and, in particular, for such imaginative and fun events as world-class jazz at the Townhouse and dinner at the Columbia Zoo. In addition, we thank the USC doctoral students (our IB scholars of the future) who pitched in and helped out with all the administrative and logistical tasks.

Our gratitude also goes to several individuals and organizations who were especially instrumental in making this conference a reality. First to be acknowledged and thanked is Professor W. R. Folks, Director of CIBER, University of South Carolina. Without his personal encouragement and the financial support provided by CIBER, the conference and the resulting books would still be a dream rather than a reality. James F. Kane, then Dean of the College of Business Administration of the University of South Carolina, must also be acknowledged for providing the College of Business Administration's support for this effort. We also gratefully acknowledge ARCO Chemical Company, Phillips Petroleum Foundation, and the U.S. Department of Education whose financial support was crucial to the conference and research project. In particular, Jack Johnson and Thomas Lambrix receive our thanks for believing in the worth of our project and conference.

A special note of appreciation goes to Patricia G. Lobenstein, past Managing Editor, *Journal of International Business Studies*. She did an excellent job of editing the many papers prepared for the conference, and bringing them together as an integrated manuscript. Likewise our gratitude goes to Kenneth J. Scott, former Director, and Catherine Fry, Director, and the USC Press staff for their expertise and patience in making our emerging vision a tangible reality.

Brian Toyne
Douglas Nigh

International Business

1

Foundations of an Emerging Paradigm

Brian Toyne and Douglas Nigh

The fields of business and international business (IB) inquiry are experiencing a period of transformation. Increasingly, they are seen as a relational process that is an inextricable part and expression of the societies from which they emerge and in which they subsequently evolve (e.g., Granovetter 1985; Mattsson, chapter 9; Wartick, chapter 3). This social process view of business is in sharp contrast to the dominant economic view that assumes economic and social separation [Gilpin 1987]. Advocates of the social process perspective go so far as to argue that a fuller and richer understanding of business organization can only be obtained by gaining a more comprehensive understanding of the social-embedded business process [Schumpeter 1926; Baumol 1968; Toyne 1989].

This book explores the state of IB inquiry. A major conclusion that emerges from the many strands of theorizing and research presented in the following sections and their collective analysis is that a distinctive conceptualization of IB is taking shape. A second conclusion is that the emerging importance of IB as a distinctive, unified, systematic body of knowledge requires a restructuring of institutional arrangements and incentives as they relate to how IB scholars, researchers, and educators fulfill their responsibilities. This conclusion is addressed in a second book, *International Business: Institutions and the Dissemination of Knowledge.*

BACKGROUND: PARADIGMIC CONFLICT IN THE SOCIAL SCIENCES

Like the social sciences and the various business disciplines that collectively define business activity, IB inquiry is experiencing paradigmic conflict. The reasons for this conflict are fully explored in the following sections. However, before embarking on this discussion, first it is necessary to clarify what is meant by the term "paradigmic conflict."

Phillips [1987, p. 205] notes that a paradigm is a theoretical framework (i.e., an abstraction or representation of the real world) that " . . . determines the problems that are regarded as crucial, the ways these problems are to be conceptualized, the appropriate methods of inquiry, the relevant standards of judgment, etc." Also, according to Reynolds [1971], a "new" paradigm:

1. represents a new conceptualization of a particular phenomenon;
2. suggests new problems for solution (raises questions not asked before);
3. frequently explains phenomena that previous paradigms were unable to explain; and
4. suggests a new research strategy or methodological procedure for gathering empirical evidence to support the paradigm.

To summarize, the term "paradigmic conflict" refers to the challenge posed by a "new" conceptualization or abstraction of a studied phenomenon. However, the emergence of a new paradigm does not mean that the phenomenon under investigation has necessarily changed. It may simply mean that the way in which the phenomenon is abstractly represented has changed. Nor does it mean that the "new" paradigm replaces existing paradigms. The paradigms may be incommensurable and, if so, offer alternate views of reality that add richness to our understanding (e.g., quantum and Newtonian mechanics; psycho-analytic and medical models of mental disorder).

International business is not alone today in grappling with paradigmic conflict. In many social and professional sciences, dominant paradigms are facing increasingly strong contenders. The extensiveness of the current paradigmic conflict in the social sciences should come as no surprise given the earlier conflict in the physical sciences. Our conceptualizations of the social world and of the natural world affect and reinforce one another [Casti 1989; Mirowski 1988; Phillips 1987]. Below we sketch the character of the paradigm conflict in certain disciplines.

In economics, Mirowski [1988] leads a pragmatist institutionalist challenge to a neoclassical economics he characterizes as a "bowdlerized imitation of 19th century physics" [1988, p. 5]. Institutionalist economics argues that neoclassical economics is based on an outdated Cartesian conceptualization of a mechanically deterministic and static world. The institutionalists contend that social institutions such as money, markets, and property rights cannot be reduced to mere epiphenomena of individual constrained optimization calculations (as the neoclassical orthodoxy would have it). Rather Mirowski argues "Institutions can be understood as socially constructed invariants that provide actors who participate in them with the means and resources to cope with change and diversity: this is the nonmechanistic definitions of individual rationality" [1988, p.132]. Such arguments between institutionalist and neoclassical

economists are not new. What is new is (1) the strength of the dissatisfaction with the neoclassical orthodoxy and its attempts to answer such challenges by tinkering at the margins and (2) the growing body of modern economic theorizing that reflects the influence of pragmatist philosophy.

In sociology, Peter Berger recently considered withdrawing his famous invitation to sociology [1963 and 1992]. He finds sociology today to be afflicted with parochialism, triviality, rationalism, and ideology. In particular, he highlights the subjectivist-objectivist epistemological debate in sociology. He takes a stance in opposition to the Marxists, feminists, and multiculturalists and their belief that objectivity is impossible and that sociologists should expressly operate as advocates [1992, p. 17]. In addition, he decries the adoption of the rational action paradigm of economics by many sociologists. (See, for example, the rational choice sociology of James Coleman [1990 and 1992].) Berger argues that the assumption that ordinary social action is guided by rationality will retard the development of our understanding of social behavior.

This example of the encroachment of economic approaches into sociology is part of a larger redefinition of the boundary between economics and sociology [Swedberg 1990]. After decades of ignoring each other, economists such as Gary Becker have begun to take on traditional sociological topics using traditional economic approaches. Other economists like George Akerloff have started using sociological insights in their work. Meanwhile, sociologists like Harrison White and Mark Granovetter have begun to take on traditionally economic topics using sociological approaches. In developing a new economic sociology, Granovetter [1985, p. 487] argues that economic actions are embedded in concrete, ongoing systems of social relations and that economic institutions are social constructions. (Also see Swedberg 1990, pp. 96–114.) Here we can see the effect that the interaction between two disciplines has on the paradigmic conflict in each. Within each discipline, we see today serious debates concerning appropriate domains and methods of inquiry.

In anthropology, Fox [1992] comments on aspects of paradigmic conflict dealing with epistemological assumptions and unifying theoretical frameworks. He views science with its objectivity and its openness to validation and refutation as the one international language capable of providing objective knowledge of the world. He accuses other anthropologists of abandoning science by extending the traditional cultural relativism of anthropology to embrace cognitive relativism as well. Fox sees these anthropologists as preaching to graduate students that "all knowledge is gender or class or culture relative (as though this were somehow a new idea!) and that science as we know it is a male white European enterprise, and so tainted and of no more value than magical incantations" [1992, p. 49]. In addition, he laments the fragmentation of the anthropology that he thinks should be a synthesizing, holistic science of mankind. Fox comments on the struggle of those few anthropologists like him who are trying to develop a unified discipline of anthropology—a neo-Darwinian synthesis that would "put together the primate and mammalian past with the archeological record and the ethnographic present under the aegis of evolutionary theory" [1992, pp. 50–51]. To date, the relativistic, cultural deterministic orthodoxy has prevailed and remains strong.

Paradigmic conflict is also evident in the business discipline of marketing. Hunt [1983, 1991] reviews the crisis literature that questions the underlying philosophical foundations of marketing. Hunt supports a postpositivist/modern empiricist science and rejects the relativistic/constructionist science of Anderson [1983] and Peter and Olson [1983].

In education, an area of inquiry like business with a professional practitioner constituency, Guba [1990] advances an alternative paradigm dialogue, in which the constructivist paradigm with its relativist ontology and its subjectivist epistemology challenges the more established postpositivist paradigm with its realist ontology and objectivist epistemology.

As the above examples indicate, the paradigmic conflict in the social sciences, of which business and international business are parts, revolves around basic philosophy of science issues concerning ontology, epistemology, and methodology, as well as issues regarding the proper domain of a particular discipline. Essentially, the challenge is to the reductionistic abstraction of human beings that is made in order to study the manifested consequences of their actions. Put differently, reductionism has resulted in a thousand points of understanding about human behavior that lack illumination. What is missing in the pursuit of understanding humans, and what is being sought by an increasing number of scholars, is a framework (paradigm) that can help transform the thousand points of understanding into a coherent source of illumination. The challenge is to understand human beings and their creations as complex, multi-level, integrated, reciprocally-interactive, recursive, self-referential, learning entities.[1]

As a field of study, IB draws on the various social sciences and their sub-branches for guidance, inspiration, and paradigmic structure and focus. Thus, it should not be too surprising to find that IB inquiry is also undergoing systemic change. To better understand what the search for a more holistic paradigm within the social sciences and business disciplines might hold for future IB research and education, we first present a brief historical overview of the field of IB education and research, and its paradigmic roots. We then present a paradigm (or vision) that conceptualizes IB as an evolving (or emerging) multi-level, hierarchical system.

INTERNATIONAL BUSINESS AS A FIELD OF INQUIRY AND EDUCATION

The embryonic field of IB was viewed more as an extension of business education than as a distinct field of inquiry. When founded in 1958, for example, the Academy of International Business (AIB) was named the Association for Education in International Business, and had the following three major purposes [Fayerweather 1986, p. 4]:

> Three significant purposes were apparently unanimous with the group. Each member wanted (1) contacts for information and exchange of ideas among colleagues in the field and particularly for advancement of school or training curricula and the general improvement of education with respect to IB; (2) a central organization which could perhaps control, sponsor, or guide research activities to provide additional information; and (3) an organization to which they could look for both dissemination and furtherance of available knowledge about international business and a professionalization of this broad area.

This view is still held by many business scholars today. Essentially, they argue that IB inquiry is not a distinct field of scientific study since it does not ask unique questions (see Toyne, chapter 2). It is merely an extension of the inquiry undertaken by the business disciplines. Also, most business schools seeking to "internationalize" business education focus their energies on modifying the content of business programs, not the discipline-entrenched structures of their institutions (e.g., departments of finance, management, and so on). Even many AIB members view the AIB as secondary to their disciplinary associations.

Nonetheless, several things occurred in the intervening decades that call into question the basic assumptions underlying IB inquiry and IB education. First, the recommendations of the Carnegie-Ford reports of 1959, which have had a profound influence on both business education and business inquiry, are being challenged. Second, the world of business has become increasingly complex because of its growing interconnectedness and interdependence at the global, regional, national, industrial, firm, and individual levels. Third, the body of knowledge and experience associated with

the practice of IB has grown during the intervening years, is widely disseminated, and is used by both IB practitioners and researchers.

The Carnegie-Ford Reports

As noted by Toyne [1993], the current emphasis on functional specialization and logical empiricism by business scholars is traceable, in part, to the Ford-Carnegie reports published in 1959. For example, the Graduate Management Admissions Council (GMAC) has succinctly stated the following [1990, p. 15]:

> In the three decades since the "revolution" codified in the Gordon-Howell and Pierson reports [prepared for the Ford and Carnegie Foundations], business schools have reached ever-higher levels of consumer popularity and academic respectability ... The academic disciplines of management have also matured, with rigorously refereed scholarship in hundreds of journals and increasingly sophisticated doctoral education programs. No longer characterized by the mundane descriptive analysis of the 1950s, the disciplines of the management school are now side by side with those of the arts and sciences. Ground-breaking work that uses academic theory to change management practice has been done in such fields as investment theory, consumer behavior, competitive strategy, and organization behavior ... These institutional and intellectual accomplishments have made graduate schools of management especially important components of their universities.

A consequence of the search for respectability has been an emphasis on research by the various business disciplines in the United States that are *collectively* assumed to define business activity and, increasingly, business purpose. Since the epistemology of this research is logical empiricism, the emphasis on determinism, and thus reductionism,[2] has led to the entrenchment of the business disciplines, a focus on similarities, and the use of methodologies borrowed from the physical sciences. In other words, the business disciplines became highly specialized, protective of their domains, and increasingly preoccupied with methodological issues [Toyne 1993]. Moreover, although members of the business disciplines increasingly recognize IB practice, most members of the business disciplines see it only as an opportunity to exercise what Kuhn [1970] referred to as "normal science." To disciplinary purists, IB is merely "internationalized" management, "internationalized" marketing, "internationalized" finance, and so on.

The effects of specialization in business research eventually spilled over into the classroom as highly arcane business courses. It was, and still is, widely assumed that practitioner and student alike will somehow internalize the separate bodies of knowledge and arrive at a comprehensive, integrated understanding of business both as output and process.[3] However, Bedeian [1989], Daft and Lewin [1990], Porter and McKibbin [1988], GMAC [1990], and others have raised serious questions concerning the efficacy of the Ford-Carnegie paradigm upon which much of modern U.S. business education and research is based. Collectively, these critics question the ability of the present education-research system to deliver on the kind of education required in the years ahead. In particular, Porter and McKibbin and the report published by GMAC argue that the massive and interconnected changes transforming the environment of business, such as globalization, rapid technological change, and increasing demographic and cultural diversity of the workforce, require different education and research approaches. More specifically, the GMAC report notes that during periods of rapid and fundamental change, it is more important to define business outcomes in terms of process. This latter point, of course, is not a rejection of what has been gained by focusing on essentially a single output of the business process, i.e., the firm. Indeed, the changes reflected in the post-1990 accreditation requirements of the

AACSB support the argument that a more comprehensive approach that encompasses both perspectives is needed for a better understanding of business activity.

Complexity, Interconnectedness, and Interdependence

In contrast to the business reality of the 1980s and 1990s, the reality of the 1950s, 1960s, and even the 1970s, could be represented as simple, straight forward and stable, and conceptualized using Newtonian principles (unidirectional cause-effect, atomistic phenomena).[4] From this perspective, the relationship between the firm and higher levels of the business process (industry, government, society) could be assumed stable (unchanging). In other words, the rate of boundary condition change occurring within these higher levels that directly or indirectly affected firm-level practice and choice could be ignored.[5]

However, major changes did occur during these three decades in both the environment and nature of IB (i.e., in form and practice) that finally demanded a more explicit understanding of the interactive, recursive nature of national business processes[6] and the emerging IB process that these dynamic interactions were bringing about. For example, students of IB can no longer ignore the historical roots and long-run effects that have irreversibly affected governments, industries, firms, and individuals. Nor can they ignore the impact that technological and communication changes are having on national business processes, the linkages between the levels of these processes, and the indeterminacy of their outputs (e.g., the internal relations of geographically dispersed operations of firms, and the ability to be in "two places simultaneously" because of advances in communications).

Despite these developments, IB—like domestic or nation-bound business—is viewed primarily as a firm-level phenomenon. Additionally, mainstream business scholars (and economists interested in firm-level economic theory) think in terms of categories of business organizations that are assumed to share *similar* characteristics (e.g., exporters, multinationals, global companies, industry leaders, industry followers). Such a firm-level approach is useful in situations that are stable and socio-culturally homogeneous. However, because of treating human activity as divisible and discrete (reductionistic), neither business inquiry nor IB inquiry have developed systematic methods for analyzing (or thinking about) complex, interactive, dynamic (or learning-dependent recursive) human processes. By focusing on output, business scholars have also biased their studies to the study of the attributes of aggregated sets of firms.

Essentially, they ignore the process that actually produces the organizations they study and instills them with meaning. Methodologically, the insistence on assuming human activity as determinate, and thus reductionistic, encourages both the production and borrowing of increasingly sophisticated statistical techniques for interpreting what are ultimately distributions of independent events (e.g., enterprises). It also results, as Marshall [1920] noted many years ago, in causality errors. He argued that new wants give rise to new activities, and not vice versa (i.e., firms and industries evolve to satisfy emerging wants rather than new wants emerging because of firm and industry activities).[7]

Additionally, the Anglo-American "ideal" of economic liberalism (separation of the political and the economic) has become so removed from reality that the study of business activity, particularly IB activity, can no longer be based on this simplifying assumption. Governments have intervened more-or-less continuously and consciously in the affairs of companies by attempting to regulate their activities, attract their investments, and "capture" the employment they provide. Currently, they are also highly involved in creating larger and larger trading blocs to satisfy the market appetites of companies, and to alter the "rules of the game"

in favor of their particular national (or regional) goals. That is, governments are central players in their national business processes, and in the emerging IB process. They rightly assume that they can modify the behavior of firms (see Boddewyn, chapter 2, and Root, [1993]). For example, as the emergence of the pollution control industry testifies, governments, as extensions of their respective societies, can be central players in the creation of global industries.

Likewise, firms participate in the political processes of nation-states. Firms have certain basis of power that allow them to influence the outcomes of political processes. These include their size, market power, and control of certain knowledge, technologies, and employment opportunities. Although the objectives of firms and nation-states can be congruent, this is not necessarily the case. Firms may have ideologies, objectives and goals that are at odds with those of nation-states (e.g., authoritarianism versus democracy, efficiency versus effectiveness, profit versus social welfare). International firms influence the government decisions and the national business processes of both the home countries from which they emerge and the host countries in which they participate (e.g., see Toyne and Martinez 1988).

Again, the situation is not one sided. The last three decades have also been witness to the fact that firms involved in IB are themselves affected by the business processes of their host countries. For example, the multinational enterprise of the 1960s is not the global or transnational company of the 1990s. Despite the advances made in technology and communications and their cumulative influence on business practice, these firms have changed and are changing because of their interaction with other national business processes and their abilities to learn from these interactions (for example, Bartlett and Ghoshal [1989] and Kogut [chapter 8] both hint at this possibility).

Finally, and just as importantly, international "interaction" is no longer concentrated and discrete, involving just a few public and private organizations within any particular society. Because of technology (e.g., transportation and communications), education, and the growing interconnectedness and interdependence of nation-states, this interaction is increasingly diffused, spanning all levels of society and an increasing portion of the phenomena within these levels. *If for no other reason, the environment in which IB is embedded has changed in fundamental ways, requiring a reevaluation of the abstracted, reductionistic, static paradigms that have guided IB education and research until now* [Toyne 1994].

Knowledge, Experience and the Practice of IB

The practice of IB has also changed because people learn, and as a consequence of learning, create new tools, new internal and external organizational arrangements, new ways of looking at "old activities," and so on. Importantly, they modify their ideas of reality, modify their goals, and modify their behavior in the *very act* of learning. This is true of both business practitioner and business researcher. Yet, U.S.-derived theories of management, marketing and finance are silent on the influence that learning, the available pool of knowledge, and the transfer of information may have on a particular society, its business process, and the organizations and practices this process engenders; the processes of change are essentially ignored as subjects of investigation.

As an example, the study of business and IB can no longer be viewed as a U.S. phenomena. Asian and European scholars are increasingly interested in the study of business. The national culture of the researcher influences the research questions asked and theories developed [Hofstede 1994]. Thus, the involvement of Asians and Europeans in business inquiry reverberates with the "world views" that are inimitably a part of their indigenous business processes (e.g., Austrian economic school of entrepreneurship, neo-mercantilism of Germany and Japan) [Toyne 1994].

INITIAL PARADIGMS OF IB

To understand the field of IB in its present form it is useful to examine the paradigms that have dominated and guided much of IB inquiry for the last three decades. Importantly, paradigms do not just impose restrictions on the questions raised and the methodologies used to answer them. Besides prescribing the width, breadth, depth, and quality of the knowledge gained, they also influence the education, skill requirements, and socialization of both researchers and practitioners alike [Toyne 1994]. For example, of the major social sciences, economics plays the dominant role in business education and thus IB education. Although a deep understanding of anthropology, political science, psychology, and sociology would provide a richer and more complete understanding of different national business processes and their outputs, these sciences are not stressed, if indeed they are even included in graduate business and IB programs. The reason for this bias is partly a consequence of the assumption that the firm, although a product and part of a social process, is an economic device that exists apart from historical, political and social forces. It may also be the measurability of economic activity and the relative immeasurability of other aspects of human activity (see, for example, von Hayek 1989).

The Paradigmic Roots of IB Inquiry

The impetus for IB inquiry in the United States sprang from a desire to educate future U.S. international business practitioners. A handful of U.S. educators, mindful of the socio-cultural and politico-legal differences existing among nation-states, saw the need to address the issues and problems encountered when involved in international business.

Essentially, these educators adopted two paradigms to guide them in their educational efforts that are still very much evident in the arguments, thinking, and research of many IB scholars [Vernon 1964]. The first paradigm, labeled *the extension paradigm* here, emphasizes the management of functional activities "within foreign economies." The second paradigm, labeled *the cross-border management paradigm* here, focuses attention on the integration and management of operations "within the international environment and across foreign economies." Some of the characteristics of these initial paradigms are listed in Table 1.

The Extension Paradigm

When IB practice is seen merely as an extension of domestic practice, IB education and research can be readily viewed in unidisciplinary terms, and thus better left to

---

Table 1. Characteristics of the Initial Paradigms of International Business

Core Orientation
BUSINESS is firm-level activity that is reducible to accounting, finance, marketing, personnel, production, strategy, and so on for the purpose of observation, explanation, and prediction.

INTERNATIONAL BUSINESS is firm-level activity that crosses national borders and/or is conducted in a country other than the firm's home country.

Implicit/Explicit Assumptions
Business is business no matter where practiced.

Firm-level activity is to be studied using logical empiricism (determinism and reductionism).

Firm-level activity is primarily economic.

International firm-level activity is an extension or adaptation of home-country activity.

The firm's external environment can be reduced to a few dimensions and each studied separately in terms of its constraining influence on business activity.

Socio-cultural diversity at the firm-level is "managed" by reducing (or isolating) dissimilarities.

Implications for IB Inquiry
Understanding firm-level activity in an international context is gained through the extension of Anglo-American unidisciplinary paradigms, theories, concepts, methodologies, and insights (an emphasis on finding and explaining similarities not differences).

Strengths of Paradigms
Findings augment the departmentalized understanding and knowledge derived from the unidisciplinary study of business outcomes.

Both paradigms have resulted in theoretical contributions (for example, see Hennart, chapter 11).

The certification and generalizability of acquired understanding (movement toward knowledge) is supported by highly developed, rigorous methodology that seeks to establish/identify similarities (central tendency approaches).

Weaknesses of Paradigms
Emphasis is on the extension and confirmation of unidisciplinary business inquiry and the knowledge it provides. Both initial paradigms tend to reinforce ethnocentricity and disciplinary parochialism since they do not challenge the assumptions, paradigms, and theories on which their unidisciplinary inquiry is based.

Comparative business research is only a tangential interest (i.e., to be of value, the knowledge gained by this inquiry must improve on the decision-making process of firms involved in international business). Differences are viewed as contingencies or ignored.

Both paradigms raise the same questions of business, and use the same methodologies to answer these questions regardless of where observed. That is, the interconnectedness (and interaction) of multi-level societal processes, the entities they produce, and the business practices changes that arise from this interconnectedness are ignored.

functional experts. For example, Vernon recommended that IB be taught by:

> our existing functional groups—our production people, our marketing people, our control people, our finance people, and so on. I say this because, as all of you know, we have developed a body of hard conceptions and ideas within the fields of production, marketing, control, and finance. These ideas I assume, can appropriately be extended by observant men who are specialists in their fields. It would seem prudent to me to take the discipline as it exists and to see in what sense these ideas have to be adapted to the peculiar conditions of foreign environments. I think we will learn that, with suitable, sensitive adaptation, many principles we now use can be applied to the circumstances of foreign economies and will continue to be valid [1964, p. 8].

Vernon's recommendation that functional specialists should teach IB was made to avoid two kinds of risks:

> One risk is that we as IB teachers really become sloppy social anthropologists ... The other risk is of an even more subtle kind. A case or a problem is presented, wrapped about with exotically foreign names. But after you have studied the problem a bit, you realize that if you just change the names a little, the case could have taken place in Muncie, Ind. And we think of ourselves as teaching IB because we have slipped some exotic names into our problem [1964, p. 8].

From this extensionalistic perspective, much of IB inquiry is the testing of contingency theories and its output classified as "international" marketing, "international" finance, "international" finance, "international" management, and so on. At the core of this perspective is the assumption that business is business wherever practiced, only the circumstances change. Essentially, the questions raised by this paradigm are concerned with identifying those environmental factors that have a statistically significant influence on a firm's operations and its management. Simultaneously, the questions are limited to those that can be legitimately articulated within the paradigms accepted by the various business disciplines. It can be no other way. For example, Feldman, in his non-discussion of the papers by Sullivan, Boyacigiller and Adler, and Redding in chapter 7, prefers to focus on the failures of international management with respect to the paradigms used by U.S. organizational behaviorists.

The Cross-Border Management Paradigm

The second conceptualization of IB that has strongly and continuously influenced IB inquiry for at least the last 30 years deals with the problems associated with the movement of goods and capital across national boundaries and the surveying and integrating from headquarters of operations existing in more than one country. From this perspective, Vernon [1964, p. 9–10] believes that IB inquiry is distinct for four reasons:

1. IB involves both risks and opportunities of a kind not normally encountered within the domestic economy (e.g., balance of payment risks and opportunities, import restriction risks and opportunities).
2. IB requires an understanding of the vagaries and intricacies of international taxation, foreign exchange, the international patent system, and the special problems of international oligopoly pricing.
3. IB requires dealing with governments, particularly at the point of entry.
4. IB requires the development of an effective operating discipline for understanding the complexities of moving across boundaries and operating in many countries.

In Vernon's view these peculiarities raise questions not addressed by the "functional groups." At the same time, however, this paradigm suffers from the same conceptual constraints as the extension paradigm. It is a firm-level paradigm that focuses attention on normative application and description, and assumes business is business no matter where practiced. That is, it assumes that ultimately there is a single definition of business with many variants that are the result of environmental (structural) differences.

Paradigmic Synthesis

The framework developed by Nehrt, Truitt, and Wright [1970] for the preparation of "an inventory of recent and current research in international business and recommendations for further research" presents an excellent synthesis of the research implications of the extension and cross-border management paradigms. As shown in Table 2, these authors, in an exclusionary fashion, defined IB research as the scholarly study of a phenomenon that satisfies five criteria. Importantly, they viewed IB research as interdisciplinary. Unfortunately, this interdisciplinary approach to the study of IB was either ignored or overlooked by the already established and dominant "functional groups" in the United States. It is only recently that there has again been a call for an interdisciplinary approach to the study of IB, this time by Dunning [1988] and Toyne [1989].

AN "EMERGING" VISION (PARADIGM) OF IB

It was argued earlier that the social sciences and the business disciplines are seeking to reformulate the central questions guiding their respective inquiries. In attempting to do this, they are seeking new paradigms, new ways of conceptualizing the world. One possible reformation of what IB

Table 2. The Dominant Paradigm's Definition of International Business Research

- It is concerned with firm-level business activity that crosses national boundaries or is conducted in a location other than the firm's home country. (This activity may be the movement of goods, capital, people, and knowledge, or it may be manufacturing, extraction, construction, banking, shipping, advertising, and the like.)

- It is concerned with the interrelationships between the operations of the business firm and international or foreign environments in which the firm operates.

- It does not include studies devoted to economic development, development planning, foreign trade, and the international monetary system, which belong to development and international economics. Excluded also are studies of foreign legal, political, economic, and social environments. These belong to the fields of law, political science, economics, and behavioral science unless the study itself relates the environment directly to the organizational, operational, or decision-making problems of international business firms.

- It does not include studies of business activities in given foreign countries. A study of marketing channels in Turkey, whether it is done by a U.S., French, or Turkish professor of marketing, is still a study about domestic business in Turkey. This would not be international business any more than would the study of motivation levels of Portuguese workers or the study of personal income distribution in Japan, though each may be of interest to international business firms.

- As an exception to the last point, however, *comparative* business studies are included within this definition. For example, a study of pharmaceutical marketing channels in Germany, Italy, Brazil, and Japan, which makes comparisons and analyzes the causes and effects of similarities and differences, would be considered international business research although it was not concerned with the relationship between the marketing channels within each country and international business firms.

Source: Nehrt, Truitt, and Wright [1970, p. 1–2].

involves is presented on the following pages as a "new" paradigm. Simply put, this paradigm presents IB as a multi-level, hierarchical system that evolves (emerges) over time as a consequence of exchange coupled with experience, new knowledge, and learning.

A Hierarchical Process Representation of the IB Phenomenon

There are several justifications for adopting an expanded and evolving hierarchical paradigm for the study of IB phenomena and their relationships. One justification is that an expanded conceptualization of IB would add interest and challenge to current investigations. Another is that the business disciplines are expanding and recasting the domains of their fields and, since IB is at least in part an aggregation of these disciplines, it should follow suit. A third defense is that the AACSB is now stressing process rather than content, and this change will have some effect on the kinds of questions addressed by educators and researchers. A fourth and probably the most relevant justification for an expanded conceptualization of IB is that the current understanding of IB cannot advance without such an expansion; reality has changed to such a degree that "old ideas" no longer work (see, for example, Westney, chapter 6, regarding the "revolutionary" transformation of firms in recent years). More specifically, to avoid the dangers of accumulating narrowly specialized knowledge without perspective, such as is gained from increasingly specialized business functional inquiry, we need one or more new paradigms that give larger, more generalized meaning to specialized knowledge.

Delaying for the moment the discussion about the complexities of differentiating between levels of inquiry, and focusing on the more familiar unit of analysis, the firm, an expansion of the representation of the world of IB is necessary for the following interrelated arguments.

First, all conceptualizations are incomplete [Gödel's Incompleteness Theorem—Hofstadter 1979]. The firm-level representation of IB could only be made complete if the firm were placed inside yet another logical system that would resolve unanswerable questions within the original conceptualization (see, for example, Buckley 1988). However, the incompleteness of the firm-level conceptualization of IB cannot be the issue. All representations are incomplete (i.e., completeness is only achieved when conceptualization is replaced by the real world). The germane questions are: What type of incompleteness is acceptable? What level of incompleteness is acceptable? Although the answers to both questions are indeterminate over time, answers can be suggested for a particular period of time if time is used as a proxy for knowledge and the awareness (influence) that this knowledge brings to the questions being asked. For example, given today's global situation and the level of cumulated IB knowledge, is it acceptable to conceptualize IB as firm-level phenomena from an Anglo-American economic view? If the answer is to satisfy all of the social and business disciplines interested in understanding IB, the answer cannot be yes. As Toyne [1989] and Behrman in chapter 11 point out, economic motivations do not dominate all enterprise decisions. Just as an explanation and prediction of snowflakes cannot be gained solely from a study of snowflakes, nor can a study of IB phenomena yield the depth of understanding required for prediction. In both cases it requires an understanding of the process that yields these phenomena.

Second, the phenomena identified, labeled, and observed in attempting to understand, explain and predict IB and IB practice are neither identical within nor across national borders. Although all IB phenomena are indeterminate (i.e., no two firms are exactly alike), they are the products of particular social processes. Subsequently, they are affected by the business processes of their home, host, and international contexts.

The exogenization of business processes, such as is done when a firm-level conceptualization of IB is adopted, implicitly assumes that the product of a particular process is not the creation of that process, but merely affected by the process. It is then much easier to assume that IB phenomena are identical, irrespective of their origins (e.g., firm-level contingency theory—business is business no matter its source locale since the activities and outputs of doing business are modifications resulting from contextual factors). Thus, the common practice of exogenizing the business processes of nation-states results in the assumed similarities of IB phenomena (e.g., all enterprise strategists think alike regardless of their nationalities). Put more forcefully, the fundamental differences of phenomena are ignored or not examined; only their similarities are recognized and considered of interest and value.

Third, if business and IB phenomena are indeterminate yet socio-culturally distinguishable at the nation-state level, an understanding of their interaction with one another and with the business processes of different locales requires including those processes that explain their emergence, continuance, *and individuality*. Thus, the representation needs to explicitly include those processes that generate particular phenomena. That is, IB's conceptualization must not just raise questions concerned with the similarities of IB phenomena but also must raise questions concerned with their differences. Moreover, this representation must include those processes that subsequently have an influence on these similarities and differences (e.g., the educational process can both socialize and individualize people). If such an argument has force, a comprehensive and richer understanding of IB phenomena needs to be advanced than is currently available.

Fourth, the issue of entity definition is critical to a better understanding of IB [Wilkins 1986]. To observe an IB phenomenon, for example, the multinational company's (MNC) boundary must be known, since it "comes apart," and its parts relocate elsewhere with other firms that hail from other places. Thus, a relevant question is whether MNCs intruding on a new locale take on meanings similar to those given firms that have emerged from that locale's business process, or do they retain the meaning given them by the business process that created them initially (see, for example, Westney, chapter 6). To answer this and similar questions requires a much deeper understanding of business process and enterprise difference than is presently available or even sought after. Using the terminology of Salthe [1985, pp. 23–33], to recognize an entity as such it must satisfy the four criteria of entification: it must have boundaries, scale, integration, and spatiotemporal continuity. As a consequence, entities also possess individuality (indivisibility and particularity). Stated briefly, a *boundary* identifies a discontinuity with the environment that contains the entity. An entity represents "a system separate from its environment and contains those subsystems that have significant mutual interactions over some specified period" [Salthe 1985, p. 23]. *Scale* refers to the size of an entity (i.e., it must be identifiable). "A thing cannot be an entity unless it is perceived as bigger or smaller than something else" [Salthe 1985, p. 24]. *Integration* refers to the claim that "if it is at all complex, an entity must be a well-integrated cybernetic system. That is, its subsystems will be connected by information networks and feedback loops such that they are functionally integrated and more or less interdependent" [Salthe 1985, p. 26]. Finally, *spaciotemporal continuity* refers to the covariance of an entity's parts. Spaciotemporal continuity is the stability criterion, either entities do not change or they change in prescribed or predicted ways.

Fifth, what is missing from current research on IB phenomena is a theory of differences, not similarities—the methodology used to study business phenomena is a reinforcement of this argument. That is, current theory and current methodology are focused on identifying similarities, not differences among IB phenomena. What is needed to understand IB entities are theories that can explain differences, initially at the nation-state level and subsequently at the international level (e.g., what role does learning, recognized as both a socializing and an individualizing activity, play in the emergence of similarities and differences among organizations).

Sixth, to make sense of IB organizations it is not sufficient to study just the phenomena involved in IB, even if this study involves organizations from different socio-cultural contexts and consequently the product of uniquely different processes. To have explanation and prediction, the study must explicitly include an examination of *the sources* of the similarities and differences found in phenomena from different national business processes. This, of course, requires the simultaneous study of the processes that created them and are transforming them. It is insufficient to include just the immediate context (industry) within which they exist, such as advocated by Porter [1980] and the Anglo-American industrial organization theorists from whom he draws so heavily. The sciences of anthropology, political economy and sociology can contribute as much to an understanding of IB phenomena and the national business processes from which they sprang as can economics [Dunning 1988; Toyne 1989].

Root's Interaction Paradigm

Vernon [1964] was not alone in arguing for the distinctiveness of IB inquiry. In 1969, Root offered the following definition of IB that he believed distinguished it from other social and business disciplines:

As a field of study, IB is primarily directed toward the description, analysis, explanation and prediction of the actual and normative behavior of the private business enterprise as it strives to achieve its strategic and operational goals in a multinational environment. In particular, the study of international business centers on the *cross-national interactions* that create dynamic linkages among the elements comprising the international enterprise (intra-enterprise interactions) and between

the enterprise as a whole and its multinational environmental systems (extra-enterprise interactions) [author's emphasis, 1969, p. 18].

Unlike Vernon [1964], Root took a system's approach when conceptualizing the field of IB inquiry. He identified three basic environmental systems with both international and national counterparts: political, economic, and socio-cultural. Consistent with a system's representation of reality, he argued that the international-level systems exist because nation-states "communicate" with one another through political, social, cultural, economic, and business transfers and exchanges. That is, the sets of relational patterns (networks) that link nation-states are the international-level systems. Thus, according to Root, these international-level systems cannot exist apart from nation-states.

Root also visualized the international enterprise as a subsystem of a nation-state system that "internalizes" the international environment. The flows between the various parts of the enterprise (parent and foreign affiliates) occur within the constraints laid down by the governments of two or more nation-states, and the internal relations between these various parts replicate those of the international environment: political, economic and socio-cultural. Consequently, Root argued that the study of IB can be from an expanded set of different *interaction process* perspectives, and analyzed with techniques drawn from different disciplines, including "the functional business fields, the social sciences, the behavioral sciences, and mathematics" [1969, p. 25]. Such an interaction perspective is reflected, for example, in the work by Bartlett and Ghoshal [1989] and Mattsson, chapter 9.

Although Root's paradigm is much closer to "capturing" reality in its complexity, richness and hierarchical inclusiveness than the "oversimplified" firm-level paradigms that have dominated much of IB thinking and study, it does not go far enough. It lacks an underlying, unifying purpose and a "dynamic" that is needed to understand the sources of change, and the effects of change within and among the four identified systems. For example, although Root specified three environmental systems as impinging on and constraining the international enterprise system, he is silent on why they and their relationships may change over time. As such, his paradigm does not allow for either the emergence of an IB process that is apart from the national business processes, or the emergence of supra-national firms. Both eventualities are now conceivable, if not already realities. In other words, his conceptualization is static, not evolutionary.

An "Emerging" Interaction Paradigm

Table 3 describes an "emerging" interaction paradigm that is an evolving hierarchical representation of IB. At its core is the idea that business is an evolving multilevel, social-embedded process. By process

---

Table 3. Characteristics of the "Emerging" International Business Paradigm

Core Orientation

BUSINESS is an emerging, recursive, hierarchial social process, the outputs of which are indeterminate (e.g., firms, associations, etc.).

INTERNATIONAL BUSINESS is an emerging, hierarchial social process that is the result of the interaction of national business processes and their outputs. The output of this IB process is indeterminate.

Implicit/Explicit Assumptions

A particular business process evolves over time because of both internal examination and change (e.g., economic, technological, political, sociological) and its interconnectedness with other business processes is indeterminate.

Because of the hierarchical nature of the business process, all levels of a society that impact on or are impacted by the IB process are central to IB inquiry.

Phenomena at each level of the business process are expressions of current knowledge and information received from upper and lower levels.

Implications for IB Inquiry

Future business activity is dependent on learning related to such things as previous experience, self-study, transfer of and response to practices of other business processes, and environmental discontinuities arising from scientific breakthrough, etc.

IB knowledge (certified and generalized) is gained from the development and testing of theories and concepts that seek to explain and predict the outcome of the interaction of two or more social-embedded business processes.

Strengths of Paradigm

Recognizes the new "reality"—increasing complexity and interconnectedness of business processes and their outputs.

Requires increased understanding of and knowledge about the basic social sciences and the contributions they make in explaining and predicting the IB process.

Brings comparative business studies "center stage" by requiring an understanding of the evolving differences of business processes and their outputs.

Results in "new" theories and concepts that have value by contributing to a better understanding and explanation of single business processes.

Weaknesses of Paradigm

Increased sense of "uncertainty" because of the indeterminacy of elemental (e.g., government, industry, firm, individual) outcomes.

Deficiency of theories and concepts explaining the outcome and directions of interconnected organizations and systems.

Rigorous research methodology is underdeveloped.

is meant the regular, habitual activity generated by interaction of initiating conditions at any level of organization that produces continuous or intermittent output (e.g., business-related phenomena such as firms and industries) regulated by boundary conditions imposed by upper levels.[8] Also, this hierarchical process evolves intermittently because of the consequences of informed hunch, intuition, and vision (learning and inductive thinking) that can originate at *any* level in the process (i.e., above the focal level, at the focal level, or below the focal level). An example would be a group of firms (focal level phenomena) vying for market exchanges. Using Salthe's [1985, p. 75] suggestion that the "basic minimal cluster of levels required to represent fundamental interactive relationships is a triad of contiguous levels" (i.e., the focal level bounded by its immediate upper and lower levels), the idiosyncratic approaches used by these firms would be initiated by their intrinsic properties (e.g., lower level phenomena such as individuals and groups), yet regulated by industrial and governmental properties and purposes (e.g., upper level phenomena including trade associations, government agencies, supranational organizations and the consequences of their actions).

Choice of Hierarchical Levels

There are various levels of organization that describe, constrain, stimulate, and shape IB. Following in the tradition of Root [1969] and others (see, for example, non-IB scholars such as Pfeffer 1982; Miller 1978; Schendel and Hofer 1979), the hierarchical levels germane to IB inquiry extend from the individual to the suprasocietal.[9] Beyond these lower and upper levels nothing much can be said at this time concerning their boundary and initiating conditions, respectively.

Some simple criteria can be used to identify the levels most appropriate for the study of IB. Although the levels to be identified are changeable—they depend on the specific, particularized interests of the researcher—it is safe to say that the criteria

used to distinguish among them appear to be universal and appropriate for both the physical and social sciences [Salthe 1985, pp. 170–173]:

1. Phenomena at each level must be capable of being "seen" or "sensed" (e.g., product divisions, firms, nation states, EU, GATT, UN).
2. Phenomena at lower levels must be contained within (are intrinsic to) those of contiguous upper levels (e.g., individuals are in firms, firms are in industries, and so on).
3. Interactions between phenomena at contiguous levels must be capable of establishing initiating or boundary conditions. Initiating conditions are lower level constraints that give rise to focal-level processes. They are the intrinsic properties of phenomena interacting at the focal level (e.g., management capabilities, organizational slack). Boundary conditions are higher level constraints regulating focal-level processes (e.g., governments and industries contextualizing the responses of firms).
4. Functional component phenomena at the different levels must be "different in kind." That is, the levels must be incommensurable (e.g., each level serves a different function).
5. Level identification is dependent on the principle of robustness [Levins 1966; Wimsatt 1980].[10]

Using these criteria, an appropriate hierarchy of levels for studying IB with examples of their initiating and boundary conditions is shown in Exhibit 1. This hierarchy is presented as an example of one appropriate hierarchy, not the only possible hierarchy of levels for studying IB.[11] Three points about this proposed hierarchy need to be noted. First, the phenomena included in each level are observable and functionally incommensurable with phenomena in contiguous levels. Second, the proposed hierar-

Exhibit 1. Different Levels of International Business

Hierarchical Level	Examples of initiating and boundary conditions
1. Suprasocietal	The suprasocietal level imposes boundary conditions on the contiguous level of nation-states. Examples of boundary conditions include human rights, environmental concerns, multilateral trade agreements, international monetary system, and so on.
2. Societal (or nation-state level)	Nation-states are embedded in an emerging suprasocietal world and constitute the suprasocietal level's initiating conditions. These arise from the socio-cultural, economic, and political distinctiveness of nation-states and their individual and collective (regional/global) political and economic aspirations. They also constitute the boundary conditions for lower levels (e.g., laws, rules and regulations governing business, tax structures, education of the workforce).
3. Industry	Industries are embedded in national business processes and constitute initiating conditions (e.g., economic efficiency, economic specialization, satisfaction of indigenous needs/wants). They also provide the boundary conditions for lower levels (e.g., competitive intensity, technology and investment characteristics).
4. Firm	Firms are embedded in industries and constitute their initiating conditions (e.g., innovativeness, organizational capabilities, resource bases, geographic scope). Firms also constitute the boundary conditions for lower levels (e.g., policies and procedures, strategic direction, budgets).
5. Group	Groups are embedded in firms and constitute their initiating conditions (e.g., divisional focus, functional expertise, managerial capabilities and talents). Groups are also the boundary conditions for individuals (e.g., they contextualize and inform individuals concerning possible behaviors, the scope of their authority).
6. Individual	Individuals are embedded in groups, and constitute their initiating conditions or intrinsic properties (e.g., the group's potential motivation, talents, capabilities, skills and knowledge/expertise).

chy includes a self-reference [Harris 1968]. This was done by truncating the hierarchy at points where we can no longer form opinions given our particular perspective (i.e., business). Third, all of the phenomena above that of the individual are human creations, and are manifestations of available knowledge, information, and experience (general or local).

Toyne's Exchange Paradigm: IB Process as an Evolving Hierarchical System

Toyne [1989] argues that the underlying, unifying purpose of IB was sociopolitical influenced exchange. He defined IB as:

> a sociopolitical conditioned exchange process involving two or more countries and two or more social actors whose commercially motivated purpose is to either satisfy imperfectly satisfied national exchanges, or to simultaneously create and satisfy national exchanges [p. 7].

He elaborated on this definition by further proposing that the international exchange process could be conceptualized as having three dimensions: *polity-economy*, *external-internal*, and *substructure-super-structure*. Also, the purpose of the process is to achieve interorganizational exchange equilibrium through *domain consensus, ideological consensus, positive evaluation*, and *work coordination*.[12] He concluded that:

> The boundaries for international exchange, and the phenomena to be included, should be defined in economic, social, and political terms. International business, as a field of theoretical inquiry, should encompass all social, industrial, market, and government activities (economic and political) that lead to, or directly influence in some way, *international exchange* [1989, p. 13].

Toyne's conceptualization of IB presents an expanded, hierarchical conceptualization of the domain of IB inquiry, focuses attention on various but specific phenomena at different levels of organization and their relationships, and raises distinctive questions. However, it lacks a "dynamic" that explains and possibly predicts changes in the process and its output. Missing in this and the paradigms described earlier is a "dynamic" that simultaneously links IB and national business, yet distinguishes between them in fundamental ways.

The three essential elements of this "missing" dynamic are common to all levels of the business process: (1) self-interest; (2) the available pool of information, knowledge and experience;[13] and (3) learning which includes awareness, discernment, interpretation and judgment). A particular level of the business process and the various phenomena that are the output of this process change incrementally, sometimes radically, as a result of the interaction of these three elements. This, in turn, results in changes in the initiating and boundary conditions (i.e., the relationship between contiguous levels is changed).

Self-interest, articulated in economic terms by Adam Smith in *An Inquiry into the Nature and Causes of the Wealth of Nations* (1776), is at the core of most explanations dealing with business, regardless of organizational level. It is accepted by most busi-

ness scholars as the motivator or galvanizer of action. Learning is also common to all levels of organization. It is central to what individuals and organizations seek to become within an already ongoing world of ideas.[14] Finally, the world of ideas upon which individuals and organizations depend for meaning is the pool of available information, knowledge, and experience at a particular point in time.

There are two distinguishing features to national business processes (apart from the physical resource base). One is the interpretation given self-interest by individuals and organizations. The other is the available pool of information, knowledge, and experience on which individuals and organizations depend when seeking to understand what others seem to already understand. Collectively, they distinguish between national business processes because they reflect the socio-cultural and historical differences that distinguish nation-states. They also distinguish between the national and international business process, since the latter is the process that is continuously harmonizing national differences as a consequence of knowledge, information, and experience transfers. In fact, the IB process can be viewed as an "ongoing," continuous reconciliation process the purpose of which is domain consensus, ideological consensus, positive evaluation, and work coordination (see Toyne, chapter 2). The suprasocietal level can be viewed as the multinational manifestation of this reconciliation process. Its purpose appears to be to bring agreed upon interpretations of order to exchange relations among nations, partly through transparency requirements and partly through the creation of "external" impartial monitoring mechanisms that increasingly have an ability to persuade, but not yet enforce.

Self-interest, for example, is a nihilistic concept if not moderated by a societal fabric of values and beliefs.[15] Thus, to the extent that societal values and beliefs differ by nation-state, the interpretation given self-interest and the constraints imposed on individual and organizational behavior arising from this interpretation at various levels of national business processes will also differ. For example, the U.S. business person might see his or her primary "professional obligation" as the generation of a flow of dividends for stockholders, and the German businessman might see his primary goal as the creation of wealth because of his calling or *Berufung*. The same is true of the historical-based, socio-cultural influenced pool of information, knowledge, and experience on which various levels of organization depend (e.g., successful business behavior is interpreted differently by U.S. and Chinese business persons because of differences in experience).

The theoretical and research implications of this "emergent" hierarchical view of IB are explored in the introductions to the various parts of this book, and in the concluding chapter.

THE STRUCTURE OF THE BOOK

Recognition of the emerging complexity and multi-dimensionality of IB, in contrast to the increasingly specialized lines of IB inquiry, guided our partitioning of the field into the nine sections found in the remainder of this book, and led us to ask the authors of the twenty-six invited topic papers, nineteen commentaries, and four panel papers to address specific topics. Exhibit 2 lists the topics covered in this book and the authors who contributed papers.

The topics covered do not exhaust the many institutionalized and specialized directions IB inquiry is taking us. The time and space constraints of the four-day conference at which all these papers were discussed prevented us from explicitly including a number of perspectives of interest. For example, we would have liked to include an anthropological perspective, and within the business administration field, accounting and production perspectives. Although these omissions give silent testimony to the complexity of international business, they do not detract from the value of the analysis

presented here, nor from the conclusions reached concerning the emerging conceptualization of IB.

The papers presented in chapter 2 review the conceptual domain of IB inquiry. In the first topic paper, Mira Wilkins defines the field of IB inquiry in classical terms as the study of the economic-driven dynamics of the individual firm. In the second topic paper, Jean J. Boddewyn expands on Wilkins's economic-dominated firm-level view by drawing attention to the political meaning and implications of "international" and arguing that IB encompasses many levels of analysis and interpretation (i.e., from the individual to the global). In the third topic paper, Brian Toyne first identifies four possible conceptual domains of IB inquiry by the questions asked, and then proceeds to ask whether these questions are addressed by the traditional business disciplines. The three topic papers are discussed by Jack N. Behrman, Hans Schollhammer, and Tom Hench from three very different perspectives.

The papers included in chapter 3 deal with the relationship between the emerging perspectives on business and society and IB inquiry. Robert H. Hogner argues in the first topic paper that culture is the foundation of the "naturalist model" which is the emerging basis for scientific inquiry. In the second topic paper, Edward Freeman points out that social issues pertinent to IB, while embedded within the global society, exist in individual societies characterized by cultural diversity. Finally, Donna J. Wood and Jean Pasquero examine the research issues raised by expanding business and society research internationally. The three topic papers are discussed by Philip Cochran and Steven Wartick.

The papers presented in chapter 4 examine the relationship between economic theorizing and IB inquiry. Mark Casson authored the first topic paper and presents an interesting introduction by arguing that while economic theory has made a substantial contribution to IB inquiry, future economic contributions will probably not be

Exhibit 2. Topics and Authors Contained in the Book

Chapter	Topic	Paper Authors	Commentary
1.	Foundations of an emerging paradigm	Toyne/Nigh	
2.	The conceptual domain of international business inquiry	Wilkins Boddewyn Toyne	Schollhammer Behrman Hench
3.	Business and society perspectives and international business	Hogner Freeman Wood/Pasquero	Cochran Wartick
4.	Economic perspectives and international business	Casson Dunning Ozawa	Hennart Graham
5.	Political perspectives and international business	Kobrin Nigh Kuhlman	Starr Brewer
6.	Organization theory perspectives and international business	Westney Egelhoff Hedlund/Ridderstråle	Astley Ghoshal
7.	Organizational behavior perspectives and international business	Sullivan Boyacigiller/Adler Redding	Mendenhall Feldman
8.	Strategic management perspectives and international business	Kogut Doz Mascarenhas	Kim Hitt
9.	Marketing perspectives and international business	Mattsson Samiee Sheth	Gatignon Cavusgil
10.	Financial perspectives and international business	Lessard Errunza	Walter Dufey
11.	Theory and research implications for international business	Toyne Behrman Boddewyn Hennart Bhagat	
12.	The future development of international business inquiry	Toyne/Nigh	

based purely on the extension of existing (economic) theories. In the second topic paper, John H. Dunning explores what he perceives to be some of the more exciting challenges and pressing needs for research including the effects of both culture and government on MNCs and their strategic responses. Terutomo Ozawa, in the third topic paper, takes a more macro approach to the question of the relationship between IB inquiry and economic theorizing by attempting to replace dependency theory with a theory of economic development based on the experiences of newly industrialized countries. The three topic papers are discussed by Jean-François Hennart and Edward M. Graham.

The papers in chapter 5 address various political perspectives and the study of IB. Stephen Kobrin examines the concept of the state and explores the implications of the evolution of the international political system for IB theory. Douglas Nigh investigates the concepts of nation and nation-state. He examines the meaning of national identity of multinational corporations and its implications for relationships between nation-states and MNCs. James Kuhlman discusses the important role of levels of analysis in IB inquiry and argues for the consideration of levels of political entities other than the nation-state. Harvey Starr and Thomas Brewer discuss the three papers.

The three topic papers included in chapter 6 examine the assumptions and trends in organization theory (OT) and their importance for the study of IB. In the first topic paper, D. Eleanor Westney argues that while the fields of OT and IB diverged in the 1980s as a result of different interests (e.g., macro-organization theory in OT and micro-organization application in IB), the 1990s may yet see increased disciplinary interaction because of the growing complexities of international, national, and local institutional environments. In the second topic paper, William G. Egelhoff explores the contribution that an integration of information technology and organiza-

tional information-processing perspective can make to an evaluation of MNC strategy and organization design. Lastly, Gunnar Hedlund and Jonas Ridderstråle examine the theoretical potential when examining the MNC as a self-renewing organization. The discussants of these papers are Graham Astley and Sumantra Ghoshal.

The papers in chapter 7 explore the relationship that exists between organizational behavior (OB) perspectives and IB. Jeremiah Sullivan suggests in the first paper of this section that culture theories have very little chance of developing in the IB field unless the causal paradigm on which cultural theorizing is presently based is replaced with the purposive paradigm underpinning economic theory. In the second topic paper, Nakiye Boyacigiller and Nancy J. Adler first discuss the ill-defined construct of culture, and then proceed to explore the reasons for the emergence of the field of international OB. In the last of the three topic papers, S. Gordon Redding initially examines the progress made in recent years in clarifying issues in comparative OB theory, and then discusses the relevance and epistemology of this work and its future direction as a discipline. The three papers are then discussed by Mark Mendenhall and Daniel C. Feldman.

Chapter 8 explores the relationship between strategic management research and IB inquiry. In the first topic paper, Bruce Kogut examines what he terms the "evolutionary theory of the multinational corporation" in which organizing and technological capabilities are accumulated over time in response to the home and international environment. Yves Doz, in the second topic paper, argues that the resource-based paradigm in strategic management and the growing recognition that firm-specific intangible capabilities provide the most distinctive competence offer a series of research issues deserving of further inquiry by IB scholars. Lastly, Briance Mascarenhas identifies four perspectives relevant to international competition and examines their combined ability to suggest further inquiry. The three topic papers are then discussed by W. Chan Kim and Michael A. Hitt.

Chapter 9 explores the relationship between marketing and IB inquiry by examining such issues as the failure of international marketing to develop a common body of theory-based knowledge. In the first paper, Lars-Gunnar Mattsson addresses the relationship between the paradigmic orientations of marketing and IB, and how differences and similarities in these orientations influence the ability of marketing scholars to make important contributions to the development of IB knowledge. In the second paper, Saeed Samiee examines the development of international marketing and offers a conceptual framework that differentiates international and domestic marketing. Lastly, Jagdish Sheth argues that international marketing has not generated its own theory or constructs because of its contextual focus. The three papers are discussed by Hubert Gatignon and S. Tamer Cavusgil.

Chapter 10 examines the relationship between financial perspectives and IB inquiry. The first topic paper by Donald R. Lessard reviews the various roles of finance in international business. He explores the extent to which financial factors give rise to comparative advantage, affecting the competitiveness of certain firms. Further he investigates the aspects of financial management that give rise to competitive advantage among firms. The second topic paper, written by Vihang R. Errunza, examines emerging markets—those of developing countries. He reviews important differences between developed and emerging markets and trends in the development of emerging markets. He argues that emerging markets and firms from emerging markets will play an increasingly important role in international business. The two papers are discussed by Ingo Walter and Gunter Dufey.

Chapter 11 presents four papers by Rabi Bhagat, Jack N. Behrman, Jean J. Boddewyn, and Jean-François Hennart that ex-

amine the viability of IB inquiry to develop into a distinct field of inquiry given its lack of a unifying definition and its current and foreseeable dependency on the paradigms, theories and constructs of economics, political science, sociology, and the business disciplines. Also reported is the panel discussion that took place, including audience remarks.

The final chapter summarizes what we believe are the theory and research implications of the IB paradigm we see emerging.

In each chapter, we provide an introduction that gives our views as to why the topic(s) were selected; what we believe each paper's highlights to be; what we believe the discussants have to say; and finally, our comments and opinions about the significant issues developed in each section. It needs to be clearly understood that neither the reader, the authors, nor the discussants may hold similar views.

The topic papers and the commentaries follow immediately after our opening comments. Hopefully, our remarks will aid the reader to more quickly isolate the key issues in each paper, and to see their significance concerning the various IB paradigms presented earlier.

The references for each paper are combined and listed at the end of each section. This was done to reduce unnecessary duplication of individual citations.

NOTES

1. We would like to acknowledge the suggestions made by Tom Hench (see chapter 2) in private communications with one of the editors that humans are also reciprocally-interactive and self-referential.

2. Reductionism assumes that it is desirable to interpret a phenomenon in terms applicable to its parts. It focuses exclusively on *initiating conditions*, ignoring *boundary conditions* [Salthe 1985, p. 304].

3. Although Schendel and Hofer [1979, p. 5] addressed this issue, and offered the strategic management paradigm as the integrating solution, their focus was, and still is, on only one of the outputs of the business process—the firm.

Moreover, the paradigm was normative/prescriptive, static, and grounded in determinism.

4. Robinson [1981] provides an account of the development of IB after World War II—from the two-actor era of the postwar decade, through three-actor and four-actor eras, to the multi-actor era of the 1980s and beyond.

5. Upper levels of the business process can be viewed as contextualizing, informing, selecting from among possible behaviors, governing, regulating, or controlling the results of lower-level processes (see, for example, Salthe 1985, p. 84). These constraining attributes (which include the creation of appropriate organizations) can be viewed as stable when the rate at which they change is slower than the rate at which the focal-level process changes.

6. For purposes of explication, national business process and social-embedded business process will be used interchangeably. However, it should be recognized that in the same way that using national borders to define cultural groupings is not correct, defining social-embedded business processes by national borders may be equally wrong.

7. It might be more accurate to visualize the want-activity relationship as reciprocating, not unidirectional (see Toyne 1989).

8. Biology's contributions to our understanding of processes have been used to articulate the characteristics of the national and international business processes described as the "emerging vision." This representation, of course, has its limitations, but they appear to be less serious than for an inorganic representation.

9. It's interesting to speculate that perhaps someday the levels below individual, such as organs and cells, may be considered germane to IB inquiry. (See, for example, Hofstadter 1979, and Varela, Thompson, and Rosch 1991.)

10. For example, if we detect the same things in two different ways we increase our confidence of their reality—they are robust to perceptual confidence.

11. As Salthe [1985, p. 168] points out, the identification of the specific levels are dependent on the interests and needs of the researcher. For example, the level above firm may more appropriately be family of firms (e.g., keiretsu) rather than industry for certain IB researchers.

12. Domain consensus refers to the extent to which a country or group of countries and their enterprises are permitted to enter into the national exchange process of another country or group of countries. Ideological consensus refers to the agreement among exchange participants concerning the nature and appropriateness of the approaches to be used when satisfying a specific exchange or array of exchanges. Positive evaluation refers to the judgment by the exchange participants concerning the rules governing the exchange process. Work coordination refers to the patterns of exchanges, cooperation, and coordination agreed to by the international exchange actors [Toyne 1989, p. 12].

13. Knowledge is used here in both its broadest sense—what Hirsch [1987] termed "cultural literacy" and its most rigorous sense—certified and generalized knowledge. Information refers to the information collected and used by focal-level phenomena when making decisions. Experience is idiosyncratic to a particular focal-level phenomenon.

14. As noted by Oakschott [1975, p. 37], "[t]he starting-place of doing is a state of reflective consciousness, namely, the agent's own understanding of his situation, what it means to him. And, of course, it is no less *his* situation even though it may be a concern with what he understands to be the situation of another or of others."

15. Smith did not support a nihilistic concept of self-interest. A fuller and more accurate understanding of his concept of self-interest in *Wealth of Nations*, for example, can be obtained from his earlier book on ethical behavior, *The Theory of Moral Sentiment*. Also Hirschman [1984] points out that in the design of its institutions, society has two dangers when it comes to the balancing of self-interest and civic spirit. In addition to making insufficient demands on morality and public spirit, society may make excessive demands on morality and public spirit.

REFERENCES

Anderson, Paul F. 1983. Marketing, Scientific Progress, and Scientific Method. *Journal of Marketing* 47(4): 18–31.

Bartlett, Christopher, and Sumantra Ghoshal. 1989. *Managing Across Borders: The Transnational Solution*. Cambridge, MA: Harvard Business School Press.

Baumol, William. 1968. Entrepreneurship in economic theory. *American Economic Review*. Papers and Proceedings of the 80th Annual Meeting, 58(May): 64–71.

Bedeian, Arthur G. 1989. Totems and taboos: Undercurrents in the management discipline, Presidential Address, Academy of Management Meeting, August.

Berger, Peter L. 1992. Sociology: A Disinvitation? *Society* 30(1): 12–18.

Berger, Peter L. 1963. *Invitation to Sociology: A Humanistic Perspective*. New York: Doubleday.

Buckley, Peter J. 1988. The limits of explanation: Testing the internalization theory of the multinational enterprise. *Journal of International Business Studies*, 19(2): 181–193.

Casti, John L. 1989. *Paradigms Lost: Tackling the Unanswered Mysteries of Modern Science*. New York, NY: Avon Books).

Coleman, James S. 1992. *Rational Choice Theory: Advocacy and Critique*. Newbury Park, CA: Sage Publications.

Coleman, James S. 1990. *Foundations of Social Theory*. Cambridge, MA: Harvard University Press.

Daft, Richard L. and Arie Y. Lewin. 1990. Can organization studies begin to break out of the normal science straitjacket? An editorial essay. *Organization Science*, 1(1): 1–9.

Dunning, John H. 1988. The eclectic paradigm of international production: A restatement and some possible extensions. *Journal of International Business Studies*, 19(1): 1–31.

Fayerweather, John. 1986. A history of the Academy of International Business from infancy to maturity: The first 25 years. *Essays in International Business*. Columbia, SC: College of Business Administration, University of South Carolina, No. 6, November.

Fox, Robin. 1992. Anthropology and the "teddy bear" picnic. *Society* 30(1): 47–55.

Gilpin, Robert. 1987. *The Political Economy of International Relations*. Princeton, NJ: Princeton University Press.

Graduate Management Admission Council (GMAC). 1990. *Leadership for a Changing World: The Future Role of Graduate Management Education*. Los Angeles, CA: Graduate Management Admission Council.

Granovetter Mark. 1985. Economic action and social structure: The problem of embeddedness. *American Journal of Sociology*, 91(3): 481–510.

Guba, Egon G. (editor) 1990. *The Paradigm Dialogue*. Newbury Park, CA: Sage Publications.

Harris, M. 1968. *The Rise of Anthropological Theory*. New York, NY: Crowell.

Hirsch, E.D., Jr. 1987. *Cultural Literacy: What Every American Needs to Know*. Boston: Houghton Mifflin Company.

Hirschman, Albert O. 1984. Against parsimony: Three easy ways of complicating some categories of economic discourse. *The American Economic Review*, 74(2): 89–96.

Hofstadter, Douglas R. 1979. *Gödel, Escher, Bach*. New York, NY: Vintage Books.

Hofstede, Geert. 1994. Management scientists are human. *Management Science*. 40(1): 4–13.

Hunt, Shelby D. 1991. *Modern Marketing Theory: Critical Issues in the Philosophy of Marketing Science*. Cincinnati: South-Western Publishing Co.

Hunt, Shelby D. 1983. *Marketing Theory: The Philosophy of Marketing Science*. Homewood, IL: Richard D. Irwin.

Kuhn, T.S. 1970. *The Structure of Scientific Revolution*. Chicago: The University of Chicago Press.

Levins, R. 1966. The strategy of model building in population biology. *American Science*, 54: 421–431.

Marshall, Alfred. 1920. *Principles of Economics*, 8th ed. London: Macmillan, 76.

Miller, J.G. 1978. *Living Systems*. New York, NY: McGraw-Hill.

Mirowski, Philip. 1988. *Against Mechanism: Protecting Economics from Science*. Totowa, NJ: Rowman and Littlefield.

Nehrt, Lee, Frederick Truitt, and Richard Wright. 1970. *International Business Research: Past, Present, and Future*. Bloomington: Bureau of Business Research, Indiana University.

Oakeshott, Michael. 1975. *On Human Conduct*. Oxford: Clarendon Press.

Peter, J. Paul and Olson, Jerry C. 1983. Is science marketing? *Journal of Marketing*, 47(4): 111–125.

Pfeffer, J. 1982. A variety of perspectives, *Organizations and Organization Theory*. London: Pitman, Chapter 1.

Phillips, D.C. 1987. *Philosophy, Science, and Social Inquiry*. New York, NY: Pergamon Press.

Porter, Lyman W. and Lawrence E. McKibbin. 1988. *Management Education and Development: Drift or Thrust into the 21st Century*. New York, NY: McGraw-Hill.

Porter, Michael E. 1986. *Competition in Global Industries*. Boston, MA: Harvard Business School Press.

Porter, Michael E. 1980. *Competitive Strategy: Techniques for Analyzing Industries and Competitors*. New York, NY: The Free Press.

Reynolds, Paul D. 1971. *A Primer in Theory Construction*. New York, NY: The Bobbs-Merrill Company, Inc.

Robinson, Richard D. 1981. Background concepts and philosophy of international business from World War II to the present. *Journal of International Business Studies*, 12(1): 13–21.

Root, Franklin R. 1993. Is international business a discipline? *Academy of International Business Newsletter*, Fall.

Root, Franklin R. 1969. A conceptual approach to international business. *Journal of Business Administration*, 1(1): 18–28.

Salthe, Stanley N. 1985. *Evolving Hierarchical Systems: Their Structure and Representation*. New York, NY: Columbia University Press.

Schendel, Dan E. and Charles W. Hofer (eds.). 1979. *Strategic Management: A New View of Business Policy and Planning*. Boston, MA: Little, Brown and Company.

Schumpeter, J. 1979 [1926]. *The Theory of Economic Development*. 2nd. edition. New Brunswick: Transaction Press.

Swedberg, Richard. 1990. *Economics and Sociology*. Princeton, NJ: Princeton University Press.

Toyne, Brian. 1994. International business scholarship: What are the essentials? Presented at the Second Michigan State University Roundtable. East Lansing, MI. Accepted for publication by the Michigan State University Press.

Toyne, Brian. 1993. Internationalizing the business administration faculty is no easy task. In S. Tamer Cavusgil, ed. *Internationalizing Business Education*. East Lansing, MI: Michigan State University Press: 45–64.

Toyne, Brian. 1989. International exchange: A foundation for theory building in international business. *Journal of International Business Studies*, 20(1): 1–17.

Toyne, Brian and Zaida L. Martinez. 1988. Enterprise behavior within an international exchange context. Presented at the Academy of International Business Annual Meeting, San Diego, October.

Varela, Francisco J. Thompson, Evan; and Rosch, Eleanor. 1991. *The Embodied Mind: Cognitive Science and Human Experience*. Boston, MA: MIT Press.

Vernon, Raymond. 1979. The product cycle hypothesis in a new international environment. *Oxford Bulletin of Economics and Statistics*: 255–267.

Vernon, Raymond. 1966. International investment and international trade in the product cycle. *Quarterly Journal of Economics*, 80(1): 190–207.

Vernon, Raymond. 1964. Comments. *Education in International Business*, Stefan H. Robock and Lee C. Nehrt (eds.). Bloomington: Graduate School of Business, Indiana University: 7–10.

von Hayek, Friedreich A. 1989. The pretence of knowledge. *American Economic Review*, 79(6): 3–7.

Wilkins, Mira. 1986. Defining a firm: History and theory. In Peter Hertner and Geoffrey Jones, eds. *Multinationals: Theory and History*. Brookfield: Gower Publishing Company.

Wimsatt, W.C. 1980. Robustness, reliability and multiple determinism in science: The nature and variety of a powerful family of problem-solving heuristics. In M. Brewer and B. Collins, ed. *Knowing and Validating in the Social Sciences: A Tribute to Donald T. Campbell*. San Francisco: Jossey-Bass.

2

The Conceptual Domain of
International Business Inquiry

EDITORS' COMMENTS

There is no wide agreement on what constitutes the conceptual domain of international business (IB) inquiry. With notable exceptions [Nehrt, Truitt, and Wright 1970; Root 1969; Toyne 1989; Vernon 1964], the IB literature is remarkable for its absence of discourse on such central questions as: What is IB? What kinds of phenomena are appropriately termed IB phenomena? How do IB activities and relationships differ from non-IB activities? How can the IB process be distinguished from other social processes? Which organizations should be referred to as IB organizations? In short, what is lacking in the extant literature is the questioning of *what is the proper conceptual domain of the construct labeled "international business."*

We therefore thought it apropos to ask the authors of the first three topic papers to address this central question. More specifically, we asked them to explore such basic issues as the conceptual boundaries of IB, the phenomena and relationships researched, and the ontological and epistemological assumptions made when building and testing theories within this conceptual domain. They were also asked to examine the diversity of perspectives (e.g., economic, political, sociological), the levels of analysis (e.g., nation-state, industry, enterprise, individual) increasingly found in the literature, and demonstrate the degree to which these varying perspectives and their attendant assumptions and theories are commensurable, and where and how they contribute to the growing body of knowledge on IB. Collectively, the six papers included in this chapter address many of these issues.

Wilkins responded with "a very personal perspective on where we are and where we should be going [as a field of study]" [p. 31]. In her paper, she points out that her archival research of firms led her to the conclusion that the field of IB should be defined "in terms of the dynamics of the individual firm" [p. 32]. According to Wilkins, firm-level activity that crosses national borders gave rise to IB. In her words, "the field of international business is a sub-set of the study and analysis of business enterprise; it must be linked with a viable and rich theory of the firm" [p. 34]. Since she equates the multinational enterprise and international business, she offers Buckley's [1990] and Pitelis and Sugden's [1991] works on multinational enterprise as evidence in support of a definable field of IB, a body of knowledge that constitutes a discipline.

In Wilkins's view, what distinguishes the sub-field of IB from the field of business is the *"firm that extends over borders"* [p. 35]. Thus, her definition agrees closely with those provided by Vernon [1964] and Nehrt, Truitt, and Wright [1970] and discussed in the opening chapter. Moreover, her focus is on the uncertainties that are introduced because of the need to operate under different cultures (translated as a cost of information), currency regimes and national sovereignties.

Boddewyn's conceptualization of IB is also primarily economic in nature. However, unlike Wilkins, he argues for a multi-level, integrative conceptualization of the domain of IB. At the same time, he limits what can be considered "business" by arguing that "I do not think that conceptualizing the domain of a particular societal institution, such as the family or international business, requires throwing in the 'whole kitchen sink' of all its determinants, processes and outcomes." Thus, importantly, he explicitly recognizes and accepts the notion that all domain definitions are somewhat arbitrary and incomplete.

Essentially, he argues that his definition of IB is an elaboration on Fayerweather's 1969 definition that refers to international business as "business processes intersected in some way by national borders" [1969:5]. At the same time, however, he avoids the theoretical implications of Fayerweather's insinuation that IB requires that some attention be given to the processes involved and the effects that national borders may have on these processes. In fact, they differ sharply in that Fayerweather appears to view business as a process while Boddewyn views it as an institution (or, perhaps more correctly, an outcome of a process).

At the same time, Boddewyn's definition differs from that of Wilkins by asserting that IB is not limited to the firm. In his view, the domain of IB encompasses many levels of analysis and integration that ultimately must contribute to a better understanding of firm-level behavior. As he points out, "Dunning's eclectic paradigm [1988a] already integrates the firm (ownership advantages), industry (internalization advantage) and nation (locational advantage) levels" [p. 60].

In the third paper, Toyne explores which of four schools of thought discriminate between business and IB by raising unique or distinct questions about the latter. For strictly explicative purposes, he classified these four schools of thought as substantialism, extensionalism, universalism, and resolutionalism, and uses them to demonstrate how different orientations and paradigms influence our view of reality, and thus the questions we ask of this reality. Extensionalism and resolutionalism have as their underpinnings the extension/cross-border management paradigms and the multi-level, emerging interaction paradigm discussed in chapter 1, respectively. Substantialism, on the other hand, refers to either applied research (i.e., the application of knowledge to solve important problems) or a research agenda that is developed as a consequence of practice. Finally, universalism refers to the paradigm that assumes human beings are subject to universal laws.

He concludes that while all four schools of thought contribute importantly to the body of IB knowledge, only resolutionalism contributes uniquely. Three reasons are presented for this conclusion. First, the emerging interaction paradigm is fundamentally different from those guiding research in other fields of business inquiry. Second, the findings and contributions gained as a consequence of resolutionism contribute in a meaningful and significant way to the body of business knowledge. Finally, these same findings and contributions also have pragmatic value.

Schollhammer makes several points in his commentary of the three topic papers that are certainly worthy of note. First, he describes Wilkins's approach to delineating the IB domain as "institutional." He then notes that Boddewyn postulates that the configuration of a domain ought to be based on theoretical constructs, and describes Boddewyn's delineating approach as a "transaction/process." Finally, he views Toyne's approach "as fluid, multifaceted and dependent on the existence of meta-level theoretical constructs" [p. 78].

Schollhammer also identifies several shortcomings in each paper. For example, he notes that Wilkins specifies no constraints or boundary conditions for IB as a domain of inquiry, and excludes all IB activities that do not require foreign-based assets. In the case of Boddewyn, he questions the advisability of using a series of definitions as the means for formulating a conceptualization of the IB domain, and his failure to relate these definitions to existing theoretical constructs. Finally, contrary to what he observed earlier, he sees in Toyne's elaborations a zealous effort to departmentalize a very complex, multifaceted set of issues into separate, exclusive compartments. However, unlike Behrman's conclusions, to be discussed next, Schollhammer finishes on

a positive note by stating that the diversity of views and the existence of competing theories of IB are clear indicators of a healthy development of the discipline.

In his discussion of the three topic papers, Behrman takes a different tact by suggesting that what he missed in the three topic papers was a careful assessment of those areas of inquiry of interest to the "stakeholders" in IB. As he puts it, to exclude these stakeholders will make "any recommendations coming out of IB inquiry irrelevant or vapid" [p. 83]. Moreover, the domain of IB is essentially undefinable, since to do so will inject significant potential error from the standpoint of one or more of the major players.

Essentially, Behrman is troubled by any attempt that artificially limits or reduces IB inquiry. That is, like Hogner (see chapter 3), Behrman would like to see IB re-embedded in a societal context—two views that are in agreements with the position taken in chapter 1. In Behrman's view, "if IB is not a *policy* discipline, it is irrelevant" [p. 86]. Thus, Wilkins's economic-driven, firm-level definition lacks relevance for corporate or governmental practitioners of policy. He further argues that Boddewyn's definition of the domain of IB is based on a set of assumptions regarding the behavior of firms that cannot be found in "reality." Thus, Boddewyn's definition "begins with a nonentity and remains unrealistic throughout the paper because of this unnecessary constraint" [p. 85]. Finally, Toyne's approach is "academic 'scoping' based on highly suspect distinctions, as far as policy/practice is concerned" [p. 86].

In his critique of the papers by Wilkins, Boddewyn, and Toyne, and the commentaries by Schollhammer and Behrman, Hench notes in his opening remarks that the IB domain question can only be fully appreciated within the broader undercurrent of debate that is currently "raging" in both the social and the physical sciences. The question of domain, he argues, must be answered within a Newtonian, Relativity,

Quantum Mechanics, and Chaos Theory context and our growing ability to examine more complex abstractions because of the tools we have developed and use. He further argues that there is sufficient evidence to suggest that the three lead authors and two commentators are, to some extent, mixing their paradigms. Perhaps it would be more accurate to say that they are simultaneously attempting to hold fast in what is familiar (e.g., the deterministic and reductionistic extension and cross-border management paradigms discussed in chapter 1) while seeking a more holistic understanding of a world that has become more diverse, complex, and ambiguous.

Hench continues by discussing the various paradigms underpinning the three topic papers and two commentaries. For example, he suggests that Wilkins's paradigm reflects the "quintessential Newtonian 'mechanical' approach to domain construction. Boddewyn's paradigm, while aligned with the traditional Newtonian-based paradigms of business and management, introduces a number of anomalies that seriously challenge the very viability of those paradigms (e.g., our inability to draw nicely defined boundaries around the phenomena of interest, and the possibility of multiple "best ways" of doing things). In the case of Toyne, Hench believes that his paradigm appears to be more reflective of contemporary science (i.e., human beings modify their thinking, reasoning, and behavior as a consequence of learning) since it is emergent.

With regards to the two commentaries, Hench suggests that Schollhammer and Toyne are not so far apart as Schollhammer apparently believes. He notes, for example, that Schollhammer began his critique by reaffirming his belief in the need for any academic discipline to delineate its domain and specify its boundary conditions, and then takes Toyne to task for doing so.

Hench also suggests that Schollhammer appears to be missing the essential point that the complexity and diversity he discusses might be the harbinger of a new paradigm. As for Behrman, Hench suggests that, with the exception of Toyne, he came closest to reflecting the principles of the emerging paradigm. By eschewing reliances on the traditional discipline of economics as the conceptual foundation of IB, Hench suggests Behrman presents a compelling argument for a holistic view of the reality of IB.

Overall, these papers illustrate very well the need for new and more clearly defined paradigms for the field of IB, a clearer articulation of the assumptions that each paradigm makes, and more consistent terminology in the field. In this regard, we suggest that the three paradigms introduced in chapter 1 are a good start in this direction.

A review of the three topic papers, and three commentaries as a group raises additional issues and questions that go beyond those suggested by the papers individually. First, there appears to be general agreement that IB is a distinct, if not unique domain of inquiry. As acknowledged by Schollhammer and argued by Boddewyn, Toyne, and Hench, there also appears to be a shift occurring in the way business in general and IB in particular are viewed and examined.

Second, the conflicting views presented by the topic authors and commentators suggest that there is considerable room for more dialogue, a dialogue that without question would be both constructive and salutary. Such dialogue should be welcomed since the failure to understand or communicate is evidenced in the need for rejoinders by Wilkins, Boddewyn, and Toyne. Although, as Hench asserts, the failure to communicate can be attributed, at least in part, to the mixing of paradigms, it might also be a consequence of unwittingly mixing levels of abstraction.

The Conceptual Domain of International Business
Mira Wilkins

I

Books and articles on international business (IB) now number in the thousands, if not tens of thousands. In arts and sciences faculties, economists, sociologists, political scientists, historians, geographers, psychologists, and philosophers have provided and continue to dispense offerings. Art historians and English professors feel free to comment on how major corporations "exploit."[1] Law professors have, on a more scholarly basis, made major contributions to the literature. Practically every business school in this country (and many abroad) has one, if not several, specialists in IB (some institutions have many more such experts).

Employees of domestic and international governmental agencies, as well as of "think tanks," churn out descriptive and prescriptive documents. The *Journal of International Business Studies* (*JIBS*), the *CTC Reporter* (in 1991 renamed *Transnational Corporations: A Journal of the United Nations Centre on Transnational Corporations*), and a coterie of added serials monitor the writings and contribute to enlarging the total. Professional associations, including the Academy of International Business and a myriad of others, hold lengthy discussions on a multitude of aspects of IB. There is a growing second- (and even third-) generation of scholarship, explaining what has been said in times past; there are reprint series containing important articles. It is little wonder that confusion exists on what is (and should be) the sphere of IB studies. Thus, the conference that Brian Toyne and Doug Nigh convened came at an appropriate juncture.

My paper is not another one reporting or analyzing what has been said and written. Instead, I offer a very personal perspective on where we are and where we should be going. What are the fundamental conceptual issues in the field of International Business at the start of the 1990s? What ought to be the domain of IB?

My perspective emerges from the vantage point of over three decades of research; I feel as though I have grown up with the controversies and debates on IB, and in the course of doing so I have formed strong and perhaps, some will think, dogmatic opinions that I want to share with you herein.[2] This essay, to repeat, takes an unequivocal position on what the field of IB should contain. Since my views are shaped by my own experience, and since with the immense growth of the field that vantage point may not be well known, I am taking the liberty herein to combine a little bit of autobiography with my argument.

My interest in IB began in the late 1950s and my first book on the subject was published shortly afterwards [Wilkins and Hill 1964]. What got me involved was a sense that this was a significant subject—significant in the light that it cast for an understanding of the world in the twentieth century. I have never swayed from this belief.

In the late 1950s, I went to Detroit as a research associate for Allan Nevins's project on Ford Motor Company history. In the course of my study, I came across an extraordinary collection of documents in the Ford Motor Company archives on its worldwide operations. In its domestic business a great many matters were accomplished in conversation, orally. Before the jet airplane and the international telephone, however, in IB most strategic decisions and the process by which they were made were written down. Travelers would write to their superiors at home. Subsidiary heads would send reports and in their letters ask questions about basic concerns; crucial topics would be examined in correspondence; directives and suggestions would go from home office to managers abroad. In the

Ford files in Dearborn (and then later in Ford files in countries around the world) I found rich evidence on how one large and major business operated internationally. Ford's sixth car built was exported. In its second year of existence (1904), Ford made a direct investment in manufacturing abroad. Subsequently, the company expanded worldwide. In its archives was a record of the economic and political history of the world in the twentieth century from the view of one company that wanted to make and sell automobiles. The available data were remarkable.

As I read this material in the Ford Archives, I wanted a conceptual foundation. I wanted theory. Was Ford Motor Company typical or atypical? I read everything I could find that seemed relevant. There was a huge literature on international capital flows, yet it was unsatisfactory for my purposes because it was not institutional. It did not deal with *company* behavior. There was also a great deal available on combines and cartels. This was useful, but was so concerned with competitive structures that it ignored what was happening inside firms; moreover, it took for granted that business behavior was motivated by anticompetitive aims. There was a Marxian literature on companies, imperialism, and exploitation. It assumed foreign investment was stimulated by capital surpluses; that business and home country politics always went in tandem. None of these books and articles coincided with anything that I was uncovering in the Ford Motor Company archives.

In addition, there was a long-standing body of writings on foreign direct investments. Initially in connection with balance of payments compilations in the 1920s, and subsequently, independently of balance of payments calculations (albeit reconciled to them), the U.S. Department of Commerce had assembled, and continues to this day to gather, materials on foreign direct investments. In the 1920s and 1930s, a number of books had dealt with the nature of business investments over borders. These were help-ful, but they were not based on company records.

In reading all this material and in my archival research, I had begun to define the field of IB in terms of the dynamics of the individual firm. I continue to do so today. I do recognize that others may wish to include in the subject the world of business, the international economy, and the political and social environment faced by the international firm. These topics are highly germane (a company does not operate in a vacuum), but over the years it has seemed to me that what research on IB must consider first and foremost (and what is our unique contribution) is the study of enterprise: the international-multinational-transnational-global business-enterprise-firm-company-corporation. (As is now common in the literature, I use the words international, multinational, transnational, and global interchangeably and the words business, enterprise, firm, company, and corporation interchangeably as the second part of the clause.)

As I studied the histories of firms, the importance of the evolution of their strategies became apparent. Over time firms change; many grow; some merge and/or acquire other firms; some fall by the wayside. Firms enter and exit from particular home and host countries (and particular functional activities and product lines). Early in my thinking about IB, I realized that for a full understanding of business activity at any point of time, the firm must be seen as an evolving entity, a dynamic unit. It is impossible to understand today's complex multinational enterprises (MNEs) without a knowledge of their background.

To return, to my inquiries from the late 1950s and early 1960s: I discovered then that it was not only economists who had dealt with the firm over borders. Historians, political scientists, and what were once called by the more general name "social scientists" had written at length on "imperialism;" on bankers and diplomacy; and more specifically on such topics as United Fruit's corruption of local governments in Central

America. The influence of Hobson's and Lenin's volumes on imperialism and Hilferding's work on finance capitalism was substantial—although more on historians, and political and social scientists than on economists or business school professors. I was surprised a few years ago when a prominent economist—who will remain unnamed—commented on the absence of a lengthy literature on business and government relationships and proposed a volume of selections from *Foreign Relations of the United States*, dealing with the long history of business-government interactions. *Foreign Relations of the United States* is a serial publication of U.S. State Department correspondence; every specialist in American diplomatic history has used this basic source; diplomatic historians—long before the late 1950s—had tapped it to comment on IB relationships.

In the 1950s, there appeared some excellent archive-based histories of particular MNEs (the first two volumes of the history of the Standard Oil Company [New Jersey] were published in 1955 and 1956). While I found them of immense value, these (and other) business histories did not reach beyond the role of the individual firm. They failed to generalize.

When I read the books and articles on IB that were written before 1959, I discovered a gold mine in the contributions of legal scholars. Their work provided numerous insights on international law, international diplomacy, and antitrust matters. By the early 1960s, many more individuals were becoming interested in IB. In 1962 I embarked on a study of the history of American business abroad—motivated by my desire to obtain a more general context for what I had been finding in the specific case of Ford Motor Company.[3] Charles Stewart and George B. Simmons [1964] compiled a 600 page bibliography of writings on IB.

The approach of Stewart and Simmons was comprehensive. They dealt in turn with comparative business systems; government and international operations; and the firm in international operations (which included

parts on industrial organization, business organization, sociological and psychological aspects, U.S. management abroad, comparative management, direct foreign investment, labor-general, etc.), and finally there was a section on nations and regions. There was no heading on the theory of the international firm—for in the early 1960s there was no available theory of the international firm. Most of the articles and books that Stewart and Simmons included had been published in the 1950s and 1960s.

What is important is that all through the twentieth century the role of business over borders, of IB (as I am now defining it), has been a subject for academic attention in the United States and in Europe. Life by no means began with Stephen Hymer.[4] I was convinced by the early 1960s that MNEs were neither unique in the post-World War II years nor was the literature about them new to such recent times.

Yet, the questions that scholars have been asking in the last three decades (1960–1992) are novel. The answers found also are fresh. The literature that is available now is far different, far more enriching, far more helpful to understanding, than the scholarship existing at the end of the 1950s, when I first embarked on my studies, or in 1964, when the Stewart and Simmons volume was published.

This notwithstanding, British historian D. K. Fieldhouse wrote, "by the early 1980s . . . it was now widely, if not universally, accepted that Multinational is merely shorthand for a wide range of capitalist enterprises which share only one common and non-definitive feature: that beyond there is fundamental diversity camouflaged under an umbrella term" [1986:26]. Brian Toyne [1988], in what he calls a "maverick's view," agreed; "IB lacks a fundamental, comprehensive, and unifying construct."

Both of these statements sadden me. I could not disagree more. I do not believe that with all the writings of the last three decades (and all that prior to the last thirty years) that the field has developed no basic tools for understanding, has made no conceptual advances, and that there is really no field at all. I want to take on these assertions and ask, where are we now? What do we know that we did not know three decades ago? Is there a fundamental, comprehensive, unifying construct? Do we have a field—or are we talking about "fundamental diversity camouflaged under an umbrella term?" I believe there is a definable field, a body of knowledge that constitutes a discipline.

Recently, at the start of an article published in *JIBS*, Peter Buckley began by stating: "It is now generally agreed that an established theory of multinational enterprise exists" [1990:657]. He cites his own work to substantiate this. Likewise, Christos Pitelis and Roger Sugden, in an introduction to their new book take for granted that there is a theory of MNE universally accepted that they believe should be modified; they write that new work "may no longer justify total reliance on a transaction costs explanation of the transnational corporation" [1991:11]. Thus, Buckley's view and that of Pitelis and Sugden contrasts sharply with that of Fieldhouse and Toyne. I do not share with Buckley the exact dimensions of what the "established theory"of MNE is, nor do I believe that a transaction costs explanation of MNE behavior has totally suppressed all other theoretical approaches. I do concur that the literature today contains many of the basic ingredients for understanding and analyzing the multinational firm and for such a core theory.[5]

II

What are those ingredients? What exactly should we be looking at as we define the conceptual domain of IB? It is not a neat, formal scientific theory that we should be seeking when we discuss this subject; we will never find that; the material is too complex to be straitjacketed into highly formalized models. Instead, we need to define the "field" and thereby establish a construct that provides a core of explanations. We can begin with the question "What is a field?"

A field, I would suggest, is an arena that provides understanding of materials within defined parameters—whether broad or narrow. History is a field. A historian studies history. Particular historians study ancient history; within that subdiscipline, a historian might study the monetary policies of ancient Rome. Each constitutes a field, one broad, the other two increasingly narrower. Similarly, economics is a field. Economists share a broad knowledge of economics. Particular economists study macroeconomics. Within that subset, economists might specialize in money and banking. In my view, the field of IB is a subset of the study and analysis of business enterprise; it must be linked with a viable and rich theory of the firm.

If we are seeking to comprehend IB, we should not roam into diversions and study a dozen other related and tangential matters for their own sake, because they are somehow vaguely relevant. Rather, we should concentrate on the nature and the dynamics of business as an institution as it moves and operates over borders. The dictionary definition of institution is: "an organization . . . devoted to the promotion of a particular object . . . ." I have no problem with this definition. Business is devoted to the object of producing goods and/or services, with the aim of making profits. If we study the business, our inquiry has focus.

I am totally convinced that a MNE is the same as any business enterprise *except* that it operates under more than one national sovereignty. Thus, a student of IB must know everything that a pupil of domestic business learns in terms of the growth of, the management of, and the strategies and structures of the firm, the markets of the firm, as well as the rules of local, state, and national governments.

If we are examining U.S.-headquartered businesses, we are used to dealing with firms that expect to make profits; with state enterprises in other countries sometimes profits are not anticipated. The firm we are investigating is our starting point. We want to know what its strategies are. We want to know how it is organized. We want to know the market or markets it seeks to serve.

To study firms in different countries is *not* in my mind what the field of IB is all about. Instead, the consideration should be of the *firm that extends over borders*. To explain such an enterprise, the researcher on IB must know more than the student of a purely domestic entity.

As a firm moves over national frontiers, to reach new markets, to find new sources of supplies, to extend existing operations, to add to its revenues and to its bottom line (in the most typical case), it encounters materially different circumstances from the purely domestic firm, circumstances that influence its destiny. It is affected by what it faces and often, in turn, influences the locality and at times even the foreign country in which it does business. In this context, and more specifically, an IB is different from a domestic one in that under most circumstances it meets with a higher level of uncertainty, based on its operating under the jurisdiction of more than one national government. Often the point is made that unlike the domestic firm it encounters different cultures. That is not necessarily the case (the cultural identity between Detroit, Michigan, and Windsor, Canada—a short drive across the river—is surely closer than the cultural links between Detroit and Miami). Yet, the notion of culture can be subsumed under the rubric of uncertainties. Indeed, as business moves farther afield internationally, the cultural gap does widen; uncertainty increases. The costs of information rise.

Another crucial matter is that IB requires operating under more than one currency regime (and currency again is a function of government). To do business under more than one currency alters strategic activities.[6]

The core of what we ought to accept is that the complex modern firm is the basic starting point of study in the field of IB and that operating under different national sovereignties creates special problems, the most fundamental *general* ones being a higher level of uncertainty and the variety in currencies.

Today's firms that we investigate are typically multiplant, multifunctional, multiproduct, multidivisional enterprises. They have a background of experiences. Decision making in the firm is never isolated; it is made in the context of both past and present practices. The essential contribution of business history to the discipline of IB is twofold. First, it provides context. Are present day events new or do they have precedents? As I look at the contemporary literature, I read about "new forms"—contracts, joint-ventures, interlocking strategic interrelationships—and I am appalled at how little history such commentators know. The second contribution of business history is even more important. Business history teaches us that a theory of the firm must provide a dynamic frame of reference, to show transitions, evolution, background, growth, and contraction, and to indicate how decision making takes shape over time, that learning occurs. It is impossible to understand domestic or international business today without knowledge of process, change, and complexity. A theory of MNE must be dynamic and cumulative. Yet, it cannot be linear. Because of uncertainty, the future will not follow in a straight line from the past. Indeed, the study of business history shows the uneven path. A satisfactory theoretical framework covering IB activity has to take into account that while every decision (each transaction) is discrete, where the decision lies in a sequence of prior ones is of profound importance.

A theory of MNE is *not* the same as a theory of foreign direct investment (FDI). This equation has caused immense confusion. A theory of MNE, an understanding of the MNC, comprises knowledge of the behavior of the entire firm—not merely its activities as a maker of investments. It is legitimate to define a MNE as a firm that operates over borders, i.e., makes direct investments. Once we have done that, we must go on with a deeper scrutiny. The MNE transmits over borders a package of attributes; direct investments are only one of these.

FDIs set the minimum requirements; they separate a firm that operates in one country from one that operates outside its headquarters country. Once a firm has moved over borders, made a direct investment (no matter how small), I want then to view the evolution of its many types of activities abroad. Some activities will enlarge its direct investments and others will involve strategies that do not require the firm itself to extend more extensively over national frontiers.

The growth and seasoning of a MNE cannot be understood without a broad interdisciplinary background. While I argue that we must narrow the core to the study of the firm over borders, this narrowing, while highly focused, still calls on insights and research from many different traditional disciplines.

When we deal with the firms' operations over border, and after we have established our core focus, we want to ask: which firms expand over borders; why, where, when, and how does a firm expand (or contract) internationally? In the process of answering these queries, we can respond to a large number of additional ones. The literature on IB of the last several decades (including the sizable amount published on the history of IB) gives us a frame of reference to answer these questions. When I read my daily newspaper and learn of the multinational expansion of particular firms in particular places, or the retreats from IB, I feel very comfortable that I can in broad terms explain the strategies. When colleagues and students (and journalists and government officials) ask me why an individual MNE would follow a particular strategy, or about the location chosen for a new investment, or about the timing of a decision, or whether the approach that the MNE took was typical or atypical, I believe that my readings in the field, especially those works written in the past thirty years, provide me a basis for replying to the questions superior to others who have not read as much in the field.

Do I accept a grand general theory of IB? Do I think that internalization or trans-action cost theory offer the final answers? My response may seem unsatisfactory to many of you, but I am content with it. The function of theory is to provide understanding, to give a framework for analysis. If we have approaches that improve our understanding, we have something highly rewarding. Internalization and transaction cost theories do help explain many facets of IB behavior. They may not (in their present state) aid us in discerning all aspects. As stated earlier, I think a neat, mathematically perfect model is impossible to find. Instead, I favor first and foremost a theoretical structure that incorporates a view of the firm as an evolving entity and looks at process, a theory that is dynamic, since it seems to me that past conditioning must be taken into account.[7] Economists are discussing at length path dependency;[8] I would like to see such an approach incorporated into an economic theory of the multinational firm. Recently, the phrase has been repeated (and used in a book title) "the past as a foreign country." Perhaps, students of IB might think about the past in those terms—although I do not want to take the parallel too far (since the past is known, or can be known and established), while in foreign countries of the present there is much that takes place that is unanticipated and cannot be determined before it occurs.

Leaving that aside, too often economic theory, in the interest of elegance (or purely by neglect), has lacked dynamism. In the papers that follow in the course of this conference, we will hear about economic theories of MNE (you will hear about the applications of industrial organization theory, game theory, networking, about internalization, about transaction costs, about the eclectic paradigm; you may hear about Schumpeterian applications, about entrepreneurial behavior within the firm). I do not want to repeat in this opening paper what you will get from others' presentations and in other panel sessions. What I do want to argue is that for any theory of MNE to contribute to the field, it must concentrate on the firm *per se* and must be dynamic; be an economic theory since we are dealing with an institution that operates in this sphere of endeavor; and correspond to and give us help in explaining an evolving entity that functions in a world where change is the norm. It must be a theory tailored to the particulars of MNE, not a grafting activity.[9] Often, however, new developments in economics can be (and should be) appropriately incorporated into theories of multinational behavior.[10] To the extent that research and theory enrich our understanding and our analysis, they are of great merit.

The heart of our discipline, what we want to teach our students, is an approach to, a means of understanding, one of the most significant institutions in today's world. We can debate at length on the "power" of the multinational, but it seems undebatable that this entity is (and I believe will continue to be in the twenty-first century) a vital institution in the world economy. We want to teach our students what is behind the international expansion (or contraction) of business enterprise—the which, why, where, when, and how of the story. We want our students to understand which companies participate in IB, why a business enterprise exists, where the firm chooses to expand, what options it has (and when it adopts those options) in expanding or not expanding, and how its management goes about making strategic decisions. The literature of the past thirty years has provided us the basis for systematic responses on these matters. Given the present day world, we want a theory of the firm that comprises the international firm as the general case and the domestic one as the specific case (see Casson [1987:1] and the work of Alfred Chandler [1977, 1990]).

Our approach to theory cannot be one that merely looks at the firm as a set of inputs and outputs. It has to look at the enterprise as a governance structure. As we study why decisions are made and carried out we must consider what happens within the firm as well as in the firm's relationships to external markets. We will have to make assumptions, simplify, yet ultimately we must relax our assumptions and be sure that our theoretical structure corresponds to the realities at hand.

What then specifically have we learned over the past three decades? What exactly is the progress we have made toward such an understanding? First, we know something about which firms engage in business over borders. Most experts in the field have come to recognize that not all firms expand internationally; most of us accept the proposition that in order to succeed abroad, because the firm is extending its internal governance and thereby acquiring new costs, a business must have some advantage in international activities. Moreover, once abroad, the firm faces new uncertainties that are presumably higher than those of firms already established in the host country; such inherent disadvantages must be offset by the MNE's advantage(s).

While the advantage that the MNE has can be capital, much more often it lies elsewhere—in the firm's technology and name recognition, in its products and processes, in the existence of internalization *itself*, in the resulting economies of scale and scope, in the generalized and functional managerial experience—or more likely, in a combination of these frequently inseparable aspects of the large modern enterprise. Given the acceptance of the idea of advantage, we can explore the types of advantages that a MNE might have. We have learned that such advantages may differ from one nation's firms to another and may not be sustained over time. A scrutiny of advantages helps us to understand which firms invest abroad and more important, which continue to be active abroad. A firm may perceive that it has advantage and yet not, in fact, have that advantage and not succeed.

We know that if a firm moves abroad and is to be competitive abroad, it must maintain its advantage or assume new advantages. Recent work by Professor Tetsuo Abo [1994] on the application-adaptation paradigm opens up a new way of thinking about multinational enterprise. If a firm is to be successful abroad, clearly it must come to terms with conditions in the host country; but if it adapts too much, it might dissipate its advantage. This is a fascinating insight.[11]

We have also learned that it is not useful to talk in the old-fashioned language of the world of antitrust that assumed all business enterprises were out to eliminate competition (and collude). Nor do we want to see the MNE as merely an allocator of capital; this is but one of the firm's functions. Mark Casson [1990] has pointed out recently that the orientation of much of the current literature has been on the firm as a mover of technology. What seems to me to be even more important is that businesses carry over borders a "package" including capital, technology, products, processes, marketing methods, administrative procedures, management, and so forth. All of these have to be perceived in the context of the individual firm and its advantages. The trade mark is a particularly important advantage (see Wilkins [1992, 1994c].

Depending on how we define "technology," it is legitimate or illegitimate to concentrate on technology. If it is defined in strictly hardware terms (new inventions translated into viable products and processes), then a technological approach has limitations. On the other hand, it can be defined to embrace "social technology" including management methods. Broadly defined, the package of attributes transmitted might be viewed in terms of technology transfer. What is crucial is to study the entire firm as it extends over borders (and see advantages within the context of such an enterprise).

I find myself impressed with the new literature that sees the large scale firm as an economizing rather than a monopolizing unit. This is not to say that all large firms are more efficient than smaller ones; it is to say that by definition (with rare exceptions) the firm that carries on business over borders must be larger than the firm that serves a single local market.[12] Firms that can ben-

efit from economies of scale and scope have advantages in doing business over borders.

If we view the large firm as an economizing unit, this presses us to look specifically at the ways by which the firm is able to create efficiencies (and its solutions to inherent inefficiencies of extended governance); it makes us pay attention to the management of resources. If we recognize that the firm is not able to sustain a move over borders unless it has some advantage, we can look at that advantage as predatory, or alternatively in terms of efficiencies. The latter has seemed a more fruitful approach. The application-adaptation paradigm of Professor Abo then takes on more meaning.[13]

Part of the answer to questions on which firms extend over borders must lie in which firms have had success in international activities. Presumably, firms that find international endeavors to be "good business" will persist in their business abroad, enlarging their activities.

Advantages, to repeat, can change over time. They are relative to the particular host country in which the entry and expansion are undertaken; are always linked with opportunities abroad; and always must be weighed against the disadvantages of extending the firm.

By definition, a MNE operates in different countries; countries are governed and so a good theory of MNEs must deal with the firm's relationships within a sovereign state. The literature has, it seems to me, moved away from the naive beliefs inherent in the earlier political science writings that multinationals must be either instruments of the state (home or host) or directors of the state (home or host) policy, or that they totally transcend governments (in either a benign or a malign manner) to a more complex and realistic evaluation of business and governmental actors with different goals that may overlap or may conflict under different circumstances and in different times. Sovereignty can be at bay for short periods, but the norm of today (and of times past) is that the enterprise conforms to the requirements of sovereign state policies.[14] In discussions of the interactions between the MNE and governments, the bargaining model has been developed and has proved a fruitful way of looking at many of the relationships (see Behrman and Grosse [1990]).

Sometimes, however, the bargaining model is deficient since it assumes the existence and need for firm-government bargaining. This may not be the case. The student of MNE should see the firm as an independent actor; in certain of its decisions and operations it has little contact with governments (and merely pays taxes and conforms to host state laws). In others, these contacts are extensive. Particular kinds of firms in particular countries in particular types of activities will have more or less government contact. A knowledge of which firms interact in which ways is part of the understanding of IB. Likewise, relationships between the MNE and governments are better understood when the reason multinationals make direct investments is known.

When we turn to analyze why a firm extends over borders, we can identify particular motivations—to reach markets and to obtain sources of supply. Yet, this reveals nothing about the precipitating motive(s), nor about where the investment is made, or when it is made, or how it is made. We know that firms can invest to obtain markets based on purely economic considerations (opportunities, competitor's behavior, etc.) or based on politically created causes (state-erected barriers to trade, for example). We also are aware that a firm can find similar sources of supply in different locales and that it can buy from outsiders or produce itself (i.e., make an investment).

I believe that an economic theory of the firm that helps answer questions about why, where, when, and how, must form the basis for our discussions and for an introduction for students to IB. To repeat, we have to turn to an *economic* theory of the firm, because we are dealing with an institution that is an economic entity—that carries on fundamental economic activities. The economist, however, must incorporate in the theory constraints on choices (bounded rationality) that are based not only on (external) market considerations and internal governance constraints but also on governmental actions. There is no reason why this is not possible. The modern economist recognizes uncertainties and lack of full information. Even in elementary economic classes, we talk about government as an important actor in the economic system. A firm's choices are molded by households, by considerations internal to the firm, and in many instances by governmental actions. Insights of organizational behavior theorists, political scientists, and business school professors (in dealing with bargaining), as well as from public choice economics, can enrich the economic theory of the firm.

I do not believe it is always appropriate to separate the political from the economic in providing an analytic framework. Political actions create economic costs and benefits. A decision maker in a firm makes choices and evaluations. Tariff and nontariff barriers to trade are often spurs to specific investment strategies of multinationals. The political action of governments in raising barriers to trade creates economic costs. Likewise, if a manager perceives an unfriendly government (or the possibility of expropriation), those political considerations can be easily translated into true economic costs. A decision not to invest based on such rationales is both political and economic. An economic theory of the firm must take into account such circumstances.

While the field of business and politics is far from new, in the last few decades the work of political scientists on bargaining interactions and of public choice economists on the nature of governmental decision making, pushes us to see the state as complex. Thus, as we analyze business and state relationships, we are dealing with two multiunit institutional structures. Business in its domestic and international relations does not interact with a single government national policy but rather with a range of policies from multiunit governments—policies that furthermore alter over time.

Where a firm invests can be explained in terms of economic opportunities, the standard battery of considerations that location theories offer, in some cases by "follow the leader strategies," but also in terms of the uncertainties that are created by operating under any particular sovereign government. A company that sees opportunities in many places may, because of politically created economic conditions (blocked remittances, for example), not be in a position to gain from an investment. Transaction cost theories suggest that *ceteris paribus* firms will invest in more familiar over less familiar locations (familiarity, information, ease in negotiations, lowers the costs of uncertainties) and firms will have better success in familiar over less familiar locations. Business history, however, teaches us that "perceptions" of familiarity may not correspond to the realities of familiarity.[15]

MNEs may find opportunities in one place and time, but not in another. A theory of MNEs must not only deal with which firms go, why they go, and where they go abroad, but also with the matter of timing. When a firm makes investments, they can vary based on circumstances within and exterior to the firm. The behavior of competitors can influence investment timing. A construct that aids us in understanding the nature of the MNE recognizes that the expansion of firms is not inevitable; a firm does not expand everywhere and certainly not all at once; there is sequence and priorities; understanding of the core firm, its past experience, learning processes, and present milieu help explain its activities. Early choices often serve to explain subsequent strategies. Patterns that evolve *within a firm* affect the future paths taken. Likewise, the theorist must never forget that the world changes so external opportunities must be there (there must be real choices) for any firm to make choices.

The work of the past decades has helped us to understand what companies can do and what they cannot do, what they will do and what is very unlikely. Likewise, the literature has helped explain the "how."

Firms have options not only in making decisions to expand or not to expand, and where and when to expand, but in the methods and means—and with which product lines. By methods and means we are talking about greenfield operations and joint-ventures, about acquisitions, about sources of finance (within the company, external to the company—at home, in the host country, or in a third country), about partial alliances, about licensing, about numerous possible approaches to an opportunity.

Once the core of a firm's behavior has been understood then a variety of other related subjects seem appropriate in an IB program. Too often, the field of IB has a need to gather in all related subjects; I think this is part of the immaturity of the *field in the business school curriculum*. We should not be presenting students with a "grab bag" assortment of knowledge. Most IB textbooks, for example, begin with a discussion of Heckscher-Ohlin and comparative advantage. Why? Because some of our best students of multinationals learned that when getting their Ph.D.s; it was part of the baggage that they brought to the discipline. Now is the time to cast this off. IB must begin with the firm and what we know about it. We must concentrate on providing answers to the fundamental questions of the growth and characteristics of the modern MNE.

Industrial organization theorists pushed us to look at industry structures. This did *at one time*, I would suggest, form a highly valuable building block in our knowledge. It became clear that there were certain behavior patterns that were industry-specific, "advantages" that were associated with certain industries. Yet, I would argue that the firm-oriented approach is far superior to the industry one. This means that if we begin with the firm, we can ask of that firm what facets of its behavior are common to the industry in which it is engaged, always recognizing that many of our modern firms produce products in many industries. Assuming we can legitimately classify a firm into a particular industry category, it is clear firms in a specified industry have in the past behaved in their international businesses in entirely different manners. An approach based on the development of the firm, its past history and experience, accepts that as a given. If we have a core theory of the firm, there is no mystery in the fact that while Ford and General Motors both developed vast international operations, there were substantial differences in the specific ways that these two automobile companies did business abroad. On another level, however, Ford, General Motors, Toyota, and Renault may have more in common in their international pursuits than they have with small American, Japanese, and French furniture makers. In short, we begin with the firm, albeit we enrich our knowledge of firm behavior by using more generalized research.

Likewise, advantages change and advantages can relate to countries and periods. In studying American business abroad I was struck by the absence of expansion of textile firms; yet, in doing research on the history of British and Japanese companies abroad, many of their earliest MNEs were in textiles. A core concept of advantage makes this understandable.[16]

Similarly, students of the history of American business abroad find nothing comparable to the Canadian real estate firms that extended over borders. Here again, a flexible concept of MNE can explain the differences.[17]

If we accept that the MNE is a firm operating over borders, we do not have to deal (and indeed should not deal) only with manufacturing operations. Firms produce goods and services; the behavior of firms in providing services over borders lies within the core concept that we are studying.[18] We need to study all kinds of firms as multinationals, wherever we find the institution. Trading companies and banks as MNEs are important topics. Thus, it is legitimate to segregate and ask does the sector (manufacturing, trading, banking) make a difference—and in what manner?

Why do we need a core theory and a core concept? What does it add? Why not let the field remain an interdisciplinary collage of different approaches: economic theories, political science theories, comparative business structures, business and society studies, comparative cultural experiences, etc.—i.e., no field at all. The reason we need to aim for a real field, for a core theory and set of core concepts it seems to me is that we can do so and have made great progress in that direction, that there now does exist a fundamental basis for the understanding of one of the most important institutions of modern times, and that we do not need to offer a patchwork quilt.

III

I want to provide a baker's dozen of examples on how a core theory helps. The examples that follow are heterogeneous yet practical. They relate to business school students who will work for MNEs and to business school students who will be employed by home or host governments of multinationals. Some of these examples cover public policy questions. It seems to me that because IB programs have not yet adopted and not yet accepted a core of understanding, egregious errors have been made, particularly by those students who have been employed by governments that are hosts to multinationals. The education on the nature of, the history of, and the theory of MNE by students who have become policy makers in third world countries has been nothing short of dreadful. Because students are not taught about how the IB functions, because they have been provided undigested information shaped neither by sound empirical research nor by a dynamic core theory of how and why businesses operate over borders, there have been numerous misunderstandings.

Taxes. Do MNEs avoid taxes? If so, how? Is tax avoidance important to their behavior? If one understands the nature of decision making by multinationals and the rationales behind transfer pricing, the answers can help us design the right questions to deal with the specific issues at hand.

(Transfer pricing is necessary in large domestic as well as multinational firms; there is nothing nefarious about transfer pricing *per se*.) Discussions of strategies and structures of multinationals cast important light on how to evaluate tax and tax motivated behavior.

Attracting MNEs. The possibilities of a less-developed country government attracting a MNE. If a student is able to analyze the behavior of multinationals and has knowledge of what motivates strategies, the basis for its location decisions for example, it is possible to predict whether there is or is not a possibility of attracting a particular firm.

Cheap labor. Do most multinationals seek cheap labor? What makes labor cheap? An understanding of why a MNE invests abroad puts the many discussions of "cheap labor" in perspective.

Foreign direct investments. International investment, international finance, and international sources of capital can be channeled through the MNE. MNEs are not the only conduit for the transfer of international capital. Indeed, because of the lack of understanding of MNE there has been an immense confusion of MNE with other sources of foreign capital. Students with a core theory of MNE recognize the basis for such mix-ups and can explain that only one of the activities of the MNE is that of a mobilizer and allocator of capital. It is not merely a channel for capital flows across borders, but can turn domestic capital (through borrowings in the host country) to productive purposes. A holist theory of the firm recognizes that the institution has to be evaluated in terms that go far beyond the movement of capital to a host nation and the dividends and interest the firm sends abroad.

Technology transfer. Do MNEs serve to diffuse technology in the host country? Do they pluck technology from advanced countries, leaving the latter at a competitive disadvantage? We know now (from many studies) a great deal about multinationals and technology transfers. A student with a core knowledge of multinational behavior can make perceptive evaluations in responding to these questions—being careful of course to be sure how technology is defined.

Trade. What effect does MNE activity have on international trade? The effects are complex—and multidirectional. In the modern world a sizable proportion of international trade is now conducted by and within MNEs. No one today who discusses trade policy can afford not to be knowledgeable on the behavior patterns of MNEs.

Costs and benefits to the host and home countries of multinationals. If a national government (particularly in a host country) is aware of multinational firms' behavior, expectations on costs and benefits should be more realistic.

Efficacy of regulations. If a student knows the rationales behind multinational strategies and structures, he or she will as an employee of a MNE or of a government that is instituting the regulations be better able to evaluate the effectiveness of and the distortions induced by government interventions.

Efficacy of incentives. When will incentives work and when will they fail? A student who is aware of how MNEs make decisions will be able to judge government incentive programs.

Business and politics. If a student has a fundamental understanding of the dynamics of a MNE's motivations and activities and recognizes the economic and political constraints on its power, its political interactions become explicable and in a broad sense predictable.

Joint-ventures and strategic alliances. A theory of MNE helps explain when and why joint-ventures and strategic alliances are choices (or second-best alternatives) rather than 100% owned operations abroad, and when and why the firm often considers full control the more desirable choice. A MNE has many options; exports (or imports), licenses, joint-ventures, 100% ownership, and combinations thereof. Sometimes the options are real; sometimes they are not (because of limiting constraints). The student of MNEs has a good means of evaluating which approach will be chosen under which circumstances—in the vast majority of cases.

Rhetoric and reality. The student of MNEs, having learned a great deal about the nature of firms, will at the same time be in a position to know how often rhetoric about the multinational departs from reality.[19] The absence of a core of understanding about MNEs often becomes the reality of bad decision making (by governments and by multinational managers as well). Misinformation, unsupported rhetoric, frequently creates a reality that the student of multinationals should be able to understand.

Uncertainty. The student with a fundamental understanding of multinationals knows that linear analysis is faulty, uncertainty in both domestic and even more in IB is inevitable, surprises are to be expected, and what exists today will not exist in the exact same form tomorrow. Internal and external markets are imperfect. Transactions have costs—in particular, information costs. A student that takes into account the history of MNEs learns to expect and to anticipate uncertainties (even though because they are "uncertainties" they cannot by definition be specifically identified).

We are, in short, arguing in this paper that a core conceptual foundation on which, why, where, when, and how businesses operate over borders not only provides academic satisfaction, but has practical applications. The academic satisfaction lies in the attraction of comprehension. The practical application lies in the fact that training in IB, as suggested above, provides students with knowledge that can be employed later in their careers.

IV

I am arguing—to repeat—that the field of IB must begin with a study of the IB firm and its behavior. The core knowledge our students should have lies in the history of

and the present day strategies of business enterprises that extend themselves over borders. We are interested in the internal workings of the firm (the transactions within the firm) and its experiences as it encounters outsiders. The student needs not only descriptions but theoretical analysis. He or she needs to be able to extend descriptions to the more general case. Because what goes on within a firm is affected by what goes on in the world outside the firm, this approach while focused and integrated has a great deal of breadth. The student must know a great deal about world economic history to understand the decisions of managers of MNEs. Sometimes choices made within the firm and within the market are free to be made; sometimes the constraints preclude choice (and there is only a single viable response possible). The domain of IB must concentrate on the firm *per se*. It must define the phenomenon. In its definition it must recognize the multiplicity of relationships that a single firm has; the MNE not only makes direct investments but it exports, it enters into contracts, it engages in many different kinds of business arrangements. It has relations with many outsiders (suppliers, dealers, customers). The single construct that integrates the field of IB is the nature of the business firm and the wherewithal of its performance. Theory must focus on the firm as such and not muddy the waters with miscellany. We must concentrate on interpreting this highly important complex organization.

Has all the research been done in understanding the nature of the multinational firm? Not by any stretch of the imagination. A number of uncharted paths seem to me necessary to explore in order to enlarge and enrich the conceptual domain of IB. Let me present some of the matters that still puzzle me.

1. We live in world of fluctuating exchange rates. As a business historian, I have dealt with earlier periods of fluctuating exchange rates; I feel secure in explaining be-

havior when fluctuating exchange rates were exceptional, or when fluctuations were small. Today, fluctuating rates are the norm and the variations are substantial. Does this systematically affect the strategies of MNEs? If so, how? (What are the effects on the timing of initial investments, reinvested earnings, joint-ventures, trade versus investment decisions, licensing decisions, etc.). How do we take into account the many other factors that affect strategies, weighing these with the effects of exchange rate fluctuations? Are there legitimate generalizations on MNEs' responses? Robert Aliber has argued that when currencies are strong, direct investments increase; when weak, they slow. This seems too general. I was fascinated to see that Lipsey [1991], based on empirical evidence, has found that floating exchange rates have a systematic effect on trade within the firm. I find myself uncertain in trying to chart many of the other relationships between currency fluctuations and MNE behavior. Much more firm-specific research needs to be done.

2. Is there an investment equivalent to dumping? If Japanese firms manufacturing automobiles in the U.S. make no profits in their U.S. business (which seems to have been the case in the past few years), could this be interpreted as equivalent to dumping?

3. Much more systematic research needs to be done on firms from small countries compared with those from larger ones. There are clear differences in behavior patterns.

4. Are there systematic ways of looking at host countries and MNEs?[20]

5. One of the most important argu-

ments for the advantage of MNEs over arms' length relations is associated with the reduction of information and negotiating costs. We need more studies of the significance of such costs in decision making. Transaction cost theories of the firm become extremely helpful.

6. Today we are seeing MNEs that are holding companies. Firms such as Hanson PLC that trade in companies on an international scale need to be analyzed within the existing theories. What are such firms' advantages?

7. The modern world has immense complexities of strategic alliances, cooperation among giants. How do these compare with some of the past cartel relationships? What are the advantages and disadvantages of partial interconnections? Scholars of today's alliances need to do more historical analysis to evaluate these arrangements.

8. One of the truly open areas for research on multinationals is related to trade. In the early days, students of MNEs saw exports and investments as alternative strategies. It became clear that many firms that would have preferred to export made foreign direct investments in manufacturing abroad in order to reach particular markets (sometimes these decisions were precipitated by tariffs and other barriers to trade; sometimes they were based on transport costs, nearness to customers, and so forth).[21] The new questions are more complex. Firms make or buy some parts of a product abroad and import other parts. Trade in both final and intermediate products takes place within the firm. The nature of trade within the firm is now

open to scrutiny.[22] We still do not know exactly when firms internalize trade, when contractual relations are the norm, and when arms' length trade is appropriate. These activities have changed over time—even within particular industries. Thus, for many years major oil firms integrated crude oil extraction, transportation, refining, and marketing.[23]

When OPEC countries took over their national production activities, new contractual relationships evolved between the oil ompanies and their crude oil suppliers. At the same time, the amount of oil sold on spot markets increased dramatically. Slowly, a number of *producing countries' companies* (Kuwait Oil Company, the Venezuelan state oil company, for example) started to follow the pattern of the earlier MNEs, integrating forward into refining and marketing in the consuming countries. What are the economics of internalized trade in the oil industry? Will we see more integration (by host state firms) or more spot market transactions and why? To answer these questions, we need to know more about the economies involved in a multinational enterprise's vertical integration. We need to know what is the effect on world prices of internalized versus contracted versus spot transactions. When third world countries took over bauxite supplies once owned by multinationals, there have been suggestions that prices fell dramatically. Was this based on the nature of the institutional relationships or on other considerations? Students of MNE need to focus on the institutional structure of trade in commodities and differentiated products—and

where and how internalized trade fits into the evolution of international trade.

9. There need to be more studies of investments by MNEs for information and other strategic considerations.[24] Once we have defined a company as a MNE, i.e., if it has made any direct investments at all (no matter how small), then it is important to cover the entire spectrum of its activities—all of its strategic alliances. We should not be fettered to definitions of MNE that are too rigid or too constricting.

10. Domestically and internationally, one of the most important (in my view) new developments in the twentieth century is of "satellite firms." By satellite firms, I mean independent businesses that depend on giant enterprises for survival. They include parts suppliers, dealerships, gas stations; small firms that sell all their production on contract to Sears Roebuck; independent soft drink bottlers; and hotels that are franchised by a major hotel chain. In dealing with MNEs, it is important to consider when, how frequently, and why satellite firms are employed rather than internalized activities. Are the patterns the same domestically as internationally? My current reading of the core of MNE theory would suggest major similarities in pattern (albeit with some variations, for example, with the large firm encouraging its reliable domestic suppliers to follow it in multinational expansion).

11. Researchers need to pay more attention to the development of organizational structures: International divisions, product divisions, regional structures, grids. MNEs have become huge. In

1990, General Motors' 761,400 employees was more than double that of any other firm. Daimler-Benz had 376,785 employees; IBM, 373,816; Siemens, 373,000; Ford, 370,000; Unilever, 304,000; Fiat, 303,238; and Hitachi (the largest in terms of employment of the Japanese multinationals), 290,811. Is there an optimum size of employment? In past decades while sales of every one of these multinationals (except Fiat) had more than doubled and in one case (Daimler-Benz) more than tripled, and in another case (Hitachi) almost quadrupled, employment had grown far slower (and in the cases of Ford and Fiat had actually decreased): in 1980, GM had 746,000 employees; Daimler-Benz had 183,000; IBM, 341,000; Siemens, 344,000; Ford, 427,000; Unilever, 300,000; Fiat, 343,000; and Hitachi, 143,000.[25] How do firms manage such vast employee networks? How often are changes in organizational structures needed? What is the experience with particular forms of organization? In the 1990s, "restructuring" became even more important; cutbacks in employment became the norm.

12. People who write on the history of MNEs are assumed not to be using theory—if they do not cite particular theorists and theories. Theorists do not know how to incorporate in their theories the dynamic processes that historians find. While there has been a great deal of progress in integrating history and theory, there is still a formidable gap.

13. Over the past three decades, there has been a proliferation of works on the history of MNEs.[26] Yet, these writings on MNCs have not been fully incorporated into the mainstream of the field of IB (aside from the footnote on page 1 of textbooks). Few courses have been taught on the history of MNEs.[27] There needs to be an effort on the part of those writing in the field and those already in the field to put this important literature into the curriculum of graduate IB programs.

14. Students of MNCs should try to separate the literature on MNEs from that on FDIs. As indicated earlier, the topics are different. The subject matter for the student of foreign direct investment is that of investment alone. The study of MNEs is that of the entire enterprise.

15. Likewise, students of MNEs have to be sure that when they examine foreign investment that there is a differentiation between those investments made that carry control or the potential for control and those that are made for purely financial reasons (portfolio investments). Banks can, for example, be studied as MNEs (as institutions) and as financial intermediaries (makers and facilitators of portfolio investments).

Above, I have given a multitude of promising and important areas of inquiry for the future. There are many other research topics that will enlarge our understanding. In our studies, we need to figure out more ways to give our faculty and our students access to top level decision making within multinationals. Theory must emerge out of evidence and help us make sense of the evidence. We need to aid our students in designing meaningful studies based not on aggregates but on internal behavior of individual companies. When we are dealing with this field, as I have maintained throughout this paper, we must emphasize that our starting point is the nature and growth of the firm. We should be offering our students both descriptive and analytic studies. We should be teaching the currently available economic theories (internalization theories, transaction cost theories, theories that come out of the business history literature), those that begin with the firm, explaining where the theories are enriching and adding to them where they are deficient. Most of all, we should be seeking to focus on the multinational enterprise *per se*. That is what is distinctive about our area of inquiry.

NOTES

1. At a summer, 1991, gathering on world history at the University of Utah, an art historian was sure that he knew all about the activities of multinationals. The "politically correct" approach to MNEs is to see them as part and parcel of the history of "victimization."

2. Some ideas expressed in this essay are original to its author; many, however, are derived from the work of others. Although I am not summarizing the literature, I express a deep debt of gratitude to countless academic colleagues in the United States, Europe, Canada, Japan, and in Latin America, who have contributed to shaping my views.

3. My two-volume history of American business abroad would subsequently appear (Wilkins 1970; 1974).

4. On the tendency among economists to believe that life began with Hymer's 1960 MIT dissertation, see the excellent anthology by Casson (1990). Business International Corporation, which became a forum for discussions on contemporary IB, was formed in 1954. Fayerweather's book (1960) was very influential in its day—yet, unlike the work of Hymer, it has not been perceived as path-breaking. But, the economist will say, there was no *theory* of MNEs as firms before Hymer. Before Hymer, in fact, there were many contributing ideas in the 1950s; an article and book by Edith Penrose (1956, 1959) and a seminal article by Alfred Chandler on the rise of big business (1959), for example, represented building blocks as significant as the 1960 work of Hymer. There was also all the pre-World War II literature (including R.H. Coase's [1937] article, which Hymer introduced in 1968 into the literature on MNEs); materials *relevant* to the

development of a theory of MNEs by no means started with Hymer.

5. Belassa (1990) referred to Dunning's *Explaining International Production* as a "monumental work." Dunning has spent his academic career seeking to understand the MNE. Surely, his works contribute to our understanding. So, too, the three decades of writings on MNEs by Vernon and Kindleberger—both of whom published their first works on multinational enterprise in the 1960s—along with a legion of other scholars have added immeasurably to development of an analytic framework.

6. It could be argued that there are numerous other differences related to governments—differences in trade policies, in industrial policies, etc., that are faced by the firm that is involved in cross-border operations. Yet, a MNE that operates (through FDI) within a host country and undertakes no international trade could operate without being affected—on a regular basis—by either the home or the host nation's *trade* policies. By contrast, a MNE must ultimately remit profits and thus the differences in currencies are a perennial unique feature affecting IB. (Even in the days when extractive companies would export from third world countries and receive revenues in hard currency and not convert their profits into local currencies, foreign exchange matters were important since local payrolls had to be met in local currency.)

7. In the early 1970s I tried to develop such a construct (1974:414–422), reprinted more recently in my anthology (Wilkins 1991: 149–158). As my research after the early 1970s on the history of FDI in the United States progressed, I discovered there was a part of the history of *British* multinational enterprises in particular that failed to conform to my model of the development of American MNEs (Wilkins 1988b:259–282). I would have to make modifications were I to write a more general approach. On the other hand, I continue to feel satisfied with this model vis-à-vis U.S. enterprise (although I would add the insights of much of the recent litera ture). I have felt content enough with this construct to believe that in its broadest manner it applies beautifully to the history of Japanese business in the United States (Wilkins 1990:585–629). A number of economists now recognize that a theory of the firm must be dynamic. Some fail, however, to incorporate the contributions of business historians *in their theoretical framework*.

8. The concept of path dependency originated with economist Brian Arthur and economic historian Paul David at Stanford University. While at origin it dealt exclusively with technology, it is now being used in wider contexts. Path dependency suggests that prior choices set a path and alternative (in David's terms superior) paths may be precluded because of the choices earlier made.

9. Some attacks on economic theories of the MNE are on straw men: No serious student of MNE believes that the modern giant enterprise operates under conditions of perfect competition, indeed much of the work on the theory of MNEs by economists is based on market imperfections. Sometimes, however, there exists among economists a "grafting" on to existing bodies of knowledge, for example, assuming that one can explain MNE by subtracting exports from imports (but in 1991, once again, no serious student of the economic analysis of MNE believes that).

10. This is not only true of the work on path dependency mentioned above, but on substantial other research efforts. Thus, as another example, the studies being done on property rights have important implications for the theory of MNE; likewise, recent work on contestable markets is very applicable to a theory of the giant multiproduct MNE. It is the newer developments in economics that ought to be continually tested for applicability, while older analyses found deficient ought to be once and for all abandoned—rather than belabored (there is still too much "beating of dead horses").

11. The research by University of Tokyo Professor Tetsuo Abo (and his team) began with a core knowledge of multinational behavior. They assumed that a firm that moved abroad had advantage. With Japanese MNEs in the automobile industry, they felt that advantage (or at least an important part of the advantage) lay in plant management. They knew that as a firm moved abroad it could replicate what it did at home, or adapt. Yet, if the Japanese automobile companies in the United States adapted too much to U.S. production practices, they would lose their advantage. Professor Abo's research has come up with some splendid insights on the general problems of MNEs in host countries.

12. There have been a number of interesting studies of the experiences of small firms over borders. Often the process of moving internationally begins when a firm is still small (this is

particularly true of firms headquartered in small countries). I do not deny the participation of small firms in the process of multinational expansion; nonetheless, for sizable FDI, over time, firms almost by definition become large.

13. Work by economists, especially Oliver Williamson, on firm governance has proved stimulating to students of MNE.

14. I have been saying this for many years. The last sentence of my 1974 book reads: "Over time, the U.S.-controlled multinational corporation has overcome obstacles to become both giant and formidable but, as in the past, it still must bow to the power of national sovereignties" (Wilkins 1974:439). Alex Rubner (1990) discusses the myth of the power of MNEs. He argues that the left (Stephen Hymer and Charles Levinson) and the not-so-left (Howard Perlmutter and Eldridge Haynes) both erred in assuming the power of MNEs.

15. In my present research on the history of foreign MNEs in the United States, I found that often British firms *assumed* familiarity with the American market (after all, Americans spoke English and U.S. law took its point of departure from British origins); many were surprised at the immense differences that existed between the United States and the British market, differences that they discovered only after the firms had made sizable investments—and differences that affected their ability to compete in the United States.

16. Many students of IB have assumed symmetry by industry in international expansion. The assumption was based on observations made by Hymer that certain industries were characterized by "cross-investments." Research of more depth, and historical research, has disclosed a considerable amount of asymmetric behavior—that can be explained by a range of differences in firm-specific advantages—sometimes but not always linked with "stages in development."

17. I have tried to deal systematically with differences in home countries of MNEs (Wilkins 1986a; 1988a; 1991).

18. See the splendid article by Boddewyn, Halbrich, and Perry (1986). There has been an assumption in much of the literature that service MNEs are new, as is the study of such MNEs. I have always believed that the field of international enterprise studies must include the study of all business over borders, not simply the manufacture of goods abroad (see Wilkins 1970; 1989). In 1983, Kindleberger wrote an article

on "International Banks and International Business in Historical Perspective". The literature on banks as MNEs grows by leaps and bounds, showing that banks have long histories as multinationals (see Jones 1990; 1993).

19. *After* the core theory has been taught, it may be wise to offer students the rhetoric of mistaken analysis. I say this with some reservations, because too often the mistaken approaches have been taught as a core rather than as they should be taught. I have strongly advocated teaching a core analysis and rejecting approaches that fail to cast light on the nature of the firm. I had a graduate student recently, a retired executive with some thirty-five years of high level experience in Latin America and elsewhere for a major American oil company. He knew a great deal about the operations and business of this single multinational firm. In writing an international studies master thesis on IB in Latin America he found most useful his reading of Celso Furtado, Daniel Chirot, Fernando Cardoso and Enzo Faletto, and Andre Gunter Frank. As one can imagine none of these authors helped him understand the MNE *per se*; they did, however, aid him in understanding why there existed the opposition to MNEs in Latin America. Perhaps such authors should be read in IB classes and programs—as influences on the *rhetoric* of the third world governments and as creating part of the environment of the MNE. In the 1990s these authors may have less influence in the third world than they had in earlier years, yet the residual of their influence does remain.

20. In putting together my anthology (1991), I could not find an article that dealt in a systematic fashion with "comparative hosts." I wanted to find an historical essay that dealt with the complex ways in which firms from various home countries make choices to invest in different national locales and how they behave in these locales. I have written a paper entitled "Hosts to Transnational Investment—A Comparative Analysis" (1994b; see also 1994a).

21. Raymond Vernon identified the motive of "defending" a market as key in market-oriented manufacturing operations. In my historical work, I have found this a common motive, except I have preferred not to see investments as "defensive," arguing that a company has the choice not to invest—thus, the investments can be seen as aggressive in that the firm seeks out the market and the investments are a way of coping with the inability to reach the market or enlarge the market share through exports. The difference is semantic; not one of basic motivation.

22. The most exciting work on trade within MNEs has been done by Robert Lipsey (see Kravis and Lipsey 1989).

23. The integration was not uniform; few companies had an exact balance of crude oil production with refining capacity. Some had excess of crude; some bought crude. All the major companies had a strategy of integration.

24. Such minority investments crop up often in the study of the history of MNE. Recently in writing on the history of FDI in the U.S., I have dealt with the varieties of business entries into America, trying to segregate foreign portfolio from direct investments. Usually the differences are clear: portfolio investments are purely financial; FDIs are made by MNEs with an eye to business strategies. There are occasional problems related to minority interests. For example, in the early 1920s, Du Pont owned a sizable portion of General Motors and wanted to obtain financing for it. The time, however, was not right to go to outside capital markets (the U.S. was in the midst of the post-World War I recession). Instead, Du Pont turned to a British firm, one of the predecessors to Imperial Chemical Industries. Over the years, Du Pont and this predecessor of ICI had cooperated in agreements related to markets and technological interchanges. Management of the two firms was on "friendly" terms. Du Pont suggested that the British firm make a sizable investment in General Motors, which it did. Should this investment be classified as portfolio or FDI? Since it was under 10% the U.S. Department of Commerce would not classify it as FDI. The British firm was not the largest single investor and could hardly have exercised control. Moreover, since the British firm's main reason for the investment was purely financial, it could be argued that this was a portfolio investment. On the other hand, this was an investment by a British MNE; the British company did place two representatives on the GM Board of Directors; the large size of the investment (about 4% of GM stock) might possibly mean potential influence, if not control; the investment would not have been made had there not been the prior relationship between Du Pont and the British firm; and the investment could be seen as part of a business-related strategy, linked with its relations with Du Pont. Whether one classifies this as FDI is a "statistical" matter. For the student of MNEs, the investment is important as part of the

IB of the British firm—and of the strategies employed.

25. 1990 figures are from *Fortune*, July 29, 1991, p. 245; the 1980 figures are from U.N. Centre on Transnational Corporation, *Transnational Corporations in World Development, Third Survey* (New York: United Nations, 1983, p. 357). Sales figures in billion U.S. dollars (1980, 1990) were GM (57.7, 125.1); Daimler-Benz (17.1, 54.2); IBM (26.2, 69.0); Siemens (17.6, 39.2); Ford (37.1, 98.3); Unilever (24.2, 40.0); Fiat (24.2, 47.8); Hitachi (13.0, 50.7).

26. This mirrored the general growth of the literature on multinationals (see the articles reprinted in Wilkins 1991).

27. Geoffrey Jones at the University of Reading is virtually alone in teaching a course on the history of the multinational enterprise.

■ ■ ■

The Conceptual Domain of International Business: Territory, Boundaries, and Levels
Jean J. Boddewyn

Most textbooks on international business (IB) start with a rather perfunctory definition of this activity and institution.[1] This is seldom the case in other fields of inquiry, such as marketing, economics, political science, and anthropology, where there have been prolonged and even heated discussions of their proper contents and modes of analysis. It may simply be that IB textbook authors assume that the nature of "business" has been amply grasped in previous courses, and that a brief definition of "international" will suffice to differentiate IB from its domestic counterpart.

This essay explores the conceptual domain of IB in terms of (1) constituting elements[2] to be observed and explained, (2) boundaries, and (3) appropriate levels of analysis. Successive definitions will be developed in this process.

EPISTEMOLOGICAL CAVEATS

In handling this assignment, I will tackle the combined words of "international business" literally. However, the fact that many schools of *business* have renamed themselves schools of *management* has added a confusing element to the titles of international courses, programs, and textbooks. Besides, the words "global" and "transnational" have come to substitute for "international" in an often indiscriminate or arbitrary manner.[3] Regarding the validity of these new terms, I will limit myself to quoting Kogut [1989:388]: "It seems fair to ask what is the analytical value of prefacing 'strategy' with the word 'global.' What is distinctive in the international context, besides larger market size, is the variance in country environments and the ability to profit through the system-wide management of this variance."

Kogut's quotation introduces the word "management." However, I decline to discuss "international business *management*" because this constitutes a separate topic, as is well evidenced by the fact that there are separate (and usually more advanced) courses and publications focusing on it. Besides, one cannot analyze IB management without first defining *what* is being "managed."

My starting and even dominant perspective *is economic in nature*. "Business" is fundamentally an economic institution (activity, function, process, etc.) even though, like other institutions, it is affected by, and in turn affects other societal institutions such as the polity, the community, the social structure, the system of values, and the physical environment (see Parsons and Smelser [1956]). Nobody would deny that the family has economic determinants and effects; yet, it is not centrally conceptualized and analyzed as an economic institution. Similarly, the economy and its business subset are institutions embedded in society, but their functions are not predominantly understood to be political, social, or cultural in nature.

I am fully aware that business is affected by countless factors, including "humanity's propensity to truck and barter" (Adam Smith's assumption, which itself has been challenged by anthropologists and psychologists), and that international business may contribute to world peace as well as to harming the world's physical environment. However, I do not think that conceptualizing the domain of a particular societal institution, such as the family or IB, requires throwing in "the whole kitchen sink" of all its determinants, processes, and outcomes. No field of action and inquiry is defined in such a total manner as far as I know.

Still, it will be necessary *at some point* to relate the economic conceptualization of international business to other societal institutions and to noneconomic perspectives. I will do so *to some extent* (1) when contrasting the concepts of "nation" and "state," which have crucial cultural and political denotations that must be considered when conceptualizing international business, and (2) when analyzing "levels of IB analysis." However, I will not provide a definition of international business that would amount to defining it in terms of "business and society," of all its stakeholders, and of their multiple and changing interactions.

I must add one further comment about the economic emphasis of my definition. A fundamentally economic institution, such as IB, can be studied under different "economic" perspectives. I am not relying exclusively on the tenets of "neoclassical economics," nor do I accept without limit all of its assumptions, such as optimizing behavior and efficiency. However, I do associate business with "the profit motive" because I cannot conceive of business individuals and organizations not intending primarily to "do well" financially, even if they end up also "doing good (or bad)," and even if they have additional motivations such as power, self-actualization and the well-being of mankind. Actually, I am much more inclined to analyze business and its international variant in the context of the disciplines of political economy and economic sociology—as will be evident in my discussion of the political and sociocultural dimensions of the nation-state.

Even so, this broadening of the economic analysis of IB may still be considered to be too ethnocentric because relying on "Western" and particularly "Anglo-Saxon" views of economic activity—with their peculiar emphasis on the market system (and its rational, impersonal and contractual bases) which is far from being common around the world (see below) and is even rejected for being alien to other types of society.

My comparative studies have long alerted me to this pitfall; and I realize that business involves more than rational, impersonal, contractual relations—both within the firm and between firms. Still, all "modernist" scientific inquiry imposes rationality on its subjects, even though it is only one way of "understanding" them. Thus, Louis T. Wells, Jr. pointed out, during a workshop at the 1991 AIB Annual Meeting, that the concept of the obsolescing bargain (credited to Raymond Vernon) constituted a real progress in interpreting international business-government relations because it superseded the prior interpretation that less developed country (LDC) governments repudiated prior investment agreements simply because they were irrational. Yet, we can also agree that the rational obsolescing-bargain model does not fully explain the phenomena of contract repudiation, renegotiation, and expropriation.

Besides, the "market-system" was not invented by Anglo-Saxons or broadly defined Westerners, even though they have been the ones who theorized about it and practiced it the most. Economic historians and anthropologists have traced its manifestations and evolution in many places and distant times. Right now, it is the dominant "recipe" for restructuring the world's economic order—both domestically and internationally—even though it remains in conflict with mercantilistic (e.g., protectionism and strategic-trade theory) and other ideologies (e.g., Islamic socio-economics). Therefore, it is acceptable in my opinion to associate international business with the market system and its "negotiated" characteristic (see below).

Finally, I realize that this essay represents an "academic" exercise—namely, defining a field of *inquiry*—which does not capture all the dimensions of a field of *action*, such as IB. Even so, it is a daunting task whose outcome, as developed in this essay, may not satisfy anybody. At least, I have accepted to grab the bull by the horns and the tiger by the tail, fully aware of the dangers involved. The other essays on the conceptual domain of international business, on the one hand, provide complementary perspectives that address some of the elements left out of my definition. On the other hand, I believe that this essay provides an *explicit* analysis of the concept of "international business," which is left implicit or underdeveloped in the other essays.

TERRITORY: THE MEANINGS OF "INTERNATIONAL" AND "BUSINESS"

Most definitions of IB refer in some way to "business that crosses borders" or, as Fayerweather [1969:5] put it, to "business processes intersected in some way by national borders." Therefore, we need to examine both terms, separately and in combination.

Business

In the IB literature, "business" is usually understood to encompass "trade and investment." Under *trade*, a good or service produced in one country is sold or rented to an unrelated party abroad (e.g., an independent foreign distributor or customer) or to a related one (e.g., a foreign subsidiary involved in intracompany trade). As such, international trade includes not only exporting and importing but also foreign licensing, franchising, leasing, subcontracting, management contracts, and turnkey projects. In the latter cases, the firm in the home country is really selling to, or buying from, another party located abroad, either title or possession regarding a technology, skill, or made-to-order facility.

Investment[4] refers to situations where the producer of the good or service transfers some or all of the necessary factors of production (raw materials, capital, labor, technology, skills, reputation, etc.) to another country where complete or partial production will take place under its control of these combined factors of production.

This distinction between trade and investment is deceptively simple, however. Thus, Oman [1984] has challenged the classification of international licensing, franchising, management, and turnkey contracts, subcontracting and some other "new forms" of international involvement, as amounting to trade. For him, these operations often constitute investment because they are not spot transactions that realize value already created and that involve no risk for the seller and no control by the seller, subsequent to the sale. They may also amount to investment because they include the acquisition of rights to the new value to be created in the host country and to the resulting future income—as with a licensing agreement providing for fees linked to the future sales of goods or services utilizing the licensed technology abroad.

I do not fully subscribe to Oman's arguments because plain exports can also involve some risk (nonpayment and foreign-exchange fluctuations, for example), some post-sale control (for instance, export controls designed to ensure that sales to "friendly" countries do not end up in "enemy" countries), and some lasting relationships with foreign buyers and suppliers, so that spot transactions often fold into future ones. The form assumed by a revenue flow should not determine whether a transaction amounts to a sale or an investment. That a landlord does not ask a tenant to pay rent in the form of an up-front lump sum or of a fixed regular amount but through a flexible amount based on the tenant's fluctuating income does not necessarily transform the apartment rental into an "investment" in the tenant in any strict legal sense of that word.

Still, Oman has rightly pointed out that the contractual relations involved in IB, a favorite focus of transaction-cost and internationalization theory, are more complex than a simple distinction between "markets" (linked to trade) and "hierarchies" (linked to investment) would seem to imply. Indeed, trade and investment are often interrelated, as evidenced by discussions of the investment-creating function of trade (e.g., building a factory at home in order to export) and of the trade-creating function of investments (Drucker [1989]). Is a singer like Julio Iglesias performing in concerts throughout the world in international trade, investment, or both? He is clearly "trading" his singing in foreign spot markets, but has to move his "firm-specific resources, assets, advantages and factors of production"— namely, his person—across borders in order to sing in different countries, so that he is also in foreign direct "investment."

This problem is not proper to the production of services [Boddewyn et al. 1986] but extends to international "network" firms that farm out and orchestrate the design, manufacturing, distribution, revenue-collection, and servicing of their manufactured products by other companies located in various countries, as in the case of Galoob Toys [Wilson and Dobrzynski 1986]. Such "networking" involves much more than the subcontracting of various functions across borders—a simple case of trade—since the orchestration of foreign subcontractors involves frequent overseas travel to supervise and motivate them in their locales. Clearly, the international-network firm crosses borders with its skills—hence, it is a case of investment—but without transplanting them overseas under

its ownership or even control; nor does it charge subcontractors for these skills, as in management contracts.

Similarly, international alliances between competing multinational enterprises (MNEs) amount to investment—these firms are not simply contracting for their foreign allies' goods or services. Instead, they use alliances to implement coherent international policies and strategies through other entities, in order to add value and/or to control outputs in several countries—an acceptable definition of "investment," according to Peter Buckley and Mark Casson (see Boddewyn et al. [1986]).[5]

So far, this definition of business in terms of trade and investment echoes Richard D. Robinson's early distinction ([1964b] cited in Aharoni [1971]) between *transactions* (as in exports and imports) and *firms* crossing borders, with investment clearly linked to the latter, but without equity being always required to achieve presence and impact in foreign countries. Therefore a preliminary definition of our domain can be worded as follows: "International business" refers to trade and investment crossing borders, but with certain IB activities straddling both dimensions.

This wording reflects the interest recently expressed in the Uruguay Round to include some aspects of investment under GATT rules, which had been limited to trade in the postwar period. However, international trade and investment are *not* synonymous in nature and extent with "international economic transfers" because the latter also include private "unrequited" transfers (e.g., immigrants sending money back home, or retirees collecting their pension checks abroad) as well as governmental (e.g., foreign aid) and intergovernmental (currency swaps, loans, funding of international organizations, etc.) transfers of goods and funds. The implication of this distinction is that IB covers only *privately negotiated* trade and investment, plus governmental transactions *negotiated* (rather than imposed) between governments as well as between governments and independent firms (whether privately or governmentally owned).

There are problems with this "negotiated" qualification, however. In the first version of this essay, I had added the qualifier "at arm's length" in order to differentiate bargained market transactions from those based on command or tradition (Polanyi [1944]; Smelser [1976:119–23]). This is not an idle distinction when it comes to defining international business.

I would guess that some international economist has sorted out what is truly "business"[6] in international trade and investment, but I have not come across such a study. Hence, I will limit myself to a discrepancy uncovered a few years back [Boddewyn and Falco 1988]. We were trying to determine the size of the *market sector* around the world—that is, those *domestic* buyer-seller transactions ruled by negotiation (usually called "bargaining" in economic anthropology), rather than by command or tradition. At the conclusion of our investigation, only about 20% of the world's population and income could be linked to "bargained market transactions"—which can be roughly equated with "business"—*within* the 150+ domestic economies of the world around 1983.

The relative size of *international* "negotiated" business is likely to be much larger because it is possible to "market" *to* nonmarket economies through international trade (e.g., to the old Soviet Union) even though "marketing" is not allowed *within* these economies. This situation has obviously changed on account of recent shifts away from command economies toward market systems, that allow more private trade and investment with and within the emerging market economies.[7]

On second thought, I do not think that it is necessary to add "at arm's length" because the distinction between market (where negotiations take place), command and tradition, as the bases of economic exchange systems, is sufficient for my purpose. This qualifier forced me to exclude "intracompany transfers at administered prices," which loom large in modern international trade and investment, and which is routinely included in international statistics. However, it could be mentioned, in support of my earlier qualifier, that governments often try to impose "arm's length prices" in computing import-export prices and corporate income taxes.

This qualifier also obscured the fact that negotiated market exchanges are frequently embedded in social and political *relationships* (both national and international) as well as in value systems (Toyne [1989])—as is evidenced by steady patterns of relationships with foreign distributors and suppliers, of colonial-type relationships among certain countries, of free-trade area agreements, and of affinities among markets (Ohmae's "Triad" argument [1985]). In such situations, negotiation does not take place for each transaction, but it is embedded in longer-lasting relationships involving *both* "spot" and "futures" transactions. I think that the expression "*negotiated* trade and investment" is flexible enough to cover both types of transactions, without having to specify it. Keeping these reservations in mind, I would reword my earlier definition as follows: "International business" refers to *negotiated* trade and investment crossing borders, but with certain IB activities straddling both dimensions. As such, IB is smaller in scope than "international economic activities/exchange."

International

This word has the meaning of "crossing borders," but what do "borders" stand for, and what are their implications for IB?[8] They refer to the boundary lines between nation-states. Implicit in this definition is the notion that borders act as *barriers* to international trade and investment. The implication is that if the world were made up of only one nation-state, there would be no *inter*national business. The creation of new nation-states (usually, former colonies) as well as the break up of old ones (e.g., the USSR and Yugoslavia), conversely, generates more *inter*national business, all else being equal—for example, barring autarkic policies or economic integration.[9]

"Nation-state," however, is an expression conjugating two very different concepts. *Nation* refers first and foremost to "a community of sentiments" often linked to ethnic, language, and religious factors with a relatively long history (Mellor [1989 chap. 1]; Taylor [1985:125]; see also Douglas Nigh's paper in this volume). Thus, one can speak of a "Jewish nation" spread all over the world for some 20 centuries, while the "Polish nation" has been repeatedly divided among several states in recent centuries. Similarly, discussions of "nationalism" revolve around those ideological/cultural elements that make one group of people feel as "we" against "them" on account of shared tradition Fayerweather [1969:88–96]). Hence, a nation-state can include various "nations" such as the Czechs and Slovaks of Czechoslovakia, the French and English of Canada, and the four parts of the "United Kingdom" (England, Scotland, Wales, and Northern Ireland)— for short or long periods of time, and with or without a federal system allowing for greater autonomy of these "nations" within the nation-state, as with the Swiss cantons.

The concept of nation, however, has also an economic dimension—as is well revealed by the title of Michael Porter's recent book on *The Competitive Advantage of Nations* [1990]. His "determinants of national advantage" [71]—factor conditions; demand conditions; related and supporting industries; and firm strategy, structure and rivalry—are essentially economic in nature. They reflect the fact that, within the borders of each nation-state, there is a particular bundle of resources, skills, and wants that determine "the wealth of nations" (Adam Smith) as well as their competitiveness vis-à-vis other nations (Kogut [1991]). After borders are redrawn, these economic bundles change, as happened following Singapore's split from Malaysia.

When boundaries are essentially economic, as among U.S. states and regions ruled by the Interstate Commerce Clause, factors of production and goods tend to move to equalize the supply and demand differentials among them, thereby redrawing these *permeable* boundaries [Clark 1991:8]. Most economic analyses of international business focus on this very phenomenon as firms are perceived to cross borders in search of cheaper or better factors of production, unsatisfied customers, etc., *thereby homogenizing markets*—all the way to "global markets."

Altogether, the concept of *nation* emphasizes economic and sociocultural variables rather than political ones (Lenway and Murtha [1991]). This particular coloration helps explain the partial validity and great popularity of Levitt's [1983] "globalizing markets" and of Ohmae's [1990] "borderless world" views, which rest upon the notion that, in the face of more homogenous consumer segments around the world, nation-states do not matter very much anymore because they share similar purchasing power, preferences, and lifestyles— like "The United Colors of Benetton." We are currently witnessing this "globalization" phenomenon which is reversible, however ("Buy National" outbursts).

Challenging this "homogenizing" view is the notion of the *state* which constitutes a compulsory association with a territorial basis [Weber 1964:156], where the government, as the immediate agent of the sovereign state, exercises potential supreme power (physical coercion) above all other political actors also endowed with power. States draw finite boundaries around the national segments of world economic activity. These borders interfere with the free movement of factors of production, intermediate products, and final goods and services, because political boundaries are less permeable and often more permanent than economic ones (Clark [1991]).

The existence of *states* thus creates "political spaces" which increasingly do not overlap with the economic and sociocultural ones found within and across *nations* [Kobrin 1990; 1994]. As Kindleberger put it: "It seems likely that the optimum economic area is larger than the nation state, the optimum cultural area is smaller, and the optimum political area . . . identical with it" [1975:358–359].

This political dimension is more complex in its implications for the nature of and theorizing about the IB field. Without political boundaries, there would be no *international business*—only trade and investment ruled by "locational" economic and sociocultural factors. As Grosse and Behrman [1992] put it forcefully: "Examination of the international activities of companies, which assumes governments as 'given' or unchanging, takes the 'national' out of *inter*national, and leaves the analysis as a simple extension of [universal or generic] firm and market theories . . . Therefore, a theory of IB must be a theory of obstructions to markets (interventions and distortions), flows of information, movements of people, etc. *imposed by national governments.*"

Without government intervention, there is only a one-world market explainable under universal economic and strategic theories. It is precisely the existence of contrasting national economic orders (that is, "political economies" contained within state borders), together with the concomitant assertion of governmental controls and of business devices to avoid or exploit them, that distinguish international business from domestic business [Supple 1989:3].

In this view, the crossing of national borders through trade, investment, and alternative modes of entry into other sovereignties transforms radically an economic and sociocultural act into a political one. Hence, the political dimension of IB is not an "add on" to its economic and sociocultural dimensions *but fundamentally defines it* (Boddewyn [1988]; Boddewyn and Brewer [1991]).[10]

This situation is somewhat acknowledged in Dunning's eclectic paradigm [1988] and in the related literature on transaction costs and internalization, to the extent that the market imperfections generated by governments both hinder and facilitate interna-

tional trade and investment (Boddewyn [1988], Brewer [1991]).[11] It is much more explicit in Doz' [1979; 1986] strategic analysis of the tension between "global integration" (ruled by economic considerations) and "national responsiveness" (to governments). Mira Wilkins, in her introductory essay in this chapter, also recognizes the crucial impact of sovereignties.

Therefore, "international business" assumes three conceptual dimensions. First, international business incorporates an *economic* dimension which is quite amenable to theories of: (1) the "macro" absolute and comparative advantages of home and host nations, and (2) their firms' "micro" competitive advantages, which can be expressed in many ways (e.g., Bartlett and Ghoshal's [1989] as well as Hamel and Prahalad's [1988] emphasis on economies of scale, scope, and learning). This economic dimension usually retains the emphasis on inter*national* in the expression "international business."

Second, IB includes a *sociocultural* dimension which is mostly developed in the comparative, cross-cultural, international-marketing and international-management literatures. Here, the meaning of "international" is subject to tensions well articulated by Perlmutter's [1969] concepts of ethnocentricity, polycentricity, and geocentricity, and endlessly discussed in the "standardization vs. adaptation" literature (Jain [1989], Walters [1986], Wind and Douglas [1986]), and in the international-marketing papers in this volume.

Mentioned earlier, extreme emphasis on the economic and sociocultural dimensions of international business leads to a shift in the meaning of "international" to "global"—as in discussions of "the globalization of markets," found in the marketing and finance (capital and foreign-exchange) literatures. A more moderate recognition of the importance of these dimensions has led to the resurrection of the U.N.'s concept of "transnational" (Bartlett and Ghoshal [1989]), which acknowledges that "national" matters but that there are also "global" imperatives so that the overarching philosophy is one of "Think globally, act locally."[12]

Third, IB has a fundamentally *political* dimension because the act of "crossing borders" is first and foremost a political act—whether in compliance, competition and/or partnership with more or less sovereign governments (Boddewyn [1992], Boddewyn and Brewer [1994]). This dimension leads to state business," where "nation-state" refers to political economies exhibiting varying "differentials" (the economic and sociocultural dimensions) and "permeabilities" (the political dimension)—as argued by Clark [1991].

Consequently, theories of IB will have to be built around these three conceptual dimensions; and an expanded definition of our field reads as follows: "International business" refers to negotiated trade and investment *that join nations and cross state barriers*, but with certain IB activities straddling both *sets of* dimensions.

As Kobrin points out in this volume, there are uncertainties about the viability of contemporary nation-states. A plurality of political structures—subnational, regional, supranational, and global is aborning (Mellor [1989:49–52]). Ohmae [1990: 182–185] refers to "the interlinked [global] economy" where subnational regions (e.g., California's Silicon Valley and Belgium's Flanders), cities (e.g., New York, London, and Tokyo) and supranational regions (e.g., the European Community and the North American Free Trade Area) are emerging as major competitors and cooperators in IB, challenging the political role of traditional nation-states.

This undoubtedly is happening and likely to keep growing. However, it may amount more to the creation of new "nations" than of new "states," according to the distinction made earlier. Besides, in its purely political aspects, this development will multiply political structures rather than eliminate them, thereby *both* complicating the conduct of IB and increasing the opportunities for IB firms to arbitrage

and leverage these multiple political structures (Kogut [1985b]).

THE BOUNDARIES OF INTERNATIONAL BUSINESS

The definition of IB as "crossing borders" is usually understood in terms of relatively explicit flows (inward and outward) and stocks (domestic and foreign) of factors of production, intermediate products, and final goods and services. However, there are subtler interactions among nations and states, that may be subsumed under the IB concept.

For example, Robinson [1978:17] broadened the concept of IB to include *all private and public business activities affecting the persons and/or institutions of more than one country*. In this perspective, purely domestic U.S. firms, with no direct international involvement, are in IB because they are ultimately affected by what happens outside the U.S.—bad crops, rising interest rates, fluctuating exchange rates, embargoes, new technologies, etc.—on account of the U.S. economy being a relatively open one. Thus, Robert Reich recently observed that:

> The global economy is tightly linking our citizens to the citizens of other nations— with ties as strong as, if not stronger than the economic connections binding us to one another within our borders. Talented and well-educated Americans grow wealthier as the emerging world market rewards them for their problem-solving skills. Unskilled Americans grow poorer as they are forced to compete with millions of unskilled workers from around the world who are eager to work for a small fraction of American wages [1992:25].

Most U.S. teachers of IB are not actively involved in international service trade and investment since they do not regularly teach overseas. However, they could lose their jobs if their students decided to get an international-business education abroad. Are they then in international business because they are exposed to such international developments? Similarly, a United States franchisee of McDonald's may seem to be involved only in domestic business, but his or her future is affected by how McDonald's, as the franchiser, chooses to allocate its resources between the United States and foreign markets—recently slipping and fumbling at home but doing well abroad [Therrien 1991]. Again, is that McDonald's franchisee in international business because it is indirectly impacted by it? And what about the company that seriously considers going international but then decides not to do so for valid reasons (Aharoni [1971] discussing Perlmutter [1969]): is it in international business too?

These questions reveal the fuzzy limits of the concept "international." European practitioners and scholars have long been puzzled by the typically U.S. dichotomy between "domestic" (at home) and "international" (abroad, overseas, foreign). For them, all business is really international on account of the economic interdependence of European nations with each other and with the rest of the world.[13] Recent discussions of the shift from "*international* competition" to "*global* competition" also reflect the realization that few major industries and firms are now sheltered from what is happening abroad in terms of risks and opportunities (Drucker [1989:115–139]). Robinson had already argued that "domestic business" is a subset for the internationally-oriented firm—with the former "simply a special case in which the relevant variables are weighted in a unique manner. The variables remain the same, even though some be assigned zero values" [1978:30].

Even if it were true that *all* industries and firms are directly or indirectly in IB, one could still choose to limit the study of IB to "borderland" activities where differential pressures and permeabilities among nation-states are felt *explicitly, directly, and measurably*; while excluding the "heartland" where such elements "will be determining factors in the *general* market conditions, *albeit hidden ones*" [Clark 1991:17, emphasis added]. This distinction echoes Fay-

erweather's point that "the contact points between people, companies and activities located within two countries do not necessarily take place at the border" [1969:5]. The internationalization, transnationalization, or globalization of most firms will ultimately reduce the importance of this distinction between borderland and heartland—also called the "hinterland," the land behind the border areas.[14]

THE BOUNDARIES OF THE INTERNATIONAL FIRM

Previous comments about what to include within the concept of international business have already raised questions about the boundaries of IB firms—or of any firm for that matter.

Economists have been derided endlessly for treating organizations as "black boxes" with definite walls separating them from their environments and from other firms. Transaction-cost and internalization theories also imply well defined boundaries between external "markets" and internal "hierarchies," both ruled by explicit contractual relationships.

Most descriptions and analyses of international companies, such as multinational enterprises, refer to their measurable limits—number of subsidiaries, employees, assets, sales, and profits worldwide, etc.—as if they were finite creatures with clear boundaries. Besides, the ownership advantages of the eclectic paradigm as well as the competitive advantages stressed in strategic analysis sharply distinguish one firm from another. Even discussions of the complex relations *within* "transnational" and "heterarchical" corporations [Bartlett and Ghoshal 1989; Hedlund 1986] tend to set them apart from other firms.

Reality, however, is much more complex than that. Notwithstanding the recent interest in international alliances, consortia, and networks, firms have long had *relationships*—not just one-time or spot transactions—with other companies, both domestic and foreign, through distributorship agreements, cartels, cross-licensing, the pooling of patents, subcontracting, interlocking directorships, cross-ownership, etc. (see Mira Wilkins's essay in this chapter). As Richardson observed, most firms are not "islands of [internally] planned coordination in a sea of market relations," but are frequently linked together in patterns of cooperation and affiliation [1972:883,895]. Legal issues regarding the liabilities of parent companies for the actions of their independently incorporated subsidiaries and affiliates also illustrate the permeability of a firm's boundaries (the Bhopal disaster). As Dunning put it:

> The boundaries of firms are becoming more difficult to delineate. Firms both co-operate and compete with each other. They are linked by webs of trust, tradition, commitment and contractual relationships, as well as by ownership. Mutual tolerance, reciprocity and forbearance are features of networks. Increasingly, economic activity is taking the form of a system of incomplete hierarchies and markets in which the interest of one firm or market is determined by the success of the system or groups of which it is part [1991:4].

Hence, the borders of IB firms are no less permeable than those of countries—maybe even more so [Kogut 1991:33]. One research implication follows from this realization. Studies of IB firms must expand their confines beyond the prevalent but narrow views of ownership and firm-specific advantages (as found in economic analysis), of internal resources and capabilities (as found in strategic analysis), and of headquarters—subsidiary as well as subsidiary-subsidiary relationships (as found in discussions of the "transnational and heterarchical solutions"). These studies treat IB firms (particularly MNEs) as islands rather than as parts of semi-internalized networks or as related parts of "galaxies" (Dunning [1988b:328]).

I am not advocating the study of networks *per se*—this is already being done (Contractor and Lorange [1988]; Forsgren [1989])—but rather a broader conceptualization and operationalization of the IB

firm's boundaries now expressed in terms of firm-specific advantages, resources, and capabilities *narrowly* measured by size, technological intensity, market share, and the like. The IB firm is larger than the latter measures imply so that our research must learn to capture its truer if more fluid dimensions.

LEVELS OF IB ANALYSIS

The previous discussion has included "macro" concepts such as trade and investment as well as "micro" ones such as the IB firm's resources, governance structure, and relationships. This raises the question of the appropriate level(s) to study and research IB.

Mira Wilkins's introductory paper is somewhat perplexing in this respect. She states repeatedly that: "The field of international business is a subset of the study and analysis of business enterprise; it must be linked with a viable and rich theory of the *firm* . . . Its focus should be on the firm that extends across borders . . . Its study must *begin* with a study of the IB firm, its nature, behavior, and growth" [p. 34].

Her statements are perfectly understandable, coming from a *business* historian—a field that distinguishes itself from economic history precisely by focusing on individual firms and particular business institutions, functions, and practices, rather than on aggregate developments such as the evolution and current constitution of U.S. foreign trade and investment. Besides, *business* schools were created for the purpose of applying other disciplines—economics and the other social sciences—to the management of *firms*.

To be sure, she acknowledges that other disciplines are most "germane" to the study of the IB firm, and she even privileges economic theory because "the MNE is an economic institution." However, she refuses to equate the study of IB with that of the world of business, the international economy, and/or the political and social environments of the international firm—all background rather than focal elements in her opinion.

This is a defensible view although two

objections are in order. First, the "international firm" to which she refers explicitly is the "multinational enterprise" (or equivalent appellations used nowadays). She may be simply using and emphasizing her own background and great expertise in the historical study of that particular IB "institution." However, it would seem that other types of IB firms belong properly to the domain of IB: exporters, importers, freight forwarders, customs brokers, export-management companies, etc.—even purely domestic firms impacted by international competition, as was argued before.

Second, if international business is an "institution"—as she argues repeatedly if vaguely—it would seem perfectly appropriate to study it at various levels, as is done with other institutions.[15] The "firm" level, after all, is only one level of institutional analysis (see Perrow [1986 chap. 5]). For that matter, Dunning's eclectic paradigm [1988a] already integrates the firm (ownership advantages), industry (internalization advantages), and nation (locational advantages) levels. Additional ones can also be considered: the product (e.g., Vernon's "international product life cycle"), the project or venture (many bargaining analyses belong here), the function (e.g., international marketing), the network (alliances are relevant here), the individual/personal (e.g., studies of IB careers and of "centric" attitudes à la Perlmutter), and—of course—the global (as in discussions of the shift toward global competition) levels.

Therefore, I would argue that the domain of IB is not limited to the MNE or to other types of IB firms for that matter. It does encompass many levels of analysis and integration, even though there are real conceptual and methodological problems when "mixing variables of different levels of explanation without defining mediating mechanics" [Macharzina and Engelhard 1991:27]. Hence, my final definition of our field: "International business" refers to negotiated trade and investment that join nations and cross state barriers, *as performed by firms (private and public) operating and interacting at various personal, organizational, product, project, function, network, industry, global and other levels.*

Even if nobody agrees with this definition, this conceptual exercise should help everybody think about what to include and exclude when studying "international business," although different definitions are acceptable for different scholarly purposes.

NOTES

1. There are exceptions, such as Richard D. Robinson's thoughtful distinction between domestic and international business (1977: 17–19) and John Fayerweather's discussion of the meaning of "national borders" (1969:5).

2. *A conceptual framework* spells out the constituting elements of the phenomenon studied, fixing attention upon what is to be first observed and then explained. *Propositions* are assertions about relationships between concepts or variables, which are used to build a *model* which can be evaluated both in terms of its internal logical consistency and its utility for purposes of analysis, but not of its truth or falsity. In contrast, a *theory* is composed of hypotheses, and purports to explain relationships which exist in the real world (Riggs 1970:106–107; see also Bacharach 1989).

3. For discussions of the meaning of "international, global, and transnational," see Bartlett and Ghoshal (1989), Hamel and Prahalad (1988), Drucker (1989), Morrison (1990), and Sundaram and Black (1992).

4. I am, of course, focusing on foreign direct investment rather than on foreign portfolio investment. How "control" is achieved constitutes an important issue, but is extraneous to this analysis (see the U.N. definition in endnote 5 for a more recent definition of "control," however). What is transferred abroad is not always obvious. It has been observed that U.S. foreign direct investors have seldom invested much original capital abroad, serving instead as "capital former" rather than as "capital transferor" by raising money abroad. Thus, they have really transferred a skill and/or reputation rather than funds.

5. The terminology used here echoes a little known definition emanating from the United Nations, although I am not primarily concerned with defining "transnational corporations" or "MNEs" for that matter: "The term 'transna-

tional corporation' as used in this Code means an enterprise, comprising entities in two or more countries, regardless of the legal form and fields of activity of these entities, which operates under a system of decision making, permitting coherent policies and a common strategy through one or more decision-making centers, in which the entities are so linked, by ownership or otherwise, that one or more of them may be able to exercise a significant influence over the activities of others, and, in particular, to share knowledge, resources and responsibilities with the others" (United Nations 1982:3).

6. The word "business" (busy-ness) is notoriously vague in the English language—as it is in French where *les affaires* simply means "things to do." Schools of business and MBA programs abroad have had problems finding a local-language equivalent for "business." They tend to fall back on words like commerce, applied economics, administration, and *gestion* (management). For an old but still pertinent discussion of "business," see Keezer (1930).

7. This distinction between domestic and IB reflects the old battle cry of the eighteenth-century French Physiocrats, *"Laissez faire, laissez passer,"* which embodied both notions of "let do" (allow free domestic enterprise) and "let pass" (allow free international trade and investment), unencumbered by government intervention of the mercantilist type.

8. An illuminating analysis of national boundaries and their relationships to international marketing is provided by Clark (1991) in his paper presented at the 1991 AIB Annual Meeting. See also Kobrin (1990), and his chapter in this volume.

9. It is not clear whether the creation of common markets and economic unions results in the elimination of international trade and investment among their member countries. For example, after 1992 or 1999, will there still be "international" business between France and Germany?

10. This view contrasts with Porter's (1990: 680–682) treatment of government as a passive constraint on international business, with little or no strategic interests and capabilities of its own (Lenway and Murtha 1991).

11. *Market imperfections* are created (e.g., protectionism) or tolerated (e.g., cartels) by governments—that is why they are labeled as

"unnatural"—while *market failures* reflect "natural" uncertainty, bounded rationality, monopolies based on unique competencies, unintended externalities, and the like.

12. Taylor (1985:29) refers, in a related vein, to "a national scale of ideology, a local scale of experience and a global scale of reality."

13. It is worth remembering that, historically, "business" in the sense of bargaining through the market system started as "international" business in the form of "long-distance" trade, because "domestic" exchange was ruled by norms of reciprocity or command (Polyani 1944).

14. Drucker (1989:126) illustrates this process: "A hundred years ago, the Germans had to learn to manage even a strictly local firm—say a cigar maker in Hamburg—as a national business. Otherwise, a cigar maker from Munich or Stuttgart would take away their local market. Fifty years ago, every American—say an adhesives company in Massachusetts supplying local offices and banks—had to learn to manage itself as a continental business. Otherwise, an adhesives manufacturer from southern California would suddenly appear and take over its 'regional' market. At present, even the small sausage maker in Belgium has to learn to run his firm as a 'European' business. Otherwise, a sausage maker from Spain will take over his national market. Increasingly, firms will have to learn to see themselves as transnational businesses. Otherwise, a Japanese, a Korean, a German, a Canadian or an American will push them out of their own home market." Drucker had originally discussed the *world* economy in his well known 1986 article, but he shifted to the *transnational* economy in his 1989 book.

15. "Institution" is a notoriously amorphous concept. "It connotes a way of thought or action of some prevalence and permanence, which is embedded in the habits of a group or the customs of a people . . . Institutions fix the confines of, and impose form upon, the activities of human beings . . . Arrangements as diverse as the money economy, classical education, the chain store, fundamentalism and democracy are institutions." [Hamilton (1930:84)]. See also Scott (1987) for a discussion of institutional theory as applied to organizations, while D. E. Westney addresses institutions in this volume.

■ ■ ■

International Business Inquiry: Does It Warrant A Separate Domain?

Brian Toyne

I feel it is safe to say that international business (IB) researchers, as a group, have ignored questions about the domain of their inquiry. For example, Wilkins argues that a discussion of this domain is at best trivial. It was established many years ago and consists of the firm. Thus, she would have us believe that IB research is concerned with gaining a better understanding of the relationship between the firm and the international and foreign environments in which it operates, and the adjustments and adaptations it needs to make to its activities as a result of these interactions.

She is, of course, entitled to this view, especially since it is given as a personal view. What troubles me, however, is the idea that a substantive, socially defined phenomenon, the firm, is the *alpha* and *omega* of IB inquiry. We need to remember that the domain of a particular inquiry, whether implicitly assumed or explicitly stated, restricts as much as it focuses the research activity. So a discussion of domain is important, if for no other reason than to clarify which phenomena and relationships are to be studied and what questions are to be asked about these phenomena and relationships.

What I like about the literature in such diverse fields of business inquiry as marketing, management, and organization theory is the willingness of their scholars to enter into frequent debate concerning the domain of their particular inquiries and the knowledge (truth) they seek. Essentially, they admit that the state of knowledge and the process by which this knowledge is gained must undergo constant scrutiny because the knowledge gained suggests other ways of looking at a particular field or a phenomenon within a field. The usefulness of such debate is that it clarifies what is worth "knowing." In effect, truth, at least for these scholars, is not viewed as "revealed"

or "given," but emergent. They constantly question what they are doing, partly because of the future indeterminacy of human activity, partly because of the complexity of human-created phenomena, and partly because of the advances anticipated in their methodologies.

In this paper I attempt to enter into a similar debate by examining four conceptual domains of IB, as represented by four schools of thought that underpin much of what we do as IB theoreticians and researchers. While these schools of thought are neither collectively exhaustive nor individually exclusive (at least at the level of the individual researcher), they are, in my judgment, representative of the orientations assumed by IB researchers when examining the IB phenomenon.

To accomplish this purpose, I first describe a triangular, three-level framework that has been used to model a field's system of inquiry.[1] I then use this framework to discuss the four domains of IB inquiry in terms of the phenomena and relationships examined, the meaning sought concerning them, and the importance and uniqueness of contributions thus made to the general body of business knowledge. I conclude by presenting a brief overview of IB inquiry in terms of its origins and obstacles I see as potentially inhibiting the field's future development.

IS IB INQUIRY A SCIENCE OR AN ART?

The organization of thinking, reasoning, and research is often represented as a three-level (triangular) framework consisting of (1) the substantive level, (2) the scientific level, and (3) the metalevel (e.g., van Gigch and Pipino [1986]).

1. The *substantive level* of inquiry is devoted to the formulation and solutions of organizational problems. At this level, managers and

policy makers are concerned with the value of knowledge they have in order to fulfill their decision-making responsibilities. The inputs to this level of inquiry are received from the scientific level in the form of theories, models, and methodology.

2. The *scientific level* of inquiry is an enterprise in which propositions are generated, as product or as process. At this level of inquiry inputs are received from the metalevel, consisting of orientations, paradigms, metaphors, and methodology.

3. The *metalevel* of inquiry consists of the assumptions and world-views of the actors (managers, policy makers, theorizers, and researchers) concerning the subject of inquiry, and the meaning to be sought (i.e., the interpretation and emphasis given empirical positivism, operationalism, and pragmatism). It provides the paradigms, metaphors, and methodology used at the scientific level of inquiry.

Figure 1 presents these three levels of inquiry and their relationships to one another. Unfortunately, these distinctive levels of in-

Figure 1. Systems of Inquiry: A Triangular View of IB Inquiry

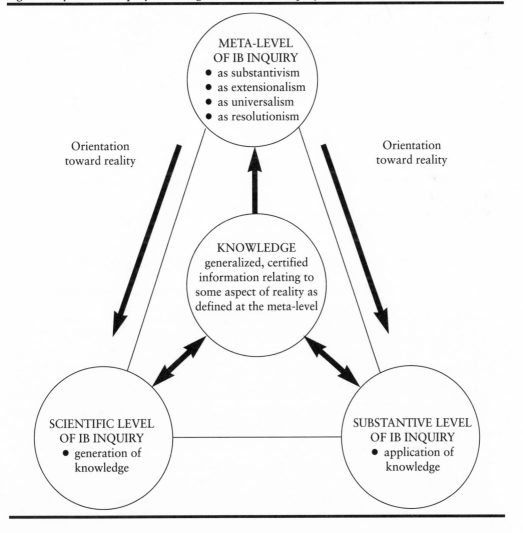

quiry and their relationship to one another are often indistinguishable in the minds of researchers and are not made clear in their work.

At the substantive level, IB inquiry is an art in the same sense as engineering is an art. It is the application of the knowledge created at the scientific level. At the scientific level, IB inquiry is more akin to physics in the same sense that physics is related to engineering. Its purpose is to seek a particular truth—the laws and theories that give meaning to the conceptual domain of the construct known as IB—that is based on a particular conceptualization of reality. At the metalevel the various conceptualizations of reality are given expression: questions such as, what is IB? what kinds of phenomena are appropriately labeled IB phenomena? and how can the IB process be distinguished from other social processes? are raised and answered.

The impetus for IB inquiry can be from either the meta- or substantive-levels. When directed from the former, the process yields theory. When directed from the latter, it yields empirical generalization and description. The reason for this is that substantive-driven inquiry lacks a specific, theory-building purpose or capability.

Since IB inquiry is viewed here as a scientific enterprise, the purpose of which is theory building and theory testing, its domain must be defined in terms that find their origin, expression, and meaning at the metalevel of inquiry. Thus, IB inquiry cannot be separated from the conceptualizing act. Moreover, since we deal with human behavior, which is fundamentally indeterminate, or emerging, IB inquiry is more interested in the discovery of midrange theories that have sufficient explanatory and predictive power to be of value until overwhelmed by the future thinking, reasoning, and behavior of humans (i.e., until human discernment, learning, judgment, and action negate the premises upon which the theories are based).[2]

While the domain of IB inquiry can be established in metalevel terms, it does not establish the uniqueness of IB inquiry as product or process. Essentially, IB inquiry can be legitimately claimed by an already well-established and well-defined field, such as economics, marketing, organization theory, or strategic management. This, of course, would imply that IB inquiry is either in a preparadigmatic stage, or is not a unique scientific enterprise; a situation that will remain true so long as we insist on taking a substantive view of what we do, or that our inquiry remains empirical, descriptive, or strictly theory-testing (i.e., dependent on the metalevel underpinnings of other distinctive inquiries).

IB AS SCIENTIFIC INQUIRY

In her opening paper, Wilkins referred to an unpublished paper I wrote which stated that "international business lacks a fundamental, comprehensive, and unifying construct" [Toyne 1988]. The following is the paragraph from which this statement was taken:

International business has several deficiencies that weaken its claim to be a distinct field of inquiry, and its ability to develop theory. First, international business lacks a fundamental, comprehensive, and unifying construct. Second, it is treated primarily as an extension of the business disciplines. Third, it is dominated by the "managerial relevance" paradigm that guides much of the research undertaken by these disciplines. As a consequence of these deficiencies, there has been no serious effort to develop a "grand" theory of international business, or a set of "middle-range" theories. This has not only resulted in the development of an increasingly fragmented body of knowledge, it has also exposed us to serious threats, in the form of encroachment, from the business disciplines concerning the legitimacy of our claim to a distinct field of inquiry.

While I still believe this, it need not be the case. As I will argue later, IB inquiry has the potential to make unique contributions to the body of knowledge concerning the social phenomenon known as business.

In order to establish the domain of IB inquiry, two questions need to be answered. The first deals with the conceptualization of the construct IB. The second deals with the meaning sought of this conceptualization. Thus, the domain of IB inquiry involves more than the articulation of the boundaries and content of the construct known as IB, such as presented by Wilkins and Boddewyn in their papers. Of necessity, it also involves the articulation of the "truth" to be gained as a product of the IB inquiry process. The domain of IB inquiry establishes the boundaries of IB, the phenomena and relationships studied, the questions asked of these phenomena and relationships, the methodologies used in answering the questions, and the rules used when interpreting the results. It also establishes the product value produced by making clear the purposes for which the body of knowledge is being sought.

The articulation of the conceptualization of IB, and the meaning sought, does not mean that its domain is "fixed" for all times. As mentioned earlier, the domain of any inquiry should be under continual scrutiny and revised as the accumulated body of knowledge dictates and as human beings modify their thinking, reasoning, and behavior as a result of this body of knowledge.

The remainder of this paper explores these two questions using the four schools of thought identified in Figure 1. Because of space restrictions this examination will be limited. However, the unevenness of this examination should not be interpreted as suggesting that one school of thought is more important than another. Each contributes in a very meaningful and significant way to the body of knowledge dealing with business as process and product.

THE CONCEPTUALIZATION OF IB

In contrast to the single domain approaches taken by Wilkins and Boddewyn, the approach presented here assumes:

(1) there are multiple conceptual domains of IB inquiry; (2) each domain is established by a particular "school of thought" that seeks a particular body of knowledge; (3) the theorizing and research undertaken by members of each school of thought provides an important, but incomplete understanding of IB; and (4) IB is a social process.

The first three assumptions are discussed in detail in the remainder of the paper, while the last needs to be elaborated on here. Boulding [1978] and Klein [1977] explained, business can be viewed as a multilevel interactive societal process. Accordingly, a particular society's business process and the products of this process are the result of the dynamic interaction of that society's population in terms of (1) its economic, legal, political, and sociocultural heritage, (2) the institutionalization and organization of its business activities, and (3) the way it handles change and the effects of change. Further, the comparative business literature is sufficiently developed to suggest that the way business as process and product is evolving in one society differs significantly from the way it is evolving in another society. If taken from this perspective, IB also can be described as a multilevel, dynamic, and interactive social process, the outcome of which is the reconciliation of the evolving differences in the business processes of two or more societies. Macrolevel examples of International Business as a social process are the processes entered into by countries in order to reconcile their economic, political, and legal differences. The protocols and the organizations created are the products of these processes. An example is the internal adjustments made by a company to handle the environmental diversity it encounters when operating in two or more countries. The precise way that IB is defined for the purpose of scientific inquiry will depend on the meaning to be sought of the interaction-reconciliation process.[3]

THE MEANING SOUGHT OF THE DOMAIN OF IB INQUIRY

Figure 1 lists the four metalevel schools of thought that I believe represent the various definitions given the nature, scope, and content of IB inquiry.[4] For discussion purposes, they are labeled *substantivism*, *extensionalism*, *universalism*, and *resolutionalism*. By *substantivism*, I mean the study of firm-level activity that crosses national boundaries or is conducted in a location other than the firm's home country. By *extensionalism*, I mean the confirmation of the product of business inquiry undertaken in one societal setting when extended to another societal setting. By *universalism*, I mean the search for universal laws concerning the business-related nature and behavior of human beings and the organizations they create, irrespective of their societal origins. By *resolutionalism*, I mean the search for a body of theories that explain and predict the interaction-reconciliation process and its outcomes that stems from the existence of significant differences in the business-related nature and behavior of human beings and their organizations who are from separate and distinct societal settings. While it will be shown that these four schools of thought contribute importantly to the body of knowledge dealing with the phenomenon known as IB, the question posed here is whether any of these schools of thought can lay claim to providing IB inquiry its uniqueness, as product or process.

Neither the question nor its answer is trivial. Each school of thought sets the stage for what is done by researchers, even by educators, managers, and policy influencers. It establishes the domain of IB inquiry and thereby determines whether it is important and unique. This is because a particular school of thought is not based exclusively on a theoretical argument but on an ideological one as well. Each school of thought entails a belief system concerning the nature and behavior of human beings, including the social organizations they create and the significance they attach to business. Each is therefore similar to what Kuhn [1962] has called a paradigm. As Kuhn demonstrates, intellectual commitments are held tenaciously and seldom can be dislodged by logic or by contrary evidence, and as Gilpin puts it, "these commitments or ideologies

allege to provide scientific descriptions of how the world *does* work while they also constitute normative positions regarding how the world *should* work" [1987:26]. That this is especially true in the social sciences is well established in the literature (see, for example, Hunt [1990]; Phillips [1987]).

A school of thought includes a particular language and culture, and determines the state of knowledge, the stage of inquiry, and the special conditions of the particular problem studied. Thus, it gives unique expression to the three dimensions of meaning: *logical positivism*, *operationalism*, and *pragmatism* [Kaplan 1964].

Logical positivism asks the question: What are the phenomena and relationships studied, and what are the questions asked of these phenomena and relationships if substantivism, extensionalism, universalism, or resolutionalism is adopted as defining IB inquiry?

Operationalism asks the question: What needs to be done to believe substantivism, extensionalism, universalism, or resolutionalism? How are the phenomena and their relationships to be measured?

Finally, *pragmatism* asks the question: What will be done if substantivism, extensionalism, universalism, or resolutionalism is believed? Pragmatism is not action or contemplation, practice or theory, expediency or principle. It is the value attached to the knowledge gained as a result of scientific enterprise [Kaplan 1964:43]. Thus, the way IB is conceptualized, and the meaning sought by the questions asked, are "part and parcel" of the school of thought adopted.

IB Inquiry as Substantivism

As substantivism, the focus of IB inquiry is on some phenomenon, usually the firm. Its purpose is to gain a better understanding of the interplay between this phenomenon and the relevant dimensions of the international and foreign environments in which it is a part. More specifically, it is an open-ended and one-sided process of inquiry, the purpose of which is the study of the adjustments/adaptations that firms from one societal-defined business process need to make to their behavior when intruding on other societal-defined business processes. By open-ended, I mean that IB inquiry as substantivism is common to all branches of the social sciences (e.g., anthropology, economics, history, political science, psychology, sociology) and the business disciplines. Thus, the meaning given the firm, and the questions asked of the firm and its relationship with its external environment, are reflections of these branches and disciplines; their ideologies, their various states of knowledge, their stages of inquiry, and the questions they ask. The methodologies used to answer these questions are also just as varied and just as legitimate.

By one-sided, I mean that this form of IB inquiry assumes the firm is a major (if not sole) transfer agent of foreign innovation, technology, and managerial know-how. Largely ignored are the modifying and intervening roles played by other social phenomena, such as media, industry and business organizations, and government, and their effects on societal-defined business processes. The difference between "The firm is part of society" and "Society includes the firm" is a real one and could be an important one: the first puts the firm as the focus of attention and the second society.

In a world rapidly becoming interdependent, culturally, economically, politically, sociologically, and technologically, the focus on the firm has resulted in a body of knowledge of considerable value to firms as they embark on activities in other social milieu. We now have a better understanding of the economic reasons for the multinational enterprise (MNE) (e.g., Buckley and Casson [1976], Dunning [1988b], Hymer [1976]); the social responsibility of MNEs (e.g., Donaldson [1989]); the MNE-nation-state relationship (e.g., Behrman and Grosse [1990], Boddewyn [1988], Moran [1985]); the management of MNE-nation-state conflict (e.g., Gladwin and Walter [1980]); and

the within-and across-country management of capital, human resources, marketing, and manufacturing (e.g., Ricks, Toyne, and Martinez [1990]).

Importantly, IB substantivism has progressed beyond a parochial concern with understanding the behavior of U.S. firms. We are now aware that a firm's interaction with its international and foreign environments may yield multiple outcomes, each of which can be linked, at least in part, to the societal-defined business process from which the firm springs. For example, there appear to be U.S., Japanese, and German outcomes.

It has also progressed to a point where some have expressed concern over the absence of an interdisciplinary unifying theme [Dunning 1989; Hawkins 1984; Toyne 1989]. Dunning, for instance, called for a more interdisciplinary approach to the study of the firm and its behavior. Implicitly, he argued that there is a common, unifying construct that engenders a set of common questions that should be jointly researched. However, such a possibility is somewhat problematic. First, unlike economics and organization theory, the business disciplines have not focused on building a theory of the firm. Indeed, they seek to answer fundamentally different questions; a situation that is becoming progressively clearer as they become increasingly specialized and less interested in the firm and its management [Toyne 1992]. Second, IB substantivists are seeking to answer questions of substantive value, not scientific value. Simply put, their research is empirical, descriptive, and applied. Although contributing to inductive reasoning, they do not in and of themselves extend the body of knowledge by building theory.

IB substantivists have given scant theory-building attention to the more macrolevel events affecting and shaping the IB process, and thus the phenomena of their inquiry. Because of their focus, their inquiry is limited to those dimensions of the environment that are specified as important by the firm at any point in time. Mainly ignored are such things as the interaction of national markets, national industry policies, national foreign policies and agreements, and the modifying effects that these interactions may have on particular business processes, and thus on the international behavior of firms that have emerged, or are emerging from these processes. Since the focus is on the firm, circumstances, not the reasons for the circumstances, are of primary interest. Thus, the IB substantivists' understanding of the firm and its activities is limited, and they end up being "surprised" by the changing nature and behavior of the phenomena under investigation. By insisting on a firm-level conceptualization of IB they end up studying the outcomes of change, not the reasons for change.

The emphasis on the firm is the result of bias. There are, of course, many researchers (primarily microeconomists) who believe that a satisfactory theory of IB must "ultimately" be a firm-level theory [Buckley 1988; Rugman 1985]. To them, "scientific" means accepting the firm as the necessary and sufficient foundation for IB theory. However, as Kaplan has observed, although it is plausible to understand macro phenomena in micro terms, the argument that it is necessary is specious [1964:322]. Another source of bias is what Kaplan terms "the search for entities and structures rather than for processes and functions." In this regard, von Hayek was echoing Kaplan when he suggested that what is treated as important is that which is accessible to measurement. This often leads to the demand that our theories must be formulated in terms that refer only to measurable magnitudes [1989:3].

The weakness of focusing primarily on substantive phenomena, such as the firm, can be illustrated using an analogy employed by Kaplan [1964:11]:

> There is a story of a drunkard searching under a street lamp for his house key, which he had dropped some distance away. Asked why he didn't look where he had dropped it, he replied, "It's lighter here!"

The key, in our case, is a fuller and richer understanding of the IB process with the end result being theories, concepts, and metaphors of scientific and substantive value. The firm, no matter how visible it may be, is not necessarily the correct foundation on which to build an argument concerning the domain of IB inquiry and the uniqueness of its contributions. The firm is a unit of analysis. It is an interactive outcome of a social process, not the process itself. However, a study of firm-level activity is not so removed from the actual location of the key. The firm, as Wilkins notes in her paper, has no meaning in a vacuum. Its meaning and significance are only made clear within a tapestry of social relationships; it is the woof and weave of the tapestry, not the individual threads, that convey meaning.

IB substantivism leaves these relationships, and the questions asked of them, unspecified. It is the various branches of the social sciences and the business disciplines interested in the firm as a social phenomenon *within* their domains of inquiry that give meaning and significance to the firm and the relationships studied. More specifically, they identify the important questions to be asked and the methodologies to be used. They also provide the language and culture of the inquiry process itself and the body of knowledge to be used and augmented. That is, the firm has no scientific meaning without referring to one of these branches or disciplines. Unfortunately, these various branches and disciplines, while borrowing from one another, do not communicate with one another; nor are they individually or jointly involved in developing a coherent body of knowledge.

Although some may take issue with this argument, I believe that we can all agree with Kaplan's recognition of the value of inductive research. He states that:

> the pattern of search, we feel, should be closely related to the probability of the thing sought being in the place where the seeker is looking. But the joke may be on us. It may be sensible to look first in an un-

likely place just *because* "it's light here." We might reasonably entertain one hypothesis rather than another because it is easier to refute it as false, or because it will eliminate a greater number of possibilities, or because it will show us more clearly what steps to take next [1964:17].

The next step, that of theory building, has not occurred, nor can it occur. IB substantivists do not question the existence of the firm but merely seek to understand how firms handle the managerial issues and problems they face when intruding on other socially prescribed business processes. Unlike microeconomists, for example, they ignore the theory-building *why* question. The positivistic philosophers of science claim that "A scientific explanation may be regarded as an answer to a *why* question" [Hempel 1965:334 (emphasis added)]. The realist school goes even further and maintains that the *how* question must be answered along with the *why* question for explanation to occur [Keat and Urry 1975:31]. To explain and predict (i.e., theory), the antecedent conditions to the phenomenon need to be identified and their linkage to the phenomenon specified.

IB Inquiry as Extensionalism

As extensionalism, the purpose of IB inquiry is the confirmation of the scientific product of business inquiry developed in one societal setting when extended and tested in another societal setting. Like substantivism, extensionalism is open-ended and one-sided. It is open-ended because it too is common to all branches of the social sciences and to the business disciplines. It is one-sided because it is primarily interested in testing homespun theories and concepts in different societal settings.

Adler [1983] and Boyacigiller and Adler [1990] have termed this form of inquiry parochial. It is parochial, but only to the extent that IB extensionalists are interested in extending and replicating the questions they have posed in one societal setting to another societal setting. They are guided by the values, norms, paradigms, theories, metaphors, and methodologies that have been agreed upon by their colleagues. More specifically, they want to know if the theories and concepts arrived at as a result of studying some aspect of the business process embedded in one societal setting (e.g., the United States) are equally applicable in all societal settings. However, this stream of inquiry can be viewed as augmenting our knowledge by providing a better assessment of the boundaries and parochialism of the theories and concepts being developed within specific societal settings and within specific fields of inquiry. This does not detract from the value of their work. To the contrary, IB extensionalists contribute significantly to our understanding of business as a social process. Their work has considerable substantive value. However, their work simply isn't producing a coherent, comprehensive, and certified body of knowledge dealing with the phenomenon known as IB.

IB extensionalists do not provide "natural" or comprehensive arguments for the uniqueness of IB inquiry. They generally resort to "artificial" arguments [Kaplan 1964:50–51]. Here, artificial, in contrast to natural, means that the various attributes claimed to provide IB inquiry its uniqueness are self-serving. The attributes argued as providing IB inquiry its uniqueness are not significantly related to attributes conceptualized elsewhere in our thinking, causally or statistically. They serve the specific needs of the various branches of the social sciences and the business disciplines. For example, it has been suggested that the uniqueness of IB inquiry can be established by referring to some aspect of the IB context, such as culture, foreign exchange, national borders, or (somewhat in the same vein) national polity. That is, they seek to justify the work they do in language familiar and acceptable to their "domestic" colleagues (e.g., international finance and international marketing researchers seeking to legitimize their work in the eyes of their domestic colleagues). Importantly, they unnecessarily impose a structural-functional perspective regarding human beings and the organizations they create [Donaldson 1985]. They are not describing the totality of IB, nor are they interested in doing so.

In short, IB extensionalism is the practice of normal science undertaken by researchers embedded in one societal setting in terms of the questions asked and the interpretation given particular findings [Kuhn 1962]. *More pointedly, IB extensionalists are interested merely in foreign situations not IB*, nor in developing a comprehensive and coherent body of knowledge explaining business.

IB Inquiry as Universalism

As universalism, the purpose of IB inquiry is the search for universal laws concerning the nature and behavior of human beings and their social creations. In contrast to IB extensionalism, which reveals societal differences, IB universalism reveals societal similarities. Essentially, universalists assume that all peoples are the same "under the skin," only the circumstance in which they find themselves differ. Thus, variations in their behavior and the social organizations they create are the result of *contextual differences*.

IB universalism is merely one of several scientific endeavors undertaken to arrive at universal theories. While IB may provide opportunities for the discovery of universal "truths" concerning human beings and the business processes and organizations they create, IB is not essential to the universalist's work. That is, universalists do not have as their primary focus an understanding of the IB process. Like most economists, they are not interested in process, only outcomes.

Unfortunately, universalists oversimplify reality in order to develop prescriptive theories. Universalism assumes away the possibility of an "inner, emergent person." In the strictest sense, it is a structural-functionalist approach. Universalists seek to explain variations in the nature and behavior of human beings and their social creations in terms of structures, functions, roles, and processes. Alternative, axiomatic

assumptions (i.e., assumptions that cannot be refuted), such as the social action argument that views human creations and activities in terms of actors, goals, situations, norms, and meanings, are either considered false or ignored.

Universalists also ignore, or de-emphasize, the pragmatic dimension of the domain of meaning when remarking on the scientific enterprise of others. For example, while essentially correct when suggesting that IB extensionalists are parochial, they ignore the value of the knowledge that extensionalists produce. Extensionalists make significant contributions to our understanding of human beings and their social creations by clarifying the power of their explanations in other societal settings.

Pragmatically, U.S. managers want to know what are the limits of the theories, concepts, and principles they presently use and how they need to modify them in order to be successful. Also, if parochialism is inherent to human beings, then it too is worthy of study by universalists. If extensionalists can be faulted, it is only for not making clear the boundaries and orientation of their inquiry and the scientific value of their product in terms understandable to others. This is also true of universalists. Boyacigiller and Adler [1991], for example, call for a more open and tolerant regard for the work of others. As noted in the conclusion to their paper, they call for universally applicable theories, regiocentric theories, intercultural theories, and intracultural theories. This, of course, requires discourse by members of the four schools of thought being discussed here.

IB Inquiry as Resolutionalism

As resolutionalism, the purpose of IB inquiry is the search for theories and concepts explaining the emergent, socially based interaction-reconciliation process that arises when two socially distinct business processes and their creations come into contact. That is, IB inquiry can be viewed as the study of those processes and outcomes that give rise to the resolution of meaningful (significant) societal differences. It argues that IB is a unique social process and therefore worthy of separate study. Essentially, it has a unique set of questions that are not being asked by the other three schools of thought. Initially viewed as a microlevel phenomenon (see, for example, Adler [1983]; Adler and Bartholomew [1992]; Black, Mendenhall, and Oddou [1991]; de la Torre and Toyne [1978]), the interaction-reconciliation process is increasingly recognized as common to all substantive phenomena and all levels of analysis (e.g., joint ventures, mergers and acquisitions, licensing and distribution arrangements, government foreign relations).

International business resolutionalism does several things that the other schools of thought are neither prepared to do nor capable of doing. First, it expands the domain of International Business inquiry by focusing on the interaction and resolution of societal differences at the microlevel, the micro-cum-macrolevel, and the macrolevel. Second, it places emphasis and value on a better understanding of these levels by calling attention to the economic, legal, political, and social interdependencies of societies, and the business processes by which these interdependencies are created and maintained. Its emphasis is on understanding the process by which societal differences are reconciled within and between phenomena that are either simultaneously involved in two or more societal-defined business processes or that are in meaningful contact with other societal-defined business processes. Thus, the firm remains a central phenomenon of IB inquiry, except now it is viewed as an interactive, societal transforming mechanism that is, itself, transformed by its interactions. Finally, resolutionalism places equal emphasis on understanding unintentional as well as intentional outcomes and the processes that produce these outcomes. For example, it can be argued that substantivism and extensionalism limit themselves to the study of intentional outcomes (as seen from a firm's perspective). Unintentional outcomes, such

as the transformation of the bridging mechanisms as a result of the reconciliation process and the emergence of stakeholder groups where none existed prior to the conduct of international business, are, of course, major sources triggering change. In fact, unintentional outcomes may represent the act of reconciliation.

Resolutionalism also argues for a catholicity of outlooks. This is in contrast to extensionalism and universalism which tend to espouse the idea that any other view is acceptable as long as it is the one they support. They are wrong, however, when they insist on a single view, a single school of thought. The validity of their positions and arguments does not depend on the alienation of other positions and arguments. Substantivism, extensionalism, and universalism contribute important but limited insights into the IB process. The more we know about the adjustments and adaptations of phenomena from one societal business process when intruding on other societal-defined business processes, the more we know about the explanatory and predictive limitations of parochial theories and concepts, and the more we know about the universal aspects of human beings and their social creations, the more insights we gain on which to base our studies, our inquiry. Thus, all four schools of thought contribute to the body of knowledge explaining IB. However, resolutionalism establishes IB inquiry as unique and distinctive, in terms of product and process, if for no other reason than that the other schools of thought do not have the same domain of inquiry, nor do they ask the same questions. Resolutionalism wants to know *why* and *how* the nature and behavior of human beings and their social organizations are transformed as a result of their international interactions.

THE ORIGINS AND FUTURE OF IB INQUIRY

The discussion so far suggests that international business inquiry provides the various branches of the social sciences and the business disciplines opportunities to extend their "puzzle-solving" or "normal science" activities.[5] At the same time, IB inquiry also has the potential to address unique questions, develop a unique body of knowledge that can be linked to the general but fragmented body of knowledge dealing with business, and to present this body of knowledge in a more coherent, integrated fashion. However, this does not mean that a unique and coherent body of knowledge will emerge. Although the reasons for this are many, they can be understood by briefly reviewing what has been done so far and what seems to be ahead.

Prior to the 1950s, IB was treated as an economic closure phenomenon at the microlevel. That is, IB researchers primarily focused on identifying and describing the issues and problems confronting firms that reconciled macrolevel disparities in national demand and supply conditions (e.g., exporters, importers).[6] If asked to explain what they were doing, they would probably have said that they were interested in identifying and describing *who* accomplished the reconciliation task and *how* it was accomplished. However, by focusing on *who* and *how* questions, these researchers were not providing a basis for theory construction. They accepted the economic explanation for trade, did not question the existence of exporters (e.g., why some firms exported and others did not), and sought to understand empirically the managerial issues and problems exporters faced when seeking to accomplish their trade task.

Although not contributing to IB theory, or to the field's legitimacy as a distinct and unique inquiry, this "preliminary work" was important to the future development and definition of IB inquiry for two reasons. First, it established the firm as the unit of analysis. Second, it demonstrated that the business disciplines, particularly finance and marketing, could make worthwhile (albeit parochial) contributions.

The field was redefined in the late 1950s by economists who recognized the growing policy importance of U.S. foreign direct investments (FDI) via the MNE phenomenon. The U.S. trade position was unchallenged, so it was not of concern to policy makers. However, the MNE was a "new" phenomenon, research funds were available, and its importance for foreign policies of the U.S. and European countries was clear. The MNE was also seen as an agent inhibiting or aiding in the industrialization of the "underdeveloped" world, depending on the observer's particular point of view.

The scholars responsible for the "ground-breaking," seminal research on the MNE were mostly U.S. economists who, because of their parochial, insular, and policy-driven perspectives, were quick to recognize the "uniqueness" of this phenomenon and its policy implications. They naturally described the phenomenon in U.S. economic terms, imbued it with a U.S. interpretation of world events, and placed the phenomenon within a scientific framework predicated on a U.S. social science belief system (ideology) that advocated reductionism, determinism, logical empiricism, and economic liberalism [Gilpin 1987; Lastrucci 1963; Popper 1961; Zetterberg 1954]. Consequently, these scholars not only redefined IB, the questions to be asked, and the methodologies to be employed to answer these questions, they also imbued the phenomenon with normative liberal economic implications (e.g., what was good for the MNE and the United States was also good for the rest of the world; the political and economic spheres of human activity are to be treated separately). Significantly, the important *why* question was asked concerning the emergence and existence of the MNE. Hymer's monopoly advantage explanation of FDI [1960] and Vernon's product-cycle hypothesis [1966] were not only seminal explanations of the MNE, they also provided a much needed theoretical legitimacy to the study of IB.[7]

With the MNE firmly established as a legitimate unit of analysis (albeit economic),

IB inquiry quickly attracted a community of researchers whose research traditions were well established in their respective business disciplines. To paraphrase Kuhn [1970:10], their research was based upon the past achievements that their particular disciplines acknowledged as supplying the foundation for their further practices. Thus, these researchers were "peripheral and radical" in the sense that they were interested in a phenomenon that was not of central concern to their domestic colleagues. They were "traditional" in the sense that the questions they asked, and the knowledge and methodologies they employed to answer these questions, were guided by the paradigms, theories, metaphors, and methodologies accepted and used by their colleagues. Consequently, most IB researchers were, and still are, mere extensions of their business disciplines and engrossed in normal science or puzzle solving.

The 1980s and 1990s have been witness to a growing, and as yet, unvoiced crisis in IB inquiry. The central reason for this crisis can be discussed in the context of three rather obvious (but not exhaustive) trends: (1) the emergence of coalitions (strategic alliances) and their implications for the study of firm-level activities in general, and IB in particular; (2) the increasing need to address the relationship between macroeconomic and political policy issues and firm-level behavior and activities; and (3) the internationalization of the business disciplines. The first example raises questions concerning the metatheoretical underpinnings of business inquiry, the second questions the assumptions underpinning liberal economics, and the third questions the viability of IB inquiry given the psychology and the sociology of behavioral inquiry. As Kaplan has noted:

> The fragmentation of a science into "schools" is by no means unknown even in as rigorous a discipline as mathematics; what is striking in behavioral science is how unsympathetic and even hostile to one another such schools often are [1964:29].

The Emergence of Transnational Coalitions

Although the emergence of transnational coalitions in the 1980s is viewed primarily as a response by MNEs to global environmental trends, it could just as easily signal the emergence of a new form of IB activity *that does not require the extension and adjustment of functional activities across national borders*. In its extreme form, this phenomenon suggests that functional extension and adjustment, FDI, and control are not needed of any particular firm. The essence of transnational coalitions involves *contracted and administered relationships, knowledge and technology transfers*, and the *cartelization of world markets*. Is this exclusively economics? Certainly not. Is it IB as presently conceived and defined? Certainly not. So what is it?

What distinguished the MNE from the exporter was FDI and the transfer and cross-national control of business activities (thus, the initial justification for IB extensionalism and the eventual emergence of IB universalism). What distinguishes the transnational coalition from the MNE is the increasing reliance on social relationships, the transfer of knowledge, skills, and technology, and the lack of foreign direct investment and the need to transfer and cross-nationally control functional activities. Fundamentally, the study of transnational coalitions involves law, organization theory as it relates to economic and political power, social relationships, organizational boundaries, and corporate-level strategy. Thus, it is more akin to the administrative definition of the firm suggested by Wilkins [1986b:80–95].

The implications of the transnational coalition for IB inquiry are many and raise serious questions concerning the appropriateness of a definition of IB that limits research to a study of firm-level activities that have been artificially reduced to finance, manufacturing, marketing, and so on. For example, it requires periodically redefining the domain of IB inquiry. This, in turn, suggests that IB substantivism fails to capture the *totality*, the *essence* of IB. Perhaps even more fundamental, this emerging phenomenon also raises uneasy questions concerning the nature and scope of business inquiry in general, and whether or not business should be treated as a set of distinct functional activities. By viewing business as a marketing function, a production function, or a finance function, are we missing out on an opportunity to raise and answer questions of similar portent to those tackled by economists, sociologists, and political scientists? Has IB inquiry unnecessarily limited its importance by insisting that it is either substantivism, extensionalism, or universalism with the clear disciplinary demarcations that these schools of thought entail?

Macrolevel Economic and Political Issues and IB Inquiry

In recent years, the ability of IB inquiry to make meaningful contributions to the debate on U.S. competitiveness has become increasingly questionable. In general, government policy makers and industry representatives turn to economists and political scientists for answers. There are both theoretical and institutional reasons for this deficiency. Without a comprehensive understanding of the symbiotic linkages between macro and micro phenomena, IB substantivists can only address microlevel situations on a contingency basis. They ignore the dynamic and evolving relationship between firm-level activity and society. Consequently, when asked to make recommendations, their answers are not just more of the same but with greater intensity, they are highly temporal and localized. Unlike economists and political scientists, business researchers are unable to predict changes in business behavior as a result of fundamental changes in the structuring of the environment. Because of the meaning sought as substantivism, extensionalism, and universalism, IB inquiry simply does not ask questions that will provide this knowledge.

IB researchers are constrained in their understanding of a basically holistic, societal phenomenon by self-imposed departmentalization of their inquiry and focus on microlevel analysis and theorizing. For example, although Vernon's original work pointed to the need to include a societal-level interpretation of IB, this symbiotic linkage between firm and environment was subsequently overlooked or ignored by IB researchers. Thus when national and industry-level competitiveness issues are at the forefront of public and private concern and debate, business and IB researchers find themselves unable to come to grips with these concerns because of a lack of a unifying conceptualization of business as a social phenomenon, a lack of appropriate theory, a lack of an appropriate methodology, and an inability to work together because of metalevel barriers and institutionalized obstacles.

Internationalization of Business Disciplines

In the 1960s, the U.S. business research community became engrossed in establishing its legitimacy within a university setting by defining business schools as schools of applied science. That is, considerable time and effort have been spent since 1959 on implementing the recommendations presented in the Gordon-Howell and Pierson reports sponsored by the Ford and Carnegie foundations. Their recommendations were inward-looking and resulted in a shift towards systematic research [Daft and Lewin 1990:4]. Theory-building and theory-testing have become paramount (basic, not applied science now rules the roost), and departmental barriers have been erected and reinforced.

IB inquiry is at a crossroads with respect to the business disciplines. It can either develop a scientific and socially relevant perspective that adds to human understanding and knowledge in the future, or it can limit itself to artificially and fragmented disciplinary elements and eventually be overwhelmed by the narrowly defined basic-science interests of the business disciplines as expressed in IB extensionalism and IB universalism. Inevitable internationalization of these disciplines can only accentuate this problem. Put differently, the business disciplines only describe parts of the elephant, not the entire body. Who, if substantivism, extensionalism, and universalism are pursued to their logical conclusions, will be in a position to give us some idea of what the elephant looks like?

While the lack of an overarching, unifying conceptual definition of IB has not stopped many of us, on an individual basis, from exploring other phenomena and relationships, the work itself highlights the difficulties facing the IB academic community. By insisting that IB inquiry be defined in substantive, extensional, or universal terms, we are increasingly aware that our academic and research organizations (e.g., institutions of higher learning, associations, and academies), and the rewards and sanctions these organizations impose, are obstacles to our inquiry. For example, the growing emphasis on narrowly defined, discipline-constrained inquiry as a result of increasing specialization, current internationalization trends, and the lack of "departments of IB" that encourage a more holistic view of business, restricts our inquiry to artificially and narrowly defined domains of inquiry. As noted earlier, the business disciplines are not interested in understanding the IB process. They are only interested in foreign situations to the extent that these situations provide them the opportunity to practice "normal science." The ultimate result of the encroachment of the business disciplines through a process of "internationalization" does not provide any encouragement for believing new perspectives and new knowledge will materialize.

This exposes IB researchers to the distinct possibility of becoming extinct. While many IB researchers welcome the "legitimizing" effect that the internationalization of their "mother" disciplines will have on their academic and research status, IB researchers interested in understanding the "totality" and "essence" of IB as a unique social process could end up as institutional "orphans."

SOME FINAL THOUGHTS

When does a particular field of inquiry become respectable? When does it become recognized as worthy of support? I would suggest that this occurs when three things are made clear. First, when it can be demonstrated that it is working from a perspective that is fundamentally different from those already being explored by other fields. This, I believe has been accomplished in this paper. Second, when it can be demonstrated that its contributions are linked to other fields of inquiry and thus contribute in a meaningful and significant way to a better and more comprehensive and integrated understanding of the nature and behavior of human beings. This too has been done by comparing the questions asked by the four schools of thought identified and discussed here. And third, when it can be demonstrated that the contributions have value. This, has been done here.

What is lacking is not a deficiency of interest in IB. What is lacking is a common knowledge generating purpose. This, unfortunately, will not be gained so long as those interested in IB seek to answer questions that originate from entirely different metalevel sources. It can only be achieved when the questions asked of IB have a common, unifying purpose.

NOTES

1. There are, of course, other ways of interpreting the scientific process. The reason for using this particular framework is its ability to make clear the distinctions I am stressing between metalevel inquiry, scientific inquiry, and substantive inquiry.

2. Another detailed discussion of this view is presented in the opening chapter of this volume.

3. The argument here is not determinism or indeterminism. Kaplan notes that such debate does "not assist inquiries into any particular causes, nor do demonstrations of an 'ultimate indeterminacy' prevent us from trying to learn more than we now know about such determi-

nants as there are" (1964:21). Thus, the gaining of knowledge is an unfolding, emergent act, not an ultimate act.

4. In a previous paper (1989) I identified three schools of thought. The first can be viewed here as representing what I refer to a substantivism. The second was comparative business inquiry. Here, this school can be viewed more as a methodology employed by universalism. The third was essential microeconomics. Here, this school of thought can be viewed as represented under the umbrella of substantivism.

5. This section presents an abridged, but modified version of what was argued in my unpublished paper (1988).

6. In private correspondence, Mira Wilkins was most helpful by pointing out that the MNE was studied prior to the 1950s. However, what I am referring to here is concerned with deliberate efforts to develop theory, not historical description. That these studies are extremely important is not denied, nor should they be ignored. They contribute to the inductive reasoning process involved in theory building.

7. See, for example, Dunning and Rugman (1985) and Horaguchi and Toyne (1990).

■ ■ ■

COMMENTARIES
Hans Schollhammer

Discussion of "The Conceptual Domain of International Business"

The Importance of Domain Considerations

The most central issue for any academic discipline is the delineation of its domain and the specification of boundary conditions. Delineating the domain of a discipline creates a basis for suggesting appropriate areas of inquiry and for assessing the relevance of theoretical as well as empirical studies as contributions to the accumulation of discipline-specific knowledge and its application in a professional setting. It is the construct of a domain that gives conceptual and empirical studies their meaning. Domain considerations are inextricably linked to theory building—whether by deductive

or inductive means—and to the cumulative development of knowledge. The delineation of a domain of inquiry entails the specification of boundary conditions—whether in a closed or open system context—and it is only with clarity about these boundary conditions that it is possible to assess the comparability of diverse studies that focus on specific domain issues.

Given the significance of domain considerations for the dynamic development of a discipline one has to applaud the efforts of Mira Wilkins, Jean Boddewyn, and Brian Toyne for providing us with their conceptualizations of the internatnional business (IB) domain. At the same time one has to notice, with some unease, that their conclusions about the scope of the IB domain and its boundaries are quite different. In light of the intensity of academic concern with IB phenomena, and in view of the growing volume of studies dealing with these issues, it seems surprising that the question about the conceptual domain of IB remains unsettled and that the answers to this question reflect so little commonalty. For reviewing this triple effort I chose two approaches: a comparative analysis followed by an assessment of each study's contribution or shortcoming from the perspective of its ability to provide a foundation for further theory building and to guide empirical investigations.

A Comparison of Three Perspectives

To facilitate a comparative review of the three studies I used several classifications. A summary of this analysis is presented in Table 1. The most crucial dimension concerning each analysis is the choice of the critical constituent element for characterizing the IB domain. For Wilkins the critical element is the internationally operating firm in the pursuit of an economic purpose. She delineates the IB domain strictly from an institutional perspective; namely the individual firm as actor in the IB arena. Since her focus is so clearly on the institution of the firm and the structure (Gestalt) of the firm's international involvement in a dynamic context, I characterize

Table 1. The Conceptual Domain of International Business: Three Perspectives

Perspectives	Constitutional Condition and Boundary Constraints	Dominant Issues	Conceptual Foundation/ Direction for Theory Building	Ambiguities and Shortcomings
Mira Wilkins: institutional perspective	National boundaries; firms operating under more than one sovereignty, control over foreign-based assets through direct investments "no matter how small"	The multinational firm, its evolution structures, strategic orientations, and environmental interactions; coping with uncertainties, regulatory constraints, currency diversity	Theory of the multinational firm	Vague characterization of MNC; narrow focus; ignore cross-border economic transactions not linked to firms' control over foreign based assets
Jean Boddewyn: transaction perspective	Cross-border "negotiated" economic exchanges in the form of trade and investments among independent organizational units with varying degrees of structural complexity; market obstructions by governmental authorities	Rationale for cross-border transactions; adaptive processes	Eclectic, advocacy of adoption of conceptual constructs from economics, political science, sociology, and other fields	Ambivalence about key concepts such as "negotiated"; ignores non-negotiated cross-border business transactions such as intra-firm exchanges; very broad domain conceptualizing without specific direction for theory building
Brian Toyne: multi-dimensional perspective	Firm-level border crossing business transactions; environmental diversity among sovereign nation states	Four dominant sets of issues labeled substantialism, extensionalism, universalism, resolutionalism; focus on transactions as well as comparative institutional/environmental business aspects	Conceptual diversity stress on theory-driven (deductive) domain conceptualization	Lack of domain integration, diffuse foci; overemphasis on categorization and separation instead of integration

her approach to the configuration of the IB domain as "institutional." In contrast, Boddewyn defines the IB domain strictly from the perspective of cross-border business transactions in the form of trade, investments or other factor transfers among independent organizational entities. Boddewyn thus uses a transaction-process perspective for delineating the IB domain. Toyne adopts from the outset not an empirical but a normative stance. He postulates the configuration of a domain of inquiry driven by and congruent with theoretical constructs. He identifies with a scheme that differentiates between substantive, scientific, and metatheoretical level inquiries and suggests that only the latter is domain determinant. He also suggests the fragmentation of IB as a domain because of four schools of thought, each focusing on different aspects of IB as a domain of inquiry. The issue is further complicated by Toyne's perceived necessity to also include macrolevel international economic and political issues, and new forms of cross-border, interfirm alliances.

While Wilkins and Boddewyn present the IB domain as determined by institutional actors, i.e., multinational enterprises (MNEs), or cross-border business transactions, Toyne presents it as fluid, multifaceted, and dependent on the existence of metalevel theoretical constructs. Each of the three scholars specifies the domain in a different way; each stresses a different set of constituent conditions and diverse foci of inquiry. In light of the volume of studies on IB issues since the late 1950s, it is surprising that there exists so little commonality in defining the field—let alone in theorizing about the most central issues. Arguably the absence of a reasonable degree of unanimity concerning the IB domain hampers not only theory building but also focused empirical research.

Mira Wilkins's Perspective of the IB Domain

Wilkins's studies focusing on the transformation of major U.S. companies into MNEs have shown that the operational activities of these firms are the major engines driving the expansion of IB transactions. For her the domain of IB is specified by the cross-border activities of these internationally operating firms "no matter how small" [p. 36 in this volume]. Mira Wilkins accepts the notion that a necessary characteristic of a MNE is the acquisition and control over foreign-based assets, to engage in transborder business activities, in making strategic choices about the rationale (why), the timing (when), the location (where), and the operational modes (how) of these activities and the firm's interaction with constituents of the economic as well as political environments [p. 39 in this volume]. Apart from a vague efficiency criterion as the source of a sustainable competitive advantage, Wilkins specifies no constraints or boundary conditions for international business as a domain of inquiry. Delineating the IB domain by focusing on firms with just two essential attributes, namely cross-border transactions that serve an economic purpose and the control over foreign-based assets through direct investments, is insufficient and a major shortcoming of Mira Wilkins's conceptualization. Her notion that a multinational enterprise (MNE) is a multinational enterprise is unrealistic, misguides empirical studies, and ignores a degree of differentiation among firms that has been advocated since the very beginning of an intensified analysis of this type of firms. For example, Steiner and Cannon [1966] used the term MNE for firms "doing business in two or more countries in such a *volume* that its well-being and growth rests on more than one country" [6]. Aharoni [1971] advocated to differentiate among multinational firms using structural, behavioral, and performance characteristics. If the conceptualization of the IB domain is predicated by the existence of multinational enterprises, it is necessary to define with greater precision the nature of this type of firms as an object of inquiry.

Another shortcoming of the way Mira Wilkins delineates the conceptual domain of IB is the exclusion of IB transactions in which participating firms do not acquire foreign-based assets that are under their direct control. A significant volume of international transactions involves firms that operate in a single national context. Indirect exporting or importing, international licensing, strategic alliances among firms based in different countries, or other contractual arrangements are forms of international engagement that do not necessarily involve control over foreign-based assets through direct investments. To argue that these types of engagements are not to be considered as part of the IB domain is not justifiable.

By not paying attention to the extraordinarily diverse nature of MNEs and by seemingly excluding IB transactions that do not require the involvement of firms with FDI, Mira Wilkins provides us with a rather fuzzy delineation of the IB discipline. The primary purpose of being concerned with delineating a discipline domain is to provide a foundation for theory building and theory testing. To the extent that the delineation of a conceptual domain is vague or is not generally accepted, the development of a reasonably unified theory is hampered and the comparability of empirical studies seriously impaired. Mira Wilkins recognizes the linkage between domain conceptualization and theory building. She suggests what types of issues the theory should address, and she advocates the development of a "core theory" [p. 41 in this volume] that explains (and predicts?) "which firms go (international), why they go, where they go abroad, and the matter of timing" [p. 40 in this volume]. In one way or another these questions have been addressed with a conceptualization that John Dunning [1973; 1980;1981] labeled an "eclectic" theory. Was it this eclectic theory Mira Wilkins had in mind when she stated "that there now does exist a fundamental basis for the understanding of one of the most important institutions of modern times [the MNE], and that we do not need to offer a patchwork quilt"? [p. 41 in this volume] Yet instead of offering the outlines of a "core theory," Wilkins in the very next sentence

provides us with "a baker's dozen of examples" a core theory might address: Do MNEs avoid taxes? Do they exploit factor cost differentials? Are they agents of technology diffusion? Inquiries along these lines have significant practice relevance, but they do not lead to an overarching theoretical construct.

In my opinion, Mira Wilkins's analysis of the conceptual domain of IB is too limited and too vague. She focuses exclusively on the operational activities of MNEs, and no attempt is made to impose any meaningful boundary conditions as to what constitutes a MNE as the principle structural element in Wilkins's conceptualization of the IB domain.

Jean Boddewyn's Perspective of the IB Domain

Jean Boddewyn's review of the IB domain results in a series of definitions that aim to encompass all economic exchanges (in contrast to noneconomic exchanges) across national boundaries. The delineation of the conceptual domain of IB thus centers on cross-border transactions (processes) in the form of trade in goods, services, and the transfer of production factors (investments). Boddewyn stresses two boundary conditions: the cross-border transactions are to be "negotiated" (and "at arm's length" in an earlier version of the study) and they may involve a variety of actors such as individual persons, private or public organizations and groupings among firms (consortia and alliances). For Boddewyn the conceptualization of the IB domain is clearly centered on cross-border economic transactions, and the institutions involved in the transactions are only of interest to the extent that they provide a specification of the level of analysis. In Boddewyn's view the IB domain is specified by the array of cross-border transactions, not by the institutions involved in these transactions. Cross-border transactions have not only economic but sociocultural and political ramifications; these issues are part of the IB domain also. Also, Boddewyn wrestles with "the boundaries of IB" [pp. 57–58 in this volume] and comes to the conclusion that there are no objective boundary constraints. He realizes that in an economically interdependent world, "purely domestic U.S. firms, with no direct international involvement, are in IB because they are ultimately affected by what happens outside the U.S." [p. 57 in this volume]. Boddewyn raises some other issues such as the difference between nation and state. Boddewyn believes that in an IB context, the nation as an element of analysis is largely irrelevant since in the political sphere only the state and its agencies are able to obstruct access to markets. Boddewyn then quotes Grosse and Behrman [1992] claiming "a theory of IB must be a theory of obstruction to markets" [p. 56 in this volume]. In view of Boddewyn's much broader conception of the IB domain, one has to wonder why he accepts this statement unchallenged?

In my opinion, Boddewyn's conceptualization of the IB domain—presented as a series of definitions—is a rather questionable exercise. On the one hand, he aims to be all-inclusive by emphasizing the entire spectrum of cross-border transactions at different levels of institutional involvement. On the other hand, only "negotiated" business transfers are to be considered part of the IB domain. Yet, non-negotiated, intrafirm, cross-border transfers constitute an ever-growing proportion of the totality of international business transactions. Although the U.S. Tax Code may provide evidence for the fiction that intracompany, cross-border transactions are "negotiated," in the context of "creative accounting" this is actually meaningless. There is every indication that a significant proportion of cross-border transactions does not meet the standards suggested in Boddewyn's definition of the IB domain.

If the purpose of concern about the conceptualization of the IB domain is to provide a foundation for theory building and theory testing, then Boddewyn's effort falls short of one's expectations. Practically no effort is made to relate the proposed definition of IB to existing theoretical constructs,

such as Dunning's "eclectic" theory, or to the delineation of new conceptualizations such as an international extension of industrial organization theory, population ecology, resource-based strategic management models, and others. In addition, Boddewyn's analysis of the IB domain reflect a degree of ambivalence that is disconcerting, especially coming from someone who has spent a lifetime contributing to this domain of inquiry. There is also a concern about boundary conditions: is "negotiated" or "arm's length" an appropriate qualifier for cross-border trade and investment flows? Boddewyn drops the "arm's length" qualifier "on second thought" but retains the term "negotiated" cross-border trade and investment as the defining element of the IB domain because the qualifier "is flexible enough to cover both, 'spot' and 'futures' transactions, without having to specify it" [p. 54].

Brian Toyne's Perspective of the IB Domain The title of Toyne's analysis suggests that it is questionable whether IB should be considered as a separate domain or merely as an integral part of the general business discipline. In the end, this question is resolved in favor of IB as a separate domain because of three reasons that are presented in a not very convincing manner. First, a unique perspective that is fundamentally different than those already being explored by other fields. Second, contributions linked to other fields of inquiry, and third, demonstrable value contribution to the accumulation of knowledge [p. 75]. For reaching his conclusion about international business as a unique, separate domain of inquiry, Toyne uses two analytic concepts: first, a threefold differentiation among methodological approaches for categorizing domain-relevant insights, and second, the presentation of four schools of thought labeled substantivism, extensionalism, universalism, and resolutionalism that reflects "the nature, scope, and content of IB" [pp. 65–66 in this volume].

Although one might argue about the appropriateness and the descriptive validity of these labels, I see Toyne's elaborations as a zealous effort to departmentalize a very complex, multifaceted set of issues into separate, exclusive compartments. Assuming we could agree on a group of studies that have made a significant contribution to our understanding of IB issues, I believe we would be unable to agree on categorizing these studies by using Toyne's classification schemes. Even if some substantive value could be found in Toyne's categorizing effort, one must challenge some of his assertions. First, the claim that domain separation must be established in metatheoretical terms and that IB substantialists "do not . . . extend the body of knowledge by theory building" [p. 67 in this volume]. Theory development can proceed in an inductive as well as a deductive manner. Eisenhardt [1989] points out, studies that are merely descriptive can well be used as elements in the development of an overarching theory. Theory building is a dynamic, evolutionary, interactive process, and the existence of competing theories (four schools of thought) is a sign of a healthy development of a discipline. Second, Toyne seems to suggest that domain conceptualization should be congruent with theoretical constructs, and it is because of a lack of congruency between domain and theoretical perspectives that he arrives at the rather negative assessments of IB inquiry as substantivism, extensionalism, and universalism. Toyne's characterization of these "isms" tends to be without factual support and without explicit reference to specific studies. Given the shortcomings Toyne attributes to the four schools of thought that reflect the substantive issues of the IB domain, one has to wonder how he nevertheless comes to the conclusion that IB has become a respectable, unique domain [p. 75 in this volume]. However, this assessment is immediately negated by the last paragraph in Toyne's analyses in which he laments the absence of a "common knowl-edge generating purpose" and the existence of too many metatheoretical sources of the IB domain.

In Conclusion

The commonalty among the three studies that focus on the conceptualization of the IB domain is that they agree on the existence of a separate domain. However, each study delineates the domain in a different manner and from a different perspective. Each presents a rather different perception of the nature, scope, and of the substantive issues to be covered in IB. Mira Wilkins's domain configuration rests on a structural-institutional element, namely the internationally operating firm and its disposition over foreign-based assets. From a theory building perspective, this view of the IB domain leads consequently to a theory of the MNE. In my opinion, that is a too narrow configuration of the IB domain, since not all cross-border economic transactions are taking place in the context of international operating firms. Boddewyn's definition of the IB domain centers on all conceivable border crossing trade and investment flows as long as they are "negotiated" and take place between independent organization entities. For Boddewyn, IB encompasses macrointernational economic, political, and sociocultural considerations. He thus provides the broadest possible delineation of the domain, since it focuses not only on the entire spectrum of cross-border transfers but also on their direct and indirect effects in a micro- and macroeconomic setting. Boddewyn does not call for a unified, domain-congruent IB theory, but emphasizes the integration or adaptation of existing theoretical constructs from several disciplines among the complementary or competing IB theories. For Toyne the delineation of the IB domain is a function of the existence of a metalevel conceptualization, and he seems to deplore that, in spite of a massive volume of IB studies, no comprehensive, inclusive, domain-congruent theoretical conceptualization has emerged. Instead, Toyne points out that IB is a fragmented domain; domain-relevant phenomena are studied from four rather different perspectives and for very different purposes.

A book by Joseph McGuire [1964] starts with the observation that "business is a practice in search of a theory." The remainder of the book enumerates a rather large number of theories of business, and McGuire concludes with the observation that there does not—probably will not—exist a theory of business as such. The same observations apply to IB as a unique and distinct domain of inquiry. IB is a complex domain with a series of competing theories concerned with different substantive issues. If one surveys the evolution of the conceptual foundations of the IB discipline one notices that over time different questions and conceptualizations become dominant and provide an impetus for a broad stream of analyses of IB phenomena. During much of the 1960s the predominant concern of those studying IB issues was to establish the differences between firms involved in IB transactions and those operating in a single national setting. During the 1970s the dominant IB concern shifted to the question: what induces firms to "go international" or to expand their international operations? Studies in response to this question culminated in the advocacy of an "eclectic" theory that centers on location-, firm-, industry-, and management-specific advantages as drivers of the internationalization process of firms. Since the mid 1980s another question has become a dominant focus of IB studies: the strategic choices of firms engaging in, or involved in international operations and their effect on firm performance. Each of the different questions has led to competing theoretical constructs and a wide array of empirical studies. The newer theoretical conceptualizations concerned with IB issues focus on how firms use a given resource base [Tallman 1991], exploit leverage and arbitrage opportunities [Kogut 1985a], and the impact of strategic choices as determinants of firm performance [Doz and Prahalad 1991].

The three studies demonstrate that there are valid reasons for considering IB as a unique, distinct domain of inquiry. There are clear differences about the scope and boundaries of the IB domain that result in a diversity of theories. In my view, the diversity of perspectives and the existence of competing theories of IB are clear indicators of a healthy development of the discipline.

Jack N. Behrman

Discussion of "The Conceptual Domain of International Business"

The papers presented by Professors Wilkins, Boddewyn, and Toyne are wide-ranging, stimulating, and come at the question from quite different directions. Mira Wilkins is more historical (as would be expected), illustrating the dynamic nature of international business (IB); Jean Boddewyn is more analytical, searching for an inclusive definition; and Brian Toyne categorizes, seeking an exclusive definition, which provides sufficient differences from other business and international topics to permit the development of a unique discipline for IB.

Each of the three focuses more on subject rather than on *methods* of IB inquiry, but all are concerned with the place of IB theory in defining the scope and methods of IB research. The absence of an established theoretical structure *that is not a derivative of microeconomics* is an obstacle but not crippling—a subject I address in chapter 11 of this volume.

Attacks on definition and the conceptual domain have come from the viewpoint of "what IB does," "problems that IB executives face," "concerns raised by others involved," or "issues examined by IB professors." Since each author recognizes that these aspects are themselves changing in nature and scope, a precise definitional construct is difficult—the target is dynamic, expanding, and contracting. Only Boddewyn tries his hand at a definition.

The very nature of business (domestic

or international) is that it is changing—from its own efforts to be innovative, to meet competition, and to respond to changes in government policy and in the environment. This means that a theory must encompass purposeful and divergent change *and* at the same time recognize that all change is interactive. The ancient Chinese *Book of Changes* (the *I Ching*) makes it quite clear that change is unpredictable and interrelated. The pattern of change is more complex—changes within IB practices and the technologies in international production change the environments around the world, inducing changes on all types of IB.

It is feasible to fix a domain for *inquiry*; it may not be feasible to fix a domain of *practice*, save in the broadest of terms; this leaves the discipline open to "invasion" from overlapping problem areas. This, however, is the nature of the "real world"—nothing is wholly isolated; all things and events are connected; IB is an integral part of the world, and the world of the universe, and it cannot be otherwise. Therefore, any attempt to conceptualize a *domain* that restricts the scope of inquiry excessively automatically leads to irrelevance for policy.

The domain of inquiry, therefore, is a domain set by the inquirers *but* should it not be in response to the potential audience? Yet, this audience itself is shifting—not only from country to country (as with the entry of China, Eastern Europe, and the Balkans into the world economy)—but also within each country according to the issues. For any business discipline, there are four major audiences: students and professor—students of the discipline, practitioner—students involved in the arena, government officials (at all levels) concerned with public policy implications of business activity (in macro-micro and domestic-global terms), and nongovernment entities that seek to alter or enhance the roles of business in society or the environment.

I missed in each of the papers a careful assessment of the impact *on the domain* of the various "stakeholders" in IB. It will be of no value, for example, to define the dis-

cipline in a way that excludes public policy initiatives or responses or makes any recommendations coming out of IB inquiry irrelevant or vapid. (Much from the economic profession has become vapid because of an insistence that the world should reflect the models used and the assumed "oughts" rather than the other way around; e.g., government interventions seen as market "distortions." There are in fact no "distorted markets" except in the minds of economists. Every market responds automatically to *all* of the elements impinging on it, and for economists to argue that governments create "distortions" is not to recognize that they are a legitimate player in all markets—at least as they see it.)

Equally, to define the discipline so that issues of imperialism or social responsibility across borders are voided would not be responsive to the concerns of observers in many countries of the world over IB activities—concerns with which IB executives must deal.

To limit the domain to "what IB executives deal with" potentially excludes issues with which they *should* be concerned but are not—as was and is the case with many environmental issues. To emphasize only the environment is to eliminate the contributions to the improvement of firm activity that would result from sound analysis of the operations of firms internationally.

Therefore, the "domain of IB" is multifaceted—formed by multiforces in a multinational, multigovernment, multiorganizational world composed of multicultures interacting in response to multiexpectations of the future based on multiperceptions of the past and of present pressures and conditions. The "domain of IB" is not definable, even conceptually, without injecting significant potential error from the standpoint of one or more of the major players, based on their own cultures, education, and value sets. Thus, "Capitalism" is essentially Scotch/Anglo-Saxon/American in concept and has not been fully accepted anywhere, including in these nations.

It is feasible for a group of academics to

define an accepted scope of inquiry for their "discipline," but they should recognize that it may be considered insignificant or useless. Even so, disagreements will remain as events proceed, and such disagreements are necessary to keep inquiry alive and relevant. There also is danger in attempting any relatively tight conceptualization, since some highly important issues may be excluded which are "over the horizon" in time or in scope. A look at each paper shows these observations are appropriate.

Wilkins's Domain

Mira states her preference for a definition of "the field of IB in terms of the dynamics of the individual firm." She states, "others may wish" to include political, governmental, and environmental aspects, which are "highly germane," *but* "the study of enterprise" should be first and foremost. She leaves unanswered what the content of the "international, multinational, transnational, global" aspects of the firm is, however, which distinguishes it from other enterprise, except to state that "business over borders" has long been a subject of academic attention—asserting a *selection* by academics. "Academic preferences" are not a description of a domain in practice or policy.

She agrees that there should be a definable domain, and contradicts Toyne's view that the field "lacks a fundamental, comprehensive, and unifying construct," by asserting that there is "a definable field, a body of knowledge that constitutes a discipline." [p. 34] She cites Buckley's assertion that "It is now generally agreed that an established theory of multinational enterprise exists." [1990:657] Not only is there no such agreement—save for those pursuing particular interests in *economic, microtheory of the firm*—but also those theories are so *partial* as to have little meaning for defining a "holistic" discipline.

Her efforts to define a "field" are clearly related to what academics do—"A historian studies history." [p. 34] History is what occurred in the past, and it is both un-

known and unknowable—contrary to Mira's assertion. Note the sage's comment that "It is difficult to predict the future but impossible to predict the past." The past is what historians (and others) *say* or *perceive* that it was, and this perception changes with each new contribution. So historians *define* the *field* of inquiry—and there are infinite approaches and segments to research, leaving many subfields suitable for academic inquiry—*and* consequently determine publishability. History itself, however, does not wait on academic definitions—for example, it can be demonstrated that, to understand history, we must also understand the impact of the future on the present.

Her second approach is to look at "what business does"—i.e., "the nature of and the dynamics of business as an institution as it moves and operates over borders." [p. 34] This involves problems of national sovereignty—thus, *differing governments* is the distinguishing character of IB's domain. This qualification, however, is *not* acceptable in the "established theory" of Buckley and *all* other IB theory where there is no room for government intervention in firm behavior.

She accepts, further, that IB firms face higher uncertainty because of different governments and cultures, but insists that "we must narrow the core to the study of the firm over borders." [p. 36] Again, this is a research-discipline definition, not a *domain* of IB. The rest of her argument rests on her concept of theory, which takes in my other paper.

In sum, I interpret Mira's view to be that the domain of IB is what we (you? me? which?) academics decide to study based on *economic* theory of the firm—plus some environmental aspects—regardless of the relevance of the research for the corporate or governmental practitioners of policy.

Boddewyn's Domain

Jean begins at the other side of the issue, asserting with Kogut that the distinctive element for IB is "the variance in country environments." [p. 50] When he produced his definition of IB in his first version of his paper in this chapter, however, it is a legal-economic one based on *"arm's length negotiated* trade and investment crossing borders . . ."" (These comments remain relevant even though Jean has dropped the limitation, for the concept is fundamental to the economic theory of markets as espoused by American economists.)

Nowhere does he define "arm's length," and he is exonerated, at least by the IRS, which has stated in its regulations that "Arm's length means arm's length." The concept, however, comes from the rules of competition in "free markets" and implies that full information is exchanged (or is at least freely available) *and that no other past or anticipated future relationships exist between buyer and seller*. There are, of course, few if any transactions in which both parties so act, and they are clearly not the style of corporate transactions. All business builds on *relationships*, that is, "with arm's linked." All over the world, *the network works*!

His definition thus begins with a nonentity and remains unrealistic throughout the paper because of this unnecessary constraint. His assertion in the first version of his paper that IB is "not commensurate with all economic activities that cross borders, but only with bargained exchanges, even if 'bargaining' does not take place for each transaction but is embedded in longer-lasting relationships" does not relieve this restriction sufficiently, for relationships are not incorporated in his further explanations.

Furthermore, this definition gives to the economists (and microeconomic IB theory) the sovereign hand in delimiting the discipline—a result the rest of the paper rejects.

Jean draws some quite necessary distinctions between the concept and role of a "nation" and those of a "state." I will not review these, but some cautions are due on his generalization that a "nation" emphasizes economic and sociocultural variables rather than political ones. (1) Tribal nations were clearly political (and military) in nature, but we would not call them "nation-

states;" they took no ownership in specific resources but protected their "area." (2) The Jewish, Polish, and Arab "nations" have existed even without territory or any unified economic capability, leaving them wholly social entities, based on ethnic characteristics. (3) The Palestinian nation has exercised political and quasi-military power without an economic base and without a territory. These are, however, modifications of a useful distinction.

They do, however, suggest a modification of Kindleberger's view; Jean quotes him as saying that the optimum economic area is clearly larger than the nation-state, and the optimum cultural (ethnic) area is smaller. I would think, however, that it is now recognized that the optimum political area is also probably much smaller than the economic arena—i.e., coterminous with the ethnic community. We face economic integration, ethnic consolidation, and political disintegration around the world. The implications for IB are serious—and not necessarily unfavorable—but require a merging of economic, commercial, social, psychological, political, and security analysis.

When Jean comes to his final definition, modifying it to encompass all of the significant features of IB, he includes a congeries of elements that are not definitional at all but constitute an invitation to inquire into virtually anything—especially since the limiting "arm's length" qualifier is not operational. In an effort to establish a domain relevant to practice, he ends up with no useful distinctions at all for the field of IB. This is the result I expected—an inability to delimit activities relevant to what business does, for they fit within no specific "international" constraints in practice *other* than those imposed by different governments and ethnic-cultural environments—both change over time.

Toyne's Domain

Brian states unequivocally that the purpose of defining any domain of inquiry is to focus *and* limit the scope and method of research. Therefore, the domain under consideration is an academic exercise for academics. The error of this approach is decisively shown by Herman Hesse in *The Glass Bead Game* [1969], an account of a future research institute set up by European government to "model the world" to assist in government policy making; its activities became so "focused and restricted" that it became nothing but a highly complex, methodological "game," enjoyed by researchers and selected invitees—wholly irrelevant to the policy objectives sought in its creation; consequently, the institute was terminated.

The rest of Brian's paper is, in my view, an exercise in academic "scoping" based on highly suspect distinctions, as far as policy/practice is concerned. In my view, if IB is not a *policy* discipline, it is irrelevant. From the *Journal of Irreproducible Results* comes a lovely comment on the methods used in irrelevant research—"If a project is not worth doing, it is not worth doing well."[1]

Now to the substance of Brian's argument, which is based on a three-level conceptualization of policy research, policy formation and implementation (substantive), theoretical reasoning and recommendations (scientific), and underlying assumptions as to the "oughts" and ultimate meanings to be sought (metalevel). He asserts that at the policy level, IB is an *art*, but at the scientific level it is a derivative of physics; while at the level of assumptions it has no distinguishing features.

Clearly business and government policy is an art, though many seek to inject "an objective science" into it through quantitative analysis and modeling. At the "science" level, he accepts too readily the economic paradigm of mechanical physics—I assume it is "mechanical" that he refers to, since present astro- and theoretical physics is quite metaphysical—which has defined the economic theory paradigm so as to lead to some harmful ideological policies, such as those pursued by Reagan and Bush in the U.S. and Jeffrey Sachs in Poland and now Russia.

The purpose of science *is* to seek truth, but science *is* based on metaphysics, and is also an art, relying on "revelation" to change the scientific paradigms. The purpose of the search "for truth" in economics—and its derivative in business theory—has been narrowed to maximization concepts (coming from mechanical physics). Maximization has been delimited to *efficiency* in generating production and revenue. *No* aspect of socioeconomic-political life is *solely* concerned with maximization (there are too many trade-offs required) or with efficiency—not even in the production plant. Microeconomic and business theories have fixed on a goal (profit maximization) that is wholly inadequate in representing what business does when policy is the focus. The substitution of "optimization" widens the objective to undefinable and uncontainable concepts when realistic specification is attempted.

There are several other socioeconomic-political objectives besides efficiency that should be explicitly recognized in policy deliberations, as I have analyzed elsewhere, equity, participation, creativity, stability, and autonomy [Behrman and Grosse 1990: 17–21]. I would now add a concern for the future in care of the *environment*, *compassion* in national catastrophe or trauma, and social and individual *responsibility*. For further discussion, see my other paper in this volume.

The goal of efficiency has clearly distinguished economics, which prides itself in not being "soft" like the other social sciences, by being "quantitatively, scientifically" grounded. But this is a chimera! The separation and distinction are false. "Everything is connected." It would be equally or more useful to search for the *relationships and connections* than to seek only for "distinguishing" characteristics, especially since the world runs on relationships, and to disregard them is an academic exercise.

The world of policy-practice is not neatly separated into pockets of activities named by the various academic disciplines. One's intellect (logic), emotions (feelings), body (senses), and psyche (soul) are all inseparably involved in every act and decision. It also is better to be "totally aware" than so focused as to be "asleep" to the myriad elements that impinge on and are affected by one's actions.

The absence of theory does not prevent sound policy-practice; it only prevents extension of academic publication. The German caution is worth remembering, "Theory is supposed to work, but doesn't; Technik works, but no one knows why." In any case, rather than descriptive observations *not* leading to theory, as Brian asserts; theory can *only* come from *some* observation and is validated *only* by observation. Theory that does not work in practice is not good theory! Brian admits all of this in the next paragraph. While he recognizes the need for "purpose," he nonetheless continually side-steps *what it is* in IB inquiry; it can come *only* from a value-system (metatheoretical), which is unexamined either in economics or business curricula or research—for example, does it lead to the achievement of a "new world order" or to "sustainable growth" or what? How does IB fit into this objective? What are the meta-level assumptions? (Whatever they are, they have a spiritual, moral content; and such matters are not even whispered in schools of business.)

Brian then turns to four schools of thought on the domain of IB, (1) cross-border and multidomestic activities, (2) hypothesis testing in several nations, (3) testing in all environments to achieve generalizations or universal validity, and (4) processes of reconciling remaining differences. He criticizes each as inadequate in distinguishing the domain when they cannot be more than different segments of the larger domain. It requires all four to encompass the relationships of business, governments, and the environment.

None of these *could* provide uniqueness to IB inquiry, for all four are applicable to *any* international activity, including weather prediction, postal services, or health care. Any claim by any one of these for uniqueness is false and is asserted merely for the desire to "professionalize" the participants, permitting them to set the criteria by which their performance will be judged—a privilege that we are removing even from the medical and legal professions.[2]

Equally, a claim by IB participants that they are in some sense unique, or face unique elements or factors (such as extreme uncertainty) is false. A dichotomy represented by "logical positivism," "operationalism," or "pragmatism" also misses the field. The definition of the questions asked and the phenomena studied can be done academically *or* by *any* inquirer! Once again, however, all three are needed to operate in a domain; while they are *necessary*, they are not *sufficient*.

These three jargon-words can be simplified as—subject definition, methodology, and recommendations-results. To separate these, as is often done in academic articles (focusing solely on methodology without reference to subject-definition or applicability of results), is to increase the irrelevance of the project, regardless of how "well done."

Jargon can lead us astray, by inducing an air of precision when it does not exist—for example, Brian's reliance on Kaplan (whom I find a weak reed in the several quotes from him) on the concept of "pragmatism." The common use of the word makes it identical with what Kaplan says it is *not*—i.e., action, practice, and expediency—or, *results*, regardless of how achieved or whether the results are in some other sense desirable. Pragmatics is *what works*, as Chairman Deng intended, when he called for a "pragmatic policy," for an end to ideology, and for the Chinese to "seek truth from facts." To raise pragmatics to a "value-laden concept" is to place values at the lowest level of ethical-moral categories, for pragmatics is below "desirable results" in an ethical (societal) sense, and further below "acceptable intent" in a moral (personal obligation) sense.

Yet, it is at these levels that society as a whole functions; only if they are included can the domain of inquiry be considered "sufficient"—as is well shown by Wall Street of the 1980s. To be so inclusive makes it clear that the inquiry is *not unique* and cannot be, for it is but one iteration of the multiple relationships that make up the entire national, international, and global society.

When Brian moves to an assessment of what IB theory has achieved, much too much is claimed for the narrow, economic-based efforts of Hymer, Dunning, Buckley, et al., which have prevented the discipline from evolving its own theory. They have been too concerned to join economics as a "hard science" rather than to be relevant to our clients. This, however, is not feasible when, as Brian recognizes, "there appear to be U.S., Japanese, and German outcomes." [p. 67 in this volume] Economic theory is an Anglo-American invention based on its culture *and* metalevel assumptions as to "the good life" and the way "economic man" *should* rationally behave.

His observations on "substantivism" do not always hold—e.g., on their lack of contribution to theory and focus on outcomes rather than process or analysis of causes. My view is that Robinson, Fayerweather, Dunning, Vernon, Aharoni, and others have been much broader, not surprised by change, and offering many avenues for development of theory that were rejected by those seeking to remain in the paradigm of economics and at the level of the firm. His further indictment of substantivists as focusing on observable phenomena, or those yielding to certain techniques, is appropriate but not telling; no one with any policy sense would recommend relying solely on phenomenological inquiry.

His final criticism of substantivism is still harder to accept not because any one approach is *partial*, but because the citations are simply in error. The entire focus of the initial research by the NBER on business cycles was empirical and substantivist *but* driven by "theory-building questions of causation"—quite the contrary to Brian's assertion. Further, *no* scientific explanation can be regarded as an answer to the *why*

question of intent (contrary to the assertion from Hempel); it is only an attempt to gain acceptance to a potential answer to a *how* caused question. As Einstein said, "All I want to know is *how* God did it; all the rest is detail." It would be a foolish question *why* God did it; it is not a scientific question in the sense of "objective, observable."

No astro- or theoretical physicist probing for the Grand Unified Theory (as Stephen Hawking of Britain) is asking the why question—only *how*. All questions of *why* get into the arena of *intent* and of *will*. Neither of these is objective or observable, since they come from within and are melded inextricably with hidden and unknowable forces or considerations. Any selection of *an* intent is still selective.

As to extensionalism, I will merely say that the indictment misses the mark again— there is no reason why it *should* produce "a coherent and comprehensive body of knowledge;" that is not its purpose. The assertion that "IB extensionalists are interested merely in foreign situations not IB." [p. 70 in this volume] is, of course, incorrect; rather, to the extent that they are simply comparative, that is *why* they can be called "extensionalists." It is a bit too cute to indict a group for being what it is defined to be.

Universalists do *not* "assume that all peoples are the same 'under the skin'"—if they did, there would be no reason for inquiry; the assumption is a hypothesis to be tested. Where differences are shown, the inquiry must move to "resolutionalism." Next, they are indicted for "oversimplifying . . . in order to develop prescriptive theories" [p. 70]. Substantivists were indicted for *not* building theory; universalists are indicted for trying and failing—due to simplifying. All theory is simplification; in fact, science has a rule that the simpler theoretical explanation is the one to accept—a posture that is, however, highly questionable. Finally, I simply do not understand the statement that "Like most economists, [universalists] are not interested in process, only outcomes." [p. 70] I count the statement invalid for either group—both are much interested in process, for there one finds the proximate *causes,* the *hows,* which are a better view of the similarities and differences than mere results.[3]

Resolutionalism is, of course, *uniquely* distinct from the other three, asking questions different from the others, *but,* that does not make it *preclusive.* It should be included with the others. Neither it, nor any of the others, "establishes IB inquiry as unique and distinctive" because it asks different questions. *All* ask different questions and use approaches common to other disciplines, so how do they provide a unique IB domain?

Turning to the "origin and future" of IB inquiry, I find still more inadequacies. The assertion that the "ground-breaking" research on the MNE was parochial, insular, and policy-driven, etc., is simply a misreading of the literature (not cited by Toyne). The first extensive, empirical post-WWII scholarly assessment of *U.S. Private and Government Investment Abroad* [1960] was admittedly policy oriented but included a 150 page examination of "Direct Private Foreign Investment,"[4] which first examined organizational forms, then characterized the transfer of resources, assessed economic effects, then described U.S. government promotional policies and analyzed host-government policies—all without *any* implication that U.S. policy or corporate approaches were "correct." Subsequent research by Behrman, Dunning, Fayerweather, Robinson, Vernon, and others was not infected with Toyne's ethnocentric virus in terms of scope—but in terms of methodology and culture-bound questioning.

Conversely, Toyne's claim that the (theoretical) contributions of Hymer and Vernon set major directions for subsequent multinational corporations (MNCs) research is overblown. There was then, and is now, no *need* for a "theoretical legitimacy" to conduct policy research. The best evidence is that there *is* no theory—whether accepted or not—that comes close to explaining IB phenomena. An inquiry is justi-

fied by its purposes, as Toyne recognizes; and its results are validated by proper procedures (judged by readers and colleagues, who *may* use theories for purposes of assessment). The absence of a theory merely says that we do not *yet* see the flow of causal events clearly enough to simplify them into an abstraction—as is recognized in the emerging "theory of chaos," which is a search for the (implicit) order in what now seems unordered.

Policy makers will seldom be found referring to theory to explain or justify their decisions or their decision-process. Contrarily, when they do rely on theory, they become temporarily blind or entranced, only to find they have been following advice of dead economists (living or not). A minister of the fallen socialist government of Jamaica some years back confessed to his audience that they had learned some bitter lessons—one being that there were three quite different ways to ruin a government, the first was through drink, and this was the quickest; the second was through sexual affairs, and this was the most pleasant; but the surest was to follow the advice of economic "experts."

Theoretical abstractions validate the research *only* in the eyes of the profession. Therefore, once again, academics can define a domain any way they wish. It can be done for their own convenience or egos, or for service to those who are practicing the discipline or are affected by these activities—and that means both business and government (national and intergovernmental) officials and those who are involved in all facets of action and reaction of doing and receiving.

Further, it appears to me we should humbly consider our efforts here as mere tentative beginning. The domain of IB—if there is one, and whatever it is—is operative in many nations, states, and cultures with quite different views. All should be involved in any such conceptualization—after all, our academy *is* multinational.

Finally, Toyne comes to the conclusion that IB is "a basically, holistic, societal phenomenon." [p. 74] If it is fully understood as such, then there is *little* basis on which to *delimit* a domain, and any effort by either *Americans or academics* (as distinct from others involved) to do so on their own is unwarranted on its face.

If there are some tentatively useful results from this conference, they should immediately be subjected to "substantivist," "extensionalist," "universalist," *and* "resolutionalist" inquiries by academics and practitioners from around the world.

At that point we might begin to understand that "everything is connected" and start trying to make substantive contributions to the ills and problems faced by the world as it deals with and is affected or benefited by business. The more help we can get in this from others similarly concerned the better—whether in or outside the IB curriculum, outside departments of management, or of business schools in other disciplines, or in government or business. This approach should produce some distinguished academics, familiar with varied methodologies, and who would be unsatisfied to remain within a neat and distinctive academic discipline but quite comfortable in the messy limbo of policy.

IB should take the lead within business schools to broaden the outlook of all disciplines (professors, curricula, and students), to meet the increasing criticism that they are behind the times and the needs of decision makers.

On a personal note, I entered the field in the late 1950s *because* it was wide open and permitted diverse forays into the mysteries of corporate and government policy and the difficulties of implementation. I would not have enjoyed my career nearly so much doing what others now apparently want to fix as the domain of IB.

NOTES

1. Academics talking to academics makes for publication and promotion, which may make the research "worth doing" but does not do much policy improvement. Most of what *JIBS* has been publishing is of this nature; its articles are stereotyped and frequently reflect "a methodology seeking a data base;" conclusions are so limited as to be useless. I find *The Economist, International Economy, Foreign Affairs,* and the new *European Affairs* much more useful for my own work on policy issues; even the *CJWB* has improved significantly, coming from a less-than-scholarly approach.

2. This, of course, is the problem facing business schools in their interaction with U.S. corporations, which say that the schools have forgotten who the customer is. A profession, by definition, is supposed to know more about what the customer needs—medicine and law—than the customer does, and therefore can and should set the standards of quality and performance. Business schools—as all others—operate in a market (which business professors should fully understand), and no market permits the producer to fix the standards in production and exchange. Academics have, therefore, turned to serving each other and themselves, defining success as publication and promotion (both of which subgroups control), rather than serving those who are practicing or preparing for practice in the discipline.

3. The fact that jeans are sold in many countries is the event-result. Any comparison includes a host of other observations on who the customers are, what channels of distribution are effective, prices and qualities, other clothing competition, social lifestyles, transmission of ideas, fads, and so on. Some will even ask what are the proximate causes of these aspects, attempting to get at the why question.

4. See Mikesell (1960). Noted section by J. N. Behrman (pp. 77–230).

Thomas J. Hench

The Domain of International Business: Paradigms in Collision

The basic premise of my critique is that we cannot understand the papers and commentaries in this and the subsequent chapters without first understanding the changing context in which they are presented. By this I mean the broader social, scientific, and epistemological context in which they are embedded. In short, the three topic papers by Wilkins, Boddewyn, and Toyne, and the two commentaries by

Schollhammer and Behrman cannot be fully understood without a clear understanding of the paradigms upon which they are based. I argue in the following pages, the papers by Toyne and Behrman are grounded in fundamentally different models of social reality than are the papers by Wilkins, Boddewyn, and Schollhammer.

The Broader Context

The questions posed for the conference on *Perspectives on International Business: Theory, Research and Institutional Arrangements* have a familiar ring to them. Indeed, the question of "the appropriate domain of international business (IB)" is the same question that is asked by all areas of inquiry in their formative stages. Yet, as familiar as this question may be, its full significance for IB inquiry can only be understood in the context of the much broader undercurrent of debate currently raging in the social and the physical sciences.

Whether described as confrontations of modernism vs. postmodernism, of Einstein vs. Bohr, of strategic choice vs. determinism, or of networks vs. hierarchies, the basic elements of these confrontations are the same. They reflect a fundamental questioning of the world around us, and how, as a consequence of the knowledge and understanding we have gained, our view of the world is changing. They also reflect, perhaps to a lesser but still important degree, our growing ability to examine more complex abstractions because of advancements in the tools we use. As such, these confrontations reflect a collision of paradigms of Kuhnian proportion [Kuhn 1970].

The Paradigms Defined

The paradigm that has dominated the social sciences until recently is commonly described as the Newtonian view of the universe. In this view, reality is essentially simple, ordered, determinate, and material. It exists independent of human discernment and understanding. It operates according to a system of atemporal, strict, and absolute natural laws that can be discovered and ob-

served through the judicious application of logical positivism and the *scientific method*. Empirical and rational analysis are its touchstones to understanding.

As in the physical sciences, this paradigm assumes axiomatically that our social reality consists of indestructible and elemental building blocks that tend to exist in or near equilibrium—and all phenomena within this reality can be defined in terms of their matter or motion. Everything can be reduced to a system's initial conditions and trajectory. If we know how the individual parts of a system work, then we also know how the whole works. Everything fits into a tidy, little package.

In contrast, a new paradigm is emerging that presents an entirely different view of our social reality. It is evolving out of the three scientific revolutions that occurred in the physical sciences in the twentieth century—Relativity, Quantum Mechanics, and Chaos/Complexity Theory. Instead of a social world of absolutes that exists completely independent of us, we are now confronted with a world that depends in part upon how we, as sentient, learning human beings, engage that world. Instead of a material world comprised of indestructible and elemental building blocks, the social world we create is seen as a transitory manifestation of our energy and information (knowledge) [Prigogine and Stengers 1984; Wheatley 1992]. Instead of a social world described in Newtonian terms as simple, ordered, and determinate, this world is seen as being much more complex, interconnected, interdependent, and indeterminate. Instead of operating in accordance with absolute natural laws, it operates in accordance with fields of energy and quantum probabilities. Instead of existing at or near equilibrium, this paradigm views reality as existing in a constant state of flux and change—"far-from-equilibrium"—where "Order [arises] out of chaos" and the total system is comprised of indeterminate periods of *both* order and disorder [Prigogine and Stengers 1984; Jantsch 1980].

There is of course some danger in attempting to explain "social" phenomena in terms of "natural" sciences. However, recent discoveries have demonstrated that certain important properties are *common* to both "natural" and "social" systems [Jantsch 1980; Prigogine and Stengers 1984; Gersick 1991; Laszlo 1991; Wheatley 1992], particularly with regard to change and evolution. Therefore, it may be that earlier distinctions between these two types of phenomena are no longer relevant, at least with regard to their dynamic properties. It may be that these earlier distinctions had more to do with the "values" of a Newtonian mechanical view of the world than with the actual differences between the two systems. If this is the case, then my use of the "natural sciences" to explain certain "social" phenomena is much more defensible.

It is obvious that the Newtonian paradigm and the emerging paradigm describe entirely different—and sometimes incompatible—social realities. Yet, taking our cue from the physical sciences, we know that each paradigm is effective and appropriate *within limitations* (e.g., Newtonian mechanics holds for "material" objects of ordinary magnitudes and velocities less than the speed of light, while Quantum Mechanics is more appropriate for energy fields and their complex interactions). Each must be applied to the appropriate phenomenon of interest. Similarly, each paradigm is *inappropriate* if applied to the wrong phenomenon of interest.

But are these differing views of social reality important to our understanding of the conceptual domain of IB? I believe they are. The paradigm adopted by a particular social scientist has a direct bearing on the way he or she views social reality. It affects the assumptions made about human beings, the organizations people create, the types of questions people ask, and the methodologies and measurements people use to answer these questions. Therefore, it is very important for IB theoreticians and researchers to be aware of the limitations and assumptions of the paradigms they use, and the implications of these paradigms for the

phenomena being studied. Unfortunately, this often does not appear to be the case in the study of IB and complex organizations. Probably because of the relative recency of this newly emerging paradigm, and our uncertainty over its scientific implications (e.g., boundaries, research methodologies), we are mixing paradigms.

Mixing Paradigms

If we look closely at the question of the conceptual domain of IB and the arguments presented about what it should or should not be, we are presented with strong evidence that the authors are indeed mixing paradigms. Yet, the need for a new paradigm *is* emerging as a consequence of a fundamental change in how IB is conducted throughout the world. From the view of the IB practitioner, the world has indeed changed [Bartlett and Ghoshal 1989]. The prescriptions from the past no longer work. Yet many IB researchers appear to be trying to understand these changes through the precepts and assumptions of a paradigm that may no longer be relevant to our field of inquiry.

It is widely recognized and accepted that most management theory, and IB by extension, is grounded in the principles and concepts of Newtonian mechanics and its derivative social science, neoclassical economics (see Teece [1990]; Bygrave [1989]; and Hambrick [1990])—a point Hogner addresses in chapter 3 of this book. As noted above, Newtonian mechanics and the laws of motion were designed to explain exactly the linear relationships between two interacting inert material objects. Yet, even within the "appropriate" realm of the Newtonian paradigm, not all solutions are determinate. For instance, introduce a "third-body" into a classical gravitational problem and it is no longer solvable in exact terms [Briggs and Peat 1990]. This "three-body" problem is simply too "complex" to be solved exactly. It involves indeterminate, nonlinear feedback loops with reciprocal interactions that make only "approximate" solutions possible. Furthermore, as more "bodies" are added, its approximations become increasingly less predictable [Briggs and Peat 1990; Gleick 1987; Stewart 1989; Wheatley 1992]. The same is true of classical trade theory when the two-country model is replaced with an n-country model.

Thus, even if the fact is overlooked that international firms are *not* inert material objects, but made up instead of sentient, learning human beings, it is not easy to overlook the fact that all international firms are subject to an almost unimaginable array of influences—certainly far more than what can be usefully accommodated in any "two-body" problem. Consequently, the n-body example should at least give researchers cause for serious questioning of Newtonian approximations within the IB domain.

Yet the legacy of the Newtonian world view is seen everywhere in organizations and organizational thinking—international and domestic alike. As Wheatley comments, "We manage by separating things into parts, we believe that influence occurs as a direct result of force exerted from one person to another, we engage in complex planning for a world that we keep expecting to be predictable, and we search continually for better methods of objectively perceiving th[at] world" [1992:6].

Throughout the three-day conference, several similar criticisms were raised: such as the difficulty of predicting a specific outcome for a single international firm; of identifying well-defined boundaries between nations and states, or between domestic and international firms; of differentiating between "arms length" versus "arms linked" negotiations; and of separating knowledge exploitation from knowledge creation. Also heard was the need for holographic organizations and shared visions to replace fragmented, parochial, command, and control hierarchies. Yet, most of the prescriptions for solving these newly identified problems appeared to be little more than simple linear extensions of traditional Newtonian thinking. Thus, even as IB scholars begin to see the world using this newly emerging paradigm, they continue to try to explain this "new" reality with constructs and tools developed for the "old" reality. Therefore, as Toyne suggests, we must examine not only our ontological assumptions but also our epistemological assumptions.

The Unique Challenge of IB and the Need for a New Paradigm

The uniqueness of IB is not necessarily to be found in the differences of its parts and those of domestic business. Rather, I propose that the difference between domestic and IB—and thus IB's uniqueness—rests with the *qualitatively* higher levels of complexity and ambiguity that exist in the domain of IB. The idea of describing IB as a simple, predictable, and homogeneous interaction of physical "objects" must be abandoned. In this regard, there are no especially useful constructs for dealing with the complex and ambiguous diversity of IB, or of differentiating IB from domestic business.

At the risk of oversimplification, the simple, predictable Newtonian world of absolutes is being abandoned for one of complexity and ambiguity. What is emerging is a world of relationships, where all *meaning* exists *in relation*, and matter and energy are essentially one and the same phenomenon. In this new view structure is nothing more than information (knowledge) made manifest [Wheatley 1992]. Thus, where once *structure* was viewed as providing meaning—and thus information—it is now seen as the other way around. Information creates structure and becomes the central organizing element of that structure [Wheatley 1992].

Accordingly, the central issue of organizations thus shifts from one of planning and control to one of *learning*, and the two are profoundly different. Instead of controlling nature, the emphasis shifts to one of understanding nature. The idea of a mechanical "fit" is increasingly being replaced by more of a notion of "harmony," of being in synchronous motion with nature's continuous ebbs and flows [Capra 1976;1983].

93

If as Jantsch [1980], Prigogine and Stengers [1984] and others have suggested the world is evolving to ever higher levels of complexity, then *IB inquiry is central to our understanding of our emerging social world*. The knowledge gained from IB inquiry anticipates and/or clarifies our understanding of the domestic arena as it too evolves to ever higher levels of complexity (*Editors' note*: See Hennart's paper in chapter 11).

Thus, given the emerging social paradigm and the *qualitative* uniqueness of IB, it should come as no surprise that the concern for networks and heterarchies, for relationships instead of structure, for holographic organizations, for information creation instead of simple information processing, and for "matrices of the mind" and more have all found their greatest expression and their greatest reception in the field of IB. The field of IB truly reflects the latest in contemporary scientific thought as well as science's attempt to find *meaning* and *value* in the complex, ambiguous world that surrounds us.

Scholars adopting the Newtonian paradigm traditionally attempt to identify differences between systems by focusing on the differences between their individual parts. In contrast, those scholars adopting the emerging paradigm are learning to differentiate between systems by observing the behavior of the *whole*. In complex dynamic systems, of which international firms must be considered a part, the actions of the individual parts are essentially indeterminate, providing no reasonable basis for making comparisons across systems. It is only at the global level of behavior that systems display subtly discernible patterns—and even then only when observed over long periods of time. In Chaos Theory, for example, this principle has led to the concept of "local indeterminacy and global stability" [Gleick 1987; Briggs and Peat 1990]—a curiously similar idea to the now familiar International Business refrain, "Act global, think local." Logically, the two are not so far apart.

Though not all participants at the conference would agree that a new paradigm is emerging or needed, the words used to describe the contemporary realities of International Business seem to belie such sentiments. Vestiges of this new paradigm were evident everywhere at this conference, especially in the papers presented in this chapter. At every turn we heard talk of the impact of time (e.g., Wilkins) on organizational structure and performance—a decidedly non-Newtonian concept. We also heard talk of fuzzy and ambiguous boundaries, of complex realities and *relations* that were more important than contracts (see Behrman's commentary here). There also were: calls for a broader, more holistic view of the *whole* ("it [was] the woof and the weave of the tapestry, not the individual threads, that convey[ed] meaning" (see Toyne, p. 68 in this volume); calls for multiple levels of analysis (see Toyne, Behrman, and Boddewyn in this chapter); and, finally, reminders that International Business was, after all, a social process not a material object (see Toyne in this chapter too).

A new paradigm *is* emerging in both the physical and the social sciences. And within this new paradigm is a unique contribution for International Business to make—the study of the management of complexity, diversity, and ambiguity. As I explore the contributions of Wilkins, Boddewyn, and Toyne, the need for this new paradigm and the contribution it can make will become even more apparent.

Mira Wilkins's Conceptual Domain of IB

Wilkins adopts a very traditional, Newtonian approach in her description of the conceptual domain of IB. Accepting what can be described as the classical view, she asserts that the domain of IB is firm-specific, dynamic, grounded in economic theory, concerned with institutions that move and operate across borders, inclusive and responsive to evolution and ongoing change, and tailored to the particulars of the multinational enterprise (MNE). With the exception of including *time* as a critical factor in her construct, Wilkins's suggestion for the domain of IB reflects the quintessential Newtonian "mechanical" approach to domain construction.

By focusing on only one element of IB—the international firm—Wilkins appears to accept the reductionist assumption that by looking at only parts of a total system the findings can be extrapolated to explain the whole. Based on what we now know about the behavior of such complex systems [Gleick 1987; Briggs and Peat 1989; Wheatley 1992] as MNEs, such an exercise now seems largely inappropriate. To borrow a phrase from Toyne, such an approach is likely to "only describe parts of the elephant, not the entire body." [p. 75]

Wilkins's analysis also appears limited by her insistence that IB must be grounded in economic theory—a concept shared by Boddewyn in his paper, as well as by Casson in his paper and as presented in chapter 4. Wilkins accepts the *a priori* role of economics as her basic starting point because she sees the MNE as "an institution that is an economic entity . . . carr[ying] on fundamental economic activities" [p. 39]. Certainly this is correct as far as it goes. This does not, however, necessarily justify the role of economics as the integrating discipline for IB. Such a conclusion seems untenable in light of what has been learned from contemporary science and the nature of generative processes. Assuming that Wilkins reasons are similar to those argued by Casson, such shortcomings become readily obvious.

The reasons presented by Casson during the conference were: (1) economics provides a general theory of choice under conditions of scarcity, (2) it exploits the principle of optimization, and (3) it exploits the concept of equilibrium to simplify the discussion of interpersonal relationships. Close examination of each point, however, demonstrates just the opposite of what is intended; economics is not an appropriate foundation for the conceptual domain of IB.

First, the idea of "choice under conditions of scarcity" is primarily concerned with only one dimension of business activity—the *efficient* allocation of resources. Economics deals with the distribution of wealth *that has already been created*. It is not necessarily adept at explaining the creative process by which wealth is actually created. Arguably, while efficiency is an important dimension of business enterprise, it is certainly not the only aspect of interest—nor is it even the most important. Indeed, I believe that there is a much more compelling case to be made that the preeminent purpose of business is the creation of new knowledge. This is similar to what Norman [1968], Nonaka [1989] and others have suggested (see also the topic paper by Hedlund and Ridderstråle, and the commentary by Ghoshal in chapter 6). It is only after new knowledge and value have been created that it is appropriate to be concerned with the efficient allocation of resources and other such "choice[s] under conditions of scarcity."

Business enterprise is first and foremost a *generative process*. That is, it is a process of discovery and creativity. Unfortunately, economics has little to teach us about such processes. It is widely recognized that classical economics has very little to tell us about the value creating processes of innovation and entrepreneurship, the creative engines of enterprise [Teece 1990; Kirchoff 1992]. Consequently, one must seriously question the efficacy of basing the study of IB—or, indeed, of any form of business—primarily on the limited perspective of economics.

Further, the argument that economics is a good integrating discipline because it "exploits principles of optimization" also rings false. By definition, any theory of optimization implies some level of linear relationships. However, the evidence to date suggests that such complex, dynamic systems as MNEs are nonlinear. Therefore, simple optimization models have little with which to enlighten us in the world of IB. Finally, the contention that economics "exploits equilibrium concepts to simplify the discussion of interpersonal relationships" also rings hollow. It is now known that complex mechanisms such as business organizations live "far-from-equilibrium" [Prigogine and Stengers 1984], only intermittently passing through periods of seeming stability and equilibrium. Once again, economics is only capable of giving us a very partial explanation of IB, leading us to ultimately question Wilkins's and others' reliance on economics as the defining discipline of IB. (*Editors' note*: See Behrman's panel paper in chapter 11 for other arguments supporting a less important role for economics).

Yet, there are at least two aspects of Wilkins's domain definition that are of particular value. The first is her inclusion of evolution and change over time. Contrary to the Newtonian concept of a clock-like universe that works the same in either direction, Wilkins reminds us that time is critical in the study of business. Time is not reversible. The clock cannot be turned back, nor a decision completely reversed. There is an arrow to time [Prigogine and Stengers 1984] and it goes forward from the past to the future. Ultimately, this has important implications too for the irreversible nature of creativity and decision making and the consequence of path dependencies on organizations (*Editors' note*: see Kogut's paper in chapter 8). The inclusion of *time* as a consideration of the domain of IB also places it squarely in line with contemporary thinking in physics, chemistry, biology, nonlinear thermodynamics, and evolution [Prigogine and Stengers 1984; Hawkins 1984].

In addition, Wilkins also singles out the presence of 'higher levels of uncertainty' as a defining characteristic of IB—even more so than with domestic business. This fits very closely with the suggestion that IB's *uniqueness* is in its overall level of complexity, diversity, and ambiguity. Though Wilkins did not necessarily intend to make the same point as I do, I do believe that her assessment of the level of uncertainty inherent in IB is correct—and also supportive of my point.

Clearly, a close examination of Wilkins's domain definition suggests a common concern for many of the same issues as outlined

above. In providing the definition that she does, however, Wilkins demonstrates her faith that the answers sought will emerge as an extension of existing paradigms. Though neither time nor complexity is particularly well explained by those paradigms, Wilkins makes it clear that her faith in a solution rests with the entrenched Newtonian paradigm.

Jean Boddewyn's Conceptual Domain Of IB

While Boddewyn ultimately remains aligned in his thinking with the traditional Newtonian-based paradigms of business and management, his line of reasoning introduces a number of anomalies that seriously challenge the very viability of those paradigms. In quick order, Boddewyn introduces the reader to the convolutions and reversals inherent in trying to draw clear distinctions in a world marked by complexity and ambiguity. It is clear from Boddewyn's treatment of such concepts as "negotiated" trade versus "arm's length" transactions, of "nations" versus "states," the definition of the "IB firm," and the potential confusion implicit in the seemingly straightforward definition of "crossing national borders," that there are certain obvious limits to our ability to draw nicely defined boundaries around our phenomena of interest.

Boddewyn also undermines the sovereignty of the Newtonian paradigm by raising the specter of cultural ethnocentrism in IB. If there is, according to natural laws, "one best way" for conducting business, then that concept is threatened if we admit that there are potentially as many variant ways of conducting IB as there are cultures in which to conduct it. In short, this line of thinking opens Pandora's box to the same view suggested by Toyne that IB is a social process. Though this should not be "news" in such a *social science* as IB—or in any of the management sciences, for that matter— it nevertheless seems to be a statement that is often made without fully comprehending its consequences.

Nonetheless, Boddewyn's purpose in introducing these issues was not so much to confuse the reader or to undermine the appropriateness of the Newtonian paradigm as it was to seek clarity for his own definition of the conceptual domain of IB:

> "International business" refers to negotiated trade and investment that join nations and cross state barriers, with certain IB activities straddling both sets of dimensions, and *as performed by firms operating and interacting at various personal, organizational, product, project, function, network, industry, global, and other levels* [p. 60 in this volume].

Boddewyn's "starting and even dominant perspective *is economic in nature*" [p. 50 in this volume]. This places him alongside Wilkins. His reasons appear to be both rational and pragmatic. From the rational perspective, Boddewyn holds that "'Business' is fundamentally an economic institution" [p. 50 in this volume] again echoing the sentiments of Wilkins. From a "pragmatic" perspective, Boddewyn commented that "you have to start somewhere" in response to a comment from Behrman dismissing economics as a foundation for IB.

Beyond this economic issue though, Boddewyn appears to go further than Wilkins in his own inclusion of multiple levels of analysis. He also goes further than Wilkins in his consideration of sociocultural and political implications for the conceptual domain of IB. However, Boddewyn explicitly stops short of providing a "definition of IB that would amount to defining it in terms of 'business and society,' of all its stakeholders, and of their multiple and changing interactions" [p. 51 in this volume]. Clearly, while he continues to flirt with many of the difficulties that have lead others to abandon the simplifying assumptions of the Newtonian paradigm, he draws the line at too inclusive a definition of IB.

Brian Toyne's Conceptual Domain Of IB

Of the three papers in this chapter of the book, Toyne's paper was the only one that appeared firmly rooted in the insights of contemporary science and how they might apply to the world of IB. However, I use the qualifier "appeared" because he never states explicitly that he intends to make such a linkage to contemporary science or a new paradigm. Yet, even a cursory look at his arguments suggests strongly that such a linkage is there to be made. He is unequivocal when he states that "human beings modify their thinking, reasoning, and behavior as a result of this body of knowledge [information]" [p. 65]. (*Editors' note:* Toyne elaborates on this point in his rejoinder.)

Though largely lost on the participants of the conference, four important messages concerning the nature of IB inquiry and whether or not it warrants a separate domain were articulated by Toyne. Although these points are not individually original, collectively they represent an important message worth noting. Unfortunately, much of that message can be lost if too much time is focused on the classification scheme Toyne uses to explain why earlier attempts at defining a conceptual domain for IB were inadequate. While his classification system is open to criticism, it simply is not the most critical aspect of Toyne's presentation.

Probably the single greatest contribution of Toyne's presentation is his call to establish an appropriate conceptual domain of IB in *metatheoretical* terms. He based this assertion on the assumption that "Since IB inquiry is viewed here as a scientific enterprise [and he appears to accept as a given that it is], the purpose of which is theory building and theory testing [a premise that most of us would be comfortable in accepting], its domain must be defined in terms that find their origin, expression, and meaning at the metalevel of inquiry. Thus IB inquiry cannot be separated from the conceptualizing act" [p. 64 in this volume]. Toyne seems fully aware that "the way IB is conceptualized, and the meaning sought by the questions asked, are 'part and parcel' of the school of thought adopted" [p. 66 in this volume]. Thus, without necessarily taking sides in this issue of paradigms in collision, Toyne vividly reminds us that the assumptions we make and the theories that we apply do make a fundamental difference in how we go forward. This is not a lesson that should be quickly forgotten.

The second major contribution of Toyne's work is his explanation of the limitations of the "firm" as the appropriate unit of analysis for IB and the fact that the firm itself is a social phenomenon. Once again, while this is not necessarily new, it seems that it is a lesson that needs restating: "The firm is a unit of analysis. It is an interactive outcome of a social process, not the process itself. . . . The firm, as Wilkins notes in her paper, has no meaning in a vacuum. Its meaning and significance is only made clear within a tapestry of social relationships; it is the woof and weave of the tapestry, not the individual threads, that convey meaning" [p. 68 in this volume]. Though the full significance of this statement is deceptively subtle, its implications speak volumes.

To begin, Toyne calls our attention to the fact that not only is the firm—and by inference, IB—the result of a social process, but also the result of an *interactive* process. This strongly suggests that instead of the simple, unidirectional cause and effect typical of a Newtonian-based paradigm, IB is subject to a much more complex, *interactive* cause and effect relationship that cannot be exactly modeled within the constraints of the Newtonian paradigm. Furthermore, the suggestion that IB is a social process instead of a material object is decidedly "outside" of the Newtonian domain.

Toyne's tapestry analogy also suggests yet a third contribution to the debate on the domain of IB: the necessity of *comprehending the whole*. Taken in context, this indicates a noticeable tilt in the direction of holism and away from the traditional reductionism of the Newtonian paradigm. His strong implication is that any understanding of the individual parts of a system must be preceded by an understanding of the whole. A simple example to make this point is the impossibility of understanding the gestalt of a jigsaw puzzle by first looking only at its individual parts. It simply cannot be done. If, however, one first understands the overall image of the jigsaw puzzle, then one can very quickly understand the relationships among the individual parts. This is exactly opposite the traditional Newtonian mode of analysis.

Finally, Toyne provides an interesting and compelling logic of when and why a particular field of inquiry becomes respectable—and by inference, why IB is worthy of such respect as a separate field of inquiry:

> First, when it can be demonstrated that it is working from a perspective that is fundamentally different than those already being explored by other fields . . . Second, when it can be demonstrated that its contributions are linked to other fields of inquiry and thus contribute in a meaningful and significant way to a better and more comprehensive and integrated understanding of the nature and behavior of human beings . . . And third, when it can be demonstrated that the contributions have value [p. 75 in this volume].

Because of the criticism Toyne received during the conference concerning his classification scheme, it is not clear that he made his case for the uniqueness of IB as compellingly as he would have liked. Indeed, as suggested earlier and consistent with the criteria outlined by Toyne above, it is possible that an even stronger case for the uniqueness of IB inquiry can be based on the complexity and ambiguity inherent in the IB process. Nonetheless, in light of his own arguments and given the seeming close association of the substantive, extensional, and universal terms as described by Toyne with Newtonian models, there should be little doubt about the correctness of his assertion. "By insisting that IB inquiry be defined in substantive, extensional, or universal terms, we are increasingly aware that our academic and research organizations, . . . and the rewards and sanctions these organizations impose, are obstacles to our inquiry" [p. 75 in this volume]. In a world of changing and shifting paradigms, it is the anomalies of the past that give rise to the paradigms of the future. As such, these anomalies become impediments to progress when we persist in trying to examine them within the shortcomings of the existing paradigms.

This, I believe, is the problem confronting scholars of IB when defining the conceptual domain of IB inquiry. I also believe it is the problem to which Toyne is trying to alert us. We are well advised to take his message to heart—something that Professor Schollhammer apparently failed to do in his commentary.

Hans Schollhammer's Commentary

Schollhammer began his critique by reaffirming his belief in the need of any academic discipline to delineate its domain and to specify its boundary conditions—as well as the need for continuing theory building. It is both surprising and ironic that he failed to understand that Toyne was making much the same point. Schollhammer also criticized Boddewyn's presentation on the grounds that "if the purpose of concern . . . is to provide a foundation for theory building and theory testing, then Boddewyn's effort falls short of one's expectations. Practically no effort is made to relate the proposed definition of IB to existing theoretical constructs" [p. 80]. Finally, Schollhammer criticized Wilkins's work on the grounds of being too narrow and too restrictive: "Apart from a vague efficiency criterion as the source of a sustainable competitive advantage Wilkins specifies no constraints or boundary conditions for IB as a domain of inquiry" [p. 78].

In his conclusion, Professor Schollhammer further comments on how each presenter delineated the conceptual domain of IB "in a different manner and from a different perspective." Yet, instead of seeing this as a potential problem, he sees it as a sign of health:

The three studies demonstrate that there are valid reasons for considering IB as a unique, distinct domain of inquiry. There are clear differences about the scope and boundaries of the IB domain that result in a diversity of theories. In my view, the diversity of perspectives and the existence of competing theories of international business are clear indicators of a healthy development of the discipline. [p. 82]

In the face of all this diversity, Schollhammer appears to be missing an essential point. When he states that "IB is a *complex* domain (emphasis added) with a series of competing theories concerned with different substantive issues" [p. 82], he seems to be overlooking the possibility that all of this complexity and diversity might indeed be the harbinger of a new paradigm; not simply a healthy reflection of an old paradigm.

Jack Behrman's Commentary

In many ways, with the exception of Toyne's presentation, Professor Behrman's commentary came the closest in reflecting the principles of the emerging paradigm. Eschewing reliance on the traditional discipline of economics as a foundation for the conceptual domain of IB, Behrman presents a compelling argument for a holistic view of the pluralistic reality of IB—where relationships, networks, and a wholly interconnected world are the fundamental realities with which any conceptual domain of IB must contend. Indeed, while Behrman recognizes the need for theoretical domains for conducting academic research, he appears far more concerned that IB focus on issues of policy or praxis—the combination of theory and practice—and less concerned with the narrow distinctions that are made for "academic" purposes.

Behrman closes his remarks with a call for academics and practitioners alike to:

start trying to make substantive contributions to the ills and problems faced by the world as it deals with and is affected or benefited by business. The more help we can get in this from others similarly concerned the better—whether in or outside the IB curriculum, outside of departments of management, or of business schools in other disciplines, or in government or business. This approach should produce some distinguished academics, familiar with varied methodologies, and who would be unsatisfied to remain within a neat and distinctive academic discipline but quite comfortable in the messy limbo of policy [p. 90].

Though it is not clear that Behrman realizes just how close he comes to describing what reality is like when viewed from the emerging paradigm—*a satisfying but messy limbo*—it is clear that he is making a plea for a different reordering of priorities than those implied by the traditional, "economic" model of IB. If Behrman's assessment is correct, then the old approach will certainly not take IB where he believes it needs to go. As a new paradigm emerges in IB, I believe the visions of Behrman and Toyne will point the direction in which the conceptual domain will lead.

I also believe that each in his own way is alerting us to the pending arrival of a new understanding of IB. I further believe that this new understanding will be based on a radically different view of social reality. It will be far different from the view held at the start of this century and different from the view that shaped most of our earliest thinking in IB and management alike. Finally, even though the emergence of this new paradigm went largely unnoticed at the conference, I also believe it provided both the central justification for the conference and the explanation of why no simple, single, unifying construct could be agreed upon for defining the conceptual domain of IB.

We are still in a period of transition from the old paradigm to the new one and may remain so for many more years to come. However, until such time as this new paradigm is fully accepted, or some other paradigm similar to it, I believe that no single answer concerning the conceptual domain of IB is likely to emerge.

REPLIES

Mira Wilkins

Business in the phrase "international business" can mean business "activities" or business "enterprise." My approach is a normative one: it is focused on *the firm*, the enterprise. Understanding of the IB firm is unique and special to our field, and, I argue, provides our contribution to knowledge. I have no problem with Hans Schollhammer's description of my view as that of an institutional perspective.

While my approach is focused, it is *not* narrow, nor is it vague. Thus, Jean Boddewyn wants to include exporters, importers, and so forth. If the exporter has any foreign presence, I would include it. If it merely functions out of a New York office with no extension of the *firm* over borders, I would exclude it.

Schollhammer criticizes me in one paragraph for being too all-inclusive and in the next for not being inclusive enough. My approach is to consider the *evolving* firm, thus the phrase foreign direct investment "no matter how small." This takes into account beginnings and growth. Once a foreign direct investment (FDI) occurs, I believe we should *then* look at *all* the firm's international engagements, not simply FDI. I plead "not guilty" to the second "shortcoming" of excluding all the other engagements. Also I plead "not guilty" to the charge that I do not *explicitly* pay attention to the "extraordinarily diverse nature of multinational firms." It is this *very diverse* activity that I believe must be understood. I agree with Schollhammer 100% that domain considerations are "inextricably linked to theory building" and that core theory helps us to deal with these issues. My approach differs *fundamentally* from that of Boddewyn and Toyne; *my focus is on the firm*.

Toyne suggests that my form of inquiry assumes "the firm is a major ... transfer agent of foreign innovation, technology, and managerial know-how." I am a business historian; I know from my research that particular individual firms were and are major transfer agents. Indeed, it is my argument that the firm as a conduit and intermediary is our particular interest. Societal constraints are vital in determining when, why, or even whether a firm is able to be a transfer agent.

I have emphasized throughout my paper that theory must be dynamic. This is the true contribution of the business historian. My paper stresses the importance of uncertainty, of nonlinear circumstances. A focus on the firm deals with strategies shaped over time by conditions internal and external to the enterprise.

Basic to my argument is that IB studies have been *too* general in the past. Here we have this marvelous subject—the "multinational enterprise." We are the experts. We are the ones who should know something. Yet, regrettably our field has often lacked focus. This is why I want to reiterate the point that our inquiries should be firm-oriented, that we should seek explanations on why and how this important institution functions.

As we consider the domain of IB, what drives our deliberations? Is the answer, as Jack Behrman suggests, driven by the provider, the professor? Or is it driven by the audience (students, business executives, government officials), or by public policy considerations? I believe that it is our responsibility as "providers" to present a core of understanding that is enduring rather than *ad hoc*, to present a paradigm that leads to comprehension. I do not see the function of university education as that of solving each short-term problem (putting out fires), but rather that of giving context, a basis for problem solving, and general knowledge. It is our assignment to seek to provide a core theory that helps us handle a range of different issues. As an historian of MNE, I know that an adequate theory must be dynamic, must emphasize complexities, and change; it is essential to place the multinational in its "political setting."

Yet, do we have any basis for generalization? Has all our study been for naught? Behrman takes the approach that theory is sterile and does not lead to understanding. I do not agree. Theory enriches understanding. And, even Behrman concedes that it is worth looking for the "flow of causal events . . ." I remain convinced that the domain of IB *should be* a search for understanding and

explaining the evolving, complex firm as it moves over borders over time and does business under a variety of different national sovereignties.

Jean J. Boddewyn

This first session of the conference was lively and got the ball rolling even though "domain" questions never came up again. It may be that such an endeavor is pointless or undoable—what W. C. Fields used to call "an insurmountable opportunity." Still, domain problems will continue to surface whenever novel forms of IB do appear, as when countertrading with foreign governments became significant. With that thought in mind, I would like to justify, clarify, and extend some of the arguments made in my paper, in answer to Jack Behrman's and Hans Schollhammer's strongly articulated critiques.

First, let me point out they did *not* offer any alternative *explicit* definition of IB, but limited themselves to probing some of my criteria and arguments, with much validity in some cases.

Second, the discussants argued that my definition was *not sufficiently* focused on the "firm," oriented to "policy" issues, and driven by "theory" (as recommended by Brian Toyne in his paper). This is true, but it does not help define the IB domain. What "firms" are they talking about? "Policies" about what? "Theory" of what? These three otherwise essential dimensions need a *preliminary focus* which, in our case, can only be "trade and investment crossing borders"—not any firms, not all international economic relations, and not world welfare.

Third, my discussion of "negotiated" trade and investment—which I had thought of qualifying as taking place "at arm's length"—was strongly challenged, and rightly so. Yet, there has to be some way of including only what is "business" in "international *business*"—whether you call it negotiated, private, market, or whatever. I am still struggling with the appropriate wording, however.

I certainly agree that more is involved than "*arm's-length transactions*," and that *relationships* are often developed among IB actors. However, Jack Behrman's suggestion that "arms-linked" constitutes a more realistic term to use is too warm and fuzzy, in my opinion. Even love and marriage—the epitome of an arms-linked behavior and institution—are full of negotiations because people are different and do change in the context of evolving situations. Therefore, IB is replete with transactions *and* relationships *but both are negotiated*, either in spot or future contexts.

Finally, Hans Schollhammer questioned most appropriately my ambiguous treatment of *intracompany transfers as part of IB*. After further thought, I think that all of them can be treated as IB transactions/relationships. The first (easy) case involves a firm, like IBM Corporation, shipping computers to IBM France for resale in France. Since the *ultimate* purpose of the transfer is a negotiated sale to the French, this cross-border trading activity can readily be considered to be "international business."

More complex is the second case of a U.S.-owned maquiladora to which U.S. parts are shipped to be transformed in Mexico and returned to the U.S. parent company for ultimate sale to a *U.S.* customer. Parts and finished products crossed the U.S.-Mexican border, but *within the same company*: is that transfer a "negotiated trade?" Yes it is, to the extent that the "relationships" between the U.S. and Mexican divisions of the same company, like all relationships, involve negotiations—as I just argued above.

A second justification for including the maquiladora type of transfer is because, as Robinson [1964b] put it, those relationships among business activities (the transfer, the production, and the ultimate negotiated sale) that are conducted within different countries "fall within the field of IB so long as they relate to *both* domestic and foreign persons or institutions." In other words, the ultimate sale negotiated *within* the United States depended on investment and trade conducted *across* the U.S.-Mexican borders.

If anyone can think of a better justification, please let me know because I think that "domain" questions are important and answerable.

Brian Toyne

The critiques by Schollhammer and Behrman are interesting because of their contrasting opinions concerning the arguments I advanced in my paper. Behrman seems to view the issues raised by historians and philosophers of science as inessential, arbitrary, even downright wrong. He appears to ascribe to the view that IB inquiry should be an applied, policy-driven science, not a basic science. Unlike Behrman, Schollhammer offers no alternative view, except to note in an unconvincing and substantially unsupported manner that: (1) there is no theory of International Business (which I believe most of us would agree with); and (2) that the questions asked of the firm have changed over the years (without explaining why they have changed). Although not offering a definition of the domain of international business and its boundary conditions, the examples towards the end of his paper suggests he supports a firm-level view similar to that offered by Wilkins. His criticism of her definition is one of degree, not form. He took a management perspective, she took an economic perspective.

Behrman argues value-laden policy should guide our inquiry; he objects to the fundamental rules that are part and parcel of the scientific method—particularly the tiresome replication required to certify knowledge. He objects to the *why* question. The value of the *why* question is clear—it is not asked of God, but of nature. It seeks to understand the linkage of yet to be discovered antecedents and current behavior. The question "Why does a firm internationalize?" is fundamentally different from "How does a firm internationalize?" Although the former is scientifically expansive, and the latter scientifically restrictive, both need answering to have a complete understanding of the internationalization process.

As to his charge that my purpose was to justify the development of a unique discipline for IB, I readily admit that this was the case. However, I disagree with his implication that this is "an academic exercise for academics," and therefore irrelevant. There are at least four reasons for this disagreement. First, to identify and understand the implications of the assumptions that underpin and guide much of our theorizing and research is not irrelevant.

The way we view reality is fundamental to the questions asked. To view the headquarters-subsidiary relationship as a parent-child relationship is certainly different from viewing it as one of evolving interaction between competency centers. The two views engender different policy and research questions and require different observations. This, of course, does not necessarily mean that one perspective is superior to the other.

Second, it is not irrelevant to classify research. Classification schemata are fundamental to explanation—even policy makers use them. They help reduce confusion, identify gaps in understanding, assist in the systematic investigation of phenomena, and facilitate in the retrieval of knowledge. However, I readily admit that a particular classification scheme can be questioned, indeed should be questioned.

Third, I believe we can all agree that it is not irrelevant to ask if a particular stream of research is important or unique. What can and should be questioned and debated are the criteria used to measure the value of research. In this regard, Behrman appears to have a more limited set of criteria than I do. I argue that IB inquiry is both an applied and a basic science, the importance and uniqueness of which must be measured in terms of the contributions it makes to the

generalized, certified body of knowledge about business, and used by both practitioners and academicians. Behrman appears to argue that IB inquiry should be an applied science that satisfies the practitioner's knowledge needs.

A fourth reason for focusing on the uniqueness of IB inquiry is that, like practitioners, academicians also reside in the "real world." They too are subjected to constraints (e.g., budgets, peer pressures) and subject to within and across departmental rivalries. Like practitioners, they too must justify their existence, their work. What better way is there to meet these challenges than to demonstrate that IB researchers not only contribute importantly to the body of knowledge about business, but also uniquely? This argument, of course, is based on my firm belief that there is much more to IB than what is examined by the traditional business disciplines.

Schollhammer's complaint that I contradict myself is forced—he takes some of what I said out of context and overlooks some of what I did say. In fact, it is relatively easy to show that he too appears to contradict himself. For example, on the first page of his commentary he expresses "some unease, that their conclusions about the scope of the IB domain and its boundaries are quite different." He further states "it is surprising that there exists so little commonalty in defining the field—let alone in theorizing about the most central issues. Arguably the absence of a reasonable degree of unanimity concerning the IB domain hampers not only theory building but also focused empirical research." These two statements suggest that he seeks "single-mindedness." Yet, he contradicts himself by stating elsewhere: "In my view, the diversity of perspectives and the existence of competing theories of IB are clear indicators of a healthy development of the discipline." [p. 82]

I agree with his remarks, although they appear to be contradictory. As I noted, a multiplicity of views is required if a more complete understanding of IB is to be gained. The important, but fragmented, knowledge gained as a result of substantivism, extensionalism, and universalism is incomplete and can be legitimately claimed by the traditional business disciplines and the social sciences. To be a distinct field, IB inquiry must contribute uniquely to a better understanding of business, and this, I suggested, arises from our study of the interaction of socially embedded business processes and their outcomes.

Both commentators correctly noted that inductive reasoning leads to theory and that descriptive studies contribute importantly to this activity. I couldn't agree more. However, there must be a theory building purpose behind these types of studies for this to occur. Substantive research does not *inherently* lead to theory.

Both commentators erroneously assumed that my intent was to reduce IB inquiry to a set of exclusive, reified schools of thought. This was not my goal. Nor was it my intent, as stated by Schollhammer, to suggest that IB should be considered a separate domain from the business discipline in general. My goal was to show that there are multiple conceptual domains of IB inquiry, each established by a particular school of thought and leading to a particular body of knowledge about business. That these bodies of knowledge can and need to be integrated is explained within my paper.

An inquiry's domain describes the reality to be explained or theorized about. That I call attention to the metalevel of inquiry reflects my belief that all human activity, including scientific inquiry, is embedded within a sociocultural context [Gould 1981] and thus conditioned by our current biases, prejudices, understanding, and knowledge. We like to believe we are objective and removed from the reality we study, but we are not. Put simply, reality is what we say it is. What we say it is determines the questions asked and the principles governing and shaping the interpretation of observations. This latter point is evident in the papers by Wilkins, Boddewyn and Behrman. The questions their realities engender differ in nature, not just degree.

Humans are learning animals. Thus, the reality that they create is not exclusively mechanistic and deterministic (Newton) or relativistic (Einstein). It is fundamentally evolutionary. Yet, our view of this reality is strongly influenced by our current value-laden, metalevel understanding of reality (quantum mechanics and chaos theory). Old data were not discarded when Copernicus's reality replaced Ptolemy's reality. What did change was the way the old data were interpreted. Also, the questions asked of Copernicus's reality are fundamentally different from those asked of Ptolemy's reality. This, I believe, occurs when IB inquiry is viewed as either substantivism, extensionalism, universalism, or resolutionalism.

REFERENCES

Abo, Tetsuo. 1994. *Hybrid Factory.* New York: Oxford University Press.

Adler, Nancy J. 1983. A typology of management studies involving culture. *Journal of International Business Studies,* 14(2): 29–47.

Adler, Nancy J. and Susan Bartholomew. 1992. Academic and professional communities of discourse: Generating knowledge on transnational human resource management. *Journal of International Business Studies,* 23(3): 551–569.

Aharoni, Yair. 1971. On the definition of the multinational corporation. *Quarterly Review of Economics and Business,* 11(2): 27–37.

Bacharach, S. B. 1989. Organizational theories: Some criteria for evaluation. *Academy of Management Review,* 14(4): 496–515.

Bartlett, Christopher A. and Sumantra Ghoshal. 1989. *Managing Across Borders: The Transnational Solution.* Boston: Harvard Business School Press.

Behrman, Jack N. and Robert E. Gross. 1990. *International Business and Governments.* Columbia, SC: University of South Carolina Press.

Belassa, Bela. 1990. Review of John Dunning, *Explaining International Production. Journal of Economic Literature,* 28(June): 708.

Black, J. Stewart, Mark Mendenhall, and Gary Oddou. 1991. Toward a comprehensive model of international adjustment: An integration of multiple theoretical perspectives. *Academy of Management Review*, 16(2): 291–317.

Boddewyn, Jean J. 1992. Political behavior research. In Peter J. Buckley, editor, *New Directions in International Business: Research Priorities for the 1990s*, 81–87. Brookfield, VT: Edward Elgar.

Boddewyn, Jean J. 1988. Political aspects of MNE theory. *Journal of International Business Studies*, 19(3): 341–363.

Boddewyn, Jean J. and Th. L. Brewer. 1994. International-business political behavior: New theoretical directions. *Academy of Management Review*, 19(1): 119–143.

Boddewyn, Jean J. and J. J. Falco. 1988. The size of the market sector around the world. *Journal of Macromarketing*, 8(1): 32–42.

Boddewyn, Jean J., M. B. Halbrich, and Anne C. Perry. 1986. Service multinationals: Conceptualization, measurement and theory. *Journal of International Business Studies*, 17(3): 41–57.

Boulding, Kenneth E. 1978. The legitimacy of the business institution. In Edwin M. Epstain and Don Votaw, editors, *Rationality, Legitimacy, Responsibility*. Santa Monica, CA: Goodyear.

Boyacigiller, Nakiye and Nancy J. Adler. 1990. The parochial dinosaur: Organizational science in a global context. *Academy of Management Review*, 16(2): 262–290.

Brewer, Thomas L. 1991. Market imperfections, government policies, and foreign direct investment theory. Washington, DC: Georgetown University, School of Business Administration. Mimeo.

Briggs, J. and F. D. Peat. 1990. *Turbulent Mirror: An Illustrated Guide to Chaos Theory and the Science of Wholeness*. New York: Harper and Row.

Buckley, Peter J. 1990. Problems and developments in the core theory of international business. *Journal of International Business Studies*, 21(4): 657–665.

Buckley, Peter J. 1988. The limits of explanation: Testing the internalization theory of the multinational enterprise. *Journal of International Business Studies*, 19(2): 181–93.

Buckley, Peter J. and Mark Casson. 1976. *The Future of the Multinational Enterprise*. London: The MacMillan Press.

Bygrave, W. D. 1989. The entrepreneurship paradigm (I): A philosophical look at its research methodologies. *Entrepreneurship Theory and Practice*, (Fall): 7–26.

Capra, F. 1983. *The Turning Point: Science, Society and the Rising Culture*. New York: Bantam Books.

Capra, F. 1976. *The Tao of Physics*. Boston: Shambhala.

Casson, Mark, editor. 1990. *Multinational Corporations*. Aldershot: Edward Elgar.

Casson, Mark 1987. *The Firm and the Market*. Cambridge: The MIT Press.

Chandler, Alfred D. 1990. *Scale and Scope*. Cambridge: Harvard University Press.

Chandler, Alfred D. 1977. *The Visible Hand*. Cambridge: Harvard University Press.

Chandler, Alfred D. 1959. The beginnings of "big business" in American industry. *Business History Review*, 33:1–31.

Clark, Terry. 1991. International boundaries and international marketing: A survey of major concepts. South Bend, IN: Notre Dame University, College of Business Administration.

Coase, Ronald H. 1937. The nature of the firm. *Economica*, 4:386–405.

Contractor, Farok and Peter Lorange, editors. 1988. *Cooperative Strategies in International Business*. Lexington: Lexington Books.

Daft, Richard L. and Arie Y. Lewin. 1990. Can organization studies begin to break out of the normal science straitjacket? *Organization Science*, 1(1): 1–9.

de la Torre, Jose and Brian Toyne. 1978. Cross-national managerial interaction: A conceptual model. *Academy of Management Review*, 3(3): 462–474.

Donaldson, Lex. 1985. *In Defence of Organization Theory*. Cambridge: Cambridge University Press.

Donaldson, Thomas. 1989. *The Ethics of International Business*. Oxford: Oxford University Press.

Doz, Yves. 1986. *Strategic Management in Multinational Companies*. New York: Pergamon Press.

Doz, Yves. 1979. *Government Control and Multinational Strategic Management.* New York: Praeger.

Doz, Yves. and C. K. Prahalad. 1991. Managing DMNCs: A search for a new paradigm. *Strategic Management Journal,* 12:145–164.

Drucker, Peter F. 1989. *The New Realities.* New York: Harper and Row.

Drucker, Peter F. 1986. The changed world economy. *Foreign Affairs,* 64(4): 768–791.

Dubin, Robert. 1978. *Theory Building.* New York: The Free Press.

Dunning, John H. 1991. Governments-markets-firms: Toward a new balance? *The CTC Reporter,* 31(Spring): 2–7.

Dunning, John H. 1989. The study of international business: A plea for a more interdisciplinary approach. *Journal of International Business Studies,* 20(3): 411–436.

Dunning, John H. 1988a. The eclectic paradigm of international production: A restatement and some possible extensions. *Journal of International Business Studies,* 19(1): 1–31.

Dunning, John H. 1988b. *Explaining International Production.* Boston: Unwin-Hyman.

Dunning, John H. 1981. *The Eclectic Theory of the Multinational Corporation.* London: Allen and Unwin.

Dunning, John H. 1980. Toward an eclectic theory of international production. *Journal of International Business Studies,* 11(1): 9–30.

Dunning, John H. 1973. The determinants of international production. *Oxford Economic Papers,* November: 289–336.

Dunning, John H. 1958. *American Investment in British Manufacturing Industry.* London: Allen and Unwin.

Dunning, John H. and Alan M. Rugman. 1985. The influence of Hymer's dissertation on the theory of foreign direct investment. *American Economic Review,* 75(2): 228–244.

Eisenhardt, Kathleen M. 1989. Building theory from case study research. *Academy of Management Review,* 14(4): 532–550.

Fayerweather, John. 1969. *International Business Management: A Conceptual Framework.* New York: McGraw-Hill. Expanded in his book, *International Business Strategy and Administration.* Cambridge: Ballinger, 1978;1982.

Fayerweather, John. 1960. *Management of International Operations, Text and Cases.* New York: McGraw-Hill.

Fieldhouse, D. K. 1986. The multinational: A critique of a concept. In Alice Teichova, et al., *The Multinational Enterprise in Historical Perspective.* Cambridge: Cambridge University Press.

Forsgren, Mats. 1989. *Managing the internationalization process.* New York: Routledge.

Gladwin, Thomas N. and Ingo Walter. 1980. *Multinationals Under Fire: Lessons in the Management of Conflict.* New York: John Wiley and Sons.

Gersick, C. J. G. 1991. Revolutionary change theories: A multilevel exploration of the punctuated equilibrium paradigm. *Academy of Management Review,* 16(1):10–36.

Gilpin, Robert. 1987. *The Political Economy of International Relations.* Princeton: Princeton University Press.

Gleick, J. 1987. *Chaos: Making a New Science.* New York: Penguin.

Gould, Stephen Jay. 1981. *The Mismeasure of Man.* New York: W.W. Norton and Company.

Grosse, Robert and Jack N. Behrman. 1992. Theory in international business. *Transnational Corporations,* 1(1): 93–126.

Hambrick, D. C. 1990. The adolescence of strategic management, 1980–1985: Critical prescriptions and reality. *Perspectives on Strategic Management,* 237–253. New York: Harper and Row.

Hamel, Gary and C. K. Prahalad. 1988. Creating global capability. In Neil Hood and J. E. Vahlne, editors, *Strategies in Global Competition,* 5–39. New York: Croom-Helm.

Hamilton, W. H. 1930. Institution. In E.R.A. Seligman, editor, *Encyclopedia of the Social Sciences,* 8: 84–89. New York: MacMillan.

Hardin, Garrett. 1986. *Filters Against Folly.* New York: Penguin Books.

Hawking, S. W. 1988. *A Brief History of Time: From the Big Bang to Black Holes.* NY: Bantam Books.

Hawkins, Robert G. 1984. International business in academia: The state of the field. *Journal of International Business,* 15(3): 13–18.

Hedlund, Gunnar. 1986. The hypermodern

MNC—A heterarchy? *Human Resource Management*, 25(1): 9–25.

Hempel, C. G. 1965. *Aspects of Scientific Explanation*. New York: Free Press.

Hesse, Herman. 1969. *The Glass Bead Game*. NY: Holt, Rinehart & Winston.

Horaguchi, H. and Brian Toyne. 1990. Setting the record straight: Hymer, internalization theory and transaction cost economics. *Journal of International Business Studies*, 21(3): 487–494.

Hunt, Shelby D. 1990. Truth in marketing theory and research. *Journal of Marketing*, 54(3): 1–15.

Hymer, S. H. 1976:1960. *The International Operations of National Firms: A Study of Direct Foreign Investment*. Ph.D. thesis, Massachusetts Institute of Technology, first published Cambridge, MA, 1976.

Jain, Subash C. 1989. Standardization of international marketing strategy: Some research hypotheses. *Journal of Marketing*, 3(1): 70–79.

Jantsch, E. 1980. *The Self-Organizing Universe*. Oxford: Pergamon Press.

Jones, Geoffrey. 1993. *British Multinational Banking*. Oxford: Oxford University Press.

Jones, Geoffrey, editor. 1990. *Banks as Multinationals*. London: Routledge.

Kaplan, Abraham. 1964. *The Conduct of Inquiry: Methodology for Behavioral Science*. New York: Harper and Row.

Keat, R. and J. Urry. 1975. *Social Theory as Science*. Boston: Routledge and Kegan.

Keezer, D. M. 1930. Business. In E. R. A. Seligman, editor, *Encyclopedia of the Social Sciences*, 3: 80–87. New York: MacMillan.

Kindleberger, Charles. 1984. International banks and international business in an historical perspective. Reprinted in his *Multinational Excursions*, 155–170. Cambridge, MA: MIT Press.

Kindleberger, Charles. 1975. Size of firm and size of nations. In John H. Dunning, editor, *Economic Analysis and the Multinational Enterprise*, 342–362. New York: Praeger.

Kirchoff, B. A. 1992. Entrepreneurship's contributions to economics. *Entrepreneurship Theory and Practice*, 16(2): 93–112.

Klein, Thomas A. 1977. *Social Costs and Benefits of Business*. Englewood Cliffs, NJ: Prentice-Hall.

Kobrin, Stephen J. 1990. *The Impact of Transnational Integration on States and the State System*. Philadelphia, PA: University of Pennsylvania, Wharton School.

Kogut, Bruce. 1991. Country capabilities and the permeability of borders. *Strategic Management Journal*, 12(Summer): 33–47.

Kogut, Bruce. 1989. A note on global strategies. *Strategic Management Journal*, 10:383–389.

Kogut, Bruce. 1985a. Designing global strategies: Comparative and competitive value added chains. *Sloan Management Review*, Summer: 15–28.

Kogut, Bruce. 1985b. Designing global strategies: Profiting from operational flexibility. *Sloan Management Review*, 26(1): 27–38.

Kravis, Irving B. and Robert E. Lipsey. 1989. Technological characteristics of industries and the competitiveness of the U.S. and its multinational firms. Working Paper No. 2933, April, National Bureau of Economic Research, Cambridge, MA.

Kuhn, Thomas S. 1970. *The Structure of Scientific Revolutions*, Second Edition, revised. Chicago, IL: University of Chicago Press.

Kuhn, Thomas S. 1962. *The Structure of Scientific Revolutions*. Chicago: University of Chicago Press.

Lastrucci, Carlo L. 1963. *The Scientific Approach*. Cambridge: Schenkman Publishing Co., Inc.

Laszlo, E., editor. 1991. *The New Evolutionary Paradigm*. New York: Gordon and Breach Science Publishers.

Lenway, Stephanie A. and Thomas P. Murtha. 1991. *The Idea of the State in the International Business Literature*. Ann Arbor: University of Michigan. Working paper.

Levitt, Theodore. 1983. The globalization of markets. *Harvard Business Review*, May-June: 92–102.

Lipsey, Robert. 1991. Foreign direct investment in the United States and U.S. trade. In *The Annals of the American Academy of Political and Social Science*, 516 (July): 76–90.

Macharzina, Klaus and Johanna Engelhard. 1991. Paradigm shift in international business research. *Management International Review*, 31(91): 23–43.

McGuire, Joseph. 1964. *Theories of Business Behavior*. Englewood Cliffs: Prentice-Hall.

McKelvey, B. 1978. Organizational systematics: Taxonomic lessons from biology. *Management Science*, 24: 1428–1440.

McKelvey, B. 1975. Guidelines for the empirical classification of organizations. *Administrative Science Quarterly*, 20: 509–525.

Mellor, R. E. H. 1989. *Nation, State and Territory: A Political Geography*. New York: Routledge.

Mikesell, Raymond F., editor. 1960. *U.S. Private and Government Investment Abroad*. Eugene: University of Oregon Press.

Moran, Theodore H. 1985. *Multinational Corporations: The Political Economy of Foreign Direct Investment*. Lexington, MA: Lexington Books.

Morrison, Allen J. 1990. *Strategies in Global Industries*. New York: Quorum Books.

Nehrt, Lee, Frederick Truitt, and Richard Wright. 1970. *International Business: Past, Present, and Future*. Bloomington: Indiana University Graduate School of Business.

Nonaka, I. 1989. Experiences of Japanese MNCs. In Christopher A. Bartlett, Yves Doz, and Gunnar Hedlund, editors, *Managing the Global Firm*. London: Routledge.

Norman, R. A. 1968. Managing tomorrow. Unpublished speech. Lancaster, PA.

Ohmae, Kenichi. 1990. *The Borderless World: Power and Strategy in the Interlinked Economy*. New York: Harper Business.

Ohmae, Kenichi. 1985. *Triad Power: The Coming Shape of Global Competition*. New York: Free Press.

Oman, Charles. 1984. *New Forms of International Investment in Developing Countries*. Paris: Organization for Economic Cooperation and Development.

Parsons, Talcott and N. J. Smelser. 1956. *Economy and Society*. New York: Free Press.

Penrose, Edith. 1959. *The Theory of the Growth of the Firm*. New York: Wiley.

Penrose, Edith. 1956. Foreign investment and the growth of the firm. *Economic Journal*, 64(June): 220–235.

Perlmutter, H. V. 1969. The tortuous evolution of the multinational corporation. *Columbia Journal of World Business*, January-February: 9–18.

Perrow, Charles. 1986. *Complex Organizations*. New York: McGraw-Hill.

Phillips, D. C. 1987. *Philosophy, Science, and Social Inquiry*. New York: Pergamon Press.

Pitelis, Christos N. and Roger Sugden. 1991. On the theory of the transnational firm. *The Nature of the Transnational Firm*. London: Routledge.

Polanyi, Karl. 1944. *The Great Transformation*. New York: Rinehart.

Popper, Karl R. 1961. *The Logic of Scientific Discovery*. New York: Science Editions.

Porter, Michael E. 1990. *The Competitive Advantage of Nations*. New York: Free Press.

Porter, Michael E., editor. 1986. *Competition in Global Industries*. Boston: Harvard Business School Press.

Prigogine, I. and I. Stengers. 1984. *Order Out of Chaos: Man's New Dialogue With Nature*. New York: Bantam Books.

Reich, R. B. 1992. Is Japan really out to get us? *New York Times Book Review*, February 9: 1ff.

Richardson, D. B. 1972. The organization of industry. *Economic Journal*, 82(September): 883–896.

Ricks, David A., Brian Toyne, and Zaida L. Martinez. 1990. Recent Developments in International Management Research. *Journal of Management*, 16(2): 219–253.

Riggs, F. W. 1970. *Administration in Developing Countries*. Boston: Houghton Mifflin.

Robinson, Richard D. 1978. *International Business Management*. Hinsdale: Dryden Press.

Robinson, Richard D. 1964a. Joint ventures or transnational business. *Industrial Management Review*, 6(1): 59–65.

Robinson, Richard D. 1964b. *International Business Policy*. New York: Holt, Rinehart and Winston.

Rubner, Alex. 1990. *The Might of the Multinationals: The Rise and Fall of the Corporate Legend*. New York: Praeger.

Rugman, Alan M. 1985. Internalization is still a general theory of foreign direct investment. *Weltwirtschaftliches Archiv*, 121(3): 570–575.

Scott, W. R. 1987. The adolescence of institutional theory. *Administrative Science Quarterly*, 32: 493–511.

Smelser, N. J. 1976. *The Sociology of Economic Life*. Englewood Cliffs, N.J: Prentice-Hall.

Steiner, George A. and Warren M. Cannon. 1966. *Multinational Corporate Planning*. New York: MacMillan.

Stewart, Charles F., and George B. Simmons. 1964. *A Bibliography of International Business*. New York: Columbia University Press.

Stewart, I. S. 1989. *Does God Play Dice: The Mathematics of Chaos*. Cambridge, MA: Basil Blackwell.

Sundaram, A. K. and Black, J. S. 1992. The environment and internal organization of multinational enterprises. *Academy of Management Review*, 17(4): 729–757.

Supple, Barry. 1989. Introduction: Multinational enterprise. In A. Teichova et al., editors, *Historical Studies in International Corporate Business*, 1–6. New York: Cambridge University Press.

Tallman, Stephen B. 1991. Strategic management models and resource-based strategies among MNEs in a host market. *Strategic Management Journal*, 12: 69–82.

Taylor, P. J. 1985. *Political Geography: World-Economy, Nation-State and Locality*. New York: Longman.

Teece, David J. 1990. Contributions and impediments of economic analysis to the study of strategic management. *Perspectives on Strategic Management*, 39–79. New York: Harper Business.

Therrien, Lois. 1991. McRisky [McDonald's]. *Business Week*, 21(October): 114–122.

Toyne, Brian. 1992. Internationalizing the BA faculty is no easy task. In S. T. Cavusgil and A. Yaprak, editors, *Internationalizing Business Schools and Faculty*. Michigan State University.

Toyne, Brian. 1990. The international dimension of business and society. *1990 Proceedings*, compiled by Donna J. Woods and William E. Martello. International Association for Business and Society.

Toyne, Brian. 1989. International exchange: A foundation for theory building in international business. *Journal of International Business*, 20(1): 1–17.

Toyne, Brian. 1988. A maverick's view of the state of international business inquiry. Unpublished paper.

Tsoukas, Haridimos. 1989. The validity of idiographic research explanations. *Academy of Management Review*, 14(4): 551–561.

United Nations Centre on Transnational Corporation. 1983. *Transnational Corporations in World Development, Third Survey*. New York: United Nations.

United Nations. 1982. Work related to the formulation of a code of conduct: Definitions and scope of application. New York: Commission on Transnational Corporations, Report E/C.10/1982/6, 5 June.

van Gigch, J. P. and L. L. Pipino. 1986. In search of a paradigm for the discipline of information systems. *Future Computing Systems*, 1(1): 71–97.

Vernon Raymond. 1966. International investment and international trade in the product cycle. *Quarterly Journal of Economics*, May: 190–207.

von Hayek, Friedrich A. 1989. The pretense of knowledge. *The American Economic Review*, 79(6): 3–7.

Walters, Peter G. P. 1986. International marketing policy: A discussion of the standardization construct and its relevance for corporate policy. *Journal of International Business Studies*, 17(2): 55–69.

Weber, Max. 1964. The Theory of Social and Economic Organization. New York: Free Press.

Wheatley, M. J. 1992. *Leadership and the New Science*. San Francisco: Berrett-Koehler Publishers.

Wilkins, Mira. 1994a. Comparative hosts. *Business History*, 36(January): 18–50.

Wilkins, Mira. 1994b. Hosts to transnational investment—A comparative analysis. In Hans Pohl, ed. *Transnational Investments from the 19th Century to the Present*, a supplement to *Zeitschrift für Unternehmensgeschichte*, 81:25–69.

Wilkins, Mira. 1994c. When and why brand names in food and drink? In Geoffrey Jones and Nicholas Morgan, *Adding Value: Brands and Marketing in Food and Drink*. London: Routledge.

Wilkins, Mira. 1992. The neglected intangible asset: The influence of the trade mark on the rise of the modern corporation. *Business History*, 34(January): 66–95.

Wilkins, Mira, editor. 1991. *The Growth of Multinationals*. Aldershot: Edward Elgar.

Wilkins, Mira. 1990. Japanese multinationals in the United States: Change and continuity, 1871–1990. *Business History Review*, 64(Winter): 585–629.

Wilkins, Mira. 1989. The History of Foreign Investment in the United States to 1914. Cambridge: Harvard University Press.

Wilkins, Mira. 1988a. European and North American multinationals, 1870–1914: Comparisons and contrasts. *Business History*, 30(January): 8–45.

Wilkins, Mira. 1988b. The free-standing company, 1870–1914: An important type of British foreign direct investment. *Economic History Review*, 2nd series, 41(May): 259–282.

Wilkins, Mira. 1986a. The history of European multinationals: A new look. *Journal of European Economic History*, 15(Winter): 483–510.

Wilkins, Mira. 1986b. Defining a firm: History and theory. In Peter Hertner and Geoffry Jones, editors, *Multinationals: Theory and History*. Aldershot: Gower Publishing Company.

Wilkins, Mira. 1974. *The Maturing of Multinational Enterprise: American Business Abroad from 1914 to 1970*. Cambridge: Harvard University Press.

Wilkins, Mira. 1970. *The Emergence of Multinational Enterprise: American Business Abroad from the Colonial Era to 1914*. Cambridge: Harvard University Press.

Wilkins, Mira. and Frank Ernest Hill. 1964. *American Business Abroad: Ford on Six Continents*. Detroit, MI: Wayne State University Press.

Wilson, J. W. and J. H. Dobrzynski. 1986. And now, the post-industrial corporation. *Business Week*, 3 (March): 64–71.

Wind, Yoram and Susan P. Douglas. 1986. The myth of globalization. *Journal of Consumer Marketing*, 3(Spring): 23–26.

Zetterberg, Hans L. 1954. *On Theory and Verification in Sociology*. Stockholm: Almqvist and Wiksell.

3

Business and Society Perspectives and International Business

EDITORS' COMMENTS

Business and Society as a field of study has a lot in common with IB inquiry. As Steve Wartick says in his commentary below, if they are not siblings, they're at least first cousins. Given the similarities, we thought that IB might have something to learn from Business and Society and vice versa.

We asked the topic authors to examine the various business and society frameworks that have been developed and, in particular, their ontological, epistemological, and human nature assumptions. We asked the authors to assess the ability of the business and society theories, classification schemes, and models to contribute to the systematic body of knowledge of international business and cross-societal interaction. In this evaluation, we invited the authors to select for review any or all of the various components of the field of business and society—business ethics, corporate social performance, stakeholder and issues management, business and government, etc.

As a group, the five papers make one particularly noteworthy point: international business, business, and the economy are embedded in society and future IB inquiry should reflect this reality. In the first topic paper, Bob Hogner begins by placing international business inquiry itself squarely within its own societal and scientific context—one of changing world views (from modern to post-modern) and changing ideas of "scientific reality and corresponding models of legitimate scientific method" (from a positivist paradigm to naturalist paradigm). Hogner argues "The destruction of philosophical positivism signaled an end of the positivist paradigm for the entire scientific world. We in the social and management sciences are today living through these changes." [p. 121]

Hogner sees most of economics, management, and international business studies today as still connected with the maintenance of the traditional positivist paradigm. Yet the drift toward the naturalist paradigm is affecting inquiry in economics, economic anthropology, economic sociology, and business and society. Here we find more evidence of the paradigmic conflict we discussed in chapter 1.

A particularly important aspect of Hogner's "naturalist drift" is the shift from the economy as disembedded from society to the "economy in society" model, which Hogner develops from Polanyi's theory of social and economic transformation. Hogner contends, "Economy as a sphere of patterned behavior is inseparable from society. Economics as the conceptual model for understanding the provisioning of society is inseparable from other social science modelling of it. Economy does not exist distinct from the whole of society just because economics, driven by long abandoned stories of a physical world, chooses to model it as such." [p. 124]

Hogner sees the historical context of IB inquiry, "emergent out of positivism but retaining a holistic, institutional, process perspective," as bridging the changes in world views and paradigms currently underway. Whither IB inquiry? Hogner holds out a couple of choices: decline in continuing allegiance to positivism or substantive change in the process and form of IB leading to a "more human, social, moral, humane, and more political" science [p. 130].

In the second topic paper, Ed Freeman gives particular emphasis to business ethics; indeed, Freeman labels his field Business,

Ethics, and Society, or BES. Freeman asks, "Why have BES scholars and executives been silent so long, for the most part, on global moral issues?" [p. 131] He finds his answer in (1) the "problem of two realms" in which business theory and business ethics have developed along separate tracks and (2) the tremendous complexity inherent in the internationalization of business.

Freeman argues that business is seen by business theorists and executives as essentially economic and "its political, social or cultural effects, not to mention its moral effects, can safely be bracketed and dealt with on the side or at the margin" [p. 132]—a domain that BES scholars have made their own. Freeman decries this cleavage into two realms and the failure to see the possibilities in understanding business as the greatest of all social institutions. Like Hogner, Freeman finds promise in a re-embedding of business (and business inquiry) in society.

For Freeman, the internationalization of business has generated immense challenges to BES inquiry. The multiplicity of value issues, the variety of different cultural/ethical systems, and the rise of truly global issues have taxed standard BES ways of thinking. For Freeman, "Their development was never intended to take account of the complexity inherent in today's world, or if it was the result was facile." [p. 133]

What can BES contribute to international business inquiry and practice? Freeman examines what he calls a key underlying assumption of IB: moral relativism. "From the fact of cultural relativism, that cultures differ on many matters, IB theorists deduce that moral reasoning across cultures simply cannot occur." [p. 134] Freeman condemns this deduction as false and notes that it serves to ensure that the two realms of business and ethics remain separated.

Moral relativism also reinforces the view of business as competition and of ethics as "stone tablets." Yet Freeman argues that business is just as much about cooperation as about competition and "ethics is conversation about what we can agree upon how to live. There are no ultimate foundations ... The conversation is open textured, although at times we are sure enough of ourselves to codify some rules of thumb, traced in pencil rather than chiseled in stone." [p. 135]

In the end, Freeman recommends that BES work on giving an account of a "domestic" U.S. corporation in multicultural terms (race, gender, sexuality, culture). "If we can overcome our inability to deal with race, gender, and ethnicity in the U.S. we can create our corporations in a way that makes them more effective around the world." [p. 131] This suggestion echoes a resurgent interest in international business inquiry—the increased recognition and investigation of differences within a country—and is consistent with our ideas concerning the embedded multi-level nature of IB processes.

In the third topic paper, Pasquero and Wood take a different perspective and focus on what Business and Society needs to do to internationalize its inquiry. Like Freeman, they acknowledge that Business and Society has had largely a domestic or uninational orientation over the past two decades, but emphasize that the trend recently is toward more international business and society inquiry.

To guide the Business and Society scholar in his or her internationalization, Pasquero and Wood provide a number of classification schemes with accompanying explanations—the types of international research; the dimensions of the issues faced by international business and society; the objectives of international business and society research; and the benefits of international business and society research.

Much of what they recommend can be seen as extentionalism—one of the four schools of thought concerning the domain of IB inquiry that Toyne identified in his chapter 2 topic paper.[1] Pasquero and Wood argue that the two theoretical benefits from internationalizing Business and Society research are "(1) tests of the appropriateness of American models of business and society relationships and processes when applied to other cultures, and (2) tests of the robust-ness (novel perspective, relevance, applicability) of our ideas." [p. 151]

They take four mainstream concepts in Business and Society (stakeholders, business and government relations, business ethics and corporate social performance), assess the face validity and symbolic or structural equivalence of each, and the implications of extending the concept to other societal settings.

With some concluding practical advice to business and society scholars on how to improve their own international expertise, Pasquero and Wood bring the discussion back to the role of academics in society. "The purpose of international study goes beyond what the academic community gains from the constant extension of its interests into outer spheres. Through meeting, understanding, and explaining others to ourselves and to our peers, we [international business and society researchers] hope to help prepare for a better world." [p. 159]

In his commentary, Cochran first links Hogner's distinction between a positivist paradigm and a naturalist paradigm to Isaiah Berlin's distinction between hedgehogs and foxes. In looking at writers, thinkers, and human beings, in general, Berlin [1986: 1–2] sees hedgehogs who relate everything to a central vision, "a single, universal, organizing principle, in terms of which alone all that they are and say has significance" and foxes who "pursue many ends, often unrelated and even contradictory, ... related by no single moral or aesthetic principle." Cochran sees those trained in finance, accounting, and economics as typically hedgehogs and those in Business and Society, IB, and organizational studies as typically foxes. This characterization raises some interesting sociology of knowledge questions with regard to the mechanisms of selection and adaptation that might be operating to generate finance hedgehogs and Business and Society foxes. We'll have more to say in the concluding chapter on the nature of the business and social science disciplines and the possibilities of multidisciplinary inquiry in international business.

Cochran also addresses the two sets of contending forces in the world today—centripetal and centrifugal. The increased integration of the European Union and the North American Free Trade Agreement members coexist with the devolution of the USSR and Yugoslavia. Cochran sees evidence of both more monoculturalism worldwide and increased multiculturalism, or increased sensitivity to diversity. The implications for business ethics are significant. Cochran sees global consensus existing or building about a number of important ethical issues and is heartened by Freeman's assertion that ethical relativism has been completely discredited. Yet he sees the need for more work on the reconciliation of ethical absolutism and multiculturalism.

In his commentary, Wartick calls for moving from the study of "business and society" to "businesses in societies" since "the traditional unisocietal conceptualizations of the interface between business and society are inadequate for international analysis." [p. 166] Wartick sees the most important impact of globalization on business and society inquiry as the need to put business activity back into the context of societies.

This dissatisfaction with the status quo in Business and Society inquiry (most clearly seen in the Hogner and Freeman papers) is also evident in IB inquiry. Wartick looks at the two areas of study and asks how they might coevolve. First he looks at what Business and Society and IB have in common. "The two fields share a perspective of business that extends across functional areas and does not artificially limit analysis to some narrowly defined domain. The two fields share an interest in how the business environment both promotes and limits certain business activity." [p. 170]

We see other similarities. Business and Society has always investigated phenomena at many levels—from the level of an entire society down to the level of the individual. As we suggest in chapter 1, just such a span

of levels (from suprasocietal to individual) is what IB inquiry should involve in the future. In addition, both fields are inherently multidisciplinary. Wartick writes "You don't have to be an anthropologist, a sociologist, a philosopher, an economist, and a political scientist to understand and appreciate Business and Society ... scholarship, but it would certainly help." [p. 165] The same could be said about international business.

Both areas are hot topics and growth areas in business schools and in professional associations. Both are, as Wartick argues, "at risk of being trivialized by those in business schools who believe that our fields are most properly absorbed into the functional areas." [p. 171] The call for everyone to teach the international dimension of their subject is paralleled by the call for everyone include ethics and public policy analysis in their functional area of study.

How will the two fields coevolve? We find the "businesses in societies" framework quite consistent with our ideas of international business as an evolving, multilevel, socially embedded process. Likewise we find business and society's tradition of questioning the status quo in inquiry and practice as compatible with our vision of the future of international business.

To conclude, as first cousins, IB and Business and Society do seem to have much in common and much to learn from one another as they develop. One common challenge we face has to do with the concept of society—which still plays a critical role in Wartick's "businesses in societies" framework. Too often to date we have assumed that society is the functional equivalent of nation-states—a concept investigated in chapter 5.

NOTES

1. Extentionism is the confirmation of the scientific product of business inquiry developed in one societal setting when extended and tested in another societal setting.

International Business Studies: Science, Society, and Reality

Robert H. Hogner

Therefore, at times of revolution, when the normal scientific tradition changes, the scientist's perception of his environment must be re-educated—in some familiar situations he must learn to see a new gestalt.

[Thomas Kuhn 1962]

My introduction to International Business Studies (IBS) came in the early 1970s. I was a graduate student and assistant for an interdisciplinary international business (IB) seminar and had the opportunity to present some research findings in that seminar. I had "walked through" U.N. data looking for statistical signs of potential multinational corporation (MNC) expropriation activity. A spirited discussion about the "method of science" I used followed my presentation. There was intense specific criticism from some professors for not having used the hypotheses development, acceptance, and rejection model that was normal science. Varying sides were taken, and a memorable time ensued.

What I remember most about the event was the morning seminar in urban anthropology. There, we were discussing the application of models of sociocultural behavior—rituals, fetishes, myth and symbols, rites, etc.—to understand urban culture. Transferring morning knowledge to the afternoon, I was only a graduate student and already marginalized between two cultures of science.

I did not know then, and only partially know now, the depth of the social and scientific changes underway, making themselves a part of my world view. Earlier, as an undergraduate physics major, I easily accepted as normal the new science necessary to understand optical holograms. Now other forces were shaping my world and scientific view. New chapters in science's storybook were opening.

History was weaving its fabric. Social and political discontent of the period raised deep questions about the purpose of science. That questioning, for those just sprouting "scientific inquiry buds," altered forever our vision of normal science. Science, for us, could not exist except deeply embedded in its social context. The political, historical, cultural, social, economic—even moral—aspects of scientific inquiry were not dimensions to be added to science. They were not wizard's grains thrown in the mix, coloring an otherwise rational endeavor. They *were* science.

What could economics and economic institutions "in reality" *be* except social entities deeply woven into a cultural fabric? They were artifacts of our being, symbolisms created by us, about and for social purposes. Our apparent reality, our science, was becoming different.

The thesis developed here is simple. It has three parts: First, within the last part of this century there has emerged, some say reemerged, a new world view in Western society. This view directly challenges the modernist reality, a mechanistic, individualistic, rationalistic reality.

Second, this new world view emerged alongside basic changes in scientific reality and corresponding models of legitimate scientific method. These paradigmatic shifts were recognized first in the hard sciences, then in the social sciences. A new paradigm is building. A new scientific reality associated with "provisioning" for human society (economics, management, etc.) is forming.

Third, IBS exists in the old and new paradigms. Its relations with (neo)classical economics and management on one hand, and its holistic focus on institutional processes on the other, position it so. It must abandon that marginal position. Cleavages opened by paradigm shifts open, then close.

These ideas are addressed by examining how the changing nature of science, society, and even what we know as reality form a basis for change in IBS. First, I address the theme that a new paradigm for reality and scientific understanding and method is, indeed, emerging. These changes are linked to basic shifts in understanding the world around us. The nature of our physical reality, the interconnectedness of human societies, and the relation of those societies to their natural environment are all a part of these changing perceptions.

Second, I show how these emergent ideas and "paradigmatic shifts" have already had an impact on science. I portray the unresolved underlying tensions remaining from the evolution of positivist science, specifically economics and the other social sciences, as forming the conditions for these developments. Their impact is shown by the evolution of new models of social science inquiry and knowledge-building systems.

Finally, I ask, of what consequence is this for IBS? Ideas, as Berger suggests, "do not survive by virtue of their truth, but rather by virtue of their relationship to specific social processes" [Berger 1965]. IBS is on an evolutionary path guided by such processes. New questions arise and demand answers, both answers *and* questions previously unknowable in the old paradigm. The process of restructuring IBS to allow for these new answers should provide for a stronger and more beneficent science.

Beyond these questions, beyond the explicitness detailed above, a theme develops. IBS, the social and management sciences of which it is part, and the broader scope of science itself, including the so-called hard sciences, are all story-telling systems. The stories we tell ourselves and others across the academic campfires of *JIBS, American Economic Review,* or *Physics Today* are just that: stories about our lives which we hope make sense of our past, present, and future. Indeed, these concepts—past, present, and future—are stories within themselves.

That they are stories does not identify them as "only stories." We should not lose sight of their usefulness, for they do put us in touch with one another and enable us to avoid an avalanche of ideas/data that the consensus of time has for this moment in history ruled irrelevant. They place us in context—political, social, cultural, and so on—and for those of us for whom science story telling is a vocation, they entertain as well.

On the other hand, let us not forget they are, indeed, "only stories." We should not lose sight of their fundamental essence as such. Much, if not all, of what we speak of in IBS or the other social sciences simply does not exist as empirical reality. An outline of such a reality may exist in the hard sciences, although they are a much easier vocation than the social and management sciences.

We have created it all. Physics, chemistry, and disciplines offer students a *tangible* science.[1] Those scientists have created most of it, because a flame or acid can burn, or electricity can shock. However, no IBS class is structured with a lab (3-credit lecture; 1-credit lab) to *touch* a market, or *see* a corporation.[2] These are unknowables whose shapes take place only within the stories we tell.

This, then, is a story about a story.

SCIENCE, SOCIETY, AND CULTURE: AN OVERVIEW

[I]n some important respects, though by no means all, Einstein's general theory of relativity is closer to Aristotle's than either of them is to Newton's.

[Kuhn 1962]

What we experience in the world around us becomes dependent both upon the perception process and upon the needs of the historical period in which we find ourselves. It is an individual experience, shaped by our uniqueness. It is also a social experience, shaped by general understandings about the limits of possibility, that is, the prescripts of reality. This is true regardless of the institutional context in which we find ourselves: butcher, baker, or M.B.A. maker.

An example is worthwhile. Major portions of Euro-American cultures centuries ago abandoned the notion that the world is a dynamic and mystical cosmos. A more scientific reality emerged: the world is a determinable plane, floating in a still mystical cosmos. Slowly, a "round planet reality" emerged to take the place of the obsolete world view. As did the flat-earth idea, the "round planet reality" influenced our language, our images of global politics, awareness, and issues.

A "round planet" provides us with a metaphor for surviving in our day-to-day reality. For some of us, however, there is a mythology to a "round planet" and a "reality" to an irregularly shaped planet, one whose shape is in continual, if barely perceived, flux. There are still others who now really *know* better. They are the glassy-eyed theoretical physicists and astrophysicists—and perhaps meta-physicists—we encounter across the university commons. Their weirdness is real: they now "know" the world is indeed embraced in a dynamic and mystical cosmos.

The point is that in the latter part of this century we gathered an enormous amount of scientific thinking and data about the world around us. This process occurred in a reality where humanity was seen at the center of a controllable, determinable, and rational world/universe. Scientific inquiry was integral to that world view and was directed toward determining and controlling the "external." That *story* is changing.

This prior world view, which we labeled "modernism," is a scientific tradition delimited by *positivism* and *reductionism*. Positivism links scientific reality to what is measurable. Reductionism dictates that reality will be prescribed through understanding smaller and smaller parts of the whole.

The scientific principles from these two delimiters are the boundary markers for modernist reality. They are summarized in Table 1.

In each science's domain, a highly valued system of beliefs has developed. A supposed beneficent, if unrelated, consequence of science's prescripts was that these systems gave the industrial sector greater predictive power and immediate control over the natural environment.

This was true, as well, for the development of the social sciences. Each of the social sciences, carving out an area of reality for itself, assumed a structure built around modern scientific determinism and empiricism. Each retained the services of the "modernistic principles of science." Each assumed a posture of overlaying models of the physical world on social and human processes. Each, in a flash of the wizard's

Table 1. Reality Delimiters of Modernism

Objectivism	The basic elements of nature are purely objective in character and measurable.
Externalism	Reality is exhausted by the external side of being.
Locomotionalism	Motion is prescribed only through locomotion; i.e., "becoming" or anything "hidden" is beyond reality.
Mechanistic Determinism	Causation comes from external sources.
Reductionism	All apparent "wholes" are reducible to their parts.
Sensationism	All experience is rooted in perception, and all perception is measurable sensory perception.

Adopted from Griffin (1988)

wand, allowed these models to adopt an objective reality. In each, these stories, these structures of reality-based inquiry, paradigms, achieved a status that Kuhn was later to call "normal science."

In this new normalcy an unapparent purpose developed. Control of the social environment, that is, of humanity and society, developed. Control, an expression of human domination over the world and its inhabitants—including fellow humans—unfolded not as an incidental externality, but as a subtheme of scientism itself. The apparent reality, however, was still of science engaged in a system of knowing.

The drive *to know and control* in greater and greater detail the smaller and smaller parts of the physical and social world forced change. Assuming a dominant position of ideological prescription of truth, Paz [1990] refers to this as the religion of scientism. With their drive to know, predict, and control, modernistic sciences carried the seeds of their own destruction. Their linkage with the industrialization process imposed immeasurable impact upon the world's ecosystem. Slowly, social and knowledge systems developed the realization of their own linkages with an outside and changing reality. Indeed, as we will explore, science's inside and outside boundaries themselves have disappeared.

In the physical sciences, first and notably in physics, classical mechanistic notions gave way to Einstein-induced relativism and the mysticism of quantum physics. The ideas so developed—the new world view—are presented in Table 2.

Every principle of modernism is now topsy-turvy. Causality, linearity, rationality, and reductionism are recognized as elements of a past reality. This has been true for a long time in physics and in popularized adaptations of Einstein's reality. Now these ideas have changed our basic perceptions of social and physical reality.[3] As one way of seeing, the world was swept away, and another emerged. "What were ducks in the scientist's world . . . [became] rabbits afterwards" [Kuhn 1962:111]. These changes, and their references, the metaphysics of the Middle Ages, are summarized in Table 3.

The sweep of positivism left untouched many areas of inquiry. In the physics of optics, for instance, the positivist, Newtonian reality of color was based on breaking down the spectrum into its components. Newton's victory was neither total nor lasting, for it allowed Edwin Land's twentieth century experiments verifying color-based perception as a dynamic process, one of the mind-interpreting boundary condition changes. We now know Goethe was at least partially correct. "Knowing" color in the new science is not totally to be achieved by measuring a stream of data, but rather by answering the question "What is the human experience of color?" [Berman 1981:186].

Today, debate emerges on the hearing process. What does it *mean* to understand that the ear not only collects data but also creates its own sounds to better enable the hearing process? We find that sight and sound are not stories in themselves, but rather that story, storyteller, and story preceptor shaping, after the movie title, *The Never-Ending Story*.

In the social sciences, positivism had swept away most remnants of naturalistic science. Duck stories abounded. Threads of

Table 2. The New Physical Reality

Being	Wave/particle duality. Existence cannot be defined as a singularity.
Movement	Discontinuous, leaping. "Quantum leap."
Causality	Undefinable, across "Newtonian" time and space.

Adopted from: Zohar (1990).

Table 3. World View Comparisons

MIDDLE AGES	MODERN	POST MODERN
Universe: earth at center, geocentric, closed, with outer sphere God.	Universe: heliocenric.	The world is knowable only through our perceptions and in its context.
Explanation: teleological, everything, God excepted, in process of "becoming."	Explanation: atomistic, linear.	Living systems are not reducible.
Matter: continuous.	Matter: atomic.	Wholes have properties parts do not have.
Motion: forced or natural, requires a cause.	Motion: describable.	Time and reality are interrelated through circuitry.
Time: cyclical, static.	Time: linear and pro- gressive.	Mind/body and object/subject are two aspects of same process.
Nature: alive, organic.	Nature: mechanistic, known through reduci- ble inorganic parts.	Fact and value are inseparable.

Adopted from Berman (1981).

holistic inquiry remained only as off-center inquiring systems. As modernism's twilight approached, however, and as Goethe's ideas formed a basis for a new reality of color, these threads of naturalistic inquiry re-emerged in management, economics, and other social sciences. Rabbit stories emerged.

THINKING ABOUT MANAGEMENT AND ECONOMICS

If some good economists espouse positivism, the question arises how economics[4] would be different without it. He [the economist] would be more serious about analyzing his introspection. Right now introspection comes in through the back door. He would recognize his metaphors and his stories. Right now he calls them models and time series, thinking himself superior to the humanists. He would reassess his devotion to value-freedom, without abandoning the distinction entirely. Right now the values run the wizard's show from behind the curtain. He would be less enamored of utilitarianism. Right

now utilitarianism seems to most economists to be the same as thinking. [McClosky 1989:236]

The sense of what has been presented above is that something important, if not revolutionary, is happening in our world. We have abandoned positivism in philosophy and in the old stories of the hard sciences. Man-nature and nature-universe ideas that only two decades ago were not seriously challenged today stand abandoned. Explanations in popular culture are common: Chernobyl, rain forest destruction, McDonald's, Alar. Not as common is the simple observation that these changes in world view are parallel with more basic changes in philosophical and scientific world views.

As scientists in management, the social sciences, and IBS we should not be surprised that we also are touched by these forces. The world of science we have entered is not "fixed once and for all by the nature of the environment, on the one hand, and of science on the other. Rather, it is determined jointly by the environment and . . . [a] particular normative-scientific tradition . . ." [Kuhn 1962:111].

That is the nature of, the story of, science, society, and change.

In this section, I will examine the resulting changes we see in economics and allied social and management sciences. I will direct this analysis to explore what these changes are and how they have transformed some sciences. Finally, I will examine the relation of these changes to broader philosophical, social, and institutional changes. This allows reflection in the final section about what this all means for the field of IBS.

The Social Science Shift

The positivist world of the social scientist is a mechanistic world whose existence rests on three assumptions. First, the positivist *knows* that a reality exists: it is the atomistic and determinable world of observable data. Second, the positivist *knows* that the social systems may be understood through knowing their smallest and there-

fore most easily measurable elements. This understanding is then extended to continuously broader systems. Finally, the positivist *knows* that he and his science are separated from the world of observable reality, which is achieved through controllable experiments and by assuming a position of value-free inquiry.

The devolving positivist model of scientific inquiry and the evolving naturalist model of scientific inquiry, post-positivism, may be differentiated along five principal axioms and are presented in Table 4.

The Newtonian positivist world view formed the womb for the conception and development of liberal economics. Later, the shift of physics away from mechanism toward understanding energy and entropy caused economics to focus on price and value determination [Mirowski 1988]. Today, the world of traditional economics, and so the bulk of management and IBS, is connected with the maintenance of that paradigm. The changes that the new paradigm imposes on science and society are summarized in Table 5.

Table 4. Contrasting Positivist and Naturalist Paradigms

AXIOMS ABOUT	POSITIVIST PARADIGM	NATURALIST PARADIGM
The nature of reality.	Reality is single, tangible, and fragmentable.	Realities are multiple, constructed and holistic.
The relationship of knower to the known.	Knower and known are independent, a dualism.	Knower and known are interactive, inseparable.
The possibility of generalization.	Time- and context-free generalizations are possible.	Only time- and context-bound working hypotheses (idiographic statements) are possible.
The possibility of causal linkages.	There are real causes, temporally precedent to or simultaneous with their effects.	All entities are in a state of mutual simultaneous shaping, so that it is impossible to distinguish causes from effects.
The role of values.	Inquiry is value-free	Inquiry is value-bound.

Source: Lincoln and Guba (1985: 37).

Table 5. Societal Implications of World View Ideas

WORLD VIEW "ANCHORS"	lead to	WORLD VIEW REALITIES
PRE-MODERN WORLD		
Time: cyclical, static.		Progress: alien concept, only change.
Understanding: holistic thought, continuous.		Economy: integrated into world experience.
Being: continuous.		Self: social.
Matter: mystical, holistic.		Nature: mystical, part of being.
MODERN WORLD		
Time: linear.		Progress: growth in "detached" economic sphere.
Understanding: linear, atomistic.		Economy: distinct "market."
Being: inorganic, mechanistic.		Self: mind/body separation, individual.
Matter: atomistic, determinable.		Nature: separate, to be dominated.
POST-MODERN WORLD		
Time: circuitous.		Progress: "Sustainability," revelation, wisdom.
Understanding: holistic.		Economy: societal integration.
Being: transcendent.		Self: person/society; mind/body identity.
Matter: relational.		Nature: co-dependency, experientially revealed.

Sources: Berman (1981); White (1964); Adas (1989); Boorstein (1983).

The changes detailed above were not complete. Elements of the prior view remained. Holistic and naturalistic inquiry developed as an integral part of anthropological inquiry. In economics, institutionalist science ridiculed and was ridiculed by "mainstream" economics. Social and evolutionary economics developed in parallel with institutionalist science. The development of these sciences, and their great thinkers—Pierce, Dewey, Veblen, Ayres, Myrdal, Galbraith—took place, however, in a world different from mainstream economics.[5]

The destruction of philosophical positivism signaled an end of the positivist paradigm for the entire scientific world. We in the social and management sciences are today living through these changes.

We can witness these paradigm changes, or attempted changes, in economics, economic anthropology, sociology, and the management sciences themselves. Where they occur they are driven not only by science but by society itself. The model of social and scientific change outlined in the first section of this paper specifies that world view changes leading to the abandonment of positivism—scientific and as a reality—are interrelated with broader societal changes. What are these factors?

The Societal Shift

I portray the societal context of this change by the "economy in society" model. The model is based largely upon the theory of social and economic transformation developed by Polanyi [1944;1947;1957;1977] and summarized in Table 6.

Polanyi's view of the transformation of society from its antecedent form to its market form was one of a "disembedding" process. It is a fracturing of communication between those *things* in reality considered economic and those considered social.

History shows us that any society's "provisioning" process is largely an invisible process [Stanfield 1989]. Economy in "modern" society becomes separate—visible and no longer embedded in a web of social relations—either in ideology [Reddy 1984;1987] or in the process of patterned behavior that the "science of economics" delimits as its field of observable reality.

Economic forces mechanically signaled a path to the now rational and measurable goal of progress. Progress, defined as the measurable economic growth factor, became a primary social concern. Economic forces and the economy itself first became "reality" [Frederick 1983]. These economic forces, seen to promote social justice, took on moral characteristics [Ayres 1944].

The disembedding process is parallel to the linearity, reductionism, social progressiveness, and determinism of positivism. A holistic, enchanted world [Berman 1981] was fractured. In its place came a world of society and economy. The disembedded world Polanyi described *is the first one on the planet in which an economy existed.* This is not a small point. It led to integrating the two lines of thought we are developing. The changing world view surrounding science was related to the *process* of life and livelihood, what economics describes as economic and social relations.

We can evidence these changes in four areas of scientific inquiry. Each of these— economics itself, economic sociology, management's business and society, and economic anthropology—experienced and

Table 6. The "Economy in Society" Model

1. Prior to the advent of market economy and free market society, society's human relations and its relations with nature were embedded in a constellation of societal forces. What are considered "economic forces" were indeed present, but inseparable in concept and action from tensions in the social fabric.
2. The evolution of society into what we know as market society occurred through the transformation of capital, humanity, and nature—money, labor, and land, or natural resources—into economic commodities. They became disembedded.
3. The evolution of society into what we know as centralized planning and societies transformed these same social goods into political "commodities," goods subject to influences of privilege, power, and bureaucracy.
4. These social goods—nature, humanity, and capital—are commodities only in fiction. They have no objective reality as economic goods except of a symbolic character as defined by the prevailing world view.
5. Both command and market structure economies evolved from the same world view: a determinable, linear, and mechanistic physical, social, and natural world.
6. The process of disembedding capital, humanity, and nature set loose forces that offered unparalleled social, political, and environmental dislocation.
7. The immediate reaction was to begin protective and reactionary measures—reform. These measures continue through today. They are efforts to deeconomize and depoliticize—to reembed into society—labor, nature, and capital.
8. The world view change of the type discussed here—towards a holistic, socially connected, ecological existence—is experienced integral with the social structure changes detailed above.

continues to experience the paradigm shift differently and with different effects. Each, to varying degrees, shares in common what we will call the naturalistic drift.

The Naturalist Drift in Economics

The positivist world, to a large degree, has maintained itself best in economics. This world view has five principles of reality. They are summarized in Table 7.

These principles are the mainsprings of contemporary economics. They tell us little about the world, at least as we are growing to know it. However, they do tell us a lot about how we came to understand the world in the manner we did. This world view has received considerable critical attention. Here are a sampling of these perspectives.

> There neither exists, nor is there a social need for, a distinct body of economic thought. Just as "an economy" cannot be viewed by its participants as a separate social institution, so economic thought cannot be viewed as distinct from total social knowledge. [Wisman 1988:58]

> Natural law cosmology blinded economists to the ethical nature of their discipline. [Wisman 1986:34]

> International economic law is a set of myths . . . but the effect of myth is to sanctify one way of knowing events in the world. [Tarullo 1985:547–548]

> To see the world from a Smithian perspective, and to judge human behavior and social institutions from such a perspective is to make a mockery of social science. The practice of this social science is far from benign; it can only aid in the destruction of all desirable human relationships. [Kaun 1984:40]

> Adam Smith's invisible hand performs a little-noticed function. It is as if God told us: "Don't be afraid, my child, of apparently trespassing against my commands. I have so arranged everything that you are justified in neglecting morality in this particular case." [Dumont 1977:61–62]

> That formalism inhibits scholarly understanding of past economies is not its most urgent defect. It also obscures understandings of the present. [Stanfield 1989:272]

> That is why "price theory" and "price mechanism" are terms of derision in institutionalist circles, not because institutionalists are ignorant of neoclassical theory, but because "price theory" and "price mechanism" are terms of myth and magic. [Dugger 1989:609]

> The economy is not like the solar system. The economy is not given to man. It is an artifact . . . made through our efforts to apprehend it, to know and effectuate policy to ward it off. [Samuels 1989:130]

> The price system has a meaning for human life and destiny which none but astrologers any longer impute to the social system. . . . No one would aver that the meaning of price is a physical actuality like the moons of Jupiter. . . . We talk of the laws of supply and demand, but in truth there is only one law: the law of the interrelatedness of all purchases and sales. In economics as in mechanics every action has its equal and opposite reaction. Is this just? Is the solar system just? [Ayres 1944: 29–35]

Mainstream economics, describing and promoting the workings of the liberal economic system and trying to describe a process of provisioning and social reproduction, created an objective reality out of their stories of economy and economic forces. The paradigmatic "deep structure" at work was linked to an eighteenth and nineteenth century conventional wisdom. Descriptions based in science—but also story telling and myth—of the provisioning process underway in industrial capitalism became objects themselves. An "economy" developed, but not as a conceptual framework for understanding the "process" or patterned behaviors within society. It became an "object" existing in the deepness of a socially constructed reality.

Further, the social ordering established by the economics and economists places the economy in a protected position. The economy is "natural," evolutionary, self-regulating, and, reflecting an eighteenth and nineteenth century understanding of moral as well as solar systems, *just* [Dugger 1989; Samuels 1989; Stanfield 1989; Tarullo 1985].

Faith, substituting for science, produces a reality in which market activity "creates order out of chaos" and supply and demand coordinate society "naturally" [Kornai 1990]. Spiritualism may dictate that the price system at work in industrial capitalism has a meaning for human life and destiny. What we know about our physical, moral, and social existence offers not a hint.

The laws of mechanics tell us that for every action, there is a reaction. Physics and astronomy tell us that the moon revolves around the earth, and the tides result. The laws of market economics tell us of "the law of interrelatedness of all purchases and sales" [Ayres 1944:35]. The solar system, balls on a pool table, and the tides are not *just*. Neither, by their existence in social science stories, are the workings of a market economy.

Further, reliance upon the rapidly disintegrating, liberal, economic model forces a view that there is something "out there" called an economy. Economy as a sphere of patterned behavior is inseparable from society. Economics as the conceptual model for understanding the provisioning of society is inseparable from other social science modeling of it. Economy does not exist distinct from the whole of society just because economics, driven by long abandoned sto-ries of a physical world, chooses to model it as such.

The Naturalist Drift in Economic Anthropology

Economic anthropology has drifted between naturalist and positivist views, rather than drifting toward naturalist ideas. Here a war developed to prevent positivism from making further inroads into the science. The debate between the positivists and the naturalists[6] opened with Marshall Sahlins's "Political Power and the Economy in Primitive Society" [1960]. The first major battle, however, began with the publication of George Dalton's "Economic Theory and Primitive Society" [1961].

Each of these analyses, however, found its origin in Karl Polanyi's earlier essays. Polanyi's model included the assumption that the ethnocentric views of the nature of humanity, community, and economic life embedded in market society are inapplicable for understanding life cross-culturally or historically. Polanyi further asserted that market-centered views severely limited an understanding of the range of life- and freedom-giving opportunities available to us at any given historical moment.

Polanyi's positions were integrated into the substantivists' attacks and counterattacks on the formalists' positions. The debate expanded further to include the debate over integrating values and policy considerations into scientific analyses. The debate closed, unresolved, in 1969.

David M. Lewis, analyzing this debate,

Table 7. The Reality of Economics

First,	an economy exists, separate and distinct from the rest of society.
Second,	the economy, as with the rest of society, is part of a determinable and reducible mechanistic system of the natural social world.
Third,	as a reducible and determinable part of society, an "economy" known in greater and greater detail illuminates more and more about ourselves, society, and nature in general.
Fourth,	"knowing" the economy can be achieved without knowing the larger society.
Fifth,	"knowing" the economy can be achieved by assuming the position of an observer, i.e. one who is separate from and unaffected by the facts collected.

draws heavily upon Popper and Kuhn for modeling the science, the story, of the debate. In brief, his main points are:

1. The formalist-substantivist controversy is a manifestation of mutually contradictory "paradigms." . . . At the heart of these opposing paradigms are diametrically opposed conceptualizations of the individual and of the individual's relation to the source of order . . .

2. In terms of an historical geography of ideas . . . these "paradigms" can be related rather distinct intellectual traditions. In this regard, the formalist position is a manifestation of the British/Anglo-American intellectual tradition, while the substantivist position is a manifestation of an essentially Germanic intellectual tradition.

3. In terms of the fundamental problems of method . . . these antithetical "paradigms" can be understood as reflecting, on one hand, an adherence to the project of science established in the Enlightenment and, on the other hand, the opposition to the fundamental tenets of that project. . . . [T]his opposition rests on the belief in "environmental" relativism, primarily but not exclusively a cultural and historical relativism.

4. The recognition of these paradigms suggests that behind the question of the applicability of formal economic theory there is a much more complex methodological problem. . . . Epistemologically, the problem revolves around the question of how credible knowledge is to be determined. Anthropologically, it revolves around the question of humanity and its relation to the order of things—including the conscious representation of that relation in the order of things. [Lewis 1983:2–3]

There are two paradigm "faults" which arise in this model. *First*, there is the debate over the appropriateness of using the models of physics and mechanics to the social sciences. Here emerge on one side the positivists, integrating these models into their search for the natural universals of social life. On the other side emerge the historicists, the naturalists, taking a holistic, intuitive, and qualitative (as opposed to quantitative) approach. *Second* is the debate over the possibility of a nonnormative social science. Lewis sees this battle first erupting in 1904 when Jaffe, Sombart, and Weber took over as editors of *Archive für Sozialwissenshaftlen und Soziopolitik*. In direct opposition to Smoller's program in the *Verein für Soziopolitik* for a normative social science, they announced a new editorial policy of separating discussions of policy from those of "science" [Lewis 1983:112].

These differences are basic to understanding the unresolvable controversy between formalists and substantivists. They are critical to understanding why today adherents to either the formalist or the substantivist positions practice different sciences.

The Naturalist Drift in "New Economic Sociology"

Similar forces of change are being felt in sociology. Zelizer [1988] and Swedberg, Himmelstrand, and Brulin [1986] have identified a "new economic sociology." This new science arose from one that either "surrendered the market to economists" or "further bolstered the dominance of a market model by adopting analytic tools for their own [sociologists'] research" [Zelizer 1988:616]. Zelizer describes this new effort as one that goes beyond critical sociology, a science of "cataloging complaints." New economic sociology is an effort "to disturb the alleged moral and social neutrality of the market . . ." [617]. It is an effort to complicate the simplistic, positivist, view of economic life.

The broad sweep of change underway in sociology, but connected with interdisciplinary change, Zelizer argues, takes on three different orientations:

1. The "boundless market" model: an ideological critique of the power of the market that centers on the destructive social, moral, and cultural effects of commoditization.
2. The "subordinate market" model: a more fundamental rejection of the accepted instrumentalist paradigm of markets by demonstrating the ongoing cultural, structural, and historical constraints of the supposedly autonomous market.
3. The "multiple markets" model: the market as the interaction of cultural, structural, and economic factors. [Zelizer 1988:618]

Further evidencing the broad sweep of change is a change of vocabulary. Terms found in the literature include: "the culture of consumption," "money and liberty," "market culture," "the social meaning of money," and so on.

Institutionalizing this shift has already taken place: George Washington University has its "Center for the Study of Market Processes," the University of California at Santa Barbara has its "Center for Economy and Society," the Russell Sage Foundation has a program in "behavioral economics," and Boston University has the "Institute for the Study of Economic Culture."

The paradigmatic shift in economic sociology has had its false starts, i.e., old science masquerading as new. Etzioni's recent work [1988] and the associated development of the "Society for the Advancement of Socio-Economics" has been characterized as an attempt to build a "new science" from foundations in sociology and economics. Etzioni integrates into the positivist framework a model of human activity that is rational and economic on one hand, and on the other hand is moral and ethical.

The problem within economic sociology is far deeper than cosmetically adding a "moral dimension" to the preexisting paradigm. It requires a "theoretical revolution,"

a replacement of the "mechanistic assumptions at the hub of orthodox economics" [Hodgson 1991:12]. It requires more than repackaging economics as "*Economics-Lite®.*"

The Naturalist Drift in Management

With his 1985 presentation entitled "The Normative Factor in Corporate Social Analysis," Frederick opened the "naturalist" dialogue within the field of SIM.[7] Frederick's thesis was "our work as teachers and researchers is inherently normative, compelling us to form and declare moral judgments concerning the issues we study" [Frederick 1985:1]. It led to proposing a model of business and society thought called corporate social rectitude, or CSR_3. CSR_3 "embodies the notion of moral correctness in actions taken and policies formulated" [17].

CSR_3 quickly became a focus of intense discussion within the management field. Frederick, recognizing the politicizing the discussion had undergone, issued the "Normative Manifesto" for studying SIM. The manifesto called for integrating values and policy questions into the study of societal processes and outcomes. It also proposed the study of how "liberating, life-giving humane values can be encouraged to grow and expand in all directions and to all people" [Frederick 1988:5]. It called for, in summary, a normative science assuming advocacy positions.

The unrest within management expressed in Frederick's "manifesto" evolved. The tension was evidenced in Logsdon and Palmer's questioning of the value basis for issues management as a corporate policy tool. There they questioned "issues management analysis" as a means for livelihood in the business and society field. This questioning was based in the negative societal outcomes (as judged by the authors) emanating from the corporate implementation of the technique [Logsdon and Palmer 1988].

Freeman [1989] provided another step. As poet and pragmatist—feeling and value-laden professionals—he suggested that those in the management sciences stop being scientists and become CRITS (Committee for Critical Studies in Management). It was a call for a holistic and naturalistic science, what Lincoln terms a constructivist [Lincoln 1990].

Each of these business and society authors expressed the same four themes. First, each recognized the business and society field as inherently value-laden. Second, each raised the issue of self-deception brought about by failing to recognize the value content of the academic profession. Third, each addressed how this self-deception resulted in academics committing fraud upon society and their students. Finally, each prescribed a path for developing a fully socialized and humanized livelihood for academe: a path that recognizes the social, cultural, and moral context of our sciences.

What we can surmise from this is that business and society as a science is undergoing a metamorphosis. The origin of this change for business and society lies in the "science tensions" and in the broader social tensions produced by the "disembedded" economy. This new paradigm may already be formed in business and society. All we need to do is recognize its new normalcy.

INTERNATIONAL BUSINESS STUDIES

The greater interdependence of the world . . . [has] raised concerns about our management of the 'international commons.' [Behrman and Grosse 1990]

The above quote appears in an IBS text section analyzing the social, ethical, and political issues of IB. It raises issues, concepts, and tensions far deeper than a textbook on IB can be expected to explore. There is, for example, no commons, no interdependence, in a positivist reality. Who should manage that commons, and toward whose ends? That is a premodern, or a postmodern question, but certainly not one for Milton Friedman or Jeffrey Sachs. Interdependence conflicts with the individualistic world view woven into traditional economic modeling.

We can, after study and introspection, understand a dynamic and holistic model of world interdependence. I can guarantee, however, that without extensive qualifying footnoting, reducing substantive content to nil, there will be no equations in the model.

These issues, concepts and tensions have been the subject of the preceding analyses. Here IBS now regains the focus. What will, or should, IBS be as a new world view develops? Whose purposes will, or should, it serve? And as, or if, a new paradigmatic structure emerges, what will be its "circuitry" with other sciences, with a changing structure of scientific inquiry, and with humanity and its institutional structures? In general it is asked: What is the appropriate relationship between IBS and its world? This question, and the preceding ones buried in it, I hope to begin to answer here.

IB: Some Emergent Tensions

We would be surprised if, after we found the "naturalist drift" in the cited sciences, we did not find similar tendencies in IBS. Indeed, these tendencies are seen, but to a lesser extent than found elsewhere. This phenomenon leads us to the heart of answering the questions posed above.

Behrman and Grosse in their 1990 IBS text noted above raise some concerns. The issues facing IB for them include the standard economic, political, and organizational ones as well as those arising from the technological, economic, social, cultural, and political process of IB operations. For them, IB concerns embrace not only efficiency and profitability but also a concern for peoples of the world and the "worldwide effects of environmental degradation" [1990:331]. It is but a short leap from "IB needs to be socialized."

Kefalas raises a similar set of concerns, albeit in a restricted "single issue" case. Kefalas, using the issue context of "bioeconomics," directly challenges the "four pillars" of conventional economic wisdom: (1) growth is the answer to all problems; (2) scarcity is the basic economic problem; (3) there is perceived to be an infinite store of natural resources; and (4) equation-based economics has modeling capability [1990:137–141].

Kefalas offers no extension of the discussion to broader IB or IBS questions. Its selection as an issue, however, raises these topics for discussion.

Dunning has recognized the need for a changed paradigm in IBS [1980;1988; 1989]. However, he proposes that IBS change through the process of adopting techniques and perspectives from those sciences sharing similar paradigms. This approach will assure that IBS becomes more focused and that its methodologies will be seen as more legitimate within economics departments. The question remains: will it be relevant to the world? Dunning's call is for a continuation of a positivist IBS science. Does that portend: "International Business Studies: Ever Positivist, R.I.P.?"

Boddewyn's analysis of "Multinational Enterprise (MNE) theory" [1988] assures us that if the "ever positivist" headstone is raised, at least one significant warning, one paradigm disturbance, will have been issued beforehand. That Boddewyn is about to engage in paradigm disturbance is signalled early in the work.

> The purpose of this exercise is not to develop an interdisciplinary theory of the multinational enterprise . . . but rather to enrich Dunning's eclectic paradigm. . . . Still, the concluding section of this paper comments about the possible contents of a broader MNE theory. [Boddewyn 1988: 341–342]

Boddewyn's proposal for enriching the eclectic model is to transform it through developing an interdisciplinary IBS theory.

Dunning's eclectic model was interdisciplinary, but only by integrating disciplines whose basic assumptions are mirrors of positivism. Boddewyn proposes integrating disciplines whose models share to one degree or another the "naturalist drift." These different sciences and world views will, when integrated into IBS, challenge its underlying assumptions about science and re-ality. To Boddewyn, IBS needs to be a broad, interdisciplinary science. It is a science where market and other "economics-based" models serve to limit, rather than expand, understanding. Further, in reintegrating the question of values and policy into science, IBS has among its tasks the responsibility to raise what Boddewyn calls social welfare questions.

The new IBS paradigm, as Boddewyn lays it out, is one that is holistically focused on social behaviors and a social institution—in this case, IB. Further, it is a science that integrates raising and answering policy and value questions into its purposes.

Toyne's [1989] proposal for theory building in IBS advances the prospects for discussion. Toyne presents exchange theory as a "unifying construct for the study of IB" [2]. IBS, here, focuses inquiry on a *social* institution involving *social* actors.

The resulting "social institution" of IB is in a political economy. Thus, power, the domain of political science and economy, the domain of economics are important but only two of a wide matrix of social and cultural factors necessary for understanding Toyne's IB.

Boddewyn and Toyne's works do represent a "paradigm disturbance." Those who view "better science" allied with concepts such as "specificity," "determinability," "measurability," "scientific objectivism" and other foci of positivism will object, an objection coupled with a longing for old stories and the old campfire days. It is also a longing for the continuing classroom applicability of notes gathered as a graduate student.

Within the emerging tension is an assumption not possible in prior social and scientific realities. The "new IBS" will have a more expansive view. It will be less deterministic, less reductionistic, and, in coincidence with a changing world and world view, more meaningful. A more expansive view will provide a deeper, richer, and more complete understanding of IB than did the "old IBS." Further, in Boddewyn's work especially we see the possibility of a value-free science abandoned, and, as recalled from Frederick's CSR₃, a call for an explicitly value-based science of IBS.

IB Studies: Some Unresolved Tensions

IBS has begun the process of bringing to the surface the issues and concerns raised by other sciences. Questions associated with the emergence of a postpositivist, naturalist, or constructivist paradigm are emerging. A full shift, however, demands answers to some questions. Answers to these questions will help define what IBS is to be as a science. IBS is in an evolutionary state, changed from only a few years past.

First, we will need to ask: "How has IBS recognized that at its core it is an artifact of culture?" How has it dealt with its holistic focus, with nonlinearity as a unifying world concept, with the nonseparability of fact and value, and with the perception/relation basis of knowing reality? How has it resolved the inseparability between scholar/researcher/consultant and student/worker/executive/peasant? Between observer and subject? Answering those questions tells us how the field has recognized and is resolving its interpenetrating relationships with changing world view systems. We will then know how the science recognizes its own character as a cultural symbol system.

Second, we need to ask: "How has IBS recognized its nature as a social endeavor?" Do IBS scientists view themselves as social actors? Do they have values, feelings, and community in their livelihood—on-the-job asking, answering, knowing, teaching, and writing—as well as in their personal lives? These answers tell us how the science has recognized and ordered its humanness and humanity among its purposes.

Third, we need to know: "How has IBS recognized the political nature of its undertaking?" There is a "Why?" behind every question asked by IBS. Science can be used for (1) value-free understanding;[8] (2) social control; (3) social engineering; (4) advocacy of the underprivileged to the powerful—to afflict the empowered; (5) education of the

underprivileged—to empower the afflicted; or (6) revolution [Firestone 1990:119]. The choices—such as what questions are to be asked or left unanswered, or who will receive the fruits of our labor—are always there. What choices are to be recognized? What choices are to be made? These answers lead IBS to recognize the political currency of knowledge, then lead to resolving the moral responsibilities arising out of that recognition.

Fourth, we need to know: "How has IBS recognized the historical nature of its undertaking?" Positivism-driven separateness and reducibility drove wedges into a unified world view. Specification and factual knowledge increased, but at the expense of understanding. Historical forces originating from that paradigm impose a similar structure on IBS. The history of this emergent science is now being written. A conversation with its history will provide a stronger base for resolving the choices IBS has before it.

Finally, we need to know: How has IBS ordered itself as a "knowing system"? We see that the charted domain increasingly is focusing on "world society's provisioning process." However, missing answers, wrong answers, even missing questions about the science's undertaking have resulted in extraordinary—pardon the expression—opportunity costs. Blinded by positivism and ideology, we miss a lot.

Certainly world capitalism existed as the primary form of "world society's provisioning process" by the early 1900s. Subsequently, new world orders have emerged. The dominant theme of this age is social welfare. However, what Polanyi referred to as the "obsolete market mentality" has maintained its affliction on the field. For example, we know not, excepting ideology, how cooperatives, socially owned, and privately owned enterprises work differently in "international exchange." We know far less about how they differentially provide social welfare.

We know—not from IBS and certainly not enough—about major "international exchange" in certain goods and services. Have we ordered our science so that inquiry must go elsewhere if we wish to "know" about international exchange processes associated with weapons, drugs, sex, food? A science centered on questions comforting to the empowered serves willy-nilly as a conduit of both misery and affluence.

Maybe that is good. I think not, for the "dark side" is a part of our humanity, culture, and society. Individually, we may get away with ignoring such inconvenient topics. Our lives are short and inconsequential. At the community level that strategy may work for a short period. At the international level, presumably the domain of IBS ... well, we are bearing the consequences today.

CONCLUSION

Where does that leave IBS? I believe where, at the onset of this paper, we intended to be: knowing more, but with many more questions than we had when we started.

First, we have placed science itself in its cultural, social, and historical flow. We know that science and reality are not bound by but rather change over time. We also know that these changes sometimes occur to an extraordinary degree, shifting an entire age's social and scientific reality. We also know that we are experiencing such changes today.

Second, we have placed social science in general, and economics, economic anthropology, economic sociology, and management studies' business and society into a model of social and scientific change. We know that their tensions and troubles are part of a broader sweep of social and scientific change. We also know that some very specific social and scientific forces can be associated with these changes.

Third, we can place IBS into that matrix of science and society. IBS's historical context, emergent out of positivism but retaining a holistic, institutional, *process* perspective, bridges the changes underway. We also know that a continuing allegiance to a

past ideology and world view may decrease its value as a knowledge system.

Finally, we know that engaging the full paradigm shift will require substantive change in the process and form of IBS. If it works, if IBS assumes a new "normalcy," it will be more human, social, moral, humane, and more political. In short, it will be a better and stronger science.

NOTES

1. I wonder about the ethics of teaching students that electrons, for example, exist in objective reality rather than only in a useful story.

2. This will be true until virtual reality enables us to walk through a country's export stream. Then a virtual physical reality will simulate the nonexistent physical reality of such data.

3. The driving forces within positivism induced this switch. This was not a "data-induced" change. Paradigms—the reality of the world view—are not provable theorems. They define what exists. Within that reality, the sciences do their work.

4. This section is adopted, in part, from Hogner 1990.

5. A historical irony is worth noting here. While Adam Smith and others of his era embraced the emerging world view to "more adequately explain the world," their science was still naturalistic, holistic, and, in its origin, mystical. Galbraith has been criticized for his naturalistic and institutionalist approach. Both Galbraith and Smith were, in many respects, similar in their science. Both looked out their windows and explained the world around them. Galbraith, however, stands taller than did Smith. He is not so heavily laden with the occult and medieval mysticism as was Smith.

6. Within economic anthropology the formalists (positivists) and the substantivists (the naturalists).

7. "SIM" is its title as a division in the Academy of Management. Scholars in the field have recently formed the International Association for Business and Society. I will refer to it here as business and society.

8. We may question the degree that this, indeed, can exist as a phenomenon. Available space forces answers to be searched out elsewhere.

■ ■ ■

Managing in a Global Economy: From Relativism to Multiculturalism

R. Edward Freeman

SECTION I

The recent wave of concern with business ethics has given new life to scholars working in the field of business, ethics, and society (BES). From the Wall Street scandals to the Valdez spill, managers and scholars alike have renewed interest in understanding the normative and societal aspects of business, rather than focusing exclusively on the positive and economic dimensions.

A second, seemingly unrelated, trend gives added weight to the need to develop new ways of understanding BES, and this is the manic focus on competitiveness in general and international competitiveness in particular. From xenophobic speeches by executives and politicians to attempts by every major business school to "internationalize" the curriculum, there is ample evidence that the U.S. business community is trying to join, at long last, the real world.

In becoming more attuned to the mysteries of International Business (IB), value confrontations move to the forefront. When the theories, concepts, and models are primarily seen as economic and value-neutral, major problems loom on the horizon.

This paper suggests a way to think about BES in a global context. Ironically, by exploring an issue that has gained major attention in the United States, multiculturalism, we can find ways to understand complex IB issues.

In section II, I examine how BES has become globalized and suggest some barriers to the straightforward application of current ideas in the field to these global concerns. Section III analyzes the underlying assumption of moral relativism that is prevalent in IB. Section IV critically outlines one alternative proposed by Thomas Donaldson and suggests some limitations. Section V explains how multiculturalism can

work as a framework for IB. The irony in this paper is strong, for it suggests that if we can overcome our inability to deal with race, gender, and ethnicity in the United States (U.S.) we can create our corporations in a way that makes them more effective around the world.

SECTION II

It is only recently that scholars in BES have turned their attention to global issues. "International Fever," currently an epidemic in business schools, swept through BES with the establishment of two new international professional societies. There are a number of reasons for the emergence of these issues on a global scale. However, first it is important to understand why it took so long. Why have BES scholars and executives been silent, for the most part, on global moral issues?[1]

The Problem of Two Realms

Business theory[2] and business ethics, or BES, have developed along separate tracks during this century. There is a deep-seated belief among business school faculty and executives that business and business theory are amoral. Business is seen as solely, or primarily, an activity best described by the metaphors and tropes of economics.[3] Consider the statements by two IB scholars.

In chapter 2 Mira Wilkins says:

> What I do want to argue is that for any theory of MNE to contribute to the field, it must concentrate on the firm *per se* and must be dynamic; be an economic theory since we are dealing with an institution that operates in this sphere of endeavor; and correspond to and give us help in explaining an evolving entity that functions in a world where change is the norm. [pp. 36–37 in this volume]

Jean Boddewyn says:

> My starting and even dominant perspective is *economic in nature*. "Business" is fundamentally an economic institution (activity, function, process, etc.) even though, like other institutions it is affected by, and in turn affects other societal institutions such as the polity, the community, the social structure, the system of values and the physical environment (cf. Parsons and Smelser [1956]). Nobody would deny that the family has economic determinants and effects; yet, it is not centrally conceptualized and analyzed as an economic institution. Similarly, the economy and its business subset are institutions embedded in society but their functions are not predominantly understood to be political, social or cultural in nature. [pp. 50–51]

So business in general, and IB in particular, is economic, and its political, social or cultural effects, not to mention its moral effects, can safely be bracketed and dealt with on the side or at the margin. This margin has become the semiexclusive domain of BES scholars. Figure 1 is a simple picture of how the relationship between business and ethics is supposed to work. BES scholars play the role of bridge building between the real stuff of business and the ephemeral stuff of ethics and social theory.

BES scholars have accepted this role which leads to their existence reinforcing the status quo. BES becomes an apologist for business theology. As long as there are two distinct realms, even two distinct connected realms, we will continue the hegemony of economics and economists and we will fail to see the possibilities in understanding business as the greatest of all social institutions. The Two Realms Problem is a significant barrier to more workable narratives about business in a global economy, or in the real world.

The Social Realm as Complex

The forces that led to the globalization of business have enormous implications for BES. Here are a few examples that are far from exhaustive, but which show how our relatively narrow conception of business and ethics are challenged.

First of all, technology in general and information technology in particular have made communication much simpler and more intense. Cross-cultural communication is increasing. On a recent trip to Indonesia I was struck by the number of satellite dishes—in the jungle—all of which received CNN. Inexpensive and intense cross-cultural communication puts business on stage throughout the world, and it brings a multiplicity of value issues into stark relief. Indonesians with access to CNN are treated to the ethic of development and consumption—the revolutions in Eastern Europe and the Gulf War—all in real time. The social realm becomes much more complex. Usual cultural practices, such as nepotism (in our terms; "caring for family" in theirs), come into question, with dire consequences. The government and business leaders in Indonesia are leading a new drive against "corruption." However, it isn't so simple

Figure 1. The Problem of Two Realms

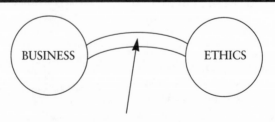

BUSINESS, ETHICS AND SOCIETY

since the very meaning of the term, "corruption," is up for grabs.

Secondly, U.S. managers, for example, have been exposed to a variety of different cultural/ethical systems. The level of difference is astonishing. From Maoist/Confucianism, Shintoism, Islam, Hinduism, and the relatively minor variations of U.S. ethics found in other cultures, managers and theorists are exposed to a panoply of systems that are not comparable. If the only response is determined by the two realms problem, i.e., that business is amoral, then it is easy to see how businesses that see themselves in profoundly moral contexts[4] will come into conflict with those which see things differently.

Finally, a number of social issues have taken on global proportions, so that it is no longer sensible to address them solely within the boundaries of the nation-state. For example, the environment has become a truly global issue. We have no conceptual apparatus we can use to ask simultaneously how we can have an effective and profitable business, do the right thing, and save the Earth.

It is small wonder that a standard application of the BES ways of thinking fall short. Their development was never intended to take account of the complexity inherent in today's world, or if it was the result was facile.

For instance we could look at the multinational corporation (MNC) in terms of the corporate social performance model, but we would have difficulty in specifying social performance across cultures, or standardizing within a multicultural society. We could try to give an account of an organization's stakeholders, but without specifying them more completely by culture we would have at best a laundry list.

Even an argument like Milton Friedman's breaks down here as different cultures have different senses of "ownership" and those which are similar to Western ones, have different structures and roles for debt and equity partners. So, we are left in a world where the building blocks of our

conceptual apparatus in BES (community, employee, supplier, customer, owner, manager) and the decision rules that we apply to these building blocks are up for grabs.

SECTION III

The problem of two realms and the increasing complexity of the social realm neatly fit with a key underlying assumption in IB: moral relativism (or, to be more precise, the continuum from moral imperialism to moral relativism).

Moral Relativism

How should global managers deal with tricky ethics issues, where the answer that they would give in their home culture is not necessarily the answer given in the host culture? Vernon and Wells are symptomatic of a refusal to engage in moral discourse. They claim:[5]

> In practice, experienced managers are aware that they are largely on their own when they confront conflicting demands from different states and when their rights are challenged outside the home jurisdiction. Accordingly, when conflicting commands from different governments converge on the desk of the unit manager in a multinational enterprise, the tendency is to try to bridge, fudge, or compromise the issue, not to highlight it. When a foreign-owned unit operating in some distant land is discriminated against by the national government—when it is denied the research subsidies its local competitors are receiving, or the right to sell its local output to government agencies—the usual reaction is to avoid dealing with the issue on the level of principle.

While this situation may be ameliorated slightly because of principled stands on trade, even the recent debacle in the auto industry illustrates a failure to deal with a multiplicity of "moralities" in a more than rudimentary way.

The standard argument begins with the usual whine when ethics are mentioned: "but whose ethics do you use?" Since "I have my ethics and you have your ethics," we are at an impasse. The clever manager or theorist points out that even if we have some political process to determine "our ethics," there is no such process for deciding between Indonesian ethics and American ethics.

The roots of moral relativism are well known, and except for a recent revival, due to a misunderstanding, of so-called postmodernism, moral relativism has been completely discredited.[6] From the fact of cultural relativism, that cultures differ on many matters, IB theorists deduce that moral reasoning across cultures simply cannot occur. Of course this deduction is false, but it is false in an interesting way. Just as "I have mine and you have yours" is a rhetorical move to close off discussion, so moral relativism functions to ensure that the two realms of business and ethics remain separated. Such a move reinforces at least two common misunderstandings about business and ethics.

Cowboy Capitalism

The first follows from the problem of two realms. If business is separable from the social world, and if its separation is a "fact," then concepts, theories, and models that are "scientific" must accept and explain this fact. One of the "facts" of business is that it is fundamentally, essentially, at heart about competition. Business is hostile to ethics precisely because it depends on a view of humans as self-interested and a view of business as trying to put "the other guy" out of business. According to this view, which I have called "cowboy capitalism," the appropriate metaphors for business are warlike. Managers are to be understood as "lonely warriors on the battlefield of global business competition." As we all know there is no real ethics of war.

I have argued elsewhere that cowboy capitalism is mistaken on a number of grounds, that business and capitalism are first and foremost about cooperation, creating value for stakeholders, promise keeping, truth telling, and relationship building.

Such a view of business is not hostile to ethics, and in fact, is compatible with most ethical systems in the world today. I want to claim, at least, that such a view of business can serve as a basis for a cross-cultural conversation in a way that cowboy capitalism cannot. The response to this claim is that any way of understanding capitalism and business is culturally determined, and if it is to serve as a basis for a global business ethic, it is tantamount to moral imperialism, the imposition of one culture's morality on another, usually accomplished only in conjunction with the coercive power of the state. Such a response misunderstands the nature of ethics, as do most IB theorists.[7]

Ethics as Stone Tablets

The dominant view of ethics in IB is that it is best understood as a set of individual values or principles that may be socially or culturally determined. Such values or moral principles are inscribed on stone tablets and applied whenever the real world parcels out a moral issue, usually in the form of some Scylla and Charybdis. While there are few if any serious BES people who would endorse this view there is a correlate that still gives rise to the relativism/imperialism continuum as the only choices available.

This view sees the task of the BES theorist as essentially descriptive or as descriptive as possible. Clifford Geertz is the model for doing cross-cultural work, and BES people take his warnings about ethnocentrism seriously. You have to be careful in using the concepts of Peoria to describe Samoa. In fact there may well be such an indeterminacy about description that little can ever be said about ethics across cultures. Consequently the normative force of much BES work is comparatively inconsequential.

I offer a different view of ethics: essentially a pragmatist's view. Ethics is first and foremost about how we are going to live. Who counts in the "we" is an open question. It is always on two levels, personal and social. Individuals want to understand and give meaning to their lives, to see some common threads, life plans, or at least the capability to give order or choose chaotic actions for themselves. They also want to live with others, to seek solidarity. If they don't and their "personal ethics" are too far out of whack, then others, a "them," will call the individual to account. There is always an "us" and a "them." Ethics is about including more people in the "us" and less in the "them."

So, ethics is conversation about what we can agree upon about how to live. There are no ultimate foundations, and we are all ethnocentric in the sense that we start from where we are and work outwards. The conversation is open-textured, although at times we are sure enough of ourselves to codify some rules of thumb, traced in pencil rather than chiseled in stone.[8] So to the old relativist's saw "When in Rome do as the Romans do," and the imperialists' "When in Rome do as we do in Peoria," I have a different response. The relativists don't respect themselves as part of a larger "us," and the imperialists don't respect the Romans as part of that larger "us." Ethics as conversation responds with a "new saw" that goes, "When in Rome do as we and the Romans can agree upon." Seeing business as cooperative, friendly to ethics, based upon truth telling, promise keeping, value creating, and relationship building, is a good start on a conversation with the Romans, though they may well have a different starting point, making more conversation, rather than less, necessary.

Cultural relativism doesn't end conversation for IB scholars. It provides the basis for a starting point. With this in mind "ethics and IB" become a rich area of study, done in detail, not the abstract.

SECTION IV

Before proposing some rather concrete suggestions for an ethics conversation in IB, I want to deal with an alternative to ethics as conversation. This view sees ethics as fundamentally normative. Ethics prescribes how the world should be and how actors, or moral agents, should conduct their lives. Such a view has a long history and culminates in Kant's dictum to treat others as ends in themselves and never as mere means.

There is much wisdom in this view, and it has recently been applied in a deep and thoughtful manner to IB by Thomas Donaldson [1989] in *The Ethics of International Business*.[9] Donaldson argues that the language of human rights is a good starting point for discussions about international human rights. He proposes that we take the list of rights from the U.N. Declaration on Human Rights and similar documents that have been agreed to by a vast majority of states, and that we form a list of important rights. Whether a particular business practice or a decision made by a multinational manager is morally correct will depend crucially on how well it stacks up against those rights.

Donaldson proposes a two-pronged algorithm to determine whether a practice is justifiable. A practice (P) that is impermissible in a home country may be permissible in a host country if that practice violates no important human rights and it is necessary to follow P in order to do business in the host country.

Such a test rightly, to my mind, picks out petty bribery to expedite business as morally permissible when it is part of a system of compensation to low-paid government officials and when it violates no important human rights. Similarly Donaldson's system makes doing business with profoundly racist societies morally impermissible, even where acting in racist ways are necessary to do business in a country, simply because these practices violate basic human rights.

While most IB scholars must be unaware of Donaldson's work (which would go a considerable way to enrich the conversation in this field), let me try to argue that Donaldson's work does not go far enough. I have two objections to Donaldson, which are essentially objections to the sole use of the language of rights, espoused in Kantian terms. The first objection is that rights language and human rights charters that are couched in such language assume a view of the moral subject as independent, autonomous, and capable of action. In other words, it assumes what some would call a fully situated subject and abstracts from that subject its essence, in this case "autonomous action." Morality, on this view, is about the limits of our action, how far we may permissibly go, or when our actions affect others. Donaldson claims that we may go only so far as human rights and our own sense of morality allow us.[10] The problem is that we are not of one mind about what is a subject. Seyla Benhabib has suggested that the idea of an autonomous individual, and a concomitant morality of rights, is based on a notion of the self that is largely male, defined by separation from others rather than by connection to them.[11] Suffice it to say that feminist theorists and others working on so-called minority discourse have called the language of rights into question in an important way.[12]

The second objection is that the application of rights language as the only standard assumes that individuals have already decided to be moral—to take the moral point of view. I believe that such an assumption denies the validity of the experiences of many who are struggling to find a possibility to create meaning in their lives. The first part of ethics, finding meaning in our lives, goes hand in hand with being responsible for the effects of our actions on others. There are many in society who, like Emma Bovary from Flaubert's novel, simply see no possibility for the creation of a meaningful life. Morality for them simply does not come up. We need to explore definitions of morality that can be inclusive, that can allow the participation of a multiplicity of cultures within our society, especially those which have been historically oppressed. It is such a counterpoint that I wish to explore in juxtaposition to an exclusive reliance on the morality of rights.

SECTION V

I suggest a return to basics. I suggest that the building blocks of BES be redefined to take account of the realities of IB. Happily, a kindred task is being undertaken elsewhere in the humanities under the code word "multiculturalism." Multiculturalism is a view that starts with the premise that most of our "knowledge" is fixed in the sense that the 1919 World Series was fixed. Whether something is knowledge largely depends on the race, gender, sexual orientation, and culture of the author, with the winners all "just happening" to be white Western males. Multiculturalism seeks to address what we might call "monoculturalism" by a politics of inclusion, by including others' work who are explicitly not white, Western males.[13]

Henry Louis Gates, Jr. defines the issue:

> Ours is a late-twentieth century world profoundly fissured by nationality, ethnicity, race, class, and gender. The only way to transcend those divisions—to forge, for once, a civic culture that respects both differences and commonalty—is through education that seeks to comprehend the diversity of human culture. Beyond the hype and the high-flown rhetoric is a pretty homely truth: There is no tolerance without respect—and no respect without knowledge. Any human being sufficiently curious and motivated can fully possess another culture, no matter how "alien" it may appear to be. [1992:15]

Ironically Gates is talking about American society. So, the argument can be made that a fundamental deficiency is present in our BES models, namely that they do not take account of race, gender, sexual orientation, and culture. The result is a fissuring of knowledge and practice, or a politics of exclusion. A less kind view would be that the stakeholder model of BES is facile in the sense that it does not account for multiculturalism. More ironic still is the fact that if we can give an account of a "domestic" corporation in multicultural terms, the groundwork will have been laid for a more complete way of understanding

BES issues in IB. Let me try to sketch such a view.

The Multicultural Firm

Corporations have stakeholders, and these stakeholders have a number of important dimensions. Figure 2 details at least some of these dimensions. The usual way of managing stakeholder relationships is to manipulate the interests of stakeholders along the horizontal role dimensions of "customer," "supplier," "employee," etc. One way of formulating BES models is to say that stakeholders have certain rights, values, and relationships that determine their level of participation in determining the "affairs of the corporation." (Such is the argument Bill Evan and I have suggested in a paper in Bowie and Beauchamp, *Ethical Theory and Business*, and in a paper in the *Journal of Behavioral Economics*.)

At minimum we need to add the vertical dimensions to this argument in which in addition to their traditional stakeholder roles, stakeholders can be conceptualized, prioritized, and legitimized in terms of race, gender, sexual orientation, etc. I call this view the "Melting Pot View of BES." The task of any corporation is to understand its stakeholders in terms of the particularities represented by the vertical dimensions. The politics of management take on something akin to the task of melding together acute differences.

There is a second competing way to apply multiculturalism to the corporation. I call this view the "Minority Culture View" of BES which recognizes that the standpoint of a minority culture, African American culture, is in fact multicultural in some sense. Gates reminds us:

> For whatever the outcome of the culture wars in the academy, the world we live in is multicultural already. Mixing and hybridity are the rule, not the exception. As a student of African American culture, of course, I've come to take this kind of cultural palimpsest for granted. Duke Ellington, Miles Davis, and John Coltrane have influenced popular musicians the world over. Wynton Marsalis is as comfortable with Mozart as with jazz. Anthony Davis writes in a musical idiom that combines Bartok with the blues. In the dance, Judith Jameson, Alvin Ailey, and Katherine Dunham all excelled at "Western" cultural forms, melding these with African American styles to produce performances that were neither, and both. In painting, . . . and in literature, . . . African American culture, then, has been a model of multiculturalism and plurality. It is this cultural impulse, I believe, that represents the best hope for us, collectively forge a new, and vital, common American culture in the twenty-first century. [1992:xvi–xvii]

Figure 2. Outline of a Multicultural View of BES

		Race	Gender	Sexuality	Culture
			Dimensions		
Stakeholders	Stockholders				
	Customers				
	Employees				
	Suppliers				
	Community				
	Government				
	Etc.				

I suggest Gates's view of African American culture as multicultural is important for the modern corporation. If we perform a similar task on others who have been "minoritized" we will find a similar phenomenon. The Minority Culture View of BES says we should study minority cultures to find ways that differences have been forged together, ways that "us and them" have been turned into "us." This is a completely different approach from studying the dominant culture of the U.S. multinational to find what can work elsewhere in the world. This view also says that until we can solve the problem of the lack of diversity of our own domestic organizations along the vertical dimensions in Figure 2 we shall make little progress in the larger world.

I want to end this brief sketch with some claims in the form of propositions or assertions.

1. The multicultural firm encourages an ongoing conversation about the meaning and consequences of race.
2. The multicultural firm encourages an ongoing conversation about the meaning and consequences of gender.
3. The multicultural firm encourages an ongoing conversation about the meaning and consequences of sexuality.
4. The multicultural firm encourages an ongoing conversation about the meaning and consequences of culture.
5. The multicultural firm has nontoken members of different races, genders, sexualities, or cultures at all levels of management.

What I have suggested can be more simply stated as "race, gender, sexuality, and culture count" in understanding IB along ethical dimensions, precisely because it should count in business theory in general. The problem of building ways to understand the difficult global moral issues of today is no different from understanding and coming to terms with the real world: the multicultural real world. I have offered no panacea, nor even a guideline for how to proceed. I have merely, and tentatively, suggested that any starting point must take account of the world as we find it with race, gender, sexuality, and culture determining to a large extent the "haves" and the "have nots." A conversation without paying attention to these differences will not matter.

NOTES

1. This is not quite right. They believe they are silent because they choose to ignore the moral force of their actions. Executives, or more accurately still, business theorists' pictures of executives, for the most part, see themselves as morally neutral captains steering the economic engines of the world. Additionally, the Foreign Corrupt Practices Act engendered some rather heated point-counterpoint on international ethical issues.

2. I use "business theory" as a term to encompass the disciplines generally taught in business schools. While there would be disagreements at the margin, most of these disciplines are simply applied economics. I have in mind finance, decision analysis, marketing, accounting, organization theory (some varieties) and others. There is no currently accepted "critical approach" that questions the fundamental assumptions of economics.

3. Of course, to use the phrase "the metaphors and tropes of economics" is to signal that I will have nothing to do with the elevation and deification of economics-as-narrative into economics-as-science. I rely primarily on the arguments of Donald McCloskey and his followers.

4. A profoundly moral context is one in which the participants see themselves engaged in moral actions, regardless of the rightness or wrongness of the action. "Moral" is being used, more or less, in a purely descriptive sense here.

5. R. Vernon and L. Wells, *Managers in the International Economy*, Englewood Cliffs, NJ: Prentice Hall, 1981, 4th edition, at 106.

6. See Freeman and Gilbert (1989) for a more thorough development and discrediting of moral relativism.

7. Of course, I realize that the "correct" way to say this is that IB theorists work with a different "theory-in-use" of the concept "ethics." But, since I want to urge that theory is

the rhetoric in front of the politics I have put the point as I did in the text.

8. This view of ethics is essentially found in the work of John Dewey, Richard Rorty, and other philosophical pragmatists.

9. My deep and abiding respect for this line of reasoning and for Donaldson is evidenced by the preface I wrote for his book. I am critical here in the sense that I want to show how ethics as conversation leads to a different view of business, and how it can solve some unresolved problems in so-called normative ethics. I am explicitly not critical in a "tearing down" sense. A world in which Donaldson not Freeman is taken seriously is a vast improvement over our current one.

10. This is because a practice is not permissible even if it violates no basic human rights just because it is permissible in the host country. A practice that is impermissible in the home country, violates no important human rights, and is *not* necessary to follow to do business in the host country is, according to Donaldson, impermissible.

11. S. Benhabib, "The Generalized and the Concrete Other: The Kohlberg-Gilligan Controversy and Moral Theory" in Eva F. Kittay and Diana T. Meyers (editors), *Women and Moral Theory*, Towota, NJ: Rowman and Littlefield, 1987, pp. 154–177.

12. Of course, this doesn't count against Donaldson's view specifically so much as it does the genre in which he is working. As far as rights talk applied to IB, Donaldson is as good as it gets.

13. Now multiculturalism has engendered a huge media outburst with charges ranging from killing the University to politicizing all that we hold dear to a hegemony of "political correctness." All of these charges rest on a misreading of most multicultural theory. No one is suggesting that we throw out Plato and Shakespeare, at least no one I have read. Rather they suggest that we read these authors critically, in the same way that we might read Alice Walker, Virginia Woolf, and James Baldwin, profoundly influenced by their race, gender, and sexuality.

■ ■ ■

International Business and Society: A Research Agenda for Social Issues in Management
Donna J. Wood and Jean Pasquero

Not surprisingly, most of the issues that have occupied SIM (for social issues in management) scholars for the past two decades have been essentially domestic ones: corporate political action, regulation, charitable giving, community relations, public affairs, issues management, business ethics, and so on, all U.S.-oriented. Yet, since its institutionalization in U.S. business schools in the early 1970s, the field of business and society (or SIM—the two terms will be used interchangeably in this paper) has had a slim but important international component. Currently, the rise of the global economy and the massive shifts in the worldwide political order have made it imperative for SIM scholars to examine and reshape their field carefully in light of international realities.

In this paper we first describe the role international issues and research have played to date in the SIM literature. We then examine the global, cross-national, international, and home dimensions of SIM research, as well as the primary objectives of such research. Next, a number of benefits of developing the international dimension of SIM research are explored, including perceptual, theoretical, practical, and ethical benefits. Then, using several key concepts in the SIM field (stakeholders, business-government relations, business ethics, and corporate social performance), we build a preliminary research agenda for international SIM, testing the concepts in the international domain according to several theoretical criteria. Finally, we offer practical advice on how SIM scholars can increase their international expertise and conclude with a note on the special challenges of international SIM research.

HISTORICAL AND CURRENT STATUS OF INTERNATIONAL BUSINESS AND SOCIETY

International themes—though not central to the field—have long been present in SIM research. Of particular significance historically was the emerging research stream addressing issues of corporate irresponsibility or crime abroad [Post and Baer 1980]. Swiss-based Nestlé's marketing practices for infant formula in third world countries, ITT Corporation's alleged involvement in overthrowing the Chilean government, the Japanese-Lockheed bribery scandal, and corporate indifference to apartheid in South Africa were some of the early international SIM cases that held the interest of scholars. Yet, attention to such cases focused almost exclusively on U.S. multinational corporations (MNCs). Even the Nestlé case was written up from the perspective of Abbott Labs (see Molander 1980). Corporate social performance was another early stream of international research in SIM [Preston, Rey, and Dierkes 1978; Sethi 1978; U.S. Department of Commerce 1979]. Its focus was clearly more comparative, more cross-national. But despite a few significant works, however, it never achieved the prominence of works in business ethics. Outside of these two areas of interest, international research in SIM was even more occasional and certainly more fragmented, so that no research stream could really emerge. In short, the international dimension of business and society has never been totally absent from this field. Despite a few high-visibility international cases it has long received only marginal attention.

The picture is now somewhat different. In the past few years, the international aspects of business and society have increased in importance and have commanded more scholarly attention. The founding of new professional associations such as IABS, the International Association for Business and Society, and EBEN, the European Business Ethics Network, indicates the strength of scholarly interest.

A cursory review of the recent literature points to four areas of interest. One is the continuation of the earlier work in International Business (IB) ethics and corporate social performance. Another is the emergence of new streams of international research related to public policy. The third area is concerned with methodological issues in cross-national research. The final area includes a variety of topics at the crossroads of SIM and other management disciplines, indicating the rich cross-fertilization that the field is currently undergoing. Not all of this research is comparative, but a growing part of it is, and all of it deals with international aspects of the relationships between business and society. A few examples will illustrate these trends.

Recent research in IB ethics includes cases—some involving no U.S. firms at all—that have been written about the *maquiladora* industries at the Mexican border [Russell 1984], Japanese MNC involvement in South Africa [Paul 1992], or the differing cultural interpretations of issues such as monetary gifts to business associates and government officials [Fadiman 1986]. Likewise, a flow of international studies has begun to appear on corporate social reporting [Dierkes 1980; Dierkes and Berthoin Antal 1986], corporate social responsiveness [Berthoin Antal 1991], and corporate social performance in countries such as Canada [Clarkson 1988], Great Britain [Moore and Richardson 1988], and Japan [Mafune 1988].

Work on comparative public policy is now well established in at least two new areas: environmental regulation [Kelman 1981; Peterson and Wade 1985; Badaracco 1986; Vogel 1986; Mahon and Kelley 1988] and business-government relations [Wilson 1985; Dierkes, Weller, and Berthoin Antal 1987; Tiffany 1987; Wilks and Wright 1987; Ring, Lenway, and Govekar 1990]. Related research has occurred in the area of corporate political involvement [Lenway and Ring 1991]. Work on methodological issues draws from both inside the field of

SIM and from related fields, like comparative politics, comparative sociology, and IB [Dierkes, Weller, and Berthoin Antal 1987; Wright, Lane, and Beamish 1988].

Illustrative of the convergence between SIM and other management functions, recent international work has appeared on Swiss ecological marketing strategies [Dyllick 1989], MNC crisis management [Nigh and Cochran 1991], the Canadian collaborative roundtables for implementing sustainable development [Pasquero 1991], stakeholder involvement in hydroelectric projects in Czechoslovakia and Hungary [Wood 1992], and comparative work on more traditional topics like issues management or philanthropy [Pasquero 1989; 1991b]. Other significant work has appeared in compendia such as the recent book edited by Karen Paul [1991] on contemporary issues in business and society, where seven of the twelve entries deal directly with international issues.

How can we explain this new appeal of the international domain? To a large extent, American SIM scholars are merely catching up with the pace of world economic and political events. In the economic realm, MNCs have become omnipresent; some of the U.S.'s largest corporations earn a majority of their returns abroad; foreign investors now own major American corporate landmarks and invest heavily in U.S. businesses. Further, political events such as Europe 1992, the opening of Eastern Europe and the Soviet Union, the North American Free Trade Agreement, the Persian Gulf war, the unification of the two Germanys and possibly of the two Koreas, and the upcoming absorption of Hong Kong into mainland China have dramatically emphasized the global significance of corporate activity. SIM scholars have little understanding of the degree to which their concepts and models are culture- and time-bound, and thus are at present unable to bring much explanatory power to bear on the non-U.S. business and society issues that are raised by these world events.

Another reason for the new interest in international SIM is a recognition that many social problems relevant to business are truly international, even global, in scope. Pollution is perhaps the most obvious of global social problems, but it is by no means the only one. Terrorist activities, diseases such as AIDS, and radioactive fallout from defective nuclear plants do not respect national borders. The materialist wealth of capitalist societies is subject to emulation, envy, or repulsion throughout the world, stirring up vast social forces for political change. Long-standing social problems such as poverty and illiteracy continue to affect the world's social, political, and economic orders, as has the emergence of global production and distribution strategies. For example, the growing discrepancy between the limited political power of national states and the supranational economic power of MNCs is fast casting the seemingly dormant issue of business-government relations in an entirely new light. In short, the field of SIM has been forced to turn its attention to relationships between business and a variety of societies, and to the social, ethical, and political problems and issues deriving from the interconnectedness of today's multinational economic and political environments.

Finally, North American (particularly U.S.) feelings of insecurity should not be discounted as a factor driving increasing interest in international SIM. Central cultures are not usually interested in peripheral ones; they focus attention on themselves. Traditionally, American scholarship in the social sciences has been rather isolationist [Hollander 1981]. However, in a time when the U.S. is stagnant, federal debt is staggering, foreign investment in the U.S. economy increases, and all the world seems poised to challenge and overturn U.S. economic dominance, it should not be surprising that a sense of insecurity, inadequacy, and frustration would drive U.S. business scholars into the international domain. This new interest can be interpreted as a search for efficiency in a world where time-tested solutions are no longer adequate, and where efficiency itself may not be the most desired objective.

It is not mere curiosity seeking; it reflects a growing awareness of the need for U.S. businesses to share the world's resources and to compromise with others who also hold economic and political power.

Although significant efforts are being made to produce international research in SIM, progress occurs slowly, for this arena of research is arguably the most demanding of all. Technically, this "international" research exists at several levels, which can be ranked in ascending order of complexity (see Table 1).

At Level 1 is simple international research conducted on a single foreign country. The objective is to understand the core of a social political phenomenon as it is experienced in a country unfamiliar to the researcher. This is the case of most anthropologists, or that of the SIM scholar returning from a sabbatical abroad with notes on a particular topic. Level 2 is comparative international research. The same phenomenon is studied in two or more countries, by a single researcher or a team of researchers. The research design remains informal and no attempt is made to compare systematically the elements of the phenomenon under study. Work on each country is usually published in separate chapters. A concluding chapter highlights the main similarities and differences between the countries in the sample, but mostly in a discursive, argumentative way. Level 3 is standardized cross-national research, where research is conducted in two or more countries, but in a systematic way. The same conceptual cat-

egories, however broadly defined, must be applied, and the same data types must be gathered in each country. A common research design is imposed across all countries. Research can be quantitative or qualitative, but in all cases it requires central coordination. At Level 4 is what has been called transnational research [Kohn 1987]. In this type of research, each nation in the sample is considered as a component of a larger international system. The objective lies beyond understanding how the behavior of a particular phenomenon and its explanation can be generalized across a variety of nations. The objective is to understand how this phenomenon is tied to relationships encompassing clusters of several nations. Development of research at this level is still in its infancy.

Overall, what distinguishes international research, especially in its higher levels, is that it combines all the difficulties of the other types and adds its own as well. These difficulties are now well documented [Heller 1988; Punnett 1988]. At each level, the research pitfalls—problems such as language barriers, cultural differences in values and customs, unfamiliar symbols and behaviors, familiar symbols and behaviors that carry a different interpretation in other cultures, and different social and organizational structures—become more complex and demand more effort of the researcher to overcome. SIM scholarship, traditionally more qualitative by nature, adds yet another layer of complexity to classic cross-national work. The sobering conclusion is

Table 1. Levels of Complexity of SIM International Research

Level	Description of Complexity
1. Simple international	One foreign country, not comparative.
2. Comparative international	Two or more countries, informal comparisons.
3. Standardized cross-national	Two or more countries, formal comparisons.
4. Transnational	One phenomenon, one or more clusters of countries.

that SIM international researchers face what is probably the most difficult type of research, since it combines the triple hurdles of international work, comparative work, and field work (for a more complete treatment, see Pasquero 1988).

Yet, despite the difficulties of doing this sort of research, there are numerous rewards, which we will discuss below. For now, it is sufficient to observe that the volume of work in international SIM is growing, and that this trend is to be applauded and nurtured.

WHAT IS THE INTERNATIONAL DIMENSION OF BUSINESS AND SOCIETY?

Many disciplines concern themselves with international affairs, so that we must first distinguish the focus of international business and society, or SIM, as the field is coming to be known. Economics tends to emphasize exchanges of goods and services or contractual relationships in international contexts. Traditional management disciplines such as accounting, marketing, or human resources concern themselves with various aspects of operating efficiency. SIM, in contrast, focuses on public policy processes, interorganizational relationships, and ethics as they relate to the governance and operations of corporations. This corporate/management focus is in contrast to sociologists, who study macroglobal issues, and to political scientists, who study the development and operation of international orders and regimes, without particular reference to corporations or to management.

We contend that international business and society issues focus on four dimensions (see Table 2): the global dimension, the cross-national dimension, the international dimension, and the home-country dimension.

Each dimension has different value for business and society studies, and each focuses on different phenomena. Social issues and problems exist in every dimension, and a single issue may exist in more than one dimension. We explore these four dimensions further in the sections that follow. To illustrate how a social issue can exist in multiple dimensions, we will trace a single example—environmental protection—through the four dimensions and show how different research questions arise with respect to this issue at each level. Note that despite the similarity of some terms, issue dimensions (Table 2) must be distinguished conceptually from levels of research complexity (Table 1).

THE GLOBAL DIMENSION

The global dimension of business and society has to do with identifying and understanding those structures, processes, trends, events, issues, and problems that (1) are common to many or all countries, and/or (2) are not country-specific, that is, they cannot be linked to any particular country, and/or (3) that reverberate throughout the world or through major re-

Table 2. Dimensions of International Business and Society Issues

Dimension	Descriptor
Global	Worldwide issues, trends, impacts (more free-flowing and broad)
Cross-national	Exchanges/interactions/comparisons between or among countries
International	"Them"
Home-country	"Us"

gions of the world. For example, global SIM research might address questions such as these: How are business-government relationships being redefined around the world? What are the common social/political issues facing global corporations? Are there common strategies for managing such issues? How are countries contributing to the development of international law affecting business activity? What roles do business organizations play in broad global social problems such as pollution, poverty, illiteracy, and disease? How does worldwide religious activity (e.g., Moslem fundamentalists, Catholic liberation theologists) affect economic development, political events, social values and practices, and, in consequence, MNCs around the world? How do MNCs manage their relationships with global (non-country-specific) stakeholders?

If we were to study the global dimension of environmental protection (see Speth [1987]), we might, for example, borrow from the biologists' efforts to trace the actual flow and effects of pollutants from their sources through their transmission media (air, water, soil) to their destinations, and then see if a relationship existed among the severity of damage within countries, the assessment of company responsibility for creating the problem, stakeholder awareness and action, and business and governmental responses to the problem. Or we might, instead, investigate global efforts to impose voluntary controls on pollution-creating activities, efforts such as the Montreal Protocol on Substances that Deplete the Ozone (see Getz 1991a), or the recent United Nations agreements on transnational shipping of hazardous substances and on export of toxic wastes (see Mahon and Kelley 1988). Additionally, one could research the ways in which different countries have or have not implemented global directives such as the Brundtland report on sustainable development. As a final example, we could study the structure and strategies of global environmental protection activist groups such as Greenpeace, or the processes by which a country—specific geographical feature—for example, the Amazon rain forests—comes to be seen as a global resource of interest to people everywhere.

THE CROSS-NATIONAL DIMENSION

The cross-national dimension of business and society is concerned with exchanges, interactions, and relationships between or among countries. The distinction between cross-national and global dimensions of business and society is that the former term focuses on specific, identifiable relationships, while the latter term concerns broader, more ambiguous, more widespread ones. (The difference may reflect our theoretical inability to deal with complex, multiple, simultaneous exchanges and thus be a difference of degree rather than type.)

Research questions in this dimension might concern corporate involvement in obtaining bilateral or multilateral protectionist trade agreements between nations, the formation and operation of multicountry governing bodies such as the European Union and their effects on business activities, the development of social issues originating in one country but directly affecting another (for example, U.S. tobacco sales to Third World countries; see Davidson 1991), the implications of a country's use of large numbers of workers from another (usually Third World) country (e.g., Turks in Germany, Indians in Britain, Mexicans in the U.S., North Africans in France), or the social and political effects of across-the-border manufacturing or assembly of products to be sold in the nonproducing country.

The cross-national dimension of environmental protection contains numerous issues and questions for study. Two-country SIM issues are perhaps the easiest to identify—issues such as the U.S.-Canadian battle over acid rain or the Hungarian-Czechoslovakian controversy over preservation of a wetlands and a freshwater aquifer. One could also research bilateral or multilateral agreements, for example, to restrain cross-border shipments of hazardous materials or to protect common water sources. Even more interesting, perhaps, would be to study the social and political antecedents and consequences of the *nonexistence* of such agreements where ecological analysis suggests they would be beneficial.

THE INTERNATIONAL DIMENSION

For corporate managers, the international dimension of business and society is normally concerned with "host country" issues. For SIM researchers, it involves understanding and learning from relevant processes, structures, relationships, and issues in other countries.

There are so many relevant questions that can be asked at the international level that it is difficult to select a few to exemplify this dimension. In essence, any research question that is appropriate at the domestic level can also be appropriate at the international level, the idea being, "This is how it works here, this is how we handle it, how do you deal with it?" As one example, researchers working on the international dimension of business and society could ask questions such as this: How do economic, health care, and government organizations interact—or divide the labor—to deal with complex problems such as AIDS? In the U.S., the burden for health care is placed primarily on business organizations and their insurance providers. In other nations, health care is the job of government. In still other nations, no societal institution is responsible for health care. These different arrangements have implications for managing the impacts of major health problems and for MNC employee benefit programs. Other examples of relevant international research topics are almost innumerable: the nature of corporate involvement in public policy processes, voluntarism and charitable giving practices in various countries, corporate governance structures, the role of central planning and/or state-owned enterprises in national economies, regulatory concerns and practices, the nature of social and political issues and of corporate re-

sponses to them, the role of the media in providing awareness and information of social issues, and much more.

If we were to study the international dimension of environmental protection, we might ask, for example, about the processes and technologies other countries use to dispose of their wastes, or about the allocation of responsibility for waste generation and disposal among businesses, government, other institutions, and citizens. We could inquire about the nature and extent of pollution control regulation in other nations. Or we could research the existence and impacts of environmental protection interest groups and their strategies for interacting with corporate polluters. We would be looking for structures, processes, strategies, values, and conditions that could profitably be compared and contrasted with our own to help us gain a better understanding of how various countries deal with pollution.

THE HOME DIMENSION

Finally, the home dimension of business and society studies is concerned with relevant phenomena in the domestic environment. Because much of the existing literature in SIM is U.S.-oriented, we simply direct the reader's attention to the multitude of studies conducted on public policy and business-government relations, issues management, stakeholder relations, business ethics and values, and so on. (See Kahn 1990, for a recent review of the ethics literature; Donaldson 1989, for a theoretical approach to IB ethics; Preston 1986, for a review of business and public policy; and Wood 1991a;1991b, for overviews of SIM research in other areas.)

Domestic-oriented research is related to international-oriented research in two ways: as an input and as a beneficiary. In both cases, it requires answering an important question: How close are American models and frameworks to American reality? If much of American work in business and society, for example, is based on what could be argued as a fictional conflict between business organizations and government, or on a powerfully symbolic but unreal idea about the role of neoclassical economics in managerial decision making, then our findings cannot usefully be applied to comparative or global research because they do not reflect domestic reality.

Conversely, international research can help home country researchers come to a better understanding of their topics or solve some of their research puzzles. For example, international research would help to decipher little-researched behavior codes, such as the significance of the role of lawyers or of the pervasiveness of government regulations in American business practice. Or, it could shed light on the issues of day care, cooperatives, and alternative forms of governance in American corporate society. Actually, every culture can ask such questions of its own research. Foreign models shed new light on home research and are one way (which is discussed later) of criticizing it and assessing its validity.

To complete our environmental protection example, studying the home dimension of this issue would involve asking essentially similar questions to those asked in the international dimension. The intent, however, would be to specify and understand "how we handle it," thus establishing baseline empirical data and analytical models for comparison with international, cross-national, and global findings.

OBJECTIVES OF AN INTERNATIONAL DIMENSION OF BUSINESS AND SOCIETY RESEARCH

In an important sense, international business and society is no different from other areas of social-science-based scholarly study; its objectives are to describe, explain, and understand social phenomena. We believe, however, that international business and society studies should give special emphasis, at least at this time, to *understanding* phenomena of interest.

Description and explanation. Social science disciplines tend to downplay descriptive research in favor of explanatory studies. At this early point in our field's maturation process, however, description should be as legitimate as explanation. We do not know enough at the international, cross-national, and global levels to construct variable-based theory that would lend itself to quantitative explanatory research. As examples of relevant descriptive research, it would be fruitful to describe networks of personal and organizational relationships as they define societal processes in other countries, or the weight of historical processes in shaping today's cultural and social structural patterns, or the social processes of collaboration and competition as they shape interorganizational relationships in various countries.

Three focuses for descriptive international SIM research stand out. First, we need to know more about the actual *behaviors* of corporate, governmental, and voluntary groups and organizations. Second, research should focus on *practices* (processes, normal procedures, policies) of such groups and organizations. Third, a focus on macrolevel sociopolitical *patterns*—international regimes and their impact on MNCs, for example—would be useful. Descriptive studies of behaviors, practices, and patterns can be accomplished in the context of single-event case studies, a particular management problem such as how to manage responses to a specific social issue, or a variety of other settings. What is important is to obtain high-quality, realistic descriptive material on relevant aspects of international business and society relationships so that theory building can proceed inductively.

Understanding (verstehen). SIM is an area of study characterized by the importance of values and symbols. The importance of these symbolic features is even more evident at the international or cross-national level. Therefore, "understanding" as *verstehen* (that is, understanding not only observed behaviors and practices but also the meanings and symbols attached to them and to concepts describing them, as well as the context in which they occur and are used) should be a prime research objective.

In many areas of interest, striving for *verstehen* may be a great deal more productive than efforts to determine causal variable relationships, which are so often elusive even in the better-defined social science disciplines.

As examples of international SIM research questions that would be oriented to *verstehen*, consider the following: What values underlie business-government relations in various countries, what meanings are attached to these relations, and what symbols are used to capture these meanings? When international managers experience ethical conflict because of competing value systems, how do they attempt to understand and resolve their problems? How should the concept of a business community be understood across different countries? How can a foreign manager distinguish between probusiness and antibusiness behavior among a company's stakeholders? What is the implicit hierarchy of social obligations expected of a large corporation in various cultures? Under what circumstances will a given corporate behavior be judged as benign, indifferent, or intolerable by its main stakeholders? Why should a company pay attention to powerless stakeholders? What is the role of religion in basic business relationships? What are the absolute taboos of corporate behavior, and conversely, just how flexible are the limits imposed by the ambient culture on corporate behavior? Answering each of these questions properly will generally be of greater help to managers and researchers alike than the often-ambiguous evidence of causal relationships.

BENEFITS OF DEVELOPING AN INTERNATIONAL DIMENSION OF BUSINESS AND SOCIETY RESEARCH

There are four classes of benefits to be gained from studying the international dimension of SIM—perceptual, theoretical, practical, and ethical benefits. These are discussed below.

Perceptual Benefits

Escape from Ethnocentricity. The primary reason to study the international dimensions of business and society is to escape the ethnocentrism that too often characterizes our thinking and research. Ethnocentrism is the tendency to apply one's own research frameworks, viewpoints, values, or cultural interpretations to the study of other cultures without examining their fit in the other cultures. From a foreign point of view (Canadian, European, and even more if non-Western), it is evident that much of the research done in the U.S. is particular to that country. Not only is the research done in the U.S. on U.S. companies and governments, but the models and frameworks used appear to be rooted in U.S. structure, culture, symbols, and understandings. Some U.S.-based frameworks can be extended outside the U.S. borders, and some can be adapted, but some do not seem to be generalizable. Some, indeed, are viewed as extreme curiosities by scholars and managers in other countries.

This problem is not unique to U.S. research. In any country, the ethnocentrism of research parallels the idiosyncrasies of that society's processes, structures, values, or issues. The bias of ethnocentrism is not particular to any one nation. We focus here on U.S. ethnocentrism because the U.S. is virtually the only source of ideas and theory on topics relevant to the study of business and society. One reason is that more research on these topics is published and publicly accessible in this country than in any other country. Not that business and society issues are not discussed in other countries; in fact they are, and more often than not, they have been discussed for longer than in the United States. For example, debate on the respective roles of government, business, and society, and on the proper relationships among them, has been raging in Europe for at least a century, if not more.

In the past three decades, most non-occidental countries have been experimenting with one form or another of a vast array of political, social, and economic arrangements that have very little in common with those of the United States. For example, critical ideal-types like national planning, social security, socialism, social democracy, neo-corporatism, industrial democracy, nationalizations, public enterprise, privatization, welfare state, politicized unions, tripartism, etc., have all been invented and applied outside the U.S. In each case, the introduction of these arrangements has led to a redefinition of the relationship between business and society.

In most countries, unfortunately, academic research at the corporate level on these issues has been scarce, difficult to locate, and inaccessible to most unilingual American researchers. The unavailability of foreign sources, however, is no proof that U.S.-based research is generalizable to foreign settings. Conversely, the staggering variety of manifest business and society relations outside the U.S. does not necessarily entail that the relevance of U.S. findings, especially at the more structural levels, is limited to the U.S. territory. We contend that international research in business and society issues is the prime way for testing this generalizability. To illustrate, following are some examples of research areas in which American frameworks would be considered as culture-bound by foreign scholars.

Governmental Legitimacy. To a non-American scholar, the area of business and government is one where the ideological biases of American literature show perhaps most clearly. U.S.-based research reveals a permanent tension between the rhetoric of self-interest (a central tenet of much American literature, seldom questioned) and the observation of political and collective realities. For example, many SIM textbooks appear not to explain the reality of government's place and role in economic life, but to justify that government may indeed have a legitimate place in society and in the oversight and control of business behavior. Much SIM research, therefore, is cast in a defensive framework and results in self-limiting outcomes. Counterexamples that standard frameworks cannot explain are simply overlooked. Researching government-related business (e.g., state-owned business

in the U.S.), for instance, appears as a scholarly form of bad taste.

The Issue of Nationalism. In the U.S., "nationalism" is considered a destructive force, particularly when it is observed in other countries. By contrast, in many other parts of the world—in Canada for example—nationalism is often viewed as a positive force. The main reason for this difference is that foreign cultures do not define nationalism in the same way as American culture does. For Americans, nationalism is but a dangerous form of collective irrationality. It is associated with either militarism, parochialism, or backwardness. It is conceived as a superstitious attachment to a territory, frozen institutions, or a sometimes glorious but long-gone past. In international relations, nationalism is equated to a self-serving justification of anti-Americanism. It is condemned for appealing to the emotional side of people, and for being the prime device used by demagogues, despots, or dictators to manipulate entire populations. In brief, for the American psyche, nationalism is bad.

That nationalism has a dark side cannot be denied. To many populations in search of an identity, however, and especially to those in the process of reconstructing a shattered identity, nationalism is a driving force. It thrives on personal and public pride in one's country's heritage, accomplishments, culture, and potential. It is turned toward the future. Paradoxically, politicians will use appeals to their common heritage to help populations break away from the very weight of this heritage, to demonstrate that the present difficulties are not a product of fate, but of passing circumstances that a collective effort can overcome. Nationalism in these conditions cannot be simply dismissed as a dysfunctional form of tribalism. It must be understood as a permanent exhortation for individual and collective achievement, most often economic achievement.

A lack of awareness of these differences leads to two consequences. First, foreign nationalism is misunderstood in the U.S. and is systematically condemned for what it often is not. Second, American nationalism itself is systematically ignored in mainstream SIM research and thus we understand and acknowledge little about its nature and consequences. Americans may prefer to define the concept as the more acceptable "patriotism," thus placing it squarely within the individual consciousness and avoiding the issues of economics and management that arise with the societal concept of nationalism. The study of nationalism is therefore abandoned to a few reckless political scientists or anthropologists. The net result is that the import of economic nationalism as a central element of individual and collective behavior is nearly totally absent from American research on business and society relations.

Protectionism. Protectionism is a societal departure from the standard microeconomic model, and thus falls in the province of SIM studies. In recent years, U.S. management literature has focused much attention on the cry for "improving U.S. competitiveness in global markets," in part through forging new business-government partnerships and protecting U.S. manufacturers' domestic markets—an interesting idea for a supposedly free-market, antinationalistic nation. Protectionist measures are quite common in the U.S, as well as in the EC, Japan, and other trading nations. How can SIM scholars fully grasp the issue of protectionism among the U.S., the EC, and Japan, without fully understanding the cultural and structural bases for the cross-accusations these partners exchange over various oceans? Here, in fact, is a fruitful area in which to study the effects of nationalism (either explicit or implicit) on public policies relating to business.

Stockholders vs. Stakeholders. As a final example, the idea that stockholders are naturally the principal stakeholders with which business management must be concerned is a peculiarly American idea (and is not even true in the U.S. domestic environment, though much SIM literature attempts

to defend against the fiction that it is true). In other societies, various types of enterprise-stakeholder core relationships can be observed: for example, the domination of German boards of directors by top management, bankers, and lawyers and the active participation of labor in corporate governance; the relationships among powerful ministries, peak industry associations, and large companies in France or Japan; the extended family networks supporting and being supported by companies in Taiwan and Africa; or the near-equivalence of government and large business enterprise in Chinese and former Soviet industries.

The ongoing argument between American SIM scholars and neoclassical economics is reflected again and again, in stakeholder theory, in ideas about nationalism and protectionism, in questions of governmental legitimacy, and in other areas as well. This argument makes it difficult for U.S. SIM scholars to escape ethnocentrism even when attempts are made to internationalize the research agenda. Internationalizing business and society research might have an unexpected payoff in providing evidence for the construction of a valid, coherent, comprehensive, non-neoclassical theory of the firm and of business-society relationships.

Theoretical Benefits

In this category, the most important benefit is that international SIM research will help U.S. scholars to assess our home-grown theories of how business organizations and social systems interact. To this end, international research provides three tests:

1. *A test of the universality of our models.* If American models do indeed reflect American reality, to what extent do they also reflect reality in other countries? How much of what we know and think is compatible with conflicting or competing foreign models?

2. *A test of how well we understand*

our familiar issues and frameworks. Grasping an alien reality enables a scholar to have a more thorough understanding of his/her familiar topics and environment. It also probably makes them seem less complex than they otherwise appear. Paradoxically, distancing breeds both depth (in terms of better understanding) and simplification (in terms of being able to see more clearly the broad structural patterns of social phenomena). Some of the best insights into national cultures and values are the work of foreigners; e.g., de Tocqueville on America, or American scholars on European neocorporatist states.

3. *A test of the robustness of our new ideas.* How robust are our new ideas when taken into the international context? Testing (either logically or empirically) our ideas in the international domain gives us a new sense of perspective (How novel is this idea, really?), a keener sense of relevance (Is the idea useful in explaining or understanding other cultures?), and a better sense of applicability (Is this idea realistic?). Wartick and Wood (forthcoming), for example, take this sort of approach in testing the concepts of corporate social performance in international settings. Berthoin Antal [1991], in her cross-cultural study of corporate responses to youth unemployment in Great Britain and Germany, found differences in perspective, relevance, and applicability of the concept of corporate social responsiveness, and thus was able to mold a better theoretical understanding of this U.S.-originated concept.

In addition to these theoretical assessment functions, international SIM research

is a rich source of new ideas and insights into business and society relationships worldwide. Scholars can import "sensitizing concepts" and guiding questions from abroad. For example, after witnessing the collapse of some giant East German companies following German reunification, an American scholar could come home and start raising questions about the minimum requirements expected of social and political networks to sustain the permanence of economic organizations. Another sensitizing concept would be that of network reconstruction, this time applied to the case of American corporations experiencing a turnaround. Alternatively, a European scholar interested in corporate philanthropy could return home from a U.S. visit and devise a fresh project based on the American concept of "community." Research methods also can be imported; for example, much of the current North American craze for qualitative methods has European origins. Finally, as we mentioned earlier, looking abroad for ideas and theoretical perspectives may provide SIM scholars with viable alternatives to the neoclassical/utilitarian bogeyman, allowing them to move forward, finally, toward a more comprehensive theory of business-society relationships.

Practical Benefits

Studying international aspects of business and society will yield practical benefits in our interactions with students and clients. An important payoff will be seen in better teaching. Teaching is the art of conveying concepts through comparison, and developing a sense of proportion and judgment among students. With a significant body of international SIM research and thinking to draw upon, professors can explain U.S. concepts more clearly by contrasting them with relevant foreign concepts. Further, students can be exposed to new frameworks and ideas that they might encounter or find useful later in their careers. Cases based on overseas and cross-national issues can be developed and taught to help students grapple with the tough international management problems that inevitably arise.

Furthermore, international business and society study will have practical benefits in better understanding. Scholars will become more sensitive to the issues faced by our nationals working abroad, as well as those faced by foreign students in our classrooms and foreign managers in our communities. We may become better able to use the expertise of foreign students and managerial colleagues in a more meaningful and productive way.

Ethical Benefits

Finally, as professionals, and even more as educators and scholars, we have a moral duty to contribute to the construction of a better world, a world where barriers to intercultural communication—often the source of avoidable conflicts—can be better controlled and perhaps overcome. Granted, in the international arena, conflict will always be with us, and so will barriers to communication. Conflict—particularly the nonviolent forms—can even be constructive on occasion. Much conflict, however, is merely destructive and is based on misunderstanding. Which of us has never revised her/his own prejudices upon hearing a foreign student or colleague tell a different story from the one we knew about an issue? Internationalizing our SIM curriculum and knowledge base is a prime way for us to make a meaningful ethical contribution as educators and knowledge producers.

Additional ethical benefits result from internationalizing our research and teaching. International research establishes better communication among scholars around the world. We can develop more solid information and more rigorous theory with which to influence our students' ethical judgment processes. We can offer less prejudiced counsel to our clients. In virtually every aspect of academic professional life, there is a payoff to increasing our knowledge and understanding of international social issues

and international business and society relationships.

A PRELIMINARY RESEARCH AGENDA FOR INTERNATIONAL BUSINESS AND SOCIETY

Throughout this paper we have given examples of internationally oriented SIM research questions that need to be addressed. Here we attempt to develop a more systematic understanding of underresearched topics in international SIM and of questions that are not yet well understood. In the previous section, we noted these two theoretical benefits to be obtained from internationalizing business and society research: (1) tests of the appropriateness of American models of business and society relationships and processes when applied to other cultures, and (2) tests of the robustness (novel perspective, relevance, applicability) of our ideas. In the following subsections, we examine several of the core concepts and frameworks of the business and society literature and point to areas in which, from an American perspective, international research could provide such tests. Our analysis relies on the following questions to guide it:

> *Logical or face validity*—Does the concept apply at all in foreign settings?
> *Symbolic and structural equivalence*—Does the concept mean the same thing in other cultures? Does it look like the same thing?
> *Implications*—Theoretically, what becomes possible when the concept is applied to foreign settings? What still needs to be known?

Stakeholders

A corporate stakeholder is defined as "any group or organization that can affect or is affected by the achievement of the firm's objectives" [Freeman 1984:24]. The concept of stakeholder has also been used to connote persons, groups, or organizations having an interest or stake in an issue domain [Gray and Wood 1991]. Earlier we discussed the "stakeholders vs. stockholders" problem as an example of how our North American concepts would look different if applied in foreign settings. Here we take a closer look at the concept of "stakeholder" itself, in both the organizational and the issue contexts, to see if anything about it changes when considered in the international arena.

Face Validity. The term "stakeholder" expresses a structural relationship between a person, group, or organization, and a business enterprise or social/public issue. On the one hand, stakeholders of a company have an interest in what that company does; on the other hand, stakeholders of an issue have an interest in how that issue evolves and is handled. These structural relationships are likely to look different in various cultures, but there is no reason to suspect that there are cultures where stakeholders do not exist at all, or where the idea expressed by the concept would be completely foreign. In fact, the term primarily connotes an open-systems interconnectedness among people and organizations, the very heart of social organization everywhere.

Equivalence and Implications. Nevertheless, the concept of stakeholder will not mean the same in every culture. One important cross-cultural difference is in the question of *who are a firm's primary stakeholders.* U.S. thinking focuses first on stockholders, employees, suppliers, customers, and government, and then extends to community, environmental protection groups, consumer groups, minority activists, and a host of other organizations and interest groups. In Germany and France, a business firm's core stakeholders would more likely be thought of as employees first, and then, perhaps in a different order, customers, bankers, government, and competitors. In Haiti, key corporate governmental stakeholders might include—in addition to the U.S. federal government and the national governments of other economic partners— the former military government, and the democratically elected government, for-

merly in exile. In many African countries, the government, the bureaucracy, and the extended personal networks of managers would be given priority.

Another cross-cultural difference will be found in the question of *who has a right to intervene in business affairs.* Stakeholders are normally defined in terms of the interests they hold in business activities or in the resolution of social issues. However, people and groups with interests do not necessarily have the right to act—that is, formal access to public policy processes—to achieve those interests. An obvious example is the South African apartheid system, in which black workers certainly had interests in business operations but no legal right to act in those interests or to challenge business management. Another example would be the environmentalists of mid-1980s Hungary, who had definite interests in development of the Danube River but who had no official legitimacy and thus no legal right to exist, much less to intervene in the government's plans [Wood 1992].

A third cross-cultural difference will be *the degree to which stakeholders are integrated into management decision-making processes.* U.S. boards of directors are dominated by executives of the company and elite outside directors. Workers or union representatives almost never have a place on a U.S. board. The German codetermination system, however, routinely places a Worker Council representative on the corporate board of directors and requires decision-making consultation between labor and management. By law, French corporations have to consult their employee-run workers' councils on all matters pertaining to working conditions, which can extend to investment and disinvestment policy when these are likely to affect working conditions. Canadian law now provides for the consultation and decision-making participation of local communities on environmental issues for all large federally financed capital projects. In Quebec, occupational health and safety policy is determined by joint employer-union committees at both the sectoral and corporate levels.

Beyond the realm of cross-cultural differences, we are now observing the operations of *global stakeholders*, not tied to a particular country but active in many. This by no means invalidates or changes the concept of stakeholder, but it has implications for the way we think about stakeholders and the way we incorporate them into theory.

Finally, increasing the number of stakeholders means an increase in the complexity of their interrelationships. U.S. stakeholder models, for example, typically incorporate "government" as a key stakeholder, and more complex models break down this generic category into the specific federal, state, and local entities that are most relevant to the firm. In the global arena, the governmental stakeholder category of a MNC could represent one hundred or more national governments and their various departments or ministries; a huge number of state, regional, and local governments; revolutionary governments and governments-in-exile or in-waiting; and international governing organizations such as the European Commission or the United Nations. Taking the stakeholder concept global means broadening the concept to include many more stakeholders as well as types of stakeholders not normally found in North America. Furthermore, an MNC deals with intricate political and legal relationships among many of these various government bodies. This reticulated character of international stakeholders adds a new dimension of complexity to corporate stakeholder relations.

For SIM researchers, taking the stakeholder concept international cannot be a mere extension of American models. The level of complexity is multiplied many times, both quantitatively and qualitatively. New elements must be added to the stakeholder concept, new properties must be studied. It may be the best stimulus for revitalizing this currently dormant (and one

might add, now disappointingly common-sensical) conceptual tool.

Business-Government Relations

There is no commonly accepted definition of business-government relations, but the term refers to structural or behavioral connections, or exchanges, between business organizations and government organizations, and the effects that each institution has on the operating environment of the other. Earlier we gave several examples of research questions that could be asked about business-government relations in the international domain. Here we examine the concept itself to see how it can be applied internationally.

Face validity. On the surface, all we need to achieve face validity for this concept cross-culturally is to observe business (or economic) organizations, government organizations, and some relationship between them. To the extent it is possible to use "business" as a generic, noncapitalistic, non-Western term connoting organizations engaged in economic activity, then we can identify business-government relations virtually anywhere.

Equivalence. The study of business-government relations is predicated on the way each of these three elements is conceptualized. Forms of business that are marginal in the U.S. may occupy center stage in other cultures. For example, to what extent is it possible to consider as equivalent research units a large private bank in the U.S., and an equally large, democratically run credit union in Quebec, each filling the same economic purposes? Defining the concept of government is another source of concern. For example, to what extent should European neocorporatist structures, which are run by private parties (mostly unions and employer associations) be considered as part of government? To what extent should the personalized states of Africa [Médard 1983] or Italy [Balducci 1987] be considered the conceptual equivalents of the classic impersonal bureaucratic states of western tradition? As for the problems of business-government relations, thorny questions of equivalence arise with cultures in which the limits between state and private ownership, and especially the limits between state and private control, are uncertain. What is government, what is business, and what is the relationship between the two in economic organizations of which both are owners and managers, and in which both are parties to internal exchanges of resources? The appropriate equivalent in this case may be that of the private joint venture rather than that of the segregation between public and private interests.

Implications. Much more research needs to be done on the role of history, ideology, and values in shaping business-government relations in various nations. One important path is to conduct cross-cultural and global research to determine the various shapes of business-government relations, and then to engage in metaanalysis so that general theoretical principles can be extracted. Further, as multicountry and even global forms of governance become more commonplace, researchers will need to describe and understand the similarities and differences in business-government relationships at this level.

Raising the question of the equivalence of our concepts, research units, and theoretical partitioning of the reality in foreign settings opens the door to a critical look at their true significance, not only as universal concepts, but also as valid American concepts to explain American reality. Myths may be revealed about the way American scholars conceptualize their country's economic environment. One potential myth is that of the so-called adversarial relationship between business and government in the U.S., which might well appear as an epiphenomenon masking an otherwise well-entrenched structure of government support to business.

Business Ethics

Velasquez [1992:1] defines business ethics as "applied ethics. It is the application of our understanding of what is good and right to that assortment of institutions, technologies, transactions, activities, and pursuits which we call 'business.'" Is business ethics something that can be applied to international business and society relationships? What does the international dimension do to enhance our understanding of this concept and its applicability to managerial practice?

Face validity. As a description of a relationship between values and evaluations, or even more simply as a set of rules about how people (and organizations) are to relate to each other, business ethics can be observed in any cultural setting. In terms of content (what those values are) and form (how the evaluations are conducted), differences will be found cross-culturally.

Equivalence. Perhaps more than any other concept that we are considering here, there will be differences in business ethics around the globe. The difficulty is not that observable manifestations of ethical behavior will vary, although they do; it is that the very essence of the concept of ethics itself may be totally heterogeneous across cultures. The debate between ethical absolutism and ethical relativism is not new, but it is far from being closed. Anthropology shows that the debate is fueled not so much by various degrees of cynicism concerning the assessment of good and bad, but by variations among the ways cultures define their identity. Indeed, the present "discourse on business ethics" is considered by many scholars outside the U.S. as yet another example of American exceptionalism.

Each country shares a concern for business ethics, but it casts the debate in different terms. Finding equivalent definitions of ethical behavior may thus at best be a very hazardous task, even among western nations. For example, in one challenging framework, ethics are a reflection of idiosyncratic national traditions, which makes comparisons virtually meaningless. According to that framework, in the U.S., what is ethical is what is fair, within a contract-like exchange among equals; in France, what is ethical is a behavior that is faithful to the moral requirements of the particular craft to which a person belongs, within a time-tested tradition that can be traced back over generations; in Holland, ethical behavior is behavior based on an objective analysis of facts, within a consensual decision-making process where individual pressures are absent [D'Iribarne 1989].

Implications. Scholars such as Getz [1991b] and Wood [1991c] point out the extreme difficulty of saying anything definitive about business ethics in the global context. Some business ethicists (e.g., Donaldson and Dunfee 1991), however, are working to establish the existence of universal ethical principles—for example, equal employment opportunity—which apply to business behavior while accommodating a position of cultural relativity with respect to business ethics situations that are not in the domain of universal principles.

This problem is much more than semantic; it describes the dilemmas facing international managers who experience culturally based value conflicts in their work. For example, what is considered a bribe in America may be seen as an obligation of the higher-status person in Kenya, a token of respect or courtesy in Japan, a friendly gift in Mexico, a charitable gesture to underpaid bureaucrats in Thailand, a political necessity in Saudi Arabia, or an incentive to remove administrative barriers in Indonesia. Further, even in the case where "universal principles" could be established, there may be cultural differences in what kinds of beings are eligible to be fully human and are therefore subject to the principles.

A great deal of research is needed on international, cross-cultural, and global ethics and values. George W. England's [1975] cross-national study of managerial values, for example, needs to be updated, expanded, and replicated. Research such as Wokutch [1982] has conducted on the social change activities of religious organizations could be very profitably expanded into international domains. Efforts to rationalize the study of international business

ethics, such as those of Donaldson and Dunfee [1991], should be continued, even though they may come to a different stance than the universalism intended.

Corporate Social Performance

Corporate social performance (CSP) is defined as "a business organization's configuration of principles of social responsibility, processes of social responsiveness, and policies, programs, and observable outcomes as they relate to the firm's societal relationships" [Wood 1991a:693].

Face validity. One obvious problem with transferring this concept abroad is that corporations do not exist in all cultures. Another problem is that even when corporations do exist in other countries, their formal structure and governance procedures can vary considerably, making it difficult to assess both the "social" and "performance" aspects of the concept. Nevertheless, because this is a structural conceptualization rather than a value-filled one (see Wartick and Wood [forthcoming] for a more extensive discussion), we can observe the three components of CSP—the principles, processes, and consequences that link business organizations to the societies in which they operate.

Equivalence. As with business-government relations and business ethics, CSP will have different meanings in different cultural contexts. Because it is a structural framework expressing relationships rather than "shoulds" or "oughts," it is to some extent dependent upon cultural values for its content and specific measurements and assessments. Further, different legal-political structures will cause variations in both the conceptualization and outcomes of corporate social performance. For example, many of the corporate programs associated with social responsibility in the United States are considered as current operations in Europe simply because they are mandated by law. In addition, what makes the issue of equivalence even more difficult to settle is that the concepts of CSP are constantly evolving. The diffusion of management innovations across nations, especially among Japan, the U.S., and Europe, makes it difficult to assess which behaviors are truly typical of any one nation. At the same time, equivalence may be misleading, because the same observable socially responsible program or behavior may have a very different salience from one nation to the next. In the absence of a broad statistical base, typicality and saliency of CSP components—the basic ingredients of international comparisons—may be elusive.

Implications. Again, the challenge here is to assess to what extent the heterogeneity of observable instances and assessments of corporate social behavior across cultures is a reflection of deep structural differences or is simply a surface phenomenon tied to contingent factors. Constructing objects of study that are valid across cultures is therefore an urgent need before undertaking international comparisons. From an American perspective, this probably means "reconstructing" our research objects as we now know them.

This effort would go a long way toward redefining the role of business, and especially the role of the corporation, in American society. With the advent of the postcommunist world order and the collapse of the Soviet Union, the old reference points have vanished. Indeed, the social performance of the American corporation will continue to be judged partly in relation to traditional American ideals. But it also will be compared to that of its Japanese or European counterparts, which have a longer tradition of embeddedness within their social political structures. In other words, the test of corporate social performance will no longer be American vs. Communist business; it will be American vs. social democratic business, and this latter test is more stringent, because it is more realistic.

In sum, the SIM field would benefit enormously by extending its concepts, frameworks, research methods, and research questions into international, cross-cultural, and global dimensions. In the next section

we consider some of the practical steps that can be taken to accomplish this objective.

INCREASING THE INTERNATIONAL EXPERTISE OF BUSINESS AND SOCIETY SCHOLARS

As the knowledge base of business and society expands to include international and global domains, those who create that knowledge must themselves make changes in their own experience and approach to their subjects. Both personal investment and organizational commitment are needed for SIM scholars to make the transition from a domestic focus to an international one. Specifically, investment and commitment in most of the following areas will be necessary.

Develop a sense of context. An issue being researched cannot be isolated from its historical context (it is the end result of a heritage), its structural context (it is constrained by its interdependencies with neighboring structures), or its cultural context (it is shaped to some extent by the values and symbol systems of the cultures in which it exists). This frame of mind is the single most distinctive characteristic of the scholar interested in international issues. It can be developed at home on home issues (for example, always be prepared to explain *why* American public decision making is done the way it is). In addition, it is good practice to develop a keen awareness of the diversity of the various structural and cultural aspects of collective life at work both at home and abroad; the links between a society's structure and culture; and the links between the sociopolitical context of a firm and its behavior.

Start with a research puzzle and think "foreign." A research puzzle is a discrepancy between one's expectations and one's observations. A good starting base consists of detecting foreign corporate behaviors that do not fit the American model and then asking how the discrepancy can be explained. Here are some examples: Why is the capture of regulatory agencies a sin in the U.S. and a virtue in Europe? What is the rationale for not privatizing profitable state-owned enterprises operating exclusively in the competitive sector? How can cooperative organizations like customer-owned credit unions in Quebec, which are subject both to the social constraints of democratic management and to the economic constraints of a competitive market, be more profitable than their capitalist counterparts operating in the same market? How could continental European companies get away with their presence in apartheid South Africa when their Anglo-Saxon counterparts could not? Why is corporate litigation so prevalent in the U.S. when it is not in comparable industrial countries?

Read the IB literature. International business studies have much in common with business and society studies (see Toyne 1990). Like SIM, they also deal with government policy and cultural patterns; they often face the same issues and obstacles to research as do SIM studies; they are not yet well developed theoretically. Despite these problems, some conceptual contributions of IB can be useful for SIM (e.g., in the area of political risk analysis), as is much of the anecdotal material on which IB textbooks seem to thrive. Furthermore, reading the IB literature is a good way to acclimate oneself to international thinking and to learn about the problems and opportunities that are being faced by international managers.

Get exposure to at least one other culture. Two points are particularly relevant here. First, learn a foreign language. (To paraphrase H. L. Mencken, "If French is too hard for starters, take up British first.") Nothing else is so useful for learning cross-cultural differences in symbols and meanings. Language and thinking/perceiving patterns are tightly linked; it is impossible to truly understand another culture without knowing its language. Even a passing acquaintance with another language or two can be enough to increase one's awareness of the vital role language plays in cross-cultural differences.

Second, spend time in a foreign country. A two-week vacation or conference trip abroad is better than nothing, but it will not provide a solid basis for understanding intercultural similarities and differences. In fact, from a scholar's perspective, a short stay abroad can do more harm than good by implanting superficial and false impressions about "how things are done" in other countries. Frequent short-term travel to one location is better; as colleagues come to know and trust each other, deeper information may be shared and more learning can take place. The best solution for scholars is to live abroad for six months or more, conducting research and staying in close contact with scholars of the host country. A long stay in a foreign country is educational on many counts: linguistic mannerisms and idioms are learned, questions can be asked again as new information is attained, customs can be observed in many settings and across a broad sample of people, and the visiting scholar (who is now the "foreigner") experiences cycles of emotional and intellectual connection and distancing with the host culture: euphoria and depression, confusion and understanding, similarities and differences, judgment and acceptance. A sabbatical is a good way to start. Subsequent joint research projects will keep the experience alive.

Get training in comparative research methodology. Even for purely descriptive research, some training in comparative research methodology is warranted. Such training draws attention to the opportunities of international research and helps one develop the "reflex" skills needed to function in international environments. Quantitative comparative methodology is usually the best place to start, for it builds on basic concepts that are familiar to most researchers, and it provides all the benchmarks for high-quality research in the international field. Qualitative research methodology expertise can then be developed through a familiarity with the issues faced routinely in this type of research.

Problems such as reactivity, validity, selective perception, cultural "filters" on observations, data recording and analysis, and ethical dilemmas facing the researcher are perhaps magnified when the qualitative research project is undertaken internationally. Eventually, comparative qualitative research methodology becomes a must for any international SIM research which seeks to go beyond the level of statistical description.

Teach a class or a course on a foreign process or issue. In international business and society, as in any other discipline, teaching is the best way for the teacher to learn. An easy progression would be to start with one class, then write a case (perhaps with the help of foreign students), then develop an elective course. Topical examples for a single class lecture or a case, on which literature is readily available, include the following:

a. Contrasting environmental protection policies in the U.S. and the United Kingdom (U.K.)
b. Comparing nuclear power policy in the U.S. and France.
c. Understanding Germany's "market social economy."
d. Understanding Canada's "elite accommodation process" (insiders' lobbying).
e. Understanding Italy's underground economy.
f. Understanding the Japanese government's "developmental" industrial policy.
g. Understanding the social functions of corruption in the Third World.
h. Understanding Africa's "parallel" micromarkets (off-market markets).
i. Understanding corporate social accounting in Europe.

It is best for scholars to work within their own areas of expertise. There is a wealth of books on foreign processes (e.g., in the environmental protection area), written in English by American scholars. Although their conclusions may be (and often are) criticized by foreign scholars, they are rarely faulted for major errors, and they provide the easiest access to expertise in the international dimensions of business and society. Depending upon the topic, there is often more literature written by American scholars on foreign countries than by nationals of these countries (in the SIM field, the U.S. research-producing machine is by far the most extensive in the world).

Another avenue to learning is to internationalize the existing curriculum in business and society. Using comparative material—contrasting U.S. material with material on foreign countries—is perhaps the best approach, although some courses are now including global-level content (e.g., global environmental problems and solutions). U.S.-written cases on foreign topics are becoming more plentiful and add a practical, realistic dimension of complexity to SIM internationalization efforts. Foreign students can be a valuable resource as well for giving a foreign perspective on a typical American issue or for researching an issue in their home country.

Join forces with foreign scholars. Teaming up with foreign colleagues can be a shortcut approach to cross-cultural research; each colleague conducts the relevant research in his/her own country, and papers are written together. This approach can go a long way toward solving the language and cultural barriers that haunt this type of research. Nevertheless, it is a high-risk and often frustrating proposition. Casual teams may not work well together; cultural barriers may still exist between the researchers themselves; communication channels may be slow and very costly. Cross-cultural team research is most likely to succeed when the team scholars have durable institutional support, for example, a teaching and research covenant between two universities, possibly with accords of cooperation at the national and international levels.

Do research on nonmainstream topics in the U.S. Not all scholars interested in extending their research base into comparative work can commit to long-term overseas strategies. For those who cannot, a perfectly acceptable alternative strategy is available. Many of the benefits of international comparative work can be obtained at minimum risk by researching nonmainstream topics in the U.S. For example, one easy way to get a flair for cross-cultural research is to research issues relating to marginal cultures in the U.S. (e.g., ghetto economics, minority pressure groups, migrant labor). Other approaches are to research American expatriate managers back home and foreign expatriate managers posted in the U.S., or to research U.S.-based divisions responsible for foreign operations or the adaptation of foreign divisions to the U.S. environment. Yet another idea would be to trace corporate practices in social issues management from U.S. headquarters out to their foreign subsidiaries, or to research the transformation of SIM practices between foreign headquarters and their U.S.-based subsidiaries. Financing such research is easier and cheaper. Eventually this work may provide access to international research networks.

CONCLUSION

For business scholars, few trends are more exciting—or threatening—than the rise of a global business environment. In this paper we have shown how research on the international dimensions of business and society is filled with opportunities. We have tried to conceptualize this emerging field into research purposes and levels of analysis. We have demonstrated the benefits of international research for teaching, research, and practice. We have laid out exemplars of research topics. We have also indicated some of the difficulties of this kind of research—the threatening side of it. Solutions to these difficulties have been suggested, and some of them require nothing more than researching the U.S. business environment with a keener eye.

Overall, we hope to have conveyed the sheer joy of international research. For many of us, studying the international dimensions of business and society is as much a philosophical choice as it is a trade. We have shown how the international, cross-cultural, and global dimensions of social issues, business-government relations, business ethics, and more can add a richness to SIM theory, an integrity (e.g., a freedom from ethnocentricity), and a generalizability that the field currently lacks. The purpose of international study goes beyond what the academic community gains from the constant extension of its interests into outer spheres. Through meeting, understanding, and explaining others to ourselves and to our peers, we hope to help prepare for a better world. Researching the international dimensions of business and society is therefore one avenue to fulfilling the highest expectations of academics.

■ ■ ■

COMMENTARIES
Philip L. Cochran

*Future Directions in International
Business and Society Research*

International research in the Business and Society, or SIM, field is a relatively new phenomenon, as Wood and Pasquero note, and it will become more important in the future. I am, therefore, particularly encouraged that a conference devoted to exploring the theory, research, and institutional arrangements of International Business (IB) should include a session on SIM perspectives.

The SIM field certainly can learn from the IB field. The SIM field is rapidly moving into the international arena and is beginning to adopt many of the research techniques pioneered by the IB area. If some of the domain of the IB field is absorbed by the functional areas within the colleges of business then the IB field may have to shift its domain toward that of the SIM field.

Evidence of such domain shifts in both fields can be seen in the 1990 founding of a new professional association, the International Association for Business and Society (IABS). IABS held its first international conference in Leuven, Belgium (1991). The format of the conference was designed not only to present research papers but also to give participants an opportunity to participate in international research ventures in Europe.

World Views

Historically, within colleges of business there have been two very different and distinct world views. One view, which Hogner calls the Positivist Paradigm, sees the entire world through the lens of a single paradigm. The other view, which Hogner calls the Naturalist Paradigm, uses a wide range of theories and observes the world through a variety of different lenses.

This dichotomy in world views is hauntingly reminiscent of the distinction made by Isaiah Berlin in his famous essay "The Hedgehog and the Fox."

> There is a line among the fragments of the Greek poet Archilochus that says: 'The fox knows many things, but the hedgehog knows one big thing.' Scholars have differed about the correct interpretation of these dark words, which may mean no more than that the fox, for all his cunning, is defeated by the hedgehog's one defence. Taken figuratively, however, the words can be made to yield a sense in which they mark one of the deepest differences that divides writers and thinkers, and, it may be, human beings generally. For there exists a great chasm between those, on one side, who relate everything to a single central vision, one system less or more coherent or articulate, in terms of which they understand, think and feel—a single, universal, organizing principle in terms of which alone all that they are and say has significance—and, on the other side, those who pursue many ends, often unrelated and even contradictory, connected, if at all, only in some *de facto* way, for some psychological or physiological cause, related by no single moral or aesthetic principle; these last lead lives, perform acts, and entertain ideas that are centrifugal rather than centripetal, their thought is scattered or diffused, moving on many

levels, seizing upon the essence of a vast variety of experiences and objects for what they are in themselves, without, consciously or unconsciously, seeking to fit them into, or exclude them from, any one unchanging, all-embracing, sometimes self-contradictory and incomplete, at times fanatical, unitary inner vision. The first kind of intellectual and artistic personality belongs to the hedgehogs, the second to the foxes; and without insisting on a rigid classification, we may, without too much fear of contradiction, say that, in this sense, Dante belongs to the first category, Shakespeare to the second; Plato, Lucretius, Pascal, Spinoza, Hegel, Dostoevsky, Nietzsche, Ibsen, Kafka are, in varying degrees, hedgehogs; Herotodus, Aristotle, Horace, Erasmus, Molière, Goethe, Pushkin, Balzac, Joyce are foxes. [1986: 1–2]

In this sense those trained in finance, accounting, and economics tend to be hedgehogs. Those trained in organizational behavior, IB, and SIM tend to be foxes. The former adhere to what Hogner called the Positivist Paradigm. The latter espouse what he calls the Naturalist Paradigm. Clearly the authors of the other papers in this chapter adhere to the Naturalist Paradigm. All are foxes.

The Collapse of the Positivist Paradigm

The Positivist Paradigm, however, might be on the verge of collapse. Hogner, in a much broader and wider ranging discussion, basically argues this point. The thrust is narrower in scope and looks primarily at the Positivist Paradigm as it appears in colleges of business. For my purposes, the Positivist Paradigm is summarized as that body of theory which suggests that the only reason for the existence of the corporation is to maximize the return to the shareholders.

The emergence of the modern era in finance (the heart of the Positivist Paradigm in business schools) began with a series of powerful papers published some forty years ago. These papers transformed the academic area of corporate finance from a descriptive field to an energetic normative area. It is not within my scope to trace the evolution of the finance area here, but it covered such critical areas as the irrelevance of dividends, the efficient markets hypothesis, the capital asset pricing model, and so on. In business schools it resulted in the emphasis on finance. In the business world it leads to an emphasis on Wall Street. It reasonably could be argued that the emergence of finance as a normative discipline eventually lead to the acquisition, merger, and leverage binge of the 1980s.

Within colleges of business, the effect of this paradigm has been almost imperialistic. Some subscribe to the Positivist Paradigm and teach in business schools; they are rather blunt in their opinion that all research within schools of business must conform to this paradigm. These are the hedgehogs of schools of business. For them descriptive research, international research, ethics research, and such are either suspect or simply wrong because this research is not consistent with this unitary view of the world.

However, a series of recent and forthcoming articles (chief among them Fama and French [1992]) seriously question some of the fundamental tenets underlying this field. For example, the concept of beta as the sole variable for explaining stock returns may well be dead. The death of beta is a serious, perhaps fatal blow to the capital asset pricing model.

This has lead some researchers in the finance area to suggest that finance might be on the verge of a major paradigm shift. It is felt that the field might have to return to its descriptive roots. Others are examining the anthropology literature for new models. For example, an article by Frankfurter and Lane [1992] examines the Kwakiutl Potlatch and notes connections between this Pacific Coast Native American ceremony and the dividend policies of modern corporations.

As Hogner notes, such a paradigm shift may lead to a reevaluation of the role of business in society. It might lead to a greater degree of consensus on basic principles. Whatever the results of this possible paradigm shift, the next several years hold the promise of being dynamic and interesting years for academe.

Cowboy Capitalism vs. Cooperative Capitalism In his paper, Freeman coins the term "cowboy capitalism" to describe the prevailing view that the business environment is an environment of unbridled competition. Though Freeman does not use this language, it is obvious that this view of the environment of a capitalist economy is derived from the Positivist Paradigm. Freeman argues that if business is modeled after the Positivist Paradigm then the metaphors of war would seem appropriate.

He is correct. Sun Tzu's *The Art of War* [1971], B. H. Liddell Hart's *Strategy* [1974], and Machiavelli's *The Prince* [1907] are important and classic treatises on military strategy. They also are often required reading in doctoral seminars in corporate strategy. They are all normally sold in the strategy sections of publishers' booths at academic conferences.

Freeman is also correct when he suggests that the metaphor of business competition as war leads to little if any role for ethics. In previous centuries, there was a military field of ethics. However, twentieth century military strategy now includes the carpet bombing of cities and the doctrine of mutual assured destruction. This doctrine of taking the war to the civilian populations has effectively signaled the end of military ethics.

The good news is that the military metaphor for business competition is simply wrong. Business competition is very different from military competition. War is by its very nature a negative sum game; it is destructive competition. While there may be winners in a war, the average participant in a war is worse off than before. In business competition, while there may be losers, the average participant is better off. Business competition is creative and constructive. It is cooperative competition. It is a positive sum game. The failure of the general public and the media to grasp this simple point has in large part lead to the generally poor image of business and to such idiotic economic policies as protectionism.

A theory of cooperative capitalism could be based on a Naturalist Paradigm. It would recognize that business activity is a positive sum game. In a positive sum game, there is not only a role for ethics but a positive need for ethics. In a positive sum game there is a surplus that must be divided among the participants. Ethics can address the manner in which this surplus should be divided. Thus, Freeman is correct when he contends that "[s]eeing business as cooperative, friendly to ethics, based upon truth telling, promise keeping, value creating, and relationship building is a good start. . . ." [p. 135] Business must be viewed in this manner if there is to be a role for ethics in business.

Toward a Stakeholder Theory of the Firm
Freeman, Wood, and Pasquero call for a stakeholder view or model of the firm. Hogner contends that the liberal economic model, which assumed the economic and social spheres were separate and distinct, is in the process of disintegrating.

The concept of stakeholder was defined by Thompson [1967] as "those groups which make a difference" and by Freeman [1984] as "any group or individual who can affect or is affected by the achievement of the organization's objectives."

Aoki [1984:7] contends that the traditional theories of the firm have in common the assumption that the firm is being managed "in the sole interests of a particular group of its participants, identified as either shareholders, managers, or workers. They try to capture the essence of the firm by focusing their analytical attentions on the utility maximization of a dominant class of participants. . . ."

In a more recent article Aoki [1990:24] suggests a "J-model" (for Japanese model) theory of the firm that seeks to balance owner and employee interests. He contends that the success of the Japanese firm is a function of the fact that it balances the needs of the stockholders with those of the employees. He further recognizes that this J-Model "is perhaps fated to be subsumed under the yet to be developed general theory of the firm. . . ."

More recently, Kotter and Heskett [1992] have suggested what amounts to a three dimensional extension of Aoki's model. They contend that firms which pay attention to their major stakeholders (customers, employees, and stockholders) show much higher rates of increase in sales and in profits than do firms which satisfy only one or two of their major stakeholders. Brenner and Cochran [1991] have recently proposed an even broader theory based upon satisfying the competing demands of an even broader range of stakeholders.

Theories of corporate social responsibility are derived from theories of the firm. The neoclassical theory of the firm, based upon the Positivist Paradigm, leads inexorably to narrow views of corporate social responsibility such as that espoused by Milton Friedman. He equates proper management behavior with decisions based primarily upon economic value tradeoffs and profit maximization. Given this premise, one is led to the conclusion that firms have no ethical obligations beyond those to their shareholders. For this reason, Milton Friedman argued "there is one and only one social responsibility of business—to increase its resources and engage in activities designed to increase its profits so long as it stays within the rules of the game . . ." [1962:133].

Ethics: Performance Enhancing vs. Performance Harming
Do ethical business practices lead to greater profits or decreased profits? Is corporate social responsibility related positively or negatively to corporate financial performance? This has been a topic of some interest in the SIM literature. Cochran and Wood [1984], Aupperle, Carroll, and Hatfield [1985] among others have explored this issue empirically. The overall conclusion seems to be that there may be some slight positive correlation between corporate social responsibility and financial performance.

The anecdotal support for this positive relationship stems from stakeholder theory. If firms have good relationships with various stakeholder groups then those groups are less likely to oppose the firm's economic activities. If, for example, Exxon desired to engage in drilling or transporting oil in any environmentally sensitive areas then all the major environmental groups would surely oppose their initiative.

However, it is all too easy to get hung up on this dichotomy. One of Milton Friedman's [1970] key critiques of the concept of corporate social responsibility revolves around the argument that if an activity will yield a profit then it should be pursued for its own sake and not on the basis of "corporate social responsibility." He argues that any activity which is pursued strictly on the basis of corporate social responsibility must lose money.

In one sense he is correct. In a perfectly rational world, producing a safe product, creating a fulfilling work environment, and hiring and promoting women and minorities should be done not only because it is the right thing to do but also because it will enhance the firm's bottom line. But the world is not perfectly rational. Prejudice, bias, bigotry, and discrimination have plagued mankind for all of recorded history. They are strong motivators. Firms that engage in such practices almost certainly earn less money over the long run than do firms which do not.

But in another sense, he is wrong. While it is encouraging that on average good ethics lead to higher profits, this is not and cannot be the only justification for engaging in such activities. One can show counterexamples where good ethics lead to reduced profits. There may be powerful arguments for engaging in ethical behavior. Ethics must dominate profits, not vice versa.

Reconciling Cultural Relativism with Ethical Absolutism

We are operating today in a world that, in Berlin's [1988] words, is simultaneously being pulled together by centripetal forces and being torn apart by centrifugal forces. We see the possibility of a North American Free Trade Area. On the other hand we see the disintegration of the Soviet Union, the splintering of Yugoslavia, the possible separation of Quebec from Canada, and calls for home rule in Scotland.

These two forces (centripetal and centrifugal) are operating in the arena of ethics as well. On one hand we may be entering a world of global monoculturalism. Freeman, here, discusses satellite dishes in the jungle of Indonesia which receive CNN. This is part of a worldwide phenomenon. Today most consumer products are designed and built for consumers worldwide. In the future, movies and television, manifestations (for better or worse) of national cultures, will increasingly be produced for worldwide audiences. This inevitably will lead to greater cultural homogeneity or to monoculturalism, and would repeat the experience of the U.S. over the bulk of this century. Today, thanks to CNN, ABC, CBS, and NBC the U.S. culture is becoming more homogenous. I can clearly remember an era in which U.S. culture was more diverse. Twenty-five years ago I had never been east of Montana. The culture shock I faced going to college in Boston was severe. I literally couldn't understand the Long Island or Alabama dialects of some of my new classmates. Today the regional dialects and accents are muted.

Today I am more comfortable in London or Seoul than I was in Boston or New York in the mid-1960s. In virtually any major city worldwide in addition to watching CNN on a Sony television, I can stay at a Hilton, rent a Toyota from Hertz, eat a Big Mac, use my MasterCard, and purchase an *Economist*.

The cynic may decry this commonization or democratization of the world. However, the firms that succeed in the world marketplace are those that have proven themselves to be the most efficient suppliers of consumer wants in human history. Just as the supermarket forced the corner grocery store out of business, the most efficient manufacturers, retailers, and service providers will prevail in the long run. The net result will be a world in which most products and services are similar. The twenty-first century will see the emergence of a reasonably homogeneous market and this in turn will result in a reasonably homogeneous culture.

At the same time, we see the parallel emergence of multiculturalism and its sensitivity to diversity and multiple "voices." Women and minorities are beginning to break into the ranks of senior management of U.S. firms. This trend is occurring in firms in other developed countries as well, albeit with a lag in certain countries. Thus as we enter the era of monoculturalism we must simultaneously become more sensitive to and aware of multiculturalism. These trends are not as contradictory as they might seem on the surface. We must, as Freeman notes, reframe the issue. We must find a new basis for conversation.

I contend that on the level of ethics we will see something very similar. We have already seen a growing global agreement on a wide range of basic issues. Slavery is no longer legal anywhere. Women have the right to vote in most societies and equal rights in the more progressive societies. According to Fukoyama [1989], given the fall of Marxism, democratic capitalism has been all but universally accepted as the only viable organizing system for modern industrial society. Is there any intelligent person who believes that apartheid is the wave of the future, that the handicapped will be hidden away in institutions, that child labor will become common, or that the emphasis on workplace safety is a passing fad?

Modern business must operate in a wide range of different cultures, each with its own perspectives on ethical issues. Reconciling the seemingly contradictory trends of accepting diversity, but insisting on ethical absolutism, will be a major challenge to business in the next several decades.

I am encouraged, therefore, by Freeman's contention that "moral relativism has been completely discredited." I only wish that this message was more widely disseminated. It concerns me that Wood and Pasquero contend that "the debate between ethical absolutism and ethical relativism is not new, but it is far from being closed." [p. 154] Clearly the arguments that demonstrate the death of moral relativism are not widely known or accepted.

International Business/Business and Society Links   The fields of IB and SIM have emerged independently. They have separate domains. Historically they have examined different research questions. Just as clearly, these two academic fields are drifting toward a common center. They may never meet in this center but each can learn from the other.

The SIM field, as argued earlier, is becoming more global in scope. I would go so far as to contend that in the future there will be less and less significant SIM research that is not international in scope. I suspect that most, if not all, future doctoral dissertations in the SIM area will explore SIM phenomena from a multinational perspective.

Though all politics might be local, all issues are now global. Freeman further notes that the environment is now a global issue, but so is virtually any other issue that concerns business. Now, employee privacy, consumerism, and ethnic diversity are all global issues. Because of the trend toward monoculturalism, any social, political, or legal issue that begins to affect business operations in one country will probably soon affect business operations in other countries.

The IB field is, paradoxically, beginning to suffer from its own success. As colleges of business increasingly attempt to internationalize their curriculum, the various functional areas within the college attempt to internationalize their offerings. As a result, there is the distinct possibility that independent, stand-alone IB courses will be eliminated.

The IB area may have to ally itself with the SIM area. The two are currently linked in the new AACSB accreditation requirements which state that "both undergraduate and MBA curricula should provide an understanding of perspectives that form the context for business. Coverage should include: ethical and global issues; the influence of political, social, legal, regulatory, environmental, and technological issues; and the impact of demographic diversity on organizations."

Key Research Areas I suspect that every researcher could outline a different set of key research areas. I would contend, however, that in the future most SIM research must be international, cross-national, or transnational. Just as it is of little interest or importance to compare corporate governance practices in Pennsylvania with those in California, future studies which just focus on the U.S., Great Britain, or Japan will seem terribly provincial and not very useful to firms operating in a wide range of countries. Some of the key areas of international SIM research in the next decade probably will include the following areas.

Business Ethics. A number of researchers such as Freeman and Donaldson are mapping out important new areas in the area of IB ethics. The attempt to reconcile ethical absolutism with multiculturalism will be very important to this emerging field.

Corporate Social Performance. Freeman notes that the concept of corporate social performance, slippery enough within the context of a single culture, becomes extremely difficult when dealing with a firm that has operations in many countries.

Corporate Governance. There is some cross-national work in the area of corporate governance. However, much more remains to be done. A new journal devoted entirely to the area of corporate governance, *Corporate Governance, an International Review*, is scheduled to begin publication.

Corporate Social Responsibility. What might be considered responsible within one culture might not be within another. Responsibilities can be compounded by the demands of international agencies, and responsibility to whom becomes much more critical in the international arena.

Corporate Crime. I am aware of little work outside the U.S. and Australia on corporate crime. Is there, for example, any Japanese literature on corporate crime? If so, how does it compare to the U.S. literature?

Government Relations. The relations between firms and governments vary widely throughout the world. Wood and Pasquero contend that SIM researchers traditionally have a too narrow focus when it comes to questions dealing with business and government relations.

Public Affairs/External Relations. Once again, little is known about the international dimensions of public affairs.

Stakeholder Theory. Stakeholder theory is an area that has only recently emerged in the international arena. I would like to suggest that a third dimension be added to Freeman's Figure 2 which would include various countries and cultures as well as supranational entities.

In conclusion, I would like to reiterate my basic premise that the fields of IB and SIM have similar histories and are currently facing similar problems. Each has the opportunity to learn from the other and, perhaps in a synergistic fashion, each can significantly strengthen the other.

Steven L. Wartick

From "Business and Society"
to "Businesses in Societies":
Comments on the Papers by Hogner,
Freeman, and Wood and Pasquero

You do not have to be an anthropologist, a sociologist, a philosopher, an economist, and a political scientist to understand and appreciate Business and Society or SIM (Social Issues in Management) scholarship, but it would certainly help. The papers by Hogner, Freeman, and Wood and Pasquero illustrate why this assertion is true.

Each of the authors was given the task

of examining the various SIM frameworks and theories that have been developed; their ontological, epistemological, and human nature assumptions; and their ability to contribute to the systematic body of knowledge on International Business (IB) cross-sectional interaction. Hogner begins this exercise by contrasting positivist and naturalist paradigms. Freeman engages us in conversation relating to multiculturalism and ethics. Wood and Pasquero focus most directly on the field of SIM by providing a bridge between what is and what could be. If three more papers from SIM scholars were requested, additional insights might be provided. However, the works from Hogner, Freeman, and Wood and Pasquero do provide an accurate view of the breadth of current topics relating to the internationalization of business as reflected in SIM study.

More to the point, the three papers, when considered collectively, present an interesting contrast of how SIM scholars (like those in many other areas of business study) are grappling with the impact of globalization on their field of inquiry. From its beginnings as a field in the late 1950s and early 1960s, SIM has continually recognized the importance of the international arena (see Fritzsche and Wartick [1987]). As in most areas, however, the international arena was considered to be more tangential than central to the crucial questions of the day. It wasn't until the middle or late 1970s that international SIM topics pushed their way to the forefront of scholarly inquiry, and it was not until a decade later that the study of the international dimension of SIM started to take on a life of its own.

As suggested by the title of these comments, what we are seeing now is a "competing framework" approach as we move from the study of "business and society" to the study of "businesses in societies." The earliest form of the competition between these two perspectives can be found in the early 1960s. After the widespread 1950s argument about the proper role of American business (see Bowen [1953], Galbraith [1958], Levitt [1958], and Friedman [1962]), two University of Washington scholars offered competing analyses of SIM questions. Withers [1966], in his book entitled *Business in Society*, saw the field through a management theory lens: changes in society meant changes in management planning, leadership, staffing, control, and organization. McGuire [1963] in his book entitled *Business and Society* took an institutional approach; the interaction between and among dynamic societal institutions led to changing roles and responsibilities for business. McGuire's perspective won out and for twenty years the institutional approach dominated the field. Now, with the increasing globalization of business and the wide variety of institutions which appear to influence businesses which operate in multiple societies, the "businesses in societies" perspective has reemerged. Simply put, those who see the field becoming "businesses in societies" believe that the traditional unisocietal conceptualizations of the interface between business and society are inadequate for international analysis.

This competition between frameworks is more than just semantics, more than just the discovery of a comparative approach to analysis, and more than just different applications of old concepts. The competition is a challenge to SIM scholars to rethink the fundamental tenets of their field and to fully integrate international/transnational/global considerations into their frameworks. The competition contains a call for SIM scholars to reexamine their assumptions and methods in order to develop studies which more fully address the complexities attendant to the internationalization of business.

The three papers presented in this session of the conference reflect the developing "businesses in societies" side of the competing frameworks. Each paper continues to adhere to the field's standard definitions of "business" and "society," i.e., that business is a process of converting inputs into outputs and that society is the functional equivalent of nation states. These definitions allow for treating as variables such matters as: (a) public versus private ownership of property, (b) productive versus redistributive business activities, (c) alternative types of legal or structural organizational forms, (d) "shared values" within and among interest groups, and (e) intrasocietal power distributions. Beyond adhering to the basic definitions of "business" and "society," however, the three papers take off into alternative views of what the "businesses in societies" framework could or should be.

Each paper, for example, is primarily targeted at a different level of abstraction. Hogner maintains an institutional level of generalization. Freeman's discussion of ethics pertains mostly to individuals within organizational contexts. Wood and Pasquero focus most directly on organizations within varying societal contexts.

The three papers differ in their approach as well. Hogner appears to be a SIM insider looking out at other areas, Freeman is an insider looking into the core of SIM method, and Wood and Pasquero are insiders looking around at SIM accomplishments and deficiencies.

Without doubt, these differences in levels of abstraction and approaches are key factors which underlie the authors' views of how business should be put back into society. When Hogner presents his perspective of "businesses in societies" as a contrast of the positivist idea of disembedding the economy and the naturalist notion of the "economy in society" model, he is describing a fundamental change in SIM method. When Freeman makes a parallel point with his criticism of "cowboy capitalism" and his advocacy of a pragmatic, interactionalist framework for ethics analysis, he is calling for change in the way that we conceptualize it. When Wood and Pasquero develop their view of "businesses in societies" by examining the "symbolic and structural equivalence" which result when current concepts (i.e., stakeholders, business-government relations, business ethics, and corporate social performance) are extended

from the American experience to the international arena, they advocate change in traditional constructs, variables, and theory.

Of all of the impacts which globalization has had (and could have) on SIM study, this common theme of putting business activity back into the context of societies is the most important. At some point, there may be global principles which transcend the economic, social, political, and technological dimensions of any single society. At some point, all nations of the world may adhere to the same economic, social, political, and technological precepts. The authors of these three papers argue that until that time comes, however, SIM scholarship must attempt to incorporate societal contexts or, at the very least, acknowledge when these contexts are being ignored. This contention appears to be the central theme which unites the three works, and it is a theme which SIM scholars should carefully consider.

Beyond this general "businesses in societies" theme there are four more specific topics which are addressed in the papers and are especially relevant for this conference: (1) the status quo in SIM study, (2) the centrality of economics, (3) the relationship between SIM and IBS, and (4) the implications of "businesses in societies" for IBS. The remainder of my comments will focus on these four topics.

The Status Quo in Business and Society Study

Each of the three papers expresses a dissatisfaction with the status quo in SIM study. Each argues that in one way or another what we are doing in SIM research is simply inadequate to understand, explain, and predict the interface between business and society in the international arena.

According to Hogner, the problem lies in epistemology. The positivist paradigm calls for objective, separable social scientists who rely on value-free reductionism to measure mechanistic relationships among smaller and smaller variables. The reality of globalization calls for holistic analyses which relate to larger and larger entities and place business performance in the context of time and values (values of the "knower" as well as values of the "known"). Drawing from the physical sciences as well as from economics, anthropology, sociology, and management studies, Hogner argues effectively that we have moved in the wrong direction and that the emerging naturalist paradigm is bringing SIM study back on target.

Freeman focuses specifically on business, ethics, and society (BES) and states his concern over the status quo in the context of "the problem of the two realms." For Freeman, the issue is conceptualization. In SIM study (and in business practice), business and ethics are viewed as separable entities which somehow interact. The key research questions are how does business influence ethics and how does ethics influence business? With technological development, multicultural exposure, and cross-societal issues attendant to globalization, discussing ethics as some separable entity which exists on the margins of business practice results only in superficial analysis. Thus, according to Freeman, it is no "small wonder that a standard application of the BES ways of thinking fall short. Their development was never intended to take account of the complexity inherent in today's world, or if it was the result was facile." [p. 133] Like Hogner, Freeman suggests that current thinking in SIM is simply inadequate when placed in the international arena.

More so than either Hogner or Freeman, Wood and Pasquero target the breadth of SIM study in their dissatisfaction with the status quo. After looking at both the levels of complexity of international SIM research and the major dimensions of international SIM issues, they conclude that scholarship in our area falls short on the basis of description, explanation, and understanding. For Wood and Pasquero, the need is for an escape from the ethnocentricity which characterizes SIM scholarship (see their discussions of governmental legitimacy, na-

tionalism, protectionism, and stockholders versus stakeholders). Unlike Hogner and Freeman, however, Wood and Pasquero do not call for scrapping and replacing existing paradigms or conceptualizations. Instead, they argue that "the SIM field would benefit enormously by *extending* its concepts, frameworks, research methods, and research questions into international, cross-cultural, and global dimensions" (emphasis added). [p. 156] Their central point, however, is still the same as Hogner and Freeman's: the status quo in SIM scholarship is simply inadequate to address the realities of globalization.

Collectively, these three papers offer valid criticism of the status quo in SIM. It also should be noted, however, that SIM scholars never seem happy with the status quo. In fact, most would acknowledge that the field itself is premised on challenging the status quo. When others argued shareholder dominance in the 1980s, we opened the discussion of stakeholder importance and corporate governance. When others were glorifying the business practices of the 1980s, we were asking questions about business ethics. When others tried to ignore the managerial implications of public policy development, we incorporated these limits into decision making analyses. By being slightly more than irreverent toward the status quo, SIM scholarship has raised a number of critical research questions.

Further, most would agree that the "search for a paradigm" in SIM which Preston [1975] identified nearly two decades ago continues as we move through the 1990s. Unlike other fields of business study which adopt and embrace a central academic religion and then define themselves vis-à-vis others using some narrowly constructed central paradigm, SIM scholars have never felt such a need. The downside is that the field will never be mistaken for a discipline. The positive side is that through multidisciplinary approaches to answering important research questions, we now have a breadth and depth of knowledge about business ethics, corporate social performance, and public/social policy implications of managerial decisions which were probably not achievable under the rigidity of a common academic theology.

My concern, though, is that we should not be too quick to discard or even substantially revise the existing frameworks and concepts which have led to the successes in SIM scholarship until we more thoroughly understand the consequences of doing so. Must the naturalist paradigm replace the positivist paradigm or can they coexist as complements rather than substitutes? Similarly, must pragmatism prevail over idealism especially in conversations relating to ethics and morality? Is the importance of the internationalization of SIM principles, concepts, and methods merely an issue-specific concern for matters such as environmentalism? Answers to these questions must remain for others to address, but they are important considerations attendant to the authors' dissatisfaction with the status quo of SIM study.

The Centrality of Economics

A second topic addressed in each of the three papers relates to the manner in which economic motivation gets treated in IB study (as well as most other areas of business study) as the only thing that matters for business organizations. Hogner tackles the issue at the institutional level of analysis by citing a number of scholars from diverse disciplines who are challenging the "spiritualism" and "protected position" which underlie the centrality of economics in business activity. Freeman connects the overemphasis on economics to the "deep seated belief among business school faculty and executives that business and business theory are amoral, [and that] business is seen as solely, or primarily, an activity best described by the metaphors and tropes of economics." [p. 131] Implicit in much of the argument by Wood and Pasquero is their concern with the "powerfully symbolic but *unreal* idea about the role of neoclassical

economics in managerial decision making" (emphasis added) [p. 146].

For those outside the area of SIM, caution should be exercised before jumping to the conclusion that these scholars, as well as others in the field, believe that economics is never important to business activity, and should therefore be *disregarded entirely*. Although sometimes overstating their case, SIM scholars have always recognized the imperative of economic performance in business organizations (see Carroll [1979]). Still, there is indeed a long-standing tradition among SIM scholars which says that ignoring the social, political, and technological dimensions of business enterprise or relying solely on economic interpretations of these dimensions of business enterprise results only in superficial analyses. On the level of the firm, economics is certainly a major consideration, but it is not the only consideration. SIM scholars will argue that business organizations have never been economic organizations exclusively and that for most societal concerns the social, political, and technological dimensions of business activity are just as important as its economic dimension. Within the field, whenever the economic dimension of business becomes overemphasized something of a "family squabble" ensues, centered around reasserting the multidimensionality of business.

I am drawing attention to this point because the implications for internationalizing SIM study are enormous. As the SIM field moves toward internationalization, the importance of all sides to business activity must be reaffirmed. I believe it is for this reason that Hogner, Freeman, and Wood and Pasquero each make their case against overemphasizing the economic dimension of business enterprise. The uniqueness of SIM study rests not with telling economists what they already know or even arguing about narrowly constructed conclusions. The uniqueness rests with factoring into the analysis additional dimensions of business activity that are no less important to management. For SIM scholars it is critical to know the economic costs and benefits of locating a plant in a particular part of the world, but it is no less important to understand the social, political and technological implications of the decision for the host country, the home country, and transnational alliances. Others try to make us become economists, but we refuse. Simply put, SIM scholars choose to be something other than economists. This point seems well worth reiterating and reemphasizing in the context of international SIM study.

The Relationship Between Business and Society Study and International Business Study

A third specific topic considered in each paper involves reflection on where SIM and IB stand vis-à-vis one another in terms of the issues raised by the authors. For example, Hogner suggests that SIM study is slightly ahead of IB study in relation to the shift from a positivist to a naturalist paradigm. Through the work of Frederick, Logsdon and Palmer, and Freeman, Hogner suggests that: "the new paradigm may already be formed in Business and Society. All we need to do is recognize its new normalcy." [p. 127] Conversely, through the works of Dunning and Boddewyn, Hogner sees only the beginning of a paradigm disturbance and concludes that: "we know that engaging the full paradigm shift will require substantive change in the process and form of IB study. . . . If IB study assumes a new 'normalcy' . . . it will be a better and stronger science." [p. 130]

In relation to matters of ethics, Freeman sees SIM as much advanced beyond IB understandings. Freeman argues that: "the dominant view of ethics in IB is that it is best understood as a set of individual values or principles which may be socially and culturally determined . . . [but] there are few if any serious BES people who would endorse this view." [p. 134] The mere description which Freeman sees in current IB study of ethics is "comparatively inconsequential." SIM study goes well beyond descriptive points to include normative analysis.

Wood and Pasquero appear to be at an entirely different point from either Hogner or Freeman. For Wood and Pasquero, IB study is a source of knowledge for SIM just as, by implication, SIM should be a source of knowledge for IB. They suggest that SIM scholars should spend more time with the IB literature and texts. Both the anecdotal and conceptual contributions of IB can be of great benefit to SIM scholarship as it seeks to internationalize. Wood and Pasquero suggest more interaction among international scholars and within international scholarship.

Although all three papers make valid points, Wood and Pasquero appear, in my opinion, to be more on the right track than Hogner or Freeman. Cross-fertilization between the two fields is attractive. The two fields share a perspective of business that extends across functional areas and does not artificially limit analysis to some narrowly defined domain. The two fields share an interest in how the business environment both promotes and limits certain business activity. For example, what we in SIM can learn from IB's understanding of political risk assessment seems just as important as what IB might learn from SIM understandings of corporate social performance. In short, if SIM and IB are not siblings, they are at least first cousins.

A problem with both Hogner and Freeman is that the conclusions they relate regarding SIM study (more so than IB study) are arguable at best. Evidence of the shift to a naturalist paradigm in Business in Society seems to me to be far less developed than Hogner suggests. The importance of the CSR_3 notion of Frederick is still being debated, and the Logsdon and Palmer interpretation of issues management as amoral has little theoretical or empirical foundation. There is no doubt that Freeman's case for multiculturalism has merit; but the jury is still out, as evidenced by Freeman's own comments relating Donaldson's alternative to a pragmatic, interactionalist, conversationalist framework. Until these matters are more thoroughly resolved within SIM, I am hesitant to use them as bases for comparing our field to IBS.

The Implications of "Businesses in Societies" Study for IBS

The final topic discussed in each of the three papers is best articulated through two questions. Given the view of "businesses in societies," what are the implications for IBS? What are the contributions revised SIM study can make to IB study?

Hogner sees the implications in the form of "unresolved tensions" relating to how IB has recognized that (1) at its core, it is an artifact of culture, (2) it is fundamentally a social, political, and historical undertaking, and (3) it is ordered as a distinct "knowing system." Freeman's answer to these questions comes in the form of a conceptualized multicultural firm which recognizes the variables of race, gender, sexuality, and culture in their stakeholder analyses. Wood and Pasquero see improved explanation and understanding resulting from SIM study, incorporating IB understandings through such techniques as starting with a research puzzle and thinking "foreign" or getting training in comparative research methods.

Collectively, the three papers present all combinations of possible change for the two fields. Hogner suggests that IB scholars need to change by reconsidering what they are doing and why. Wood and Pasquero suggest that SIM scholars need to change by rethinking their concepts, frameworks, and methods. Freeman says that both areas are deficient.

Should we heed the suggestions for change offered in the three papers? It seems that we have come full circle to the question of disturbing the status quo. The positivist in me still wants to know what new insights for SIM, and now IB, come from the naturalist paradigm. The idealist in me still wants to know what new insights come from extending stakeholder analysis to incorporate race, gender, and sexuality (culture, I understand, but I wonder if it isn't already being adequately addressed) into a conceptualization of a multicultural firm. The traditionalist in me still wants to know whether extending SIM concepts to more of a cross-societal level will clarify or distort business performance in any given societal context. In short, the answer to whether we should heed the suggestions made in these three papers rests with our perceptions of the likely value added attendant to each of the author's recommended changes.

Concluding Comment

The contributions of the three papers discussed in these comments will not go unnoticed by SIM scholars. The movement of SIM to "businesses in societies" is an important topic for scholarly debate. The contributions of these works for IB study should be thoroughly considered as well since what the authors say is no less important for IB scholars.

Answering the question of who we are in both IB and SIM is not inconsequential. Both areas, it seems to me, are at risk of being trivialized by those in business schools who believe that our fields are most properly absorbed into the functional areas. "Everyone ought to teach and research the international dimension of their field" is a call with which IB has been dealing for years. "Everyone ought to include ethics and public policy analysis (i.e., SIM) in the teaching and research of their field" is a call we are hearing more and more from the those in the functional areas. Idealistically, we can live with these calls. Realistically, we know that integrating either field into the functional areas of business study results in significant losses of both breadth and depth.

The organizers and supporters of this conference on the "Perspectives of IB" should be complimented for their efforts and recognition of this problem. SIM scholars should learn from this endeavor.

REFERENCES

Aoki, Maasaahiko. 1990. Toward an economic model of the Japanese firm. *Journal of Economic Literature*, 27: 1–27.

Aoki, Maasaahiko. 1984. *The Co-operative*

Game Theory of the Firm. New York: Oxford University Press.

Aupperle, Kenneth E., Archie B. Carroll, and John D. Hatfield. 1985. An empirical examination of the relationship between corporate social responsibility and profitability. *Academy of Management Journal*, June: 446–463.

Ayres, Clarence E. 1944. *The Theory of Economic Progress*. Chapel Hill: University of North Carolina Press.

Badaracco, Joseph L., Jr. 1986. *Loading the Dice: A Five-Country Study of Vinyl Chloride Regulation*. Boston, MA: Harvard Business School Press.

Balducci, Massimo. 1987. *Etat Fonctionnel et Décentralisation: Leçons a Tirer de l'Expérience Italienne*. Bruxelles: Editions Story-Scientia.

Benhabib, Seyla. 1987. The generalization and the concrete other: The Kohlberg-Gilligan controversy and moral theory. In Eva F. Kittay and Donna T. Meyers, editors, *Women and Moral Theory*. Towota, NJ: Rowman and Littlefield.

Berger, Peter. 1965. Towards a sociological understanding of psychoanalysis. *Social Research*, 32(Spring).

Behrman, Jack N. and Robert E. Grosse. 1990. *International Business and Governments*. Columbia, SC: University of South Carolina Press.

Berlin, Isaiah. 1988;1953. *The Hedgehog and the Fox: An Essay on Tolstoy's View of History*. New York: Simon and Schuster.

Berman, Morris. 1981. *The Reenchantment of the World*. Ithaca, NY: Cornell University Press.

Berthoin Antal, Ariane. 1991. Corporate social performance: Rediscovering actors and their organizational contexts. Unpublished doctoral dissertation, Technical University, Berlin.

Boddewyn, Jean J. 1988. Political aspects of MNE theory. *Journal of International Business Studies*, 19(3): 341–364.

Bowen, Howard R. 1953. *The Responsibilities of the Businessman*. New York: Harper.

Brenner, Steven N. and Philip L. Cochran. 1991. The stakeholder theory of the firm: Implications for business and society theory and research. *International Association for Business and Society Proceedings*, 449–467.

Carroll, Archie B. 1979. A three-dimensional conceptual model of corporate social performance. *Academy of Management Review*, 4: 497–506.

Clarkson, Max B. E. 1988. Corporate social performance in Canada, 1976–1986. In Lee E. Preston, editor, *Research in Corporate Social Performance and Policy*, 10: 241–265. Greenwich, CT: JAI Press.

Cochran, Philip L. and Robert A. Wood. 1984. Corporate social responsibility and financial performance. *Academy of Management Journal*, March: 42–58.

Dalton, George. 1961. Economic theory and primitive society. *American Anthropologist*, 63: 1–25.

Davidson, D. Kirk. 1991. Marketing cigarettes in third world countries: Is this the Nestlé of the nineties? *International Association for Business and Society Proceedings*, 517–526.

Dierkes, Meinolf. 1980. Corporate social reporting and performance in Germany. In Lee E. Preston, editor, *Research in Corporate Social Performance and Policy*, 2: 251–290. Greenwich, CT: JAI Press.

Dierkes, Meinolf and Ariane Berthoin Antal. 1986. Whither corporate social reporting—Is it time to legislate? *California Management Review*, 28(3): 106–121.

D'Iribarne, Philippe. 1989. *La Logique de l'Honneur: Gestion des Enterprises et Traditions Nationales*. Paris: Seuil.

Donaldson, Thomas. 1989. *The Ethics of International Business*. New York: Oxford University Press.

Donaldson, Thomas and Thomas W. Dunfee. 1991. Integrative social contracts theory: Ethics in economic life. Working Paper No. 91–156, Department of Legal Studies, The Wharton School of the University of Pennsylvania.

Dugger, William M. 1989. Instituted process and enabling myth: The two faces of the market. *Journal of Economic Issues*, 23(2): 607–615.

Dumont, Louis. 1977. *From Mandeville to Marx*. Chicago: University of Chicago Press.

Dunning, John H. 1989. The study of international business: A plea for a more interdisciplinary approach. *Journal of International Business Studies*, 20(3): 411–436.

Dunning, John H. 1988. The eclectic paradigm of international production: A restatement and some possible extensions. *Journal of International Business Studies*, 19(1): 1–31.

Dunning, John H. 1980. Towards an eclectic theory of international production: Some empirical tests. *Journal of International Business Studies*, 11(1): 9–31.

Dyllick, Thomas. 1989. Ecological marketing strategy for Toni Yogurts in Switzerland. *Journal of Business Ethics*, 8: 657–662.

England, George W. 1975. *The Manager and His Values*. Cambridge, MA: Ballinger.

Etzioni, Amitai. 1988. *The Moral Dimension*. New York: The Free Press.

Fadiman, Jeffrey A. 1986. A traveler's guide to gifts and bribes. *Harvard Business Review*, (July-August): 122–136.

Fama, Eugene and Kenneth R. French. 1992. The cross section of expected stock returns. *Journal of Finance*, 47(2).

Firestone, William A. 1990. Accommodation: Toward a paradigm-praxis dialectic. In Egon G. Guba, editor, *The Paradigm Dialogue*, 67–87. Newbury Park, CA: Sage.

Frankfurter, George and Bill Lane. 1992. *The Rationality of Dividends*. Greenwich, CT: JAI Press.

Frederick, William C. 1988. Response to the ethics and politics of business school education: Updating the Frederick/Vogel dialogue. Academy of Management Meetings, Anaheim, CA.

Frederick, William C. 1985. Towards CSR3: The normative factor in corporate social analysis. Academy of Management Meetings, San Diego, CA.

Frederick, William C. 1983. Corporate social responsibility in the Reagan era. *California Management Review*, Spring: 145–157.

Freeman, R. Edward. 1989. Let's disband the Academy of Management. *SIM News*, Autumn: 4–8.

Freeman, R. Edward. 1984. *Strategic Management: A Stakeholder Approach*. Boston: Ballinger.

Friedman, Milton. 1962. *Capitalism and Freedom*. Chicago, IL: University of Chicago Press.

Fritzsche, David J. and Steven L. Wartick. 1987. The international dimension of business and society. In Karen Paul, editor, *Business Environment and Business Ethics: The Social, Moral and Political Dimensions of Management*, 51–60. Cambridge, MA: Ballinger.

Fukoyama, Francis. 1989. The end of history. *The National Interest*, 16(Summer): 3–18.

Galbraith, John K. 1958. *The Affluent Society*. New York: Houghton Mifflin.

Gates, Henry Louis. 1992. *Loose Canons*. New York: Oxford University Press.

Getz, Kathleen. 1991a. Response to international regulation: The Montréal protocol on substances that deplete the ozone layer. *International Association for Business and Society Proceedings*, 245–255.

Getz, Kathleen. 1991b. Values in international codes of conduct. *International Association for Business and Society Proceedings*, 538–550.

Gray, Barbara and Donna J. Wood. 1991. Collaborative alliances: Moving from practice to theory. *Journal of Applied Behavioral Science*, 27(1): 3–22.

Griffin, David R. 1988. Introduction: The reenchantment of science. In D. R. Griffin, editor, *The Reenchantment of Science*. Albany, NY: State University of New York Press.

Hart, B. H. Liddell. 1974;1929. *Strategy*. New York: New American Library.

Hodgson, Geoffrey M. 1991. The evolution of economies and the temporal dimension: Is neo-classical theory a limiting case? *Joint International Association for Research in Economic Psychology/Society for the Advancement of Socio-Economics Conference* Stockholm, June 16–19.

Hogner, Robert. 1990. We are all social: Institutional perspectives on the place of SIM in management and society. *International Association for Business and Society Meetings*, San Diego, CA.

Kahn, W.A. 1990. Toward an agenda for business ethics research. *Academy of Management Review*, 15: 311–327.

Kaun, David E. 1984. The economist's theory of

ideology: Competing views. *Economic and Industrial Democracy*, 5: 25–50.

Kefalas, Asterios G. 1990. *Global Business Strategy: A Systems Approach*. Cincinnati, OH: South-Western.

Kelman, Steven. 1981. *What Price Incentives? Economists and the Environment*. Boston, Mass.: Auburn House.

Kornai, Janos. 1990. *The Road to a Free Economy*. New York: W.W. Norton.

Kotter, John P. and James L. Heskett. 1992. *Culture and Performance*. New York: The Free Press.

Kuhn, Thomas S. 1962. *The Structure of Scientific Revolutions*. Chicago: University of Chicago Press.

Lenway, Stefanie A. and Peter S. Ring. 1991. Strategic predisposition and firm strategies: Implications for foreign policy makers. *International Association for Business and Society Proceedings*, 152–169.

Levitt, Theodore. 1958. The dangers of social responsibility. *Harvard Business Review*, 36: 41–50.

Lewis, David M. 1983. *The formal-substantive controversy: A critical analysis*. Doctoral dissertation, Indiana University. University Microfilms: 8317110.

Lincoln, Yvonna S. 1990. The making of a constructivist: A remembrance of transformations past. In Egon G. Guba, editor, *The Paradigm Dialogue*, 67–87. Newbury Park, CA: Sage.

Lincoln, Yvonna S. and Egon G. Guba. 1985. *Naturalistic Inquiry*. Newbury Park, CA: Sage.

Logsdon, Jeanne M. and David Palmer. 1988. Issues management and ethics. *Journal of Business Ethics*, 19(4): 8–17.

Machiavelli, Niccolo. 1907. *The Prince*. New York: The National Alumni.

Mafune, Yonosuke. 1988. Corporate social performance and policy in Japan. In Lee E. Preston, editor, *Research in Corporate Social Performance and Policy*, 10:291–303. Greenwich, CT: JAI Press.

Mahon, John F. and Patricia C. Kelley. 1988. The politics of toxic waste: Multinational corporations as facilitators of transnational policy. In Lee E. Preston, editor, *Research in*

Corporate Social Performance and Policy, 10:59–86. Greenwich, CT: JAI Press.

McClosky, Donald N. 1989. Why I am no longer a positivist. *Review of Social Economy*, 47(3): 225–238.

McGuire, Joseph. 1963. *Business and Society*. New York: McGraw-Hill.

Médard, Jean Francois. 1983. *The Creation of Political Order in Uganda*. Nairobi, Kenya: Harare, Zimbabwe: CREDU.

Mirowski, Phillip. 1988. *Against Mechanism*. Totowa, NJ: Rowman and Littlefield.

Molander, Earl. 1980. Abbott Laboratories puts restraints on marketing infant formula in the third world. *Responsive Capitalism: Case Studies in Corporate Social Conduct*. New York: McGraw-Hill.

Moore, Christopher and Jeremy J. Richardson. 1988. The politics and practice of corporate responsibility in Great Britain. In Lee E. Preston, editor, *Research in Corporate Social Performance and Policy*, 10:267–290. Greenwich, CT: JAI Press.

Nigh, Douglas W. and Philip L. Cochran. 1991. Crisis management in the multinational firm. *International Association for Business and Society Proceedings*, 214–227.

Pasquero, Jean. 1991a. Supraorganizational collaboration: The Canadian environmental experiment. *Journal of Applied Behavioral Science*, 27(1): 38–64.

Pasquero, Jean. 1991b. Trends in international corporate philanthropy. In Karen Paul, editor, *Contemporary Issues in Business and Society in the United States and Abroad*, 225–257. Lewiston, KY: The Edwin Mellen Press.

Pasquero, Jean. 1990. Trends in international corporate philanthropy. *International Association for Business and Society Proceedings*, 252–261.

Pasquero, Jean. 1989. A cross-country comparison of national and corporate public issue agendas: Exploring the convergence hypothesis. *Academy of Management Best Papers Proceedings*, 323–327.

Pasquero, Jean. 1988. Comparative research: The case for middle-range methodologies. In Lee E. Preston, editor, *Research in Corporate Social Performance and Policy*, 10:181–209. Greenwich, CT: JAI Press.

Paul, Karen. 1992. The impact of U.S. sanctions on Japanese business in South Africa: Further developments in the internationalization of social activism. *Business & Society*, 31(1): 51–58.

Paul, Karen, editor. 1991. *Contemporary Issues in Business and Society in the United States and Abroad*. Lewiston, KY: The Edwin Mellen Press.

Paz, Octavio. 1990. *The Other Voice*. New York: Harcourt Brace Jovanovich.

Peterson, Michael R. and Larry L. Wade. 1985. Environmental pollution policy in Japan: A public choice hypothesis. In *Public Policy Across Nations: Social Welfare in Industrial Settings*, 71–90. Greenwich, CT: JAI Press.

Polanyi, Karl. 1977. *The Livelihood of Man*. Edited by H. W. Pearson. New York: Academic Press.

Polanyi, Karl. 1957. The market economy as an instituted process. In K. Polanyi, C. M. Arensberg and H. W. Pearson, editors, *Trade and Markets in Early Empires*. Glencoe, IL: The Free Press.

Polanyi, Karl. 1947. Our obsolete market mentality. *Commentary*, February: 109–117.

Polanyi, Karl. 1944. *The Great Transformation*. Boston: Beacon Press.

Popper, Karl R. 1966. *The Open Society and Its Enemies*. Princeton, NJ: Princeton University Press.

Popper, Karl R. 1957. *The Poverty of Historicism*. New York: Harper and Row.

Post, James E. and Edward Baer. 1980. Analyzing complex policy problems: The social performance of the international infant formula industry. In Lee E. Preston, editor, *Research in Corporate Social Performance and Policy*, 2: 157–196. Greenwich, CT: JAI Press.

Preston, Lee E. 1986. Business and public policy. *Journal of Management*, 12(Yearly review): 261–275.

Preston, Lee E. 1975. Corporation and society: The search for a paradigm. *Journal of Economic Literature*, 13: 434–453.

Preston, Lee E., Françoise Rey and Meinolf Dierkes. 1978. Comparing corporate social performance—Germany, France, Canada, and the U.S. *California Management Review*, 20(4): 40–49.

Punnett, Betty Jane. 1988. Designing field experiments for management outside North America. *International Studies of Management and Organization*, 18(3): 44–54.

Reddy, William M. 1987. *Money and Liberty in Modern Europe*. Cambridge: Cambridge University Press.

Reddy, William M. 1984. *The Rise of Market Culture*. Cambridge: Cambridge University Press.

Ring, Peter Smith, Stefanie Ann Lenway, and Michele Govekar. 1990. Management of the political imperative in international business. *Strategic Management Journal*, 11(2): 141–151.

Russell, James W. 1984. U.S. sweatshops across the Rio Grande. *Business and Society Review*, 50(Summer): 17–20.

Sahlins, Marshall. 1960. Political power and economy in primitive culture. In Gertrude E. Dole and Robert L. Caneiro, editors, *Essays in the Science of Culture*. New York: Thomas Y. Cromwell.

Samuels, Warren J. 1989. The methodology of economics and the case for policy diffidence and restraint. *Review of Social Economy*, 47(2): 113–133.

Sethi, S. Prakash. 1978. An analytical framework for making cross-cultural comparisons of business responses to social pressures: The case of the United States and Japan. In Lee E. Preston, editor, *Research in Corporate Social Performance and Policy*, 1: 27–54. Greenwich, CT: JAI Press.

Speth, James Gustave. 1987. An environmental agenda for world business. *Across the Board*, 24(March): 21–26.

Stanfield, J. Ron. 1989. Karl Polanyi and contemporary economic thought. *Review of Social Economy*, 47(3): 266–279.

Swedberg, Richard, Ulf Himmelstrand, and Göran Brulin. 1986. Economic sociology: Past and present. *Current Sociology*, 35: 1–21.

Tarullo, Daniel K. 1985. Logic, myth, and the international economic order. *Harvard International Law Journal*, 26(2): 533–552.

Thompson, James. 1967. *Organizations in Action*. New York: McGraw-Hill.

Tiffany, Paul. 1987. Japanese corporate lobbying in the United States: Strategy and structure.

Paper presented at the Academy of Management annual meeting, New Orleans, LA, August 11.

Toyne, Brian. 1990. Contributions of international business to the international dimension of business and society debate. *International Association for Business and Society Proceedings,* 447–453.

Toyne, Brian. 1989. International exchange: A foundation for theory building in international business. *Journal of International Business Studies,* 20(1): 1–17.

Tzu, Sun. 1971;500 b.c. *The Art of War.* Translated by Samuel B. Griffith. London, England: Oxford University Press.

U.S. Department of Commerce. 1979. *Corporate Social Reporting in the United States and Western Europe.* Report of the Task Force on Corporate Social Reporting. Washington, DC: U.S. Government Printing Office.

Velasquez, Manuel G. 1992. *Business Ethics.* 3d edition. Englewood Cliffs, NJ: Prentice Hall.

Vernon, Raymond and Louis Wells. 1981. *Managers in the International Economy.* 4th edition. Englewood Cliffs, NJ: Prentice Hall.

Vogel, David. 1986. *National Styles of Regulation.* Ithaca, NY: Cornell University Press.

Wartick, Steven L. and Donna J. Wood. Forthcoming. *International Business and Society.* Cambridge, MA: Blackwell.

Wilks, Stephen and Maurice Wright, editors. 1987. *Comparative Government-Industry Relations: Western Europe, United States, and Japan.* Oxford, UK: Clarendon Press.

Wilson, Graham K. 1985. *Business and Politics: A Comparative Introduction.* Chatham, NJ: Chatham House Publishers, Inc.

Wisman, Jon D. 1988. The dominance of consensual over technical rationality in Confu-

cius' socio-economic thought. *International Journal of Social Economics,* 15(1): 58–67.

Wisman, Jon D. 1986. The renaissance of natural law cosmology: Free markets and fettered minds. *International Journal of Social Economics,* 13(10): 26–37.

Withers, William. 1966. *Business and Society.* New York: Appleton-Century-Crofts.

Wokutch, Richard E. 1982. Ethical investment policies and activities of Catholic religious orders. In Lee E. Preston, editor, *Research in Corporate Social Performance and Policy,* 4:157–188. Greenwich, CT: JAI Press.

Wood, Donna J. 1992. Dams or democracy? Stakeholders and social issues in the Hungarian-Czechoslovakian hydroelectric controversy. *International Association of Business and Society Proceedings,* Leuven, Belgium, June.

Wood, Donna J. 1991a. Corporate social performance revisited. *Academy of Management Review,* 16: 691–718.

Wood, Donna J. 1991b. Social issues in management: Research and theory in corporate social performance. *Journal of Management,* 17(2): 383–406.

Wood, Donna J. 1991c. Toward improving corporate social performance. *Business Horizons,* 34(4): 66–73.

Wright, Lorna L., Henry W. Lane, and Paul W. Beamish. 1988. International management research: Lessons from the field. *International Studies of Management and Organization,* 18(3): 55–71.

Zelizer, Viviana. 1988. Beyond the polemics on the market: Establishing a theoretical and empirical agenda. *Sociological Forum,* 3(4): 613–634.

Zohar, Danah. 1990. *The Quantum Self.* New York: Quill/William Morrow.

4

Economic Perspectives and International Business

EDITORS' COMMENTS

As noted in the opening chapter, economic assumptions and theory have dominated IB thought, particularly in terms of firm behavior. However, there is growing disagreement between those who advocate an economic-driven approach to the study of international business (IB) and those who champion a more holistic approach that gives equal weight to the other major social sciences.

Since we wanted to give particular attention to the role that economic thought has played and will continue to play in the development of the field of IB, we asked three leading contributors to the IB economic literature to explore what they saw as some of the challenges facing economists interested in IB phenomena. As their papers reveal, they did this from three very interesting and somewhat different perspectives. At the same time, however, as the two commentators point out, there are several common themes to their discussions. There is also a common call for a more inclusive, if not holistic, understanding of IB.

In the leadoff paper, Casson presents a theme that is certainly worthy of attention, particularly in light of the ideas presented in the opening chapter. While acknowledging the substantial contribution made by economic thought to our understanding of firm-level economic behavior in an international context, Casson's central argument is that conventional economic theories of IB are a special case of a more general theory that should become the focus of future development. Supportive of recent trends in the social sciences that are remarked on in the opening chapter, he develops a convincing argument that the development of this general theory requires an integration of economic theory and theories of organizational behavior.

Casson notes that three streams of economic thought are present in what he refers to as the modern IB theory: internalization, industrial organization theory, and location theory. However, he correctly points out that a "serious misunderstanding is that these three streams of thought are collectively [assumed] sufficient to analyze any international business issue." [p. 184] According to Casson, IB is inherently multidisciplinary since IB problems cannot be neatly packaged and classified as either economic, political, or social. In his view, it would be more correct to view IB inquiry as an eclectic discipline that is based on an "eclectic paradigm" capable of accommodating "newly relevant inputs."

Casson continues by recommending that optimization should be the unifying assumption for developing a more general theory. Optimization, he argues, is well established in economics, and has made significant inroads in political science and sociology. However, to solve the paradigmatic conflicts inherent to multi-disciplinary research, he suggests that the contributing disciplines need to standardize the postulates of individual optimization.

Given our interest in IB phenomenon at all levels (individual, group, organization, societal, suprasocietal), we question whether Casson's suggested adoption of the assumption of individual optimization will contribute to improved understanding at all levels. Certainly some economists who have adopted an evolutionary perspective in trying to understand economic change would have their doubts. (See Kogut, chapter 8.) The coevolution of technology, business organizations, and societal institutions, for example, seems to exhibit a strong path dependence and the assumption of individual optimization doesn't help much in predicting outcomes. Further, the outcomes reached at any particular point in time are not globally optimal.

In his paper, Dunning picks up on Casson's argument for increased communication among the social sciences by suggesting that "culture . . . is likely to become center-stage in much of IB research over the next decade." He even goes so far as to predict that "an increasing number of cross-disciplinary strategic alliances will be concluded in the 1990s." [p. 194]

Dunning advances two reasons for a shift from uni-disciplinary research to multi-disciplinary research. First, the changing characteristics of intra- and inter-firm relationships require either an extension or reappraisal of internalization theory, or both. Second, the extent and location of firm activity requires a more systematic treatment of both culture and government. He then proceeds to identify three "fronts" of inquiry along which progress can be made: (1) the dynamics or developmental aspects of international production; (2) the more explicit accounting of a nation's culture as a component of its comparative advantage; and (3) the changing composition of the "universe" of multinational enterprises (MNEs) and the ability of countries to attract inbound MNE activity.

In the third topic paper, Ozawa advances the argument that economic explanations of IB are formulated in accordance with the theorist's perceptions of reality. To buttress this argument, he suggests that the realities on which Western economists, Latin American economists, and Asian Pacific economists base their explanations of international trade and the role of multinational companies are fundamentally different. For example, Western explanations of international trade have been dominated by Adam Smith's economic liberalism exemplified by Ricardian comparative advantage. Also, the Marxian dependency view has dominated the arguments of Latin American countries regarding the role played by multinational corporations in the economic development of their countries. Finally, Ozawa suggests that the experience of the Asian Pacific economies can be explained using yet a third perception of reality, namely the emulation paradigm. That is, a "follower" or "latecomer" economy can emulate and learn from a more advanced economy.

In the case of the Asian Pacific reality, the Marxian idea of the leader as exerting malicious dominance and the laggard as displaying pathetic dependence is replaced with a teacher-learner relationship that sees the learner as responding in a positive, emulating fashion to the challenges of the leader. As examples of the outcomes of the Marxian and emulation realities, Ozawa notes that the inward-looking, import regimes fits the former, and the outward-looking, export promoting regimes fit the latter.

In his commentary on the three papers by Casson, Dunning, and Ozawa, Hennart notes that culture is a "common thread" that links the three topic papers. Thus, while commenting on each paper separately, he focused most of his attention on the socialization theme common to the three papers. For example, in his discussion of Casson's contribution Hennart focuses on Casson's discussion of socialization based on guilt or shame as a control method for managing subsidiaries, and continues the discussion by examining the various costs of socialization. He concludes by challenging the suggestion that socialization, when contrasted with price and monitoring, is the most efficient control tool.

In the case of Dunning's paper, Hennart focuses his attention on Dunning's suggestion that an authoritarian hierarchical relationship is giving way—in part at least—to a cooperative heterarchical relationship. Noting that the concept of heterarchy relies on socialization, he continues his discussion by exploring why heterarchy should eventually prevail, and whether culture can be incorporated in our [economic] IB theories. Like Casson, he concludes that

recent empirical work on Japanese practices shows that these practices can be explained in economic terms. However, he fails to explain why the Japanese were able to craft more effective institutional arrangements to control opportunism and foster cooperation.

Finally, in discussing Ozawa's paper, Hennart acknowledges that while Ozawa's primary effort was focused on presenting a theory of economic development which might replace dependency theory, he would restrict his comments because of space limitations to the impact of culture on development. In order to do this, Hennart first focuses the reader's attention on the lowering of the costs of exchange necessary for economic development to occur, and then proceeds to explore the three main ways by which these costs can be lowered: socialization; hierarchy; and property rights. By doing this, Hennart is able to point out that Japan, Taiwan, Korea, Hong Kong, and Singapore used substantially different approaches in achieving economic development. In contrast, Ozawa had argued that the strongly collective-welfare minded governments of the five countries were instrumental in the economic development of their countries.

Graham adds yet another dimension to the discussion of the three topic papers by focusing his commentary primarily on the cooperative networks of organizational entities discussed by Dunning and Ozawa, and the trust and reputation ideas explored by Casson and Dunning. He starts off by remarking that much of what the three authors wrote about invoked memories of a series of seminars he attended in France during a two-year period in the early 1980s. These seminars, led by the industrial economist Jean-Pierre Ponssard, introduced him the French concept of *filière* (i.e., a network of economic agents whose undertakings are interdependent but not necessarily under common ownership or control). French economists theorize that neither hierarchical control associated with internalization nor arm's length transactions associated with an auction market is necessarily the optimal way to organize relations among agents in *filière*.

Noting the lack of citations bearing French names, Graham suggests that the three authors wrote their papers without apparently realizing that French economists and industrial policy planners had already developed the literature in the area that they describe as needing development. Consequently, in Graham's words, "there is some case to be made that Casson, Dunning, and Ozawa run the risk of rediscovering that which the French have already discovered." [p. 229] He then continues, however, by contrasting the Anglo-Saxon and Asian mind sets with that of the French in such areas as the geographic scope of networks, the role of intervention, and the underlying motivations for such inquiry.

A review of these five papers as a group raises several additional issues and questions that go beyond those suggested by the papers individually. First, without detracting in any way from the discussions presented by the three topic authors, Graham's remarks concerning the French concept of *filière* are important for several reasons. First, of course, is the well recognized failure by both U.S.-bound business and IB scholars to actively seek out and examine "foreign" knowledge, information, and experience, particularly when in a foreign language or journal. Another is the failure to more closely examine "foreign" interpretations of events and relationships (i.e., the orientations, paradigms, metaphors, and theories used by foreign business scholars). Finally, another reason, and one noted by Graham, is the failure to "remember" what has gone before, and to assume too quickly that what we are now witnessing is invariably new. As one of the editors notes elsewhere [Toyne 1994], international colloquy among business scholars is not just desirable, it is increasingly necessary because business scholarship has become global in scope and content. However, such colloquy requires a passion for knowledge from all possible sources combined with a tolerance

for "foreign ideas." There is, of course, such dialogue among scholars from the main social sciences, and there needs to be more among business scholars.

Second, the contributions of Casson, Dunning, and Ozawa are essentially examples of the extension or cross-border management paradigms discussed in chapter 1. The two core assumptions of these paradigms are (1) business is business wherever practiced, only the situation or external circumstances change, and, (2) as a consequence, there is a propensity for business practices to converge. The commentary by Hennart supports such a view. However, the commentary by Graham appears to support the assumptions underpinning the emerging interaction paradigm (e.g., business is a socially embedded process, and it and its output change because of culturally-defined self-interest and bounded learning that occurs as a consequence of interacting with other business processes and their outputs). In fact, Dunning's and Hennart's commentary on Japanese organizations and Japanese practices can be viewed as examples of culturally-defined learning.

Third, although their primary focus is on the firm, Dunning, Graham, and Ozawa explicitly bring to the forefront the pressing need to develop a more comprehensive, multi-level understanding of IB, as discussed by Boddewyn and Toyne in chapter 2, and the editors in chapter 1. The roles of government and society in contextualizing, informing, and selecting possible behaviors of the business process and the organizations this process create are increasingly clear. Yet, they remain difficult to include because of the paradigmic foundations of most business theorizing and research.

Finally, Dunning and Casson are suggesting, perhaps obliquely, that progress can only be made by entering into partnership with scholars from the other social sciences and business disciplines. While not going so far as to recommend interdisciplinary scholarship, they do see a clear need for at least multidisciplinary scholarship (albeit led by economists).

Economic Theories of International Business:
A Research Agenda
Mark Casson

Economic theory has made a substantial contribution to international business (IB) studies, but it remains an open question whether future analytical developments should be based purely on the extension of existing theories. Further, extensions may encounter diminishing intellectual returns. This paper argues that conventional economic theories of IB should be considered as a special case of a more general theory and that this general theory should become the focus of development in future. The paper argues, furthermore, that a general economic theory of IB can encompass many issues outside the traditional domain of economic applications. This is because economic principles are far more general than is currently believed.

Economics can be defined as either a *field of study* or a *method of study*. As a field of study economics is concerned with production, employment, trade, finance, and so on. Key aspects of IB operations clearly fall within economics as a field of study. But how much insight into them can be gained by using economics as a method of study?

Economics is often defined as the study of choice under conditions of scarcity [Robbins 1932]. Because choice affects almost areas of human behavior, this provides ample scope for "economic imperialism"— extending the application of economic methods outside the field indicated above [Hirschleifer 1985].

Indeed, some economic imperialists would argue that almost all the social and political phenomena encountered in IB can be successfully analyzed in economic terms. By this they mean that any given phenomenon can be interpreted as an equilibrium outcome resulting from the interaction of individuals rationally pursuing well-defined personal goals.

There is, however, a problem with implementing this agenda, and this is that economics has considerable difficulty handling the emotional dimension of relations within a social group [Etzioni 1988]. This is significant for economics because such relations are crucial in enforcing intragroup coordination, and so have a major impact on the overall performance of a group.

The development of an adequate economic theory of social groups would remove many of the current limitations in applying economic analysis to IB phenomena. Such groups are important on the factory floor. The ability to coordinate work groups is widely regarded as a competitive advantage of Japanese firms. A key issue in IB is how far such skills are transferable overseas. The engineering of loyalty in widely dispersed groups is a crucial factor in reducing the problems of cross-cultural management in multinational firms (MNEs). Social groupings based on education and religious affiliation can be an important influence on the attitudes of the business elites from which many top managers are recruited. At the other extreme, grouping based on local community and trade union membership can be significant in uniting local opposition to foreign investor's activities.

A historical perspective reinforces this point. IB activity antedates the creation of formal institutions—the firm and the nation state—which dominate IB today. These institutions merely codify and bureaucratize activities which for centuries were carried on informally by social groups. As late as the nineteenth century extended families such as the Rothschilds had a dominant role in European finance. In contemporary Asia the overseas Chinese and Indian communities still have an important role in international trade. Some of the world's major firms, such as Seimens and Pilkingtons, have striven hard to maintain the culture of a family firm. High-technology firms such as IBM and 3M have invested heavily in corporate cultures based on personal respect, even though they have no "family tradition" to draw on. In all these cases it is not the formal organizational structures and the legally binding contractual arrangements that govern economic performance, but the "invisible infrastructure" of social relations.

Investigation of group phenomena seems particularly timely. Over the past twenty years economic research on foreign direct investment (FDI) has concentrated on explaining the scale and direction of multinational expansion at the country and industry level. Concepts such as "internalization" and "ownership advantage" have played an important role. How exactly, though, do internal markets work [Hennart 1986,1991; Williamson 1985]? If firms are merely networks of intermediate product markets then why are authority relations still so important relative to negotiation within many large firms? How can salaried managers of subsidiaries be effectively motivated to make internal markets work for the overall benefit of the firm? Issues of this kind open up the interface between economic theory and theories of organizational behavior. It is disappointing that these two bodies of theory often seem to provide conflicting accounts of the same phenomenon rather than complementary accounts of different phenomena. This is because economics has hitherto ignored the emotional dimension of group behavior, while organizational behavior has underestimated the impact of material incentives on individual behavior. One solution is for economics to embrace emotional factors more fully; other solutions are briefly considered in the section, Comparism with Behaviorism.

Similar issues emerge when the dynamics of ownership advantage are considered. Ownership advantages have to be continually recreated for a firm to maintain supernormal profits. Most technological advantages are created through team-based corporate R&D, and the efficiency of teamwork depends on the level of trust, which influences the willingness to share information and to be honest about it. A high-trust culture therefore supports group-centered learning.

Other advantages may stem from the patronage of the source government—for example, through the award of defence contracts with commercial spin-offs, and protection of the domestic market. Patronage is the result of coalitions between influential people, each of whom brings to the negotiating table the resources or the votes that he (or she) controls. A viable coalition must prevent people deserting to form rival coalitions with other parties instead. Thus the formation of a coalition requires considerable trust among its members—as does the enforcement of the resulting deal, which is often informal (and occasionally illegal). Trust between the negotiators, based on shared cultural values, is thus crucial in explaining which of the possible coalitions emerges successfully, and hence who the winners and the losers from government patronage turn out to be.

The creation of ownership advantage is, of course, at the heart of recent debate over international competitiveness [Porter 1990]. The preceding remarks suggest that the key to this long-run macrolevel issue lies in short-run microlevel phenomena connected with contractual arrangements in social groups. This means that research into international competitiveness may well have to be based on a refinement of earlier analysis of internal markets. The concept of internal market, however, will have to be extended to include any market internal to a social group. The role of high-trust culture in the operation of internal markets will have to be considered more fully as well. This brings the argument back to the point made at the outset—economic analysis must take more account of the emotional dimension if it is to fulfill its potential as an imperialist social science. Existing theories of IB must be extended if they are to cope with issues of this kind.

The rest of the paper is organized as follows.

The next section examines the "state of the art" and shows how current economic theories of IB synthesize three main strands of theory. It is argued that these three strands can be used in quite different combinations to analyze different issues. More significantly, it is shown that further strands can be added in order to widen the range of issues that the theory can address. Some of these strands may draw upon ideas from outside the usual domain of economics.

The third section demonstrates that any successful synthesis needs a common core of assumptions to achieve consistency between the different strands. The existing synthesis relies heavily on the idea of profit maximization by the firm. Although some critics claim to dispense with profit maximization, the hypotheses they generate hinge on a very close approximation to it. However, a wider synthesis will have to replace corporate profit maximization with utility maximization because of the need, amongst other things, to analyze the agency problems encountered in the management of large firms.

The fourth section argues that the success of utility maximization as a theoretical postulate derives not from the narrowly utilitarian view that preferences are autonomous, nor from the restrictive view (favored by many economists) that expectations are rational, but simply from the view that people optimize. Optimization is advocated as the key assumption that will reconcile different strands of theory within a wider synthesis.

The fifth and sixth sections derive predictions from the idea that theories of individual and group behavior can be synthesized. Particular stress is placed on the role of group leaders in providing entrepreneurial vision and in building up mutual trust between members of a group. The seventh section focuses on IB applications of the proposed synthesis. The emphasis is on explaining how cultural aspects of internal organization impinge on the competitive performance of the firm. Other applications—for example, to the political economy of business-government relations—are considered too.

The eighth section compares the optimization approach with syntheses based on alternative standardizing assumptions, and in particular with the assumptions of sequential rule-based decision-making associated with the behavioral approach. The final section summarizes the main conclusions.

CURRENT THEORY: A BRIEF REVIEW

Although this paper may be interpreted as calling for a radical change in economic theorizing, it can also be viewed as merely spelling out the consequences of continuing a movement that is already underway in IB studies. This section shows that previous work on the economics of IB has already successfully adapted and then synthesized different streams of thought. The main novelty of the proposal, so far as IB theory is concerned, is simply that this process should be extended to include microanalysis of group behavior. Existing insights contained in other disciplines should be adapted so that they can be expressed more rigorously in economic discourse, and then synthesized with established streams of economic theory.

Three main streams of thought are present in the modern theory [Buckley 1983; 1988]: internalization theory, which is a subset of transaction cost theory; industrial organization theory, with its emphasis on market structure; and location theory, which is a mixture of conventional trade theories based on comparative advantage and tariffs, and "geographical" theories based on economics of scale and transport costs.

These streams of thought were first successfully combined by the Canadian economist Stephen Hymer. Drawing on Coase [1937], he explained how the logic of multinational organization is governed by the internalization of international markets in intermediate products [Hymer 1968]. Drawing on Bain [1956] and Dunning [1958], he explained how the profitability and growth of MNEs reflect their possession of monopolistic "ownership" or "competitive" advantages such as proprietary technology, brand names and other firm-specific assets [Hymer 1976]. It was, however, left to others to synthesize all of these components into a single framework related to institutional economics rather than to Marxist theory.

Advantages such as technology have "public good" characteristics [Johnson 1970]. As different plants embody the advantage in goods supplied to different market areas, internalization leads to *vertical* integration in the *intermediate* market, but *horizontal* integration in the *final* product market.

Internalization of technology markets affords two key benefits [Casson 1987 chap. 1]. It overcomes "buyer uncertainty" about the quality of the advantage, and it solves the problem of coordinating collusion amongst licensees with potentially overlapping market areas.

Successful collusion is possible because of the barrier to entry that the monopolistic advantage creates. This establishes a crucial link between ownership advantage and internalization. Ownership advantages create a situation where quality uncertainty and opportunities for collusion allow internalization economics to flourish. (Although instances of backward integration in resource-based industries show that internalization can occur for other reasons too.) The simplicity of this link was lost in Kindleberger's early exposition of Hymer's thesis [Kindleberger 1969] because he based the entire theory on the quite superfluous assumption that there are costs of doing business abroad which the MNE requires an advantage to overcome. While this assumption may be valid for first-time investors, it is not true of experienced repeat investors, so there is no gain in realism to offset the cost of complicating the theory in this unnecessary way.

There is a widespread misunderstanding about the way that the three streams of thought identified above have to be combined. The fallacy is that each stream is a necessary element in the economic analysis of any IB issue. Yet, it is quite clear that some issues can be successfully tackled using just one of them and others by using only two. For example, a theory of location based on transport costs may be quite sufficient to explain why a German cement company would prefer to source its French customers from France rather than by export from Germany. It is only when one inquires why the firm can successfully bid away the customers from French competitors in the first place that the other streams of thought have a significant contribution to make.

An even more serious misunderstanding is that these three streams of thought are collectively sufficient to analyze any IB issue. For example, if the issue is to explain the European propensity to make acquisitions rather than greenfield investments in the U.S., the role of international banks in funding the market for corporate control is clearly relevant, which means that the theory of finance has a significant contribution to make. It is true that in the past the theory of finance had only limited success in explaining the gains from multinational operation in terms of the kind of economics of diversification enjoyed by a mutual fund. This does not mean, however, that it cannot contribute in other ways. Any branch of economics is potentially relevant to IB—it simply depends on the issue it is desired to explain.

If this point is accepted then it is clear that IB is an essentially eclectic discipline, drawing on different streams of theory and synthesizing them as appropriate on a case-by-case basis. It may be useful to develop an "eclectic paradigm" that provides a checklist of relevant theoretical inputs [Dunning 1988], but as new phenomena emerge it is likely that the paradigm will have to enlarge to accommodate newly relevant inputs. Recently, for example, the paradigm has been extended to include elements of corporate strategy [Dunning 1991]. The inclusion of microanalysis of group behavior can therefore be considered, if desired, as yet another extension of the "eclectic paradigm."

OPTIMIZATION: A STANDARD FOR THEORETICAL UNIFICATION

Economists outside IB often regard the synthesis of complementary theories as a rather trivial matter. They prefer analysis of an abstract problem to synthesis directed towards a real-world problem. Quite apart from the challenging complexity of real-world problems, this attitude overlooks the purely analytical difficulty of synthesizing theories based upon different assumptions. Thus conventional trade and location theories ignore transaction costs, while internalization theory presupposes them. It is no trivial task to effect a synthesis between them.

A synthesis can in fact be achieved because both theories are ultimately based upon profit-maximization. Within this common framework, a synthesis can be constructed in which transaction costs affect mainly the ownership structure and other factors affect mainly location choice [Casson 1979].

This problem of finding a common framework increases as the range of phenomena to be explained widens. Thus to explain how internal markets are actually managed it is necessary to examine the "agency problem" of motivating managerial employees [Arrow 1985; Holmström 1979].

Agency theory is based upon individual utility-maximization rather than corporate profit-maximization. To integrate this theory with others it is necessary to rationalize profit-maximization in terms of utility-maximization by the owners of the firm. Utility-maximization rather than profit-maximization therefore becomes the overall framework within which synthesis is achieved.

Utility-maximization is an extremely general theoretical framework. It does not really commit the theorist to the philosophy of utilitarianism, because utility can simply be defined as "that which people maximize." In conditions of scarcity, as assumed in economics, people actually *optimize*; they

maximize subject to constraints. It is thus the assumption of optimization rather than a commitment to utilitarian philosophy that characterizes economics as a method of study.

The assumption of optimization is essentially immune to refutation. By itself it implies nothing. It is only when combined with assumptions about preferences and constraints that it yields predictions. Optimization, therefore, is an assumption made to extract meaning from other assumptions, rather than to predict anything itself. It is in the combination of assumptions that the predictive power of the theory lies. Optimization is simply a standardizing assumption that guarantees consistency in economic discourse.

ENDOGENOUS PREFERENCES AND SUBJECTIVE INFORMATION

How is it then, it could be asked, that the economic method seems so much more successful in some areas than others? Optimization models, for example, seem to be more successful in explaining financial behavior than in analyzing human resource management and government-business relations. It is argued below that this is mainly because of the unimaginative way in which economic principles are normally applied. The difficulties are not inherent in the method, but in the culture of the economics profession that influences how the method is applied. It could reasonably be claimed that there is no problem in International Business Studies (IBS) that is not amenable to economic method provided there is sufficient flexibility in the way the economic model is specified.

In conventional economics, optimization is normally combined with two other assumptions that are of much more dubious standing. The first is that individual preferences are autonomous and stable, and the second that decision makers correctly perceive constraints.

The first of these assumptions is widely believed to be crucial in giving economic models predictive power [Becker and Stigler 1977]. This is because if preferences could change erratically then any kind of behavior could be rationalized, not as an intelligent response to scarcity, but as a consequence of preference change. While allowing erratic preference change may undermine predictive power, however, specifying a plausible mechanism of preference change may actually enhance it. Such mechanisms are particularly important in explaining individual adaptation to group norms [Akerlof 1980]. Strict adherence to an assumption of autonomous and stable preferences effectively disqualifies economics from analyzing group behavior, because of the role of social interaction in effecting preference change. Conversely, the modeling of preference change equips economics to analyze group behavior as the aggregate outcome of optimizing responses to mutual influence within the group. It can be justifiably claimed that such analysis of group behavior is potentially more rigorous than that at present afforded by other social sciences.

The second dubious assumption, that constraints are correctly perceived, appears at its most extreme in the Walrasian theory of markets, where the uniform price is known to all transactors. Even where uncertainty is acknowledged, the range of possible states over which uncertainty exists is assumed to be known. Thus while uncertain events are recognized, totally unexpected events never occur. The agent can therefore calculate in advance how he would respond to each possible outcome, and what inferences he would draw from its occurrence. Thus all substantive learning is completed before any decision is made. Only the decision and its outcome occur in real time.

It is this absence of substantive learning that is at the root of the accusation that economic theory is essentially static. Many economic models are dynamic in the sense that they chart the movement of variables over time. They remain static, though, in so far as decision makers cannot change the

mental models with which they operate over time.

Taking explicit account of learning thus has important consequences for the nature of economic modeling. Individuals with different backgrounds may well have different learning experiences and so work with different models of the environment. Thus they may interpret the same raw data in different ways and so reach different decisions in the same situation.

To achieve greater realism in economic modeling it is therefore necessary to combine the postulate of optimization with assumptions about mechanisms of preference change and model change. The danger is that the ensuing models will be so complex that the simplicity and parsimony of traditional economic models will be lost.

In the research agenda outlined in this paper it is assumed that preference changes and model changes are affected by the leaders of social groups. Leaders are respected individuals who can use their influence to standardize members' preferences and to standardize the models they use. Preferences are manipulated by moral rhetoric; this rhetoric is in turn predicated on a particular mental model that the leader claims is supported by his (or her) exceptionally wide experience of life.

The reason why conventional economic models work reasonably well in areas like finance is that the assumptions of autonomous stable preferences and correct perception of the environment are fairly realistic in this context because the self-interest of well-informed individuals is the driving force. Conversely, the reason they do not work well in areas like human resource management and government-business relations is that group-centered behavior, reflecting the manipulation of preferences and the engineering of mental models by leaders, has an important influence on outcomes. Individuals are influenced by group loyalty and by conformity with the opinions of the leader and their peers. Indeed, it is interesting that economics is least successful in analyzing just those financial issues—such as the causes of panics and crashes—where assumptions such as correct perception of the environment are demonstrably false, and where group-centered behavior—such as conformity with "market sentiment"—is most important.

THE ECONOMICS OF SOCIAL GROUPS

From an evolutionary perspective, the reason why people's preferences and models are manipulable is likely to be that this enhances the competitive performance of groups. This section reviews some well-known reasons why individuals affiliate to groups. It also examines the circumstances in which leadership is especially crucial for group performance.

Transaction cost theory identifies at least six useful functions of a group.

(1) A system of rights and obligations can be established to coordinate individual actions. These can range from standardized customs and conventions to a full-fledged system of individual property rights. The rights reflect mutual recognition between members of the group, in the sense that each member accepts the legitimacy of other members' rights, and recognizes an obligation to respect them.

(2) Individual ownership encourages intragroup trade based on the voluntary exchange of property rights; since trade exposes people to risks of default, arrangements for the enforcement of contracts must be made within the group. Trade in turn sustains a division of labor in production based upon specialization according to comparative advantage.

(3) Groups encourage teamwork: production teams function best as social groups because social contact enhances the flow of information between team members. This is a special case of the more general point that groups promote a common language, and establish institutions for regulating communication, that sustain the information flow necessary for economic coordination.

(4) Members gain access to nonexcludable public goods, such as defence, which can be financed using universal contributions—normally, though not necessarily, obtained coercively through taxation. The protection of individual property and the enforcement of contracts can be organized in a similar way.

(5) Insurance can be provided through the pooling of risks—either through informal mutual assistance or formal contracts of insurance.

(6) Group-centered collusion affords increased bargaining power against members of other groups.

Other benefits follow indirectly from the improved security—both internal and external—associated with (1)–(6) above.

(7) Increased predictability of the individual member's environment reduces the strategic complexity of the decisions that have to be made. Simple mental models can be used because certain possibilities can be disregarded. This reduces the stressfulness of decision making and increases the probability that a correct decision will be made.

(8) Increased predictability also reduces the risks associated with any decision, and so reduces the anxiety about what the outcome will be. It also reduces the need for costly organization of insurance.

(9) Reduction of stress and anxiety frees resources for learning activities. *Ex ante* learning through

experiment and play avoids painful ex post learning from mistakes. Faster learning also improves group productivity.

In the light of these remarks it is easy to explain how narrow self-interest will induce people to coalesce into groups. What is difficult to explain, though, is how narrow self-interest will induce people not to cheat on each other after they have joined. There are certain cases where enlightened self-interest may sustain cooperation, but in general there is no substitute for leadership activity.

The main situation where enlightened self-interest may sustain cooperation is where interactions between group members are repeated an indefinite number of times [Axelrod 1984; Kreps and Wilson 1982]. This means that a cheat may expect to be punished by a victim next time they meet. The conditions most favorable to this mechanism are found in small, stable, and compact groups. In small groups repeated interaction with the same partner is more likely because the number of possible pairings is small. In a stable group an offender is less likely to leave before his next encounter with a victim. In a compact group it is easier for the victim to identify and pursue the offender. Reputation effects are also likely to be stronger in a compact group, since it is more likely that independent eyewitness will be available to provide corroboration for the victim's claims. Reputation also spreads spontaneously through gossip in a compact group, and will quickly reach everyone when the group is small.

Another possibility is that group members are genetically related and have a genetically-determined preference for altruistic acts that promote the survival chances of their own genes. Some sociobiologists argue that enlightened self-interest based on repeated interaction and genetically-determined altruism are the only reasons why people show consideration for other members of a group [Dawkins 1989].

In practice, however, nonselfish behav-ior is often observed when these restrictive conditions do not apply. Thus game theory and sociobiology, as presently formulated, cannot provide a complete explanation of cooperation within social groups. There is a missing factor. This paper seeks to identify the missing factor with leadership activity within the group [Casson 1991a].

LEADERSHIP STRATEGIES

A leader needs to be trusted, for otherwise the followers will attempt to resist manipulation. In a highly centralized group the leader may act as a planner, exercising direct authority over followers. In a decentralized group, of the kind assumed above, this option is not available. The leader must choose between two main strategies: to invoke formal legal procedures to discipline members, but these are often costly because of the difficulty of collecting evidence; or to use emotional manipulation to persuade members to discipline themselves.

Emotional manipulation can take several forms [Casson 1991b]. Within a corporate context, one of the most important appears to be the engineering of respect. Members punish themselves for cheating by losing a sense of respect. In this context cheating may refer to breach of contract, slacking at work, misrepresentation of information, or even violent criminal acts. Contracts are enforced, effort is elicited, truth is guaranteed, and peace assured because members fear the loss of respect.

Various forms of respect can be distinguished: for example, self-respect, peer-group respect, and the respect of the group as a whole. A desire for self-respect associates guilt with cheating, whereas peer-group respect involves a sense of shame. So far as the group as a whole is concerned, cheating can result in loss of status. By and large, individual offenders are better informed about their own actions than are their peers, who are in turn better informed than the group as a whole. Thus self-respect is a more reliable incentive for honesty than peer-group respect, which in turn is more reliable than status, because the emotional sanctions are based on more accurate information.

If the leader can standardize the membership on an ethic of respect then members will be keen to interact with each other because they will be confident that they will not be cheated. Nonmembers will be anxious to join because of the good external reputation that the group acquires. Conversely, if the leader cannot standardize members on respect, then those who are honest will be taken advantage of by those who cheat. The honest members will therefore avoid interaction-reducing group productivity—and tend to leave, giving the group a bad reputation which makes it difficult to replace them. Thus leaders who cannot standardize their groups on respect must have recourse to formal procedures instead—otherwise they will lose membership until loss of critical mass makes the group extinct.

Different environments present different incentive problems for the leader of a group. Leaders therefore face strategic choices in adapting the group ethic to the system of natural incentives that prevails. Assuming that the leader, unlike the followers, has autonomous preferences, the choice of ethic will reflect the interaction between the leader's preferences, the nature of the environment, and the size, stability, and compactness of the group.

Leaders can also influence the kind of model that members use in reaching their decisions. Leaders often take responsibility for managing the external relations of the group, and are therefore in a good position to present a distorted picture of the group's environment should it be advantageous to do so.

A leader who portrays the environment as stable helps to legitimate custom and tradition, while someone who portrays it as dynamic and evolving encourages innovation instead. An incompetent leader may portray the group's environment as hostile in order to excuse his own mismanagement, while a competent leader may do the reverse in order to help people feel secure.

It is more difficult for a leader to distort the picture of the internal environment, however, because members have independent evidence against which to check it. Because the scope for manipulation is somewhat lower in this context, there is more scope for diversity, as each individual generalizes from his own unique subset of experiences within the group.

So far as economic performance is concerned, an important set of beliefs is about the structure and the membership of the group itself. While small groups are often structured to allow direct relations between the leader and the followers, in large groups these relations are typically mediated by an elite. Further intermediation can lead to additional levels in the social hierarchy. A leader who promotes the view that no one can rise beyond their present level clearly discourages ambition. If, in addition, people in the lower strata are considered incompetent and unimaginative, then innovative ideas formulated at these levels are likely to be disregarded too. Such elitist attitudes also encourage the centralization of economic power and the allocation of resources to prestigious megaprojects favored by the elite.

By choosing to promote an appropriate combination of beliefs the leader can engineer a highly entrepreneurial culture within the group [Casson 1990 chap. 4]. Such a leader needs to display confidence in his or her own judgement, however, because by inspiring an entrepreneurial attitude people are encouraged to question that judgment by thinking for themselves. A weak and incompetent leader, in contrast, will favor more centralized control, since it provides the ability to monitor dissidents and prevent their criticisms from gaining popular support.

IB APPLICATIONS

The ideas articulated above do not, of course, have a specifically international flavor. They can, however, be applied to a range of issues including the creation of ownership advantages, the performance of joint ventures, and cultural barriers to technology transfer. This section focuses on two main areas: the internal organization of the MNE, and the international political economy of government-business relations. These areas have been chosen to minimize overlap with previously published applications, such as Buckley and Casson [1988; 1992].

Internalization theory indicates that an internal market can be organized in several ways. One method requires internal prices to be set centrally—sometimes using headquarters' estimate of comparable external prices. Another method requires the prices to be set by negotiation between different divisions of the firm, often through separate bilateral bargains. A third approach—which involves partial decentralization—requires the headquarters to set a quantity plan and divisions to bid competitively to carry out parts of the plan as subcontractors. There are a number of issues here—the extent of the decentralization, the intensity of internal competition between subsidiaries, and the question of whether outside firms are allowed to play a real role in winning business from internal divisions if their price is right.

Transaction cost theory can be used to derive predictions about which method of internal organization is likely to be most efficient according to the type of industry [Casson 1990 chap. 2]. A straightforward application of this theory would imply that all firms in a given industry (apart from those whose exit is imminent) will adopt the efficient method. Yet evidence suggests that leading firms can coexist in the same industry using different methods. In an international context one possible explanation is that firms of different nationalities are "free-riding" on different source-country cultures. Each culture legitimates a certain system of values linked, perhaps, to an ideal type of organization, with which it pays each firm to conform up to a point. The top management of each firm therefore faces a trade-off between the claims of culture-free economic logic on the one hand and cultural

conformity on the other. Different managements will identify different equilibria depending both on the nature of the true trade-off, and their own culturally specific view of where the trade-off lies. The equilibrium will depend on a mixture of factors, some identified by conventional internalization theory and other reflecting the specifics of source-country culture.

It could be objected, of course, that cross-country comparisons of this kind can be handled using existing organization theories, and that giving these comparisons an economic dimension is superfluous. The present paper rejects this argument: indeed it is precisely on this point that one of the major claims for the theory can be staked out. For without a transaction cost perspective it is difficult to fully understand the function of multinational organization in the first place. If the function is not fully understood, it is difficult to analyze how different cultures will help or hinder the performance of this function, and hence difficult to predict how the compromise with source country culture will be made.

A theoretical synthesis based on the optimization approach can illuminate the business-government interface as well. Economic theories of rent-seeking lobbying, of coalition formation, and of interparty rivalry in a democracy all show the relevance of individual optimization in political life [Mueller 1989]. Individuals with similar interests coalesce into political groups to avoid duplication of effort in disseminating information and in order to improve their own bargaining power. Political groups require internal enforcement mechanisms to achieve coordination, just as do firms; hence the aspects of organizational behavior analyzed above apply to them as well. There are important differences, of course—political groups do not maximize profits, they do not "employ" ordinary members in the same sense as a firm, and the structure of "intermediate product flow" within the group is much simpler than in the typical firm. On the other hand, intergroup rivalry in political life is not too dissimilar from that of firms. Political parties, for example, are competing for the right to form a government which, in a constitutional democracy, is periodically offered as a prize awarded through the voting system. This is not too different from large firms tendering for a contract—particularly if the contract is to operate a natural monopoly such as a national utility industry.

In business-government relations, the policies of the government are typically those of the party in power (unless the civil service bureaucracy is too strong for the party to control it). Thus business-government relations involve one type of group— the firm—interacting with another type of group—the political party. Neither group can expect the other to accept a deal that leaves them worse off than before. Thus, in the context of foreign investment in less-developed countries, economists have tended to focus on the unacceptability of many host government requirements imposed upon firms—particularly in the 1960s and 1970s—while political scientists have tended to focus on the "sweeteners" offered by investors to governing factions in order to get these requirements relaxed on an unofficial basis. The divergence between the interests of the governing faction and the interests of the population they are supposed to represent reflects the discrepancy between individual and social optimization which occurs when high transaction costs inhibit competition from alternative coalitions.

In IB, of course, two political groups are often involved—the host government and the source government. Except in times of war these two governments are not in direct competition with each other for the control of the same territory. But there is still a measure of conflict over the distribution of the gains from trade, investment, and technology transfer between the two countries. National cultures may well influence the way this conflict is perceived. One government may believe that distribution must conform to certain principles of natural justice (such as equal shares), while the other may perceive distribution simply as the outcome of an adversarial bargaining situation in which the economically strongest party (which has the widest range of options) gets the largest share. Again, one government may perceive trade as a zero-sum game, in which distribution is the key issue, while the other may perceive it as a positive-sum game in which maximizing the volume of trade through liberalization is the dominant issue. Such cultural differences will affect the strategies pursued by the two governments and hence the actual distribution of the gains between them.

Thus, once again, optimization provides a framework within which different aspects of group behavior can be synthesized. It is more difficult to assess the magnitude of this contribution in the political context, however, because it is not immediately obvious which particular empirical generalizations are awaiting explanation from a theory of this kind. Further empirical work on the political economy of IB is probably required before the value of this approach can be properly assessed.

COMPARISON WITH BEHAVIORISM

Economic imperialism has been justified above on the grounds that the optimization postulate is a convenient standard on which to synthesize theories of individual and group behavior. It has not been claimed, however, that this is the only standard on which a suitable synthesis can be based.

Nevertheless, most alternatives seem distinctly inferior to the approach advocated here. In particular an approach which takes a purely organic view of social groups fudges the issue of why any individual should wish voluntarily to join the group and why, having joined, they would comply with group norms. The main strength of the organic view is that it harnesses metaphors (typically derived from biology) to analyze the structure and organization of a group from an evolutionary point of view [Mc Kelvey 1982].

A more powerful alternative to the optimization approach is the behavioral one. The behavioral approach stresses rule-governed behavior. Such behavior is not necessarily in conflict with optimization, since the results of optimization can often be expressed as a rule. A demand curve, for example, can be interpreted as a rule by which optimal purchasing decisions are governed by price stimuli. The difference between the theories lies not in the use of rules, but whether the rules that are used are optimal or not.

The behavioral approach suggests that decisions are made by evaluating alternatives sequentially, rather than simultaneously as in the optimization approach. A suboptimal rule may be adopted simply because it is the first acceptable alternative to be considered [Simon 1983]. Of course, the fact that optimization alone implies nothing may be exploited to provide a rationalization of practically any rule. Thus the chosen rule may be reinterpreted as optimal by arguing that mental resources are scarce, so that the cost of considering further alternatives outweighs the expected benefits involved. Choice of rule is then predicted by, say, defining a set of possible rules, ranking them in order of simplicity, and arguing that search begins with the simplest and proceeds until the optimal degree of complexity has been reached.

This example illustrates the general point that in many cases the optimization and behavioral approaches simply provide a different kind of language in which to express the same idea about individual behavior. Thus when a behaviorist talks about the internal state of the system as mediating stimulus and response, the optimization theorist would talk of differences in preferences and mental models mediating responses instead.

There is, however, an undoubted difference of emphasis in the two approaches, in the sense that optimization theorists regard individuals as inherently more adaptive than do behaviorists. This is reflected in the fact that behaviorists stress quite simple patterns of response to non-price stimuli, while optimization theorists stress more subtle responses oriented to prices. This difference means that behaviorists perceive the drive towards efficiency as occurring more at the system level than at the individual level. Adaptation occurs through Darwinian-style competition eliminating the less-well adapted members of the system rather than by everyone adapting successfully, as a conventional application of optimization theory would suggest.

The unconventional application of optimization theory set out in this paper does not carry such a strong implication, however. It allows for the possibility that the mental models used by individual decision makers may not be well adapted to the environment, particularly if the individuals concerned are poorly educated, or recent entrants to the environment, or if the environment itself has unexpectedly changed. This more flexible use of the optimization postulate further undermines the substantive differences between the optimization and behavioral approaches.

The tentative conclusion that emerges from this discussion is that while conventional optimization theory and conventional behavioral theory are rival approaches—in the sense of offering different standards on which to synthesize the analysis of individual and group behavior—a more flexible kind of optimization theory differs from sophisticated behavioral theory mainly in form rather than in content. The difference is in the language used, rather than what the language signifies in terms of observable behavior. In some respects this not unexpected, since model differences relating to purely unobservable aspects of individual decision making should not lead to irreconcilable differences in predictions.

SUMMARY AND CONCLUSIONS

This paper has set out an agenda for developing an IB theory that integrates individual and social aspects of behavior within an optimization framework. The aim is to

Table 1. Comparison of Two Theoretical Approaches

Dimension	Type of approach	
	Narrow neoclassical	General optimisation
Fundamental principle of behaviour	Optimisation*	
Individual preferences	Autonomous*	Manipulable
Model of environment	Correct*	Over-simplified
Access to information	Equal	Unequal*
Costs of enforcing legal contracts	Zero	Large*
Advantages of internalisation	Zero	Large*
Engineering of trust through moral rhetoric	Impossible*	Feasible
Role of individual differences in preferences and mental models in stimulating entrepreneurial behaviour	None*	Significant

Note: *indicates an assumption of conventional economic theories of international business.

develop an economic theory of social groups which can be applied to both firms and nation states—and eventually to all the other groups, such as trade unions, which are important in international affairs. IB problems are inherently multi-disciplinary—few, if any, occur neatly packaged as purely "economic," "political," or "social." At present, multidisciplinary research involves the researcher grappling with conflicting paradigms. This problem would be solved if all the contributing disciplines standardized on the postulate of individual optimization. There are other postulates which could be used as a standard, but optimization has a "head start" because it is not only well established in economics but has made significant inroads into other social sciences—notably politics, but more recently sociology too [Coleman 1990]. In any case, the consequences of choosing one standard rather than another may not be so acute as might at first appear, particularly since optimization by itself implies nothing that is inconsistent with alternatives such as behaviorism.

A practical point in favor of the proposed agenda is that it simply continues a process of theoretical development that is already underway. Established theories of IB already mark a significant departure from the narrow neoclassical approach that characterized economics some twenty-five years ago. Table 1 compares the narrow neoclassical approach with the general optimization approach proposed in this paper. The comparison involves eight dimensions, and it can be seen that in half these dimensions the transition to the general optimization approach has already been made. It is probably true that the easiest changes have been the first to be made, so that in terms of effort the process is not yet half complete. On the other hand, progress almost certainly generates increasing returns, in the sense that the value of each new transition is increased by growing synergy with the transitions that have already been made. Thus although the marginal cost of further theoretical development may be increasing, the marginal benefit is almost certainly increasing too.

■ ■ ■

Micro and Macro Organizational Aspects of MNEs and MNE Activity
John H. Dunning

The contributions by economists to our understanding of the determinants of foreign production and the growth of the multinational enterprise (MNE) have taken two different but complementary forms. The first attempts to identify and explain the unique characteristics of the MNE qua MNE; while the second has tried to explain the determinants of the foreign value-added activities of MNEs irrespective of whether they are due to their multinationality. Over the years, the distinction between these approaches has become increasingly blurred with the result that some of the richness of the two strands of thought has become devalued in unnecessary and fruitless controversy. In this paper, we shall take as given the reader's knowledge of the basic tenets of the micro theories of the MNE and the more macroaccented theories of MNE activity (including theories of foreign direct investment, or FDI[1]); and shall concentrate on what the author, at any rate, perceives to be some of the more exciting challenges and pressing needs for research in each area over the next decade of so.

THE ECONOMICS OF THE MNE: A MICROORGANIZATIONAL PERSPECTIVE

Apart from the pure modeling of the MNE—a task that, no doubt, will continue to fascinate the economist in the twenty-first century—and what, to some pure theorists, is the only legitimate contribution he can make to the debate—it is likely that in the future economic analysis, by itself, will play a less dominant role in theorizing about the MNE than it has done in the past. At the same time, economic analysis, in conjunction with other disciplines, especially organizational theory, seems set to offer several new and existing insights into both the determinants of MNE behavior and the interaction between MNEs and other economic agents.

It seems probable that an increasing number of cross-disciplinary strategic alliances will be concluded in the 1990s. This is because to understand properly the form, content, and consequences of the emerging globalization of economic activity, the international business (IB) scholar needs to be much more eclectic in his intellectual foraging. In particular, although the word can be easily overplayed, culture—by which is meant the ethos of a particular group of people, as revealed, *inter alia*, by their attitudes, ideologies, values, and social mores, and the private and public institutional framework that gives expression to this ethos—is likely to become center-stage in much of IB research over the next decade or more.

Most surely, the most significant contribution by microeconomists to our understanding of the MNE, qua MNE, is the application of internalization theory (or as it is sometimes more appropriately called, the internalization paradigm) to explain cross-border hierarchical transactions. Yet, in many ways, such an analytical perspective, which stems from the twin disciplinary stables of Ronald Coase and Oliver Williamson, although developed to explain the emergence and growth of the MNE, has made greater inroads into the theory of the multiactivity firm than the theory of MNE *per se*. This is because, true to its neoclassical tradition, its main tenets take some of the more interesting influences on the behavior of MNEs, *qua* MNEs, as exogenous variables; the result of which is that many of the aspects of market failure, which are uniquely cross-border, have received less attention than those which are not.[2]

There are, of course, exceptions. The response of firms to imperfection in international capital and exchange markets has long occupied the attention of finance scholars. But, industrial organization theory, as extended to explain the interface between the behavior of firms and the structure of regional or global market structures in which they compete, has made very little allowance for the kind of parameters that are fixed when the firm operates in a country, but must be considered variable between countries, or between groups of countries. The MNE is different from the uninational multiactivity firm precisely because it operates within different national or location bound environs. Indeed, as an organizational entity or system of cross-border relational interactions, one of the main tasks of a MNE is to understand, reconcile, and assimilate into its own corporate culture, a miscellany of disparate country or regional, ideologies, perceptions, laws, and regulations, in a way that best advances its global strategies. Behind the identification and evaluation of the different kinds of cross-border market failure that may both prompt the internationalization of value added activity and determine its form, lies the questions "Why," or "What causes markets to fail?" Are these market impurities technical and *culture neutral*, or do they arise specifically because of the costs of establishing and maintaining transactional and other commercial relationships that, more often than not, are *culture related?*

Different perceptions of time and punctuality in Spain, Jordan, India, and Canada may affect the interfirm transaction costs of the procurement of (say) a TV set. Differences in values of workers toward authority, incentives, loyalty, teamwork, and commitment in Japan, the United States, and Nigeria may affect the costs of maintaining labor productivity and discourage or encourage shirking. Differences in laws and regulations in Sweden, Pakistan, and Colombia, with respect, e.g., to the environment, mergers, and property rights may create a "constitutional uncertainty" in trade and FDI, which pose coordination problems of a special type for interacting economic agents.[3]

While the determinants of some of these culturally related transaction costs are idiosyncratic—or even firm specific—others may be generalized about; and it is the identification and evaluation of these generalizations that has prompted multidisciplinary coalitions among scholars, with the objectives and form of the alliances being determined by the "lead" discipline. Taking, as an example, economics as the lead discipline, the economist needs to join forces with management, organizational, and legal scholars, and these, in turn, may need an input from other disciplines interested in the make-up of a country's culture[4] and the way in which particular systems of governance can handle them.

Intrafirm Relationships

It is our contention that such a networking of scholars is necessary to appreciate better and explain both intra- and interrelationship firms now being forged; and indeed, the interface between the two.

One of the features of the last decade, which seems set to dominate intellectual discussion in the 1990s, is the nature of the dynamic interplay between cooperative and combative transnational modes. For example, organizational scholars are now questioning the concept of the *hierarchy* as the main mechanism for organizing commercial, nonmarket transactions, at least in large global firms. In pointing to MNEs such as IBM, SKF, and ICI, in which key resources and capabilities are geographically dispersed, cross-border flows of knowledge, information, and ideas are multidimensional, communication is lateral, and there is a strong sense of shared values and mission among the different parts of the organization, the interplay of decision taking is better described as a *heterarchy*.[5]

Yet, if the culturally related cross-border costs of internal decision taking are complex enough as one moves from a series of dyadic and unidimensional relationships to a network of cooperative relationships geared to advancing the global strategy of the hierarchical core, imagine the additional complications that arise in balancing the economies of organizational integration with those of organizational localization in situations where intrafirm communication is multidimensional, lateral, and between multiple centers of decision taking. This is one reason why the systems approach taken by Mark Casson and others in dissecting the core attributes of large MNEs of the 1990s offers considerable promise for economic and business analysts.[6]

At the same time, the identification and measurement of culturally related transaction costs, and an analysis of the way in which these might be surmounted, circumvented, or minimized, remain largely uncharted territory. Many of the empirical advances so far made in this area rest on the differences perceived between the microorganizational practices of Japanese MNEs and those of their Western counterparts.[7]

While some attention has been given to the organizational differences between European and North American MNEs, most scholarly effort has so far sought to explain technical rather than culturally related differences, and rarely have these been embodied into either particular or general theories of MNE behavior. Indeed one suspects that may have been one of the reasons why scholars, businessmen, and politicians have made so little headway in explaining much of the conflict that arose between MNEs and the governments of host developing countries in the 1960s and 1970s. Frequently, in their negotiations, the two parties were on completely different cultural wavelengths, and, because of this, they misunderstood or mistrusted the other's objectives and actions.[8]

As an increasing number of MNEs emerge from a non-North Transatlantic culture, and as more cooperative ventures are now involving partners from South East Asia, Latin America, and Eastern Europe, one might expect a greater diversity of cultural interaction, which might be expected to raise intra-firm transaction or relational costs[9] except where the introduction of new, and culture free, organizational methods may lessen hierarchical or heterarchical tensions.

It is not the purpose of this paper to detail the intercountry, cultural differences that might add to intrafirm organization costs. Instead we wish to explore the premise that firms which are best able to identify and reconcile such differences, and utilize them to their gain, are likely to acquire a noticeable competitive advantage in the global marketplace. Borrowing from Lipsey [1991], we shall refer to such ownership (O) specific advantages as cultural competitive advantages, or as is more relevant to the macrotheory of MNE activity, the comparative advantage of national cultures or attitudes. The third section, Macroorganizational Theories, will explore this notion in more detail.

The outcome of such MNE management may show itself in various ways, well beyond the organization of decision taking *per se*. These include the types of innovation and product strategy adopted, the location of production, and the methods of advertising and training methods employed. In particular, the techniques and capability of a MNE to transfer its intrafirm domestic organizational capabilities to a foreign location may rest on the transaction costs associated with the adaptation of these methods, or the costs of replanting them in an unfamiliar or uncongenial environment. The literature recognizes that organizational methods (particularly those which may require substantial modification to well-established practices—e.g., industrial relations procedures), take much longer and are likely to be more expensive to transplant than machine intensive production techniques and processes [Kogut 1990; Kogut and Parkinson 1992]; and that the extent and speed of the transfer are likely to vary according to the cultural distance between the investing and recipient country and the experience of the investing firm in the foreign country [Franke, Hofstede, and Bond 1991].

Studies of the governance of Japanese and U.S. corporate activity have highlighted the differences in the cross-border market failure experienced by the two groups of firms and their organizational responses to them.[10] As to the major differences, two, in particular, might be highlighted. These are first the production systems employed, and second the structuring of the internal labor market (which includes such considerations as the recruitment, training and allocation of labor within the firm, compensation and promotion systems and their incentive and motivational effects) [Lincoln 1992].[11]

As to the first, we may compare and contrast the Toyota Production System (TPS) adopted by some of the large Japanese MNEs in fabricating (and especially in the motor vehicles sectors), and the Mass Production System (MPS)—sometimes call "Fordism"—which their U.S. counterparts pioneered later this century.[12] Each differently affects both the production and relational costs of value-added activity. At the same time, each system demands adherence to a different set of rights, objections, and responsibilities, the nature and character of which is at least partly culture specific, even though this specificity may not necessarily be linked to a particular country.[13]

Secondly, Japanese firms appear to strive to minimize relational costs by encouraging a sense of group loyalty, commitment to equality, and a strong work ethos; the Americans rely more on the "carrot" of monetary incentives, the "stick" of unemployment, and the written contract between the two or more parties to an agreement.

The options available to U.S. and Japanese MNEs to respond to unfamiliar cultural environments are broadly the same. First, they might try to avoid potential combative situations altogether by adapting to local customs (this is likely to be practiced where the conflicts are relatively unimportant, and/or can only be resolved by the localization of organizational methods). Second, they may avoid conflict by exercising direct control over the areas where such conflict is serious enough to undermine the long-term strategy of the firm. However, the emphasis on these alternative routes differs in the two groups of firms. While, e.g., in the past, U.S. affiliates have largely conformed to local personnel practices (except in respect to incentives), Japanese MNEs, while being prepared to localize their wage systems, have strongly inculcated the management of their affiliates with the philosophy of Japanese working practices and industrial relations. Moreover, while U.S. MNEs prefer U.S. expatriates to be in charge of their sales and marketing functions, Japanese MNEs are more likely to have Japanese nationals employed in either the top or second-to-top position in finance and accounting, production, and in the purchasing department [Dunning 1993a].

Of course, the extent and complexity of intrarelational transactions, both between different parts of a MNE system and within a particular affiliate, will vary with the extent and form of foreign value added activities. In the main, the globalization of Japanese MNEs is still in its infancy. In 1989, the foreign production of their leading industrial companies averaged less than 10% of their total production; the corresponding figure for U.S. MNEs was 29%. Probably less than 2% of the total R&D undertaken by Japanese MNEs is currently conducted outside Japan. The corresponding figure for U.S. MNEs in 1989 was 10%.[14] Up to now, the local value added content of Japanese affiliates in most European countries is considerably less than that of U.S. or other European MNEs. As this rises, and it is rising, both the number of transactions and the likelihood of higher relational transaction costs also are likely to grow. Thus, the real test of the capability of Japanese MNEs to internationalize the kind of competitive cultural advantages that initially helped them establish a premier position in some world markets, remains to be seen [Gittleman and Dunning 1992; Dunning 1993].

In general, however, there are several reasons to believe that, relative to pure production costs, the transaction costs of economic activity[15] will continue to rise in the 1990s—whatever their organizational form may take. We have also suggested that part of the transaction costs of firms associated specifically with their cross-border operations will also become relatively more significant, and that any systemic economies of scope, scale, or flexibility may well be outweighed by the costs of culture specific intrafirm decision taking. Whether this does in fact occur depends on the ability of firms from different cultures to overcome the relational costs of technological advances and environmental change, and the pace and pattern of the globalization of production. Any advances in the theory of the MNE, qua MNE, must then surely await a better understanding of (a) the content of these costs, (b) how they vary according to the particular characteristics of countries, industries, and firms, and (c) what is the appropriate organizational route for replacing, surmounting, or minimizing them, relative to the benefits they confer.

Interfirm Relationships

In some ways, however, a more needful area of research, and certainly a no less challenging one, is that which arises from the growth of cross-border strategic business alliances (SBAs). Although not new, the motivation and character of these nonequity ventures has changed over the last decade. As with FDI, at least within the Triad, the objective of many SBAs is to *acquire* a competitive advantage, while the selection of partners; the concordance of management goals, attitudes and strategies; and the synergy of capabilities have become more important ingredients of success.

Interfirm alliances are of especial interest to the scholar of the MNE because they open up new organizational modes that possess some of the features of markets and hierarchies, but also some of their own. Although they are part of a hierarchical strategy of the participating firm and may be driven by market imperatives (particularly in the final goods markets), they do not fit

neatly into Williamsonian or Coasian paradigms.

Both the rationale for and the implications of SBAs, for our theorizing about the MNE, have been discussed extensively in the literature[16] and this paper will not repeat what has already been written. Instead, it will make just two points. The first is that, viewing the multiactivity firm as an initiator and organizer of a system of transactional linkages, increasing attention is now being given to the nature and form of these linkages *as a competitive or ownership (O) specific advantage in its own right*. Secondly, in our complex technological age, it would seem that not only are fewer and fewer transactions of intermediate products being conducted at arms length but that the nature of the interface between differently owned firms—be it one between buyers, sellers, or buyer and seller—is increasingly taking on the characteristics of an intrafirm relationship.

This *de facto* convergence between the two sets of relationships reflects changes in both. On the one hand—as in a marriage—the real binding force of an interfirm alliance rests not in the formal terms of the agreement but on the trust and forbearance established between the two parties. On the other, as we have already seen, the complexities of organizing a global firm suggest that an authoritarian hierarchical relationship is giving way—in part at least—to a cooperative heterarchical relationship. Such a relationship is governed less by authority and more by the need to benefit from a sharing exchange of ideas, knowledge, and values between parts of a heterarchy, so that the heterarchy, as a system, may flourish.

Obviously, the notion of intra- and interfirm cooperation—replacing interfirm contractual or intrafirm hierarchical relationships—can be pushed too far; and it is easy to wax lyrical about the benefits of cooperation while, in practice, intra and intercorporate rivalry conflict and strife abound. Two points might be made, however. The first is that technological developments and changes in the world economic environment are exerting an increasing pressure on firms to cooperate along and between value added chains if they are to compete effectively in the global market place. The second is that the organization and management of transaction intensive assets is becoming as important a competitive advantage as that of the "harder" assets of resources, technology, and human skills.

In this approach, which is echoed in the writings of various scholars, one is clearly influenced by the difference between the Japanese (or should we call it the Far Eastern) way of conducting business relationships and most of the U.S. and European way. Again, the literature is replete with examples of the way in which the Japanese MNEs conduct their interfirm relationships, especially with their supplier and industrial customers in such sectors as engineering and autos.[17] Words such as trust, loyalty, commitment, reciprocity, forbearance slip easily off the tongue, but those who have observed, not just the Japanese way, but that of all successful MNEs, cannot be but impressed by the attention given to the minimizing of culturally related transaction costs—including in this instance intercorporate cultural differences—as a prime target for success.

A recent analysis of the influence of alternative mechanism of interfirm transactions and governance on the success of firms—and particularly of Japanese automobile firms in Asia—is set out by Okada [1991]. He argues very strongly that the cooperative interface between Japanese MNEs and their suppliers, not just in the *production* of auto components, but in the *innovation* of new products, production processes, and organizational structures, stands out in marked contrast to the arms length and often adversarial relationships that frequently exist between U.S. firms and their suppliers.[18] For example, in a number of defense related sectors in the United States, it is argued that rather than adopting a cooperative stance towards the design and

manufacture of components and subassemblies, contracting firms view their suppliers as potential (if not actual) competitors.

What specifically, though, do the changing mechanisms of cooperative interaction (Okada prefers this word to transactions) have to do with the theory of the MNE *qua* MNE? Simply this—and let me state it in terms of the emerging globalization of Japanese business. If one accepts that at least part of the success of Japanese firms in world markets is due to the way in which they handle their domestic (i.e., intra-Japan) interfirm relationships, the question arises whether the Japanese engaging in foreign production can successfully export these relationships and/or adapt them to the cultures of the host countries. Putting it rather differently, if the Japanese modes of governance are successful both inside and out of Japan, to what extent can U.S. and European firms emulate or improve on them; or, indeed, innovate new methods even more appropriate to their own corporate needs?

One thing seems to be sure. The theory of the MNE needs to embrace more explicitly both intrafirm and interfirm relationships. While the markets versus hierarchies conundrum remains central, the focus of the 1990s seems likely to shift to the alternative forms of interactions formed by, or within, hierarchies (or heterarchies) and the way in which these affect the competitive position of the participating firms. It also is precisely in this area of research that a juxtaposition of different disciplinary approaches is needed, even though the *tools* of the economist provided by internalization theory, transaction costs, agency theory, and modern industrial organization theory offer an excellent framework for analysis.

MACRO-ORGANIZATIONAL THEORIES

In contrast to scholars concerned with explaining the conduct and behavior of MNEs, qua MNEs, others are more interested in explaining the growth of the foreign value activities of MNEs. Clearly, MNEs possess many characteristics *other* than their multinationality *per se*. As firms become more global, though, the attribution of their behavior to any one set of characteristics is becoming increasingly difficult. Any explanation of a country's changing propensity to be home or host to MNE related activity, however, needs to consider variables other than those that interest the microtheorist.[19] Moreover, at a meso or macro level of analysis, some variables exogenous to the microtheorist require explanation themselves.

Here again, however, the features that distinguish the determinants of the foreign from the domestic value activities of MNEs lie in the different national environments in which they produce and, just as the economist needs to join forces with organizational *et al* scholars to understand the way in which firms organize their cross-border activities, so some appreciation of the theory of political science is necessary to inject an element of reality into explanations of MNE activity. For the purposes of our discussion, we shall deliberately confine the boundaries of political science to the role of the state as a form of governance of economic activity geared to the political goals of the authorities currently in power.

If the internalization paradigm, modified by an appropriate theory of strategic behavior, is the contribution of the economist to explaining the distinctive characteristics of FDI or the MNE, the eclectic paradigm as modified by the introduction of a theory of political economy is at least a good starting point to explaining all kinds of MNE activity. It is only a starting point, however, and in the light of both technological and environmental change, needs frequent reconsideration and reformulation. In particular, we would foresee progress along three fronts. The first concerns the dynamics or developmental aspects of international production. There are various strands to this emphasis. Some interesting work is currently being done by Ozawa [1992a] and others on the interaction between inbound and outbound MNE

activity and the course of economic development and restructuring.[20] This includes the evaluation of the relevant O specific advantages of MNEs and location bound assets of countries. It also includes the way in which MNEs choose to organize the interaction between these two sets of advantages, in the light of their international strategies and as countries proceed through various stages or phases of development such as those identified by economic historians [Rostow 1959], business analysts [Porter 1990], and development economists [Chenery, Robinson, and Syrquin 1986]. Add to the staging of a country's development that of the internationalization or multinationalization process of firms, and one has the rudiments of a theory of the development and the restructuring of MNE activity.

A second and related line of progress concerns the suggestion by some scholars (e.g., Lipsey [1991]) to take account more explicitly of a nation's culture as a component of its comparative advantages. They also suggest acknowledgment that as a country moves through various stages of its development, and depending on its structure of resources and capabilities, the demands on the entrepreneurial and work culture of its people change. The culture best suited to advancing the needs of producers and consumers in the information and service economy of the 1990s is not the same as that needed for a mass production manufacturing economy of the 1960s and 1970s, or that for the early stages of contemporary industrialization. The ability of a country to identify and sustain the culture most appropriate to its resources and capabilities, and to make the necessary adaptations to that culture as its resources and capabilities (and the market for them) changes, will give it an important head start on its competitors as a location for MNE activity.

The third front of progress, and again it is related to the other two, rests in the theory of asset accumulation and/or agglomeration in explaining both the changing composition of the universe of MNEs and ability of countries to attract inbound MNE activity. Here one is involved, at a micro or macro level, with the way in which firms network with each other to the benefit or costs of the strategic groups or countries of which they are part. The relevant analytical techniques are partly those of the economics of technological change, in the Schumpeterian tradition (e.g., Pavitt [1987]; Cantwell [1989,1990]) and partly those of the economies of geographical agglomeration [Porter 1990]. However, the concept of technological accumulation needs to be widened to include all kinds of firm specific resources, including those of organization, learning, and experience; those to do with establishing and nurturing cooperative interfirm relationships [Okada 1991]; and those which relate to the degree to which a firm can sustain its privileged asset position [Dierickx and Cool 1989].[21] It could, then be hypothesized that the growth of MNE activity is positively related to the capacity of MNEs to accumulate and effectively control an international portfolio of competitive advantages in the most cost effective way.[22]

At the same time, the location of MNE activity and its competitiveness, vis-à-vis indigenous firms, is also likely to be influenced by the ability of countries to offer and build up the (complementary) assets required by MNEs. Certainly, in the advanced industrial nations, there is reason to suppose that the availability of technological and social infrastructure necessary to support the core assets of MNEs is a powerful inducement both to attract inward investment and to facilitate outward investment.

The interaction between MNE activity and the accumulated assets of a nation, via, e.g., technological transfer and competitive stimulus, has long been of interest to scholars, but is only now beginning to be formalized. In Dunning [1993b], the author has attempted to set out how this interaction *may* vary between the phases of development of a country. While, without knowledge about the kind of MNE activity and the locational characteristics of the countries concerned, the path of interna-

tional production cannot be predicted, it is possible to identify and evaluate the variables likely to influence the changes in the accumulated inward and outward investment stock over time.

Advances in the explanation of MNE activity seem likely to focus as much on factors exogenous to MNEs than those endogenous to it. In a lecture delivered at the University of Lund, Sweden, in 1989 (later published in Dunning 1990) I argued that perhaps too much emphasis had been given in the 1970s and 1980s to organizational issues, and too little to changes in the external environment, in influencing both the extent and form of MNE activity. I suggested that there were three centrally important variables. The first is the course of world economic development itself; the second is technological progress that was itself partly influenced by multinationality of firms, and the third was the role of governments in affecting the ownership, locational, and internalization (OLI) configuration facing firms.[23] We propose for the remainder of the paper to limit our comments to the last factor, which is also the third of the strands of thought to which reference was earlier made.

While by their actions governments affect and are affected by the behavior of all firms, it might reasonably be hypothesized that in a world increasingly dominated by MNE activity, these actions should take account of both the presence of such activity and its likely consequences. While the theory acknowledges this, it is perhaps not given the explicit attention it deserves. For, in a variety of ways, governments shape both the competitive advantages of domestic MNEs and the attraction of their location bound assets to inbound investors. As is most dramatically revealed in the course of the last decade, they can influence fundamentally the way in which economic activity is organized and the ethos of their constituents towards such wealth influencing variables as savings, work, innovation, entrepreneurship, income distribution, quality of demand, and so on.

Scholars like Porter [1990] would prefer to view governments as setting the framework within which a country's competitive advantages are created and sustained. Because their actions may (but not necessarily will) represent an alternative organizational form of the governance of resource allocation from that offered by markets or firms and/or may considerably influence the conduct of both firms and markets, we consider that this variable deserves special attention.[24] While this has been the case for many years, it may be argued that, in a global economy where the capabilities for production have to be created as well as the goods and services arising from such capabilities; where these capabilities can be moved across national boundaries with increasing ease; and where the markets for intermediate and final products are becoming more costly to create and to operate efficiently, then the responsibility of national governments is increased. If this is correct, then any theory of MNE activity that does not explicitly seek to understand and explain the role of governments, not just as another variable, but, like the market, as an organizational entity is, in its own right, bound to be deficient.

The way in which the distribution of the governance of economic activity between governments, firms, and markets impinges on the competitive strengths and weaknesses of firms and countries in their final goods market, and the strategic and organizational response of MNEs to these advantages, offers several challenges to the economist. Several well-established analytical tools are available. Though mainly applied to explaining the choice between markets and hierarchies, transaction cost analysis can no less be applied to the reasons for which, and the extent to which, governments, directly or indirectly, may influence resource allocation.[25] The principles underlying strategic trade policy can be extended to other areas of government germane to MNE activity.

At the same time, these tools require the complementary assets of other scholars. It is impossible, for example, simply to transfer Japanese or Korean government policies out of their environment to say Spain or Nigeria and expect them to work. Some knowledge of the competitive theory of government behavior and of political institutions, not to mention wider issues of culture identified earlier, is necessary. All this may not be good news to the "pure" economist; however, for many years now, the IB scholar has argued for an interdisciplinary approach to his subject, simply because the key difference between international and domestic business issues lies in the legal, political and cultural characteristics which separate nations from each other.

CONCLUSIONS

This rather speculative paper has tried to identify some—and only some—of the lacunae in the theories of MNE and MNE activity and to suggest some of the avenues for further research in the 1990s. The paper has suggested that the changing characteristics of intra- and interfirm relationships are requiring an extension and/or reappraisal of certain aspects of internalization theory, while the future explanation of the extent and location of MNE activity requires more systematic treatment of the role of cultural and government related variables in affecting the OLI configuration facing MNEs and their strategic response to it. In both parts of the paper, the need for an interdisciplinary approach has been stressed. Lest I might be accused of watering down the intellectual content of a single discipline, let me say this is far from my intention. What I have in mind is for the assets of a core discipline, e.g., organization theory, economics, political science, marketing *et al* to be combined with the complementary assets of related disciplines. Only then will a systemic and holistic explanation of our subject matter be a realistic possibility.

NOTES

1. For recent reviews of these different approaches see Cantwell (1991) and Dunning (1992b).

2. A point made at some length, but from a somewhat different perspective to that taken in this paper by Strange (1988), Behrman and Grosse (1990), Eden and Hampson (1990), Yarbrough and Yarbrough (1990), Schmidtchen and Schmidt-Trenz (1990), and Grosse and Behrman (1992). For an analysis of the various approaches to identifying and evaluating the interaction between IB and governments see Boddewyn (1988;1991).

3. The concept of the territoriality of law resulting in a heightened amount of risk specific to international transactions is developed by Schmidtchen and Schmidt-Trenz (1990). In this paper, the authors argue that many of the specific properties of cross-border transaction can be traced to constitutional uncertainty caused by the different national legal and regulatory systems.

4. The term in the sense defined above or taking Webster's definition as the skills, arts, etc., of a given people at a given period of time.

5. As recently discussed by Hedlund and Rolander (1991) and Hedlund and Kogut (1993).

6. Other approaches include that of Hedlund and Kogut (1993), who suggest that the modern MNE is better received as a professional organization than as a bureaucracy; and that rather than thinking of the headquarters of the firm as being the brain with its subsidiaries being the links, it would be more helpful to conceive of the firm as a brain where all parts of the organization contribute to the thinking as well as the action.

7. The literature on this subject is vast. For a contemporary examination of such practices, especially as they affect intrafirm organizational costs, see several essays in Kogut (1993).

8. This point is enlarged upon in Buckley and Casson (1991).

9. As we shall explain later, we prefer the term relational costs, as many intra- and interfirm costs have only a distant bearing on specific transactions. Indeed, much more work is needed on the different kinds of costs arising from the establishment, substance and implementation of ongoing commercial relationships.

10. See, for example, Dunning (1986, 1992a), Schmitter (1988), Gustafsson and Williamson (1989), Weiermair (1990), Fruin and Nishiguchi (1993), Lindberg, Campbell and Hollingsworth (1992), and Lincoln (1992).

11. These differences are similar to those suggested by William Ouchi in 1977 in distinguishing two measures of administrative control,

viz., behavioral and output control. Ouchi argued that the former was necessary to ensure that the performance expected of people was actively achieved; whereas, the control of output was less dependent on idiosyncratic human behavior, and could be adjusted by some kind of mechanical or electronic device, to achieve expected performance.

12. The decline in hierarchical integrated mass production and mass distribution systems, and a labor-capital accord in the form of tacit informal understandings and collective bargaining practices between large industrial oligopolies and no less bureaucratic trade unions, has been fashioned by a series of events over the last 30 years. These have included a rebellion by labor unions against the monotonous and repetitive character of narrowly defined tasks, a rise in the educational qualifications and expectations of many workers, the world economic recession of the 1970s, the introduction of new and flexible techniques of manufacturing and information systems, the greater attention paid by consumers to the quality and variety of goods and services purchased, the demobilization of national oligopolies as competition has become global, and the greater pressure on firms to engage in cross-border joint ventures and strategic alliances, e.g., to exploit unfamiliar markets and/or to gain technological synergy, or exploit scale economies. All these events have necessitated a reconceptualization of the nature of production, and have dramatically affected the form of intra (and interfirm) relations. Toyotaism is one attempt to come to grips with these environmental changes, although, in turn, it is requiring several modifications to meet the new technical, organizational and environmental challenges of the 1990s (Weiermair 1990; Fruin and Nishiguchi 1993).

13. For an excellent account of these differences, see Fruin and Nishiguchi (1993). In particular, the authors emphasize the importance attached to the mutuality of networking relationships, the specificity of transaction rights being separated from the residual rights of ownership, and the concept of embeddedness, which refers to the accumulation of the relational goodwill arising from the continuous interaction of people, institutions and institutional environments over time. For an explanation of differences in U.S. and Japanese corporate structure in terms of economics of trust see Casson and Nicholas (1989).

14. Data of these kinds are contained in the U.S. Department of Commerce (1991) and UN (1992).

15. Defined as costs of producing a good or service in a perfect market.

16. See e.g., some excellent contributions in Contractor and Lorange (1988) and Buckley (1993).

17. See those identified in note 10.

18. Again, examples can be found to the contrary, particularly in sections in which there is a strong Japanese presence.

19. It will be observed that in the first part of the paper, we dealt with only organizational issues except in so far as these were affected by the location of value added activities we did not deal with location issues *per se*.

20. We use the word restructuring to cover the development of already industrially developed countries (which embrace mostly the OECD countries).

21. According to Dierickx and Cool (1989), the sustainability of a firm's accumulated assets depends on how easily assets may be substituted or imitated. This, in turn, is linked to the characteristics of the asset accumulation process, e.g., the extent to which there are asset mass efficiencies, interconnectedness between assets and the speed of erosion, e.g., by obsolescence, of asset values. In the light of the argument set out earlier, we might add the form and content of relational assets to these characteristics.

22. Resource-based theory is also relevant to this discussion (Wernerfelt 1984; Barney 1991; Mahoney and Pandian 1992), but the concepts of rent yielding resources needs to be broadened out to incorporate rents which may arise from the accumulation of relational competitive advantages.

23. For a further elaboration of this concept see Dunning (1990, 1991a and b).

24. See also Chapter 5 of this volume.

25. Since writing these paragraphs, I have come across an extremely interesting contribution by Eden and Hampson (1990) which identifies several different kinds of failures specific to cross border markets. Some of these are economic; others relate to distributional conflicts and security dilemmas. All are relevant to the kind of arguments I am making in this paper.

■ ■ ■

Images, Economies of Concatenation, and Animal Spirits—Dependency vs. Emulation Paradigms
Terutomo Ozawa

Following Kenneth Boulding [1956], I begin with the proposition that the *image* of reality (how we perceive the world around us and how we interpret the *messages* therefrom) governs our thinking and behavior. Since reality is in a state of constant flux, our images also must change. Our perception, however, often lags behind a sudden change in reality. Without exception, economic theories of international business (IB) are formulated in accordance with theorists' perceptions of the global economy; that is, models are built in theorists' images of reality. In this regard, there is no *absolute* truth about reality; it all depends on our perception and interpretation.

So far as IB activities (trade and invest-ment) are concerned, two fundamental images of the world economy have dominated our thinking over more than a century; one image was perceived and bequeathed by Adam Smith in the tradition of economic liberalism and the other by Karl Marx in the philosophy of socialism.

As we know, Smith developed a sanguine, probusiness view of the world against the backdrop of the buoyant dynamic era of incipient capitalism he witnessed in Glasgow, where merchants, shippers, and bankers all prospered by importing an ever-rising amount of tobacco from Virginia and the West Indies in exchange for Glasgow products such as silk, leather, and iron. "Glasgow belonged to him; it was his laboratory and its merchants were his teachers."[1]

On the other hand, Karl Marx was forming a different image as he observed the turbulent period toward the end of the Industrial Revolution in which income distribution had been increasingly polarized into astronomical wealth and abysmal poverty. Marx saw two classes emerge from the unbridled growth of capitalism—the bourgeoisie and the proletariat. Thus the phenomenon of class struggle he perceived came to underlie his analysis.

Interestingly, the two schools have impacted our thinking of trade and investment in a rather diametric fashion. In the main, Smithian economic liberalism has come to dominate the way we think of international trade, as best exemplified by the Ricardian doctrine of comparative advantage. On the other hand, the Marxist school has so far been very strong in conceptualizing the role of foreign investment in Third World countries—namely, the neo-Marxist dependency theory buttressed especially by Latin America's experience.[2] The latter state exists partly because the dependency theory has not encountered any viable and equally persuasive theoretical alternative that is empirically based on some positive relationship between multinational corporations (MNCs) and the host country's economic development.

Yet the recent experiences of the rapidly growing Asian Pacific economies with inward foreign investments give us a whole new perspective. MNEs can serve as powerful jump-starters for growth in the labor-driven phase of economic development. Indeed, the Asian Pacific is presenting itself as an *ideal* laboratory—another Glasgow— for theorizing the positive interaction of foreign investment with local development. The purpose of this paper is to capitalize on this godsend opportunity for conceptualizing a new analytical framework, what may be called an emulation paradigm, that it is hoped can serve as an antithesis to the dependency theory.

TOWARD THE EMULATION THEORY OF MULTINATIONAL CORPORATION-FACILITATED DEVELOPMENT

New Messages from the Asian Pacific

A recent newsletter, *Transnationals* [Oct. 1991:1], of the United Nations Centre on Transnational Corporations (UNCTC) is upbeat on foreign direct investment (FDI) in Asia:

> Growing from $3 billion in 1980 to $16.5 billion in 1989, annual investment flows to Asia quintupled in the last decade. Taken together, 21 Asian countries now receive about a half of all flows to the developing world. The growth was especially sharp in the late 1980s, mirroring a surge in Japanese investments.
>
> Four newly industrializing economies— Hong Kong, Singapore, the Republic of Korea and Taiwan Province of China— drew half of all 1980s inflows to Asia. Indonesia, Malaysia, the Philippines and Thailand—all members of the Association of South-East Asian Nations—received 26 percent. China accounted for 19 percent, with inward investment growing 13 times between 1982–1988.

The outcome of such a phenomenal infusion of foreign investments into the Asian Pacific has been a *concomitant* explosive economic growth and trade expansion throughout the region.

The neo-Marxist dependency theory— and its widely held image of capitalism— does not fly in the face of the symbiotic relationships that exist between MNCs and the developing host countries in the Asian Pacific and the crucial role played by the former as jump-starters for development. In fact, the Asian experiences present several "paradoxes": (1) an undreamed-of rise in wages and household incomes and even the occurrence of labor shortages in the labor-driven stage of development (the very stage viewed by radical economists as the *worker-exploiting* one), (2) a very fast accumulation of domestic savings and investable surpluses at home despite—or rather because of—a heavy dependence on foreign MNCs in labor-driven manufacturing and exports, (3) a relatively equitable income distribution, and (4) the quick emergence of labor-seeking multinationals from the very developing countries (notably the newly industrializing countries or NICs) which themselves were only a short time ago labor-surplus and low-wage economies. Some rapidly developing economies are joining the ranks of multinational employers of low-wage workers from their less-developed brethren, spreading employment opportunities.

All these empirical revelations (facts) are adamantly contrary to the visions of the neo-Marxist dependency school. The economic miracles in the Asian Pacific are thus flashing new messages that demand a change in the fast-obsolescing image of the global economy still held not only by radical economists but also by some orthodox theorists of contemporary IB.

Back in 1950, for example, Taiwan, Hong Kong, and Singapore had about the same income as in Kenya, Pakistan, and Bangladesh. War-torn South Korea had a much lower per capita income. Yet Singapore and Hong Kong now enjoy per capita incomes higher than those of Spain and Ireland, and South Korea's income exceeds Portugal's [World Bank 1991]. The so-called new NICs (Thailand, Malaysia, and Indonesia) are also catching up rapidly. Even South China, centered on the special economic zones in the provinces of Guangdon, Fujian, and Hunan, has been booming at an astonishing pace. In Guangdon, for example, real rate of growth has been 12.5 percent per year over the past ten years, with per capita GDP now reaching the level of $2,000 a year, thanks largely to the phenomenal rise in inward FDI, especially from Hong Kong and Taiwan.[3]

One thing clear about the Asian miracles is that all of them began to see their incomes rise phenomenally after they adopted *an outward-looking, export-promoting course of development, which opened up some significant segments of their economies for FDI and trade.* There is good reason for a close correlation between outer orientation and FDI-triggered growth in the Asian miracles, as will be detailed below. Indeed, their vigorous growth is *unthinkable* without the involvement of MNCs as investment financiers, entrepreneurial organizers, technology providers, and connectors with the world market.

DEPENDENCY VS. EMULATIVE DEVELOPMENT

Marx vs. Smith et al.

Given the above-described phenomenon of MNC-facilitated development in the Asian Pacific, a theoretical void clearly exists; we have no theory of MNCs as facilitators of economic development that can capture this explosive growth made possible by the symbiosis of multinationals and the local host economies, no theory that can replace—and serve as an antithesis to—the dependency theory. Hence, I like to propose what may be called an emulation paradigm of MNC-facilitated economic development, a thesis 180 degrees opposite to the Marxist dependency theory.[4]

The first fundamental difference is that unlike the dependency school which derives its theoretical underpinning from Marxism, the emulation paradigm draws on economic liberalism and technological dynamism— the ideas of free markets and individual initiative originally espoused by Adam Smith and the notions of innovation and latecomers' catch-up developed by Joseph A. Schumpeter [1934;1961], Thorstein Veblen [1939], and Alexander Gerschenkron [1962].

First, it is worth recalling an incisive observation made by Adam Smith more than 200 years ago:

> Private people who want to make a fortune, never think of retiring to the remote and poor provinces of the country, but resort either to the capital, or to some of the great commercial towns. They know that where little wealth circulates, there is little to be gotten; but that *where a great deal is in motion, some share of it may fall to them.* The same *maxims* which would in this manner direct the common sense of

[individuals] . . . should make a whole nation *regard the riches of its neighbours as a probable cause and occasion for itself to acquire riches.* A nation that would enrich itself by foreign trade, is certainly most likely to do so when its neighbours are all *rich and industrious.* (emphases added) [1776;1908:378]

This statement, though deceptively simple and elementary, contains so much truth. Any underdeveloped country, if it is really serious about raising its standard of living most effectively as a member of the international community, should open up its economy judiciously so as to *align* the direction of its development effort mostly with the advanced countries so that it can *avail itself of opportunities to trade, interact with, and learn from them—that is, to feed on their lush pastures* [Ozawa 1992a].

Indeed, ever since the Industrial Revolution in England ushered the world into the present modern economy fundamentally built on science and technology, industrialization in the rest of the world, wherever successful, has been essentially a *derived* phenomenon, in the sense that a "follower" or "latecomer" economy can emulate and learn from the already advanced ("leader" or "teacher") economies. Continental Europe succeeded to industrialize by following Britain's footsteps through commercial contacts and conscious efforts for learning and emulation [Landes 1969]. So did the United States at the start of industrialization: "When the U.S. began to industrialize in the nineteenth century, she was following a path which had been blazed earlier by Great Britain. Much of the technology which was introduced into America during this period was in fact borrowed from that country, with varying degrees of modification" [Rosenberg 1972:59]. More bluntly put, "America started off as a copier" and "stole British technology" [Thurow 1985:1]. America, however, quickly pioneered by introducing numerous innovations in the area of mass production and mass marketing. So did the Soviet Union in its modernization efforts by adding some significant improve-

ments [Gerschenkron 1962]. Likewise, Japan's economic miracle in both the pre- and post-World War II periods was based on this same mechanism of learning and emulation under the hegemony of the Pax Britannica early on and under that of the Pax Americana more recently. Both hegemonies created a concatenation of "leader-follower" or more appropriately "leader-challenger" links among the aspiring nations.

The Smithian notion of what may be hereafter identified as *economies of concatenation* thus jibes with Joseph A. Schumpeter's theory of economic development [1934] when the latter is interpreted in an international context. In Schumpeter's vision, innovators' initial advantages are doomed to be competed away as hordes of "imitators" quickly move into the newly developed market or industry, and this process of emulation and learning is the very elixir of wide-spreading development and growth—and the cause of a business cycle.[5]

Although Schumpeter did not elaborate on the diffusion process of innovations, emulators themselves may eventually turn into innovators as they incrementally improve and perfect the existing ways of "making new combinations" or even come up with drastically new approaches. Here lies the possibility of a change in the global captains of industry. In this regard, Thorstein Veblen's thesis of latecomer advantages [1919] is highly relevant. He emphasized the peculiar advantages of Germany and Japan as latecomers to global industrialism. Alexander Gerschenkron [1962] reiterated "an advantage of backwardness;" latecomers can compensate for their weak position in terms of new institutional arrangements. They are able to spare the expense of reinventing wheels and escape from being stuck with obsolete technology since they are in a position to choose among and pick the latest technologies "off the shelf."

When the basic ideas of Smith, Schumpeter, Veblen, and Gerschenkron are synthesized into *a model of emulative development,* we can state that *the more advanced the leader economy is, the greater the opportunities for the challengers to catch up rapidly* (provided that the follower has a social capacity to mobilize its population for the challenge of emulation, as will be discussed below). The advanced countries are the rich reservoirs of industrial technology, information, experiences, finance, and purchasing power which the challengers can tap. They provide the promising export markets from which the less developed countries can earn foreign exchange with which to pay for the imported capital goods needed for industrialization. Nowadays, furthermore, these trading and learning opportunities are all the more expanded, because the advanced countries themselves take the initiative to make use of hierarchical relations and structural differences (in technology, factor endowments, and per-capita incomes) by way of their MNCs' activities and their official development aid (ODA) programs. Thus, not only the followers (as stressed by Adam Smith) but also the leaders themselves can gain from this structure of hierarchical relations, *a structure that creates opportunities for the less developed to emulate the advanced—and for the advanced to transfer, for both commercial and altruistic (humanitarian) reasons, their knowledge and skills down the hierarchy*. These two-way flows of benefits are the manifestations of *economies of concatenation in economic development*.

What is more, the potential for exploiting the economies of concatenation has greatly expanded in the recent past because of ever-improving means of international communication and transportation—and of national economic management. That is to say, the *pace of catch-up* has been accelerating. It took the United Kingdom nearly 60 years (1780–1838) to double its per capita output; the United States, 47 years (1839–1886); Japan, 34 years (1885–1919); Turkey, 20 years (1857–1877); Brazil, 18 years (1961–1979); South Korea, 11 years (1966–1977); and China, only 10 years (1977–1987) [World Bank 1991]. A similar trend is observable in the average rate of real wage increases: "While it took English workers seventy years to raise their real earnings by roughly 150%, Korean manufacturing workers achieved a comparable gain in about 20 years (from 1955 to 1976). In just one decade, 1969–1979, real wages in Korea rose by more than 250%" [Amsden 1989:197]. These phenomena unequivocally demonstrate the working of what I like to identify as *the principle of accelerating catch-up in income*. I also would like to posit that this is all happening mainly because of the ever-expanding economies of concatenation in development that are created—and reaped—by IB activities.

The principle of accelerating catch-up in income operates because knowledge or information is basically borderless and travels fast. IB activities, along with international education activities (i.e., overseas studies and research by students and scholars), not only bridge the gaps in knowledge, that is, equilibrating Wallasian-type knowledge arbitrage, but also lead to synergistic creations of "new combinations" in knowledge, that is, disequilibrating (gap-creating) Schumpeterian-type knowledge advancement. The former type of knowledge transfer is prevalent between advanced countries and developing ones, while the latter type is more frequently observed among the advanced countries. So far as the developing countries are concerned, this essentially means that "the options and prospects facing latecomers [at least, initially] are necessarily influenced by what is going on in pioneers" [Bell 1987:2], although latecomers themselves often turn into path-breakers in the course of catching up and surging ahead [Abramovitz 1986].

What, then, would the neo-Marxist dependency school say to this? According to their view, the outer-oriented developing economies are subjugated to exploitation by foreign capital and left helplessly impoverished as foreign capital siphons off the surpluses (profits) extracted from local labor. In fact, so far as the exploitation of labor by capital is concerned, it first occurs at home and then spreads overseas. The exploitation of labor is thus universal and nondiscriminatory; both domestic and foreign labor are exploited.

Furthermore, any IB exchange between the advanced and the less advanced is considered "unequal exchange" and a *zero-sum* game, since development and enrichment at one pole (i.e., the advanced world) are inextricably coupled with underdevelopment and impoverishment at the other (the Third World). Thus any hierarchical relationship between the advanced and the developing countries creates only exploitative opportunities for the former, polarizing their welfare positions. Here, the law of uneven development and polarization governs; instead of gap-closing (as envisaged in the principle of accelerating catch-up in income), gap-widening continues.

As far as the hierarchical structure of the world economy is concerned, the dependency school postulates that only the *dominant-dependent* relations (which I would characterize as maliciously dominant and pathetically dependent) exist between the advanced and the less advanced, and not the *leader-challenger* (leading with goodwill and ardently challenging) relations we can observe in the Asian Pacific. Here lies an enormous *perceptive* difference in images of the global economy between the two sets of relations.

This Marxist mind set has been retained by Latin American economists. Their common view is well expressed by Theotonio Dos Santos [1970:231]:

> In analyzing the process of constituting a world economy that integrates the so-called "national economies" in a world market of commodities, capital, and even of labor power, we see that the relations produced by this market are unequal and combined—unequal because development of parts of the system occurs at the expense of other parts. Trade relations are based on monopolistic control of the market, which leads to the transfer of surplus generated in the dependent countries to the dominant countries; financial relations are, from the viewpoint of the dominant powers, based on loans and the export of

capital, which permit them to receive interest and profits, thus increasing their domestic surplus and strengthening their control over the economies of the other countries. For the dependent countries these relations represent an export of profits and interest which carries off part of the surplus generated domestically and leads to a loss of control over their productive resources. In order to permit these disadvantageous relations, the dependent countries must generate large surpluses, not in such a way as to create higher levels of technology but rather *superexploited manpower*. The result is to limit the development of their internal market and their technical and cultural capacity, as well as the moral and physical health of their people. We call this combined development because it is the combination of these inequalities and the transfer of resources from the most backward and dependent sectors to the most advanced and dominant ones which explains the inequality, deepens it, and transforms it into a necessary and structural element of the world economy (emphases added).

Dos Santo's view once epitomized the fusion of ECLA (the United Nations Commission on Latin America) structuralism and neo-Marxist dependency theory that "became the accepted way to describe Latin American economic relations, not only among radical intellectuals but among commentators, government officials, the military, and politicians" [Sigmund 1980:35]. We can find many variants of dependency theory (for example, Baran [1957]; Furtado [1976]; Amin [1976]; and Frank [1967]).

Outer-oriented vs. Inner-oriented Regime

Can we really observe such behaviors of foreign investors as described above in the Asian Pacific? Clearly not. Indeed, the Asian experience—and the emulation paradigm—turn the Marxist dependency school on its head; *the very exposure of a labor-surplus economy to the forces of IB enriches (instead of impoverishes) that economy's national income and raises (instead of lowers) wage rates, because labor is superactivated instead of superexploited.*

A critical question then, needs to be answered: Why is it that MNCs, supposedly the ruthless vanguards of international capitalism in neo-Marxists' perspective, behave in such a manner to promote local economic development as they do in the Asian Pacific? Didn't they prove to be malicious "octopuses" in Latin America?

One fundamental difference between the two developing regions is that the currently booming Asian economies all have turned to global market forces much earlier and more decisively than their Latin American counterparts by opening up labor-intensive manufacturing activities to the world. In fact, they have connected import substitution with its subsequent phase of export promotion in a particular industry as a sequential development process of comparative advantage. The rapidly developing Asian economies, initially Japan, then the NICs (Singapore, Hong Kong, Taiwan, and South Korea), the new NICs (Thailand, Malaysia, Indonesia, and the Philippines), and the "new" new NICs (China, and possibly, India, Pakistan, Sri Lanka, and Bangladesh) have gone, and are currently going or attempting to go, through the labor-driven stage of development by adopting outward-looking, export-promoting (OL-EP) policies for FDI in varying degrees.

What is crucial for export-focused development is that inward foreign investment needs to be made in such a manner that the developing host countries' *existing* or *potential* comparative advantage can be fostered and fully maximized, that is, in a comparative-advantage-augmenting fashion. Let's call this *the principle of trade augmentation through MNCs*. Here, the notion of protrade FDI (and that of antitrade FDI) introduced by Kojima [1975;1985] is quite relevant. The beauty of the OL-EP regime is that it automatically attracts protrade FDI rather than antitrade FDI, since it eagerly promotes the export sector (comparatively advantaged one) with a variety of incentives (including the establishment of export-pro-

cessing zones). Trade augmentation naturally follows through FDI, magnifying the power of trade.

The OL-EP approach also enables the developing country to go through multiple phases of industrial upgrading gradually, each phase compatible with its corresponding factor endowments (capital-labor ratios) and technological capacity in an unjumbled manner. This evolutionary path fits the Smithian notion of an optimal sequencing of development ("a natural order of things") starting from the initial stage of labor-intensive, low-skill manufacturing or from the initial stage of natural resource extraction and moving on to the subsequent stage of relatively physical-capital-intensive industrial activities and finally to the more advanced stage of human-capital-intensive growth. After all, the nation grows by upgrading its structure as its factor and technological endowments change with the accumulation of physical and human capital (relative to resources and "raw" labor). *The higher the per capita gross national product, the larger the per capita stock of physical and human capital relative to that of resources and the larger the per capita stock of human capital relative to that of physical capital.* The economy continuously evolves to develop new comparative advantage by shifting from technologically less sophisticated, low-productivity products to more sophisticated, higher-productivity industrial activities requiring a large input of human capital [Chenery 1960]. This orderly process of development and trade may be called *the principle of stages-compatible structural upgrading*, a principle brought into operation under OL-EP policy. The recent Asian experiences all delineate the close interrelatedness between FDI, dynamic comparative advantage, and structural upgrading, along the paths of their rising human- and physical-capital/resource proportions and technological progress.

Indeed, a high correlation between outward orientation and supergrowth has been empirically confirmed (mainly based on the Asian experiences) [Balassa 1989; World Bank 1991]. The causative links between those two phenomena, however, still are left unexplained. The above-identified prin-

industrialization" [1970: 234]. The one-sided IL-IS policy creates lucrative opportunities for both MNCs and local elites to collude and enrich their own interests at the

Figure 1. Upward Spiral Process

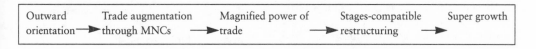

Outward orientation→ Trade augmentation through MNCs → Magnified power of trade → Stages-compatible restructuring → Super growth →

ciples of trade augmentation through MNCs and of stages-compatible structural upgrading, taken together, can thus provide one possible inside mechanism for this black box as shown in Figure 1.

(How this upward-spiral type of process is also accompanied by the mechanisms for wage hikes, an unskewed income distribution, and the accumulation of local capital will be discussed below).

In contrast, as we all know, Latin American countries until very recently had long pursued inward-looking, import-substituting (IL-IS) policies—without any connecting links with export promotion. Under such totally inward-oriented policies, factor prices are grossly distorted in favor of comparatively disadvantaged, inefficient, white elephant industries, at the cost of discouraging the development of comparatively advantaged labor-intensive light industries that can create employment opportunities for the masses. Once the nation allows any inward FDI, monopoly-rent-seeking MNCs from the capital-intensive, technologically sophisticated industries in the advanced countries are naturally attracted only to such protected (comparatively disadvantaged) local markets. Wrong policy thus attracts wrong MNCs. In fact, Dos Santos himself admits that what he calls "traditional decadent oligarchies" in Latin America are responsible for the willingness of "the national bourgeois governments to facilitate the entry of foreign capital in order to supply the restricted national market, which is strongly protected by high tariffs in order to promote

cost of the masses—hence, the phenomenon of "superexploited manpower." The masses are exploited by decadent local elites who constitute the "internal interdependent 'colonial' centers" as much as by foreign capitalists who represent the "metropolitan centers" [1970:234].

The way out of such "combined development" is to move away from inward-looking jingoistic policies toward outward-looking, export-focused ones. This outer-oriented trade/FDI regime is crucial if a developing host country is to attract stages-compatible investments from MNEs. Latin American structuralism has been the very outcome of their own IL-IS approach; the OL-EP regime can lead to a *new* structuralism (i.e., the "outer orientation-super-growth" structure) as evidenced in the Asian Pacific.

Resigned Dependency vs. Mobilized Emulation

In addition, there is another fundamental difference between the neo-Marxist dependency theory and the emulation paradigm. As stressed earlier, the former regards the leader as *maliciously dominating* (or oppressor) and the laggard as *pathetically dependent and helplessly manipulated (or oppressed) at the will of foreign capitalists.* In sharp contrast, the emulation thesis is built on the *challenging spirits and aggressive strategies* pursued on the part of the followers. It is not the dominant-and-dependent relationship but the leader-and-challenger (or teacher-and-learner) relationship.

In this regard, what Simon Kuznets [1968:100] emphasized is relevant:

> Without continuous economic relations between the "laggard" and the more advanced countries, the drive toward modern economic growth is not likely to be generated in the former. It follows that the "opening up" of the laggard countries by the threat of force on the part of the advanced countries is a *prerequisite* for the spread of economic growth to the former.
>
> This pattern seems simple enough, but it is true only for countries at *widely different* levels of economic and social development and hence of power. It finds classic corroboration in the "opening up" of Japan and the spread of modern economic growth to that country. (emphases added)

The "threat of force" (the show of force displayed by "black ships" in the fearsome bombardment of Japanese ports) is obviously no longer permissible. But Kuznets's observation is still quite pertinent for the present-day world in two respects; (1) economic contacts between the advanced and the laggard serve as a powerful "wake-up" call or a trigger for emulation, and (2) the gap in economic and social development between the two is a positive asset, *if properly exploited*, for the enhancement of the laggard's and the world's economic welfare; the larger the gap, the more powerful the stimulant—namely, the greater the potential for economies of concatenation.

This way of interpreting the role of interaction in spreading industrialism and modernization is also clearly postulated in Arnold J. Toynbee's famous thesis of *challenge and response* [1934:277–78]. "The function of 'the external factor' is to supply 'the inner creative factor' with a perpetual stimulus of the kind best calculated to evoke the most potently creative variations."

Highly motivated economic agents (constituents) are then necessary if the society, in aggregate, is capable of reacting creatively to external stimuli. On this point, the Smithian market system or the "invisible hand" apparatus is envisaged to work because each individual relentlessly pursues his or her "selfish" interest. Here the implicit assumption is that each individual is a highly motivated challenger in response to external stimuli or a demonstration effect. In *The Theory of Moral Sentiments*, Adam Smith had the following image of individuals:

> The poor man's son, whom heaven in its anger has visited with ambition, when he begins to look around him, admires the condition of the rich. He finds the cottage of his father too small for his accommodation, and fancies he should be lodged more at his ease in a palace . . . It appears in his fancy like the life of some superior rank of beings, and, in order to arrive at it, he devotes himself forever to the pursuit of wealth and greatness. To obtain the conveniences which these afford, he submits in the first year, nay, in the first month of his application, to more fatigue of body and more uneasiness of mind, than he could have suffered through the whole of his life from the want of them . . .
>
> He studies to distinguish himself in some laborious profession. With the most unrelenting industry he labours night and day to acquire talents superior to all his competitors. [1759:259–260]

If all individuals were as much *self-motivated* as Smith envisioned, the entire society could operate at the maximum level of motivation and emulation. The challenge-and-response mechanism would always work perfectly. Yet not all individuals are necessarily so highly self-motivated. Social engineering for emulation may thus be required.

Interpreted in this manner, my analysis directly links up with what Mark Casson is emphasizing in his paper: the emotional aspect of a social group. The strength and effectiveness of response to challenges (external stimuli) on the part of the laggard countries are no doubt conditioned by its cultural and socio-psychological characteristics.

Social mobilization at the emotional level is required for a latecomer so as to form a "disciplined" society that can take advantage of—and by so doing, close—

gaps (technological, institutional, and economic), and exploit economies of concatenation. In this regard, the latecomer cannot afford to run a "soft state." This point was stressed by Gunnar Myrdal [1968:67]. A *prerequisite* to economic development "the success of planning for development requires a readiness to place obligations on people in *all* social strata . . . It requires, in addition, rigorous enforcement of obligations, in which compulsion plays a strategic role."

In other words, the engineering of loyalty in widely-dispersed groups [Casson] is a crucially important social task required of any aspiring developing country. The fast-growing Asian Pacific economies, on the whole, have been successful in "engineering" disciplined managers and workers by maintaining the appropriate incentive and disciplinary socio-economic apparatuses. The governments (mandarins and bureaucrats, if not politicians) of Japan, Taiwan, South Korea, Singapore, and Hong Kong have been relatively corruption-free and strongly collective-welfare-minded. They have succeeded in building "hard states" by Myrdal's criteria.

It may be said that economic development requires four basic wares: "hardware," "software," "humanware,"[6] and "spiritware." The importance of spiritware cannot be overemphasized as a driving force for modernization. I like to use "spiritware" interchangeably with the phrase, *animal spirits*, although Karl Marx and John Maynard Keynes used it in somewhat different contexts. Marx [1867:325–26] explained how "mere social contact begets in most industries an emulation and a stimulation of the animal spirits that heighten the efficiency of each individual workman." Keynes [1936:161] described an "irrational" investment behavior that reflects "a spontaneous urge to action rather than inaction," causing an outward shift of the "marginal efficiency of capital." My use of this phrase, "animal spirits," though it refers to a human urge to action, is closer—and indeed, similar in its focus on the socio-emotional aspect of em-

ulation—to Marx's, but rather at the mobilized national level than at the microlevel of a team work on the factory floor. The nationally mobilized or engineered animal spirit to challenge the leader is a key explanatory factor in the emulation paradigm.

Internalization vs. Cooperative Affiliation

The forms of investment adopted by MNCs have dramatically diversified from the conventional type of whole or majority ownership (that excludes any local participation in equity interest and decision making) to a great variety of forms, the latter now collectively called "new forms of investment" [Oman 1984]. The new forms include minority-owned joint ventures, licensing agreements, subcontracting, management and marketing contracts, and other non-equity types of contractual arrangements in which local interests are able to participate in both ownership and decision making.

FDI is obviously not an arm's-length transaction unconsciously coordinated by the market mechanism, but an activity managed—and internalized—within a particular organization. *Hierarchies* thus substitute for or transcend *markets*. This way of thinking is in line with, and an extension of, the transaction cost theory originated in Ronald H. Coase's work [1937]. The complete internalization postulate, however, applies to the conventional old type of multinationals whose overseas operations are wholly or majority controlled and where *command and hierarchical control* replace *the price mechanism and contracts*.

Yet a third modality of economic coordination exists; the networking of cooperative and affiliate transactions [Richardson 1973] or what may be called *links*. In this third genre, *interagent trust and reciprocity* [Polanyi 1977; Goldberg 1980; Casson 1990] and long-term legal contracts serve as the most effective binding "glue" of transactions. Indeed, interpersonal relational advantages and costs are weighing more and more heavily than ever before on the firms' operating costs, especially in component-based assembly industries where the outsourcing of intermediate goods—hence, relational exchanges between suppliers and assembler—is the most critical aspect of production. My discussion thus connects with Dunning's emphasis on relational transaction costs as opposed to pure production costs.

In this regard, new forms of investment, as adopted in the Asian Pacific in particular, are strongly governed by the binders of trust and reciprocity as the underlying transactional principles. This is in the main perhaps explainable in terms of the cultural influence of Confucianism in the region, the dominant Asian investment position of Japanese industry, and the rising role of overseas Chinese businessmen as intraregional investors. The Asian NICs follow transactional modalities that are strongly characterized by this third approach. (Here again, my analysis converges with Casson's and Dunning's in touching on the cultural and emotional aspects of IB.)

Another key difference between the conventional and the new forms of investment is that the former is aimed at extracting residuals (or surpluses) from overseas ventures by combining investors' capital with local factors (whether natural resources or labor supply), whereas the new forms are designed to sell some specific corporate assets such as technology and managerial and marketing skills and capabilities as inputs for local production in a relatively unbundled fashion [Hennart 1991b]. The latter thus avoids the most serious source of conflict with the host country, namely the extraction and repatriation of surplus from the local economies, the phenomenon that constitutes the core mechanism of exploitation of local resources envisioned by Marx.

Until recently, unfortunately, Latin American countries had long been exposed to the conventional wholly owned operations of monopoly/monopsony power-yielding multinationals from the advanced Western countries, especially in mines, utilities, and plantations, as legacies of their colonial days. Those multinationals were

essentially the exploiters of the surpluses of extractive ventures. Indeed, combined with the "gunboat" diplomacy of the United States in the pre-World War II period, Western MNCs were the vanguards of economic imperialism that turned Latin America, especially Central America, into a hodgepodge of "banana republics." Hence, quite understandably, the whole region suffered a hang-up about inward foreign investment. The image of MNCs as monstrous octopuses and oppressors of local economies thus was formed throughout the region, and expropriations and nationalizations of foreign-owned assets became commonplace in the 1960s and 1970s.

In contrast, the Asian Pacific, and East Asia in particular, has come to develop a different—somewhat more benign—image of MNCs. The Asian countries were fully aware of the monopoly/monopsony power (the "Mr. Hyde" side) of giant multinationals but were cognizant of the latter's efficiency-enhancing power (the "Dr. Jekyll" side) as well.[7] As is well known, throughout the early postwar period the Japanese government was instrumental in assisting Japanese industry to deal with powerful Western MNCs in its efforts to acquire valuable corporate assets (mainly modern technology) through licensing agreements without jeopardizing Japan's economic sovereignty [Ozawa 1974]. The successful Japanese formula clearly had a significant impact on the neighboring Asian countries' policies toward technology imports and MNCs. Through the demonstration effect in policy formulation, the whole region— first East Asia and then Southeast Asia— soon developed confidence about interacting with foreign multinationals (mostly via new forms of investment) and benefiting from such contact [Linder 1986; Enos and Park 1988; Amsden 1989].

Moreover, MNCs hosted by the developing Asian countries have quite different *modus operandi* from those experienced by Latin American countries. Joint ventures and nonequity contractual types of investment are most prevalent and sharply on the

Table 1. Differentiating Features of Two Paradigms

Component	Dependency Paradigm	Emulation Paradigm
Inferential base	Latin American experience	Asian Pacific experience
Ideology	Marxism	Liberalism
Global hierarchy	Oppressor of growth	Stimulant to growth
Operative principle	The law of uneven development and polarization	The principle of accelerating catch-up in income
		The principle of trade augmentation via MNCs
		The principle of stages-compatible industrial upgrading
	Diseconomies of concatenation	Economies of concatenation
Regime	Inward-looking, import substituting (IL-IS)	Outward-looking, export-promoting (OL-EP)
State	Soft state	Hard state
Labor	Superexploited	Superactivated
Response mentality	Resigned dependency (weak animal spirits)	Mobilized emulation (strong animal spirits)
Operative mode of MNCs	Internalization (old form of investment)	Cooperative affiliation ("new" forms of investment)

rise in the Asian Pacific, especially in labor-intensive manufacturing.[8] As will be explained below, there is good reason for this trend, and the new forms are serving as jump-starters for local development as they enable the developing host countries to reap the benefits of the new forms of investment, that is, *to secure necessary inputs for local industrial activities without totally surrendering reinvestable local surpluses to foreign interests.*

Viewed in the above light, the contours of major differences between the dependency and the emulation paradigms have emerged. Table 1 summarizes their differentiating characteristics of the two paradigms.

THE LABOR-DRIVEN STAGE OF ECONOMIC DEVELOPMENT AND MNCS

As pointed out earlier, economic development proceeds step-by-step along the path of factor growth and structural change (i.e., the principle of stages-compatible structural upgrading). The role of MNCs as facilitators of growth changes *pari passu* with the evolving stages of development.[9] The stages approach can be tied to the "stages theory of competitive development" recently introduced by Michael Porter [1990]. He observes that "despite the diversity of most economies, we can identify a predominant or emergent pattern in the nature of competitive advantage in a nation's firms at a particular time" [1990:446] by way of four distinct stages: (1) factor-driven, (2) investment-driven, (3) innovation-driven, and (4) wealth-driven. But "the first three stages involve successive upgrading of a nation's competitive advantages and will normally be associated with progressively rising economic prosperity," while "the fourth stage is one of drift and ultimately decline" [1990:546].

The Asian NICs have only recently graduated from the labor-driven (that is, factor-driven) stage and are well on their way to the investment-driven phase of building some key industries (such as steel, petrochemicals, and automobiles) and even on the threshold of the innovation-driven phase in some limited areas of the high-tech sectors, notably consumer electronics and biochemical/engineering. On the other hand, the new NICs located in Southeast Asia are in the middle of the factor-driven (resources/labor) stage, and the "new" new NICs (China, Pakistan, Bangladesh, and Sri Lanka) have just begun to enter the labor-driven stage in earnest.

Interestingly enough, the open-door

policy for MNCs has so far proved extremely effective in jump-starting the engine of development in those host economies that adopted the OL-EP labor-driven strategy. Indeed, there are many good reasons why this is the case. In the first place, such a strategy is fully in line with the power of trade envisaged in both the Smithian "vent-for-surplus" theory [Myint 1958] and the Heckscher-Ohlin (H-O) factor proportions theory [Ohlin 1933]. At the start, the developing host country usually supplies labor from its unemployed (mostly urban) and underemployed (mostly rural) labor pool at low wage rates (a process also postulated by Arthur Lewis [1954] in his model of unlimited labor supply). With the help of MNCs, a labor-surplus economy initially develops a comparative advantage in labor-intensive, technologically standardized manufactures, as envisaged in the H-O model.

The more labor-seeking FDI flows in, however, the sooner the disappearance of unemployment, if not underemployment. The MNCs-magnified power of H-O trade (i.e., under the principle of trade augmentation through MNCs) is then seen in a surprisingly rapid growth of wages, a more equitable income distribution, and a rising amount of exchange earnings from exports. This is a full reflection of the so-called "Stolper-Samuelson factor-price-magnification" effect [1941]. The demand for labor would rise quickly, pulling up local wages and soon even creating a tight labor market, albeit at relatively low wage rates by international (or advanced countries') standards. The end result is not "superexploited manpower" but superactivated manpower.

Ironically, along with the success of labor-driven exports that leads to an appreciation of the home currency, rising wages will eventually undermine the price competitiveness of their developing countries' exports. A rising incongruity between the quickly rising capital-labor endowment proportions and the labor-intensive nature of low value-added manufactures develops, creating what may be called *the principle of increasing factor incongruity*. The upshot of

all this is the emergence of low-cost-labor seeking manufacturing investments from the rapidly developing countries (especially, the Asian NICs) into other developing countries (such as China, Malaysia, Indonesia, and the Philippines) where labor supplies are still plentiful at low wages.

Interestingly, labor-driven manufacturing will also lead to a higher rate of savings at home. This is not only because wage rates will rise but also because *household* incomes will rise even faster, since more employment opportunities open up and many more *members* of a household (e.g., mothers and adolescent children) can earn incomes. Given the appropriate incentives for savings, rising household incomes become an important source of funds for industrialization.[10] The conventional analysis usually focuses only on wage rates and neglects the role of rising household incomes, even at relatively low wage rates, in raising the standard of living and generating domestic savings (reinvestable surpluses) in developing countries. This is especially true where the family serves as a basic collective production and consumption unit. What is more, the residuals (surpluses) of local manufacturing can remain in the local economy when MNCs adopt the new forms of investment, as mentioned earlier.

This income-raising mechanism of comparative-advantage-based trade can also moderate or even avoid a skewed income distribution between the "haves" (capitalists) and the "have-nots" (workers), since the H-O type of trade raises the return to an exporting country's abundant factor (workers), while restraining a rise (or even reducing) the returns to its scarce factor (capital and land).

Furthermore, when the multinational manufacturers who produce labor-intensive products or components usually operate in monopolistic markets where product differentiation occurs in physical (e.g., different models and functional features) or marketing (e.g., brand recognition through advertising) characteristics, the marginal value product of labor diverges from the value of marginal product, and they can earn *monopolistic* profits that come from the pockets of consumers in the final good market. These monopolistic profits are in essence the Schumpeterian innovation rents.

It is different from the *monopsonistic* profits that can be extracted from the employment of local workers when the wage rate is set along the supply (average-wage) function of labor instead of the marginal input (marginal-wage) function. The latter may be distinguished as the Ricardian resource rents.

Since the supply function of labor in a labor-surplus economy is very flat over a considerable range and then begins to slope upward only slowly (that is, a very high supply elasticity) in the early stages of development, any Ricardian resource rents that appear as wage rate starts to rise are relatively insignificant, especially compared to the Schumpeterian innovation rents. In other words, under these circumstances MNCs' profits, even under the conventional type of FDI, come mostly from the Schumpeterian innovation rents or the marketing end (i.e., from the pockets of consumers) of their vertical chain of value-added activities rather than the Ricardian resource rents or the production end (i.e., from the sweat of workers) [Ozawa 1992b]. The value-added chain of multinationals in modern industry is on the whole becoming more and more heavily skewed toward—and concentrated on—the final goods market than to the labor market, although a shifting of production to a lower wage location does help raise the monopolistic profits, since lower production costs lead to an expansion of markets.

In fact, many multinationals with well-established brand names (such as Sony, Siemens, Philipps, Nike, Reebok, YKK, and the like) in the final consumers' markets in the advanced countries may well be able to pay—and as a matter of fact are paying— wages relatively higher than the average local wages because of their ability to *cross-subsidize* the labor-intensive production side by the higher value-adding marketing side of their operations. Such an act may be dubbed a "Robin Hood" effect, since these multinationals are capable of "robbing the rich (in the advanced countries' markets) and giving to the poor (in the developing countries' labor markets)"—at least in the form of expanded employment opportunities.

For example, one may wonder why China, still a stubborn holdover of communism and perhaps the most likely believer in the Marxist dependency theory, is so eager to encourage inward FDI, thereby risking itself to imperialist exploitation. Most foreign multinationals in China, however, not only from the West and Japan but especially from Hong Kong and Taiwan, are highly export-oriented and adopting the new forms of investment such as joint ventures, subcontracting, and output sharing. The way they operate, these multinationals are indeed "robbing the capitalist consumers and giving to the communist workers," as they straddle their labor-driven manufacturing and exporting activities between China and the West, profiting more from the Schumpeterian rents and "sharing" them with the host in terms of providing employment opportunities. No wonder, then, they receive a blessing from Beijing.

MNCS AND HOST GOVERNMENT IN THE HIGHER-ORDER STAGES OF DEVELOPMENT

Despite the sanguine scenario presented above about the favorable interaction between MNCs and the developing host countries when the latter are in the labor-driven stage of development, there is no guarantee that this symbiosis and relative harmony can continue to prevail as the host economies move to higher-order stages of development, that is, the investment-driven and then the innovation-driven stage.

When the country reaches the threshold of higher-order stages, more physical capital, and more skill-intensive (human-capital-intensive) industries are to be built. The government must provide physical infrastructure (communications and transportation), training and education (both software and hardware), public health, R&D finance and incentives, and other "public goods." As compared to the labor-driven stage, which can be left largely to the dictates of the market with the minimum selective involvement of government (since the industries developed in such an early stage are highly competitive light industries where economic concentration is minimum), the development of more advanced industries entails an appropriate management of externalities (market imperfections), since education and training (which are the causes of positive externalities) are now the key industrial inputs, along with the minimum scale of operation required by indivisible capital investments and the accompanying economies of scale. The government is thus called upon to provide the *stages-appropriate* institutions and infrastructure investments and programs to foster the sequential development of dynamic comparative advantage [Dunning 1988b, 1991d; Ozawa 1987; World Bank 1991].

Besides, the developing countries are not likely to maintain the initial open-arm attitude toward MNCs adopted during the early labor-driven phase of industrialization. State involvement in terms of fiscal, trade, and industrial competition policies is expected to rise as the developing host economies begin to graduate from the early-phase development and strive to move up to higher value-added, more science-and-technology-based activities. The recent change in Malaysia's incentive program for MNCs is a prime example:

Malaysia unveiled a 1992 budget that scraps certain foreign investment incentives and creates others in a bid to develop more home-grown industries.

The 45.45 billion ringgit ($16.5 billion) budget, up 18% from this year's spending plan, is designed to ease the transition to industries with greater export capabilities. The plan abolishes tax breaks for firms with five-year "pioneer" status, pivotal in transforming the agriculture-based economy to one led by manufacturing. Induce-

ments such as tax abatements for export performance will be given only to firms at least 70%-owned by Malaysians. To encourage investment in high-risk businesses based on new and sophisticated technology, venture-capital firms will be offered tax incentives.[11]

Another example is South Korea. Other than in labor-intensive manufacturing, it has scarcely depended on inward FDIs. As has been the case with Japan, the Koreans have been taking advantage of licensing agreements and sharply stepping up R&D efforts to improve on imported technologies and come up with their own innovations [Enos and Park 1988; Amsden 1989]. As we all know, technological and educational activities (knowledge adoption, adaptation, and creation) inevitably generate a great deal of discrepancy between social and private benefits/costs. They also require human capital (scientists, engineers, and technicians) as inputs; inputs that the private sector alone cannot adequately create without foresighted assistance from the government. After all, education is the foundation for both innovative and adaptive activities.[12]

Furthermore, at the higher-order stages of development, the nature of interaction with foreign MNCs also changes dramatically. The multinationals in capital-intensive, R&D-based, oligopolistic industries have a strong monopolistic need to control the ownership of corporate assets (technology and access to markets) in order to recoup the ever-rising burden of R&D and market development.[13] On the other hand, the host countries become less willing to let foreign MNCs monopolize the higher-productivity high-tech industrial sectors under whole or majority ownership. The relationship between the host governments and MNCs becomes far more complex as the developing countries endeavor to build higher value-added industries.

CONCLUSIONS

The recent demise of communism in Eastern and Central Europe will surely help discredit the Marxist dependency theory, especially as these newly "marketizing" countries (NMCs) eagerly seek the help of multinationals from the West. Indeed, Latin American countries themselves are casting aside the dependency paradigm and moving away from their IL-IS stance by opening up their economies for freer trade and investment. They are making their economies more promarket and freer from direct government ownership and control.

Given these rapid recent changes in the world economy, a theoretical void clearly exists. We have no well articulated theory that can replace the neo-Marxist dependency theory. We thus need an antithetical paradigm that can explain the *positive* role of multinationals as promoter for growth in developing countries. Focusing on the recent experiences of MNCs-facilitated industrial expansion in the Asian Pacific, the emulation paradigm presented above is an attempt to fill the theoretical lacuna by accentuating the important functions of IB as they are performed during the labor-driven stage of development.

Whether the emulation paradigm is heavily dependent on region-specific factors, such as culture, political stability, and historical accidents—hence inapplicable to other regions—remains to be seen. A particular region may indeed enjoy certain competitive advantages because of the economies of concatenation generated by socio-economic/politico-cultural factors unique to that region. In this regard, the competitive advantage of *regions* may be another important research topic (only partly explored above) in addition to the "competitive advantage of nations" and the competitive advantage of "global industries" and of "global firms" [Porter 1980; 1985;1990].

NOTES

1. Sir Alexander Gray, *Adam Smith*, the Historical Association, General Series, G. 10: London, 1948: 5, as quoted in John F. Bell (1953:156).

2. Marxism has seen its own evolution in theoretical constructs. Aboriginal Marxists, Karl Marx and Lenin, argued that the export of surplus capital under colonialism would eventually encourage economic development in backward countries as part of a global capitalist system. The neo-Marxists of the mid-twentieth century, notably Frank (1967) and Amin (1976), explained the persistent underdevelopment and continuing post-colonial dependence of the developing countries on their former metropolitan nations and in terms of what is known as the dependency theory. For excellent surveys on radical perspectives, see for example, Brewer (1990), Johns (1985:259–282), and Meier (1984:133–143).

3. The South China Miracle. A great leap forward, *The Economist*, 5 Oct 1991, pp. 19–22.

4. The arguments presented here draw and expand on Ozawa (1991;1992a;1992b).

5. Interestingly, both Marx and Schumpeter foresaw the inevitable spread of modern production to latecomers but the latter paid more attention to the imitators' capacity to emulate the innovators.

6. The word "humanware" was introduced in Haruo Shimada (1988).

7. A distinction between endogenous (cognitive) and exogenous (structural) market imperfections is made in Dunning and Rugman (1985). The efficiency-enhancing property of the MNC as an organizer of economic activities is related to the former (i.e., reduction of transaction costs), while the monopoly-power aspect of the MNC to the latter (i.e., barriers to entry).

8. Minority and majority participation in joint ventures have been the prevalent form of foreign involvement in most countries, despite the abolition of restrictions on foreign ownership (UNCTC Newsletter 1992:2).

9. Similar views are expressed by Dunning (1991a) and Cantwell and Tolentino (1990).

10. For example, Japan effectively mobilized household savings into investment through its postal savings program with a tax incentive; Singapore used the Central Provident Fund Scheme under which workers and their employers are required to set aside a given proportion of their monthly earnings.

11. "Malaysia alters incentives mix," *The Wall Street Journal*, 4 November 1991, p. A 16.

12. In reference to America's experience, Nathan Rosenberg (1972:35) observes: "Not only did American society devote a large pro-

portion of its resources to inventive activities; it is also apparent that the human resources of the country were well-equipped through formal education with the skills which might raise their productivity as inventors and as successful borrowers and modifiers of technologies developed elsewhere."

13. The relationship between technological accumulation and internationalization of business activities is explored in Cantwell (1989).

■ ■ ■

COMMENTARIES

Jean-François Hennart

Comments on Economic Theories of International Business

It is obviously impossible to do justice to three very rich and stimulating papers in the space allotted. Consequently, I will limit myself to selected comments on some of the issues raised by the three authors. Culture, both company culture and national culture, is a common thread through these three papers, and it is to this theme that I will devote most of my comments.

ECONOMIC THEORIES OF INTERNATIONAL BUSINESS: A RESEARCH AGENDA

The goal of Mark Casson's paper is to show that by relaxing some of the assumptions of narrow neoclassical theory the economic theory of international business (IB) can deal with phenomena, such as the microanalysis of groups, which are an important part of IB but difficult to handle within the framework of traditional neoclassical economics. Relaxing these additional assumptions is nothing but the continuation of a trend that was started when IB theorists abandoned the fiction of zero transaction costs so as to make economics more useful for their purposes. In the process they established the foundations of an evolving theory of IB.[1]

As Casson argues, the usefulness of economics for IB is still limited by two of its as-

sumptions: (1) that individual preferences are autonomous and stable, and (2) that decision makers correctly perceive constraints. Clinging to these two assumptions has made it difficult to address issues such as human resource management and firm-government interactions as in these two areas "group centered behavior, reflecting the manipulation of preferences and the engineering of mental models by leaders, has an important influence on outcomes" [p. 186 in this volume].

Casson explores some of the avenues that open when these two assumptions are relaxed. Assuming that preferences are not autonomous makes it possible to consider the role of social interaction in changing them. Casson starts with the paradox of groups as public goods: it pays for individuals to join groups, but it also pays for them to free ride, and in so doing, destroys the group. The fear of retaliation will prevent free-riding if there is repeated interaction between the members of the group. In practice, nonselfish behavior is often observed even in the absence of repeated interaction, and this can be attributed to "leadership activity within the group." Casson suggests that a leader has the choice between two modes of control in a decentralized group: he can invoke formal legal procedures or emotional manipulation (socialization) to persuade members to discipline themselves.

Casson identifies three strategies of socialization: those involving the inculcation of guilt, shame, or status consciousness. He argues that guilt is a more reliable incentive for honesty than shame, which is in turn more reliable than status. This is because guilt involves self-monitoring, while shame involves monitoring by a small group, and status involves monitoring by a larger group. Offenders are better informed about their own actions than are peers, while peers in turn are better informed than society as a whole. Casson also notes that it is crucial that leaders be able to standardize the group. Otherwise, cheaters will be able to take advantage of the honest members. Leaders who are not able to standardize their group will resort to formal modes of control.

Casson's interesting treatment raises a number of questions. First, while it may be useful to think of socialization as furthered by a "leader," this is only a first approximation. Company culture is indeed often established by entrepreneurs, but no particular individual can be singled out as responsible for fostering other forms of socialization. Guilt, for example, is inculcated in Western societies both in the form of religion and in the form of general morality. It is not clear that these efforts at socialization are purely self-serving. For example, inculcating "civic virtues" in schools does not benefit any particular political party, but is instead a general public good like justice or defense.[2]

Hence one possible difference between socialization based on "guilt" and socialization based on "shame" is that they are undertaken by different groups. Shame systems are generally established in smaller units than guilt systems. In the United States for example, shame systems are developed at the level of the firm or that of the profession. Socialization of police officers seems to be based on shame, not on guilt, as suggested by the fact that policemen have a tendency to protect one another, even to the point of failing to volunteer information if it might lead to the conviction of a fellow officer. On the other hand, guilt is inculcated at the national (schools) or even the international (religions) levels.

Casson describes the two control alternatives facing leaders of decentralized groups as consisting of legal procedures and socialization. Surprisingly, there is no mention of prices. Control through prices, in the form of commission payments or profit centers, is another way of controlling employees whose behavior is difficult to direct or observe, but also probably those who are difficult to socialize. For example, California packers, who had to deal in the 1900s with a transient and heterogeneous labor force, used a piece rate system that absolved managers of the need to supervise and socialize

workers who, given their heterogeneity and transient membership in the labor force, would have been costly to socialize [Brown and Philips 1986].

Casson's argument that guilt systems are more efficient than shame systems, though persuasive, raises additional questions. It would appear that the typical "company spirit" in Japanese firms is based on shame. Yet, if guilt systems are more efficient than shame systems, why don't Japanese firms instill guilt?

Perhaps the beginning of an answer can be found by looking at the costs of socialization. One can think of three aspects of this cost. The first one is the cost of inculcating it. The cost of instilling guilt may be higher than that of instilling shame, because guilt is a more complex feeling than shame. The second aspect, mentioned by Casson, is the potential cost of standardizing the group. It is possible that the costs of heterogeneity are greater for some systems than for others. One can argue, for example, that Japan's homogeneous population encourages the use of shame systems, while these systems are costly to establish in a highly heterogeneous country like the United States.[3] A third dimension of the cost of socialization is the type of biases they engender. A side effect of shame systems is a tendency towards conformity and intolerance towards outsiders. In societies like Japan this leads to rigid conformity and xenophobia. In firms it engenders "groupthink" and the "not invented here" syndrome [Janis 1972]. Is it just a coincidence that IBM, one of the more "socialized" of U.S. companies, has had such hard times developing software, a product that requires creativity and individuality [Judis 1991]? On the other hand, guilt is an individualistic system of control. A person motivated by guilt "answers to a higher authority" than the group leader. This puts more constraints on the group leader who is prevented from doing as he or she pleases by the very morals he or she has encouraged in others. The tribulations of U.S. "televangelists" are a case in point.

Casson then presents two applications of his ideas to two IB topics, the internal organization of the multinational enterprise (MNE) and the international political economy of government-business relationships. Casson's treatment of the internal organization of the MNE is short. Casson lists three ways in which internal markets can be organized: (1) prices can be set centrally by headquarters; (2) prices are set by negotiation between divisions; and (3) headquarters set a quantity plan, and divisions bid competitively to carry out parts of the plan as subcontractors. Since this is an area which John Dunning, in his paper discussed below, sees as requiring an extension and reappraisal of internalization theory, let me suggest some ways in which this extension and reappraisal can be made.

A good starting point is the early views of some internalization theorists that internalization consists of replacing failing external markets by "internal markets." Rugman [1981:28], for example, has argued that "the internal prices (or transfer prices) of the firm lubricate the organization and permit internal markets to function as efficiently as a potential (but unrealized) regular market."

Other authors have more nuances in their views of what constitutes an "internal market." Buckley [1983:65] argues that an internal market involves both a "hierarchical, administrative solution" and "a decentralized system based on decentralized shadow (transfer) prices." One major question that can be addressed to that literature is that if external markets fail, why should internal market not fail as well? Indeed, interviews of profit center managers by Eccles revealed that they thought the external market to be more efficient than the internal one [Eccles and White 1988]. The question raised by Buckley's argument is which of the two organizing methods used in firms—internal prices or hierarchy—explains why firms can be more efficient than markets, and if it is the use of internal prices, then why do firms use hierarchy?

To clarify the debate, it may be useful to describe, by analogy with an "external market" what an archetypal "internal market" should look like. If the raison d'etre of firms is to replace external by internal markets, then one would expect to see employees (or at a minimum work groups) organizing their interaction through prices; they would sell their output to headquarters (HQ) on the "corporate market" through any of the three pricing systems described by Casson and they would be paid from the difference between their costs and their revenues. In short, both the form and amount of their income would be indistinguishable from what it would be if they were self-employed subcontractors.

How close are firms from this "ideal type"? Not very. An overwhelming percentage of intra-unit transactions are not directed by prices but are organized by hierarchical directives, directly voiced by superiors, formalized in standard operating procedures, or internalized through indoctrination. Only one-fourth of U.S. employees participate in schemes where their salary is directly linked to their output (through piece work or commission), and this percentage is declining; for most of them output-linked compensation makes up only part of their pay [Seiler 1984]. Similarly, few inter-unit interdependencies are mediated by prices. Many smaller firms are functionally organized, and hence do not use any of the three types of internal markets listed by Casson. Even in large firms, transfers between independent profit centers are singularly limited. While 249 of the 291 largest U.S. firms studied by Vancil had transfers between separate profit centers, these transfers made up only 10 percent of their sales [Vancil 1978:176]. In only four of the 13 firms studied by Eccles could the managers choose between internal and external transactions [Eccles and White 1988]. In the archetypal model of the firm as an internal market, heads of profit centers would be rewarded in proportion to the profits made by their division. In practice, the rewards of profit center managers seem to deviate considerably from what they would be if these managers were self employed. Because there is no mechanism for translating the impact of the present behavior of the head of a subsidiary on the subunit's future income stream, managers are rewarded for short-term performance; they also have considerable leeway for manipulating their rewards by "cooking the books." Performance standards are often not challenging, and they are asymmetrical. Lastly, the size of the rewards is often limited upwards [Merchant 1989].[4]

It makes intuitive sense to assume that firms will succeed when markets fail not because they mimic markets, but instead because they introduce a totally different mode of organization. This mode of organization is hierarchy [Hennart 1986;1991a]. Hierarchy is an organizing method that can be described as the imposition of direct behavior constraints. Under hierarchy, an individual is paid a fixed amount, independent from his market-measured output, to "do as told."[5] Hierarchy provides the solution to market failure because it breaks the link between individual rewards and (failing) prices and replaces defective price signals by managerial directives. The weaknesses of hierarchy are the dual of its strengths: dissociating rewards from performance results in shirking and in failure by the employee to collect rele-vant information and to show initiative. Hence firms must constrain the behavior of their members either through external constraints, i.e., directing and observing behavior, or by socialization.

If hierarchy is the solution to market failure, why do firms use "internal prices?" My view is that managers reintroduce prices to counteract the most glaring weaknesses of hierarchy, shirking and lack of initiative. Prices are used when behavior control (either through monitoring or socialization) would incur high costs. The result is a hybrid system in which both prices and hierarchy are used simultaneously [Hennart 1993]. Examples are salary plus commission schemes, or profit centers subject to head-quarters' directives. Although these schemes have some features of markets, they differ from markets in the sense that price constraints are supplemented by a heavy dose of behavior constraints. For example, the contracts signed by British manufacturers with their overseas sales agents at the turn of the century contained a mix of price and behavioral constraints: agents were paid by commission, but the contracts also imposed behavior constraints in the form of minimum amounts of showing, traveling, and advertising the agent was required to do, and a minimum level of stock he was obliged to hold [Nicholas 1983].

Earlier I have defined hierarchy as an organizing method that directly constrains behavior, in contrast to the price system that does it indirectly. Direct control of behavior can be external (monitoring) or internal (socialization). Monitoring requires that the employee be told what to do, and be observed doing it. External monitoring is costly when the employer has less knowledge of the production function than the employee. When output is easy to measure, price controls can be reintroduced, but when it is not, the best solution is internal control of behavior (socialization) [Ouchi 1979]. By investing resources in persuading employees to internalize the employer's values, or by selecting employees who already have those values, the firm can persuade employees to feel that "what they want to do is the same as what they have to do" [Kanter 1972]. Socialization economizes on information and monitoring costs: socialized employees need not be told what to do (they will deduce from the philosophy of the organization the rules appropriate for any situation) and they need not be monitored. Hence this solution is ideally suited for changing circumstances. On the other hand, socialization involves very high setup costs and, as noted above, has potentially deleterious side effects.[6]

Some observers of the MNE have argued that socialization is increasingly used as a control mode in MNEs [Hedlund 1993]. One crucial element of Bartlett and Ghoshal's "transnational solution" [1989] is a switch from external monitoring and price controls towards socialization, which the authors describe as "the 'global glue' that counterbalances the centrifugal processes of the transnational structure and processes."[7] Bartlett and Ghoshal's book contains fascinating discussions of how MNEs foster socialization through extensive programs of management development as well as frequent rotation of managers among the units. They note, for example, that Unilever spends $170 million (U.S.) per year on management development [164] and that as much as 5 percent of Unilever's management positions are held by expatriates [191] at substantial cost, since maintaining an expatriate manager costs from two to ten times as much as hiring a local manager. They do not mention, however, other potential costs of socialization, such as the biases described above.

That socialization should be recommended as the most efficient tool to manage foreign subsidiaries is somewhat paradoxical. While the cost of all three control methods (price, monitoring, and socialization) should increase with physical and cultural distance, I would expect that the increase in the cost of socialization would be the highest, followed by that of monitoring, with the additional cost of using price constraints the lowest. Foreign environments are likely to be quite different from domestic ones, so that employees posted in foreign countries will have an information advantage over HQ, making centralized decision making less efficient, and privileging systems—like price control and socialization—that rely on "on the spot" decisions. Of these two, socialization would seem to be most affected by physical and cultural distance, since it relies on personal interactions and communications, and consequently the cost of implementing socialization should rise dramatically as spatial dispersion and cultural heterogeneity increase. Did Bartlett and Ghoshal underestimate the costs of fostering socialization? Is their conclusion biased by the idiosyncrasy of their nine-firm sam-

ple? Or are there important factors ignored by the theory? Clearly we need more research in this area.

MICRO AND MACRO ORGANIZATIONAL ASPECTS OF MNES AND MNE ACTIVITY

In this very stimulating piece, John Dunning tries to identify "some of the lacunae in the theories of the MNE and MNE activity and to suggest some of the avenues for further research" [p. 202]. Dunning's paper is divided into two sections. The first deals with the microtheory of the MNE, while the second addresses the macrotheory of the MNE, the part of the theory that explains "a country's propensity to be home or host to MNE-related activity" [p. 200]. Because of space limitations, I will limit my comments to the first part.

According to Dunning, changes in the characteristics of intra- and interfirm activity are requiring an extension and reappraisal of certain aspects of internalization theory. As far as intrafirm relationships are concerned, internalization theory needs to incorporate the concept of culture. Also, the theory needs to reflect the fact that, due to the complexity of organizing a global firm, "an authoritarian hierarchical relationship is giving way—in part at least—to a cooperative heterarchical relationship. Such a relationship is governed less by authority and more by the need to benefit from a sharing exchange of ideas, knowledge and values among parts of a heterarchy, so that the heterarchy, as a system, may flourish" [p. 198].

Dunning sees a shift in interfirm relationships towards cooperation. Here the Japanese are supposed to lead the way with their greater emphasis on cooperation than on arm's length adversarial relationships, and this is providing them with a "cultural competitive advantage" [p. 196].

Two remarks can be made in this context. First, the concept of heterarchy relies on socialization, and, as argued above, it is not clear why socialization should be the preferred organizing method in MNEs. Second, one must be careful to delineate better what in the practices of Japanese MNEs is culture-specific (non-imitable by outsiders), and what is not.

As Hedlund [1992] notes, socialization plays a key role in heterarchies, being the glue that protects heterarchy from mere anarchy. It is clear that socialization can be an efficient control tool in ethnocentric MNEs, as shown by MNEs like Philips and L. M. Ericcson who successfully use teams of homogeneous, home country expatriates to run their subsidiaries.[8] As I argue above, however, this method would seem to be the most expensive way to organize a geocentric MNE, i.e., an MNE where promotion ladders are truly global and where socialization has to work across cultures.

Can culture be incorporated into transaction cost theory, and if so, how? In a recent article Doz and Prahalad [1991] argue that the presence of "cultural differences" between U.S. and Japanese contracting practices proves that the culturally biased assumptions of transaction cost theory make it unsuitable to address managerial issues. They write that [48]:

> Transaction cost analysis has proven useful in analyzing specific types of interorganizational analysis in a North American context such as relationships between U.S. firms and their suppliers, vertical integration [Monteverde and Teece 1982; Stuckey 1983] and joint ventures with rigorous constraints on the nature of the joint venture [Hennart 1982]. Transaction cost analysis, however, does not explain relationships between Japanese firms and their suppliers, a relationship built on mutual trust and on a belief that the joint benefits (in contrast to self interest) are worth pursuing in a win framework over the long term. [Dore 1983]

Is opportunism purely culture-specific? Can transaction cost theory be applied in non-U.S. contexts? How easy will it be to incorporate culture in our IB theories?

Recent empirical work on Japanese procurement practices provides some answers to these questions. In a recent article reviewing the procurement practices of the Japanese automobile industry, McMillan [1990] shows that these practices can be explained in economic terms, and are not qualitatively different from many practices used in U.S. industry. For example, Japanese automobile assemblers attempt to reduce reliance on a single supplier by using dual sourcing (like U.S. firms), and they use a two-tier hierarchy of suppliers, as do U.S. aircraft makers (but not, until recently, the U.S. car industry). McMillan concludes that [52]:

> There need be nothing mysterious about how Japanese business practices work, nor need the success of the Japanese system be explained by things uniquely Japanese like the Shinto-Confucian ethic or Japan's consensus culture. Rather, Japanese industry can be understood as having attained, as the end point of an evolutionary process, a complex system of incentives to which firms respond rationally.

Similarly, the conclusion drawn by Asanuma [1989] from his study of manufacturer-supplier relationships in Japan is that "these relations are to be explained in economic rather than cultural terms based on the relation-specific skill accumulated by suppliers as well as ratings exercised thereon by the core firm."

In short, while particular conditions in Japan seem to have encouraged the development of advanced contractual forms, evidence from Japanese procurement contracts does not support the view that the basic assumptions of transaction cost theory are culture-specific. There is strong evidence that the cooperative nature of Japanese supply relationships does not arise from inherent differences between Japanese and Americans in their propensity towards opportunism, but rather from the fact that the Japanese have crafted more effective institutional arrangements to control opportunism and foster cooperation. There is no reason why, with some adaptations, these arrangements could not be implemented by non-Japanese outside Japan. In fact they already are.[9]

In this interesting paper, Terutomo Ozawa seeks to build from the experience of Southeast Asian countries, and especially from that of the Newly Industrialized Countries (NICs) of Taiwan, Korea, Hong Kong, and Singapore, a theory of economic development that might replace dependency theory. According to Ozawa, dependency theory cannot account for the explosive growth of the NICs. Ozawa presents an interesting theory of how MNEs can propel host countries towards fast economic growth. Space considerations prevent me from discussing at length his theory, so my comments will be limited to his treatment of the impact of culture on development and to the alleged superiority of the "new forms of investment."

Ozawa argues that economic development requires a "hard state" and that the governments of Japan, Taiwan, South Korea, Hong Kong, and Singapore, are strongly collective-welfare-minded. What I find striking, however, is not the similarities among these three countries, but the contrasts. Economic development arises from increasing specialization, and this specialization is made possible by exchange. Hence one necessary condition for development is the lowering of the cost of exchange, i.e., transaction costs [North 1986]. The costs of exchange are those of informing parties of the potential gains of exchange, of enforcing the terms of exchange, and of reducing bargaining [Hennart 1982]. If one looks at the panoply of organizational forms used in firms as an analogy, then there are three main ways by which the costs of exchange can be lowered.

The first one is socialization. With this method, all parties to the transaction can be incited to collaborate and not to cheat out of regard for some sense of collective ethic.

That ethic can be established at the firm, clan, or country level. Japan seems to have successfully harnessed such an ethic. An alternative method is hierarchy. Cooperation is then ordered through fiat. The autocratic systems of Singapore and (until recently) Korea are examples. A third way to reduce the costs of exchange is by establishing property rights. When property rights are well established and enforced, and competitive markets are maintained, the price mechanism will coordinate the behavior of the parties and make exchange and specialization possible. Economic development can be achieved by all three methods. Which is the least costly will hinge on the characteristics of the country and those of the transactions. In practice, all three methods will be used simultaneously, although in different proportions.

Taiwan and Hong Kong, for example, seem to have relied more heavily on the market mechanism than Korea or Japan. In Taiwan and Hong Kong, exchange and specialization has been obtained through a network of nimble, entrepreneurial firms coordinating their activity through market prices. To a novice observer, creative traffic patterns and uncontrolled pollution suggest a low level of collective orientation and discipline, at least compared with Japan. The hierarchical component seems higher in Korea, a country that has based its development on large, hierarchically organized conglomerates. All methods are efficient as long as they match the characteristics of the transactions to be undertaken: Korea's hierarchical firms have a comparative advantage in producing goods manufactured in capital-intensive plants using stable technologies, while Taiwan's and Hong Kong's industrial structures are better suited to quick response, custom-made goods produced in small series.

Ozawa also suggests that the "new forms of investment" such as joint ventures, subcontracting, and output sharing provide greater benefits to host countries than the traditional old forms of investment. This view comes from seeing MNEs as "rent extractors": the greater their ownership stake, the greater the share of locally generated profits that they take out from host countries. A lower stake means, however, lower incentives to commit resources. A technology seller who takes an equity stake in the host country (as opposed to one who sells unbundled technology) has built-in incentives to perform an efficient transfer, since he is paid from the output of the plant using the technology. Hence, it may be true that the share of the profits of the venture that is captured by the MNE is lower the lower the MNE's equity stake, but it does not follow that the host country's gain is higher the lower the MNEs stake, which is what happens when MNEs use the "new forms" of investment. When the new forms of investment are freely chosen, we would expect them to be the most efficient transfer mode. When they are forced upon the parties by governments, the resulting inefficiencies will more than make up for a decrease in the share of the profits that accrue to the host country. Hence by imposing these new forms of investment the host country may end up with a slightly bigger piece of a much smaller pie [Hennart 1989].

NOTES

I am indebted to Mark Casson and the participants of the conference for useful comments.

1. See my comments for the session on Theory and Research Implications for IB in this volume.

2. The financing of this public good varies across countries: in some, ministers are state employees (Switzerland), in others churches are tax-exempt (the United States).

3. Standardizing does not come cheap, especially in culturally heterogeneous countries like the United States, as shown by Toyota's considerable investment in screening applicants for assembly line positions at its Kentucky plant. Successful applicants underwent 18 hours of testing and only one in 67 applicants was hired (Wallace 1991).

4. In his study of the ways U.S. firms motivate profit center managers, Merchant notes that: (1) "many profit center managers are rewarded for attaining a budgeted profit target

they are virtually certain to attain" (p.35); (2) 66 percent of the managers interviewed admitted they had "managed earnings" through accounting or operating methods (p.173); and (3) in eleven out of twelve firms studied the size of the manager's bonus was limited to 30–140% of a manager's salary and/or was limited by the size of the bonus pool, itself determined by overall corporate performance (Table 2.4). Compensation in internal markets is therefore quite different from that in external ones.

5. Note that hierarchy is defined here as a "method of organization" and is not synonymous with the firm or with upper managers (as in Chandler's term of "managerial hierarchies").

6. Note that, contrary to Doz and Prahalad's assertion (1991:149), the presence of socialization does not invalidate transaction cost theory, for absent opportunism there would be no need to invest in socialization.

7. "Coordination and control in the transnational organization are accomplished as much through the socialization of its members as through formal systems" (Bartlett and Ghoshal:209).

8. Graduates of Stockholm Royal Engineering School and the "Dutch Mafia" recruited from Dutch engineering schools.

9. The same can be said for the so-called "loyalty" of the Japanese work force. As Florida and Kenney (1991: 388) argue, "this long held cultural effect is also a product of organizational practice," namely careful screening and selection.

Edward M. Graham

Comments on Papers by Mark Casson, John Dunning, and Terutomo Ozawa

It is a pleasure to serve as commentator on the papers by Professors Mark Casson, John Dunning, and Terutomo Ozawa. Each of these three eminent scholars has been a leader in the development and synthesis of economic theories of IB. Each author presents a paper delineating where, in his view, these theories should now be going. While the authors do in some cases attempt to break some new ground, such path breaking is not really the central mission of the papers; the mission is to identify where the new ground lies rather than to break new pathways into it.

Against this standard, the authors by and large succeed. While they do identify new ground in need of exploration, in my view, some ground is left out of their vision. I shall expand on this later.

Although each of the papers is very different, to a large degree each focuses on the internal characteristics of firms and, especially in the papers of Dunning and Ozawa, the characteristics of what might be called cooperative networks of organizational entities, where these entities are not necessarily related to each other in the sense of having common ownership. Dunning rightly emphasizes the role that governments might have in creating advantages within these networks, noting that governments in some cases are best viewed as internal entities within the networks rather than external players. Ozawa notes that what are viewed as traditional, ownership-linked MNEs are often the core entities in a much larger international network of organizations, wherein local entities within a particular host-nation economy might remain under local ownership. Both Dunning and Ozawa note the growing importance of strategic alliances among MNEs and related organizational entities, including alliances among or between entities that might be thought of as rivals.

Much of what these authors write about invokes memories by this commentator of two years spent in France in the early 1980s, where I attended seminars led by Jean-Pierre Ponssard about industrial economics. These seminars introduced me to the French concept of the *filière*.

This concept, articulated by French economists during the 1970s, is more than superficially similar to ideas expressed in these three papers. To the French, the *filière* is a network of economic agents ("firms," if you like, plus the government) whose undertakings are interdependent but which are not necessarily under common ownership or control. French economists postulate that neither hierarchical control associated

with "internalization" (these economists don't use this term, but they understood the concept) nor "arm's length" transactions associated with an auction market is necessarily the optimal way to organize relations among agents in the *filière*. Cooperative non-hierarchical modes of organizational relations might therefore dominate more traditional modes.

To the devotees of the *filière*, the importance of the network as a whole lay in the dynamics of interaction among the constituent entities. Significant economies were achieved via these dynamics, including many of those associated by Casson and Dunning in their papers with such ideas as "trust" and "reputation." Of utmost importance, though, was innovation and, most especially, the relationship between innovation by one entity in the *filière* to the innovative activity of other entities.

To French planners, insights from studying the *filière* are to be applied normatively. Much time has been spent over many years by French indicative planners attempting to determine what are the key nodes of innovation within a *filière* in the sense that innovation in these nodes stimulates further innovation elsewhere in the network. To an Anglo-Saxon economist, what the French are doing in this regard is attempting to determine where the deviations between social and private returns to innovation (i.e., cases where innovation creates significant externalities) are greatest. These cases, to both the French and the Anglo-Saxon mind sets, are those where public subsidy or other forms of public intervention are most warranted. The French analyst is more inclined actually to attempt such an intervention than is the Anglo-Saxon one; the Anglo-Saxon by contrast is likely to argue that while a case can be made theoretically for intervention, in practice governments will always get it wrong and screw it up, and so theory must be overridden on practical grounds. To some extent, John Dunning's paper is all about trying to change this mind set.

The French economist might argue,

however, that there is more to stimulation of innovation than simply identifying where the divergence of public and private returns is the greatest. Externalities, they would argue, cannot be captured by just anyone, and indeed much of the strength of the *filière* lies in the relationships among organizational entities that enable such capture to be maximized. Thus, French industrial policy is not simply identification of what activities to support; rather, it concerns itself with the structure of economic activity. The long reach of the concept of the *filière* can most recently be seen in the attempts of former French Prime Minister Edith Cresson to reorganize the holdings of Thomson SA, notably by spinning off the consumer electronics and home appliance division and putting these under the control of the French atomic energy agency while retaining Thomson CSF under Thomson SA.

These somewhat distant (to me, at least) concepts lying behind French industrial policy are echoed in the three papers we are presently considering. Given the lack of citations bearing French names (with the exception of J.-F. Hennart, whose career has largely taken place in the United States) in the references of any of the three papers, however, there is some case to be made that Casson, Dunning, and Ozawa run the risk of rediscovering that which the French have already discovered. If so, it wouldn't be the first time that the English have planted their flag on what they thought to be undiscovered terrain, only to learn later that the French had already been there. Professor Ozawa couldn't be guilty of this precisely, given that he isn't English; but my point is still valid, I suspect.

There are of course, key differences in the French concepts and the ones of Casson, Dunning, and Ozawa. French industrial planners tend also to be French nationalists, and little room exists in their thinking if a *filière* crosses out of French territory. By contrast, Ozawa in particular seems to be describing *filières* that span much of East Asia, wherein national boundaries are of decreasing relevance. Nonetheless, a little

nationalism does creep into Ozawa's paper. There are hints of Kojima's "bad" (in Kojima's terms, trade substituting) multinationals versus "good" ones (trade reinforcing); the bad ones seem to be mostly American in origin, and the good ones Japanese. Nowhere in Ozawa's present paper is there reference to "flying geese," and this lack is probably a blessing. But, the concept is still there.

Much of what motivates Dunning's as well as Ozawa's paper in fact is the rise of Japanese MNEs. Without question, Japanese organization is different from Western organization. The type of macro organizational entities that exist in Japan (the much debated *keiretsu*) is the subject of much controversy (e.g., Does the tight "family" of firms that constitute a *keiretsu* lead to enhancement of efficiency? Do these families constitute "unfair" barriers to entry to outsiders?). The controversy surrounding the *keiretsu* prompts one to ask questions of Ozawa that the present paper doesn't fully answer. For example, is Ozawa describing the extension throughout Asia of the *keiretsu*? Or is it something else?

Even more fundamental questions however can be asked. Not the least of these is, whether the new forms of multinational organization that are being observed really are, after all, that new? The French, for example, originally used as the model of the *filière* the structure of certain industries in the United States, e.g., the combined semiconductor/computer industry ("l'industrie informatique") and the aerospace industry, where cooperative relations between legally nonrelated firms created (in French eyes, at least) a *de facto* entity that was much bigger than any of the nominal parts. A number of observers have noted that although by most classical definitions the U.S. aerospace firm Boeing doesn't even qualify as a "multinational," as long ago as the 1960s Boeing began to build an international network of affiliations with subcontractors that collectively looks suspiciously like today's "new" MNE. As the French themselves say, "la plus ça change, la plus rien est changé."

As I said at the beginning of this commentary, the three authors ignore terrain that ought to be included. In this, they are joined by the French economists who invented the idea of the *filière*. All three authors (and their French predecessors) are so enamored of cooperative relationships among organizational entities and what might be called the economics of harmony that they tend to forget other Anglo-Saxon descriptive terms for organizational relationships that are very harmonious: cartels and monopolies.

I have three comments to make. First, whereas there doubtless are significant static and dynamic economies associated with networking and harmony, these economies do not override the fact that monopolies and cartels can be highly inefficient organizational forms. They are most especially inefficient in a dynamic sense: The empirical literature is quite clear on the point that monopolies and cartels do not foster rapid technological or organizational innovation. This point was, during the 1970s and early 1980s, largely forgotten by French indicative planners enamored of the *filières* (and, more recently, by Ms. Cresson). In attempting to build strong French *filières* in dynamic industries (e.g., telecommunications), the French have too often created cozy and uncompetitive networks of local monopolies.

Second, Japan is not one giant network of firms working as a harmonious team. Indeed, in those sectors where Japanese firms are acknowledged to be the most formidable of the world's competitors, rivalry among competing firms, or perhaps competing *keiretsu*, is intense. If one looks inside the Toyota network, one indeed does see harmony and trust. If one looks at Toyota's relationships with Nissan, however, "harmony" and "cooperation" are not words that spring to one's lips. In the early 1980s, several articles appeared that contrasted the structure of French industry with that of Japanese industry and concluded that the main difference was the relations between erstwhile competitors in France

which tended to be far more cozy than in Japan. Indeed, in Japan, the number of competing groups of firms in major industries is significantly higher than in France.

Further, in Japan where monopolies or cartels predominate (for example, in the construction industry), Japanese firms do not lead the world in terms of their competitiveness. "Toyota-ism" is a great organizational paradigm and offers lessons of the most positive sort for those who study the economics of the organization. Japan is not, however, simply the land of "Toyota-ism" and "kamban"; it is also a land of "dango." "Dango" is a Japanese word denoting a price-fixing, bid-rigging cartel that no one should want to imitate. "Toyota-ist" organizations exist in Japan, not the least of which is Toyota and its network of suppliers and other affiliated firms. But there is plenty of "dango" in Japan as well.

The third point is that to understand IB from an economic point of view, one must take into account strategic rivalry among firms. This might seem to some observers to be a self-serving statement coming from this particular commentator, given that much of my own work has centered on rivalry. I am not, however, alone in my lamentation. In a conference held at the National Bureau of Economic Research in Cambridge on foreign direct investment (FDI), Raymond Vernon stressed that much of the spread of IB by U.S.-based firms can be accounted for by these firms mimicking the international moves of their domestic rivals. This point was indeed made by Stephen Hymer in his pioneering works on FDI, just as Hymer might be seen as the first to apply "Coasian" thinking to IB. The recent international expansion of Japanese firms seems to conform to Knickerbockian notions of "follow-the-leader," a matter not touched upon by Ozawa. Alexis Jacquemin, one of continental Europe's leading industrial economists and currently advisor on industrial policy to EC President Jacques Delors, recently has published an article in which he argues that *all* FDI is "strategic" (i.e., is driven by interfirm rivalry); he cites my work as pioneering in this regard.[1] I am not sure that I myself would go quite as far as Jacquemin in advocating "strategic" investment as the wellspring of IB, but all three papers under discussion here can be roundly criticized for failing to consider interfirm rivalry at all as an explanator of IB.

Rivalry among firms goes much further than explaining IB, though. It is a driving force for innovation and for other efficiency-enhancing activities of organizations. In the view of many, it is a very important explanator in its own right of the success of Japan and other East-Asian economies. I personally take some exception to certain observations of Ozawa regarding this success, in particular the claim that the policies of these nations have always been "outward" in orientation. Japan and Korea, for example, certainly have not been particularly "outward" with respect to encouraging foreign-based multinationals to locate productive capacity inside their territories, nor have they been at all "open" with respect to importation of products competing directly with the output of favored home-based producers. They may have been "outward" in terms of promoting competitiveness of these producers by encouraging exports. My key point, however, is that in pursuing quasi-protectionist policies, Japan and Korea have fostered high degrees of rivalry among domestic producers. Would these producers have been as dynamically competitive had there not existed substantial rivalry within the home markets, i.e., if favored firms had been granted cozy domestic monopolies as have been created in certain Latin American countries? One doubts it, and hence one is led to consider the nature of competition within these nations as an explanator of success as well as "outward" orientation.

NOTES

1. Comment by Alexis Jacquemin in *Kyklos* 42 (4), pp. 495–513, entitled "International and Multinational Strategic Behaviour."

REFERENCES

Abramovitz, Moses. 1968. Catching up, forging ahead, and falling behind. *Journal of Economic History* 46(2):385–406.

Akerlof, G. A. 1980. A theory of social custom, of which unemployment may be one consequence. *Quarterly Journal of Economics* 94:719–735.

Amin, Samir. 1976. *Unequal Development: An Essay on the Social Formations of Peripheral Capitalism*. New York: Monthly Review Press.

Amsden, Alice H. 1989. *Asia's Next Giant: South Korea and Late Industrialization*. Oxford: Oxford University Press.

Arrow, K. J. 1985. The economics of agency. In J. W. Pratt and R. J. Zeckhauser, editors, *Principles and Agents: The Structure of Business*. Boston: Harvard Business School Press.

Asanuma, Banri. 1989. Manufacturer-supplier relationships in Japan and the concept of relation-specific skill. *Journal of the Japanese and International Economies* 3:1–30.

Axelrod, R. 1984. *The Evolution of Cooperation*. New York: Basic Books.

Bain, J. S. 1956. *Barriers to New Competition*. Cambridge: Harvard University Press.

Balassa, Bela. 1979,1989. The changing pattern of comparative advantage in manufactured goods. *Review of Economics and Statistics* 61(May):259–266. Reproduced in *Comparative Advantage, Trade Policy and Economic Development*. New York: New York University Press.

Baran, Paul. 1957. *The Political Economy of Growth*. New York: Monthly Review Press.

Barney, Jay. 1991. Firm resources and sustained competitive advantage. *Journal of Management* 17:99–120.

Bartlett, Christopher and Sumantra Ghoshal. 1989. *Managing the Global Firm: The Transnational Solution*. Boston: Harvard Business School Press.

Becker, G. S. and G. J. Stigler. 1977. De Gustibus non est Disputandum. *American Economic Review* 67:79–90.

Behrman, Jack N. and Robert Grosse. 1990. *International Business and Governments*. Columbia: University of South Carolina Press.

Bell, Clive. 1987. Development economics. In J. Eatwell, M. Milgate, and P. Newman, editors, *The New Palgrave: Economic Development*. New York: Norton.

Bell, John F. 1953. *A History of Economic Thought*. New York: Ronald Press.

Boddewyn, Jean J. 1991. International business political-behavior research: Assumptions, categories and propositions. New York: Baruch College (CUNY). Mimeo.

Boddewyn, Jean J. 1988. Political aspects of MNE theory. *Journal of International Business Studies* 19:341–363.

Boulding, Kenneth. 1956. *The Image. Knowledge in Life and Society*. Ann Arbor: University of Michigan Press.

Brewer, Anthony. 1990. *Marxist Theories of Imperialism: A Critical Survey*. London and New York: Routledge.

Brown, Martin and Peter Philips. 1986. The decline of the piece-rate system in California canning. *Business History Review* 60(Winter):564–601.

Buckley, Peter J., editor. 1993. *Cooperative Forms of TNC Activity*. UN Library on Transnational Corporations. London: Routledge.

Buckley, Peter J. 1991. Multinational enterprises in less developed countries: Cultural and economic considerations. In P.J. Buckley and J. Clegg, editors, *Multinational Enterprises in Less Developed Countries*. London: MacMillan.

Buckley, Peter J. 1988. A theory of co-operation in international business. In F.J. Contractor and P. Lorange, editors, *Cooperative Strategies in International Business, 31–53*. Lexington: Lexington Books.

Buckley, Peter J. 1988. The limits of explanation: Testing the internalisation theory of the multinational enterprise. *Journal of International Business Studies*, 19(2):181–193.

Buckley, Peter J. 1983. New theories of international business: Some unresolved issues. In M. C. Casson, editor, *The Growth of International Business, 34–50* London: Allen and Unwin.

Buckley, Peter J. and Mark C. Casson. 1992. Organising for innovation: The multinational enterprise in the twenty-first century. In P. J. Buckley and M. C. Casson, editors, *Multinational Enterprises in the World Economy: Essays in Honour of John Dunning*. Cheltenham: Edward Elgar.

Cantwell, J. C. 1991. A survey of theories of international production. In C. Pitelis and R. Sugden, editors, *The Nature of the Transnational Firm*. London: Routledge.

Cantwell, J. C. 1990. The technological competence theory of international production and its implications. Discussion Papers in International Investment and Business Studies, Series B. No. 149. Reading: University of Reading.

Cantwell, J. C. 1989. *Technological Innovation and Multinational Corporations*. Oxford: Basil Blackwell.

Cantwell, J. C. and Estrella E. Tolentino. 1990. Technological accumulation and third world multinationals. Discussion Paper No. 139. Department of Economics, University of Reading, Series B, vol. III (1990;1991).

Casson, Mark. 1991a. Modeling the multinational enterprise: A research agenda. *Millennium*, 20:271–285.

Casson, Mark. 1991b. *The Economics of Business Culture: Game Theory, Transaction Costs and Economic Performance*. Oxford: Clarendon Press.

Casson, Mark. 1990. *Enterprise and Competitiveness: A Systems View of International Business*. Oxford: Clarendon Press.

Casson, Mark. 1987. *The Firm and the Market: Studies in Multinational Enterprise and the Growth of the Firm*. Oxford: Blackwell.

Casson, Mark. 1979. *Alternatives to the Multinational Enterprise*. London: MacMillan.

Casson, Mark and S. Nicholas. 1989. The economics of trust explaining differences in corporate structure between the U.S. and Japan. Discussion Papers in Economics Vol. II No. 219. Reading: University of Reading.

Chenery, Hollis B. 1960. Patterns of Industrial Growth. *American Economic Review*, 50(4): 624–654.

Chenery, Hollis B., S. Robinson and M. Syrquin. 1986. *Industrialization and Growth*. Oxford: Oxford University Press.

Coase, Ronald H. 1937. The nature of the firm. *Economica*, 4:386–405.

Coleman, J. S. 1990. *Foundations of Social Theory*. Cambridge: Belknap Press.

Contractor, Farok J. and Peter Lorange, editors. 1988. *Cooperative Strategies in International Business*. Lexington: Lexington Books.

Dawkins, Richard. 1989. *The Selfish Gene*, second edition. Oxford: Oxford University Press.

Dierickx, I. and Karl Cool. 1989. Asset stock accumulation and sustainability of competitive advantage. *Management Science*, 35: 1504–1511.

Dore, Ronald. 1983. Goodwill and the spirit of market capitalism. *British Journal of Sociology*, 34:459–482.

Dos Santos, Theotonica. 1970. The structure of dependence. *American Economic Review*, 60(May):231–236.

Doz, Yves and C. K. Prahalad. 1991. Managing DMNCs: A search for a new paradigm. *Strategic Management Journal*, 12:145–164.

Dunning, John H. 1993a. The governance of Japanese U.S. manufacturing affiliates in the UK: Some country specific differences. In Bruce Kogut, editor, *Country Competitiveness: Technology and the Organization of Work*. Oxford: Oxford University Press.

Dunning, John H. 1993b. Japanese and U.S. manufacturing investment in Europe: Some comparisons and contrasts, GSM Working Paper Series No. 93–01, Rutgers University, Newark, NJ.

Dunning, John H. 1992. *Multinational Enterprises and the Global Economy*. Workingham, Berkshire: Addison Wesley.

Dunning, John H. 1991a. Dunning on Porter: Reshaping the diamond of competitive advantage. University of Reading. Mimeo.

Dunning, John H. 1991b. Governments-markets-firms: Towards a new balance? *The CTC Reporter*, 31(Spring):2–7.

Dunning, John H. 1991c. The eclectic paradigm of international production: A personal perspective. In C. N. Itelis and R. Sugden, editors, *The Nature of the Transnational Firm*, 117–136. London: Routledge.

Dunning, John H. 1991d. Governments and multinational enterprises: From confron-tation to cooperation? *Millennium*, 20:225–244.

Dunning, John H. 1990. *The Globalization of Firms and the Competitiveness of Nations*. The Crafoord Lectures 1989. Lund: University of Lund.

Dunning, John H. 1988a. *Multinationals, Technology and Competitiveness*. London: Unwin Hyman.

Dunning, John H. 1988b. *Explaining International Production*. London: Unwin Hyman.

Dunning, John H. 1986. *Japanese Participation in British Industry*. London: Croom Holm.

Dunning, John H. 1958. *American Investment in British Manufacturing Industry*. London: Allen and Unwin.

Dunning, John and Alan M. Rugman. 1985. The influence of Hymer's dissertation on the theory of foreign direct investment. *American Economic Review*, 75(May):228–232.

Eccles, Robert and Harrison White. 1988. Price and authority in inter-profit center transactions. *American Journal of Sociology*, 94 (Supplement):17–51.

Eden, L. and F. O. Hampson. 1990. *Clubs are Trump: Towards a Taxonomy of International Regimes*. Working Paper, 90–02. Ottawa: Carleton University Centre for International Trade and Policy Studies.

Enos, J. L. and W. H. Park. 1988. *The Adoption and Diffusion of Imported Technology: The Case of Korea*. London: Croom Helm.

Etzioni, A. 1988. *The Moral Dimension: Towards a New Economics*. New York: Free Press.

Florida, Richard and Martin Kenney. 1991. Transplanted organizations: The transfer of Japanese industrial organization to the U.S. *American Sociological Review*, 56:381–398.

Frank, A. Gunder. 1967. *Capitalism and Underdevelopment in Latin America*. New York: Monthly Review Press.

Franke, R. H., Geert Hofstede and M. H. Bond. 1991. Cultural roots of economic performance: A research note. *Strategic Management Journal*, 12:165–173.

Fruin, M. and T. Nishiguchi. 1993. Supplying the Toyota production system: Making a molehill out of a mountain in Japan. In B. Kogut and Van den Bulcke, editors, *Country Competitiveness: Technology and the Organizing of Work*. Oxford: Oxford University Press.

Furtado, Celso. 1964. *Development and Underdevelopment*, translated by R. De Aguiar and E. Drysdale. Berkeley: University of California Press.

Gerschenkron, Alexander. 1962. *Economic Backwardness in Historical Perspective.* Cambridge: Harvard University Press.

Gittleman, M. and John H. Dunning. 1992. Japanese multinationals in Europe and the United States: some comparisons and contrasts. In M. W. Klein and P. J. J. Welfens, editors, *Multinationals in the New Europe and Global Trade.* Berlin: Springer-Verlag.

Grosse, Robert and Jack N. Behrman. 1992. Theory in international business. *Transnational Corporations,* 1:93–126.

Gugler, P. 1991. *Les Alliances Strategiques Transnationales.* Fribourg: Editions Universitaires.

Gustafsson, B. and O. Williamson, editors. 1989. *The Firms as a Nexus of Treaties.* London: Sage.

Hedlund, Gunnar. 1993. Assumptions of hierarchy and heterarchy. In D. E. Westney and S. Ghoshal, editors, *Organization Theory and the Multinational Corporation.* NY: St. Martin's Press.

Hedlund, Gunnar and Bruce Kogut. 1993. Managing the MNC: The end of the missionary era. In G. Hedlund, editor, *Transnational Corporations and Organization,* UN Library on Transnational Corporations. London: Routledge.

Hedlund, Gunnar and D. Rolander. 1991. Action in heterarchies—new approaches to managing the MNC. In C. A. Bartlett, Y. Doz and G. Hedlund, editors, *Managing the Global Firm.* New York: Routledge.

Hennart, Jean-François. 1993. "Explaining the 'swollen middle': Why most transactions are a mix of market and hierarchy," *Organization Science,* vol. 4, no. 4, November, 529–547.

Hennart, Jean-François. 1991a. Control in multinational firms: The role of price and hierarchy. *Management International Review,* 31(Special issue):71–96.

Hennart, Jean-François. 1991b. The transaction cost theory of the multinational enterprise. In C. N. Pitelis and R. Sugden, editors, *The Nature of the Transnational Firm.* London: Routledge.

Hennart, Jean-François. 1989. Can the *new forms of investment* substitute for the old forms? A transaction costs perspective. *Journal of International Business Studies,* 20(2):211–233.

Hennart, Jean-François. 1986. What is internalization? *Weltwirtschaftliches Archiv,* 122(4): 791–804.

Hennart, Jean-François. 1982. *A Theory of Multinational Enterprise.* Ann Arbor: University of Michigan Press.

Hirschleifer, J. 1985. The expanding domain of economics. *American Economic Review,* 75:53–68.

Holmström, B. 1979. Moral hazard and observability. *Bell Journal of Economics,* 10:74–91.

Hymer, Stephen H. 1976. *The International Operations of National Firms: A Study of Direct Investment.* Cambridge: MIT Press (previously unpublished doctoral dissertation, 1960).

Hymer, Stephen H. 1968. The large multinational "corporation": An analysis of some motives for the international integration of business. *Revue Economique,* 19(6): 949–973. Reprinted in translation by N. Vacherot in M. C. Casson, editor, *Multinational Corporations.* Aldershot: Edward Elgar.

Jacquemin, Alexis. 1989. International and Multinational Strategic Behaviour. *Kyklos,* 42(4): 495–513.

Janis, Irving. 1972. *Victims of Groupthink.* Boston: Houghton-Mifflin.

Johns, R. A. 1985. *International Trade Theories and the Evolving International Economy.* New York: St. Martin's Press.

Johnson, H. G. 1970. The efficiency and welfare implications of the international corporation. In C. P. Kindleberger, editor, *The International Corporation.* Cambridge: MIT Press.

Judis, John. 1991. Innovation, a casualty at IBM. *Wall Street Journal,* October 17:A23.

Kanter, Rosabeth. 1972. *Commitment and Community.* Cambridge: Harvard University Press.

Keynes, John Maynard. 1936. *The General Theory of Employment, Interest and Money.* NY: Harcourt, Brace.

Kindleberger, C. P. 1969. *American Business Abroad.* New Haven: Yale University Press.

Kogut, Bruce, editor. 1993. *Country Competitiveness: Technology and the Organizing of Work*. Oxford: Oxford University Press.

Kogut, Bruce. 1990. The permeability of borders and the speed of learning across countries. In J.H. Dunning, B. Kogut and M. Blomstrom, editors, *Globalization of Firms and the Competitiveness of Nations*. Lund: Lund University Institute of Economic Research.

Kogut, Bruce and H. Parkinson. 1993. The diffusion of American organizing principles to Europe. In B. Kogut, editor, *Country Competitiveness and the Organization of Work*. Oxford: Oxford University Press.

Kojima, Kiyoshi. 1975. International trade and foreign investment: Substitutes or complements. *Hitotsubashi Journal of Economics*, 16(1):1–12.

Kojima, Kiyoshi and Terutomo Ozawa. 1984. Micro- and macroeconomic models of direct foreign investment: Toward a synthesis. *Hitotsubahsi Journal of Economics*, 25(1): 1–20.

Kreps, D. and R. Wilson. 1982. Reputation and incomplete information. *Journal of Economic Theory*, 27:253–279.

Landes, David S. 1969. *The Unbound Prometheus*. Cambridge: Cambridge University Press.

Lenin, V. I. 1939. *Imperialism: The Highest State of Capitalism*. New York: International Publisher.

Lewis, W. Arthur. 1954. Economic development with unlimited supplies of labour. *The Manchester School of Economics and Social Studies*, 12(May):139–191.

Lincoln, J. R. 1993. Work organization in Japan and the United States. In B. Kogut, editor, *Country Competitiveness and the Organization of Work*. Oxford: Oxford University Press.

Lindberg, L. N., J. L. Campbell and J. R. Hollingsworth. 1992. Economic governance and the analysis of structural change in the American economy. In J. L. Campbell, J. R. Hollingsworth and L. N. Lindburg, editors, *The Governance of the American Economy*. New York: Cambridge University Press.

Lipsey, R. 1991. *Economic Growth: Science and Technology and Institutional Change in the Global Economy*. Toronto: Canadian Institute for Advanced Research CIAR Publication No. 4, June.

Mahoney, J. T. and J. R. Pandian. 1992. The resource based view within the context of strategic management. *Strategic Management Journal*, 13:363–380.

McKelvey, W. 1982. *Organisational Systematics: Taxonomy, Evolution, Classification*. Berkeley: University of California Press.

McMillan, John. 1990. Managing suppliers: Incentive systems in Japanese and U.S. industry. *California Management Review*, Summer:38–55.

Meier, Gerald M. 1984. *Leading Issues in Economic Development*. New York: Oxford University Press.

Merchant, Kenneth. 1989. *Rewarding Results: Motivating Profit Center Managers*. Boston: Harvard Business School Press.

Monteverde, Kim and David Teece. 1982. Supplier switching costs and vertical integration in the automobile industry. *Bell Journal of Economics*, 13:206–213.

Mueller, D. C. 1989. *Public Choice II*. Cambridge: Cambridge University Press.

Myint, Hla. 1958. The "classical theory" of international trade and the underdeveloped countries. *Economic Journal*, 68(June): 317–337.

Myrdal, Gunnar. 1968. *Asian Drama: An Inquiry into the Poverty of Nations*. New York: Pantheon.

Nicholas, Stephen. 1983. Agency contracts, institutional modes, and the transition to foreign direct investment by British manufacturing multinationals before 1939. *Journal of Economic History*, 68(3):675–686.

North, Douglas. 1986. The new institutional economics. *Journal of Theoretical and Institutional Economics*, 142:230–237.

Ohlin, Bertil. 1933. *Interregional and International Trade*. Cambridge, MA: Harvard University Press.

Okada, Y. 1991. Cooperative sectoral governance strategies of Japanese automobile multinationals in Asian countries. Niigata-Ken: International University of Japan. Mimeo.

Oman, Charles. 1984. *New Forms of Interna-*

tional Investment in Developing Countries. Paris: OECD.

Ouchi, William. 1979. A conceptual framework for the design of organizational control mechanisms. *Management Science*, 25(9): 833–848.

Ozawa, Terutomo. 1992a. Foreign direct investment and economic development. *Transnational Corporation*, 1(February):27–54.

Ozawa, Terutomo. 1992b. The "paradoxes" of labor-driven economic development in Pacific Asia: Multinationals as the sinews of growth. Paper presented at the Fifth International Conference on World Trade and MNEs in the 21st Century, Taipei Grand Hotel, Taipei, Taiwan, Republic of China, May 4–6.

Ozawa, Terutomo. 1991. The dynamics of pacific rim industrialization: How Mexico can join the Asian flock of the "flying geese." In R. Roett, editor, *Mexico's External Relations in the 1990s.* London: Lynne Rienner.

Ozawa, Terutomo. 1987. Can the market alone manage structural upgrading? A challenge posed by interdependence. In J. H. Dunning and M. Usui, editors, *Structural Change, Economic Interdependence and World Development.* Basingstoke: MacMillan.

Ozawa, Terutomo. 1974. *Japan's Technological Challenge to the West, 1950–1974: Motivation and Accomplishment.* Cambridge: MIT Press.

Pavitt, Keith. 1987. International patterns of technological accumulation. In N. Hood and J. Vahlne, editors, *Strategies in Global Competition.* New York: John Wiley.

Polanyi, Karl. 1977. *The Livelihood of Man.* New York: Free Press.

Porter, Michael E. 1990. *The Competitive Advantage of Nations.* New York: Free Press.

Porter, Michael E., editor. 1985. *Competition in Global Industries.* New York: Free Press.

Porter, Michael E. 1980. *Competitive Strategy: Techniques for Analyzing Industries and Competitors.* New York: Free Press.

Richardson, George B. 1972. The organisation of industry. *Economic Journal*, 82:883–896.

Robbins, L. 1932. *The Nature and Significance of Economic Science.* London: MacMillan.

Rosenberg, Nathan. 1972. *Technology and American Economic Growth.* New York: Harper and Row.

Rostow, W. W. 1959. *The Stages of Economic Growth.* Cambridge: Cambridge University Press.

Rugman, Alan. 1981. *Inside the Multinationals: The Economics of Internal Markets.* New York: Columbia University Press.

Schmidtchen, D. and H. J. Schmidt-Trens. 1990. New institutional economics of editors, *Jahruch für Neue Politische Ökonomie, vol. 9.* Tübingen: J. C. B. Mohr.

Schmitter, P. C. 1988. Sectors in modern capitalism: modes of governance and variations in performance. Paper presented at a Conference in honor of Evio Tarantelli on *Markets, Institutions and Cooperation: Labor Relations and Economic Performances*, Venice, October 20–22.

Schumpeter, Joseph A. 1934:1961. *Theory of Economic Development*, translated by R. Opie. New York: Oxford University Press.

Seiler, Eric. 1984. Piece rates vs. time rates: The effect of incentives on earnings. *Review of Economics and Statistics*, 66:363–375.

Shimada, Haruo. 1988. *Hyumanueya no Keizaigaku* (The Economics of Humanware). Tokyo: Iwanami.

Sigmund, Paul E. 1980. *Multinationals in Latin America: The Politics of Nationalization.* Madison, WI: University of Wisconsin Press.

Simon, H. A. 1983. *Reason in Human Affairs.* Oxford: Blackwell. International transactions. In E. Boettcher, S.K. Harder-Dorneich and D. Schmidtchen,

Smith, Adam. 1759;1976. *The Theory of Moral Sentiments*, edited by D. Raphael and A. Macfie. Oxford: Clarendon Press.

Smith, Adam. 1776;1908. *An Inquiry into the Nature and Causes of the Wealth of Nations.* London: Routledge (1776). New York: E.P. Dutton (1908).

Stolper, W. F. and Paul A. Samuelson. 1941. Protection and real wages. *Review of Economic Studies*, 9(November):58–73.

Strange, S. 1988. *States and Markets.* Oxford: Basil Blackwell.

Stuckey, John. 1983. *Vertical Integration and*

Joint Ventures in the Aluminum Industry. Cambridge: Harvard University Press.

Thurow, Lester C. 1985. *The Management Challenge: Japanese Views*. Cambridge: MIT Press.

Toyne, Brian. 1994. International business scholarship. The essentials. Paper presented at the Second Michigan State University Roundtable. East Lansing, MI.

United Nations. 1992. *World Investment Report 1992: Transnational Corporations as Engines of Growth*. New York: United Nations, Transnational Corporations and Management Division of Department of Economic and Social Development.

United States. Department of Commerce. 1991. *U.S. Direct Investment Abroad. 1991 Benchmark Survey Preliminary Results*. Washington: Bureau of Economic Analysis.

Vancil, Richard. 1978. *Decentralization: Managerial Ambiguity by Design*. Homewood, IL: Dow Jones-Irwin.

Veblen, Thorstein. 1939. *Imperial Germany and the Industrial Revolution*. New York: Viking Press.

Veblen, Thorstein. 1919. *The Vested Interests and the State of the Industrial Arts: The Modern Point of View and the New Order*. NY: B. W. Huebsch.

Wallace, Allan. 1991. Competitive advantage in the automobile assembly industry. Unpublished manuscript, University of South Carolina.

Weiermair, K. 1990. Globalization, the diffusion of technology and new forms of organization. Toronto: York University. Mimeo.

Wernerfelt, B. 1984. A resource based view of the firm. *Strategic Management Journal*, 5:171–180.

Williamson, O. E. 1985. *The Economic Institutions of Capitalism*. New York: Free Press.

World Bank. 1991. *World Development Report*. Washington DC: World Bank Publications.

Yarbrough, B. V. and R. M. Yarbrough. 1990. International institutions and the new economics of organization. *International Organization*, 44:235–260.

5

Political Perspectives and International Business

EDITORS' COMMENTS

In the study of international business, political actors and processes have never been merely an afterthought or sideshow. Instead, a major stream of IB inquiry has sought to understand the relationship of economic and political actors—at both micro and macro levels.[1] IB scholars have contributed to our understanding of political risk management, international business-government relations, international business and national development, and international political economy.

As Nigh notes in his paper, the study of IB and indeed most social sciences have been profoundly affected by their development in a world that has been largely defined as a world of nation-states. Given our theme of unearthing underlying assumptions of IB inquiry and holding them up to the light for examination, we thought that the "nation-state" was a prime candidate for investigation. Further, with the nation-state comes the modern state system and questions concerning the nature of and possible changes in the international system.

In the lead paper, Kobrin explores the "state" part of the nation-state and challenges IB's assumption that "political authority is, and will be, organized in terms of the post-Westphalian system of territorially defined sovereign states" [p. 243]. Kobrin asks some very basic questions about the relationship of economics and politics, markets and states, international business and the international political system—questions that Nigh, Kuhlman, Starr, and Brewer use as a starting point for their own contributions in this chapter.

In reviewing the nature of the modern state, Kobrin singles out *territoriality* as a particularly salient feature. Since states claim sovereignty over a particular geographic territory, borders as boundaries both enclose and define the state and separate one state from another.

Kobrin goes on to emphasize the development of national markets within the borders of the state. He reviews the processes by which the national level came to overshadow the local/regional or transnational levels of economic activity—up to the first half of the twentieth century. While this view has merit, we would add that it's important to remember that all three levels are in play at all times, even if one is more dominant.

The symmetry during this time period between the territorial scope of political authority (the state) and economic activity (the national market) is important for Kobrin, since for the larger states, their territory is big enough for their national firms to exploit economies of scale in production and distribution and to recoup investments in technological development.

In the latter part of the twentieth century, however, Kobrin argues that the movement of integrated markets from a national to transnational level introduces a basic mismatch between political and economic geography.

In his comments at the conference, Kobrin admitted to being somewhat of a technology determinist. For Kobrin technological development plays a key role in moving economic activity to the transnational level in two ways. First, advances in transportation, communication, and information processing make it possible for firms to integrate activities on a global scale. Secondly, the cost of developing the next generation technology in many industries is so high that returns need to be generated on a worldwide basis to make the investment feasible.

Given this transnational economic development, Kobrin asks "are territorial states becoming outmoded as a means of organizing political authority? Are we witnessing the early phases of a transition analogous to the decay of feudalism and the rise of the modern sovereign state in Europe: the onset of the development of a 'post-modern' form of political organization?" [p. 249] Kobrin answers these questions in the affirmative, "The modern state and the modern state system are fundamentally and inherently geographic. Once discrete borders and territoriality are compromised, in both practice and principle, the meaning of both unit and system must change." [p. 254]

Given his framing of the questions of concerning change in the international system, Kobrin goes on to consider what this postmodern system might look like. He and other contemporary observers, however, are taking on a very big question. In looking back at the development of the modern state, Mann [1993, p. 87] notes "The modern state has emerged in forms intended by no one and has in turn transformed all their [economic, political, military, ideological actors] identities and interests."

Nonetheless we applaud Kobrin's attempt to discern the future path of the modern state and the modern state system and its implications for international business. As George Steiner said, "To ask larger questions is to risk getting things wrong. Not to ask them at all is to constrain the life of understanding." [quoted in Von Laue 1987, p. 2]

We think Kobrin is on the right track in conceptualizing the international system as a social network, although we prefer to think of social networks in the more basic terms of social network analysis. "A social network consists of a finite set or sets of actors and the relation or relations defined on them" [Wasserman and Faust 1994, p. 20]. The relational tie among social actors may be of a cooperative nature, as Kobrin suggests, but need not be. The types of relational ties can be quite varied and can include those of a conflictive nature, for example. Still one important point here is that power comes from one's position in a social network as well as resources that one controls.

In his paper, Nigh picks up on Kobrin's investigation of the nation-state by first emphasizing that the state is an *organization* with its own infrastructure and personnel. He goes on to focus on the "nation" part of nation-state—the part that is less commonly understood and the part that tends to produce most of the confusion as to what exactly a nation-state is. He identifies two important components of the nation, one involving certain commonalities of language, religion, customs, or heritage among a population and the other involving the will of a population to perceive themselves as a nation.

Nigh stresses the close connection between the development of the nation and the state. Whether or not certain commonalities exist among a population, the state seeks to build a community of solidarity among the population within the territory it controls in order to secure and maintain its legitimacy. The state builds an "Us" within its borders and emphasizes the distinctness of its citizens interests in relating to "Them," the citizens of the other states.

The extent of this nation building process varies greatly across the states in the world. Nigh observes "In some states, the national building process is far advanced and continues each day. In others states, the process has barely begun. Unlike pregnancy, nationhood is not an all or nothing proposition. A state can be a little bit a nation." [p. 259] Thus as various authors draw the line as to what degree of nationhood qualifies for categorization as a nation, we get varying lists as to what qualifies as a nation-state.

Nigh goes on to review the role of national identity in the nation building process and identifies two sources of individual attachment to the nation-state: the sentimental and the instrumental [Kelman 1969]. Yet identification with the nation-state may be just one of many identifications made by an individual.

Picking up on a theme introduced by Kobrin, Nigh asks what national identity might mean for a multinational corporation, operating in a home country and one or more host countries. Nigh argues that a MNC can be considered to have a national identity—one that reflects the individual national identifications of its top management team. The national identity of an MNC can change over time and can vary greatly from company to company. More importantly, this national identity influences the MNC's relationships with various nation-states.

Nigh brings this concept of national identity of the MNC to bear on the debate concerning the extent to which a corporation will make contributions to the competitiveness of a nation-state—part of the "Who is Us?" debate initiated by Reich [1990]. He develops two key questions that need to be answered. First, "to what extent do the resources within the territory controlled by the nation-state matter to the multinational in its pursuit of its objectives, relative to other territories?" [p. 267] This question is very much in line with traditional bargaining power formulations of MNC - nation-state relations and links nicely with the instrumental sources of attachment to the nation-state.

Nigh adds, however, an important second question, "To what extent do those who control the MNC identify with the nation-state, relative to other identifications?" [p. 267] This question links nicely with the sentimental sources of attachment to the nation-state.

Like Kobrin, Nigh wrestles with the implications of the increased transnational economic activity for relations between economic and political actors, but does so at a level lower than the system level. In doing so, however, he highlights the importance of developing a better understanding of the processes by which the state and civil society influence one another.

In the third topic paper, Kuhlman makes three particularly notable points.

First, he asserts that IB is an interdisciplinary field of inquiry that should draw on all the social sciences. In fact, we believe that IB will find more intellectual nourishment going back directly to scholarly work in the behavioral and social sciences (e.g., economics, political science, psychology) rather than getting behavioral and social science concepts, theories, and methods filtered through largely uninational-oriented business disciplines (e.g., finance, organization behavior, marketing).

Second, reflecting his political science background, Kuhlman stresses the importance of levels of analysis sensitivity in the study of IB. He argues that "markets and politics interact within and between themselves at differing levels of analysis. The global political economy is a multilevel system in which issue variance will account for simultaneously operating levels of the system involved." [p. 269] Finally he goes on to question Kobrin's ideas concerning the end of the territorial state and argues that "Issues of autonomy and independence are compromised only in the sense that they are being negotiated constantly between the nation-state and actors at levels both above and below it in a kind of global hierarchy." [p. 271] Where Kobrin sees a change in kind, Kuhlman sees more continuity in the dynamics of the current system.

In his commentary, Starr also addresses Kobrin's views on the demise of the territorial state. He thinks Kobrin puts too much emphasis on territoriality as *the* defining characteristic of the sovereign state, rather than one dimension of a more complex concept. Starr goes back to Herz [1957] who first predicted the demise of the territorial state due to its inability to protect against the delivery of nuclear weapons, but later recanted [Herz 1968] when "He recognized that the allure and power of the territorial state as a mode of organization transcended his earlier argument regarding defense, to issues of identity, recognition and status" [p. 275].

Introducing the Deutsch's [1957] idea of security communities, Starr notes that in its pluralistic form, "states need not give up independence or territorial integrity to achieve significant levels of integration or to benefit from the positive processes that can occur with interdependence. Territorial boundaries, sovereign claims to equality, independence, and consent can co-exist with high levels of interdependence and transnational activities." [p. 276]

In the end Starr finds Kobrin's arguments flawed in two major ways. First, he argues that Kobrin underestimates the extent to which states have always had to contend with interdependence—from the very beginnings of the Westphalian system. Second, even with a shift in the balance of the "Westphalian trade-off," toward more interdependence, Starr argues that states have developed a array of regulatory mechanisms to manage this interdependence and have demonstrated a remarkable ability to adapt to changing conditions.

In his commentary, Brewer begins with a review of some core concepts of political analysis: value allocation, power, conflict, cooperation, interests, ideology, and institutions and then follows with a typology of the subfields of political science: international political economy, international security studies, national/subnational political systems, cross-national comparative politics, political philosophy, and political methodology. Arraying these subfields against IB transaction types and managerial functions, Brewer creates a matrix which he uses to analyze the topic areas in which IB research has incorporated a certain political dimension and where it has not. This proves to be an interesting exercise. The most important result is that there are so many empty or sparsely populated cells in the matrix, indicating many opportunities for future studies addressing certain aspects of the relationship between politics and IB. Brewer returns to the core values and identifies a point worth noting about value allocation: "although there has been tremendous attention given to the impact of IB on the distribution of economic and political values in society, relatively little attention has been given to the impact on the distribution of other values" (such as enlightenment, affection, beauty, well-being). [p. 284] Behrman makes a related plea in his commentary in chapter 2 and his paper in chapter 11 for IB to go beyond economic efficiency to include consideration of such human objectives as creativity, participation, stability, and compassion.

As a group, the five papers in this chapter highlight the need for a more comprehensive paradigm in IB inquiry. As suggested in chapter 1, IB needs a more encompassing paradigm that incorporates all levels of society and its interactions with other societies. That is, the political dimension of society can no longer be treated as exogenous to IB inquiry. It must be viewed as endogenous to an evolving process.

To this end, the five papers in this chapter advance the study of IB and politics in important ways. The nature of a key concept, the nation-state, has been clarified. Our understanding of the importance of the coevolution of state and nation for international business has been enhanced. The nation has been called an "imagined community" [Anderson 1983] since the size of this community is so much larger than the communities individual's identified with in the past. Given the key role of the state in building the nation, how might a global "imagined community" be developed? Further, some see the development of "virtual communities" linked only through electronic communication networks. An interesting question here is how important such geographically dispersed virtual communities will become in meeting human emo-tional needs and what effect they will have on the "imagined community" of the nation.

Also in these five papers, we find a most provocative and sophisticated debate on impact of transnational economic development and interdependence on the future of the modern state system. Are we at the dawn of a new postmodern international system, as Kobrin argues? Or can the current system of sovereign territorial states continue to adapt to increasing interdependence without even a significant change in its organization, as Starr argues? What are the implications for international business inquiry?

Finally, it's obvious that ideas presented in this chapter concerning the interdisciplinary nature of IB inquiry and the need for a framework that incorporates multiple levels of analysis (from the world to the individual) are quite consistent with the emerging interaction paradigm of IB we presented in chapter 1. IB as a field of inquiry needs to pursue its study of business and politics within a framework that allows for the simultaneous operation of multiple levels of analysis.

NOTES

1. To be more precise we should acknowledge that the term "economic actors" refers to actors whose behavior is predominantly but not exclusively in the economic arena and that the term "political actors" refers to actors whose behavior is predominantly but not exclusively in the political arena. For example, although states are political actors, at times states produce and distribute goods.

Transnational Integration, National Markets, and Nation-States
Stephen J. Kobrin

Robinson [1967:1] defined international business (IB) as "governmental and private business activity that affects persons or institutions of more than one national state, territory, or colony." It is this intervention of borders that gives legitimacy to the study of IB; any claim to uniqueness on the part of the IB literature ultimately reduces to the simultaneous operation of multinational firms across a number of different economic, cultural, and political entities.

A concern with politics and government has always been integral to the study of IB.[1] Behrman [1972], Fayerweather [1975], and Vernon [1971], among many others, dealt directly with nation-states and nationalism early in the development of the field. At the risk of oversimplification, a threefold categorization of the role that politics and states have played in the IB literature is possible:

1. *Firm-state interaction.* This includes the political risk literature, much of the work on bargaining, analyses of expropriation and "nationalism," and a good deal of the discussion of the role of foreign investment and the multinational enterprise in development.

2. *Strategic management.* Although this literature certainly overlaps firm-state interaction (e.g., bargaining), discussion of government takes place in the larger context of firm strategy and industry structure.

3. *International political economy.* IB scholars have contributed to the discussion of the impact of Multinational Enterprises (MNEs) as transnational actors on the state-centric view of the international political system: the liberal-realist argument in political science.

Although there are some important exceptions, in all three cases the IB literature deals with politics in terms of policy: problems of government control and jurisdiction. Despite all of the usual disclaimers, the political risk literature focuses on prediction and management of policy constraints that can be imposed on firms by governments. The emphasis of the strategic management literature is the trade-off between pressures

to integrate globally and what Doz [1980:27] calls the political imperative, "the adjustments made necessary by the demands of host governments."[2]

Even writers such as Behrman and Vernon, whose work is more directly concerned with politics *qua* politics, deal primarily with the erosion of government control and policy effectiveness. A major political theme in both of their works is extraterritoriality, the impact of the direct control of a subsidiary by a parent located in another country on the effectiveness of host government policy; the problem of overlapping jurisdictions [Vernon 1971:271].

Several authors have focused on integrating politics and the IB literature. Bodewyn, for example, argues that Dunning's eclectic paradigm should include politics; that "market imperfections may also be enacted through political behavior" [1988: 357]. Lenway and Murtha [1994:26] survey conceptions of the state in the IB literature, concluding that "theory concerning the attributes and elements of such structures (states) provides a powerful tool for organizing, predicting and explaining countries' economic strategies and policies, and their implementation capabilities." Although the scope of both papers is relatively broad, their focus is clearly on the state as an institution: on the motivation for, sources, and effectiveness of government policy and control.[3]

A fundamental tenet of the IB literature is that the political environment is a variable; the *idea* of the state, however, is a given or parameter. It is assumed that political authority is, and will be, organized in terms of the post-Westphalian system of territorially defined sovereign states. With few exceptions,[4] sovereignty is discussed operationally in terms of the *degree* of control exercised by the state, rather than conceptually. There is a corresponding assumption in the literature that territorially organized and defined national markets are the basic units in the international economic system.

In this paper, I will use a fundamental IB concept to question these basic assumptions about the organization of political and economic institutions. A focus of the strategic management literature is the simultaneous economic and technological pressures multinational firms face to integrate globally and the political (and social) pressures to fragment strategy, to respond to national differences. I will attempt to turn this concept of the integration-fragmentation trade-off "on its head" to examine the impact of economic and technological pressures to integrate globally on the very concept of the territorial organization of economics and politics, of national markets and modern sovereign states.

I will argue that increasing pressures to integrate transnationally raise questions about the viability of the primary existing modes of organizing economic and political institutions. In short, politics is integral to IB theory, and the implicit assumptions about politics and government underlying much of that literature may no longer be valid. In the remainder of this paper I will develop that argument in detail and explore its implications for IB theory. I will begin by making the assumptions discussed above explicit: by outlining the salient features of modern nation-states, national markets, and the international political system.

NATION-STATES

The sovereign state, which is but one of a number of historical modes of organizing political authority, arose from the decay of the feudal system in medieval Europe and became dominant in the sixteenth century. The modern state differs significantly from other Western modes of political organization, both Empire and feudal.[5] First, it is *territorial*, requiring clear and discrete borders and unambiguously defined geography. Second, it has a monopoly of authority (and force) within its territory. Third, it is not subject to a higher authority, such as an emperor or pope. As Watkins [1968:50] notes, "The state is a territory in which a single authority exercises sovereign powers."

Tilly [1975:27] has characterized the European nation-state as: (1) exerting control over a well-defined and continuous territory, (2) relatively centralized, (3) differentiated from other organizations, and (4) reinforcing claims through a monopoly of force. It is critical for my purposes to note that states and the state system are fundamentally *territorial*:

> "Modern states ... are all *territorial* in that they explicitly claim, and are based on, particular geographic territories, as distinct from merely occupying geographical space, which is true of all social organisations ... Its sovereignty is thus defined in terms of its territory ... This territory is typically continuous and totally enclosed by a clearly demarcated and defended boundary ..." [Anderson 1986:117]

Borders as boundaries are of the essence, they define both states and the very concept of the sovereign state. "Sovereignty must be bounded: a world of sovereign states is a world divided by boundaries" [Taylor 1985:105].

Medieval "states" differed markedly. Their territories were often discontinuous, borders ill defined and ambiguous, and sovereignty itself not based on territory [Anderson 1986:117]. "Medieval Europe comprised a cosmopolitan patchwork of overlapping loyalties and allegiances, geographically interwoven jurisdictions and political enclaves ... there was no clear demarcation between the domestic and external spheres of organization, no sharp dividing line between 'public territories' and 'private estates'" [Camilleri 1990:13]. Organizing political authority on the basis of a clearly defined and "more permanent political geography" represented a significant change from the feudal system [Johnson 1982:41].

The essential characteristic of the international system of sovereign states, formalized with the treaty of Westphalia (1648), is the absence of any central authority; it is decentralized and anarchic [Waltz 1979:88]. It is a system based on sovereignty and "self-help," with no central or higher authority to whom states can turn for protection.

NATIONAL MARKETS

Although the term *national market* is used frequently in the IB literature, little thought is given to its meaning. It is important to distinguish the creation of national markets from the rise of the market system in Europe. Long range trade and an "international economy" existed long before national markets, which were built up inside of, and in opposition to, that larger system in the late seventeenth and eighteenth centuries [Braudel 1984:322].[6]

The creation of a national market involves two primary processes: (1) internal consolidation or the removal of internal barriers to the free flow of goods and services, and (2) the separation of the domestic (the national) from the international through the establishment of meaningful and discrete economic borders over which political authorities have some measure of control. Thus, Braudel defines a national market as:

> "A political space transformed by the state into a coherent and unified economic space, . . . a system of internal mechanisms and connections with the outside world . . . a large-scale economy, territorialized so to speak, and sufficiently coherent for governments to be able to shape and manoeuvre it to some extent." [Braudel 1977:99; 1984:294]

After consolidation of national power, European governments viewed their economies as sources of revenue, of taxes and loans [Koenigsberger 1987:102]. However, it was the creation of national markets though the imposition of discrete borders and internal consolidation that allowed the exercise of real national economic sovereignty.

The basic organizing principle of national markets (and nation-states) is territoriality, "asserting and attempting to enforce control over a specific geographic area" [Sack 1981:55]. The development of the national economy was an attempt to circumscribe economic activity within the boundaries of the state and exert control over economic actors and transactions through control over territory [Braudel 1977:99].

It is important to note that national markets were created by relatively mature states [Price 1988:43]. Braudel [1984:287] argues that there was nothing spontaneous about the "welding together" of a number of autonomous economies against the resistance of feudal authorities, cities, regions, and foreigners.[7] It involved an active process of creation by political authorities, "there was inevitably behind the national market a centralizing political will—fiscal, administrative, military, or mercantilism." The very term "national market" defines an economic institution in political terms.

To this point, I have been using national market in the context of trade, in terms of an area in which gains can be achieved from specialization and the free flow of goods and services. (I have also been using national market as an economic area under the control of political authorities.) By the late nineteenth century, however, the term national market began to take on additional meaning as firms began to feel pressure to *integrate* operations over a larger area to remain competitive.

Until the 1870s most industries were subject to constant returns to scale. Manufacturing technologies developed after that date differed significantly in that they allowed the exploitation of economies of scale and scope; they required large scale production in order to obtain the lowest unit cost [Chandler 1977; Porter 1973]. As Chandler notes, the combination of developments in manufacturing with those in transport and communications resulted in a revolutionary change in the nature of business enterprise:

> "As a result of the regularity, increased volume, and greater speed of the flows of goods and materials made possible by the new transportation and communications systems, new and improved processes of production developed that for the first time in history enjoyed substantial economies of scale and scope." [1990:8]

The linkage of basic science and technology and the institutionalization of technological development by industry, which began to emerge late in the nineteenth century [Landes 1969:323,325], also exerted pressure to integrate markets over a larger geographic area. By the mid-twentieth century, rapidly increasing research and development expenditures necessary to remain technologically competitive in many industries became as, if not more, important than mass production economies as a motivation for integration. To paraphrase Scherer, the costs of research and development projects became so high that a large national market was necessary to justify the investment [Scherer 1974:48].

Gradually, the idea of first a regional and then a national market as the minimum geographic area required for efficient business operations came into being. As Porter concludes regarding the United States, "Much of the subsequent success of the national economy rested on the existence of a large domestic market that made the fruits of industrialization available . . ." [Porter 1973:40]. For the first time, a large national market provided a competitive advantage in terms of manufacturing efficiency (and later technological development).

In the first half of the twentieth century, the geographic territory bounded by the borders of the larger states contained adequate demand to allow the efficient operation of business firms, both in terms of manufacturing scale economies and (later) technological development. Furthermore, and perhaps more important, both states and markets were organized territorially. Nation-states and national markets coexisted within the same borders. Political and economic controls were exercised through control over geographic territory bounded by discrete, unambiguous, and meaningful borders. A symmetry existed between political and economic geography; at least in the larger countries, there was a correspondence of both scope and organizing principle. As we shall see, that symmetry was soon broken.

TRANSNATIONAL INTEGRATION

The technological revolution of the late nineteenth century resulted in the expansion of the geographic scope of integrated markets to allow firms to fully exploit scale economies. To some extent (and more so in Europe than in America), this involved international integration through trade; "If a country wanted to participate in the new world that was opening up, it had to release trade and commerce from these ridiculously small economic territories" [Price 1988:43].

Truly integrated international markets, however, awaited the revolutionary post-World War II developments in transport, communications, and electronic information processing. "The new telecommunications technologies are the electronic highways of the informational age, equivalent to the role played by railway systems in the process of industrialization" [Castells and Henderson 1987:6].

In the postwar era, the most important vehicle for transnational integration has been the multinational firm. As John Fayerweather [1969] observed over two decades ago, firms integrate globally—they standardize products, rationalize production, and centralize and/or coordinate research and development—when the benefits of integration exceed the limited recognition of national differences. As the literature is well developed on this point, I shall do no more than summarize the arguments.[8]

In many industries, the scale of efficient production in terms of fixed capital and the cost, complexity, and risk of technological development have increased to the point where even the major national markets are too small to support efficient business operations. In Ohmae's terms, there has been a dramatic shift from a variable to a fixed cost environment in production and research and development (R&D). This new logic, "forces managers to amortize their fixed costs over a much larger market base and this drives them to globalization" [Ohmae 1990:7]. In many industries, markets must be integrated across borders to allow a plant of minimum efficient scale or to support competitive R&D efforts.

I argued elsewhere that even though manufacturing economies of scale are an important determinant of transnational integration in several major industries, (automobiles and construction equipment, for example), it is technology that dominates as a motive for cross-border integration [Kobrin 1991]. The costs of developing new commercial technologies—both product and process—in industries such as microelectronics, computers, jet aircraft, and telecommunications have grown to the point where even dominant firms in the largest markets cannot afford them based on expected sales in a single country. Transnational integration is necessary to compete technologically.

The sharp increase in mergers, collaborative arrangements, strategic alliances, and joint ventures over the past decade illustrates the changes taking place in the economic and technological structure of many industries. This new wave of cooperative agreements reflects the difficulty that even the largest firms from the largest economies have integrating markets transnationally on their own through Foreign Direct Investment (FDI).[9] As Fusfeld and Haklisch [1985:60] note, "Global competition and limited resources have changed the way companies engage in R&D. Gone are the days when a technology based company—even the largest—could rely on internally generated and financed research projects alone."

In many strategic industries it is becoming increasingly unlikely that any single firm, regardless of its size and competitive position, has the resources or capabilities to deal with the "next generation" of product or process technology.[10] It is important to note that this structural change is taking place at the level of the industry and economy, even though it is manifest in the multinational firm. The clear implication is that even the largest of the world's economies are too small to support competitive levels of technological development in many leading industries.

The expansion of the size of integrated markets needed to support competitive business operations—from local, to regional, to national, to transnational—has been a gradual evolutionary process that began with the manufacturing revolution of the 1870s and the institutionalization of industrial research and development at the end of the nineteenth century. What is revolutionary is not the expansion of the scope of markets, but that expansion in relation to the way the world is organized politically: the developing asymmetry of economic and political geography.

Kindleberger [1975:359] has argued that there may be different "optimal sizes" for political and economic areas; "It seems likely then that the optimum economic area is larger than the nation-state, the optimum cultural area is smaller, and the optimum political area ... identical with it." His statement reflects the growing asymmetry between political and economic institutions, between markets and states. Although international trade certainly constrains national policy autonomy, it is generally supportive of the concept of national markets and nation-states. As we shall see, transnational integration is not. It erodes the very foundations and meaning of national markets. It is to that subject that I now turn.

NATIONAL MARKETS UNDER FIRE

The two primary attributes of national markets are consolidation and the separation of the domestic from the international economy; the removal of internal barriers to the free flow of goods and services and the imposition of discrete and meaningful borders. Put more formally, the creation of national markets involved extending the geographic *scope* of economic activity and establishing territoriality as the basic *principle of organization* of economic institutions.

At this point both the scope and mode of organization of national markets are threatened by technologically driven transnational integration. The scope of national markets, the geographic territory of even the largest nation-states, is no longer sufficient to allow for competitive industrial activity, primarily competitive levels of technological development. As argued above, markets in many of the leading or strategic industries are inherently transnational.

It is of more fundamental importance that territoriality is losing meaning as the organizing principle for markets; borders are rapidly becoming irrelevant as economic frontiers. As Brunn [1984:162] notes, the emergence of "space adjusting technologies" makes boundaries less important. Borders are being blurred or eroded as, "formal boundaries have lost much of their importance with instant telephone linkages, satellite images, computer processing of international data and images, and global television reporting."

If borders are to have meaning in an economic sense, national governments must be able to exert a reasonable degree of control over flows of goods, funds, information, and people across them. Governments must be able to exert territorially based control over economic actors and over the economy. Technological developments, particularly in telecommunications and information processing, have severely compromised that control and thus the meaning of borders and national markets.

Only a few examples are necessary to make the point. A senior officer of AT&T has described a vision of short term developments in cellular communications where a satellite network will link mobile phones worldwide, with a tracking capability that will allow any phone to be reached at any time in any place.[11] When that is achieved, the geographic organization and control of telephone communications will be virtually irrelevant. Telephone numbers will have to be assigned to individuals rather than by area and city, and government control over personal communications will be severely eroded.

Satellite imaging is another example. What do borders mean when the United States or Russia can scan any territory in the world and obtain detailed information about resources, industrial activity, troop movements, patterns of land use and urbanization, and the like? It is entirely possible that the U.S. government using a satellite may know more about the distribution of resources in Argentina than that country's government. Similarly, it is virtually impossible for any government to control the transborder transmission of data electronically when huge amounts of information can be sent in an instant via computers and satellites. Clearly, information, "a basic resource as important as land, labor and capital have been in the past," can no longer be contained within national borders [Blumental 1988:534].

Perhaps the best and most directly relevant example of the irrelevance of geography and territoriality as the organizing principle of economic activity is financial markets. When one says that financial markets are global, it implies considerably more than the linking of national markets. The financial market is global in the sense that transactions take place in an electronic network. Borders and territoriality are virtually irrelevant.[12] Government control over flows of funds and thus the value of currencies or monetary policy is very limited.

As Wriston [1988;1989:71] has observed, the change in the organization of financial markets is a result of technology:

> "Our new international financial regime differs radically from its precursors in that it was not built by politicians, economists, central bankers or finance ministers, nor did high-level international conferences produce a master plan. It was built by technology . . . Today, information about all countries' diplomatic, fiscal, and monetary policies is instantly transmitted to more than two hundred thousand screens in hundreds of trading rooms in dozens of countries . . . The entire globe is linked electronically with no place to hide."

Borders are clearly losing meaning as economic boundaries. Ohmae makes the point well: "On a political map, the boundaries between countries are as clear as ever. On a competitive map, showing the real flows of financial and industrial activity, those boundaries have largely disappeared" [1990:18]. The implications are all pervasive as markets are no longer geographic spaces but have become global networks [Nye 1990:8]. "The space of places is being superseded by the space of flows." Economies may still have spatial forms but their logic is increasing placeless [Castells and Henderson 1987:7].

In summary, there are a number of reasons to question the viability of national markets as the basic unit of economic organization. First, they are too small; they do not provide sufficient scope for competitive economic activity. Second, national economic borders are increasingly less meaningful. Both arguments mean that the distinction between domestic and international economic activity is losing meaning. Last, there is reason to question the presumption of the territorial or geographic organization of economic activity and markets; the information and telecommunications revolution has resulted in electronic networks replacing geographic proximity in many instances. Both the scope and basic organizational principle of national markets are increasingly irrelevant.[13]

Nation-states, however, remain the basic unit of political organization. The nation-state still defines the scope of political authority, and territoriality is still its basic organizing principle. The result is a considerable asymmetry between both the scope and mode of organization of political and economic institutions. Kindleberger once concluded that, "the nation-state is about through as an economic unit" [1969:207]. Waltz responded that, "If Charles P. Kindleberger were right . . . then the structure of international politics would have to be redefined. That would be necessary because economic capabilities cannot be separated from the other capabilities of states" [1969:94]. That question must now be addressed.

THE FUTURE OF THE TERRITORIAL STATE

The relationship between the disintegration of the feudal system and the rise of the modern territorial state is complex and certainly not monocausal. There is little question, however, that developments in military technology, the spread of monetary payments for services and goods, and the rise of markets and the market system played a major role [Koenigsberger 1987; North and Thomas 1973; Tilly 1975]. The modern state evolved as a political institution that was consistent with social and economic organization from the sixteenth through the twentieth centuries. A number of authors have raised what, by this point, should be an obvious question. Given the tendency towards global integration of technology and the economy, are territorial states becoming outmoded as a means of organizing political authority? Are we witnessing the early phases of a transition analogous to the decay of feudalism and the rise of the modern sovereign state in Europe: the onset of the development of a "post modern" form of political organization?

During the first wave of interest in the multinational corporation (MNC) in the late 1960s there were a number of predictions that the state would "wither away" in the face of the economic efficiency of integrated MNCs. Ball, for example, argued that states were, "Archaic concepts unsympathetic to the needs of our complex world" [1969:165]. As noted above, Kindleberger saw a conflict between optimal economic and political areas and argued that the nation-state is neither sacrosanct nor eternal. "If the scale of political efficiency changes, why should not the national state follow the county not into oblivion but into the museum of antiquarian interest with the city-state?" [1975:361].

Ball, Kindleberger, and others such as Robinson envisioned the development of supranational economic and political institutions that would be isomorphic with the MNC [Kindleberger 1975:360; Robinson 1964:224]. Other observers have questioned the continuing significance and viability of territorial states. Tilly's conclusions to an extensive study of the formation of the nation-state in Europe are worth quoting:

> Perhaps the European national state grew up at a scale roughly matched to the markets, capital, communications, and productive organization of the seventeenth or eighteenth centuries, but increasingly irrelevant to the scale and manner of independence prevailing in the twentieth century. Perhaps control of a contiguous territory was peculiarly advantageous to the land- and water-bound technologies of the European state-making eras, but an obstacle to full exploitation of technologies of flight, electric power, and electronic information-handling. [1975:638]

Similarly, Brunn [1984:161] labels the state an industrial-era phenomenon and wonders if we are in the midst of a transition, a "watershed" to some sort of global geopolitical organization.

Others disagree sharply. Falk argues that the "deconstruction" of the modern state is both premature and misleading. "Territorial states remain the predominant political actors in our world, even if their interactions are becoming bewilderingly complex and increasingly extraterritorial in their operational reach, and despite the fact that their capacity for autonomy is being multiplied and cumulatively eroded" [1990:61].

Similarly, Keohane and Nye criticize modernist writers who, "see our era as one in which the territorial state . . . is being eclipsed by non-territorial actors such as multinational corporations, transnational social movements, and international organizations" [1987:727; 1989:3–5]. They argue that neither the traditionalist nor the modernist framework is adequate to understand the impact of technological and economic changes, the impact of "complex interdependence."

Although there is certainly a relationship between technico-economic and political change, it is very unlikely that transnational economic institutions will create trans, or supra, national political entities. If the past is any guide, the process works in quite the other direction. National markets were created by nation-states; they developed *after* the consolidation of national political institutions. The process has been inverted in the creation of transnationally integrated markets.

Although certain postwar international institutions and organizations such as the World Bank, the International Monetary Fund (IMF), and the GATT were created to facilitate and organize international economic activities, there are few, if any, transnational political institutions. The one major exception might be the European Union, but even there it can be argued that the reality of economic integration drove whatever political consolidation has, or is, taking place. As Keohane and Nye have observed [1987:739], international organizations have generally functioned as facilitators in the context of regimes rather than as lawmakers.

Although we are clearly in the midst of a revolutionary transformation in the scope and mode of organization of economic institutions, and in the relationship between economics and politics, it is far too early to dismiss the nation-state as the primary mode of organization of political authority, or primary unit of political allegiance. In an article on the impact of technological change on the world economy, Blumental [1988:545] concluded that although technology is making the notion of national sovereignty obsolete in much of economic affairs, "regardless of where the technology moves, nation-states will continue to exist for a long time to come and more important, will behave as if they continue to control key economic events a great deal more effectively than actually may be the case."

Agreement that states will not wither away to be replaced by transnational political institutions does not imply that current structures are immutable. States have evolved continuously over the last four hundred years, and the question at hand is whether the changes we are witnessing are those of kind or degree? Can territoriality be maintained as the cardinal organizing principle in the international political system when it has been compromised in the international economic system? Can nation-states maintain their meaning when national markets are losing theirs?

These questions form the core of one of the central arguments in international political economy, the differences between the neoliberal and neorealist paradigms (see Keohane [1986]). There is no question that developments in the past two decades have compromised the sovereignty and autonomy of states. The rise of transnational organizations (the MNC is the prototype) as autonomous actors in world politics affects the relationships and interactions between states and the ability of any given state to influence others [Keohane and Nye 1977]. Similarly, in a later work Keohane and Nye [1989:24–25] argued that "complex interdependence" may well transform the nature of relations among states.[14]

The question, however, is the impact of these changes on states and the state system. Is the glass "half empty or half full?" At the end of the day, are sovereign states still the dominant actors in the system or are we in the midst of a revolutionary transformation in the nature and meaning of nation-states?

It is certainly possible to take a position between these two extremes, to conclude that although states' power and sovereignty are compromised by economic and technical integration, they remain important actors in world politics. In a recent book, for example, Rosenau [1990:247,256] argues that the dynamics of postindustrialism will result in a multicentric world, that is, "a paradigm that neither circumvents nor negates the state-centric model but posits sovereignty-bound and sovereignty-free actors as inhabitants of separate worlds that interact in such as way as to make their coexistence possible."[15]

The question is whether these changes are of degree or kind. Will the nation-state of the twenty-first century be functionally equivalent to that of the nineteenth or twentieth? Can the symmetry between economic and political institutions be restored, and if so, what implications does that have for the organization of political authority? In many strategic industries, markets are larger than those of even the largest nation-states and are no longer organized in terms of contiguous geography. The question is What is the impact of these changes on states and the state system?

THE END OF TERRITORIALITY?

There are critically important differences between interdependence resulting from relatively free flows of trade and investment (the extension of a market system across national borders that links national markets) and the transnational integration of markets motivated by scale considerations. Cooper [1968] defines trade-based integration in terms of the sensitivity of economic events and policies in one country to what is happening in its trading partners. (Keohane and Nye [1989:12] define interdependence in terms of vulnerability as well as sensitivity.)

The primary issues created by interdependence revolve around a trade-off between the gains from cooperation and the potential loss of autonomy in terms of a nation's freedom to frame and implement economic policy. As Rosecrance [1986:14] notes, "In the past, trade was a tactical endeavor, a method used between wars, and one that could easily be sacrificed when military determinants so decreed."

If increasing fixed costs drive transnational integration the benefits are likely to be discontinuous. As few, if any, national markets are large enough to sustain technological development in main-frame computers, telecommunications, or jet aircraft, firms and governments face a zero-one choice rather than a trade-off: to integrate across borders to develop a market of sufficient size to support R&D costs or to abandon such efforts. As Hobsbawm [1990:25] observes, the nineteenth century world economy was "*international* rather than cosmopolitan" (emphasis original). Transnational integration fuses rather than links national markets; it transforms the underlying economic structure of industry.

I will argue that the transnational integration of markets is a change of kind rather than degree. It does not merely constrain the economic autonomy or independence of states, but rather compromises autonomy or independence as meaningful constructs. It is not simply that determining the national origin of products or exerting national control over technology has become more complex or difficult. Rather, the concepts themselves have lost relevance or meaning. The link between economics and politics is the loss of meaning of the concepts of borders and territoriality.

Reich [1990;1991a] has asked two revealing questions: Who is us?, and Who is them? What is an American, Japanese, or German firm?, and is the question even relevant? Is the IBM notebook computer designed, produced, and at least initially sold in Japan an American or a Japanese product? What about the Honda Accord station wagon designed in the United States for the American market and produced in Honda's U.S. plants with a high level of local content? Is it an American or a Japanese car? The real question given the degree of integration of firms and markets in these industries is whether it matters, whether the question is even relevant?

One can go even further and ask about the origin and control of technology. If the Hitachi-Texas Instruments cooperative agreement to develop large capacity memory chips is successful, is the technology American or Japanese? Which government has the right to exert control over its use and dissemination? If neither firm (or economy) can deal with the cost, risk, and complexity of the technology on its own, is the concept of national origin and control of technology even meaningful?

Again, the underlying issues involve not only the size or scope of markets but the meaning of borders and territoriality. In many industries, governments are able neither to control flows of ideas, information, or even funds across borders nor to exert control over economic actors through control over geographic territory. The existence of contiguous geography is increasingly irrelevant economically. The basic concept of autonomy or independent control over territory is compromised.

The integrated multinational firm serves as a metaphor for changes taking place in international political and economic systems. Take the example of a vertically integrated automobile firm. The question is how one values a subsidiary, say in Mexico, producing engines that are shipped to assembly plants in several other countries. To the extent the subsidiary is dependent on other units in the firm for products, technology, and outlets its value does not flow from its assets or capabilities as an independent company. Rather, its value is a function of its integration into the transnational system; of its relationships with other units on whom it is dependent for inputs and the disposal of outputs.

In an analogous fashion, the appropriate metaphor for the international political system is evolving from the "organized anarchy" of independent, functionally equivalent states to a social network where integration rather than interdependence links constituent units. In this sort of world, independence and sovereignty, control over territory and borders, will become less meaningful.

THE INTERNATIONAL SYSTEM AS A SOCIAL NETWORK

In the past, economic, and thus political, power has been *relative*, a function of resources—land, population, and minerals as well as industry and technology—controlled by one state compared to others. As a result of transnational integration, power is becoming *relational*, a function of how well states manage their interrelationships in a transnational network. The issue is one of managing cooperation. The idea of maintaining independence is rapidly becoming ephemeral.

As noted above, states do not appear to be withering away and will remain the basic units of organization of political authority and of individual attachment. However, national power in the sense of technological competence and provision for domestic economic and political welfare will come less from independence or sovereign control over territory and more from managing cooperation, from a state's position in an international social network.

In a recent book, Reich [1991c:172] describes both large international firms and national economies in terms of "global webs." "Barriers to cross-border flows of knowledge, money, and tangible products are crumbling; groups of people in every nation are joining global webs. In a very few years, there will be virtually no way to distinguish one national economy from another except by the exchange rates of their currencies—and even this distinction may be on the wane."

Ghoshal and Bartlett [1990] argue that the MNC should be seen as an interorganizational network, that social network theory is both a useful and appropriate tool for modeling that entity. Although I will not pursue the idea in any depth here, interorganizational theory would seem to be an appropriate model of the emerging global economy as well. Networks and markets are very different mechanisms for coordinating economic activity [Powell 1990]. Networks are inherently *relational* and they entail reciprocal interaction; the "basic assumption of network relationships is that one party is dependent on resources controlled by another, and that there are gains to be had by the pooling of resources" [Powell 1990:303].

As Hughes [1989:286–87] has observed, once economies become interlinked the meaning of national competitiveness becomes increasingly complex:

> If global interdependencies predominate, then no economy may encompass the whole of one industry or even the whole of

one product . . . firms' success will depend on the competitiveness of firms in other economies who are producing other parts of the same product. In addition, firms' success will also depend on their global network, not on their performance in a single economy alone . . . Put simply, the overall health of the economy will depend, in part, on how good it is at producing it's part of various products and on the value of those 'parts' relative to other parts.

It is important to distinguish national economic interests from the national economy. As Reich [1991c:153] notes, "To claim that corporate nationality is becoming irrelevant is emphatically not to argue that, in the global economy toward which we are rapidly heading, national economic interests have ceased to exist or ceased to matter." Similarly Hobsbawm [1990:175] argues that the changes that have occurred do not imply that the economic functions of states are likely to fade away.

National markets, however, are losing meaning; they are becoming too small to support competitive enterprises and their borders are eroding. In an interdependent and integrated global economy, large and important parts of which are not organized territorially, national economic interests will be achieved increasingly through managing cooperation; though exploiting the web or network to the advantage of the citizens of the state.

The transition from independent national economies to a global economy, or even from trade based interdependence to integration, is a change of kind rather than degree. The transnational integration of markets compromises not only policy independence and autonomy, but the basic concept of the territorial organization of economic institutions. The remaining question is the impact on nation-states.

THE NONTERRITORIAL STATE?

We are currently in the midst of transformation of the world political-economy that may be as significant as the transition from feudalism to the modern state system.

As Hobsbawm observes [1990:174–175], "At present we are living though a curious combination of the technology of the late twentieth century, the free trade of the nineteenth, and the rebirth of the sort of interstitial centres characteristic of world trade in the middle ages."

Modern nation-states are essentially territorial, and one must question the meaning of the term *state* in a world where territoriality is rapidly losing meaning. If the concept of independence and sovereignty—the idea of control over a clearly defined territory—looses meaning, is it anachronistic to use the term *state* to describe existing political units? A world characterized by economic integration, cooperation, and reciprocity and the blurring of borders—both economic and political—is not consistent with a system comprised of independent, sovereign, and in Waltz's [1979] terms, functionally equivalent states.

The modern state and the modern state system are fundamentally and inherently geographic. Once discrete borders and territoriality are compromised, in both practice and principle, the meaning of both unit and system must change. It is easier to foresee change, however, than to discern the outlines of a postmodern economic or political system.

One problem is that we tend to view change as linear in terms of a forward pointing arrow of time. In fact, the modern era of territorially defined sovereign states and national economies may be an exception; diffuse geography and internationalism may well be the rule. As Hobsbawm notes [1990:25], we may be returning to what constitutes normalcy over a broader sweep of time. "(F)rom the eighteenth century to the years following World War II, there seemed to be little space and scope in the global economy for those genuinely extraterritorial, transnational or interstitial units which have played so large a part in the genesis of a capitalist world economy and which are today once again so prominent . . ."

A number of authors (Bull [1977] and Lapham [1988], for example) have suggested that the postmodern political and economic system be interpreted in terms of a medieval analogy. First, as has been discussed, medieval borders were diffuse and jurisdictions overlapped. Neither political nor economic authority (or institutions) were completely territorial. Second, in the medieval period, "the world, or transnational, environment was primary, the domestic secondary" [Rosecrance 1986:77].[16] Third, and related to the second, elites—the nobility—were international. Their attachment was to the pan-European "transnational system" rather than to a given territory. Fourth, there was no clear distinction between private and public property and authority. Last, there was a belief in the ideal of the Roman Empire, a need for authority at the center, for an emperor or pope.

The analogy is apt, even if easily overextended. The current organization of international financial markets and the evolving irrelevance of the national origin of products or technology, indeed the role of national markets and nation-states in an integrated global economy, can easily be described in terms of overlapping jurisdictions and diffuse geography. Behrman and Vernon's earlier concern with extraterritoriality can be generalized to an erosion of the very concept of territoriality in politics as well as economics.

As noted several times in this paper, the system of bounded, independent, national economies and sovereign, independent states may well have been exceptional. We appear to be returning to the norm of the primacy of the international over the domestic. Although one would not want to stretch the comparison between executives of the modern transnational firm and the medieval nobility too far, the parallels in their allegiance to a broader system are obvious. Although the modern chief executive of a MNC is still very much the citizen of his or her home country, the conflict of transnationalism with that of nationalism is increasing dramatically.

Similarly, the discussion of the rise of

private transnational actors in international politics certainly raises questions about the clear distinction between private and public authority that is characteristic—at least in theory—of the modern state. Last, we are seeing the rise of transnational political and economic institutions (e.g., the European Union) and a need for some sort of authority at the center, short of real supranational institutions. Many of the world's most pressing problems such as the drug trade, the environment, and use of the oceans, in addition to the economic problems discussed in this paper, simply cannot be solved at the national level. They are inherently transnational.

Although nation-states will be here for some time to come as the basic units of political authority and legitimacy, their function and structure, and the structure of the international system, are in the process of evolution. The very basic concepts of sovereignty and territoriality are eroding to the point where their meaning is in question.

IMPLICATIONS FOR INTERNATIONAL BUSINESS

I began this paper by noting that the intervention of national economic and political borders are what fundamentally distinguishes the study of IB. If the very idea of the national market and the nation-state is compromised, if the boundaries between the domestic and international blur, the impact on the field has to be profound. In this concluding section I will do no more than raise a number of brief questions about the implications of the transition to a postmodern political and economic system on IB.

What will home and host country mean? Despite all of the discussion of the evolution of transnational enterprise, the vast majority of multinational firms are just that. They are multinational in the same sense as the original use of the term in reference to the Hapsburg and Ottoman empires. Both were multinational yet there was no doubt that the centers of power in each were Turkish and Austrian. What will a true

transnational firm in a postmodern transnational political system look like?

If national economic objectives are to be obtained through the exploitation of cooperative relationships, through the international social network, how will that affect the global strategy of the firm? What will be the strategic relationships between MNCs and the countries in which they operate? In the nearer term, the nature of political risk for the MNC will change radically. Up to this point, most discussion of political risk involves one firm and one country, typically a MNC and a host country. Increasingly, firms will find themselves caught between competing objectives of two or more countries attempting to exert control over transnational technology, for example. In fact, given the dramatic increase in alliances, one would expect political risk situations to involve multiple firms and countries.

Most important is the issue of social control over business firms and economic activity. The question is obvious, but difficult. To this point, the primary vehicle for the exercise of social control over economic actors has been the nation-state. In a transnationally integrated world, how will social objectives be determined and who will exercise control?

NOTES

1. Robinson began his well-known text with a discussion of nationalism, "It is extremely unlikely that one can come to grips effectively with the pressures and conflicts inherent in the international movement of capital, skills, technology, and goods without an appreciation of the essential nature of nationalism and the cluster of interests represented in that notion" (Robinson 1973:1).

2. Doz goes on to note that international interdependence has made countries, "more vulnerable to external factors and their traditional domestic economic policies less effective" (1980:27). In a later paper, he undertakes a more extensive examination of the problems posed for government policy by MNCs and global markets and presents a complex categorization of government policies and firm responses (1986).

3. When Boddewyn discusses sovereignty, it is in terms of MNCs "evading, eroding or capturing national controls" (1988:359).

4. One notable exception is Richard Robinson (1964:224) who argued that "multinational relationships . . . are conducive to the weaving of an even large fabric of common interest and loyalty, thereby eroding the *concept* of national sovereignty and conflicting national interests" (emphasis added). Robinson saw the possibility of a supranational authority as a solution to the problem.

5. Territoriality, in the sense of a geographic division of political power did not apply to either the Roman Empire or medieval Europe (Taylor 1985:96).

6. During the early middle ages, the self-sufficient manor was the primary mode of economic organization in Europe. However, by the twelfth and thirteenth centuries, the reemergence of towns and settling of spaces between manors led to increasing factor diversity and the gradual move from a domestic to a market economy: the growth of trade. In Braudel (1984:94) and North and Thomas (1973:55,66), Braudel argues that patterns of price variations, which were visible quite early, are, "a sign that a network of markets was established in Europe at a very early stage." He notes that a general order in price variations was observable in the fifteenth, sixteenth, and seventeenth centuries, well before the development of national markets (Braudel 1984:75). Reich (1991c:13) also notes the relatively recent development of national markets, arguing that a national economy whose members see themselves as succeeding or failing together would be seen as novel as recently as the seventeenth century.

7. On the eve of the French Revolution, for example, a cargo of timber in route from Lorraine to the Mediterranean would have encountered thirty-four separate duties at twenty-one stops (Schama 1990:190).

8. For a review see Bartlett and Ghoshal 1989, Kobrin 1991, and Porter 1986.

9. The impetus for these alliances is complex; one motivation is certainly market access, the need to obtain a secure foothold in each of the legs of the "triad." (Thus, Fujitsu's acqui-

sition of ICL reflected the importance of the European computer market.) However, in a number of the agreements—e.g., Texas Instruments/Hitachi and Fujitsu/ICL—the importance of the cost and risk of technological development as a motivator was made explicit in corporate statements.

10. Comparing *Business Week* data on R&D intensity for twenty-one U.S. industries for 1978 and 1988 reveals an average increase in R&D expenditures/sales of 32%. (*Business Week* (2 July 1979):52–72 and *Business Week* (20 June 1989):178–232.)

11. Talk by Dr. Blaine Davis at the Wharton School's International Forum, Philadelphia, 6 September 1990.

12. The centers of financial markets are always referred to as Tokyo, London, and New York, never Japan, the U.K., and the U.S.

13. As Hobsbawm (1990:173–174) observes, "The nation today is visibly in the process of losing an important part of its old functions, namely that of constituting a territorially bounded 'national economy' which formed a building block of the larger 'world economy' . . . [T]he . . . basic units in the international division of labour are transnational or multinational enterprises of all sizes, and by the corresponding development of international centres, and networks of economic transactions which are, for all practical purposes, outside the control of state governments."

14. They attribute three primary characteristics to complex interdependence: multiple channels connect societies, the absence of a clear hierarchy of issues on the international agenda, and limits on the use of military force.

15. He goes on to observe that sovereignty-free actors, "have no territory to protect for the boundaries that differentiate them from their environments are abstract, dependent on economic processes or the bounds of social cohesion rather than on land . . . "

16. As Rosecrance has observed (1986:77), the transformation from the medieval to the modern period involved a reordering of the priority of domestic and international realms to assert to primacy of the former. understanding but also to effective public policy.

■ ■ ■

Who's On First?: Nation-States, National Identity, and Multinational Corporations

Douglas Nigh

It should come as no surprise that the nation has loomed large in the study of international business (IB). Just as the word "nation" is embedded in the term "international business," so too is the study of IB embedded in the development of the social sciences in the nineteenth and twentieth centuries. Economics, political science, and sociology, among other disciplines, have been profoundly affected by their development in a world that was defined predominantly as a "world of nation-states."[1]

In "Transnational Integration, National Markets, and Nation-States," Kobrin [this chapter] focuses on the "state" part of nation-state. He identifies sovereignty over territory as the essence of the modern state.[2] I would only add for clarity that the state is a differentiated, centralized *organization* with formally coordinated parts. As an organization, "the state unifies and makes distinctive the political aspects of social life, sets them apart from other aspects, and entrusts them to a visible, specialized entity" [Poggi 1990:20].

Kobrin goes on to explore the implications of transnational economic integration for the future of the territorial state. Kobrin asks what will *home* and *host* country mean, as the world political economy evolves from the modern state system to the post-modern transnational political system that he sees coming.

This question is closely related to those raised by Robert Reich in "Who Is Us?" and "Who Is Them?" [1990;1991a]. Reich raises the issue of the relationship between the competitiveness of a nation and the competitiveness of the multinational corporations (MNCs) domiciled in that nation. Reich's answer to "Who is us?" is "the American workforce, the American people, but not particularly the American corporation" [1990:54]. For Reich, the home country of a MNC doesn't matter and gov-

ernment policy should reflect that it doesn't matter.

In this paper, I'd like to look more closely at the "nation" part of the nation-state. I will examine the meaning of the national identity of MNCs and its implications for the relationships between nation-states and MNCs. I will investigate such relationships particularly with regard to issues related to the competitiveness of nation-state.

First, I will examine the concept of nation and its relationship to nationalism. From this discussion, the relationships among nation, state, and nation-state will be clarified. It turns out that much of the lack of consistency as to what a nation-state is derives primarily from a lack of clarity as to what a nation is.

Using identification theory, I will next explore what, if anything, national identity might mean for a MNC or its members and how national identity might affect the behavior of MNCs. This discussion will provide one useful way of thinking about the meaning of nationality for MNCs.

I go on to jump into the "Who is us?" debate, in which I'll argue that recognizing the existence of competing identities (both national and nonnational) is an important first step in sorting this all out.

THE NATION AND NATIONALISM

What is a nation? This is not an easy question to answer.[3] Walter Bagehot, who characterized the nineteenth century as one of nation-building, observed "We know it when you do not ask us, but we cannot very quickly explain it or define it" (quoted in Hobsbawm [1990:1]).

Attempts to define a nation have tended to start with two dimensions, one revolving around *culture* and the other around *will*. Meinecke's [1970] distinction between *cul-*

tural nation (Kulturnation) and *political* nation (Staatsnation) is a good example. For Meinecke, the cultural nation is a social entity whose members feel a sense of belonging together based on certain commonalties of culture-common language, common religion, common heritage, common customs. In contrast, "The political nation centres on the idea of individual and collective self determination and derives from the individual's free will and subjective commitment to the nation" [Alter 1985:14]. The political nation is founded upon the equality of its members and is an expression of their will to perceive themselves as a nation.

Gellner's two preliminary definitions of a nation—the *cultural* and the *voluntaristic*—echo this distinction.

1. Two men are of the same nation if and only if they share the same culture, where culture in turn means a system of ideas and signs and associations and ways of behaving and communicating.
2. Two men are of the same nation if and only if they recognize each other as belonging to the same nation. In other words, nations make the man; nations are the artifacts of men's convictions and loyalties and solidarities. A mere category of persons (say occupants of a given territory or speakers of a given language, for example) becomes a nation if and when the members of the category firmly recognize certain mutual rights and duties to each other in virtue of their shared membership of it. It is their recognition of each other as fellows of this kind that turns them into a nation, and not the other shared attributes, whatever they might be, which separate that category from non-members. [1983:7]

Again these two dimensions are reflected in what are termed the *objective* and *subjective* criteria for defining nations, which are reviewed and critiqued by Hobsbawm [1990]. Objective criteria for nationhood have been based on single attributes such as common language or common ethnicity or on combinations of these attributes and others such as common history or common territory. Subjective criteria go back to Ernest Renan's 1882 lecture "What is a nation?," in which he answered "The nation is a daily plebiscite" [Hobsbawm 1990:7]. Again in this case we see that it is the individuals' consciousness of belonging to a nation that creates the nation.

Hobsbawm also makes the distinction between the *nationalist* concept of the nation and the *revolutionary-democratic* concept that parallels Meinecke's cultural nation and political nation. "The equation state = nation = people applied to both, but for nationalists the creation of political entities which would contain it derived from the prior existence of some community distinguishing itself from foreigners; while from the revolutionary-democratic point of view, the central concept was the sovereign citizen-people = state, which in relation to the remainder of the human race constituted a 'nation'" [1990: 22].

Nationalism and Nation-States

While highlighting important elements of the nation, these ideas involving the commonalties and the will of a population provide only a good starting point for our examination of the nation. We need to consider more explicitly the nation's relationship to the state. This is best done by starting with nationalism, the political principle that holds that the political and national unit should be congruent [Gellner 1983:1; Hobsbawm 1990:9]. From the perspective of nationalism, the desired state of affairs is the nation-state. The territory of the state is identical with that inhabited by the members of the nation. In the nation-state, state equals nation, with one state per nation and vice versa.

In addition, nationalism holds that the political duty of the members of the nation to the state that represents them overrides all other public obligations [Hobsbawm 1990]. The claims of citizenship in the nation-state take priority over the claims of humanity in general and over smaller or larger political units (cf. Walker and Mendlovitz [1990]).

The development of nations and that of states are closely connected. In some cases, the development of the nation preceded the development of the nation's state. In such cases, various commonalties of culture discussed above were used to legitimate claims for the creation of a state, indeed, a nation-state. Commonly cited examples here would include the Germans, Italians, and Poles. Yet here the political will to create a communal state was decisive [Alter 1985:16]. Indeed the role of the state in nation-building even in these cases where strong commonalties did exist prior to the creation of the state was quite significant. As Massimo d'Azeglio said at the first meeting of the parliament of the newly united Italian kingdom, "We have made Italy, now we have to make Italians" [Hobsbawm 1990:44].

In other cases, the nation developed afterwards as a consequence of the creation of the state. Here, France, England, and the United States would be good examples. "In these three states, a process of domestic political transformation generated the nation as a community of politically aware citizens equal before the law irrespective of their social and economic status, ethnic origin and religious beliefs" [Alter 1985:15]. Through mass education, the introduction of "official" languages, the introduction of judicial uniformity, and other means, the state seeks to build a nation—to build that sense of belonging together, a sense of "us" as opposed to "them." Yet it is difficult to build something out of absolutely nothing. That's why states that are successful in building nations usually have some commonalties of the population that can serve as a base for nation building. The process of convergence within the state's territory may take a very long time and, indeed, may never happen in certain states.

The above discussion points to the importance of the state in understanding what a nation is and how the two dimensions of nation might be integrated. A nation is a relative large collectivity of people which (1) due to various commonalties of a cultural, linguistic, religious, or political nature, has developed a consciousness of its unity and particular interests, and (2) demands the right to political self-determination, or has already achieved such through a nation-state [Alter 1985:17]. It is states and nationalisms that create nations rather than the other way around [Hobsbawm 1990:10; Gellner 1983:55].

The above discussion concerning the nature of the nation sheds some light on the various meanings given to the nation-state. For example, how can we live in a world of nation-states when Tilly argues that very few European states have ever qualified as nation-states and, in particular, Great Britain, Germany, and France *never* have [1990:3]? The answer is that Tilly is defining the nation-state as "state=nation" where nation is a people that share a *strong linguistic, religious, and symbolic identity*. Others take a less strict view of nationhood, allowing weaker senses of belonging together among the populations of states to qualify as nations and thus the states that are congruent with such nations to qualify as nation-states. The extreme is the use of nation-state to refer to any state, regardless of whatever sense of belonging together its population might possess.[4]

So we see there are degrees of nationhood in states around the world today. In some states, the nation building process is far advanced and continues each day. In other states, the process has barely begun. Unlike pregnancy, nationhood is not an all or nothing proposition. A state can be a little bit a nation.

We turn now to examine the nation-building process of states and the development of national identity in individuals.

NATION-BUILDING AND NATIONAL IDENTITY

Nation-states build nations to establish and maintain their legitimacy.[5] The supreme coercive power of the state alone is not enough to ensure the continued existence of the state. This coercive power is made more secure and its exercise more effective to the extent the population of the state acknowledges the legitimacy of the state's commands and accepts the nation as the community that most nearly embraces all aspects of their lives [Bloom 1990:56]. The nation-state thus seeks to build a community of solidarity within the territory it controls.

The nation, however, differs in size and scope from the actual communities people have identified with throughout most of history [Hobsbawm 1990:46]. Benedict Anderson [1983] calls the nation an "imagined community"—but still one that can fill the *emotional* void for the loss of real human communities. The state uses nationalist sentiment as the major emotional component in developing loyalty of its citizens to the nation-state.

Kelman [1969] argues that an individual's loyalty or attachment to the nation-state may be rooted in sentimental or instrumental considerations.

> An individual is sentimentally attached when he sees the system [nation-state] as representing him—a being, in some central way, a reflection of himself. For the sentimentally attached, the system [nation-state] is legitimate and deserving of his loyalty because it is the embodiment of the group in which his personal identity is anchored. [280]

For the sentimentally attached person, national identity is a dominant component of personal identity.

An instrumentally attached individual sees the nation-state as an effective means for achieving his own ends and those of fellow citizens. "For the instrumentally attached, the system is legitimate and deserving of his loyalty because it provides the organization for a smoothly running society in which individuals can participate to their mutual benefit and have some assurance that their needs and interests will be met" [Kelman 1969:281]. These two sources of attachment to the nation-state, *sentimental* and *instrumental*, are not mutually exclusive and can exist in varying combinations in one individual.

Bloom [1990] argues that identification is the major psychological mechanism involved in the process that creates and sustains an individual's attachment and loyalty to the nation-state. "Individuals actively seek to identify in order to achieve psychological security, and they actively seek to maintain, protect and bolster identity in order to maintain and enhance this psychological security which is the *sine qua non* of personality stability and emotional well-being" [53].

For an individual to identify with a nation-state, the individual must actually experience the nation-state and this experience must involve symbols of the state (e.g., individuals, institutions, ideas) that either (1) present an appropriate attitude in situations of perceived *threat*, or (2) behave *beneficently* towards the individual. Identifications with such symbolic representatives of the nation-state may be formal or informal, constitutions or ballads. Social rituals in which people communicate together about commonly held identification provide reinforcement. These rituals and communications act to socialize the child into being a national citizen [Bloom 1990:61–62].

Thus individuals seek to protect and enhance the identifications they have made, and to the extent a group of individuals share a common identification, the potential exists for that group to act together to protect and enhance that shared identity [Bloom 1990:50]. At the level of the nation-state, a national identity will exist when a mass of people residing therein "have made the same identification with national symbols—have internalized the symbols of the nation—so that they may act as one psychological group when there is a threat to, or possibility of enhancement of, these symbols of national identity" [Bloom 1990:52].

Bloom [1990] goes on to argue that actual conflict and external threat are not necessities for individuals to identify with the nation-state.

> The nation-state into which the infant is born as citizen is in a state of permanent

competition with its international environment. Other countries are competitors in the great international game. It is clear, therefore, that there is a further inherent dynamic in the contemporary images of international political competition to create us/them, in-group/out-group perceptions and attitudes in terms of domestic national citizens versus international aliens. [74]

Identification with the nation-state is just one of various identifications an individual may make. Hobsbawm [1990] argues that national identification does not exclude nor is it necessarily superior to the remainder of the set of identifications that constitute the social being [11]. Bloom [1990] argues that the nation-state possesses significant advantages over other collectivities that might compete for the loyalty of its citizens. These include a monopoly of legitimate force within its territory and control over the mass media and educational institutions.

Hobsbawm [1990] acknowledges the importance of modern mass media's capability to make national symbols part of the every day life of the individual. "The evolution of the British royal family into a domestic as well as public icon of national identification, would have been impossible but for the modern mass media, and its most deliberate ritual expression was actually devised specifically for radio—later adapted to television: The royal Christmas broadcast" [142].

He also highlights the state's use of sports teams to engender national identification. National sport teams are particularly effective due to "the ease with which even the least political or public individuals can identify with the nation as symbolized by young persons excelling at what practically every man wants, or at one time in life has wanted, to be good at. The imagined community of millions seems more real as a team of eleven named people" [143].

The nation-state has many opportunities to touch directly the lives of individuals every day—in ways that potentially develop the individuals' identification with the na-

tion-state, but so do other entities. Which identification will prevail in any given situation? Bloom [1990] lists the following factors that will affect loyalty in any given situation.

a. Individual psychological traits.
b. Degree to which identification has been evoked.
c. Intensity and perceived reality of communications and propaganda.
d. The general reaction and discourse of fellows who share the same identification.
e. The sanctions and constraints possessed by the entity claiming the individual's loyalty [73].

This discussion of multiple identities and conflicting loyalties leads us to a consideration of the national identity of the MNC.

NATIONAL IDENTITY AND MULTINATIONAL CORPORATIONS

Members of the MNC have national identities, which vary in intensity. Members of the board of directors, top executives, and workers each identify to some extent with a nation-state. For an individual, to avoid national identity is extremely difficult in the world today.[6]

In what sense then can a MNC have a national identity? Here I'll argue that we have to look at those in the MNC who set the corporate objectives and strategies—top managers. If the top management team shares a common national identity, then decisions in the MNC will reflect the *influence* of actions taken to protect that national identity from threats or to take advantage of opportunities to enhance that national identity.[7]

If the top management team shares a strong identification with the same nation, then we would expect the national identity of the multinational to be strong and clearly identifiable. To the extent that identifications with *different* nations are represented or individual national identifications are *weaker*, then we would expect the national identity of the MNC to be weaker.

It's instructive to go back to Perlmutter's [1969] classic article, "The Tortuous Evolution of the Multinational Corporation." From this article, we certainly do get the idea that MNCs have national identities and that the nature of these identities varies across both space and time. Different MNCs have different dominant identifications and those of a particular multinational enterprise (MNE) can change over time. Below we'll review what Perlmutter has to say about national identity as a part of his definition of multinationality and the orientation of headquarters to subsidiaries in the international company.

Perlmutter identifies three primary attitudes among international executives toward building a MNE: ethnocentric, polycentric, and geocentric [1969:11]. He later adds a fourth: regiocentric [Heenan and Perlmutter 1979]. He examines how identification, among other characteristics of the organization, varies across these four ideal types.

For the ethnocentric MNC, "executives in both headquarters and affiliates express the national identity of the firm by associating the company with the nationality of the headquarters: this is 'a Swedish company,' 'a Swiss company,' 'an American company,' depending on the location of the headquarters" [Perlmutter 1969:12]. The ethnocentric multinational has the same national identity throughout the organization—one strongly related to the *home* nation, in which the headquarters is located.

Top executives in the polycentric MNC begin with the assumption that "the part of the firm which is located in the host country should be as 'local in identity' as possible" [Perlmutter 1969:12]. He characterizes the identification of the whole corporation as one composed of strong identifications with each nation in which the company operates. For example, the executives of the French affiliate have a strong national identification with France. "One consequence (and perhaps cause) of polycentrism is a virulent ethnocentrism among the country managers" [Perlmutter 1969:13]. How the many national identities of the one organization are sorted out when the MNE has to speak with one voice or act as one organization is not really addressed. It is clear that the headquarters executives identify with the home country, which is their location, but it's also clear that the multinational has other competing strong national identifications.

Perlmutter characterizes the identification of the geocentric multinational as a "truly international company but identifying with national interests" [12]. At its core, this identification is supranational, i.e., the world, or at least extranational, i.e., the world of the international company. This geocentric identification is shared by executives in both headquarters and subsidiaries. Perlmutter, however, acknowledges the reality of the world of nation-states in which these geocentric firms operate by having them operate "within legal and political limits," and act as "good citizens" of the nations in which they operate [13]. What happens when the "national interests" with which the geocentric multinationals supposedly identify happen to conflict is again not really addressed here. The image you get here is that these executives in geocentric multinationals have moved beyond any identification with a nation-state; they're more citizens of the world, who acknowledge that nation-states still matter to the rest of the world and therefore to the geocentric multinational too.

The addition of the regiocentric MNC seems to have been made in response to developments in Western Europe. "Despite the continued nationalism of Western European countries, a European team is established with a Eurocentric view. Such an approach has the merit of anticipating emerging politicoeconomic communities, such as the expanded Common Market" [Heenan and Perlmutter 1979:20]. In the regiocentric multinational, the identification is not with any single nation-state but with an entity above the level of any one nation-state—the emerging "nation" of Europe, if you will.

To summarize, reflecting the national identities of its top executives who have effective strategic control, a MNC can be considered to have a national identity. Such national identities vary from company to company, and over time such national identities can change.

But what about a particular nation-state—the *home* country?

To what the extent will a particular MNC identify with its home nation? In what ways will such identification affect the relationship between the multinational and the home nation-state? These questions lead us to the "Who Is Us?" debate.

"WHO IS US?"

In two articles, Robert Reich asked first "Who Is Us?" and then "Who Is Them?" Answers have included "They Are Not Us," "We Are Us," and "We Are All 'Us'." Reich [1991b] has replied "Who Do We Think They Are?"[8] Rattled off like that, the titles reminded me of Abbott and Costello's famous "Who's On First?" routine.

Reich [1990] asks "who is us? Is it IBM, Motorola, Whirlpool, and General Motors? Or is it Sony, Thomson, Philips, and Honda?" [53]. More generally, what is the relationship between the competitiveness of the United States and the competitiveness of U.S.-based MNCs? Is the nationality of a corporation irrelevant?

Reich argues that "we" are the American worker and American people and that the American corporation is no longer "us" [1990:54]. He sees American corporations as global corporations with multinational identities. He argues that these corporations have increasingly located *outside the United States* activities that matter to the competitiveness of a country, such as technologically sophisticated manufacturing that provides good jobs and world-class products that can be sold worldwide.

At the same time, corporations outside the United States have been establishing operations in the United States. These foreign-owned corporations in the United States,

Reich contends, have as much potential to contribute to American competitiveness as the American-based multinationals. They can site high-wage, high-productivity, research-intensive activities in the United States. Reich prescribes the development of national policies that reward any global corporation (regardless of home country) that invests in the American workforce [1990:60].

I think we can see that this debate of "Who is us?" reflects a mode of thinking with strong links to nationalism. This us/them, in-group/out-group distinction is at the core of the nation building and maintenance that goes on within the nation-state. "Who is us?" matters in a world of nation-states because those in the in-group are treated very differently than those in the out-group. Reich [1991c] in his later work tries to finesse the us/them dichotomy by calling for a "positive economic nationalism, in which each nation's citizens take primary responsibility for enhancing the capacities of their countrymen for full and productive lives, but who also work with other nations to ensure that these improvements do not come at other's expense" [311]. It is a sort of "we are us *and* them."

Multinational Corporations and Nation-States

I'd like to examine the issues Reich raises by first asking "To what extent will a multinational corporation make decisions in the interests of a particular nation-state?" Part of the answer lies in the usual sources of power brought up in the IB literature that addresses the relationship between the MNC and the nation-state from a bargaining power perspective (e.g., Fagre and Wells [1982]; Lecraw [1984]; Moran [1985]; Kobrin [1987]; Lecraw and Morrison [1991]). Although focused on MNC-host country relationships, the model is generally applicable to MNC-nation-state relationships. The nation-state has certain sources of potential power that it can use to induce the MNC to do what it wants. Basically these derive from having certain resources related to controlling a particular territory—resources demanded by the multinational. Commonly cited examples would include natural resources; market size, growth, and sophistication; relatively inexpensive, productive workers. Likewise the multinational has certain sources of potential power *vis-à-vis* the nation-state. MNC resources that the nation-state would value would include technology and capability to generate exports. There are, of course, many nation-states and many MNCs, so the extent to which desired resources (or roughly equivalent substitutes) are controlled by one or only a few, as opposed to the many, provides a source of power. Also, this literature makes a point of emphasizing that relative bargaining power can change over time (e.g., Vernon [1971;1980]; Jenkins [1986]).

My intention here is not to review critically the bargaining power model but rather to argue that this approach is related to *one* of the two sources that Kelman [1969] identifies as the root of attachment or loyalty to the nation-state, *viz.*, the *instrumental*. To the extent the MNC sees the nation-state as an effective vehicle for achieving its own ends, then the multinational will exhibit an attachment to the nation-state. If the multinational sees access to the markets, people, natural resources, etc., of a particular territory as important in achieving its objectives, then it will exhibit some loyalty to the nation-state that controls that territory as long as the nation-state permits circumstances that enable the multinational to achieve its objectives.

I see this instrumental or pragmatic attachment of the MNC very much reflected in discussions about multinationals attending to nation-state *interests*. Any multinational can find it in its interest to take into account the nation-state's interests in working out a mutually beneficial arrangement. Any multinational can be committed to a nation-state because that nation-state is critical to its sales, profit, or other objectives.

Commitment to a nation-state, however, can also stem from Kelman's second source of attachment or loyalty, the *sentimental*.

IB has not paid as much attention to the role that sentimental attachment plays in the MNC's acting in the interest of the nation-state.[9] Sentimental attachment is evidenced in the commitment to cultural values reflective of national identity and the commitment to the role of national identity, linked to national symbols. I have argued above that individual members of the MNC and the MNC itself have national identities. The nature of the *national identity* of the MNC is an important influence on the extent to which the MNC will make decisions in the interest of the nation-state.

Consider the situation in which all top executives have made strong identifications with the home nation-state. As a result of this identification, the MNC will take actions to defend or enhance this national identity. Even though this MNC's achievement of its objectives may be only slightly dependent on the access to the home nation-state's territory and resources therein, the MNC will take actions in the interest of the home nation-state.

To summarize, an analysis of the extent to which a MNC will act in the interest of a nation-state needs to take into account the sentimental as well as the instrumental sources of attachment to the nation-state.

National Competitiveness and the Multinational

To return to the particular issue at the heart of Reich's concerns, the competitiveness of the nation-state, I first want to emphasize one point that demonstrates the particular relevance of national identification to this issue.

The nation-state cares about its economic performance. As Poggi [1990:28] argues, in society today, the primacy of the economic performance is demonstrated by the extent to which judgment of political success depends on economic success. Further, the rivalry among nation-states has extended from a military sphere to include an economic one as well. Threats to a nation-state are no longer seen as coming solely from military/political sources, but also from economic. Recalling that threats to national identity are triggering mechanisms that motivate action to defend that nation, I think we can see the particular relevance of identity when it comes to national competitiveness.

I'll also argue here that the competitiveness of a nation is shorthand for the international economic competitiveness of one nation-state *vis-à-vis* other nation-states. Thus competitiveness is a relative concept like power.[10] The implication for a MNC is that, in dealing with state expectations regarding contributions to competitiveness, it will find itself caught in the middle between the objectives of two nation-states.[11] Motorola cannot improve the competitiveness of the United States, Japan, and Germany in cellular phones—all at the same time. If it puts its research and development activities in the United States, it's not putting them in Japan or Germany. If it builds a sophisticated manufacturing facility in Japan and creates high paying jobs there, it's not building that plant in the U.S. or Germany.

I'll argue further that it is most likely that the MNC's contributions to national competitiveness will be judged by that nation-state *vis-à-vis* its main economic rivals. For example, the United States would judge a MNC's contribution to American competitiveness against contributions to Japanese competitiveness.

In international competition, it's likely that the nation-state will eventually want know not "Are you committed to us?" but "Are you committed to us *first*?" or at least more to us than to our major rivals.

Most multinationals are headquartered in a developed nation-state in the Triad. While the national identity of a MNC conceptually has nothing necessarily to do with where the headquarters is located, in practice it does since most headquarters are in the country in which the corporation got its start, in which its owners and managers first developed operations, made sales, hired em-ployees, etc. Consequently, the top management of the corporation tends to be heavily represented by executives whose national identifications are with the nation-state in which the company has its headquarters.

Thus, we'll find some MNCs that identify quite strongly with the home country and other multinationals that identify more weakly. Perhaps multinationals based in Japan and France would be good examples of those with strong national identity, while those based in the United Kingdom and the United States might tend toward weaker national identity. The nature of the interactions between top business executives and government officials of the nation-state is likely related to this cross-national variation in national identification.

Further the trend toward increased transnational economic integration does imply some weakening in the commitment of multinational executives toward their home nation-state. The top executives with effective strategic control of the MNC do have a number of identifications with other social entities, such as the MNC itself, the set of companies making up a global industry, a worldwide managerial class, or a profession. Just as identification provides the glue of national solidarity for the nation-state, it can serve a like function for other social entities and create us/them, in-group/out-group perceptions and attitudes in terms of the company, industry set, managerial class, or profession vs. the rest of the world. The relative strength of such competing identifications influences the extent to which the MNC will act in the interest of any particular nation-state. As the non-national identifications strengthen, MNCs are less likely to act to enhance the national competitiveness, as the home nation-state desires.

Perhaps it is in the United States that we are first seeing instances in which non-national identifications are dominating national identifications that were weaker to start with. Kapstein [1991/92] has suggested that the question "Who is us?" is distinctively American. "I have never heard colleagues from Japan or France or Germany ask a similar question of *their* corporate identity" [56]. It may also be, however, that the United States is the bellwether country for a worldwide trend.

American Competitiveness and American Multinationals

I'll conclude this section by looking at the specific case of American competitiveness and American multinationals. As of today, are U.S.-based multinationals "us?" What is the relationship between the competitiveness of the United States and the competitiveness of the U.S.-based multinationals?

First let's examine whatever instrumental attachment American multinationals might have. Most U.S.-based multinationals are still heavily dependent on activities in the United States. They have a definite interest in a continued effective use of resources in the United States to achieve corporate objectives. In 1988, operations in the United States accounted for 78% of total assets, 70% of total sales, 74% of total employment of U.S.-based multinationals. "All these shares were actually higher than they were in 1977, the reverse of what one would expect if the links between the domestic economy and U.S. multinationals were precipitously disappearing" [Tyson 1991:38]. In the manufacturing sector, Tyson [1991] also presents evidence that the American multinationals locate their "higher end" jobs and operations in the United States. Likewise, the vast majority of R&D facilities and spending are in the United States. Overall the case seems strong that U.S.-based MNCs have a significant attachment to the United States based on instrumental considerations.

What about any sentimental attachment U.S.-based MNCs might have? The national identification of most American multinationals seems to be with the United States. Most members of the board of directors and most top managers of American multinationals are Americans. "According

to a recent survey by the executive search firm Korn Ferry reported in *The Economist*, the proportion of the top 1,000 firms with a non-American on the board has declined from a recent peak of 17 percent in 1982 to only 12 percent in 1990" [Tyson 1991:40].

Still we don't really have any direct evidence as to the relative strength of identification with the nation-state, United States of America, versus identifications with other social entities, including other nation-states. The identifications of executives of American multinationals and their influence on MNC decisions affecting American competitiveness seems to me to be in need of systematic research to secure some evidence that goes beyond the anecdotal. Here issues related to their perceptions as to the credibility of any economic competitiveness threat to the United States would be relevant since these would be related to their motivation to defend the national identity.

To summarize, based on the existing evidence, American-based multinationals on the whole still seem to be "us" and play a large role in contributing to the competitiveness of America. Still serious empirical research on these issues has yet to be published.

What about foreign-owned companies with operations in the United States? As of today, are they "us"? What role, if any, do they play in contributing to the competitiveness of America? Briefly, both the instrumental and sentimental attachments of the foreign-owned multinationals to the United States are weaker than those of American multinationals. In general, the resources within the territory controlled by the United States matter less to these multinationals than to American-based multinationals. Further, the national identification tends to be with a country other than the United States—in some cases, quite strongly; in other cases, less so. When push comes to shove (and when it comes to international economic competitiveness, nation-states sometimes force it to this stage) and these MNCs have to choose—have to declare first loyalties, it's less likely that they will choose to act so as to improve the national competitiveness of the United States.

Still here too we really have little evidence concerning the strength of competing identifications for these multinationals and their effect on American competitiveness.

CONCLUSION

In this paper, I have tried to bring the nation back into the nation-state and some non-economic psychological considerations back into an understanding of IB behavior. I have argued that MNCs have national identities that influence their relationships with nation-states.

I have argued that important core questions in examining the extent to which a MNC will make contributions to the competitiveness of a nation-state are the following:

- To what extent do the resources within the territory controlled by the nation-state matter to the multinational in its pursuit of its objectives, relative to other territories?
- To what extent do those who control the MNC identify with the nation-state, relative to other identifications?

Finally, I have noted that we need serious empirical studies that investigate these questions. The "Who Is Us?" debate has been largely one of contending anecdotes. As in many areas of research, gaining access to the relevant sources of data presents a considerable challenge. Nevertheless, empirical research in this area truly has the potential to contribute not only to IB understanding but also to effective public policy.

NOTES

1. Mann (1986:2) argues that a nation-state model has dominated sociology in that it has largely conceived of "society" as an unproblematic, unitary totality and taken polities, or states, as its society, its total unit for analysis. Additional examples would include the focus of economics on the wealth of nations (really states), national economies, and international trade and the dominance of the state-centric view of international politics in political science.

2. Poggi considers the adjective "modern" in "the modern state" to be redundant, arguing that the essential features of the modern state are not found in large scale political entities other than those which began to develop in the early-modern phase of European history (1990:25). Tilly takes another tack defining state more broadly and uses the term national state to characterize what is generally referred to as the modern state (1990:2). In this paper, state will be used to refer to the modern, or national, state; state will not be used to refer to such forms of coercive organizations such as empires and city states.

3. The literature on nations and nationalism is quite large. See Smith (1973, 1983, and 1986) and Hobsbawm (1990) for bibliographies and guides to the literature.

4. I suspect that in the American context we use the term nation-state in the sense of national state simply to distinguish it from state, as in one of the 50 states in the United States of America. Also in English we sometimes use the term nation simply to mean a territorial state as in Adam Smith's *The Wealth of Nations*.

5. On nation-building, see Rokkan, Saelen, and Warmbrumm (1973) for a bibliography.

6. In *The Political Life of Children*, Robert Coles writes "Nationality is a constant in the lives of most of us and must surely be worked into our thinking in various ways, with increasing diversity and complexity of expression as our lives unfold. As soon as we were born, in most places on this earth, we acquire a nationality, a membership in a community. Our names, often enough, are recorded in a roll, made part of a government's records. The infant knows nothing of this event, but the parents certainly are aware of it, and what they know and feel, as citizens, as subjects, as comrades, is communicated to the child in the first years of life. A royal doll, a flag to wave in a parade, coins with their engraved messages—these are sources of instruction connect the young person to a country. The attachment can be strong, indeed, even among children, wherever a flag is saluted, the national anthem sung. The attachment is as parental as the words imply—homeland, motherland, fatherland . . . Nationalism works its way into just

about every corner of the mind's life" (1986:59–60).

7. The top management team or upper echelons perspective on organizations links certain upper echelon characteristics (psychological and observable) to strategic choices and organizational performance (Hambrick and Mason 1984). National identity could readily be considered part of the *psychological* upper echelon characteristics, reflecting as it does certain values that affect strategic choice. National identity does have a more readily observable counterpart, viz., nationality, that could be considered part of the *observable* upper echelon characteristics.

8. See for the articles listed, see Reich (1990), Reich (1991a), Tyson (1991), Kapstein (1991/92), Thomsen (1992), Reich (1991b). Also see Reich's book (1991c) and Hu (1992).

9. IB does have some history of addressing the impact of nationalism on multinational corporations, as opposed to the usual concern with national interests. This was a continuing interest of John Fayerweather (1975; 1978).

10. See Wrong (1979), Lukes (1986), and Mann (1986) on the nature of social power.

11. See Nigh and Cochran (1987) for an issues management framework that addresses this "caught in the middle" phenomenon for multinational corporations.

■ ■ ■

The Levels of Analysis Problem Again: Community and Regionalism in the Global Political Economy
James A. Kuhlman

DISCIPLINES AND LEVELS

Foremost in the consideration of theoretical and institutional implications of the appearance of a distinct field of international business (IB) is the awareness of the need for interdisciplinarity. Two mutually reinforcing factors have determined the interdisciplinary nature of IB as a field of study: one is the methodological determinism of the fact that business as a discipline or school was established for the purpose of drawing upon all the social sciences in analyzing the behavior of the firm; second, IB by definition involves cross-border activity of firms which demand consideration of the global political economy, itself an interdisciplinary conceptualization and field of study now quite developed.

What interdisciplinarity itself predisposes one to consider is the levels of analysis complexity in any given problem area. IB cannot be limited to consideration of the political economy of the firm alone. Individual, group (team), institutional, sectoral, communal, provincial, state, multinational

state and multistate national, regional, and global actors are involved. In other words psychological, sociological, and even anthropological dimensions of politico-economic behavior are implied aspects of the field.

It is an introductory thesis of this essay, in part in response to the perceptive essay of Kobrin herein, and, in part inherent in the central question raised within this book, that there is a levels of analysis bias to the concept of political economy as an environmental paradigm within which we suppose IB occurs (in theory, in practice, and in research). By organizing his approach to IB and one of its problem areas, namely transnational integration, into national markets as well as nation-states, Kobrin answers this bias by explicitly raising markets to the same degree of significance as politics. The organizing concept of markets, in contrast to politics, in the context of the global political economy requires the realization of actor levels other than the national or nation-state at which behavioral analysis can be accomplished.

The concluding thesis of this essay, namely that IB as a field of study is essentially a redundancy, contains an inevitable logic leading to the notion that *market* as an organizing concept is a more productive vehicle than is *politics* in studying the contemporary world system. Markets in a macroanalytic framework make it clear that "international" is best considered as the environment in which business occurs, not simply as a specialized field of business. McKibbin and Sachs [1991] and Dicken [1992] offer a variety of approaches illustrating markets playing roles similar to that of politics in previous historical periods.

In recent times it has been fascinating to note that an aspect of sovereignty within European Community debates over final formulation of EC-92 plans is now termed "subsidiarity." The language of the Maastricht Treaty refers to rights of member states in relation to commission action "only if and in so far as the objectives of the proposed action cannot be sufficiently achieved by the member-states and can therefore, by reason of the scale or effects of the proposed action, be better achieved by the Community." That these rights are given an economic, more specifically an IB reference, namely subsidiarity, is new and interesting to say the least.

The implications of using "international" as a designation of the environment in which markets (and politics) operate today for business theory, research, and institutionalization will be taken up in conclusion. Sufficient at this point is the acknowledgment that politics and markets, independently or relationally, require a sensitivity to levels of analysis. For the time being IB will be referred to as a field, but the logic of this essay will lead to an approach by which business theory, research and institutions all can benefit from viewing business in an international environment that demands interdisciplinary as well as cross-cultural skills.

Though Lindblom [1977] made one of the clearest conceptual demarcations of politics and markets, he remained oddly attached to the political as a preferred descriptive as well as prescriptive tool. With a preface noting that "the greatest distinction between one government and another is in the degree to which market replaces government or government replaces market," he concludes that, "The large, private corporation fits oddly into democratic theory and vision. Indeed, it does not fit" [Lindblom 1977:356]. What leads Lindblom in effect to prefer government or politics over markets as an organizing principle is the levels of analysis problem again. As the presumption that politics involve only governmental actors leads to a nation-state bias in descriptive and prescriptive analyses, so also in this case does the presumption that markets involve only corporations as actors lead to bias, bias against the firm as it obviously cannot compete with the territorial state and its government in the provision of sovereignty and its guarantees of status and prestige, equality and autonomy, as pointed out by Siverson and Starr [1991:16].

Kobrin makes a substantial contribution in freeing market as an organizing concept from this vertical logjam in levels of analysis. Williamson [1975] in a different context makes a similar point when he notes a distinction between markets and hierarchies. Here the notion of markets as a concept of micro theory is not sufficiently microanalytic for Williamson: "Market organization is the province of economists. Internal organization is the concern of organization theory specialists. And never the twain shall meet" [1975:ix]. The point to be made in this paper is that markets and politics interact within and between themselves at differing levels of analysis. The global political economy is a multilevel system in which issue variance will account for simultaneously operating levels of the system involved. Issues of market relevance may call into question decision makers (centralized or decentralized), information (of a command or competitive nature), incentives (moral or material), and even property rights (public or private) in a manner differently from that of issues of political relevance.

The implications of this awareness for the field of IB study, its theory, research, and institutionalization, are the subject of this book. The immediate task herein is to examine the nine major points in Kobrin's analysis. Though in substantial agreement with the approach and conclusion in Kobrin, I hope to modify and expand somewhat on his analysis, using principally the perspective of a political scientist who engages in IB theory and research and teaching partly as a result of the aforementioned commitment to interdisciplinarity and awareness of multilevel systems, and partly as a response to events in my area of interest, now alternatively is labeled as the former Soviet empire, ex-USSR, or CIS (Commonwealth of Independent States) and Eastern or East-Central Europe. These regions will be identified herein as the T-Group (for *Transitional Economies* of *Eur-Asia*).

NATION-STATES, NATIONAL MARKETS, AND TRANSNATIONAL INTEGRATION

Kobrin correctly notes that the international system of sovereign states is "a system based on sovereignty and 'self-help'" but perhaps oversimplifies the system when he characterizes it as one "with no central or higher authority whom states can turn to for protection." [p. 244] In fact geography and ideology may be conceived as structurally and functionally providing central or higher authority in many respects for states in a Westphalian system. Structurally there are examples of multinational states and multistate nations each with a legal status in the international system of sovereign states which confounds the simple notion of congruence between nationality and statehood. Divided nations and multiethnic empires have masqueraded as so-called sovereign states throughout the Westphalian period. The notions of central and higher authority somewhat insensitize one to the fact that nationalism can suffer as

well as sustain itself in an international legal system based on sovereignty. Communism and nationalism, as ideologies, have been used variously to claim central authority or higher order, existing along side of sovereignty.

This softness to the concept of sovereignty has implications for the field of IB in much the same way that it has implications for another interdisciplinary field, that of political geography. Jackson and Samuels [1971] overall evidenced the awareness of geographers and political scientists alike of an aspect of the environment in the international system apart from the purely regional. There is an implicit recognition throughout the essays in Jackson and Samuels that even in the first half of the twentieth century, as noted by Kobrin, there was not "a symmetry [existing] between political and economic geography." This understanding, namely that some of the symmetry assumed in the past may not have been there and may explain "breaks" in the system (structural and nonstructural violence), develops into an explicit acknowledgment that "the problems which are of highest priority vary greatly from place to place as does the way they are perceived by people and the methods that are used to deal with them" [Dohrs and Sommers 1976].

That multidisciplinary theory and research endeavors were first to uncover the asymmetries is not surprising, since we have already noted the levels of analysis bias inherent in disciplines. Kobrin alerts us to the symmetry "soon broken" in his discussion of transnational integration. There is an argument developed at this point in his analysis, however, which seems to say that as markets expanded over larger geographic areas, from regional to national, a trend was being set which would inevitably dissolve the symmetry between political and economic geography.

That argumentation logically leads to Kobrin's point that transnational integration "erodes the very foundations and meaning of national markets" [p. 247]. Suffice it to say at this point that the possibility of simultaneously operating system levels seems to be excluded from the analysis. Put simply, in the context of the EC, is there necessarily the implication of the end of national markets? Was there no national market operating in the context of transnational integration of a CMEA (Council for Mutual Economic Assistance) or a USSR model? Is the trend itself clearly in one direction in the contemporary international system? Can community, nationalism, and regionalism, all prevalent in current world affairs, continue concurrently?

Could it be that national markets, in which there exists a symmetry between political and economic geography, continue to be viable for some functional tasks and resulting issues but not for others? It may be clear in problem areas such as ecology that pressures for integration over a larger geographic area than national markets are predominant. MacNeill, Winsemius, and Yakushiji [1991] make such a case in discussing the "meshing of the world's economy and the earth's ecology." They make equally pressing points, however, on how industrialized nations, especially the triad, can take unilateral and regional steps to solve environmental problems, measures that would also improve microeconomic efficiency and national competitiveness.

NATIONAL MARKETS UNDER FIRE, FUTURE OF THE TERRITORIAL STATE, AND END OF TERRITORIALITY?

Keeping in mind that IB as a field of study is in question here, Kobrin might lead one to conclude at this point that there is no reason for such a separate field of business study, since "the distinction between domestic and international economic activity is losing meaning" [p. 249]. In other words, as someone would have it, all business is essentially the same. If "borders are being blurred or eroded" [p. 248], then such exercises as engaged in by Bartlett and Ghoshal [1989] and their construction of a matrix in which "Multinational," "International," "Global," and "Transnational" models for business functions, are some-

what pointless. Managing across borders that are increasingly blurred and eroded is irrelevant. Ohmae's approach to a "borderless world" [1990] might more accurately be seen as challenging national borders, while still acknowledging other borders. In this sense we might question, along with Kobrin, national economic borders as geographic organizers of economic activity and markets, but still conceive of the relevance of other geographic borders, e.g., cities, counties, provinces, and other sub-national units, as well as supranational communities and regions.

Markets, their consolidation and their competitiveness, are symmetrical with political levels below and above the nation-state. More and more the question asked concerns the most appropriate level for given functional tasks and problem solutions, rather than the question which level is now obsolete. Territoriality has been redefined in the international political and economic systems, but that is not quite to say, as does Kobrin, that it has been "compromised" in the international economic system and therefore probably cannot be maintained in the international political system.

As to the "end of territoriality" itself, it may be possible to have transnational integration unifying national markets without eliminating the territorial nation-state because the latter still serves a useful purpose to its subnational political and economic actors, and in turn benefits from their IB activity. Issues of autonomy and independence are compromised only in the sense that they are being negotiated constantly between the nation-state and actors at levels both above and below it in a kind of global hierarchy. Joint ventures are a form of IB activity that involves just such a process.

The multinational, global, international, and transnational models of cross-border management in Bartlett and Ghoshal [1989] are shown in a subsequent companion volume [Bartlett and Ghoshal 1992] to be much more complicated operational constructs, since certain functions within the business enterprise may adopt one model and other functions may require yet another. For example, a corporation may want to multinationalize its human resources organization, but globalize its finance division. Furthermore, it is conceivable that companies with different regional foci in the same industry will adopt different operational models for the same functions, i.e., the culture itself will configure the organizational structure. So not only function and location, but perhaps also size, nature of the competition, etc., will factor into organizational solutions for cross-border problems. Joint venture organizations are ideal laboratories for business theory, research, and institutions to probe the multidisciplinary and multilevel (in my mind, the "international") environment of business.

THE INTERNATIONAL SYSTEM AS A SOCIAL NETWORK, THE NONTERRITORIAL STATE, AND IMPLICATIONS FOR IB

Seeing the "international system as a social network," Kobrin stresses the "*relational*" dimension of transnational integration. But is this relational nature of the international system a "becoming" characteristic or an "always has been" but not accepting feature among political scientists and economists? Kobrin makes a point that, "In the past, economic, and thus political, power has been '*relative*'" [p. 252]. Yet, political economies in the history of the international system, such as colonialism (which were not then referred to as political economies), serve as examples of the relational roles of nation-states operating simultaneously with relative power roles. Luard [1976] demonstrates from an historical and sociological perspective the enduring notion of the international system as a social network. His description of differing "international societies" over time performing similar sociological functions, stressing relational roles of actors at various levels of the system types, is instructive.

Perhaps the point is best made by David Wightman [1984:31]: "In short, 'have concept, will travel' is not enough; within every social scientist, and every international political economist, there should be a historian struggling to get out." Strange introduces her collection of *Paths to International Political Economy* by noting that "part of the strength and interest of international political economy is that it is the antithesis of 'area studies,' and deliberately sets out at least to look at the system as a whole" [1984:xi]. Perhaps if social scientists, ideally together in multidisciplinary endeavors, had been looking "at the system as a whole" for some time, the notions previously raised about simultaneously operating levels of analysis (and actors) would have precluded the current debate on demise of the territorial state.

But what about the concept of a nonterritorial state? Here is where several divergences from the observations of Kobrin previously bring me to convergence with his observation that "diffuse geography and internationalism may well be the rule" of time [p. 254]. Possibly my earlier disagreements with his argument can be explained by a misunderstanding of his oft-repeated dichotomy of "international" and "domestic," as in, "We appear to be returning to the norm of the primacy of the international over the domestic" [p. 254]. If one simply views these as a levels of analysis problem, wherein the global political economy encompasses processes international in kind by actors subnational, national, and supranational, the problem is solved.

The implications of all this for IB (theory, research, and institutional arrangements) are indeed profound, but the parallel with implications of "international" studies for political science as a discipline is brought to mind. Debates over theoretical boundaries (paradigms), research strategies (methodology), and institutional arrangements ("fad, fantasy or field?") raged between political scientists and international studies scholars. The arguments continue, but for the most part solutions in each case are found principally in understanding the levels of analysis problem. International studies as a distinct field of political science sustains itself because certain issues can be best theorized, researched, and institutionally approached by international perspectives. As noted above, the international perspective in turn requires interdisciplinary theory, research, and institutional arrangements. Another way of saying this is that borders between disciplines have been as detrimental to international understanding as have borders between nations. One of the best literary examples of this resolution is Dell's observation that, "For more than two hundred years liberal economists have been striving to persuade governments of the need for enlarged and benevolent sentiments" [1987:3]. He proceeds simply to "the need for multidisciplinary study."

In a more crass sense, however, it is also clear that international as a special field of any discipline, political science or sociology or economics, is simply a way to "sell" the salience of one's view (theory), inquiry (research), or piece of the budget pie (institution). It is not by accident that International Studies has become the field designator in that it implies the plurality of disciplinary approaches necessary to understanding inter-nation relations. Political science theory and research on public administration, voting behavior, constitutional law, and other fields of inquiry are routinely pursued in an international environment. So it should be and will be with all fields of business inquiry.

A REGION IN QUESTION

Were there one book to recommend for reading by leaders (at the levels of sectors, cities, regions, republics, independent states, federated states, regional associations) of the Transitional Economies of Eur-Asia, I would have it be Gore's *Regions In Question*. "First, within territorial regional planning [as opposed to functional regional planning] the territorial units at various spatial scales—the nation, the region and the district—are *all* treated as organisms. To apply the organic analogy exactly, it is

necessary to consider the nation state as a living organism and analyze how its parts, like the organs and cells of a rat, are interrelated in a spatial hierarchy within the nation state" [1984:230].

As attractive as territorial regional planning has been and continues to be among T-Group economists, Gore successfully uncovers its "adherence to the spatial separatist theme," shared also by functionalist.

The fallacy in both the functionalist and territorial paradigms for regional planning rests with the fact that, "They each attempt to achieve a more desirable spatial pattern of 'development' through changing the spatial distribution of infrastructure, economic activities and urban population or through changing the spatial pattern of interaction between areas" [Gore 1984:211]. This shows the situation in which "to serve the territorial interest at one level, you have to *override* the territorial interests at the level immediately below" [Gore 1984:228]. The problem is encountered in the transnational integration process also.

The spatial separatism encountered in Europe's situation is illustrative. Europe now confronts an Eastern question (where does West stop and East begin?), a Western question (now that there is no common enemy, will the triad regions develop regional patriotism—economic and political—in competition with one another?), and a German question (what role for a re-unified Germany within the EC?). An all-encompassing question arises here: will market forces or political forces provide the answers to the previous three questions?

An initial approach to this principal inquiry would be to look for boundary reformulations. An interesting case already presents itself in the appearance of the Pentagonal (Austria, Czecho-Slovakia, Hungary, Italy, and Yugoslavia), a re-creation of sorts of economic association under the Austro-Hungarian Empire. It was alternately referred to as the Danubian Group. It became the Hexagonal with the inclusion of Poland. It then regrouped as the Central

European Initiative (CEI) with the dissolution of Yugoslavia and the inclusion separately of Croatia and Slovenia, though not Serbia or other former republics.

Yet another case is presented by the Economic Cooperation Organization (ECO) represented by Azerbaijan, Iran, Pakistan, Turkestan, Turkey, Tajikistan, and Uzbekistan. The attempted creation of the Commonwealth of Independent States (CIS) itself has produced a historical series of additions and subtractions. Within the core of the CIS, the Russian federation and its sixteen to twenty "sovereign" or "autonomous" constituent parts are constantly adjusting borders and boundaries economically and politically.

The point to be made in conclusion here is that IB as an interdisciplinary field of inquiry may be specially suited to the levels of analysis sensitivity apparent in an evolving international system. Tracking systemic change across time and space at all levels will be a complex task. Considering business as a school of study whose fields of inquiry are best theorized, researched, and institutionalized in an international environment by multidisciplinary teams will expedite the task.

■ ■ ■

COMMENTARIES
Harvey Starr

How to Manage Interdependence? The State in a Multicentric/Transnational World

DEMISE OF THE TERRITORIAL STATE REVISITED, AGAIN

In his paper, "Transnational Integration, National Markets and Nation-States," Stephen Kobrin returns to a question that has been at the heart of numerous theoretical (and methodological) debates in the study of international relations: the continuing relevance of the sovereign state in both the practice and analysis of world politics.[1] This question strikes at the core issues of international relations: the nature of the international system, the nature of the key components of that system, and the question of change in the international system.

With the freedom afforded the role of discussant, I will outline a few possible responses to Kobrin's challenge to the centrality of the state. This role also provides the flexibility to indicate that I both agree and disagree with Kobrin's main arguments. While I agree with the notion that interdependence has affected, and continues to affect, the workings of the formally anarchic Westphalian state system including the nature of state sovereignty, I disagree with the manner in which Kobrin has formulated some of his questions, as well as a number of his conclusions.

We have been pointed in essentially the correct direction; however, I think there are flaws in some of his basic assumptions, and the structure and characterization of the issues. Rather than look at the either/or proposition that transnational forces (in whatever form) diminish the state, or that the growth of interdependence (in whatever form) must reduce the relevance of the state, I prefer to see the issue as the co-existence of states and transnational forces (as argued by Rosenau [1990]). The key question should be how to manage interdependence in a world of both states and a variety of non-state, transnational actors.

Challenging the continued centrality of the state has an extensive and honorable history. For example, John Herz [1957] predicted the demise of the territorial state because it could no longer provide the protection which, he argued, had been the basis for the selection of different forms of human organization. The territorial state, he proposed, would be replaced by the "bloc," a much larger mode of organization, dominated by a single power, and the only form of organization capable of existing in a bipolar world of nuclear superpowers. In essence, Herz argued that the strategic interdependence of states (which could no longer maintain a "hard shell" against the penetration of nuclear delivery systems), would lead to the demise of the territorial state and lead to the emergence of blocs as the central actors.

A decade later Herz [1968] recanted. He recognized that the allure and power of the territorial state as a mode of organization transcended his earlier argument regarding defense, to issues of identity, recognition, and status. Indeed, smaller and smaller units had been clamoring for the establishment of independent states of their own, to permit them a legitimate institutional basis for interacting in the global system. We see, paradoxically, a more vigorous version of this argument in Rosenau's [1990] discussion of the fragmentation of contemporary states into smaller separatist units (each unit, however, desiring a new state of its own). This response to Herz's original commentary also brings into question Kobrin's discussion, where he too makes territoriality *the* defining characteristic of the sovereign state, rather than one part of a more complex concept.

A FIRST CUT: TRANSNATIONAL CHALLENGES TO STATE-CENTRIC MODELS

The challenge to the centrality of the state can also be found in those theories, models, or perspectives of how to think about international relations or world politics that have challenged the Realist view of international relations. Many of these challenges to Realist models specifically question the Realist assumption that the sovereign state is the only actor of consequence in world politics; and that the security of the state, as measured by military capability dominates the agenda of all states in the "anarchic" Westphalian system.

The stress on the state as the only consequential actor is most strenuously challenged by the various models of *transnational relations* deriving from, or reflected in, the work of Keohane and Nye [1972;1977;1989]. Keohane and Nye's formulation of "com-

plex interdependence" (which I think is an unfortunate term) refutes the notion that only states count and argues that there are numerous other consequential actors and interactions, there no longer exists a set hierarchy of issues dominated by the concerns of military security, and complex interdependence precludes the use of military force among a number of states [1977:24–25].

In this formulation we find some basic arguments as to how interdependence constrains the behavior of sovereign states, yet in no way argues that sovereignty or territoriality have become irrelevant. Keohane and Nye introduce a theme that Rosenau [1990] subsequently takes much further: that important consequences flow from the behavior of non-state actors. These include international or intergovernmental organizations (IGOs), nongovernmental organizations (NGOs), what Huntington [1973] has called "transgovernmental organizations" (the interactions and transactions of governmental bureaus and offices across states, without the knowledge and/or approval of high-level governmental decision makers), and even individuals. All these other non-state actors, *because* they exist within an interdependent system, are able to affect the other actors in the system, even the most "powerful" states. Because entities within an interdependent system are sensitive and vulnerable to each other [Keohane and Nye 1977:11–19], even the smallest can produce significant outcomes on some issues at some times (see Ward and House [1988]). This argument—that other consequential actors exist—however, is quite different from arguing that territorial states are no longer important, or are in the process of disappearing or becoming irrelevant.

A number of transnationalist writings fall into this trap, foreseeing an international system where transnationalist forces bring about some sort of evolutionary change in the nature of the territorial, sovereign state. Rosenau [1990], on the other hand, claims that a multicentric system of "sovereignty-free" actors has grown up alongside a state-centric system composed of "sovereignty bound" actors. Kuhlman, in his response paper to Kobrin, critiques Rosenau's side-by-side conception, preferring instead to see the two systems integrated in a multilayered structure. However, Rosenau's key argument stands: that the state centric system exists, will continue to exist, and will continue to have important effects on non-state actors. Despite his massive evidence demonstrating the existence and importance of the multicentric system, and powerful transnational forces,[2] Rosenau is not arguing that this demonstrates an evolutionary process eventuating in the disappearance of the state.

Rosenau's work supports Keohane and Nye's complex interdependence framework and its arguments linking power and interdependence. States continue to exist and even are "powerful" in certain contexts and under certain conditions. However, non-state actors, not constrained or bound by sovereignty (which imposes responsibilities as well as rights) may be more "powerful" than states in other situations: power is relational and contextual, and the military capabilities of states are *not* fungible across issues. Power in its various forms of control over actors and control over outcomes (see Hart [1976]) is not zero sum. The ability of other types of actors to wield influence does not mean states are no longer able to do so. This only means that there are many other forms of influence, deriving from many different types of capabilities.

How is power to be managed under conditions of interdependence? Not necessarily by states using military force. Thus, we have the second component of complex interdependence:

> The agenda of interstate relationships consists of multiple issues that are not arranged in a clear or consistent hierarchy. This *absence of hierarchy among issues* means, among other things, that military security does not consistently dominate the agenda. Many issues arise from what used to be considered domestic policy, and the distinction between domestic and for-

eign issues becomes blurred. (Keohane and Nye [1977:25], emphasis in original)

The third element of complex interdependence concerns the non-use of force by states. It rests on the social-communication integration theory of Karl Deutsch [1957] and the Deutschian concept of "security community," which is the product of social integration. Increased transactions between societies at a variety of levels (and thus including transnational relations which bypass the high level interaction of governmental leaders) produce responsiveness and feelings of community. These derive from the mutual gain brought about by increased interdependence. By definition, integration is the process by which increasing interdependence is managed in a positive way—without exploitation, with gains to all parties, and with the expectation of compliance to the demands and needs of the other parties *without* even considering the option of military force or the threat of force.

Thus, while integration theory and research challenge several of the basic assumptions necessary for Realism on both the theoretical and behavioral levels—that states are in a constant "struggle" for power and military security because of the nature of the anarchic system that generates the need for self-help, with war as the ultimate recourse among states—the existence and sovereignty of states are not challenged. States manage interdependence through the creation of security communities.

Importantly, Deutsch indicates that while there have been amalgamated security communities, where states integrate fully into a new state (e.g., the Swiss cantons), security communities may also be "pluralistic." This means that states need not give up independence or territorial integrity to achieve significant levels of integration or to benefit from the positive processes that can occur with interdependence. Territorial boundaries, sovereign claims to equality, independence, and consent can coexist with high levels of interdependence and transnational activities. While the supranational character of various European Union IGOs does indicate the possibility of systematic reduction of the sovereignty of EU members, the debate and resolution of the European Monetary System issue (with Britain retaining the sovereign element of consent through the option not to join) continues to demonstrate the coexistence of integration and sovereignty.

A SECOND CUT: HOW DOES A/THE SYSTEM WORK?

At the risk of oversimplification, recall that Kobrin argues the territorial state is becoming outmoded because territoriality and sovereignty imply borders, and that borders are made inconsequential by the transnational integration of markets. Kobrin's heading, "National Markets Under Fire," translates into "Territorial States Under Fire." Kobrin is basically asking whether or not borders remain relevant. Similarly, in his response paper, Nigh asks "what will home and host country mean?" Nigh raises Robert Reich's question—"Who is Us?" and "Who is Them?" In this section I wish to come at "how to manage interdependence?" from another angle, questioning the interpretation of system and borders implicit in Kobrin's paper, and arguing that the ideas of "national markets" or national economies are at least "quasi-myths."[3]

Let us begin with some observations about systems in general and then the international system as one type of social system. Only in this way can we understand the *inherent* tension between the concept of the sovereign state and the interdependence within which states have existed for 500 years. We need to keep in mind the "ecological triad" developed by Harold and Margaret Sprout: entity, environment, the entity-environment relationship. The entity-environment relationship is concerned in part with how environments affect the opportunities afforded to entities, as well as how they affect the willingness of decision makers in those entities to make choices.

These relationships are not deterministic. While environments provide possibilities and help set probabilities, they must be perceived by decision makers.[4]

All systems, by definition, are composed of interacting elements of some kind. These interactions are characterized by interdependence, which simply means that actions or events in one part of the system have effects and consequences in the other parts of the system. The units within a system are sensitive and vulnerable to each other.[5] The elements of a system have a structure: they can be arrayed along various hierarchies according to their attributes; patterns of their interactions can be discerned. In their concern with system stability, various analysts have discussed the consequences of disturbances within systems, and how such disturbances are handled. In a classic work, Rosecrance [1963] analyzed a series of historical European systems in terms of the "regulators" that existed to take care of the demands being placed on the system.

The feudal condition that existed in Europe following the disintegration of the Roman empire was, in part, characterized by both the local organization of political authority and local economy. The development and interaction of the political, military, technological, economic, and religious factors that eventuated in the rise of state-like actors, also increased the size and interaction between these entities (for a brief overview, see Russett and Starr [1992:52–56]; Tilly [1990]). That is, groups of entities that exhibited only the most rudimentary elements of a system were increasing the interactions and interdependencies that would create a true system.

In the formative stages, from around 1100 to 1648 (the date of the Peace of Westphalia and the nominal beginning of the modern state system), this system developed a supposedly dual hierarchical structure: (1) a political or temporal structure based on feudalism and the hierarchy of loyalty that hypothetically culminated with the

Holy Roman Emperor and (2) a spiritual structure that was based on the hierarchy established by the Catholic Church. In Rosecrance's terms, the same hierarchies that helped structure the system also worked as systemic regulators, to resolve conflicts and handle other demands and disturbances.

The establishment of the Westphalian state system threw off these two centers of authority. The distinction of this new system, states with "sovereignty," was that the units in the system were each ruled by a prince for whom *no* legitimate source of higher external authority existed.[6] Thus, from the beginning of the Westphalian system, the state actors *were* in a system; by definition they were linked by various types of economic/commercial, military, political, and social interdependencies. Because they were interdependent units in a system *without* a formal central authority, the states needed to develop new types of regulators so that they could prosper, could do what they needed to do, could get what they needed from each other in a world where nothing is distributed equally (goods of various types, including "security").

The development of mechanisms such as international law to facilitate the interactions of the states, as well as informal sanctioning mechanisms such as the balance of power, indicate that the states *were indeed in an interdependent system* that required regulating mechanisms. The growth of states depended in large part on the growth of commerce and its need to expand ever outward, as well as the way in which commerce linked separate political entities in interdependent networks. Erstwhile European monarchs used the dynamism of commerce to obtain the wealth and capital needed to defeat the nobles, consolidate their rule, and create areas of internal order (the "capital" in Tilly's [1990] title), despite the fact that commerce always put them into contact with others and was hard to "control." McNeill [1982] persuasively argues that it was the opposition to commerce (and all it entailed, including the necessary

linkages and interdependencies) that led to the stagnation of imperial China. Both McNeill [1982] and Kennedy [1987] clearly indicate the potential China had to outstrip the formative European system in the 1400s and 1500s, but failed to do so.

Gilpin [1987:10–11] delineates the tension that has *always* existed between states and markets:

> On the one hand, the state is based on the concepts of territoriality, loyalty and exclusivity, and it possesses a monopoly on the legitimate use of force. Although no state can long survive unless it assures the interests and gains the consent of the most powerful groups in society, states enjoy varying degrees of autonomy with respect to the societies of which they are a part. On the other hand the market is based on the concepts of functional integration, contractual relationships, and expanding interdependence of buyers and sellers ... For the states, territorial boundaries are a necessary basis of national autonomy and political unity. For the market, the elimination of all political and other obstacles to the operation of the price mechanism is imperative. The tension between these two fundamentally different ways of ordering human relationships has profoundly shaped the course of modern history and constitutes the crucial problem in the study of political economy.

This long citation supports one of Kobrin's basic premises, the tension between territorially defined states and transnational markets. However, Gilpin's observations also indicate that markets have always linked states, and states have always had to manage the interdependence generated by commerce.

Kobrin's idea that "national" markets or economies at some point in time stood separate from systemic interdependencies is untenable (somewhat like Hobbes's "state of nature"). From the beginning, states were interdependent. Their notion of sovereignty had to deal with externalities (sensitivity and vulnerability). Rather than note how interdependence erodes sovereignty, the question is, how have states managed interdependence at different points in time under different conditions? There *has always* been a tension between markets and sovereignty, between economics and politics.

A FINAL CUT: THE "WESTPHALIAN TRADE-OFF"

Returning to the Sprouts's ecological triad, and the ideas of opportunity and willingness, we have an alternative way to look at the relationship between sovereignty and interdependence. A state can be seen as an entity that exists within an environment. This environment sets the "menu for choice" for the decision makers of the state. (The decision makers are nested within a set of environments, each of which provides possibilities or opportunities and cues that affect the probability of choice, or willingness.) Interdependence is a significant component of this environment, with the possibilities and probabilities of state choice shaped by its externalities. The question is: How do states adapt themselves to their environments? What parts of these environments produce sensitivities to which states are most vulnerable? How are these to be managed or handled?

In the same way the multicentric system of non-state, sovereignty-free transnational actors also forms part of the environment of the territorial state. States must react and adapt to the constraints that such actors and actions place on them as well. The mechanisms for dealing with system demands and disturbances changes with the change in system structure, especially the distribution of resources (economic or military). For example, the main regulatory mechanism of the post-1945 period until the mid-1980s was the strategic balance of terror between the superpowers. This regulatory mechanism was one version of the balance of power process, that is, a deterrence process. It usefully regulated not only the conflict behavior between superpowers, but between the allies of each. Within large blocs of states order was kept by superpowers. Outside the blocs, because there were *two*

superpowers, the system provided the possibility of support against whichever superpower attempted influence, and thus the possibility of superpower conflict and the possibility of the escalation of that conflict. Thus, the superpower balance actually permeated into all areas of systemic order.

With the disappearance of one of the superpowers, the system structure and the possibilities it provided changed; there is a different menu facing decision makers. There is also the need for regulatory mechanisms to take the place of the balance of terror. An incipient "new world order," which is simply the traditional notion of collective security, is seen by some as a way to manage world security order. In the same way, the end of World War II brought about not only a capitalist world economic system, but a supposedly alternative economic system of socialist states. Within the context of the Cold War, the Western economic system required regulatory mechanisms. Western states produced a network of formal and informal rules, norms, and patterns of behavior along with IGOs to deal with many economic issues or "regimes."

The evolution of regime-like mechanisms to deal with mutual problems, interdependent linkages, externalities, and collective goods (see Russett and Starr [1992: chaps. 16–17]) indicates how states adapt to their environments. Rather than the state-to-state military treaties of the nineteenth century which dealt with strategic interdependencies, the post-1945 regimes dealt primarily with economic issues, and explicitly included non-state actors (IGOs and NGOs) in an attempt to manage the coordination needs of some regimes, and the more difficult cooperation needs of other regimes (see Stein [1983]; Keohane [1984]). To continue, the whole hegemonic-leadership regime literature is about *changing conditions*, how mechanisms are created to regulate the system and help maintain order which are affected by change, and how they are modified to deal with change.

In sum, different issues and problems, involving different mixes of collective and private goods, call for different modes of organization and regulatory mechanisms. The formally anarchic condition of the international system makes this process more complex. However, this has *always* been the case. Since 1945, many of the attempts to adapt to and deal with growing interdependencies have indicated the degree of flexibility possible without centralized authority or guidance (e.g., Ostrom [1990]). One of the advantages of central authority is a mechanism for clearly delineating rights and responsibilities among the members of the system; who is expected to do what or for whom under what conditions. As noted, such mechanisms are in place to allow a system to function smoothly, to facilitate the interactions of the constituent units, and permit them to do what they need to do.

One of the purposes of the concept of sovereignty—an abstract legal condition that characterizes states—was to delineate as clearly as possible in a decentralized system who was responsible for what (the notion of jurisdiction over people and territory). The development of international law served the same purpose of delineating rights and responsibilities. Every form of interdependence made this process less clear and more difficult, yet more necessary. With ecological externalities the territorial demarcation of states loses much of its meaning for some purposes. However, the territorial boundaries still indicate which government is responsible for what behavior of which people where.

In this sense, the questions raised by Kobrin about the national origin of products, about whether an IBM notebook is an American or Japanese product, are not necessarily the correct set of questions to ask if one is questioning the continued relevance of the territorial state. These "us" and "them" questions concern the legal issues of jurisdiction and responsibility for impeding or facilitating trade. Such questions of coordination or control (e.g., the origin and control of technology) are dealt with by states, international law, and regimes. They are dealt with through bargaining, whether

with bilateral diplomatic contacts, or through the forums provided by IGOs which exist or are created to deal with a specific functional issue (as is central to the regime literature).[7]

It is fair to ask at what point can systems (or organizations) no longer adapt to their environments; when the organization or structure of the system is dysfunctional for such adaptation. Has a system composed of sovereign territorial states reached such a point? One reason for discussing the work of Herz was to indicate that the territorial state continued to thrive even when the territorial aspect of security was no longer relevant to state survival. Sovereignty provided other benefits—of status, prestige, and entry into the arena of global politics—with the benefits of legal equality and autonomy. Sovereignty as a legal concept also helps to identify rights and responsibilities. The discussion of integration and Deutschian security communities also serves to indicate that high levels of interdependence can connect states through a variety of transnational linkages, but *not* lead to the disappearance of the state, or even a significant alteration of its organization in order to adapt to changing conditions.

The adaptation of the state to growing networks of interdependence has indeed led to a shift in the balance of what Russett and Starr [1992:440] have called the "Westphalian trade-off":

Interdependence and the idea of sovereignty, which carries the formal and legal assumption of autonomy and equality among states, *do not mix well*. Look again at the Peace of Westphalia. The statesmen and leaders who fashioned this settlement were creating agreements that met the needs of that time. Very clear *trade-offs* were made between autonomy and self-control on the one hand and the lack of order inherent in the anarchic international system on the other ... The Westphalian trade-off stressed independence and autonomy; interdependence stresses collective problems and solutions. The balance has been changing, especially in the decades since World War II; the trade-off has come to stress the need to reduce the formal anarchy of the system in order to solve the problems of interdependence. (emphasis in the original)

While Kobrin identifies some of the forces that have been responsible for the trade-off, he is wrong about the consequences. In adapting to an evolving menu for choice, the leaders of states have crafted regulatory mechanisms that are seen to be useful for dealing with contemporary interdependencies working through IGOs, NGOs, and learning how to craft bargains in situations where interdependence predominates (e.g., Keohane and Nye [1989]) and where state relations are defined within pluralistic security communities.

NOTES

1. This section head combines and paraphrases the two articles by John Herz written a decade apart: "The Rise and Demise of the Territorial State" (1957) and "The Territorial State Revisited—Reflections on the Nature of the Nation State" (1968).

2. Which includes all the transactions and linkages that constitute and indicate the emergence of international integration.

3. In a critique of the "Who is Us?" thesis presented by Reich, Kapstein (1991/92:56) argues: "The power of the home state over the multinational has not diminished; if anything, it has continued to increase. Corporations have not become anational, multinational, or transnational; they remain wedded to their home governments for both political and economic reasons. The question 'Who is Us?' is an interesting one, but it is not asked by business executives."

4. The three basic relationships the Sprouts develop as alternatives to determinism are: environmental possibilism, environmental probabilism, and cognitive behaviorism. For elaborations of these ideas as well as how my model of opportunity and willingness derived from them, see Starr (1978 and 1991); Most and Starr (1989); Siverson and Starr (1991).

5. According to Keohane and Nye (1977: 12), "Sensitivity involves degrees of responsiveness . . . how quickly do changes in one country bring costly changes to another, and how great are the costly effects?" Sensitivity indicates how quickly and to what extent, changes in one part of the system create effects in the other parts. While, "sensitivity means liability to costly effects imposed from outside before policies are altered to try to change the situation," vulnerability "can be defined as an actor's liability to suffer costs imposed by external events even after policies have been altered" (1977:13).

6. Kennedy (1987), for example, argues that the lack of a suzerain and an imperial principle of organization distinguished the European system in the mid-1500s from the other existing political systems in China, India, the Islamic world, Russia, or Japan.

7. This point is illustrated by the comments of Kapstein (1991/92:56) who notes that: "In general, large corporations are not only aware of the identity of their home country, they wish to maintain a close relationship with the government. Only the state can defend corporate interests in international negotiations over trade, investment, and market access. Agreements over such things as airline routes, the opening of banking establishments, and the right to sell insurance are not decided by corporate actors who gather around a table; they are determined by diplomats and bureaucrats."

Thomas L. Brewer

Perspectives on Relationships between Politics and International Business

In this paper, I intend to outline a domain of interdisciplinary analysis focused on the relationships between politics and international business (IB), thus suggesting key analytic issues for theory and research, and briefly and selectively summarizing some of the previous work that has been done. Additionally discussed are the papers concerning politics and IB by Kobrin, Nigh, and Kuhlman.

My analysis begins with the basic concepts of political analysis which define politics and power and summarizes the subfields of political science. This provides a framework for reviewing the IB literature in general and for discussing the previously noted papers in particular. This commentary is not intended to be a standard, or comprehensive, or necessarily even a balanced critique. Rather, the objective is to relate the papers explicitly to the larger themes discussed throughout this book.

THE NATURE OF POLITICS AND POLITICAL SCIENCE

In broad terms, there are three widely accepted notions of the basic nature of politics. These three notions of politics are overlapping and complementary; they emphasize different aspects of related phenomena.

One conceptualizes politics as a value allocation process within society (e.g., Lasswell and Kaplan [1950]; Easton [1971]). This conception of politics views values as human preferences, which are shaped and shared within the political system. One earmark of politics is therefore a struggle over the distribution of values; politics is conflict-ridden. Politics, in this view, is a social process, and governments are an important determinant of "who gets what, when, and how" [Lasswell 1958] in society. A second notion of politics focuses more narrowly on politics as the exercise of power in human relationships (e.g., Dahl [1984]). There is an emphasis on conflicts of interests and behavior, as one actor tries to induce another actor to do something it would otherwise not do. Threats, sanctions, promises, and rewards are all central to these relationships. Politics, in this view, is a strategic process, and governments are strategic actors in power relationships.

A third notion of politics emphasizes its collective decision-making aspects (e.g., Deutsch [1988;1966]). Political processes are mechanisms whereby societies try to undertake collective actions in pursuit of objectives. Politics, in this view, is a public problem-solving process, and governments are goal-seeking actors.

Power is either explicitly or implicitly a central concept in all of these definitions of politics; however, the notions of power reflected in each are quite different [Brewer

1992; Hart 1976; Keohane and Nye 1977; Knorr 1975]. In the first, power is exercised when a government or other political actor affects the allocation of values in society; powerful political actors are those that have an impact on the extent to which and ways in which people either enjoy value gratification or suffer value deprivation. In the second view of politics, power is exercised when one actor induces another to do something that it otherwise would not have done; powerful actors are those that change another actor's behavior by threats and promises. In the third notion of politics, power is exercised when an actor achieves an objective; powerful actors are those that tend to achieve their objectives.

It is, furthermore, common to distinguish between *potential* and *actual* power—a distinction that is relevant to all three notions of power. In each instance above, the definition of power is phrased in terms of actual power, that is the exercise of power. Potential power, on the other hand, refers to the (unexercised) ability to affect the allocation of values, induce others to behave differently, or achieve objectives. This distinction between actual and potential power is important because a common analytic error in the analysis of political power is to attribute actual power on the basis of potential power. In particular, the unqualified term *power* is often used in reference to the control over resources—such as military forces, populations, or economies—on the part of governments. Although such resources may be mobilized by governments in the exercise of actual power in any one of the three senses above, the mere possession of such resources does not in itself constitute (actual) power.

In addition, it should be noted that power can be described in terms of such variables as its scope, domain, and other features. The extent of power can—in principle—be measured in terms of the numbers of people affected, the amount of change in behavior, the frequency of achievement of objectives, and other indicators.

Business, governmental, and other actors in political processes not only exercise power and become involved in conflicted relationships with other actors, they also become involved in cooperative relationships. They may form temporary or permanent alliances on a broad range of issues, they may establish ad hoc partnerships on specific occasions, or they may engage in other forms of cooperative behavior.

Politics—no matter how defined—is about more than power, conflict, and cooperation, however; it is also about interests and ideology. Political actors are assumed to exercise (or to try to exercise) power in pursuit of a mixture of self-interested and ideologically based objectives. Similarly, self-interest and/or ideology can provide the sources of conflict and cooperation. Ideology itself can, of course, be merely a rationalization and camouflage for self-interest.

Finally, politics is about human institutions—more or less regularized patterns of behavior, which can be formal, as in bureaucratic organizations, or informal, as in widely accepted norms about what is permissible and impermissible behavior.

These are some of the core concepts of political analysis: value allocation, power, conflict, cooperation, interests, ideology, institutions. Such concepts are utilized in a variety of subfields of the discipline of political science. The subfields can be briefly identified as follows: international relations (including international political economy and international security studies), national/subnational political systems, cross-national comparative politics, political philosophy, and political methodology.

POLITICS AND INTERNATIONAL BUSINESS: THEORY AND RESEARCH

If the subfields of political science, on the one hand, are combined with the traditional categories of IB transactions and managerial functions, on the other hand, the resulting matrix (in Table 1) reveals a diverse variety of potential foci of analytic at-

Table 1. Matrix for Enhancing the Political Dimension in IB Research

International Business Variables	Political Variables (Political Science Fields/Subfields)					
	(A) IPE International Political Economy	(B) IS International Security Studies	(C) COMP Comparative Studies	(D) N/SN National and Subnational, Country Specific Studies	(E) PHIL Political Philosophy	(F) METH Methodology
Types of Transactions						
(1) Trade						
(2) FDI						
(3) Monetary						
Managerial Functions						
(4) Production						
(5) Marketing						
(6) Finance						
(7) Human Resources						
(8) Public Affairs						
(9) Policy/ Strategy						

tention to the interactions between politics and IB.

The summary of the relevant IB literature in Kobrin's paper [1992] can be placed within that matrix: Kobrin summarizes "the roles that politics and states have played in the IB literature" as follows:

- firm-state interaction: political risk, bargaining, Foreign Direct Investment (FDI)/Multinational Enterprises (MNEs) in development;
- strategic management: firm-government interactions in the context of firm strategy and industry structure;
- international political-economy: impact of MNEs on state-centric international political systems.

The first body of literature in the list is predominantly in cell 2-D of Table 1, which includes both the impact of governments on MNEs and vice versa.[1] The second body of literature is predominantly in cell 9-D, but is focused on the impact of governments on MNEs. The third body is in 2-A, with an emphasis on the impact of MNEs on governments. Added to the list might be literature on the politics of trade (1-A), with an emphasis on the impact of business on government, and the politics of international finance (3A), with an emphasis on the impact of government on finance. There is a smattering of IB literature found in other cells in the matrix.

However, the following ("relative") gaps are apparent. Column E, political philosophy, and Column F, political methodology, have been neglected. The traditional concerns of political philosophy, such as justice, are not much in evidence in the IB literature. Nor has there been much awareness of the diverse ways in which quantitative data on political variables can be generated. Both represent open-ended avenues for scholars to pursue of the interactions between politics and IB. Rows 4, 5, and 7 are less fully explored than other rows. These columns and rows, then, are some of the vertical and horizontal "dimensions" that could be more extensively de-

veloped by future studies of the relationship between politics and IB.

It is much more difficult to describe, classify, and critique the IB literature in terms of the key concepts of political analysis identified at the outset of this paper, but several summary observations are possible. One is that although there has been tremendous attention given to the impact of IB on the distribution of economic and political values in society, relatively little attention has been given to the impact on the distribution of other values.[2] Second, although there has been great attention paid to the power of firms, there has not been sufficient attention paid to the distinctions and dimensions of the power noted above. Third, whereas the overwhelming emphasis has been on conflicts between governments and MNEs, there has been little concern with cooperation—except for the occasional normative nod to the desirability of it.[3] Fourth, the IB literature is replete with concern about the interests of firms, but not much has been said about their ideologies.[4] Fifth, concerns about the institutions of the nation-state, as well as regional and universal inter-governmental organizations are scattered throughout the IB literature.

COMMENTS ON PAPERS

A central focus of Kobrin's paper is political institutions—especially changes in the nation-state system and to a lesser extent inter-governmental (international) organizations. He argues that "pressures to integrate transnationally raise questions about the viability of the primary existing modes of organizing economic and political institutions" and that "the implicit assumptions about politics and government underlying much of that [the IB] literature may no longer be valid." [p. 244] These are core issues of political science as well as IB research and theory. His paper is solidly within the international political economy subfield of political science, with implications for other subfields as well. The implications of his paper clearly extend across all of the types of IB transactions and managerial functions represented by the rows of Table 1 herein. In short, the explicit content of Kobrin's paper is at the core of the intersection of IB and politics and the implications of his paper include many aspects of both domains of analysis.

Kobrin's paper is also interesting because of its attention to several of the analytic issues concerning the concept of power that was introduced at the outset of the present paper. For instance, he distinguishes a nation-state's political power as a relative function of control over resources, and its power as a relational phenomenon reflecting how well relationships in transnational networks are managed. This is an important distinction that can be and is used by Kobrin to gain insight into revolutionary changes that are occurring in the international political economy.

Kobrin further argues that the transnational integration of markets "compromises autonomy and independence as meaningful constructs." Whether such power-related constructs as "autonomy" and "independence" have lost their utility in the analysis of the intersection of politics and IB may be arguable; however, the point that the meaning of some of our most basic analytic terms need to be reexamined is a point well stressed.

Similarly, the nature, the extent, and the forms of national government "controls" (i.e., power) over cross-border flows is surely a central set of analytic issues that warrant continual re-examination in IB and international political economy research and theory building.

Some additional lines of research and theory building that might be stimulated by Kobrin's paper include concerns with other types of fundamental changes in interests and ideologies, as well as changing patterns of cooperation and conflict, that would ensue from the trends he describes. Furthermore, an examination of the value allocation effect of those trends could be a promising line of inquiry. This is an issue that Kobrin alludes to in his conclusion, and

one which I reflect on in the conclusion of this paper. But first a few words about the papers by Nigh and Kuhlman.

Nigh's paper complements Kobrin's paper. Whereas Kobrin focuses on the implications of MNCs for the state in the nation-state, Nigh focuses on the nation. A nation can be thought of as a symbol of identification and as a group of people who identify themselves as belonging to the same national group. Therefore, the nation is, as Nigh appropriately treats it, a psychological-social-cultural phenomenon with important economic and political underpinnings and consequences.

Two core sets of questions are immediately raised about the relationships between national identities, on the one hand, and MNCs, on the other: To what extent and in what ways do MNCs affect national identities? To what extent and in what ways do national identities affect MNCs? Nigh explores these and other aspects of the relationships between national identities with commendable insight and evidence.

Two additional analytic issues add to the interest in those relationships: first, perhaps MNCs not only have national governments (i.e., states) "at bay," they also have national identities (i.e., nations) "at bay," as people inside and outside MNCs become confused about "who is us?" and "who is them?" As Nigh notes, the distinction between "them" and "us" is central to people's national self-concepts. To the extent that MNCs undermine and change people's notions of who the "us" and the "them" are, the MNCs are truly revolutionary forces in the world of nation-states. A second line of inquiry concerns a possible cause-effect relationship in the opposite direction: What impact is the reassertion of national identities in the former Soviet Union, in the former Yugoslavia, and in other parts of the world likely to be on the structure and operations of MNCs?

Kuhlman's paper also develops a key analytic issue in the Kobrin paper, namely a "level of analysis" problem. The analysis of the relationship between national governments and MNCs (like the relationship between political systems and markets more generally) requires a consideration of the behavior of actors at more than one level—for instance, macro-level analysis of national governments and micro-level analysis of MNCs.

One can easily take level-of-analysis issues further by examining relationships between politics and IB. Each of the two relevant disciplines already contains numerous levels-of-analysis. In the IB literature, theories of foreign direct investment (FDI), for instance, include: product-level analyses (the "product life cycle" theory), transaction-level and firm-level analyses ("internalization" theory), and industry-level analyses ("industrial organization" theory). In political science, at least three levels of analysis are explicit in the sub-fields as identified in Table 1.

The papers in this chapter have focused on the national and international levels of analysis in their consideration of politics, and they have focused on the firm level of analysis in their consideration of business. Many other combinations of levels of analysis in consideration of the relationships between politics and IB are also possible—and evident in the existing literature. I challenge other scholars to consider novel combinations of levels of analysis in their research within those relationships as they undertake work on any given topic.

CONCLUSION

I conclude with yet more questions—and an expression of hope.

Kobrin ends his paper with the following question: "In a transnationally integrated world, how will social objectives be determined and who will exercise control?" [p. 255]. These are questions of political analysis—including political philosophy and political power—*par excellence*. They raise additional questions about collective decision-making processes, about the allocation of values in society, about political institutions. Such questions could surely be-

come a core concern of theory and research concerning the relationships of politics and IB in the future.

As research and theory building efforts continue, there is hope that both political science scholars and IB scholars will be committed to continued involvement and reciprocal scholarly growth. In any case, I am confident that those scholars who address issues in the interdisciplinary domain involving politics and IB will be working on a number of the most socially important and intellectually intriguing issues in the future of IB research and theory.

NOTES

1. The literature on the relationships between politics and IB has included a concern with both the impact of the political environment on IB and the impact of IB on politics. IB scholars tend to be more interested in the former, while political scientists are more interested in the latter. Both, however, are surely important and interesting domains of analysis, and both are within the scope of the conference, the panel, and this paper.

2. A convenient starting point for the examination of such effects could be the list of human values developed by Lasswell and Kaplan (1950)—that is, power, enlightenment, wealth, well-being, skills, affection, righteousness, and deference. One could add beauty (i.e., aesthetic values) to the list.

3. The bargaining literature, of course, includes at least an implicit concern with cooperation (and sometimes an explicit concern); otherwise, the generalization about the literature holds.

4. The dependency literature is an important exception.

REFERENCES

Alter, Peter. 1985. *Nationalism*. London: Edward Arnold.

Anderson, Benedict. 1983. *Imagined Communities: Reflections on the Origin and Spread of Nationalism*. London.

Anderson, James. 1986. The modernity of states. In James Anderson, editor, *The Rise of the Modern State*, 1–20. Atlantic Highlands, NJ: Humanities Press International, Inc.

Bagehot, Walter. 1887. *Physics and Politics*. London.

Ball, George W. 1969. Cosmocorp: The importance of being stateless. *Atlantic Community Quarterly*, 6.

Bartlett, Christopher A. and Sumantra Ghoshal. 1992. *Transnational Management*. Homewood, IL: Irwin.

Bartlett, Christopher A. and Sumantra Ghoshal. 1989. *Managing Across Borders*. Boston, MA: Harvard Business School Press.

Behrman, Jack N. 1972. The multinational enterprise and nation states: The shifting balance of power. In A. Kapoor and Philip D. Grub, editors, *The Multinational Enterprise in Transition*, 411–425. Princeton: Darwin Press.

Bloom, William. 1990. *Personal Identity, National Identity, and International Relations*. Cambridge: Cambridge University Press.

Blumental, W. Michael. 1988. The world economy and technological change. *Foreign Affairs*, 66:529–550.

Boddewyn, Jean J. 1988. Political aspects of MNE theory. *Journal of International Business Studies*, 19(3):341–363.

Braudel, Fernand. 1984. *The Perspective of the World. Civilization and Capitalism: 15th-18th Century*. Vol. 3. New York: Perennial Library, Harper and Row.

Braudel, Fernand. 1977. *Afterthoughts on Material Civilization and Capitalism*. Baltimore, MD: The Johns Hopkins University Press.

Brewer, Thomas L. 1992. *American Foreign Policy*. 3d ed. Englewood Cliffs, NJ: Prentice-Hall.

Brunn, Stanley D. 1984. Future of the nation-state system. In Peter Taylor and John House, editors, *Political Geography: Recent Advances and Future*, 149–167. London: Croom Helm.

Bull, Hedley. 1977. *The Anarchical Society*. New York: Columbia University Press.

Business Week. 1989. How R and D spending pays off. June 20:178–232.

Business Week. 1979. R and D spending at 683 companies: Another record year. July 2:52–72.

Camilleri, Joseph A. 1990. Rethinking sovereignty in a shrinking, fragmented world. In R. B. J. Walker and Saul H. Mendlovitz, editors, *Contending Sovereignties: Redefining Political Community*, 13–44. Boulder, CO: Lynn Rienner Publishers.

Castells, Manuel and Jeffrey Henderson. 1987. Techno-economic restructuring, socio-political processes and spatial transformation: A global perspective. In Jeffrey Henderson and Manuel Castells, editors, *Global Restructuring and Territorial Development*, 1–17. Beverly Hills, CA: Sage Publishers.

Chandler, Alfred D., Jr. 1990. *Scale and Scope: The Dynamics of Industrial Capitalism*. Cambridge: The Belknap Press.

Chandler, Alfred D., Jr. 1977. *The Visible Hand: The Managerial Revolution in American Business*. Cambridge: The Belknap Press.

Coles, Robert. 1986. *The Political Life of Children*. Boston, MA: The Atlantic Monthly Press.

Cooper, Richard N. 1968. *The Economics of Interdependence: Economic Policy in the Atlantic Community*. New York: McGraw-Hill Book Company.

Dahl, Robert A. 1984. *Modern Political Analysis*. 4th ed. Englewood Cliffs, NJ: Prentice-Hall.

Dell, Edmund. 1987. *The Politics of Economic Interdependence*. New York: St. Martin's Press.

Deutsch, Karl W. 1988. *The Analysis of International Relations*. 3d ed. Englewood Cliffs, NJ: Prentice-Hall.

Deutsch, Karl W. 1966. *The Nerves of Government*. 2d ed. New York: The Free Press.

Deutsch, Karl W., et al. 1957. *Political Community and the North Atlantic Area*. Princeton, NJ: Princeton University Press.

Dicken, Peter. 1992. *Global Shift: The Internationalization of Economic Activity*. London: The Guilford Press.

Dohrs, Fred E. and Lawrence M. Sommers. 1976. *World Regional Geography: A Problem Approach*. New York: West Publishing Co.

Doz, Yves L. 1986. Government Policies and Global Industries. In Michael E. Porter, editor, *Competition in Global Industries*, 225–266. Boston, MA: Harvard Business School Press.

Doz, Yves L. 1980. Strategic management in multinational companies. *Sloan Management Review*, 21.

Easton, David. 1971. *The Political System*. New York: Knopf.

Fagre, N. and Louis T. Wells, Jr. 1982. Bargaining power of multinationals and host governments. *Journal of International Business Studies*, 13(2): 9–23.

Falk, Richard. 1990. Evasions of sovereignty. In R.B.J. Walker and Saul H. Mendlovitz, editors, *Contending Sovereignties: Redefining Political Community*, 61–78. Boulder, CO: Lynn Rienner Publishers.

Fayerweather, John. 1978. *International Business Strategy and Administration*. Cambridge: Ballinger.

Fayerweather, John. 1975. A conceptual scheme of the interaction of the multinational firm and nationalism. *Journal of Business Administration*, 7:67–89.

Fayerweather, John. 1969. *International Business Management: A Conceptual Framework*. New York: McGraw-Hill.

Fusfeld, Herbert I. and Carmela S. Haklisch. 1985. Cooperative R&D for competitors. *Harvard Business Review*, November-December:60–76.

Gellner, Ernest. 1983. *Nations and Nationalism*. Ithaca: Cornell University Press.

Ghoshal, Sumantra and Christopher A. Bartlett. 1990. The multinational corporation as an interorganizational network. *Academy of Management Journal*, 15:603–625.

Gilpin, Robert. 1987. *The Political Economy of International Relations*. Princeton, NJ: Princeton University Press.

Gore, Charles. 1984. *Regions in Question: Space, Development Theory and Regional Policy*. London: Methuen.

Hambrick, Donald C. and Phyllis A. Mason. 1984. Upper echelons: The organization as a reflection of its top managers. *The Academy of Management Review*, 9(2):193–206.

Hart, Jeffrey. 1976. Three approaches to the measurement of power in international relations. *International Organization*, 30(2): 289–305.

Heenan, David and Howard Perlmutter. 1979. *Multinational Organization Development*. Reading, MA: Addison-Wesley.

Herz, John. 1968. The territorial state revisited—reflections on the future of the nation-state. *Polity*, 1:11–34.

Herz, John. 1957. The rise and demise of the territorial state. *World Politics*, 9:473–493.

Hobsbawm, Eric J. 1990. *Nations and Nationalism since 1780*. Cambridge: Cambridge University Press.

Hu, Yao-Su. 1992. Global or stateless corporations are national firms with international operations. *Columbia Journal of World Business*, Winter:107–126.

Hughes, Kristy S. 1989. The changing dynamics of international technological competition. In David Audretsch, Leo Sleuwaegen and Hideki Yamawaki, editors, *The Convergence of International and Domestic Markets*, 269–293. Amsterdam: North-Holland.

Huntington, Samuel. 1973. Transnational organizations and world politics. *World Politics*, 25: 333–368.

Jackson, W. A. Douglas and Marwyn S. Samuels, editors. 1971. *Politics and Geographic Relationships: Toward a New Focus*. Englewood Cliffs, NJ: Prentice-Hall.

Jenkins, Barbara. 1986. Reexamining the obsolescing bargain. *International Organizations*, 40:139–165.

Johnson, R. J. 1982. *Geography and the State: An Essay in Political Geography*. New York: St. Martin's Press.

Kapstein, Ethan B. 1991/92. We are us: The myth of the multinational. *The National Interest*, Winter:55–62.

Kelman, Herbert C. 1969. Patterns of personal involvement in the national system: A social-psychological analysis of political legitimacy. In James N. Rosenau, editor, *International Politics and Foreign Policy*, rev. ed. New York: The Free Press.

Kennedy, Paul. 1987. *The Rise and Fall of the Great Powers*. New York: Random House.

Keohane, Robert O., editor. 1986. *Neorealism and Its Critics*. New York: Columbia University Press.

Keohane, Robert O. 1984. *After Hegemony*. Princeton, NJ: Princeton University Press.

Keohane, Robert O. and Joseph S. Nye, Jr. 1989. *Power and Independence.* 2d ed. Glenview, IL: Scott, Foresman and Company.

Keohane, Robert O. and Joseph S. Nye, Jr. 1987. Power and independence revisited. *International Organization,* 41:725–753.

Keohane, Robert O. and Joseph S. Nye, Jr. 1977. *Power and Independence.* Boston, MA: Little, Brown and Co.

Keohane, Robert O. and Joseph S. Nye, Jr., editors. 1973. *Transnational Relations and World Politics.* Cambridge: Harvard University Press.

Keohane, Robert O. and Joseph S. Nye, Jr. 1972. *Transnational Relations and World Politics.* Cambridge: Harvard University Press.

Kindleberger, Charles P. 1975. Size of firm and size of nation. In John H. Dunning, editor, *Economic Analysis and the Multinational Enterprise,* 342–352. New York: Praeger Publishers.

Kindleberger, Charles P. 1969. *American Business Abroad.* New Haven: Yale University Press.

Knorr, Klauss. 1975. *The Power of Nations.* New York: Basic Books.

Kobrin, Stephen J. 1991. An empirical analysis of the determinants of global integration. *Strategic Management Journal,* 12:17–32.

Kobrin, Stephen J. 1987. Testing the bargaining hypothesis in the manufacturing sector in developing countries. *International Organization,* 41(4):609–638.

Koenigsberger, Helmut G. 1987. *A History of Early Modern Europe 1500–1789.* London and New York: Longman Press.

Kuhlman, James A. 1992. The levels of analysis problem again: Community and regionalism in the global political economy. In this book.

Landes, David S. 1969. *The Prometheus Unbound.* Cambridge: Cambridge University Press.

Lapham, Lewis H. 1988. Leviathan in trouble. *Harper's Magazine,* September.

Lasswell, Harold D. 1958. *Politics: Who Gets What, When and How.* New York: New American Library.

Lasswell, Harold D. and Abraham Kaplan. 1950. *Power and Society.* New Haven: Yale University Press.

Lecraw, Donald J. 1984. Bargaining power, ownership, and profitably of transnational corporations in developing countries. *Journal of International Business Studies,* 15(1): 27–43.

Lecraw, Donald J. and Allen J. Morrison. 1991. Transnational corporation host country relations: A framework for analysis. *Essays in International Business,* 9(September).

Lenway, Stefanie Ann and Thomas D. Murtha. 1994. The state as strategist in international business research. *Journal of International Business Studies,* 25(3):513–535.

Lindblom, Charles E. 1977. *Politics and Markets: The World's Political-Economic Systems.* New York: Basic Books.

Luard, Evan. 1976. *Types of International Society.* New York: The Free Press.

Lukes, Steven. 1986. *Power.* Oxford, UK: Basil Blackwell.

MacNeill, Jim, Pieter Winsemius, and Taizo Yakushiji. 1991. *Beyond Interdependence.* New York: Oxford University Press.

Mann, Michael. 1993. *The Sources of Social Power. Volume II: The Rise of Classes and Nation-States, 1760–1914.* New York: Cambridge University Press.

Mann, Michael. 1986. *The Sources of Social Power: Volume I: A History of Power from the Beginning to A.D. 1760.* Cambridge: Cambridge University Press.

McKibbin, Warwick J. and Jeffrey D. Sachs. 1991. *Global Linkages: Macroeconomic Interdependence and Cooperation in the World Economy.* Washington: The Brookings Institution.

McNeill, William H. 1982. *The Pursuit of Power.* Chicago: University of Chicago Press.

Meinecke, Friedrich. 1970. *Cosmopolitanism and the National State.* Princeton, NJ: Princeton University Press.

Moran, Theodore H. 1985. Multinational corporations and developing countries: An analytical overview. In T. H. Moran, editor, *Multinational Corporations: The Political Economy of Foreign Direct Investment.* Lexington, MA: Lexington Books.

Most, Benjamin A. and Harvey Starr. 1989. *Inquiry, Logic and International Politics*. Columbia, SC: University of South Carolina Press.

Nigh, Douglas and Philip Cochran. 1987. Issues management and the multinational enterprise. *Management International Review*, 27(1):4–12.

North, Douglas C. and Robert Paul Thomas. 1973. *The Rise of the Western World: A New Economic History*. Cambridge: Cambridge University Press.

Nye, Joseph S. Jr. 1990. *Bound to Lead: The Changing Nature of American Power*. New York: Basic Books.

Ohmae, Kenichi. 1990. *The Borderless World*. New York: Harper Business.

Ostrom, Elinor. 1990. *Governing the Commons*. Cambridge: Cambridge University Press.

Perlmutter, Howard. 1969. The tortuous evolution of the multinational corporation. *Columbia Journal of World Business*, January/February:9–18.

Poggi, Gianfranco. 1990. *The State: Its Nature, Development, and Prospects*. Palo Alto, CA: Stanford University Press.

Porter, Glenn. 1973. *The Rise of Big Business*. Arlington Heights, IL: AHM.

Porter, Michael E. 1986. Competition in global industries: A conceptual framework. In Michael E. Porter, editor, *Competition in Global Industries*. Boston, Mass.: Harvard Business School Press.

Powell, Walter W. 1990. Neither market nor hierarchy: Network forms of organization. *Research in Organizational Behavior*, 12:295–336. Stamford, CT: JAI Press.

Price, Victoria Curazon. 1988. *1992: Europe's Last Chance?* Occasional Paper 81. London: The Institute of International Affairs.

Reich, Robert B. 1991a. Who is them? *Harvard Business Review*, March-April:77–88.

Reich, Robert B. 1991b. Who do we think they are? *The American Prospect*, Winter:49–53.

Reich, Robert B. 1991c. *The Work of Nations*. New York: Alfred A. Knopf.

Reich, Robert B. 1990. Who is us? *Harvard Business Review*, January-February:53–64.

Robinson, Richard D. 1973. *International Business Management*. New York: Holt, Rinehart and Winston.

Robinson, Richard D. 1967. *International Management*. New York: Holt, Rinehart and Winston.

Robinson, Richard D. 1964. *International Business Policy*. New York: Holt, Rinehart and Winston.

Rokkan, Stein, K. Saelen, and J. Warmbrunn. 1973. Building states and nations: A selective bibliography of the research literature by theme and by country. In S. N. Eisenstadt and S. Rokkan, editors, *Building States and Nations*. Vol. 1. Beverly Hills, CA: Sage.

Rosecrance, Richard. 1986. *The Rise of the Trading State*. New York: Basic Books.

Rosecrance, Richard. 1963. *Action and Reaction in World Politics*. Boston: Little, Brown and Co.

Rosenau, James N. 1990. *Turbulence in World Politics*. Princeton, NJ: Princeton University Press.

Russett, Bruce and Harvey Starr. 1992. *World Politics: The Menu for Choice*. 4th ed. New York: W. H. Freeman.

Sack, Robert D. 1981. Territorial bases of power. In A. D. Burnett and P. J. Taylor, editors, *Political Studies from Spatial Perspectives*, 53–71. London: John Wiley.

Schama, Simon. 1990. *Citizens: A Chronicle of the French Revolution*. New York: Vintage Books.

Scherer, Frederic M. 1974. Economies of scale and industrial concentration. In Harvey Goldschmitt, H. Michael Mann and J. Fred Weston, editors, *Industrial Concentration: The New Learning*, 16–54. Boston: Little Brown and Co.

Siverson, Randolph M. and Harvey Starr. 1991. *The Diffusion of War: A Study of Opportunity and Willingness*. Ann Arbor, MI: University of Michigan Press.

Smith, Anthony D. 1986. *The Ethnic Origins of Nations*. Oxford, UK: Basil Blackwell.

Smith, Anthony D. 1983. *Theories of Nationalism*. 2d ed. NY: Holmes and Meier.

Smith, Anthony D. 1973. Nationalism: A trend report and bibliography. *Current Sociology*, 21(3):7–185.

Starr, Harvey. 1991. Joining political and geographic perspectives: Geopolitics and international relations. *International Interactions*, 17:1–9.

Starr, Harvey. 1978. *Opportunity* and *willingness* as ordering concepts in the study of war. *International Interactions*, 4:363–387.

Stein, Arthur A. 1983. Coordination and collaboration: Regimes in an anarchic world. In Stephen D. Krasner, editor, *International Regimes*. Ithaca, NY: Cornell University Press.

Strange, Susan, editor. 1984. *Paths to International Political Economy*. London: George Allen and Unwin.

Taylor, Peter J. 1985. *Political Geography: World-Economy, Nation State, and Locality*. London and New York: Longman.

Thomsen, Stephen. 1992. We are all *us*. *Columbia Journal of World Business*, 26(4):7–14.

Tilly, Charles. 1990. *Coercion, Capital, and European States, AD 990–1990*. Oxford, UK: Basil Blackwell.

Tilly, Charles. 1975. Western state-making and theories of political transformation. In Charles Tilly, editor, *The Formation of National States in Western Europe*, 601–638. Princeton, NJ: Princeton University Press.

Tyson, Laura D'Andrea. 1991. They are not us: Why American ownership still matters. *The American Prospect*, Winter: 37–49.

Vernon, Raymond. 1980. The obsolescing bargain: A key factor in political risk. In M. B. Winchester, editor, *The International Essays for Business Decision Makers*. Dallas, Texas: AMACOM.

Vernon, Raymond. 1971. *Sovereignty at Bay*. New York: Basic Books.

Von Laue, Theodore H. 1987. *The World Revolution of Westernization: The Twentieth Century in Global Perspective*. New York: Oxford University Press.

Walker, R. B. J. and Saul H. Mendlovitz. 1990. Interrogating state sovereignty. In R. B. J. Walker and S. H. Mendlovitz, editors, *Contending Sovereignties*. Boulder, CO: Lynn Reiner Publishers, 1–12.

Waltz, Kenneth N. 1979. *The Theory of International Politics*. Reading: Addison-Wesley.

Ward, Michael D. and Lewis L. House. 1988. A theory of the behavioral power of nations. *Journal of Conflict Resolution*, 32:3–36.

Wasserman, Stanley and Faust, Katherine. 1994. *Social Network Analysis: Methods and Applications*. New York: Cambridge University Press.

Watkins, Frederick. 1968. State: The concept. *International Encyclopedia of the Social Science*. New York: Macmillian.

Wightman, David. 1984. Why economic history? In Susan Strange, editor, *Paths to International Political Economy*. London: George Allen and Unwin.

Williamson, Oliver E. 1975. *Markets and Hierarchies: Analysis and Antitrust Implications*. New York: The Free Press.

Wriston, Walter B. 1988;1989. Technology and sovereignty. *Foreign Affairs*, 67:63–75.

Wrong, Dennis H. 1979. *Power: Its Forms, Bases, and Uses*. Oxford, UK: Basil Blackwell.

6

Organization Theory Perspectives and International Business

EDITORS' COMMENTS

Much of the impetus for the growth of international business inquiry emanated from the development, after World War II, of a particular organization—the multinational corporation (MNC). Understanding the why and how of the multinational still occupies a lot of our time. In fact, in considering the conceptual domain of IB in chapter 2, Wilkins takes the position that IB should study first and foremost "the international-multinational-transnational-global business-enterprise-firm-company-corporation." [p. 32] While we disagree with Wilkins's position on the exclusive centrality of the business enterprise, we do acknowledge the continued importance of this organization in IB inquiry.

To advance our understanding of the role of organization in IB inquiry we wondered what organization theory (OT) might contribute to the discussion.[1] Thus, we asked our topic paper authors to critically examine the various OT theories—to identify the concepts and theories that held out the most potential for advancing IB thought. Where should we draw the line between organization and environment? What conceptualizations of organization and of environment are useful for IB inquiry?

We felt that in the past the mainstream OT theories have perhaps helped us understand better a hospital in Middletown, USA, but were not very enlightening when it came to international business organizations like the multinational corporation. Their conceptualizations seemed to falter when confronted by the complex reality of the multinational. We were looking for more from recent OT theorizing.

Our expectations were fulfilled. The authors of the three topic papers enrich our understanding of IB phenomena. Since their discussions are based essentially on contrasting paradigms, their observations and comments provide a basis for considerable, yet varied, theoretical and empirical contributions in the years ahead.

In the lead paper, Westney sees the potential for a mutually beneficial relationship between OT and IB, but judges this potential as unfulfilled to date. She sees each ignoring the other—in different ways. OT has mostly ignored phenomena of interest to IB, e.g., multinational corporations and international organizational alliances. Meanwhile, IB inquiry is stuck in the OT world of the 1960s and 1970s (contingency theory and resource dependence theory) and has ignored more recent OT developments, e.g., organizational ecology and institutional theory.

Defining OT as the application of general social theories to organizations, Westney notes that, like IB, OT is an applied and interdisciplinary field of study, drawing as it does on sociology, economics, and psychology. Unlike IB, however, OT does not go down to an individual or group level of analysis. OT leaves that for organizational behavior (OB). OT does go up to levels of analysis higher than the level of the individual organization—as we argue IB should.

Indeed, Westney argues that the development of population ecology and institutional theory constitutes something of a revolution in OT due to their shift of level of analysis from organization up to population or field, as well as their challenge to previous underlying assumptions of rationality and choice, and their enriched conceptualization of the environment.

In her review of organizational ecology, Westney points out its roots in biological ecology and its model of natural selection. Frankly, given the rapid pace of change in the social environment, compared to that of the natural environment, we side with the critics of organizational ecology and believe that it has little to offer the development of IB theory.[2] Thus we don't share Westney's enthusiasm for organizational ecology.

More promising, we believe, is institutional theory, which analyzes "the ways in which organizations in shared environments come to adopt patterns that are externally defined as appropriate and are reinforced in their interactions with other organizations" [p. 305]. Particularly noteworthy is this theory's richer, institutional conceptualization of an organization's environment and its emphasis on the interpenetration of organization and environment. As Westney explains, "This interpenetration is the key both to environmental constraints on organizational change and to environmental pressures for the diffusion of organizational structures and processes" [p. 306].

Yet the complex reality of the multinational corporation overwhelms institutional theory too. If the multinational corporation is considered to be *an organization*, characterizing its environment is problematic. For example, review the definition that Westney provides for organizational field (those organizations that, in the aggregate, constitute a recognized area of institutional life: key suppliers, resource and product consumers, regulatory agencies, and other organizations that produce similar service or products) and try to determine for yourself General Electric's organizational field.

More promising for institutional theory is to consider a part of the multinational as the organization, e.g., the subsidiary, with the rest of the multinational becoming part of the environment. Thus, as Westney explains, institutional theory has something to contribute to our understanding of subsidiary structure resulting from the competing isomorphic pulls of the host country organizational field, the home country organizational field, and perhaps a transnational organizational field. (Also see chapter 1.) At present, the potential for institutional theory to contribute to our understanding international business phenomena seems to come mostly when it draws the line between organization and environment somewhere at a level below that of the whole multinational.

Finally, Westney raises a very interesting point that IB scholars should at least consider what role the academic field of IB itself may play as an institution that legitimizes certain organizational practices. Here she argues that institutional theory can also be used as a basis for understanding how IB inquiry influences IB practice—the very phenomena we are trying to understand.

The second topic paper is by Egelhoff, a researcher who is certainly quite attuned to the complex reality of the multinational. He examines how emerging information technologies (IT) affect the information processing capabilities of multinationals and their ability to implement global and transnational strategies. Expanding on his past information-processing models, Egelhoff develops a framework relating the reach (national unit, regional unit, global product unit, global corporation) of an MNC's IT and its range (routine vs. nonroutine, sequential vs. reciprocal information processing). He then applies the framework to scheduling manufacturing on a regional rather than national basis and to coordinating R&D on a global basis.

Of particular note is Egelhoff's introduction of rich, sticky, hard-to-transfer information. This raises the question of what difference, if any, is there between organizational information and organizational knowledge. Polanyi [1958, 1966] argues that knowledge has a dimension that is tacit and cannot be articulated or codified and is transferred only by face-to-face interaction and direct experience.[3] The capability of any IT technology, even video conferencing, to substitute for face-to-face meetings is questionable.

In the third topic paper, Hedlund and Ridderstråle definitely want to move from information processing to knowledge creation, innovation, and a theory of the self-renewing MNC. In reviewing four theoretical perspectives on the MNC (transaction cost, imperfect competition, internationalization process, and information processing), Hedlund and Ridderstråle find two common shortcomings: (1) these theories focus on the exploitation of the existing rather that on the creation of the new and (2) they neglect systemic attributes and emergent properties.

They find more promise in evolutionary theory of the firm and in the case-study grounded theories of MNC's by Hedlund, Bartlett and Ghoshal, Doz and Prahalad, and White and Poynter. They suggest that contribution of evolutionary theory is its focus on change over time; its limitation is its lack of interest in internal processes, organization, and management. The case studies that led to theorizing about the heterarchy, the transnational, the multi-focal MNC, and the horizontal MNC are both their strength and weakness. While empirically grounded, this grounding is really rather limited.

Developing some ideas in the tradition of organizational learning, Hedlund and Ridderstråle make the distinction between programs of exploitation and programs of creation in organizations and investigate how we can structure a MNC to combine these two activities that seem to have conflicting requirements. The emphasis here really is on laying out the possibilities open to an MNC, formulating relevant questions, and developing some tentative propositions.

They identify four key issues: the degree of separation in exploitation and creation; the level at which separation takes place; the methods of coordinating exploitation and creation activities; and the sequencing of exploitation and creation. Particularly noteworthy is their emphasis on four levels of analysis: the country, the organizational unit, the group, and the individual. "It is the multi-level interaction between choice of emphasis, separation and sequencing that make the problem of combining creation and exploitation particularly difficult and interesting" [p. 343 in this volume]. Such a conceptualization involving multiple interacting levels is quite compatible with the ideas we present in chapter 1 on the nature of the emerging international business paradigm.

Hedlund and Ridderstråle judge traditional organization theory to be too focused on organizations as exploiters. We agree with them that the MNC, which must combine exploitation and creation—the MNC, in which the diffusion of knowledge and the operation in a variety of environments is most apparent—will likely serve as a stimulus for a reformulation of our general theories of the firm and organization. As Hennart points out in chapter 11, sometimes theorizing about international business phenomena leads rather than follows *country-bound* theorizing about business phenomena, because the characteristics necessitating theoretical development are most pronounced in the international domain.

In the end, not surprisingly, Hedlund and Ridderstråle bring it all back to the heterarchy and detail the superiority of heterarchy over hierarchy for the MNC that both exploits and creates.

In his commentary, Astley argues that in order to enhance operating flexibility and innovation, the "subunit and organizational boundaries in MNC's are becoming increasingly blurred, or are disappearing altogether" [p. 354 in this volume] and argues for the relevance to IB of certain higher levels of analysis.

In examining this blurring of organizational lines, Astley starts with the MNC's "closest" environment, the organization set, those organizations with which it has a direct link. He observes that as the MNC enters into collaborative arrangements with these organizations, its boundaries begin to blur. Moreover, as highlighted by Hedlund and Ridderstråle, the creation

activities lead to more of these collaborations.

Astley then moves on to the analysis of higher levels of action sets, organizational fields, and the nation-state, and again demonstrates the blurring of MNC boundaries with other organizations. For Astley this blurring is a necessity for the MNC's viability.

In contrast to Astley, Ghoshal argues that the three topic papers: "reflect a field of inquiry that is inconsistent in its assumptions, incoherent in its approach, and stagnant in its direction." [p. 361 in this volume]. He challenges OT scholars' interest in IB by raising such pointed questions as "How do we interpret the differences in assumptions and approaches among the three papers . . . ? Why do we find, among these established and well-known scholars, such careful avoidance of each other's work?" [p. 363 in this volume]. Apparently, Ghoshal wants a field where scholars subject each other's ideas to empirical testing and theoretical challenge. Thus, whether through selection or synthesis, the multitude of theories reflecting differing assumptions and approaches would be reduced over time. This stance suggests, or at least argues, for paradigmic/theoretical closure, or an increasing "narrowness" in view; a trend that is opposite to the one emerging in most fields of inquiry, including IB inquiry [see chapter 1].

Faced with this particular critique of their papers, it is quite revealing to note only Egelhoff made the effort to respond to Ghoshal's comments. This failure to respond provides even more evidence of the lack of dialogue that Ghoshal decries.

Egelhoff makes two particular noteworthy points in his reply to Ghoshal's comments. First, Egelhoff characterizes the OT field of inquiry as consisting of multiple paradigms. He asserts that progress is made within rather than across paradigms. Second, he provocatively argues that "empirical testing and serious theoretical challenging within paradigms are simply not cost efficient activities to engage in. Reviewers of most publications will generally reject such tedious work as lacking novelty and not making a meaningful contribution to the field." [p. 366 in this volume]. Thus, in Egelhoff's opinion, existing OT paradigms are succeeded by *new paradigms, not necessarily better paradigms*, as researchers seek to publish more and relieve intellectual boredom. Here again we are reminded of the importance of our own structures and processes for generating and disseminating IB knowledge and the consequences of progress in our field of study.

To conclude, the prognosis for major contributions from mainstream organization theory to improved understanding of IB phenomena is guarded. As Astley argues, "What is needed is the development of new perspectives that are distinctively international in nature" [p. 361 in this volume].

This book represents an effort by us and our contributors to make some substantial progress in determining just what "distinctively international" means in terms of the domain, theories, and methods of international business inquiry. In chapter 1, we present our most recent thinking on international business as an evolving multi-level, socially embedded process.

Certainly in this chapter we get a better sense of what it means to be embedded in society—now conceptualized more clearly as sets of related organizations that inter-penetrate and influence one another. These sets can transcend national boundaries. It's interesting to note that the Business and Society scholars [see chapter 3] have made in-creasing use of the stakeholder concept. While not exactly congruent with either the organization set [see Astley] or the organizational field [see Westney], the organization's stakeholders provide a similar organizational conceptualization of the relevant environment of a particular organization. Also pertinent to this discussion is Mann's [1986] conceptualization of societies as "constituted of multiple and intersecting sociospatial networks of power" [1986, 1].

As we noted in our introduction to chapter 5, such network conceptualizations of IB phenomena are promising. Yet questions remain. For example, in order to advance IB theory and understanding, what entities should be considered as actors or nodes in the network and also what relations among actors should be examined?

NOTES

1. In this chapter, organization theories coming more out of a sociological tradition are considered. As Westney notes in her paper in this chapter, economics has also contributed some organization theories. The more economics-rooted organization theories are addressed somewhat in this chapter, but also in chapters 4 (Economic Perspectives), 9 (Strategic Management Perspectives), and 11 (Theory and Research Implications for IB).

2. In addition to the critics noted by Westney, see Elster (1989), chapter VIII.

3. See Nonaka (1994) for a recent discussion on the distinction between information and knowledge.

Organization Theory Perspectives and International Business

D. Eleanor Westney

Any effort to assess the relationship between organization theory and the field of international business (IB) must be primarily a projection of its possibilities rather than a celebration of its achievements. The field of macro-organizational theory usually identified by the business school acronym of Organization Theory (OT) has largely ignored the cross-border organizational phenomena that lie within the purview of IB—most notably the multinational corporation (MNC), cross-border organizational networks such as strategic alliances, and competition in the same markets between firms nurtured in different societies. On the other hand, one could argue that IB's treatment of organizations was strongly "imprinted" by the contingency theories that dominated OT in the late 1960s and early 1970s when IB was institutionalized, and that IB has tended to ignore subsequent developments in OT[1]—which have emerged largely in reaction to contingency theory and have remained highly critical of it.

Any applied field[2] in the social sciences has a love-hate relationship with theory. The conceptual categories and the simplifying assumptions developed in theory are needed to organize the empirical investigation of complex social phenomena that lies at the heart of an applied field, but all too often they seem to those in the field to squeeze the life and identity out of the very phenomena they purport to explain. The ambivalence of those working in applied fields toward theory is exacerbated by the fact that the activities of "theory building" confer far more academic status than the application of theory to complex problems (or the rejection of the relevance of theory to problems). Those in applied fields resent the fact that developments in theory seem to be driven more by conceptual, ideological, and political factors internal to the community of theorists than by the problems and demands of application. Adding to the uneasiness of those in applied fields is the fact that the relationship between theory and application tends to be asymmetrical and largely the responsibility of those in the applied fields; either they carefully apply a single theoretical paradigm to problems and issues in the field (usually concluding with some useful suggestions for future amplification of the paradigm, which are ignored by theorists) or they draw eclectically from several paradigms to address a particular issue in the field and risk being scorned by theorists for superficiality.

The inherently difficult relationship between the applied field of IB and OT has been exacerbated by the fact that organizational analysis in IB and the trends in OT moved in opposite directions during the 1980s. Researchers in IB increasingly set their level of analysis below the level of the firm as a whole to focus on the study of businesses and product lines within the MNC; OT increasingly moved above the level of the individual organization to populations or fields. IB researchers expressed a certain disinterest in (and even distaste for) the study of formal structure, in favor of the analysis of informal processes [Hedlund 1986; Bartlett 1986]; OT focused increasingly on organizational forms and structural isomorphism (similarity in structure across organizations). To the extent that IB built on OT in the 1980s to analyze strategy and structure in MNCs, it employed the approaches if not the vocabulary of the frameworks of the late 1960s and early 1970s that focused on the individual organization: contingency theory (the Integration-Responsiveness framework; the work by Egelhoff [1982;1988] on an information-processing approach to MNC structure) and political economy or resource dependency models (a recent example being Ghoshal and Bartlett [1990]). While these paradigms continued to play a role in OT during the 1980s, they were overshadowed by developments in macro-organization theory—the analysis of organizations and their environments epitomized by organizational ecology and institutional theory. Many would argue (this author included) that the IB literature constituted an amplification of the OT frameworks, but it was rarely read and still more rarely cited by those working in OT.

Yet the organizational may well see a growing interaction across the two fields. A recent volume of edited papers on OT and the MNC [Ghoshal and Westney 1992], growing out of an 1989 workshop involving leading organization theorists and a number of those in IB who work on organizational aspects of the MNC, sets out some efforts to bridge the two fields and calls for greater interaction in the future. In the 1992 edition of Scott's review of organization theory, the multinational enterprise (MNE) draws a paragraph of discussion as an organization operating in multiple environments—a very small nod in the direction of IB, but perhaps a harbinger of things to come. Those who study MNCs increasingly recognize that the growing complexities of international, national, and local institutional environments call for finer-grained ways to analyze those environments than the two-variable characterizations (such as pressures for global integration versus pressures for local responsiveness) that dominated the 1980s.

This paper focuses on the macro-organizational paradigms of the 1980s and their potential for the IB field. It reviews the two major paradigms—organizational ecology and institutional theory—and suggests some areas for future research that could make important contributions to both fields.

I. WHAT IS "ORGANIZATION THEORY?"

The potential relationship between the applied field of IB and the realm of Organizational Theory (OT) is complicated by the fact OT itself is one step removed from the rarefied realms of pure discipline-based theory. Indeed, OT can be seen as the application of general social theories to the study of organizations and is itself strongly influenced by developments in the "purer" fields of psychological theory, economic theory, and sociological theory. In other words, both IB and OT are interdisciplinary fields, and both encounter, to very different degrees, the problems of being eclectic and "applied" in a highly specialized, discipline-based world.

Moreover, there are interesting parallels in the somewhat ambiguous institutional position of IB and OT. IB has a somewhat precarious formal institutional base: IB departments or groups in business schools tend to be small and increasingly precari-ously situated, as growing numbers of business schools argue that the need to internationalize all fields of management makes separate IB departments or groups obsolete [Dunning 1988]. OT's institutional position is even more ambiguous: OT has never had a distinct institutional base. In discipline-based departments, OT is part of the larger applied subfields of organizational sociology or social psychology. Management schools have long had OB (organization behavior) departments or groups, but not OT departments. Those who are defined as being in OT join OB groups or Strategy groups.

In fact, while the structure of the panels for the conference on which this volume is based reflects professionally institutionalized distinctions between economic theory, OT, and organization behavior, the boundaries that divide OT from OB and economic theory are very fuzzy, and not only in terms of OT scholars' institutional "home base." In practice, the distinction between OB and OT tends to be a business school phenomenon, perhaps mirroring the much more strongly institutionalized division between micro- and macroeconomics. OB and OT are distinguished in terms of levels of analysis: OB operates primarily at the level of the individual and the group and has historically been closely allied with social psychology, whereas OT works at the level of the organization and its environment, or more recently organizations and their environments, and has been most closely allied with sociology.

However, most analyses of the intellectual lineage of OT include elements of OB and of economics. For example, Scott's widely used overview of OT (first published in 1981, and now in its third edition) identified two major cradles of OT, formed virtually simultaneously at the beginning of the 1950s. One was at Columbia University, under Robert Merton, and was firmly anchored in sociology; the other was at the Carnegie Institute of Technology, under Herbert Simon, and was from the beginning an interdisciplinary group in which, in

Scott's words, "economic models of administrative behavior were modified and enriched by the insights of psychologists and political scientists" [1992:9]. In OT, these two streams are identifiable to this day in the dominant approaches to the field. One set of perspectives is rooted in sociology (and, at least in their origins, in sociology departments, although several of the leading exponents of each perspective and many of their students have been recruited to business schools): contingency theory and political economy and resource dependency approaches in the 1960s and early 1970s, population ecology and institutional theory emerging in the late 1970s and dominating the field in the 1980s. Another set of perspectives is anchored primarily in economics, including transaction cost theory, principal-agent theory, and the newest addition, the resource-based view of the firm. Theorists working in these two broad arenas tend to be aware of each other's work, but conversations across the two are complicated by the marked differences in paradigms. Reflecting the structure of the panels at this conference and the proclivities of the author, this paper will focus on the more sociologically based OT paradigms.

This is not the place for an extended recapitulation of four decades of OT; such analyses have been provided by other, better-qualified writers (e.g., Perrow [1973]; Pfeffer [1982]; Scott [1992]). We shall instead pick up the tale in the late 1970s, when in the span of little more than two years several works appeared that became touchstones in the redefinition of the terrain of OT in sociology. Aldrich and Pfeffer's 1976 review article compared the natural selection and the strategic choice perspectives on the interaction between organizations and their environments, prefiguring their subsequent work on population ecology and resource dependency. Hannan and Freeman's 1977 article, "The Population Ecology of Organizations" appeared in the *American Journal of Sociology*. The Meyer and Rowan article "Institutionalized Organizations: Formal Structure as Myth and Ceremony" appeared in the same year and the same journal.

The two emerging perspectives symbolized by these works—population ecology and institutionalization theory—represented radical departures in terms of level of analysis and underlying assumptions from the organization—environment literature that had developed from the early 1960s through the early 1970s. Their emergence can be explained by growing dissatisfaction with the assumptions of the various forms of contingency theory that dominated OT in the 1960s and early 1970s and with their characterization of the environment, as epitomized by James Thompson [1967] and by Lawrence and Lorsch [1967]. Contingency theory had extended the search for causal explanations of structural and process regularities beyond variables within the individual organization to the organization's environment, and built on the assumption that an organization adjusted its structure to its environment. That environment was analyzed by characterizing it as "high" or "low" on a range of attributes, such as uncertainty, e.g., Emery and Trist [1965] and Lawrence and Lorsch [1967]; heterogeneity, also called complexity or diversity, e.g., Lawrence and Lorsch [1967]; and concentration of resources, e.g., Thompson [1967]. There clearly were limits on how many variations on theory-building could be played on this approach to linking organizational structure to an environment characterized as a score on a set of attributes.

Moreover, some organizational sociologists were increasingly dissatisfied with contingency theory's underlying presumption of rationality and choice, epitomized by Thompson's series of propositions [1967], most of which begin with the phrase "under norms of rationality." The political economy or resource dependency approach that developed through the 1970s focused on understanding more clearly the nature of environments and their effects on organizations by analyzing resource flows between a focal organization and the other organizations in its environment in terms of power rather than simply technical rationality. However, it maintained the presumption of strategic choice that undergirded the dominant contingency theories. It was this last presumption that the emerging paradigms challenged, as they moved the level of analysis from the individual organization to the population or field.

II. ORGANIZATIONAL ECOLOGY

Organizational ecology draws upon the natural selection model of biological ecology [Aldrich 1979:27]. It postulates that the capacity of organizations to change is limited both by internal and environmental constraints, and that organizational change over time takes place primarily through selection, that is, the replacement of one organizational form by another. The selection process involves, of course, the "death" or disbanding of organizations of a given form and can be studied in organizational "death rates." Moreover, the founding of organizations and their survival chances are both strongly affected by the numbers of other organizations of the same species (density dependence), as well as by competition with different organizational forms that use the same resources.

The appropriate level of analysis is not the individual organization but populations of organizations. In their 1989 book on organizational ecology, Hannan and Freeman look back over a decade of work in this paradigm and identify three levels of analysis: the demography of organizations (i.e., the study of the organizational analogue of births and deaths—foundings and disbandments—for each organizational form); population ecology (how these "vital rates" in one population are affected by other populations); and community ecology (the study of a set of interacting populations within a bounded environment, a concept that draws on earlier sociological work by Amos Hawley using the concept of ecosystem succession—see for example Pennings [1982] and Astley [1985]. Much of the empirical work

in organizational ecology has concentrated on the first level: the demography of organizational populations, including Argentinean and Irish newspapers [Carroll and Delacroix 1982; Delacroix and Carroll 1983; Carroll 1988]; labor unions [Hannan and Freeman 1977,1984; Hannan 1988]; voluntary service organizations in Toronto [Singh, Hourse, and Tucker 1986; Tucker, Singh, and Meirland 1990]; wineries in California [Delacroix, Swaminathan, and Solt 1989; Delacroix and Solt 1988; Swaminathan and Delacroix 1991; Delacroix and Swaminathan 1991]; trade associations [Aldrich and Staber 1988; Aldrich, Staber, Zimmer, and Beggs 1990]; Manhattan banks and U.S. insurance companies [Hannan, Ranger-Moore and Banaszak-Holl 1990]; and semiconductor firms [Hannan and Freeman 1989:224–38; Freeman 1990]. Like demography itself the field has developed a strong focus on methodological issues, building longitudinal data sets of vital rates and developing sophisticated analytical and modelling techniques.

Fewer studies have attempted to move to the analysis of the relationships across populations of organizations and of community ecology [Singh 1990]. What work there is has focused on competition across forms and has tended to concentrate on comparing specialist and generalist organizations (e.g., Hannan and Freeman's work on labor unions, which looks at births and deaths of craft versus industrial unions). Community ecology has been least developed of the three levels (for an early example of work at this level, see Pennings [1982]).

Much of the recent work in organizational ecology has focused on explaining the patterns revealed by most of the demographic studies of the 1980s, particularly the pattern of density dependence, that is, the fact that rates of founding and dissolution are closely linked to the number of organizations in the population. Founding rates tend to increase over time as the number of organizations increases, but only up to a certain point, when founding rates decline with further increases in density; mortality rates fall with increasing density to a certain point, after which they rise as density increases (for detailed exposition of these concepts and the problems involved in their measurement, see Hannan and Freeman [1989]). Organizational ecologists attribute this density dependence to legitimation processes (the form itself becomes more widely accepted as the population grows) and competition for resources that constrains unlimited growth.

Organizational ecology has drawn severe criticisms within sociology (see, Young [1988]; Meyer [1990]; Perrow [1991]), partly on the grounds that the biological analogy is simply misguided for organizations, which often have no clear "births" (especially when the "organization" is a subsidiary of an existing organization), no genetically programmed life span or clear indicators of "death," and no genetic code that enables researchers unambiguously to identify an "organizational form." It has also been criticized for "black-boxing" organizations, that is, ignoring the differences that exist within a "form" as defined by its products [Young 1988; Meyer 1990]. While those who study individual organizations are willing to give the paradigm credit for highlighting constraints on organizational adaptation and explicating the reasons for organizational inertia, they believe that the basic premise of change by selection rather than adaptation is overstated, has not been seriously tested, and makes the paradigm irrelevant to their concerns [Doz and Prahalad 1992].

The gulf between IB and this particular OT paradigm is widened by the fact that virtually none of the work published in organizational ecology to date deals with populations of interest to those who study IB.[3] Very few of the empirical studies have tackled populations characterized by high levels of foreign direct investment or export-based competition from foreign firms.[4] One exception is the study by Hannan and Freeman of the semiconductor industry in the United States from 1946 to 1984, and it is worth looking more closely at this study be-

cause it reveals some of the reasons why this paradigm does not resonate within the IB field. The growing competitive presence of Japanese firms, even in the time period covered by the study, is not mentioned in Hannan and Freeman's presentation of the data in their 1989 book and rates three sentences in John Freeman's 1990 article on the study: "More recently, however, Japanese firms have entered the world market. Their success is the subject of much consternation in the United States. They are subsidiary in form and, indeed, look much like the American firms that previously lost dominance in the industry to the independent firms" (Freeman 1990:68).

The subsequent analysis separates independent firms from subsidiaries, on the presumption that "subsidiary status should lower the exit rate of semiconductor firms" [68]. The reader is left to assume, however, that Japanese firms have been included in the data set with other, U.S.-based subsidiaries, although that is never made explicit, because of the manner in which the data on the population of semiconductor firms were assembled. Hannan and Freeman built their data set from listings in the *Electronic Buyer's Guide*, and they describe the source and the process as follows: "This is a sourcebook used by industrial purchasers of electronics components that lists various products and the firms manufacturing them . . . We coded a form's entry date as the first year in which it sold any semiconductor device . . . The exist date was the last year it offered any semiconductor for sale . . . We treated a hiatus [in listing] of two or more years as an exit followed by an entry" (Freeman 1990:69).

Presumably foreign firms offering devices through the *Guide* were so coded, because they fit the definition of form, which is customarily defined in this paradigm (in contrast to most work in organizational sociology) by the output—in this case, semiconductors.

However, to those in IB, there are significant differences in "form" between a U.S. firm offering semiconductor devices designed and manufactured in the United States; a U.S. firm selling devices produced in an offshore subsidiary; a foreign firm offering devices designed and manufactured abroad, so that its U.S. "organization" is a sales office; and a U.S. firm that is a "hollow corporation" selling devices manufactured to its design by independent offshore companies. Moreover, one would think that these distinctions would not be solely of parochial concern to a handful of IB specialists. The implications for the "carrying capacity" of the niche over time obviously differ across these three types of organizations. Clearly some investigation of the relationships of these different populations or subpopulations would be highly relevant to the debates over national competitiveness and the effects of foreign direct investment (FDI).

Although work to date in this paradigm has said little that speaks to those concerned in the IB field, neither biological analogy nor population-level theorizing is totally absent from studies of IB. The most recent example is Michael Porter's *The Competitiveness of Nations*, where the underlying framework has striking similarities to the organizational ecology paradigm, although it is highly doubtful if Porter is aware of the existence of the paradigm.

Porter makes an explicit, though admittedly passing, reference to the biological model in the conclusion to the presentation of his theoretical framework in Part I of the book: "An analogy to biological evolution can be drawn. This literature stresses selective survival rates of species confronted with a given environment. In international competition, however, success grows out of the ability of firms to innovate and effective firms sustain advantage for decades in the face of external change. There are subenvironments in different nations (and in cities or regions within nations) that are more favorable ones for innovation. In biological terms, some habitats lead to stronger and more resilient species that are able to roam. They prosper in other habitats compared to those species that have evolved there" (Porter 1990:174).

The parallels between Porter and organizational ecology go beyond the concept of a selection regime; they include the assumption that the appropriate level of analysis is not the individual organization but a more aggregate level (for Porter, this is the industry, which is very close to the prevailing definition of population in the ecological paradigm) and the assumption that inertia is the natural condition of firms.[5]

However, Porter differs in two aspects, neither of which is logically incompatible with the ecological paradigm but which would challenge the prevailing mode of thinking within it. One difference is Porter's assertion that certain environments *select for* the organizational capacity for innovation and change. These are not environments with high variability or fluctuation (the characterization of environments used in Hannan and Freeman [1989 chap. 12] for example, in their discussion of environments that would favor specialist versus generalist strategies), but environments in which complex, mutually reinforcing, and presumably incremental changes in factor conditions, demand conditions, related and supporting industries, and the dominant modes of rivalry and organization create a selection regime that favors innovation. The second difference from the prevailing ecological mode of thought is Porter's view that while organizations are largely determined by their shared environments, they have some ability to select environments in which to immerse themselves—not necessarily in the classic framework of strategic choice (picking businesses) but in the framework of IB (picking geographic locations). Here, Porter remains much more an environmental determinist than most recent writers on MNCs: a firm has only one "choice" for its "home base," or in the words of organizational ecology, its basic selection regime, the environment that will select for its basic attributes and competencies.

Porter's main empirical focus—the mapping of internationally competitive industries and industry clusters in each of eight nations—clearly differs substantially from the approach of organizational ecologists. He does not provide a demography of the firms in the industries he analyses; indeed, with the exception of one chapter, in which he looks closely at four industries (one each from Germany, the United States, Japan, and Italy), the reader interested in knowing what firms operate in the industry will search in vain for systematic information. His extensive comparative mapping of industries, however, opens some potentially fruitful avenues of research in the organizational ecology paradigm, research that might help the paradigm break out of its current overdevelopment of methodology at the expense of theory while simultaneously contributing to a deeper understanding of some key issues in IB.

Even in Porter's own discussion, the concept of an environment that selects for innovation is unclear. It could mean one of two things: that the environment is selecting for an organizational form that produces innovations in products and processes, with relatively little (or relatively slow) change in basic form, *or* that the environment is selecting for organizations that can change their organizational structures and processes over time—Protean organizations characterized by measurable change and evolution (Porter himself tends to imply both characterizations). The first would be easily assimilable into the current organizational ecology framework; the second would challenge its basic assumption of organizational inertia as a generalizable characteristic. Porter has provided a very precise and empirically based identification of industries whose international competitiveness over time suggests strongly that their firms operate in an environment that is selecting for innovation. If we accept, as a working premise, that his identification is valid, then a researcher could take one or more of those industries and examine more closely the organization populations and certain key organizational characteristics, to test which of the previous characterizations of the innovative organization seems to prevail. If even in these industries the re-

searcher can find little evidence of changing organizational structures and processes then it would provide powerful support for the ecologist's presumption of organizational inertia (which ecologists have not shown much interest in testing). This means moving beyond the current definitions of "form" in organizational ecology, which provide only two basic alternatives: the very concrete "yellow pages" common sense definition (a semiconductor firm, a hospital) and the very abstract specialist versus generalist distinction.

The committed organizational ecologist would doubtless find it more interesting to make a different use of Porter's industry mapping: to examine domestic population dynamics in an industry that is strongly competitive internationally, compared to one that is not. Do the population dynamics in an industry change when firms in that industry are able to "roam" into other environments? Or do only the larger organizations take advantage of the potentially expanded niche offered by foreign environments, and therefore births of organizations in the domestic environment in that industry are unaffected (large organizations grow larger, but the domestic niche continues to constrain new formations)? What about the population dynamics in industries subject to high levels of inward foreign direct investment and imports, either directly or indirectly through high levels of FDI and imports in customer or supplier industries? This kind of research would provide a lens on the effects of international competition that is somewhat more finely honed than the aggregate national statistics so often used to assess the impact of MNCs and of international trade.

Let me recapitulate the possible research venues where the methods of organizational ecology and the concerns of IB might fruitfully interact:

a. The analysis of the organizational demographics of an industry characterized by global competition (e.g., the U.S. semiconductor in-

Table 1. Classification of Sub-populations in an Industry

	Locally-owned Firms		Foreign-owned firms	
	Independent Firms	Subsidiaries of diversified firms	Independent Firms	Subsidiaries of diversified firms
Local production only				
Offshore production only				
Domestic and offshore production				

dustry studied by Hannan and Freeman), but deepening the analysis by using finer-grained categories incorporating some of the frameworks of IB. For example, an analysis of the semiconductor industry could use the classification shown in Table 1.

Of course, using twelve categories instead of two (independent versus subsidiary, as in Freeman's analysis) means that the data must be distributed across more categories, with the consequent danger that the numbers in one or more cells become too small for statistical analysis.

b. Analysis of the organizational demographics of an internationally competitive industry that is putatively selecting for innovation, compared to one that is not, looking for changes in the organizational form over time.

c. Population dynamics in an industry that is internationally competitive in one country, compared to those in the same industry in another country of comparable size where the industry is not internationally competitive.

d. Population dynamics in an industry that is internationally competitive in one country, compared to those in another noncompetitive industry in the same country.

e. Population dynamics in industries subject to high levels of inward FDI and imports, either directly or indirectly (through high levels of FDI and imports in customer or supplier industries).

f. Community ecology in a community with hosting significant inward FDI.

Will the prospects for fruitful IB research in the organizational ecology paradigm turn at least some researchers in IB to the methods and concepts of organizational ecology, or will IB simply await the awakening of the ecologists to the possibilities of their field? One of the main attractions to IB researchers of the ecological approach may be an extremely pragmatic one: organizational ecology has demonstrated once again the power and versatility of a theoretically constructed data set. Each organizations ecology data base has yielded multiple publications, and this proliferation of publications has done much to establish the visibility and importance of the paradigm in OT. It is a demonstration that should not be lost on the IB community, even those who reject this particular paradigm.

III. INSTITUTIONAL THEORY

Whereas organizational ecology looked to the natural sciences for concepts, frameworks, and even methodologies, institutional theory is firmly rooted in social theory, both classical and contemporary. In its concern for the influence of the state and its portrayal of organizations as social structures embedded in and shaped by a larger social and cultural system, institutional theory draws on a long tradition of work in sociology, including Parsons, Selnick, and Gouldner. However, as DiMaggio and Powell [1991] point out, the institutional paradigm that has developed in organizational sociology since the late 1970s draws heavily on more recent general theories of the social construction of reality (particularly Berger and Luckman [1966], but also Giddens [1979; 1984]).

Institutional theory analyses the ways in which organizations in shared environments come to adopt patterns that are externally defined as appropriate and are reinforced in their interactions with other organizations. Thus isomorphism—that is, structural similarity across organizations—is a central concept for institutional theory. Isomorphism is a concept that is also encountered frequently in organizational ecology, but there it is not problematic: isomorphism within a population is seen as a natural outcome of selection. For institutional theorists, isomorphism within an organizational field has two basic drivers: it is produced by external "institutional agencies" in the environment that try to shape organizations into appropriate forms, such as regulatory agencies, professional societies, or consulting firms, and by the processes whereby those within organizations come to take certain externally validated structures and processes for granted or to value them as ends in themselves.

The most influential framing of the nature of the environmental pressures toward isomorphism is undoubtedly that of DiMaggio and Powell, who proposed three categories of institutional isomorphism: *coercive* isomorphism, where organizational patterns are imposed on organizations by a more powerful authority, usually the state;

normative isomorphism, where "appropriate" organizational patterns are championed by professional organizations; and *mimetic* isomorphism, where organizations respond to uncertainty by adopting the patterns of other organizations defined as "successful" in that kind of environment [1991:150–54]. More recently, Scott [1987; 1991] identified seven isomorphic processes. Three are analogues of the DiMaggio and Powell categories: "*imposition* of organizational structure" is equivalent to coercive isomorphism, "*acquisition* of organizational structure" to mimetic isomorphism, and "*authorization* of organizational structure" to normative isomorphism. Scott adds the "*inducement* of organizational structure" (where an organization that lacks power to impose patterns on other organizations instead offers inducements such as funding, or certification); "*incorporation*" (where "organizations come to mirror or replicate salient aspects of environmental differentiation in their own structures"); "*bypassing* of organizational structure" (where institutionalized and shared values can substitute for formal structure); and "*imprinting*" (period effects on organization, where an organizational form retains some of the patterns institutionalized at the time its industry was founded). "Imprinting" has been explored at the industry level by Stinchcombe [1965] and at the country level by theorists of late development [Gerschenkron 1962; Dore 1973; Cole 1978] and by some recent work in international management on country effects on the competitiveness of firms [Kogut 1987;1991; 1994].

Three of Scott's seven processes—imposition, authorization, and inducement—emphasize the role of external institutional agencies; while another three (acquisition, incorporation, and bypassing) emphasize the role of those inside the organizations, whose acceptance of certain patterns isomorphic with other organizations in the environment is shaped in sustained interactions with other organizations who share those patterns. The seventh process, imprinting, encompasses elements of both external and internal drivers. As institutional theorists emphasize, the environment is not only external to the organization; the environment also *enters* the organization. As Scott has pointed out: "The beliefs, norms, rules, and understandings are not just 'out there' but additionally 'in here.' Participants, clients, constituents all participate in and are carriers of the culture" [1983:16]. Organizations and environments "interpenetrate," and this interpenetration is the key both to environmental constraints on organizational change and to environmental pressures for the diffusion of organizational structures and processes. For Scott, himself a major contributor to this paradigm, "perhaps the single most important contribution of institutional theorists to the study of organizations is their reconceptualization of the environments of organizations" [1991:165].

Institutional theory, like population ecology, works at a level of analysis above the individual organization, although the units of analysis continue to be organizations. But in this paradigm the appropriate level of analysis for the environment is neither the society as a whole nor the organization-set of any single "focal" organization,[6] but some intermediate level. The term applied to this level varies: "interorganizational field" (proposed by Aldrich [1972]); "interorganizational network" [Benson 1975]; "industry system" [Hirsch 1972]; "organizational field" [DiMaggio and Powell 1983]; and "societal sector" [Scott and Meyer 1983]. Usage in the institutionalization literature seems to be converging on "organizational field," which DiMaggio and Powell define as:

> those organizations that, in the aggregate, constitute a recognized area of institutional life: key suppliers, resource and product consumers, regulatory agencies, and other organizations that produce similar service or products. The virtue of this unit of analysis is that it directs our attention not simply to competing firms, as

does the population approach of Hannan and Freeman [1977], or to networks of organizations that actually interact ... but to the totality of relevant actors. [DiMaggio and Powell 1983:148]

Scott [1991:173] adds to the field a category of organizations that is in fact used by DiMaggio and Powell but not included in their formal definition: "professional or trade associations, and other sources of normative or cognitive influence."

In the last few years empirical research building on the institutional paradigm has blossomed. Some recent publications include an analysis of how internal organizational processes that apparently fit the "garbage-can model" of organizational choice in individual firms can produce virtually identical outcomes in an institutionalized organizational field [Levitt and Nass 1989]; a study of mimetic behavior in corporate philanthropy [Galaskiewiesz and Wasserman 1989]; the institutionalization of financial reporting systems in the U.S. Fortune 200 [Mezias 1990]; change over time in the U.S. radio broadcasting industry in the institutionalized conventions for transactions across sets of organizational actors [Leblebici et al. 1991]; the processes involved in the development of an organizational field in the context of U.S. art museums [DiMaggio 1991]; and a comparison of the structure and interorganizational relationships of large business groups in Japan, Korea, and Taiwan [Orru, Biggart, and Hamilton 1991]. There is, obviously, a very great range in the kinds of structures or practices that can be investigated using this paradigm.

This kind of empirical work has focused the energies of those working in the paradigm on understanding the complex interactions between the strategic behaviors of individual organizations and the environments that shape and are shaped by those behaviors. Scott has emphasized that institutionalization involves both normative and cognitive processes [1991] that limit strategic choice, and instrumental, end-oriented processes that entail strategic choice: those in organizations choose to adopt certain structures and processes that confer legitimacy in the eyes of key external constituencies, because this increases the organization's access to resources, or because use in other organizations is identified with "best practice." Institutionalization theory occupies the middle ground between the presumption of organizational inertia that undergirds the organizational ecology paradigm and the strategic choice assumptions of paradigms that work at the level of individual organizations and below.

As such, it should have considerable appeal for those who study organizations in the field of IB. To date, however, as in population ecology, the investigation of cross-border organizational phenomena has apparently had little appeal for those working in the institutional paradigm. Its literature is as bereft of such work as is organizational ecology. One reason may well be the strong emphasis on the role of the state in the construction of organizational fields, an emphasis that has been embraced by those who feel that the study of business firms in the United States has long been neglectful of the role of government [Fligstein 1990], but one that reinforces the long-standing proclivity of organizational sociology to regard national boundaries as boundaries of the environment. Another reason may be that it has only been recently that those working in the paradigm began to assert its relevance to business organizations. Early expositions differentiated between institutional environments—where institutional processes were essential because of great uncertainty about efficiency criteria, such as schools, universities, public bureaucracies, and social service organizations—and technical environments, where efficiency criteria were clearer and institutional isomorphism less relevant, such as manufacturing firms (e.g., Meyer, Scott and Deal [1983]). More recently, however, this distinction has been modified (e.g., Scott [1991]): all organizations are seen to be subject to both technical and institutional pressures, to varying degrees [1991]. Some

writers have gone farther and insisted that researchers must recognize the institutionalized elements even of the most "technical" aspects of environments, on the grounds that "utility maximization, satisficing, income maximization, profit maximization, risk, power, even interest itself are all institutionally contingent" [Friedland and Alford 1991:245].

Despite the lack of attention to the MNC and other cross-border organizational phenomena in the institutional paradigm, however, there are a number of IB issues in which investigation could provide promising venues for deepening the paradigm. One of the issues that institutional theorists have recently identified as important for future research is that of the effects of competing isomorphic pulls [Scott 1991]. The problem of the standardization versus localization of subsidiary organization is one that seems ideal for such research. As early as 1970, Brooke and Remmers identified what they called the "mirror effect" in the MNC:

> The foreign subsidiary will naturally have a much simpler organization, but it is likely to mirror head office to some extent ... This mirror effect may not be produced by instructions from head office, but by an almost unconscious development along the lines of communication. [1970:40,41]

In the language of institutional theory, the MNC parent organization is the source of strong isomorphic pulls on the structure and processes of the subsidiary. These are very likely to be strongly influenced by the home country organizational field in which the parent is operating. There is considerable literature in IB on the structures and strategies of MNCs based in different societies, from the relatively early work on European MNCs by Franko [1976] and Japanese MNCs by Tsurumi [1976] to the discussion in Bartlett and Ghoshal [1989] of the contrasting modal patterns of European, U.S., and Japanese MNCs. The institutional paradigm provides a way to combine the work on home country effect on MNCs with an analysis of the competing isomorphic pulls on subsidiary structure from the local organizational field and the home country organizational field, mediated through the parent (see Westney [1992] for a more detailed discussion).

The discussion of this issue requires the recognition of a third category of organizational field in addition to the home and host country, one that crosses borders and is composed primarily of large multibusiness MNCs, some of which have multifaceted and complex interrelationships (they are simultaneously customers for some products, suppliers and even partners for others, and competitors for still others) and some of which have no direct relationships but are significant reference points, positions reinforced by (or even generated by) a number of institutional agencies, including multinational consulting firms, leading business schools, and increasingly international business media. This field also exerts isomorphic pulls on parents and subsidiaries that can be orthogonal to the pulls exerted by home and host country fields.

In this view, therefore, MNC subsidiary structure should be understood in terms of competing isomorphic pulls on large complex organizations that participate in several organization fields—and the plural form "organizations" is significant, since the paradigm focuses attention not just on one organization but on the set of organizations that participate in the same field (in this case, in the same array of fields). This is also a useful framework in which to consider the current debate in IB between the integrated network model of the MNC put forward by several of those working most closely with MNC organizational structure and processes over the last decade [Hedlund 1986; Prahalad and Doz 1987; Bartlett and Ghoshal 1989] and the home base model that has long been a staple of theory of the MNC and has been most recently espoused by Michael Porter [1990].[7] The integrated network model posits that a subsidiary can simultaneously be a legitimate "insider" within its local country or regional field, re-

sponding to the pressures of that field, and an "insider" within the MNC, transmitting those local pressures and isomorphic responses that have analogues or potential analogues in other fields to other subunits of the MNC system. Porter's version of the home base argument is an explicit repudiation of the network model: it posits that in any business an MNC can have only one home base, and that it must therefore put its business headquarters in the most advantaged location [Porter 1990:606].

Assuming that the argument is not simply one of different levels of analysis (the integrated network operating at the level of the MNC as a whole, Porter's argument at the level of the individual business or product line), we can translate the debate into institutional terms. Porter's argument, in this framing, has two aspects. One, which Porter clearly articulates, is that a subunit of an MNC will not be a legitimate insider in a country field unless it is isomorphic with autonomous local firms in itself possessing autonomy in strategy formation and technology development [Porter 1990:613]. The other, which requires much more translation to articulate it in institutional terms, is that an organization is isomorphic with its local field of customers, related and supplier industries, and institutionalized modes of organization and competition. It cannot respond to field pulls and institutionalized responses generated elsewhere in the MNC system. Subunits of an MNC will only be driven to isomorphism with pressures from other country fields—to demanding customers, more advanced components suppliers, more effective patterns of rivalry and cooperation—if they lack the capacity to respond autonomously to their own immediate fields because technology development and strategy formation are driven by a subunit in a different, better-endowed field, a "Hollywood."

The integrated network model can be interpreted in two different ways in terms of institutional theory. One is that an organization that operates simultaneously in different organizational fields can transfer and adapt its responses to isomorphic pressures in one of its fields into another. The other is that the third level of organizational field described above—the cross-border field—creates a set of isomorphic pressures that preempt those from country fields and confer legitimacy on organizations that adopt certain structures and processes regardless of whether they conform to local patterns. Indeed they may well change, over time, the institutionalized local patterns. In other words, the institutional paradigm suggests that investigation of the competing explanatory power of the network versus the home base model of the MNC requires the analysis of organizational fields.

The issue of what institutionalized patterns confer "insider" status on MNC subsidiaries and what changes occur over time is of broad and growing interest in the IB field, although the question tends to have been raised more explicitly by those outside the field (e.g., Reich [1991]). Organizational field-focused analysis of the incorporation of MNC subsidiaries into national organizational fields and the comparative analysis of changes in organizational fields over time as cross-investment by MNCs increases would be of great value both to the OT literature and to IB.

A related issue, for which the institutional paradigm can be useful, is that of cross-border learning: when is a pattern developed in one institutional context transferrable to another? Institutional theory complements work at the more microlevel of cross-border organizational learning by directing attention to *patterns* within a field and how institutional agencies within a field legitimate certain patterns. For example, in certain organizational fields in the United States learning from Japan has become a legitimate organizational activity; learning from, say, Italy or Brazil is not. Within Latin America, however, learning from Brazil may well be a more widely accepted practice. Such patterns will clearly affect the ability of MNCs to transfer learning across subsidiaries, although they will not necessarily determine it. Institutional theory would suggest that the analysis how certain patterns of organizational learning are institutionalized and the role of MNCs in that "institutionalization project" would be an important complement to the increasingly important work on the transfer of organizational technologies across borders.

This brings us to a final area where institutionalization theory raises some important issues for IB—but perhaps issues that are somewhat less congenial than those outlined above. The field of IB is itself potentially an "institutional agency" engaged in legitimating certain organizational structures and practices. The concept of the heterarchy or the transnational is simultaneously an ideal type of the MNC in the Weberian sense of an abstract concept (like bureaucracy) that enables researchers to identify the defining characteristics of a particular mode of organization, and an ideal that is interpreted by managers as a portrayal of future best practice. As an applied field, IB cannot escape the fact that its theories will be taken, despite any disclaimers by their originators, as normative theory. And indeed many of those working in IB are strongly motivated to produce normative theory—to improve practice, and to see the best test of a theory as its ability to produce change in organizations [Schein 1987]. While this makes some in the OT community suspicious of the concepts and the research in IB and contributes to the lack of communication across the fields, these aspirations on the part of IB researchers should not ascriptively discredit their work or preclude their ability to analyze their own role in the "structuration" of cross-border organizational fields. Indeed, one of the most challenging prospects for the IB field as a whole is to understand the role it plays in influencing as well as analyzing IB—and the institutional paradigm provides a way to do this in a wider theoretical context.

IV. CONCLUSION

Despite the longstanding lack of fruitful interaction between OT and IB in the past, there are grounds for optimism for the future—at least for those who view the prospect of such interaction with optimism. One can argue that both OT and international management (IM) have been somewhat myopic in the 1980s—although each field would find it easier to identify the shortcomings of the other. One of the puzzles of the 1980s is why, in spite of the fact that the analysis of large-scale organizational change over time has ostensibly moved to the center of the OT paradigms of the 1980s (especially population ecology and institutional theory), little use has been made of these frameworks to address the pressing issues of macro-organizational change in the 1980s: is an organizational revolution underway in the industrialized societies of the world, and if so, what are its main parameters and drivers? If not, why is the perception that firms have been undergoing a period of virtually revolutionary transformation so widespread (for example, Drucker [1988]; Kanter [1989]; Handy [1989])?

In the United States, the 1980s witnessed what has been touted in the business press as an organizational revolution: the "downsizing" of companies not only in their blue-collar workforce but, on an unprecedented scale, in their middle management and staff ranks; internal reorganizations to bring different functions into closer interaction and alignment; and major changes in relationships with suppliers, customers, competitors, and even the state. This last type of change can be interpreted as bringing the environment into the technical core of the firm, through the introduction of shared quality programs, joint technology development, Just-in-Time delivery systems, shared computer and information systems, and a growing resort to cooperative political strategies—a repudiation, at least on the face of it, of the longstanding premise of contingency theory and resource dependency that an organization is driven by a desire for autonomy and a need to shield its technical core from the environment. These changes are being led, at least according to the business press, by major MNCs such as Ford, IBM, Motorola, and Xerox.

In Japan, the business press from the mid-1980s has been filled by articles proclaiming "the death of Japanese management," as the large firms that have embodied Japanese management face changing labor markets, social values, and the challenges of internationalization.[8] These changes are being led by Japan's major MNCs, such as Honda, Sony, and even the firm of one of the gurus of Japanese management, Matsushita. In Europe, the business press features stories about the organizational changes necessitated by the integration of the European market and the move of Eastern Europe and Russia to market-based economies. And there too the large MNCs are in the vanguard of developments (see for example the discussion of European integration as being pushed primarily by a coalition of Europe-based MNC managers and Brussels-based "Eurocrats"; c.f. Sandholz and Zysman [1989]; Thimm [1989]). Yet macro-organization theorists have been very slow to address the questions of how to assess more rigorously the scale and dimensions of these "organizational revolutions," to analyze their similarities and differences across societies and regions, and to understand their causal dynamics and the role played by MNCs and cross-border organizational phenomena. The analysis of cross-border organizational phenomena in populations of organizations and organizational fields will become inescapable in OT in the coming decade.

The myopia in the field of IB was of a different sort. The growing importance of cross-border phenomena in the 1980s raised a serious challenge to the intellectual and institutional bases of the field [Dunning 1988]. As internationalization became increasingly relevant to what had been domestic and parochial firms and to domestically-oriented business school fields alike, IB began to lose its exclusive claim to the analysis of cross-border business. Scholars in the IB field were quicker to recognize the growing impact of the international on the domestic than the growing impact of the domestic on the international. The exploding literature in the late 1980s on country competitiveness was largely driven from outside IB, from political economy (e.g., Reich [1989]), from strategy (e.g., Porter [1990]), and from economics (e.g., Krugman [1991]). Perhaps in reaction to the earliest days of the field, when IB was seen primarily as a field concerned with understanding foreign business environments, those working on strategy and organization in IB concentrated from the mid-1970s and through the 1980s on the emergent properties of MNC networks and the model of the MNC as transcending the constraints of any single country environment, including its own home country.

Only recently have scholars in the field[9] recognized that a theory-driven, detailed institutional comparative analysis of business environments will be necessary to address some of the key organizational questions in the field, such as: are increasingly international environments producing convergent models of MNC organization, or are increasingly competition-conscious governments and differentiated regional agglomerations (or industrial districts) producing greater impediments to MNC convergence? Are MNCs able to transcend their home country environments or will they be increasingly affected by the constraints of home country environments? What levels of diversity are sustainable across firms within a global business and across businesses within international firms?

In the 1990s, both OT and IB will be drawn to increasingly detailed comparative analysis of the interactions of organizations and environments, work that will require considerable deepening of existing paradigms within each field and perhaps the development of new paradigms. Both fields will be the poorer if more attempts to build bridges between them are not made.

NOTES

1. The "integration-differentiation" framework of Lawrence and Lorsch has been reconstructed as "pressures for global integration" versus "pressures for local responsiveness" in the literature on multinational strategy (Bartlett 1986; Prahalad and Doz 1987) or "global-multidomestic" strategies. For recent use of this kind of framework to examine the "fit" between environment or strategies for coping with the environment and organizational structure; see for example Roth, Schweiger, and Morrison (1991); Martinez and Jarillo (1991).

2. By "applied field" I mean any field that focuses on one institutional sphere and is closely identified with understanding and trying to solve problems in that sphere. By this definition, IB is an "applied field" (like urban development, industrial sociology, or corporate strategy); ironically, "applied economics" is not.

3. One paper by a noted organizational ecologist, Jacques Delacroix, provides an interesting beginning in the application of the paradigm to IB issues: it takes as the organizational form the subsidiary of U.S. manufacturing companies, and looks at their formation and disbanding in Europe from 1903 to 1974 (Delacroix 1992).

4. For a recent move in this direction, however, see Delacroix (1992).

5. Porter's description of the factors behind organizational inertia parallels the discussion in Hannan and Freeman (1977): "Firms would rather not change. Particularly in a successful firm, powerful forces work against modifying strategy. Past approaches become institutionalized in procedures and management controls. Specialized facilities are created. Personnel are trained in one mode of behavior. Self-selection attracts new employees who believe in the existing ways of doing things and are particularly suited to implementing them . . . Information that would challenge current approaches is screened out or dismissed. Individuals who challenge established wisdom are expelled or isolated. As an organization matures, its need for stability and security seems to rise . . . The difficulty of innovation means that it is often 'outsiders' to the firm, the industry, the established social structure, or based in other nations, that are the catalysts for innovation . . . Whether the role of outsider can be played by firms *within* the nation instead of those from other nations will

have much to do with whether a nation's indus-try will advance" (Porter 1990:580–581). Note that this last sentence, with its implicit assump-tion that the "outsiders" are *firms*, not individu-als brought in to change existing firms, fits with the selection approach of organizational ecology.

6. William Evan proposed in the mid-1960s the concept of the "organization-set," an ana-logue of the "role-set" in social psychology, to describe the organization's "interactions with the network of organizations in its environment" (1971:178).

7. Porter's home base model has much in common—although unacknowledged by Porter

himself—with the older characterization of the MNC as exploiting the location advantages of its home country in Ray Vernon's concept of the MNC and the product life cycle and in Dunning's eclectic theory of the MNC.

8. See for example the special issue of *Pure-jidento*, a leading Japanese business journal, in April 1987, titled, "'Nihonteki Keiei' no Hokai," "The Collapse of Japanese-style Man-agement."

9. See for example recent work by Bruce Kogut, including Kogut (1987) and his 1994 edited volume on *Country Competitiveness and the Organisation of Work*.

■ ■ ■

The Implications of Information Technology for Coordination and Communication in Multinational Corporations
William G. Egelhoff

The modern MNC is one of the most complex forms of organization to manage and coordinate. Generally encompassing wide product, geographic, and cultural dif-ferences, the MNC faces information-pro-cessing and communication requirements that challenge existing organizational capa-bilities. Neither is this situation a static one. The new strategies and organizational de-signs being discussed by MNC theorists [Hedlund 1986,1993; Prahalad and Doz 1987; Bartlett and Ghoshal 1989] and in-creasingly experimented with by MNCs would appear to require different and often difficult to achieve information-processing capabilities. An important question is where and how the new ITs that have primarily emerged over the past decade, might mod-ify and expand the existing information-processing capabilities of MNCs. IT can be broadly thought of as a combination of computer and telecommunications tech-nologies.

Much of the current literature address-ing this issue tends to be more visionary than conceptually grounded or empirically

based [McFarland 1984; Drucker 1988; Keen 1987]. It generally emphasizes the technological possibilities, while paying less attention to organizational constraints and limitations. It also tends to suggest widely conceived solutions or opportunities, with-out linking these to the specific problems MNCs face or the specific competitive ad-vantages to be gained. This literature has been useful in identifying the broad poten-tial of IT, but less useful in responding to the specific needs of MNCs.

The present paper seeks to address some of these shortcomings by first propos-ing and then illustrating a conceptual framework that facilitates linking IT poten-tials to specific MNC opportunities and needs. It will do this by building off of an existing information-processing model of MNCs, which presently is structural and or-ganizational in nature and contains little IT content. By better integrating IT potential with existing MNC information-processing capacities and requirements, it is hoped that the proposed framework will help to guide empirical research on where and how IT can usefully modify the existing information-processing capabilities of MNCs and relax some of the constraints MNCs currently encounter when they attempt to implement the new global and transnational strategies.

REVIEW OF RELEVANT ORGANIZATIONAL INFORMATION-PROCESSING THEORY AND IT THEORY

Since a thorough review of the two literatures that support the proposed framework would exceed the limits of this paper, the present discussion will be confined to material of direct interest. The reader will be referred to additional sources for a more complete coverage of the underlying material.

An Information-Processing Perspective of MNCs

Recently, I proposed and outlined in some detail a specific information-processing model of MNCs. The model and its conceptual foundation will be briefly described here and then combined with IT concepts in the next section to create the proposed framework. [Egelhoff, 1991] The model rests on a foundation of concepts and arguments put forth by Thompson [1967], Galbraith [1973;1977], Tushman and Nadler [1978], and Egelhoff [1988]. It is a more specific operationalization of the general information-processing approach to organizational design described by Galbraith [1973]

and Tushman and Nadler [1978] which is shown in Figure 1. The general information-processing approach says that strategic and environmental conditions surrounding an organization create information-processing requirements between subunits of the organization and between subunits and specific parts of the environment. Features of an organization's design (e.g., its structure, degree of centralization, planning systems, and control mechanisms) influence the kind and degree of information-processing capacity the organization can use to address these requirements. Organizational effectiveness is a function of the quality of fit between an organization's information-processing capacities and the information-processing requirements it faces.

I argue that information-processing needs to be measured along multiple dimensions in order to evaluate meaningfully fit between information-processing capacities and requirements. The requisite variety and complexity of MNC strategy and organizational design demanded by global competition [Nohria and Ghoshal 1990] needs to be meaningfully represented by the information-processing framework, if this approach is to be useful. While logical and appealing, the information-processing approach can frequently be criticized for employing operational models that are too simple or underdefined for the phenomena they seek to represent. I also suggest four

Figure 1. The General Information-Processing Approach to Organizational Design

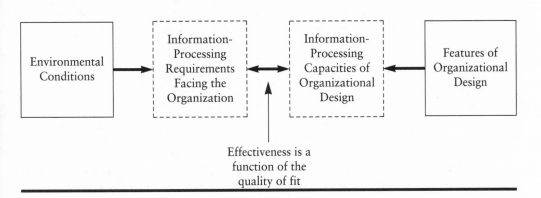

Effectiveness is a function of the quality of fit

Figure 2. The Process Dimensions of MNC Information Processing

		Interdependency between Parties to an Information-Processing Event	
		Sequential	Reciprocal
Routinism of an Information-Processing Event	Routine	**Routine-sequential information processing** Example: Deciding on a routine change in the price of a product	**Routine-reciprocal information processing** Example: Deciding how to handle an expatriate manager's request for reassignment back to the parent company
	Nonroutine	**Nonroutine-sequential Information processing** Example: Exploring the possibility of selling a customer products not available in the local subsidiary, but available in another subsidiary	**Nonroutine-reciprocal information processing** Example: Deciding on the long-range level of R&D support for a major product line

dimensions or types of information processing that are appropriate at the macro level of MNCs. These are shown in Figure 2, along with an example of each type of information-processing.

Routine information processing deals with inputs that are frequent and homogeneous. It transforms them under conditions of high certainty and assumes that goals and means-ends relationships are well known. Rules and programs (including organizational policies, SOPs, and standard methods) are examples of information-processing mechanisms that provide routine information-processing capacity. Nonroutine information processing deals with inputs that are either unique or infrequent and heterogeneous. It transforms them under varying degrees of uncertainty about goals and/or means-ends relationships. An example of a nonroutine, information-processing mechanism is hierarchical referral (processing information up and down the chain of command).

The distinction between sequential and reciprocal information processing reflects the kind of interdependency that exists between the parties to an information-processing event. This distinction is based on Thompson's [1967] topology of the three different forms of interdependence that can exist between organizational subunits (pooled, sequential, and reciprocal). Information processing is sequential to the extent that information flows in a predetermined direction across parties to an information-processing event. Information processing is reciprocal to the extent that information flows back and forth between parties in a kind of give-and-take manner that has not been previously determined. It is important to realize that the routinism and interdependency axes are Gutman-like scales. Thus, mechanisms capable of providing nonroutine information processing can also provide routine information processing, but usually at a lower volume and/or at a greater cost than mechanisms specifically designed to provide routine information processing.

Figure 3 shows how a variety of frequently used information-processing mechanisms can be measured in terms of the kind and degree of information-processing capacity each provides. The development and logic underlying this measurement are described in more detail [Egelhoff 1991]. Figure 3 only contains two clear references

Figure 3. The Capacities of Information-Processing Mechanisms

	Sequential Information-Processing Capacity		Reciprocal Information-Processing Capacity
Routine Information-Processing Capacity	Rules & programs (H) Single-cycle planning (H) Post-action control (H) Stand-alone computer systems (H)		Integrated database computer systems (H)
	Vertical information systems: assistants, clerical staff, & planning staff (M)	Steering control (M) Multi-cycle, interactive planning systems (M)	
Nonroutine information-Processing Capacity	Hierarchical referral (L)		Horizontal information systems: Direct contact (L) Task forces (M) Teams (M) Integrating roles (L) Matrix designs (M)

Note: The letters in parentheses indicate relative volumes of information-processing capacity H = High, M = Medium, L = Low.

to IT. Stand-alone computer systems are shown as providing high volumes of routine—sequential, information-processing capacity (as is required by a host of routine information-processing applications, such as payroll processing). Integrated database computer systems are shown as providing high volumes of routine-reciprocal, information-processing capacity (as is required by such applications as managing interdependent inventories across multiple locations).

It is likely that additional IT information-processing mechanisms that are potentially important to information processing in MNCs (such as E-mail, EDI-electronic document interchange, teleconferencing, video conferencing) can also be placed within this figure and thereby matched to certain kinds of information processing requirements. They might also interact with some of the organizational, information-processing mechanisms shown in Figure 3 and modify or enhance the present information-processing capacity of a mechanism. This is not the thrust of the present paper, but it describes what is meant by in-

tegrating organizational and IT information-processing mechanisms.

Some Relevant IT Concepts

The new information technologies are potentially very important to MNC strategy and MNC organizational design. They tease the mind with new sources of competitive advantage, ranging from location-independent work [Keen 1991] to offering totally new information services to customers. The former allows MNCs to exploit more fully differences in factor costs and keep up with changes in comparative advantage around the world. The latter expands opportunities for differentiating products and services and facilitates the evolution of a firm from competing with firm-specific advantages based in a single country (often the parent country) to competing with more globally based firm-specific advantages [Kogut 1985].

In an interesting assessment of the potential for IT in transnational organizations, Keen [1991:8] states that, "the degree of flexibility in the IT base [of a firm] will increasingly determine the flexibility of the organizational base." If this is true, it is also important to know where and in what manner the existing organizational base of an MNC can be most readily modified by changes in the IT base. It is the ability to integrate the more rapidly developing IT base with the more elaborated and entrenched organizational base in MNCs and focus both on overcoming critical problems facing the firm that will determine how important the IT base is to a company. Developing a conceptual framework for observing this is the thrust of the present paper.

There is relatively little empirical research that links IT to strategy and organizational design concerns in MNCs. Chismar and Chidambaram [1992] studied the association of telecommunications usage with type of organizational structure and degree of centralization in MNCs. They found no association with organizational structure, but there was some evidence that firms might be using telecommunications to increase centralization of decision making. Keen [1991] conducted extensive unstructured interviews in MNCs and reports that management's concerns regarding IT, strategy, and organizational design are wide-ranging and only weakly understood or articulated. Manheim [1992] also conducted unstructured interviews in 60 MNCs, and he concludes that three major foci are emerging that require increased cross-functional coordination in firms: the order cycle, the product development cycle, and customer relationship management. He suggests that IT will be critical to providing this coordination and that the cutting edge of the field lies with T/TSS (task/team support systems). Roche [1992] states that a review of the IT literature reveals that it has little to say about the subject of HQ-subsidiary and subsidiary-subsidiary coordination.

Despite the shortage of empirical research on IT in MNCs, interesting work has been developing in the broader IT field that has organizational content. IT has been linked to organizational interdependencies [Rockart and Short 1989], different communication demands in R&D settings [Allen and Hauptman 1987], centralization [Keen 1987], and levels of innovation in R&D communities [Rice and Love 1987]. To a large extent, this work is characterized by a lack of underlying theory that might serve to integrate it with itself or with other non-IT organizational research. In fact, after reviewing the field, Steinfield and Fulk [1987] pointed out that most empirical IT research to date has proceeded inductively and that there is a shortage of theory to guide IT research. Huber [1990] attempted to address this void by developing a range of IT hypotheses based on a variety of logics from organization theory. Yet, the eclecticism of such an approach is a major shortcoming, and it hinders integrating IT research into more powerful theories about organizations.

The present paper argues for a different approach, that of directly extending an existing theory about organizations to encompass IT concepts. To facilitate this extension and interface with IT, the proposed framework borrows from the recent work of Keen [1991], who identifies the "range" and "reach" of an IT base or platform as useful conceptual dimensions for defining what the IT platform can do for information processing in an organization. Reach refers to the locations that the IT platform can link, while range refers to the kinds of information (written, verbal, images) that can be "directly and automatically shared across systems and services" [39]. Reach is especially important and often difficult to attain in MNCs, where physical and cultural distances between locations tend to be greater than in other organizations. Range is also an important notion, because at the macro level of MNCs information processing is multidimensional and one type of information processing can't generally substitute for another. The next section will integrate these concepts with some of those already discussed to create the proposed conceptual framework.

A CONCEPTUAL FRAMEWORK FOR EVALUATING THE IMPACT OF IT ON INFORMATION PROCESSING IN MNCS

Figure 4 shows the proposed framework for defining and measuring the range and reach of an MNCs IT platform. Reach is defined in terms of four different levels of integration that commonly characterize MNC activities. The first is where activities are primarily integrated at the level of each country or foreign subsidiary. If a computer and telecommunications system were designed to integrate locations within a single country or foreign subsidiary, we would say the reach of the IT platform is at the national unit level. Some MNCs attempt to integrate many activities at a regional level (e.g., Europe), and this requires an IT platform with a regional reach. Finally, MNCs can attempt to integrate activities at a global level. As Figure 4 indicates, this can be done (1) globally within each product division, but not across product divisions, or (2) globally across all locations in a company, even across those in different product divisions. Integrating activities at the global product division level means a company could have separate, incompatible IT platforms for each product division. Integrating at the global corporation level, on the other hand, means the company needs a single, fully compatible IT platform.

Range in the proposed framework is defined in terms of the four types of information processing previously described under the MNC information-processing model. The order shown does not represent a continuum, as it does for the reach dimension. Rather, IT platforms can conceivably provide varying degrees of reach for each of the four types of information processing. This means that reach will have to be described separately for each of the types of information processing included in the range of an IT platform.

This conceptualization of the range of an IT platform differs significantly from that employed by Keen [1991]. He tends to describe the range of a platform in terms of the modes of communication provided by the platform (written, verbal, images) or in terms of the types of IT technologies employed (telephone, FAX, E-mail). While both are straightforward ways of defining an IT platform, neither can be readily related to the differing strategic and environmental conditions with which organizations must cope. It is the argument of this paper that IT technologies must first be linked to organizational, information-processing capacities, which can then be linked to information-processing require-

Figure 4. Range and Reach of MNC's IT Platform

	Reach			
Range	National Unit	Region	Global Product Division	Global Corporation
Routine–sequential information processing				
Routine–reciprocal information processing				
Nonroutine–sequential information processing				
Nonroutine–reciprocal information processing				

ments stemming from specific strategic and environmental conditions. This approach places all information processing explicitly within the context of an organization.

The four types of information processing used to define range in Figure 4 can be readily and meaningfully used to measure both the information-processing requirements that emanate from MNC strategy and the information-processing capacities that are associated with MNC organizational design [Egelhoff 1991]. If the information-processing capabilities of an IT platform can be measured with the same framework, it should facilitate linking these capabilities to the strategy and organizational design of an MNC.

The following section will attempt a kind of preliminary test of the utility and integrative powers of the proposed framework. It will use the framework to describe the information-processing implications of a number of the primary IT technologies and applications that can be found in MNCs today.

EXAMPLES OF IT IN MNCS

This section illustrates how the proposed framework can be used to measure and understand a variety of IT technologies and applications in MNCs. It also discusses where IT technologies and applications are in need of change to fit changes in MNC strategy and organizational design. In Figure 5, a

Figure 5. Some Applications of IT in MNCs

Range	Reach			
	National Unit	Region	Global Product Division	Global Corporation
Routine–sequential information processing				
Manufacturing scheduling	x ⟶			
Sales order analysis	x ⟶			
Financial reporting				x
Routine–reciprocal information processing				
Global CAD			x	
Nonroutine–sequential information processing				
E-mail	x ⟶⟶⟶⟶⟶⟶⟶⟶⟶⟶⟶⟶			⟶
Fax				x
Nonroutine–reciprocal information processing				
New product development	x ⟶⟶⟶⟶⟶⟶⟶		⟶	

Note: "X" represents current reach of IT platform supporting an application. The arrow shows how reach will be required to change to support the application in the future, as a result of changes in strategy.

number of specific examples of IT technologies and applications in MNCs are positioned on the framework shown in Figure 4. They include manufacturing scheduling, sales order analysis, financial reporting, global CAD (computer aided design), E-mail, Fax, and new product development. This set of technologies and applications is based on examples of IT found during recent exploratory research in seven U.S. MNCs by the author and on other recently reported applications of IT in MNCs. It overlaps heavily with IT areas identified by Manheim [1992] and Roche [1992] as most important to MNCs.

Routine-Sequential Information Processing

The most prevalent examples of IT applications requiring largely routine-sequential information processing appear to be manufacturing scheduling, sales order analysis, and financial reporting. Manufacturing scheduling and sales order analysis today are frequently done at the subsidiary or national unit level, but with the advent of European integration, many MNCs are planning to extend the reach of the IT platform supporting these activities to the regional level. The information-processing capacity that currently handles these requirements is largely provided by traditional computer systems and software packages that often vary from one subsidiary to the next within a company.

Some MNCs, such as globally oriented chemical companies, have pursued regionally integrated marketing or manufacturing strategies for some time. In this case, their IT platforms may have been originally created with regional reach, which implies standard or compatible hardware and software within a region. The majority of MNCs, however, probably have yet to extend the reach of such systems to the regional level.

Financial reporting is an application that also requires largely routine-sequential information processing, but appears already to be integrated electronically at the global corporate level in most MNCs. A good description of Merck's move to a global financial reporting system can be found in Roche [1992:99]. Firms that don't have global reach in their IT platform for financial reporting systems appear to be moving in this direction. This requires common software, compatible equipment, and communications for electronic data exchange across all of the primary financial subunits in a company.

All of the above applications require routine-sequential information processing from the IT platform. That is, the information inputs are well understood and repetitive, and processing tends to take place in a prescribed, sequential manner. The primary problems associated with extending reach to the regional level seem to include incompatibilities between existing national unit systems and concern over losing local responsiveness. It is likely that moving the reach of many routine-sequential, information-processing systems from the national unit to the regional level will significantly shift power and influence from the former to the latter. In one large MNC that had recently installed a regional level sales and bid analysis system, the French sales manager said he wasn't getting any new information from it. Yet, it was apparent that European regional management would now be able to compare bids and sales (including margins and the ratio of successful bids) across all subsidiaries in Europe. A later section will discuss one of these applications, manufacturing scheduling, in much greater detail.

Routine-Reciprocal Information Processing

Global CAD (computer aided design) is provided as an example of an application that largely requires routine-reciprocal information processing. For example, in semiconductor firms, circuit designers around the world often share common software design tools and are interconnected by satellite. This allows them to work interactively on designs. A circuit design can be worked on in the United States, sent electronically to Japan where it is combined with another design, sent electronically back to the U.S.

where the completed design is tested by computer simulation, before being sent electronically to Europe for manufacturing. Different activities can be done at various locations to take advantage of special skills and lower factor costs. Information inputs, however, must be codified and standardized so that their integration can follow a routine process. Interdependency between the design locations can be either reciprocal or sequential, but the described IT platform is capable of handling reciprocal interdependency.

The above is a good example of location-independent work [Keen 1991], which is possible because the supporting IT platform has global reach and is capable of providing reciprocal information processing. Keen [1991] describes a similar, but slightly different example. A number of U.S. insurance companies have moved certain back office operations, such as claims processing, to Ireland. The advantage is lower factor costs, represented by a large, well-trained pool of relatively inexpensive labor. Data is gathered in the United States, transferred electronically to Ireland every night (when communication costs are low), worked on in Ireland, and transferred electronically back to the United States the following night. As with CAD, the information processing here is routine. It is, however, largely sequential, while the global CAD systems tend to have more reciprocal capability. The former is naturally less expensive to implement than the latter. Thus, IT technologies can readily support a variety of location-independent work, involving either sequential or reciprocal interdependencies between locations. The nature of the information processing, however, must be routine. That is, the information inputs must be well understood and repetitive.

Nonroutine-Sequential Information Processing

Existing IT applications involving non-routine information processing are more difficult to identify, simply because they are nonroutine. E-mail and fax are not applica-tions, but examples of IT technologies that largely provide nonroutine-sequential information processing in MNCs. Fax can readily transfer low volumes of information globally across a company, or even between companies, since it is a globally compatible system defined by international telecommunications standards and agreements.

E-mail can transfer higher volumes of information, but today largely operates within national units. In many MNCs, however, it is being extended into a global compatible system. There is some evidence that E-mail may on occasions provide reciprocal information processing between parties [Rice and Love 1987], although international time differences probably constrain this to information processing within a region. Between regions, E-mail provides largely sequential information processing.

Nonroutine-Reciprocal Information Processing

New product development emerged as an application undergoing rapid change in most of the sample companies. Still largely conducted at the national unit level, IT generally plays only a modest role in managing and coordinating new product development activities. Task forces, teams, integrating roles, and large amounts of direct contact between interdependent individuals are the primary information-processing mechanisms used to provide the high levels of nonroutine-reciprocal information processing required to support innovation and new product development. Co-locating product development activities facilitates lots of face-to-face meetings. Increasingly, however, R&D is being globally dispersed in many MNCs. This hinders face-to-face meetings and greatly increases the cost of providing the existing forms of nonroutine-reciprocal information processing between interdependent activities (largely through increased business travel). There would appear to be considerable opportunity here to use IT technologies to provide significant levels of nonroutine-reciprocal information processing between activities in order to reduce the firm's reliance on costly business travel and other non-IT information-processing mechanisms. This requires the IT platform to extend its range to include significant nonroutine-reciprocal information-processing capacity with a reach that can be extended to the global product division level. Video conferencing appears to hold the most promise for providing the kind of rich, nonroutine-reciprocal, information processing that this activity requires, but to date there is little evidence of it being used for this purpose. Other applications in MNCs that currently require large amounts of conventionally provided nonroutine-reciprocal, information-processing capacity are strategic planning and crisis management.

The next two sections will discuss in more detail the application of IT to the manufacturing scheduling problem and the new product development problem. By narrowing our focus to specific problems and discussing how the IT platform needs to be modified to address them, the reader should get a better understanding of how the proposed framework might be used.

IT AND THE MANUFACTURING SCHEDULING PROBLEM

Optimizing manufacturing on a European rather than a national basis is a problem (or opportunity) that currently faces many U.S. MNCs. It is obviously encouraged by the Europe 1992 initiatives, that have removed barriers to the free flow of goods and services in the region. The problems and opportunities associated with coordinating international manufacturing have been discussed elsewhere [Flaherty 1986; Greene 1989]. The purpose of this section is to link requirements for such coordination to the IT platform.

Three of the author's sample firms still had largely national or local manufacturing strategies. That is, each major country had its own manufacturing, which supplied most of its sales requirements. All three were now shifting to more of a regional

manufacturing strategy in order to benefit from better economies of scale and in some cases lower factor costs. We will ignore the strategic planning problem of deciding which plants to phase out, which ones to expand, and which products to make in a plant, since IT appeared to be playing little if any role in this highly political process. These decisions required large amounts of nonroutine-reciprocal information processing between local subsidiary managements and parent HQ staffs and managements. This was largely being met by lots of face-to-face meetings or direct contact, special task forces and project teams, and the establishment of special integrating roles and staffs. These are the organizational, information-processing mechanisms shown in the lower right-hand corner of Figure 3. In all three cases, the companies were either creating or strengthening the role of a European regional HQ (located in Europe). This structural change greatly increases the nonroutine-reciprocal information-processing capacity that can be brought to bear on these problems, since it moves the key decisions and decision makers geographically and organizationally closer together.

The problem to be considered here, however, is how to schedule and otherwise manage an integrated European manufacturing circuit, once it is established. To date, this information-processing requirement has been separately met within each national subsidiary. Order entry systems, logistics systems (purchasing, supply, transportation), and manufacturing scheduling systems all tend to be compatible and designed to operate and exchange information at the national level. Financial accounting systems tend to be more standardized across subsidiaries, but manufacturing cost accounting systems may be different. Each subsidiary would have its own computers, software, and telecommunications system. Generally, they will vary from subsidiary to subsidiary. There are good reasons for this. Prior to 1992, prices of equipment and software vary considerably across Europe, there are local pressures to deal with certain suppliers, and a supplier's level of service can vary widely from country to country.

Looking back at Figure 4, it is apparent that the part of the IT platform which supports manufacturing scheduling in these three companies is largely providing routine-sequential information processing at the national unit level. It consists of local computers, software, and telecommunications systems, perhaps with some local EDI (electronic document interchange with selected local suppliers and/or customers). As a result of going from a national to a regional manufacturing strategy, these companies now want to extend the reach of their IT platforms from the national unit level to the regional level for manufacturing scheduling. In general, they do not want to alter the range of the IT platform, since routine-sequential information processing is perceived to be the most economical way to handle manufacturing scheduling.

While extending the reach of the existing IT platform one level may seem a fairly straightforward task, two kinds of problems revealed themselves during the interviews. The first has already been alluded to and consists of the incompatibilities of the existing national level systems. Here the cost of extending the reach is directly related to the nature and extent of the incompatibilities. Changing equipment and software have fairly identifiable capital and training costs. To what extent and at what cost underlying systems and processes might have to change is more difficult to estimate. For example, parts numbers may differ, material flow tracking systems may differ. When incompatibilities are too great or costly to be overcome (especially in the short run), it appears that information may have to be "portaged" (manually or otherwise transferred) from one part of the IT platform to another.

The second type of problem encountered is more subtle and deeply embedded in the work flows of the organization. It can best be illustrated with the following hypothetical example. Assume that the reach of the IT platform has been successfully extended to the regional level for manufacturing scheduling. Sales and inventory information are electronically conveyed to a central computer, which produces monthly manufacturing schedules. These schedules optimize economies of scale and factor costs across the European manufacturing circuit.

Now, however, a problem develops. It seems that the large German subsidiary had developed flexible ordering arrangements with certain large customers. These customers place regular monthly orders, but while the customer's product is still being run on the manufacturing line, the German plant calls the customer to see if it wants to adjust the order quantity. This last-minute information processing between supplier and customer saves setup costs for the German plant and leaves the customer with minimal raw material inventories. The German subsidiary developed this practice as several of its most important customers moved toward just-in-time manufacturing. Under the old decentralized strategy, no one outside of the German subsidiary was aware of this practice or was impacted by it. In fact, when the designers of the new European-wide manufacturing scheduling system talked to the systems analysts in Germany, the latter were not even aware that this practice had evolved. There was nothing about it in the written policies and procedures. Now the sales and manufacturing managers in Germany are saying that this kind of flexibility in servicing the customer's needs is critical to retaining the large customer business (which only exists in Germany). Other European subsidiaries have evolved different local adaptations to fit better the peculiarities of their markets, all of which hinder successfully extending the IT platform to the regional level for manufacturing scheduling.

The information systems people in the company may reply that there is no problem in extending the IT platform to the regional level, but that the manufacturing people should "get their act together." This reply, however, illustrates a problem the present paper is attempting to address. The IT platform should not be considered as successfully extended until it is supplying the kind of information processing required by the task. This view requires that IT be integrated with the organizational—as opposed to the technical—information-processing requirements of a firm. It also implies that modifying the IT platform in a firm cannot be solely or even primarily the responsibility of the information systems people.

This example illustrates a kind of problem that will be very common as MNCs attempt to move from a number of national strategies to a European strategy. It is useful to view this problem more conceptually. When an MNC largely pursues national strategies, there tends to be relatively loose coupling [Weick 1976] or low interdependency between foreign subsidiaries. Little communication or information processing across subsidiaries is required. This loose coupling between subsidiaries facilitates the development of a tight coupling between each subsidiary and its local national environment (just as we saw between the German plant and its large customers). Such tight coupling with the local environment is generally regarded as the primary advantage of having a collection of different national strategies. International scholars would say this MNC has a multidomestic or multinational strategy [Bartlett and Ghoshal 1989] and refer to the advantage of tight coupling with the national environment as local adaptation [Prahalad and Doz 1987].

The new European regional strategy, however, calls for much tighter coupling between the European subsidiaries. As in the above example, this tight coupling between subsidiaries can conflict with the local adaptation that already exists in the national subsidiaries. Bartlett and Ghoshal [1989] argue that increasingly successful transnationals will need to achieve a tight coupling simultaneously between subsidiaries and within local environments. If this is true, extending the reach of national IT platforms to the regional level must largely be accomplished without destroying the local flexibilities of the present platforms. The above example is, at its core, an information-processing problem, and there is probably an information-processing solution to it. The temptation in most organizations, however, is going to be for the parent or regional HQ to tell the subsidiaries that they must give up some local flexibilities in order to support regional optimization. This is especially true if problems surface after the IT platform has already been extended, as in the above example.

In order to address the above problem of retaining local flexibilities while realizing regional efficiencies as the reach of the IT platform is extended, MNCs are going to have to tackle more complex information-processing problems than they are probably envisioning. Perhaps a portion of the German plant's capacity could be reserved for certain customer orders and left out of the European scheduling system. Or, perhaps, the German plant still adapts to local customer changes, verbally informs the European HQ of these changes, and the HQ uses some simple heuristic to manually adjust manufacturing schedules for the current period to accommodate the change. Notice that this latter approach actually extended the range—not of the IT platform, but of the wider, total, information-processing platform supporting manufacturing scheduling—to include a small amount of routine-reciprocal information processing between the German subsidiary and the regional HQ. This is a more costly form of information processing, but it may be justified by the value of the local flexibility it provides.

A recommendation that seems to follow from this example is that extending the IT platform to the regional level in MNCs should be done within the wider context of modifying and extending the total information-processing platform, and this requires the heavy participation of subsidiary and HQ people from all of the affected functional areas. If this design task itself exceeds the available information-processing capacities of the organization, it may be wiser to extend the IT platform more incrementally and, in the short run, fill in the gaps with other forms of information processing, even if they are more costly. This option is more feasible when IT is organizationally managed as a part of the wider, organizational, information-processing context.

IT and the Problem of Coordinating Dispersed R&D Efforts

A second important problem for IT that emerged from the exploratory research interviews is how to coordinate an MNC's globally dispersed R&D activities. Increasingly there is a trend toward replacing differing local products with global products, where there is a much higher level of common technology, even though the end products may appear different. This requires new product development to be coordinated across different subsidiaries and different R&D sites. Even where products have been centrally developed (generally in the parent country) and sold as relatively standardized products around the world (e.g., pharmaceuticals), there is a growing diffusion of R&D activities around the world. Many U.S. MNCs attempt to have a major R&D site in Europe and Japan, as well as in the United States. Two of the sample companies had recently established Japanese R&D sites, and the others were significantly growing their Japanese R&D. All of the companies had significant European R&D efforts and several were rapidly expanding them. The primary motivation for this seems to be to exploit better strengths or abilities that have developed at a certain site or in a particular country and to develop products in and for lead markets (which may not be the parent country).

The trend toward global R&D has been described in the international and technology management literatures [de Meyer and Mizushima 1990], but its implications for information processing and IT are not well documented or understood. Probably the most striking example of IT supporting global R&D efforts is in semiconductor companies, where designers around the world often work with common software design tools and are interconnected via satellite. Impressive as this example is, however, it is not the solution to the primary problem now facing most globally dispersed R&D efforts.

From the interviews with R&D managers in the seven sample companies, it is apparent that information-processing requirements in the R&D area have been changing dramatically. Until very recently, R&D was largely done at the national unit level. Generally new product R&D was done in the United States, and finished designs were transferred overseas, where minor local modifications might be made. In a few industries (e.g., the U.S. auto industry), major foreign subsidiaries did their own R&D and developed unique products for their own markets. In both cases, the creative parts of the R&D process, which require large amounts of nonroutine-reciprocal information processing between interdependent subunits, were entirely within a single country. International technology transfer only occurred with finished designs, where most data can be readily cod-ified (in blueprints, specification lists, etc.) and primarily transferred with large amounts of routine-sequential and nonroutine-sequential information processing (see Figure 3 for the kinds of mechanisms required).

What is happening today is that R&D is increasingly being conducted at the global product division level and the creative processes and tasks are being shared across borders. While there is still a need for routine-sequential and nonroutine-sequential information processing (for status reporting, budgetary control, and the transferring of codified technical information), the requirement for nonroutine-reciprocal information processing has exploded. Deciding how to divide tasks between dispersed project teams, how to keep parallel work compatible, and what to do when problems are encountered are examples of requirements for nonroutine reciprocal information processing across the interdependent R&D

sites. In most of the sample companies these requirements had developed recently, were growing rapidly, and the companies did not appear very knowledgeable or experienced in coping with them.

The primary mechanisms being used to provide this information processing were frequent international telephone calls and business trips (facilitating direct contact and meetings). There was also a heavy use of E-mail and fax, although it appeared there was usually a 12-hour lag between message and reply. This raises the question of whether E-mail and fax can provide non-routine-reciprocal information processing internationally, or if the time problem downgrades them to nonroutine-sequential capability. Teleconferencing was also used by most of the R&D areas.

One of the sample companies had recently brought together from different subsidiaries a team of design engineers to work for six months on a new family of semiconductor chips. Given that the circuit designs themselves can be readily transferred electronically, it would appear that the need to exchange richer kinds of information prompted this arrangement. At the present time, it does not appear that IT can provide the large amount of nonroutine-reciprocal information processing required to coordinate the many complex and subtle interdependencies that exist within a creative process. Instead, shared intraorganizational data bases seem to do a much better job providing coordination between creative processes that take place at different locations.

A striking feature of the R&D areas of MNCs is that they are laced with committees and task forces at all of the significant levels of the hierarchy (top management, middle management, laboratory professional). As Figure 3 indicates, committees and task forces are important providers of nonroutine-reciprocal information processing in organizations. A problem arises, however, when members are physically distant from each other. The sample companies were largely bringing people together for

these many meetings with airplanes. As a result, several of the R&D managers interviewed seemed to be operating beyond what might be considered a reasonable and sustainable level of business travel.

A growing literature is emerging that deals with the subject of rich and hard-to-transfer information. Williamson [1975] long ago recognized "information impactedness" (the difficulty or cost of transferring hard-to-transfer information from one organization or subunit to another) as an important contingency factor to consider when organizing tasks and relationships. Since then, Daft and Macintosh [1981] have determined that the equivocality or ambiguity of information influences the way it is processed in organizations, and Daft and Lengel [1986] and Daft and Weick [1984] have further explored how organizations deal with rich information. Recently, von Hippel [1991] has proposed the notion of "sticky information" as being particularly appropriate for R&D settings. He concludes that it is often easier to move the decision to the source of sticky information than it is to move the information to a distant decision maker. Interviews in the sample companies would seem to suggest that the global dispersion of the R&D process increasingly leads to separate locations engaging in shared decision making on sticky information. Significant levels of face-to-face meeting between decision makers is how most firms attempt to handle this situation.

Teleconferencing and video conferencing would appear to be the IT technologies that hold the most promise for providing the kind of nonroutine-reciprocal information processing that face-to-face meetings are currently providing. Teleconferencing is being used for coordinating R&D, but only in a supplemental way. Its limitations are that it is difficult to conduct across multiple time zones and issues involving trust or understanding may be especially difficult to communicate. Interviews with R&D managers in the sample companies frequently revealed that heightened competition and shorter technology cycles have pushed many R&D subunits to operating at their limits, with little or no slack in the system. As a result, things were constantly going awry, plans and objectives (often involving other locations) were continually being revised, and there was a tremendous need for trust and understanding across interdependent R&D subunits.

None of the seven companies had tried to use video conferencing for international R&D meetings, although one company was about to try it. In most of the other companies there was an interest in video conferencing, no experience with it, and no immediate plans to use it. Interestingly, most of the companies seemed to use video conferencing in the United States, primarily in the sales and marketing area.

Thus, international R&D efforts are running up against a constraint that primarily consists of limited nonroutine-reciprocal information-processing capacity. They are currently trying to meet these requirements with telephone calls and travel. The direct costs of this are great, and the indirect costs (time delays, errors, and human punishment) would appear to be extremely great. The firm that could use IT to substitute out a good deal of individual travel and relax this constraint on R&D information processing should have a significant competitive advantage. As product development cycles continue to shorten, the cost of time delays in R&D becomes even greater. Some combination of telephone, fax, E-mail, teleconferencing, and video conferencing would seem appropriate for addressing this situation, but none of the companies appeared to be seriously working on it.

CONCLUSION

Future Directions for Research

As stated in the introduction, research on IT and MNCs is in its infancy. As a result, there are probably multiple paths along which future research can constructively proceed. The principal observation to be made here is that to date exploratory research of an inductive nature has dominated the field. Since the phenomenon under study is changing rapidly, such research continues to find and report new developments. What is still lacking, however, is any real theory about IT in MNCs. There is a compelling need for underlying theory that can guide the successive rounds of observation and serve to integrate them.

Theory may also be important for another reason. Not only is much of the research on IT in organizations inductive by nature, but it frequently appears to use opportunistic, as opposed to random sampling of the population. Given the sensitivity of the subject and the difficulty in gaining access to firms for detailed case studies, this situation is understandable. It means, however, that theory is especially important, because it provides a line of deductive reasoning that serves as a check on otherwise inducing theory from observations that may not be representative of the population the theory will be applied to.

Weick [1984] has suggested that IT researchers look to organization theory studies for prototypes that may be useful for their own purpose. It is true that constructs, variables, and measures are more developed in organization theory. It also appears that many of the research questions IT theorists seek to address are organizational in nature. To the extent that this is true, Weick's advice would seem to have merit. This paper has attempted to use an organizational, information-processing perspective to understand better the design of an IT platform, in order to relate it better to a firm's strategy and organizational design. The utility of the proposed framework was weakly tested, using several available examples. It appears to merit further development. More specifically, the framework seems to be suitable for comparing the information-processing capacities of specific IT technologies with the information-processing requirements emanating from characteristics of a firm's strategy.

More detailed study of specific IT technologies in MNCs should allow their information processing capacities to be more accurately described by the proposed framework. The capacity of an IT technology is also likely to be contingent on characteristics of the organizational context within which it operates. For example, significant prior familiarity and trust between individuals may allow them to substitute video conferencing for face-to-face meetings, even when information is rich [Daft and Weick 1984] or sticky [von Hippel 1991]. Or perhaps the degree of differentiation [Lawrence and Lorsch 1967] between interdependent subunits influences the degree to which IT technologies can substitute for other, more costly forms of organizational information processing. Specifying the interaction effects between IT technologies and organizational context should become an important thrust for IT research; the proposed framework would appear to facilitate such research.

Other theories about organizations might also provide useful conceptualization for IT research. Transaction cost theory [Casson 1987; Hennart 1982] should be particularly useful for evaluating the economic substitution of IT technologies for other forms of communication and the opportunities to create firm-specific advantages based on the deployment of IT. Institutionalization theory [Westney 1992; this chapter] might serve as a basis for studying the diffusion of IT technologies within industries and geographical regions. Once again, these are subjects that are of current interest to IT users and researchers, and existing organizational perspectives would appear to provide useful paths to addressing them.

An appropriate observation with which to conclude this section might be that research which seeks to address the subject of IT in MNCs needs to be multidisciplinary. Research teams that encompass a knowledge of MNCs, organization theory, and IT might well be a preferred design for studying the subject.

The Implications of IT for MNCs

Above all else, the new information technologies portend change for MNCs.

While they are not the sole or even the primary cause of this change, it is doubtful that the movement toward regional and global strategies could have proceeded as far as it has without them. The new technologies provide additional degrees of freedom that in some areas can overcome existing constraints on the way IB is conducted. Mapping out where these areas are and designing the IT platform that can overcome the constraints is the principal task facing practitioners and researchers.

The preceding section has highlighted two broad areas where new applications of IT will probably have the most impact on IB. The first deals with providing large amounts of new, routine-sequential, information-processing capacity between subsidiaries and regional and global HQs, as was illustrated by the regionalization of manufacturing scheduling. This change is already well under way, and in areas like Europe, it will significantly alter competitive strategy. The new, information-processing capability provides tremendous potential to centralize coordination of many routine activities. The previous constraint in this area used to be the cost of communications and the timeliness of information. The new technologies coupled with political change have largely overcome this constraint. The new constraint that now limits or determines how far regional or global integration can go is how to retain sufficient local flexibility and adaptation in the face of such integration. This new constraint may not be as amenable to an IT solution as the previous constraint.

Consider two of the examples already touched upon. The first example is the manufacturing scheduling problem involving the German subsidiary's desire to tightly couple its schedule to the demands of certain large customers. IT theorists have suggested that distributed data processing addresses this kind of hierarchical or two-level allocation problem. Yet, if the German subsidiary is allowed sufficient flexibility to be frequently able to reoptimize its own production schedule without disturbing the rest of the European manufacturing circuit, there is clearly going to be some cost or degree of suboptimization at the European level. Deciding how to make this and similar trade-offs lies outside of the realm of IT and more in the area of organizational governance and strategic management.

Next, consider the previously discussed sales and bid analysis system one of the sample companies recently installed in Europe. The system allows sales and various characteristics of bids by the European subsidiaries to be analyzed in a readily comparable manner. Subsidiary management was skeptical that they would learn much from this and appeared apprehensive of how regional HQ management might use such comparisons. Clearly, HQ management is now going to be much better informed about what is actually going on in the sales process at the subsidiary level. The availability of such information may begin to create changes in the local sales and bidding processes that are unanticipated, and perhaps undesirable. In other words, the mere availability of information can conceivably threaten local autonomy in ways that designers of the IT platform have not been concerned with.

The general implication for MNCs is that changing the information-processing capacities of an IT platform at the regional and global levels will lead to changes in information flows and decision making, and this can produce behavioral changes that go far beyond those envisioned by the designers. It can involve significant changes in the roles and power of subsidiary and HQ managements. Struggling with and attempting to manage this kind of change is undoubtedly going to be one of the chief tasks that will preoccupy MNC managements for the next decade.

The second broad area where new applications of IT are likely to have a substantial impact on IB is less certain than the first. It deals with the ability of IT technologies to provide large amounts of relatively inexpensive, nonroutine-reciprocal, information-processing capacity at the regional and global levels of the organization. New strategies, such as global new product development, tend to require large amounts of this kind of information processing. Today, this is largely provided by physically bringing information processors together. In many MNCs, this approach has probably reached its economic or physical limit. If the new IT technologies can electronically bring information processors together without sacrificing the important characteristics of nonroutine-reciprocal information processing, this type of information processing can be expanded and more of the new strategies can be implemented.

Unlike the previous area, technical and political constraints may still be significant impediments to expanding nonroutine-reciprocal, information-processing capacity. The cost of using existing transmission technologies is generally high, and local public telephone and telegraph companies (PTTs) sometimes prevent international video conferencing. The most important long-run issue, however, is probably how well meeting electronically can substitute for meeting physically. It may well be that some interaction of IT with features of organizational design and organizational behavior will yield a significant new source of nonroutine-reciprocal, information-processing capacity between physically distant information processors. It seems equally likely that such a system won't be general or easily duplicated. Instead, like superior process technology in some Japanese semiconductor firms, it is likely to be some complex interaction of equipment, technology, management practices and procedures, and individual capabilities and behavior. Seeing such a system at work does not mean that one can fully understand it or readily copy it. If this is true, there may be significant potential for developing long-run, firm-specific advantages in this part of the IT platform. Once again, the most successful work in this area is likely to be highly multidisciplinary—a significant barrier in its own right.

This paper has sought to use an information-processing perspective of organizations to reflect in a more deductive way on some of the important implications of the new information technologies for the strategic management of MNCs. While admittedly incomplete, it is hoped that this approach will facilitate research and understanding in this emerging area.

■ ■ ■

Toward a Theory of the Self-Renewing MNC
Gunnar Hedlund and Jonas Ridderstråle

Established theories of the multinational corporation (MNC) and its management, in our view, suffer from a neglect of aspects of innovation, renewal, and change. In the present paper, we will briefly review some important streams of research and argue that they share a preoccupation with the exploitation of given advantages and assets and only marginally deal with the creation of new sources of competitiveness. Some recent contributions go some way in addressing this latter problem, but they are neither solidly empirically founded, nor articulated clearly in theoretical terms. Drawing on studies in organization theory and of innovations, we will analyze the different requirements posed by *exploitation* on the one hand, and *creation* on the other. Alternative ways of combining the two in an MNC will be posed, and conclusions concerning a theory of the self-renewing MNC will be drawn.

Although we will occasionally touch on such issues, attributes of *systems* (national, regional, industry-wide, firm-university, etc.) of innovation will not be in focus. Thus, we will not really discuss the important question of the relative merits and intricacies of interaction between, for example, a system relying on novelty springing from small and new firms and later being exploited in larger corporations, on the one hand, and a system wherein large corporations handle both tasks, on the other. We assume that the innovative capability of the large MNC is indeed a relevant problem. The results of the contemporary competitive process in shifting leadership between firms and nations certainly seem to support such a claim. Particularly in the case of large Japanese firms, we appear to witness a capability to learn and innovate rapidly and also hints of organizational philosophies and techniques embodying such ambitions (quality circles, kai-zen, etc.). Many MNCs may be losing opportunities inherent in their assets and geographical spread.

THEORETICAL PERSPECTIVES IN INTERNATIONAL BUSINESS RESEARCH

Four research traditions dominate the academic discussion of the MNC. We will label them the *transaction cost* approach, the *imperfect competition* approach, the *internationalization process* approach, and the *information processing* approach, respectively.

The *transaction cost* approach includes analyses building on Coase's [1937] and Williamson's [1975] work. Significant contributions are Buckley and Casson [1976], Teece [1977], Rugman [1981], Hennart [1982], Magee [1977], Casson [1987]. Whether the starting point is in the concept of "transaction costs," "internalization," or "appropriability," the logic is the same. The characteristics of a given transaction or activity are analyzed, and conclusions are drawn as to the effective (and thereby probable) governance form. The latter is conceived of in terms of market or hierarchy, intermediate forms being considered in greater depth in later contributions. We will not debate these deductions, although there is scope for such a critique. For our purposes, the important point is that the analysis *assumes a certain given transaction*. It is not a matter of *generating new* transactions, nor of finding ways of combining several transactions with each other. This latter fact points to another characteristic of the transaction cost frameworks: they generally take one individual transaction or one well-defined activity as the basic unit of analysis. The systemic properties of sets of transactions are left aside, as are the consequences of these for appropriate governance form. (See Winter [1991:91] for a discussion related to this point.)

Imperfect competition is a reason for the existence of MNC in the early work by Hymer [1960;1976]. Dunning combined aspects of transaction cost theory with analysis of imperfect competition in his "eclectic theory" [Dunning 1979]. Other noteworthy contributions are by Caves [1982], Knickerbocker [1973], and Graham [1978]. The basic idea is that MNCs form around firm-specific advantages of a monopolistic nature. These are derived from the home country and later lead to exports abroad. The selection of form of foreign expansion strategy is then driven by considerations similar to those emphasized in the transaction cost approach, and by competitive imitation, hostage strategies, etc. Here, the salient point is the *origination in a given home-country-based advantage*. Analysis is not in terms of later generation of *new advantages*, nor is there much discussion of *how* even the original advantage was created. Thus, there is a lack of dynamism in the theory, and the role of "foreign" environments for innovation is not discussed.

Combined, the transaction cost and imperfect competition approaches provide an understanding of why MNCs exist at all and of the extension and boundaries of the firm. However, the theories are more applicable for early stages in the life of a MNC, when there are more givens in terms of product technology and when the crucial question is, indeed, how to exploit these givens rather than how to create new ones.

One may object to the claim that these theories neglect innovation by quoting the repeated references to high technology as a key ingredient in multinational business. Furthermore, imperfections in markets for technology figure in many discussions in the logic of transaction cost analysis. However, and again, the analysis takes this technology as given and does not concern itself with the problem of producing it in the first place.

Research on *internationalization processes*, while often relating to the two previous approaches, adds a dynamic element and a greater emphasis on the company level detail. In the product cycle model of Vernon [1966], the assumption is that high income countries generate innovations (see also Burenstam Linder [1961]), which are first exported to, then manufactured in, and finally possibly imported from other countries. The cycle is for a *given innovation*, or product, and it is assumed that it comes from the home country of the MNC. Similarly, research in Scandinavia [Luostarinen 1979; Johanson and Vahlne 1977] concluded that there was a progression ("establishment chain") of markets and modes of involvement to gradually more distant places and more committing forms of establishment. The basic and rather stable source of competitiveness is, however, as in the imperfect competition approach, a home-country-derived advantage. Learning and knowledge figure in these theories, but primarily about markets and firms rather than about final products. Furthermore, the learning strategies are imbued with bounded rationality [Simon 1955; Cyert and March 1963], and there is little scope for conscious efforts to speed up learning in the models.

Vernon [1979] departs substantially from the analysis in his earlier work, posing the "global scanner" as a model of an MNC that utilizes its global reach more ambitiously. However, the emphasis is exactly on scanning rather than doing and on more rapid exploitation rather than on the emergence outside the home country of new innovations. Sandén and Vahlne [1976] propose an "advantage cycle," where product-based advantages are replaced by those associated with international distribution. Kogut [1983] provides a taxonomy of "sequential advantages," and "learning" is one of them. However, in none of these contributions is there much discussion of what the implications are of the scope for utilizing the global network of the MNC for innovation. The new advantages occur only in later stages of the internationalization process ("sequential" to earlier ones), and they are somehow incidental and not primary.

The *information processing* approach builds on ideas most clearly expressed in Galbraith [1973]. For analyzing the MNC, Egelhoff [1982] is the paradigmatic statement. Here, the logic is to start from the nature of information processing demands and deduce appropriate organizational responses. Again, one assumes that these demands are *given*, known. They are, furthermore, conceived of in rather simple terms. Galbraith speaks explicitly of the *amount* of information, rather than, for example, its complexity, novelty, dispersion, comprehensibility, etc. (Egelhoff [1991] suggests a multidimensional view of information processing requirements, moving the analysis to more dynamic issues.) Although such simplifications may be justified for the sake of analytical parsimony, the consequence is that the organization is seen essentially as a filing system. Given bits of information are combined into categories and ordered in hierarchical classification systems. It is, we believe, significant that Galbraith refers to "*vertical* information systems" (our emphasis) as one way of addressing the processing demands, relegating the lateral possibility to the realm of theoretical ideas too difficult to implement for human beings.

Thus, the underlying notion is of a given task, implying given information and processing of information, and with certain consequences for division of work and use of managerial coordination systems. It is *not* one of *knowledge* or of *creation*, where meaning rather than bits of information is

managed, and where novelty rather than the processing of givens is the objective. (For a discussion of the difference between information processing and knowledge creation see Nonaka [1990;1991].)

THE COMMON SHORTFALLS: INNOVATION AND "SYSTEMICITY"

The four traditions have been reviewed in a sketchy fashion not doing justice to their contributions and focusing on their shortcomings. Thus, the above is somewhat of a caricature. For example, Casson [1990] contains several contributions extending the internalization approach to questions of innovation in MNCs. Still, it is fair to say that the various explicit theoretical logics all share two properties that make them less suitable for the analysis of the modern MNC.

First, they all in one way or another focus on the *exploitation of givens*, rather than on the *creation of novelty*. These givens are also mostly defined in narrow terms such as a transaction, a home-country-based, firm-specific advantage, or an amount of information processing to be handled. (The exceptions are those contributions emphasizing the "globality advantage" of the MNC, but they are mostly silent on the theoretical as well as managerial consequences of such a broader conception.) We have argued elsewhere [Hedlund and Rolander 1990] that the requirements for exploitation and creation strategies, respectively, differ substantially, and we will pursue that argument below.

It could be argued that empirical research shows that the hypothesized pattern of R&D in the home country gradually being exploited abroad indeed is the one that most closely describes reality, and that the idea of the global innovator is an unrealistic dream. However, primarily through the massive wave of cross-border acquisitions, MNCs are presently internationalizing their R&D function (see Håkansson and Nobel [1991] and Casson [1990 Ch 8], for some empirical trends). Furthermore, even if what is called central R&D is located in the "home country," input of knowledge and expertise from other units is increasingly required. (See Bartlett and Ghoshal [1989] for many telling examples.) Also, the theoretical silence on how even a narrow national innovation actually occurs within an MNC (or before the company can claim this status) needs to be filled. Porter [1990] and associated analyses (for example Sölvell, Zander, and Porter [1991]) go some way in addressing this question, but there is little on the consequences for internal company organization and management processes in this stream of research. Finally, and returning to the point on existing empirical research, the globalism of strategic resources and critical inputs may be underrated by studies conducted in terms as crude as the location of R&D units and formal headquarters. Close inspection of individual cases often reveal an amazing richness of crucial "foreign" input. For example, the Swedish company Alfa-Laval, formed in 1883 around the invention of the separator, is still a world leader in this and related fields, and a cursory look at published data would lead one to assume that the core of the company is and always has been Swedish. However, in a number of ways, foreign units of the firm and external agents have been immensely important in the company's history. For example (see Åman [1992]):

—In 1893, the "Alfa patent" was acquired from the company's then German sales agent, forming the basis not only for the first half of the company name but also for the new generation of separators.

—In 1917, the U.S. subsidiary invented the milking machine, which later became a main (in many periods *the* main) income earner for the company.

—In the 1930s, the plate heat exchange technology was developed in the German subsidiary. This became the third core product of Alfa-Laval.

The *second* and related shortcoming of existing theories is the *neglect of systemic attributes and emergent properties* of the MNC, by focusing on narrowly defined units of analysis (one transaction, one product, one advantage, a quantity of information). Innovation in itself often involves new *combinations* of different elements. Structures optimal for the exploitation of one element may hinder its involvement in a new context. Some MNCs today are reconsidering their divisionalized, product-based structure ("M-form") for this reason.

Also along the regional dimension, such interaction is critical, which is the more pertinent point for the MNC. One subsidiary may possess a certain product technology, another manufacturing know-how, and a third the largest market for the product. They all have to collaborate in its creation and commercialization. Such utilization of the strengths of the entire network is not consistent with thinking of the MNC as a set of bilateral links between one "center" and a number of "subsidiaries." A kind of research not referenced above builds exactly on this image, and numerous studies of "HQ-subsidiary relations" have been made. The most prominent variable studied is the autonomy of the subsidiary. (For reviews, see Van den Bulcke and Halsberghe [1984]; Gates and Egelhoff [1986]; and Martinez and Ricks [1989].) Obviously, this notion is less valid today.

The various forms of "atomism" inherent in the established approaches, combined with the focus on exploitation of givens, gives a machinelike, mechanistic view of the firm. To the extent that the theories have given birth to managerially useful—or at least nontrivial and comprehensible—tenets, these imply a rational actor model [Allison 1971] of decision making. The top manager analyzes the characteristics of the problem at hand and comes up with a solution to be implemented further down the organization. A long tradition of research at least from Burns and Stalker [1961] and Lawrence and Lorsch [1967] has documented the ineffectiveness of such "mechanistic" approaches to relatively complex and dynamic environments and problems. Models of the MNC therefore should capture the action and strategies emerging (cf. Mintzberg and Waters [1985]) from the interlinked MNC network as well as those emanating from the intentions of top managers. (See Doz and Prahalad [1987] for a plea for more such process oriented models and outlines of a specific model.) In a related vein, prescriptions for MNC management need to take into account the likely shift in the role of top management from a master decision maker to an architect of a global infrastructure with built-in decision making and innovation capability.

The fact that the theoretical ideas dominating the analysis of international business (IB) have not focused on issues of innovation and renewal in no way detracts from these traditions' value in addressing the problems with which they were developed to deal. Furthermore, we see attempts to extend the approaches of transaction cost analysis [Casson 1990] and information processing [Egelhoff 1991]. We believe interesting results will follow from this. However, doing justice to the properties of innovation and change will, we believe, force the adoption of new viewpoints with regard to the units of analysis ("transaction" being less appropriate, for example) and primitive concepts (for example, "knowledge" coming into focus and "opportunism" receding somewhat).

RECENT CONTRIBUTIONS TO A
DYNAMIC THEORY OF THE MNC:
EVOLUTIONARY ECONOMICS AND
SPECULATIVE MODELS OF THE MNC

There are important streams of research, outside the realm of IB and analysis of the MNC, that provide fertile ground for constructive theoretical work. Analysis of technological change is the most important such stream. A fundamental source is Nelson and Winter [1982]. Often building on this, but adding in particular significant aspects that focus on firm-specific resources and attributes of technological trajectories, authors such as Rumelt [1984], Wernerfelt [1984], Pavitt [1985;1991], Cantwell [1989], Burgelman and Rosenbloom [1989], Cohen

and Levinthal [1989], Kogut [1987], Kogut and Zander [1991], and Teece, Pisano, and Shuen [1990] contribute to an evolving evolutionary theory of, as Winter [1991] puts it, "firm-specific dynamic capabilities."

With some important exceptions, these contributions have not generally taken the existence and properties of the MNC as central. Those that have, furthermore, have not concentrated on the problems of internal organization and management, which seem to be central in understanding innovation and change. Rumelt, Schendel, and Teece [1991] emphasize this "new attention to internal organization." They also argue for the importance of knowledge management in a broad sense. Interestingly enough, for an assessment of the applicability of the more general economic theories to innovation in the MNC, they claim that "Where the coordination and accumulation of knowledge is key, and where patterns of belief and attitude are important, other disciplines (than economics) will have more to say" [27].

The problem, therefore, is not simply a matter of extending general economic theories to the MNC. A second and recent body of knowledge seems to complement the insights gained from such perspectives, by more explicitly researching the internal organization of the MNC and by questioning (mostly implicitly) the Panglossian assumptions of efficient selection inherent in many of the evolutionary and related theories. A number of authors have suggested models—some positive and some more normative—of the MNC going some way in addressing the problems of innovation and systems connectedness. Although by no means identical, and based on different kinds of empirical and conceptual research strategies, they all tend to emphasize similar matters: learning and synergy on the basis of geographically differentiated capabilities, complex and multidimensional organizational structures, roles for individual units shifting over time, new role sets for managers at all levels in the MNC, increased importance for aspects of human resource management and information systems, critical importance of managing innovation in the MNC, departure from a simple center-periphery model of the company, and lateral relationships between units.

Representative of this research stream are the concepts of the "heterarchy" [Hedlund 1986;1992], the "transnational" [Bartlett 1986; Bartlett and Ghoshal 1989], the "multifocal MNC" [Doz 1986], and the "horizontal MNC" [White and Poynter 1990]. All these authors have at least to some extent been involved as consultants to MNCs. Their empirical research consists mostly of in-depth case studies. The results, therefore, are likely to score high on current relevance and grounding in the details of reality. It is somewhat curious that this type of research, usually prone to produce mundane and "conservative" conceptions, has led to ideas sometimes criticized as being unrealistic and "visionary" in the sense of close to delusions. Not necessarily rejecting the latter possibility, a more optimistic interpretation is that empirical research on the modern MNC provides the richest ground for theorizing about a new, more dynamic theory of the firm *in general*. A central problem for the theory of the firm as well as for theories of organization in a more detailed sense is to consider the *diffusion of knowledge* and the *variety* of environments in which the firm operates. The MNC is arguably the institution where these conditions prevail most critically. (See Hedlund [1992] and concerning decentralized information, Radner [1989].)

The promising marriage of nose-to-the-ground empirical research and ambitious conceptualization notwithstanding, these later views of the MNC suffer from two deficiencies. First, empirical grounding is sparse and impressionistic, and perhaps colored mainly by the pioneers among the MNCs rather than a more representative sample. Second, theoretical articulation is still not very cohesive. This may be because the phenomena elude capture in simple theoretical frameworks, but it also could reflect their novelty, or the theoretical

immaturity of the researchers themselves. In the following, we will try to add to the theoretical discussion by first identifying the prerequisites of organizational exploitation and creation, respectively, and then investigate how these two necessary capabilities of a self-renewing firm may be combined within one MNC.

PROGRAMS OF EXPLOITATION AND CREATION

In line with our discussion in Hedlund and Rolander [1990], we may look upon strategy as patterns of action over time. Here, two different aspects can be identified. First, we have *programs of exploitation*, where the primary aim is the effective utilization of given resources and the appropriation of value stemming from current activities, as discussed within the existing paradigms. Second, there are *programs of creation*, where the focus is to seek opportunities for the future. Exploitation aims at capturing the current potential, whereas creation aims at changing the future potential. The latter could take the form of evolutionary or incremental changes as well as more revolutionary shifts and include both market, product, technological, and service development, separately or in new combinations.

A similar notion can be found in March [1991]. Discussing organizational learning, he uses the two terms exploitation and exploration. Although exploration or experimentation could be regarded as synonymous to creation, we have a specific reason for choosing the latter alternative. Creation better seems to capture a process of active construction rather than only tapping into existing resources or opportunities. Our view is close to the enactment process described by Weick [1969:64]: "the human *creates* the environment to which the system then adapts. The human actor does not *react* to an environment, he *enacts* it." However, we would like to stress even more the actual creation of new domains. As we see it, enactment is the process by which all organizations "interpret" the environment. Most authors (including Weick) seem to suggest that how and what firms enact could be the result of company history. However, as we see it, enactment could also take place more independently from past events, guided by norms and routines aiming at the future. Creation symbolizes these latter cases. The term is meant to capture activities such as exploration, experimentation, search, combination, variation, risk taking, play, and discovery. Exploitation, on the other hand, includes refinement, selection, implementation, execution, etc (cf. also March [1991:71]).

By adding aspects of proaction to Wieck's enactment framework, one might argue that we contradict the implication of his argument, that meaning is retrospective and organizations indeed may be captives of their past. On the other hand, whereas Weick is describing how these processes work, we are more interested in the normative aspects of firms enacting the environment— how enactment could be geared toward future opportunities. In our view, routines for creation-oriented enactment are essential to most organizations. Mere retrospective enactment, i.e., exploitation-oriented, could push the firm into becoming a self-producing and closed system, as argued by Maturana and Varela [1980]. There is a clear risk that these companies will bear close resemblance to what Morgan [1986] characterizes as "egocentric organizations," unaware of the systemic wisdom, destined to see what happens instead of trying to shape what happens.

Rather than regarding exploitation and creation as two separate categories, however, it is better to envision them as two endpoints on a continuum. Although it is hard

to position clearly all types of activities, Figure 1 tries to provide some guidance. It is clear that most organizations have routines for the types of activities represented at the left hand side, but few firms have developed routines for creation. Part of the explanation may be that exploitation routines are easier to articulate and transfer within the organization, whereas creation routines may be more tacit, thus harder to transfer and imitate. (Of course, these routines are also harder for the researcher to spot.)

Most action patterns would show signs of both exploitation and creation. Even in activities such as innovation or entrepreneurship, which easily could be confused with creation programs, elements of exploitation can be found in most cases. Creation is not the responsibility of a single unit or function, for example the R&D department, of the firm. Emphasis on either one of these processes varies, and should vary, from one activity to another and over time for the organization as a whole. It is the role of management to ensure that a climate facilitating adequate levels of creation is upheld company-wide in all activities.

Exploitation and creation are not only intraorganizational processes. The company also is involved in activities of both kinds when interacting with other firms, i.e., competitors, customers, suppliers. By use of relationships, contractual or less formalized, with various actors in the external network, the firm can get access to information that may be used for internal exploitation or creation activities. The interaction process itself could be characterized in terms of the above. Depending, therefore, upon the strategic focus of the firm, environmental search and cooperation will take on different forms.

Figure 1. The Exploitation-Creation Continuum

Exploitation   Creation

$\longleftarrow$ ————————————————————————————————————— $\longrightarrow$

Repetition   Refinement   Selection   Search   Exploration   Combination   Experimentation

PROBLEMS IN BALANCING ACTIVITIES OF EXPLOITATION AND CREATION

Although emphasizing creation might be justified for the reasons outlined, it should be clear that concentrating solely on these types of actions will make the firm vulnerable. Without exploiting the newly created advantages, the firm will reap only the costs without gaining any returns, and it risks never attaining critical mass in competencies, markets, or production. On the other hand, applying a narrow focus on exploitation, the company will risk being crowded out by more inventive competitors, as the lead gained by original advantages diminishes over time. Hence, maintaining a balance between activities of creation and exploitation is essential.

This might sound like a trivial statement, but given the nature of exploitation and creation it is easier said than done, particularly when considering the fact that these activities compete for scarce resources. Two main forces counteract the possibilities to maintain an appropriate balance.

First, there is a built in resistance in organizations to the unknown and the uncertain [Cyert and March 1963]. The outcomes of creation activities are less certain, more remote in time, and less obvious than is the case with exploitation activities. Moreover, as argued by March [1991], organizations learn from experience how to divide resources between the basic types of activities, and this distribution, in turn, has a short-term as well as long-term effect. The feedback loops of exploitation consequences are quicker and more precise, and thus adaptive processes generally improve exploitation more rapidly than creation. In the long run, activities of exploitation will tend to crowd out creation activities, when not countervailed by proper management responses.

In summary, there is a tendency for organizational routines [Cyert and March 1963; Nelson and Winter 1982] to become more and more rigid, inflexible, risk averse, bureaucratic, and less creation-oriented over time (cf. for instance Downs [1967]). Williamson [1975:200–201] seems to interpret this as a sign of the large, complex organization not being fit to deal with innovation. "Since innovation, in relation to production, tends to be untidy, innovation—which is a poorly structured, high-risk activity—may not be an activity which the large, mature bureaucracy is constitutionally well-suited to handle."

A logical implication of the argument is that the mature organization should stick to exploitation and leave creation to others. One potential strategy for the MNC could be to use the international network of, for instance, suppliers as extraorganizational innovators, licensing or buying technology from them, or simply buying the innovative firms. The multinational could subsequently reap the profits from exploiting these innovations globally. Apart from the fact that the large firm would lose any potential benefits from economies of scale in R&D, the most important objection to the strategy of totally externalizing creation oriented activities has to do with the difficulty of dissociating knowledge from its use.

How would the firm be able to spot potentially successful innovations when not involved in R&D itself? As noted by Pavitt [1991], among others, technology to a large extent is tacit, cumulative, and firm specific. The firm can not only look into the environment and pinpoint interesting innovations or actors. Without elements of creation and a knowledge base of their own, they will not see the opportunities. For self-renewal to take place, where to look and what to look for must not be totally restricted by the organizations' competencies of the past and present.

The *second* factor that complicates upholding a fruitful balance has to do with the fact that exploitation and creation put different demands on the company, organizationally and strategically as well as managerially. This seems especially true when considering the geographically and organizationally dispersed MNC. Effective exploitation on a global scale is in itself so complex that aspects of innovation may be thwarted. Global rationalization, which is one raison d'être for the MNC, creates inflexibilities which are difficult to combine with the openness required by creation. For global scanning to be effective, management has to rely on systems for search, combination or experimentation in multiple directions, geographically as well as cross-departmentally. These systems generally differ significantly from those associated with increasing operational efficiency. The difference is probably greater than for national firms, since the geographical distribution of assets and roles of leadership will often differ between exploitation and creation. This inhibits linking the two activities by physical proximity and also forces the design of more formal and complex systems rather than only organic natural coordination.

THE RELATIVE EMPHASIS ON CREATION AND EXPLOITATION IN THE MNC

As we have argued, there are powerful mechanisms pushing organizations to emphasize exploitation at the expense of creation. In addition to the reasons enumerated by March [1991], the possibility to harvest the rewards of an innovation on a world-wide basis reinforces this tendency. It also could be argued that the global network capabilities of the MNC are primarily operational, lending themselves to exploitation. For example, by fine-tuning currency management and factory loading, global demand for a product can be satisfied with greater profits for an MNC than for a set of national firms [Kogut 1983]. The size and attendant bureaucracy of the established MNC also tend to produce a bias to stick to organizational routines and standard procedures [Cyert and March 1963; Nelson and Winter 1982].

There are, however, also aspects favoring creation particular to the MNC. First

and foremost, the international spread of the MNC means that it has access to a greater *diversity of inputs* than national firms. The likely benefits of investing in search are therefore greater. The benefits are even greater if the inputs are likely to be *complementary* and/or *combinable*.

Baba and Imai [1991] emphasize how "systemic innovation," i.e., innovation that generates novelty in many and diverse fields, is a key characteristic of many recent technological developments. Taking one step further and following Schumpeter, we may introduce the concept of *combinative innovation capability* to denote an organizational capability to combine several different technologies, or aspects of a technology. It seems as if scientific and technological trends are opening increased possibilities for such innovation. For example, optics and mechanics are merging with electronics, chemistry with biology, biology with genetics, genetics is becoming "modularized" through recombinant DNA technology, etc. Since the geographical locus of innovation varies between such potentially combinable fields, the MNC is in a position to benefit from an active role.

Indeed, we hypothesize that the MNC is the *primary* actor for such technology combinations. Baba and Imai propose that "cross-border networks" of related but legally independent firms may have the advantage. However, their empirical evidence pertains primarily to internal Japanese networks, and some of the network participants are in fact very closely related to each other (Matsushita and JVC). They also agree that more integrated units (such as an MNC) would fare better than the looser networks when "the extent of the market is large and its rate of change high." We conclude, therefore, that the logic of systemic and combinative innovation implies a tendency to push creative activities to MNCs and increase their likely returns on investment in creation.

The question of the creation/exploitation trade-off can be posed in terms of returns to scale. The lure of exploitation is that, in the short run, it mostly seems to give substantial marginal revenues at low marginal costs. Adding one more country to the list of markets becomes rather inexpensive when you have such experience of adding countries, whereas developing a completely new product seems less attractive in the short run. One may also make the stronger argument that exploitation is associated with stable or increasing returns to scale (cf. the arguments in recent trade theories), whereas in innovative activities "small is beautiful," at least more so. Coordination costs, arguably higher for creation than for exploitation, furthermore increase with geographical distance, so that the MNC should concentrate on exploitation both because of its size and because of its global reach.

On the other hand, it can be argued (see Baba and Imai [1991]) that systemic innovation suggests the possibility of increased returns to scale in innovation. The "first" product in a supposed product cycle is rapidly improved and extended by adding functions given by technologies different from the original one, and those firms that can invest in the total system of innovations will gain at the expense of those who only are able to benefit from one component of the system, usually for a very short time. Sustained involvement in innovation on a broad front and much experimentation are necessary in order to keep up in this race. It can be added that the well known association between environmental rate of change and a system's necessary capacity for change and/or innovation should push the MNC in the direction of creation. March [1991], in his analysis of the dynamics of competition, concludes that in cases where relative position matters a great deal, there is a tendency to force all competitors to more "exploratory" behavior. We would argue that global competition is increasingly such a race for dominant relative position. At least global managers see it that way. They may be responding to the dynamics of increasing

returns and systemic innovation, in addition to personal ambitions to be the biggest in the world.

We so far have not discussed the effects of the relative "maturity" of the industry. It seems that in the extreme case of science not yet having given rise to commercializable products at all, there is no reason to expect the MNC to be the most effective institutional haven. Silicon Valley conditions, with intensive interaction among individual entrepreneurs, small firms, universities, and advanced likely users, are probably better. In commodity type industries, there may be little room for innovation anyway. Therefore, the interesting case is the "in-between" one. Here, there exist a world-wide demand and some basic products, but there is still room for innovation both in products and production processes.

It should be noted, however, that the emergence of systemic innovation and "hybrid technologies" mean that the very concept of industry maturity becomes problematical. The product or industry life cycle as a model may need thorough revision, partly because large companies are finding ways to "demature" their businesses. As we have argued, those most likely to see the opportunities for such rejuvenation are MNCs.

No simple overall conclusion about the appropriate balance between creation and exploitation follows from the discussion above. The case for creation in the MNC seems to be stronger: in relatively turbulent industry environments; where relative position is important; where there is potential for combinative or systemic innovation; where combinable inputs differ between countries; where a relatively mature industry can develop by introducing elements of new technologies; and, when the company is already established in a diverse set of environments. At the very least, it can be concluded that the MNC does not escape the necessity to invest in creation, and this requirement becomes more ominous because of some important developments in technology and the structure and logic of global competition.

DIFFERING REQUIREMENTS FOR ACTIVITIES OF EXPLOITATION AND CREATION

As indicated earlier, one of the major problems in combining activities of exploitation and creation is that they require different modes of organizing and varying management principles. The list of differences in requirements could be made infinitely long and rich in detail. However, in outlining the main characteristics of the exploiting and the creating MNC, respectively, we will restrict our discussion to four important aspects.

Overall organization. Adam Smith [1776;1953] argued early for specialization or division of labor in his famous pin-making example. The basic argument regarding increased efficiency and clarity of responsibility also was reinforced later from a sociological perspective by scholars such as Weber [1947] and Durkheim [1964], applied in scientific management by Taylor [1911], and has come to have a great influence on the way we envision organizations. The reasoning is closely coupled to the notion of a hierarchical organization. (The concepts are far older than some 200 years and can be found in chapter 18 of Exodus in the Bible and in the writings of the ancient Greeks, Dionysus the Areopagite and Xenophon.)

In the truly exploiting organization the operating system can be prespecified because the output of the processes is given and eternal. Therefore, the firm will adapt a hierarchical mode of organizing. Headquarters will take on the role of a resource allocator, specifying and handing down tasks for subsidiaries to implement. The locus of strategic initiative will be centralized to headquarters, which will act as the brain of the firm, whereas the pool of subsidiaries will make up the body. Each subsidiary will have a specific task to perform, and this task will be determined by supervising managers. As a consequence, the firm will be heavily dependent on the skills of these individuals to develop the "right" strategy and allocation mix and on experts in the fields underlying the competitive advantage of the company. Individual roles and tasks are rigidly defined and tend not to change over time, which makes it relatively easy to change personnel, although not at the management and expert level where "defections" could be detrimental. Finally, the career paths are mirrors of the way of organizing, in that people tend to enter the organization within one functional speciality, such as marketing or production, and advance vertically within the same speciality. The separation of strategy and implementation will tend to produce separate careers for "doers" and "thinkers," those merely operating and those strategizing.

Much critique of specialization of labor and rigid hierarchical solutions has come to center around worker dissatisfaction (cf. Roethliesberger and Dickson [1939]; Child [1977], among others), or the limited ability of the structure to handle heavy loads of information in a complex and turbulent environment (cf. Burns and Stalker [1961]; Lawrence and Lorsch [1967]). Although these points are important, the main reason for creation activities not "fitting" within the hierarchical configuration relates to another fact. In order for knowledge creation to take place, people with various skills or competencies must work together, and the clustering of appropriate sets of cooperating individuals must shift over time.

The main form of organizing activities in the creation oriented firm will be to use project teams. The firm will bear similarities with the operating "adhocracy" as described by Mintzberg [1979]. These projects could be regarded as temporary networks of diverse competencies in the organization, often also involving actors in the environment. Headquarters will be more a catalyst, promoting new ideas and projects, than a resource allocator. Subsidiaries will be regarded as strategic partners with wills and creation skills of their own. The different parts of the organization will work together and form projects around ideas that could originate from any node, mainly in the intraorganizational network, rather than one (headquarters-HQ) pushing it down the others' throats. Thus, in a sense the distinction between headquarters and subsidiaries will become less relevant. In most projects, the small group or team will be a crucial level of organization, in that the group will constitute the heterogeneous (in terms of competencies) unit needed for creation-oriented experimentation, combination, etc.

Moreover, rather than relying on top management as the sole designer of strategy or concepts, members of the group will take on different roles, such as the ones described by Roberts and Fusfeld [1981] and others regarding innovation projects: idea generators, entrepreneurs, champions, and gatekeepers. Ideally, top management will act as sponsors and coaches to these projects, securing legitimacy and financial backing. Subsidiary roles as well as individual ones are broadly, and more organically, defined and may shift from project to project. The subordinate in one project may well head another project later, when called for by the situation and specific competencies needed. This system depends to a large extent on career patterns where employees not only move vertically, but also horizontally across departmental boundaries. In this way, the individual will come to possess a rich variety of competencies.

Coordination methods. The second important aspect that tends to distinguish exploitation from creation concerns the methods used to coordinate the different types of activities. Hierarchy in itself is a means for integrating activities, and indeed the formal structure in an exploiting multinational will have a major impact on coordination. Decisions and communication flow vertically through an established chain of command. The firm will use formalized procedures and roles in efforts to make employees behave as predictably as possible. The main basis of power will be coercive or

calculative, and there is a tendency towards bureaucratic and mechanistic [Burns and Stalker 1961] structures. The main problem for management becomes to ensure efficiency, build an organizational memory around existing skills, and attain consistency in behavior.

To ensure efficiency the firm will use a number of integrating methods. First, the organization will try to control performance by general standards or statements. "Our subsidiaries should have a ROCE (return on capital employed) of 15% this year." Second, to realize the performance target, management may specify mechanisms in plans, telling employees or subsidiaries what to do: "To attain 15% in ROCE, reduce production costs by 10%, and introduce the new model of black birds." At its extreme, planning could become so formalized and rich in detail that it tells workers exactly what to do or how to behave. To achieve this homogeneity, it is vital for the firm to train and indoctrinate their personnel. That is, when new employees enter the firm they are immediately socialized into the culture of the organization, without the firm trying to learn from the new individual. A two-way approach could easily disrupt the stability of the exploiting system. Hence, organizational norms will be focused on economy, efficiency, and homogeneity.

The creating MNC works distinctively differently. Whereas the formal, hierarchical structure is the key to integration in the exploiter, informal process is the most important vehicle for coordination in the creator. A flat configuration will require intense horizontal communication, mainly face-to-face but also in form of horizontal information systems (cf. Hagström [1991]). Norms will differ in at least two respects, as compared to the exploiting firm. First, normative coordination will be the primary basis for integration [Etzioni 1961]. Second, the content of norms differ in that there is an emphasis on originality, eccentricity, and heterogeneity. As suggested above, the main processes in the creating multinational depend on diversity to enable combination and on obsession with experimentation or exploration of new opportunities. Hence, streamlined organization and personnel with rigid norms, focused on short-term profits and efficiency, would be inconsistent with creation.

To prevent the organization from breaking down or falling apart, the method used to coordinate creation struggles will take on a different nature, more subtle and focused on the lateral dimension. Socialization in the form of extensive traveling and informal communication among employees will be key mechanisms. "Know who" will become as important as "know how." Moreover, people entering the organization will not find themselves having to adjust to the corporate culture at once. Rather, to increase the knowledge base and learning potential, this will be a process of the organization and the individual interacting, learning from one another.

Criteria of action. A third aspect that separates exploitation from creation relates to criteria used for action, partly originating in differences in organizational goals. While a hallmark of the exploiting MNC is the pervasiveness of economic rationality, a more creation-oriented firm is multirational. For instance, personal freedom to keep on experimenting, searching, or exploring may be as important as financial prospects.

Managers and employees in the exploiting MNC tend to regard the strategy as a set of decision rules. These rules will regulate risk propensity, the type and magnitude of new investment, and the direction of search for future prospects. The focus will be on minimizing risk and maximizing some aggregate goal function, usually simply profitability. Rules for search routines and new investments will focus on upgrading existing skills and competencies, rather than looking for something new.

In the creation-oriented organization, strategy will be more of a tacit belief system. The search for novelty with uncertain outcomes will make the firm more prone to accept high risks. This is not so much an explicit choice of always going for high risk projects, but more a natural consequence of the way the firm operates. The same is true as regards the view of profitability and time horizon. Creation requires accepting uncertainty about risk level and assessments of consequences in time. Perhaps one could say that the exploiter works in a domain of risk and the creator in one of ignorance, where even objectives are debatable.

Relations to the environment. Exploiters regard the environment primarily in terms of constraints, and changes in it are looked upon as discrete interruptions rather than a continuous buzz of challenges. The changes are characterized as intrusions rather than sources of livelihood and opportunity. The firm seeks deep coverage in narrow niches related to existing competencies, primarily to control other actors or dependence on scarce resources (cf. Pfeffer and Salancik [1978]). When the technological core is threatened, they seek to protect this by buffering or smoothing the environment (cf. Thompson [1967]). The firm is seldom involved in external cooperation, as the risk of leaking some of the information underlying the given advantage is considered too great.

As opposed to exploiters, creation-oriented firms view the environment primarily as a source of knowledge. The area covered is broader, to get access to new competencies and information. Consequently, external search routines are less constrained than in the exploiting MNC. More time will be spent on searching for and enacting new opportunities. Generally, the organization will be involved in extensive external cooperation. It will use strong and weak links with customers, as described by von Hippel [1976], or suppliers (cf. Axelsson [1987]) to develop new products or get access to new inputs. The organization engages in mutually beneficial, symbiotic search in a global network, where relations often are based upon personal contacts and trust.

To sum up, the main points in our discussion are presented in Figure 2 below. The

Figure 2. Requirements for Exploitation and Creation Activities

	Exploitation	Creation
Overall Organization		
— Basic mode of organization	Hierarchy	Project-based
— Role of headquarters	Resource allocator	Catalyst
— Role of subsidiaries	Implementers	Partners
— Key personnel	Top management	Task forces
— Individual roles and tasks	Clearly defined/Permanent	Broadly defined/Changing
— Role of management	Supervisor	Sponsor/Coach
— Career path	Vertical	Shifting
Coordination mechanisms		
— Degree of formality	Formal	Informal
— Communication processes	Vertical	Horizontal
— Basis for integration	Calculative/Bureaucratic	Normative/Laissez-faire
— Norms	Economy	Originality
	Efficiency	Eccentricity
	Homogeneity	Heterogeneity
	Indoctrination	Socialization
Action criteria		
— Goals/Rationality	Economic	Multirational
— Meaning of strategy	Decision rule	Belief system
— Attitude toward risk-taking	Low risk	High risk
— ROI-perspective	Short run	Long run/No run
— Focus of search-routines and investments	Existing skills and competencies	News skills and competencies
Relation to environment		
— View to environment	Given constraints/Competitive	Knowledge-source/Symbiotic
— Coverage	Niche	Broad
— Objective associated with cooperation agreements	Independence and control	Access to new information
— Nature of cooperation	Contractual/Formalized	Voluntaristic/ Less formalized

natural question to pose is how we can structure an organization to combine activities of exploitation with activities of creation, to exploit givens as well as create novelty for the future.

Space and the difficulty of the issue do not allow full discussion of the questions raised concerning the optimal combination of the two types of action. We will focus on four related issues, which seem essential in the context of MNC management.

1. The *degree of separation* in creating and exploiting, for units and individuals within the organization.

2. The *level* at which separation takes place (countries, organizational units, groups, individuals).

3. The *methods of coordinating* creation and exploitation with each other, given that there is some separation.

4. The *sequencing* of creation and exploitation activities.

Although the literature on MNCs is not very explicit at all about these questions, there is a more general literature on the problems involved in organization theory, cybernetics, and parts of economics. March

[1991] contains a succinct and brief review, which we will not try to add to here. It also provides a discussion to which we will relate in several ways. A first, fundamental point in March's paper, and in the computer simulations it reports, is the complex interaction between learning at the individual level and at the level of the organization as a whole. The insights about the sometimes counterintuitive results of this ecology of knowledge creation seem relevant for the wider context of MNC management. The relation between individual and organizational learning is mirrored, sometimes with similar processes of interaction, in the relation between learning at the level of individual units (such as country "subsidiaries") and at the level of the MNC as a whole. Extending March's model, we propose that at least four levels need to be considered: the country, the organizational unit within the MNC, the project group, and the individual. It is the multilevel interaction between choices of emphasis, separation, and sequencing that make the problem of combining creation and exploitation particularly difficult and interesting.

THE DEGREE OF SEPARATION OF CREATION AND EXPLOITATION ACTIVITIES

Since the requirements for the two activities differ so much, there is a strong argument for assigning special units to each one of the tasks. There are, however, also a number of reasons to perform them in close conjunction.

First, clear separation creates difficulties in communication that may lead to irrelevant creation, "stupid" exploitation, and delays in moving ideas to commercialization. The difficulties in making "listening posts" in high-tech locations such as Silicon Valley effective testify to the problems of separating thinking and observation from action. A company has to be active in more "mundane" business activities to become privy to what really goes on in such environments.

Second, the source of creation is often

in exploitation. As Rosenberg [1986] has shown, the notion of science leading to practical innovations needs to be modified. Often, many significant advances come from tinkering in daily work; in our language, from those busy exploiting rather than from those more freely creating. The importance of customer input and initiative in development [von Hippel 1976] also forces the two aspects together.

Third, the motivational consequences of assigning a unit or an individual to only exploitation may be disastrous. The problem is analogous to the disenchantment of those businesses honored with "dog" and "cash cow" status and given corresponding treatment and respect in the heydays of portfolio management, à la the Boston Consulting Group.

Fourth, fargoing specialization assumes that one knows where the likely profitable sources of novelty are. The exploration part of creation is endangered if certain countries or businesses are declared uninteresting. The "global scanner" [Vernon 1979] stakes its claim to fortune on exactly being able to scan globally, not only in certain places.

Finally, in the MNC the risk of, for example, a specialized R&D unit being ignored by the rest of the company is particularly great. The benefits of its activities are uncertain and distant in time as well as space. Thus, the cultural conflict between functions like R&D and marketing is aggravated in the MNC by the geographical distance between the functions following from a policy of assigning specialized roles.

For all these reasons, we see significant risks in the declaration of subsidiary roles. It may well be useful to think about the probable contributions in terms like those suggested by Bartlett and Ghoshal [1986], but it would be dangerous to cast the characters in sharp profile. We therefore hypothesize that the MNC increasingly will have to build its adaptive capability on the principle of "redundancy of functions" rather than on "redundancy of parts" [Emery and Trist 1973]. That is, the corporation should contain many units capable of *both* creation *and* exploitation, rather than units specialized in either direction. One can see the change from functional to divisional ("M-form") organization as one historical step in this direction. It now seems that the M-form encounters its own problems of inertia and conservatism, having to do with technology convergence, systemic innovation, and obstacles to the flow of knowledge across geographical frontiers. Thus, if the M-form merged the creation and exploitation functions *within one business*, the challenge now is to combine these functions *also across* related businesses and within as well as across *countries or regions*. The key word here is "also."

An empirical example from our ongoing research on global innovations may illustrate the problems in allocating subsidiary roles and separating creation from exploitation. The picture, if more than an unusual exception, seems to cast doubt both on a rigid application of Bartlett and Ghoshal [1986] and on a generalization of Porter's [1990] view of "industrial Hollywoods," although more on the latter.

Figure 3 shows the location of sophisticated demand (educated consumers, rich array of product features, many areas of product use, demand for high quality, publicly imposed standards, etc.) and sophisticated supply (technically competent firms, access to related technologies, educated workforce, local, relevant scientific community, and educational system, etc.) for a large Swedish MNC in a consumer durables industry. The empirical detail pertains to the development of a new line of products catering to an emerging area of demand, expected by the company to extend the boundaries of the industry. Four essential points are worth emphasizing:

1. The *location of sophisticated demand differs from the location of sophisticated supply*. For example, there is advanced know-how in the United States, but the U.S. consumer does not seem willing to pay for it, whereas there appears to be a market in Japan. This requires the firm (in whose structure the same competence profile is mirrored) to either move supply capability, or to find mechanisms of mobilizing it over distance to Japanese and, later, European problems and demand.

2. Both for demand and for supply, *the centers of gravity in terms of sophistication and expertise seem to be moving*. This makes any reliance on the present distribution risky. For example, the temptation to invest in the present U.S. "supply Hollywood" has to be tempered by the emergence of a future European center.

3. *Parts of the supply competence are located on different continents*. Depending on the type of use of the products involved, all three continents hold leading positions. Further complications arise in that there are some crucial components originating in a related technology, for which the competence is most

Figure 3. Where is Hollywood? The assessed location of critical knowledge in the development of a new product in an electrical engineering company

	Present	Future
Sophisticated demand	Japan	Japan and Europe
Sophisticated supply	1. USA 2. Japan	1. Japan (2. Europe?)

developed in Japan, for reasons quite distinct from the logic of the industry in question.

4. Some of the technologies and products involved are clearly in the traditional domain of the industry, whereas others are dominated by other firms. *No firm in the industry can hope to master all of the crucial elements in the development of the new line totally on its own*. Thus, intra- and interindustry collaboration, or at least close supplier relationships, will be required. These necessarily will extend across the continents.

The picture becomes even more complicated if we consider that the competence and demand profiles differ for other product areas within the firm. Clearly, "Hollywood" is all over the place, and it does not seem likely to coagulate into one spot even in the future, after competitive blood has flowed. Within the company, a mobilization of a tricontinental system of differentiated capabilities is required. To try to "rational-ize" this into a likely and stable future center of gravity appears risky, to say the least. Although he is commenting upon a slightly different problem, Nelson's [1991:71] warning seems justified: "If the 'rationally choosing' view of technological advance is misguided, the 'rationally choosing' view of organizational change is even more so."

THE LEVEL OF SEPARATION

Any discussion of degree of separation will appear unduly abstract unless the level at which the attendant specialization occurs also is specified. Comparisons between organizations are difficult since one company may select to specialize by assigning the tasks of innovation to one specific country subsidiary, whereas another specializes by forming a global project team of researchers, and a third by establishing permanent R&D units in all subsidiaries. Much of the debate in practice revolves around questions concerning which of such solutions to adopt. Figure 4 suggests a framework for differentiating among com-

Figure 4. Levels of Specialization of Creation and Exploitation

Level of specialization	Degree of specialization on exploitation and creation activities	
	HIGH	LOW
Between country subsidiaries	Differentiated country roles "Leaders and Implementers"	Innovation potential in all countries "Kanton Model"
Between units within HQ and subsidiaries	Functional structure Independent business units Dog and star departments "Maverick enclaves"	Product/consumer divisions Engineers on factory floor "A to Z responsibility"
Within projects and small groups	Part responsibilities Sharp interfaces Sequential process "Relay approach"	Whole responsibility Overlapping interfaces Parallel process "Rugby approach"
Between individuals	Specialist careers Deep Knowledge "Holmes and Watson"	Multifunction or generalist careers Broad knowledge "Renaissance company men"

pany profiles in this respect. For the sake of simplicity, we consider the case of an MNC with only one basic product and only one subsidiary in each country. The examples of manifestations of propensities to separate exploitation and creation at a given level are not meant to be exhaustive. The labels attached to the solution are imprecise attempts to convey the gist and atmosphere characterizing an organization betting, consciously or unconsciously, on the particular approach. Please note that we are referring to *separation of* creation and exploitation, and *not* on specialization *within* each category.

For a given MNC, there are two different ways of composing a "separation formula" on the basis of our crude categories. In reality, firms will of course mostly select (or find themselves blessed or cursed with) less extreme positions on each of the separation scales. In addition, they could of course specialize in other dimensions than the exploitation/creation one, and *within* these dimensions. For example, the "Kanton model" (after the Swiss "Kanton," a small self-governing community within the Swiss federation) is fully compatible with *different* R&D mandates in every subsidiary. The point is that every subsidiary has *some* innovation task.

Probably, the pure cases of extreme separation or combination of creation and exploitation are both less viable. The extreme specializer becomes a machine of tightly programmed entities, all with their different programs. A perfect hierarchy is required, first to split the organization up optimally and then make the pieces work together. The general arguments sketched above against a "redundancy of parts" solution applies to this case. The extreme of renaissance men running around in multifunctional and global teams with no clear structural haven is also rather a danger than a feasible vision. Innovation requires a certain depth and persistence not easily combined with simultaneous attention to daily routine problems. Therefore, the argument for redundancy of functions needs to be

tempered. However, the low separation option in itself is less extreme, since it implies a combination of activities (a both/and) rather than their exclusion (an either/or). It also provides a more "natural" way of coordinating the activities. If linking exploitation and creation is a problem of complex reciprocal interdependence, traditional information processing logic [Thompson 1967] would lead us to conclude that they are best internalized within the same unit (or even individual). The case for "organic" approaches is mostly made for creationlike activities. We would go further and hypothesize that organic coordination mechanisms are also effective when there are crucial interdependencies between creation and exploitation.

The two extremes are likely to be adapted to different innovation styles. Pure separation is consistent with science-driven and radical innovation, whereas pure combination is more likely to lead to marginal innovation on the basis of technological practice and user demands. However, the hypothesis of systemic/combinative technology providing for "leaps through breadth" rather than through depth would imply that the specializer is losing even this edge. The "appropriability regime," as emphasized by Teece [1986], also affects the relative attractiveness of the strategies. Where patent protection is cheap and effective, conditions may not necessitate heavy investment in "complementary assets." This has more to do with exploitation.

The anatomy of separation differs between corporations, but it is possible to discern some more general patterns. Figure 5 gives a rough characterization of large European, U.S., and Japanese MNCs' profiles. Reservations about averaging, estimating, guessing, and pure ignorance are offered gladly. Also, the figure does not consider that the relative *emphasis* on and *type* of creation/exploitation may differ between the contexts.

A profile such as the Japanese one would, on the basis of the arguments above, make one suspect a massive output of in-

Figure 5. Specialization of Creation and Exploitation Activities in European, US, and Japanese MNCs

	Degree of specialization		
Level of specialization	HIGH	MEDIUM	LOW
Between country subsidiaries	Japan	USA	Europe
Between units within HQ and subsidiaries		Japan USA Europe	
Within projects and small groups	USA	Europe	Japan
Between individuals	USA	Europe	Japan

cremental, combinative innovations strongly based on customer input from the units in the countries specialized on creation, i.e., from Japan. The Western profiles would be geared to infrequent thrusts of more science-driven innovation, in the U.S. case more clearly inspired by home country conditions than in the European one, where there is more scope for multiple sources of innovation. The differences are less clear at the intermediate level of organizational structure than at the macrolevel of country roles and the microlevel of organization of teams and individual careers. One reason may be that the basic structure of the firm is influenced primarily by historical demands for exploitation. Creation has been a structural "add-on" in all MNCs. Special R&D units may be broken up by product divisions, which happens in Japanese as well as Western firms. However, the coupling of R&D to manufacturing and marketing, and the focus on continuous improvement in all functions in Japanese firms, justify characterizing the Japanese pattern as slightly less specialized at this level as well. (See Hedlund and Nonaka [1991] for a discussion of differences in knowledge management between Japanese and Western firms.) Another reason for the similarity at the organizational level may be offered by institutional theory. A mix of co-

ercive and mimetic isomorphic pressures may well account for the apparent homogeneity.

The dominating organizational fashion during the past few decades has been to adopt what we have termed the "from A to Z responsibility" solution. Product (usually) divisions with their own R&D and sales and market research resources have replaced functionally or geographically oriented structures. This has facilitated inter*functional* collaboration. The consequences for inter*national* linkages are debatable. The intended improvements in rapid international technology transfer seem not to have materialized to the extent hoped for [Davidson and Haspeslagh 1982]. Other purely structural experiments in combining efficiency with flexibility and innovation similarly have shown mixed results, at best. The matrix structure, conceptually an attractive proposition, generally has not fared well recently in terms of adoption by MNCs.

Our tentative hypothesis is that the balancing of creation and exploitation is *not* primarily solved by manipulating the lines of division in the formal structure. The relative importance of structure is greater for calibrating the *type of exploitation* intended; for example, whether primarily to utilize local market power or the possession of unique product technology. The choice between functional and other types of structure may also bias the type of creation. As at other levels, separation (functional specialization) will generally lead towards "big leap" innovation.

METHODS OF COORDINATION AND SEQUENCING ISSUES

The most important aspect of coordinating creation and exploitation has already been discussed. Charging a unit or individual with both tasks is in itself a powerful integrating device. This solution, on the right side of Figure 4, is probably preferred when there are strong two-way interdependencies between creation and exploitation activities. Examples are when product design is intimately connected with manufacturing technology, or when sales techniques should significantly influence choices in product technology. The best mode of coordination within units is relatively "organic," built on physical co-location and informal networks. However, the close mutual coordination in cross-functional teams, for example, does not occur automatically, but has to be managed. Critical here is the role of upper management in encouraging formation and composition of project teams and providing them with adequate resources. Encouraging mobility of personnel and upholding communication among parts of the organization is also crucial.

The principle of internalizing reciprocities is, however, difficult to implement in an MNC, because geographical distance weakens all the mechanisms integral to the mutual coordination mode: co-location is by definition often impossible; personal networks are harder to form; common language and the transfer of tacit knowledge becomes problematic; etc. Efforts are often spent trying to compensate for this by adding more complex formal systems and technology. De Meyer [1991] documents cases illustrating the relative futility of such strategies, in the absence of well developed informal systems and personal contacts. Also, as we hinted at in the discussion of the

exploitation bias of formal structure, it is very difficult to specify exactly what needs to be internalized for creation. The openness and uncertainty inherent in such activities mean that the relevant units and individuals will vary from context to context. Therefore, creation is homeless in comparison with exploitation. Or, rather, the problem is continuously to define and redefine homes for it, drawing on resources and formal structures that may be set up primarily in a logic of exploitation. Thus, an archetypal mechanism for coordination becomes *the temporary, multifunctional and international project, with resources drawn from the operational (for exploitation) structures of the firm.*

There are well known problems of *interfunctional* communication. In the MNC, an interesting complicating factor is that the *international* dimension is added. Projects may be classified as in Figure 6, and "project management" will mean different things in the four cases.

When combining creation and exploitation, one is almost always forced to link what are traditionally called functions to each other. For all but those MNCs very dependent on one market (usually the "home" one), this will lead to international composition of the projects. Markets are usually more spread around than manufacturing locations and R&D units. The pioneers in terms of technical renewal may not be where those potentially benefitting most from (or having to adapt most to) their innovations are. There is, therefore, a drift in the MNC aspiring to innovation towards the most complex corner in Figure 6, where interfunctionalism is combined with internationalism. Traditions will dictate which aspect will present the most serious problems. Japanese firms will probably find functional integration easier than international, and vice versa for Western firms. The tendency will be for projects to deviate from the perhaps ideal combination: to global functionalism for the Western, and to national multifunctionalism for the Japanese MNC.

Figure 6. Types of Project Groups, with Examples

	Mainly *intrafunctional* coordination	Also *interfunctional* coordination
Mainly *national* coordination	Project in the national R&D laboratory	Development project with one country's lead customers and local factory
Also *international* coordination	Global factory rationalization project	Global new project launch project

When creation and exploitation are relatively specialized and clearly separated, there will be a greater reliance on formal coordination mechanisms such as planning systems, marketlike relations with internal pricing mechanisms, clear specification of roles in any mutual projects, formal coordinating bodies and conflict resolution mechanisms, etc. In this case, however, temporary projects may serve to bring the respective emphases together constructively. It will be more difficult than in an MNC where the basic structure is more balanced initially, but perhaps even more necessary.

In addition to the global project, we see three other key models for coupling creation and exploitation. The first one is what may be termed *organizational relay* (cf. Takeuchi and Nonaka [1986]). Centers of innovation and development pass on ideas and prototypes, or perhaps even products marketed in key markets, to units with more implementing roles. We have questioned this model above from several angles. It is likely that required reciprocity is replaced by imposed sequentiality, with delays and risks of attempts to export irrelevant products, badly adapted to various local demands and not benefiting from the potential availability of global development ideas and resources. When leadership is very clear and covering all functions of the firm, it may be the most desirable model, however.

A second alternative is the *independent business* unit model. New ideas are incorporated in new units with responsibility for development as well as commercialization

and later rationalization. Many companies do this with projects they consider outside the normal scope of the business, but prefer to integrate most initiatives in the basic structure, such as within a product division, at least after the most exploratory phase is over. In the MNC, the "3M solution" of launching masses of fledgling companies would mean the spawning of micro-MNCs. At the extreme, this will probably be a very wasteful model, and in the long run it would undermine the incentives and interest of the bulk of the organization to contribute resources to the procreation of its rapidly independent offspring. These incentive and culture problems may be addressed separately, however, so this is a solution that should be studied more.

A third mechanism, partly integral to some way of managing projects, is to have *individuals move with the phases of the projects or businesses*. Thus, an engineer responsible for the design of a prototype follows his idea and becomes at least partly responsible for its manufacturing, and later its sales. Balancing interfunctional and international concerns thus becomes internalized in an *individual*, rather than in an organizational unit or an overseeing body. In the MNC, this principle, even more than the previous ones, necessitates intense dedication to facilitating transfers of personnel (*not* only "managers"!) across organizational and geographic boundaries. It may be a superior solution when scale-up efforts do not qualitatively change the problem, and when largely tacit knowledge guides the interaction between creation and exploitation. Writing a scientific paper is an example.

The question of the *sequence* of creation and exploitation has already surfaced several times above. The product cycle hypotheses, as well as more general theories of stages of corporate and industry growth, hypothesizes initial creation to be followed by increasingly sophisticated and multifaceted exploitation, with the firm's competitive advantage shifting accordingly. Our general argument has been that creation should be given a more prominent place in "mature" circumstances. We have also questioned, as have many others (see, for example Takeuchi and Nonaka [1986]) the "microsequentialism" in "relay approaches" of product development. Here, we would just propose that the sequencing of activities, and the level at which one sequences them, is a neglected and critical issue. For example, should there be periods when the MNC concentrates on one or the other, or a more even distribution over time?

THEORETICAL CONCLUSIONS: HETERARCHY AND THE N-FORM CORPORATION

Our discussion can be summarized in some main points, which we believe are crucial in developing a better understanding of the dynamism of MNCs and which suggest parts of a framework for analyzing the issues involved.

1. Existing theories of the MNC generally focus on the MNC as an exploiter of given advantages, an optimizer around given transactions, or an efficient processor of given information. They do not analyze in any depth questions of innovation, in spite of sometimes giving superior technology and monopolistic advantages deriving from technology a prominent place in the explanation of why MNCs exist at all. The "original" advantage is assumed rather than ex-

plained, and the later renewal of the corporation through new innovations is even less considered in the fundamental logic of the theories.

2. The imbalance in the theoretical and, to some extent, practical treatment of innovation in MNCs can be put in terms of the partly conflicting logics of *exploitation* and *creation* activities, respectively. Every organization needs both, and two main difficulties are raised in this connection. First, there is a tendency for exploitation to drive out creation. Second, the strategic, organizational, and managerial requirements of the two activities differ substantially. For MNCs, the potential for creation is enhanced by the scanning, learning, and combination potential provided by the extended and diverse global organizational network.

3. Combining exploitation and creation raises difficult questions of relative emphasis, degree, levels of separation and specialization, methods of organizational coordination, and sequencing.

4. There are great risks in pushing *separation* so far that exploitation and creation are decoupled. Therefore, assigning very specific and stable "subsidiary roles" in this sense is probably not desirable. Many issues are obscured unless the *level* of specialization of exploitation and creation is also considered. Four critical levels need to be evaluated: the country, the organizational unit, the project group, and the individual. MNCs from different countries exhibit different tendencies, and this affects the type and rate of innovation. Strictly separating creation from exploitation, at all levels, is likely to lead to infrequent but sub-

stantial innovations based on, usually, home country conditions and to difficulties in rapid commercialization, particularly internationally. A lower degree of specialization will tend to produce more incremental innovations, with a rapid flow of products transferred quickly across the globe.

5. *Coordination* of exploitation and creation is most effectively achieved through assigning both tasks to a given organizational unit. Low separation, therefore, and structuring according to the principle of redundancy of functions, may be the basic design choice. The geographical extension, the variability of the environment, and the unpredictability of combinative options, however, preclude the specification of clear and stable clusters of units, individuals and countries to be so combined. More specific mechanisms of coordination, in line with the logic above, include investments in technical information systems to facilitate complex interunit and interindividual communication systems for personnel rotation, intensive use of global and interfunctional projects, the establishment of independent business units outside the regular structure, and having individuals transfer along with the progression of projects. The global project becomes a fundamental unit of action, replacing management of and through a formal structure of units and stable responsibilities.

The MNC balancing the demands of exploitation and creation becomes a beast much more difficult to capture in the conceptual nets of traditional organization theory than the basically exploiting one assumed in the more formalized literature on MNCs. This may be one explanation for the relative lack of theoretical underpinnings in the speculative writings on MNC management. Some recent contributions attempt to relate the analysis of the MNC to more basic organizational theory. (See pieces in Ghoshal and Westney, eds., [1992]; Ghoshal and Bartlett [1990].) We would suggest that a promising avenue, in addition to these, may be to focus on the self-renewing capability of the MNC. This, however, takes us into theoretical domains rather different from those of such areas as network analysis, institutional theory, resource dependency models, or even evolutionary economics (although there is more in the latter that seems directly applicable). Rather than such very worthwhile efforts, this strategy forces us to reconsider some of the fundamental tenets of our theories of the firm and organization. A better understanding of the creative potential of the modern MNC may even provide ideas for reformulation of the general theories, rather than just for extensions to and exceptions for the MNC.

Two conclusions at this more general theoretical level seem to follow from our discussion. *First*, innovation and creation, or for that matter simply more alert exploitation, cannot be provided by optimal configuration of a corporate hierarchy. Instead, what we have earlier termed a *heterarchy* seems to be a better model for self-renewal. It is important to note that we are *not* posing heterarchy as the archetype of pure and extreme creation. More anarchical or "adhocratic" [Mintzberg 1979] structures fit better here. Instead, heterarchy provides a way of thinking about the *integration* of exploitation and creation. There *is* clear super- and subordination, but not universally (over all issues for a given agent) or eternally. (See Hedlund [1992] for detailed arguments on this and the following point.)

To substantiate the contentions above thoroughly would require a lengthy discussion. Here, only an outline can be attempted. First, it is interesting to note how in most of the literature "hierarchy" is taken as obvious in terms of both meaning and superiority as organizing principle. Simon's [1962] celebrated paper has met with very little critique and much unreflective acceptance and citation. We have tried to show elsewhere how Simon's arguments build on assumptions of stability and non-complex interaction between parts of a system. Arrow [1974:68–70] also states without much ado that "it is cheaper and more efficient to transmit all the pieces of information once to a central place than to disseminate each of them to everyone," and "[f]or the same reasons of efficiency, it may be cheaper for a central individual or office to make the collective decision and transmit it." It is significant, we believe, that there now appear papers by economists explicitly questioning the universality, or even commonality, of hierarchy as an efficient information processing device. See Radner [1989], for an example. On the basis of a simple mathematical example akin to Simon's [1962] famous watchmaking one, Radner arrives at conclusions concerning the implications of "decentralized" information remarkably close to our own: "if there are hierarchies embedded in the patterns of information processing, *there are many overlapping ones*" (our emphasis [45]). Both Radner and Arrow, by the way, speculate on the social, religious, and ontological sources of and reasons for hierarchy, rather than the economic ones. We would agree, and argue that the inventor of the word, Dionysus the Areopagite [Hedlund 1992] surpassed the muddled definitions and implicit biases of most organization theory in his characterization of the celestial hierarchy. We have inherited a whole web of interlinked precepts, and the irrelevance of some of these in a modern, industrial context is the reason organizational hierarchies seem to be crumbling. We are forced to invent new words such as "transnationals" and "heterarchies."

Trying to "disentangle" the idea of hierarchy, we can, following Hedlund [1992], distinguish between three fundamental structures in an organization: a *structure of* authority and social seniority, *a structure of action*, and *a structure of knowledge.* The *social structure* is mostly organized in a pyramidlike fashion, with clear super- and subordination in terms of respect, rewards, status, etc. One of the main virtues of this is that there is a clear way of rewarding behavior useful to the organization. The *action structure* increasingly is *not* congruent with the social one. The old idea, that people at the top (or at *head*quarters) have strategic wisdom and those further down (or in the *sub*sidiaries) implement, is breaking down. One reason for this is that God (the CEO) does not any longer know everything, nor can he usefully integrate all the pieces. Thus, the properties of the *knowledge structure* are central to our argument. Only under the most simple and stable conditions can the knowledge of an organization be structured in a stable hierarchy. Much less will it mirror, other than during short periods of stability, the social and action structures. In other words, hierarchy in the sense of coinciding structures may be a solution for exploitation, but not for creation.

Disentangling the concept of hierarchical organization is more necessary the greater the change and geographical and organizational diffusion (see, Hagström [1991]) of knowledge and capacity for strategic actions. Thus, the MNC active in fields of rapid and geographically widely extended technical and market change is a prime candidate for such disentanglement. The social structure may be kept rather simple, traditional, and stable, whereas the action and knowledge ones cannot. The formal organization could be seen as the "home," from which individuals disappear and to which they may return, or at least *belong to* and where they can *be located and found.* Much real action, however, will take place outside this structure, often in project or other temporary forms. This may make it possible to "promote" and reward people without taking them away from what they know best, and to impress upon the "top managers" that they are not necessarily paid for interfering in present work—best done and led by others—but for past performance and for a number of more catalytic roles (initiate projects, "know who," set broad directions, ensure investments in recruitment, rotation, and research, etc.).

The heterarchy, therefore, *may* entail a very traditional formal structure. One does not attempt to cover all complexity through organizational boxes and arrows. Our argument of separate structures of knowledge, action, and social position seems to be one way of explaining the tendency in the transnational corporation of Bartlett and Ghoshal [1989] to de-emphasize "anatomy" and emphasize "physiology" and "psychology."

It is interesting to note that Aoki [1990] poses a disjunction between a hierarchy for rewards and one for information processing as a key element in his theory of the Japanese firm. In our view (see Hedlund and Nonaka [1991]), the proclivity for rapid and continuous improvement in many Japanese corporations may be associated with this heterarchical property. The mere fact of disentangling the issue also allows us to make sense of the many conflicting claims concerning, for example, centralization and formalism in the Japanese firm: The social hierarchy is centralized and formal, whereas the information processing one is not. We would argue that one needs to go further and distinguish between the knowledge and action structures.

Also in the context of the MNC, questions of centralization take on another meaning. Hagström [1991;1992] suggests that in "the Wired MNC" (the MNC intensively using modern information technology) the notions of *closeness* (access, not geography!) to headquarters and core systems and of *demand* for control from auxiliaries (not subsidiaries!) partly replace the notions of centralization and supply of control, respectively. We interpret this as a reflection of the need, at the nodes, to link into the complex and fluid systems of knowledge stocks and flows, and to be considered in the diffused system of strategic action.

It might be suggested that Galbraith's [1973] arguments, extended by Egelhoff [1991], provide the same perspective as the one we have advanced. We see two main differences. First, the formal structure is still considered primarily an information processing device, whereas we attribute other roles to it. Particularly in Galbraith, the structure is one of the chief instruments. Other methods are resorted to only when the formal structure is not adequate. Second, the concepts of information and processing are, in our view, more problematical and multidimensional than even the richer treatment in Egelhoff [1991] implies. For example, the need to turn information into knowledge, and to create and enact rather than only process and react on environmental stimuli, imply closer links between exploitation and creation (including between manufacturing and R&D), a potential for continuous organizational relocation and relinking of resources, and greater attention to the role of parties external to the firm in the renewal process.

Second, the equally powerful and generally accepted connection between transaction cost considerations and the multidivisional form of organization (M-form) is cast in a dubious light. It is not necessary here to repeat the critique above of assuming given and discrete transactions. However, the implications of this critique for the view of corporate governance form need further discussion. Here, we will indicate two lines of argument of possible relevance for this question.

Companies seem to be reconsidering their multidivisional organization because of technological convergence between product areas, opening possibilities for combination in new products (cf. Pavitt, Robson, and Townsend [1989]). One example is Kodak's launch of "photo CD," combining chemical photography and electronics. Also at the marketing end, brand name and distribution economies tend to pull divisions closer, often after a long period of ever-increasing differentiation. It could be argued that creation is inconsistent with the focus on *dividing* up givens, which is the essential process in the emergence of the M-form. Dividing something known rarely produces anything new. But *combining* knowns may produce novelty. Perhaps one can pose the *N-form hypothesis* as a heuristic for further theoretical work. "N" here stands for novelty, and comes after "M." The basic properties of the N-form would, we argue, be those of the heterarchy.

The second point concerns the implications of this idea for a theory of corporate governance. The M-form hypothesis, as the general logic of transaction cost economics, sees the firm as an institutional response selected by a process of elimination in competition or by forethought, in order to optimize for a certain problem. In the N-form, the firm is rather a selecting institution, a meta-institution in terms of the previous logic. Top management in the M-form is a substitute for a capital market and owners. In the N-firm its role is much more active, concerned with integration as much as with differentiation, with "multiplication" by combining elements as much as with division, and with social and technological architecture more than with financial architecture. This speculative conceptual hunch could be shrugged off more easily if it was based only on *a priori* theoretical arguments against static assumptions. However, to us the picture of large MNCs working more on internal synergies and (successful) top management as an involved actor in realizing them seems to conform to what actually happens. MNCs act as self-renewing systems and theories need to reflect this.

■ ■ ■

COMMENTARIES
W. Graham Astley

The Blurring of Organizational Boundaries in Multinational Corporations

Two of the papers in this session deal directly with the evolving structure of multi-national corporations (MNCs). Egelhoff's paper examines the role of information technologies in enhancing coordination and communication within MNCs, while Hedlund and Ridderstråle investigate how MNCs can be structured in order to promote innovation. The third paper, by Westney, is pitched at a more macrolevel of analysis and deals with the potential for applying the abstract perspectives of organization theory to current problems and issues within international business (IB). However, Westney's paper focuses specifically on the interface between organizations and their environments, and so pertains indirectly to the operations of MNCs.

Rather than discuss each of the papers separately, I will try to draw on certain themes addressed by the papers and, where possible, integrate their insights. I will do this in the context of an overall thesis, advanced by this paper: subunit and organizational boundaries in MNCs are becoming increasingly blurred, or are disappearing altogether, in order to enhance operating flexibility and innovation within MNCs. In his 1990 annual report, Jack Welsh commented that in redesigning General Electric he was trying to create a "boundaryless organization—by knocking down the walls that separate us from each other on the inside and from our key constituencies on the outside" [Rose 1990:162]. In Welch's vision, this would involve replacing vertical hierarchies with horizontal networks, breaking down functional boundaries with interfunctional teams, forming strategic alliances with suppliers, customers, and even competitors, and recognizing no distinctions between domestic and foreign operations.

The rationale for dissolving boundaries is that boundaries make organizations rigid and unresponsive, and, in a world of rapid technological change, short product life cycles, and global competition, greater operating flexibility and the capacity to innovate are increasingly necessary [Hirschorn and Gilmore 1992]. The present paper investigates the issue of boundaries in terms of the degree and type of interdependence, or coupling, between the activities of different subunits and between organizations and their environments.

THE EVOLUTION OF MNC STRATEGY

Perlmutter [1969] contended that MNCs may be described as "ethnocentric" (home-country oriented), "polycentric" host-country oriented), or "geocentric" (world oriented) toward international competition. Ethnocentric multinationals centralize authority in their headquarters and apply similar management processes, operating procedures, and performance criteria to their foreign operations. Polycentric multinationals, in contrast, begin with the assumption that since host-country cultures and competitive environments are fundamentally idiosyncratic, local managers must be given considerable autonomy to operate their subsidiaries. Finally, geocentric multinationals adopt a worldwide approach in both headquarters and subsidiaries. The firm's subsidiaries are thus neither dependent satellites nor independent operating units, but collaborative partners attempting to integrate local with worldwide objectives as part of a coherent global strategy.

Perlmutter [1969] postulated an evolutionary movement from ethnocentrism to polycentrism to geocentrism. He argued that firms tend to be ethnocentric when they first venture abroad, but their highly standardized approach creates social and political repercussions and inhibits competitive innovations. This often leads to the adoption of a polycentric approach designed to achieve a more intensive penetration of local markets, the acquisition of better information about customers, and more host-government support. Finally, firms become more geocentric as they realize the need to mobilize resources on a worldwide scale to take advantage of interdependencies among national markets and to retaliate against rivals who use different competitive tactics in different markets to create a global strategic advantage. Variations on Perlmutter's evolutionary model have certainly been pro-

posed, both with respect to the sequence in which different stages appeared historically [Bartlett and Ghoshal 1989:49–55], and with respect to regional differences in evolutionary patterns, e.g., differences between U.S., European, and Japanese MNCs [158–165]. Despite such variations, Perlmutter's model serves as a useful heuristic for the subsequent argument of this paper.

MNC STRUCTURE: INTERDEPENDENCE, COUPLING, AND BOUNDARIES

Egelhoff's paper introduces the distinction between tight and loose coupling and applies these notions to the interdependencies existing between foreign subsidiaries, and to the interdependencies existing between subsidiaries and their local environments. In other words, the activities of an MNC's internal subunits can be tightly or loosely coupled, and the operations of an MNC and its external constituents can be tightly or loosely coupled. The type of coupling existing at these two boundaries—subunit and organizational—have implications for an MNC's operating flexibility and its capacity to innovate. In order to explore these implications, this section examines the type of interdependence and degree of coupling associated with Perlmutter's [1969] three MNC strategies.

The Ethnocentric Multinational

The highly centralized and standardized operations of ethnocentric multinationals suggest an organizational structure that is geared to what Hedlund and Ridderstråle's paper describes as "exploitation"— a mechanistic, static, inflexible structure that is ill-suited for creative innovation. The specialized operations of subunits are linked through sequential interdependencies. Like cogs in a machine, subunit activities are tightly coupled. All of the organization's component elements are set in place to produce an integrated functioning of the whole system. Each subunit's autonomy is minimized in a tightly coordinated pattern of collective action—a monolithic organization whose internal parts mesh like a set of well fitted gears. At the same time, efficiency is enhanced by "buffering" the organization's technical core from environmental disturbances [Thompson 1967]. The resulting combination of functionally specialized subunits and environmental buffers means that both subunit and organizational boundaries are clearly defined. Table 1 summarizes these characteristics of the ethnocentric multinational.

The Polycentric Multinational

The autonomous subsidiaries of polycentric multinationals suggest a pattern of "pooled" interdependence. They are what Glassman [1973], Weick [1976], and Orrok and Weick [1990] describe as "loosely coupled systems." Such loose coupling makes the organization more flexible in responding to changing environments. In this view, allowing subunits to act relatively independently promotes flexibility through localized adaptations while minimizing the ramifications of change in the rest of the organization. The resulting structure of polycentric multinationals, as Egelhoff's paper indicates, is a combination of loose coupling among subsidiaries, but tight coupling among each subsidiary and its environment. This implies clearly defined boundaries between autonomous subunits, but blurred boundaries between the organization and its environmental constituents (see Table 1).

The Geocentric Multinational

In the geocentric multinational, subsidiaries engage in collaborative interactions in the attempt to integrate local with worldwide objectives, and this suggests that they are linked through "reciprocal" interdependencies [Thompson 1967]. Local flexibility is combined with global integration by tightly coupling subsidiary activities but in a way that preserves flexibility. Such "flexible coupling" [Astley and Zajac 1991] implies a high degree of interdependence among subsidiaries, but also a pattern of interdependence that is constantly changing. This situation differs from that found in the mechanistic structures of ethnocentric multinationals where subsidiaries and headquarters are linked together in a rigid, predefined system of relationships. In these mechanistic structures, coordination is achieved through plans and schedules. In flexibly coupled structures, ad hoc decision making substitutes for planning and enhances adaptability by allowing personnel to respond to changes as they occur. This is achieved by increasing the amount of communication across subunit boundaries, in effect blurring those boundaries through the use of cross-functional teams and other lateral integrating devices that facilitate learning [Hayes, Wheelwright, and Clark 1988; Hayes and Jaikumar 1988; Nemetz and Fry

Table 1. Strategy, Interdependence, Coupling and Boundaries in Multinational Corporations

Strategy	Type of Subunit Interdependence	Degree of Coupling		Permeability of Boundaries	
		Inter-Subunit	Organization-Environment	Subunit	Organizational
Ethno-centric	Sequential	Tight (Mechanistic Coupling)	Loose	Clearly Defined	Clearly Defined
Polycentric	Pooled	Loose	Tight	Clearly Defined	Blurred
Geocentric	Reciprocal	Tight (Flexible Coupling)	Tight	Blurred	Blurred

1988]. This creates a more adaptive organization whose tight coupling and responsiveness to environmental constituencies, in turn, blurs organizational boundaries (see Table 1).

FLEXIBILITY AND INNOVATION IN MNCS: THE DISSOLUTION OF SUBUNIT BOUNDARIES

Flexibility

If it is true that MNCs are progressively adopting geocentric structures, what is the competitive advantage afforded by these structures? One advantage of coordinating activities across the globe is the economies of scale that can be achieved by serving homogeneous world markets [Hout et al., 1982; Levitt 1983]. Perhaps more important, however, are the advantages deriving from what Kogut [1985] termed "operating flexibility." Kogut [1989:384] summarized these advantages in the following manner: "The value of such flexibility rests not only on exploiting differentials in factor, product, and capital markets, but also on the transfer of learning and innovations throughout the firm, as well as the enhanced leverage to respond to competitors' and governments' threats." Thus, MNCs may, among other things, shift production capacity between countries, adjust transfer prices to minimize taxes, arbitrage informational imperfections across national borders, and benefit from government subsidies intended to encourage local investment.

According to Kogut [1989:384], the key to achieving operating flexibility is to "coordinate flows within a multination network." As Bartlett and Ghoshal [1989 chap. 1] argued, the challenge is an organizational one, which they suggest can be met by the "transnational" MNC with its integrated, yet flexibly coordinated, network. "Heterarchic" structures with their multiple, geographically dispersed centers achieve a similar result [Hedlund and Rolander 1990]. I agree with Egelhoff that such organizational structures can be profitably analyzed from an information pro-

cessing perspective. I would suggest further, that the archetypal geocentric MNC would, to use Egelhoff's terminology, possess an information network with global "reach"— one that transcends national and geographical boundaries. In addition, such MNCs likely would rely increasingly on "nonroutine, reciprocal information processing" that achieves flexible coupling through "horizontal information systems": mechanisms of coordination such as task forces, teams, integrating roles, etc. that span across and blur subunit boundaries.

I would contend, in addition, that information technology blurs vertical boundaries as well as horizontal boundaries. A reliance on lateral, cross-functional information processing and communication entails decentralization. Knowledge is disseminated throughout the organization rather than being the exclusive province of top managers, so intelligent decision making takes place at all levels. On the other hand, centralized coordination and control may coexist with decentralized decision making. Applegate et al., [1988] pointed out that information technology allows top management to monitor data at the lowest organizational levels without using an extensive chain of command. Computers assume many of the communication and coordination functions that middle managers previously performed, so that control systems no longer have to be embedded in hierarchical reporting relationships. Decentralized decision making can thus exist simultaneously with centralized control and integrated coordination [Keen 1986]. This results in organizations with tightly coupled structures, but they are not rigid mechanistic systems. Instead, they are intelligent, adaptive systems characterized by their dynamic flexibility and learning capabilities [Hayes, Wheelwright, and Clark 1988].

Innovation

Hedlund and Ridderstråle's paper also points to the need for blurring subunit boundaries, though for different reasons. They reject the mechanistic model traditionally adopted by MNCs because it is too rigidly focused on the exploitation of current operations and stifles creativity and innovation, especially "systemic innovations" that involve multiple technologies or require cooperation among different subunits. Instead of the compartmentalized, hierarchically coordinated, subunits of the mechanistic model, they advocate greater use of lateral relationships, cross-functional collaboration, and the elimination of boundaries between "doers" and "thinkers." Most significantly, these authors advocate against the separation of the exploitation function from the creation or innovation function. For example, such separation might lead to innovations that are difficult or impossible to implement or exploit and would prevent modifications introduced in the implementation process from generating innovative advances. Finally, the authors recommend not just the elimination of boundaries among functional specialities but also the elimination of geographical boundaries among activities located in different countries.

The elimination of boundaries not only enhances the creativity necessary for innovation to occur, it also increases the speed at which innovations can be developed and commercialized. For example, so-called concurrent engineering is a method of circumventing the inevitable delays that occur when different stages of product development are handled sequentially by different functional departments. Concurrent engineering involves tearing down the walls between departments, especially between design and manufacturing. Personnel of different functional specialties are then located in close proximity in identical cubicles. When a project starts up, the engineers, in effect, play musical cubicles so that they work side by side and constantly compare notes. This process dramatically reduces the time needed to introduce products to market, which is essential in an environment of short life cycles. The results are even more impressive when personnel from different

functional specialties share the same data bases, as in computer-integrated manufacturing. This eliminates the time-consuming downloads and uploads encountered as data is passed from one department to another.

Concurrent engineering and computer-integrated manufacturing are specific examples of a more general philosophy that competitive advantage accrues to those companies that minimize the time taken to develop innovations [Stalk 1988; Bower and Hout 1988; Stalk and Hout 1990]. Companies that are successful in this endeavor resist the tendency to divide responsibilities among functionally specialized units, or to measure and reward different functional specialties or divisions according to different criteria. When this occurs, subunits focus suboptimally on their localized objectives with the result that a coherent strategy fails to materialize. This problem is especially acute in MNCs where integration across different areas, products, functions, and strategic orientations is a mammoth task [Bartlett and Ghoshal 1989]. The solution is to eliminate barriers to communication and encourage more interactive and cooperative working relationships by dissolving or deemphasizing the boundaries that compartmentalize activities into subunits.

FLEXIBILITY AND INNOVATION IN MNCS: THE DISSOLUTION OF ORGANIZATIONAL BOUNDARIES

Organization Sets

The boundaries between MNCs and their environments are also blurring as they become members of larger collectivities. These collectivities can be analyzed at different levels, the lowest of which is what Evan [1967] referred to as the "organization set." An organization set consists of those organizations with which a focal organization has direct links, such as suppliers, distributors, subcontractors, competitors, etc. If transactions with these organizations are mediated through the marketplace, MNC boundaries remain relatively clearly defined. However, if the MNC enters into a collaborative arrangement with these organizations, e.g., licensing, joint ventures, strategic alliances, etc., some merging of the two decision-making bodies occurs with the result that the MNC's boundaries start to blur.

I agree with Hedlund and Ridderstråle that creation- or innovation-oriented firms are more likely to enter into such collaborative arrangements. Friedman [1983], for example, observed how the use of "just-in-time" inventory controls by Japanese auto makers encouraged active collaboration with their suppliers, in contrast to the arm's length relationships that have traditionally existed between U.S. auto makers and their suppliers. Collaboration gives suppliers much greater design and production access to the auto makers and encourages the exchange of technical know-how. As a result, Japanese producers benefit from innovations that suppliers introduce into their components, as they work jointly with suppliers on the design of autos. This cooperation stands in marked contrast to the aloof relationship that less-innovative U.S. producers have maintained with suppliers.

Such collaborative relationships are becoming increasingly important in a global environment where innovation increasingly involves systemic technologies, since MNCs often rely on each other to supply "complementary assets" [Teece 1987]. Both because these technological systems encompass many different expensive technologies, and because shorter product life cycles are increasing rates of technological obsolescence, single companies are rarely able to keep abreast of all relevant technical developments [McKenna 1985]. Instead, they may use what Hamilton [1985] described as an "options strategy," entering into multiple strategic alliances, but with the intention of terminating alliances if the technology they yield proves unpromising, or possibly substituting in-house production if the technology develops successfully. In this way, cooperation affords MNCs greater strategic

flexibility, in addition to enhancing innovative capability.

Action Sets

At a level of analysis higher than that of the organization set, the membership of MNCs in "action sets" [Aldrich 1979:280] further blurs organizational boundaries. An action set is a group of organizations formed into a temporary alliance for a limited purpose. The concept of action set refers to an interacting group of organizations, in contrast to the concept of organization set which is explicitly centered on a focal organization. Membership in action sets represents a more fundamental adaptation to the environment than does membership in organization sets because organizational autonomy and localized objectives are partially subordinated to the pursuit of collective goals. The creation of organization sets may be interpreted simply as an extension of managerial control across organizational boundaries in the sense that Pfeffer and Salancik [1978] discuss joint ventures as mechanisms for managing environmental dependence and maintaining organizational autonomy. Being part of an action set, on the other hand, implies some loss of an MNC's autonomy.

Action sets are, thus, multilateral coalitions with their own collective properties and dynamics. Action sets may, however, emerge from the convergence of several organization sets. For example, the systematic usage of strategic alliances over time may produce larger coalitions with their own collective properties and dynamics. Thus, IBM's pursuit of an options strategy in forming alliances with a multitude of software producers, chip makers, and communications firms has resulted in the creation of a broad coalition of producers promoting IBM-compatible systems. Consequently, rivals must compete not just against IBM but against a whole group of interlinked firms that may exchange know-how and jointly disseminate their innovations. Faced with this prospect, competitors are forced to join opposing coalitions, as Sun, Unisys, and others have done in backing AT&T's computer software as an alternative to IBM's. Such coalitions need not be limited to firms in the same industry: the Japanese keiretsu, which have been so crucial in that country's global presence, are coalitions of manufacturers, banks, insurers, and trading companies [Gerlach 1987]. In such instances, adaptation to the environment is a truly collective phenomenon, in which conventional MNC boundaries begin to lose their significance.

Populations, Fields, and Communities

Westney's paper directs us to levels of analysis even higher than that of action sets. For example, the notion of a population of organizations—organizations of the same "form" that share a common environmental "niche"—draws our attention to a level of analysis above that of a group of organizations that directly collaborate. Populations are relevant to organizational innovation because organizations of the same form are part of what McKelvey [1982] refers to as the same "intercommunicating competence pool." That is, they freely transmit managerial and technical know-how (perhaps by hiring each other's personnel) and thus readily adopt each other's innovations. Westney also draws attention to institutional theory's notion of an "organizational field"—an aggregate of organizations that do not necessarily interact but, nevertheless, through their social roles, constitute a recognized area of institutional life. The concept of an organizational field is broader than the concept of a population since it refers not just to competing firms but to the totality of constituencies relevant to an organization's functioning. Nevertheless, there are similar implications for innovation. As Westney points out, through "normative isomorphism," firms are led to adopt new actions that are championed by professional organizations, and through "mimetic isomorphism," organizations follow the lead of more successful or innovative organizations in the same organiza-

tional field. Ghoshal [1988], for example, demonstrated how normative and mimetic isomorphism induced Korean firms to adopt similar innovations in environmental scanning practices.

Westney also draws our attention to community ecology—the study of multiple, interdependent populations that coexist as a functionally integrated system. Westney's reference to Porter's [1990] notion of "industry clusters"—groups of related and supporting industries—is germane here. Porter ascribes a central role to industry clusters in establishing and maintaining a nation's competitiveness: their mutual exchange of products, ideas, technical know-how, etc., provides a critical mass of expertise that fosters innovations not available to countries lacking such industrial configurations. Along these lines, Krugman [1986:13] described how interindustry linkages can generate "external economies"—those increases in an industry's productivity that are derived from technological advances occurring in other industries. Such linkages are of two types: vertical inputs, as when the products of one industrial sector are used as components in another, and horizontal spillovers, as when techniques developed in one sector find application in another. The contemporary importance of such external economies further reinforces the idea that MNCs operating in complex technological and global environments cannot be regarded as autonomous, self-sufficient, clearly bounded entities; their existence is inextricably tied to that of external parties so that boundary permeability becomes a prerequisite of their successful functioning and ability to innovate.

Nation-States

Westney points out that institutional theory draws our attention to yet a higher level of analysis: that of the nation-state, or even interacting nation-states. The state influences the actions of MNCs through "coercive isomorphism"—the imposition of power and authority—though such influence is clearly a two-way process [Vernon

360

1971]. This is, perhaps, the central fact of the MNC's existence, and constitutes the peculiar subject matter of IB. Competition among MNCs is not simply rivalry between firms based in different countries; it is competition that occurs in environments that are shaped by governments in ways that further national interests. Such environments are politically and institutionally defined, either through negotiations between different countries [Prestowitz 1988], or through negotiations between countries and MNCs [Reich 1991b]. Nation-states, as well as firms, should be regarded as strategic actors; nations, themselves, possess strategies [Scott 1985]. Again, there are clear implications for innovation in state-MNC interactions. Through industrial policy, the state can foster innovation and enhance the competitiveness of its home-based firms. The classic example is provided by Japan's MITI that helped coordinate favorable taxation policies, funding arrangements, resource allocation decisions, and trade policies. Japan's current targeting of high technology sectors clearly illustrates the important role the state can play in enhancing corporate innovation [Patrick 1986]. This is another important way in which MNCs are opening up or dissolving their boundaries.

CONCLUSION

The three papers in this session have captured important facets of the pressures and contingencies which MNCs are currently facing. As Egelhoff implies, the importance of information technology is undeniable: it is the new global infrastructure. As Hedlund and Ridderstråle argue, in a dynamically changing system of world markets, creation or innovation has become more important than ever. I agree with Westney, however, that organization theory has had little to contribute to the analysis of such issues, or to the field of IB in general. I suspect, also, that the application of extant theoretical perspectives such as organizational ecology and institutional theory will only take us so far in understanding global

phenomena. What is needed is the development of new perspectives that are distinctively international in nature. Discerning what "distinctively international" actually means is, I believe, the major challenge currently facing the field.

The present paper suffers from some of these same limitations. Many of the trends described above apply to all organizations, not just MNCs. I would argue, however, that the issue of boundaries is probably more critical for MNCs than for domestically oriented firms, simply because of the sheer complexity of managing these behemoths. If it is true, as Bartlett and Ghoshal [1989] and Hedlund and Rolander [1990] contend, that the strategic problems facing MNCs are, today, multidimensional in nature, then the creation of flexibility and the capacity to innovate emerge as high, if not the highest, priority needs for the managers of MNCs. This paper has argued that the key to enhancing flexibility and innovation in geocentric multinationals is to dissolve boundaries, both subunit boundaries and organizational boundaries, in an attempt to open up these organizations to the complex, dynamically evolving, global environment.

Sumantra Ghoshal

Of Cakes, Clothes, Emperors, and Obituaries

Individually, each of the three papers presented in this panel is interesting and there is much one could discuss about the ideas and advocacy Gunnar Hedlund and Jonas Ridderstråle, Eleanor Westney, and Bill Egelhoff have put before us. Collectively, however, they reflect a field of inquiry that is inconsistent in its assumptions, incoherent in its approach, and stagnant in its direction. Strong words, these, and not in keeping with the tradition of polite discourse and mutual admiration that we have established for ourselves, but I believe they need to be said. This conference will not serve its purpose unless all of us confront the reality that collectively we represent a field that appears to be considerably poorer than the sum of the individuals who contribute to it.

Eleanor's disdain for contingency theory is manifest. Her dissatisfaction with the assumptions of rationality and strategic choice underlying contingency theory provides the foundation for her advocacy that population ecology and institutional theory should serve as the anchors for future research on organizational and environmental aspects of international business (IB). This is in sharp contrast to Bill's explicit focus on contingencies and fit, and his efforts here to extend his information processing model to the topic of how information technologies might be used in multinational corporations (MNCs).

Gunnar's discomfort with the notion of fitting anything to anything is just as obvious as that of Eleanor's. Pushing further along his own advocacy of the heterarchy model, he has now provided a framework that distinguishes structuring for exploitation of capabilities versus structuring for creation of capabilities and clearly links the notion of heterarchy to this later, superior approach. His conceptualization of knowledge creation is also very different from Bill's framing of the information processing tasks. This does not place Gunnar in Eleanor's corner, however, for his arguments are firmly grounded in the implicit assumption of strategic choice and of rationality, albeit in constrained ways—assumptions that are sharply at variance from the underlying logic of ecological determinism or even that of passive surrender to the institutional forces of conformity. While the authors and others in the audience can fault my analysis for being insensitive to nuances in the arguments that reveal common grounds, I would argue that those nuances are secondary to the broader and clearer reality: we have here three papers that make very different assumptions about both the organizational realities in MNCs and about the usefulness of different theories in illuminating those realities.

Such differences could be a reflection of either intellectual vigor or of stagnation. One could argue that such divergent approaches are the first sign that the field is indeed beginning its transition from an atheoretical stage; further reflection and empirical exploration will gradually lead to conceptual clarity and theoretical convergence. Such hopes are belied, however, by the fact that all three authors have been advocating the same ideas over the past seven to ten years without either confronting competing perspectives or modifying their own views. The theoretical perspective in Bill's paper remains the same as in his 1982 ASQ article. Eleanor made basically the same points in her presentation to the AIB's annual meeting in 1988. She has added population ecology as a potential theoretical anchor, but primarily on the ground that this may help IB researchers in the publish-or-perish game. While Gunnar has added to both the conceptual richness and the literature grounding of the heterarchy model, the model itself is not dissimilar to the proposal he presented in his 1986 HRM paper. In an intellectually vibrant and energetic field, these ideas would have been picked up, subjected to empirical testing, and challenged on theoretical grounds so as to ultimately lead to a process of selection from, or some integration across, the diverse perspectives. None of that has really happened. Neither have the authors themselves referred to each others' ideas. If Eleanor feels contingency theory has run its course, she cannot possibly be comfortable with Bill's work continuing within that paradigm. She pointedly avoids that question; nor have others either contributed to or challenged these arguments. That, to me, is a sign of stagnation. This stagnation is not limited only to those working on organizational aspects of MNCs. Most of us, I suggest, are continuing to dig our own little holes, mostly piling up conceptualization upon conceptualization, unencumbered by either the discipline of empirical verification or the discomfort of theoretical challenges that are necessary to provide consistency, coherence, and direction to IB related research.

As a Johnny-come-lately to the field, it is audacious enough of me to raise this issue; I will not make the situation worse by trying to analyze why we are in this state, and what we must do to get out of it. While there are other panels in this conference where these issues may be the focal point of discussions, I believe that we may benefit from discussing the topic here, in the specific context of organization theory applications to research on MNCs. How do we evaluate the current state of research on this topic? How much progress have we really made? How do we interpret the differences in assumptions and approaches among the three papers that have been presented? Why do we find, among these established and well-known scholars, such careful avoidance of the contradictions in each other's work? If the purpose of the conference is to take stock of where we are and to chart a course for the future, open and honest discussions on these questions may well prove to be more valuable than nitpicking debate on the specific content of the papers.

All of that having been said, I will now proceed to the more traditional task of discussants by raising some nitpicking points. Here are some questions and issues I would like Gunnar, Eleanor, and Bill to think about and, perhaps, comment on.

CAN'T WE HAVE THE CAKE AND EAT IT TOO?

I believe that the conceptual distinction Gunnar makes between organizing for capability exploitation and organizing for capability building is a useful one, and it represents a distinct step forward in the evolution of his work. I am uncomfortable, however, in the way he has conceptualized the two as opposite ends of a spectrum. Is it possible that these are not mutually exclusive (at any level of analysis) and that an either/or framing of the two may prove to be as erroneous as the either/or framings that have dominated academic work on strategy and management in the past, such as between cost and quality, short-term and long-term, task and team orientation, centralization and decentralization, and so on?

Based on our recent case research in companies like Andersen Consulting, KAO, Cartier, Intel, Caterpillar, ABB, and a few other companies, Chris Bartlett and I have argued elsewhere that the dimensions of capability (or knowledge) creation and exploitation may be more fruitfully considered as orthogonal (see Table 1).

Andersen Consulting, for example, had historically developed excellent processes for exploiting its capabilities in the systems integration field though extensive early and ongoing socialization of its professional employees ("Andersen Androids") and created highly standardized and formalized procedures for obtaining and executing projects, and for forming and managing project teams. With its target market changing from systems integration to business integration, the company is now confronting the need to build new capabilities in the fields of strategy and change management, while protecting its ability to execute efficiently the

---

Table 1. Capability Exploitation or Capability Building?

Capability (or knowledge) creation

- Intel ⟶ ● KAO
- Cartier

- Andersen Consulting
- Caterpillar

Capability (or knowledge) exploitation

relatively standard and proceduralized information technology work that still provides the bulk of the firm's revenues.

Intel, in contrast, had largely considered itself in the innovation rather than the exploitation business, focusing almost exclusively on creating pathbreaking new designs to sustain its growth and profits. Its internal management processes almost reflected what Seymore Cray had said of Cray Research: "We keep very good documents on all our designs to ensure that we never follow them again in the future." In the recent past, under the leadership of Andy Grove, the company has been strengthening its exploitation capabilities-developing skills for high volume manufacturing and for effective marketing, for example—but without sacrificing its innovativeness.

Finally, KAO appears to have built its spectacular success on the strength of its ability simultaneously to create and exploit knowledge. The company's gradual progression from the businesses of soaps and detergents to cosmetics to floppy discs and, at the same time, its increasing penetration in each of these businesses, provides a copy book example of multidimensional organizational competence.

Gunnar clearly recognizes the need for both of these capabilities, but he sees such simultaneity as being achieved through specialization and sequencing. This is indeed one possibility, and Andersen consulting appears to be adopting this approach. However, in the cases of both Intel and KAO, it appears that the companies are succeeding in creating management processes that allow each unit, and ultimately each individual, to pursue both creation and exploitation at the same time. Space limitations prevent me from elaborating the processes and, in any case, these specific descriptions may not be particularly relevant for the more general questions I have for Gunnar. What is the basis for his argument that the two sets of tasks create different strategic and organizational demands? Is he being a bit carried away by his excellent critique and deconstruction of Simon's arguments? Is a hierarchy really appropriate for exploitation, as he seems to imply? Is the heterarchy, in its pure form, really efficient in creating capabilities? Perhaps the lateral coordination and information sharing in a heterarchy can be combined with a strong corporate top management (as appears roughly the case in KAO) to build the capability of having the cake and eating it too?

DO THESE CLOTHES FIT THE EMPEROR?

As for Eleanor's advocacy of population ecology and institutional theory as the future anchors of research on MNCs, my first question to her is: Are you really serious about these proposals? The question is rude but relevant, and she invites it by the suggestion that the attraction of one of these theories is the possibility of multiple publications. Given her stature in the field, her suggestions are likely to be taken seriously. I know she is serious about institutional theory, but does she really believe that the ecological model has much to offer to researchers interested in the kind of issues she deals with in her paper?

It has been argued by others that publication of the Hannan and Freeman book can be seen as the event that first signalled the gradual waning of the population ecology paradigm. The book revealed the limits of the ecological model, as applied to organizational analysis, and the only significant theoretical advances it reported appeared to dilute even further the initial strong assumptions of Hannan and Freeman, thereby making the theory more and more like the ones it had challenged and hoped to replace. The only theoretical construct of any significance that seemed to survive and prosper was "density dependence" which, one could argue, states in rather complicated terms a concept that is really quite simple and what theorists describe as not counterintuitive ("obvious" for laypeople). Like the life cycle models of the 1960s, the concept of density dependence approximately fits most large temporal data sets, but cannot predict anything nor reveal any real exceptions (which, being counterintuitive, would be of value). Why should IB scholars adopt this paradigm at the tail end of its life cycle, when the limitations of the approach have become so obvious?

Even if one could somehow overcome the problem of how to define populations when dealing with international organizations, what kind of questions could one pursue with this model, and what would be the value of such research? Eleanor presents some research ideas but avoids the issue of value. Considering her first proposal, for example, even if one could clearly create the fine grained categories she proposes, why would a study of the demographics of units within those categories be of any use? She refers to the paper by Jacques Delacroix that looks at the demographics of European subsidiaries of American MNCs: in what way does that study contribute to anything of any significant interest to IB researchers?

Turning to institutional theory, I agree with her that this is potentially an area where collaboration between the fields of OT and IB can be fruitful. Here too, however, one confronts some disturbing signs. There has been little substantive theoretical progress within what Powell and DiMaggio call the "new institutionalism" since DiMaggio and Powell explicated the three key processes of isomorphism in their 1983 ASR paper. Since then the field appears to be specializing in review articles, creating subcategories, and incorporating diverse idea streams into a grand synthesis that has a place for every assumption, every question, and every methodology. DiMaggio and Powell's introduction to their recent edited volume is indeed a hair's breadth away from grand theory. During the same period, as the book itself reveals, there has been little empirical work and even less that has provided any new practical or theoretical insights, and little effort to identify how the ideas in the theory might be operationalized or falsified.

Yet, if I share Eleanor's expectations of a potentially fruitful alliance, I do so only to the extent that explicit framing in institutional terms, with a focus on the interactions between context and action that it implies, is, I believe, useful for future research on MNCs. At present, some IB researchers focus on the environment, ignoring organizations, while others look inside organizations, but the environment, in their studies, "is cardboard," as Don Lessard once described the book Chris Bartlett and I had written. Few in the IB field focus on the interactions between the institutional structure of the environment and internal actions or lack thereof in organizations. Eleanor exhorts us to focus on these interactions, and I believe she is right in claiming that such a focus will be helpful in building the next frontier of IB research.

In doing so, however, we may actually benefit from our ability to use multiple theoretical perspectives without becoming a prisoner of any one. Eleanor believes that unsystematic and "eclectic" use of different theories has led to IB scholars being "scorned by theorists for superficiality." Yet, perhaps the theories she would like us to use "systematically" do not fit the rich and complex phenomena we study. Built by scholars with little exposure to MNCs and designed to address questions that are of limited relevance to IB, perhaps the clothes she urges us to use simply do not fit our emperor. We can take the clothes and abandon the emperor, but that will be more an acquisition of us by OT and not the alliance she would like to see. Alternatively, like Gunnar, we may focus our energies on creating new clothes, tailored to our needs, using some off-the-shelf items when we find an opportunity. Given the very different approaches I see between Gunnar's and Eleanor's papers, this is a question I address to both of them: which of your two approaches—systematic grounding in a single existing theory versus eclectic use of different strands of theory to suit our questions and to build our own theoretical infrastructure—should we take, and why?

WHY ARE YOU IGNORING YOUR OBITUARY?

Finally, of Bill I ask the question explicitly that Eleanor asks implicitly in her paper. She, like Pfeffer, Scott, and others, is clearly sympathetic to the view that contingency theory has reached its limit on "how many variations on theory-building could be played on this approach to linking organizational structure to an environment characterized as a score on a set of attributes." Yet Bill persistently ignores this call for an obituary on contingency theory. Why? It has been years since Donaldson's answer to this question underwhelmed the OT community. The question has now been clearly put on the IB table by Eleanor and Bill's explicit answer to the question is vital both for justifying his own ongoing work and those of others (including me) who are following in his footsteps.

Gunnar, too, raises a challenge for Bill. Is information processing, by itself, an obsolete concept that should now be replaced by the concept of "knowledge management" (including both creation and exploitation of knowledge)? Would such a change, which is not a play of words, but a real departure in our conceptualization of what organizations do or should do with information, require any fundamental rethinking of the information processing model proposed so long ago by Galbraith? More specifically, will Bill reconsider how specific IT systems are or should be used, if the organizational task is not information processing but "information value-adding," as proposed by Gunnar?

REPLY

William G. Egelhoff

Response to Sumantra Ghoshal

In his lively comments, Sumantra raises a number of serious issues that can only be-

gin to be addressed here. First, his observation that the three articles somehow reflect "a field of inquiry that is inconsistent in its assumptions, incoherent in its approach, and stagnant in its direction." [p. 361] In general, human understanding and knowledge tend to progress more within paradigms than across paradigms. Thus, at the collective level of a field consisting of multiple paradigms, it is not surprising to find inconsistency, incoherence, and little overall movement in a particular direction. Nor are contradictions and inconsistencies between paradigms signs of poverty within a field.

More damaging by far is the charge that the field is characterized by inadequate empirical testing and too little theoretical challenge. I agree, but doubt that more of either is likely to lead to a more consistent and coherent field. Instead, it is likely to lead to stronger and better developed paradigms, with more consistency and coherency and more change and movement within paradigms. This would be a richer and more worthy field to be working in. Persistence in pursuing existing paradigms, however, (by the three authors as well as others) is not what hinders empirical testing and theoretical challenge. By and large, empirical testing and serious theoretical challenging within paradigms are simply not cost efficient activities to engage in. Reviewers of most publications will generally reject such tedious work as lacking novelty and not making a meaningful contribution to the field (explicit dimensions on most review forms). Yet, as indicated already, it is paradigms—not a field of multiple paradigms—that need to progress. As Kuhn [1970] indicates, most work that tests and extends a specific paradigm has little to do with novelty.

Now let me turn to a second issue, whether it is not time to accept the death of contingency theory (not as a teaching subject, but as a paradigm worthy of continuing empirical research and theoretical development). Since the debate between positivism and antipositivism [Donaldson 1985] has filled volumes without converting either side, that tact needs to be avoided here. The obituaries of contingency theory are not nearly as convincing as the demise of published contingency theory research would suggest.

As Sumantra points out, paradigms such as contingency theory have seldom been overturned by convincing empirical testing or the challenge of a superior theory for explaining the same phenomenon. Instead, many who once worked within a given paradigm when it was in vogue, such as contingency theory, simply shift to a new paradigm that usually addresses different issues and problems. This shift seldom occurs because an individual observes some discontinuity in his or her empirical data or becomes aware of a new theoretical explanation for the given subject area (both scientifically valid reasons for shifting to a different paradigm). Instead, much shifting from one paradigm to another occurs as individuals seek better publishing opportunities or to relieve the boredom of pursuing the same intellectual path. Both are understandable pragmatic reasons for abandoning paradigms, but neither are valid scientific reasons to declare a paradigm dead.

A major problem with all paradigms is that progress (as measured by published new ideas and findings) levels off and declines, and this makes further research in a paradigm less rewarding. As a result, there is considerable shifting to new paradigms as researchers attempt to catch a paradigm's progress curve when its slope is steepest and ride it before it declines. There are reasons, other than inertia, that hold researchers to paradigms with declining progress curves. These tend to be the awareness of empirical evidence and/or theoretical underpinning supporting a given paradigm. Both tend to be relatively weak within the field of organizational study, and generally can't overcome the effect of a downward sloping progress curve. This is not a direct response to Sumantra's query, why one should continue to work within a contingency theory paradigm. A direct response would require laying out the empirical evidence and theoretical underpinning for the paradigm—a task too long for this brief rebuttal. The above comments, however, do address why obituaries about contingency theory are popular. In a perfect world, death, in a scientific sense, should lead to an obituary. In a less than perfect world, obituaries often precede and contribute to the death of a paradigm. As scientists, we really need to learn to ignore them.

REFERENCES

Aldrich, H. E. 1979. *Organizations and Environments*. Englewood Cliffs, NJ: Prentice-Hall.

Aldrich, H. E. and J. Pfeffer. 1976. Environments of Organizations. *Annual Review of Sociology*, 2: 79–105.

Aldrich, H. and U. Staber. 1988. Organizing business interests: Patterns of trade association foundings, transformations, and deaths. In G. Carroll, editor, *Ecological Models of Organizations*, 111–126. Cambridge, MA: Ballinger.

Aldrich, H., U. Staber, C. Zimmer, and J. J. Beggs. 1990. Minimalism and organizational mortality: Patterns of disbanding among U.S. trade associations 1900–1983. In J. Singh, editor, *Organizational Evolution: New Directions*, 21–52. Newbury Park, CA: Sage Publications.

Allen, Thomas J. and Oscar Hauptman. 1987. The influence of communication technologies on organizational structure. *Communication Research* 14(5): 575–587.

Allison, G. T. 1971. *Essence of Decision: Explaining the Cuban Missile Crisis*. Boston: Little, Brown.

Åman, P. 1992. *Towards a Global Firm*. Stockholm: IIB.

Aoki, M. 1990. Toward an Economic Model of the Japanese Firm. *Journal of Economic Literature* Vol. XXVIII, March: 1–27.

Applegate, L. M., J. I. Cash and D. Q. Mills. 1988. Information technology and tomorrow's manager. *Harvard Business Review* 66(6): 128–136.

Arrow, K. J. 1974. *The Limits of Organization*. New York: W. W. Norton.

Astley, W. Graham. 1985. The two ecologies:

Population and community perspectives on organizational evolution. *Administrative Science Quarterly* 30: 224–241.

Astley, W. Graham and Edward J. Zajac. 1991. Intraorganizational power and organizational design: Reconciling rational and coalitional models of organization. *Organization Science* 2: 399–411.

Axelsson, B. 1987. Supplier Management and Technological Development. In Håkansson, H., ed., *Industrial Technological Development. A Network Approach*. London: Croom Helm, pp. 128–176.

Baba, Y. and K. Imai. 1991. Globalization and Cross Border Networks of Japanese Firms. Paper presented at the conference: Japan in a Global Economy—A European Perspective. Stockholm, September 5–6.

Bartlett, Christopher A. 1986. Building and managing the transnational: The new organizational challenge. In M. E. Porter, editor, *Competition in Global Industries*, 367–404. Boston: Harvard Business School Press.

Bartlett, Christopher A. and Sumantra Ghoshal. 1989. *Managing across borders: The transnational solution*. Boston: Harvard Business School Press.

Bartlett, Christopher A. and Sumantra Ghoshal. 1986. Tap your Subsidiaries for Global Reach. *Harvard Business Review* 64(6):87–94.

Bendix, R. 1956. *Work and Authority in Industry*. Berkeley: University of California Press.

Benson, J. K. 1975. The interorganizational network as a political economy, *Administrative Science Quarterly* 20: 229–249.

Berger, P. L. and T. Luckmann. 1966. *The Social Construction of Reality*. Garden City, NJ: Doubleday.

Bower, Joseph L. and Thomas M. Hout. 1988. Fast cycle capability for competitive power. *Harvard Business Review*, 66(6): 110–118.

Brooke, M. Z. and H. L. Remmers. 1970. *The Strategy of Multinational Enterprise*. New York: Elsevier.

Buckley, Peter J. and Mark C. Casson. 1976. *The Future of the Multinational Enterprise*. London: Macmillan.

Burenstam Linder S. 1961. *An Essay on Trade and Transformation*. New York, NY: John Wiley.

Burgelman, R. and R. Rosenbloom. 1989. Technology Strategy: An evolutionary process perspective. In Burgelman, R. and R. Rosenbloom, eds., *Research on Technological Innovation, Management and Policy*. Vol. 4. JAI Press, Greenwich, CT, pp. 1–23.

Burns, T. and G. M. Stalker. 1961. *The Management of Innovation*. London: Tavistock.

Cantwell, J. 1989. *Technological Innovation and Multinational Corporations*. London: Basil Blackwell.

Carroll, G. R., editor. 1988. *Ecological Models of Organizations*, Cambridge, MA: Ballinger.

Carroll, G. R. and J. Delacroix. 1982. Organizational mortality in the newspaper industries of Argentina and Ireland: An ecological approach. *Administrative Science Quarterly* 27: 169–198.

Carroll, G. R., J. Delacroix, and J. Goodstein. 1988. The political environments of organizations: An ecological view. In B. M. Staw and L. L. Cummings, editors, *Research in Organizational Behavior, Vol. 10*, 359–392. Greenwich: JAI.

Casson, Mark C. 1990. *Enterprise and Competitiveness: A Systems View of International Business*. Oxford: Clarendon Press.

Casson, Mark C. 1987. *The Firm and the Market*. Cambridge: M.I.T. Press.

Caves, R. E. 1982. *Multinational Enterprise and Economic Analysis*. Cambridge, MA: Cambridge University Press.

Child, J. 1977. *Organization: A Guide to Problems and Practice*. London: Harper and Row.

Chismar, William G. and Laku Chidambaram. 1992. Telecommunications and the structuring of U.S. multinational corporations. *International Information Systems* 1(4): 38–55.

Coase, R. H. 1937. The Nature of the Firm. *Economica*. 4: 405–448.

Cohen, W. and D. Levinthal. 1989. Innovation and Learning: The two faces of R&D. *Economic Journal* September: 569–596.

Cole, R. E. 1978. The late-developer hypothesis: An evaluation of its relevance for Japanese employment patterns. *Journal of Japanese Studies*, 4(2): 247–265.

Cyert, R. and J. G. March. 1963. *A Behavioral*

Theory of the Firm. Englewood Cliffs, NJ: Prentice-Hall.

Daft, Richard L. and Robert H. Lengel. 1986. Organizational information requirements, media richness and structural design. *Management Science* 32(5): 554–571.

Daft, Richard L. and Norman B. Macintosh. 1981. A tentative exploration into the amount and equivocality of information processing in organizational work units. *Administrative Science Quarterly* 26(2): 207–224.

Daft, Richard L. and Karl E. Weick. 1984. Toward a model of organizations as interpretation systems. *Academy of Management Review* 9(3): 284–295.

Davidson, W. H. and P. Haspeslagh. 1982. Shaping a Global Product Organization. *Harvard Business Review* 60(4): 125–132.

Delacroix, J. 1992. The European subsidiaries of American multinationals: An exercise in ecological analysis. In S. Ghoshal and D. E. Westney, editors, *Organizational Theory and the Multinational Corporation*. London: MacMillan.

Delacroix, J. and G. Carroll. 1983. Organizational Foundings: An Ecological Study of the Newspaper Industries of Argentina and Ireland, *Administrative Science Quarterly* 28: 274–291.

Delacroix, J., A. Swaminathan and M. E. Solt. 1989. Density dependence versus population dynamics: An ecological study of failings in the California wine industry. *American Sociological Review* 54: 245–262.

de Meyer, Arnoud. 1991. Tech talk: How managers are stimulating global R&D communication. *Sloan Management Review* 32(3): 49–66.

de Meyer, Arnoud and A. Mizushima. 1990. Global R&D management. In Heidi Vernon-Wortzel and Lawrance H. Wortzel, editors, *Global Strategic Management: The Essentials,* 439–455. New York: Wiley.

DiMaggio, P. J. 1991. Constructing an organizational field as a professional project: U.S. art museums 1920–1940. In W.W. Powell and P. J. DiMaggio, editors, *The New Institutionalism in Organizational Analysis,* 267–292. Chicago: University of Chicago Press.

DiMaggio, P. J. 1988. Interest and agency in institutional theory. In Lynne G. Zucker, editor, *Institutional Patterns and Organizations: Culture and Environment*. Cambridge, MA: Ballinger.

DiMaggio, P. J. 1983. The iron cage revisited: Institutional isomorphism and collective rationality in organizational fields. *American Sociological Review* 48: 147–160.

DiMaggio, P. J. and W. W. Powell. 1991. *The New Institutionalism in Organizational Analysis*. University of Chicago Press.

Donaldson, L. 1985. *In Defense of Organization Theory: A Reply to the Critics*. Cambridge: Cambridge University Press.

Dore, R. P. 1983. Goodwill and the spirit of market capitalism. *British Journal of Sociology* 34(4): 459–482.

Dore, R. P. 1973. *British Factory Japanese Factory*. Berkeley: University of California Press.

Downs, A. 1967. *Inside Bureaucracy*. Boston, MA: Little, Brown.

Doz, Yves L. 1986. *Strategic Management in Multinational Companies*. Oxford: Pergamon Press.

Doz, Yves L. 1981. Headquarters influence and strategic control in MNCs. *Sloan Management Review* 23(1): 15–29.

Doz, Yves L. and C. K. Prahalad. 1992. Managing MNCs: A search for a new paradigm. In S. Ghoshal and D. E. Westney, editors, *Organizational Theory and the Multinational Corporation*. London: MacMillan.

Doz, Yves L. and C. K. Prahalad. 1987. A process model of strategic redirection in large complex firms: The case of multinational corporations. In Pettigrew, A., ed., *The Management of Strategic Change*. Oxford: Basil Blackwell, pp. 63–83.

Drucker, Peter. 1987. The coming of the new organization. *Harvard Business Review* 66: 45–53.

Dunning, John H. 1988. The study of international business: A plea for a more interdisciplinary approach. *Journal of International Business Studies* 20(3): 411–436.

Dunning, John H. 1979. Explaining changing patterns of international production: In defence of the eclectic theory. *Oxford Bul-*

letin of Economics and Statistics 4(November): 269–295.

Durkheim, Émile. 1964. *The Division of Labor in Society.* trans. Simpson, G. New York, NY: The Free Press.

Egelhoff, William G. 1991. Information-processing theory and the multinational enterprise. *Journal of International Business Studies* 22(3) 341–368.

Egelhoff, William G. 1988. *Organizing the Multinational Enterprise: An Information Processing Perspective.* Cambridge, Mass: Ballinger.

Egelhoff, William G. 1982. Strategy and structure in multinational corporations: An information processing approach. *Administrative Science Quarterly*, 27(3): 435–458.

Elster, Jon. 1989. *Nuts and Bolts for the Social Sciences.* New York: Cambridge University Press.

Emery, F. E. and E. L. Trist. 1973. *Towards a Social Ecology. Contextual Appreciations of the Future in the Present.* London and New York: Plenum Press.

Emery, F. E. and E. L. Trist. 1965. The causal texture of organizational environments. *Human Relations* 18(1): 21–32.

Evan, W. M. 1967. The organization-set: Toward a theory of interorganizational relations. In J. D. Thompson, editor, *Approaches to Organizational Design,* 173–191. Pittsburgh: University of Pittsburgh Press.

Etzioni, Amitai. 1961. *A Comparative Analysis of Complex Organizations.* New York: Free Press of Glencoe.

Flaherty, M. Therese. 1986. Coordinating international manufacturing and technology. In Michael E. Porter, editor, *Competition in Global Industries.* Boston: Harvard Business School Press.

Fligstein, N. 1990. *The Transformation of Corporate Control.* Cambridge, MA: Harvard University Press.

Franko, L. 1976. *The European Multinationals: A Renewed Challenge to American and British Big Business.* Stamford, CT: Greylock Publishing.

Freeman, J. 1990. Ecological analysis of semiconductor firm mortality. In J. Singh, editor, *Organizational Evolution: New Directions,*

53–77. Newbury Park, CA: Sage Publications.

Friedland, R. and R. R. Alford. 1991. Bringing society back in: Symbols, practices, and institutional contradictions. In W.W. Powell and P. J. DiMaggio, editors, *The New Institutionalism in Organizational Analysis,* 232–263. Chicago: University of Chicago Press.

Friedman, David. 1983. Beyond the age of Ford: The strategic basis of the Japanese success in automobiles. In John Zysman and Laura Tyson, editors, *American Industry in International Competition: Government Policies and Corporate Strategies.* Ithaca: Cornell University Press.

Galaskiewicz, J. and S. Wasserman. 1989. Mimetic and normative processes within an interorganizational field: An empirical test. *Administrative Science Quarterly* 34(1): 454–479.

Galbraith, Jay R. 1977. *Organization Design.* Reading, MA: Addison-Wesley.

Galbraith, Jay R 1973. *Designing Complex Organizations.* Reading, MA: Addison-Wesley.

Gates, S. R. and William G. Egelhoff. 1986. Centralization in headquarters-subsidiary relationships. *Journal of International Business Studies* 17(2): 71–92.

Gerlach, Michael. 1987. Business alliances and the strategy of the Japanese firm. *California Management Review* Fall: 126–142.

Gerschenkron, A. 1962. *Economic Backwardness in Historical Perspective.* Cambridge: Harvard University Press.

Ghoshal, Sumantra. 1988. Environmental scanning in Korean firms: Organizational isomorphism in action. *Journal of International Business Studies* 19(1): 69–86.

Ghoshal, Sumantra and Christopher A. Bartlett. 1990. The multinational corporation as an interorganizational network. *Academy of Management Review* 15(4): 603–625.

Ghoshal, Sumantra and D. Eleanor Westney, editors. 1992. *Organization Theory and the Multinational Corporation.* London: Macmillan.

Giddens, A. 1984. *The Constitution of Society.* Berkeley: University of California Press.

Giddens, A. 1979. *Central Problems in Social*

Theory. Berkeley: University of California Press.

Glassman, Robert B. 1973. Persistence and loose coupling in living systems. *Behavioral Science* 18: 83–98.

Gouldner, A. 1954. *Patterns of Industrial Bureaucracy*. New York: Free Press.

Graham, E. M. 1978. Transatlantic investment by multinational firms: A rivalistic phenomenon? *Journal of Post Keynesian Economics* 1(1): 82–99.

Greene, Alice H. 1989. Globalization: Reality or trend? *Production and Inventory Management Review and APICS News* 9(12): 24–25.

Hagström, P. 1991. The "Wired" MNC: *The Role of Information Systems for Structural Change in Complex Organizations*. Stockholm: IIB.

Håkansson, L. and R. Nobel. 1991. Foreign research and development in swedish multinationals. *Research Policy*.

Hamel, G. and C. K. Prahalad. 1990. The core competence of the corporation. *Harvard Business Review* 68(3): 79–91.

Hamilton, William F. 1985. Corporate strategies for managing emerging technologies. *Technology in Society* 7: 197–212.

Handy, Charles. 1989. *The Age of Unreason*. Cambridge: Harvard Business School Press.

Hannan, M. T. and J. Freeman. 1989. *Organizational Ecology*, Cambridge: Harvard University Press.

Hannan, M. T. and J. Freeman. 1984. Structural inertia and organizational change. *American Sociological Review* 49: 149–164.

Hannan, M. T. and J. Freeman. 1977. The population ecology of organizations. *American Journal of Sociology* 82: 929–964.

Hannan, M. T., J. Ranger-Moore and J. Banaszak-Holl. 1990. Competition and the evolution of organizational size distributions. In J. Singh, editor, *Organizational Evolution: New Directions*, 246–268. Newbury Park, CA: Sage Publications.

Hayes Robert H. and Raj Jaikumar. 1988. Manufacturing's crisis: New technologies, obsolete organizations. *Harvard Business Review* 66(5): 77–85.

Hayes Robert H., Steven C. Wheelright and Kim

B. Clark. 1988. *Dynamic Manufacturing: Creating the Learning Organization*. New York: Free Press.

Hedlund, Gunnar. 1992. Assumptions of hierarchy and heterarchy: An application to multinational corporations. In Sumantra Ghoshal and D. Eleanor Westney, editors, *Organization Theory and the Multinational Corporation*. London: Macmillan.

Hedlund, Gunnar. 1986. The hypermodern MNC: A heterarchy? *Human Resource Management* 25: 9–35.

Hedlund, Gunnar and I. Nonaka. 1991. *Models of Knowledge Management in the West and Japan*. Research Paper 91/9, Institute of International Business, Stockholm.

Hedlund, Gunnar and Dag Rolander. 1990. Action in heterarchies: New approaches to managing the MNC. In Christopher A. Bartlett, Yves Doz, and Gunnar Hedlund, editors, *Managing the Global Firm*, 15–46. London: Routledge.

Hennart, Jean-François. 1982. *A Theory of the Multinational Enterprise*. Ann Arbor: University of Michigan Press.

Hirsch, P. 1972. Processing fads and fashions: An organization-set analysis of cultural industry systems. *American Journal of Sociology* 77: 639–659.

Hirschorn, Larry and Thomas Gilmore. 1992. The new boundaries of the "boundaryless" company. *Harvard Business Review* May-June: 104–115.

Hout, Thomas, Michael E. Porter, and Eileen Rudden. 1982. How global companies win out. *Harvard Business Review* September-October: 98–108.

Huber, George P. 1990. A theory of the effects of advanced information technologies on organizational design, intelligence, and decision making. *Academy of Management Review* 15: 47–71.

Hymer, S. H. 1960, 1976. *The International Operations of National Firms: A Study of Direct Foreign Investment*. Cambridge, MA: M.I.T. Press.

Johanson, J. and J-E. Vahlne. 1977. The internationalization process of the firm-A model of knowledge development and increasing market commitments. *Journal of International Business Studies* 8(2): 23–32.

Kanter, R. M. 1989. *When Giants Learn to Dance*. New York: Simon and Schuster.

Keen, Peter G. W. 1991. *Shaping-the Future: Business Design Through Information Technology*. Cambridge: Harvard Business School Press.

Keen, Peter G. W. 1987. Telecommunications and organizational choice. *Communication Research* 14(5): 588–606.

Keen, Peter G. W. 1986. *Competing in Time: Using telecommunications for competitive advantage*. Cambridge, MA: Ballinger.

Knickerbocker, F. T. 1973. *Oligopolistic Reaction and Multinational Enterprise*. Boston, MA: Graduate School of Business Administration, Harvard University.

Kogut, Bruce, editor. 1994. *Country Competitiveness and the Organization of Work*. New York: Oxford University Press.

Kogut, Bruce. 1991. Country capabilities and the permeability of borders. *Strategic Management Journal* 12(Special Issue): 33–48.

Kogut, Bruce. 1989. Research notes and communications: A note on global strategies. *Strategic Management Journal* 10: 383–389.

Kogut, Bruce. 1987,1988. Country patterns in international competition: Appropriability and oligopolistic agreement. In N. Hood and J. E. Vahlne, editors, *Strategies in Global Competition*, London: Croom-Helm.

Kogut, Bruce. 1985. Designing global strategies: Profiting from operational flexibility. *Sloan Management Review* Fall: 27–38.

Kogut, Bruce. 1983. Foreign Direct Investment as a Sequential Process. In Kindleberger, C. P. and D. Audretsch, editors., *The Multinational Corporation in the 1980s*. Cambridge, MA: The M.I.T. Press, pp. 38–56.

Kogut, Bruce and U. Zander. 1991. Knowledge of the firm, combinative capabilities, and the international replication of technology. *Organization Science*. 3:383–397

Krugman, Paul R. 1986. Introduction: new thinking about trade policy. In Paul R. Krugman, editor, *Strategic Trade Policy and the New International Economics*, 1–22. Cambridge, MA: MIT Press.

Kuhn, T. S. 1970. *The Structure of Scientific Revolutions*, Second Edition. Chicago: University of Chicago Press.

Lawrence, Paul R. and Jay W. Lorsch. 1967. *Organization and Environment*. Homewood, IL: Irwin.

Leblebici, H., G. Salancik, A. Copay, and T. King. 1991. Institutional change and the transformation of interorganizational fields: An organizational history of the U.S. broadcasting industry. *Administration Science Quarterly* 36(3): 333–363.

Levitt, B. and C. Nass. 1989. The lid on the garbage can: Institutional constraints on decision making in the technical core of college-text publishers. *Administrative Science Quarterly* 34(2): 190–207.

Levitt, Theodore. 1983. The globalization of markets. *Harvard Business Review* May-June: 92–102.

Luostarinen, L. 1979. *The Internationalization of the Firm*. Helsinki: Acta Academic Oeconomicae Helsingiensis.

Magee, S. P. 1977. Information and multinational corporations: An appropriability theory of direct foreign investment. In Bhagwati, J., editor, *The New International Economic Order: The North-South Debate*. Cambridge, MA: M.I.T. Press.

Manheim, M. 1992. Global information technology: Issues and strategic opportunities. *International Information Systems* 1(1): 38–67.

Mann, Michael. 1986. *The Sources of Social Power. Volume 1, A History of Power from the Beginning to A.D. 1760*. New York: Cambridge University Press.

March, J. G. 1991. Exploitation and exploration in organizational learning, *Organization Science* 2(1): 71–87.

Martinez, Zaida L. and David A. Ricks. 1989. Multinational parent companies' influence over human resource decisions of affiliates: US firms in Mexico. *Journal of International Business Studies* 20(3): 465–488.

Maturana, H. and F. Varela. 1980. *Autopoiesis and Cognition: The Realization of Living*. London: Reidl.

McFarlan, F. Warren. 1984. Information technology changes the way you compete. *Harvard Business Review* May-June: 98–103.

McKelvey, Bill. 1982. *Organizational Systemat-*

ics: *Taxonomy, Evolution, Classification.* Berkeley: University of California Press.

McKenna, Robert. 1985. Market positioning in high technology. *California Management Review* 27: 82–108.

Meyer, J. W. and B. Rowan. 1977. Institutionalized organizations: Formal structures as myth and ceremony. *American Journal of Sociology* 83: 340–363.

Meyer, J. W. and W. R. Scott. 1983. *Organizational Environments: Ritual and Rationality.* Beverly Hills, CA: Sage.

Meyer, J. W., W. R. Scott, and T. E. Deal. 1983. Institutional and technical sources of organizational structure: Explaining the structure of educational organizations. In J. W. Meyer and W. R. Scott, editors, *Organizational Environments: Ritual and Rationality,* 45–70. Beverly Hills: Sage Publications.

Meyer, M. 1990. Notes from a skeptic: From organizational ecology to organizational evolution. In J. Singh, editor, *Organizational Evolution: New Directions,* 298–314. Newbury Park, CA: Sage Publications.

Mezias, S. J. 1990. An institutional model of organizational practice: Financial reporting in the Fortune 200. *Administrative Science Quarterly* 35(3): 431–457.

Mintzberg, H. 1979. *The Structuring of Organizations: A Synthesis of the Research.* Englewood Cliffs, NJ: Prentice Hall.

Mintzberg, H. and J. A. Waters. 1985. Of strategies, deliberate and emergent. *Strategic Management Journal* 6(3): 257–272.

Morgan, G. 1986. *Images of Organization.* Newbury Park, CA: Sage.

Nelson, R. R. 1991. Why do firms differ, and how does it matter? *Strategic Management Journal* 12(Special Issue, Winter): 61–74.

Nelson, R. R. and S. G. Winter. 1982. *An Evolutionary Theory of Economic Change.* Cambridge, MA: Belknap Press.

Nemetz, Paul L. and P. W. Fry. 1988. Flexible manufacturing organizations: Implications for strategy formulation and organizational design. *Academy of Management Review* 13: 627–638.

Nonaka, Ikujiro. 1994. A Dynamic Theory of Organizational Knowledge Creation. *Organization Science* 5(1): 14–37.

Nonaka, I. 1991. Managing the firm as an information creation process, Working paper, Institute of International Business and Hitotsubashi University. In Meindle et al, editors, *Advances in Information Processing in Organizations,* Vol. 4. Connecticut: JAI Press.

Nonaka, I. 1990. Managing globalization as a self-renewing process: experiences of Japanese MNCs. In C. A. Bartlett, Y. Doz, and G. Hedlund, editors, *Managing the Global Firm.* London: Routledge, pp. 69–94.

Orrok, J. D. and Karl E. Weick. 1990. Loosely coupled systems: A reconceptualization. *Academy of Management Review* 15: 203–223.

Orru, M., N. Woolesey Biggart, and G. G. Hamilton. 1991. Organizational isomorphism in East Asia: Broadening the new institutionalism. In P. J. DiMaggio and W. W. Powell, editors, *The New Institutionalism in Organizational Analysis.* Chicago: University of Chicago Press.

Patrick, H., editor. 1986. *Japan's high technology industries: Lessons and limitations of industrial policy.* Seattle: University of Washington Press.

Pavitt, K. 1991. Key Characteristics of the Large Innovating Firm. *British Journal of Management* 2(1): 41–50.

Pavitt, K. 1985. Technology transfer among the industrially advanced countries: An overview. In N. Rosenberg and C. Frischtak, editors, *International Technology Transfer: Concepts, Measures, and Comparisons.* New York, NY: Praeger, pp. 3–23.

Pavitt, K., M. Robson, and J. Townsend. 1989. Technological accumulation, diversification and organisation in UK companies, 1945–1983. *Management Science* 35(1): 81–99.

Pennings, J. M. 1982. Organizational birth frequencies: An empirical investigation. *Administrative Science Quarterly* 27: 120–144.

Perlmutter, Howard. 1969. The tortuous evolution of the multinational corporation. *Columbia Journal of World Business* 4: 9–18.

Perrow, C. 1991. Organizational theorists in a society of organizations. Address to the Section on Organizations and Occupations,

American Sociology Association Annual Meeting, Cincinnati.

Perrow, C. 1979. *Complex Organizations*, second edition. New York: Random House.

Pfeffer, Jeffrey R. 1982. *Organizational and Organization Theory*. Boston: Pitman.

Pfeffer, Jeffrey R. and Gerald R. Salancik. 1978. *The External Control of Organizations: A Resource Dependency Perspective*. New York: Harper and Row.

Polanyi, M. 1966. *The Tacit Dimension*. London: Routledge and Kegan Paul Ltd.

Polanyi, M. [1958] 1962. *Personal Knowledge*. Chicago: The University of Chicago Press.

Porter, Michael E. 1990. *The Competitive Advantage of Nations*. New York: Free Press.

Prahalad, C. K. 1981. An approach to strategic control in MNCs. *Sloan Management Review* Summer: 5–13.

Prahalad, C. K. and Gary Hamel. 1990. The core competence of the corporation. *Harvard Business Review* 90(3): 79–93.

Prahalad, C. K. and Yves Doz. 1987. *The Multinational Mission: Balancing Local Demands and Global Vision*. New York: Free Press.

Prestowitz, Clyde V. 1989. *Trading Places: How We Are Giving Our Future to Japan and How to Reclaim It*. New York: Basic Books.

Prigogine, I. 1976. Order through fluctuation: self-organization and social system. In E. Jantsch and C. H. Waddington, editors, *Evolution and Consciousness*. Reading, MA: Addison-Wesley.

Radner, R. 1989. Hierarchy: The Economics of Managing. *Marshall Lectures, University of Cambridge*, Oct 25–26. (To appear in Journal of Economic Literature.)

Reich, Robert B. 1991a. *The Wealth of Nations*. New York: Alfred A. Knopf.

Reich, Robert B. 1991b. Who is them? *Harvard Business Review* March-April: 77–88.

Rice, Ronald E. and Gail Love. 1987. Electronic emotion: Socioemotional content in a computer-mediated communication network. *Communication Research* 14(5): 85–108.

Roberts, E. B. and A. R. Fusfeld. 1981. Staffing the innovative technology-based organization. *Sloan Management Review* Spring: 19–34.

Roche, E. M. 1992. *Managing Information Technology in Multinational Corporations*. New York: Macmillan.

Rockart, John F. and James E. Short. 1989. IT in the 1990s: Managing organizational interdependence. *Sloan Management Review* Winter: 7–17.

Roethliesberger, F. J. and W. J. Dickson. 1939. *Management and the Worker*. Cambridge, MA: Harvard University Press.

Rose, F. 1990. A new age for business. *Fortune* October 8: 156–164.

Rosenberg, N. 1986. The impact of technological innovation: A historical view. In R. Landau and N. Rosenberg, editors, *The Positive Sum Strategy*. Washington DC: National Academy Press, pp. 17–32.

Rugman, A. M. 1981. *Inside the Multinationals: The Economics of Internal Markets*. New York, NY: Columbia University Press.

Rumelt, R. P. 1984. Towards a strategic theory of the firm. In R. D. Lamb, editor, *Competitive Strategic Management*. Englewood Cliffs, NJ: Prentice-Hall, pp. 556–570.

Rumelt, R. P., D. Schendel, and D. J. Teece. 1991. Strategic management and economics. *Strategic Management Journal* 12(Special Issue, Winter): 5–30.

Sandén, P. and J.-E. Vahlne. 1976. Multinationella företag-jätteödlor utan framtid? (Multinational firms-great saurians without future?) *Ekonomisk Revy* 3.

Sandholz, W. and J. Zysman. 1989, 1992: Recasting the European bargain. *World Politics* 42(1): 95–130.

Scott, Bruce R. 1985. National strategies: key to international competition. In Bruce R. Scott and George C. Lodge, editors, *U.S. Competitiveness in the World Economy*, 71–143. Boston: Harvard Business School Press.

Scott, W. R. 1992. *Organizations: Rational, Natural, and Open Systems*, third edition. Englewood Cliffs, NJ: Prentice-Hall, Inc.

Scott, W. R. 1991. Unpacking institutional arguments. In W. W. Powell and P. J. DiMaggio, editors, *The New Institutionalism in Organizational Analysis*, 164–182. Chicago: University of Chicago Press.

Scott, W. R. 1987. The adolescence of institutional theory, *Administrative Science Quarterly*, 32: 493–511.

Scott, W. R. and J. W. Meyer. 1983. The organization of societal sectors. In J. W. Meyer and W. R. Scott, editors, *Organizational Environments: Ritual and Rationality*, 129–153. Beverly Hills: Sage Publications.

Simon, H. A. 1955. A behavioral model of rational choice. *Quarterly Journal of Economics* 69: 99–118.

Simon, H. A. 1955, 1962. The architecture of complexity. *Proceedings. Amer. Philosophical. Soc.* No. 106, pp. 467–482.

Singh, J. V., editor. 1990. *Organizational Evolution: New Directions*. Newbury Park, CA: Sage Publications.

Smith, A. 1776/1953. *The Wealth of Nations*, Book I, Chicago: Henry Regnery Company.

Sölvell, Ö. and I. Zander. 1991. Strategies for global competitive advantage: The home based MNE vs. the heterarchical MNE. Paper presented at Annual EIBA Conference, Copenhagen.

Sölvell, Ö., I. Zander, I. and M. E. Porter. 1991. *Advantage Sweden*. Stockholm: Norstedts.

Stalk, George. 1988. Time-The next source of competitive advantage. *Harvard Business Review* 66(4): 41–51.

Stalk, George and Thomas Hout. 1990. *Competing Against Time: How Time-based Competition Is Reshaping Global Markets* New York: Free Press.

Steinfield, Charles W. and Janet Fulk. 1987. On the role of theory on research on information technologies in organizations. *Communication Research* 14(5): 479–490.

Stinchcombe, A. L. 1965. Social structure and organizations. In J. March, editor, *Handbook of Organizations*, 142–193. Chicago: Rand McNally.

Takeuchi, H. and I. Nonaka. 1986. The New New Product Development Game. *Harvard Business Review* January-February:137–146.

Taylor, F. 1911. *Principles of Scientific Management*. New York, NY: Harper and Brothers.

Teece, David J. 1987. Profiting from technological innovation: Implications for integration, collaboration, licensing, and public policy. In David J. Teece, editor, *The Competitive Challenge: Strategies for Industrial Innovation and Renewal*. Cambridge, MA: Ballinger.

Teece, David J. 1986. Profiting from technological innovation: Implications for integration, collaboration, licensing, and public policy. *Research Policy* 15(6): 285–305.

Teece, David J. 1977. Technology transfer by multinational firms: The resource cost of international technology transfer. *Economic Journal* 87(June): 242–261.

Teece, David J., G. Pisano, and A. Shuen. 1990. *Firm capabilities, resources, and the concept of strategy*. CCC Working Paper 90–8, Center for Research on Management, University of California, Berkeley.

Thimm, A. 1989. Europe 1992-opportunity or threat for U.S. business: The case of telecommunications. *California Management Review* 31(2).

Thompson, James D. 1967. *Organizations in Action*. New York: McGraw-Hill.

Tsurumi, Y. 1976. *The Japanese Are Coming*. Cambridge, MA: Ballinger.

Tushman, Michael L. and David A. Nadler. 1978. Information processing as an integrating concept in organizational design. *Academy of Management Review* 3: 613–624.

Van den Bulcke, D. and E. Halsberghe. 1984. *Employment Decision-Making in Multinational Enterprises: Survey Results from Belgium*. Working Paper No. 3., Geneva: International Labour Office.

Vernon, Raymond. 1979, The product cycle hypothesis in a new international environment. *Oxford Bulletin of Economics and Statistics* 41(4): 255–267.

Vernon, Raymond. 1971. *Sovereignty at Bay*. New York: Basic Books.

Vernon, Raymond. 1966. International investment and international trade in the product cycle. *Quarterly Journal of Economics* 80(2): 190–207.

von Hippel, Eric. 1991. The impact of sticky data on innovation and problem-solving. Sloan School of Management Working Paper #3147–90–BPS.

von Hippel, Eric. 1976. The dominant role of users in the scientific instrument innovation process. *Research Policy* 5: 212–239.

Weber, M. 1947. *The Theory of Social and Economic Organization*. In T. Parsons, editor, translators Henderson and Parsons. New York, NY: Oxford University Press.

Weick, Karl E. 1984. Theoretical assumptions and research methodology selection. In F. W. McFarlan, editor, *The Information Systems Research Challenge*. Boston: Harvard Business School Press.

Weick, Karl E. 1976. Educational organizations as loosely coupled systems. *Administrative Science Quarterly* 21: 1–19.

Weick, Karl E. 1969. *The Social Psychology of Organizing*. Reading, Mass: Addison-Wesley.

Wernenfelt, B. 1984. A resource based view of the firm. *Strategic Management Journal* 5(2): 171–180.

Westney, D. Eleanor. 1992. Institutionalization theory and the MNC. In Sumantra Ghoshal and D. Eleanor Westney, editors, *Organization Theory and the Multinational Corporation*. London: MacMillan.

White, R. E. and T. A. Poynter. 1990. Organizing for world-wide advantage. In C. A. Bartlett, Y. Doz, and G. Hedlund, editors,

Managing the Global Firm. London: Routledge, pp. 95–113.

Williamson, Oliver E. 1975. *Markets and Hierarchies: Analysis and Antitrust Implications*. New York: Free Press.

Winter, S. 1991. On coase, competence, and the corporation. In O. E. Williamson and S. Winter, editors, *The Nature of the Firm*. Oxford: Oxford University Press, pp. 179–195.

Young, R. C. 1988. Is population ecology a useful paradigm for the study of organizations? *American Journal of Sociology* 94(1): 171–193.

Zald, M. N. 1970. Political economy: A framework for comparative analysis. In M. N. Zald, editor, *Power in Organizations*, 221–261. Nashville: Vanderbilt University Press.

Zucker, L. G., editor. 1988. *Institutional Patterns and Organizations: Culture and Environment*. Cambridge, MA: Ballinger.

Zucker, L. G. 1987. Institutional theories of organization. *Annual Review of Sociology* 13: 443–464.

7

Organizational Behavior Perspectives and International Business

EDITORS' COMMENTS

During the last twenty years, considerable progress has been made in clarifying the conceptual and empirical issues touched upon by international organizational behavior (IOB) researchers. Thus, the authors of the three topic papers for this chapter were asked to identify and examine these issues in order to provide IOB scholars a clearer idea of what is being done, the questions being asked, the assumptions being made, and the methodologies being used. That is, the papers, in keeping with the other theoretical/research papers included in this book, focus on such issues as the ontological, epistemological, and human nature assumptions that are being made, and the limitations these assumptions impose (if any) on our understanding of individual and group behavior and interaction within international organizations and between international organizations and other individuals and groups. They also identify and discuss to varying degrees the core issues receiving most research attention at this time, and the methodological problems associated with these issues as they relate to the basic theoretical, conceptual assumptions being made by the researchers.

In the leadoff paper, Sullivan argues that cultural research has been overly causal; it provides description, but is not useful. In his view, cultural values and organizational structure should not be treated as causes, but rather as sets of conditions under which some phenomena may occur. He further suggests that multivariate correlation designs should be used to examine complex processes. In a vein similar to that used in the opening chapter, Sullivan also argues that what is needed is tolerance for a combination of theoretical approaches: "economists draw[ing] on culture theory and culturists pay[ing] attention to economic issues." [p. 393]

At the root of Sullivan's discussion is the logical empiricism versus relativism argument, or the reductionism versus holism. In addition, Sullivan's position is that IB research on culture simply describes; it does not aid in predictions as would be done in purposive theory. Sullivan agrees with Triandis that our understanding of culture is inadequate and suggests several ways to improve on this understanding.

In the second paper, Boyacigiller and Adler trace the development of organizational behavior (OB) with an emphasis on its failure to include an international perspective, especially in the face of the emerging globalization of business. The authors suggest that traditional organizational behavior has tended to ignore the external environment, a logical assumption when reductionism is assumed. The authors further indicate that a lack of understanding of the culture construct inhibits the integration of OB and IB. In their view, the three areas that provide opportunities for developing an international field of OB are: (1) IB research not considered by OB researchers; (2) issues considered by neither; and (3) OB research not integrated into IB inquiry. Boyacigiller and Adler identify several issues that they believe need additional research and which are of utmost relevance to both fields. The emerging transnationals and the "parochialism" of the motivation theory developed in the U.S. are examples of issues that need to be considered from new perspectives.

Redding presents an extensive review of, and well articulated statement on, the field of comparative organizational behavior. After an extensive review of the litera-

ture, Redding concludes that the various fields within comparative organizational behavior appear to exhibit different rates of progress toward more fully explicated middle range theory. Only one grand theory, Hofstede's cultural consequences, is presented as having empirical grounding.

This failure to produce a grand theory provides the backdrop for Redding to examine the debates which have appeared in the literature about comparative OB, and suggests that 30 years of work has shed little light on the complex problem of the influence of culture on organizational behavior. Central to his argument is the observation that the main body of comparative work conforms to the empirical positivism approach and is therefore unadventurous. He recommends that a more sociological approach be used. However, because of the dominance of the field by the empirical positivism paradigm of economics, the question of the legitimacy of this type of research is raised. The threat of intellectual imperialism of the empirical positivism approach is a main focus of the argument presented, but Redding stops short of advocating a radical new paradigm, calling instead for an incremental shift based on middle-range theorizing. In this regard, Redding offers several specific suggestions.

Mendenhall, in the first of the two commentaries pleads for a more interdisciplinary approach to cross cultural research and for more tolerance within the field. He suggests that the field of cross-cultural management is at a crossroads. One path ("the familiar") follows the tradition of atheoretical empirical studies. Without utilizing theory as a base, little is learned from these descriptive studies. The "higher path" sorts out the empirical data to make sense out of it. Such theoretical perspectives are beginning to show up in academic journals. However, in Mendenhall's opinion, the road of empirical opportunism is still being followed far too often.

Mendenhall notes that the topic papers all point to a common goal: a field of rich, complex theories and diverse, vigorous methods. They identify the goal, but not the path by which it can be reached. Mendenhall believes that a number of things might help achieve this goal. First, adding to the field of knowledge must become more important *vis-à-vis* career goals in order to deviate from the easier empirical opportunism studies that are all too common today. Second, more interaction must take place outside the small "cliques" of researchers to provide more diverse inputs. Third, the field needs a new outlet for research which will allow for the types of research that are being proposed.

Feldman's discussion of the papers by Sullivan, Boyacigiller and Adler, and Redding focuses on the reasons for the failure of international management (IM) to make a more substantial impact on OB. He suggests that a central reasons for this is that there has been "too much approach, and not nearly enough arrival." [p. 446] He then offers seven specific reasons for this particular deficiency: (1) difference in the level of analysis preference; (2) different views on what are important context factors; (3) differences in preference for level of description and prediction; (4) differences in preference for kinds and size of samples; (5) differences regarding what constitutes a testable model; (6) differences in the kinds of data analysis preferred; and (7) differences in how findings are typically presented.

As a prescription, Feldman offers several specific areas where IM research might have an impact on OB. He also suggests the conditions under which comparative studies are more likely to be well received. Of these, perhaps the most important is that the "differences" found in the international arena must be systematically different from the results found in the domestic arena. Somewhat in line with Redding, Feldman suggests that middle range theory might be the best that can be expected at this time in order to reconcile the abstract approaches of IM with the more specific, content oriented approaches of OB.

Together, the five papers present a reasonably complete picture of the central issues and challenges facing those involved in IOB research. Importantly, these issues and challenges also need to be addressed by all IB scholars, since they are innate to most of the theorizing and research conducted under the conceptual umbrella of IB. Briefly, the questions raised by these papers include the following: (1) Do the paradigms currently used by most IB scholars inhibit or limit the questions asked of IB phenomena and their relationships? (2) What is the role of culture? (3) Should economics dominate the field of IB, or should there be greater receptivity to the contributions that the other major social sciences can offer? And finally, (4) What can IB scholars do to gain intradisciplinary accord and understanding?

In many ways, IOB is more advanced in its adoption of a more inclusive, interaction paradigm than the other disciplines represented in this book. Yet, because of IOB's preference for a non-process, micro-level focus, Boyacigiller and Adler are able to assert that the "external environment is ignored" (i.e., human behavior is the consequences of lower-level intrinsic traits and attributes and individual culture-bound learning as discussed in chapter 1). This exogenization of the environment in which individuals and groups are embedded arises in part from the constraining influence that the extension and cross-border management paradigms continue to have had on the questions being asked.

Culture, of course, is central to IOB theorizing and research. It is also of increasing importance in other branches of IB inquiry (see, for example, Dunning, 1995). Yet, as Sullivan suggests, very little progress has been made in explaining its role in the behavior of the phenomena and relationships studied. Here, again, the problem, perhaps, can be traced to the paradigmic foundations of IB inquiry. Fundamentally, culture is often assumed to be an unchanging, intervening force or factor that is neither an inextricable part of a social process nor a consequence of this process when, in fact, it is both.

Redding and Sullivan join Casson and Dunning by suggesting that alternative explanations are required and a more tolerant attitude be taken for different approaches. However, unlike Casson, Dunning, and Sullivan, who argue for a multidisciplinary approach lead by economics, Redding suggests that sociology should replace economics as the dominant social science. Nonetheless, acceptance of such a recommendation would be equally restrictive, since it too relegates the other social sciences, such as anthropology, to lesser roles. This, of course, gets to the heart of the controversy presently raging among these sciences, and described in the first chapter. That IB is in the middle of this controversy can no longer be ignored. It too must take the recommendations of such people as Casson, Dunning, Redding, and Sullivan seriously. It is equally important, however, to have an explicit understanding of the implications of such recommendations for IB the-ory building, theory testing, and empirical research.

In concluding this chapter's introduction, we need to briefly discuss the difficulties that are characteristic of the uneasy relationship that exists between U.S.-bound disciplinary scholars and their IB counterparts, These difficulties are articulated very well by Feldman in his commentary. Although directed at IOB scholars, we feel his comments have considerable weight for all disciplinary branches of IB inquiry. Intradisciplinary accord and understanding can only be gained through repeated attempts at dialogue. However, as already noted elsewhere, such colloquy requires a passion for knowledge from all possible sources combined with a tolerance for "foreign ideas" from both sides. There is, of course, such dialogue among scholars from the main social sciences, and there needs to be more among business scholars.

Theory Development In International Business Research: The Decline Of Culture

Jeremiah Sullivan

INTRODUCTION

The goal of science is to produce statements that tell us something about the way the world really is [Newton-Smith 1981; Suppe 1977]. We call such statements explanations; they consist of descriptions, statements of cause and effect, and prediction. Although some models exist to guide theory development in international business (IB) and management research, most explanatory theories have been borrowed from anthropology, economics, and psychology. They take two forms; *purposive* (involving predictions of actions based on firm or manager goals, wants, or intentions) and *causal* (involving stimulus-response and stimulus-organism-response kinds of statements). Purposive theories are rooted mostly in economics, and causal theories come from psychology and from anthropological models of culture.

In this paper I will review the literature on the nature of theories and point out the strengths and weaknesses of purposive and causal theory paradigms. Then I will narrow the discussion and focus on culture theories as they are applied in international management (IM) research within the causal paradigm. I will argue that culture theory stands very little chance of developing in the field of IM studies for the following reasons:

1. Culture theorists have reached a dead end in the causal paradigm. They must shift to the purposive paradigm if they are to survive.

2. Culture theories offer weak explanations of managerial behavior and do not account for changes in behavior.

3. Advocates of the purposive paradigm (economists) are dominant in international research and are actively pushing for only one paradigm (theirs) to be legitimized in the field.

However, I also argue that the coming decline of culture theory will lead to problems for IM research, for the following reasons:

1. Lay persons will continue to see national character and cultural values as influencing cross-national managerial behavior. Unlike physicists, social scientists ignore lay theories at their peril.

2. Anomalies in economic theories can be explained by culture theory. Without culture theories, the managerial audience for international research will become even more disenchanted with the field. Moreover, problems in economic theories regarding explanation and prediction will go unresolved. Nevertheless, culture will not be saved unless theorists change dramatically in the way they interpret culture and its effect.

CURRENT THEORIZING ABOUT THEORIZING

If theory development in IM research is to proceed, some sense must be made of theoretical perspectives. In other words, we should understand what a theory is, and isn't, before undertaking to develop one.

A review of relevant literature reveals a remarkable lack of unanimity as to what a theory is. Drawing on logical positivist and empiricist thinking, some researchers define a theory as a set of laws or lawlike generalizations capable of explaining and predicting phenomena [Hunt 1976]. Laws are unre-stricted universal generalizations [Michalos 1980] applicable to each manager in general. This traditional view of theories, however, is by no means dominant in the social sciences. Other definitions stress the heuristic value of theories—simplifying devices that guide research. Baumol [1959] defines a theory as a structure describing the workings of and relationships among various aspects of some phenomenon in a manner that simplifies chaotic reality.

In between these two views of theories as laws or simplifying heuristics lies a multitude of other definitions. Theories are instrumental sentences useful for making inferences about the way the world is [Duhem 1954]. In this sense theories are answers to questions, a collection of sentences providing understanding for someone curious about something. By the same token, theories are linguistic devices identifying the invariant amidst the variant [Suppe 1977]. Or they can be conjectures about law—like relations subject to falsification [Popper 1968].

In sum, theories can be laws, tools for providing useful, simple answers to questions, inference-making machines, idealizations, or outright guesses about the way the world is.

Roots of Current Views

How did such diversity come to be, and how does it affect theory development? To begin with, physiological processes were shown to conform to the general laws of mechanics by the mid-nineteenth century. This led such influential scientists as Hermann Helmholtz to proclaim the basic unity of all the sciences [Mandelbaum 1971]. This unity implies that phenomena, including human behavior, must conform to universal laws of the kind developed in theoretical physics. To explain phenomena is to state the law generating them. Metaphysical recourse is not appropriate. The laws are real and causal—not mental constructs. Twentieth century positivism, empiricism, and rationalism have their roots in Helmholtz's view of theories as laws.

A second nineteenth century view of theories was that of Ernst Mach. Since human mental processing of data can alter it, human theoretical statements are likely to be not identifications of real laws but instead mental creations that simplify and regularize beliefs about the world. These belief packages approximate true knowledge and offer the best tool for relating human belief to true knowledge. In recent years this perspective has come to be called the *Weltanschauungen* view of theories [Suppe 1977]. Since theories are human creations, they are influenced by the social environment of the theorists. They are not identifications of laws, but can be lawlike descriptions of the way the world is. Rorty [1979] has characterized the two definitions of theories by referring to two kinds of knowing, knowing *that* and knowing *of*. The law-seeking positivist wants to say, "I know that ... " The *Weltanschauungen* theorist wants to say, "I know of ... "

The theories of behavior discussed in this paper are of both kinds. Purposive microeconomic theories have been described as laws or lawlike generalizations [Rosenberg 1976], while anthropological, sociological, and psychological theories are defined as creative but nonetheless scientific abstractions about causal relations in reality [Manicas 1982].

Need for Abstract Theory

To be meaningful, a theory should contain both abstract (nonobservable) and empirical phenomena [Ryan and O'Shaughnessy 1980]. Abstractness is necessary for theoretical development to allow deduction to occur. One states the abstract theoretical generalization and then makes deductions and predictions from it. A theory simply stating generalized specifics about a manager does not allow explanations about diverse phenomena. Thus to use equity theory to say, "A manager tends *in some cases* to seek transactions in which the benefits minus the costs of the buyer are equal to the benefits minus the costs of the seller" is not to state a theory abstract enough to deduce

predictions applicable to most managers in most situations. Instead, the statement is simply an empirical generalization—a general observation [Kaplan 1964; Schlenker 1974]. Compilation of empirical generalizations is a first, not last, step in the development of higher-order theories (applicable to managers in general in most situations, including international situations) which state abstract, underlying regularities capable of providing interesting and useful explanations of behavior. In the next sections, I will characterize many social psychological theories as not very theoretical but rather as empirical generalizations about observed judgment, preference, and choice rules employed by managers as they ponder a decision. Therefore, the development of higher-order theories of individual management behavior in international settings requires that generalizations about choice rules be incorporated in more abstract statements about regularities of which the rules partake, no matter what the setting. The same kind of criticism can be made of purposive theories, which are often stated as microeconomic laws derived from axiomatic statements, but which really describe observed decision strategies which managers may or may not use, depending on the task facing them. In sum, management theories need to be more abstract to cover regularities of behavior in most settings. If international research shows that such theories cannot be developed, then microlevel generalizations focused on specific international settings are all that can be expected.

CAUSAL AND PURPOSIVE THEORIES OF MANAGEMENT BEHAVIOR

In this section we will examine the major types of individual behavior theories: purposive and causal. However, other kinds of theories do exist. Instead of focusing on individual behavior, some theorists stress groups or dyads. Similarly, social theorists emphasize demographic and economic characteristics of classes or aggregates.

These researchers develop causal theory for social groups rather than for individuals. In contrast, Bass [1974] assumes that choice behavior is characterized by substantial randomness.[1] By this he means two things: (1) that people are indeed random in their behavior (and thus lawlike causal theories are not conceivable) or (2) that the number of variables affecting behavior is too great to allow causal theories to be constructed (thus lawlike theory is not practical).

To some extent, Bass acts as if people have random behavior generators in their brains, and he builds a model of decision making based on this phenomenon. His stochastic theory predicts behavior but has nothing to say about the purposes or causes of such behavior. Most management theorists, however, have avoided a stochastic approach to scientific theorizing. Instead, they apply already developed purposive and causal paradigmatic theories.

Presuppositions of Purposive and Causal Theories

Before looking at each kind of theory in turn, let us briefly examine and compare the presuppositions underlying both as shown in Table 1.

Generally, purposive theory presumes that managers as individuals are rational, and that a rational person seeks to attain as much satisfaction of wants and purposes as possible [Henderson and Quandt 1958]. It is important to note that microeconomic theorists are referring to *individuals* as being rational rather than simply to aggregates of people. Rosenberg [1976] has made a convincing argument that microeconomic theory is indeed a theory about individual behavior and not about individuals generally speaking. Thus research on individual managerial behavior in multinational firms, for example, may not reveal anything about the firms-level activities.

Causal theory, in contrast, is based on the view of humankind as responsive not to internal wants but to the external environment or to mental manifestations of the environment. Situations, tasks, contexts, perceptions, cultural values, and attitudes are seen to invoke behavior. To be sure, many theorists mix causes and purposes together in a variety of behavior models. Some

Table 1. Presuppositions of Purposive and Causal Theories

Purposive Theory Presuppositions	Causal Theory Presuppositions
The researcher's goal is to predict behavior.	The researcher's goal is to identify the causes of behavior.
Humans are viewed as exercising free will.	Humans are viewed as constrained by environmental and internal limitations.
Human wants are uncaused; they emerge out of the will.	Humans wants are caused.
Human purposes (wants) cause behavior.	Human purposes (wants) justify behavior but do not cause it.
Research foci should be on desires, demographics, roles, etc.,—on anything that may signal purposes and predict behaviour.	Research foci should be on environmental, physical, cultural, and mental stimuli causing behavior.

researchers also have attempted to improve purposive theory by tying purposes to mental phenomena usually considered causal. The result has been models and theories of great complexity that are exceedingly difficult to understand—let alone test.

Purposive Theories

Purposive theories of human action are very old. Until recently theorists believed that humans all have the same bundle of needs in all contexts and that therefore human purposes and actions would be quite predictable. In the early nineteenth century, German Romantic philosophers began asking themselves where purposes came from. They developed the concept of the will as the source of human wants and actions. While admitting the influence of external phenomena, they saw the highest type of human as in touch with his/her will and responding accordingly. If humans could free themselves from their environment, their wills would direct them, and since all wills partake of the universal will, all people would act in universal harmony.

In England during this period, a quite different group of philosophers (e.g., Bentham, James Mill, J.S. Mill) also were seeking the source of human purposes. In place of the will there emerged from their work the concept of utility, a notion as vague as "will" but less associated with metaphysics. It is this concept that now is at the center of microeconomic theories of behavior. These theories define human economic purpose as utility maximization.

Microeconomic Theory Such theories concern themselves with an individual's desire for well being, often expressed in terms of bundles of utility. The assumption is that a manager has a purpose, and the purpose is always to maximize or somehow optimize utility through the use of his resources to acquire control over the environment. Microeconomic or welfare theory is silent as to the causes of the manager's purpose. Indeed, economics in part is described as the study of human purposes and actions, not causes

[von Mises 1962]. Those researchers who study purposes do not focus on the will but instead look at psychological, physiological, genetic, moral, economic, demographic, legal, and social phenomena. These phenomena are rarely offered as causes of purposes and actions but rather as predictors of purpose or actions. Cultural values, then, may or may not influence a manager, depending on his task and the setting. Whatever the case, though, it is his will, not his culture, that determines action. Culture is only a possible predictor.

Axiomatic Nature Predictive formulae take many forms, depending on how the researcher describes the process of utility maximization. Sometimes marginal utility is examined. Sometimes utility for attributes of decision options is stressed. Perhaps expected utility or subjective expected utility is calculated. Since no one believes these models describe causes, the formula chosen does not matter. Its ability to predict is all that counts. Sometimes the researcher will casually refer to the independent variables and their combination as the "decision strategy" of the managers—as if his or her action actually was caused by the formula being carried out in the manager's mind. But they really only mean that the formula models the exercise of purpose.

What all these researchers have in common is a shared faith in the truth of a number of axiomatic statements (1) about humans as purposive creatures and (2) about the process humans follow to carry out purposes. Take decision theory, for example, as expressed by expected value, expected utility, or subjective expected utility models. Von Neumann and Morgenstern [1944] demonstrated mathematically that expected utility maximization is a theorem that is derivable from a number of axioms having to do with an individual's expectations and preferences. The problem is that thirty years of research have revealed that the axioms are by no means self-evident truths [Shoemaker 1982]. Humans systematically deviate from the intuitively sensible and logical axioms of von Neumann and Morgenstern. Decision theory, then, cannot be viewed as verified because of its derivability from axioms. This does not mean, of course, that it can't be supported in some other way (e.g., empirical research).

Problems with Purposive Theory

The problems with purposive microeconomic theory of managerial behavior involve (1) its focus on prediction only, (2) its emphasis on laws derived from axioms, and (3) its failures to be predictive. In the first place, prediction, while an important goal of science, is not enough. If it were, the Ptolemaic theory of the heavens, which allows reasonably accurate predictions, would never have had to be replaced by the Copernican theory. The Copernican theory is only marginally better at predicting, but it offers an explanation of the process of heavenly movement which is much closer to reality than Ptolemy's. Economic theorists have stressed prediction as the be all and end all of economics [Friedman 1953], when clearly the cause of economic science also requires description and causal explanations [Rosenberg 1976]. Thus, in addition to predicting managerial behavior, purposive theories also need to *explain* the process of managerial deciding.

The second problem is the emphasis on axioms as the basis for purposive theory. It is not axiomatic that a manager—or even managers in general—is rational and purposive in all—or even most—situations. Too much evidence has built up showing that humans can deviate from rationality and cope quite nicely [Nisbitt and Ross 1980; Kahneman, Slovic and Tversky 1982]. Any theorizing about behavior process in international settings, therefore, should specify when rational purposive theory based on economic models applies and when it doesn't. Finally, as for failures in prediction, purposive theories built up from nonaxiomatic axioms are not likely to predict all of the time. In organizational research, hypotheses often are not supported, and rarely are variances of more than 25 to

35% explained. The sources of these failures are usually labeled as methodological. It may be that they are really theoretical problems with purposive theory.

Causal Theories

Such purposive theories often focus on action and not on the process through which a variety of stimuli evoke thinking about action and action itself. This section defines causal theory, especially in contrast to purposive theory, describes the need for causal theories of managerial behavior, and discusses the problems of psychological and anthropological theories that currently serve as causal theories of individual managerial behavior in IB.

Causality   Causality involves a statement of initial conditions or events that explain a subsequent event or condition. Explanation can be expressed as a lawful relation or a probabilistic relation. Causal relationships have four characteristics [Nagel 1962]. First, they exhibit uniformity and consistency. Whenever the cause occurs, the effect occurs or is likely to occur. Second and third, causality embodies spatial and temporal contiguity. Causes are close to effects in space and precede them in time. Fourth, cause-effect relationships are asymmetrical. This means that the cause causes the effect, but the effect does not or did not cause the cause. In cognitive and social psychology asymmetry is a problem, since mental events, such as beliefs or attitudes, can cause behavioral intention, while behavioral intention can in turn cause certain attitudes or beliefs to form.

Causal Research in Managerial Behavior   Causal theories are explanatory in a way purposive theories are not. Causes are answers to the questions, "Why did decision action X occur?" or "Why did the manager think Y about decision action X?" Purposes are answers to the question, "What goal was attained by the occurrence of decision action X?" This differentiation is based on the differing presuppositions described above. In purposive theory humankind is made up of active, willing creatures seeking to carry out goals. In causal theory, humans are responsive creatures, reacting to their environment.

Causes can be stated in a behavioral way, such that a particular state or stimulus determines the actions of a particular actor. This kind of causality, especially in the form of the behaviorism of B.F. Skinner, seems explanatory, but in fact tells us very little about the way a manager behaves. It focuses on actions caused by other actions or environmental entities. Although behaviorism is studied by some researchers, most decision making researchers do not devote much effort to it. Of greater interest is the S-O-R model of causal theory [Bagozzi 1980], in which environmental stimuli (S) evoke mentalistic activity (O) which in turn leads to behavioral intent or response (R). This shift from S-R causal models of behavior to the S-O-R kind is but one manifestation of a modern scientific focus on the process (rather than the fact) of causality and the probabilistic (rather than lawlike or deterministic) nature of causal relations. Structural equation models, which describe S-O-R processes, are only beginning to appear in international managerial research.

Psychology and Causality Social and cognitive psychologists want to discover causal relationships so that they can establish basic principles that will explain the phenomena of psychology [Mills 1969]. This same explanatory goal has led management researchers to employ psychological theories in a variety of experiments seeking to identify causal relations. Typically, a theory is stated and hypotheses offered regarding a manager's actions which can be expected if the theory is explanatory and predictive. Take the example of self-perception theory. The theory states that "individuals come to 'know' their own attitudes, emotions, and other internal states partially [sic] by inferring them from observations of their own behavior and/or the situation in which this behavior occurs" [Bem 1972:2]. The word

"partially" is vague but important. It implies that self-knowledge can be derived from causes other than observations of their own behavior.

The method of self-perception researchers is to test theory under varying conditions. In this way knowledge is accumulated regarding when self-perception theory is explanatory and when it isn't. The same kind of procedure occurs for the other cognitive and social psychology theories. The problem is that these theories are becoming highly complex and unwieldy. Moreover, (e.g., cognitive dissonance theory) attempts to incorporate anomalies into a theory are often ad hoc or post hoc. The result in organizational behavior and motivation research is a mishmash of theories, almost none of which have been tested outside the United States or in multinational or international environments.

THE NEED FOR PURPOSIVE CULTURE THEORY

Organizational behaviorists, whether discussing national or corporate cultures, tend to focus on artifacts, perspectives, values, and assumptions [Deal and Kennedy 1982; Schein 1985; Geertz 1973; Kluckhohn and Strodtbeck 1961]. Artifacts are the overt expressions of an underlying belief system. For example, calisthenics in a Japanese firm may indicate a culture-bound commitment to group harmony. Supporting the artifacts are perspectives, the shared rules and norms that prescribe acceptable behavior in specific situations; and values, the beliefs that guide the development of goals, ideas, standards, and perspectives. At the very base of culture systems are sets of assumptions about humankind, society, the world, truth, time, space, and so forth. Although calls occasionally are made to study the organizational impact of these assumptions, most culture-bound research focuses on norms and values within a causal theory paradigm as implicit drivers of observed behavior. I say implicit because most of this research is correlational in nature, and it is never clear whether values cause attitudes/behavior or the other way around.

Why are Japanese workers so quality conscious? Culture theorists explain this phenomenon in terms of cultural values, stressing allegiance to familylike institutions and resulting feelings of company loyalty that lead to (cause) an enhanced concern with avoiding defects that could affect company image and reputation [Ouchi 1981]. However, as Professor Kazuo Koike of Hosei University points out, "The secret of Japan's success is not a peculiar work ethic that extols intense loyalty to the company . . . In fact, according to a well-designed survey of 11 countries conducted by the Japanese Federation of Electrical Machine Workers Unions, the Japanese rank relatively low on measures of interest in the company and the job" [Koike 1990:28]. The intense and fruitful emphasis on reducing defects in big company production facilities is due more to elaborate training than to culture, according to Professor Koike. "It is unfortunate that some Western observers have ignored this point, trotting out cultural argument to explain Japan's achievements" [28].

Koike's worry is that an easy reliance on cultural values as a direct cause of behavior will mask a more complex process which, once understood, offers a richer understanding. Like most organizational researchers, he sees studies of structure, power, information flows, motivation, and leadership as offering a better explanation of Japanese work behavior than culture. Cultural values are important elements of the *overall context*, but they are not causal. In other words, nothing can happen without culture, just as fish cannot swim without an ocean, but nothing *must* happen even with culture. Even with value-driven loyalty in place, Japanese employees may not focus on reducing defects and improving quality. Other organizational, group, and individual elements will determine (or more likely simply influence) that behavior. The term "influence" is probably better than "determine" here, since it makes no sense to say

that a certain kind of structure causes behavior. It simply correlates with behavior, suggesting that information about company structure has a certain rhetorical value in the minds of employees as they develop guides to behavior. They think about the way things are in their firm and are persuaded to form guidelines such as: IF (X) THEN (Y).

What I am suggesting is that neither cultural values nor organizational structure should be treated as causal. Both provide sets of information that persuade employees to think and act in certain ways (in other words, to have purposes) under certain conditions. However, the intensity and rhetorical power of cultural values' information usually is not as great as that concerning structure, compensation, etc.

The paradigm that should govern cross-national research, then, is a modified purpose theory rather than causal theory. Some American behaviorists, however, in contrast to their colleagues in other countries, rely solely on cause-identifying experiments in their research. Their training often has been in the causal paradigm that guides research in psychology, and they apply the paradigm to organizational studies. When they do cross-national studies, they face severe constraints on the complexity of experimental designs that can be undertaken, so they rely on simple designs. Nationality is used as an independent variable which is a proxy for cultural values. Other variables are usually not manipulated, and even if they are, no theorizing about interaction effects is done. So impoverished is this model that only a few international culture studies are accepted for publication in leading organizational behavior (OB) journals in a given year.

In sum, experimental research on OB rarely is cross-national. The causal paradigm creates conditions in which such research would not have high payoffs. Consequently, we know very little about such things as the generalizability of American motivation and leadership theories to settings in other nations, particularly nations where the cultural context is very different. We do not need studies that take the easy route and treat the cultural context as *causal*. Instead, we need studies that test OB theories cross-nationally. Since the causal paradigm hinders such tests—requiring as it does elaborate experiments—and since it makes more sense to think of organizational variables as providing information to employees forming rules and purposes rather than as causal stimuli, a paradigm shift to purpose theory is needed.

Cross-national organizational research should employ multivariate correlation designs (e.g., structural equation modeling) to explore complex processes in which sets of information about compensation, working conditions, leader characteristics, and so forth influence employee development of rules and purposes, which in turn are hindered or helped in their impact on behavior by environmental constraints and characteristics (e.g., cultural values, company norms, task complexity). In this approach employee attitudes are replaced as an important variable by employee inferences, judgments, rules, preferences, and intentions. Research questions to be asked are: What kinds of information and conditions dominate the formation of preferences? How are preferences modified by cultural values and norms? What kinds of rules then emerge? Existing theories can provide guides to this research. For example, it may be that the power of need theory explanations (in motivation research) varies across nations while those of leadership theory do not. Until the paradigm shifts and too—simple cultural value experiments fade from the scene, we will not have the will or the means to know much about the universality of OB theories.

EXISTING THEORIES OF CULTURE

Culture theories pursue science in terms of identifying relationships among environmental, cognitive, and behavioral phenomena. While those in an interpretationist paradigm are content to describe networks and patterns calling it "understanding," others go a step further and describe human purposes within a process of environmental antecedents and behavioral consequences. Although purposes are the focus of attention, the causal paradigm dominates, since researchers tend to write up their findings in terms of the causes of purposes and their effects. A third group rarely mentions purposes at all, and concentrates on environmental, demographic, institutional, historical, and economic causes of mental events indicative of cultural beliefs and values.

Aside from interpretationists, culture researchers conduct causal inquiries. While interpretationist cultural theorists sometimes offer brilliant insights, their work does not fit in with the reigning purposive and causal paradigms in management and organizational research. Few interpretationist studies have appeared in the leading business journals, and I will not discuss interpretationism in depth. However, an increase of interpretationist work would be welcome in IB research. A number of theorists have written extensively on how to conduct this kind of research, and the interested reader would do well to read Gareth Morgan, *Beyond Method* [1983], Peter Frost et al., *Organizational Culture* [1985], Alan McFarlane, *The Culture of Capitalism* [1987], Henry Steele Commager, *The American Mind* [1950], and D. Lawrence Kincaid, *Communication Theory, Eastern and Western Perspectives* [1987]. I must note, however, that the chances are low of this kind of work getting published in management and business journals dominated by economists rooted in the purposive paradigm.

What kinds of theories make up the causal paradigm in cultural research?

Cultural Materialism [Harris 1980]. The idea here, based on Marx, is that modes of production and reproduction determine cultural values and culture-bound behavior.

Sociobiology [Wilson 1975]. Sociobiologists relate culture to the gene pool. In its most common form, genetically predetermined cultural traits are turned on or off by environmental switches [Harris 1980]. Thus pan-human sets of values exist, but they only become operational as a "culture" when stimulated by environmental forces. If an American manager lived in Japan for many years, he would (of necessity) begin to exhibit values supposedly "Japanese." These are really universal values in human nature but only brought into salience by peculiar Japanese conditions.

Structuralism [Levi-Strauss 1963]. Structuralists study the psychological superstructure of the sociocultural system. They try to identify mental aggregates common within a culture which drive belief and social behavior.

Psychological Anthropology [Benedict 1934]. Theorists here seek to identify national character or enduring personality types that generate behavior. A related group, cognitive anthropologists, studies common sets of plans, rules, scripts, and schemata that govern behavior [Goodenough 1970; Parsons 1967].

These are the major causal paradigms in culture theory, although other, less comprehensive approaches could be named. One will not see studies of managerial behavior and organizational functioning appear regularly in ASQ, AMJ, or JIBS. For example, take the well-known and widespread Japanese valuing of consensus in organizations. Here is how culture theorists would deal with it. It could be a response to demographics—in crowded Japan it pays to avoid antagonizing others. It could be a human trait brought to dominance by Japan's moist climate, which favors rice production and team play to produce rice. It could be caused by a Japanese mental superstructure in which concepts of "self" and "other" can only have meaning in terms of each other (the tangled logic of the causal chain could be worked out, and undoubtedly someone has done it). Consensus could be spurred on by a preponderance of warm, communal personality types in Japan. In fact, variations of these explanations of Japanese consensus have appeared regularly in books, working papers, a few journals dedicated to

culture studies, and conference papers— William Ouchi's *Theory Z* is the most well known of these. They do not appear in the scholarly business journals, however.

Although researchers in the purposive paradigm have not examined Japanese consensus, they probably would reject cultural explanations and concentrate on microeconomic maximizing explanations under constraints. For example, consensus behavior could be viewed as optimal in organizations in highly oligopolized and heavily regulated industries such as Japan's. In these kinds of conditions, cooperation pays off more than competition, and "To get along, go along" becomes a rational strategy in dealing with colleagues, suppliers, and clients. A sociologist might focus on power. Japan's history has been bloody, and the Japanese have learned that order and prosperity have come when strong centralized authorities prevailed. What looks like consensus behavior in this view is really submissive behavior among Japanese who accept the need for highly verticalized power relations in society and do not question them because of their obvious benefits. In these two theoretical explanations, consensus behavior is not really caused. Rather it is chosen by most Japanese because, given the nature of economic life and the horror that can emerge in disorderly Japanese social existence, it is in one's interest to value consensus behavior. Traditional causal culture research does not describe consensus in this manner, although the emerging interpretationist paradigm could.

Evaluation of Culture Theory

If we take commonly used criteria for evaluating a theory and apply them to culture theory, its weakness becomes readily apparent, as also do the reasons why it is so frequently applied [Chapman and Jones 1980].

Intended reference. Do cultural values as an explanation tell us much about reality? Not really, since we rarely learn about organizational conditions in which culture is weak or strong, especially in comparison with organizational culture.

Parsimony. How simply does culture explain observed behavior? Clearly this is its strength—culture is a very parsimonious explanation.

Internal Consistency. Do the elements avoid contradicting each other? Often sets of cultural values do not hang together very well. For example, as we noted above, Japanese managers are said to seek consensus in decision making because of cultural values emphasizing harmony. They also are viewed, however, as culture-bound in their need to establish vertical relations and clear authority, a sign of a strong power orientation [Sullivan 1992]. How do values of harmony and verticality square with one another? Rarely do culture studies probe such interactions to establish the internal consistency of a culture theory.

Heuristic value. Does the theory foster further fruitful empirical research? Culture explanations often are offered as if there were a direct causal link between the cultural value and stimulus and the behavioral response. Implicit is the suggestion that no greater understanding can be gained by further work. The danger here can be illustrated by research on Japanese lifetime employment [Sullivan and Peterson 1991]. Cultural explanations see it as a response to Japanese values centered around the obligations of leader to follower, parent to child, or master to servant. Over the past 20 years little empirical work has been done to test what appears to be an accepted truism, but a study conducted by my colleagues and me suggests that lifetime employment is a managerial control tool that is not rooted in culture [Sullivan and Peterson 1991]. However, more research is needed, but is not likely to be done since the cultural explanation is parsimonious, convenient, and seems to settle the problem.

Compatibility. Does the theory correspond to an established metatheoretical perspective? Culture theory is tied closely to the causal theory paradigm described above, in which humans are viewed as responsive rather than purposeful, passive rather than active, and value-driven rather than calcu-

lating. This rootedness is another reason for its survival.

Action orientation. How much does it tell us about managerial actions? Well-developed culture theories, such as that of Hofstede [1980], which describes a culture along four dimensions, offer quite a bit of information on expected behavior of managers. However, Hofstede's work is rare in its degree of elaboration. Usually culture is presented as a driver of attitudes that may or may not have any influence on behavior.

Other criteria could be listed, but by now it is clear that the strengths of culture theory lie in its parsimony and compatibility with metatheory emerging out of a belief in determinism. Its explanatory value is weak and researchers usually do not attempt to tie their work on one dimension of culture to other dimensions. Moreover, cultural explanations do not foster further research, and they often explain attitudes rather than behavior. Japanese scholar Dorinne Kondo has noted that workplace behavior, while influenced by cultural values, is more likely to be explained by such things as ideologies, policies of government and organizations, and power relationships [Kondo 1990]. These may be highly differentiated across nations, but not because of cultural differences. Instead, different historical conditions, institutional arrangements, and economic conditions have greater explanatory power.

This is not to say that culture does not count, because it does, but "culture's consequences" [Hofstede 1980], probably, have been overstated. The American valuing of individualism, for example, may seem to explain American organizations' tendency to monitor individual more than group performance and to reward individuals rather than groups. But how does one explain the oft-noted habit of Americans to form groups, both formal and informal, both at work and during leisure time? Could it be that cultural values have changed? Do culture researchers find this troubling? Or is it that, while individualism flourishes, American companies do not monitor individuals for cultural reasons but simply because it is easier than monitoring groups? These are the kinds of questions with which culture research ought to deal and usually does not.

CULTURE AND THE BATTLE OF PARADIGMS

An important distinction between the social and natural sciences revolves around the existence of theoretical consensus [Kuhn 1970]. This consensus, called "shared paradigms" by Thomas Kuhn, exemplifies the natural sciences and is absent in the social. One consequence of the absence is that social science theorists in economics, anthropology, psychology, organizations, and management shift from testers of theories to advocates of their paradigm, and social science becomes more prescriptive than the incremental accumulation of unassailable knowledge [Watson 1967]. As Robert Friederich notes, "Advocates of alternative models talk past one another, for there is . . . no fully institutionalized framework of substantive assumptions that both accept. Personal factors, aesthetic predilections, the age, role, and private interests of individuals, and subspecializations all are involved. Persuasion rather than proof is king" [Freiderichs [1970:2] cited in Roth [1987:124]).

In this kind of environment "normal science" takes a back seat to battles among competing paradigms [Ritzer 1975]. What this means is that knowledge advancements born of shared consensus about what and how to study give way to political, ideological, and individual struggles for eminence. The hard work of operationalizing and manipulating concepts is haphazard, and different research streams yield incommensurable data with conflicting results that go unresolved [Eckberg and Hill 1979]. Culture theorists cannot prevail in this battle as it unfolds in IB research. The leading journal, the *Journal of International Business Studies*, publishes mostly the work of economists, for whom cultural values are in the realm of "tastes" and thus are unworthy of study. Researchers trained in the economic paradigm dominate IB research groups at leading universities. Moreover, the rigor of econometrics provides a greater rhetorical impact for research findings than the less elaborate and more informal methods of cultural theory.

The relevant economic theories of international trade, foreign investment, and multinational corporate actions are incomplete, flawed, often ad hoc, and occasionally downright wrong. It makes no difference, as long as the defenders of the economic paradigm remain dominant. To be fair, their argument is a powerful one. Economic theories are often elegant and coherent, guided by a few defensible metatheories of human nature, and they have had many successes in noninternational settings and, in earlier periods, in international settings, too. None of these claims can be strongly made by culture theorists. What is not acceptable is the next step taken by some economists, although rarely in print. They argue, as paraphrased by Paul Roth, that "if the absence of a paradigm-inspired consensus is the central obstacle to normal science, and normal science is the royal road to scientific achievement, then there is a rationale for insisting that one method predominate 'for the good of the field'" [Roth 1987:126–127].

Under the guise of fostering better science, some economists in IB research would eliminate weak-sister paradigms. Culture theory has been a suitable first candidate for elimination, but one suspects that organizational and managerial theories are also on the short list. I find this unacceptable, since the basic needs of science are discourse and multiple perspective [Roth 1987; Feyerabend 1975]. The gradual elimination of competing ideas from JIBS and other journals will lead inevitably to sterility in theory and triviality in findings. However, the protests of a few are unlikely to have any effect.

The Problem of National Character

With the publication of Ralph Waldo Emerson's *English Traits* in the mid-nineteenth century, the concept of national character emerged. The idea is that each society has in it a kind of average enduring propensity for thought and feeling that signals membership in that culture and drives behavior. National character is thought by some to be widespread enough to influence many actions, especially in business, and thus to be worthy of study.

American national character was described in Henry Steele Commager's *The American Mind* [1959]. The typical American is optimistic and takes for granted the preeminence of the United States as the happiest and most virtuous of all societies. According to Commager, the American's character is "material, his thinking quantitative, his genius inventive, experimental and practical" [410]. He (or she) is "careless, good natured, casual, generous, and extravagant" [410]. With a low respect for authority, he is individualistic but will conform to conventions, believing that change should be evolutionary rather than revolutionary. A trace of Puritanism colors the American's faith in thrift, industry, and the association of salvation with material prosperity. He believes in democracy, equality, freedom, virtue, and the importance of courage in defense of a worthy cause.

What is one to make of this list, originally written in 1950? Is it a catalogue of traits Americans *ought* to have if they want to call themselves American, or is it a set of traits they generally *do* have? When does one acquire such a character? How? Can an immigrant become an American by an act of will, or are the traits gradually learned until they begin to cause behavior?

Foreign observers often note these traits as typical of Americans, yet what leads them to say that a person's behavior is "American" rather than attribute it to individual personality or social surroundings? If an American negotiator is good natured, experimental, and quantitative with a Japanese executive, is it because he is an American or because he is John Smith trying to cope in a given environment and with a given task? Even if almost all Japanese who encounter John Smith believe that his behavior is culture-bound, does that mean it is? John Smith may not think so, knowing in his heart that he is really ill tempered, conventional, and nonrigorous in other settings. Observation of him over time and situations may bear him out. Moreover, his behavior in Japan may be driven by Japanese expectations of how Americans are supposed to behave rather than by national character. Also, Japanese explanations for his behavior may be convenient simplifications drawn from a stereotype and ignorant of all the instances when he has violated the stereotypic American.

It is virtually impossible to explain behavior as cultural to science. Competing explanations are almost always equally defensible, and there is usually no way to set up critical experiments to test theories against one another. Yet it is equally clear that national character is a meaningful concept and that it does influence the behavior of some people in some situations at some times. In addition, foreign observers will not cease to use national character as an explanation simply because social scientists reject it. Those scientists may shake their heads in scorn of lay theorists and wait, like physicists did, for the public to accept the "truth" of alternative theories but they will have a long wait. Social science has not had the predictive successes of physics which would earn it credibility. Social science theories that survive tend to have common sense roots, emerging out of observations any thoughtful person could make.

What we have, then, is a situation in which culture and national character theories will endure in the popular wisdom, although they will be ignored by the economists and quantitatively focused researchers who dominate IB scholarship. Unlike physics, the public will not eventually come around to complex, often counterintuitive, and sometimes bizarre theories of some social scientists (e.g., the microeconomic theory of decision making in which a manager perfectly processes every scrap of information available and fits it to every need he or she has or anticipates having). We can expect a research paradigm to emerge in which academic theories become progressively dissociated from the everyday world. Here is another example: Theories of the multinational firm are focusing more and more on explanations drawn from utility maximization, agency theory, and transactions theory which ignore cultural, political, and historical influences on corporations. These theories are already overly complex and generate incomprehensible, nitpicking papers in the literature. Eventually everyone will become bored with all the hair splitting, and new ideas will emerge (I expect chaos and catastrophe theories soon to make their mark). The problem is that theory development will not occur. Rather, theory exhaustion will drive the process. The public will ignore the social scientists, who will ignore each other.

The reemergence of culture as a dominant explanation of international managerial behavior will solve nothing, but the abandonment of culture will speed the process of decay. What is needed is tolerance, tolerance for other paradigms and other ways of explaining. Tolerance is also needed for other methodologies, such as Likert scales and surveys. And tolerance is needed for essaylike discourse in which researchers tell the story of their investigations in national culture and business behavior. A broad, rich discourse in international research that encompasses multiple perspectives with none dominant offers the best chance for developing a paradigm that is both interesting and enduring. Moreover, a paradigm in which economists draw on culture theory and culturalists pay attention to economic issues is likely to generate theories and hypotheses that have predictive value, modeling as they do the way the world really works in all its causal and purposive dimensions. Predictive success generates public acceptance, which is crucial to the survival of research.

FINANCE THEORY, RISK, AND CULTURE

The reigning theories of finance revolve around the concepts of efficient markets, random walks, and rational expectations. The idea of a random walk states that, after adjusting for the long-run growth of the economy, the price of a stock is not predictable [Malkiel 1981]. The likelihood of its going up is the same as that of its going down. Thus the history of a stock's price movement contains no useful information, nor does a forecast of a firm's future performance. The efficient market idea states that the stock market almost instantaneously reflects past information and forecasts in a stock's current price. No prediction can occur based on new information available to everyone, since the price will reflect that information at once. Rational investors in this situation will recognize that the only way to target a desired return from a portfolio is to decide on the level of risk they wish to accept.

Risk is the probability of loss. Specifically, it is "the chance that expected security returns will not materialize" and that stock prices will fall [Malkiel 1981:185]. Risk, then, is the probability that the probability of financial returns is overestimated. The higher the probability is, the more likely that the expected return is too high. Risk is a subjective phenomenon, different for each person. Finance theorists, however, have created an operational definition, a price's variance over time relative to market variance (beta measures). This is convenient but not conceptually sound unless evidence can be gathered that subjectively derived risks of a large number of people regarding a stock are correlated with the variance over time and that investors demand higher returns to compensate them for higher risks.

While the beta measure of risk is useful and does roughly correlate with returns over time, its failure to capture risk fully is well known [Malkiel 1981]. Many examples exist of investors suddenly lowering their risk assessments and buying overpriced stocks to their eventual detriment. Failures to adjust risk in the face of changing betas have been noted, as have assignments of risk to a stock that is wildly different from beta information. Investors in the Japanese stock market during the late 1980s, for example, acted in ways which suggest that cultural values may have influenced their risk assessments rather than objective evidence. By late 1989 the stock prices on the Tokyo Stock Exchange may not have reflected economic values so much as a collection of cultural beliefs brought to bear on collective investor behavior.

Here is a cultural theory to augment finance theory. Instead of prices being unpredictable, one can theorize that in X context, cultural value Y will be energized in large numbers of investors, with Z heuristics being employed to estimate a stock's risk, with A impact on the stock's price. In American and Japanese contexts, then, with all other variables constant, a stock's U.S.-required price might be thirty dollars and its Japanese price forty dollars. Finance theory assesses risk based on what is known (past variance), with the underlying assumption that individuals do the same. Culture theory, however, assumes that people judge risk based on what is known, expected, and desired, and that their expectations and desires are heavily influenced by cultural values. According to Malkiel, investors probably assess risk in terms of expectations regarding national income, interest rates, and inflation. These expectations are subject to cultural values. In Japan, inflation expectations are almost always higher than warranted, while in America they have been lower at times. Japanese tend to be a pessimistic people relative to Americans, and their inflation projections are likely to be extreme. This culture-bound judgment will influence risk assessments, which in turn will impact required returns. In the global inflationary period of the 1980s, the Japanese stock market should have offered higher returns than the U.S. market. It did. In the 1990s, as long as most Japanese stock market activity is engaged in by Japanese

rather than U.S. and other investors, returns should continue to be higher than in America if culture-bound inflation worries persist. Will they? No one is likely to bet on it based on culture theory alone.

Here we come up against the problems with cultural explanations. Japanese do seem to overweight negative scenarios about the future relative to Americans, but the causal chain from differing culture-bound habits and values to higher demanded returns in the stock market is virtually impossible to establish and test. The culture model is underdetermined and thus weak in explanatory value. Predictions made based on the model would be little more than guesstimates. Among many things missing from the model are data on the *rates* at which culture-bound pessimism influences Japanese expectations about income and interest rates as well as inflation—and similar data for Americans. Moreover, since culture theory is rooted in causal paradigms, it would have to be shown that these rates of impacting on expectations are stable over time and are not changed by outcomes. Culture is not much of an explanation if it is caused by economic events.

Culture theory offers intriguing insight into stock market behavior in different countries. No rich explanations are likely to emerge nor are the predictions defensible. Economists show no interest in it, even though the evidence seems overwhelming that Japanese and American investors differ along cultural lines in their risk assessments. This sad state of affairs is likely to continue.

HOW TO SAVE CULTURE

The ongoing development of theories in IB research is likely to result in the decline of culture theories as the purposive paradigm and economic theories becoming even more dominant, yet if everyone in the whole world, save for a few hundred economists defending their theory, believes that culture studies count, then they do count, and culture studies of management ought not to disappear from the pages of the scholarly journals.

Another reason why culture should survive is that it adds explanatory power to economic theory. First, culture as a variable is asymmetric, whereas economic variables often are not. After all, market share, number of niches in which a firm competes, type of strategic focus, risk proneness, and so forth are all both causes and effects of each other. National culture fosters understanding of the *processes* of strategy-setting in MNCs, about which economic theory is silent.

Culture theories have their limitations. They provide simple explanations that do not rest on axiomatic, lawlike statements, as economics does. They are also more like empirical generalizations, since they do not state abstract, underlying regularities, as economics does. For example, economics is based on the idea that self interest is the driving force behind all purposive actions. Culture theories usually state values (e.g., individual freedom in the United States) which some people tend to have in some situations. Nevertheless, an understanding of the relationship between culture and managing international operations enriches scholarly discourse and offers useful insights to practicing managers.

How can culture be saved? Here are some suggestions for scholars:

Shift to the purposive paradigm. Researchers should treat culture as an information-providing, causelike (but not causal) input to managerial processes of judgment and purpose formation. It is only one of a number of organizational, economic, social, and personal inputs.

Develop structural equation models. Sometimes cultural values are exogenous and perhaps sometimes they are endogenous. For example, American managers often make unilateral decisions in response to a cultural valuing of individual "lone wolf"

behavior. Culture here is exogenous. Yet in bureaucratic organizations, this valuing may be muted by a highly formal task environment. In this case, culture is an endogenous variable. Researchers need to begin doing culture research, using economic/psychometric methodology which accommodates these complex relationships.

Examine value change as well as the impact of values. Sometimes organizational culture can influence mangers to modify their national cultural values. It would be nice to know how this happens (or indeed if it happens). Also, as political and economic conditions change, cultural values change in business. This process should be studied to identify values that are variant and those that are invariant, if any.

Demand access to journal boards. Reviewers act to defend their paradigm first. The advancement of knowledge or interesting discourse are only of secondary importance. Culture theorists must fight their way on to journal boards so that their position can be defended. As I have noted above, this action will be good for all parties in the long run. Discourse will improve, and problems in economic theory can be resolved.

Test management theory, not culture theory. What I mean by this is that researchers should test motivation, leadership, and communication theories cross-culturally, using culture as a meditating variable. The goal, after all, is to understand managing, not culture. Most motivation theories were developed in the United States. They may have limited international application. Only testing will reveal their universality.

NOTE

1. While Bass's theorizing refers to consumers, his paradigmatic approach clearly is applicable to all individual choice behavior, including that of managers.

■ ■ ■

Insiders and Outsiders: Bridging the Worlds of Organizational Behavior and International Management

Nakiye A. Boyacigiller and Nancy J. Adler

> Insiders and Outsiders, unite. You have nothing to lose but your claims. You have a world of understanding to win. [Merton 1973:136]

To what extent does organizational behavior (OB), as a discipline, contribute to our understanding of cross-cultural and international management (IM)? Similarly, to what extent do cross-cultural and IM studies contribute to our fundamental understanding of OB? The answer to these two questions is not yet positive: while progress has been made in both directions, to date, it has been insufficient. Yet, because business has become dramatically more international, OB research must also become more international to retain any semblance of relevance. In this paper, we call for the accelerated development of a new international field of OB. To develop such a field, a marriage must be created between OB and IM (see, Negandhi [1975]). Rapid changes in the external environment make such a conceptual marriage imperative. However, fundamental epistemological, conceptual, and methodological dilemmas continue to impede this needed integration.

In this paper, we first discuss the development of the fields of OB and IM, including fundamental assumptions underlying each. We then address a trenchant problem inhibiting development of the field: the ill-defined culture construct. Based on this discussion, we then directly explore the creation of a new international field of OB. We suggest investigating phenomena in the new field which have previously been underrecognized or ignored in traditional OB. Two such phenomena are the emergence of transnational organizations and the increasing importance of developing countries. Both of these trends in the external environment are used as examples, with the meaning of each being reviewed for the new international field of OB. Based on these changes in the external environment, we recommend reconceptualizing traditional OB. The topic of motivation is used to exemplify such a reconceptualization. The paper concludes by suggesting the type of literature that should emerge in the new, globally based field and by drawing attention to those exemplars that currently exist.

THE FIELD OF ORGANIZATIONAL BEHAVIOR

OB studies human behavior within organizations. Historically, the study of OB developed in the United States and therefore focused primarily on the behavior of Americans in U.S.-based organizations.[1] In essence, OB has evolved as a domestic discipline implicitly masquerading as a universal, or "mainstream," field. By contrast, an international field of OB, while including the historically developed U.S.-based literature, would go beyond this domestic tradition to include a) the behavior of people in organizations within a single culture (intracultural management), b) the behavior of people compared across a number of cultures (comparative management), and c) the behavior of people working in organizations that interact with more than one culture (intercultural management). Whereas some theories would describe phenomena unique to a particular culture or region (domestic or particularistic theories), others would be universal (that is, constant across all cultures). Similarly, whereas some theories would apply to unicultural settings, others would describe the behavior of people interacting with two or more cultures. Although we are currently labeling this more comprehensive field as "international organizational behavior," the label itself is an artifact of the present time and place. International OB, is in fact, organizational behavior. All other forms of OB are simply subsets of international OB.

Inherent in traditional OB are a number of characteristics, particular to its era and place of development. For example, the unit of analysis in traditional OB has typically been the individual or the group. This has distinguished OB from the field of organization theory (OT), which has primarily studied the behavior of organizations themselves, and has thus taken the organization as the unit of analysis. However, contrary to subdivisions within academic fields of inquiry, actual phenomena in organizations result from reciprocal relationships between the individual, the organization, and its environment [Schneider 1985; Weick 1979].

> Because reciprocal rather than unidirectional cause and effect relationships predominate, the OB researcher must make judgments about the proper focus for theory and or research. The two major foci of choice are the individual and his/her group and the organizational work context. However because these foci are in reciprocal relationship, a concentration on any one level frequently makes it appear that the other levels are irrelevant. [Schneider 1985:575]

Some traditional OB researchers have conducted studies integrating issues across the micro (OB)/macro (OT) gap, however they remain in the minority.[2]

While needing to be more multilevel in its analysis, the traditional field of OB has, in fact, been inherently interdisciplinary, with foundations largely in psychology and to a lesser extent in sociology, anthropology, economics, and political science [Roberts, Hulin and Rousseau 1978]. In addition, based on its managerial orientation along with its historical focus on profit making organizations, OB has clearly developed as an applied social science. From its inception, the field has been characterized by applied research primarily focused on outcome variables of greatest interest to managers. These include studies on such topics as motivation, job satisfaction, and turnover, many of

which have been conducted with few theoretical underpinnings [Staw 1984].[3] While some scholars have criticized the field for exhibiting what they describe as an excessive managerial orientation [Baritz 1960; Mechanic 1963; Pfeffer 1982], others have stressed OB's status as a subfield of a professional discipline—management—and have persuasively called for even greater managerial relevance (see, for example, Bennis [1987]; Lawrence [1991]; Van de Ven [1989]). To the benefit of the field, tension has continued unabated between the simultaneous demands for theoretical development and increased relevance.

Clearly traditional OB is still a relatively young field in a preparadigm stage of development [Pfeffer 1985].[4] Based on Kuhn's [1970] definition of scientific inquiry, Pfeffer [1985:379] has described OB as lacking "consensus on exemplars, styles of inquiry, and the major substantive issues that characterize a field at a more advanced stage of development." Pfeffer [1985] has further argued that just as scholars' methodological and theoretical choices have colored the development of the field, so have their ideological biases; even though these have only rarely been discussed.[5] This, of course, would include the American bias brought to the field by its primarily U.S.-trained and based founders and scholars. If, as Steers[6] has argued, OB research has become stuck on issues at the margin, with methodological rather than theoretical considerations dominating research agendas, then progress towards the consensus that Pfeffer [1985] calls for will not be easily achieved.

ORGANIZATIONAL BEHAVIOR AND INTERNATIONAL BUSINESS

As a discipline, international business (IB) is the study of business conducted across national borders or in multiple national locations, often times by multinational corporations (MNCs):

> MNCs differ in kind as well as in degree from domestic corporations [Doz and Pra

halad 1991; Sundaram 1991]. Unlike domestic enterprises, MNCs coordinate the activities of geographically dispersed and nationally distinct affiliate organizations to serve a common cause in culturally, historically, economically, socially, ideologically, and politically heterogeneous environments. [Caproni et al. 1991:3-4][7]

By definition, IB is contextual. It specifically includes the external international environment in which firms conduct business; that is, the international context in which firms are embedded. It is precisely the nature of this embeddedness in an external, international environment that has distinguished IB from other areas of management inquiry.

Similar to the split between organization theory and OB, IB historically has also focused on macro level issues—the firm's relationship with its external international environment—rather than on microlevel issues—the role of individuals and groups within the organization (see, for example, Bartlett and Ghoshal [1989]; Egelhoff [1988]; Kogut and Singh [1988]; Stopford and Wells [1972]; Vernon [1966]). Studies on microlevel OB issues have often been labeled comparative or cross-cultural management [Adler, Doktor and Redding 1986; Kelley and Worthley 1981; Ronen 1986; Tung 1986]. While consistently exploring the influence of culture on the behavior of people in organizations, cross-cultural management studies have rarely included macrolevel variables and thus have failed to integrate national, industry, and strategic level considerations into their analysis. In forming a truly international field of OB, it would thus be necessary to expand the current microlevel perspective of OB to include systematically both international and macrolevel variables.

Context: The External Environment

In contrast to IM, traditional OB has tended to ignore both the external environment and firms' embeddedness in it. While dysfunctional for the field's current development, this oversight is not surprising. The majority of the social sciences, including OB in its traditional U.S.-based formulation, have followed primarily a natural science model, and thus have been acontextual in their development. The natural science model "presents scientific knowledge and truth as though they were transcendent and hence independent of any particular society or historical period" [Sampson 1978:1332]. The natural science model is therefore "necessarily ahistorical and acontextual because facts and truths are defined in universalistic ways, disregarding any particular and concrete sociohistorical standpoint" [Sampson 1978:1333]. By contrast, if OB had followed a historical model of science, rather than the natural science model, it would view organizational phenomena as distinctly located in time and space [Sampson 1978:1333].

Further exacerbating the decontextualization of OB has been the theoretical separation of OB from organizational theory. Not only has this separation led to oversimplified models in both fields but, equally important, to contextual factors being underemphasized in OB.[8] Fortunately, leading scholars have recognized this split between OB and organizational theory and are increasingly conducting integrated multilevel research (cf. Chatman [1989]; O'Reilly, Chatman, and Caldwell [1991]). Given that studies embedded in an international context are a natural extension of multilevel research, this greater integration bodes well for the internationalization of both OB and organizational theory.

An additional influence increasing OB's decontextualization has been its domination by American scholars and research. The United States, defined by Hall [1981;1976] as a low context culture, traditionally under emphasizes contextual factors. Moreover, because the post-World War II situation in the United States gave it one of the most stable economic, political, and social environments, the majority of U.S. management scholars found it neither necessary nor interesting to include external environment variables in their studies. To some extent, the stability of the external environment rendered it strangely invisible. The implicitly assumed absence of contextual relevance in OB and its explicit presence and acceptance in IB form the crux of the differentiation between the two fields. Unfortunately, therein also lies one of the fundamental blocks to their conceptual integration.

Barriers: Time Lags and a Lack of Cross-field Learning

A truly international field of OB will derive from both OB and IB. However, to date, attempts to create this new field have been plagued both by time lags and by a lack of cross-field learning. Time lags occur when scholars use dated models and theories. Unfortunately, this has been common since, in much of the original international OB research, scholars simply replicated U.S. domestic research in non-U.S. settings.[9] The lack of cross-field learning is reflected in the limited impact that IB research has had on theory development in OB. Traditional (primarily U.S.-based) OB scholars have tended to ignore IB research (see, Triandis [1992]). This is not surprising given both the minimal international training most OB students receive in U.S. doctoral programs [Nehrt 1987] and the paucity of international articles published in the most prestigious U.S. OB journals [Adler 1983; Godkin, Braye and Caunch 1989; Peng, Peterson and Shyi 1991].[10] Fortunately, some leaders within the field of OB are beginning to recognize the need for cross-field learning. For example, recent special issues of the *Academy of Management Review* [1991], the *Strategic Management Journal* [1991], *Organizational Science* [1992], and *Academy of Management Journal* [1995] on international theory development testify to an appreciation of IB as a substantive (and substantively different) area of inquiry for management scholars.

Thus, to create a truly international OB, scholars must refrain from regarding traditional OB research as the primary source of theories. IB has contributions to make to OB that are not mere extensions of domestic U.S. research to non-U.S. contexts. While proceeding from a solid theoretical foundation is essential, international research can provide OB with conceptual and empirical developments that in some cases complement, in others contradict, and in all cases enrich the previously overly narrow domestic U.S. paradigm. For example, cultural synergy, historically studied in multinational enterprises (MNEs), can inform the study of cultural diversity in domestic OB research [Adler 1991; Van Mannen and Laurent 1991].

Time lags and barriers to cross-field learning have always existed between the two disciplines. However, this decade's rapid globalization has made their consequences both more salient and more problematic. Thus, rather than assuming that learning is unidirectional, scholars should assume that learning is reciprocal between both of the existing fields (OB and IB) and the newly emerging international field of OB, as shown in Figure 1.

Caproni et al. [1991:3] underscore this imperative, based on their own research on sense making in international organizations:

> Despite their attention to sense making in MNCs, international management scholars have rarely formally applied theories and models of sense making developed by organizational theorists. Similarly, organizational theorists have produced numerous studies on organizational sense making but have paid minimal attention to international organizations and the global organizational environment.

Caproni et al. [1991:3] further suggest that: "regarding organizational theory and international management as separate fields retards progress in achieving a more general understanding of organizational phenomena ... "[11] Clearly, both IB and domestic OB scholars need to consult each other to develop the new field.

In addition to time lags and barriers to cross-field learning, the culture construct remains a trenchant problem inhibiting inte-

Figure 1. Cross-Field Learning

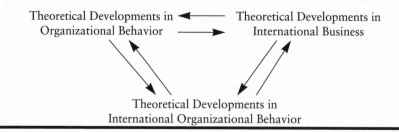

gration of OB and IB. The following section addresses the role of culture in OB research.

THE CULTURE CONSTRUCT IN ORGANIZATIONAL BEHAVIOR

The last decade has seen a resurgence in research focused on culture. Bellwethers, such as the publication of Hofstede's [1980a] *Culture's Consequences*, the JAI series on *Research in International Comparative Management*, and the phenomenal increase in publications on Japanese management, reflect a burgeoning academic and popular interest in culture. However, this increased attention has underscored the many problems inherent in culture-based research (see, Child [1981]; Roberts [1970]; Roberts and Boyacigiller [1984]; Redding [in this chapter]; Sullivan [in this chapter]). Among the most critical problems are:

1) the under emphasis on the nation-state in organizational science research;
2) the confusion about the appropriate level of cultural analysis;
3) the unrecognized reality of multiple cultural realities;
4) the lack of recognition of the multiple definitions of culture, each reflecting a different paradigm or theoretical frame; and
5) the poorly differentiated parallel concepts of organizational culture and ethnic or national culture.

Each problem will be discussed separately although in reality they are interrelated. First, the nation-state, as a construct and as a variable, has been under emphasized in organizational science research (for exceptions, see Boyacigiller [1990]; Carroll and Huo [1986]; Rosenweig and Singh [1991]). Moreover, of studies embedded in an international context, most still equate cultural differences with national differences [Child 1981; Roberts 1970; Roberts and Boyacigiller 1984]. This despite daily reports of ubiquitous ethnic and regional cultural differences that are not nationally delimited. For cross-cultural research to be valuable, scholars need to include nation-state characteristics and clearly delineate their effects on organizational phenomena from those of cultural variables. Simultaneously focusing on national and cultural variables in the same research design will allow the field to clarify the impacts of both sets of constructs. For instance, a study on turnover might include such national variables as unemployment rates, insurance coverage, and training policies along with such cultural variables as uncertainty avoidance, individualism, and activity orientation. An excellent example of this simultaneous focus is Parkhe's [1991] study of strategic alliances which clearly delineates meta-, macro-, meso-, and microlevels of diversity. As shown in Table 1, Parkhe [1991:584] integrates five levels of constructs and variables: societal culture, national context, corporate culture, strategic direction, and management practices and organization.

Second, given changes in the external environment, the appropriate unit of analy-

Table 1. Levels of Global Strategic Alliances

CONCEPTUAL LEVEL	PHENOMENOLOGICAL LEVEL	DIMENSION OF DIVERSITY	SOURCES OF TENSION
Meta	Supranational	Societal culture	Differences in perception and interpretation of phenomena, analytical process
Macro	National	National context	Differences in home government policies, national industry structure and institutions
Meso	Top management	Corporate culture	Differences in ideologies and values guiding companies
Meso	Policy group	Strategic direction	Differences in strategic interests of partners from dynamic external and internal environments
Micro	Functional management	Management practices and organization	Differences in management styles, organization structures of parent firms

Source: Adapted from Arvind Parkhe (1991) "Interfirm Diversity, Organizational Learning and Longevity in Global Strategic Alliances," Journal International Business Studies 22(4): 584.

sis has become increasingly problematic. Regional economic blocs (most often multi-national, although not always) have emerged as significant economic units. At the same time, a number of nations have fragmented into subgroups of ethnic rivals. In addition, organizations spanning na-tional borders—transnationals--have be-come more pervasive. The field therefore needs to develop consistent approaches for assessing the cultural, economic, and legal forces impacting OB at the ethnic, national, regional, and transnational levels.

Third, the reality of multiple cultural identities needs to be recognized [Brannen 1992; Gregory 1983; Phillips et al. 1992;

Sackmann 1991]. As Phillips et al. [1992:2] report:

> we must recognize that the *cultural group with its distinctive mindset* need not be delimited solely by national or organizational boundaries, but may overlap, be superimposed upon, or even nested within any single organization or set of organizations. In addition to the fact that these multiple cultural groupings exist in our complex organizational environments, we must also recognize that individuals can and do maintain simultaneous membership in any number of these groups.

While multiple roles and role conflict have been a component of role theory in traditional OB for years [Kahn et al. 1964], the international OB literature has rarely incorporated this powerful theoretical structure to investigate and explain the issues involved in multiple cultural memberships. Notable exceptions are role theory's limited use in the expatriate adjustment literature (see Black, Mendenhall, and Oddou [1991]) and in studying the CEO in international joint ventures [Shenkar and Zeira 1992].

Given changes in the external environment, the reality of multiple cultural identities is continuing to become more salient, not less. For example, as nonhierarchical networks of individuals and organizations gain prominence relative to traditionally structured hierarchies, the national culture of parent company managers no longer dominates the thinking patterns of managers in foreign subsidiaries [Adler and Bartholomew 1992b; Hedlund 1990]. The multiple cultural identities and roles of parent and host country managers express themselves simultaneously. The culturally conditioned cognitive patterns of both parent and host country nationals influence decision making and day-to-day organizational behavior. Nonhierarchical cross-cultural interaction, rather than single culture dominance, therefore defines organizational dynamics in today's networked firms. While much remains to be learned about how best to facilitate cultural synergy, recognition of these issues has increased the importance of cross-cultural cognitive studies that are based on cultural interaction and synergy rather than on traditional patterns of cultural dominance [Adler and Bartholomew 1992a; Adler, Doktor, and Redding 1986; Cox and Blake 1991].

Fourth, and most fundamental, many organizational scholars have not fully appreciated that multiple views of culture exist within the social sciences, with each reflecting an alternative paradigm or theoretical frame (see, Pondy et al. [1983]). As Sackmann [1991:7] observes:

> Although anthropologists, sociologists, organizational theorists, and managers use the same term and similar definitions, the meanings that they associate with culture are not always the same. This is due to the different contexts and respectively different assumptions associated with these contexts. They are related to differing interests regarding culture and lead to different expectations about what the concept can accomplish. Hence different lenses have been used to explore the theoretical base of culture, to explain its impact, to study it and to apply it to organizations.

Clearly, definitions of culture vary because culture is not the exclusive domain of anthropologists, but rather is studied by political scientists (see, Almond and Verba [1963]; Thompson, Ellis, and Wildavsky [1990]), psychologists (see, Bond [1988]; Rohner [1984]) and sociologists (see Alexander and Seidman [1990]; Peterson [1979]) as well as management theorists.

Even among the core cultural discipline—anthropology—the definitions of culture vary. For example, for cultural materialists, culture is behavior that is determined by techno-environmental factors [Harris 1964;1979]. By contrast, functionalists define culture as an instrument through which human needs are met [Malinowski 1939;1944]. Alternatively, symbolic anthropologists define culture "as a set of control mechanisms, plans, recipes, rules, [and] instructions for the governing of behavior" [Geertz 1973:44]. As shown in

Table 2. The Major Anthropological Approaches

ANTHRO-POLIGICAL APPROACH	MAIN FOCUS OF STUDY	MAIN REPRESENTA-TIVES	MAJOR INTERESTS IN RESEARCH	ASSUMPTIONS/ ASSERTIONS
Cultural Evolution	Culture is a complex whole which includes cognitive behavioral, and material aspects acquired by human beings	C. Taylor (1871; 1903)	Search for grand laws for evolution and origins	Educated are superior to "primitive" people who have fallen from grace
Historical Particularism	Physical anthropology facts, traits, and elements	F. Boas (1896; 1940)	Collect data in situ and discover their sui generis principles	Anthropology should be historical, inductive, and scientific The individual is an important unit of study
	"supraorganic" (the non-individual)	A. L. Kroeber (1917)	Discover patterns and configurations of culture (search for a grand theory)	Anthropology is history (rather than science) Individuals are subordinate to culture
Functionalism	Discover the structure of a natural system and try to understand how each part functions in relation to the system	A. R. Radcliffe-Brown (1952, 1957)	Social structure is an abstraction from behavior (no interest in psychological or biological aspects)	Culture concept is less meaningful than the concept of social systems
	Culture is the set of rules for fitting people together into a system		Study of social structure to determine the function in terms of how well it serves the well-being of a group	Anthropology is science People are organized in systems that constitute wholes whose parts contribute to their wholeness
		B. Malinowski (1939; 1944)	How do the various ele-ments of culture contribute to the whole? Interested in psychological, biological, and social needs	Culture is an instrument through which human needs are met (seven basic needs)

Table 2. *Continued*

ANTHRO-POLIGICAL APPROACH	MAIN FOCUS OF STUDY	MAIN REPRESENTA-TIVES	MAJOR INTERESTS IN RESEARCH	ASSUMPTIONS/ ASSERTIONS
Cultural Materialism	Culture is observable behavior	J. Stuart (1955)	Environmental and techno-environmental influences	Anthropology is science
	"Culturology" (culture exists independent of human beings). Culture is the continuum of interacting elements even though individuals are carriers of cultural tradition	L. White (1959)	Science of culture	Ecology is determining influence on culture and its evolution
	Culture is behavior	M. Harris (1964)	Collective behaviors	Culture is behavior that is determined by technoenvironmental factors
Cultural Idealism: ● Psychological Anthropology	Culture is integrated whole with consistency	R. Benedict (1934; 1942)	Culture is a determinant of personality	Culture is consistent pattern of thought; action is integrated whole
		M. Mead (1939)	Culture is different styles of life	Culture is the personality of its members and determines the personality of its members
	"Superorganic"	A. L. Kroeber (1917)		
	Culture is something internalized by human beings as a world of meaning	E. Sapir (1917)		The language a person internalizes affects the way the world is perceived
● Ethnography	Cultural descriptions based on language	J. P. Spradley (1972) H. Garfinkel (1967)	Use of ethnoscience to study the insiders' view	
● Structuralism	Collective unconscious	C. Levi-Strauss (1920; 1949)	Psychological aspects of structure, fundamental structures of the mind	History is alive in people's recollections
● Symbolic Anthropology	Culture is primarily a system of symbols	C. Geertz (1973) V. Turner (1967)	Combination of emic and etic descriptions	Symbols are involved in social processes they become associated with human interests, purposes, ends, and means

Source: Adapted from Sackmann, Sonja (1991) "Cultural Knowledge in Organizations" Sage: Newbury Park, CA. 10–12

Table 2, not only do the definitions of culture vary, but the underlying assumptions and research questions each suggests vary as well. In turn, each of these definitions has different implications for management and for the types of questions management scholars can pursue. For example, cultural materialism could lend itself most easily to the work of population ecologists, while symbolic anthropology would lend itself most easily to cognitive theories in OB [Kleinberg 1989].

Does the field of OB need a single concept of culture? Cross-cultural psychologists continue to debate the importance, or lack thereof, of a single construct of culture for the development of their discipline [Jahoda 1984; Rohner 1984; Segall 1986]. Jahoda [1984] and Rohner [1984] believe that cross-cultural psychology needs a shared understanding of the meaning of culture for requisite clarity in the field (also see Triandis [1992]). In contrast, Segall [1986] argues that a shared or global concept of culture is totally unnecessary. Given the preparadigm stage of development of OB and the complexities inherent in the culture construct, it is unlikely that OB scholars will agree on a single definition of culture capable of serving all interests. Progress could be made, however, by more consciously using the definitions selected, and by testing competing cultural hypotheses, based on various theoretical frameworks, within the same research study. While not focused exclusively on culture, an excellent example of this type of research strategy is Hamilton and Biggart's [1988] use of cultural, market, and authority patterns as explanations of organizational growth and structure in South Korea, Taiwan, and Japan.

Within the international OB literature, there is currently a predominant reliance on two conceptualizations of culture, that of Kluckhohn and Strodtbeck [1961] and of Hofstede [1980a], with most of the recent empirical work using Hofstede's four dimensions.[12] Given the disparate theoretical traditions within OB and international OB, one would expect greater variety in our conceptions of culture. While both Hofstede's [1980a] and Kluckhohn and Strodtbeck's [1961] conceptualizations have significant merit, few scholars exhibit sufficient sensitivity to the underlying assumptions inherent in each.[13]

Hofstede's dimensions have greater meaning when one becomes familiar with the questions that they are based on. As Hofstede [1990:104] states, "The national culture scores in *Culture's Consequences* only describe differences between countries: their absolute value has no meaning." Even more grievous is that so many scholars are basing their studies on a single research instrument that in the author's own words: "represents an accidental compilation of questions derived from secondary analysis of a bank of survey material developed for other purposes" [Hofstede 1990:104]. That so much of cross-cultural research has been based on Hofstede's work is unfortunate. Not because Hofstede's work is without merit—he has made a very important contribution to the field—but rather due to the often inappropriate use of his work.[14] As Hofstede [1990:105] himself notes:

> To prospective researchers on national and ethnic culture differences, I recommend that they develop their own survey instruments aimed at the particular kind of people they want to study. More interesting than replications using an unsuitable IBM questionnaire is to compare the dimensional structures obtained with different instruments on different populations, but across the same countries.[15]

While others have argued that there are weaknesses in Hofstede's measures [Dorfman and Howell 1988; Roberts and Boyacigiller 1984], this is not our objective here. Rather, we simply urge our colleagues to put more effort into understanding the culture construct, rather than borrowing what may be an inappropriate instrument.

Fifth, further complicating the issue of culture's definition in organizational research are the parallel concepts of organizational culture and ethnic or national culture (see Enz [1986]; Laurent [1991];

Schneider [1988]). The organizational culture literature was created primarily by traditional OB scholars in the 1980s (see, Frost et al. [1985;1991]; Smircich [1983]). Given the U.S. origin of many of the organization culture scholars, the organization culture concept itself became implicitly embedded in American cultural values [Adler and Jelinek 1986; Kirkbride 1987].[16] These scholars often ignored national, industry, and ethnic culture and thus gave undue credence to internal organizational issues [Schein 1985]. Their focus on organizational culture has been at the expense of a better understanding of the external environment [Jelinek et al. 1983].[17] Since the external environment interacts with the internal environment in influencing and explaining organizational behavior, organizational culture explanations have been limited and the field of OB has been impoverished by the scholarly separation of internal organizational dynamics from those external to the firm. This is especially important if, as Hofstede and his colleagues posit, organizational and national cultures are "phenomena of different orders" [Hofstede et al. 1990:313].

The debate about what culture is and how it should be used in research is a seminal issue that has engaged some of the best minds in anthropology, psychology, sociology, and political science. It is time for OB scholars to embrace the dialogue and argue culture's definition and role rather than ignoring culture or facilely accepting a particular operationalization within the organizational literature.

INTERNATIONALIZING ORGANIZATIONAL BEHAVIOR

This section focuses on three areas that provide significant opportunities for developing a truly international field of OB. To date, none of the three has been sufficiently incorporated in the OB literature. The first area includes those issues that have received attention by IB scholars but have yet to be theoretically developed from a rigorous OB perspective. The second area includes those issues that are theoretically important and relevant and yet, for a myriad of reasons, have been neglected by both IB and OB scholars. The third area includes those topics that have been addressed in the traditional OB literature but have not been extensively studied from an international perspective. Examples of each of these three areas will be presented: first, from IB, the emergence of transnationals and contemporary models of national competitiveness; second, well developed in neither discipline, management in developing countries; and third, from traditional OB, the study of motivation. These examples illustrate how cross-field learning can be used to create the new international field of OB, while simultaneously enriching both of the root disciplines.

Using International Business to Strengthen Organizational Behavior Scholarship

As discussed previously, research on MNEs has dominated the field of IB, with such scholarship focused primarily on the macro or strategic level. OB, with its decontextualized focus on microlevel issues has failed to confront many of the issues of rapid globalization inherent in today's business dynamics. This section uses some of the noteworthy advances in international strategy to investigate the current pattern of OB scholarship and to suggest directions for future research.

Transnationals. In *Managing Across Borders: The Transnational Solution*, Bartlett and Ghoshal [1989:16] suggest that to compete effectively firms must simultaneously "develop global competitiveness, multinational flexibility, and worldwide learning capability." As they posit, such transnational competitiveness depends on: "forces for global integration" and therefore "the need for efficiency" [1989:5]; "forces for local differentiation" and therefore "the need for responsiveness" [1989:8]; and "forces for worldwide innovation" and therefore the "need for learning" [1989:12]. Using these key strategic capabilities, Bartlett and Ghoshal [1989:15] define three types of firms and suggest a fourth composite type, the transnational.

As shown in Table 3, an expanded version of the transnational model can be used to outline the recent history of OB and to suggest future directions. As discussed previously, OB has focused primarily on domestic (U.S.) organizations. Given OB's implicit assumption of universality (inherent in most Western social sciences), much of the traditional cross-border OB research has simply attempted to extend domestic (U.S.) studies to the general (or "universal") case. In Bartlett and Ghoshal's [1989] terminology, this is equivalent to traditional OB having taken a global approach: that is, to the field having attempted to build parsimony through creating centralized, integrated global theories. Not surprisingly,

Table 3. Organizational Behavior Viewed through the Transnational Model

	DOMESTIC	MULTI-NATIONAL	GLOBAL	INTER-NATIONAL	TRANS-NATIONAL
CORPORATE FOCUS	Focus on operations in one country	Build strong local presence through sensitivity and responsiveness to national differences	Building cost advantage through centralized global-scale operations	Exploiting parent company knowledge and capabilities through worldwide diffusion and adaptation	Simultaneously combining national responsiveness, global efficiency, and worldwide learning capability
DOMINANT FORCE	Domestic focus	Multinational flexibility	Global competitiveness	Learning capability	Transnational mentality
ORGANI-ZATIONAL DYNAMIC	Domestic dominance	National responsiveness through local differentiation	Efficiency through global integration	Worldwide innovation through learning capability	Organizational capability through transnational mentality
ORGANI-ZATIONAL BEHAVIOR SCHOLAR-SHIP	Primary focus and research sites domestic	Comparative management research and single culture studies	Research conducted implicitly or explicitly assuming and/or concluding universality	Research on organizational learning (however, not international), viewed as a subfield or domestic organizational behavior	New transnational field of organizational behavior and cross-cultural management studies

Based on the conceptual model in Bartlett, Christopher A. and Sumantra Ghoshal (1989).

given the history of the field, these integrated theories have been based on implicit assumptions of universality more frequently than has such universality been proven to exist. By contrast, comparative management scholars—who, in fact, represent a subset of IB more that an integral part of OB—reflect a multinational orientation. Paramount in the comparative literature is the attempt to document local differences and thus respond to the exigencies of national responsiveness. In addition, another subset of traditional OB scholars has investigated organizational learning strategies and capabilities, however, they have rarely studied any form of cross-border behavior. This subset therefore reflects a domestic orientation. To the extent that domestic organizational learning research is disseminated abroad it represents Bartlett and Ghoshal's international approach. Bartlett and Ghoshal's [1989] transnational model would suggest a need to integrate the various substreams of OB and IB within the context of multicultural cross-border scholarship. Transnational OB, similar to transnational management, would simultaneously reflect the needs for global integration (universality), national responsiveness (cultural specificity), and learning capability (change and development). Specifically, transnational OB would:

(1) Focus on *cross-cultural interaction* in addition to, and as distinct from, cross-cultural comparison;

(2) Focus on *creating a worldwide multicultural organizational culture* rather than continuing to refine the ways of imposing the headquarters' organizational culture on local operations in each country. The issue is one of creating a global synergistic organizational culture, not of imposing any specific national culture on firmwide operations;

(3) Focus on *creating organizational cultures that simultaneously respect and value different national*

styles of organizing and managing while also creating and maintaining a shared transnational corporate culture. The focal question becomes *when* to be nationally responsive and *when* to act in integrated fashion worldwide, not *whether* national responsiveness or global integration should dominate;

(4) *Expand scholarship on organizational learning and capability to multicultural and cross-border firms*; and

(5) *Relegate research on domestic organizations to a subset of the broader field* of organizations with cross-border activity.

National Competitiveness. With the emergence of transnationals, the nature of national competitiveness has shifted dramatically. In *The Competitive Advantage of Nations*, Michael Porter [1990a;1990b], among others, observed that "the increasingly global nature of competition renders traditional comparative advantage theory insufficient for understanding nations' international patterns of trade" [1991:22–23]. As firms acquire a more global perspective (or, as Bartlett and Ghoshal [1989] would say, a more "transnational mentality") in choosing where they source raw materials and manufacture and market products and services, their success becomes "de-coupled" from the factor endowments of any particular country [1991:22]. However, while success depends less on basic factor endowments in a firm's home country, the capabilities "of particular countries do shape patterns of competitive success" [1991: 22–23]. According to Porter [1991:23], "sustained international competitive advantage results from ongoing improvement and innovation, not from static advantages"; or, in Bartlett and Ghoshal's terms, from the organization's learning capability. In presenting his model of national competitiveness, Porter [1991:24] suggests four factors, in addition to government policy and pure chance, that countries can use to facilitate "high and rising levels of productivity in individual industries":

Factor Conditions: The country's position in basic factors of production such as labor, land, natural resources, and infrastructure. Also included are highly specialized and advanced pools of skills, technology, and infrastructure tailored to meet the needs of particular industries;

Demand Conditions: The nature of the home-market demand for the output of local industries. Particularly important is the presence of sophisticated and demanding local customers who pressure firms to innovate and whose needs anticipate needs elsewhere;

Related and Supporting Industries: The presence (or absence) in the country of supplier industries and other related industries that are internationally competitive; and

Firm Strategy, Structure and Rivalry: The conditions in the country affecting how companies are created, organized, and managed, as well as the nature of domestic rivalry.

What can Porter's model contribute to international OB? First, it is a model for defining the macrolevel external environment within which microlevel OB takes place. As such, it offers a way to recontextualize OB. Second, in stating that "No one managerial system is universally appropriate … ," Porter's model [1990b:81] explicitly rejects universalistic one-best-way approaches. Thus, it explicitly accepts the reality of national differences, and thereby suggests nationally differentiated variables—in addition to culture—to add to comparative management studies.

Third, Porter [1990b:73] states that the essence of a "nation's competitiveness depends on its capacity to innovate and upgrade" and that "innovation and change are inextricably linked" [1990b:75]. While traditional OB and organizational development scholars have studied organizational change and resistance to change, they have rarely incorporated cultural dimensions into their models, such as assessing a na-

tion's proclivity to accept or to embrace change. In most instances, similar to Porter's model, these traditional literatures have assumed that change is good. However, two of the major cross-cultural models—that of Kluckhohn and Strodtbeck [1961] and Hofstede [1980a]—document that cultures vary markedly in their valuing, and thus in their acceptance, of change. Both the OB literature and the strategy literature could be enhanced by studies of organizational change, framed within Porter's model and incorporating appropriate cross-cultural dimensions.

Fourth, Porter's model challenges motivation scholars to incorporate external environmental exigencies. For example, Porter [1990b:89] states that firms must "seek out the capable competitors as motivators. To motivate organizational change, capable competitors and respected rivals can be a common enemy." This suggests research linking individual and group level motivation with macrolevel factors in the firm's competitive environment. It thus suggests multilevel research. Similarly, Porter's model calls for a new type of transnational leadership, and thus implicitly for new types of leadership research.

Fifth, Porter's model implicitly calls for research on perception, selective perception, and sense making in the global environment. For example, Porter [1990b] states that "we need a new perspective" [74] and admonishes executives that "adopting a global perspective is important to creating competitive advantage" [89]; and that they must "establish early warning systems" [89]. Clearly cognitive studies on how managers acquire and change perspectives are critical to understanding in the type of globally competitive environment that Porter describes.

Sixth, Porter's [1991:26] emphasis on the importance of mobile factors, in particular ideas and highly skilled individuals, to global competitiveness has multiple implications for many human resource management (HRM) functions—including recruiting, selecting, training, developing, and career pathing—along with such classic OB topics as motivation and leadership. According to Porter [1991:26], mobile factors are drawn to the location—the country—where they can achieve the greatest productivity and thus obtain the highest returns. Porter [1991:26] suggests the same features that make a country an attractive home base for a firm also help it attract mobile factors. Porter's model thus forces OB scholars to incorporate external factors, including national and industry level characteristics into their investigation of microlevel OB and HRM issues.

Seventh, Porter's model suggests a whole series of new questions for scholars studying expatriation. For example, Porter [1990b:92] states that, "To take advantage of foreign research, companies must station high quality people in overseas bases and mount a credible level of scientific effort." This implies that firms must select expatriates primarily to achieve innovation and learning goals. Similarly, his model suggests that firms should establish effective systems of communication with expatriates while they are abroad, and, equally important, plan their reentry to enhance organizational learning and thus organizational capability. To date, this has not been the case: expatriates have tended to be treated as out-of-sight and out-of-mind, while reenterers have tended to be ignored as a source of organizational learning (see, Adler [1981]; Adler and Ghadar [1990]).

Similarly, Porter's [1990b:93] admonishment that "circumstances in the home nation must support innovation; otherwise the company has no choice but to move its home base to a country that stimulates innovation and that provides the best environment for global competitiveness. There are no half measures: the management team must move as well" suggests a strategic aspect to cross-border transfers that has rarely been studied in the OB or HRM literature (see, Adler and Ghadar [1990]).

Eighth, Porter's model has implications for much more sophisticated approaches to managing cross-cultural teams, as well

as for expatriation, than previously envisioned. For example, Porter [1990:75] states that innovation, the key to his model, "comes from effort and from openness and from looking in the right place unencumbered by blinding assumptions or conventional wisdom. This is why innovators are often outsiders from a different industry or different country." A primary purpose for expatriation thus becomes innovation, not as has been the case too frequently in the past, transferring technology or accomplishing a particular job abroad. Similarly, one of the primary reasons for forming multinational corporate teams and boards becomes fostering innovation through leveraging the cultural diversity. Both with expatriation as well as with multinational teams, cultural differences must be accepted and valued rather than ignored or minimized. Given that most expatriation research has focused on adaptation and most research on multicultural teams has focused either on minimizing differences or on minimizing problems perceived to have been caused by such differences [Adler 1991], Porter's model suggests the need for a totally different type of cross-cultural research. Such research would focus on valuing and using cultural diversity; that is, it would study cross-cultural interaction as a source of cultural synergy and thus as a source of innovation (see, Adler [1991 chaps. 4,5]). As Porter's model clearly states, the issue is not "how to copy others' ideas," but rather how to create new ideas—innovation—out of the combination of different ideas.

While not the focus of this chapter, it should be noted that international OB has much to offer Porter's framework. For example, traditional models of motivation suggest that people are motivated by a set of factors, only one of which is economic (in Porter's terms "obtaining highest returns"). Moreover, cross-cultural models of motivation strongly suggest that people's willingness to change locations—and especially countries—varies by ethnic background. People from more individualistic countries are most likely to be mobile, whereas people from more collectivist cultures (and therefore embedded in extended families) would be least likely. Perhaps, given the assumptions embedded in his model, it is not surprising that Porter is an American, and therefore from the most individualistic and domestically mobile culture on earth.

Using Issues Neglected in Both Organizational Behavior and International Business

Recently, Austin [1990], Jaeger and Kanungo [1990], and Kiggundu [1989] each published excellent books on management in developing countries. After years of neglect, this burgeoning interest in developing countries is welcome. Austin [1990 chap. 1] argues that developing countries are very significant as buyers, suppliers, competitors, and capital users in what has become a highly interdependent world economy. Rapid development in Asia—highlighted by the impressive economic growth rates of such developing countries such as Indonesia, Malaysia, Taiwan, Thailand, and South Korea—has drawn significant attention in both the popular and scholarly press. One only has to witness the current interest in including second and third world countries in the major economic blocs to appreciate their importance. For example, the European Economic Community has considered the possibility of including Eastern European members; the United States has put negotiations on the "fast track" to include Mexico in the North American Free Trade Agreement; and Japan continues to invest heavily in the rapidly developing countries of Southeast Asia.

For the full potential of each country to be achieved as well as that of the economic blocs, much more needs to be learned about managing in developing countries. Kiggundu [1989:xvi] offers a vivid explanation of the importance of understanding the management systems in the developing world and increasing their efficacy:

> Although the world is experiencing the greatest technological advances in the history of civilization, and although it is en-

joying the greatest wealth so generated, the challenges of underdevelopment continue to defy the best solutions the world has to offer. Consequently, an estimated three-quarters of the world population still lives under human conditions characterized by underdevelopment, deprivation, oppression, fear, and hunger, and faces challenging administrative problems in trying to survive. Increasing global interdependence implies, among other things, that the burden and consequences of underdevelopment must be borne by citizens of the world regardless of where they live or work.

Unfortunately, many of our management tools, largely developed in North America and Europe, are inappropriate for developing countries. Marsden [1991] directly attributes the declining economic performance of Third World economies, in part, to inappropriate Western training approaches and inflexible postindependence bureaucracies (see also Srinivas [1990; 1992]). Scholarly work on developing countries has attempted to develop indigenous management practices as well as assist managers from developed countries to understand better the intricacies of managing in developing countries. While a general discussion of developing countries clearly masks significant differences among such countries, important patterns exist.

The greatest differences between developed and developing countries are contextual. Table 4 summarizes the variation in economic, political, demographic, and cultural context by level of development. Developing countries provide seemingly insurmountable challenges to managers. They are economically characterized by weak infrastructures, the lack of a skilled labor force, and low technological levels. They tend to be politically unstable. Culturally, developing countries tend to be characterized by rigid social structures, distinct gender roles, strong religious influences, and high levels of cultural diversity. Demographically, they experience high birth rates and thus have a relatively young populace [Austin 1990 chap. 3].

Table 4. Summary of Political, Cultural, Economic, and Demographic Variables
By Level of Development

| | | DEVELOPMENT LEVEL (GDP PER CAPITA) | | |
		LOW	MIDDLE	HIGH
Political Factors	Instability	High	Medium	Low
	Institutions	Weak	→→→	Strong
	International Links	Dependent	→→→	More autonomy
Cultural Factors	Social Structures	More rigid	→→→	Less rigid
	Religious Influence	Stronger	→→→	Weaker
	Gender Roles	Very distinct	→→→	Less distinct
	Language	High diversity	→→→	Low diversity
Economic Factors:*				
● Natural Resources	Importance to Economy	High	→→→	Lower
	Availability	Underdeveloped	→→→	Developed
● Labor	Skilled Human Capital	Scarce	→→→	Abundant
	Unskilled Labor: % Workforce in Agriculture	72%	44%	6%
● Capital: Domestic	Income Levels	$280	$1,810	$14,430
	Savings Rate: % of GDP 1987	15%	25%	21%
	Income Skewedness	Medium	High	Low
	Financial Institutions	Weak	→→→	Strong
	Inflation: Avg. 1973–83	14%	29%	8%
	Capital Flight	Outflow	→→→	Inflow
● Capital: Foreign Exchange	Trade Deficits	Medium	High	Low
	Commodity Export Line	Narrow	→→→	Broad
	Exchange-Rate Volatility	Low	High	Low
	Foreign Debt Service As % of Exports	21%	21%	2%
	Concessional Foreign Aid	Recipient	←←←	Donor
● Infrastructure	Physical Infrastructure	Weak	→→→	Strong
	Information Availability	Low	→→→	High
● Technology	Technological Levels	Low	→→→	High
	Industry Levels	Dualistic	→→→	Unitary
	Technology Flows	Recipient	→→→	Supplier
Demographic Factors	Annual Pop. Growth Rates (1980–87)	2.8%	2.2%	0.6%
	Age Structure	Young	→→→	Older
	Urbanization (% of total 1987 pop.)	30%	57%	77%
	Migration	Low	High	High
	Life Expectancy	54	65	76

*High-income oil exporters are excluded.
Source: Austin, J. (1990): *Management in Developing Countries*. New York: Free Press: 41, 57, 62, and 69.

In addition to external environmental challenges, people in developing countries hold values that often diverge from those on which traditional OB has been based. While developed countries tend to be characterized by relatively low uncertainty avoidance, high individualism, low power distance, and high masculinity, developing countries tend to exhibit relatively high uncertainty avoidance, low individualism, high power distance, and relatively low masculinity [Hofstede 1980a; Jaeger and Kanungo 1990]. In addition, while the traditional OB literature assumes free will [Harris and Moran 1979; Kluckhohn and Strodtbeck 1961; Stewart 1972] and a low-context orientation [Hall 1981;1976], both reflective of U.S. cultural values, most developing countries are characterized by the opposite: determinism and a high-context orientation [Boyacigiller and Adler 1991]. Furthermore, in comparing traditional and modern values Kahl ([1968:6] as quoted in Davis [1971:13]) has stated that traditional societies are characterized by values that are "compulsory in their force, sacred in their tone, and stable in their timelessness" in contrast to values in modern societies that are "rational and secular, permit choice and experiment . . . and stress individual responsibility."

GOING BEYOND TRADITIONAL OB SCHOLARSHIP: MOTIVATION IN DEVELOPING COUNTRIES

Kiggundu [1989:170] presents a stark picture of motivational problems in developing countries:

> available evidence suggests that motivational problems are pervasive across organizations in developing countries. Even under the best of times, these organizations are hard to manage or work for. They have heterogeneous membership, limited resources, diffused goals, weak management systems, and inadequate incentives and are highly politicized. These factors may contribute to the problems of low motivation among employees.

While motivation has arguably been one of the most researched topics in traditional OB [Roberts and Boyacigiller 1983; Staw 1984], significant international and cross-cultural questions remain, especially regarding developing countries. After reviewing studies on motivation in developing countries,[18] Kiggundu [1989:170] concluded that for developing as well as developed countries, "motivation is not caused by a single factor but is the result of complex psychological, sociocultural, economic, political, and organizational processes." Herein lies the challenge and opportunity for organizational scholars. While the motivational issues that emerge in developing countries manifestly combine external and internal forces that cross levels of analysis, traditional motivational theories have neither the breadth nor the depth to address them. Traditional U.S.-based motivational theories, with their lack of contextual embeddedness and individualistic orientation [Staw 1984], miss much of what is most salient about the nature of work and motivation in developing countries. As Staw [1984:650] states:

> one of the most severe challenges to conventional theories of work motivation has come, not from motivation theorists but from organizational sociologists doing cross-cultural work (e.g., Cole [1979]; Ouchi [1981]) . . . these comparisons have highlighted what could be a fundamental omission in our motivation theories . . . regardless of whether the driving force is thought to be prior reinforcement, need fulfillment, or expectancies of future gain, the individual is assumed to be a rational maximizer of personal utility.

Organizational theories, like other outcomes of cognitive behavior, are influenced by scholars' cultural values [Hofstede 1980b;1991]. Many theories of motivation, having been developed in the United States by Americans, represent American values regarding free will and individualism along with the United States' low-context culture [Boyacigiller and Adler 1991; Hofstede 1980b; Laurent 1983; Newman 1972; Stewart and Bennett 1991]. These values are not coincident with those in most developing countries and therefore theories based on such values lack applicability in most economically developing areas of the world (see, Shenkar [1985]). People in developing countries are much more likely to exhibit collective rather than individualistic values. Individuals from developing countries are more likely to accept higher levels of determinism than those from developed countries. Similarly, they are also more likely to integrate contextual factors into their conscious decision making. Moreover, empirical evidence suggests that elements of peoples' work and nonwork lives are more closely intertwined in developing countries [Appelbaum 1984; Mehta 1978]. Thus, for motivation theories to be widely applicable in developing countries, nonwork factors must be considered. For example, in describing the work environment in India, Mendonca and Kanungo [1990:236] note:

> In a well-managed, modern plant in Bombay, 35% of the workers are invariably absent during April and May when production is at its peak. Reason? To assist their families in the villages in the usual chores before the monsoons.

Likewise, Jaeger and Kanungo [1990:292] refer to:

> the common practice in Brazil to help . . . employees with personal financial problems. For example, because of a lack of public social services, employees may have an illness in the family which puts them in a precarious financial position. The personnel departments of larger Brazilian firms regularly provide assistance to employees in such a situation, thus mitigating the impact of the employee's problems on the functioning of the firm.

Srinivas [1990] refers to the importance of including nonwork factors, such as those described above, as taking a "macro-environment-conscious" work-centered strategy.

Just as collectivism and a low masculinity orientation necessitate the inclusion of nonwork factors in motivational theories, the relative belief in determinism of people in developing societies necessitates the inclusion of tradition to explain many social phenomena. As Mendonca and Kanungo [1990:237] note:

> the test of organizational policies and procedures is not a rational consideration of their appropriateness, necessity, and validity but rather the simple fact that these policies and procedures have always existed.

Thus, such simplistic approaches as changing expectancies within an expectancy theory framework, when applying them to developing countries, will probably not lead to the theoretically anticipated outcomes. Similarly, given the very nature of determinism, it is highly unlikely that equity theory will operate in developing countries as it does in developed countries.

Current thinking in traditional OB is that the various approaches to motivation (such as need, reinforcement, equity, expectancy, and goal theories) are complementary, with different situations (dependent variables) lending themselves more to certain theoretical approaches than to others [Landy and Becker 1987]. Furthermore, recent reviews of U.S.-based theories have sought a possible metatheory to integrate the aforementioned middle-range theories of work motivation [Klein 1989]. At the same time, increasing interest has been paid to the social context of motivation [Lincoln and Kalleberg 1990; Miller and Grush 1988; Salancik and Pfeffer 1978]. While all of these developments are important for the domestic study of motivation, they are especially promising for the study of motivation in developing countries.

CONCLUSIONS

We lack a coherent and systematic body of literature that can be called cross-cultural or comparative management. Thus, if we are serious about better understanding the international dimensions of [organizational behavior and] human resource management, the time has come to make a major commitment to developing a systematic and defensible body of literature surrounding this issue. To do this, it may be necessary for many of us to explore new intellectual arenas with which we are not familiar (e.g., cultural anthropology) as a means of developing sufficient theoretical bases upon which to carry our research efforts. This is no simple task, but if we are to be taken seriously by our peers, it may be a necessary step. Only when there exists a useful theoretical base and a systematic body of knowledge will the field come into its own as a central area in the study of business administration. [Steers 1989:30]

Clearly, we need much more proactive cross-field learning between OB and IB. Fortunately, certain exemplars exist. For example, Black, Mendenhall and Oddou [1991] have combined the domestic and international adjustment literatures in an effort to build a comprehensive model of expatriate adjustment using multiple theoretical perspectives. Similarly, Earley's [1989] tying of social loafing to the underlying cultural dimensions of individualism and collectivism combines strong OB research with a foundation in cross-cultural management, on questions of both theoretical and practical interest. Yang's [1992] study of U.S. and Japanese HRM policies in manufacturing and service firms similarly combines an international perspective with a multilevel analysis of fundamental human system dynamics. Yang's [1992:2] main thesis is that "the degree to which Japanese style HRM policies are successfully adopted in Japanese firms in the United States is contingent upon the firm's industry characteristics, its organizational features and the external environment." Similarly, Horng's [1992] study of cultural differences and trust moderators of MNCs' business strategies and control options in headquarters/subsidiary relationships is noteworthy for its multilevel approach incorporating three theoretical perspectives: first, theory from IB on the behavior of MNEs within a four country environmental context; second, theory from classical OB on trust; and third, theory from international OB on expatriation.

The division between IB and OB is an unfortunate historic artifact, a division no longer useful for either conceptualization or practice. We need stronger bridges and more sophisticated means of integration, not more divisions.

NOTES

1. Although the term "American" is used to describe people in North and South America, it is used here as a shorthand to refer to people in the United States of America.

2. For an excellent international example, see Zaheer (1991).

3. See Barrett and Bass (1976) for a comparable condemnation of cross-national studies.

4. See Beaty and Mendenhall's (1990) review describing IM as a preparadigm field and documenting the paucity of recent theory building articles in American journals and the complete absence of such theory building articles in the area of international OB.

5. Similarly, Caproni, et al. (1991:27) argue that "organizational scholars are not independent disinterested observers of an objective organizational world." Caproni et al. (1991:28) explicitly suggest that: "international management scholars, through their research, teaching, and consulting, are active participants in the enactment of the MNC, the global environment and the internationalization process."

6. Richard M. Steers. Personal communication, November 1991.

7. Note that Hedlund (1990:44) recommends that we view MNCs as the organizational norm and domestic companies, or as he labels them "simpler types of companies," as the variation (see also, Caproni et al. 1991).

8. And similarly, to the influence of individual variables being underemphasized in organizational theory.

9. Examples of replication studies in developing countries—each attempting to prove universality of their underlying theoretical approach—include Alvi and Ahmed's (1987) study of the determinants of organizational commitment in Pakistan, Das and Cotton's (1988) replication of a North American power-dependence study with Indian managers, and Khaleque and Rahman's (1987) study of job satisfaction in Bangladesh. See Srinivas (1992) for further examples in developing countries.

10. This is not surprising given that most

academic management journals offering opportunities for publication are U.S. based, and have American editors and editorial boards that equate acceptable theory with the body of knowledge produced in the U.S. (Boyacigiller and Adler 1991).

11. As Caproni et al. (1991:3) suggest, other scholars holding the same point of view, include: Black, Mendenhall, and Oddou (1991), Doktor, Tung, and Von Glinow (1991), Doz and Prahalad (1991), Ghoshal and Westney (1991), and Westney (1989). See Maruyama's work (1985) for a more in-depth investigation of the role of culture in sense making.

12. Most international OB scholars are quite familiar with Hofstede's (1980) initial four dimensions (uncertainty avoidance, power-distance, collectivism/individualism and femininity/masculinity) and his basic research design (an internal survey administered initially to more than 116,000 IBM employees in 40 countries). To facilitate replication, Hofstede included his Values Survey Module as well as questions from the initial questionnaire as an appendix in *Culture's Consequences* (1980:419–426, 403–410). Hofstede, with his colleague Michael Bond, later added a fifth, non-Western dimension, Confu-

cian dynamism (Chinese Cultural Connection, 1987; Hofstede and Bond, 1988). Confucian dynamism, which measures employees devotion to the work ethic and respect for tradition, was derived in a study based on a non-Western (Chinese) instrument and an initial Chinese sample.

13. See Hoppe (1990) for an exception.

14. See the debate between Hofstede (1990) and Singh (1990a) in *Organizational Studies*.

15. For an expanded discussion, also see "A note to those considering replications" in Hofstede (1991: Appendix).

16. A very important exception is the work of scholars in the Standing Committee on Organizational Symbolism (SCOS), a primarily European scholarly association.

17. For exceptions, see those organizational scholars including national culture in their work, for example, Jaeger (1983;1986), Heenan and Perlmutter (1979), Kirkbride and Chaw (1987), La Jaunie and Sambharya (1990), and Schneider (1988).

18. See, for example, Blunt (1983), Kanungo and Misra (1985), Machungwa and Schmitt (1983), Sharma (1986), and White (1986).

■ ■ ■

The Comparative Management Theory Zoo: Getting the Elephants and Ostriches and Even Dinosaurs from the Jungle into the Iron Cages
S. Gordon Redding

I will begin with an apology for the zoological metaphor, but this all began with Schollhammer's [1969] comparative management theory jungle, and was compounded by Roberts's [1970] elephant, Adler's [1983] ostrich, and Boyacigiller and Adler's [1991] dinosaur. The subliminal notion of taming something wild might as well be acknowledged also, as it contains more than a grain of truthful insight. Iron cages are also perhaps as relevant to Western scientific paradigms and the fragmented adhocracies of academic management, as they are to rule-bound bureaucracies themselves.

The purposes of this paper are (a) to note progress over recent years in clarifying conceptual issues in comparative organizational behavior theory, (b) to review the quality of such work in terms of relevance, method, and epistemology, and (c) to consider its present condition and direction as a discipline. The field itself is that pertaining to individual and group behavior and interaction within international organizations and between such organizations and other individuals and groups. The core questions at the normative, practitioner end of the spectrum of enquiry are:

1. How to manage multicultural organizations?
2. How should the organizations of one culture adapt to the cultural environments and employees of another culture?
3. How can a host culture best accommodate the organizational practices of an outside company?
4. What organizational practices are beneficially transferable from one culture to another?

At the theoretical/ epistemological end of the spectrum of enquiry, the key issues are:

1. Ethnocentrism and naive positivism in methods of research;
2. The complexity of multiple and reciprocal determinacy;
3. The highly contingent nature of the core theory of Western organizational behavior;
4. The lack of nomothetic integration soundly based in empirical support;
5. Inadequate epistemological rigor in defining valid units of analysis for comparative social science.

It will be necessary to conclude that although progress has been made, the discipline has suffered from excessive repetition of sterile reporting, from theoretical poverty and from a lack of clear direction. The journal literature suggests that without the unifying and dominant work of Hofstede [1980;1991] it would be even more disparate and undisciplined. This theoretical anemia is seen as an extension of a larger problem in the core discipline of organization theory, viewed by some as directionless and weighed down by useless proliferation [Kochan 1983] and by others (e.g., Sullivan in this chapter) as polluted by the axiom-based and positivist paradigm espoused by Anglo-Saxon economics in its attempt to cope with its physics envy. Multidisciplinary solutions to the resolution of such problems are regularly advocated, sporadi-

cally organized, but as yet have only rarely contributed to the advance of theory.

The paper will begin with a review of the literature to 1991 before proceeding to a critique of methods, assumptions, purposes, and progress in specific organizational behavior (OB) fields. It will conclude with the outlining of an agenda and a rationale for future work.

Such an analysis is set against a background of proliferating interaction and interdependence between cultures and nations, and in such a world the businessman has increasingly urgent needs for assistance from theory. In practice he is forced to run on ahead and let theorizing catch up later if it can. It has been argued that the creation of viable global organizations depends on the redesign of much human resource management practice. Such redesign is made necessary by two forces: first, the increasing turbulence and variety of environments is directing new emphasis towards the achievement of controlled diversity and thus new organizational forms; second, the growth of information technology is affecting the fundamental design of work, making it more conceptual, and causing adjustments in the organizing of tasks, roles, authority relations, and sources of power and responsibility [Schein 1986]. The field of enquiry and of potential application of new theory is changing rapidly, thus introducing extra complexity to an already complex set of issues. Not surprisingly, it will be complexity which runs as a core theme through this paper.

THE LITERATURE IN COMPARATIVE ORGANIZATIONAL BEHAVIOR

As the purpose of this paper is a critique of the character of the literature it is not intended to provide a detailed restatement of its content. Such detailed reviews are available (e.g., Roberts [1970]; Adler [1983;1984]; Barrett and Bass [1976]; Bhagat and McQuaid [1982]; Drenth [1985]; Ronen and Kumar [1986]; Triandis [1992]; Adler, Doktor, and Redding [1986]; Boyacigiller and Adler [1991]; Dunphy and Stening [1984]; Beaty and Mendenhall [1990]; Child [1981]) as are also a number of textbooks which rest upon the incorporation of a wide literature (e.g., Adler [1986]; Ronen [1986]; Terpstra and David [1985]; Dowling and Schuler [1990]). In addition, a number of collections of papers in book form have addressed the issue of comparative management (e.g., Preston [1990]; Evans, Doz, and Laurent [1989]; Clegg and Redding [1990]; Joynt and Warner [1985]; Jaeger and Kanungo [1990]; Lammers and Hickson [1979]; Brewster and Tyson [1991]; Pieper [1990]).

It will perhaps be salutary to examine the key findings of the major reviews over a period of time, as a means of defining stages of progress and identifying areas of persistent failure, and using as guides the authoritative and comprehensive reviews of Roberts [1970], Barratt and Bass [1976], Child [1981], Adler [1983], Boyacigiller and Adler [1991], and Triandis [1992]. Other more focused critiques will then be considered in order to add depth to the definition of the current state of the art.

A REVIEW OF THE REVIEWS

The early major review by Roberts [1970] was highly critical. Describing the literature as a "morass," she cited Bass's [1965] comment on U.S. organizational research that there was one group of researchers interested in people without organizations and another group interested in organizations without people. Progress depended on some interaction but little was evident.

Her analysis divided the subject into different vantage points, namely individual behavior, organizational subunits, and organizations. Her conclusion was that studies at the individual level told us little. There were few explanations of why cross-cultural investigation was necessary at all, little innovation in approach, and a lack of standardization in design to facilitate comparison. Studies at the level of organi-

zational subunit were seen as partial, fragmented, and disconnected from a crucial larger causal context. Studies of organizations to that date suffered from conceptual poverty, from the assumption of the organization as static, and from a lack of rigorous comparison.

In Roberts's view, culture itself was poorly conceptualized and in need of a theoretical system capable of handling the many variables involved. She attacked "mini" theories of culture. She also attacked the "made in the U.S.A." stamp of much research. More sinister perhaps was her identifying of the scholarly provincialism with which she was "considerably impressed," and her warning about the limits of a single discipline. She saw a set of mutually exclusive, but potentially parallel approaches to the problem of understanding organizations and their surrounding cultures, and concluded that this is a poor design for theory building. Not much had been learned, and improvement required work in three fields: understanding behavior in a single culture; developing middle level theories to guide explorations; and seeking the relevant questions to ask across cultures.

Whitley's [1984] description of management studies as a fragmented adhocracy is relevant here and explains much of the problem of achieving coordination in theory building. His taxonomy of scientific fields classifies them by (a) degree of functional dependence, or the need for researchers to use common techniques in order to use each others' work, (b) degree of strategic dependence which is highest when there is monopoly control of a theoretical core and thus of reputation granting, and (c) degree of task uncertainty, or the uncontrollability of work outcomes. The study of management occurs in conditions of low functional dependence, low strategic dependence, and high task uncertainty, and fragmented adhocracy is the organizational response. It leads to a condition where research is personal, idiosyncratic, and only weakly coordinated across research sites, and where dependence for reputation cannot justifiably be focused on a dominant core paradigm. Individuals make relatively diffuse contributions to broad, fluid goals, these goals being in turn affected by local and environmental pressures, and by the infiltration of "lay" ideas, interests, and participants. Paradoxically however, the case made out in this paper is not so much that the discipline suffers from the looseness implied above but that the North American practice of it has been colonized by an inappropriate core paradigm which is only pseudoscientific.

The review by Barratt and Bass [1976] concentrated on four areas in industrial and organizational psychology: motivation and attitudes, management and supervision, assessment, and training and development. These overlap extensively with what is normally taken as OB, but their review deliberately omitted issues relating to the organization as unit of analysis.

They began with an epistemological caveat, to which later attention will be paid in this current review, namely the constant shifting of meaning; for instance, what is participation? They did, however, confirm the salience of culture in affecting abilities and aptitudes, but concluded that it was most dramatically illustrated in differences in perceptual processes.

Their review of the literature saw it as fragmented and in need of an integrating framework, their suggestion for which was as follows: to achieve a full understanding of a person at work in a particular country requires analysis of:

1. National socialization patterns;
2. Institutions peculiar to the country (e.g., educational structure);
3. Individual traits that are typically formed within a particular nation;
4. Predominant technology;
5. Political/socio/economic environment.

They thus advocated a very large contingency model in which specific enquiries could be embedded. For such a model to work, however, required progress on operationalizing constructs and standardizing of instruments to facilitate comparative study. The literature they reviewed yielded only a small number of studies with a clear theoretical base. The majority of studies simply reported differences or similarities without the ability to illuminate their determinants and with inadequate attention to reliability.

Child's [1981] review provided a useful parallel to that by Barratt and Bass in that it concentrated more on organizations as units of analysis. Although not central to this paper's concern with organizational behavior, it is nevertheless worthy of note for its comprehensive attempt to deal with the issue of culture as determinant of variations in organizational processes and structures.

Child began with a review of the problems associated with the use of culture in the cross-national study of organizations and identified five, namely:

a. culture is not clearly defined;
b. cultural boundaries do not necessarily overlap with national boundaries;
c. cultural factors are commonly brought in as explanatory variables without any explanation of their origins in the social history of a society or of their functioning;
d. not enough has been done to specify which components of culture are relevant to organizations, and also which aspects of organizational behavior are influenced;
e. conceptual and operational problems continue to hinder the measurement of culture.

In addition to these handicaps, culture has to compete with two other major sources of explanation: that of the "culture-free" contingency theorists, and that focusing on modes of production and especially the capitalism/socialism continuum.

As regards contingency theory, Child concluded that it may well be able to specify boundary constraints on the choice of organization but these are sufficiently wide to admit of various functional equivalents the evolution of which may be culturally affected. As regards the influence of systems of power relations such as capitalism, it is argued equally that a degree of cultural modification in the operation of economic systems becomes significant at the level of individual organizations. Thus culture remains an essential part of the explanation for international variations in organizing, and the issues return of understanding "how much" and "how."

To this end Child [1981] advocated and offered a more sophisticated model than that normally found and one which is capable of incorporating the three main fields of determinants (contingency, culture, economic system), seeing them as inevitably interconnected (Figure 1). In restating the validity of a culturalist perspective, albeit a

necessarily partial contributor to explanation, he then defined the conditions under which research progress might be made. His key points are worthy of note:

1. Culture is best seen as the normative and preferential conditions for action, not the action itself. It is the system of meaning, as distinct from the social system which is the way of organizing human action. Such a distinction is, for instance, implicit in Hofstede's [1980] definition of culture and has longstanding acceptance in anthropology [Keesing 1974]. The value of such a concept is that it allows for other noncultural variables to influence action in parallel.

2. In order to avoid culture's being a

Figure 1. Arguments from Contingency, Culture, and Capitalism

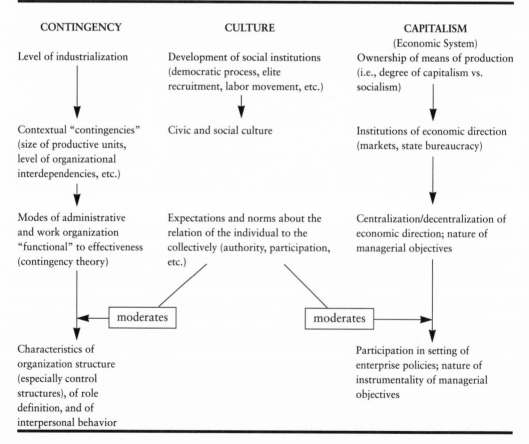

purely residual black box, it is necessary to identify in advance the cultural characteristics of a country which are considered a priori to explain organizational differences, and to demonstrate their concordance with a national boundary, rather than to infer that culture is visible in the contrasts between sets of research subject responses. These latter may well carry all sorts of nonculture effects and especially the influence of organizational environment.

3. A much richer understanding is needed of the processes of cultural influence in a society and of the stability and persistence of certain cultural transmissions. The historical emergence of a society's framework is illuminating in two senses: firstly it helps to understand the mental programming; secondly it can help to explain the development of national institutions and national distinctiveness. A richer understanding of the cultural context of OB is needed for the formulation of better hypotheses.

4. Industrialization-modernization are arguably absorbed into a nation's own tradition and are thus achieved in many different modes. This notion serves to unify the otherwise competing culturalist and "contingency" schools of thought, and should prove fertile in building necessarily more complete models, the absence of which is so regularly lamented (a point to be returned to later when considering economic culture and business recipes; see also Smith and Bond [1993]).

5. Progress in developing the "organizations within society" approach will need to come to grips with two especially intractable theoretical issues affecting the understanding of comparative OB. The first is the variation in the societal understand-ing of the meaning of authority. The second is the epistemological problem that separating culture and social structure into the two realms of thought and action does not move us forward in clarifying whether culture is an explanatory variable in its own right or a product of social structure. This of course rests upon the separate but related issue of the adequacy of theories of society.

6. In Child's [1981] view, cultural effects will be most powerful in the processes of organization relating to "authority, style, conduct, participation and attitudes," and less powerful in formal structuring and overall strategy.

Adler's [1983] "ostrich" review considered the literature from 1971 to 1980 in 24 journals and concluded that researchers were publishing very little and in a sense avoiding the problem. The ostrich accusation arose from the fact that the internationalization of business was increasing rapidly while research addressing its problems remained at the same low level. Although more books had appeared, the development of theory via the research process remained paralyzed. In the field of OB 14.1% of articles were cross-cultural, and within these 6.8% intercultural. Adler's conclusion was that cross-cultural management research remained in its infancy. The decade of the 1970s was not one of progress. The narrow domestic paradigm, at least in the United States, remained dominant.

Almost a decade later, Boyacigiller and Adler [1991] noted that the 1980s had produced no increase in the volume of cross-cultural OB articles, citing the reviews of the field by Godkin, Braye, and Caunch [1989] and Peng, Peterson, and Shyi [1991]. Exacerbated perhaps by ten more years of perceived ineptitude, they raised the metaphorical stakes from ostrich to "parochial dinosaur," as the descriptor of American organizational science. Their target, however, was not so much ethnocentrism, in which Americans might view their homebased theory as superior to others, but rather parochialism, or the simple lack of awareness about alternatives. The danger they saw for the discipline was that of becoming a fossil.

They began their review with a chilling (for Americans) expose of the massive perception that the economic success of the United States is due to the American science of management, citing Thurow [1984] and arguing instead that the two decades after World War II, which began with the United States accounting for 75% of the world's GNP, gave the United States effortless and noncompetitive monopoly profits. The alternative view is thus that success was due not to managerial know-how but to the lack of significant competition, and as the latter has grown, and U.S. GNP reduced to 22% of world GNP, so too has the threat to the implied claims of its normative theories.

Boyacigiller and Adler [1991] point to a number of institutional barriers in the discipline which are worthy of recall here, as they illuminate the practical dilemmas which stand in the way of dealing with the conceptual dilemmas.

1. Doctoral programs fail to train scholars for international research.
2. International research is more difficult and more expensive.
3. Domestic research paradigms emphasize quantification and internal validity, whereas international research tends to be contextual, to require external validity, and to be unable to offer laboratory-type, context free methodologies.
4. The review process is parochial, and reputational control maintains the status quo in the paradigm, limiting the originality of contributions.
5. The lack of a solid core of American-based references and the disdain for foreign journals prevent scholars from engineering a more

constructive paradigm shift based on respectable prior research. Thus logical empiricist methodology drives the production of knowledge and the problems and needs of managers are largely ignored.

These five strictures are made in the North American context and Boyacigiller and Adler [1991] do raise a significant point in acknowledging the fertility of European researchers in this field. This is attributed to their stronger sociological emphasis, and also to the plurality of perspectives able to combine on the basis of common respect (see also Kochan [1983]). It is perhaps also inevitable that the cultural variety of European life itself would act as a pervasive reminder that the issues are real and relevant.

A significant part of Boyacigiller and Adler's [1991]critique lay in their analysis of what they termed qualitative parochialism, a feature they illustrated by reference to American assumptions about free will versus determinism, the individualist bias, and a low-context perspective on communication, all of which are arguably manifest in the main body of management theory. Their dismal conclusion is that the discipline is trapped within geographical, cultural, temporal, and conceptual parochialism. Like organization theory, it resembles a weed patch. To turn it into a well-tended (zoological?) garden requires action. They present thirteen progressive recommendations, and they are reproduced here as Table 1.

Beaty and Mendenhall's [1990] review of what they saw as the "pre-paradigm" field of international management is also notable for its exposure of the paucity of theory building in the main U.S. journals of the discipline. Their findings were that in the Academy of Management Review from 1984 to 1988, only three out of 268 articles contributed to theory in international management. Of these, two were in strategy and one in organizational theory (OT). In JIBS, from 1986 to 1988 there were five articles, three on strategy and two in OT. There were no theory building articles in human re-

Table 1. Recommendations for a More Internationally Relevant Organizational Science

RECOMMENDATIONS	SIGNIFICANCE
Reflection	
Explicitly address the influence of cultural values on how we conceptualize organization phenomena and construct organization theories.	Helps scholars uncover neglected, over-emphasized, and overgeneralized aspects of theories.
Examine the extent to which the organizational sciences reflect U.S. cultural values.	Increases scholars' understanding of American culture and its impact on their perceptions, thoughts, and scholarship.
Action Steps for Individual Researchers	
State the cultural and geographical domain of theories and research, as well as indicate other locales in which it applies.	Minimizes implicit universalism.
Indicate the national and cultural charac-teristics of research samples.	Assists readers of the research to recognize potential limitations.
Research management systems outside the United States.	Creates new theoretical and methodological approaches not predicted on American assumptions.
Study non-U.S. management systems on their own terms (idiographic research); develop thick descriptions of organizational phenomena and the contexts in which they are embedded.	Increases the organizational forms and contexts with which scholars are familiar, as well as increasing their understanding of the uniqueness of U.S. organizational forms.
Create more multinational and multicultural research teams.	Facilitates recognition of cultural biases in theory development.
Use non-U.S. settings to frame theoretical and methodological approaches.	Expands domain of organizational theories.
Take sabbaticals in foreign countries.	Increases scholars' understanding of foreign cultures and their own cultures, including providing personal thick descriptions of the foreign sabbatical culture.
Organizational Changes	
Journal editors, reviewers, and scholars should question one another regarding thteir cultural assumptions and research domains.	Rewarding careful exposition of the geo graphical and cultural domain will check implicit universalism.
Expand editorial boards to include global representation and expertise.	Increases the perspectives represented, both substantively and symbolically.
Consider forming "global lines of business," strategic alliances, and networks among academic organizations worldwide.	Facilitates internationalization, and, thus, contributes to future relevance.
Select leaders of academic management organizations from multiple nations.	Increases perspectives and knowledge bases represented, thus facilitating frame-breaking change.

sources management, organization behavior, or general management. Qualitative methodologies were clearly disdained and "empirical opportunism" rampant.

Triandis [1992] begins his review of 400 studies by acknowledging the parochialism of American organizational psychology and its outcome—an underdeveloped theory of the way culture influences social and organizational behavior. An indicator of this is the individualist bias in much Western research and the underestimating of the importance of groups, culture and other surrounding features. His analysis of the issues which have to be faced produces the following list of research needs:

1. A rigorous analysis and operationalizing of the concept of culture, including attention to the issue of which dimensions especially influence organizational behavior.

2. The development of a model able to explain the links between culture and organizational behavior.

3. Attention to the methodological pitfalls which lie in wait for those doing cross-cultural research, and acknowledgment that it is not so much a choice of which particular method, but of which combination of methods.

4. Acknowledgment of the roles of perception and cognition in the workings of cultural influence, together with the epistemological implications for the definition of the objects of study.

5. The influence of norms in differentiating meanings of apparently common notions.

6. The antecedents and consequences of culturally varied needs, attitudes, motives and values. In this context, Hofstede's [1980;1991] work stands dominant as a working theory of culture, but Triandis nevertheless calls for a deeper understanding of Hofstede's four dimensions, and especially uncertainty avoidance and masculinity.

7. Introduction of more dynamic perspectives which illustrate the "negotiation" processes which mediate the interaction of norms, roles, values, etc. in each environment.

Triandis concludes that "our ideas are still quite vague" [54]. We are still without a widely accepted definition of culture. We cannot yet clearly separate (a) the psychological from the cultural, (b) the universal from the culture-specific, and (c) the single-case specific from the general pattern. Management systems and job designs are known to be culturally influenced but precisely how and under what conditions cannot be specified in any comprehensive way.

This review of the major reviews inevitably leads to the conclusion that thirty years' work has made little impression on the immensely complex problem of cultures and OB. There is however strong agreement on the essence of the difficulty and the nature of the failure and these may be illustrated in graphic form by relating two of the main dimensions of theory building. Figure 2 proposes that one important dimension is the interpretive-descriptive (or ethnoscience-positivism) dimension. The other is the idiographic-nomothetic dimension, or the theoretical level of analysis from micro theory to grand theory with middle range theorizing half way.

The main body of work is clustered incompetently, unadventurously, but with comfortable conformity in the positivist micro-mini theory corner. Outliers exist but in apparently unattractive territory. Understanding lies in moving upwards and outwards but this requires a more sociological perspective and immediately raises questions about research legitimacy. As Sullivan has argued in this chapter the positivist paradigm of economics has defined the norms of the science, and its reputational criteria. One might extend the argument to say that in the process it has turned effective scholars into deviants and caused at least thirty years' waste.

In such a context not much may be ex-

Figure 2. Location of the main body of Western comparative management research, with outliers and a proposed re-location

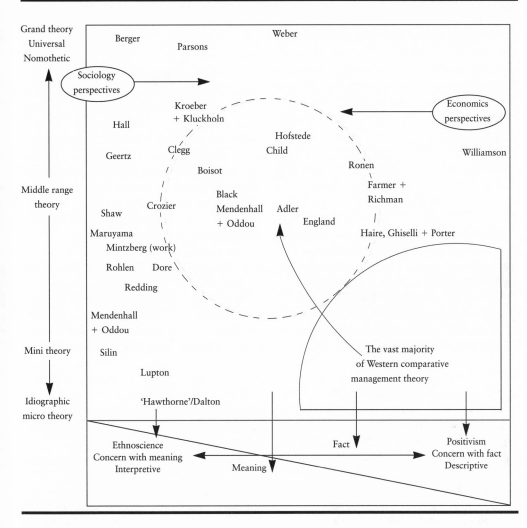

pected when we turn to examine more specifically the research on separate aspects of comparative OB. It should also be stated as previously that the analyses which follow do not pretend to review comprehensively the literature content. Instead they will concentrate on issues concerned with the process of theory building in order that a more progressive research agenda may be defined. Two general issues will first be addressed, followed by a review of progress in particular OB fields. This paper will then conclude with an examination of epistemological issues and research requirements.

The term "general issues" refers to those aspects of the study of international OB which are wider in their reach than the traditional subdivisions such as leadership and motivation. The general issues to be considered will be:

a. Intercultural relations, and
b. Human resource management seen as a whole.

More specific aspects will then be addressed, viz.:

c. Leadership;
d. Motivation-needs-attitudes-values;
e. Selection-placement-job design-training;

f. Organization development and corporate culture.

These are more focused probes into the literature than the broad review which has preceded in the early part of this paper and by sketching current knowledge boundaries they will set the stage for the final section which considers how we might proceed with finding out what we currently do not know.

INTERCULTURAL RELATIONS

Two general prescriptions pervade the field of studies in intercultural relations. The first argues by implication that managerial issues are too complex to allow precise advice on anything and the way forward is for each party to understand the other and then take such understanding into account as a contingent factor. It is what one might call a "recommended empathy" approach it is often the only real advice emerging from the many studies which describe differences in a theoretical vacuum.

A second somewhat more positive approach is to make the assumption that there is synergy to be sought in cultural variety and that mixtures can result in greater creativity, innovation, and responsiveness [Heenan and Perlmutter 1979; Adler 1981; Schein 1986; Cox and Blake 1991]. It is possible, using such work, to know whether an organization is culturally heterogeneous and to know the procedural steps necessary to achieve synergy. What we do not yet know sufficiently is how the synergy works and thus how to determine the components of the mixture. As the issue is not one of interpersonal harmony (and may in fact be a matter of using interpersonal tension creatively) it is inevitably very complex. Personality variations also enter the picture to complicate it further.

Looking at the same issue in the context of cross-cultural leader-subordinate relationships, Shaw [1990] has proposed a cognitive categorization model, building on an earlier model by Redding [1980] and the recommendation by Adler, Doktor, and Redding [1986] for cognition to be taken seriously in cross-cultural understanding. He presents a case for the cultural creation of prototypes of good/bad role behavior, and argues that effective relations are achieved when the prototypes can be adjusted to overlap. His contribution is valuable middle range theory building although it still calls for testing.

The adjustment of managers to foreign assignments is another field which has followed the pattern of being studied extensively but atheoretically, and Black, Mendenhall, and Oddou [1991] have usefully proposed new theorizing which makes use of the extensive U.S. domestic literature on transfers and adjustments. They provide a theoretical framework for international managerial adjustments which is capable of sustaining new research efforts of an improved kind.

It is of course in the field of joint ventures that intercultural relations become especially significant, and here the empirical accounts range from descriptions of problems and failures (e.g., Elashwami [1990]; Shenkar and Zeira [1990]; Nirenberg [1986]; Parnell and Vanderkloot [1989]) to claims of successful adaptation (e.g., Rehder, Smith, and Burr [1989]; Oliver and Wilkinson [1988]; Ouchi [1981]). Calling for a more rigorous approach to the study of the human resources issues in international joint ventures, the literature on which they saw as sporadic and limited, Shenkar and Zeira [1987] proposed a preliminary research framework and a set of hypotheses. This uses an open systems approach and concentrates on analyzing personnel problems.

The field of intercultural relations, which lies at the core of the most urgent practitioner problems, is beginning to focus now on middle range model building and hypothesis generation, and progress must be acknowledged.

HUMAN RESOURCE MANAGEMENT (HRM)

Laments about the failure to understand theoretically the international dimension of human resource management are regularly accompanied by claims for its increasing significance. Such claims rest on the fact of globalization and a massive growth of IB [Adler 1986; Ronen 1986] but also more subtly on the increasing strategic significance of human resources as firms enter new modes of competitive behavior [Tichy 1983; Fombrun et al. 1984; Adler and Ghadar 1990a; Evans 1986].

Adler and Ghadar [1990a] point to new approaches in managing R&D, production, marketing, and finance developed in the face of new global realities, but see no equivalent evolution of thought for international human resources systems. The issues are complex because of the variety of perceptions, value systems and interests [Horwitz 1990], and because of the changes wrought by information technology, organizational destructuring, and market turbulence [Schein 1986].

It was noted earlier that practice runs ahead of theory in complex fields, and Kidger [1991] provides some useful reflections on this in describing a converging set of HRM practices internationally. He sees increasing standardization in having personnel specialists, policy statements, job evaluation, briefing groups, quality circles, and notes an increase in resources for personnel work. He also argues that there is a closing of the gaps between Japanese, U.S., and European systems, with the Western practices drifting towards an emulation of Japanese lifetime employment ideals, teamworking, concern with quality and removal of overt status differences, citing Peters and Waterman [1982], Goldsmith and Clutterbuck [1984], Pang and Oliver [1988], and Purcell [1987]. The underlying principles in this process are summarized by Thurley [1990] as those that sponsor (1) dialogue between the social partners in the organization, (2) organizations built on a multicultural basis, (3) opportunities for participation, and (4) continuous learning by staff based on objective feedback.

The convergence hypothesis, however, is always controversial and an ample litera-ture exists to indicate that HRM practices do vary substantially in their visible manifestation (e.g., Shackleton and Newell [1991]) as well as in the underlying cognitive frameworks which affect them [Al-Faleh 1987; Hayes and Allinson 1988].

Poorly researched issues which are of current concern to practitioners are seen by Kidger [1991] as:

a. the integration of HRM with business strategy;
b. the development of a distinct corporate culture;
c. the creation in different countries of a skilled, flexible, committed workforce, adaptive to change;
d. implications of culture on commitment and on unions.

In endorsing a similar set of research aims, Schein [1986] has pointed out a crucial epistemological stumbling block, well worth noting before considering the next stages in the discipline. He points out that the meaning of such things as careers and what people get from work varies so substantially across cultures that deeply held concepts about what authority, management, and work are all about in the larger scheme of things may also vary in critical ways.

A claim can be made that a basic conceptual framework for the HRM field, based on the Harvard model [Beer et al. 1984], is widely accepted by theorists. Concern with the link to strategy has also been analyzed theoretically (e.g., Hendry and Pettigrew [1990]; Fombrun, Tichy, and Devanna [1984]). Attention has also been paid to the corporate culture/national culture interaction (e.g., Schneider [1988]). The models offered are however somewhat tentative and will require several iterations before their precision approaches the complexity of the explananda. Nor do they meet Schein's concern to include at least some ethnomethodology. Many assumptions still require empirical demonstration and it is perhaps best to conclude this consideration of the general international HRM field with

Kidger's [1991] recommendation of research questions, namely:

1. Is an international body of practices in fact emerging?
2. Do the practices have the same significance/meaning in different countries?
3. Do the differences relate to the cultural/educational/political context in such a way that needs to be understood for best practice?

LEADERSHIP

The massive Western literature on leadership has continued to be enriched with new insights as more ethnographic studies (e.g., Mintzberg [1973]; Kotter [1982]; Bennis and Nanus [1985]) supplement the earlier base of largely survey-dependent understanding (e.g., Stogdill [1977]). Moving out from this core into the international field has been mainly a matter of extending the survey-type, attitude-oriented methodologies which typify the early descriptive phase of social research and which are well summarized in Ronen [1986]. More recent research has now begun to explore the potentially much richer fields of differences in behavior patterns and in cognitive structures of the kind advocated for study by Adler, Doktor, and Redding [1986].

Doktor [1990] has presented data to demonstrate that CEOs use their time differently in Hong Kong, United States, Japan, and Korea and Stewart [1992] has similarly reported for China. Different styles for the use of authority have also been reported by Aldemir [1986] as have variations in "performance management" behavior between developing countries and Western countries by Mendonca and Kanungo [1990]. Sinha [1990] has also developed a normative model for effective leadership behavior in the Indian context. Japanese structures of leadership behavior have been extensively studied (for a review see Dunphy [1986]) and the occasional ethnographic study (e.g., Rohlen [1974];

Clark [1979]; Silin [1976]) has enriched understanding of the workings of Asian OB.

A fuller understanding will need progress on the question of differences in mental landscapes. Although Hofstede's dimensions provide a useful beginning here on approaching empirically Berger and Luckmann's [1966] social construction of reality, we are still left with only the most broad hints about the mental framework of leaders in various cultures, and there is a clear need for much more indigenous specification of meaning structures of the kind offered by Pye [1985] on authority in Asia. The contribution here of Mendenhall and Oddou [1986] in presenting a guide to the cognitive context of Japanese management is a valuable advance which contains a theory of causation. An empirical extension of such work has been reported by O'Connell, Lord and O'Connell [1990], and an equivalent for the Overseas Chinese is available [Redding 1990].

A significant empirically based investigation of this same issue is now also available [Smith et al. 1989; Smith and Peterson 1988] in which the generalizability of the notion of leadership style across cultures is tested. Using 1,177 respondents in Britain, United States, Hong Kong, and Japan, and using Misumi's notion of a distinction between a general structure in leadership and variations in its specific expression [Misumi and Peterson 1985], they discovered that, as an example, consideration in an individualist culture might mean respecting subordinates' autonomy, whereas in a collectivist culture it might mean more interaction with them. They also propose that performance and maintenance behaviors are more differentiated from each other in the United States, whereas more overlap may occur elsewhere. The balance of their internal constituents will also vary.

Research of this latter kind is clearly significant in opening up the cognitive dimension. Its potential for enriching theory is also clearly large. It is however difficult to conduct and, so far, very sparse.

MOTIVATION/NEEDS/ATTITUDES/VALUES

The essential problem in the field of understanding worker motivation cross-culturally is that we have a vast quantity of description of differences, but very little understanding of their local antecedents and causes, or of their implications for appropriate organizational and managerial responses. A comment typifying the outcome is offered by Seddon [1987] who claims: "It is likely that few appraisal systems are operating effectively in organizations in developing countries."

The large literature on the differences themselves has been well presented by Ronen [1986] and reviewed by Triandis [1992]. Beginning with the idea that motives will vary in their dependability and pliability, Triandis opens up the probability that although the structure of motive arousal may be universal to homo sapiens, the content of the standards will vary with cultural frames of reference. How this connection works is addressed hardly at all by the large literature describing variations. Except, that is, by Hofstede who has written extensively on the antecedents of value systems [Hofstede 1980] and more recently on their organizational and managerial outcomes [Hofstede 1991]. A fully worked out theory of culture and its organizational effects is thus available, but as there are inevitable trade-offs between universalism and specificity, it can only offer signposts to the deeper understanding of specific cultures. It must also be acknowledged that variations from Hofstede's set of four values may emerge to make them less universal than they currently appear. An example here is the description of a Chinese values set which suggests a different cognitive structure [Bond and Hofstede 1990; Bond 1988], and this is backed up by other work on Chinese organizational behavior [Redding and Wong 1986], face [Redding and Ng 1982], trust [Wong 1988], and group dynamics [Tang and Kirkbride 1986].

Hofstede's work has inspired a great improvement in the discipline by specifying a wide-ranging theoretical model which serves to coordinate research efforts. Two roads now lead from it. One is to examine more completely the question of universals and produce a map of value-sets indicating the way they vary in their internal distribution and weighting of factors. The other is to examine more closely the local origins of those value-sets and the mechanics of their influence on behavior in organizations. One must conclude that such work is in its infancy, although new work by Bond and Schwarz provides hope that breakthroughs may be anticipated [Bond 1991].

SELECTION/PLACEMENT/TRAINING/JOB DESIGN

It is inevitable that the paucity of more fundamental understanding of the interaction between culture and OB will weaken the precision with which more practical applications are worked out. Thus, Bhatt and Miller [1983] found the research field on questions of selection and placement to be "in disarray." There is a high failure rate in expatriate assignments [McEnery and Des Harnais 1990] and the training of expatriates is either not done or is done ineffectively [Derr and Oddou 1991; Adler and Ghadar 1988; Mendenhall and Oddou 1986; Tung 1982; Ronen 1986]. Little progress has been made on the issue of career and personal variables which will predict success in foreign assignments [Adler and Graham 1987], although a somewhat disparate literature exists (reviewed by Brislin [1981] and Kealey and Ruben [1983]).

An attempt to generalize was made by Mendenhall and Oddou [1985] who isolated four variables critical to the processes of selection and training: self-orientation; other orientation; accurate perceptions; and cultural toughness. A much more substantial advance however is now available in the comprehensive research model proposed by Black, Mendenhall, and Oddou [1991] and referred to earlier in the discussion of intercultural relations.

The training of people for work in

cross-cultural situations has been reviewed and categorized by Triandis [1992] into four approaches: self insight which helps a person to identify his/her own "cultural baggage"; attribution training or learning of the others' framework via culture assimilators; behavioral training to retune a person's receptors of stimuli; experiential training or extensive exposure to people from the new host culture. Application of these methods does however need sensitivity to collectivist/individualist differences, and there is also evidence that the sequence in which techniques are used by an individual will influence the effectiveness of a program of sensitization. There appear to be more questions than answers on the issue of cross-cultural training and its effectiveness. Is a general cultural assimilator useful? When should training be given? Who should do it? Should trainers be from the host culture or neutral? How do trainee attributes interact with training? What is the best balance of cognitive versus behavioral training?

The literature on cross-cultural training effectiveness was reviewed by Black and Mendenhall [1990] and their conclusion was that such training was capable of enhancing skill attainment, overall adjustment to a new culture and job performance, findings which augur well for more attention to this aspect of the field.

The study of job design is a potentially useful field for revealing cross-cultural differences in organizational effectiveness and the determinants thereof. It is here that some of the more dramatic contrasts exist between American and Japanese factories. Understanding remains puny, however. The Western approach to job design tends to argue that the more variety, task identity, and feedback are provided by a job the greater a worker's satisfaction [Hackman and Oldham 1980]. There is some argument, however, that in collectivist societies, motivation is likely to be influenced by task interdependence and affiliation needs [Morishima and Minami 1983], and that the nature of attachment to the organization and to a job

is significantly influenced by culturally determined frameworks of meaning [Redding, Norman, and Schlander 1992].

ORGANIZATION DEVELOPMENT AND CORPORATE CULTURE

There is clear evidence that organization development needs to be consistent with local subjective culture if it is to be effective [Preston 1987; Tainio and Santalainen 1984; Jaeger 1990; Blunt 1988; Feldman 1986; Hayes and Prakasam 1989; Rigby 1987]. Its origin as a U.S. technique, although clearly ethnocentric, does not necessarily negate its use in other cultures, but does impose a requirement for adaptation [Jaeger 1990]. Models for understanding such adaptation are available (e.g., Berry [1980], Harris and Moran [1979], Zeira and Adler [1980]) but the empirical testing and refinement of them is still pending.

A similar conclusion applies to the cross-cultural use of the notion of corporate culture. There are well-argued contentions that a corporate culture must be in tune with national culture for an organization to function well [Schneider 1988; Adler and Jelinek 1986; Soeters and Schreuder 1988] and there is some evidence to support the contention empirically (e.g., Lincoln, Hanada and Olsen [1981]; Ferris and Wagner [1985]; Misumi [1984]). There is also valuable work on adaptation of organizational culture, such as that by Ouchi and Jaeger [1978] on the emergence of Type Z as an adaptation from Types A and J.

Further progress in achieving congruence between national and corporate cultures remains dependent upon advances in conceptualization of the issues and instrumentation to foster fieldwork. Useful contributions to the latter are noted from Cooke and Rousseau [1988] and Hofstede et al. [1990].

The various fields within cross-cultural OB theory appear to exhibit different rates of progress toward more fully explicated middle range theories, and only one universal theory has reached the stage of extensive empirical grounding. The review of theoretical requirements which now follows must take as its starting points (a) the enrichment of the middle range, (b) the sponsorship of alternative grand theory, and (c) the refinement of the grand theory whose use is growing.

These theoretical issues will be addressed by examining the debating points which persist in the literature and which remain unresolved. Such debates surround the question of how knowledge should grow and are partly epistemological, partly institutional and partly methodological, usually all at the same time. As debates, they are not always overt and must be inferred from the behavior of social scientists across a wide spectrum of disciplines. They may be identified as follows:

1. The specification of the field of enquiry in terms of the key questions being addressed;
2. The specification of the field in terms of the disciplines and schools of thought being brought to bear on it;
3. The issue of alternative frameworks of meaning;
4. Questions of epistemology and causation;
5. More progressive research design.

THE FIELD IN TERMS OF QUESTIONS ADDRESSED

The more obvious questions of practitioners were identified at the beginning of this paper. Behind them lie the core research questions at the center of which is the issue of generalizability, of whether there are certain universals in the managing of organizations. A subsidiary issue is that of identifying what varies and what does not. Until we can specify the limits to generalizability, the focusing of research will remain problematic.

It is interesting that the original proponents of the convergence hypothesis [Kerr et al. 1960] have more recently acknowledged that although convergence appears to be occurring in "the ordinary business of life," or how a person gets and uses his income, there appears little coming together in the realm of the mind, the field of beliefs and values [Kerr 1983].

Those scholars who argue for a single international managerial culture (e.g., Kidger [1991]; Everett, Stening, and Longton [1982]) seem now to be authoritatively outnumbered by those who argue like Laurent [1986] that variety proliferates and that "the art of managing and organizing has no homeland," but the real questions of what does or does not vary have not been answered. Jorgensen, Hafsi, and Kiggundu [1986], Kiggundu [1990] and Jaeger [1990] have produced tentative models of conditions for transferability of organizational systems. Ishida [1986] has similarly treated the transfer of Japanese HRM practices. Fairchild [1989] has also perceptively studied the way in which culture causes a reinterpretation of the processes and structures of organizing and the consequent contrasts in the manifestation of bureaucracy. Redding and Whitley's [1990] framework for the analysis of economic systems "beyond bureaucracy" and Whitley's [1991;1992] theory of business recipes are beginning to accumulate information from Europe and East Asia which allows for a typology of organizational design clusters, each being understood in terms of a complex of cultural, sociological, and institutional determinants. Undoubtedly the new institutionalism in organizational analysis [Powell and DiMaggio 1991] is greatly enhancing understanding.

We observe an enriching of the field of questions and an ability to specify them with more contingencies and more precision. It is not intended to list them here in detail, but at least those themes that lie at the heart of the field of cross-cultural OB as it now stands and are beginning to claim attention, can be identified. They are:

1. What are the antecedents and determinants of organizationally relevant values, beliefs, attitudes, and motives in specific cultures?

2. Which clusters of values, beliefs, etc., are organizationally relevant in which national contexts?

3. How does culture interact with other factors (e.g., structural contingencies, macroeconomic systems, surrounding institutional frameworks) as part of a complex model of multiple and interacting determinants of organizational responses?

4. Can organizational responses be clustered to produce a typology?

5. How do the specifics of OB reflect the cultural predispositions and meaning systems of members?

6. How may different cultures be blended effectively at the interpersonal, hierarchical, organization structural, and operating system levels of analysis?

7. Which aspects of organizing and managing may be said to be universal and which are most affected by culture (that is, if there is such a construct as managing which can be disembedded at all).

THE FIELD IN TERMS OF DISCIPLINES AND SCHOOLS OF THOUGHT

The dangers of a field settling prematurely into a normal science straightjacket are manifest in OT, as regular warnings indicate [Daft and Lewin 1990; Gioia and Pitre 1990; Sullivan 1992] and the narrowness of focus of many studies in comparative management is a likely outcome of what is taken as normal science, i.e., publishable, in the central disciplines of OT/OB.

The complexity of the domain of study in comparative OB is significantly greater than at the core and calls for the incorporation of more explanatory variables, and more diverse models of the management process. The resulting dilemma is that a creative diversity of approaches will hinder even more the achievement of intellectual synthesis and practical research integration,

challenges which are already demonstrably problematic.

To examine the nature of this dilemma, it will be appropriate to consider some maps of how the discipline has so far diffracted, and then some proposals for holding it together with an integrating framework. We shall then be in a position to consider the wider integration initiatives which incorporate other disciplines.

Alder [1982] has usefully identified six alternative ways of doing cross-cultural research: parochial, ethnocentric, polycentric, comparative management, geocentric, and synergistic. These vary by the number of cultures involved, the way similarities and differences are approached, the basic study design and research questions, and the methodology. Synthesis is clearly not fostered in such circumstances.

Another typology by Sechrest [1977] identified three kinds of cross-cultural research: Type I studied the overall impact of culture on OB; Type II studied what specific aspects of culture had what effects, using psychological processes as the main object of study; Type III were more anthropological and attempted to study culture itself rather than concentrating on its organizational effects. His observations were that most studies were Type II. Type I studies have to compete with alternative theories claiming different primary determinants. In a comment using this typology, Bhagat and McQuaid [1982] advised beginning with Type I, to achieve some perspective, then proceeding to Type III for greater insight, then Type II for more specific understanding of cause and effect and relative weightings, an iteration between the nomothetic and idiographic which is also seen by Lammers and Hickson [1979] as the most fruitful means of pursuing understanding in this field.

Assuming that it is possible to accept such advice and dispose oneself as a researcher alternately in ethnographic and hypothesis-generating mode, then an overarching framework is still required to provide adequate perspective and to suggest necessary inputs from other disciplines. In a valuable attempt at such integration, Bhatt and Miller [1983] proposed a framework reproduced here as Figure 3.

Their Venn diagram identifies three major categories of variables: enterprise-specific, a field where organizational and managerial differences can normally be reported but not explained; location-specific, dealing with the institutional and cultural environment and connecting often with de-

scriptions of managerial practices which typify and represent that environment; international environment-related which allow the incorporation of cross-national factors affecting organizations such as trade protection, recessions, and booms, etc. They also identify fields of overlap or interaction, the most complex being at the center.

The point of such an exercise in separating fields is that each category has its own accepted research criteria, and is cap-

Figure 3. Fields and Types of Research

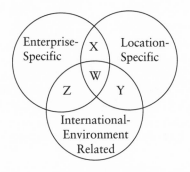

Typical Comparative Management Research

Enterprise-Specific	Variables which describe characteristics, operations, and performance of an enterprise and/or its members.
Location-Specific	Variables which describe the nature of an institutional and cultural environment in a given location that are relevant to an enterprise and/or its members.
International-Environment Related	Variables which describe the nature of the international environment affecting more than one nation at a given time.
Area X	Studies describing interactions between enterprise and its local institutional/cultural environment.
Area Y	Studies describing interactions between local and international environments.
Area Z	Studies describing interactions between enterprise and international environment.
Area W	Studies describing interactions among enterprises, their local institutional/cultural environments and the international environment.

Source: Bhatt and Miller (1983).

able of yielding valuable inputs based upon sound existing methodologies and particular disciplinary perspectives. Bhatt and Miller conclude that what is now needed is a moratorium on description and a move toward interdisciplinary theorizing.

This plea echoes that of Child [1981] noted earlier, and represented in Figure 1. There is a long history of such frameworks (c.f., Farmer and Richman [1965]; Negandhi and Estafen [1965]; Koontz [1969]), but it is only recently that researchable specifications of causation are emerging and also that interdisciplinary approaches are beginning to bear fruit. Four examples of this fusion are worthy of note.

First, at Harvard the work of Austin [1990] and Porter [1990] displays the value of combining economics and management theory within the context of international organization. Although still antisociological, with neither author acknowledging HRM as an issue, the advance in understanding of the international dimension of business remains indisputable.

Second, and also based in economics, is the work of Williamson [1975;1985] in comparative institutional analysis, with its fusion of work in economics, organization theory and contract law.

Third, is the new institutionalism in OT which enriches the core by focusing on "a broad but finite slice of sociology's institutional cornucopia" [DiMaggio and Powell 1991:9]. Within this same field is the work of Whitley [1992] on business recipes and their origins in societal institutions, under a framework intended to be a sociology of organization.

Fourth, is the program of studies on industrial democracy in Europe [International Research Group 1981] which fused the two disciplines of OB and industrial relations and proved that "an interdisciplinary, cross-national team composed of individuals with different goals, political philosophies, and research traditions can produce a product that contributes to both theoretical advancement and public policy" [Kochan 1983:634].

These advances have normally restricted themselves to the connecting of two main disciplines, but note should be taken of some initiatives which incorporate four or five main disciplines in collaboration on a complex question.

Two major projects now incorporate approaches from history, sociology, economics, OT, philosophy, and political science, to study the success of East Asian economies. The underlying assumption is a link from society's value systems to its organizations and its national performance. The projects are based at the American Academy of Arts and Science [Tu 1991] and the East-West Center [Dernberger 1989].

Progress may now be identified in matching complex questions with sophisticated frameworks, and the longstanding advocacy of multidisciplinary approaches is now providing for important advances in understanding. Whether in the longer term they will be seen as major breakthroughs remains uncertain but they clearly chart a direction worth exploring.

ALTERNATIVE FRAMEWORKS
OF MEANING

OB theory is a social science and its purpose is the understanding of behavior. Social science normally achieves its purpose by the study of meanings rather than of facts. To understand OB comparatively requires access to indigenous frameworks of meaning.

The cross-cultural OB literature offers almost nothing progressive in this regard and to get the issue back onto the research agenda may require a radical ethnographically based challenge, such as those issued by Mintzberg to management theory [1973] and to corporate planning [1990]. If leadership "means" different things in different countries [Smith, et al. 1989], if OB "means" something different in Japan [Mendenhall and Oddou 1986], if the "meaning" of organization and how you attach yourself to it is different in Asia from the West [Redding, Norman, and Schlander

1992; Yu and Yang 1992], then the eventual understanding of OB in any "meaningful" way will have to come to terms with the challenges of ethnoscience.

Nor should it be forgotten that cognitive frameworks include those that carry the mental processes of understanding and explanation, and that social science itself is a Western cultural artifact, the basic cause-and-effect notion within which is arguably ethnocentric [Maruyama 1974].

EPISTEMOLOGY AND CAUSATION

There is one central challenge which dominates the field in an epistemological sense and that is the bankruptcy of empirical positivism. More than anything else it is this which has sent the subject round in circles for thirty years. In considering that issue, it is appropriate to take note of certain questions which surround it, namely (a) the lack of a common observation language and the inevitability of relativism, (b) the imperialism of economics, (c) the weakness of the deterministic mechanical causal model and the false assumptions on which it is based, (d) the implications of causal complexity and reciprocal determinacy, and (e) the special nature of the comparative method and the compromises it entails but finds useful. After considering these issues, a more progressive paradigm shift can be defined.

The main opposition to empiricism comes from the relativist position which holds that a common observation language is impossible in social science. As Geertz [1973:5], arguing from this position, says:

> The concept of culture I espouse . . . is essentially a semiotic one. Believing, with Max Weber, that man is an animal suspended in webs of significance he himself has spun, I take culture to be those webs, and the analysis of it to be therefore not an experimental science in search of law but an interpretive one in search of meaning.

The dilemma posed by this position is that interpretive approaches resist conceptual articulation and thus systematic modes of assessment. As Geertz [1973:24] points out: "the tension between . . . the need to grasp and the need to analyse is . . . both necessarily great and essentially irremovable." Culture theory in this formulation works under three conditions: it must stay close to what it describes and cannot assume a life of its own with freedom to shape its own internal logic; second, it does not accumulate upon itself, except that an accretion of conceptual tools allows for deeper and more incisive probes into the same things; third, it cannot be predictive. The role of its theoretical concepts is to provide a vocabulary in which what a society's symbolic action has to say about that society can be expressed. Considering the superficiality of much cross-cultural management understanding, and its manifestation in the gulf between the American and Japanese organizational psyche, it is salutary to be reminded of the value of people's understanding of themselves.

Geertz' position lies, of course, at one end of the interpretive/descriptive continuum of the discipline, illustrated in Figure 2 (for a more elaborate discussion see Morgan and Smircich [1980]). It is hardly worth dilating on matters at the opposite end, as that is where we have characterized the main part of the discipline as languishing and stranded. Suffice it to say that, as Sullivan has argued in this chapter, IB research is dominated by economic theory and the purposive paradigm. The achievement of this form of intellectual imperialism by economics can be understood by way of reference to the sociology of the discipline operating as a conservative novelty-producing system with highly standardized training and certification systems, designed to train future economists to solve artificial puzzles with formal analytical techniques. Such dogmatic initiation is unchallengeable by neophytes and unchallenged by members. The end product is described by Whitley [1986:193]:

> As a result, economists share common analytical skills, a standardized symbol sys-

tem for communicating the results of analytical research, a strong consciousness of the boundaries of economics and of appropriate ways of formulating intellectual problems in the field, and an overwhelming commitment to theoretical goals and priorities since none of the skills they have acquired deal with empirical research or the problems of turning data into information.

Economics is a "partitioned bureaucracy" in which the theoretical, analytical work retains its intellectual primacy by marginalizing a number of "applied" subfields which deal with empirical uncertainty. This domination by the high priesthood of neoclassical orthodoxy is maintained with strictly controlled significance standards and criteria governing access to key resources. It is thus fortified against change [Whitley 1984;1986].

An important concomitant of this, for IB theory, is that progress cannot be achieved by attempting to change economics or by staying within its paradigm. A fundamentally new discipline is required, with a more sophisticated and relevant paradigm.

Such a move is advocated however, not so much out of pique at having been colonized, but out of a conviction that the deterministic mechanical causal model of the natural sciences is inappropriate for the enterprise of social science, and that economics in acting as a pseudoscience has avoided this issue instead of facing it.

There are three substantial objections to the unquestioning transfer of natural science rules to the human sciences: first, the purposes of the two forms of science are not identical (different purposes both require and sanction different rules of method); second, social science is value-laden and interactive; third, social phenomena vary by their meanings. These points require some elaboration.

Modern Western science follows a dominant ideology in which its core purpose is the manipulation and control of the natural world. Epistemological validity and

progress are seen in terms of prediction and control. Although this same ideology pervades extensively the human sciences, it has no monopoly [Burrell and Morgan 1979], and its legitimacy is weakened by the inadequacy of a mechanical closed system model to account for and allow control of social phenomena.

The incursion of values into the processes of social science is manifest in project design, results application, and topic biases. Judgments also enter the descriptions of phenomena, and their critical assessment. Although conventions exist to foster objectivity in description, there are limits to the formulation of universal statements. For instance, to discuss participation in the context of a society for which it has little meaning is to impose an inappropriate observation. Thus, the search for universal abstract patterns of causation is frustrated both by the observers' interaction with the object of study and by the nature of that object of study.

It was contended earlier that social reality lies in its participants' accounts of it. This requires interaction between the scientist and the object of study in ways which do not apply in the natural sciences. The introduction of participants' conceptions then seriously hinders the construction of a shared observation language for scientists. Because meanings can change, so can phenomena; predictive laws cannot remain valid. Changing phenomena will also undermine the stability of criteria set up to control the adequacy of scientific description. Nor will social groups exhibit consensus over meanings, and this makes empirical evidence contestable.

Perhaps the greatest fault, however, in the misapplication of the positivist paradigm—and this leads into our next topic, causation—is the fact that social phenomena are internally related and vary with each other. To be an employee, for instance, takes meaning from the context of having an employer and colleagues, and a surrounding organization. Change in any one of these components results in an adjustment of meaning and relationship. The nature of the phenomena is contingent upon the relationships. Cause and effect cannot be ontologically separate and the most fundamental of positivist premises collapse.

An explanation in social science is necessarily a complex of forces, with the following characteristics:

a. multiple;
b. with some more salient than others but not necessarily following precedents in other areas or at other times;
c. interconnected in complex ways;
d. influenced reciprocally by their effects;
e. analyzable via several disciplines;
f. expressed via the meaning structures of actors.

In the face of this, one obvious option is multicausality, but this can mask evasion. As Kaplan and Manners [1972:160] point out:

It often happens that multicausalism becomes, in fact, a retreat from explanation, a confession of despair, a final refuge for those who find the birth, life and death of human institutions and the intricacies of human behavior much too complex to understand.

Quite simply what is required of the theorist is to stick his neck out, as Weber [1958] did, but to do so while respecting the norms of causal explanation in social science. The first of these is to dissociate social science cause from natural science cause, seeing the latter as a particular case of the general principle of determinacy and applying it only to the unambiguous influence of external forces [Bunge 1963]. The second norm is the acceptance of complexity and nonclosure of a system. The third is to study processes as well as objects. The fourth is to use several methods to throw explanatory light from different perspectives on to a common set of phenomena.

The use of the comparative method has, in the vast majority of reported research,

been simplistic. The standard report says that, "Managers in country A believe this; managers in country B believe that. They are different. Isn't that interesting?" A variant is "We think this is why there are differences but we didn't look at that." Another is, "We think these are the implications for practice, but more research is needed on that."

It requires a return to something more radical if comparative OB as a social science is to achieve the full potential of the use of comparison which lies at its heart as a discipline. A recent treatment of this issue by Ragin [1987] offers valuable insight. He notes the qualitative/quantitative split as being more profound in social science than elsewhere and that it requires some bucking of the trend to attempt a reconciliation. Not to do so means that important research questions will continue to be overlooked or distorted.

His solution is the idea of qualitative comparative analysis, in which wholes may be compared as configurations of parts. This integrates the case-oriented and the variable-oriented approaches and allows investigators to retain the complexity of social causation while at the same time acknowledging the variety of social phenomena. The end product is the description of phenomena as clusters of features or types, and inside each type a rich pattern of interacting determinants can be analyzed. This is clearly a useful starting point for middle-range theorizing of the kind needed to move the discipline away from its tight little corner.

MORE PROGRESSIVE RESEARCH DESIGN

The first question to be addressed in considering an improvement to the present condition of international OB is whether to advocate a new paradigm or amend the present one. The encouragement of new initiatives is advocated, by Burrell and Morgan, who identified four major paradigms for the analysis of organizational life (radical humanist, radical structuralist, interpretive, and functionalist—the latter being their term for the one identified here as positivist) and said:

> We firmly believe that each of the paradigms can only establish itself at the level of organizational analysis if it is true to itself. Contrary to the widely held belief that synthesis and mediation between paradigms is what is required, we argue that the real need is for paradigmatic closure. In order to avoid emasculation and incorporation within the functionalist problematic, the paradigms need to provide a basis for their self-preservation by developing on their own account. [Burrell and Morgan 1979:230]

It is not proposed here to be swayed by such an extreme view, but simply to note that it is backed up by powerful arguments and that it confronts the problem of intellectual imperialism which runs through this paper. Two factors allow for a less extreme position: first, the kind of comparative methodology advocated by Ragin would allow for some useful fusion; second, a comparative researcher can proceed into the middle ground safely if he or she is aware of exactly what is going on, and thus chooses consciously to use something better than a single approach.

It would be inappropriate here to discuss the specifics of research design for middle-range theorizing in this field and they have been well covered elsewhere (e.g., Ronen [1986]; Pasquero [1990]). Instead, some pulling together of conclusions will be done with a summary of what it would mean to move, in terms of figure 2, from the bottom right hand corner to the center of the field. These then are the recommendations for progress:

1. Pursue the comparative method via the study of clusters of phenomena or types, the "interior" of which can be subjected to more idiographic analysis of causal linkages.
2. Search for the kinds of abstract models which can encourage multidisciplinary research by rising above the observation languages of the disciplines themselves. For instance, instead of referring to "lifetime employment" which is anchored in HRM, use the concept "form of organizational attachment" about which more general theory can be developed.
3. Use the new middle range theories now emerging in fields such as intercultural relations to go into the field ethnographically and refine the models. Find means of encouraging such nomothetic-idiographic iterations.
4. Enrich further the current grand theory of Hofstede by further probes into the societal origins of his value clusters, and in terms of outcomes, trace more explicitly the patterns of their organizational consequences.
5. Test further the existence of alternative value clusters, indigenously perceived.
6. Call a halt to closed-system, empirically based positivist reportage.
7. Encourage complex model building of the kind advocated by Child (e.g., analyzing the processes of modernization for their capacity to illuminate the culturalism/contingency debate). Do so without falling into the trap of multicausalism, i.e., have a leading idea of determinacy.
8. Avoid seeing culture as a single cause of anything and get accustomed to claiming its position as a necessary but not sufficient determinant of social outcomes.
9. Do much more ethnographic work on the crucial links between the mental world of culture and the behavioral world of organization, focusing on processes and meanings.

While all this may be going on, the practitioner questions we started with are still there, unanswered. The epistemological questions are also unanswered, but in their case it is not surprising for they can never go away. They are indicators of the need in organizational science for fusion of approach rather than entrenched specialization, and they represent the problem of coming to terms with the immense complexity of social life. Movement is now needed if understanding is to increase, and it is at least thirty years overdue. This strangest of animals has been in the wrong cage for too long.

■ ■ ■

COMMENTARY
Mark E. Mendenhall

Goals with No Paths: A Consideration of How Worlds Can Be Bridged, Declines Reversed, and Animals Caged

The papers by Boyacigiller and Adler, Redding, and Sullivan effectively delineate the root problems of the cross-cultural/international human resource management (HRM) and organizational behavior (OB) fields; they forthrightly declare what must occur for the field[1] to thrive in the future. Rather than quibble about some of the disagreements I had with some of the authors' views,[2] I would prefer to explore the recommendations they have made to scholars in order to address the persistent problems inherent in the field. Before I do this however, I would like to state a preamble to my comments.

THE FIELD AND ITS CROSSROADS

The field, in my view, is in a precarious state, and researchers in the field face a type of crossroads. At the crossroads there are two paths. One path is deeply connected to the path that the field has trod for the past thirty years, and it leads straight ahead, across a flat desert, until it disappears into the horizon. I have named this highway the "Familiar Path." The other path branches

off from the crossroads and torturously winds its way up the rocky hillside of a nearby forbidding mountain until it is lost to view. I will refer to this path as the "Higher Path."

THE FAMILIAR PATH

For the past thirty years, as the authors have stated in their papers, OB/HRM researchers interested in the international dimensions of their field, have produced a literature of empirical studies that is almost wholly atheoretical in nature. If the familiar path is chosen by the majority of us, for whatever reason, and if journal editors let the products of this philosophy of scholarship continue to appear in journals, then the field will be left with a literature that, in the words of Redding, will be limited in its reportage and insight to the fact that "Managers in country A believe this; managers in country B believe that. They are different. Isn't that interesting?" [p. 437] Without utilizing theory as a base, nothing is learned from empirical studies—the causes of differences remain underground, hidden to view.

THE HIGHER PATH

The sheer mass of the literature over the past thirty years has allowed some scholars to begin to sort out the empirical data and to make some conceptual sense of it, such that some theoretical models have begun to show up in journals such as the *Academy of Management Review* (AMR) and the *Journal of International Business Studies* (JIBS). Empirical studies that have tested these models' propositions are just now beginning to show up in journals such as the *Academy of Management Journal* (AMJ), *JIBS*, and other reputable journals. Progress is being made. That is the good news. However, the attraction to the familiar path remains strong. It is disheartening to continually review papers for the above and other journals (as well as for conferences) and to see the continuance of colleagues submitting atheoretically-based, empirical papers on areas in the field where theoretical models exist—models replete with propositions and attendant hypotheses that are waiting to be tested. Empirical opportunism was somewhat understandable when few models existed, but now it borders on the unconscionable. The question everyone in the field must ask him/herself as they stand at the crossroads is: "Will I take the higher path and be a theory-tester and a theory-builder or will I be an empirical opportunist?"

RECOMMENDATIONS TO THE FIELD

Each of the papers point to a common goal or destination—a field with rich and complex theories and diverse and vigorous methods. They point out the goal, *but not the path to reach that goal.* Each of the authors outlined remedies to the problems of the field, and in order to facilitate a quick review of these recommendations, I have classified them in an appendix to this paper, and labelled them Appendix Tables 1–5. Each table represents a "problem" category within the field; the categories deal with the areas of theory development, theory testing, research design issues, the construct of culture, and institutional realms.

The recommendations are direct quotes from the three papers; notice that all of them call for changes to occur in the field. Within each recommendation are words such as: "should," "could," "need to," "must," "do much more," "it is necessary to," "pursue," "call a halt," "find means of," "encourage," "search," "use," and "enrich." The recommendations are directional in nature—they are in essence goals for the field. The authors generally did not explore the implementation issues associated with their recommendations. How these recommendations might be implemented will be discussed below.

MAPPING THE HIGHER PATH

As I considered the recommendations of the authors, I began to ask myself the following question: What would have to happen to make their recommendations ac-

tually happen? In other words, what would the path look like that would lead to the goals they articulated? What follows are some musings and "envisionings" on my part of what must happen in the field if the field is to reach the goals delineated by Boyacigiller and Adler, Redding, and Sullivan.

THE NEED FOR PASSION

The authors have listed the barriers to their recommendations occurring, thus they need not be discussed in great length at present except to list some of them by way of example: the biases of journal editors, methodological biases by differing IB researchers, the difficulty of logistically managing international research projects, etc. Scholars in the field are aware of these issues; each of us have complained about them, and for the most part have found them to be intractable, and have lost the will to combat them.

What follows may appear to be "positive mental attitude" drivel or ill-advised cheerleading. I don't believe it is either. Rather, it is steeped in the degree to which each scholar, individually, truly cares about the field. Consider the following question: Does the field exist as a means by which one attains individual career goals (a "Familiar Path" temptation) or does one owe the field something? In other words, does the field matter to us? Is there something of importance about the field intellectually, morally, emotionally, managerially, creatively, or even spiritually, that initially led you into it, and triggered the passion in your research agenda? That passion was a necessary friend to enable the hurdles of the dissertation and the "publish or perish" tenure process to be successfully negotiated.

Many have altered the purity of that passion to fit the molds of the politics of academe and consulting contracts. I am suggesting that if we truly care about the knowledge base of the field, that *returning to that passion is a prerequisite to the commitment that will be needed to reach the goals delineated in the three papers.* The

Nike marketing slogan of late has been: "Just do it." One cannot do anything unless a very personal, very internal commitment toward something outside of oneself is solidified. Unless a majority of the scholars return to the roots of their evolution as international OB/HRM researchers, the next thirty years of research output will not be unlike that of the past thirty years.

THE BREAKDOWN OF CLIQUES

While for the most part scholars in the field are amiable towards each other, cliques exist. This is natural in any organization or field. I am a part of one. It would be possible to give them names and illustrate their memberships and their relationships to one another; to some degree these cliques have formed out of shared organizational and institutional affiliations of the past and of the present, but to some degree they also revolve around shared preferences in terms of paradigms and methodological issues.

In order to foster the kind of work suggested by the authors, the walls have to come down, and clique members have to do more than enjoy each other's company at academy mixers and paper sessions. It will be necessary to spend time with "clique outsiders" discussing our work, how we can help each other, and how we can coordinate each clique's efforts so that all are moving towards the goals mentioned in the Appendix Tables 1–5.

No doubt good-natured and heated arguments about the issues and recommendations in Appendix Tables 1–5 will occur between and within cliques. That will only lead to positive outcomes. It will take creative means to stay in touch with each other during the school year, to meet at times and places outside of scheduled Academy of Management and Academy of International Business meetings, and to work on research projects with new people. Only commitment to truly furthering the field will cause these kinds of sacrifices to be made. If they are not made, we will all likely find ourselves coming to a conference like this one

in three or five years from now. To break this cycle, cliques must be opened and interchange must occur between them.

A NEW OUTLET FOR RESEARCH

Reigniting passion for the field and breaking down cliques are very idealistic ventures, and idealistic ventures need something tangible to hang onto, otherwise their momentum dissipates. What is needed is some kind of facilitating idea around which commitment, passion, and deeper collegiality can be focused—a kind of tangible, superordinate goal or task. There are probably numerous ideas that would qualify as such a goal; I offer the following as a suggestion.

Fighting one's way onto journal boards, as Sullivan suggested we do, doesn't get at the underlying cause of the problem; namely, that people will not conduct research that (1) rises above the observational languages of the disciplines themselves, (2) involves complex model building, (3) ethnographically refines middle-range theories, (4) traces more explicitly patterns of organizational consequences of models, (5) uses multiple theoretical approaches in their research designs, (6) develops new approaches for assessing the cultural, legal, and economic forces that impact OB, or (7) ethnographically studies links between the mental world of culture and the behavioral world of the organization. Why does not more of this type of research occur? Because it does not pay to do this type of research.

From personal experience I have found that even if one is on the editorial board of international management-oriented journals, one simply does not see this kind of work coming in. Why? There is no faith that it will be published, thus people choose the "Familiar Path"—empirical opportunism.

Consider the following realities. If one gets a theory article rejected at *AMR*, where does one send it next? *JIBS*, is a likely reply. What if it is rejected there too? There is not a strong cadre of first or second tier journals that are theory development-oriented in management, let alone international management.

Where does one send a paper that utilizes ethnographic methodologies? Such papers pop up in management journals, but not enough to stop authors' wondering about such issues as: Are the editors and reviewers biased against such papers? What if I get a reviewer that doesn't value the methods I used? To truly report my data, I need longer page lengths than empirical papers; how can I edit my paper down without compromising its rigor? One sends such a paper to *Human Organization* or to *Advances in International Comparative Management*. Again, there are few other outlets that are respected.

If one employs a more traditional research design that uses complex statistical methods, one can send a cross-cultural paper to any number of first, second, and third tier journals—both in the field and outside of the field. The pay-offs are to take this route, for it is more likely that one can find a home for one's research in this way. However, focusing only on this dimension of research retards the progress of the field toward theory development.

Perhaps the field needs to provide a new outlet for quality research-quality research being any kind of research that is well done within the standards of the paradigm and methodology utilized. There is a model from which the field can draw. The Western Academy of Management is made up of a lot of people who are good at playing the research game of academe, but who like to think, argue and tinker with creative ideas. To date, many of those creative ideas were limited to paper presentations at paper sessions in the annual meeting of that organization. A group of senior members of the organization began to toy with the idea of creating a journal—a journal that would allow them to explore the edges and frontiers of management thought. Thus, the *Journal of Management Inquiry* was born. Its editorial policy is:

> to explore ideas and build knowledge in management theory and practice, with a focus on creative, nontraditional research. The journal seeks to maintain a constructive balance between innovation and qual-

ity, and at the same time widely define the forms that relevant contributions to the field can take.

There is an editor-in-chief and an associate editor-in-chief, but the journal is divided up into sections, each of which has its own editor and editorial board. This allows for division of labor in terms of reviewing papers and also allows for more scholars in the field to be part of the editorship of the journal. Its subdivisions are: *"Non-Traditional Research," "Essays," "Dialog," "Reflections on Experience," "Reviews,"* and *"Meet the Person."* A new international management/OB/HRM journal could utilize the same approach, except perhaps be made up of subsections such as *"Theory Development," "Theory Testing," "Ethnographic Studies," "Literature Reviews,"* and *"Essays/Critiques."* If the senior and prominent scholars in the field constituted the core of the editorial board, such a journal would be seen as a strong tier two journal immediately, and over time would move into the tier one level in the field.

I am a realist, though. Starting up such a new journal would take a heavy institutional commitment, money, a sympathetic publisher, review boards who were willing to sacrifice a lot of time to the field, and a few colleagues who would be willing to shoulder most of the burden of the operational aspects of the journal. But the members of the Western Academy of Management were able to overcome those same hurdles; if they did it, so can scholars within our field.

If those interested in theory-building and theory-testing, and in employing "qualitative" and nontraditional methods in doing so, knew there was such a journal, an increase in such papers would come. Such a journal presently may truly seem like a "dream of the field," but "if we build it, they will come." Perhaps submissions would come first from senior scholars who have little to lose in submitting their "off-the-edge" papers to such a journal; perhaps they will come from colleagues in other fields (anthropology, psychology, sociology), or perhaps the journal will be that institutional beacon that will trigger in us the desire to get started on doing "that study" that we have always wanted to do but never got around to doing because its "publication pay-off potential" was not high enough.

CONCLUSION

The musings in this paper are not meant as the only mapping of the "higher path." A journal may not be the answer (though I think it is a large part of the answer). I believe that something that is tangible, that can act as a facilitation device by which people will actually be motivated to follow the directions set by the authors of the papers within this session, is desperately needed in the field. I agree with Steers (quoted by Boyacigiller and Adler) when he stated that:

If we are serious about better understanding the international dimensions of human resource management, *the time has come* to make a major commitment to developing a systematic and defensible body of literature surrounding the issue. To do this, *it may be necessary* for many of us to *explore* new intellectual arenas that we are not familiar with (e.g., cultural anthropology) as a means of developing sufficient theoretical bases upon which to carry our research efforts. ... Only when there exists a useful theoretical base and a systematic body of knowledge will the field come into its own as a central area in the study of business administration. [1989: 30]

I agree with Sullivan when he stated that:

Tolerance is needed for essay-like discourse in which researchers tell the story of their investigations in national culture and business behavior. A broad, rich discourse in international research which encompasses multiple perspectives with none dominant offers the best chance for developing a paradigm which is both interesting and enduring. [p. 393]

I agree with Boyacigiller and Adler when they state that:

to create a truly international OB [field], scholars *must* refrain from regarding tra-

ditional OB research as the primary source of theories ... international research *can* provide OB with conceptual and empirical developments that in some cases complement, in others contradict, and in all cases enrich the heretofore overly narrow domestic U.S. paradigm. [p. 399]

And, I agree with Redding, when he stated that "movement is now needed if understanding is to increase, and it is at least thirty years overdue." [p. 439]

But I have no illusions that just because we think this should happen, and want it to happen, that it probably will happen. It won't. The fact that these very insightful papers have been written will not in and of itself make anything recommended in those papers occur in the real world of our field. It will only happen if we care enough to "do it." And to do it, we will have to come together as individuals, organize, and launch forays (like starting a journal, or organizing special informal group gatherings between cliques to explore other approaches) to preserve that which we hold dear, which is, the quality of the field itself. The real issue becomes, then, do we as individual scholars truly care enough about the field to do the kinds of things necessary to make the recommendations in Appendix Tables 1–5 actually happen? If we are not willing to, we might as well quit complaining and stop having these kinds of conferences. That is the choice we must make at this crossroads.

NOTES

1. In this paper, the fields of cross-cultural/international organizational behavior and cross/cultural international human resource management will be encapsulated into one, larger whole and referred to as "the field." Thus, when the term "field" is used herein, it refers to the literatures of both of these fields.

2. For example, Sullivan's view that it is necessary to test North American theories of motivation across cultures; they generally have not been shown to be very robust in predicting motivation among North American samples, so why bother taking them overseas? Perhaps what is needed is a new approach to theory-building in the area of motivation.

APPENDIX

Table 1. Recommendations that Relate to Theory Development

Encourage complex model building of the kind advocated by Child . . . But do so without falling into the trap of multi-causalisms, i.e., have a leading idea of determinacy (Redding).

Search for the kinds of abstract models which can encourage multi-disciplinary research by rising above the observation languages of the disciplines themselves. For instance, instead of referring to "life-time employment" which is anchored in HRM . . . use the concept "form of organizational attachment" about which more general theory can be developed (Redding).

Use the new middle range theories now emerging . . . to go into the field ethnographically and refine the models (Redding).

Herein lies the *challenge and opportunity* for organizational scholars. While the motivational issues that emerge in developing countries manifestly combine external and internal forces that cross levels of analysis, traditional motivational theories have neither the breadth nor the depth to address them. Traditional U.S.-based motivational theories with their lack of contextual embeddedness and individualistic orientation, miss much of what is most salient about the nature of work and motivation in developing countries . . . Thus, for motivation theories to be widely applicable in developing countries, non-work factors *must* be considered (Boyacigiller and Adler).

Table 2. Recommendations that Relate to Theory Testing

Researchers *should* test motivation, leadership, and communication theories cross-culturally, using culture as a mediating variable . . . Most motivation theories were developed in the United States. They may have limited international application. Only testing will reveal their universality (Sullivan).

Enrich further the current grand theory of Hofstede by further probes into the societal origins of his value clusters . . . trace more explicitly the patterns of their organizational consequences (Redding).

Many organizational scholars *have not fully appreciated* that multiple views of culture exist within the social sciences . . . Progress *could* be made, however, by . . . testing competing cultural hypotheses, based on various theoretical frameworks, within the same research study (Boyacigiller and Adler).

Table 3. Recommendations that Relate to Research Design Issues

The field . . . *needs to* develop consistent approaches for assessing the cultural, economic, and legal forces impacting organizational behavior at the ethnic, national, regional, and transnational levels (Boyacigiller and Adler).

Researchers *need to* begin doing culture research using economic/psychometric methodology which accommodates . . . complex relationships (Sullivan).

Sometimes organizational culture can influence managers to modify their national cultural values. It would be nice to know how this happens (or indeed if it happens) . . . This process *should* be studied to identify values which are variant and those which are invariant, if any (Sullivan).

Table 3. Continued

Pursue the comparative method via the study of clusters of phenomena or types, the "interior" of which can be subjected to more idiographic analysis of causal linkages (Redding).

Scholars *need to* include nation-state characteristics and clearly delineate their effects on organizational phenomena from those of cultural variables. Simultaneously focusing on national and cultural variables in the same research design will allow the field to clarify the impacts of both sets of constructs (Boyacigiller and Adler).

Do much more ethnographic work on the crucial links between the mental world of culture and the behavioral world of organization, focusing on processes and meanings (Redding).

In forming a truly IOB field, *it [is] necessary to* expand the current micro-level perspective of OB to systematically include both international and macro-level variables (Boyacigiller and Adler).

Table 4. Recommendations Relating to the Construct of Culture

Researchers *should* treat culture as an information-providing, cause like (but not causal) input to managerial processes of judgment and purpose formation.; It is only one of a number of organizational, economic, social, and personal inputs (Sullivan).

Avoid seeing culture as a single cause of anything and get accustomed to claiming its position as a necessary but not sufficient determinant of social outcomes (Redding).

It is time for OB scholars to *embrace the dialogue* and argue culture's definition and role rather than ignoring culture or facilely accepting a particular operationalization within the organizational literature . . . *we urge* our colleagues to put more effort into understanding the culture construct, rather than . . . borrowing what may be an inappropriate instrument (Boyacigiller and Adler).

The reality of multiple cultural identities *needs to be* recognized . . . we must . . . recognize that individuals can and do maintain simultaneous membership in any number of [cultural] groups (Boyacigiller and Adler).

Table 5. Recommendations that Relate to Institutional Realms

The division between IB and OB is an unfortunate historic artifact, a division no longer useful for either conceptualization or practice. We *need* stronger bridges and more sophisticated means of integration, not more divisions. (Boyacigiller and Adler).

Call a halt to closed-system, empirically based positivist reportage (Redding).

Find means of encouraging . . . nomothetic-idiographic iterations of middle-range theories (Redding).

Reviewers act to defend their paradigm first . . . Culture theorists *must* fight their way on to journal boards so that their position can be defended (Sullivan)

Daniel C. Feldman

When Does Demonstrating a Difference Make a Difference? An Organizational Behavior Perspective on International Management

All three of the papers in this section decry the lack of international perspective taken by mainline organizational behavior (OB) in its study of organizational life. All three want the boundaries of the field to be more receptive to an international perspective, all three want the standards of "normal science" to adjust to their approach, and all three want traditional social science to be more welcoming of the new paradigm they champion. In short, these papers all advocate the incorporation of an international approach to the study of behavior in organizations.

Why, then, has international management not made the impact on OB one might expect, especially at a time when there is such a clamor for better understanding of international business (IB)? The reason, I believe, can be quickly captured by the slogan: "Where's the beef?" Organizational behavior researchers are anxious to know the concrete findings of international management that would explain and/or predict human behaviors and attitudes. For many of them, there has been way too much approach, and not nearly enough arrival.

George Homans, writing in *Nature of Social Science* [1967], comments quite powerfully on this "too much approach, too little arrival" problem in social science:

> Sooner or later we must stop 'being about' to talk about something and actually say it. Some students get so much intellectual security out of such a scheme because it allows them to give names to, and to pigeonhole, almost any social phenomena. Much writing in social science consists of such 'orienting statements', and often they are quite useful in telling us what or how to study, but they tell us little about the thing studied. In Merton's words, they give us an approach, not an arrival. Let us not exhaust ourselves in the preliminaries lest

we fail at the consummation. We are always getting around to saying something we never actually come out with. But sooner or later a science must actually stick its neck out and say something definite. If there is a change in x, what sort of change will occur in y? Don't just tell me there will be *some* change. Tell me *what* change. STAND AND DELIVER!

It might be worthwhile, then, to look more closely here at why the international perspective has not made as many inroads into OB as these authors would like, what alternative approaches to "international organizational behavior" research might look like, and some specific content areas where an international perspective might be particularly fruitful in understanding important organizational dynamics.

THE DIFFERING PERSPECTIVES OF OB AND IB

In reviewing the articles which have appeared in international OB over the past few years, it seems there are at least seven general reasons why IB researchers have not had the powerful impact on OB that they might want, or indeed deserve.

1. *There are substantial differences in preference for level of analysis.* A major difference between OB researchers and international management (IM) researchers is in their level of analysis. OB researchers have worked most comfortably at the individual level of analysis; IM researchers have worked most comfortably at the macro level of culture. Many OB researchers have not perceived IM work as particularly germane or relevant to their own endeavors, particularly when the explicit links between culture and individual attitudes and behaviors are not demonstrated.

2. *There are major differences in what OB and IM researchers see as important context factors.* Related to the first point, IM researchers

have typically focused their attention on culture as a cause of individual behavior, and are puzzled as to why OB researchers have missed what they perceive to be a self-evident, and crucial, determinant of individual behavior. OB researchers, though, are much more convinced of the impact of the immediate situation as the major causative agent of individual actions and attitudes. To the extent that culture influences individual behavior, OB researchers see it as operating indirectly through other intermediary links—such as supervisor rewards and punishments or group norms about appropriate behaviors. Without a theory which explains how culture influences the immediate situational context, it is unlikely IM researchers will persuade OB researchers of the unique value of their work.

3. *There are substantial differences in preference for level of description and prediction.* OB researchers have been most interested in predicting, at least on the aggregate level, how employees will behave in the workplace. The peculiarities of the organization and the country have not been of much interest to OB researchers and have typically been controlled for as much as possible. In contrast, IM researchers are much more interested in describing the countries and corporations where they do their research. For IB researchers, the settings, the anecdotes, and the quotes are often very much the story. For OB researchers, the settings, the quotes, and the anecdotes are diversions, all be they interesting diversions, from the real task of the research.

4. *There are substantial differences in preference for kinds and sizes of samples.* I have noticed three very

major differences between OB and IM scholars in how they approach sampling. First, OB researchers are much more used to large data sets; drawing conclusions from small convenience samples is much more troublesome for them than for IM researchers. Second, OB researchers are much more used to higher response rates. It is unlikely that an OB study with a response rate of less than 50% would be acceptable, yet IB researchers—because of the difficulties of overseas data collection—are much more willing to go with response rates of 25%. Third, OB research—to the extent it is willing to take self-report data at face value—is only willing to accept self-report data from the respondents themselves as legitimate. In contrast, IM researchers often ask managers about how their spouses react to international assignments, or ask top executives about the cultures or practices in their firms and consider that data worthwhile. OB researchers tend to reject that kind of data outright.

5. *There are major differences about what constitutes a useful, testable model.* In OB, researchers have a tradition of taking causal modelling very seriously, and using powerful empirical analytic techniques (often to the point of overkill) for model testing. When OB models appear in the literature, they tend to be presented formally, with all relationships between variables specified and tested. In contrast, IM models tend to be more informal and operate more along the lines of a general framework. These frameworks are often overspecified, i.e., there are more predictions than variables, and many of the relationships posited are two way. Consequently, OB researchers

often are often unpersuaded by models which do not lend themselves to empirical testing, even in theory.

Particularly troubling to many OB researchers, for example, is the unclear role which culture is presumed to play in international research. Is it an independent variable, which directly influences attitudes and behaviors? Is it a moderating variable, interacting with independent variables to predict behaviors and attitudes? Is it a mediating variable, whose presence or absence influences causal chains of events? Is it a dependent variable, created as a result of various individual and situational factors combining in predictable ways? I am continually surprised at the number of papers I read and review in IM where nationality and culture are used interchangeably as independent, dependent, mediating, and moderating variables. For IM to have more of an impact on OB, it is critical that the precise relationships in its models be made explicit and testable.

6. *There are distinct differences in the kinds of data analysis preferred by OB and IM scholars.* There are at least four sets of results which are characteristically reported in OB articles. First, the scale means, standard deviations, and alphas for all variables are reported. Second, the simple correlations among all variables are reported. Third, some sort of multiple regression or analysis of variance results are reported in cases where there are multiple independent and/or dependent variables. Lastly, in cases where causal models or moderating variables are presented, one typically sees reported LISREL or moderated regression results.

In the IM literature, while the first two sets of data are generally presented, the second two sets of data are often absent. When multiple independent variables are predicted to be associated with a dependent variable, one frequently sees the author counting the number of significant correlations or running a series of t-tests or one-way ANOVAs rather than multiple regression analyses. When moderating variables are predicted, one frequently sees subgroup mean differences reported rather than moderated regression analysis. When causal models are presented, one frequently sees partial correlations reported rather than LISREL results. As a result, IM researchers perhaps convince their OB readers of the plausibility of their results, but not with high confidence.

Another area in which IM research has sometimes failed to impact the OB literature has been in its focus on the strength of subgroup differences on independent or dependent variables. While IB researchers often focus most heavily on the *differences between cultures*, OB researchers typically focus on *differences in the strength of relationships among variables* across research sites. For example, one often sees in the IM literature that there are differences in some outcome variables between two cultures. However, OB researchers are much more interested in knowing whether the relationships between dimensions of cultures and outcome variables are predictable or vary in some systematic ways. For many IB researchers, discovering mean differences is an end in and of itself; for many OB researchers, discovering mean differences is a side street which is of only passing interest off their major thoroughfare.

7. *There are distinct differences in*

how OB and IM researchers present their findings. There are at least four key differences between OB and IM researchers in how they present their findings that lead to ineffective communication between them.

First, OB researchers have a tendency to understatement and IM researchers have a tendency to overstatement. A major issue which OB researchers often have with IM articles is the promising of too much on the front end of an article and the delivery of too little on the back end. Perhaps it is a difference in personal style or perhaps it is being used to finding modest-sized results. In either event, OB scholars probably have a greater respect for understatement than for overstatement. They are puzzled by papers that present "grand theories" and 20-box, 40-arrow models on the front end with four t-tests at the back end.

In addition, OB researchers have traditionally been trained to see every flaw in their research, to err on the side of cautiousness in making inferences from their results and to identify multiple caveats in interpreting their findings. To OB researchers, IM research articles sometimes seem to overstate the results and to stint in identifying the limitations of their research findings. Moreover, at least traditionally, OB researchers have shied away from making prescriptions until there were reasonably consistent and stable results from empirical data studies. In some subfields of IM, strongly worded prescriptions have preceded systematic theory formulation and data collection.

Third, IM and OB use very different types of jargon, much of which is either incomprehensible or nonsensical to the other group. Most OB people, for example, have no idea what a "heterarchy" is, nor any clear notions of how it is identified or defined, nor much knowledge of the relevance

for this concept for understanding individual behavior and attitudes.

Last, and perhaps most importantly, IM and OB researchers have very different preferences for linearity. For example, researchers in IM try to recreate for their readers the "feel" of different cultures, and use plenty of metaphors and similes to identify nuances and shadings of meaning. This approach to reporting research is generally antithetical to conventional OB research. To use a popular culture analogy to explain this difference, IM scholars are kindred souls to *Twin Peaks*. OB people are kindred souls to *Dragnet*; just the facts, ma'am, just the facts.

WHAT TYPES OF IB RESEARCH COULD IMPACT OB?

If the basic premise of the first half of this article is correct—that OB researchers view IB research as too much approach and not enough arrival—then the corollary point is that OB researchers would like to see more concrete results from their IM colleagues. For OB researchers, simply demonstrating that Japanese managers are different from American managers, for instance, is not enough. The other half of the story is predicting when, and how, those differences will make a difference in organizational life, and whether the dimensions of difference identified in one study help us predict differences in culture across other studies.

For differences between cultures to make a difference in the organizational sciences, then, at least five conditions must be present:

1. The differences must be stable. They must not be simply artifacts of sampling or self-reports of a handful of managers speaking for their entire companies or their spouses.

2. The differences must be predictable a priori from some theory, and not simply post hoc chance empirical findings.

3. The magnitude of the differences

must be large enough to be substantively important and/or account for significant amounts of variance in organizational life.

4. The difference in culture or "internationalness" found in one study must, in some systematic way, be generalizable to multiple cultural contexts. For example, if we find American and Japanese managers differ on some attribute X, have we identified some specific dimension of culture that lets us predict the differences between Japanese and African managers?

5. The difference found in the international arena must be systematically different from the difference found in the domestic arena. For example, much of the expatriate and repatriate literature has demonstrated that these cross-cultural movers have difficult adjustment problems. However, the domestic relocation literature demonstrates the same finding. The critical theoretical question becomes, then: How does the "internationalness" of the move advance our understanding of relocation *over and above* what happens in domestic job changes?

In the past ten years, the bulk of the IM literature (excluding the philosophy of science pieces advocating the adoption of an international perspective) have focused on expatriate/repatriate assignments or on the strategic differences between domestic, international, and global-oriented businesses. While these literatures have certainly provided some of the best empirical research to date in the international management area, there are multiple other areas where an international perspective could make a difference in understanding organizational life. Below, several potential avenues for future international OB research are identified, and clustered by level of analysis.

Differences Across Individuals. One area of individual-level research which might benefit from an international perspective is motivation theory. Reasonable questions which might be asked here include: Do different theories predict individual behavior equally well in individualistic- and collectivist-oriented cultures? Does the concept of "expectancy" make any sense in nonrationalistic cultures, and if not, what types of theory predict individual behavior here? Along the same lines, consider some of the research on reward systems. Do the concepts of "internal equity" and "external equity" mean the same things across cultures, and if not, how is equity perceived in different kinds of cultures? Under what circumstances will individually-based pay systems make the most sense, and why?

To date, most of the research on individual differences in IM has been on job attitudes and has demonstrated mean differences across countries. By focusing more on individual behaviors, and by examining the ways culture moderates important individual-level processes in organizations, IM would make a major contribution to the organizational sciences.

Differences Across Groups. In the IM area, researchers have repeatedly noted that some cultures are more group-oriented than others. However, the whole area of how culture impacts group dynamics has been virtually ignored.

For example, consider the area of norm development and enforcement. The OB and social psychology literatures have focused on the impact of the immediate environment on norm-regulated behavior, such as the role that critical incidents early in the group's life play in norm formation. However, it might be possible that, depending on the culture, the culture of the country far overwhelms the immediacy of the present situation in governing within-group behavior. Another area which might benefit from an international perspective is the conformity/deviance literature. How does culture interact with group dynamics to determine whether individuals feel free to deviate from group norms, and what sanctions are likely to be attached to that deviance?

Yet a third whole area of group research which might benefit from an international perspective is decision making. How does culture interact with specific group processes to facilitate/impede critical thinking? How does culture interact with specific group processes to facilitate/impede group consensus? How does culture interact with specific group processes to facilitate/impede individuals' commitment to group activities rather than to individual activities?

Differences Across Tasks. An area virtually ignored by IM researchers has been the role that the task itself plays in determining individual attitudes and behaviors. The focus of IB research has been primarily on managers (and, occasionally, on differences among managers at different hierarchical levels), but rarely on what differences in attitudes and behaviors occur because of the work itself.

Consider, for example, the research on job design. For close to twenty years, the OB literature has assumed that five attributes of jobs are most critical in motivating workers—task identity, skill variety, task significance, autonomy, and feedback from the job itself. However, might there not be other job attributes—such as dealing with others and feedback from supervisors or customers—that might be more motivating in other cultures than in our own? Similarly, American job design scholars view group task design as the technological alternative to be taken only when the work itself cannot be divided into clear subparts and when individual-level rewards cannot be clearly distributed. Scholars in international OB might want to ask instead: How does type of culture interact with type of job design to create the highest levels of motivation and performance?

Differences Across Time. Even within the OB literature, research on the differences among individuals, groups, and organiza-

tions over time has been the poor stepchild. For instance, we know much more about the differences between midcareer employees and late-career employees than we do about how people recognize when they are changing career stages and need to behave differently; we know much more about the differences between new ventures and mature companies than we do about the processes by which firms recognize they are no longer entrepreneurial and need to change their strategies and structures.

In the international arena, differences in time are even more worthy of study because how time is perceived itself varies from culture to culture. How do cultural concepts of time influence short-run or long-run decision making or profit-orientations? How do cultural concepts of time influence individual perceptions of career stage or organizational perceptions of corporate maturity? Does the speed of individual reactions to managers' rewards and punishments vary across cultures, and why? Do positive attitudes toward jobs, bosses, coworkers decay at different rates in different cultures, and why?

Thus, we do need much more research on differences between cultures—but not necessarily along the lines this research stream has been developing to date. To keep on piling up studies that suggest Country X is different from Country Y, or that Country A is different from Country B, will not be particularly helpful in the long run. Instead, what we need now is a systematic set of dimensions along which cultures vary, and a theory which predicts when, how, and why cultural differences will influence individual- and group-level phenomena across tasks and over time.

MIDDLE-RANGE THEORY:
A MIDDLE GROUND

Conclusion

It is not coincidental that the authors of these papers all use the metaphor of the "comparative management theory zoo," full of ostriches, dinosaurs, and elephants. For most OB people, the metaphor of the IM theory zoo is an apt one, too—but for a different reason. For many OB researchers, IM is an area, like the zoo, characterized by a loud cacophony of sounds generally incomprehensible to the outside visitor; a nice place to visit, perhaps, but you wouldn't want to live there.

How, then, can we reconcile the more general abstract approaches of IM with the more specific, content-oriented approaches of OB? Perhaps some meeting on middle ground might be achieved by the development of "middle range theories," most completely described and advocated by Robert King Merton in his *Social Theory and Social Structure* [1968].

Merton's middle range theories use abstractions close enough to observable data so that empirical testing of propositions is actually possible. Middle range theories also involve *sets* of hypotheses; the hypotheses must not be "logically disparate or unconnected" [61]. Rather than providing general frameworks in which all types of phenomena can be examined at all levels of analysis, middle-range theories examine a series of relationships among a smaller *subset* of variables. Moreover, a middle range theory must increase our understanding of a phenomenon in some significant way. For example, it could specify the conditions under which previously formulated empirical laws hold (or do not hold) true, or predict and explain phenomena that were not known about before the theory was formulated. Thus, these middle-range theories may help us bridge the gap between the overarching general frameworks so valued by these authors in IM and the preference for precision and specificity so valued by mainstream OB researchers.

It is certainly obvious in reading these papers that IB researchers and OB researchers bring very different perspectives to their study of organizational life. Relying implicitly on the arguments made by Thomas Kuhn in *The Structure of Scientific Revolutions* [1962], the IB authors of these papers see gatekeepers in mainline social science as "forcing nature into conceptual boxes supplied by professional education" [3], no matter how arbitrary or irrelevant those conceptual boxes may be. For them, any current paradigm which neglects the international dimension is de facto obsolete.

However, perhaps collectivism can exist in our scientific communities in a different, and perhaps more appropriate, sense than Kuhn means. As Joseph Agassi writes in *The Journal of the History of Philosophy* [1966:351–354], collectivism in academic research can operate, not in the sense that everyone belongs to the same paradigm, but in the sense that everyone agrees on what is significant enough to deserve critical attention. Given the state of the current "international management theory zoo," perhaps that is the best we can hope for right now.

REFERENCES

Adler, Nancy J. 1991. *International Dimensions of Organizational Behavior*. Second edition. Boston: PWS-Kent Publishing.

Adler, Nancy J. 1986. *International Dimensions of Organizational Behaviour*. Boston: Kent Publishing.

Adler, Nancy J. 1984. Understanding the ways of understanding: Cross-cultural management reviewed. In R. N. Farmer, editor, *Advances In International Comparative Management*, Vol. 1:31–67. Greenwich, Conn.: JAI Press.

Adler, Nancy J. 1983. Cross-cultural management research: The ostrich and the trend. *Academy of Management Review*, 8(2): 226–232.

Adler, Nancy J. 1981. Re-entry: Managing cross-cultural transitions. *Group and Organization Studies*, 6(3): 341–356.

Adler, Nancy J. 1980. Cultural synergy: The management of cross-cultural organizations. In W. W. Burke and L. D. Goodstein, editors, *Trends and Issues in OD: Current Theory and Practice*. San Diego: University Associates.

Adler, Nancy J. and Susan Bartholomew. 1992a. Academic and professional communities of discourse: Generating knowledge on transnational human resource management.

Journal of International Business Studies, 23(3): 551–569.

Adler, Nancy J. and Susan Bartholomew. 1992b. Managing globally competent people. *Acad emy of Management Executive*, 6(3):52–65.

Adler, Nancy J., Robert Doktor and S. Gordon Redding. 1986. From the Atlantic to the Pacific Century: Cross-cultural management reviewed. In J. G. Hunt and J. D. Blair, editors, *Yearly Review of Management of the Journal of Management*, 12(2): 295–318.

Adler, Nancy J. and Fariborz Ghadar. 1990a. International strategy from the perspective of people and culture: The North American context. In A. M. Rugman, editor, *Research in Global Strategic Management: International Business Research for the Twenty-First Century*, Vol. 1. Greenwich, Conn.: JAI Press, 179–205.

Adler, Nancy J. and Fariborz Ghadar. 1990b. Strategic human resource management: A global perspective. In Rudiger Pieper, editor, *Human Resource Management in International Comparison*. Berlin: de Gruyter, 235–260.

Adler, Nancy J. and John L. Graham. 1987. Business negotiations: Canadians are not just like Americans. *Canadian Journal of Administrative Sciences*, 4(3):211–238.

Adler, Nancy J. and Mariann S. Jelinek. 1986. Is "organizational culture" culture bound? *Human Resource Management*, 25(1): 73–90.

Agassi, Joseph. 1966. Book review of *Structure of scientific revolutions*. *Journal of the History of Philosophy*, 4: 351–354.

Aldemir, M. C. 1986. The impact of cultural values upon managers' choice of social power base. *International Journal of Manpower*, 7(5):13–19.

Alexander, Jeffrey C. and Steven Seidman, editors. 1990. *Culture and Society: Contemporary Debates*. Cambridge: Cambridge University Press.

Al-Faleh, Mahmoud. 1987. Cultural influences on Arab management development: A case study of Jordan. *Journal of Management Development*, 6(3):19–33.

Almond, G. A. and S. Verba. 1963. *The Civic Culture: Political Attitudes and Democracy in Five Nations*. Princeton: Princeton University Press.

Alvi, S. A. and S. W. Ahmed. 1987. Assessing organizational commitment in a developing country: Pakistan, a case study. *Human Relations*, 40(5): 267–280.

Appelbaum, H. 1984. *Work in Non-market and Transitional Societies*. Albany: State University of New York Press.

Austin, James E. 1990. *Managing in Developing Countries: Strategic Analysis and Operating Techniques*. New York: The Free Press.

Bagozzi, R. A. 1980. *Causal Models in Marketing*. New York: John Wiley and Sons.

Baritz, Loren. 1960. *The Servants of Power*. Middletown: Wesleyan University Press.

Barrett, G. V. and Bernard M. Bass. 1976. Cross-cultural issues in industrial and organizational psychology. In M. D. Dunnette, editor, *Handbook of Industrial and Organizational Psychology*, 1639–1686. Chicago: Rand McNally.

Bartlett, Christopher A. and Sumantra Ghoshal. 1989. *Managing Across Borders: The Transnational Solution*. Boston: Harvard Business School Press.

Bass, Bernard M. 1965. *Organizational Psychology*. Boston: Allyn and Bacon.

Bass, F. M. 1974. The theory of stochastic preference and brand switching. *Journal of Marketing Research*, 11: 1–20.

Baumol, W. J. 1959. On the role of marketing theory. *Journal of Marketing Research*, 21: 413–419.

Beaty, David T. and Mark Mendenhall. 1990. Theory building in international management: An archival review and recommendations for future research. Academy of Management Annual Meetings, San Francisco, August.

Beer, M., B. Spector, P. R. Lawrence, D. Q. Mills and R. E. Walton. 1984. *Managing Human Assets*. New York: Free Press.

Bem, D. J. 1972. Self-perception theory. In L. Berkowitz, editor, *Advances in Experimental Social Psychology*, Vol.6. New York: Academic Press.

Benedict, Ruth. 1942. Anthropology and culture change. *The American Scholar*, 11(2): 243–248.

Benedict, Ruth. 1934. *Patterns of Culture*. New York: Houghton Mifflin.

Bennis, Warren. 1987. Using our knowledge of organizational behavior: The improbable task. In J. Lorsch, editor, *The Handbook of Organizational Behavior*. Englewood Cliffs: Prentice-Hall, 29–50.

Bennis, Warren and B. Nanus. 1985. *Leaders: The Strategies for Taking Charge*. New York: Harper and Row.

Berger, P. L. 1986. *The Capitalist Revolution*. New York: Basic Books.

Berger, P. L. and T. Luckmann. 1966. *The Social Construction of Reality*. London: Pelican.

Berry, J. W. 1980. Social and cultural change. In H. C. Triandis and R. W. Brislin, editors, *Handbook of Cross-cultural Psychology*. Boston: Allyn and Bacon.

Bhagat, Rabi S. and Sara J. McQuaid. 1982. Role of subjective culture in organizations: A review and direction for future research. *Journal of Applied Psychology Monograph*, 67(5): 653–685.

Bhatt, Bhal J. and Edwin L. Miller. 1983. A framework for upgrading comparative management research. *Asia Pacific Journal of Management*, 1(1):26–35.

Black, J. Stewart, Mark Mendenhall, and Gary Oddou. 1991. Toward a comprehensive model of international adjustment: An integration of multiple theoretical perspectives. *Academy of Management Review*, 16(2): 291–317.

Black, J. Stewart and Mark Mendenhall. 1990. Cross-cultural training effectiveness: a review and a theoretical frame for future research. *Academy of Management Review*, 15(10):113–36.

Blunt, Peter. 1988. Cultural consequences for organization change in a southeast Asian state: Brunei. *Academy of Management Executive*, 2(3):235–240.

Blunt, Peter. 1983. *Organizational Theory and Behavior: An African Perspective*. London: Longman.

Boas, Franz. 1940. *Race, Language and Culture*. New York: Macmillan.

Boas, Franz. 1896. The limitations of the comparative method of anthropology. Reprinted in F. Boas, *Race, Language and Culture*. New York: Macmillan, 271–304.

Boisot, Max. 1987. *Information and Organization: The Manager as Anthropologist*. London: Fontana.

Bond, Michael H. 1991. Cultural influences on modes of impression management: Implications for the culturally diverse organization. In R. A. Giacalone and P. Rosenfeld, editors, *Applied Impression Management*. London: Sage Publication.

Bond, Michael H. 1988. Invitation to a wedding: Chinese values and global economic growth. In D. Sinha and H. S. R. Kao, editors, *Social Values and Development: Asian Perspectives*. New Delhi: Sage Publications.

Bond, Michael H., editor. 1988. *The Cross-Cultural Challenge to Social Psychology*. Newbury Park: Sage Publications.

Bond, Michael H. and Geert Hofstede. 1990. The cash value of Confucian values. In S. R. Clegg and S. G. Redding, editors, *Capitalism in Contrasting Cultures*. New York: de Gruyter.

Boyacigiller, Nakiye A. 1990. The role of expatriates in the management of interdependence, complexity and risk in multinational corporations. *Journal of International Business Studies*, 21(3): 357–382.

Boyacigiller, Nakiye A. and Nancy J. Adler. 1991. The parochial dinosaur: Organizational science in a global context. *Academy of Management Review*, 16(2): 262–290.

Brannen, Mary Yoko. 1992. Your next boss is Japanese: Negotiating cultural change at a Western Massachusetts paper plant. Unpublished doctoral dissertation, University of Massachusetts, Amherst.

Brewster, C. and S. Tyson, editors. 1991. *International Comparisons in Human Resource Management*. London: Pitman.

Brislin, R. W. 1981. *Cross-cultural Encounters*. New York: Pergamon.

Bunge, Mario. 1963. *Causality*. Cleveland: Meridien Books.

Burrell, G. and G. Morgan. 1979. *Sociological Paradigms and Organizational Analysis*. London: Heinemann.

Caproni, Paula J., Stefanie Ann Lenway, and Thomas P. Murtha. 1991. Multinational mind sets: Sense making processes in multinational corporations. Paper presented at the Academy of International Business Annual Meetings, Miami, October.

Carroll, Glenn and Y. Paul Huo. 1986. Organizational task and institutional environments in ecological perspective: Findings from the local newspaper industry. *American Journal of Sociology*, 91(4): 838–873.

Chapman, A. J. and D. M. Jones. 1980. *Models of Man*. Leicester: The British Psychological Society.

Chatman, Jennifer. 1989. Improving interactional organizational research: A model of person-organization fit. *Academy of Management Review*, 14:(3) 333–349.

Child, John. 1981. Culture, contingency and capitalism in the cross-national study of organizations. In B. M. Staw and L. L. Cummings, editors, *Research in Organizational Behaviour*, 3:303–356. New York: JAI Press.

Child, John and M. Tayeb. 1983. Theoretical perspectives in cross-national organizational research. *International Studies in Management and Organization*, 12(4):23–70.

Chinese Culture Connection. 1987. Chinese values and the search for culture-free dimensions of culture, *Journal of Cross-Cultural Psychology*, 18(2): 143–164.

Clark, Rodney. 1979. *The Japanese Company*. New Haven: Yale University Press.

Clegg, Stewart R. 1989. *Frameworks of Power*. London: Sage Publications.

Clegg, Stewart R. and S. Gordon Redding. 1990. *Capitalism in Contrasting Cultures*. New York: de Gruyter.

Cole, Robert E. 1979. *Work, Mobility and Participation: A Comparative Study of American and Japanese Industry*. Berkeley: University of California Press.

Commager, Henry Steele. 1959. *The American Mind*. New Haven: Yale University Press.

Cooke, R. A. and Denise M. Rousseau. 1988. Behavioural norms and expectations: A quantitative approach to the assessment of organizational culture. *Group and Organizational Studies*, 13: 245–274.

Cox, Taylor and S. Blake. 1991. Managing cultural diversity: Implications for organizational competitiveness. *Academy of Management Executive*, 5(3): 45–56.

Crozier, M. 1964. *The Bureaucratic Phenomenon*. Chicago: University of Chicago Press.

Daft, Richard L. and A. Y. Lewin. 1990. Can organization studies begin to break out of the normal science straight jacket? *Organization Science*, 1(1):1–9.

Dalton, M. 1959. *Men Who Manage*. New York: Wiley.

Das, G. S. and C. C. Cotton. 1988. Power-balancing styles of Indian managers. *Human Relations*, 41(7): 533–551.

Davis, Stanley M. 1971. *Comparative Management: Organizational and Cultural Perspectives*. Englewood Cliffs: Prentice-Hall.

Deal, T. E. and A. A. Kennedy. 1982. *Corporate Cultures*. Reading: Addison-Wesley.

Dernberger, R. 1989. Introduction, Conference on Comparative Analyses of the Development Process in East and Southeast Asia: An integrated disciplinary approach. Honolulu, HI, East-West Center.

Derr, C. B. and Gary R. Oddou. 1991. Are US multinationals adequately preparing future American leaders for global competition? *International Journal of Human Resources Management*, 2(2):227–244.

DiMaggio, P. J. and W. W. Powell. 1991. Introduction in W.W. Powell and P.J. DiMaggio, editors, *The New Institutionalism in Organizational Analysis*, 1–38. Chicago: University of Chicago Press.

Doktor, Robert H. 1990. Asian and American CEO's: A comparative study. *Organizational Dynamics*, 18(3):46–56.

Doktor, Robert, Rosalie L. Tung, and Mary Ann Von Glinow. 1991. Incorporating international dimensions in management theory building. *Academy of Management Review*, 16(2): 259–261.

Dore, Robert P. 1973. *British Factory, Japanese Factory: The Origins of National Diversity in Industrial Relations*. Berkeley: University of California Press.

Dorfman, Peter W. and Jon P. Howell. 1988. Dimensions of national culture and effective leadership patterns: Hofstede revisited. In R. N. Farmer and E. G. McGoun, editors, *Advances in International Comparative Management*, Vol. 3. Greenwich: JAI Press, 127–150.

Dowling, P. J. and R. S. Schuler. 1990. *Interna-

tional Dimensions of Human Resource Management. Boston: PWS-Kent.

Doz, Yves and C. K. Prahalad. 1991. Managing MNCs: A search for a new paradigm. *Strategic Management Journal*, 12(5): 145–164.

Drenth, P. J. D. 1985. Cross-cultural organizational psychology: challenges and limitations. In P. Joynt and M. Warner, editors, *Managing in Different Cultures*. Amsterdam: Universitetsforlaget AS.

Duhem, P. 1954. *The aim and structure of physical theory*. Princeton: Princeton University Press.

Dunphy, Dexter C. 1986. An historical review of the literature on the Japanese enterprise and its management. In S. R. Clegg, D. C. Dunphy, and S. G. Redding, editors, *The Enterprise and Management in East Asia*. Hong Kong: Centre of Asian Studies, University of Hong Kong.

Dunphy, Dexter C. and B. W. Stening. 1984. *Japanese Organization Behaviour and Management*. Hong Kong: Asian Research Service.

Earley, P. Christopher. 1991. Organizational behavior and intercultural research: Looking into Pandora's black box. All-Academy Symposium, Annual Meeting of the Academy of Management, Miami, August.

Earley, P. Christopher. 1989. Social loafing and collectivism: A comparison of the United States and the People's Republic of China. *Administrative Science Quarterly*, 34(4): 565–581.

Eckberg, D. L. and L. Hill. 1979. The paradigm concept and sociology: A critical review. *American Sociological Review*, 44: 925–937.

Egelhoff, William G. 1988. *Organizing the Multinational Enterprise: An Information Processing Perspective*. Cambridge: Ballinger.

Elashwami, Farid. 1990. Japanese culture clash in multi-cultural management. *Tokyo Business Today*, 58(2):36–39.

England, G. W. 1978. Managers and their value systems. *Columbia Journal of World Business*, 13(2):35–44.

Enz, Cathy A. 1986. New directions for cross-cultural studies: Linking organizational and societal cultures. In R.N. Farmer, editor, *Advances in International Comparative Man-agement*, Vol. 2. Greenwich: JAI Press, 173–189.

Evans, Paul A. L. 1986. The strategic outcomes of human resource management. *Human Resource Management*, 25(1):149–167.

Evans, Paul, Yves Doz, and A. Laurent, editors. 1989. *Human Resource Management in International Firms*. London: Macmillan.

Everett, James E., B. W. Stening, and P. A. Longton. 1982. Some evidence for an international managerial culture. *Journal of Management Studies*, 19(2):153–162.

Fairchild, Erika. 1989. National culture and police organization in Germany and the United States. *Public Administration Review*, 49(5):454–462.

Farmer, Richard N. and B. M. Richman. 1965. *Comparative Management and Economic Progress*. Homewood, Il: Irwin.

Feldman, Steven P. 1986. Management in context: an essay on the relevance of culture to the understanding of organizational change. *Journal of Management Studies*, 23(6):587–607.

Ferris, G. R. and J. A. Wagner. 1985. Quality circles in the United States: a conceptual reevaluation. *Journal of Applied Behavioural Science*, 21:155–167.

Feyerabend, Paul. 1975. *Against Method: Outline of an Anarchist Theory of Knowledge*. London: New Left Books.

Fombrun, C. J., N. M. Tichy, and M. A. Devanna, editors. 1984. *Strategic Human Resources Management*. New York: Wiley.

Friedman, M. F. 1953. Methodology of positive economics. In M. F. Friedman, editor, *Essays in Positive Economics*. Chicago: University of Chicago Press.

Friedrichs, Robert W. 1970. *A Sociology of Sociology*. New York: Free Press.

Frost, Peter J., Larry F. Moore, Meryl Reis Louis, Craig C. Lundberg, and Joanne Martin, editors. 1991. *Reframing Organizational Culture*. Newbury Park: Sage.

Frost, Peter J., Larry F. Moore, Meryl Reis Louis, Craig C. Lundberg, and Joanne Martin, editors. 1985. *Organizational Culture*. Beverly Hills: Sage.

Garfinkel, H. 1967. *Studies in Ethnomethodology*. Englewood Cliffs: Prentice-Hall.

Geertz, Clifford. 1973. *The Interpretation of Cultures*. New York: Basic Books.

Ghoshal, Sumantra and Eleanor Westney, editors. 1991. *Organizational Theory and the Multinational Corporation*. New York: St. Martin's Press.

Gioia, D. A. and E. Pitre. 1990. Multiparadigm perspectives on theory building. *Academy of Management Review*, 15(4):584–602.

Godkin, L., C. E. Braye, and C. L. Caunch. 1989. U.S. based cross-cultural management research in the eighties. *Journal of Business and Economic Perspectives*, 15(2): 37–45.

Goldsmith, W. and D. Clutterbuck. 1985. *The Winning Streak*. Harmondsworth: Penguin.

Goodenough, Ward. 1970. *Description and Comparison in Cultural Anthropology*. Chicago: Aldine.

Gould, D. J. and J. A. Amaro-Reyes. 1983. The effects of corruption on administrative performance: Illustrations from developing countries. Washington, D.C.: World Bank Staff Working Papers, No. 580, Management and Development Series, No. 7.

Gregory, Kathleen L. 1983. Native-view paradigms: Multiple cultures and culture conflicts in organizations. *Administrative Science Quarterly*, 28 (3): 359–376.

Hackman, J. R. and Gary R. Oldham. 1980. *Work Redesign*. Reading Mass.: Addison-Wesley.

Haire, Mason, E. E. Ghiselli, and L. W. Porter. 1966. *Managerial Thinking: An International Study*. New York: Wiley.

Hall, Edward T. 1981;1976. *Beyond Culture*. Garden City: Anchor Press/Doubleday.

Hall, Edward T. 1976. *The Silent Language*. Greenwich Conn.: Fawcett.

Hamilton, Gary G. and Nicole W. Biggart. 1988. Market, culture and authority: A comparative analysis of management and organization in the Far East. *American Journal of Sociology*, 94(supplement): 52–94.

Harris, Marvin. 1980. *Cultural Materialism*. New York: Vintage Books.

Harris, Marvin. 1979. *Cultural Materialism: The Struggle for a Science of Culture*. New York: Random House.

Harris, Marvin. 1964. *The Nature of Cultural Things*. New York: Random House.

Harris, Philip R. and R. T. Moran. 1979. *Managing Cultural Differences*. Houston: Gulf.

Hayes, John and C. W. Allinson. 1988. Cultural differences in the learning styles of managers. *Management International Review*, 28(3):75–80.

Hayes, J. and R. Prakasam. 1989. Culture: The efficiency of different modes of consultation. *Leadership and Organization Development Journal*, 10(1):24–32.

Hedlund, Gunnar. 1990. Assumptions of hierarchy and heterarchy: With application to the management of the multinational corporation. Stockholm School of Economics, Working Paper 90/4.

Heenan, David A. and Howard V. Perlmutter. 1979. *Multinational Organizational Development*. Reading: Addison-Wesley.

Henderson, J. and R. Quandt. 1958. *Microeconomic Theory*. New York: McGraw-Hill.

Hendry, Chris and A. Pettigrew. 1990. Human resource management: an agenda for the 1990's. *International Journal of Human Resource Management*, 1(1):17–44.

Hofstede, Geert. 1991. *Cultures and Organizations: Software of the Mind*. London: McGraw-Hill.

Hofstede, Geert. 1990. Pitfalls in replicating culture surveys. *Organization Studies*, 11(1): 103–106.

Hofstede, Geert. 1980a. *Culture's Consequences: International Differences in Work-related values*. Beverly Hills: Sage.

Hofstede, Geert. 1980b. Motivation, leadership and organization: Do American theories apply abroad? *Organizational Dynamics*, 9(1): 42–63.

Hofstede, Geert and Michael Bond. 1988. The Confucious connection: From cultural roots to economic growth. *Organizational Dynamics*, 16(4): 4–21.

Hofstede, Geert, Bram Neuijen, Denise Daval Ohayv, and Geert Sanders. 1990. Measuring organizational cultures: A qualitative and quantitative study across twenty cases. *Administrative Science Quarterly*, 35(2): 286–316.

Homans, George. 1967. *The Nature of Social Science*. Cambridge, Mass: Harvard University Press.

Horng, Ching. 1992. Cultural differences, trust, business strategy and control: Testing a holistic model in the context of headquarters-subsidiary relations. Department of Management, University of Northern Iowa.

Horng, Ching and Barry Baysinger. 1991. Cultural differences, trust and their impact on business strategy and control. Academy of International Business Meetings, Miami, October.

Horwitz, F. 1990. HRM: an ideological perspective. *Personnel Review*, 19(2):10–15.

Hunt, S. D. 1976. *Marketing Theory: Conceptual Foundations of Research in Marketing.* Columbus: Grid.

International Research Group. 1981. *Industrial Democracy in Europe.* Oxford: Clarendon Press.

Ishida, Hideo. 1986. Transferability of Japanese human resource management abroad. *Human Resource Management*, 25(1):103–20.

Jaeger, Alfred M. 1990. The applicability of western management techniques in developing countries: a cultural perspective. In A. M. Jaeger and R. N. Kanungo, editors, *Management in Developing Countries.* London: Routledge.

Jaeger, Alfred M. 1986. Organizational development and national culture: Where's the fit? *Academy of Management Review*, 11(1): 178–190.

Jaeger, Alfred M. 1983. The transfer of organizational culture overseas: An approach to control in the multinational corporation. *Journal of International Business Studies*, 1(2): 91–114.

Jaeger, Alfred M. and Rabindra N. Kanungo, editors. 1990. *Management in Developing Countries.* London: Routledge.

Jahoda, G. 1984. Do we need a concept of culture? *Journal of Cross-Cultural Psychology*, 15(2): 139–151.

Jelinek, Mariann, Linda Smircich, and Paul Hirsch. 1983. Introduction: A code of many colors. *Administrative Science Quarterly*, 28(3): 331–338.

Jorgensen, Jan J., T. Hafsi, and M. Kiggundu. 1986. Towards a market imperfections theory of organizational structure in developing countries. *Journal of Management Studies*, 23(4): 417–442.

Joynt, Pat and M. Warner, editors. 1985. *Managing in Different Cultures.* Amsterdam: Universitetsforlaget AS.

Kahl, Joseph A. 1968. *The Measurement of Modernism.* Austin: University of Texas Press.

Kahn, Robert L., D. M. Wolfe, R. P. Quinn, and J. Diedrick. 1964. *Organizational Stress: Studies in Role Conflict and Ambiguity.* New York: John Wiley.

Kahneman, D. P. Slovic, and A. Tversky. 1982. *Judgement under Uncertainty, Heuristics and Biases.* Cambridge: Cambridge University Press.

Kanungo, R. N. and S. Misra. 1985. The bases of involvement in work and family contexts. *International Journal of Psychology*, 23(3): 267–282.

Kaplan, A. 1964. *The Conduct of Inquiry: Methodology of Behavioral Science.* San Francisco: Chandler.

Kaplan, D. and R. A. Manners. 1972. *Culture Theory.* Englewood Cliffs, NJ: Prentice-Hall.

Kealey, D. J. and B. D. Ruben. 1983. Cross-cultural personnel selection: criteria, issues and methods. In D. Landis and R. Brislin, *Handbook of Intercultural Training*, 1:155–175. New York: Pergamon.

Keesing, R. M. 1974. Theories of culture. *Annual Review of Anthropology*, 3:73–97.

Kelley, Lane and Reginald Worthley. 1981. The role of culture in comparative management: A cross-cultural perspective. *Academy of Management Journal*, 24(1): 164–173.

Kerr, Clark. 1983. *The Future of Industrial Societies.* Cambridge, Mass.: Harvard University Press.

Kerr, Clark, J. T. Dunlop, F. H. Harbison, and C. A. Myers. 1960. *Industrialism and Industrial Man.* Cambridge, Mass.: Harvard University Press.

Keys, J. B. and T. R. Miller. 1984. The Japanese management theory jungle. *Academy of Management Review*, 9:342–353.

Khaleque, A. and M. A. Rahman. 1987. Perceived importance of job facets and overall job satisfaction of industrial workers. *Human Relations*, 40(7): 401–416.

Kidger, Peter J. 1991. The emergence of international human resource management. *International Journal of Human Resource Management*, 2(2):149–163.

Kiggundu, Moses N. 1990. Managing structural adjustment in developing countries: an organizational perspective. In A. M. Jaeger and R. N. Kanungo, editors, *Management in Developing Countries*. London: Routledge.

Kiggundu, Moses, N. 1989. *Managing Organizations in Developing Countries: An Operational and Strategic Approach*. West Hartford: Kumarian Press.

Kincaid, D. Lawrence. 1987. *Communication Theory, Eastern and Western Perspectives*. San Diego: Academic Press.

Kirkbride, Paul. 1987. The "culture" of organizational culture research. *Asia Pacific Journal of Management*, 4(2): 124–129.

Kirkbride, Paul and Shae Wan Chaw. 1987. The cross-cultural transfer of organizational cultures: Two case studies of corporate mission statements. *Asia Pacific Journal of Management*, 5(1): 55–66.

Klein, H. J. 1989. An integrated control theory model of work motivation. *Academy of Management Review*, 14(2): 150–172.

Kleinberg, Jill. 1989. Cultural clash between managers: America's Japanese firms. In S. Benjamin Prasad, editor, *Advances in International Comparative Management*. Greenwich: JAI Press, 4:221–244.

Kluckhohn, F. R. and F. L. Strodtbeck. 1961. *Variations in Value Orientations*. Evanston: Row, Peterson.

Kochan, Thomas A. 1983. Review of *Industrial Democracy in Europe* (International Research Group, Oxford: Clarendon Press 1981). *Administrative Science Quarterly*, 28(4): 629–634.

Kogut, Bruce and Harbir Singh. 1988. The effect of national culture on the choice of entry mode. *Journal of International Business Studies*, 19(3): 411–432.

Koike, Dorinne K. 1990. *Crafting Selves: Power, Gender and Discourse in a Japanese Workplace*. Chicago: University of Chicago Press.

Koontz, H. 1969. A model for analysing the universality and transferability of management. *Academy of Management Journal*, 12(4):415–429.

Kotter, John P. 1982. *The General Managers*. New York: Free Press.

Kroeber, A. L. 1917. The superorganic. *American Anthropologist*, 19: 163–213.

Kroeber, A. and C. Kluckholn. 1952. Culture: A critical review of concepts and definitions. Cambridge, Mass.: Papers of the Peabody Museum of American Archeology and Ethnology, Harvard University.

Kuhn, Thomas S. 1970;1962. *The Structure of Scientific Revolutions*. Chicago: The University of Chicago Press.

La Jaunie, Jr., Louis and Rakesh Sambharya. 1990. Mediatory myth: An approach to managing organizational culture in MNCs. In S. B. Prasad, editor, *Advances in International Comparative Management*, Vol. 5. Greenwich: JAI Press, 211–225.

Lammers, Cornelis J. and D. J. Hickson. 1979. *Organizations Alike and Unlike*. London: Routledge and Kegan Paul.

Landy, Frank J. and Wendy S. Becker. 1987. Motivation theory reconsidered. In B. M. Staw and L. L. Cummings, editors, *Research in Organizational Behavior*. Greenwich: JAI Press, 9:1–38.

Laurent, André. 1991. Weaknesses of strong cultures in multinational firms. 8th International SCOS Conference, Copenhagen, June 26–28: 1–7.

Laurent, André. 1986. The cross-cultural puzzle of international human resource management. *Human Resource Management*, 25(1): 91–102.

Laurent, André. 1983. The cultural diversity of western conceptions of management. *International Studies of Management and Organization*, 13(1–2): 75–96.

Lawrence, Paul. 1991. Keynote address at the Western Academy of Management, Santa Barbara, California, March.

Levi-Strauss, Claude. 1963. *Structural Anthropology*. New York: Doubleday.

Levi-Strauss, Claude. 1949. *Les Structures Elementaires de la Parente*. Paris: Presses Universitaires de France. (English translation, 1969, *The Elementary Structures of Kinship*. Boston: Beacon.)

Lincoln, J. R., M. Hanada, and J. Olsen. 1981. Cultural orientations and individual reactions to organizations: A study of employees of Japanese-owned firms. *Administrative Science Quarterly*, 26:93–115.

Lincoln, James R. and Arne L. Kalleberg. 1990. *Culture, Control, and Commitment: A Study of Work Organization and Work Attitudes in the United States and Japan.* Cambridge: Cambridge University Press.

Lupton, T. 1963. *On the Shop Floor.* Oxford: Pergamon.

Machungwa, P. D. and N. Schmitt. 1983. Work motivation in a developing country. *Journal of Applied Psychology*, 68(1): 31–42.

MacFarlane, Alan. 1987. *The Culture of Capitalism.* Oxford: Basil Blackwell.

Malinowski, B. 1944. *A Scientific Theory of Culture.* Chapel Hill: University of North Carolina Press.

Malinowski, B. 1939. Review of six essays on culture by Albert Blumenthal. *American Sociological Review*, 4(4): 588–592.

Malkiel, Burton. 1981. *A Random Walk Down Wall Street.* New York: W.W. Norton.

Mandlebaum, M. 1971. *History, Man, and Reason: A Study in 19th Century Thought.* Baltimore: The John Hopkins University Press.

Manicas, P. T. 1982. The human sciences: A radical separation of psychology and the social sciences. In P.F. Secord, editor, *Explaining Human Behavior*. Beverly Hills: Sage.

Marsden, D. 1991. Indigenous management. *International Journal of Human Resource Management*, 2(1): 21–38.

Maruyama, Magoroh. 1985. Mindscapes: How to understand specific situations in multicultural management. *Asia Pacific Journal of Management*, 2(3): 125– 149.

Maruyama, Magoroh. 1974. Paradigmatology and its application to cross-disciplinary, cross-professional, and cross-cultural communication. *Dialectica*, 28(3/4):135–196.

McEnery, Jean and G. Des Harnais. 1990. Culture shock. *Training and Development Journal*, 44(4):43–47.

Mead, M. 1939. *From the South Seas.* New York: Morrow.

Mechanic, David. 1963. Some considerations in the methodology of organizational studies. In H. J. Leavitt, editor, *The Social Science of Organizations*. Englewood Cliffs: Prentice-Hall.

Mehta, P. 1978. Objective and subjective factors in employee satisfaction. *Indian Journal of Industrial Relations*, 2(13): 433–444.

Mendenhall, Mark and Gary Oddou. 1986. The cognitive, psychological and social contexts of Japanese management. *Asia Pacific Journal of Management*, 4(1):24–37.

Mendenhall, Mark and Gary Oddou. 1985. The dimensions of expatriate acculturation: A review. *Academy of Management Review*, 10:39–48.

Mendonca, Manuel and Rabindra N. Kanungo. 1990. Performance management in developing countries. In A. M. Jaeger and R. N. Kanungo, editors, *Management in Developing Countries*. London: Routledge, 223–251.

Merton, Robert K. 1973. *The Sociology of Science: Theoretical and Empirical Investigations*. Chicago: The University of Chicago Press.

Merton, Robert K. 1968. *Social Theory and Social Structure.* New York: Free Press.

Michalos, P. 1980. Philosophy of science. In P. T. Durbin, editor, *A Guide to the Culture of Science, Technology, and Medicine*. New York: The Free Press.

Miller, Lynn E. and Joseph E. Grush. 1988. Improving predictions in expectancy theory research: Effects of personality, expectancies and norms. *Academy of Management Journal*, 31(1): 107–122.

Mills, J. 1969. *Experimental Social Psychology.* New York: Macmillan.

Mintzberg, Henry. 1990. The design school: Reconsidering the basic premises of strategic management. *Strategic Management Journal*, 11(3):171–195.

Mintzberg, Henry. 1973. *The Nature of Managerial Work.* New York: Harper and Row.

Misumi, J. 1984. Decision making in Japanese groups and organizations. In B. Wilpert and A. Sorge, editors, *International Perspectives on Organizational Democracy*. New York: Wiley.

Misumi, J. and M. F. Peterson. 1985. The Performance-maintenance (PM) theory of leadership: Review of a Japanese research program. *Administrative Science Quarterly*, 30:198–223.

Morgan, Gareth, editor. 1983. *Beyond Method.* Beverly Hills: Sage.

Morgan, Gareth and L. Smircich. 1980. The case for quantitative research. *Academy of Management Review,* 5(4):491–500.

Morishima, M. and T. Minami. 1983. Task interdependence and internal motivation: Application of job characteristics model to collectivist cultures. *Tetsugaku,* 77:133–147.

Nagel, E. 1962. *The Structure of Science.* New York: Harcourt, Brace and World.

Negandhi, Anant R. 1975. Comparative management and organization theory: A marriage needed. *Academy of Management Journal,* 18(2): 334–344.

Negandhi, Anant R. and B. D. Estafen. 1965. A research model to determine the applicability of American management know-how in differing cultures and/or environments. *Academy of Management Journal,* 8(4): 309–318.

Nehrt, Lee C. 1987. The internationalization of the curriculum. *Journal of International Business Studies,* 18(1):83–90.

Newman, William H. 1972. Cultural assumptions underlying U.S. management concepts. In J. L. Massie and S. Laytie, editors, *Management in an International Context.* New York: Harper and Row, 327–352.

Newton-Smith, W. H. 1981. *The Rationality of Science.* Boston: Routledge and Kegan Paul.

Nirenberg, John. 1986. Understanding the failure of Japanese management abroad. *Journal of Managerial Psychology,* 1(1):19–24.

Nisbett, R. E. and L. Ross. 1980. *Human Inference: Strategies and Shortcomings of Social Judgement.* Englewood Cliffs: Prentice-Hall.

O'Connell, M. S., R. G. Lord, and M. K. O'Connell. 1990. Differences in Japanese and American leadership prototypes: Implications for cross-cultural training. Working paper, Dept. of Psychology, University of Akron.

Oliver, Nick and B. Wilkinson. 1988. *The Japanization of British Industry.* Oxford: Blackwell.

O'Reilly, III, Charles A., Jennifer Chatman, and David F. Caldwell. 1991. People and organizational culture: A profile comparison approach to assessing person-organization fit. *Academy of Management Journal,* 34(3): 487–516.

Ouchi, William G. 1981. *Theory Z: How American Business Can Meet the Japanese Challenge.* Reading, Mass: Addison-Wesley.

Ouchi, William G. and A. M. Jaeger. 1978. Type Z organization: stability in the midst of mobility. *Academy of Management Review,* 5:305–314.

Pang, K. and N. Oliver. 1988. Personnel strategy in eleven Japanese manufacturing companies in the UK. *Personnel Review,* 17(3): 16–21.

Parkhe, Arvind. 1991. Interfirm diversity, organizational learning, and longevity in global strategic alliances. *Journal of International Business Studies,* 22(4):579–602.

Parnell, Myrtle and J. Vanderkloot. 1989. How to build cross-cultural bridges. *Communications World,* 6(8):4–42.

Parsons, Talcott. 1968. *The Structure of Social Action.* New York: Free Press.

Parsons, Talcott. 1967. Sociological theory. *Encyclopedia Britannica,* 20:799–802.

Pasquero, Jean. 1990. Comparative research: The case for middle range methodologies. In L. E. Preston, editor, *International and Comparative Corporation and Society Research.* Greenwich,Conn.: JAI Press.

Peng, T. K., M. F. Peterson, and Y. P. Shyi. 1991. Quantitative methods in cross-national management research: Trends and equivalence issues. *Journal of Organizational Behavior,* 12(2):87–108.

Peters, Thomas J. and R. H. Waterman. 1982. *In Search of Excellence.* New York: Harper and Row.

Peterson, R. A. 1979. Revitalizing the culture concept. *Annual Review of Sociology,* 5:137–166.

Pfeffer, Jeffrey. 1985. Organizations and organization theory. In G. Lindzey and E. Aronson, editors, *Handbook of Social Psychology,* 3rd edition. Westminster: Random House, 379–440.

Pfeffer, Jeffrey. 1982. *Organizations and Organization Theory.* Boston: Pitman.

Phillips, Margaret E., Nakiye A. Boyacigiller, Michele K. Bolton, and Sonja A. Sackmann. 1992. Multiple cultural mindsets as a normal state: A cultural perspective on European organizational life. Presented at the Second International Conference of the Western Academy of Business, Leuven, Belgium, June.

Pieper, R., editor. 1990. *Human Resource Management: An International Comparison*. Berlin: de Gruyter.

Pinder, C.C. 1984. *Work Motivation*. Glenview: Scott, Foresman.

Pondy, L. R., P. J. Frost, G. Morgan, and T. C. Dandridge, editors. 1983. *Organizational Symbolism*. Greenwich: JAI Press.

Popper, K. R. 1968. *The Logic of Scientific Discovery*. London: Hutchinson.

Porter, Michael E. 1991. *Canada at the Crossroads: The Reality of a New Competitive Environment*. A study prepared for the Business Council on National Issues and the Government of Canada, October.

Porter, Michael E. 1990a. *The Competitive Advantage of Nations*. New York: The Free Press.

Porter, Michael E. 1990b. The competitive advantage of nations. *Harvard Business Review*, March/April: 73–93.

Powell, Walter W. and P. J. DiMaggio. 1991. *The New Institutionalism in Organizational Analysis*. Chicago: University of Chicago Press.

Preston, J. C. 1987. Cultural blinders: Take off before attempting international organizational development. *Organizational Development Journal*, 5:50–56.

Preston, Lee L., editor. 1990. *International and Comparative Corporation and Society Research*. Greenwich, Conn.: JAI Press.

Price-Williams, D. R. 1985. Cultural psychology. In G. Lindzey and E. Aronson, editors, *The Handbook of Social Psychology*, Vol. 2. 3rd edition. New York: Random House, 993–1042.

Purcell, John. 1989. The impact of corporate strategy on human resource management. In J. Storey, editor, *New Perspectives on Human Resource Management*. London: Routledge.

Pye, L. 1985. *Asian Power and Politics*. Cambridge, Mass.: Harvard University Press.

Radcliffe-Brown, A. R. 1957. *A Natural Science of Society*. Glencoe: Free Press.

Radcliffe-Brown, A. R. 1952. *Structure and Function in Primitive Society*. London: Dohen and West.

Ragin, C. C. 1987. *The Comparative Method*. Berkeley: University of California Press.

Redding, S. Gordon. 1990. *The Spirit of Chinese Capitalism*. New York: de Gruyter.

Redding, S. Gordon. 1980. Cognition as an aspect of culture and its relation to management processes: An exploratory view of the Chinese case. *Journal of Management Studies*, 17(2):127–148.

Redding, S. Gordon and M. Ng. 1982. The role of 'face' in the organizational perceptions of Chinese Managers. *Organization Studies*, 3(3):201–219.

Redding, S. Gordon, A. Norman, and A. Schlander. 1992. The nature of individual attachment to the organization: A review of East Asian variations. In M. D. Dunnette, editor, *Handbook of Industrial and Organizational Psychology*, Vol 4. Palo Alto: Consulting Psychologists Press.

Redding, S. Gordon and R. D. Whitley. 1990. Beyond bureaucracy: Towards a comparative analysis of forms of economic resource co-ordination and control. In S. R. Clegg and S. G. Redding, editors, *Capitalism in Contrasting Cultures*, 7–104. New York: de Gruyter.

Redding, S. Gordon and G. Y. Y. Wong. 1986. The psychology of Chinese organizational behaviour. In M. H. Bond, editor, *The Psychology of the Chinese People*, 267–295. Hong Kong: Oxford University Press.

Rehder, Robert, M. Smith, and K. Burr. 1989. A salute to the sun: Cross-cultural organizational adaptation and change. *Leadership and Organization Development Journal*, 10(4):17–27.

Rigby, J. Malcolm. 1987. The challenge of multinational team development. *Journal of Management Development*, 6(3):65–72.

Ritzer, George. 1975. *Sociology: A Multiple Paradigm Science*. Boston: Allyn and Bacon.

Roberts, Karlene H. 1970. On looking at an elephant: An evaluation of cross-cultural research related to organizations. *Psychological Bulletin*, 74(5):327–350.

Roberts, Karlene H. and Nakiye A. Boyacigiller. 1984. Cross-national organizational research: The grasp of the blind men. In B. M. Staw and L. L. Cummings, editors, *Research in Organizational Behavior*. Greenwich: JAI Press, 6:423–475.

Roberts, Karlene H. and Nakiye A. Boyacigiller. 1983. A survey of cross-national organizational researchers: Their views and opinions. *Organization Studies*, 4(4): 375–386.

Roberts, Karlene H., Charles L. Hulin, and Denise M. Rousseau. 1978. *Developing an Interdisciplinary Science of Organizations*. San Francisco: Jossey-Bass.

Rohlen, Thomas P. 1974. *For Harmony and Strength: Japanese White-collar Organization in Anthropological Perspective*. Berkeley: University of California Press.

Rohner, R. 1984. Toward a conception of culture for cross-cultural psychology. *Journal of Cross-Cultural Psychology*, 15(2):111–138.

Ronen, Simcha. 1986. *Comparative and Multinational Management*. New York: John Wiley.

Ronen, Simcha and R. Kumar. 1986. Comparative management: A developmental perspective. In B. M. Bass, P. Weissenberg, and F. Heller, editors, *Handbook of Cross-cultural Organizational Psychology*. Beverley Hills: Sage.

Ronen, Simcha and Oded Shenkar. 1985. Clustering countries on attitudinal dimensions: A review and synthesis. *Academy of Management Review*, 10(3):435–454.

Rorty, R. 1979. *Philosophy and the Mirror of Nature*. Princeton: Princeton University Press.

Rosenberg, A. 1976. *Microeconomic Laws: A Philosophical Analysis*. Pittsburgh: University of Pittsburgh Press.

Rosenzweig, Philip M. and Jitendra V. Singh. 1991. Organizational environments and the multinational enterprise. *Academy of Management Review*, 16(2):340–361.

Roth, Paul A. 1987. *Meaning and Method in the Social Sciences*. Ithaca: Cornell University Press.

Ryan, M. J. and O'Shaughnessy. 1980. Theory development: The need to distinguish levels of abstraction. In C. W. Lamb and P. M. Dunne, editors, *Theoretical Developments in Marketing*. Chicago: American Marketing Association, 47–50.

Sackmann, Sonja A. 1991. *Cultural Knowledge in Organizations: Exploring the Collective Mind*. Newbury Park: Sage.

Salancik, Gerald R. and Jeffrey Pfeffer. 1978. A social information processing approach to job attitudes and task design. *Administrative Science Quarterly*, 23(2): 224–253.

Sampson, Edward E. 1978. Scientific paradigms and social values: Wanted a scientific revolution. *Journal of Personality and Social Psychology*, 36(11):1332–1343.

Sapir, E. 1917. Do we need a superorganic? *American Anthropologist*, 19:441–447.

Schein, Edgar. 1986. International human resource management: New directions, perpetual issues, and missing themes. *Human Resource Management*, 25(1):169–176.

Schein, Edgar H. 1985. *Organizational Culture and Leadership: A Dynamic View*. San Francisco: Jossey Bass.

Schlenker, B. R. 1974. Social psychology and science. *Journal of Personality and Social Psychology*, 29:1–15.

Schneider, Benjamin. 1985. Organizational Behavior. *Annual Review of Psychology*, 36:573–611.

Schneider, Susan. 1988. National vs. corporate culture: Implications for human resource management. *Human Resource Management*, 27(2):231–246.

Schollhammer, Hans. 1969. The comparative management theory jungle. *Academy of Management Journal*, 12:81–97.

Sechrest, L. 1977. On the dearth of theory in cross-cultural psychology: There is madness in our method. In Y. H. Poortinga, editor, *Basic Problems in Cross-cultural Psychology*, 73–82. Amsterdam: Swets and Zeitlinger.

Seddon, John. 1987. Assumptions, culture and performance appraisal. *Journal of Management Development*, 6(3):47–54.

Segall, Marshall H. 1986. Culture and behavior: Psychology in global perspective. *Annual Review of Psychology*, 37:523–564.

Shackleton, V. V. and S. Newell. 1991. Management selection: A comparative survey of methods used in top British and French companies. *Journal of Occupational Psychology*, 64(1):23–36.

Sharma, B. R. 1986. *Motivational Crises in Indian Administration: A Case of Existential Sickness*. New Delhi: Indian Institute of Public Administration.

Shaw, James B. 1990. A cognitive categorization model for the study of intercultural management. *Academy of Management Review*, 15(4):626–645.

Shenkar, Oded. 1985. Organizational coordination and motivation according to Confucius and the human relations school: A comparison. *The Chinese Journal of Administration*, 38(February):1–8.

Shenkar, Oded and Simcha Ronen. 1987. Structure and importance of work goals among managers in the People's Republic of China. *Academy of Management Journal*, 30(3): 564–576.

Shenkar, Oded and Yoram Zeira. 1992. Role conflict and role ambiguity of CEOs in international joint ventures. *Journal of International Business Studies*, (in press).

Shenkar, Oded and Yoram Zeira. 1990. International joint ventures: A tough test for HR. *Personnel*, 67(1):26–31.

Shenkar, Oded and Yoram Zeira. 1987. Human resources management in international joint ventures: Directions for research. *Academy of Management Review*, 12(3):546–557.

Shoemaker, P. J. H. 1982. The expected utility model, its variants, purposes, evidence, and limitations. *Journal of Economic Literature*, 20:529–563.

Silin, Robert H. 1976. *Leadership and Values: The Organization of Large-scale Taiwanese Enterprises*. Cambridge, Mass.: Harvard University Press.

Singh, Joginder P. 1990a. A comment on Hofstede's reply. *Organization Studies*, 11(1): 106.

Singh, Joginder P. 1990b. Managerial culture and work-related values in India. *Organization Studies*, 11(1):75–102.

Sinha, Jai B. P. 1990. A model of effective leadership styles in India. In A. M. Jaeger and R. N. Kanungo, editors, *Management in Developing Countries*. London: Routledge.

Smircich, Linda. 1983. Concepts of culture and

organizational analysis. *Administrative Science Quarterly*, 28(3):339–358.

Smith, Peter B., *et al.* 1989. On the generality of leadership style measures across cultures. *Journal of Occupational Psychology*, 62:97–109.

Smith, Peter B. and M. H. Bond. 1993. *Social Psychology across Cultures*. New York: Simon and Schuster.

Smith, Peter B. and M. Peterson. 1988. *Leadership in Context*. London: Sage Publications.

Soeters, Joseph and H. Schreuder. 1988. The interaction between national and organizational cultures in accounting firms. *Accounting, Organizations and Society*, 13(1):75–85.

Spradley, J. P. 1972. *Culture and Cognition: Rules, Maps and Plans*. New York: Chandler.

Stopford, John M. and Louis T. Wells. 1972. *Managing the Multinational Enterprise: Organization of the Firm and Ownership of the Subsidiaries*. New York: Basic Books.

Sullivan, Jeremiah. 1992. *Invasion of the Salarymen: The Japanese Business Presence in America*. Westport, CT: Praeger.

Sullivan, Jeremiah and R. Peterson. 1991. A test of theories underlying the Japanese lifetime employment system. *Journal of International Business Studies*, 22(1): 79–97.

Sundaram, A. 1991. Unique attributes of multinational enterprises. An earlier version of this paper was presented at the Annual Meeting of the Academy of International Business, Toronto, October 1990.

Suppe, F., editor. 1977. *The Structure of Scientific Theories*, 2nd ed. Urbana: University of Illinois Press.

Tainio, R. and T. Santalainen. 1984. Some evidence for the cultural relativity of organizational development programs. *Journal of Applied Behavioural Sciences*, 20:95–111.

Tang, Sara F. Y. and P. S. Kirkbride. 1986. The development of conflict-handling skills in Hong Kong: Some cross-cultural issues. Working paper, City Polytechnic of Hong Kong.

Terpstra, Vern and K. David. 1985. *The Cultural Environment of International Business*. Dallas: Southwestern.

Thompson, Michael, Richard Ellis, and Aaron

Wildavsky. 1990. *Cultural Theory*. Boulder: Westview Press.

Thurley, Keith. 1990. Towards a European approach to personnel management. *Personnel Management*, 22(9):54–57.

Thurow, Lester. 1984. Revitalizing American industry: Managing in a competitive world economy. *California Management Review*, 27(1):9–41.

Tichy, Noel M. 1983. *Managing Strategic Change*. New York: Wiley.

Triandis, Harry C. 1992. Cross-cultural industrial and organizational psychology. In M. D. Dunnette, editor, *Handbook of Industrial and Organizational Psychology*, Vol. 4. Palo Alto: Consulting Psychologists Press.

Tu, Wei-ming. 1991. The rise of East Asia: The challenge of the post-Confucian states. Working paper, American Academy of Arts and Sciences.

Tung, Rosalie L. 1986. Toward a systems model of comparative management. In R. N. Farmer, editor, *Advances in International Comparative Management*, Vol. 2. Greenwich: JAI Press, 233–248.

Tung, Rosalie L. 1982. Selection and training procedures of U.S., European, and Japanese multinationals. *California Management Review*, 25(1):57–71.

Turner, V. 1967. *The Forest of Symbols*. Ithaca: Cornell University Press.

Van de Ven, Andrew H. 1989. Nothing is quite so practical as a good theory. *Academy of Management Review*, 14(4):486–489.

Van Maanen, John and Andre Laurent. 1991. The flow of culture: Some notes on globalization and the multinational corporation. In S. Ghoshal and D. E. Westney, editors, *Organizational Theory and the Multinational Corporation*. New York: St. Martin's Press.

Vernon, Raymond. 1966. International investment and international trade in the product cycle. *Quarterly Journal of Economics*, 80: 190–207.

von Mises, L. 1962. *The Ultimate Foundation of Economic Science*. Princeton: Van Nostrand.

von Newmann, J. and O. Morgenstern. 1944. *Theory of Games and Economic Behavior*. Princeton: Princeton University Press.

Watson, Robert I. 1967. Psychology: A prescriptive science. *American Psychologist*, 22(June):436.

Weber, Max. 1958. *The Protestant Ethic and the Spirit of Capitalism*. New York: Scribners.

Weick, Karl. 1979;1969. *The Social Psychology of Organizing*. 2nd ed. Reading: Addison-Wesley.

Westney, Eleanor. 1989. Institutionalization theory and the multinational enterprise. Paper prepared for Workshop on Organization Theory and the MNC, INSEAD, Fontainebleau, France.

White, L. A. 1959. The concept of culture. *American Anthropologist*, 61:227–251.

White, L. G. 1986. Managing development programs: Management strategies and project interventions in six African agricultural projects. AID Evaluation Special Study No. 38. Washington, D.C.: U.S. Agency for International Development.

Whiting, B. B. 1976. The problem of a packaged variable. In K. F. Riegel and J. A. Meacham, editors, *The Developing Individual in a Changing World*, Vol. 1. Chicago: Aldine, 303–309.

Whitley, R. D. 1992. *Business Systems in East Asia*. London: Sage.

Whitley, R. D. 1991. The social construction of business systems in East Asia. *Organization Studies*, 12(1):1–28.

Whitley, R. D. 1986. The structure and context of economics as a scientific field. *Research in the History of Economic Thought and Methodology*, 4:179–209.

Whitley, R. D. 1984. *The Intellectual and Social Organization of the Sciences*. Oxford: Clarendon Press.

Williamson, Oliver E. 1985. *The Economic Institutions of Capitalism*. New York: Free Press.

Williamson, Oliver E. 1975. *Markets and Hierarchies*. New York: Free Press.

Wilson, E. O. 1975. *Sociobiology: The New Synthesis*. Cambridge: Harvard University Press.

Wong, Siu-lun. 1988. *Emigrant Entrepreneurs: Shanghai Industrialists in Hong Kong*. Hong Kong: Oxford University Press.

Yang, John Zhuang. 1992. Americanization or Japanization of human resource management policies: A study of Japanese manufacturing and service firms in the U.S. In S. B. Prasad, editor, *Advances in International Comparative Management*, Vol. 7. Greenwich: JAI Press, 77–116.

Yu, An-Bang and K. S. Yang. 1992. The nature of achievement motivation in collectivistic societies. In S. C. Choi, C. Kagitcibasi, and U. Kim, editors, *Individualism and Collectivism: Social and Applied Issues*. London: Sage Publications.

Zaheer, Srilata A. 1992. Organizational context and risk taking in a global environment: A study of foreign exchange trading rooms in the U.S. and Japan. Doctoral dissertation. Sloan Management School, Massachusetts Institute of Technology, Boston.

Zeira, Yoram and Nancy J. Adler. 1980. International organizational development: Goals, problems and challenges. *Group and Organizational Studies*, 5:295–309.

8

Strategic Management Perspectives and International Business

EDITORS' COMMENTS

As an academic field of study, strategic management has been through some remarkable changes over the past 30 years. The evolution of business policy into strategy, or strategic management, is instructive for those interested in the development of IB as an academic field of study. In Chapter 3, we contend that IB and Business and Society have a lot in common as fields of inquiry. In strategic management, we find another intellectual link.

Strategic management, like IB, is eclectic in that it draws on a number of social sciences for intellectual sustenance. These include economics, organizational sociology, and political science. Like IB, strategic management emerged first as a teaching area in business schools and only later developed field-specific concepts, theories, and measures. Also like IB, strategic management has struggled to establish its distinct identity as a field of academic study and still contains within it factions with differing academic backgrounds, research foci, and methodological approaches.[1] Although focussing on the firm and its top management, strategic management increasingly addresses phenomena at all levels of analysis, from the individual to the suprasocietal, as we argue in this book IB should.

Given the rich recent developments in strategic management and its commonalities with IB, we thought it important for IB to tap into the latest thinking in strategic management. More than most fields, strategic management has incorporated an international dimension as central to its domain—as exemplified by its interest in global competition and national sources of competitive advantage. We asked our contributors to review critically current theoretical advances in strategic management and their potential contribution to international business understanding. We were interested in the limitations, if any, of strategic management concepts and theories, when extended into the international sphere. We also sought clarification of core paradigmatic assumptions underlying the various streams of strategic management research.

In the lead paper, Kogut explicates an evolutionary theory of the multinational corporation, in which MNC capabilities (both technological and organizational) accumulate over time in response to the home and international environment. Drawing most heavily on Nelson and Winter's [1982] evolutionary perspective on economic change, Kogut extends this perspective to suggest a framework to explain the behavior of firms engaged in international competition. He applies his evolutionary perspective to four core concerns of international business: the initial entry into a country; the choice of entry mode; managing the multinational network; and country competition.

Kogut's paper is rich in concepts, propositions, and speculations and here we will highlight only a few. First we note that one cornerstone of his evolutionary perspective is the embeddedness of business processes in the larger societal environment. This is quite consistent with our ideas presented in Chapter 1 and the Business and Society perspectives presented in Chapter 3. In Kogut's theory, home country matters because it is the environment in which the firm starts and develops initially. The firm chooses to invest in certain technological or organizational resources that fit the home country environment, eventually developing organizational routines and skills that are successful in the home country. It is these routines and skills that the firm exploits when it moves into international competition. Kogut argues "To understand international strategies requires an understanding of comparative management systems and their historical evolution." [p. 474]

Kogut introduces the concept of the option as his principal tool to examine the evolutionary path followed by a firm engaged in international competition. Using option in a more generic sense, rather than in its more precise definition in financial theory, Kogut shows how decisions are made to take into account both the uncertain future market structure and the constraints on internal resource development. Kogut's ideas here are related to but distinct from the resource-based view of the firm. He sees firm capabilities as subject to inherent decreasing returns to expansion and subject to the evolving market structure.

Kogut argues that a firms' initial investment into a country establishes a significant within-country growth option, since it can serve as a platform for subsequent expansion (e.g., new products) in that country. He goes on to demonstrate that the value of the growth option varies across entry modes, since these provide different opportunities to learn through experience and develop new organizational capabilities. Thus licensing with its low potential for learning has a low option value, while a joint venture has a high potential for learning and a high option value.

Kogut goes on to explain the second kind of option generated by investment in a foreign country—the "across-country" switching option, generated by the possibility of changing activities within a coordinated multinational network as the uncertain future unfolds. Kogut rightly warns that it's a major organizational challenge for firms to manage such flexibility effectively.

Kogut's evolutionary perspective is attractive in many ways. It emphasizes the dynamics of IB behavior in its theorizing—an often neglected aspect. It seems to capture better the complex nature of the processes and outcomes, so evident to those who have studied them in detail. It also can develop testable hypotheses (e.g., regarding the choice of mode of IB involvement), some of which contradict those derived from other IB theories, thus setting up the attractive possibility of tests of competing hypotheses.

In his paper, Doz first notes that IB and strategic management inquiry developed quite separately early on. Interests in process, rather than content, brought the two fields together. Doz argues that only with the emergence of the process school of policy research and IB research on MNC organization and management processes did the two fields begin to overlap. Yet the process-oriented MNC researchers and content-oriented strategic management researchers went down separate paths with the former increasingly eclectic in its theorizing (e.g., linking up with organization theory) and the latter increasingly dominated by economics. While disdainful of the Johnny-come-lately industrial organization (IO) explanations of global competition and MNC management, Doz sees great promise for fruitful IB/strategic management interaction due to the ascendancy of the resource-based view of the firm in strategic management. With both IB and strategic management researchers increasingly focussing on organizational capabilities as the main determinants of sustainable competitive advantage, Doz notes the challenge and opportunity for both to develop better taxonomies and measures of these organizational capabilities. Further, drawing on work on individual and organizational learning, Doz details a research agenda aimed at understanding better how firm-specific skills, capabilities and competencies are built over time.

In his paper, Mascarenhas identifies four perspectives relevant to international competition: nation centered, globalist, "glocalist," and population ecologist. The first three perspectives seem to reflect an organization's response to the traditional IB integration/responsiveness demands, with

"glocalist" roughly analogous to Doz's multifocal category. Mascarenhas goes on to examine the driving assumptions, strategy prescriptions, and industry evolution prescriptions of each perspective. He completes his paper with a brief review of some existing empirical evidence on industry evolution.

In his commentary, Kim takes Mascarenhas to task for his classification of four perspectives on international competition. Kim finds no appropriate organizing principle underlying Mascarenhas's classification system, rejecting both the key success factor and the adaptability dimensions.

Kim also gets hung up on Kogut's characterization of evolutionary theory as a fourth school of IB theorizing, really a minor point in Kogut's paper. Rather than dealing with the substance of what Kogut has to say, Kim criticizes it on the grounds that (1) evolutionary theory is not uniquely suited to address the problems of international management and (2) international management does not provide a unique testing ground for evolutionary perspectives. Kim does make one good point, however, that researchers pursuing an evolutionary perspective need to improve the definitions and operationalizations of important concepts like capability and option.

In his commentary, Hitt endorses a resource-based view of the firm, which figures heavily in Kogut's and Doz's papers. He emphasizes the importance of intangible assets, which are more difficult to imitate than tangible assets and thus enable the development of sustained competitive advantage.

For Hitt, the internationalization of the firm is international diversification. Firms undertake product diversification as well, which leads Hitt to explore the interaction of these two kinds of diversification and their relationship to firm performance, innovation, strategy implementation, and organization.

Some of his most interesting comments have to do with top management teams. In commenting on the challenges MNCs (especially product diversified MNCs) face in achieving integration and fostering local responsiveness, Hitt suggests that their top managements may have certain increased knowledge requirements. We would add here that, indeed, certain tacit knowledge needs to be embedded in the top management team for effective MNC performance. Hitt also introduces a cross-national comparative dimension in this area by arguing that the strategic decision models used by top executives differ across firms domiciled in different countries. Such a situation would be quite consistent with our perspective on the embeddedness of business processes in the larger societal environment.

IB and strategic management do have the potential to contribute much to the development of the other's inquiry. IB and strategic management, however, may take divergent paths in their future development. In strategic management, economics-based approaches are becoming more dominant, while in IB they are becoming less so.

Nonetheless, Doz's vision of a fruitful interaction between IB and strategic management seems quite possible to us. Certainly, strategic management work in the tradition of the resource-based view of the firm will contribute to IB understanding. Certainly, IB research on the organization and management of MNCs will contribute to strategic management understanding. As Rumelt, Schendel and Teece stated in their recent review and research agenda for strategic management, "What is part of the new story is that organizational processes and forms are seen as an important and perhaps as the most fundamental source of advantage, and it has taken study of the international level of competition to make a fresh contribution to our understanding of the modes of survival and ultimate success" [1994:422). Here again theorizing about IB phenomena leads rather than follows theorizing about business phenomena, because the characteristics driving theoretical development are most evident in the international domain.

NOTE

1. See Rumelt, Schendel, and Teece (1994) for a recent comprehensive effort to define the domain of strategic management.

The Evolutionary Theory of the Multinational Corporation: Within- and Across-Country Options
Bruce Kogut

The appeal of international strategic management has been its combination, however uneasy, of research in economics, organizational theory, and business history with an impressive case study tradition oriented toward managerial practice. Strictly, its heritage is not old in the sense that international strategy was only consciously identified as an area in the mid 1980s. Nevertheless, the roots of the area dig into the heartland of international business (IB).

In a review article, I identified two of these roots as the Cambridge Axis and the Reading Terminal.[1] The Cambridge Axis consists of a remarkable constellation of scholars centered around Raymond Vernon, who in the late 1960s produced a number of articles and books on themes which still dominate our field.[2] Since then, the Reading Terminal, whose work is best known through the writings of John Dunning, Mark Casson, and Peter Buckley, has stressed the importance of why a firm should itself grow across borders, while also acknowledging the role of location and ownership factors.[3]

There is another tradition with an emphasis on detailed field research on issues of managerial importance. This school, which we can label the Atlantic Alliance, includes

Yves Doz, C. K. Prahalad, Chris Bartlett, Sumantra Ghoshal, and Gary Hamel. To a large extent, this group represents the organizational side of the field. The work of Michael Porter can be seen as bridging this school with the industrial organization tradition of the Cambridge Axis.[4] Recently, this work has developed closer ties with organization theory, due to the efforts of above authors, as well as William Egelhoff, Gunnar Hedlund, and Eleanor Westney. Recent statistical work has begun to validate some of the principal precepts of this school.[5]

I would like to propose that there is a fourth movement afoot, which draws from these three areas. This approach is what can be called the "Evolutionary Theory of the Multinational Corporation," in which organizing and technological capabilities can be seen as accumulating over time in response to the home and international environment. This school of thought dates back to the turn of the century, but more pragmatically, its roots in international strategy can be traced to three different sources. The first is the body of work developing at a few research sites in Japan, where Kiroyuki Itami, Ken-ichi Imai, Tadao Kagono, Iku-jiro Nonaka, Kiyonori Sakakibara, Akihiro Okumura, and their colleagues have explicitly labeled their work as evolutionary. The second is the studies on technology and patents emanating from the University of Sussex under the direction of Christopher Freeman and Keith Pavitt; John Cantwell's work on patents and investments is one of the more important accomplishments in this tradition. The third stems from the ideas of Richard Nelson and Sidney Winter, whose work is best known in their path-breaking book *An Evolutionary Theory of Economic Development*.

If this paraphrase had not been so often used, I would be tempted to say that the development of evolutionary theory has given the impression to many that they were speaking this prose without knowing it. I have traced the history of the perspective in a book chapter, where the argument was given that the country origins of firms are consequential for determining their capabilities and the *country pattern* in trade and investment. Allow me to state the basic argument by quoting from this chapter:

> This perspective suggests a view of international competition as an evolutionary process, which begins with firms investing in organizational and technological resources which correspond to the cultural and demand characteristics of the immediate local environment. These investments result over time in organizational routines and skills which are characteristic of the country, much like the genetic pool of a population ... One way to characterize the analysis is to conceive of the strategy of the firm as the placement of investment bets on assets with future and uncertain payoffs. If all firms had the same resources at every point in time and faced the same set of opportunities, strategies would be like placing a single chip on the roulette wheel. However, the key difference is the number of chips and the odds of the game are independent at each play of the wheel over time. The inter-temporal dependence of the moves implies that eventual outcomes should be examined as they sequentially unfold from initial positions...
>
> [Consequently] in international competition firms exploit those skills and routines which drive their home market success ... In this sense, strategy is much more than the selection of product markets and technologies of production. It is, above all, the creation and maintenance of superior organizational routines which reproduce the strategy (and the organization) over time. [Kogut 1988:316–317,322]

In the strategy field, this perspective has been labeled the resource-based view of the firm.[6] This view, especially discussed by Teece, Pisano, and Shuen [1990], is essentially evolutionary in its logic, stressing path dependencies in strategy, or what I, in the above passage, call: "intertemporal dependence."[7] There is, however, one difference in our perspectives. Teece, Pisano, and Shuen argue that the resource view of the firm is incompatible with a stress on market structure, while it is consistent with the notion of the firm as being determined by transaction costs.

In the view which I wish to clarify below, market structure still remains of importance to understanding the strategy of the firm. The issue becomes one of understanding how current decisions must take into account the evolution of future market structure and the stickiness by which capabilities are built. What an evolutionary perspective calls into question is much of the logic of the economizing framework of the Williamson tradition and, to a lesser extent, of the internalization school.

It is possible to discuss the issue of the evolutionary path of firms in several different academic languages. Option theory from finance throws an important perspective on the issues of investments as platforms for future opportunities. Evolutionary theories of self-organizing systems, which are related to the formal apparatus and insights of option theory, provide useful ways to explore the notion of trajectories and competency traps. Organizational theory, in many ways, provides the most insight into the heart of the matter, that is, platforms have value because they are often organizational in character (e.g., developing a distribution system) and hard to imitate.

In what follows, I rely upon these perspectives with the recognition that justice is not rendered to any of them. My aim is to suggest a way to reorient research in the international area toward the understanding of different national organizing principles and their competitive implications. Not all questions of interest can be, or should be, fruitfully addressed by this approach. The effect of exchange rate movements on pricing decisions can be, for example, analyzed in the context of a conventional economic framework. And yet even so, as discussed later, the evolution of organizational practices may influence the pricing decision.

My focus is primarily directed at the firm, though it is necessary to relate the accumulation of organizing capabilities to national origins. To motivate the argument, we first look at a case as a way of motivating the approach. The subsequent section sketches the foundations to the overall argument. The concept of a capability as arising out of the technological resources and organizing principles of a firm is developed by linking the idea of multinational corporations (MNCs) as a network to the capability of operating flexibility. We then look at four applications: the first entry decision, the choice of entry mode, the multinational network, and country competition.

The practical implication of the development which follows is to propose that an evolutionary perspective leads to the view point that a firm is placing bets on the future through the creation of options. Two kinds of options are described: a within-country (i.e., growth) option and an across-country (i.e., flexibility) option.[8] The important question is whether a firm has the managerial capacity to design and exercise such options; this issue is linked to analyzing the network design of the MNC.

I. MOTIVATION

Let us consider why an evolutionary view of comparative management is critical to understanding strategic responses by looking at the widely used cases of Caterpillar and Komatsu.[9] These cases look at the reactions of the companies and the effects of the swings in the dollar/yen exchange rate on their competitive positioning in the earth-moving equipment industry. If we ask a class of MBA students what should Caterpillar do in response to inroads by Komatsu in the earth-moving industry, there are many possible answers. Caterpillar could set a "limit" price to restrict entry; it could advertise more or strengthen dealerships. These sorts of answers are appealing, for firms that have immediate control over these decisions.

Yet, in hindsight of case method, we know that deterrence of Komatsu would not be assured by pricing and advertising decisions. We could reason that the credibility of price cutting in the American market would be questionable, as it would hurt Caterpillar much more than Komatsu. It is not uncommon, then, to conclude that Caterpillar should retaliate by cutting prices in Japan through its joint venture with Mitsubishi.

While this conclusion is insightful, we have come a long way from believing that the ability to retaliate would be credible. For the unstated *ceteris paribus* condition in this analysis Caterpillar does not suffer a cost or quality disadvantage. If the challenger has a cost and/or quality advantage, then this short-term pricing decision is only a finger in a dike.

In the enlightened decade of the 1990s, the discussion usually proceeds further to a consideration of cutting costs and improving quality. Closing down plants, outsourcing, and switching production to non-American sites are decisions which cannot be implemented immediately, but they can be carried out within a medium term frame, a year or two. Moreover, antiquated capital equipment can be replaced by newer purchases.

These recommendations are directed toward cutting costs. The primary source of these savings is through the reduction of Caterpillar's labor force. Usually, however, the recommendation is made that Caterpillar should also try to improve quality and upgrade its models. By the time they read the Komatsu case, they also recognize that the competition is not a stationary target, but is also moving to lower its costs by internal improvement and international manufacturing.

To improve quality raises, however, a spectrum of questions which usually fall outside the confines of a class on strategy. How is quality achieved? How are models brought quickly to the market place? How are flexible manufacturing systems installed successfully without a change in organizing of work?

In consideration of these questions, three simple insights are usually gained. The first is that we do not fully understand the answers to these complex questions; we are not even sure if we know the right ques-

tions. An important task in strategic analysis is the identification of the signal amidst the noise. This task is all the harder because the differences between Komatsu and Caterpillar are many and the causal relationship between a component and performance is difficult to ascertain. Ignorance is the first major conclusion.

The second insight is that once having identified the solution, Caterpillar may not be able to implement the strategy. The adoption of new manufacturing systems may be constrained by limitation of skilled workers or by union rules. Financial institutions may be unwilling to lend sufficient capital to a strategy which cuts prices in the short run while engaging in large new capital investments. Control over institutions such as education, union contract, and financial markets is limited.

A third insight is that the short-term and medium-term actions may conflict with the long-term ambition. By the seniority system, factory closings layoff the younger workers who are the most promising candidates for retraining. Layoffs interfere with the establishment of trust required to institute new organizational changes. The success of radical strategic change, involving the alteration of work organization, depends critically upon the management of human resources.

There is a dynamic path of adjustment to the entry of Komatsu into Caterpillar's market. I have summarized these observations in Figure 1 by adapting a chart first proposed by Donald Lessard [1979] as a description of the control variables open to a firm in response to exchange rate movements. One way to understand this approach more formally is to follow Winter's [1987] suggestion that strategic discretion can be characterized as identifying the control and stock variables of a dynamic program. In the short run, the firm consists of a stock of assets which comprise both physical investments and the "knowledge" of organizing human resources. The control variables are usually such discretionary choices as quantity of production, labor

Figure 1. Lessard's Window

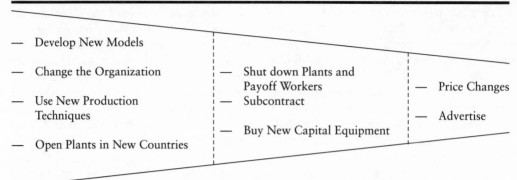

— Develop New Models

— Change the Organization   — Shut down Plants and
  Payoff Workers   — Price Changes

— Use New Production
  Techniques   — Subcontract   — Advertise

— Buy New Capital Equipment

— Open Plants in New Countries

---

supply, or advertising, but they could also be the amount of resources devoted to learning.[10] As the horizon is expanded, the firm also can also change the rate of resource accumulation by scrapping old plants and methods and investing in new facilities and ways of organizing.

In the long run, a firm may be unable to evolve a new set of strategic resources due to limitations arising from its location. Managers who are hired from the pool of American, college-educated students carry a bag of expectations: life-time employment with one firm with low starting salaries may not be one of them. In this sense, the penultimate control decision is whether to reincorporate in a new country.

It is the rarity of this decision that underscores the embeddedness of firms in their national environments. The variance and immobility of social institutions provides the fundamental insight into why differences in the performance of firms from different countries may endure for long periods of time. To understand international strategies requires an understanding of comparative management systems and their historical evolution.

II. FOUNDATIONS: CAPABILITIES, TRAJECTORIES, AND OPTIONS

To distill brutally the essay of Nelson and Winter [1982], there are six basic elements to an evolutionary perspective which addresses the issues raised in a simple case discussion:

1. Embeddedness: Knowledge is embedded in people and institutions.
2. Organizing heuristics as genes: Organizations exist as vehicles by which knowledge is replicated through proliferation of behavioral routines.
3. Path-dependent learning: The degree to which knowledge is public or tacit is dependent upon the prior accumulation of experience.
4. Trajectories and technological opportunities: Expansion of a given knowledge may exhibit increasing returns in its early use, but ultimately experiences decreasing returns.
5. Selection: The environment, through competition and government policy, favors and penalizes the use of organizing heuristics.
6. Innovation: Problem solving occurs in response to environmental signals but by use of past solutions.

To this list, we should add a seventh element, which is frequently overlooked but is implicit in Nelson and Winter's notion of routines as "truces":

7. Political impasse: Organizing heuristics represents a political ordering

of the distribution of power and authority.

It is outside the scope of this paper to explore these issues fully. I would like to trace out a few implications in order to motivate three ideas: incremental accumulation of knowledge implies a firm's current activities generate options on the future, the boundaries of the firm can be explained by factors other than market failure, and knowledge is bounded spatially within geographical borders.

It should be admitted, at the start, that a satisfactory statement of the foundation of the evolutionary approach is premature. At the heart of the mainstream of economic theory lies the notion of the individual pursuing the maximization of well-ordered preferences constrained by a given budget. There is no corresponding theory of individual choice in this evolutionary perspective, though bits and pieces have been suggested.[11] On reflection, the heart of the matter lies in understanding individual choice in reference to specific social contexts. That is, individual preferences must be seen as context dependent and not necessarily well-ordered in a uniform or *a priori* sense.

Because these issues are so difficult, most treatments of choice take a different avenue, suggested by Nelson and Winter [1982], that begins with the view of the firm as consisting of a set of capabilities, or competencies, as embodied in a stock of knowledge. This stock of knowledge is developed cumulatively. Due to differences in their experiential histories, the cumulative learning of firms displays considerable heterogeneity.

This avenue is critical for the establishment of a few important properties. First, the micro foundation must develop the perspective of how knowledge accumulated at the individual, organizational, and country levels. Second, it must explain the heterogeneity of knowledge in terms of the environment which acts to select "better" ways of doing things for a given context. And finally, it must account for why people, firms, or societies cannot easily switch to "better" practices, once these practices have been shown to be evolutionarily superior.

On examination, these issues boil down to two factors: that knowledge is temporally incremental and it is socially embedded in firms and countries. These two factors are subtly related. The distance between technologies at a given point in time presents the same issue at a distance between technologies over time. The history of technology does not show absurdly radical leaps in stages of development; quantum mechanics was not discovered in primitive societies. In a very basic sense, the physical laws of technology are permanent; the only question is the social process regulating the accumulation of knowledge required for their discovery.

Similarly, at any moment in time, the claim that new knowledge is incremental to the existing stock of knowledge is fundamental to understanding performance variations across individuals, firms, and countries. At the individual level, training and experience in a technology determines—in a very obvious way—the ability to understand new findings and to add to the body of knowledge.[12] Education is a simple recognition that knowledge is incremental.

Why can't a firm simply change by firing its workers (by early voluntary retirement or other means) and hiring workers with the new training?[13] There are, certainly, legal covenants and social contracts which cannot be violated. The experience of the 1980s shows that substantial restructuring can occur through employee turnover. Yet, these cost-cutting measures are not equivalent to altering the capabilities of firms.

To explain variations in the knowledge of performance of firms requires more than a comparison of the aggregation of the knowledge of individuals.[14] Firms, as organizations, differ in terms of the *information* which they have and can access; an extreme example is the existence of raw commodity traders who profit on imperfections in the information regarding supply, demand, and transport costs. In addition, the knowledge of the firm consists of the *know-how* regarding work organization, exercising and distributing authority, and cooperation achievement. The way a firm is organized, and the information used to inform decisions, evaluations, and actions, generates a set of capabilities which drive the strategy of the firm.

Frequently underestimated, these ways of doing things are reflected in a political ordering. Technological innovations are not radical, but reflect a fairly smooth shifting of the contour of incremental progress. A radical or distant innovation is not inherent in its physical properties, but is a question of whether the new technology, or way of doing things, represents changes in the political allocation of authority and power inside an organization.[15] What is radical for one firm may be incremental for another.

This observation becomes important in an international context if we were to explore such questions as why incumbent Japanese firms sometimes appear to be more successful in diversifying into new industries than American firms. A comparison of the experiences of Toshiba and NEC with those of GE and RCA in the area of semiconductors and computers is a case in point. In Japan, incumbent firms made the transition from vacuum tubes to semiconductors; the American industry was dominated, initially, by new foundings. A reasonable adduction is that incumbent Japanese firms shared a similar set of organizing principles and incentives which favored the exploitation of new technologies.

The effect of location on the knowledge of a firm is not limited to the influence on the structure of cooperation and authority within the organizational boundaries. As a member of an industrial network, a firm shares information as to the identity and capabilities of other actors, such as competitors, buyers, and suppliers. It also has developed a set of heuristics of how to sell, compete, or cooperate.

If knowledge could be easily imitated and acquired, then the implications of these distinctions would be uninteresting from an economic perspective. However, as stressed widely in the literature, because it is often experiential, organizational knowledge ends to be difficult to identify and communicate. A portion of the knowledge of how to organize is tacit; that is, it is *non-tradable* in markets.[16] A question of critical public policy importance is to understand the limits of the diffusion of new knowledge across borders, especially when financed by government subsidies.

That new knowledge accumulates incrementally has a radical though simple ramification: the knowledge and capabilities which a firm acquires today carries implications for the future. One way to understand the implications of this observation is to think of current investments as generating an option to have discretion over a wider set of control variables in the future. In the parlance of financial theory, the attractiveness of investing in a new activity can be decomposed into the cash flows stemming from its current use and the cash flows accrued from expanding into new markets and countries. These latter cash flows represent what Stewart Myers [1977] has called "growth options."

Growth options are characterized by three properties: uncertainty, time dependence, and managerial discretion.[17] The first property is obvious; an option is valuable insofar as it provides the right to respond to unknown and future events. Time dependence means that today's investment decision influences subsequent opportunities. It also implies that an investment in a growth option should be proprietary and difficult to imitate or preempt. Finally, the exercise of an option must be discretionary; maintaining the right to pollute or shut factories, for example, may be ruled illegal.

The analogy to options is appealing because it maps well (even in its mathematics) into what Winter [1987] meant by firm knowledge as a stock with managerial discretion over certain control variables. Zander and I [1995] have elaborated on these ideas. Figure 2 reproduces the road map to our thinking. The body of current knowledge, consisting of how to organize the firm and the information system, defines the capability set of competing in current markets. From a finance perspective, the decision whether to invest in enlarging factory size can largely be determined by net present value calculations without concern for the growth opportunities. (We might care about other options, e.g., abandonment.)

Some investments, however, build new capabilities by recombining current knowledge with new learning. We define the ability of the firm to learn in this sense its "combinative capabilities" because such capabilities reflect investment and know-how. But unlike much of the current thinking on the resource view of the firm, we view these capabilities as subject to inherent decreasing returns to expansion (i.e., diminishing technological and organizing opportunities) and the structure of the market as it evolves. In a fundamental sense, this learning capability is a bundle of options that directs the expansionary path of the firm.

The notion of options provides insight into the meaning of a "trajectory," as introduced by Nelson and Winter [1982] and Dosi [1982] under the more narrow usage of "technological trajectories." For example, the application of digital technologies has evidenced increasing returns insofar as the installation of computers has promoted the digitalization of telecommunications. (At some point, further expansion should face fewer technological opportunities.) However, as implied by the above discussion, organizing heuristics also generates a trajectory. Systems of mass production as first developed in the United States for example, were progressively expanded and applied to the organization of work.

In general, a trajectory is the expansion of a technology or organizing principle which is characterized by a path-dependent process due to increasing returns. Equivalently, it suggests that the accumulation of experience in a technology or organizing method provides a finite set of options to expand into new applications in the future. As these options are exercised, the value of a subsequent search for new applications experiences eventually declining returns. Indeed, the expansionary path of mass production appears to be far more limited in its prospects today than in the time of Henry Ford.

It is important to realize that a trajec-

Figure 2. Growth of Knowledge of the Firm

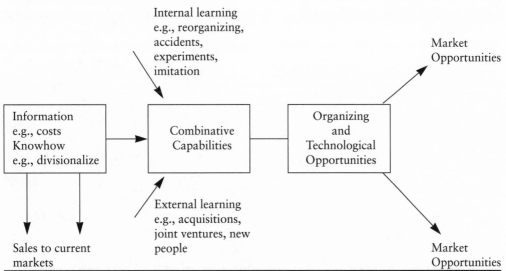

tory works both at the level of the firm and society. To the extent that experience is idiosyncratic and non-tradable, we should expect that firms will differ in their ownership of options and in their trajectories. Yet, clearly, knowledge also accumulates more broadly through spillovers, imitation, and public institutions of education and research. Moreover, many technologies are systems requiring the cooperation of many actors. For these reasons, trajectories are specific to firms, and yet are broadly shared.

We noted above that trajectories are expanding heuristics application of new technologies and methods of organization. I have argued elsewhere that methods of organization provide more potent trajectories for two reasons [Kogut 1991]. One is that a new way of organizing has greater opportunity set by cutting across many industries and markets: Taylorist principles of functional management influenced by manufacturing, financial, and service industries. Second, organizing principles tend to be harder to imitate and are allowed to diffuse; the underlying knowledge is more tacit.

These comments shed light on the important concept of "core competence," as developed by Prahalad and Hamel [1990]. Such a competence is an option, as we have described it. It has future and wide applica-

tions to multiple markets, it is proprietary, and it should be difficult to preempt.

Figure 3 presents two ways to understand a core competence depending upon the structure of the firm. As the structure of the firm changes the incentives and discretion to exercise options, Figures 3A and 3B are not equivalent. In many ways, though, these figures are simple reconfigurations of a value chain which took a sharp right turn. Despite the important turn in thinking regarding the capabilities of the firm, it would be useful to ask similar kinds of questions in either a value chain or capabilities approach to strategy.

In figure 4, I provide an example of an exercise which identifies the link responsible for generating rents by looking at the market, and then by looking at the firm's resources.[18] This process can also be reversed, by first looking at the resources of the firm and then projecting onto the market. In this latter exercise, the focus is on which link of the chain acts as a lever into future markets, which link generates economic rents, and which ones are necessary to protect rents due to transaction or internalization motivations. These approaches—mapping the market onto the firm and mapping the firm onto the market—are not mutually exclusive, quite the contrary.

Figure 3. Knowledge Base of the Firm

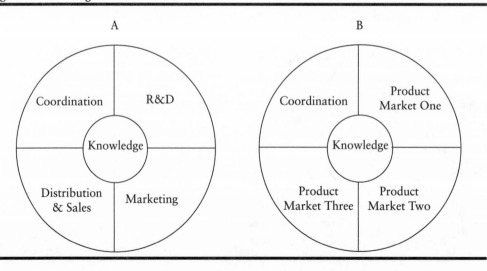

Figure 4. Value Chain Exercise

I. Product-Market Focus
(Products or services are bundles of attributes)
1. What product or service is demanded by but not available to customers?
2. What are the attributes of products or services most desired by customers?
3. To what activities or resources do they correspond? (Mapping exercise).
4. What is the capability of my firm in delivering these services relative to competitors?
5. Is my position sustainable over time and can other firms address this market better?
6. How can we improve our position? (Linkages between resources or markets, cooperative ventures, acquisitions)

II. Resource Focus—Reverse the Process
1. What activities have the greatest potential for generating features (breadth).
2. What markets will reward these features, new technologies, or services (depth).
3. What is the capability of my firm in delivering these services relative to competitors?
4. Is my position sustainable over time and can other firms address this market better?
5. How can we improve our position? (Linkages between resources or markets, cooperative ventures, acquisitions)

The trick has always been to understand the interaction between resources and the market. It is somewhat surprising that this interaction is subject to debate. In one of the two articles I wrote on the value (-added) chain, I argued:

> If the only issue were to determine demand for product attributes, strategy would simply be a market research question. But assets that underlie the production of these attributes are not easily redeployed along the value-added chain, nor is product or process imitation without uncertainty and risk . . . Strategy is thus not just the selection of profitable product markets; it is also the attempt to create a competitive advantage by investing in the link that generates the product attribute most strongly desired by consumers and which corresponds to the firm's distinctive competence relative to its competitors. [Kogut 1985a:17]

Drawing on the distinction of ownership and internalization advantages current in the international literature, it was natural to differentiate "rent-generating" activities from "rent-protecting" investments [Kogut 1984:155]. This definition of strategy, when compared to its earlier citation [see p. 471] follows logically from the notion of firm resources in the context of a specific market. The value chain is simply a heuristic by which to map the market onto the firm's resources, or vice versa.

Some of the confusion in the value chain and resource-based view debate (see Porter [1991]) may be somewhat idiosyncratic to Porter's formulation due to the minimum attention he pays to the distinction between ownership and internalization. In an otherwise appealing figure, the value chain formulation of Porter errs by putting the margin at the end. The question becomes, which activities generate economic rents or which ones protect the firm from transactional hazards? In a dynamic setting, the issue is on what links should "a firm place a bet." Current investments provide valuable options on future opportunities contingent on the evolution of market structure [Kogut 1984:155].

The notion of betting strategies returns us to the relationships among options, trajectories, and capabilities. The term "trajectory" implies that there is a core set of capabilities which generate the options on future growth. The term "option" has a wider application than a core competence

Figure 5. Organizing Principles and Capabilities

Organizing Principles	Capabilities

I. Network (Heterarchic) Organization
   Contingent Budgeting
   International Information systems
   Dispensed Control
	Operating flexibility by
	across-border coordination

II. Kanban System
   "market pull" scheduling
   multiple-manning of machinery
   Just-in-time production
	Flexible response to market
	Variety
	Cost-reduction with quality
	improvement

or trajectory, for it includes many discretionary capabilities, such as abandonment of existing operations. It is insightful to describe growth options as "platforms," which might be core in the sense of experience in a technology, but which also might be strategic in the sense of providing a venue into new markets and countries. It is also useful for our latter discussion to demark another kind of option as giving the right to "switch," such as closing down plants or manufacturing flexibly.

It would be wrong to conclude from this discussion that market structure is no longer important. The distinction between current capabilities and investments in options complicates the usual understanding of competitive positioning. It is necessary to consider not only current structure but also how it may evolve in response to the investments which firms are placing on the development of new capabilities. In this framing, the critical question becomes, how does the investment in platforms affect a firm's current positioning, and hence its short-term chances for survival and opportunity to exercise these options in the long-term?[19]

I have spent considerable time in building up these ideas even though some of them have, separately, been discussed in many literatures. This discussion has sought to stress why options are linked closely to organizing principles which accumulate experientially and which serve as expanding heuristics into new applications. In the next section, these ideas are explored by showing their relevance to four issues central to international strategy: initial investment in a country, choice of entry mode, multinational network, and country competition.

These four applications are not chosen randomly. The principles by which a firm enters a country, organizes its activities globally, and taps into country advantages define the capabilities of the MNC. Figure 5 illustrates this link between how activities are organized and the capabilities which these principles generate. A multinational network is the organizing principle behind operating flexibility. A principle of organizing, such as a Kanban system which arose in a particular national industrial context, is strategically important because it provides the capability to respond quickly to the market with requisite variety and at a competitive price. To return to the Komatsu and Caterpillar case, the reason why neither firm could respond quickly to the inroads of the other was not that they did not understand the capabilities; rather, they did not understand how to operate on the underlying organizing principles.

III. APPLICATIONS TO INTERNATIONAL STRATEGY

Initial Entry as Option

An initial investment into a country has the unique trait of being composed, potentially, of a high option content regarding future expansion. An investment in a foreign country establishes an important growth option, or what can be called a "within-country" option which, by establishing a brand label or simply knowledge of the market, provides a platform for the introduction of new products.

The investment in these options is not itself an **advantage** of being international. This kind of option applies also to an investment by a domestic firm which is diversifying within its country of origin. Though not an advantage due to being international, it has important consequences for the process by which firms expand in a foreign country. Eventually, as the foreign firm grows in the domestic market, the value of the options to launch new products or to diversify within the country becomes the same as for a purely domestic corporation.

Within-country options are significant in the international case because of the Hymer condition, that is, the first international investments are made by firms which lack the organizational knowledge and supporting assets in the foreign market. The first investment carries a large option value as it serves as a platform for subsequent expansion.

The nature of this platform investment consists in the establishment of distribution channels and brand recognition. Yet, an important element concerns the learning of knowledge specific to a country: running a corporation and foreign work force, understanding the local politics, and ultimately identifying useful practices and technologies in the local environment.

In this sense, entry into a country is a sequential process. This perspective has two implications. The first is the need to recognize that the economics of the first entry consists of the profits (or losses) from competing in the current market and of the value of this growth option. In figure 6, I have broken out these two components into cash streams as an illustration.

Second, the initial entry has important strategic implications. As analyzed first by Dixit [1989] and Dumas [1988], the first

Figure 6. Sequential Entry Strategies

- First entry
  —To sell a product
    AND
  —To build the path for subsequent products

- Issues:
  —First entry strategy
  —Leveraging strategies
  —Market Strategy Evaluation

entry decreases the likelihood of exit from a country because switching in and out of a country is costly. It pays to persevere with losses in the short run if there is a possibility (due to exchange rate or price movements) that the future may shine more favorably. Once a foreign firm enters a market, it is much more difficult to deter expansion.

Another way to understand this result is by noting that firms exercise the option to invest in a foreign country during *windows of opportunity*.[20] Such opportunities may result from exchange rate fluctuations which promote the investment in brand labels to support exports; these labels then generate growth options for future expansion. They may result from periods of deregulation when the incumbent domestic rivals are as much at a competitive disadvantage as foreign entrants. An option is an investment in future opportunity.

Choice of Entry Mode

These considerations have a direct implication for the large literature in IB on the internationalization of the firm and sequence of entry into foreign markets.[21] Johanson and Vahlne [1977] analyze the implication of "psychic distance" on the choice of entry mode. Davidson [1980b] showed that the choice of entry tends toward greater control with increasing experience in a country.

These findings are only awkwardly incorporated into a theory of transaction costs and internalization due to market failure. They are, however, readily explained by an evolutionary perspective that stresses the accumulation of knowledge as influencing the capabilities and decisions of firms. In an empirical study of the effects of variations of tacit knowledge on the diffusion of technology, Udo Zander and I have advanced the argument that the firms exist as efficient vehicles for the generation and replication of new knowledge. In one investigation [Kogut and Zander 1992], the time to transfer manufacturing technology was shown to be significantly slower when the knowledge was difficult to codify and teach; transfer was faster, the more intense the competition. When we turned to analyzing the choice of entry mode between direct investment and licensing [Kogut and Zander 1993], a technology which was complex and difficult to codify and to teach was found to be transferred within the firm.

In effect, the capabilities of the firm can be understood as generating a cost advantage *relative* to other firms for the transfer of non-codified and complex knowledge. This cost advantage defined the core boundary of the firm. Knowledge idiosyncratic to a firm tends to be non-tradable in the market.

The above conclusion leads to a rather simple proposition. *The choice of mode (e.g., licensing, marketing, direct investment) is influenced by the cost of replicating this knowledge within the firm relative to a market transaction.* This proposition is only remarkable insofar as the supporting argument does not require any statement regarding market failure or the self-interest of individuals.

These studies did not look at the larger question suggested in the above discussion, why certain technologies may be kept inside a firm because they have a high option content. This statement is consistent with the findings of Walker and Weber [1984] that technological complexity increased the likelihood of internal sourcing. Firms keep in-house new technologies with high option content.

We should expect that the option value will vary across entry modes for two rea-

sons. First, modes differ to the extent that they establish property claims to future options, such as the right to expand a technology into new markets. Second, an option often is the result of investments in experiential learning, and entry modes differ in providing the opportunities for the development of new capabilities of the foreign firm. Licensing, for example, is a way to enter a market with low fixed costs, but the licensing firm does not gain from learning by doing in the foreign country. As often noted, American brands have a reasonable share of the Japanese market through licensing or franchising. While providing an income stream, this mode of entry has limited value as a platform for expansion.

The view of experience has provided an option which carries substantial implications for acquisitions. An acquisition also provides an immediate platform and country expertise from which to launch a firm's array of existing products. For this reason, it is not surprising that acquisitions are the most common way in which direct investment is channeled across borders. *We should expect to find that acquisitions by foreign firms entering a country for the first time reveal a higher premium due to the larger proportion of value in growth options.*

On the other hand, the value of this growth option is diminished by the cost of post-acquisition integration. It can be expected that firms from countries where the culture is very different from the target market will tend to rely on joint ventures, with an option to acquire in the future, as a way to reduce these integration costs.[22] *We should expect to find that international joint ventures terminate more often through the acquisition by the foreign partner.*

These propositions differ significantly from the extant literature. In figure 7, a comparison is made between a static and platform analysis of the choice of entry mode. Usually, the standard approach is to evaluate the investment risk, the costs of control, and transactional hazards; revenues are assumed the same. In a platform

Figure 7. Knowledge Based View of Entry Choice

I. Static Comparison	Wholly-owned	Joint Ventures	License
Risk	High	Moderate	Low
Control Costs	High	Problematic	Low
Transactional Hazards	Low	Moderate	High
II. Platform Capability			
Learning	Costly	Potentially High	Low
Option Value	High	Moderate	—

approach, the option value is also considered; for purposes of illustration, the figure offers the example of learning as generating an option to expand on this acquired capability in the future. In this view, licensing looks much less attractive because the option value is generally low. If the foreign partner has a buy-out clause to a joint venture, an equity cooperative agreement can serve as a platform into a new country. Even without such a clause, if the learning can be transferred out, a joint venture is a potentially powerful way to learn about the foreign country or new managerial and organizational practices. Interestingly, a wholly-owned investment may prove not only to be an expensive way to acquire experience, it may fail to adopt new ways of doing things exactly because it is a replication of the foreign firm's organization. There are many more important implications to flush out, but it should be clear that an option perspective radically changes the traditional thinking about entry.

Multinational Network

It is important to note that an investment in a foreign country generates two kinds of options. One is a "within-country" growth option, as discussed above. The second is the "across-country" switching option provided by operating flexibility of coordinating a multinational network.

The advantage of operating across borders relative to a purely domestic firm lies not in being international; because growth options might be greater for the first time entrant into a country just means that it has a longer way to go in catching up. An international advantage is, however, captured in the ownership of options to flexibly coordinate **multinational** activities. The option value of multinationality is different from that of the benefits of geographic diversification. The benefits of diversification are created by the reduction in variance of the overall portfolio of subsidiary results.[23] An option, on the other hand, is valuable because it gives **managerial discretion** to respond profitably to the realization of uncertain events.

The strategy of operating flexibility and exercising across-country options rides upon the uncertainty in the environment and the organizational capacity to coordinate activities over borders. The value of coordinating across borders is generated by being able to respond to multiple sources of uncertainty: shifting production in response to exchange rates, exiting a country due to government policies, or learning through the transfer of new practices and innovations. The capability to respond to these uncertainties is a product of the ownership of a multinational network of subsidiaries.

Despite the wide currency of the idea of the multinational firm as a network, the evidence for its benefits has been rather thin. Doukas and Travols [1988] found that returns to acquiring firms increased for acquisitions that added to a firm's multinationality. Tsetsekos [1992] and Morck and Yeung [1991] found little evidence for such an effect. The results of Geringer, Beamish, and da Costa [1989] and Kim, Hwang, and Burgers [1989] were mixed, with some indication that performance increased with multinationality.

It should not be ruled out that the benefits of multinational switching options are not fully realized under current incentives and organizational structures. The notion of multinational flexibility provides a false aura of unconstrained managerial discretion.[24] To be consistent with an evolutionary perspective on adaptive heuristic rules, an important question is whether the managerial discretion to exercise such options exists.

By our earlier discussion of the Lessard window, it seems reasonable to suppose that a firm has easiest control in the short run over such decisions as pricing. In the long run, it may be able to build new plants or establish new subsidiaries. Intermediate to these two extremes is the possibility to shift production, or purchase new equipment.

Yet, the difficulty of identifying and managing this flexibility should not be underestimated. A firm must be able to gather the appropriate information to know when the option should optimally be exercised; even when the information is known, exercise may be hindered by organizational features that obstruct flexibility.

Consider, for example, the issue of exercising pricing flexibility across borders, a benefit of multinationality which Buckley and Casson, under price discrimination, listed as one of the major drivers to internalizing transactions across borders. Pricing flexibility appears to have developed rather slowly in MNCs, since firms tend to transfer their home pricing rules to overseas operations. These practices show up in a few popular MBA teaching cases. Caterpillar Tractor is described as using cost-plus pricing rules, with the cost estimates derived from U.S. plant experiences, "Because the company used a uniform dollar pricing policy, dealers all over the world were billed in dollars, irrespective of the origin of the machines. The prices were often based on U.S. manufacturing cost, and when the dollar was strong, the company had to engage in price-cutting" [Harvard Business School [1985]. In the mid 1980s, it switched to competitive pricing, as Komatsu began to make severe in-roads in the United States and elsewhere. Matsushita seems to be following a similar pricing rule. "In general," it is noted in the case, "the (Japanese) plant was expected to absorb the effect of any changes in its costs during the year, while the subsidiary was expected to deal with changes in market conditions **without modifying the transfer price**" [Ghoshal and Bartlett 1987].

These examples point out that managerial discretion is proscribed not only by the environment, but by the internal rules of the corporation. Over time, a firm adaptively seeks to design organizing principles and rules suited to the complexity and uncertainty of operating across many countries. In the short run, this search is localized to remaining close to the practices which it developed in its home market. In fact, Sharp [1987] found substantial persistence of suboptimal pricing rules by American corporations in the United Kingdom.

The implications of a multinational network for redesigning the organizations of the firm has been analyzed by Hedlund [1986], Bartlett and Ghoshal [1989], and Prahalad and Doz [1987]. More recently, the work of Westney [forthcoming] provides positive insight into these issues. The critical element in these approaches is the coupling of the dispersion of resources among countries (i.e., no country leads in all technologies and markets) and uncertainty regarding relative prices and the national origin of new capabilities.

There is an underestimation, which is a characteristic of organizational theory in general, of the proactive role of firms responding to uncertainty. The IB literature to its credit has not shared this presumption. For example, Ghoshal and Nohria [1989] relate the differentiation of subsidiaries in response to the uncertainty and resources of the local environment. It strikes me that understanding the multinational network as an organizational evolution in response to the diversity of national resources and the uncertainty of the environment should have important implications for understanding the structure and design of organizations in general.

Country Competition

The work of Sharp [1987], Hedlund and Aman [1983], Stopford and Wells [1972], and Franko [1976] on the slow adaptation of the organization of the firm to international markets points to the importance of understanding the national origins of MNCs. It is now understood that these structures were adaptive responses of corporations to the international environment. Through comparative research, the conventional view made two implicit assumptions: that product innovations and critical resources were located in the home country and that the firm was not already international.[25]

European companies, which had internationalized earlier under a period of high tariffs, faced a different process of adaptation to international pressures. Initial conditions and the accumulated experience differed for European companies and hence so did the path of their adaptation to international markets. European firms were organized significantly different from American firms, as the studies by Channon [1973], and Dyas and Thanheiser [1976] document. Bartlett [1986] called this effect of history the bias of "administrative heritage." In evolutionary terms, it is the outcome of cumulative and differentiated experiences, generating a property of path dependence and irreversibility.

A more subtle issue is the resource bias in this approach. Because these structures grew to sell products designed for the home market—much as an evolutionary view would expect—the adaptive problem was not seen initially as the importance of tapping into foreign resources. It is also possible that the United States held a wide leadership in technologies and market demand, and hence resources were greater in the home market. As a result, the resource abundance of the U.S. market may have crippled American corporations from developing the capability to assimilate and transfer learning from foreign countries.

These considerations raise the wider observation that because countries have differed historically in the kinds of products which they preferred and in their institutional and economic resources, they have evolved different capabilities over time. It is important to note that these capabilities are often firm-embodied, but country-specific. There is, in effect, a body of national organizing principles which tend to characterize firms derived from the same origins.[26]

This observation has many implications, but I wish to note only the implication for understanding the difference in time horizon and the investment in growth options. The ability to identify and develop activities with high option content is itself a kind of knowledge, or capability, which appears to vary by country. There may well be differences in the time horizons among firms depending on their national origins.

Even if foresight is assumed, firms may not be able to engage in forward-looking plans if the selection environment is too severe. A firm struggling to survive in the market will be unable to divert resources to projects with value that cannot be realized until the future. In part, this observation regresses to a question of the foresight of financial institutions to lend money to such projects. Clearly, given the variance in financial institutions across borders (from banking to equity based systems), the degree of foresight is likely to vary by country (see, Lessard and Perotti [1990]; Berglof [1991]; Aoki [1988]). Even if financial institutions should be endowed with foresight, the binding constraint on firms may not be financial but an inability to divert human resources to new projects with distant payoffs.[27]

An emerging argument is that country advantages may also be understood as generating trajectories which pull foreign direct investment (FDI). The traditional view has been that firms may choose to source raw materials or cheap labor in foreign markets.

Due to the work of Cantwell [1989] and others, there is also recognition that the technological leadership of certain countries draws FDI. Empirical evidence for this proposition is found by Kogut and Chang [1991] and Shan [1992] regarding pulling Japanese investment into the United States.

In this sense, the economics of a foreign investment consists of the value of learning skills in different countries. There is a more dynamic element insofar as sourcing or selling overseas permits firm participation in further development, or trajectory, of the resident countries. This enjoyment of localized spillover suggests that these investments should also be seen as platform investments generating growth options for exploitation in the local market and, if transferred, internationally.

It is an inadequately answered question why the capturing of this spillover should require a local presence. If there is a country factor in international competition, then we essentially must explain why this advantage is non-tradable. Access to financial markets is becoming less compelling as an explanation. The answer to this question easily follows from the notion of firms learning experientially and incrementally on the basis of their cumulative knowledge which define their organizing and technological capabilities. The distinction between information and know-how is useful in this regard. A local presence for tapping into a trajectory seems to be a minor issue if the knowledge is only information; it if is know-how, then we return to the importance of organizational knowledge and the importance of experience.

IV. FUTURE RESEARCH

Because the above comments were meant to describe the elements to a school of thought and its implications for international strategy, the implied research agenda can be rather wide ranging. There are a few topics which are easily within reach.

An important area of research is understanding the growth of the firm in the context of the process of birth, growth, and death in the home market. Internationalization may be seen as being squeezed from the home market (as suggested by Mascarenhas [1985]), or as the growth of successful firms that spill across borders. The work by Mitchell, Shaver, and Yeung [1991] is promising in this regard.

The internationalization of a firm in a particular country is a well-studied phenomenon. The study has tended to underestimate the sequential entry as riding on the developmental platform of the initial entry. We would expect that international acquisitions by firms investing in a country for the first time would have a positive effect on the premium of the acquiring firm's stock, contrary to domestic acquisition findings. The work by Chiu [1993] should be able to address this issue.

Despite much of the fanfare about cross-border flexibility, the documentation of this practice is still rather thin. There are formal models of production shifting across borders, but the empirical evidence is lacking. Most of the examples are case studies of the transfer of product and technological innovations, which, though interesting, give no assessment of their share of overall innovations. However, evidence for the attraction of investment into innovative areas is increasing.

An important issue is the organizational underpinning of a strategy of multinational flexibility. We have stressed the application of organizing principles to establish information systems and to structure the corporation. In many respects, there has been too much attention paid to network structures relative to the role of information systems and heuristic rules. There has been some work in the area of heuristic rules, such as Sharp's [1987] thesis on the change in pricing rules in U.S. subsidiaries in the United Kingdom, and on information systems, such as Hagströms's [1991] thesis on information systems in a large MNC.

Lastly, an area of research already in full swing is the application of evolutionary thinking to country competition. There are many examples of this approach, from Dosi, Cantwell, and Pavitt on technological trajectories, to my own research stressing the localized diffusion of organizing principles in generating long-term patterns in country competition. It is my guess that national principles of organization will prove to be the instrumental factor in understanding capabilities of countries and historical cycles in national leadership.

NOTES

1. See Kogut (1989).

2. In a wider account, we should also note the importance of industrial economic approaches, starting with Stephen Hymer but developed by Richard Caves and Charles Kindleberger; and the historical studies of Alfred Chandler and his students (especially Mira Wilkins), whose work blended well with that Vernon, Lou Wells, Lawrence Franko, and others—as the book by Stopford and Wells shows.

3. The names cited do not by any means exhaust the list, and certainly, the works of Alan Rugman and Jean François Hennart deserve mention in any wider accounting of this school of thought.

4. See Solvell (1987) for an exploration of the links between these two schools.

5. See Kobrin (1991) and Roth and Morrison (1991) for studies on the global integration/national responsiveness dimensions. Fuller and Stopford (1991) provide a rich and incisive study of the U.K. white goods industry in this vein.

6. See Barney (1986) and Dierickx and Cool (1989). See also Kagono et al., (1985:255ff) for a perceptive evolutionary discussion along the lines of the above citation, as well as the recent article by Collis (1991). In many respects, the origins of this approach lies with Aharoni (1966).

7. See the elegant work by Arthur Brian (1988) and the insightful historical interpretation by Paul David (1985).

8. These terms are taken from Kogut and Kulatilaka (1991).

9. Republished in Bartlett and Ghoshal (1992).

10. For a terse description of the mathematical approaches to these problems, see Dixit (1990, chaps. 10, 11). As evident in chapter 11, this formulation of stock and control variables under uncertainty is equivalent to the treatment of options through stochastic dynamic programming. For an application of dynamic programming to the investment decision in learning, see Kogut and Kulatilaka (1992).

11. See Mark Casson's contribution to these volumes for an economic treatment of culture.

12. See Teece (1977).

13. To a certain extent, this behavior fits the description of Japanese firms. See Dore (1986) and Whittaker (forthcoming).

14. The following draws from Kogut and Zander (1992).

15. We will not pursue this point further, but this argument is essentially Olson's (1982) explanation why political interest groups inside a country block progress. See also Boddewyn's (1988) admonition to pay closer attention to the political dimension.

16. A reader with an economics background might wonder why this avenue of development was chosen instead of an explication of the firm as a production function, with heterogeneity explained by firm effects. Implicitly, we are suggesting that these firm effects can be traced back to differences in knowledge, with the proportion of tradable and imitable knowledge reflected in a common technological shift parameter.

17. These ideas are drawn from Kogut and Kulatilaka (1994).

18. I have expanded this portion of this chapter in response to the comments of Alan Morrison who suggested a more thorough comparison of the value chain with a resource-based view perspective on the firm. As I have noted elsewhere (Kogut 1989; Kogut 1985), my perspective was influenced by Don Lessard and the general discussion (originating, I presume, from the Boston offices of McKinsey) in the early 1980s. But the article by Seev Hirsch (1976), in particular, made a strong impression on me.

19. See Kulatilaka and Perotti (1992) for an analytical treatment.

20. See Kogut and Kulatilaka (1994) for simulation results. Tsetsekos and Gombola (1992) find some evidence that investors recognize the value in the option to open and close plant operations.

21. See Root (1987) for a comprehensive coverage.

22. See Kogut and Singh (1988) for some evidence on cultural distance and entry choice

and Hill, Hwang, and Kim (1990) for a discussion of different influences on entry mode choice.

23. This diversification, because shareholders can achieve it more efficiently through capital markets, has empirically been shown to be of minor value to the multinational corporation. See Jacquillat and Solnik (1978).

24. The following is drawn from Kogut and Kulatilaka (1994).

25. The recognition of this bias was the cornerstone of Burenstam Linder (1961), Vernon (1966), and Davidson (1976). See its recent revival by Porter (1990). For an early analysis of the home country bias on a firm, see Perlmutter (1969).

26. See Chandler (1990); for an empirical test of the argument that foreign direct investment is the transfer of organizing principles across borders and that the American decline stems from the diffusion of the principles of mass production and the standardization of work, see Kogut (1992).

27. A more difficult issue is that, from a macroeconomic perspective, the struggle for survival may be common to many firms due to business cycles or the penetration by foreign firms. These issues raise important problems of how solvency is resolved under bankruptcy and whether credit can be deemed to ever short.

■ ■ ■

Strategic Management and International Business Research: An Empirical Convergence?
Yves L. Doz

International Business (IB) has long been a field in search of an identity. It was seen as an applied "appendage" to one or another discipline, depending where one sat: international economics, finance, strategy, comparative cultures, and so on. Scholars who were suspected of not being able to "make it" in the mainstream discipline went to its international application, where they could borrow concepts and theories from the main discipline and apply them to the wide-ranging opportunities offered by "IB." The teaching of IB reflected this soul searching, with courses ranging from very broad subjects such as "the world economy" to narrow techniques such as the tools of foreign trade or currency hedging.

The emergence of the manufacturing multinational as a phenomenon—however belatedly recognized by most management scholars—, the challenge it was assumed to create for nation states, and the intensification of global competition coming with freer trade and investment in the 1960s shifted the scholars' attention to the multinational company (MNC) as an institution, and to both the reasons for and the implications of the development of such an institution. IB became international management, and it had found its object of study.

Both causes and consequences of MNCs were first addressed by borrowing from economics, in the usual fashion of IB. Conventional industrial organization economics provided the starting point [Caves 1971]. The phenomenon was so rich, in its content, that multiple models were required. Economics itself was not standing still. The articulation of transaction cost economics [Williamson 1975], evolutionary economics [Nelson and Winter 1982], and agency theory [Jensen and Meckling 1976], and more broadly the development of institutional economics all shed light on the reasons for the existence of MNCs and provided some propositions on their consequences and on the management issues they are facing.

At the same time, or earlier, management scholars started to devote attention to the strategic, organizational, and management process choices made by MNCs (e.g., Fayerweather [1960], Perlmutter [1969], Fouraker and Stopford [1968], Stopford and Wells [1972]). Interestingly, the relationship between strategic management and the emerging interest in international management was not strong. This was partly due to the discrepancy between the process nature of the dominant strategy paradigm (the "concept of strategy," as articulated by Learned, Christensen, Andrews, and Bower [1965] and formalized by Ansoff [1965]), and the content nature, derived from industrial organization economics, of the emerging international management research. It is only with Prahalad [1975] and then Doz [1976] that content and process were bridged by applying to MNCs a contingency framework to the industry structure-strategic choice-organizational design-management process interactions in the context of global competition.

After briefly discussing the historical separateness of the strategic management and multinational management fields, and their distinct evolutions, this paper explores the opportunity for a more fruitful interaction between the two fields. In particular, the emergence of the resource-based paradigm in strategic management, and the growing recognition that firm-specific intangible capabilities provide the most distinctive resources, lead to the competence-based model of competitiveness which may provide an opportunity for a more explicit coverage of the two fields. The intensity of global competition, and the globalization of firms, may also, in a phenomenological sense, lead to the merger of both fields.

In the competence-based perspective of global competition, this paper proposes for debate a series of tentative research issues deserving of further intellectual investment.

IB research, before international management research, started by drawing on international trade economics and by explaining the evolution of trade flows over time. It relied mostly upon traditional macroeconomics. Moving out of the constraints of traditional comparative advantage explanations, Vernon [1966] proposed a dynamic explanation of trade flows in industrial goods based upon an international product life cycle concept integrating demand and supply considerations into a model of sequential product market and national industry development and decline as various countries developed over time. In this work

Vernon brought the analysis to the level of specific products and escaped the equilibrium constraints of economics. In a separate effort, the seminal work of Hymer [1960] brought the debate to firm-specific explanations in analyzing the reason for foreign direct investment (FDI). So did Dunning's [1958] work on U.S. investments in Britain. Building on the contributions of Hymer, Dunning, and Vernon, a whole stream of research drew upon models of oligopolistic competition to analyze the investment strategies of MNCs (e.g., Kindleberger [1969], Caves [1971], Knickerbocker [1973], Davidson [1980a]). This research stream drew upon industrial organization economics and did not challenge the assumptions of firms being similarly capable but for size. Technology differences play a key role in these models but not firm-specific competencies, a departure from Hymer's work. By identifying strong "follow-the-leader" biases in the investment behavior of companies, this work did violate the equilibrium assumptions. Firms could not be empirically shown to analytically choose the "best" course of action given the information available. Yet, the models developed by Vernon and his followers were deterministic ones. They did not place much emphasis on management direction and strategic choice to explain corporate behavior. Although clinical studies of foreign investment were proceeding in the same time frame (e.g., Aharoni [1966]), their evidence of a fairly complex behavioral decision process was not incorporated in the "Vernon" studies, which considered aggregate patterns of investments rather than individual decisions and relied on economics rather than behavioral models. In retrospect, this line of research almost prefigures the population ecology theory.

Strategic management did not make a contribution to this research, largely because strategic management research itself was in its infancy. The "concept of strategy" as formulated in Learned, Christensen, Andrews, and Bower [1965], formalized by Ansoff [1965], and expanded by Andrews [1971], was a normative process model of top management's task in formulating and implementing strategy, but not a theory, nor a framework, explaining the competitive activities of firms. The model had little theoretical content, and while the process it advocates is posited as universal, the content is situational.[1] Strategic management, thus, had little to contribute to international management research.

The main contribution came not from strategic management per se, but from business history: Chandler's (1962) analysis of divisionalization in the US industry inspired research on the strategic and structural evolution of MNCs as a complement to the stream of research on strategy and structure in domestic industries (Fouraker and Stopford, 1968, Stopford and Wells, 1972). Such research was subsequently extended to comparative studies between the US, Europe and Japan (Franko, 1976, Dyas, 1972, Thanheiser, 1972, Yoshino, 1968).

Yet, as multinational companies developed further, Hymer's seminal work took on more importance, in particular the issue of why FDI is an instrument of economic integration. Dunning, in studying U.S. investments in Europe and later in developing the "eclectic" theory of the MNC, stresses the importance of "ownership-specific" advantages in foreign investment, i.e., company-specific advantages that more than outweigh the cost of operating in an unfamiliar distant environment [Dunning 1973, 1980, 1981; Hirsch 1976]. Dunning, however, argues that such ownership advantage includes legally protected rights such as brands and patents, commercial monopolies (for example, on raw materials), or economies of scale, or "surplus" entrepreneurial capacity (building on Penrose [1959]). The mere fact of operating in multiple markets also provides for some risk reduction and income maximization opportunities, for example, through transfer pricing.

Transaction cost economics, formalized by Williamson [1975] building on Coase [1937], provided another bridge between economics and international management, by explaining why certain advantages are linked to ownership when others are not. In particular, as discussed by Arrow [1974,

1985] and elaborated by Hennart [1982] and Teece [1985], transaction cost economics contributes to an explanation of why ownership advantages are particularly important in the exploitation of technologies and even more so in the exploitation of know-how.

Transaction cost economics proved very useful in explaining the development of the MNC as an institutional form to internalize certain types of transactions and also provide a theory to determine and predict the "boundaries" of MNCs (i.e., which transactions would be internalized, which would remain market transactions). In particular, the transaction cost approach shows that non-tradeable skills, for which markets fail, may lie at the heart of MNC development.

Agency theory, with its emphasis on control issues in various forms of contractual relationships, contributed to MNC scholars by casting issues of control in "outcome" and "behavior" terms, a useful distinction. Agency theory is helpful in its provision of the "base core" economic theory of headquarter-subsidiary relationships in MNCs, against which actual practices and behaviors can be researched.

Interestingly, as the field of IB evolved toward that of MNC management, it borrowed more from microeconomics and institutional economics than from strategic management, perhaps reflecting the background of the involved researchers and the relative development of the two fields.

Both strategic management and international business were fields in search of a theory, whereas economics offered an increasingly well developed theory to pick from, and provided some structuring frameworks to analyze and interpret the complexity of the MNC phenomenon. Where strategic management provided useful structuring frameworks, such as on the relationship between strategic choices, organizational structures and management processes, the relationships between the two fields could evolve constructively.

Indeed, it is only with the development of contingency theory [Lawrence and Lorsch 1967] and the emergence of a process school of policy research (Bower [1970]; see Bower and Doz [1977] for a summary), that empirical research on the organization and management processes of MNCs started and that both fields started to significantly overlap.

Prahalad's research [1975] focused on the processes by which the management of a business perceived changing environmental demands and responded to these by redirecting the attention of managers, shifting strategic direction, and realigning power and influence process, to make these consistent with the new conditions. The work of Doz [1976,1979] analyzed on a comparative basis the management processes used in several companies, and in several businesses in each company, to manage the tensions between the needs to optimize responses to national markets and government policies and those for strategic coordination and operational integration of the firm's activities between countries. This work brought together the economics and political analysis of MNCs and drew their organizational and managerial consequences. Doz [1979,1980] also analyzed how differences in competitive positions between firms in the same industry affected their responses to the tension outlined above. Bartlett [1979] then compared the changes in the management systems and processes used by companies affected by shifts in demands for integration and responsiveness, and further extended the understanding of redirection processes. Bartlett [1981] also considered how the "institutional heritage" of a firm, embodied in its attention and action routines, constrained the development of new capabilities and constituted a form of "organizational inertia" that top management must pay attention to in strategic redirection.

The emerging multinational management paradigm coming from this cumulative work brought together several strands within the literature. It captured substance and process in a single framework which could work at various levels (industry, business, function, management process, the individual) and could be used both to assess static balances between conflicting forces and dynamic changes in balance over time [Doz and Prahalad 1991].

Independently from this line of work, combining strategic management and multinational management, a similar line of work emerged in Sweden, rooted in clinical research based upon the experience of Swedish MNCs [Hedlund 1981,1986].

In the mid-1980s, Ghoshal added a significant dimension to the research on MNC management. A detailed study of innovation processes led to the conceptualization of MNCs as "differentiated networks" in which various affiliates play different roles and the headquarters of which play a more or less central and active role [Ghoshal 1986]. This led to a more general argument conceptualizing MNCs as differentiated networks [Ghoshal and Nohria 1989] and to the application of network theory to MNC management [Ghoshal and Bartlett 1990].

In turn, this line of research provided the opportunity for more directly linking organizational theory (in particular organizational sociology and institutional theory) to MNC management. While scholars of the MNC had increasingly borrowed from organization theory, this borrowing had seldom been disciplined or systematic [Doz and Prahalad 1991]. It is only recently that the linkage has been clearly established [Ghoshal and Westney 1992]. Both institutionalization theory [Meyer and Rowan 1983; Di Maggio and Powell 1983; Zucker 1983] and the organizational power and dependence theory [Crozier 1964, Pfeffer 1977] are extremely useful to MNC scholars insofar as they provide the basis for theories (such as the Prahalad and Doz "Integration/Responsiveness" model) that can straddle various levels of aggregation, from the individual to interunit relations in a MNC, to interorganizational relations and to organizational fields.

None of these contributions, however, had a mainstream influence on the strategic management field. If anything, contributions to MNC management research were made by "dissidents" from the strategic management field who were more interested in process research than in the mainstream's increasingly analytic work of strategy researchers. This led to some interesting tensions between the fields of multinational management and strategic management [Bartlett and Ghoshal 1991; Schendel 1991] with a view of international management becoming wider and farther reaching in its eclectic theoretical base, and one of strategic management becoming increasingly hostage to economics.

Indeed, the strategic management field came to be divided between the "content" and the "process" researchers, the former taking their inspirations from microeconomics (via Michael Porter) and the latter from organizational theorists and from managers in the field. Forays by industry structure analysts into global competition and multinational management led them to conceptualizations that used new labels but were not fundamentally different from those of the MNC scholars (e.g., Porter's [1986] "configuration-coordination model"). The linkage was not very strong, and the two fields continued on largely separate paths.

With the exception of the small group of process researchers whose work is discussed above, we have so far stressed the relative separateness of the international management and strategic management fields.

However, in the 1980s, the strategic management field started to undergo a deep transformation. The dominant strategy paradigm of the 1970s and 1980s came to be challenged. It conceived of strategic management largely as a positioning exercise: deciding in which industries to compete and which type of strategy to follow [Porter 1980]. The concept of mobility barriers [Caves and Porter 1977] and that of strategic groups provided a conceptual framework to analyze competition within industries (see McGee and Thomas [1986]). Much research in strategic management was seen as paradigmatic research within the industry and competitive analysis structural paradigm.

Empirical research, however, started to cast doubt both on the significance of strategic groups in performance terms (firms in the same group may offer more variation in performance than firms belonging to different groups, see Cool and Schendel [1988]), and on the significance of industry structural analysis (according to Rumelt's [1991]

analysis, which industry a business unit belongs to seems to have very little correlation with its financial performance). Further, Rumelt's research seems to indicate that stable long-term differences between the business units competing in the same industry account for most of the variance in performance between business units. There is unexplained inertia to differences in business unit performance and industry structural conditions do not play a discriminating role.

Multinational management scholars, starting with Hymer [1960], had long stressed the importance of firm-specific assets in competitiveness as a way for MNCs to overcome the disadvantages of operating in new, less familiar, environments. Finally, strategic management researchers were willing to consider similar arguments, focusing on their own conceptualization from firm-specific "resources" to skills and know-how as the main determinants of competitive advantage.[2] More specifically, both the MNC researchers and those looking at how firms exploit technological advantages were considering integrative organizational capabilities as the key [Doz and Prahalad 1988; Nelson 1991; Teece, Pisano and Shuen 1990]. The significance of the organizational capability perspective on global competitive advantage was reinforced by the relative weakening of other factors.

Historically, both skills and markets have been differentiated. Skills were unevenly distributed between regions and firms [Hamel 1990] and may have been the result of idiosyncratic local cultivation processes [Porter 1990]. European companies created science-based inventions but suffered from a poor understanding of new markets and often failed to apply innovations to markets successfully [Doz 1992; Hamel and Prahalad 1991]. Amer-ican companies succeeded at important product and market innovations but failed to buttress initial successes with fast improvements in cost and quality. They fell prey to Japanese companies that design manufacturing and product development for speed, efficiency, flexibility, and "trial and error" market learning and product introduction [De Meyer 1991; Nevens, Summe and Uttal

1990; Hamel and Prahalad 1991]. Similarly, management skills and the underlying process disciplines were also unevenly distributed. Japanese companies developed stronger capabilities to blend diverse technologies into collective know-how that resulted in deeply rooted and widely held competencies [Prahalad and Hamel 1990], improving, for example, product integrity [Clark and Fujimoto 1990] and developing joint product, process and commercialization skills).

While these skills and competence differences have played a major role in global competitive battles [Womack, Jones, and Roos 1990; Clark and Fujimoto 1990], their importance is likely to diminish in the future as the capabilities of (surviving) firms along these dimensions tend to converge. It is unlikely that differences in management disciplines—no matter how wide a gap they create between competitors—will result in stable, sustainable, competitive advantage differences between competitors.

In a similar fashion, gaps in market access have narrowed as American, European, and Japanese firms rush to build market presence worldwide. Competitors with more or less matching market access capabilities may emerge [Doz and Prahalad 1988]. They will "cover the world" in approximately equal terms.

In summary, we observe a convergence process between global competitors taking place along several dimensions: global market access infrastructure and marketing skills, management disciplines that improve the integrity and the value to customers of the products, and competencies and technologies which allow product innovation and market creation [Doz and Hamel 1992]. However, which firms manage this convergence process most effectively depends upon where they start and what new capabilities they need. Market access may be easier or more difficult depending upon the type of products one sells and the types of markets one seeks to penetrate. The nature of the product or the service, the type of product sold, the policies of governments all play a role in making market access competencies more or less difficult.

Similarly, management disciplines may be more or less difficult to acquire and develop. Complex process skills, in which social and technical characteristics are closely intertwined and which are embedded in the organization and conditioned by its culture, may be much more unique than other skills. They may allow competitive advantage to be gained in otherwise unlikely industries (see the description of Minebea's entry into DRAMS [Collis 1991]) which would be very unattractive to a firm not having these unique competencies. Conversely, lags in management disciplines may make access to otherwise attractive industries infeasible. Most disciplines, however, may be codified and become more easily imitable and transferable by third-party channels such as consulting or engineering firms.

Beyond market access skills and management disciplines, the ability to integrate, combine, blend, and leverage multiple skills may give rise to "core competencies" in corporations [Prahalad and Hamel 1990]. These core competencies are aggregative and combinatory in nature and thus embedded in organizational capabilities. It is not the range of skills and disciplines which provide competitive advantage but the ability to blend and integrate them in imaginative and unique ways. While the notion of unique "core" competencies is not new (it can be traced back to Selznick's [1957] concept of "distinctive competence"), one observes a resurgence in the importance of the core competence concept as strategic management scholars start to draw the implications from the empirical "anomalies" detected in the analytical strategic management paradigm. Firm-specific differences in competence accumulation and leverage are hypothesized to explain the large part of the variance in business unit performance that cannot be ascribed to industry setting and strategic position in an industry.

Similarly, in the research on multinationals, the more closely MNCs come to be matched in access to labor and other production factors, in timely access to key markets worldwide and in access to management disciplines, the more the differences in their relative success comes to be understandable only in terms of the relative integrative organizational capabilities of firms [Doz and Prahalad 1988].

As the interests of the strategic management field were not, until very recently, focused on competencies as sources of competitive advantages, empirical research on this emerging paradigm is in its infancy. Such research is difficult to carry out as it is very data intensive. Analytical research faces the task of isolating company-specific capabilities from a number of traditional economic variables, such as scale or cumulative investment. Focusing on only one function (e.g., R&D), using simple proxy variables (e.g., new product sales), and restricting the research to industries where public domain statistical data are abundant (e.g., pharmaceuticals) already yield complex research designs [Cool and Dierickx 1992]. The clinical route is equally fraught with difficulties, not just in observing deeply embedded, often partly tacit, corporate processes, but also in the longitudinal analysis of these processes to establish causality [Van de Ven 1992]. The integrative nature of core competencies also lends to processes which are not easily parceled out and for which many variables may have influences [Hogarth, Michaud, Doz, and Van der Heyden 1991].

Recent research on MNCs [Ghoshal 1986; Ghoshal and Bartlett 1988, 1990; Ghoshal and Nohria 1989] contributes to this emerging line of research by identifying enabling conditions and impediments to innovation processes in MNCs. Similarly, the work of Hedlund and Rolander [1990] on the "heterarchic" MNC contributes to the same line of research. More broadly, the management of innovation and new product development researchers has made the most progress along this line, perhaps because new product development was the most obvious area of differential performance between firms and an area which made major differences in their international competitiveness [Clark and Fujimoto 1991; Nishiguchi 1992].

In sum, with an emerging agreement on

different competencies as an explanation of stable differences in business unit (and firm) performance over time, and while the characteristics of more or less competent firms begin to be identified, the process by which such competencies are built and come to differ significantly between firms are not well researched, perhaps with a few exceptions in the area of new product development.

The development of collective capabilities in organizations is not a well-researched process. Paradoxically, the absence of such process is better understood. We understand more about why some organizations cannot learn than we do about why or how some do learn.

This has led to a rich literature on strategic renewal and organizational learning, but one which may fail to address some central issues [Levitt and March 1988]. It has also led to an emerging new paradigm of the complex organization, as a network of empowered customer responsive entrepreneurs, supported by a common infrastructure and functional specialists and committed to collective, rather than purely individual success. While this vision is rich in metaphor, it is still relatively short on empirical research, perhaps because the empowered network (or its close analog the "heterarchic" MNC) are ideal types. Hence, no observable company will comprise all the key features of this model.

An interesting literature drawing upon individual learning has also emerged, analyzing why organizational contexts and processes, and how they are interpreted and felt by members of the organization, may prevent learning [Argyris 1985]. In fact, most of the literature on organizational learning transfers models of individual learning to organizations, thus dealing more with the issue of individual learning in an organizational context.

Another stream of the literature, building on Simon [1957] has been more recently developed around Nelson and Winter [1982] and others, considering organizational learning as "embedded routines" that can evolve slowly. This line of research shows the importance of learning in organizations, and the criticality of effective embedded routines to organizational performance.

The linkages between individual and organizational learning, and the various types of learning objects and learning types, that may be required as one moves from the individual to the collective level have not been researched in depth, except, again on a few examples of new product development processes [Nonaka 1991; Nonaka and Hedlund 1993]. This, however, is central to the development of a detailed understanding of how firm-specific competencies are built and honed over time. Among the key issues to be researched, are:

Moving from individual skills to collective corporate skills, in particular, motivating individuals to contribute and share their skills, transforming tacit skills of individuals into explicit skills and then embedding them into action procedures ("scripts") that can be learned by others and improved via practice, and which ultimately have become part of the tacit, but collective, routine repertoire of the corporation.

"De novo" skills vs. skill transfer. Skill transfers play a key role in MNC success, obviously. The duplication of skills in different contexts starts to be researched and to some extent understood (e.g., Japanese "transplants" in the United States, Disney in France, etc.,). The ability to develop skills *de novo,* in particular when these skills are not first developed in the home country, is less understood. More research building on Ghoshal's work is needed to better understand the "polycentric" MNCs, in particular the development and diffusion of skills (not just products) when such development is centered outside the home country of the MNC. As an example, it seems that it is quite feasible for Nissan to develop cars specially adapted to the European or the North American markets, but does Nissan develop new skills in Europe or North America that are of value to Nissan worldwide? Polycentric skill development may be even more difficult than polycentric product development.

Skill development vs. skill internalization. MNCs access skills via acquisitions,

alliances, technology partnerships, and technology transfer agreements. Although we have argued that many competencies are essentially non-tradable, acquisitions may allow access to them as a "functioning" set, and alliances may provide the means to co-practice them and learn from a skilled partner [Hamel 1991; Doz and Hamel 1992]. More research is needed on effective and ineffective skill transfers in acquisitions and alliances, particularly tacit core competencies, beyond the clinical insight provided thus far [Haspeslagh and Jemison 1991; Doz and Hamel forthcoming].

Competence cultivation. While conceptual frameworks exist (e.g., Hogarth et al. [1991]) and are rooted in well-documented case studies, the microprocesses of competence cultivation are not very well known. The emerging literature on product development teams provides a starting point (e.g., Fruin [1992]; Dougherty [1990]), the processes are neither well documented nor analyzed, particularly not in the context of MNCs. More broadly, as stressed above, the processes of organizational learning are still not very well known, particularly the processes by which effective (or ineffective) action routines are developed in organizations.

Skill mobilization and leverage. Beyond the range of skills cultivated by the firm, its ability to access, blend, and leverage them is essential.

Accessing

Access requires overcoming fragmentation. In particular, any subunit must be able to access skills cultivated in other units. Awareness of the skills developed in other units is a first hurdle. Some companies maintain "catalogues" of skills or organize internal technology "fairs," usually in the form of R&D conferences in which various subunits present and discuss their projects and findings. The "catalogue" and "fair" approaches, however, suffer from their formality: many are of the most relevant embedded skills are of a tacit collective variety, and may only be revealed and understood in practice. Mobility of key personnel between units, and/or the setting up of joint teams is thus required beyond the more formal communication and exchange processes.

Access requires more than awareness, very often co-practice too. Effective access thus also requires, on the part of the unit which has cultivated a skill, the willingness to train members of other units in the practice of their skill. Such active sharing may require the units to work in horizontal networks rather than vertical hierarchies [Aoki 1988] and to make frequent use of cross-functional interunit teams [Hogarth et al. 1991].

The lateral communication pattern requires both an ability to connect subsets of skills and an ability to contribute key skills. Depth of know-how in a specific field and an understanding of how to use this know-how in conjunction with adjacent skills are required. Control systems exclusively based on subunit performance may undermine such horizontal networking [Prahalad and Hamel 1990].

Although one can argue that participants in the lateral network should find their own benefits in the collaboration, and therefore control systems based on subunit performance should not prevent mutually beneficial cooperation, one observes that starting such horizontal networking processes usually requires some encouragement; its costs are felt before any benefits can be found. Management systems therefore need to encourage cooperation, at least initially.

Blending

Interunit teams may also be important to allow the blending of various skills to exploit new opportunities: such opportunities may become visible only once the team has acquired a deep understanding of the various skills available. Individuals, or subgroups, deeply familiar with only one subset of skills might not be in a position to conceive of the opportunity. Fragmented knowledge of skills leads to fragmented perceptions of opportunities. In other words, rather than be set up in response to a known need to blend skills for a particular purpose, teams may be assembled to become deeply familiar with a complete range of skills and to "dream up"

new applications for that range of skills. This requires that the internal debate between subunits is driven by the search for new opportunities rather than the apportioning of benefits from existing activities.

Leveraging

This requires that new opportunities be imagined which draw on existing skills, and that the whole organization be mobilized to imagine, identify, and pursue such opportunities. Leveraging assumes an ability for a person within the company to become free from perceptions based too narrowly upon "served-markets" and to constantly dream up areas where the skill mix of the company might provide competitive advantage. Although there is no surefire way to maximize the leverage obtained from existing core skills, a few approaches may improve the odds.

For example, testing one's business logic in the context of another business may lead to successful "competitive innovation," such as Canon's application of camera product logic to the photocopy market which had been previously served by Xerox as an on-premises service business. Moving from an analysis of product use to the latent functionalities served by the product may also contribute to improved leveraging, by allowing identification of poorly served markets [Hamel and Prahalad 1991]. Building a better interaction between the technologists and the market specialists may also help to identify leveraging opportunities, by providing for a more "visceral" sense of product functional integrity [Dougherty 1992].

Relying on core skills can also help reduce the cost of "experimental" leveraging, by reducing the cost of product failures. Having a few core platforms (as with Sony's Walkman where three basic platforms yield about two hundred product variations), increasing the speed and reducing the cost of new product development, achieving greater manufacturing flexibility and ramp up speed can all contribute to both making more abundant successes and making failures affordable, hence allowing for more risky "experimental" leveraging of skills. Recombining existing competencies to achieve "white space" management (a term coined by Hamel and Prahalad [1991]) may also yield new opportunities.

Both the fields of strategic management and IB have moved away from their flirtations with microeconomics and placed greater emphasis on firm-specific competencies as sources of competitive advantage. This is not such an "innovation" in the IB field as the theme of firm-specific intangible advantages has been there all along, both in research works that explain aggregate MNC behavior and in research works that analyze how they are managed. Strategic management has evolved differently from wide process models, to sophisticated, albeit disconnected from each other, analytical and behavioral models, to an attempt at synthesis more recently.

This convergence creates an opportunity for more fruitful exchanges between the two fields beyond those of the small group of scholars who would identify themselves with both fields already. At the same time, the evolution toward an intangible competence-based view of global competition opens a whole new set of avenues for MNC research, and may propel it to the leading edge of organization theory and organizational learning research. This is a challenge for the field itself, as the very same issue of skills and competence we see in companies, may come to apply to our field.

NOTES

1. It is important to note that this model was developed from the teaching and casewriting experience of its authors, and was seen primarily as a teaching tool, supporting case discussion learning, rather than as a stand-alone theory of competitive advantage.

2. Economics has faced similar issues. While the classical market equilibrium theories rules out the long-term sustainability of above average returns, the observation of firm performance suggests that some firms do maintain long-term above-average performance. Such performance can be explained only in terms of the maintenance of market power over time, as a firm develops new sources of market power when previous ones are imitated or weakened. In a situation where innovation and technology open new opportunities, superior skills, better knowledge, and greater abilities to mobilize them may underlie new market power. Skills are understood here as the collective know-how providing the firm's capability to act confidently and successfully in meeting market demand. Ricardian rents on intangible resources, in the form of temporary returns on new knowledge and proprietary know-how, rather than stable monopoly power, can explain long-term success. Further, monopoly power itself derives from "barriers to entry," and barriers to entry are often rooted in imitability difficulties.

■ ■ ■

Four Perspectives on International Competition and Industry Evolution
Briance Mascarenhas

Over the past two decades, international competition has generated an outburst of interest and research. Four perspectives relevant to international competition can be discerned: the nation-centered; the globalist; the glocalist; and the population-ecologist perspectives. These four perspectives are rooted in different literatures, vary in their assumptions and units of analysis, and provide different views of the complex and dispersed international competition. Yet these four perspectives have not been distinguished and jointly analyzed heretofore.

One objective of this study is to map out the field and interplay the diverse perspectives. Interplaying the perspectives will hopefully reduce theoretical compartmentalization that can misguide administrative practice [Astley and Van de Ven 1983], highlight central debates, and provide a nuanced understanding of international competition.

With the exception of population ecology, the perspectives have been expressed in static terms. Though these perspectives imply different industry evolution dynamics and outcomes, these longitudinal patterns have seldom been explicitly articulated. A second objective of the study, therefore, is to specify the perspectives' driving assumptions and attendant predictions for the relative profitability and survival over time of firms pursuing different types of strategy. Articulating the implicit assumptions and resulting outcomes can help to move the existing international literature from being mostly descriptive towards fulfilling the explanatory and predictive roles of theory.

This specification task is daunting, however, since a perspective's assumptions are at times unstated or unclear. Further, many of the strategies imputed to a perspective have yet to be confirmed by empirical evidence. For example, Kogut notes in his paper that, despite much fanfare about cross-border production flexibility, supporting empirical evidence is lacking. In this paper, therefore, I will try to focus on the common central theme(s) of a perspective rather than exhaustively reciting and reconciling a litany of features that might be ascribed to it.

The third objective of this paper is to evaluate the existing empirical evidence with respect to the industry evolution predictions from the four perspectives. This comparison will help to validate the various perspectives and identify areas needing further research.

FOUR PERSPECTIVES

Nation-centered

The nation-centered perspective holds that nation states are important for their special resources, nurturing abilities, or demand conditions. This perspective suggests diverse nationally tuned strategies. One strategy is to focus on the domestic market, for example, by tailoring products to local market needs or exploiting government localization pressures. Another strategy is the multi-domestic or polycentric strategy [Perlmutter 1969]. A third strategy is to enhance international competitiveness by exploiting national conditions, such as an educational system, culture, or demanding buyers at home [Porter 1990]. Such nation-based capabilities permeate less easily across than within national borders [Kogut 1991].

An implication of this perspective is that firms pursuing nationally based or nationally focused strategies will exhibit higher profitability and in the long run industries will be characterized by firms of varying sizes which exhibit these diverse strategies.

Globalist

Globalism has been popularized during the last decade: managers have been warned to think and to act "globally" or perish [Levitt 1988; *The Economist* 1989; Ohmae 1990]. In sharp contrast with the nationalist perspective, globalists hold that national differences are becoming less important due to improvements in transportation and communication, homogenization of tastes internationally, falling trade barriers, and growing scale economies.

The terms "globalization" and "global strategy" have been used to incorporate a wide range of practices [Ghoshal 1987; Mascarenhas 1992a; 1992b; Morrison 1990; Yip 1989]. Commonly imputed elements of a global strategy include extensive integration among affiliates, standardized products, widespread market participation, and centralization of some value-creating functions to capture scale economies with world volume [Day 1990]. Economies of scale occur in research and development, purchasing, production, or marketing. Large size affords scale economies and lower unit costs, barriers to competitor entry, market power in distribution, and political power. An implication of this globalization theme is that larger firms will earn higher returns and industries in the long run will consolidate into few, giant firms with worldwide scale beyond the size of individual national markets.

Glocalist

"Glocalism" has arisen as a mid-point between nationalism and globalism, rather than being an original and unique perspective. This perspective suggests that organizations experience and should balance both local responsiveness and international integrative pressures [Bartlett and Ghoshal 1989; Prahalad and Doz 1987]. At the heart of this perspective is the assumption that organizations are adaptive. One implication of the glocalist perspective is that firms in the "middle" that satisfy both international integration and local responsiveness pressures will outperform others and survive in the long run.

Population Ecologist

Population ecology is rooted in the biology literature but has been used lately to study organizations. Population-ecologist researchers, however, have examined organizations mostly in restricted sub-national or comparative national contexts. The population-ecology perspective is introduced to analyze international competition because it predicts a particular industry evolutionary dynamic and outcome that provides a contrast to the three other perspectives. Further, examining population-ecology hypotheses in the worldwide economy comes closer to the true "population" of organizations and permits an assessment of the theory's broader relevance.

According to this population-level perspective, firms have limited adaptability and the environment selects organizations with particular traits to survive. In the world economy, though, it is not clear what are the contours of the relevant environment (national, regional, or global). Carroll's resource-partitioning model [1988] suggests that as concentration in an industry increases, large generalists (i.e., multi-product, multi-market firms) emerge, catering to the market center and creating conditions that enable specialists to survive at the periphery. Thus, few generalists and many small diverse specialists are expected to thrive under increasing industry concentration, and outperform firms in the middle

Table 1. Assumptions, Prescriptions, and Predictions of Four Perspectives

	Perspectives			
	Nation-Centered	Globalist	Glocalist	Population Ecologist
Driving Assumptions	National differences are important	National differences are dwindling	Both local and international pressures need to be met	Firms have limited adaptability and the environment selects which organizations survive
Strategy Prescription	Exploit national sources of advantage and/or be nationally focused	Exploit worldwide scale beyond national boundaries	Satisfy both local and international pressures	Avoid being stuck between generalists and specialists
Industry Evolution Prediction	Proliferation of firms of diverse sizes pursuing domestic, multi- domestic, or national sources of competitive advantage strategies	Survival of few supra-national firms pursuing scale economies and the world market	Survival of firms that are both locally responsive and internationally integrated	Survival of few generalists and many specialists with industry concentration

which face competitive pressure from both sides. Further, reorganization attempts by badly-performing firms in the middle are subject to implementation risks which may hasten their failure [Levinthal 1991].

Table 1 summarizes the four perspectives' prescriptions for strategic behavior and predictions of industry evolution. Juxtaposing the perspectives highlights into two major debates, where diametrically opposed views exist.

The first debate pivots on the importance of national differences for strategy. The nationalist perspective suggests that national differences are all-important. The globalist perspective, in contrast, suggests that national differences are dwindling and strategies should transcend national boundaries as firms pursue world markets. Thus, the globalist approach implies the increasing domination by few colossal international firms, while the nationalist approach allows for the co-existence and prosperity of nationally based or nationally focused firms of varied sizes over time.

The second debate concerns the incidence and merit of the ambidextrous strategy of simultaneous adaptation to local and international integrative pressures. The glocalist perspective assumes that organizations are adaptive and implies the pre-eminence of firms that balance international integration and local responsiveness. The population-ecology perspective, however, assumes that organizations have limited adaptability and implies the emergence of few large generalists and many small specialists as industries concentrate, with the decline of firms in the middle.

EXISTING EMPIRICAL EVIDENCE

International studies of industry evolution encompassing both longitudinal data and the broad range of firms in an industry are rare. Studies of international expansion or diversification and performance are numerous and mostly show a positive relationship between internationalization and performance. These studies, however, are cross-sectional and examine only the largest

firms, while excluding the many small firms in an industry. It is unclear if the positive relationship is an intra large-firm group phenomenon or not. Consequently, their results are difficult to interpret in the broader context.

Recently, however, empirical evidence has emerged in separate longitudinal studies of two industries: oil-drilling [Mascarenhas and Aaker 1989] and appliances [Baden-Fuller and Stopford 1991]. The evidence is preliminary and incomplete: it includes inter-group comparisons of profitability but not of survival rates.

A common finding of the two studies was that firms pursuing a nationally focused, domestic strategy maintained higher returns than the more international groups. One possible explanation posits that firms investing in international expansion depress their profitability temporarily. The profitability differences, however, persisted over extended periods of time. Mascarenhas and Aaker [1989] suggested that the strong bargaining power of large customers and prestige-driven excessive overseas investment may have depressed the international group's profitability. Baden-Fuller and Stopford [1991] suggest that the barriers to international integration may have been underestimated by firms expanding internationally.

The emerging empirical evidence is consistent with one of the strategies advocated by the nation-centered perspective, the domestic strategy, and consistent with one of the strategies suggested by the ecologist perspective, the specialist strategy (i.e., single product and/or market firms). The evidence does not appear consistent with the globalist and glocalist perspectives, however.

CONCLUSION

Four perspectives relevant to international competition and strategy were identified from the literature as the nation-centered, globalist, glocalist, and population-ecologist perspectives. These four perspectives were then analyzed with respect to their different premises and prescriptions for strategic behavior. From the assumptions and strategy prescriptions of each perspective, industry evolution outcomes were inferred with respect to the relative profitability and survival of firms pursuing particular types of strategy. Existing empirical evidence on industry evolution was then evaluated relative to the predictions of the perspectives.

This approach helps to develop a nuanced understanding of international competition by interplaying the perspectives. It also helps to move the existing international strategy literature from being descriptive to becoming more causal and predictive. By specifying the disparate predictions of each perspective, it provides the basis for systematic empirical evidence to winnow out or refine the various perspectives.

The empirical evidence to date on industry evolution is scanty and incomplete. While limited evidence exists on the relative profitability of domestic versus international firms within an industry, data on the relative profitability of different international strategies (such as multi-domestic versus global) is lacking, as is data on relative survival.

The limited evidence on profitability suggests that the domestic strategy is the more profitable, partly consistent with the nation-centered and population-ecologist perspectives, but not with the globalist and glocalist perspectives. Large international firms may possibly benefit from product and geographic diversification and exhibit a higher survival rate than firms pursuing domestic strategies, but empirical evidence to date is lacking.

Additional systematic empirical research has the potential to refine or winnow out the divergent perspectives on international competition and is badly needed. For example, further research may reveal that the relevance of the different perspectives may vary across industry types or over time.

Finally, as internationalists, we should be alarmed by the preliminary evidence suggesting the higher profitability of the domestic strategy. Such evidence raises funda-

mentally uncomfortable questions. Have internationalists simply underestimated or glossed over the costs and impediments of international expansion, movement, and operation? If so, we may have to re-emphasize international obstructions rather than downplaying them. Has the compartmentalization of domestic and international research led to a narrow and misleading view of the part instead of the whole? These disconcerting questions, which are at the heart of our field, remain.

■ ■ ■

W. *Chan Kim*

Three Questions for Mapping and Developing Strategic Management Perspectives on International Business

Bruce Kogut and Briance Mascarenhas present interesting attempts to conceptually link perspectives in strategic management to issues in international management.[1] We stand to gain a lot from such attempts. International management can further progress and become enriched through its intimate connection with major theoretical developments in adjoining fields of study.

Using the Kogut and Mascarenhas papers as a basis for discussion, I will address the more general issues raised by this kind of work. At times, I may appear to be criticizing the authors; I do so only in the hope of being constructive.

COMMENTS ON THE KOGUT PAPER

Bruce Kogut's paper identifies and labels three broad streams of research in international management. It proposes that a fourth stream, the evolutionary perspective on strategy, can cast new light on the questions of internationalization, multinational network utilization, and strategic country difference exploitation in the international setting.

My comments, couched in terms of

questions, cover three aspects of the proposed marriage between the evolutionary perspective on strategy and international management. First, I ponder the meaning of the proposed classification system in which the link between evolutionary perspective and international management figures as a fourth, novel school of thought. Second, I ask about the suitability of the link. Third, I probe for potential bottlenecks in the link and suggest how these can be overcome.

1. What is the organizing principle underlying the classification system?

    I must confess to some puzzlement over the proposed classification system which begins the paper. Even on repeated reading, I am left unclear as to the organizing principle underlying the system. Is it the discipline base that separates one stream from another? Is it research methodology? Or is it problem focus? I suspect that it is problem focus that does the best job in discriminating among the proposed three existing streams: each of these studies a different problem area. The fourth, a new stream, purports to address **each** of the problem areas accorded to the first three, so problem focus cannot be the sole organizing principle.

    In general, the choice of organizing principle depends on the purpose motivating a classification system. My difficulty in understanding the organizing principle underlying the author's proposed classification system can probably be traced to the author who does not make clear his purpose in classifying the literature.

    If the purpose were to organize and redirect work in what is a fundamentally interdisciplinary field, identifying the underlying disciplines and subdisciplines that have contributed to the field is a good

beginning. A broad classification by underlying discipline would set the proper stage for the kind of cross-pollination between theory and problem area which the author proposes.

2. In what way is the evolutionary perspective uniquely suited to address the problems of international management? Conversely, in what way is international management a unique testing ground for the evolutionary view?

    Whenever a new marriage between theory and phenomenon is considered, it is necessary to contemplate the question of suitability. The theory of resort needs to be uniquely suited to explain the problem identified. Conversely, the extension of a theory to new problem areas is compelling when it contributes uniquely to the development and the generalization of the theory.

    The paper at hand deals with the first of the two sides of the research coin, the resort to theory in the face of phenomena seeking explanation. I ask the author to demonstrate in what way the problems of international management and, more specifically, those of the multinational corporation (MNC) provide a unique testing ground for the evolutionary perspective. In the absence of this demonstration, I cannot help but wonder if we are not reexamining the ground already covered by Nelson and Winter.

    If we accept the link between the evolutionary perspective and international management as a one-sided marriage in which the phenomenon seeks a theory but has nothing to offer the theory in return, then the unique suitability of the theory still remains to be demonstrated. Is there a natural juncture between issue and theory?

For each issue, internationalization, multinational network utilization, and strategic country difference exploitation, we must ask if there are other theories that might be brought to bear equally well or even better. In the absence of pressing reasons to consider **only** the evolutionary perspective, the author's call for research along this line loses some of its power and urgency.

Are the issues the author raises the most compelling ones in the field of international management today? If they are, the author might wish to articulate this point to emphasize the urgency of conducting research along the line for which he argues. If they are not, then the immediate concern of international management must be to identify the most salient issues and to concentrate research attention on them.

Here, I am tempted to explore a line of research that I think has unique promise and towards which the author has already made an important beginning. As originally pointed out by Hedlund [1986], one of the most critical challenges the multinational faces today is the intense need for voluntary cooperation across its subunits in the face of the collapse of the multinational's hierarchy. How do we meet this challenge? As we all have argued in one way or another, the disciplines of social psychology and sociology are likely to contribute a lot to answer this question. For example, applications of concepts from the literature on community might provide novel and unique insight to the specific challenge in international management outlined by Hedlund. At the same time, testing a theory of community in a setting far removed from the theory's original context may contribute significantly to the theory. Work of this kind may advance knowledge in the area and lead to new streams of thought.

3. What potential bottlenecks confront researchers who would pursue the evolutionary perspective? How might these be overcome?

Without denying the promise of a research program built on the evolutionary perspective, I would like to pause for a moment, to anticipate the bottlenecks in such a program. My focus on potential bottlenecks derives not from skepticism but from interest in making the dialogue between evolutionary perspective and international management more explicit and ultimately more fruitful.

As currently stated, the evolutionary perspective itself is very broad and lacks a clear-cut definition of terms. Words like "capability" and "option" are used without theoretical clarity. If anything and everything can be a capability, and if every corporate action can be understood in terms of an option, the perspective loses much of its explanatory power. This problem of definition currently limits the operational utility of the evolutionary perspective. A considerable effort must yet be put into clarification and refinement of the underlying concepts.

It is conceivable that insights from international management may help to overcome the current limitations of the evolutionary perspective. Organizational capabilities such as innovation diffusion or operational flexibility may be particularly well developed in the multinational corporation. The comparative study of these capabilities in a broad range of organizations, multinational and domestic, may provide researchers with a more concise understanding of this core concept and lead to further theoretical refinement. At any rate, I think it is important that the bottlenecks cited be recognized at the outset. Such recognition can only put future development on surer footing.

I end my commentary on Kogut's work with a last observation. Both here and elsewhere in his recent work, the author has shown firm commitment to mapping out a new approach to the study of international management issues. In so doing, he has gone outside of traditional fields of reference and pointed out previously unremarked linkages between disparate study areas. His framework building efforts are praiseworthy and deserve our continued attention.

COMMENTS ON
THE MASCARENHAS PAPER

Briance Mascarenhas's paper bears a striking outward resemblance to Bruce Kogut's paper. As in the Kogut paper, a literature classification is presented, a new approach is argued, and research implications are discussed. Similar to Kogut's paper, the link between international management phenomena and perspectives in strategic management is emphasized. The resemblance between the two papers extends even to the size of the respective classification systems: both have room for three existing literature streams and identify one new one.

Of course, the two papers treat different substantive areas and draw upon different theoretical traditions. Thus, where the paper by Kogut applies the evolutionary perspective to several, seemingly separate, problems in international management, the paper by Mascarenhas suggests the adoption of a population-ecologist perspective in the study of a single problem, international competition. Nevertheless, the papers' similarity—in form and logic—is such that I would repeat myself were I to go through as detailed an analysis for the second paper as I have done for the first. However, the same three questions are germane:

1. What is the organizing principle underlying the proposed classification system?
2. In what way is the proposed perspective uniquely suited to address the problems of international management?
3. What potential bottlenecks confront researchers who would pursue the proposed perspective?

For the sake of brevity, I will concentrate my comments on the classification system. The general remarks about suitability and potential limits made in reference to the Kogut paper apply equally to Mascarenhas's paper, even though the latter does not develop its alternative perspective on international management and population ecology as deeply.

The classification system suggested by Mascarenhas divides the literature on international competition into four categories. The four categories are differentiated by their underlying assumptions about the key success factors in international competition and about the adaptability of firms. This dual organizing principle does not do an adequate job of separating the literature streams discussed.

The success factor dimension is conceptually unconvincing. First of all, population ecology has little to say about the key success factors in international competition and thus appears like an apple among the success factor oranges. Second, there is overlap between the three genuine success factors: nation-centered arguments a la Kogut or Porter do not exclude globalist or glocalist views. The focus of a particular study may be the nation-state, but no author would dogmatically forego global advantages if these were to be had. Each of the three success factor arguments is a contingent statement in which industry conditions, regulatory factors, and firm-specific endowments all play a role in determining success. This contingent character makes any clear-cut separation between success factors highly problematic.

The adaptability dimension, too, does

only a partial job in distinguishing the streams. Nation-centered, globalist, and glocalist approaches all implicitly assume that firms are rather adaptable. Thus, assumptions about adaptability only separate out population ecology, casting the literature in dichotomous terms which do not support the fourfold classification presented.

I agree with the author that international management needs to pay more attention to the explanatory and predictive roles of theory. I am just not sure if the proposed classification system advances this objective. When distinctions between categories are problematic, a classification system may be vulnerable to misuse. Students outside the field of international management who do not understand the finer distinctions between research streams may be misled. I would therefore urge the author to refine his classification system, by giving more thought to the discriminatory power of the organizing principles supporting it.

Having said this, let me be the first to acknowledge that taking on complex, multilevel questions of real current significance has never been easy. The author directs our attention to one such question, international competition, and makes a commendable attempt to expose some of our most enduring assumptions about the subject. In recasting the debate about international competition in terms of the population-ecology approach, the author asks us to look at what we thought we already understood through new lenses. I find such a view worthy of further inquiry.

CONCLUDING REMARKS

As I look over the two papers once more, I am again struck by their similarity. I would like to know what prompts both authors to independently propose classification systems at this time. The act of linking a perspective in strategic management to problems in international management does not **necessarily** require an introductory classification of the literature. Conceivably, a careful answering of the questions of suitability and potential bottlenecks would suf-

fice to make a case for a particular link. Why then this concern with classification? I don't have a definite answer for this question.

Is the purpose of such classification in international management to review and map out the boundaries of the field? At what point does this mapping of boundaries become a goal in its own right, divorced from theoretical and phenomenological concerns? Under what circumstances is there a real need for such classification? In reference to institutional theory, Scott has argued that "efforts to take stock and consolidate previous contributions" only make sense when "there has been sufficient development and sufficient theoretical differentiation" [Scott 1991:164]. Are we at this stage of development in international management? The current efforts at classification would seem to suggest that this is the case. Perhaps they are right. I am, however, left with more questions than answers on this score.

I conclude my remarks by making one last observation. As the authors' discussions of strategic management perspectives on international business (IB) bring to light, the preponderance of literature in this field focuses on issues of strategy design for multinational organizations. As important as this school of research is in international management, it would seem equally important to understand how multinational organizations can go beyond questions of design to actually implement strategic prescriptions. Yet, there is a relative void of literature in this domain. As I have already touched upon, I think the rich bodies of social psychology and sociology literature could provide a valuable contribution to the development of this line of research inquiry. Such research will open the window of our understanding on managing the internal motive system of the multinational—the underlying forces that drive and motivate the individuals and subunits that comprise its global community of operations.

A Last Reflection

The process of commenting on the papers of Kogut and Mascarenhas brought to mind a discussion I once had with Cynthia Montgomery, who is now at Harvard Business School. At the time of our conversation, Cynthia was the guest editor of the Strategic Management's special issue on Strategy Content Research. Charles Hill and I had written a paper for the issue which proposed a dynamic theory of the multinational enterprise (MNE), a theory which, ironically, finds echoes in the evolutionary perspective on international management proposed here by Kogut. In the course of our conversation, Cynthia spoke to me of her experiences in being an editor. While she found reviewers' comments thoughtful and helpful, she thought that we, as scholars, could all benefit by being yet more encouraging and generous in our evaluations of prospective articles.

Now, as I reread my commentary on these two papers, I cannot help but question myself as to whether I have lived up to Cynthia's advice. When acting as an evaluator we often fail to remember the tremendous struggle authors have had to go through to resolve the conflicts in the literature and to write the paper that now sits on the desk before us. While I have tried in earnest to be fair and constructive in my reviews, perhaps I may have been too critical in my commentary. I hope this is not the case. I also hope that my commentary will serve to further spark the research of these two authors. I believe that their research has promise.

NOTE

1. Economists and organizational sociologists will forgive me, I hope, for adopting the evolutionary and population-ecologist perspectives on behalf of strategic management.

Michael A. Hitt

The Evolution of Multinational Corporations: Integration of International Diversification and Strategic Management

Bruce Kogut has provided us with an excellent review of the evolution of thought on the multinational corporation (MNC); Yves Doz explained the evolution of the field of international business (IB) in contrast with strategic management. Additionally, Briance Mascarenhas gives us an interesting evaluation of four perspectives on international competition and industry evolution. Together, they have carefully crafted the historical development of research on the MNC and IB. As they imply, the development of this field has drawn on contributions from multiple disciplines which include IB, economics, organization theory, and more recently strategic management. Some of the recent work by Yves Doz, C. K. Prahalad, Christopher Bartlett, and Sumantra Ghoshal have provided significant impetus for the development of our knowledge of international strategic management.

My comments are organized around some of the key themes in works by Kogut and Mascarenhas by discussing and, in some cases, extending a few of their ideas. I focus on the rationale for international diversification and the integration of international and product diversification, critical issues in the implementation of international diversification, organizing for international diversification, and offer some suggestions for future research in this area.

INTERNATIONAL DIVERSIFICATION: RATIONALE AND INTEGRATION WITH CORPORATE STRATEGY

Kogut effectively argues that strategy is much more than the selection of product markets and technologies for production. Instead, he suggests that it is the creation and maintenance of superior organizational routines which reproduce the strategy over time. As he aptly notes, this perspective represents the resource-based view of the firm, a perspective to which I subscribe, with a few caveats.

The resource-based view of the firm has been effectively described by Barney [1991] but the focus is on the extent which it affects international strategy or diversification. As noted by Kogut, there may be multiple explanations for a firm diversifying internationally. The primary goal is to gain a sustainable competitive advantage. To do so, international diversification may afford a firm opportunities to exploit benefits of performing more activities internally [Rugman 1979]. It allows the exploitation of interrelationships among business segments, geographic areas, or businesses in related industries [Porter 1985]. Thus, international diversification may produce economies of scale, scope, and/or experience. Furthermore, Kogut, in some of his earlier work [1984] suggested that internationally diversified firms are able to gain competitive advantage by exploitation of differences in national resources, flexibility, and bargaining power from a multinational network, in addition to economies of scale, scope, and learning. Kobrin [1991] argues that technology is the primary determinant of cross-border integration. In fact, Kobrin [1991] and Kogut [1991] both suggest that firms may need to be globally diversified and integrated in order to have appropriate resources to invest in R&D and the new technology necessary to meet or beat global competition. Doz argues that integration can occur by leveraging core competencies across geographically diversified units.

Mascarenhas offers two perspectives that promote international competition, globalist and glocalist. The globalist perspective fits well the arguments for international diversification noted above. That is, large size affords economies and other advantages such as entry barriers along with market and political power. He describes the glocalist as a mid-point between nationalism and globalism. This perspective is similar to that of transnational capability [Bartlett and Ghoshal 1988] in which firms achieve both global integration and local responsiveness. Mascarenhas also offers criticisms of these perspectives that are explored later herein.

Kogut's work on the evolution of the MNC argues strongly that gaining competitive advantage in international diversification requires leveraging international firm capabilities. He argues, in fact, that in order

to compete in international markets, firms must have a broader set of capabilities and must leverage these capabilities to gain a sustainable competitive advantage. In so doing, he and Doz discuss the notion of core competence [Prahalad and Hamel 1990]. A core competence may be defined as an organization's capability for complex problem definition and solution that results from organizational learning and the sustained accumulation of firm specific assets, skills, and heuristics [Lei, Hitt and Bettis 1996]. In line with Doz's arguments, the development of core competencies and the transfer and leveraging of this knowledge across a firm's businesses and country borders, can produce competitive advantage. Thus, core competencies can be viewed as a firm's unique set of resources (tangible and intangible). While tangible assets may be more easily imitable [Barney 1988], intangible assets oftentimes are more difficult to imitate. In order to develop a **sustained** competitive advantage, core competencies and the leveraging thereof, must not be easily imitable. Intangible competencies include differential skills, technological prowess, and organizational routines and skills. Firms, therefore, should select types and directions of international diversification that allow the leveraging of core competencies to obtain or maintain a competitive advantage.

The population-ecology perspective described by Mascarenhas partially conflicts with the resource-based view in that firms do not have strategic choices. The population-ecology perspective suggests that firms have limited adaptability and the environment selects firms with specific characteristics (e.g., skills) for survival. In other words, firms can't select types and directions of international diversification; it is an extreme external control (deterministic) perspective [Romanelli and Tushman 1986]. However, many organization theory and strategic management scholars are moving toward a more realistic perspective that integrates external control and strategic choice [Hitt and Tyler 1991].

Another extension to the Doz, Kogut,

and Mascarenhas's discussions of international diversification, is integration with other corporate strategies. One of the most common and visible corporate strategies is that of product diversification. In fact, discussion of the evolution of the multinational firm may not be complete without including product diversification. Domestic single business firms often consider international diversification as an alternative to product diversification. Until recently, however, many firms chose product diversification and expanded internationally at a later time, for reasons described later. Therefore, we may need to explore the interaction and/or integration of international and product diversification. For example, while product diversification has been a popular strategy, evidence regarding performance implications of such diversification is decidedly mixed [Hoskisson and Hitt 1990; Ramanujam and Varadarajan 1989]. A number of scholars argue that product diversification is the result of agency costs and is based on executives' attempts to spread their risk of failure and/or lower their employment risk. However, product diversification is decidedly difficult to manage and oftentimes is accomplished through acquisitions (similar to international diversification as noted by Kogut), and frequently financed by the use of debt. As a firm takes on more debt, bankruptcy risk increases. For these reasons, early gains may be realized from initial product diversification, but are offset by continued diversification further from the firm's core business. Therefore, Hoskisson and Hitt [1990] conclude that over time, product diversification has, at best, a neutral effect on firm performance.

Mascarenhas concludes that the nationalist perspective should lead to the highest performance. However, this is in conflict with the majority of research on international diversification. His conclusions are based on the results of two single-industry studies. Perhaps there are industry effects which must be realized. The theory supporting international diversification is strong.

However, Mascarenhas has added some caveats. Firms must recognize the barriers to achieving success with international diversification, prominent among those focus on implementation of the strategy. In fact, Hitt, Hoskisson and Ireland [1994] argue that there are limits to the positive benefits of international diversification, thereby providing some support for Mascarenhas.

Alternatively, most of the research on international diversification has shown a positive relationship with performance [Buhner 1987; Geringer, Beamish, and daCosta 1989; Rugman 1979]. In fact, Buhner argued that domestic product diversification appeared to be motivated more by poor performance than the desire to reduce risk. However, international diversification was motivated more by prospective market opportunities. Furthermore, Kobrin [1991] argued that multinational firms able to integrate globally (integrate across country borders by standardizing products, rationalizing production, and coordinating critical resource functions such as R&D) achieve optimal economic scale and amortize investments in critical functions over a broader base. This achievement requires effective organizational arrangements which are discussed by Kogut, Doz, and herein.

Most multinational firms have multiple and diverse product lines. As a result, they are both product and internationally diversified. Hitt, et al. [1994] argued that product-diversified firms may improve their performance by diversifying internationally. In so doing, they may be able to achieve some of the benefits of international diversification and capture synergies of product diversification. For example, international diversification may facilitate exploitation of the interdependencies across related businesses. In support, Kim, Hwang, and Burgers [1989] found that related diversified firms that were also internationally diversified were able to achieve greater profit stability than firms that were not internationally diversified. This suggests that international diversification reduces the risk of related product diversification by stabilizing returns.

International diversification may also facilitate performance in unrelated product-diversified firms. For example, Kim et al. [1989] found unrelated product-diversified firms that were internationally diversified had higher profit growth than those that were not internationally diversified. Furthermore, they found no performance differences between related and unrelated diversified firms that were internationally diversified. Thus, international diversification allows the exploitation of economies of scale and scope in unrelated firms and thereby, promotes greater profit growth. Unrelated diversified firms often cannot achieve economies of scale in domestic markets. Additionally, movement into international markets may allow unrelated firms to achieve more unique and inimitable synergies beyond purely financial synergies.

Hitt et al. [1994] also argued that international diversification affects long-term performance through its impact on innovation. For example, international diversification lowers the risks of R&D investments by spreading the opportunity to achieve returns over a broader set of markets. Thus, international diversification provides incentives for firms to innovate. Kotabe [1990] found that U.S. multinational firms with a higher level of integration and coordination on a global basis were better able to retain their innovative capabilities because they were capable of tapping various resources. Thus, we might conclude that international diversification improves the appropriability regime of innovation [Teece 1986]. It does so by increasing the firm's ability to appropriate returns from innovations before competitors can overcome the initial competitive disadvantage created by the innovation [Kotabe 1990]. Furthermore, if innovation facilitates higher performance, as argued by Porter [1985]; Grant, Jammine, and Thomas [1988]; and Franko [1989], it will provide increased incentives for greater international diversification. Therefore, there may be a reciprocal interrelationship between international diversification and innovation.

However, as noted earlier, Hitt et al. [1994] argued that there are limits to the positive outcomes of international diversification. For example, Geringer et al. [1989] found that early international-diversification efforts produced positive performance outcomes. But, as international diversification increased, the slope of the relationship with performance eventually became negative. Reasons for this inverted U-shaped relationship relate to ideas advanced by Doz and Kogut regarding implementation and organizational arrangements and those advanced by Mascarenhas regarding the difficulty of achieving global integration and local responsiveness simultaneously.

IMPLEMENTATION OF INTERNATIONAL STRATEGY

Kogut discusses several issues important for the implementation of international diversification. For example, he argues that the multinational firm must possess the capabilities to carry out activities such as advertising, adaptation of products, and efficient production of products, particularly in international markets. However, there are a number of potential complicating variables that affect a firm's ability to carry out these activities effectively. Porter [1990], for example, suggested that broad geographic dispersions increase coordination, distribution and management costs. To derive the benefits of economies of scale and scope, requires coordination and an ability to distribute goods efficiently on a global basis. Different government regulations, trade laws, and cultures across separate countries can create significant barriers to coordination. These barriers can make it difficult to transfer competitive advantages across country borders [Kogut 1985]. They reflect Mascarenhas's [in this book] arguments of problems with the globalist and glocalist perspectives. These problems are exacerbated when the firm has a diversified product line. For example, laws and regulations oftentimes may differ by product line (e.g., import limits). Furthermore, coordination must be achieved across geographic boundaries and product divisions (depending on organization structure).

As a result of these potential problems, firms may consider acquiring businesses already operating in markets they wish to enter. However, acquisitions also pose a number of potential integration problems. In fact, integration costs may be particularly acute in firms operating in countries with distinctly different cultures. In these cases, a firm may opt to form a joint venture or a strategic alliance, rather than enter the market through an acquisition. Of course, joint ventures do not necessarily offer the same opportunities for economies of scale and scope and for transferring technology. Probably the most significant implementation issues relate to the organization of multinational firms as suggested by Kogut and by Doz in this chapter.

ORGANIZATION OF MULTINATIONAL FIRMS

Bartlett and Ghoshal [1987,1988,1989] argued that internationally diversified firms must establish global integration of their international operations while at the same time allowing local operations the autonomy required to respond to idiosyncratic markets. Thus, internationally diversified firms must be simultaneously centralized (to achieve global integration) and decentralized (to allow local market autonomy). Of course, the means of achieving simultaneous centralization and decentralization are quite complex and difficult as noted by Mascarenhas [in this chapter]. To achieve the required integration and multinational flexibility [Kogut in this chapter], use of a matrix structure might be argued. On the surface a matrix structure seems to be an excellent fit to these requirements. However, this type of structure is exceedingly difficult to implement effectively. In fact, the research suggests that these structures have produced mixed results in domestic firms. Furthermore, it would be more difficult to implement a matrix structure effectively in

an internationally diversified firm. Additionally, organization theorists have long argued the importance of a fit between the organization and its environment. Thus, subsidiary structures may need to be different because of the idiosyncratic characteristics of their environment. While this argument has intuitive appeal, care must be taken because conventional western theories of fit between the organization and its environment may not be operative in different cultures and environments. Thus, we need more research to understand the appropriate fit between an organization structure and its environment within different country environments and markets.

Kogut argues for multinational flexibility, but also suggests that it may provide a false aura of unconstrained managerial discretion. He notes that managerial discretion is constrained by the firm's environment as much as it is by internal rules. Therefore, managers do not have unconstrained discretion and flexibility. This is an excellent point. These arguments are similar to the debate regarding external control and strategic choice theories of strategic decision making (see, Hitt and Tyler [1991] for a review). Similarly, firms that desire to achieve both global integration and allow local flexibility, must achieve a balance between control and autonomy. Thus, other contextual characteristics may be important in addition to structural arrangements.

Weick [1987] argued that corporate culture may be used as a substitute for centralization of authority. A strong culture helps socialize managers to use similar decision premises and assumptions, thereby aiding coordination of decentralized operations. By definition, corporate culture entails a set of ideologies and values shared throughout the organization and it regulates behavior [Kilmann, Saxton, and Serpa 1986]. Clan-type cultures appear to be the most appropriate for internationally diversified firms. They emphasize close superior-subordinate interrelationships and qualitative measures of performance. Thus, they are more effective than market cultures that place a premium on strictly defined roles limiting opportunities to share skills and learning across unit and country boundaries [Kerr and Slocum 1987; Ouchi 1980].

Corporate governance devices, such as executive incentive compensation, may be helpful for aligning managerial interests with those of the firm [Hoskisson, Hitt, Turk, and Tyler 1989; Hoskisson, Hitt, and Hill 1991; Tosi and Gomez-Mejia 1989]. In particular, hierarchical systems involving the use of subjective criteria, close relationships between members, and the selective use of financial and strategic goals may be used to promote long-term commitment. Hierarchical based systems are distinctly more effective with integration strategies than are performance-based systems. However, internationally diversified firms require both integration and responsiveness as noted. Therefore, incentive compensation arrangements may need to include an appropriate mix of hierarchical and performance-based approaches.

Horizontal coordination mechanism may also be necessary. The matrix structure is designed to integrate both the vertical and horizontal coordination. However, there may be other horizontal coordination mechanisms that would be useful. Prahalad and Doz [1987], and Bartlett and Ghoshal [1989], for example, recommended the utilization of several of Galbraith's [1973,1977] horizontal coordination mechanisms for integrating SBUs in multinational firms. These include the use of integrators, teams, task forces, and coordination committees. Teams might be used to assimilate information and monitor and refine the progress of various R&D projects across SBUs. Even more sophisticated coordination mechanisms may be useful when the interdependencies deal with multiple products and technologies. Interunit decision forums, for example, may be useful to exchange views and resolve differences between SBUs. Additionally, there may be a need to develop teams or groups composed of top managers from both corporate and SBU units.

There may be a need to examine the strategies in international SBUs within large multinational firms. Lei, Hitt, and Goldhar [1996], for example, argue that to be competitive in international markets and possibly even against international competition in domestic markets may require an integrated low cost/differentiation strategy. Such an integrated strategy necessitates a complex organization that achieves both high differentiation and high integration. Differentiation and integration can be facilitated by loose coupling, integrators, and multiunit/multifunctional teams. Loose coupling may be achieved through shared values (organization culture).

Obviously, horizontal integration devices should facilitate the achievement of complementarities across separate divisions and between divisions and corporate operations. They should facilitate the application of core competences and the achievement of economies of scale and scope, as suggested by Doz and by Kogut in this chapter. As a result, they should help to achieve synergy and competitive advantages for the multinational firms. The complexity of achieving integration while simultaneously allowing local responsiveness, particularly in product diversified firms, likely requires a combination of structural arrangements, strong corporate culture, and effective corporate governance mechanisms. It also requires more knowledge of strategic leadership in multinational firms. Thus, management of multinational firms may be informed by upper echelon theory [Hambrick and Mason 1984; Hambrick 1989].

CONCLUSIONS AND FUTURE RESEARCH

The works by Doz, Kogut, and Mascarenhas provide information on the rich history of the multinational firm, IB, some caveats to the benefits of international diversification [Mascarenhas in this volume], and opportunities to achieve integration and competitive advantage by developing and leveraging core competences across units [Kogut, Doz, in this volume]. However, theory and research from strategic management could inform the work of all three. The evolution of the multinational firm may not be complete without examination of product diversification. Furthermore, the combination of both product and international diversification (exemplifies most multinational firms) greatly complicates the management of these firms, particularly the achievement of integration. Additionally, Hitt and Ireland [1986], building on a stream of research in strategic management, found the competences most important for firm performance to vary by the type of product diversification pursued. Thus, this stream of research might inform work on core competences. Finally, at least partial explanations for the results described by Mascarenhas may be found in research on implementation of corporate strategies (both international and product diversification). While the arguments above may suggest caveats to the conclusions made by Doz, Kogut, and Mascarenhas, without more inclusive research on the theoretical domain in question, they have provided important ideas and avenues for further inquiry.

The papers by Doz, Kogut, and Mascarenhas and some of the arguments offered herein suggest a number of rich domains for future research. For example, more research on the interaction of international diversification and corporate strategies such as product diversification should be explored in more detail. Accordingly, the interaction of international diversification and business level strategies such as the integrated low cost/differentiation strategy may yield rich insight into the operation of multinational firms.

Additional research on the implementation of international diversification is required. We need to understand more about international strategic alliances and acquisitions. Furthermore, we need to have a better understanding of the tradeoffs involved in such strategic actions.

As noted by Doz and Kogut's arguments and herein, more research on the or-ganizational arrangements that facilitate implementation and operation of multinational organizations is required. In fact, our knowledge of international diversification is more advanced than our knowledge of the organizational arrangements that facilitate the implementation and management of internationally diversified firms. However, these organizational arrangements are critical to the success of international diversification. Therefore, we need to understand how to achieve the transnational capability suggested by Bartlett and Ghoshal [1988].

Boeker [1989] concluded that history and precedents play a strong role in shaping strategic action. Accordingly, our knowledge of the evolution of the multinational firm has helped shape international strategic actions. However, we seem to have a better understanding of why firms diversify internationally rather than how to implement and manage international diversification effectively.

Our knowledge of the management of multinational firms is evolving as is the operation of these firms. Hitt, Tyler, and Park [1990], for example, found differences in the strategic decision models used by U.S. and Korean top executives. While this could be predicted based upon differences in culture, country, stage of industrialization, method of capital formation, natural resource endowment, and relationships between business and government in the home country, little is known about the precise differences in strategic decision models used by executives in different countries. This knowledge becomes critical in multinational firms that employ executives from multiple home countries. Therefore, research is required to integrate our knowledge of executive strategic decision behaviors along with firm-level strategic decisions and the organizational arrangements necessary to implement and manage those operations.

Bartlett and Ghoshal [1991] called for more research that integrated theory and empirical work from both the IB and strategic management fields. I concur and view this as an opportunity to gain more knowledge about these complex and rich organizations referred to as multinational firms.

REPLY
Briance Mascarenhas

A Reflection on the Comments of Professors Michael Hitt and Chan Kim

Michael Hitt and Chan Kim raise important issues that have stimulated further thought and will undoubtedly help to develop the field of international strategy. Two of their points in particular have struck a chord in my thinking. I would like to reinforce these two points and extend them.

Hitt brings to the analysis the issue of strategy implementation. This is an important contribution since the bulk of research has focused on environmental assessment and strategy formulation, while strategy implementation has been neglected. For example, a survey of courses on international strategy which I recently conducted revealed over-emphasis on environmental assessment and strategy formulation but a paucity of material on strategy implementation. Hopefully, the importance of strategy implementation will encourage further research in the area.

Kim makes a contribution by urging us to re-think the underlying logic for the variables employed in the classification scheme. Ideally the classification scheme should be theoretically relevant and should result in categories that are mutually exclusive and collectively exhaustive. Clearly the last two conditions are not met by my classification scheme. For example, regionalization is an emerging stream of research that may deserve its own perspective status. I have relied on the use of common perspectives for several reasons. A perspective represents a complex configuration of variables, rather than relying on merely one or two. A perspective is also impersonal: individual researchers have taken multiple positions over time. Clearly, though, future reviews of international strategy research should involve more fundamental thought about the criteria to be chosen for taking stock of our field.

REFERENCES

Aharoni, Yair. 1966. The foreign direct investment decision. Boston: Harvard Business School.

Andrews, K. 1971. *The Concept of Corporate Strategy.* Homewood, Ill.: Dow Jones-Irwin.

Ansoff, I. 1965. *Corporate Strategy. An Analytical Approach to Business Policy for Growth and Expansion.* New York: McGraw-Hill.

Aoki, Masahiko, 1988. *Information, Incentives and Bargaining in the Japanese Economy.* Cambridge, MA: Harvard University Press.

Argyris, C. 1985. *Strategy, Change and Defensive Routines.* Marshfield, Ma.: Pitman.

Arrow, K. J. 1985. The economics of agency. In J. W. Pratt and R. J. Zeckhauser, *Principles and Agents: The Structure of Business.* Boston, Ma.: HBS Press.

Arrow, K. J. 1974. *The Limits of Organization.* New York: Norton.

Astley, Graham and A. Van de Ven. 1983. Central perspectives and debates in organization theory. *Administrative Science Quarterly,* 28: 245–273.

Baden-Fuller, C. W. F. and John M. Stopford. 1991. Globalization frustrated: the case of white goods. *Strategic Management Journal,* 12:493–507.

Barney, Jay. 1986. Strategic factor markets: expectations, luck, and business strategy. *Management Science,* 32:1231–1241.

Barney, J. B. 1991. Firm resources and the theory of competitive advantage. *Journal of Management,* 17: 99–120.

Barney, J. B. 1988. Returns to bidding firms in mergers and acquisitions: Reconsidering the relatedness hypothesis. *Strategic Management Journal,* 9(special issue): 71–78.

Bartlett, Christopher A. 1986. Building and managing the transnational: The new organizational challenge. In *Competition in Global Industries*, M. E. Porter, editor. Boston: Harvard Business School.

Bartlett, Christopher A. 1981. Multinational structural change: Evolution versus reorganization. In L. Otterbeck, editor, *The Management of Headquarters-Subsidiary*

Relationships in Multinational Corporations. Aldershot, England: Gower.

Bartlett, Christopher A. 1979. Multinational structural evolution: The changing decision environment in international divisions. Unpublished doctoral dissertation, Harvard Business School.

Bartlett, Christopher and Sumantra Ghoshal. 1992. Transnational management. Homewood, IL: Irwin.

Bartlett, Christopher A. and Sumantra Ghoshal. 1991. Global strategic management: Impact on the new frontiers of strategy research. *Strategic Management Journal,* 12 (Special Issue):5–15.

Bartlett, Christopher A. and Sumantra Ghoshal. 1989. Managing across borders: The transnational solution. Boston: Harvard Business School Press.

Bartlett, Christopher A. and Sumantra Ghoshal. 1988. Managing across borders: New strategic requirements. *California Management Review,* 30(1):54–74.

Bartlett, Christopher A. and Sumantra Ghoshal. 1987. Managing across borders: New organizational responses. *Sloan Management Review,* Fall:43–73.

Bartlett, Christopher and Sumantra Ghoshal. 1987. Managing across borders: New strategic requirements. *Sloan Management Review,* 28(4):7–17.

Berglof, Erik. 1991. Corporate control and capital structure—essays on property rights and financial contracts. Stockholm: Institute of International Business, Stockholm School of Economics.

Boddewyn, Jean J. 1988. Political aspects of MNE theory. *Journal of International Business Studies,* 19:341–363.

Boeker, W. 1989. Strategic changes: The effects of founding and history. *Academy of Management Journal,* 32:489–515.

Bower, J. L. 1970. *Managing the Resource Allocation Process.* Boston: HBS Division of Research.

Bower, J. and Yves Doz. 1977. Strategy formulation: A social and political process. In D. Schendel and C. Hofer, editors, *Strategic Management: A New View of Business Policy and Planning.* Boston, Ma.: Little, Brown and Co.

Buckley, Peter and Mark Casson. 1976. *The Future of Multinational Enterprise.* London: Macmillan.

Buhner, R. 1987. Assessing international diversification of West German corporations. *Strategic Management Journal,* 8:25–37.

Burenstam Linder, Staffan. 1961. *An Essay on Trade and Transformation.* New York: Wiley.

Cantwell, John. 1989. *Technological Innovations and Multinational Corporations.* Cambridge, Ma.: Basil Blackwell.

Carroll, G. R. 1988. Concentration and specialization: Dynamics of niche width in populations of organizations. *American Journal of Sociology,* 90:1262–1283.

Carroll, G.R. 1984. The specialist strategy. *California Management Review,* 26(3).

Carroll, G. R. and Jose Delacroix. 1982. Organizational mortality in the newspaper industries of Argentina and Ireland: An ecological approach. *Administrative Science Quarterly,* 27:169–198.

Caves, Richard E. 1982. *Economic Analysis and Multinational Enterprises.* Cambridge: Cambridge University Press.

Caves, Richard E. 1971. International corporations: The industrial economics of foreign investment, *Economica,* 38:1–27.

Caves, Richard and Michael Porter. 1977. From entry barriers to mobility barriers: Conjectural decisions and contrived deterrence to new competition. *Quarterly Journal of Economics,* 91:241–262.

Chandler, Alfred D. 1990. *Scale and Scope: The Dynamics of Industrial Capitalism.* Cambridge, Ma.: Harvard University Press.

Chandler, Alfred D. 1962. *Strategy and Structure: Chapters in the History of the American Industrial Enterprise.* Cambridge, Ma.: M.I.T. Press.

Chandler, Alfred D. and Herman Daems, editors. 1980. *Managerial Hierarchies: Comparative Perspectives on the Rise of the Modern Industrial Enterprise.* Cambridge, Ma.: Harvard University Press.

Channon, Derek F. 1973. *The Strategy and*

Structure of British Enterprises. Boston, Ma.: Division of Research, Graduate School of Business, Harvard University.

Chiu, Charles. 1992. Acquisitions and growth options. Thesis, University of Washington.

Clark, K. and T. Fujimoto. 1991. *Product Development Performance: Strategy, Organization, and Management in the World Auto Industry.* Cambridge, MA.: Harvard Business School Press.

Clark, K. and T. Fujimoto. 1990. The power of product integrity. *Harvard Business Review,* 68(6):107–118.

Coase, Ronald. 1937. The nature of the firm. *Economica,* 5:386–405.

Coleman, James S. 1988. Social capital in the creation of human capital. *American Journal of Sociology,* 94 (Supplement):95–120.

Collis, David. 1991. A resource-based analysis of global competition: the case of the bearings industry. *Strategic Management Journal,* 12(Special Issue):49–68.

Cool and Dierickx. 1992. "Determinants of Innovation: The Pharmaceutical Industry in the U.S., Europe and Japan, 1940–89," Working paper, INSEAD.

Cool, Karel and D. Schendel. 1988. Performance differences among strategic group members. *Strategic Management Journal,* 9:207–222.

Crozier, Michel. 1964. *The Bureaucratic Phenomenon.* Chicago, Il.: University of Chicago Press.

Davidson. 1980a. *Experience Effects in International Investment and Technology Transfers.* Ann Arbor: UMI Research Press.

Davidson, William. 1980b. The location of foreign direct investment activity: Country characteristics and experience effects. *Journal of International Business Studies,* 11.

Davidson, William. 1976. Patterns of factor-solving innovation in the industrialized world. *European Economic Review,* 8:207–217.

Day, G. S. 1990. *Market driven strategy.* New York: The Free Press.

De Meyer, A. 1991. Report on the INSEAD Manufacturing Futures Survey.

Dierickx, Ingemar and Karel Cool. 1989. Asset stock accumulation and sustainability of competitive advantage. *Management Science,* 33:1504–1513.

Di Maggio, J. and W. Powell. 1983 The Iron cage revisited: Institutional isomorphism and collective rationality in organizational fields. *American Sociological Review,* 48:147–160.

Dixit, Avinash. 1990. *Optimization in Economic Theory.* Oxford: Oxford University Press.

Dixit, Avinash. 1989. Hysteresis, import penetration, and exchange rate pass-through. *Quarterly Journal of Economics,* 104:205–228.

Dougherty, D. 1992. A practice-centered model of organisational renewal through product innovation. *Strategic Management Journal-Special Issue: Strategy Process: Managing Corporate Self-Renewal,* Summer.

Dougherty, D. 1990. Understanding new markets for new products. *Strategic Management Journal,* 11:59–79.

Doukas, John and Nickolaos G. Travlos. 1988. The effect of corporate multinationalism on shareholders wealth: Evidence from international acquisitions. *Journal of Finance,* 43:1161–1175.

Doz, Yves L. 1992. Strategies of competence accumulation within firms: A synthesis. Working Paper.

Doz, Yves L. 1981. Multinational strategies and structures in government-controlled business. *Columbia Journal of World Business,* 15:4.

Doz, Yves L. 1980. "Strategic Management in Multinational Companies," *Sloan Management Review,* 21, 2.

Doz, Yves L. 1979. *Government Control and Multinational Strategic Management.* New York: Praeger.

Doz, Yves L. 1976. National policies and multinational management. Doctoral Dissertation, Harvard Business School.

Doz, Yves L., Christopher A. Bartlett, and C. K. Prahalad. 1981. Global competitive pressures and host country demands: managing tensions in MNCs. *California Management Review,* Spring:63–74.

Doz, Yves L. and Gary Hamel. forthcoming. *The Competitive Logics of Strategic Alliances.* New York: The Free Press.

Doz, Yves L. and Gary Hamel. 1992. Alliances in technology strategies. Working Paper.

Doz, Yves L. and C. K. Prahalad. 1991. Managing MNCs: A search for a new paradigm. *Strategic Management Journal*, 12:45–164.

Doz, Yves L. and C. K. Prahalad. 1988. Quality of management: an emerging source of global competitive advantage? In N. Hood and J. E. Vahlne, editors, *Strategies in Global Competition*. London: Croom Helm.

Dumas, Bernard. 1988. Perishable investment and hysteresis in capital formation. Working Paper #44–88, Rodney L. White Center for Financial Research, University of Pennsylvania.

Dunning, John H. 1990. The globalization of firms and the competitiveness of countries. In *Globalization of Firms and the Competitiveness of Countries*. England: Craoford Lectures, Institute of Economic Research, Lund University.

Dunning, John H. 1981. *The Eclectic Theory of the MNC*, chap. 4. London: Allen and Unwin.

Dunning, John H. 1980. Explaining changing patterns of international production: In defence of the eclectic theory. *Oxford Bulletin of Economics and Statistics*, 42:269–295.

Dunning, John H. 1980. Toward an eclectic theory of international production: Some empirical tests. *Journal of International Business Studies*, Spring/Summer:9–30.

Dunning, John H. 1973. The determinants of international production. *Oxford Economic Papers*, November:289–336.

Dunning, John H. 1958. *American Investment in British Manufacturing*. London: Allen and Unwin.

Dyas, Gareth. 1972. "The Strategy and Structure of French Industrial Enterprise." Doctoral Dissertation, Harvard Business School.

Dyas, Gareth P. and Heinz T. Thanheiser. 1976. *The emerging European enterprises: Strategy and structure in French and German industry*. London: Macmillan.

Economist, The. 1989. Management brief: Managing your oyster. October 28:78–79.

Egelhoff, William G. 1988. Strategy and structure in multinational corporations: A revision of the Stopford and Wells model. *Strategic Management Journal*, 9:1–14.

Fayerweather, J. 1960. *Management of International Operations: Text and Cases*. New York: McGraw-Hill.

Fouraker, L. E. and J. Stopford. 1968. Organization structure and multinational strategy. *Administrative Science Quarterly*, 57–70.

Franko, Lawrence G. 1989. Global corporate competition: Who's winning, who's losing and the R&D factor as one reason why. *Strategic Management Journal*, 10:449–474.

Franko, Lawrence G. 1976. *The European multinational*. Stamford, Connecticut: Greylock.

Freeman, J. and W. Boeker. 1984. The ecological analysis of business strategy. *California Management Review*, 26(3): 73–86.

Freeman, J. and M. T. Hannan. 1983. Niche width and the dynamics of organizational populations. *American Journal of Sociology*, 88:1116–1145.

Fruin, M. 1992. Good fences make good neighbours. In T. Nishiguchi, editor, *Managing Product Development*. New York: Oxford University Press.

Galbraith, J. R. 1977. *Organization Design*. Reading, Mass.: Addison-Wesley.

Galbraith, J. R. 1973. *Designing Complex Organizations*. Reading, Mass.: Addison-Wesley.

Geringer, J. Michael, Paul Beamish, and Richard C. da Costa. 1989. Diversification strategy and internationalization: Implications for MNE performance. *Strategic Management Journal*, 10(2):109–119.

Ghoshal, Sumantra. 1987. Global strategy: An organizing framework. *Strategic Management Journal*, 8:424–440.

Ghoshal, Sumantra. 1986. The innovative multinational: A differentiated network of organizational roles and management processes. Doctoral Dissertation, Harvard Business School.

Ghoshal, Sumantra and Christopher A. Bartlett. 1990. The multinational corporation as an interorganizational network. *Academy of Management Review*, 15:603–625.

Ghoshal, Sumantra and Christopher A. Bartlett. 1988. Creation, adoption and diffusion of innovations by subsidiaries of multinational corporations. *Journal of International Business Studies*, Fall. 19(3):365–388.

Ghoshal, Sumantra and Nitin Nohria. 1989. Internal differentiation within multinational corporations. *Strategic Management Journals*, 10:323–337.

Ghoshal, Sumantra and D. E. Westney. 1993. Organization theory and the multinational corporation: Overview. In S. Ghoshal and D. E. Westney, editors, *Organization Theory and the Multinational Corporation*. London: Macmillan.

Grant, R. M., A. P. Jammine, and H. Thomas. 1988. Diversity, diversification, and profitability among British manufacturing companies, 1972–1984. *Academy of Management Journal*, 31:771–801.

Hagström, Peter. 1991. The wired MNC. Stockholm: Institute of International Business, Stockholm School of Economics.

Hall, G. and R. Johnson. 1970. Transfers of United Aerospace technology to Japan. In R. Vernon, editor, *The Technology Factor in International Trade*. New York: Columbia University Press.

Hambrick, D. C. 1989. Guest editor's introduction: Putting top managers back in the strategy picture. *Strategy Management Journal*, 14 (Special Issue):5–15.

Hambrick, D. C. and P. A. Mason. 1984. Upper echelons: The organization as a reflection of its top managers. *Academy of Management Review*, 9:195–206.

Hamel, Gary. 1991. Competition for competence and inter-partner learning within international strategic alliances. *Strategic Management Journal*, 12:83–103.

Hamel, Gary. 1990. Competitive collaboration: learning, power and dependence in international strategic alliances. Ph.D. dissertation, The University of Michigan.

Hamel, Gary and C. K. Prahalad. 1991. Corporate imagination and expeditionary marketing. *Harvard Business Review*, July-August:81–92.

Hamel, Gary and C. K. Prahalad. 1989. Strategic intent. *Harvard Business Review*, May-June:63–75.

Hamel, Gary and C. K. Prahalad. 1985. Do you really have a global strategy? *Harvard Business Review*, July-August:139–148.

Hamel, Gary and C. K. Prahalad. 1983. Managing strategic responsibility in the multinational company. *Strategic Management Journal*, 4:341–351.

Hannan, M. T. and J. Freeman. nd. Density dependence in the growth of organizational populations. *Ecological Models of Organizations*.

Hannan, M. T. and J. Freeman. 1977. The population ecology of organizations. *American Journal of Sociology*, 82:929–954.

Haspeslagh, P. and D. Jemison. 1991. *Managing Acquisitions: Creating Value Through Corporate Renewal*. New York: The Free Press.

Hedlund, Gunnar. 1986. The hypermodern MNC—a heterarchy?" *Human Resource Management*, 25:9–35.

Hedlund, Gunnar. 1981. Autonomy of subsidiaries and formalization of headquarters subsidiary relations in Swedish MNCs. In L. Otterbeck, editor, *The Management of Headquarters Subsidiary Relationships in Multinational Corporations*. Aldershot: Gower.

Hedlund, Gunnar and Per Aman. nd. *Managing Relationships with Foreign Subsidiaries*. Stockholm: Sveriges Mekanforbund.

Hedlund, Gunnar and D. Rolander. 1990. Action in heterarchies: New approaches to managing the MNC. In C. Bartlett, Y. Doz, and G. Hedlund, editors, *Managing the Global Firm*. London: Routledge.

Hedland and Nonaka. 1993. "Models of Knowledge Management in the West and Japan" in P. Lorange, B. Chakravarthy, J. Roos, and A. Vandeven (eds.). *Implementing Strategic Processes: Change, Learning and Co-operation*. Oxford: Basil Blackwell.

Hennart, Jean-François. 1982. *A Theory of the Multinational Enterprise*. Ann Arbor: University of Michigan.

Hill, Charles, Peter Hwang, and W. Chan Kim. 1990. An eclectic theory of the choice of international entry mode. *Strategic Management Journal*, 11:117–128.

Hirsch, P. M. 1976. Organizational effectiveness and the institutional environment. *Administrative Science Quarterly*, 20:327–344.

Hirsch, Seev. 1976. An international trade and investment theory of the firm. *Oxford Economic Papers*, 258–270.

Hitt, M. A., R. E. Hoskisson, and R. D. Ireland. 1994. A mid-range theory of the interactive effects of international and product diversification on innovation and performance. *Journal of Management*, 20:297–326.

Hitt, M. A., R. E. Hoskisson and R. D. Ireland. 1990. Mergers and acquisitions and managerial commitment to innovation in M-form firms. *Strategic Management Journal*, 11(Special Issue):29–47.

Hitt, M. A. and R. D. Ireland. 1986. Relationships among corporate level distinctive competencies, diversification strategy, corporate structure, and performance. *Journal of Management Studies*, 23:401–416.

Hitt, M. A. and B. B. Tyler. 1991. Strategic decision models: Integrating different perspectives. *Strategic Management Journal*, 12:327–351.

Hitt, M. A., B. Tyler, and D. Park. 1990. A cross cultural examination of strategic decision models: Comparison of Korean and U.S. executives. *Academy of Management Proceedings*, 111–115.

Hogarth, R., C. Michaud, Yves Doz, and L. Van der Heyden. 1991. Longevity of business firms: A four-stage framework for analysis. INSEAD Working Paper 91/55/EP/SM.

Hoskisson, R. E. and M. A. Hitt. 1990. Antecedents and performance outcomes of diversification: A review and critique of theoretical perspectives. *Journal of Management*, 16:468–509.

Hoskisson, R. E., M. A. Hitt, and C. W. L. Hill. 1991. Managerial risk taking in diversified firms: An evolutionary perspective. *Organization Science*, 2:296–314.

Hoskisson, R. E., M. A. Hitt, T. Turk, and B. Tyler. 1989. Balancing corporate strategy and executive compensation: Agency theory and corporate governance. In G. Ferris and K. Rowland, editors, *Research in Personnel and Human Resources Management*, 25–57. Greenwich, CT: JAI Press.

Hout, T., M. Porter, E. Rudden, and F. Vogt. 1982. How global companies win out. *Harvard Business Review*, September-October:98–108.

Hymer, Stephen. 1976. *The International Operations of National Firms: A Study of Direct Investment*. Cambridge, MA: MIT Press (reprint of his Ph.D. thesis, Department of Economics, MIT, 1960).

Hymer, S. H. 1960. The international operations of national firms: a study of direct foreign investment. MIT, Doctoral Dissertation, 1960, published by MIT Press in 1976.

Imai, Ken-ichi, Ikujiro Nonaka, and Hirotaka Takeuchi. 1985. Managing the new product development process: How Japanese companies learn and unlearn. In K. Clark, R. Hayes, and C. Lorenz, editors, *The Uneasy Alliance. Managing the Productivity-Technology Dilemma*, 336–376. Boston: Harvard Business School Press.

Itami, Hiroyuki and Thomas Roehl. 1987. *Mobilizing Invisible Assets*. Cambridge, MA: Harvard University Press.

Jacquillat, Bertrand and Bruno H. Solnik. 1978. Multinationals are poor tools for diversification. *Journal of Portfolio Management*, Winter:8–12.

Jensen, M. C. and W. H. Meckling. 1976. Theory of the firm: managerial behavior, agency costs and capital structure. *Journal of Financial Economics*, 3:305–360.

Johanson, Jan and Jan Erik Vahlne. 1977. The internationalization process of the firm—a model of knowledge development and increasing foreign market commitments. *Journal of International Business Studies*, 8:22–32.

Kagono, Tadao, Ikujiro Nonaka, Kiyonori Sakakibara, and Akihiro Okumura. 1985. *Strategic Versus Evolutionary Management. A U.S.-Japan Comparison of Strategy and Organization*. Amsterdam: North Holland Press.

Kerr, J. and Slocum, J. W., Jr. 1987. Managing corporate cultures through reward systems. *Academy of Management Executive*, 1(2): 99–108.

Kilmann, R. H., M. J. Saxton, and R. Serpa. 1986. Issues in understanding and changing culture. *California Management Review*, 27:209–224.

Kim, W. Chan, Peter Hwang, and William Burgers. 1989. "Global diversification strategy and corporate profit performance." *Strategic Management Journal*, 10:45–57.

Kindleberger, C. P., 1969. *American Business Abroad: Six Essays on Direct Investment*. New Haven, CT: Yale University Press.

Knickerbocker, F. T., 1973. *Oligopolistic Reaction and the Multinational Enterprise*. Cambridge, MA: Harvard University Press.

Kobrin, S. J. 1991. An empirical analysis of the determinants of global integration. *Strategic*

Management Journal, 12 (Special Issue): 96–108.

Kogut, Bruce. 1993. Knowledge of the firm and the evolutionary theory of the multinational corporation. *Journal of International Business Studies*. 24:625–642.

Kogut, Bruce. 1992. Joint ventures and the option to expand and to acquire. *Management Science*, 37:19–33.

Kogut, Bruce. 1991. Country capabilities and the permeability of borders. *Strategic Management Journal*, 12 (Special Issue):33–47.

Kogut, Bruce. 1989. A note on global strategies. *Strategic Management Journal*, 10:383–389.

Kogut, Bruce. 1987. Country patterns in international competition: appropriability and oligopolistic agreement. In N. Hood and J. E. Vahlne, editors, *Strategies in Global Competition*. London: Croom Helm.

Kogut, Bruce. 1985a. Designing global strategies: comparative and competitive value-added chains. *Sloan Management Review*, 27:15–28.

Kogut, Bruce. 1985b. Designing global strategies: profiting from operational flexibility. *Sloan Management Review*, 26(5):27–37.

Kogut, Bruce. 1984. Normative observations on the international value-added chain and strategic groups, *Journal of International Business Studies*, 15 (2): 151–167.

Kogut, Bruce. 1983. Foreign direct investments as a sequential process. In *The Multinational Corporation in the 1980s*, ed. Charles P. Kindleberger and David Audretsch, Cambridge: MIT Press.

Kogut, Bruce and Sea-Jin Chang. 1991. Technological capabilities and Japanese foreign direct investment in the United States. *Review of Economics and Statistics*, 73: 401–413.

Kogut, Bruce and Nalin Kulatilaka. 1994. Operating flexibility, global manufacturing, and the option value of a multinational network. *Management Science*, 40(1):123–139.

Kogut, Bruce and Nalin Kulatilaka. 1992. What is a critical capability? Paper presented to the Schumpeter Society conference, Kyoto, Japan.

Kogut, Bruce and Harbir Singh. 1988. The effect of national culture on the choice of entry mode. *Journal of International Business Studies*, 19:411–32.

Kogut, Bruce and Udo Zander. 1993. Knowledge of the firm and the evolutionary theory of the multinational corporation," *Journal of International Business Studies*, 24:625–646.

Kogut, Bruce and Udo Zander. 1992. Knowledge of the firm, combinative capabilities, and the transfer of technology. *Organization Science*, 3:383–397.

Kotabe, M. 1990. The relationship between offshore sourcing and innovativeness of U.S. multinational firms: An empirical investigation. *Journal of International Business Studies*, 21:623–638.

Kulatilaka, Nalin and Enrico Perotti. 1992. The Timing of a Strategic Investment. Boston University, Mimeo.

Lawrence, P. R. and J. Lorsch, 1967. *Organization and Environment*, Cambridge, MA: Harvard University Press.

Learned, Edmund P., Carl R. Christensen, Kenneth R. Andrews and Joseph Bower. 1965. *Business Policy: Text and Cases*. Irwin.

Lei, D., M. A. Hitt and R. Bettis. 1996. Advanced manufacturing technologies, organization design, and strategic flexibility, *Organization Studies*, in press.

Lei, D., M. A. Hitt and R. Bettis. 1996. Dynamic core competencies through meta-learning and strategic context, *Journal of Management*, in press.

Lessard, Donald. 1979. Financial Management of International Operations. Introduction, in *International Financial Management*, ed. D. Lessard, Boston: Warren, Gorham, and Lamont.

Lessard, Donald and Enrico Perotti. 1990. Moving toward 1992: managing the internationalization of ownership and corporate finance, in *Managing the Globalization of Business*, ed. D. Lessard and C. Antonelli, Naples: Editoriale Scientifica.

Levinthal, D. 1991. Organizational adaptation and environmental selection: Inter-related processes of change. *Organization Science*, vol. 2, No.1, February, 140–145.

Levitt, B. and J. G. March. 1988. Organizational learning. *Annual Review of Sociology*, 14, pp. 319–40.

Marston, Richard. 1989. Pricing to market in Japanese manufacturing. *Journal of International Economics*, 3, 4:217–236.

Mascarenhas, Briance. 1992a. First-mover effects in multiple dynamic markets. Research Note. *Strategic Management Journal.*

Mascarenhas, Briance. 1992b. The order of entry and performance in international markets. *Strategic Management Journal.*

Mascarenhas, Briance. 1989. Domains of state-owned, publicly traded, and privately held firms in international competition, *Administrative Science Quarterly*, December.

Mascarenhas, Briance. 1985. International strategies of non-dominant firms. *Journal of International Business Studies*, 16.

Mascarenhas, Briance and D. Aaker. 1989. Mobility barriers and strategic groups. *Strategic Management Journal*, vol. 10, 475–485.

McGee, J. and H. Thomas. 1986. Strategic groups: theory, research and taxonomy. *Strategic Management Journal*, March-April, pp. 141–160.

Meyer, J. and Rowan, B. Institutionalized organizations: formal structures as myth and ceremony. *American Journal of Sociology*, 83, 1977, pp. 340–363.

Mitchell, Will, J. Myles Shaver, and Bernard Yeung. 1991. Changing international presence in domestic and transition industries. University of Michigan, mimeo.

Morck, Randall and Bernard Yeung. 1991. Why investors value multinationality. *Journal of Business*, 64: 165–187.

Morrison, A. J. 1990. *Strategies in Global Industries: How U.S. Businesses Compete.* New York: Quorum Books.

Miller, D. and P. Friesen. 1984. A longitudinal study of the corporate life cycle. *Management Science*, 30, 1984a, 1161–1183.

Myers, Stewart. 1977. Determinants of corporate borrowing. *Journal of Financial Economics*, 5: 147–176.

Nelson, R. 1991. How do firms differ, and how does it matter? *Strategic Management Journal*, 12, pp. 61–74.

Nelson, Richard R. and Sidney G. Winter. 1982. An Evolutionary Theory of Economic Development. Cambridge, MA: Harvard University.

Nevens, T., G. Summe and B. Uttal. 1990. Commercializing technology: what the best companies do. *McKinsey Quarterly*, 4, pp. 3–22.

Nishiguchi, Toshihiro (ed.). 1992. *Managing Product Development.* New York: Oxford University Press, forthcoming.

Nonaka, I. and G. Hedlund. 1993. Models of knowledge management in the West and Japan. Working Paper.

Nonaka, I. 1991. The knowledge-creating corporation. *Harvard Business Review*, 69, 6, pp. 96–104.

Ohmae, K. 1990. *The Borderless World.* Harper and Row.

Pavan, Robert J. 1972. The strategy and structure of Italian enterprise, unpublished doctoral thesis, Boston: Harvard Business School.

Pavitt, Keith. 1971. The multinational enterprise and the transfer of technology, in *The Multinational Enterprise*, ed. J. Dunning, London: George Allen and Unwin.

Penrose, E. 1959. *The Theory of the Growth of the Firm.* Guildford: Basil Blackwell.

Perlmutter, Howard. 1969. The tortuous evolution of the multinational corporation. *Columbia Journal of World Business*, 4: 9–18.

Pfeffer, J. and G. R. Salancik. 1978. *The External Control of Organizations.* New York: Harper and Row.

Pianka, Eric R. 1983. *Evolutionary Ecology.* Third edition. New York: Harper and Row.

Porter, Michael E.. 1991. Towards a dynamic theory of strategy. *Strategic Management Journal*, 12: 95–118.

Porter, Michael E. 1990. *The Competitive Advantage of Nations.* New York: The Free Press.

Porter, Michael E.. 1986. Competition in global industries: a conceptual framework, in *Competition in Global Industries*, ed. Michael E. Porter, Boston: Harvard Business School.

Porter, Michael E. 1985. *Competitive Advantage.* New York: Basic Books.

Porter, Michael E. 1980. *Competitive Advantage.* New York: The Free Press.

Prahalad, C. K. 1976. Strategic choices in diversified mncs. *Harvard Business Review*, 54: 67–78.

Prahalad, C. K. 1975. The strategic process in multinational corporation. Unpublished Doctoral Dissertation, School of Business Administration, Harvard University.

Prahalad, C. K. and Gary Hamel. 1990. The core competence of the corporation. *Harvard Business Review*, 68(4): 79–91.

Prahalad, C. K. and Yves L. Doz. 1987. *The Multinational Mission: Balancing Local Demands and Global Vision*. New York: The Free Press.

Ramanujam, V. and P. Varadarajan. 1989. Research on corporate diversification: A synthesis. *Strategic Management Journal*, 10: 523–552.

Roach, S. 1991. Services under siege-the restructuring imperative. *Harvard Business Review*, September-October, 82–91.

Robinson, Richard D. 1978. *International Business Management: A Guide to Decision making*. Hinsdale, Ill,: Dryden Press.

Romanelli, E. and M. L. Tushman. 1986. Inertia, environments and strategic choice: A quasi-experimental design for comparative longitudinal research. *Management Science*, 32: 608–621.

Root, Franklin R. 1987. *Entry Strategies for International Markets*. Lexington: Lexington, MA.

Roth, Kendall and Allen Morrison. 1991. An empirical analysis of the integration-responsiveness framework in global industries. *Strategic Management Journal*, 21: 541–564.

Rugman, Alan M. 1981. Internalization as a general theory of foreign direct investment: a reappraisal of the literature. *Weltwirtschaftliches Archiv*, 116: 365–79.

Rugman, Alan M. 1979. *International Diversification and the Multinational Enterprise*. Lexington M. A.: Lexington Books.

Rumelt, Richard P., Dan E. Schendel, and David J. Teece, 1994. *Fundamental Issues in Strategy: A Research Agenda*. Boston: Harvard Business School Press.

Rumelt, R. 1991. How much does industry matter? *Strategic Management Journal*, 13, 3, pp. 167–185.

Schendel, D. 1991. Introduction to the special issue on global strategy. *Strategic Management Journal*, 12, pp. 1–3.

Scott, W. R. 1991. Unpacking institutional arguments, in W. W. Powell and P. J. DiMaggio, Eds., *The New Institutionalism in Organizational Analysis*, Chicago: The University of Chicago Press.

Selznick, P. 1957. *Leadership in Administration*. New York: Harper and Row.

Shan, Wei-jian. 1992. Strategic direct investment in high technology industries. Wharton School, mimeo.

Sharp, David. 1987. Control systems and decision-making in multinational firms: price management under floating exchange rates. Ph.D. thesis, Massachusetts Institute of Technology.

Simon, H. A. 1949. *Administrative Behaviour* New York: The Free Press.

Solvell, Orjan. 1987. Entry barriers and foreign penetration-emerging patterns of international competition in two electrical engineering industries, Institute of International Business, Stockholm School of Economics.

Stopford, John M. and Louis Wells, Jr. 1972. *Managing the Multinational Enterprise: Organization of the Firm and Ownership of Subsidiaries*. New York: Basic Books.

Teece, David J. 1986. Profiting from technological innovation. *Research Policy*, 15:285–306.

Teece, David J. 1985. Multinational enterprise, internal governance and economic organization. *American Economic Review*, 75, pp. 233–238.

Teece, David J. 1980. Economies of scope and the scope of the enterprise. *Journal of Economic Behavior and Organization*, 3: 223–247.

Teece, David J. 1977. Technology transfer by multinational firms: the resource costs of transferring technological know-how. *Economic Journal*, 87: 242–61.

Teece, David J., G. Pisano and A. Shuen. 1990. Firm capabilities, resources and the concept of strategy. Consortium on competitiveness and cooperation, Working Paper 90–9, University of California at Berkeley, Centre for Research in Management.

Thanheiser, Heinz. 1972. "Strategy and Structure of German Industrial Enterprise." Doctoral Dissertation. Harvard Business School.

Tosi, H. and Gomez-Mejia, L. 1989. The decoupling of CEO pay and performance: An agency theory perspective. *Administrative Science Quarterly*, 35:169–189.

Tsetsekos, George. 1989. Multinationality and common stock offering dilution. *Journal of International Financial Management and Accounting*, 3: 1–16.

Tsetsekos, George P. and Michael J. Gombola. 1992. Foreign and domestic divestment's: evidence on valuation effects of plant closings. *Journal of International Business Studies*, 23: 203–224.

United Nations Center on Transnational Corporations. 1988. Transnational corporations in world development: Trends and prospects, United Nations, New York.

Van de Ven, A. 1992. Suggestions for studying strategic process: A research note. *Strategic Management Journal-Special Issue: Strategy Process; Managing Corporate Self-Renewal*, Summer.

Vernon, Raymond. 1966. International investment and international trade in the product life cycle. *Quarterly Journal of Economics*, 80: 190–207.

Weick, K. E. 1987. Organizational culture as a source of high reliability. *California Management Review*, 29: 112–126.

Westney, Eleanor. 1992. Institutionalization theory and the multinational corporation. *Organizational Theory and the Multinational corporation*, ed. S. Ghoshal and E. Westney, London: MacMillan.

Whittaker, Hugh. 1993. New technology and the organization of work: British and Japanese factories, in *Country Competitiveness: Technology and the Organizing of Work*, ed. B. Kogut, Oxford, UK: Oxford University Press.

Wilkins, Mira. 1974. *The Maturing of Multinational Enterprise: American Business Abroad from 1914 to 1970*. Cambridge: Harvard University Press.

Williamson, O. E. 1975. *Markets and Hierarchies: Analysis and Antitrust implications*. The Free Press, New York.

Winter, Sidney. 1987. Knowledge and competence as strategic assets, in *The Competitive Challenge-Strategies for Industrial Innovation and Renewal*, ed. D. Teece, Cambridge, MA: Ballinger.

Womack, J., D. Jones, and D. Roos. 1990. *The Machine That Changed the World*. New York: Macmillan.

Yip, G. S. 1989. Global strategy . . . in a world of nations? *Sloan Management Review*, Fall.

Yoshino, M. 1968. *Japan's Managerial System*. Cambridge, Mass.: MIT Press.

Zander, Udo and Bruce Kogut. 1995. Knowledge and the speed of transfer and imitation of organizational capabilities: an empirical test. *Organizational Science*. 6:76–92.

Zucker, L. G. 1983. Organization as institutions. In S. Bacharach, editor, *Advances in Organizational Theory and Research*. Greenwich: JAI Press. Vol. 2, 1–43.

9

Marketing Perspectives and International Business

EDITORS' COMMENTS

There has been considerable debate in the marketing literature on (1) what constitute's the conceptual domain of marketing, (2) the phenomena and relationships to be studied, and (3) the field's core ontological and epistemological assumptions (see, for example, Hunt 1990). Given this background of debate, we thought it appropriate to ask three leading international marketing (IM) scholars whether they saw IM as a distinct field of inquiry, or simply as an interesting extension of marketing inquiry that provides opportunities to test theories and concepts originating in one societal setting. We went even further and asked them whether the lack of theory building (as distinct from theory testing) in IM can be traced to the core (axiomatic) assumptions underpinning marketing inquiry? In short, is IM inquiry, as distinct from marketing inquiry, doomed to remain theoretically sterile because of these assumptions? The authors were also asked to develop a framework that highlights the various orientations, paradigms, theories, and metaphors, etc., and their contrasting assumptions, questions, and methodologies, and which could be used to distinguish between the theoretical and research contributions of marketing and IM.

Mattsson, in the leadoff paper, chose to focus on the paradigms that link and underpin research in marketing and IB. By noting that exchange is common to both marketing and IB [Bagozzi 1975; Hunt 1976, Toyne 1989], he is able to argue that "if marketing academics more generally consider the nature of the exchange paradigms they use, then the limitations and opportunities of marketing studies for international business theory and practice could be clarified." [p. 527] That is, he shows how marketing and IB researchers could make substantial contributions to the development of the other's field of inquiry.

According to Mattsson, marketing researchers use either a marketing-mix paradigm or a marketing-relationship paradigm when examining exchange-related issues. The marketing-mix paradigm—a special case of the extension and cross-border management paradigms discussed in the opening chapter—is based on neo-classical micro-economic theories of monopolistic competition and theories of consumer behavior, and assumes that the role of exchange is to mutually satisfy the needs and wants of buyers and sellers. It is also static and cross-sectional, and views sellers and buyers as belonging to different systems. The seller is viewed as an external initiator who creatively manipulates or exploits an amorphous "average" buyer using a set of "action variable" in order to compete with other sellers in selling to a market.

The marketing-relationship paradigm— a special case of the emerging interaction paradigm described in the opening chapter— is based on the social exchange and social action schools of thought, among others, and assumes the role of exchange is the mutual adaptation over time of products and processes. In contrast to the marketing-mix paradigm, the marketing-relationship paradigm is dynamic and longitudinal, and sees buyers and sellers as belonging to the same system with mutual, yet changing dependencies. Thus, the relationship between seller and buyer is viewed as an interactive, incremental, learning process.

Mattsson concludes his paper by first examining the influence that the two exchange paradigms have on what is studied

and how it is studied. He then examines what could be done to improve on the academic and practical contributions of IM research to both marketing and IB.

In the second topic paper, Samiee, arguing from a marketing-mix perspective, points out that not only does the field of international marketing (IM) lack academic identity, there has also been little effort made to provide it with conceptual, theoretical, and methodological legitimacy. Thus, he saw as his central purpose the need to examine "the nature and status of IM and . . . [to develop] a conceptual framework that differentiates the domain of IM from that of domestic marketing." [p.453]

In developing his argument, Samiee evaluates the past and current status of IM research within the field of marketing, and explores three aspects of IM in his paper. First, he examines the meaning that has been attached to the term "international marketing" over the years, and concludes that there is no universally accepted definition of IM. Thus, asserting that the "lack of theoretical development in IM necessitates the adoption of a general definition," he defines IM as *the pursuit of business activities beyond a firm's home market in a cross-cultural sense.*" [p.544]

Second, he examines the relationship between IM and domestic marketing (DM) as distinct fields or disciplines. According to Samiee there are two opposing schools of thought. The first states that there is no difference between IM and DM and that "the character and elements of marketing do not change from one country to another." [p. 544] Echoing Vernon's [1964] description of the cross-border management paradigm discussed in the opening chapter, Samiee suggests that the second school of thought holds that IM is distinct from DM since there are unique issues such as standardization and countertrade, and also fundamental differences between the markets and institutions of different nations.

Finally, he offers a conceptual framework for the field, the basis of which include intermarket segmentation, market entry mode, and the management of the marketing activity according to one of three market orientations (i.e., extension, multidomestic, and global). The objective was to develop and present a conceptual framework that emphasized elements and issues not typically included in the treatment of marketing at the domestic level.

In the final topic paper, Sheth argues that IM inquiry has been primarily contextual in nature and, therefore, unable to generate its own theory or constructs to justify it as a unique school of marketing thought. He further argues, from a marketing-mix paradigmic orientation, that as a contextual practice, IM has rightfully focused on two obvious issues: how and why marketing varies from country to country. Unlike Mattsson, Sheth does not examine the linkage between IB and IM research, and how each contributes to the other's inquiry.

Although not made explicit, Sheth appears to support a multi-level conceptualization of marketing. He also appears to accept the controversial assumption that technology (more specifically, transportation and communication technologies) and regionalization are bringing about environmental convergence, and that "there will be no discipline of IM even if it was developed based on a contingency theory approach." [p. 561] He further argues that IM will be born again, but with an emphasis on global and cross-functional dimensions, and that this inquiry may become a subdiscipline or a school of marketing thought.

In the first of two commentaries, Gatignon selects to "emphasize and amplify" two areas of promising research raised by the authors of the three topic papers: (1) interorganizational relations; and (2) globalization/regionalization. Importantly, he appears to support the multi-level conceptualization of IM implied in Sheth's remarks, since his discussion is not restricted to or exclusively based on a firm-level conceptualization of IM.

Under the inter-organizational relations category, Gatignon suggests that the two central research questions raised by the three papers deal with the level of control sub-organizations must have within the firm, and across firms, and under what conditions relations should exist, especially in the form of alliances. Interestingly, Gatignon avoids discussing the theoretical and research implications of the two paradigmic orientations discussed by Mattsson. Instead, he argues for a transaction costs (micro-economic) analysis of the two particular inter-organizational issues he addresses. The discussion of both issues would have been enriched if the implications of the marketing-mix and marketing-relational paradigms had been incorporated; implications dealing with the specific questions they would engender, the specific hypotheses to be tested, and the methodologies to be used.

Under the globalization-regionalization category, Gatignon identifies three issues requiring research: (1) the standardization versus differentiation question raised by Mattsson and Samiee; (2) the revision of the diffusion theory that incorporates the interaction of populations as proposed by Sheth; and (3) the allocation of marketing resources as suggested by Samiee.

Cavusgil's commentary is simultaneously more comprehensive and more focused than Gatignon's. More specifically, Cavusgil addresses a more comprehensive list of issues than does Gatignon. He asks and then answers eight questions that deal with such widely ranging issues as the scope and distinctiveness of IM, the generalizability of IM knowledge, and the most promising directions for IM research. Yet, in sharp contrast to the multi-level conceptualization of marketing advanced by Gatignon, his remarks emphasize a firm-level and manageriallydominated conceptualization of marketing.[1] For example, when remarking on the scope of international marketing he suggests "that there are two fundamental tasks in international marketing *management*"(emphasis added by the editors). [p. 571]

A review of these five papers as a group raises several additional issues and questions that go beyond those suggested by the papers individually. First, only Samiee and Cavusgil include definitional discussions of IM. The other authors assume that the reader is aware of and also accepts the conceptualizations they implicitly advocate. This, of course, is problematic. As the discussion presented in the opening chapter suggests, there are a number of views, each of which engenders a different definition of IM.

Second, the significance of Mattsson's contribution is generally overlooked. His discussion of the marketing-mix and -relational paradigms and their influence on marketing research is somewhat ignored. However, these marketing-specific paradigms are examples of the extension, cross-border management, and interaction paradigms identified and discussed in the opening chapter. Also, Mattsson's discussion of these marketing paradigms illustrates the fundamentally different theoretical and empirical questions that these IB paradigms engender. The other four authors appear to be strongly attached to the marketing-mix paradigm that so pervasively influences most U.S. marketing thought and research.

Third, the difficulty of developing a coherent and comprehensive understanding of the research undertaken and reported on in different countries does not appear to be simply one of "coming to grips" with paradigmic, even philosophic differences. Such differences were, of course, evident in the five papers presented in this and some of the other sections in this book (e.g., the French discoveries versus the English rediscoveries remarked on by Graham in chapter 4). Nor does this difficulty appear to be one arising from a "mechanical" failure in the retrieval and acquisition of knowledge. In his paper, Mattsson clearly demonstrates not only an awareness of, but also an ability to digest and integrate into his "Scandinavian" thinking the implications of the U.S. marketing orientation and paradigms, and the marketing knowledge that this *Gestalt* has generated.

Rather, the difficulty can be traced, we believe, to one or more of the following reasons. The first, and most frequently mentioned reason is that of language. It is often argued that U.S. business scholars lack linguistic skills so cannot read the papers and books written and published in other languages. This reason has gained support in recent years as the number of business researchers in other parts of the world has grown substantially. Another reason is the "not invented here" syndrome. Simply put, conceptualizations and research findings that are not based on Anglo-American underpinnings are just not worth knowing or thinking about deeply. A third possibility is the failure of U.S. doctoral programs to incorporate (1) an awareness of and appreciation for non-U.S. contributions to the body of knowledge, and (2) the skills and knowledge needed to work with and within different orientations and paradigms using their respective questions and methodologies. As these programs have become increasingly specialized and narrow, the scholarship (e.g., reading, reflection, and research) undertaken by students of these programs has also become increasingly narrow and unsympathetic.

Finally, as the contrasting arguments presented in these papers demonstrate so convincingly, the conduct of IB research requires a fuller understanding of the paradigmic roots of the theories and streams of research in this area; an observation that has equal merit in any other area of inquiry. As Hench points out in chapter 2, we are in a period of paradigmic change and consequently tend to confuse our discussions and our research by shifting from one paradigmic orientation to another without fully addressing the theoretical and empirical implications of such shifts.

NOTE

1. His argument for managerial relevance is similar to that of Schendel and Hofer [1979] which inadvertently resulted in the premature closure of the strategic management field. Essentially, they argued that the knowledge generated as a consequence of research is only of value if it has immediate managerial relevance.

Exchange Approaches And Marketing's Contributions To International Business Research
Lars-Gunnar Mattsson

The aim of this paper is to discuss how research on marketing can contribute to the general research field of international business (IB). More specifically, issues will be raised concerning how paradigmatic orientations of academic research in marketing and in IB are related to each other. The extent to which such orientations are different or similar will influence the ability of marketing researchers to make important contributions to the development of IB knowledge and vice versa. I argue that if marketing academics more generally consider the nature of the exchange paradigms they use, then the limitations and opportunities of marketing studies for IB theory and practice could be clarified. This would be helpful in giving directions for future international marketing (IM) research. The exchange concept may serve as an integrating mechanism for IB research in general [Toyne 1989]. Exchange paradigms can be used as bridges between the micro issues of behavior of individual actors and the macro issues concerning the structure, behavior and performance of international industries and markets; issues which are of vital concern for research in marketing.

My reasoning is as follows. First, economic systems are coordinated through a *governance structure* (i.e., an institutional form such as a hierarchy, a market or some kind of intermediate contractual arrangement). Exchange is theoretically treated differently depending upon governance structure. Second, marketing as an academic field of inquiry has differentiated paradigmatic attributes depending upon type of governance structure. Especially one can distinguish between "stimulus-organism-response" (i.e., marketing mix approaches) and exchange relationships frameworks. Third, IB as an academic field of inquiry can be divided into three types of studies (e.g., Toyne [1989]): (1) Type A International operations by individual firms; (2) Type B Comparative system studies; and (3) Type C Explanations of the multinational enterprise (MNE) as an institution. Major aspects of research on IB can be linked to theories about governance structures. Fourth, research on IM is by definition related to research on IB of Types A and B. It may or may not be related to Type C in an explicit way. An important question is to what extent and how IM research contributes to IB research outside of marketing's own domain. To answer that question we need to characterize research on IM and discuss how it is linked to major streams of research on IB. Finally, with this background we are ready to discuss potential contributions from the research in marketing to IB research.

GOVERNANCE OF ECONOMIC SYSTEMS AND MARKETING EXCHANGE PARADIGMS

Markets, Hierarchies, and Intermediate Forms

Economic systems are composed of actors carrying out interdependent activities. The coordination of these activities influences the performance of the system as does also the mechanism used for this coordination. The archetypes "hierarchy" and "market" lead to different transaction cost levels, depending upon the structural and behavioral conditions included in the theory [Williamson 1985]. Costs of internalizing activities within a hierarchy can be compared to costs of externalizing activities into a market. In the market, the actors transact with each other through arm's length relations. Thus, individual counterparts are unidentified and transactions are of a nonrecurring nature. When transactions take place between identified counterparts and are of a recurring nature they are governed by "intermediate" institutional forms (i.e., legal and social norms for behavior in exchange relationships). Macneil [1980] describes this as "relational contracting." The transaction cost approach covers all three types of governance structures, thereby postulating nonrelationship exchange on markets and relationship exchanges for intermediate forms and (implicitly) in hierarchies.

Marketing as Exchange

Even if there exist many different "schools of thought" in marketing, an overriding conceptual focus is on value creation by *exchange*. Thus, exchange concepts have a wider application in academic marketing thought than that used by the specific "social exchange school" [Bagozzi 1975; Hunt 1976; Houston and Gassenheimer 1987]. Kotler states: "Marketing is a social and managerial process by which individuals and groups obtain what they need and want through creating and *exchanging* products and values with others" [1988:3] (emphasis added).

Different paradigmatic orientations in marketing research describe exchange and the systems within which exchange takes place in different ways (see Figure 1). The S-O-R/marketing mix is a noninteraction/nonrelationship approach. The focus is on the seller's marketing activities (S) and the buyer's response (R) to such activities, depending on buyer attributes (O). Interaction approaches can be subdivided into single transaction and exchange relationship approaches. The latter finally can be of a dyadic or a network nature.

The marketing mix and the single transaction approaches are consistent with market governance, given that the "market" is imperfect. (If the market is perfect, marketing itself is nonexistent). The Danish "parameter theory," developed during the 1940s and 1950s, very clearly demonstrates how the marketing mix models are related to microeconomic models of monopolistic competition and to theories of consumer behavior [Rasmussen 1955]. The exchange

relationship approaches are consistent with "intermediate" forms for governance. Dyadic and network approaches differ in terms of how the contexts of individual exchange relationships are described. Network approaches treat individual exchange relationships as interconnected, which purely dyadic approaches do not. In the history of marketing research several approaches such as the Institutional, Functional, Organizational Dynamics, Systems, and Social Exchange "schools of thought" have considered exchange relationships [Sheth et al. 1988]. Below, I will discuss some major differences between the various approaches to exchange in Figure 1.

What is the role of exchange? In microeconomic theory, the role of exchange is to "clear the market" and to lead to an optimal allocation of resources. In the marketing mix model the role of exchange is to satisfy needs and wants of buyers and sellers. The microtheoretic background of the marketing mix model makes the idea of optimal allocation of resources across the marketing mix variables an important issue. The role of exchange, while basically limited to a comparative, static perspective, also has a dynamic aspect since marketing activities may influence rate and speed of diffusion of innovations and long-term customer preferences [Rasmussen 1955]. In relationship models, exchange has a dynamic role. It influences mutual adaptations over time of products and processes. Present exchange influences future exchange. Exchange gives access to resources controlled by other actors [Pfeffer and Salancick 1978].

Within what system does exchange take place? The obvious concept to rely on here for marketing is the "market." How can the market then be defined? To quote once more from an influential textbook: "A market consists of all the potential customers sharing a particular need or want who might be willing and able to engage in exchange to satisfy that need or want" [Kotler 1988:9].

According to this definition one of the

Figure 1. Paradigmatic Orientations for Analysis of Marketing Exchange

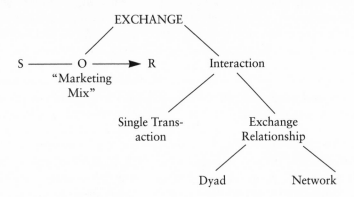

parties in the exchange, the seller, is not included in the market. This implies that seller and buyer are members of different systems, that exchange takes place at "arm's length" as in neoclassical microeconomic theory and that a specific market is delimited on the basis of substitutability. This definition is consistent with the marketing mix approach. Thus, sellers compete in selling *to* the market.

In the industrial organization (IO) literature, the market concept is used in a more supply oriented way (number of sellers, seller concentration, barriers to entry, etc. as attributes of the market structure) even if the "number of buyers" and "vertical integration" are included as structural dimensions of an "industry." The market, as defined in the marketing mix model, is in the IO-model treated as exogenous to the market structure since demand characteristics are included in "Basic Conditions" [Scherer and Ross 1990]. Also, in the IO-literature, substitutability delimits the relevant system for exchange.

In exchange relationship approaches, markets are described as systems of exchange relationships. Sellers and buyers belong in the same system. Both complementarities and substitutes are included in the network. According to the most important author in the exchange relationship tradition, exchange takes place between and within organized behavior systems, matching heterogeneous supply and demand through a complicated and dynamic sorting process [Alderson 1957].

On what level of aggregation is exchange studied? In microeconomic theory, demand response to seller activities is an aggregated response. Response is measured by the "elasticity" of price, advertising, etc. This is the basic way in which marketing mix models also view customer response. Customers with similar responses are grouped together in market segments. Response patterns refer to aggregates.

Relationship approaches take the individual exchange relationship as the basic building block of the market system. Exchange between individual actors takes place within an "environment" or in a "context." How can this environment be characterized? Is it regarded as an aggregated market structure or is it regarded as a set of other dyadic relationships? In the network approach, the individual dyad is connected to other dyadic relationships. The total market system thus becomes a network of interconnected relationships [Cook and Emerson 1978].

What is the character of the exchange? "Marketing (management) is the process of planning and executing the conception, pricing, promotion and distribution of ideas, goods and services to create exchanges that satisfy individual and organizational objectives." (Kotler [1988:11] cites this definition that was approved by the American Marketing Association in 1985.)

In the marketing mix model, the exchange is thus a creative act by the initiating seller who has at his disposal a set of action variables. The degree of interdependency between individual actors (buyer and seller) in the exchange is low. The focus is on aggregated responses during one time period.

In relationship approaches, exchange takes place through interactions between individual actors where prior knowledge about the counterpart and mutual dependency are important considerations. The relationships are developed and changed over time through activities and adaptations by both parties. Thus, the buyer is equally as active as the seller.

Who participates in the exchange? In the marketing mix model, the exchange activities are the domain of the marketing function in the organization. Typically, actors involved are the "boundary personnel" of sellers and buyers. Buyers, be they consumers or organizations, are in some models described as small groups (households, "buying centers," etc.) which means that the "O"-variable contains several actors and their relationships.

The relationship model takes a holistic view of both the interacting parties. All the different kinds of resources and functions in the firm are more or less involved and may need to be adapted for the exchange relationship to develop. This means that the internal organizational structure of both parties will be of explicit relevance for the exchange. This goes beyond the way in which the marketing and purchasing functions are organized.

Use of nonrelationship and relationship approaches to exchange. Exchange relationship approaches have been mostly used for "industrial marketing" and "marketing channels" studies. It is easy to understand that there are important interdependencies between actors in production and distribution systems and thus to see links to research

problems dealt with in industrial organizations and in interorganizational studies. On the other hand, the typical use of the marketing mix approach is for exchange between sellers and consumers. In such situations the characteristics of exchange are easier to conceptualize on an aggregated level and at arm's length, especially if we are interested in the problems of the marketing manager.

The marketing mix model dominates the academic discipline as it relates to marketing management. Within "mainstream" marketing research only the channel literature is to an important extent exchange relationship oriented. In the marketing mix model, exchange takes place within the governance structure of the "imperfect" market. Exchanges within hierarchies are in the marketing management literature treated as organizational processes *within* the selling or buying organization. Seller behavior is marketing mix related in that it deals with the (rational) planning and execution of marketing activities (S) while buyer behavior is included in the "O" variable of the S-O-R model.

However, relationship approaches are gaining ground, not only in several European countries but also in North America. Philip Kotler recently suggested that the paradigmatic development of marketing is moving "from transactions to relationships to networks" [Kotler 1991b].

In Sweden the development of the "markets as networks" approach can be seen as the result of a long-term research tradition [Johanson and Mattsson 1994]. Several recent books reporting on predominantly European IM research using network approaches have been published (see Hallén and Johanson [1989]; Ford [1990]; Axelsson and Easton [1991]). While the marketing mix and the transaction cost analyses are based on neoclassical microeconomic theory, the network approach is more related to Schumpeterian approaches such as neo-Austrian economics [Kirzner 1973] and theories about industrial change in economic systems [Dahmén 1970;1988] and in technological systems [Hughes 1987].

INTERNATIONAL BUSINESS RESEARCH

IB is concerned with business activities performed in more than one nation. The term internationalization is somewhat ambiguous since it can signify the "degree of internationalization" or the "process of internationalization." Hence, there is also a possible subdivision of IB research in static (or comparative static) and process-oriented analyses at the firm level and/or the industry/market level. Most IB studies are not process-oriented and there is rarely explicit consideration of the simultaneous internationalization processes at the micro and the macrolevels. Since Type C studies are theoretically more explicit and coherent than the other types, I will comment on them first.

Type C: Explaining IB (Multinational Enterprises)

The conventional theory explaining the existence of the multinational enterprise (MNE) is based upon theories of imperfect competition as expressed in the IO-literature and theories of internalization [Caves 1982]. Related to this, but also including location specific variables, is Dunning's "eclectic paradigm" [Dunning 1988]. It organizes three types of variables in an effort to explain the extent, form, and pattern of international production: Ownership specific advantages (i.e., variables defined within the industrial organization framework), Locational advantages and Internalization advantages.

O-advantages can be due to some specific immaterial asset or to the advantages of being a multiplant firm, and are theoretically linked to the IO analysis of imperfect competition and thus also to the marketing mix model. Reasons to internalize O-advantages are linked to various aspects of market failure and thus to the same conceptual framework as transaction cost analysis. Finally, the reasons why produc-

tion is located to a specific country, or set of countries, is explained by the existence of country-specific factor endowments and is thus related to trade theory.

Recently, efforts have been made to reorient the theory of MNE in order to accommodate some prominent features of the modern MNE and its environment [Dunning 1988; Casson 1990; Buckley 1990]. Conventional theories are, according to Casson [1990], trapped in a static mode. They take the firm's technological advantage as a datum. They have a too polarized view of contractual arrangements and do not consider the complex interorganizational structure of the international production. Furthermore, according to Casson, conventional theory does not sufficiently consider the driving force of entrepreneurship and the system nature of production. This means that too little consideration is given to complementarities between firms and the strategic behavior by individual firms. Nor is the importance of "distribution assets" in comparison with "manufacturing assets" given enough theoretical consideration. I interpret these shortcomings of the theory of the MNE as a need to use more exchange relationship oriented approaches, especially network approaches.

Type A: International Operations by the Individual Firm

The adjustment by individual firms to conditions of locations other than the home country can be of a strategic, organizational, and functional nature. The different subdisciplines of "business administration" gives input to these IB studies. There are as many paradigmatic orientations for these types of studies as there are for the subdisciplines without the "international" prefix.

Later I will discuss the international marketing (IM) literature as it relates to type A and B studies. Here I will only make some general comments using the conceptual scheme illustrated in Figure 2 which relates the content, process, and context of corporate strategy [Pettigrew 1987].

Figure 2. Dimension to Characterize Corporate Strategy Research

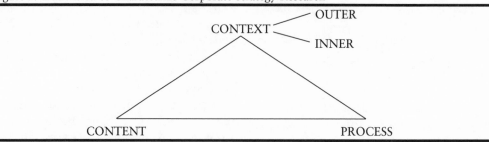

From Pettigrew (1987), p. 5.

The IO-derived strategy literature (e.g., Porter [1980]) focuses on the *content-outer context* linkage. For IB research, a typical study determines if the international market structure in an industry makes differentiation or standardization the most effective strategy (e.g., Buzzell [1968]; Porter [1986]; Levitt [1983]). Process-oriented researchers [Mintzberg 1978] emphasize the *process-inner context* linkage. How are strategic processes influenced by the way in which the international firm is organized and the characteristics of management attitudes and values? Export performance studies provide many examples of this approach (e.g., Axinn [1988]). The strategy-structure school [Chandler 1962] focuses on the link between *content and inner context*. As the international firm increases its degree of internationalization, is there a need to change the organizational structure (e.g., Stopford and Wells [1972])? The contingency theory [Lawrence and Lorsch 1967] is more interested in the adaptation of the firm's organization to differences in its environment. It is thus primarily a question of the link between *inner and outer context*. Some of the studies on standardization vs. differentiation belong here (e.g., Kotabe [1990]; Bartlett et al. [1989]).

A major Type A inquiry concerns the internationalization process of the individual firm. Here one of the most pervasive ideas is the internationalization process model explaining the firm's internationalization as a gradual, sequential increase in international extension and international resource commitments [Hörnell et al. 1975; Johanson and Wiedersheim-Paul 1975; Johanson and Vahlne 1977; Bilkey 1978]. Internationalization is driven and constrained by "experiential learning" about foreign market conditions. In terms of the content-context-process triangle, this model gives a behavioral interpretation of how the strategic *process* leads the firm to an extension-penetration sequence (*content*) whereby the firm is able to match its knowledge base (*inner context*) to the attributes of its foreign environment (*outer context*). The approach lets the theoretical nature of the process be the major explanation of internationalization behavior. The model is consistent with exchange relationship approaches and has had an important impact on the development of network research [Johanson and Mattsson 1994].

The possibilities of linking Type A and Type C studies depend upon the extent to which the underlying theories are similar, especially as they concern the exchange concept. Thus, theories on imperfect competition and transaction cost analysis link "outer context/content" A-studies to C-studies. However, when A-studies focus on strategic processes, inner contexts or outer contexts with a high degree of international interdependencies, then the conventional theory of the MNE has less to offer as base for Type A studies.

Type B: Comparative Studies

Comparative studies can have an "international" dimension in two senses. The first (and most frequent) interpretation is that differences and similarities between national systems are highlighted. The second is that national systems are more or less dependent upon each other. That is, the national systems themselves are internationalized.

Drawing upon many disciplines, researchers are comparing different national conditions for business behavior. Linked to that are also studies of governance structures and norms for business exchange. Comparative management deals with various aspects of management beliefs and behavior, organizational structure and control, different practices concerning functional areas such as manufacturing, purchasing, and marketing. Major research interests during the last couple of decades have been concentrated on the Japanese socioeconomic system compared to those in the United States and in Western Europe.

In the comparative literature on government-business interaction several themes are explored. The most prominent is how host and home governments influence MNEs. Are production factor supply conditions becoming less important than transaction cost influencing conditions as determinants of foreign direct investments [Dunning 1991]? Comparative studies focusing on conditions for exchange in different countries can obviously contribute to Type C studies that explain IB using a transaction cost or exchange relationship approach.

INTERNATIONAL MARKETING

IM is not one of the major areas for inquiry in marketing judging from the relative sparsity of published articles in leading academic journals, both the functional ones and those specializing in IB [Hampton and Van Gent 1984; Morrison and Inkpen 1991; JIBS 10-year index, Summer 1987]. A recent survey by Li and Cavusgil [1991] suggests a more positive view of the development. The infrequent publication of IM articles in the academically leading journals as reported by Morrison and Inkpen [1991]

must be interpreted to signify that the academic status of IM research is still low. Judging from the dissertation abstracts published by JIBS, marketing subjects cover only around 10% of all IB dissertation research.

In this section I will comment on three IM research subject areas: *early stages* in the firm's internationalization, *buyer behavior*, and the behavior of *highly internationalized* firms. Taken together, such studies account for a significant share of IM research, which is one reason to select them. Another reason is that the research provides examples of research that has, implicitly or explicitly used different exchange paradigms.

Early Stages

Market entry: which markets to enter? In the internationalization process model referred to above, the firm's choice is initially much constrained by lack of information. Knowledge is gradually accumulating and helps the firm to continue its extension to more distant markets. In spite of observations that this model might not be valid when the markets are already highly internationalized [Johanson and Mattsson 1988], recent studies [Nordström 1991; Lindqvist 1991] have found that it still has explanatory value even if the speed of internationalization in terms of extension and resource commitment seem to have increased. This approach, stressing the importance of experiential learning, implies that exchange relationships in networks is the major vehicle to increase market knowledge.

Marketing research literature aiming to aid rational decision making (e.g., Douglas and Craig [1983]) typically describes methods for simultaneous evaluation of entry alternatives using secondary or primary data of an aggregated, nonrelationship nature.

Market entry: which mode of entry? The comments above on the internationalization process model and its explanation of the international extension pattern are valid also here, with the addition that increased resource commitments by the seller serve to increase the level of trust in exchange relationships with buyers in foreign markets.

Mode of entry is usually treated as a distribution channel problem, one of the major areas of IM research [Albaum and Peterson 1984]. It is therefore not surprising that transaction cost theory has been used in several studies. Anderson and Gatignon [1986] use theoretical constructs from this theory to integrate the entry mode literature and to establish a set of normative propositions on the efficiency of different institutional arrangements. Anderson and Coughlan [1987] found in an empirical study that firms introducing a new product group in a foreign market tended to use already established distributor relationships even if the new product group was quite different from the established ones. Kogut and Singh [1988] found that "cultural distance" between the home market and the foreign market influenced mode of entry and gave a transaction cost related explanation for this.

Transaction cost analysis does not explicitly treat exchange behavior once a specific institutional arrangement exists. Within the "political economy" approach [Stern and Reve 1980; Arndt 1983], the effects of organizational arrangements within the channel on norms and sentiments and on channel performance can be studied. For example, Haugland and Reve [1989] found that formalization and centralization correlated with relational contracting norms (reliance, solidarity, and mutuality) and with channel cohesion. Interorganizational structure was also found to influence processes in studies by Bello and Williamson [1985] and Rosson and Ford [1982]. These and similar studies focus on dyadic exchange relationships rather than on networks.

Export performance. In a recent review, Aaby and Slater [1989] conclude that, in spite of the large number of studies, few solid general conclusions can be made. Explanatory variables describing management characteristics (commitment, attitudes/perceptions, quality) were shown to be more clearly linked to export performance than marketing strategy variables. However, the evidence is quite mixed. Thus, Cooper and Kleinschmidt [1985] and Ryans [1988] found market segmentation strategies to have explanatory value. Axinn [1988], using management and firm characteristics organized within the "adoption of innovation framework," as suggested by Reid [1983], found very limited support for this model. Cavusgil and Naor [1987] using a very broad set of 25 explanatory variables based on previous export literature found significant support for only nine. The results supported the idea that pre-export behavior [Wiedersheim-Paul et al. 1978] has predictive value, but was inconclusive as to one of the most widely researched phenomenon in the export literature, the effect on export performance of management perceptions and attitudes (e.g., Axinn [1988]; Gripsrud [1990]; Dichtl et al. [1990]).

The export performance studies referred to above focused on cross-sectional studies of the internal characteristics of the firm and its strategic choice. The exchange approach in these studies were mostly non-interactive.

Dynamic, "strategic-content rich" analyses of exporting is mostly found in more business oriented literature. For example, Kotler et al. [1985] analyzed the marketing strategies used by Japanese firms in entry and extension stages in the U.S. market. They showed how the development during early stages determines the conditions for later growth. This is also shown and analyzed within a network perspective by Mattsson [1989].

Government export promotion. A much researched problem is the impact of government export promotion policies on firm behavior. Some major findings are that export promotion mostly benefits firms with export experience [Olson 1975; Seringhaus and Botschen 1991], large firms [Grönhaug and Lorentzen 1983] or that export promotion is of secondary importance [Christensen et al. 1987]. These studies do not have any clear paradigmatic orientation, even if one explanation for the results could be of an exchange relationship nature.

Buyer Behavior

Comparative studies. Major issues in IM relate to the pattern of similarities and differences between national markets. Are between-market differences smaller or larger than within-market differences? Can international market segments be identified?

Clark [1990] proposes that "national character" research could provide an integrative theoretical framework for cross-cultural studies that are often criticised as being fragmented and without theoretical cohesiveness. Even if personality traits have not proved to have predictive value in consumer research, Clark argues that if interpreted within national systems contexts the results might improve.

An example of the importance of national system context is the study reported in Douglas [1976]. She compared American and French employed and nonemployed housewives with regard to their shopping attitudes and behavior. She found intercountry differences and behavior differences to be greater than intracountry and attitude differences. Difference in retail structure between the two countries might explain the differences in shopping behavior. Thorelli et al. [1975] discovered important similarities across countries and cultures in terms of information handling by well-educated consumers, called "Information Seekers."

Cross-cultural research on family decision making demonstrates the validity of some cultural stereotypes for marital power relationships [Green et al. 1983]. Such patterns might vary considerably within one nation [Huszag and Murphy 1984].

Studies of the attitudes of consumers in different countries towards marketing practice, consumerism, and government policies (e.g., Barksdale [1982]; French et al. [1982]) and of executives towards consumerist movements (e.g., Ryans et al. [1985]) have demonstrated some differences between countries in terms of how consumers and the business community view each other's performance.

Graham and others have used laboratory simulations in several comparative studies of dyadic negotiation processes (e.g., Graham [1985]; Adler et al. [1987]; Campbell et al. [1988]). Differences and similarities concerning the relationships between bargainer characteristics, bargaining strategy, and outcome are explored. This series of studies has identified several cultural differences, even if the findings are far from conclusive. These studies treat exchange in a dyadic, single transaction setting. Campbell [1985] is an example of a dyadic exchange relationship approach to comparative buyer studies. He found interaction in Japan to be less formal, more frequent, more open, and the atmosphere to be more characterized by trust and mutual commitment than in Germany.

Using a more traditional organizational purchasing process approach, Banting et al. [1985] compared characteristics of buying behavior in four English-speaking industrialized countries and found intercountry differences to be small within each purchase category, but differences within each country to be significant for different product categories.

Buying behavior when seller and buyer are of different nationalities. We can distinguish between the case when the buyer can have a direct contact with the seller from another country and when the product or mass-communication is the primary mediator of the exchange. In the latter case, noninteraction approaches within the "country-of-origin effects" type of studies are prevalent. In the former, case interaction studies are more important. This roughly corresponds to a distinction between consumer buying and organizational buying.

Country-of-origin effects on consumer perception and evaluation is a much researched phenomenon. Bilkey and Nes [1982], using only the country-of-origin cue found a significant effect. However, later studies that added other cues, such as retail store image and warranty [Thorelli et al. 1989] or product familiarity [Johansson et al. 1985], found interaction effects between the independent variables. Johansson [1989] discussed these interaction findings, and suggested that linkages between country-of-origin cues, such as "made-in" labels, and consumer behavior can be explained by the consumer's prior familiarity with the product and with the country of origin.

The above mentioned studies obviously relate to the marketing mix framework, since they aim to explain the influence on consumer behavior of various cues that can more or less be controlled by the sellers.

Organizational buying behavior in an international context has been a major subject for research and a vehicle to develop the interaction approach to marketing, especially in European research. The interaction approach is, of course, as valid from a seller as from a buyer point of view. The purchasing perspective dominating the early interaction studies, however, helped in discovery of the existence of dynamic, long-term supplier relationships and their importance for performance of production systems and innovative activities. A major research program, the IMP-project [Håkansson 1982], found for example, that cultural affinity strongly influenced business relationships [Hallén 1979], that relationship management skills are important determinants of buyer preferences [Ford 1984], and that purchasing behavior is strongly influenced by the functions of exchange relationships vis-à-vis production technology and technical change. Interaction perspectives on "country-of-origin effects" are thus quite different from marketing mix perspectives.

Adaptations by sellers to cultural differences in buying processes are analyzed by Murray and Blenkhorn [1985]. They focus on the international diffusion of typical Japanese supplier-manufacturer relationships due to the establishment of Japanese "transplants" in the United States. Johansson et al. [1990] studied adaptations needed by U.S. manufacturers as regards their relationships to distributors when exporting to

Japan. Other studies of internationalization aspects of purchasing and its effects on supplier-buyer relations include Davis et al. [1974], Jansson [1982], and Kotabe and Omura [1989]. In the bargaining studies reported by Graham and others [e.g., Graham 1985] both parties are of the same national origin. Bargaining in international and complex contexts has been studied for big projects by Ghauri [1983]. In Liljegren [1988], such a negotiation process is put into the context of two complementary suppliers' long-term exchange relationship.

For firms who are already highly internationalized three major and interrelated strategic problem areas are: (1) international (or "global") standardization vs. local differentiation; (2) organization of the MNE; and (3) internalization vs. externalization and interorganizational issues.

Standardization vs. differentiation. Classical articles by Buzzell [1968] and Keegan [1969] are still much quoted. More recently, the issue has been part of the debates on "globalization" of markets and of corporate strategies. Marketing program standardization is usually defined in terms of the marketing mix variables. Among these "promotion" and "product" are, not surprisingly, the most researched.

Recent review articles [Jain 1989; Walters 1986] point out that there is still no conclusive theory or practice. In fact, the debate during recent years on "globalization" makes the issue even more unsettled. Moving away from earlier simplistic notions about comparisons between scale economic advantages of standardization and revenue disadvantages of inferior adaptation to heterogeneous demand, many authors have contributed more situation- and process-specific analyses. Jain [1989], for example, suggests that the seller and the competitor market positions are important, while Douglas and Craig [1989] stress evolutionary aspects of the seller's internationalization. Rau and Prebber [1987] emphasize interdependence between markets, organizational factors, and the international diffusion of scarce, good marketing ideas. Walters [1986] lists, as positive effects of standardization, potential benefits from central coordination, more rapid diffusion of innovations and coherent international image.

There are not many studies of the actual marketing behavior by firms or the effects of standardization. Rosen et al. [1989] found that the international diffusion of major U.S. brand names was very limited. Mårtensson [1987] linked the level of product/service innovation and the control of distribution channels to successful international standardization. Mueller [1991] found that standardized advertising contained less information.

Arguments in the literature on "global" vs. "multidomestic" corporate strategies to some extent overlap arguments in the literature on standardization vs. differentiation of marketing. However, the former stress much more competitive processes on globally interdependent markets and the advantages of controlling resources for market access and flexible responses in many such markets [Hamel and Prahalad 1985; Yip 1989], while the latter are more concerned with traditional marketing mix issues.

Organization of the MNE. Kashani [1989] addressing the globalization issue suggests that the quality of management processes explains why some global marketing strategies fail while others succeed. He found, contrary to conventional wisdom, that management processes for global marketing should not be highly centralized and standardized since not enough attention is paid to the inputs of local management and the learning process across the different markets. Some studies investigate the linkages between standardization of marketing and other functions such as sourcing, manufacturing, and R&D, and find such linkages to be important [Kotabe 1990]. The ability to carry out global marketing strategies also depend upon comparative management attributes. Tse et al. [1988] found that a manager's home culture influenced IM decisions, but also that the effects of cultural differences tend to diminish.

Practice and research on the organiza-tion of the MNE in a highly internationalized world tries to find solutions to the two-sided problem of global coordination and decentralization. Bartlett et al. [1990] state that MNEs can no longer have the center coordinate a set of national subsidiaries that are largely independent of each other. Instead, the firm should be regarded as an interdependent, integrated network which can be used not only for selling to individual, more or less distant markets and to run a cost-effective production system, but also for innovation and creation of information. Formal hierarchies will become less important [Hedlund 1986]. A contemporary, highly internationalized enterprise often operates in a highly internationalized environment. This has led Ghoshal and Bartlett [1990] to analyse the organization problem in terms of an internal network embedded in an external network and Forsgren [1989] to find new roles for subsidiaries.

The studies referred to above are thus suggesting that the MNE itself is, or should become, more like a network than like a traditional hierarchy, and that a major reason for this is that the "environment" of the firm has become more like a network than like a traditional market.

Internalization vs. externalization, interorganizational issues. Contemporary practice and research on international corporate strategy is also much concerned with exchange relationships. Descriptive terms like strategic alliances, joint ventures, hybrid organizations, and strategic networks are used to characterize this [Contractor and Lorange 1988]. (In several marketing "schools of thought," and especially with applications to distribution channels and industrial marketing, such exchange relationships have been widely researched but hardly referred to in the strategy literature.) Among reasons mentioned for international cooperation between firms are: risk reduction, economies of scale and/or rationalization, complementary technologies and patents, co-opting and blocking competition, overcoming government-mandated investment or trade barrier, initial international expansion and access to resources of different kinds [Contractor and Lorange 1988:10]. Given such an extensive list, one might ask why the interest in formal cooperation has increased during the last decade [Doz 1991]. One set of explanations is barriers of a legal, economic, and organizational nature against outright mergers between already large firms of different nationalities and/or from different industries. Another type of explanation is the high costs, high risks, long time period required, and possible overcapacity created if firms pursue individual, organic growth strategies. A third is that arm's length exchange fails to create effective coordination between interdependent activities. Much of the research on joint ventures and strategic alliances concerns individual dyads and aggregates of such dyads (e.g., Harrigan [1986]; Håkansson and Lorange [1991]). However, given that firms are involved in several such partnerships, the dyads can be regarded as embedded in networks of strategic alliances, which create interdependency patterns that are different from the ones described in the traditional industrial organization literature [Mattsson et al. 1990; Hamel et al. 1989; Jarillo and Martinez 1991].

MARKETING EXCHANGE APPROACHES AND IB RESEARCH

I will comment on how different exchange paradigmatic orientations influence research on the content, contexts, and processes of IB behavior. First, I will contrast marketing mix and network approaches. Second, I will compare three dyadic exchange approaches. Finally, some suggestions will be made about what could be done to improve the on the contributions of marketing research for IB inquiry.

The Marketing Mix vs. the Network Approach

Content. The marketing mix approach concentrates on segmentation, marketing action variables in the marketing plan, and market share. The network approach fo-

cuses on selecting and handling dynamic exchange relationships and development of the firm's network positions.

Outer context. The marketing mix approach describes the outer context as consisting of customers and competitors. The customers are described in terms of organism-response attributes and are aggregated into market segments. The network approach describes the firm as embedded in a network context consisting of both complementary and competitive individual actors. The nature of the exchange relationship is an attribute of the context. This also means that existing and potential exchange relationships not only to customers, but also to other actors such as suppliers, distributors and customers' customers, are included. There is, however, a major difference between a network approach focusing only on the individual firm's own "strategic network" (e.g., Thorelli [1986]), and one in which the firm's strategic action is analysed in the context of an overall network structure [Johanson and Mattsson 1991]. In the latter case it is possible to analyse the dynamic effects of interdependencies between several sellers' strategic networks [Hertz 1993].

Inner context. The marketing mix approach focuses on the marketing function of the seller. The network approach focuses on the corporate organizational context, sometimes including some interorganizational relationships.

Process. The marketing mix approach regards the process as a rational decision making process, including use of market research information and the firm's economic control system. The network approach sees the process as influenced by interorganizational interaction and socially constructed perceptions.

The two approaches have advantages and disadvantages. The marketing mix approach is easier to operationalize for empirical studies and for practical market research, and it is theoretically linked to economic analyses. It is easier to measure actor attributes than relationship attributes.

Secondary data on industries and markets predominantly reflect criteria of substitution and not of complementarity. The network approach, on the other hand, recognizes the long-term, dynamic, and possibly innovative characteristics of interaction and does not leave out important interdependencies of a complementary nature. The network approach increases the possibility to consider interdependencies between firms in different industries and between firms located in different national markets. Through its holistic view of the firm, the interdependence between marketing and other functions of the firm is explicitly considered. This also makes the network approach better suited than the marketing mix approach to handle marketing from a dynamic production systems point of view, according to which the role of marketing is to influence and handle interdependencies between heterogeneous actors, each specializing in production/distribution of certain goods/services.

Transaction Cost, Relational Contracting, and Dyadic Interaction

Transaction cost analysis is used to explain the governance structure for the coordination of interdependent activities. The content is thus limited to a selection of one of a few alternative forms for exchange. Attributes of internal and external context are explanatory variables given by the theory (e.g., number of actors, frequency of transactions, bounded rationality). In early formulations, intermediate forms between market and hierarchy were considered unstable which is in stark contrast to the interaction and network approach that consider these the predominating ones. Transaction cost analysis does not provide any conceptual help if we are interested in studying the management and dynamics of exchange [Johanson and Mattsson 1987]. Relational contracting studies, analysing the relation between contract form, norms/sentiments and behavioral outcomes give insight into the process of relationship management. The "interaction approach"

[Håkansson 1982], however, goes further than relational contracting in its ambition to understand how short-term exchange episodes influence the institutionalization and adaptation within the relationship. Also, over time, the link of the analysis to technical and commercial interdependencies and to the strategy content and organizational structure (i.e., inner context) of the interacting parties is made explicit. Thus, we can see how the three basically dyadic exchange approaches relate quite differently to IM issues, but also differently to the marketing mix and the network approaches.

Research Methods in IM

Most IM research is nonrelationship oriented, and the major method used is cross-sectional surveys of consumer or management perceptions and attitudes. Thus, most of the studies are static in spite of the predominantly dynamic interpretation and high importance given to the term "internationalization" in management practice. When surveys concern dyadic exchange relationships they are usually not put into an explicit governance structure for the "outer context."

There are obvious difficult sampling problems for network studies, but the tradeoff in terms of increased insight into exchange relationship context might make such efforts worthwhile. Typical cross-sectional survey IM studies often suffer from vague theoretical frameworks, very high nonresponse rates, and inconclusive results. Other less traditional methods should be pursued. Case studies require deeper interaction between the researcher and firms. Such access could be quite difficult to get but will give better insights into the dynamics of IB and better bases for inductive conceptualization and theory building. It might be difficult to get such research accepted within some research communities, and the typical journal article format might not be feasible. Longitudinal case studies might be too time-consuming for researchers working under pressure to get their research ready for publication. However, there exist several good examples of extensive case studies of exchange relationships and networks (e.g., Rogers [1986]; Liljegren [1988]; Lundgren [1991]; Waluszewski [1989]). It might be worthwhile for marketing researchers to increase their use of social network analytical methods [Knoke and Kuklinski 1982] and to construct databases for analysis of network structures and network dynamics [Mattsson et al. 1990].

Need for Better Linkages to Theory and Practice

In an address to IB researchers, Daniels [1991] pleaded for more and better "linkages." Following that idea, Figure 3 shows some linkages among research disciplines, and Figure 4 some linkages among research development and real world issues. Figure 3 is obviously just illustrative of a more complicated reality. IB is shown to relate to industrial organization, organizational economics (especially transaction cost analysis), international marketing. IM is through

marketing linked to some of the same disciplines as IB. My point is that if researchers on international marketing more explicitly select and consider major linkages to other disciplines they will be able to improve on their contributions not only within their own field, but also to other areas of inquiry. An important condition for making such connections is similarities of conceptual foundations, or ability to make differences explicit, especially concerning the nature of exchange. One example referred to above is that some of the requirements pointed out by Casson [1990] for Type C studies (the role of entrepreneurship, the interorganizational nature of production systems, the importance of intermediate forms of governance, etc.) can be addressed by network approaches but hardly by nonrelationship approaches. Two other examples are: How can research on marketing contribute to the analysis of "competitiveness of nations," or to the understanding of "technological change?"

For economists working on the as-

Figure 3. Illustration of Linkages between Research Disciplines

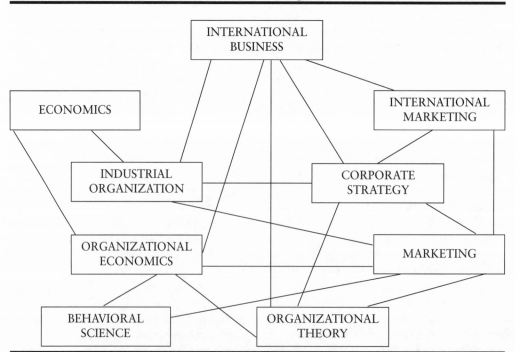

Figure 4. Linkages between Research Issues, Research Development, and "Real World" Issues

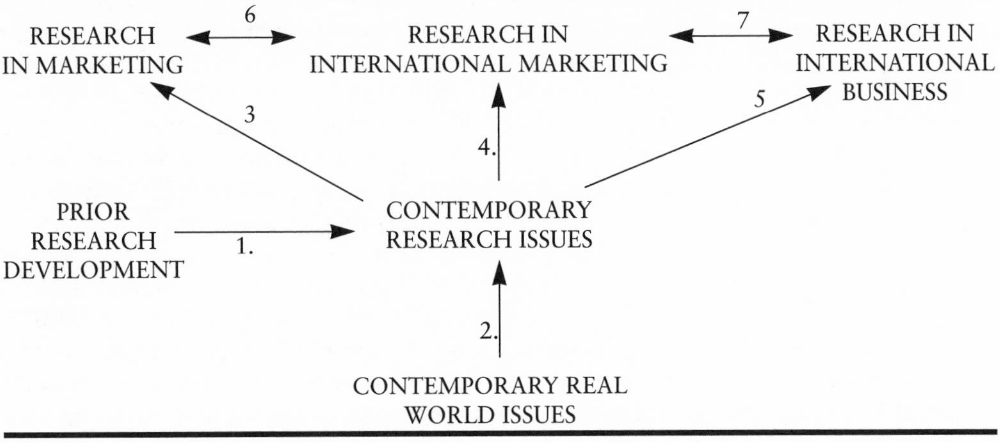

sumption of a perfect market, marketing has no role. The competitiveness of a nation's industry will, given such assumptions, be determined by production costs, and the policy recommendations will aim at decreased cost of production factors, increased productivity or devalued currency. Certainly, there is not a word about improved marketing. If advice is based upon theories of imperfect competition, then recommendations concerning how to improve an industry's marketing mix programs can be made, but the interorganizational interdependencies and the long-term, dynamic aspects of such programs cannot be handled based on this nonrelationship approach.

If an exchange relationship approach is used, there is a theoretical base to address such issues. For example, the investment nature of IM can be given a conceptual meaning [Johanson and Mattsson 1985] as can the links between marketing and technological development [Håkansson 1987, 1989; Lundgren 1991]. Two early publications in Sweden on the network approach actually addressed the role of marketing in the context of contemporary debates in Sweden on how the competitiveness of Swedish industry could be improved [Hägg and Johanson 1982; Hammarkvist et al. 1982].

Porter, in his book on the competitiveness of nations, has taken up similar ideas [1991], and Imai [1988] is among several researchers who discuss the influence of the exchange relationship networks in Japan on the international competitiveness of Japanese industry. It is interesting to note that an important interdisciplinary contribution to the debate on the competitiveness of U.S. industry has no contribution from marketing academics [Teece 1987]. Several such debates concern conditions for technological change and innovation in a country.

To create linkages between disciplines is sometimes difficult because the ideas emanating from one discipline might be theoretically incompatible with the "ruling" paradigmatic orientation in the other. The problem is aggravated if the frontiers between different national research communities in a specific discipline, such as marketing, are infrequently crossed.

Figure 4 illustrates how prior research development and contemporary real world issues influence ongoing research in IB, marketing and IM. Ideally, there should be a balanced and interactive development. If, for example, IM moves along the 1, 4 path and disregards arrows 2, 6, and 7, the result will be isolated, internal exercises without much practical relevance and with little influence outside of the specialized academic subdiscipline. If, on the other hand, all the linkages are functioning well, then a relevant and fruitful development is more likely to happen. IM research must address important, contemporary "real world issues," not because they are "hot," but because they indicate important changes in the context of IB in a wide sense.

Some such important contemporary issues relate to increased concentration within industrial specialties through mergers and divestments, increased cross-national and cross-industries interdependencies, proliferation of strategic alliances of different kinds, the demise of central planning in nations and firms, deregulation of markets, and privatization of state-owned firms and industries. Many of these changes in real world conditions have important implications for *ex-change* conditions within industrial systems and for exchange involving final consumers. The exchange conditions generally become more relationship and network like. Judging from recent research literature on IB, I get the impression that researchers in IM have not yet responded to these changes to the same extent as researchers in related field such as corporate strategy, OB, or IB in general. This indicates that for marketing, which focuses on exchange in economic and social systems, to considerably enhance its contribution to the development of knowledge about IB in the future, research in IM must put more emphasis on exchange relationship approaches.

■ ■ ■

A Conceptual Framework For International Marketing
Saeed Samiee

As international involvement of businesses has intensified and global marketing and sourcing have become commonplace, international business (IB) as a discipline has gained prominence. In response to this change, colleges and universities have begun offering courses and specialization in IB. The American Assembly of Collegiate Schools of Business (AACSB) also stresses the need for the inclusion of international components in business curricula and a gradual effort to internationalize the business curricula has necessitated faculty training in IB.[1] Historically, the study of IB at many colleges and universities preceded specialized courses such as international marketing (IM), and today many still offer only courses in IB. However, as IB has gained wider acceptance, an increasing number of institutions has begun offering courses pertaining to its functional components.

IM, the focus of this study, is a hybrid of marketing and IB. However, there appears to be no consensus as to the nature of IM as a field of study and whether it is something apart from domestic marketing. This controversy is over two decades old and, in all likelihood, it will continue unless conceptual and theoretical advances in IM are made.

The growing number of publications in scholarly journals and the plethora of new and revised IM texts and edited books illustrate the intensity of interest in IM as an area of study and inquiry by academicians.[2] In addition, several new journals that are entirely devoted to IM topics have been introduced during the last decade.[3] Concurrently, there appears to be greater interest in publishing IM articles in key marketing journals. For example, in a reversal of historical patterns, three of the seven articles published in the January 1989 issue of the *Journal of Marketing* dealt with international aspects of marketing.

Despite the level of interest demonstrated in IM, the field lacks academic identity and little effort has been expended to legitimize IM from conceptual, theoretical, and methodological perspectives. Albaum and Peterson [1984] in assessing empirical research in IM, for example, stated that "with few exceptions, existing research on IM issues is fragmentary, generally atheoretic, and not sufficiently programmatic to offer anything other than simplistic and incomplete insights into the underlying phenomenon of interest." The observation by Hawkins [1984] regarding IB research includes and is equally applicable to IM; "IB is a potpourri of functional fields . . . with occasional theorizing and conceptualizing which does not yet come together into a coherent package of received wisdom." Others have labeled IM research as "descriptive, repetitive and non-analytical" [Bradley 1987].

Meaningful research should be guided by some type of conceptual framework that relates the subject under study to parts of or to the whole field. As with other scientific research, the development of a conceptual basis for the study of IM is, by definition, a necessity. Conceptual framework(s) and theory(ies) guide hypothesis generation and research in the field. Concurrently, the lack of development of a conceptual base has hindered IM-related methodological developments (see, Bradley [1987]). The country-of-origin and advertising standardization literature are representative of this. Despite much interest and published research in these areas, no universally accepted constructs and measurement scales have been offered. The immediate result of this "lack of development" is that the "wheel is reinvented" with every new research project.

Conceptual and methodological difficulties associated with IM research have been noted in the literature (e.g., Albaum and Peterson [1984]; Bradley [1987]; Cavusgil and Nevin [1981]; Wind and Perlmutter [1977]). Not surprisingly, some fundamental issues in IM remain unanswered and controversial. Is IM, for example, a field that is apart from domestic marketing? If not, do environmental conditions significantly alter the manner in which marketing is practiced in other nations? Is dealing with these international environ-

mental conditions different than addressing them in the domestic market? What, if any, is the potential difference in the practice of marketing by large, sophisticated domestic firms and large international firms? Do global corporate philosophies and organizational structures affect the approach, planning, and implementation of marketing on an international basis? And, if so, where and how should these influences be included in the marketing literature? Acceptable responses to these questions are not likely to emerge in the absence of a conceptual framework.

The primary purpose of this study is to examine the nature and the status of IM and to better define the relationship between marketing and IM. A conceptual framework that differentiates the domain of IM from that of domestic marketing is thus developed. Such a framework can also serve as a guide for future research in distinct IM subjects. In order to examine the current status of IM and the directions of interest in IM research, an audit of major marketing journals is also conducted. No attempt has been made to link IM to IB or to explain the role of IM in IB theory.

DEFINING INTERNATIONAL MARKETING

The earliest book in IM, titled *World Marketing*, was written by Collins [1935]. However, publishing activities in IM were scant prior to the 1960s [Bartels 1962][4] and most terminologies have been developed since then. Over the years, a plethora of terminologies and jargons have been used in the IM literature and, in part, are reflected in the titles of IM textbooks. Some early scholars focused on marketing in one country (e.g., Goldman [1963]). Though the use of the term "foreign marketing" has not been widespread, numerous studies focusing on marketing in a single nation represent this notion. In addition, such titles as export marketing and comparative marketing were commonly used prior to the 1960s.

The use of "comparative" and "international" marketing gained widespread acceptance during the 1960s. Since then, the term "international" has been used to denote any and all activities pertaining to marketing beyond the domestic level. Two terminologies are commonly used to refer to marketing activities beyond the national level: international or multinational, and global. Though some authors have attempted to make a distinction between these, their definitions are imprecise and subjective. Albaum and Peterson [1984], for example, defined IM as "influences on and activities involved in marketing not only to, but also within foreign countries." Toyne and Walters [1993], on the other hand, consider marketing activities across national boundaries IM and their coordination and control within and across foreign markets as global marketing. In other words, the method of management of IM activities is central to these definitions and distinguishes international from global marketing. These definitions are typical of the literature and are somewhat broad in that they include marketing in *only one* country as IM. However, key journals in marketing have not published one-country marketing studies (e.g., marketing in the Netherlands) since 1981 when the *Journal of Marketing*, for example, published seven such articles.

There are no universally accepted definitions of IM and the literature often labels the lowest denominator of marketing activities across national boundaries as IM. Perhaps it is for this reason that "international marketing" is the most commonly used title for textbooks in this area. The lack of theoretical development in IM necessitates the adoption of a general definition. Thus, the IM definition in this study is *the pursuit of business activities beyond a firm's home market in a cross-cultural sense*. This definition includes surveys of management in a single country as regards their operations elsewhere and excludes studies pertaining to *marketing in one country*. This definition is consistent with that offered by Albaum and Peterson as well as that currently in use by the *Journal of International Business Studies* (*JIBS*) for screening purposes. For example, studies of advertising or distribution channels in India or Japan do not constitute IM, whereas a study of U.S. exporters focusing on Japan does.

INTERNATIONAL MARKETING AS A DISTINCT DISCIPLINE

Over two decades ago Bartels [1968] elaborated on whether domestic and IM are dissimilar. Apparently, the issue gained added importance as a result of extensive discussions in 1967 about the addition of IB studies to business programs. Then as now, in a central point of these discussions on "the relative merits of specialized versus integrated treatment of international and comparative aspects of business, it was acknowledged that the subject still lacked identity" [Bartels 1970].

Recognition of IM as a separate and distinct discipline from domestic marketing requires an examination of the relationship between the two areas. Meaningful conceptual frameworks and theoretical bases for studying IM are unlikely to evolve unless this relationship is defined. The nature of this relationship has been the subject of much debate over the years and there appears to be no consensus as to what this relationship is.

There are two opposing schools of thought regarding IM. Some hold that there is no difference between domestic and IM, and that the character and elements of marketing do not change from one country to another.[5] According to this school of thought, differences between domestic and IM are attributed to environmental variables. Since domestic marketing is also concerned about these variables, then, it is argued, there is no difference between the two fields. If one agrees with this viewpoint, it follows that the study of IM is a futile exercise which adds little, if any, value to the advancement of frontiers of marketing.

IM has been criticized by the proponents of the first school of thought because few differences are noted by this group between domestic and international components of marketing. Existing differences are often explained in terms of the environmental conditions within which marketing functions are performed [Bartels 1968; Boddewyn 1966,1981].[6] In general, Bartels [1968] asserted that:

1. "Marketing technology" is valid and potentially applicable everywhere;
2. Behavioral considerations in marketing among various nations are indicative of differences in marketing;
3. Marketing managers need to be aware and expect both similarities and differences relative to home markets, "but with the understanding that both are embraced within a consistent body of knowledge."

Empirical testing of the validity of this position has been rare and inconclusive. In one study, marketing practices in Ceylon, Chile, Greece, Italy, and Japan, for example, were not shown to be associated with environmental variables [Douglas and Wind 1973]. Differences among firms were explained by such firm characteristics as size and managerial attitudes. However, the authors did not make an attempt to explain managerial attitudes in terms of social and cultural norms, i.e., environmental variables. One would expect a high degree of correlation between managerial attitudes and environmental factors.

The second school of thought, on the other hand, views IM as distinctly different from domestic marketing. The proponents of this school of thought contend that the magnitude of differences in environmental variables is so great that addressing them necessarily demands a level of managerial proficiency that is not included in the body of knowledge typically taught or researched in domestic marketing. Furthermore, some topics of critical importance (e.g., standard-

ization, parallel markets, and countertrade) are only discussed in IM.[7] In addition, it is argued that there are many fundamental differences between the markets and institutions of different nations that warrant a separate treatment of the subject.

Since IM textbooks are the vehicle through which the body of knowledge in IM is conveyed, they offer valuable input regarding whether or not IM as a field of study is or has developed into something quite distinct from domestic marketing. Barring minor differences, IM textbooks have two common components: (1) the environment of IB and (2) the elements of marketing plan, the planning process, and the organizational setting. The latter is not much different in character (though it is different in substance) than that found in most marketing management books. The material covered in the former, on the other hand, is quite different from subjects generally discussed in domestic marketing textbooks. International trade theories, economic unions and market integration, the foundations of other nations' cultures and their assessment (but not psychographics or lifestyles), secondary data problems and cross-cultural marketing research issues are just a few of the major environmental topics discussed by all IM textbooks.

It might be argued that much of what is labeled as environmental analysis in IM is not really pertinent to marketing. For example, international trade flows and theories have little relevance to the development and execution of marketing plans. Description of multinational markets such as the European Union (EU), Latin American Integration Association, or the Arab Common Market is of greater assistance in the *market entry phase* than it is to the development of the short- and medium-term *marketing* plans.[8] However, many of these issues are inherently intertwined, and how a firm conducts its marketing is significantly influenced by variables that are irrelevant[9] or far less important on a domestic basis. It is then apparent that the environmental analysis portion of IB and IM bodies of knowledge significantly overlap.

EARLY IM FRAMEWORKS

Shortly after Bartels [1968] elaborated on the nature of IM, Buzzell [1968] questioned whether IM can be standardized. The thrust and motivation in standardizing IM plans may be linked to the question raised by Bartels, i.e., "are domestic and international marketing dissimilar?" Implicit in the standardization of marketing plans is some level of similarity, congruence, and even homogeneity among various national markets. The study by Bartels strengthens the conceptual base of the field from a comparative viewpoint but the one by Buzzell does not provide a conceptual base to deal with the incongruity of environmental variables. Thus, neither study resulted in the development of a meaningful theoretical base for IM.

A statement by Bartels [1970] reflects the sentiment toward IB and IM among many scholars. IB and IM, according to Bartels, "lacked academic status, scholarly respect, and sufficient theoretical content to earn a consensus on [their] substance." The development of a conceptual base is critical to theory building and research. The lack of a theoretical foundation in IB was also reported by Schollhammer [1973] in his partial review of the literature. In part, this lack of development has been blamed on ethnocentrism among marketing scholars with an eye on the domestic market [Cavusgil and Nevin 1981].

To be certain, IB scholars have made some important theoretical advances and the IB literature has fared better than IM. The IB literature has been enriched through conceptual and/or theoretical contributions by Vernon and Wells [1968] (the international product life cycle concept), by Dunning [1977] (the eclectic view of foreign direct investment), and by others who have focused on the internalization concept. Nevertheless, these theoretical developments have had limited impact on the empirical research in the field.

The IM area, on the other hand, is impoverished in this regard and lacks a theoretical base. There is no evidence of widely accepted or even debated conceptual framework(s) or theories in IM. The international product life cycle concept, despite its contribution to our understanding of product flows among groups of nations over time, is macro in nature and of little use in IM research.

To make matters more complicated, there appears to be little consensus as to exactly what constitutes a framework, a conceptual framework, or a theory within marketing. Scholars have used a variety of definitions and approaches. Some have relatively concise definitions for theory (e.g., a regression model) whereas others have focused on broader notions. Bartels [1970] presented a relatively narrow definition for conceptual framework and theory development. To build a theory, he argued, relatively concise components must be identified, their relationships defined, and generalized.[10] Later, he wrote that a conceptual framework relies on three stages of subject identification, assimilation, and conceptualization and that marketing can be viewed as either formative or adaptive.

In the IM area, several broad frameworks have been offered. Organizational typologies (ethnocentric, polycentric, and geocentric) proposed by Perlmutter [1969] have been relatively dominant in IM. Cavusgil and Nevin [1981], for example, have labeled these managerial orientations an IM framework, and nearly every IM textbook provides a coverage of these typologies. Despite the extensive mention of this framework in IB and IM since its 1969 debut, it has been the foundation of very little IM research. Wind, Douglas, and Perlmutter [1973], for example, empirically tested the relevance of these managerial orientations.

Toyne and Walters [1993] offer a similar, but more pragmatic, conceptual view of IM by focusing on philosophies of firms and their strategic orientations. In this classification scheme firms are divided into three groups depending upon whether their global view of marketing is market extension, multidomestic, or global. Although this framework has considerable merit, it has a drawback. Classification of multiproduct, multidivisional, multinational firms in these categories is problematic and tends to be more subjective than objective.

Clark [1990] proposed "that the scientific study of *national character* has value in international marketing" and might be the appropriate vehicle for developing an IM framework. National character is said to have a valid base for study and analysis of IM in that "people of each nation have a distinctive, enduring pattern of behavior and/or personality characteristics." The author suggests that national character can be used as a basis for analysis of both strategic and consumer decision making.

Despite these developments, it is apparent that conceptual frameworks and theories are still scarce and this limitation has created a barrier to a consistent and defensible explanation of the roles, differences, and similarities of IM to domestic marketing and IB. National character as the basis for studying IM involves several critical methodological issues and empirical research using this framework has not been reported thus far. In fact, Cavusgil and Nevin [1981] in their overview of the field noted that IM conceptualization has had little impact on stimulating empirical research in the field.

RESEARCH IN INTERNATIONAL MARKETING

Challenges of IM Research

Perhaps the greatest challenge in IM research is that of overcoming obstacles to gathering cross-cultural data. IM researchers must deal with methodological issues of instrument development and language, distance, and cultural barriers, as well as the cost and time involved in conceiving, designing, and executing international projects (for example, see Davis, Douglas, and Silk [1981]; Green and White [1976]; Mayer [1978]; Wind and Perlmutter [1977]). For

these reasons, IM projects are often conducted in one country by soliciting data regarding managements' views on their treatment of one or more elements of the marketing mix, the planning process, their management at the international level (e.g., advertising standardization), or by asking customers' views regarding products of foreign origin.

The issues of sampling and appropriateness of selected informants in IM projects have received little attention. Which individuals within firms are best qualified to provide reliable and valid information regarding IM activities? The majority of studies do not attempt to test internal validity of information gathered, and the accuracy of information provided by one individual regarding diverse international markets is often open to question. Dunn [1976] has suggested that much imprecise information is provided by executives; for example, "some marketing executives do not really know what is and what is not being transferred across boundaries." Although an increasing number of studies are focusing on specific industries and business unit (BU) levels, little effort is expended to validate executive responses. The validity of responses are likely to vary by the nature of the industry and BU's marketing operations, as well as by the subject matter being studied. A researcher interested in studying the effects of the EC-1992 Plan on firms' practice of marketing may find that most executives do not have detailed knowledge about their 1992-related activities.[11]

The difficulties associated with determining the influence of numerous environmental variables on IM activities are but one group of obstacles that must be overcome in IM research. The responses of firms to these differences depend upon the relative importance of and commitment to IM as well as their organizational philosophies and orientations. Coordination and control of marketing activities across markets disclose a great deal about the manner in which IM activities are performed [Kashani 1989; Quelch and Hoff 1986]. Yet, the research tradition in IM has not included orientation of firms and its influence on the conduct of IM activities. Typically, various aspects of marketing are researched from an international viewpoint without regard to this important, broader perspective.

EARLY INTEREST IN IM

Little IM research was published prior to the 1960s. The use of "comparative marketing" and "foreign marketing" terminologies was consistent with the conceptual and international involvement of firms. During the 1960s, use of the terms "international" and "comparative marketing" gained popularity. A natural extension of researching the functions of IM was to compare and contrast planning and performance of these functions among various national markets. Thus, the "comparative" approach to the study of IM became commonplace and today remains an integral part of IM literature. Interest in comparing markets, customer behavior, strategies, and management styles persists. During this decade, the "managerial" approach to studying marketing became popular and its extension to the international arena continues to be the cornerstone of much of the work being conducted in the field. Concurrent with the development of functional, comparative, and in particular, managerial orientation in investigating IM, increasing use of the terms multinational enterprise (MNE) and multinational marketing was made. During the latter part of the 1960s and early 1970s, much research was directed at understanding and explaining the activities of MNEs.

During the second half of the 1970s, as strategic planning and strategic marketing gained popularity, a considerable amount of research effort was directed towards the analysis of institutions, particularly the MNEs, and their management from these perspectives. Since the 1980s, there appears to be an intense interest in the analysis of international activities of firms from a global perspective.

There is little evidence of a definite direction in early IM research. In a review of the IM literature, Cavusgil and Nevin [1981] examined 265 articles. Although there are some gaps in their coverage, it provides a reasonable representation of quantity and areas of interest in IM research. The earliest pieces examined by the authors date to 1964, but only 26 (i.e., less than 10%) of the references were published in the 1960s. Only 19 of these studies are directly related to marketing, six (32%) of which pertained to advertising issues. No other area (e.g., distribution, standardization, exporting) had more than two entries. However, the authors left out at least four published studies dealing with the country-of-origin during this period. Thus, the country-of-origin topic appears to be a close second to advertising.

CURRENT AREAS OF INTEREST IN IM

The directions of contemporary IM research may provide valuable insights and assist in identifying components of a conceptual base. However, some observers have reported little change in the direction of IM research. For example, Terpstra [1987] noted, that according to *The International Executive*, there has been little change in the number of articles published on IM between 1970 and 1985. In addition, he noted that the distribution of topical areas has also remained the same. Previously, Albaum and Peterson [1984] reported 91 IM *empirical* studies in 23 outlets (i.e., 17 journals and 6 conference proceedings) during the 1976–82 period. These studies were classified into five marketing categories (12 subcategories) and two nonmarketing categories.[12] About 65 percent of the articles dealt with the elements of the marketing mix and 28 percent were in the buyer behavior area.

Bradley [1987] surveyed 32 journals for their IM content for the 1980–85 period. He identified 1,014 IM articles representing about 13 percent of all published studies. Articles were not classified by area of inquiry. Rather, they were carefully examined and classified into 21 elements of system exchange paradigms based upon the principal focus of each article. Not surprisingly, the majority (over two-thirds) of the articles dealt with the environment and participants. Almost half of the studies (45 percent) were at the lowest level of Bradley's scientific inquiry scale, i.e., assessment of existing knowledge.

Unlike earlier surveys of IM research, five key publications were surveyed for their IM content in the current study. These publications were selected because they represented the research thrust in marketing, have attained a prestigious position among scholars, and enjoy a wide readership base. In addition, no other major marketing and/or international journals were pub-

lished until the 1980s.[13] These journals include *Journal of Marketing, Journal of Marketing Research, Journal of Consumer Research, Journal of the Academy of Marketing Science*, and *Journal of International Business Studies.*

IM articles published in five key journals during the 1971–80 and 1981–90 periods were examined to determine the directions of interest in IM research. All articles dealing with nondomestic marketing issues are included in Table 1. Based upon the definition offered earlier, studies which provide only a one-nation perspective were excluded. As shown in Table 1, more than 55 percent of published studies during the 1971–90 period (70 percent for the 1971–80

Table 1. Studies in IM

TOPIC[1]	COUNT[2,3]		PERCENT		PERCENT
	1971–80	1981–90	1971–80	1981–90	CHANGE
General Marketing Management	12	22	24	20	83
Export-Import Studies	7	20	14	18	186
Buyer Behavior/Consumer Attitude Studies	8	11	16	10	38
Advertising and Promotion Issues	8	8	16	7	0
Country-of-Origin Studies	4	10	8	9	150
Distribution Management Issues	3	10	6	9	233
Product Market Analysis	2	6	4	6	300
Marketing Research (Review)	0	7	0	6	na
Standardization of Marketing	2	4	4	4	200
Legal, Governmental, and Public Policy Issues	1	2	2	2	100
Product Management Issues	0	4	0	4	na
Methodology Issues	1	3	2	3	300
Pricing Issues	2	0	4	0	−100
International Marketing Negotiations	0	2	0	2	na
TOTAL	50	109	100	100	118
Comparative Studies	12/50	24/109	24	22	100
Less Developed Countries Studies	6/50	8/109	12	7	33

[1]The topics are listed in order of their combined frequency of publication during 1971–90.
[2]The frequencies are based on a survey of the following journals: *Journal of Marketing, Journal of Marketing Research, Journal of Consumer Research, Journal of the Academy of Marketing Science, and Journal of International Business Studies.*
[3]*Journal of the Academy of Marketing Science* was first published in 1973 and these frequencies exclude volumes 1–4 of this journal. Only four international marketing articles were published in *JAMS* from 1977–80, however, and by implication, it is unlikely that a large number of such articles were published in the first four volumes.

period) were in four areas: general marketing management, export-import, buyer behavior and consumer attitude, and advertising and promotion studies. As compared to the 1970s, research productivity has increased in nearly every area of IM during the 1980s. However, considerably more interest was exhibited in four areas: product-market analyses, standardization issues, methodology-related topics, and distribution management issues. Interest in methodological considerations is a natural outgrowth of the demand for greater scientific rigor in IM research. The number of comparative studies and those focusing on less developed nations, however, have remained at about 30 percent of all published articles.

Some patterns with regard to topics published in various journals are evident. There is a greater concentration of export-related and country-of-origin studies in *JIBS* than in other journals. It would appear that researchers place less emphasis on bridging the gap between mainstream research in marketing and areas of interest in IM, most notably exporting studies. Research in exporting, for example, has almost invariably focused on exporters. A greater number of outlets, e.g., *Journal of Consumer Research*, have become available for country-of-origin articles as a result of bridging existing gaps. With a few exceptions, publications on topics idiosyncratic to IM, e.g., exporting, are rare in the remaining key journals. No other patterns are evident. Since their introductions in 1984 and 1985, respectively, *International Marketing Review* (IMR) and *Journal of International Marketing* (JIM) have become key outlets for IM research. Like *JIBS*, IMR and JIM have been common outlets for exporting and country-of-origin research.[14]

A CONCEPTUAL FRAMEWORK

The two schools of thought discussed earlier represent extreme views towards the conceptual and managerial status of IM. Although the core marketing decision variables remain the same, numerous additional considerations elevate IM to a much more complex planning and decision making process. To discount these differences as merely superficial changes in the environmental variables, as do the proponents of the first school of thought, is quite naive. To think of them as changing the core and the thrust of the marketing process is also unwise.

Primary considerations that significantly alter the type of marketing that is practiced in the domestic market vis-à-vis the international marketplace include the IM philosophy and the international organization of firms, the resultant pursuit of intermarket segmentation, and the market entry mode. As such, how corporations view their international markets and related activities is central to the conceptual base developed in this study. Thus, the three strategic orientations cited earlier (à la Toyne and Walters), i.e., market extension, multidomestic, and global, are central to the approach taken in this study.

Quite understandably, economic and legal environments, as well as the practice of business, vary greatly even among clusters of similar nations (e.g., developed nations). Thus it is only natural that IM plans involve considerations that are not parts of domestic plans. A view of these and other issues to be discussed in this section are presented in Figure 1. A critical mediating factor in this conceptualization is the focus on issues that are pivotal in IM. Marketing elements and issues that do not change very much from one area to another are not included.

THE CONCEPT OF INTERMARKET SEGMENTS

The foundation of contemporary marketing thought is based upon market segmentation. Market segmentation is a *necessary* and *critical* component of every marketing plan. Though segmentation is not always practiced by firms and is not applicable to all products, it is the point of departure for conceptual and managerial discussions of marketing. Adapted from the microeconomic theory of price discrimina-

Figure 1. A Conceptual Framework for International Marketing

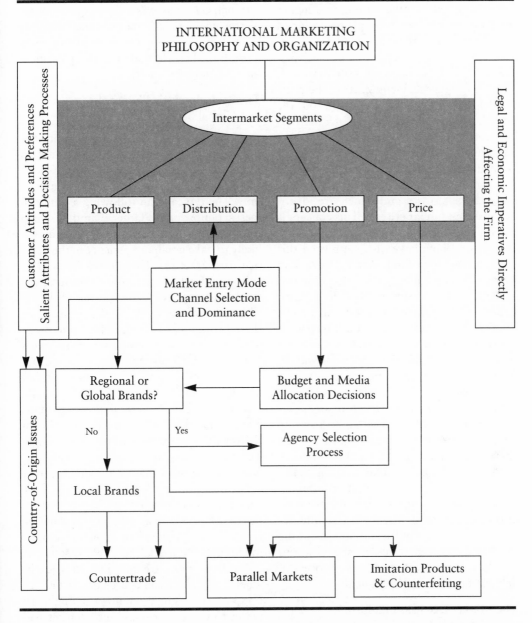

tion, market segmentation essentially acomplishes one thing. Using the relevant criteria, customers are grouped into homogeneous subsets, thereby allowing the firm to cultivate particular market niches in which fewer or no competitors are present. The theoretical model is normative in nature with the goal of profit maximization.

Competitive advantage offered to the firm using market segmentation can be significant. First, a firm may remain a quasi-monopolist in its selected market segment(s), enabling it to price its products with relative freedom from competitors. All things being equal, pricing freedom should lead to higher margins and, therefore, better BU performance. Second, by focusing on individual target markets, the firm can anticipate and react to market changes more effectively and efficiently, leading to a higher level of customer loyalty. Implementation of an effective segmentation program, however, requires the presence of a number of *a priori* conditions, including potential profits from selected segment(s). If so, the practice of IM must also be based on the identification and cultivation of intermarket segments. The concept of intermarket segments is defined as the presence of well-defined and similar clusters of customers across national boundaries that possess the same characteristics and which are identified by using similar criteria. This concept is central to Levitt's [1983] position on globalization. Others have also supported this position [Douglas and Wind 1987; Jain 1989; Kale and Sudharshan 1987; Onkvisit and Shaw 1987; Simmonds 1985; Sheth 1986]. If this position is valid and practical, then applying the segmentation concept internationally should allow the firm to standardize its marketing programs and offering(s) for each identified segment on a global basis and, by definition, achieve a higher level of *economic performance*.

However, the basis used for segmenting intermarket segments may require the inclusion of variables that are of little concern in segmenting domestic markets. For example, certain market factors that prohibit entry (e.g., export bans for certain products into some markets) or make it virtually uneconomical (e.g., significant changes in the product to meet government specification) should be considered during the process of delineating intermarket segments.

The Market Extension Philosophy and Global Segmentation

By definition, firms that are characterized as following the market extension philosophy consider international markets as secondary to their domestic activities. Though such firms may be quite sophisticated in their approaches to the cultivation of domestic markets, segmentation, and targeting, they do not proactively segment their international markets. Thus, market extension firms *do not seek to identify their intermarket segment(s)*. Since segmentation is, to some degree, a natural phenomenon, their intermarket segments are identified as a result of their IM activities in a piecemeal fashion and by default.

The Multidomestic Philosophy and Global Segmentation

Multidomestic firms consider international opportunities to be as important as their domestic markets and have established affiliates that operate with relative autonomy. The typical firm following a multidomestic philosophy is larger than that which has a market extension orientation, and is likely to have greater experience in the practice of marketing. Thus, these firms typically use market segmentation around the world independent of their other affiliates. This is understandable as the affiliates of these firms tend to develop their own products (or borrow from other subsidiaries only that which fits their perceptions of local needs and strategy). Thus, firms with a multidomestic orientation do not typically attempt to identify intermarket segments. This implies that the level of coordination of IM activities in these firms is not very high. Yet, their success in the international marketplace is in part due to drawing on their overall corporate resources and synergies. Thus, the identification and cultivation of intermarket segments by multidomestic firms is largely dependent upon how closely individual "domestic" marketing activities around the globe are coordinated. Clearly, when an affiliate is in charge of a region (as opposed to a single country) it might attempt to identify regional intermarket segments. Nevertheless, multidomestic firms are not characterized as pursuing a corporate-wide effort to identify intermarket segments.

The Global Philosophy and Global Segmentation

Firms that have adopted a global philosophy do not make a distinction between domestic and IM opportunities. Since global firms are strategically not bothered by national boundaries, their implied marketing objective is to identify intermarket segments as though there were no environmental constraints. The key ingredients in the strategy of global firms are the appropriate levels of *control and coordination* of IM activities among various affiliates. Thus, the success in identification and cultivation of intermarket segments is dependent upon how well a global firm controls and coordinates its IM activities.

Evidence of Intermarket Segments

The identification and cultivation of intermarket segments has been urged in the literature [Cunningham and Green 1984; Douglas and Craig 1983; Kale and Sudharshan 1987]. Nevertheless, there is no evidence in the literature that firms seek to identify intermarket segments. Several examples frequently used in the literature, e.g., soft drinks and fast food, are aimed at mass markets for which segmentation is not an issue. Industrial products are the most likely candidates to fit the conceptual prerequisites of intermarket segments because they satisfy common needs and their purchases are more likely to be policy-driven and rationalized by informed individuals.

THE INTERNATIONAL MARKETING
PROGRAM

The driving force behind the identification of intermarket segments is the development of standardized marketing plans which can be used globally with minimum change. However, as noted earlier, the identification of intermarket segments is neither evident from the literature nor the practice of IM. Clearly, many partially standardized approaches have been used, but there is no evidence that they have been preceded by the segmentation. Furthermore, there is no evidence that firm profitability is greater in cases where this so-called partial standardization has been employed [Jain 1989; Samiee and Roth 1992].

Thus, most firms, regardless of strategic philosophy, approach IM in a fragmented manner. Basic elements of marketing are thus planned and coordinated for each market as management sees fit. These strategies are primarily driven by *legal* and *economic* imperatives of host markets and the way customers behave which, in turn, is a function of *attitudes, preferences,* and *decision-making processes.*

As long as legal and economic differences between markets influence elements of the marketing program, it will be impossible to plan and implement completely standardized IM programs. Every element of marketing is influenced by legal constraints which vary across markets. The proponents of the school of thought viewing international and domestic marketing as equivalent are accustomed to countries, chiefly the U.S., where there are relatively few legal restrictions (e.g., price controls, advertising controls, restrictions against vertical and horizontal mergers and acquisitions) in their domestic markets. Thus, they see legal restrictions as something quite removed from the planning process and a relative nonissue.

A manager confronted with the diversity of laws in the marketplace has to resort to modifications atypical of domestic marketing. Consider that many nations have minimum or maximum markups and inflationary economies frequently exercise price controls. Product standards and regulations with regard to their safety vary considerably too. In fact, a major promise of the EC-1992 plan was the unification of existing product standards [Samiee 1990a]. The ISO 9000 standards, though less specific in the actual formulation or design of final products, represent another example in this regard. What channel intermediaries can and cannot do is also restricted in many countries. Some countries do not allow forward integration in the channel, whereas others do not allow horizontal expansion, and still some do not permit the opening of stores of a certain size or attributes [Samiee 1990b]. Promotional activities are perhaps among the most restricted in the international arena. They range from what can or cannot be advertised, where they might be advertised, what can or cannot be said in the advertisement, to banning or severely restricting personal selling and, in particular, sales promotion activities. As long as these differences persist, marketing planning in diverse, if not adverse, legal environments remains a management challenge. Thus, the belief that domestic marketing and IM are similar represents a narrow and naive view. Though it is true that marketing in a local sense would not change, its management in a global sense, driven by the firm's philosophy and international organization, is much more complicated. Marketing scholars have typically focused on relatively micro issues in marketing and have not been concerned with the influence of firms' philosophies and international organization upon the practice of marketing. In order for IM to be viewed the same as domestic marketing, this gap must also be filled.

DECISION-MAKING PROCESSES

As one might expect, preferences and salient attributes involved in purchase decisions differ among customer groups everywhere. In this context, international markets do not vary much from domestic ones. Yet, there are aspects of these factors that vary greatly from one market to another. For example, in the developing countries where demand frequently exceeds supply, salient attributes do not have the same meaning as in the more affluent, free market areas where supply almost invariably exceeds demand. Thus, even when buyer behavior or information processing models dealing with these constructs are developed in the domestic market and can be shown to be generally valid in other affluent markets, they may be inappropriate for use in the developing markets. Modified versions of models and theories are needed to better explain and predict the behavioral patterns in these markets.

Organizational decision-making processes vary greatly from one culture to another. Differences in decision making in Japan, Germany, and the United States demonstrate the magnitude of the problem marketers face internationally. In Japanese organizations, decisions are typically made by consensus. Furthermore, in many Japanese organizations decisions are made in a bottom-up fashion. In contrast, the decision making process in most other developed nations tends to be autocratic. In the United States and, particularly, in Germany, decisions are made in a top-down fashion with limited or no input from lower level employees.

Family decision-making authorities also vary considerably across national boundaries. The relative roles of family members with regard to household purchases or purchases of particular items are quite different in various markets. Children in the U.S., for example, play a major role in the purchase of such products as breakfast cereals and toys. In contrast, in many other nations (e.g., Great Britain) children command very little influence over what is or is not bought, even when they are the ultimate consumer of the product. Likewise, joint decision making by spouses, or individual dominance by husband/wife, varies across cultures (for example, see Green and Cunningham [1980]).

The identification of decision-making loci in the international markets is pivotal to the proper identification and cultivation of intermarket segments. Yet, cross-cultural knowledge in this regard is impoverished.

THE ROLE OF MARKET ENTRY MODE

Market entry mode, a nonissue in domestic marketing, can significantly influence the marketing activities of a firm. The critical importance of market entry mode in IM is demonstrated by its use as the central theme for a relatively successful *International Marketing* text [Terpstra and Sarathy 1994]. The authors make frequent reference to market entry modes and their influences on the IM processes and programs. The relative dominance of exporting research in IM addresses this aspect of the conceptual framework. However, scholarly effort with regard to the marketing influence of market entry mode is incomplete in that it does not address other patterns of market presence and strategic alliance.

The most immediate impact of the market entry mode is on international distribution decisions. The entire distribution network, its control, coordination, market penetration, and hence, other aspects of marketing are substantially influenced by this initial decision. For example, distribution through export management or export trading firms provides little control over the channel, segmentation, product positioning, product service, market research, and direct customer feedback. Though market entry mode is typically a strategic decision external to marketing, it shapes the character and scope of IM activities of the firm from the outset.

COUNTRY-OF-ORIGIN ISSUES

Another by-product of the mode of market entry is the manner in which host-market customers view the country in which a product is made and/or its location of manufacture. Country bias and the image that it projects upon products manufactured there have been areas of inquiry within IM since the mid-1960s. The body of literature in the area generally supports the presence of some bias toward products of foreign origin.

Despite dozens of published articles in this area, country-of-origin of products are typically beyond the domain of marketing. When some form of country-equity is present in the product (e.g., German quality), marketers can stress such dimensions in their promotional programs. However, the key concern regarding the country-of-origin of products is where a negative image is conveyed. Though the marketing mix can be adjusted to counterbalance some of the negative image projected by a product's country-of-origin, a marketing manager cannot singularly "correct" this problem. Market entry mode decisions are external to marketing departments and exacerbate the

problem. Clearly, it is quite likely that management considers such issues as quality of labor, country infrastructure, costs, etc., when making entry decisions. However, there is no evidence in the literature that country-of-origin *per se* is a consideration in its market entry mode deliberations.

In addition to the market entry mode, customer attitudes, preferences, and salient product attributes, uniform branding policies (i.e., regional or global brands) also influence the country-of-origin effect. Local brands may be at a disadvantage vis-à-vis those produced in areas with significant country-equity, but much greater problems are faced with regional and global brands. For example, a Sony product manufactured in Taiwan, Korea, or the United States may not be viewed in the same light as one made in Japan. The issue is quite complex and the literature in the area is both scant and inconclusive.

Continued intense interest in researching the country-of-origin issue is the result of complexities of the international marketplace. On the one hand, firms increasingly source, produce, and market their products on a global basis and, on the other, we know that customers hold certain biased views towards products manufactured in other countries. Since the marketer is typically not involved in the market entry decision process, it is the marketing manager who must correct any negative bias resulting from this choice.

REGIONAL AND GLOBAL BRANDS

The combined influence of the firm's strategic orientation, product strategy, and market entry mode determines the feasibility of establishing global or regional brands. Whereas global firms with regional or local market presence are likely to be reaching their intermarket segments with global or regional brands, multidomestic firms are more likely to be focused on local brands.

The decision to standardize marketing plans relies in part on the presence of globally or, at least, regionally recognized and positioned brands. Regional brands, such as those marketed only in Europe or Latin America, represent limited standardization. The decision to develop global or regional brands involves many other facets of the IM plan. International corporate and brand-specific communications strategies have to be developed. Advertising copies and, in particular, media choice are significantly affected by the decision to standardize brands.

The presence of reasonably standard products, brands, and positions is implicit in standardization of the marketing plan. The significance of this research issue is reflected in the IM practice of some of the best-known and managed firms. Consider, for example, the case of Procter and Gamble (PandG) in Europe. Until recently, PandG typified a company with a multidomestic orientation. As late as 1980, it sold only six products in Europe, whereas its main global competitors, Colgate-Palmolive and Unilever, dominated Europe with dozens of products and brands. Prior to the mid-1980s, Ariel, its highly successful detergent in Europe, had different product *compositions* and *positions* in various national markets. Ariel was a presoak in one country, an all-purpose detergent in another, a powerful cleaner in a third, and so on. Thus PandG was unable to benefit from media spillover and cross-border purchases in these contiguous markets. To make matters worse, price differences caused by exchange-rate fluctuations led to the creation of parallel markets for the brand as some distributors found it economically advantageous to source Ariel, though the "wrong" formulation of it, for distribution in their own market area.

Whenever firms succeed in their efforts to develop global or regional brands, they invite competition. One source of competition is through *imitation products and brands* that lead to the erosion of brand position and market share. Another form of competition results from piracy and the theft of intellectual/industrial property and goodwill (*counterfeiting*). Unauthorized distribution of products represents a third form of threat to the marketing activities of firms (*parallel markets*). These issues are generally not considered a part of the body of knowledge in domestic marketing literature and receive little, if any, coverage. However, they represent some critical considerations in IM plans and strategies.

ADVERTISING AGENCY, BUDGET, AND MEDIA DECISIONS

The types of advertising-related decisions a firm faces are dependent upon its IM philosophy. Market extension firms may leave it entirely to host-market intermediaries to manage local campaigns, or they may have limited involvement. As such, agency selection may be viewed as a local decision, and budget and media selection are fragmentary. Multidomestic firms, on the other hand, either locally or regionally, control and coordinate their own campaigns, subject to the level of coordination demanded by the headquarters. In cases where local affiliates of a multidomestic firm are completely independent of one-another and market only local brands, agency, media, and budget decisions are similar to those made in the domestic market. In contrast to other corporate philosophies, global firms are likely to focus on world-wide coordination of advertising campaigns (including positioning, production, and placement) of their global brands.

PARALLEL MARKETS

Government regulations influence all aspects of the marketing plan, whether domestic or international. However, the presence of laws which are idiosyncratic to specific markets, coupled with the firm's marketing strategy, can potentially lead to undesirable or less-than-optimum results. With the exception of some product categories,[15] firms typically have to compete on a local basis which consists of numerous local competitors. Market- or demand-oriented pricing strategy in national markets is imperative for these firms. Since firms rationalize their sourcing on a global or regional basis, they invariably face foreign exchange fluctuations. Higher prices which might result from these fluctuations cannot always be passed on to the customer, thus creating opportunities in the market for "product arbitrage" or parallel markets.[16] Likewise, some markets are subjected to price controls which further fuel parallel markets. The presence of different standards of living and disposable income in various markets further contribute to the growth in parallel markets. Parallel markets, however, cannot exist in the absence of global or regional brands. The PandG example cited earlier is typical of the predicaments that firms face, albeit PandG faced the disadvantage of having different product constituents and positions.

THE ROLE OF INTERNATIONAL COUNTERTRADE

There is an absence of conceptual treatment of countertrade in IM. In fact, most IM textbooks provide only a rudimentary treatment of this subject matter, by providing general information regarding its nature, different types, and countries demanding countertrade in return for their purchases. Czinkota and Ronkainen [1995], however, deviate from this pattern of coverage and provide a comprehensive account of the topic by allocating an entire chapter to the subject. Nevertheless, this material is descriptive and falls short of the types of conceptual and analytical advances needed in IM.

A special case can be made for passive exporters with local brands or unbranded merchandise. These entities adhere to a market extension philosophy and because of their lack of market knowledge, marketing know-how, and foreign exchange restrictions, resort to countertrade to satisfy local needs. In this vein, countertrade demands represent a *pricing* or *valuation* exercise. Thus, as noted in Figure 1, countertrade is a hybrid of pricing and absence of global or regional brands, since if the latter were present then there would be little need for countertrade.

During the past twenty years, cash-poor nations and centrally planned economies have placed an increasing amount of pressure on conducting foreign trade via countertrade.[17] Although the actual volume of countertrade is not known, it is estimated that 10 to 15 percent of the world trade is conducted via countertrade transactions. Indeed, demand for countertrade is so widespread today that some affluent nations, such as Switzerland, require some countertrade. This form of trade exerts much pressure on corporate resources and significantly influences pricing and distribution decisions.

In addition to the problems faced by organizations demanding countertrade in return for their purchases (as noted above), there is a feeling on the part of many Western firms that market share and penetration must be preserved, even if it involves countertrade. Furthermore, the nature of markets, marketing resources invested in a new product, and competitive forces in Western countries require reliable supply sources. Inasmuch as many countertrade deals are close-ended, they typically do not satisfy Western firms' demand for reliable, continuous supply sources.

RESEARCH PRIORITIES IN INTERNATIONAL MARKETING

It is evident from the analysis of IM publications in Table 1 that the pursuit of scholarship in IM is not entirely consistent with the priorities outlined in the conceptualization offered in this study. IM research priorities promoted by the present framework center on topics that only minimally overlap with the coverage of domestic aspects of marketing. The IM literature appears to be quite rich in some areas but impoverished in others. For example, the literature in exporting is quite comprehensive, but very limited in comparative exporting practice (e.g., export involvement, information use, management, and performance in Germany vis-à-vis Japan). Nor have the influences of other market entry modes on marketing been sufficiently investigated. In fact, for all marketing publications combined, exporting and country-of-origin studies constitute the most popular areas of investigation in IM. Chances are that the focus on these topics is due to the relative high speed and low cost associated with data acquisition, quite frequently from domestic sources. One would expect the presence of a higher order as the driving force behind the selection of areas of inquiry by scholars.

There are numerous research opportunities in assessing the suitability and the profit impact of both IM components and plans. Standardization and countertrade are but two examples that require more thorough investigation. The former topic is pivotal to serving intermarket segments whereas virtually no information is available on the profit impact on various channel members in the letter.

Firms with a global organization or those striving to develop a global strategy can no longer use segmentation in its traditional form. Although the concept does not change, its application does. Specifically, firms with a global or regional view of their markets must identify *intermarket segments*. This means that similar, cross-cultural market segments must be identified and cultivated in all markets where the firm has a presence. The IM literature is vacuous in this area. The critical role of market segmentation in marketing theory and practice is extended to the investigation of intermarket segments.

There are also numerous opportunities to extend knowledge gained through domestic models and theories to an international setting. Much of the country-of-origin literature has evolved independently of buyer behavior models and virtually none of the studies have fully examined the saliency of country-of-origin. One exception includes a study by Johansson, Douglas, and Nonaka [1985] in which the basic Fishbein attitude model was applied to assess the country-of-origin bias among U.S. and Japanese students.

Empirical research involving developing nations is also rare. These nations con-sume about 30 percent of world trade, but constitute more than 140 nations. Though researching developing nations may not sound or appear as prestigious and fascinating, it is of critical importance from a public policy view. In addition, IM research priorities in these markets are likely to be different than those one may encounter in the developed markets. Practitioner-oriented research dealing with distribution, product adaptation, and pricing is likely to be far more important than the more esoteric and theoretical aspects with limited managerial implication. In addition, new developments in Eastern Europe offer many research possibilities. For example, the role, impact, and significance of Eastern European markets on IM plans and strategies of firms might be assessed.

A final aspect of IM research that can benefit from additional coverage is international or foreign perspectives, particularly with regard to IM plans and strategies. Currently, much of the research is focused on the American perspective. Non-American views are increasingly important in the face of strong competition from the EU, Japan, and in particular, from the newly emerging industrialized nations. To be sure, multinational research projects tend to be expensive and time consuming. However, research in these areas is needed if IM, as a legitimate scholarly area of inquiry, is to prosper.

CONCLUDING REMARKS

The objective of this study was to develop a conceptual framework for IM with emphasis on elements and issues that are not typically included in the treatment of marketing at the domestic level. It is apparent from this conceptualization and its rationalization that, while the core marketing constructs do not change in various national markets, many critical issues in IM are not encountered in domestic markets and lead to a considerably more complex managerial task. Thus, the extreme positions held by the two schools of thought are unwarranted. Few experts would argue that the core and thrust of marketing varies from place to place. However, given the present conceptualization, it is evident that, aside from the addition of new considerations in IM, there are significant differences in marketing analysis, planning, and implementation at the international level.

Lack of conceptual and theoretical development in IM is somewhat understandable. For one thing, marketing itself lacks identity from a theoretical perspective and there is no universally accepted marketing theory. Quite naturally, it would be difficult to move marketing forward into the international arena when there are questions with regard to its theoretical status. Furthermore, scholars have focused more on methodologies and psychological and social aspects of marketing at the expense of developing the nucleus of marketing. There has been a tendency to borrow, perhaps excessively, from other fields rather than to develop our own systems and processes. In addition, the ethnocentric orientation of marketing scholars (à la Cavusgil and Nevin [1981]), as well as the greater environment in which marketing is practiced domestically, have assisted in retaining a domestic orientation over much of what is researched and published in marketing.

To complicate matters, with minor exceptions (e.g., the United Kingdom), academic research activities in the marketing discipline represent a relatively new phenomenon in much of the developed world. Demand for research productivity is not very high and, unlike the common practice in the United States, at best, there is only limited pressure on non-U.S.-based academicians to develop scholarly work. Thus, little assistance in theory development has been forthcoming from outside the United States.

The conceptualization presented in this study was developed with a specific objective in mind and independently of existing IB and marketing theories. IB and marketing theories have little in common and are difficult to converge. Each has its own weaknesses which further complicates their

convergence into a cohesive, universal IM theory. It is apparent that more conceptual and theoretical work is needed to enrich the foundation of IM.

NOTES

1. The American Assembly of Collegiate Schools of Business has developed workbooks and offers seminars for faculty training. A number of faculty workshops in IB are also offered. The Faculty Development in International Business program at the University of South Carolina, for example, has become increasingly more popular since its inception in 1989.

2. The number of IM textbooks is about three times greater than it was two decades ago. New or revised books in international marketing are regularly being scheduled for publication (e.g., Buzzell, Quelch, and Bartlett; Dahringer and Mühlbacher; Douglas and Craig; Jeannet and Hennessey; Kashani; Keegan; Samli, Still, and Hill; Terpstra and Sarathy; and Toyne and Walters).

3. These include *International Marketing Review, Journal of Global Marketing, Journal of International Consumer Marketing,* and *Journal of International Marketing.*

4. In his comprehensive review of the marketing literature, Bartels (1962) did not even include a category pertaining to IM.

5. A key marketing theoretician, Robert Bartels, for example, had much interest in the study of international business and comparative marketing systems. However, despite the many IM publications and the availability of several IM textbooks during his tenure, he frequently noted that he was at a loss as to what one may realistically teach in an "international marketing" course. Indeed, no international marketing course was offered at his institution during that period.

6. In fact, the term "environmentalism" was used by Bartels to denote relating marketing to the environment in which tasks were performed.

7. Standardization, parallel markets, and countertrade are not exclusive domains of IM and constitute marketing and business considerations in domestic markets as well. However, they are virtually ignored by general marketing textbooks. Of course, their roles in IM are much more critical and their impact on firms is more complex. Thus, it is understandable that IM has

become the primary information outlet on these subjects.

8. Naturally, market entry decisions include some key marketing considerations such as distribution and pricing. But once the decision is made, it becomes a constant in the firm's marketing plan and strategy. Nevertheless, a review of these topics provides a richer understanding of the international business environment.

9. For example, the presence of the Latin American Integration Association or the Arab Common Market will not influence domestic marketing programs of U.S. firms. Even the North American Free Trade Area is likely to have only a limited impact on domestic marketing programs.

10. Specifically, Bartels (1970) points out that theories require seven essential qualities: subject identification, basic concepts, intraconcept differences, interconcept relationships, generality, diversity, and resolution of differences.

11. The 3M Company, for example, had assigned one individual at its headquarters with the responsibility of coordinating and overseeing the firm's activities for the EC-1992 Plan. Johnson and Johnson, whose global philosophy is "multidomestic" in nature, on the other hand, reorganized its European operations to prepare for the Single Market Initiatives in Europe. However, since the reorganization took quite some time, the firm's ultimate structure had not yet emerged, and no informant in the firm can provide valid responses to research questions regarding the firm's future in Europe during the periods preceding 1993. Naturally, given an appropriate design, the researcher can identify and eliminate from the sample organizations that might have fallen in this category. However, in the absence of prior knowledge or in-depth organizational studies, it is quite likely that researchers would overlook these organizational imperatives.

12. The authors reported 112 articles of which 21 dealt with multinational corporations and foreign direct investment, which have been subtracted from the total.

13. The survey excludes journals published abroad. However, it is not readily apparent that journals excluded from the survey have had an impact in setting the tone or a direction in IM research. Other journals that might have been surveyed include: *International Marketing Review, Journal of International Consumer Marketing, Journal of International Marketing, Journal of Business Research,* and *Journal of Global Marketing.* Their relative recency and the exclusive international focus of the first three on IM topics would significantly skew the counts and the distribution of the areas of interest. In addition, general management-oriented journals such as *Business Horizons, California Management Review, Columbia Journal of World Business, Harvard Business Review,* and *Sloan Management Review* were excluded due to their typical nonacademic orientation.

14. For example, if the *IMR* articles were included in the table, the top four areas would account for 65 percent of all IM studies, with export-import studies dominating IM research (23%), followed by country-of-origin (17%), general marketing management (17%), and buyer behavior and consumer attitudes (8%). It is thus evident that the five publications used in this study are not key outlets for country-of-origin and export-import studies.

15. These exceptions include capital intensive industries and industries that face rapid pace of technology change whose products are reasonably similar, e.g., electronic storage devices and memory chips.

16. It is noteworthy that parallel markets may also involve authorized distributors across national boundaries. For example, a Swiss authorized distributor may bypass the local subsidiary and source its supply from an authorized distributor in Britain or a customer who would turn around and sell part of its purchases to other end-users. For a comprehensive account of parallel market activities see Cespedes, Corey, and Kasturi Rangan (1988), Duhan and Sheffet (1988), and Engardio, Fins, Baudoin, and Tell (1988).

17. The emphasis here is on manufactured products, as opposed to commodities for which formal international markets (i.e., commodity exchanges) exist.

■ ■ ■

The Reincarnation Of International Marketing
Jagdish N. Sheth

In this paper, I will first trace the evolution of International Marketing (IM) and its determinants and demonstrate that IM has been primarily contextual in nature and, therefore, unable to generate its own theory or constructs to justify it as a unique school of marketing thought [Sheth, Gardner, and Garrett 1988; Sheth and Eshghi 1989; Ricks, Fu, and Arpan 1974].

As a contextual practice, IM has rightfully focused on two obvious dimensions: how the practice of marketing varies from country to country (extension vs. adjustment tactics) and why it varies (cultural, social economic, political, and physiological differences) from country to country [Buzzell 1968; Levitt 1983; Quelch and Hoff 1986; Boddewyn 1981]. The second part of the paper proposes that most of the contextual determinants of IM are disappearing and, that there will be no discipline of IM even if it was developed based upon a contingency theory approach. It is even likely that IM practice as we know it today may also become less relevant as these contextual determinants become less relevant [Levitt 1983; Bartlett and Ghoshal 1989; Sheth 1995].

The final part of the paper discusses the emerging reincarnation of IM with its emphasis on global (as opposed to international) and cross-functional (as opposed to functional) dimensions. I will conclude that the reincarnation of IM holds the promise of becoming a subdiscipline or a school of marketing thought.

DETERMINANTS OF INTERNATIONAL MARKETING

International marketing refers to the understanding of marketing practices in different countries (comparative descriptions); its structural determinants anchored to national differences (comparative explanations); and deployment of country specific marketing strategies and operations by multidomestic firms (comparative prescriptions). Therefore, its primary focus is the description, explanation, and managerial control of marketing practices across national boundaries [Toyne 1989].

Compared to international trade and export marketing, IM is a more recent phenomenon [Root 1978; Yoshino 1976]. It has grown since World War II and presumably was a consequence of the demise of colonialism and the recreation of numerous independent nations. In my view, this origin for the rise of IM resulted in a number of contextual determinants for its practice and became the focus of academic research and thinking. Figure 1 displays the contextual determinants of IM.

Numerous books, monographs, and review papers have been written which document how these contextual determinants have shaped the marketing practices between countries [Ohmae 1985; Porter 1986,1990; Kotler 1991]. Therefore, it is better for me to simply focus on a few key points with respect to these determinants instead of describing them in detail.

The first four determinants (political stability, government policy, ideology driven economy, and fear of colonialism) are more responsible for the prescription of multidomestic marketing practices, therefore, there exists more anecdotal and trade literature [Ricks, Fu, and Arpan 1976] and less academic research on them. This includes such managerial decisions as selection of countries with which to do business and specific entry strategies. Most of this has required the understanding and utilization of what has been recently referred to as the fifth "P" of marketing (politics and public relations). Unfortunately, there is very little theoretical foundation underlying these determinants partly because IM has not borrowed from the social sciences, even political science.

The next three determinants (marketing

Figure 1. Contextual Determinants of International Marketing

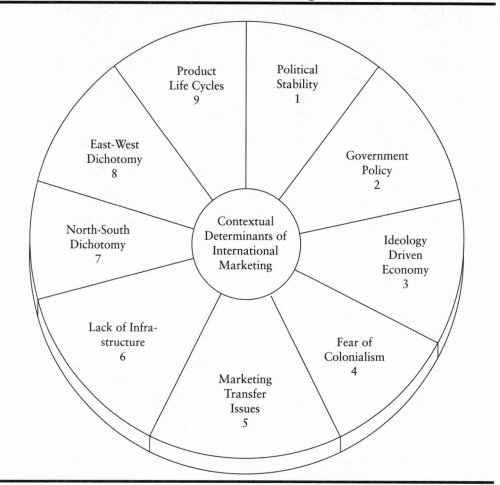

transfer issues, lack of infrastructure, and North-South dichotomy) need a little more description. Marketing transfer issues relate to the *operational* challenges of product, price, distribution, and promotion adjustments across national boundaries due to divergence in support and core value chain activities including materials, people, processes, and facilities.

Lack of infrastructure refers to inadequate availability of transportation, communications, physical, financial, natural, and human resources most especially in less developed countries. This lack of infrastructure impacts the adjustment process for the marketing mix. Finally, the North-South dichotomy refers to the "have" and

"have-not" countries of the world and is a direct reflection of the traditional economic development theories and their importance to IM practices. Academic research on these three determinants is moderately rich and seems to be grounded in the theories of economics, logistics, and public policy.

Finally, most of the academic research in IM has been focused on the last two determinants: East-West dichotomy and product life cycles. The first refers to the cultural differences between nations both at a macro and micro level of understanding and explanation [Clark 1990]. The second refers to the birth and death theories of product life cycles as they move across national boundaries [Wells 1968; Johanson and Valhne 1977]. Again, the product life cycle concept has benefitted from population ecology and biology theories as its basis and, to that extent, it seems to have at least face validity and empirical support.

This analysis clearly suggests why IM has predominately remained a contextual practice and why it has been difficult to develop a theory of IM even based upon contingency propositions: Most determinants of IM are ad hoc, dynamic, and unstable and, therefore, not subject to theory building opportunities. For example, who could have forecasted the demise of the Soviet Union (political stability), development of regional integrations (European Community (EC) '92), privatization of industries (Japan and United Kingdom) and pro-western links by Muslim states (Indonesia and Egypt)?

THE BORDERLESS WORLD

The fate of IM is closely tied to its determinants. As they change, both the theory and practice of IM must change. Ironically, it is not the *direction*, but the *existence* of most of the determinants that is increasingly under attack. Consequently, the existence of IM as we know it today is questionable.

A number of powerful macroeconomic forces are reshaping the world. They are: regional integration and the emergence of the triad power; technology advances, especially the adoption of information technologies in business operations; emergence of a free world ideology and the role of the market economy policy; and the borderless economy as a consequence of global sourcing and global competition.

These four major macroeconomic forces are also shaping the determinants of IM [Sheth 1995], and are represented in Figure 2. Together, these forces are creating a borderless world where the national boundaries are becoming either obsolete or less relevant in determining differential marketing practices. As the economic world becomes global, *inter*national differences are being supplanted by *intra*national differences, but on a global basis. In other words, in a global economy, *within-country* differences will surpass *between-country* differences. Therefore, it may be advantageous to look at different target markets within a country, but on a global basis [Sheth and Eshghi 1989; Ohmae 1990; Lamont 1991].

The regional integration of Western Europe (EC '92) and Southeast Asia (ASEAN) has recently demonstrated that nations can gain more competitive advantages by enduring alliances rather than by self reliance

Figure 2. Causes for the Borderless World

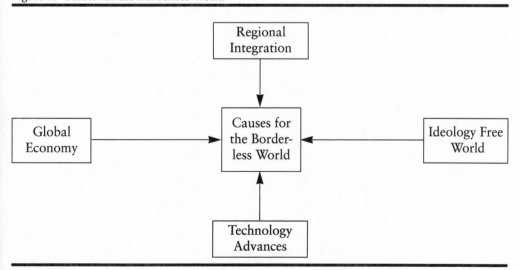

or by bilateral trade agreements [Porter 1990]. The emerging economic power of EC '92 is, in turn, creating a domino effect on the rest of the world. For example, it encourages North American regional integration between the United States, Canada, and Mexico and has encouraged Japan's attempted alignment with the ASEAN bloc. The economic blocs of EC '92, ASEAN, and North American integration have resulted in the emergence of a triad power dominating the world economy [Ohmae 1985]. It is estimated that 75 percent of world GDP and 70 percent of world trade are concentrated among these three regional economic blocs.

REGIONAL INTEGRATION

Regional integration is not a new concept. It has been practiced by kings and emperors in ancient times and by colonial powers in modern times [Kennedy 1987]. In fact, the United States, after the Civil War, created regional integration among all its states which resulted in several competitive advantages over dominant European nations such as England, France, and Germany. What is new is the emergence of three super economic powers replacing the old model of a single economic superpower ruling the world. Additionally, these superpowers are highly interdependent in their economic activities through mutual presence and mutual trade—the future of one is a lot more dependent upon the future of the others, resulting in the need for greater cooperation and understanding.

TECHNOLOGY ADVANCES

Technology advances, especially in electronics, have revolutionized business processes and practices [Guile and Brooks 1987; Gerstein 1987]. The computerization of people, machinery, and physical facilities has literally reshaped the traditional economic concepts of scale, scope, and structure. Similarly, the use of telecommunications and information technologies has reduced the time and place barriers of doing business. It is no exaggeration to suggest that the tradi-

tional marketing theories based on location (for example, the law of retail gravitation, wheel of retailing, inventory management, logistics, and physical distribution) may be obsolete when customers and suppliers can do business at anytime and from anywhere. Finally, electronic advances result in market egalitarianism.

The traditional trickle-down theory of markets (government, industrial, service, consumer) for diffusion of technology and products is being replaced by a trickle-up theory (from consumer, to services, to industrial markets). This is evidenced by the use of transistors in personal radios prior to computers; or the mass marketing of television prior to the emergence of CRTs; or the use of compact discs (CD-ROM) in personal entertainment prior to storage of library information.

As we will discuss later, this egalitarian and convergent nature of the electronics technology will challenge such well-known concepts as the diffusion of innovation theory and product-market definitions in marketing strategy.

IDEOLOGY FREE WORLD

A third macroeconomic force is the economic collapse of ideology driven nations, especially the communist countries. As governments become more pragmatic and less ideology driven, it is inevitable that many of the traditional beliefs about the role of the market economy and private enterprises will change [Drucker 1989; Burnstein 1991]. This is likely to result in privatization of the public sector, less regulation of most industries, and development of procompetitive policies to encourage innovation and efficiency in different sectors of the economy. This is bound to blur the distinction between marketing practices of profit versus nonprofit entities and industries. Also, significantly different marketing practices across nations which are based upon government trade and employment policies are likely to give way to more market based marketing practices in the future.

GLOBAL ECONOMY

Finally, and probably as a consequence of the other three macroeconomic forces, we are experiencing globalization of domestic economies, primarily through global sourcing and global competition. Marketing practices will have to be understood and adjusted to this reality of a borderless economy [Ohmae 1990]. Borderless markets emerge when four flows (products/ services/people, money, and information) are driven by market practices without government intervention [Reich 1991]. In a borderless economy, marketing practices related to procurement, marketing mix, and customer understanding are bound to change.

THE REINCARNATION OF INTERNATIONAL MARKETING

As the traditional determinants of IM go out of existence, the result is bound to be the demise of IM as we know it today; namely the description, explanation, and management of between-country differences in marketing practices.

In my opinion, IM will be reincarnated into global marketing and in the process, will result in two dimensional shifts. The first shift to global marketing will focus more on cross-functional integration and coordination and less on functional adjustments across national boundaries. The second shift will focus more on transnational similarities for target markets across national boundaries and less on international differences. This is represented in Figure 3.

FROM INTERNATIONAL DIFFERENCES TO TRANSNATIONAL SIMILARITIES

Four specific processes of transformation in the psychology and practice of IM are bound to result as a consequence of its transition to global marketing:

1. *Global Coverage.* The elitism of the diffusion of innovations from the home country to the rest of the world is replaced with the concept of global coverage. Global coverage theory is more likely to be developed because it can rely on world demographics. For example,

Figure 3. The Reincarnation of International Marketing

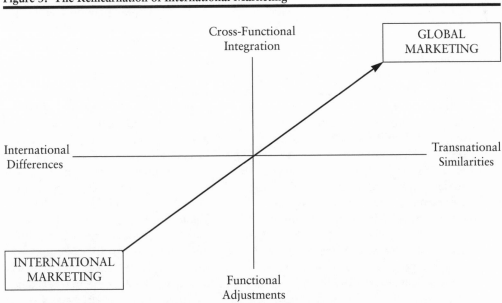

if a marketer targets its products or services to the teenagers of the world, it is relatively easy to develop a worldwide strategy for that segment and draw up operational plans to provide target market coverage on a global basis. This is becoming increasingly evident in the soft drinks industry.

2. *Mass Customization*. The concept of mass customization [Davis 1987] refers to standard platforms, but custom applications. It is also referred to as "Think Global, Act Local." It breaks the oxymoron of efficiency of mass production with the effectiveness of personalization of a product or service. Again, it is likely that we will develop a theory of mass customization in marketing that transcends national boundaries.

3. *Relationship Exchange*. In a world that is moving toward a global market economy, it is becoming increasingly necessary to rely on customer relationships to preempt competition. Emphasis on relationship exchange (as opposed to transaction exchange) allows scholars to reduce the impact of unexpected events and, therefore, capably model more consistent behavior with some well grounded theories.

4. *Trickle-Up Theory*. Technology advances created by the electronics revolution suggest that it might be best to deploy new technology in low end applications and move up to high end applications. In general, this means starting with consumer markets and moving up to commercial, industrial, and government markets. Market upstreaming becomes highly desirable to gain scale and scope advantages. Therefore, it is possible to develop a conceptual framework based on the classical theories in industrial economics [Porter 1986].

FROM FUNCTIONAL ADJUSTMENT TO CROSS-FUNCTIONAL INTEGRATION

A second dimensional shift is from functional adjustment to cross-functional integration. This is likely to generate new research opportunities for scholars in at least the four following transformation process areas:

1. *Global Accounts*. As the focus of marketing and business operations shifts from production to consumption, the need for customer orientation increases. Customer orientation suggests account by account market segmentation but on a global basis. This is already practiced in several industries and by several companies such as IBM, Procter and Gamble, and Boeing. Managing global accounts becomes a challenge for both marketing practice and academic research.

2. *Cross-Functional Consistency*. As operations get organized around global customer accounts, it becomes increasingly necessary to deploy quality consistency across all functional units. For example, the six sigma or zero defect concept is no longer limited to manufacturing or to line operations, but is extended to all functions, line and staff. A theory of consistency becomes a very viable concept for global marketing.

3. *Value Based Accounting*. Allocation of costs to different functional and business units traditionally has been based upon accepted accounting principles. Unfortunately, they are not so universally accepted, let alone practiced on a global basis. While a recent effort to utilize activity based costing (ABC) is gaining popularity, the ultimate option may be to develop a matrix which measures value to the market and its attribution to different functional and business units. Since we

have some well accepted concepts of value creation and value distribution in economics and social sciences that transcend national boundaries, it may be possible to generate a unified theory in this area.

4. *Networked Organization.* Cross-functional integration requires coordination and communication. While functional adjustments are dependent upon the contextual determinants, cross-functional integration and coordination is capable of transcending ad hoc, context-driven issues to a higher plane of conceptual theory. In other words, it has the potential to be invariant to context.

As I have outlined the reincarnation of IM into global marketing and the consequent domain of emerging research and practice, it is becoming increasingly evident that we can utilize basic concepts and theories of economic and social sciences to develop a theory of global marketing. Furthermore, this theory, if grounded on time and distance concepts, may actually not only contribute, but revolutionize a more general theory of marketing.

SUMMARY AND CONCLUSION

In this paper, I have identified why IM has remained a contextual practice devoid of a well-accepted theory. The nine determinants of IM (political stability, government policy, ideology driven economy, fear of colonialism, marketing transfer issues, lack of infrastructure, North-South dichotomy, East-West dichotomy, and product life cycles) are gradually becoming extinct as markets become increasingly borderless. The forces driving a borderless world are: regional integration, ideology free world, technology advances, and global economy. This is likely to transform IM into global marketing with less emphasis on functional adjustments across countries and differences among national and more emphasis on

cross-functional integration and transnational similarities. I have identified eight processes of this transformation: global coverage, mass customization, relationship exchange, trickle-up theory, global accounts, cross-functional consistency, value based accounting, and networked organization. All these processes of reincarnation are likely to elevate the practice of marketing from the specifics of context and anecdotes to a more generalizable theory of global marketing.

■ ■ ■

COMMENTARIES
Hubert Gatignon

Marketing Perspectives and International Business: Discussion Paper

From the three topic papers in this chapter on international marketing (IM), it becomes clear that while the majority of IM research has focused on the comparative study of differences across countries in consumers' behavior or in managerial decision making, the future rests on global marketing [Sheth, this chapter], which emphasizes simultaneous marketing management for all countries. Each of the three topic papers provides a delineation of what constitutes IM and provides a list of issues which pertain to the domain of IM research. Instead of discussing each paper in turn, I will outline the commonality of the three papers, especially in terms of IM research opportunities. Therefore, the purpose of this discussion paper is to emphasize and amplify the areas of promising research on IM issues.

Integrating these papers, I find two broadly defined categories of issues to address by research: interorganizational relations and globalization/regionalization.

INTERORGANIZATIONAL RELATIONS

The functioning of the international organization requires management, especially coordination and communication

[Sheth, this chapter], within and across functions performed by different organizations or different suborganizations [Sheth, this chapter]. This functioning creates an interorganizational network [Mattson; Sheth, this chapter]. The notion of marketing exchange is therefore extended, as discussed in Mattson's paper. New types of exchange such as countertrade are also added to the usual marketing types of exchange [Samiee this chapter]. Two types of research questions seem essential to be addressed in IM research concerning interorganizational relations: the level of control each suborganization must have on the others within the firm and, across firms, under what conditions should relations exist, especially in the form of alliances.

Control

At the extreme ends of the vertical integration continuum, the integrated company assumes the control of its subsidiaries, while a nonintegrated firm uses a simple contractual arrangement with another organization without direct investment, typically leading to a minimum level of control. Research in this area is known as the mode of entry literature. This abundant research stream has been converging recently on the theoretical framework provided by transaction cost analysis [Anderson and Gatignon 1986; Anderson and Coughlan 1987; Gatignon and Anderson 1988; Gomes-Casseres 1990; Hennart 1991]. While not all research on the internalization of the firm claims to follow this theory, many of the explanatory mechanisms proposed are similar, if not identical [Dunning 1980, 1988; Itaki 1991; Horaguchi and Toyne 1990]. Most of the empirical research so far, however, has been limited to manufacturing firms or distribution arrangements and to a small subset of control mechanisms.

Expanding the Scope of Products/Industries.

Beyond manufacturing entities and distribution-supplier relationships, it has been argued that services may offer a different perspective. For example, Erramilli [1991] shows the critical role of experience for service firms. Expanding the scope of this research might require the identification of key dimensions distinguishing services from products in order to analyze when the theory fails in its predictions, which could then be complemented by additional factors.

Expanding the Forms of Control

Transaction cost analysis predictions have been tested and supported in terms of whether a firm entering a foreign market establishes a wholly owned subsidiary or, instead chooses a partner to form a subsidiary [Gatignon and Anderson 1988]. Both options involve foreign direct investment (FDI). The degree of ownership may depend, however, upon other factors which are not inherently part of transaction cost analysis. The theory should therefore be extended to account for the degree of ownership. In fact, ownership might be just one dimension which permits control. Other ways of gaining control, with or without direct investment, should be investigated. This will expand forms of control to forms which do not involve direct investment, starting with exports and including licensing agreements. This research might require an analysis of contractual arrangements to categorize those elements which lead to some form of control.

Alliances

Although the interorganization structures discussed above are a kind of alliance, the research agenda is concerned with vertical integration questions. Alliance is a terminology typically used when concerned with horizontal integration issues, although not necessarily between competitors. Alliances, and especially international alliances, are particularly relevant in high technology industries, where costs of R&D surpass the available resource of a single enterprise. Current research on alliances is on the verge of theoretical developments which could unify the points of views found in this literature. Transaction cost analysis appears here to be a possible theoretical framework. However, some of the expanded concepts of hostages and credible commitment will be necessary to offer guarantees to the partners, since control is not enforceable due to the lack of ownership [Spekman and Sawhney 1990]. These research questions offer the possibility, not only of developing theories on alliance formation and their effects, but also of expanding the transaction cost analysis framework.

GLOBALIZATION-REGIONALIZATION

As pointed out in Sheth's paper, the IM of products and services takes a more global/regional view of world markets. This view is the direct consequence of the interrelationships that exist among consumers in the countries of the world. This recognition leads to three research issues: (1) the standardization versus differentiation question (pointed out in the Mattson and Samiee papers), (2) the revision of diffusion theory (as proposed by Sheth), and (3) the allocation of marketing resources (as suggested by Samiee).

The Standardization Issue

The debate on the globalization of markets, reopened recently by Levitt [1983], is becoming even more critical with the changes occurring in world markets, and in particular with the creation of a unified Europe. However, the proposition that "companies must learn to operate as if the world were one large market—ignoring superficial regional and national differences" [Levitt 1983] is not widely accepted within companies, nor within academia. In fact, many multinational firms do not adhere to this standardization argument: they give a large degree of autonomy to the local country marketing departments to define their own marketing mix policy.

While there is wide recognition of the cost benefits of standardizing marketing programs,[1] no consensus exists to date regarding the appropriateness of such strategies in competitive markets. A major reason

for this debate on global strategies is the lack of empirical evidence regarding the extent of the differences across countries. In addition, the critics of standardization have been focusing on differences in country characteristics. In fact, the critical factor that determines whether a particular strategy is appropriate is the market's response to the marketing mix policies. If responses are similar across countries, a similar strategy is deemed appropriate. If, however, the response coefficients (elasticities) are significantly different, a common strategy is not warranted. Therefore, the answer to the question of IM standardization depends crucially upon the differences and/or the similarities in the response functions across countries to the marketing mix instruments. Thus, it has become critical to know and understand the response function in one's country or market in order to judge the transferability of a marketing program. This understanding is obtained in part by knowing which factors explain cross-country differences in the effectiveness of a marketing instrument. For example, knowledge of the role of cultural, competitive, infrastructure or economic conditions prevailing in a country might explain differences in marketing mix elasticities across countries.

The Diffusion of Innovations

Sheth [in this chapter] points out the inadequacy of diffusion theory to explain international phenomena. Most marketing studies of the diffusion of innovations in the marketing literature have been conducted within one country. The few studies that go beyond the limits of one country examine differences in diffusion rates and patterns across countries [Gatignon, Eliashberg, and Robertson 1989; Heeler and Hustad 1980]. The theoretical explanations for these differences in diffusion are still in their infancy. A theory needs to be developed to explain why the same innovations diffuse differently across countries. Moreover, international diffusion research should not assume that the population system in which the diffusion occurs is bounded by nationality. Instead, an international theory of diffusion should consider the interactions among populations of the world to explain the timing of the introduction of one innovation across countries.

Allocation of Marketing Resources

While often discussed verbally, the issues that result from direct or indirect impacts of the actions of one subsidiary on the results of another subsidiary of the multinational (e.g., parallel imports and exports, advertising overlap) have remained analytically untouched [Duhan and Sheffet 1988; Cavusgil and Sikora 1987; Eger 1987; Clemens 1987].

The issues of multinational coordination and control which arise from such direct and indirect interactions will grow in number and importance during the 1990s, in particular within the European Community (EC). On the one hand, because the international division of markets along economic and sociocultural lines is likely to remain a feature of the IM scene, multinationals will continue to operate largely through country-based marketing/selling subsidiaries. On the other hand, national subsidiaries within the same organization will interact to an increasing extent, due to reductions in transaction costs and the removal of barriers to cross-national interactions (e.g., the single market of the EC).

Therefore, it becomes critical to build models of marketing competition for the multinational firm with domestic marketing/selling subsidiaries as well as to derive the marketing-allocation implications for the multinational firm and the implications about the extent to which the multinational should exert control over its subsidiaries' marketing actions.

CONCLUSION

In summary, the three topic papers about IM research present a converging view of its definition, agree upon the need for true theoretical perspectives, and call for a research program which I have highlighted in this discussion and which I discuss at a somewhat more concrete research level.

NOTE

1. While a distinction has been made between the standardization of programs and the standardization of the strategic process across countries (Douglas and Wind 1987), much of the debate is about the appropriateness of standardizing *programs*, as there is general agreement that the *process* is relatively country invariant (Walters 1986). Here, we used the definition of Jain, who proposes that "standardization of international marketing strategy refers to using a common product, price, distribution and promotion program on a worldwide basis" (Jain 1989).

S. Tamer Cavusgil

Marketing Perspectives and International Business: A Commentary

It is always useful to reflect periodically on the progress of an academic discipline as a field of inquiry and take stock of what has been accomplished and what new frontiers ought to be explored. In their respective papers, Drs. Mattsson, Samiee, and Sheth provide thoughtful perspectives on the evolution of international marketing (IM). Here, I will offer some reactions to these ideas. These observations are organized around a set of questions central to IM that are addressed by one or more of these authors.

Before commenting on these key issues, let me offer a general observation on the relative positioning of international marketing within the larger field of international business (IB). In my opinion, the unique explanation a marketing orientation brings to IB phenomena is the "customer/market interface." As Mattsson and other proponents of the interaction approach would argue, buyer-seller relationships represent a central construct in IM explanations. Marketing perspectives tend to focus on the enterprise's link with the external environment. As such, marketing perspectives tend to offer a certain degree of realism and a managerial orientation to IB studies. Furthermore, IM researchers tend to be less "multinational corporation-biased." That is, studies of small companies and modes of involvement such as exporting, licensing, and franchising are very common.

WHAT IS THE SCOPE OF IM?

While we may not reach universal agreement on this, it seems to me that there are two fundamental tasks in IM management. One is the understanding of and coping with the external *environment*. Compared to the domestic setting, the international environment is less familiar, less certain, and more complex for the manager to grasp. Customer expectations which may be idiosyncratic, product standards which may be less customary, distributor practices which may seem "nontraditional," are just some of the features of the external environment. These characteristics of operating in a broadened and multilayered environment simply create a more risky and less certain atmosphere within which the manager has to operate, requiring some special knowledge, skills, and cross-cultural empathy.

The other fundamental task relates to the managerial *process* of operating in multiple markets. This managerial process has three dimensions:

- between markets (e.g., domestic and export market);
- within (individual) markets; and
- coordination and control across all markets of the firm.

The first aspect of the managerial process is a natural consequence of boundary spanning or market expansion by the firm. Certain idiosyncratic issues are encountered for the first time: market access, international logistics, payments with currency differentials, and so on. The second aspect of the process has to do with the formulation of entry mode for the particular market and management of the marketing variables within the limits afforded by the chosen entry mode. Some illustrative tasks include support and supervision of distributors/agents, local adaptation or value adding, pricing for end users, and marketing communications. Finally, the third aspect of the process is the coordination and control of IM activities across all markets of the firm. This is especially a concern for the highly involved international firm which finds itself operating in a global industry.

Figure 1 illustrates the three dimensions of IM. I believe there is some convergence on this type of conceptualization by Mattsson and Sheth. Comparative studies of the environment dominated early writings in IB. In contrast, contributions explaining IM operations (Type A studies according to Mattsson's framework) have been contributed over the past 15 years.

IS INTERNATIONAL MARKETING A DISTINCT DISCIPLINE AND DOES IT LACK ACADEMIC IDENTITY?

As many others have done, Samiee raises these questions. Reviewing the literature, he argues that IM is "impoverished"

Figure 1. Scope of International Marketing

Dimension	Mattsson	Sheth
Environment	Comparative system studies (type B)	Comparative explanations
Process —Between markets	International operations (type A)	Comparative descriptions
—Within markets	International operations (type A)	Comparative prescriptions
Coordination and Control	International operations (type A)	

in terms of theoretical frameworks and "lacks a theoretical base" [p. 546]. Samiee concludes that "this limitation has created a barrier to a consistent and defensible explanation of the roles, differences, and similarities of IM to domestic marketing and IB." [p. 547]

Indeed, developing unique frameworks/propositions to explain IM phenomena would be desirable. However, I am not convinced that those of us who specialize in the international or comparative dimensions of marketing would necessarily be better off if we just constrained ourselves to our own constructs, models, and explanations. While our perspectives may differ in terms of how we look at the international business phenomena (e.g., those of the marketer vs. organizational behaviorist vs. anthropologist), firm behavior is too complex and multifaceted to be described by narrow and incomplete approaches. I believe we are better off in acknowledging the contributions of related disciplines and attempt to provide more holistic descriptions of real world, rather than locking ourselves in less relevant quarters of academic disciplines.

I think cross-fertilization is healthy. Richness of the understanding does come from competing explanations! Diversity of perspectives (economic, financial, behavioral) *does* lead to more complete and coherent explanations of IB phenomena. I think demarcation is bad; we do need an appreciation for alternative explanations of the same IB phenomena.

Furthermore, I do not believe this situation is any different in the interface between IB and other functional areas such as international finance or international management. I am not sure why IM deserves a separate academic identity that is not afforded to these other fields of inquiry.

I also feel that, the search for a distinct identity for IM is essentially an academic exercise. After all, practitioners do not cry out for such a separation. Of course, they *do* acknowledge the added knowledge and skills a manager needs to possess to be effective in the international arena. Why, then

insulate ourselves, when the real task is to bridge the gap?

Finally, I strongly believe that the distinction those of us in North America continue to make between "domestic" and "international" marketing is counterproductive. I would argue that, while there are substantial differences, this tradition has resulted in a certain degree of ethnocentrism in marketing practice and compartmentalization in marketing education. Both are detrimental to long-run economic competitiveness. In the *practice of business*, we seem to have pushed managers into relatively familiar, cozy, and predictable quarters of the home market. Despite the ongoing globalization of markets in radical ways, business executives have been led to think in terms of the domestic market alone, not making the connection to the larger, real, global market. And, in *business education*, we have continued to reinforce the artificial distinction between "domestic" and "international." Isolating and pigeon-holing the curriculum (in the form of separate courses, chapters, and separate books), or the faculty (through special designation or special departments) have also contributed to the view some of us "domestic" marketing practitioners and educators can feel sufficiently competent if they understand just the "domestic" dimension. Elsewhere, I have argued for the importance of building some bridges urgently between the so-called domestic and international, and for an "infusion" approach [Cavusgil 1991]. Other business educators seem to agree [Cavusgil, Schechter, and Yaprak 1992].

IS INTERNATIONAL MARKETING KNOWLEDGE GENERALIZABLE?

In his paper, Sheth observes that "international marketing has predominantly remained a contextual practice and . . . it has been difficult to develop a theory of international marketing even based on contingency propositions" [p. 563]. Indeed, the multidimensional nature of IM practice—involving multiple markets, industries, and entry modes—makes it difficult for scholars to propose relationships that are not context-specific. A lot of what we observe through research or consulting applies to specific instances of firm behavior under given circumstances.

In developing computerized decision support (or expert) systems for IB at Michigan State University, we had to recognize the contextual nature of IB knowledge. For example, in designing the *Country Consultant*, an intelligent database of target markets, we had to build this richness of knowledge into the software. Each piece of knowledge (either judgements or guidelines) entered into the database applies to a specific combination of:

- the market (country) of interest,
- industry/product sector,
- chosen entry mode (e.g., exporting, licensing); and
- feature (dimension of the market such as market access, property protection, marketing infrastructure).

This certainly makes knowledge generation and knowledge expression more challenging in IM. Nevertheless, it does not mean that marketing scholars should not strive toward theory building. The situation is not necessarily unique to IM or business either.

I believe marketing scholars have an obligation to investigate fundamental relationships in IM. For example, we need to better understand the marketing-strategy marketing-performance relationship in international markets and attempt to express our findings in the form of propositions and managerial prescriptions. However, such inquiries ought to adhere to generally accepted principles for knowledge creation. Unfortunately, however, we have not always done this. There are simply too many "research" efforts which fail to: start from existing knowledge as the basis for inquiries; incorporate fundamental relationships as frameworks; follow acceptable data collection and analysis procedures; and integrate findings within the specific context of the study.

My point is that we should not abandon knowledge generation because IM is so contextual. Rather, we should pay strict adherence to principles of scientific inquiry in the way we approach the challenge. In the final analysis, research findings must be integrated with what is already known and synthesized into the existing body of knowledge. While such work can be very tedious, there is no substitute to programmatic research. Otherwise, voluminous research, however interesting, may not amount to much in the way of confirmed generalizations. A case in point is the country-of-origin research. After export behavior studies, this research stream represents the most popular area of investigation by IM scholars [Li and Cavusgil 1991]. Although numerous inquiries have been completed, conclusions and implications which can be generalized across countries, industries, and consumers are scarce. About the only thing we can safely claim is that consumers **do** tend to form either favorable or unfavorable perceptions of products originating from other countries.

DOES INTERNATIONAL MARKETING NEED ITS OWN CENTRAL CONSTRUCTS AND THEORIES?

Professor Samiee offers a conceptual framework of IM and several key constructs. Both Mattsson and Sheth offer additional constructs critical to explaining IM behavior. Such efforts should be applauded. Hopefully, they and others can build upon these efforts and engage in empirical work to verify their usefulness.

An example of a key construct is the concept of "intermarket segmentation." This is defined by Samiee "as the presence of well defined and similar clusters of customers across national boundaries that possess the same characteristics and which are identified by using similar criteria" [p. 552]. Thorelli and Robinson were among the first who recognized the importance of identifying and catering to "subnational markets" which exhibited similarities across national markets. Robinson [1986] argued that "the very concept of **national marketing,** or **international marketing** . . . , may be increasingly inappropriate. We should talk, rather, of **intercultural marketing**" [6]. In a programmatic research study, Thorelli and his collaborators verified the existence of an information-prone consumer segment in several western markets.

While attempting to develop constructs and frameworks unique to IM, international marketing scholars should be open to using frameworks developed elsewhere to shed light on IM phenomena. For example, transaction cost analysis or the value chain framework offers rich explanations for IM. The value chain analysis can be a particularly helpful tool in sorting out the processes/assets/resources which provide competitive advantage for the firm and those that are most strongly valued by customers. Similarly, value chain analysis can point to those modes of entry appropriate for a market, and the types of alliances the firm may wish to initiate with overseas partners.

IS THERE A SINGLE, MOST USEFUL CONSTRUCT IN INTERNATIONAL MARKETING?

In his paper, Mattsson contrasts the "marketing mix" approach to the "network approach" as competing central constructs in IM. He finds the network approach to be capable of recognizing the "long term, dynamic, and possibly innovative characteristics of interaction and does not leave out important interdependencies" [p. 539]. This approach can also provide a more holistic view of the interdependence between marketing and other functions of the firm.

Growing evidence, initially from the International Marketing and Purchasing group (IMP) in Europe, and now from others studying relationships, suggests that the examination of business-to-business interaction can provide powerful explanations of IM behavior. As such, the network approach promises to be a key construct for

IM scholars to use. If we accept the view that relationships can be among the most enduring competencies of a firm, the network approach provides a fruitful construct for researchers.

Theory building is an evolutionary process. Each new construct or framework may provide a unique explanation which was not possible before. Gradually, with newer insights on the phenomena, we may be able to develop a more complete understanding. Therefore, we view the marketing mix and the network approaches as complementary rather than competitive explanations. Each has its own strengths and limitations.

WHAT DO WE KNOW ABOUT THE INTERNATIONALIZATION PROCESS OF THE FIRM?

Substantial work has been conducted on the process by which companies engage in boundary spanning activities. All three authors acknowledge the relevance of the internationalization process in explaining IM phenomena. For example, Mattsson classifies his research agenda by "early stages" and "highly internationalized" categories.

More empirical work on internationalization as well as meta-analysis of previous works in this area should be encouraged. Knowledge of the firm's internationalization process can be especially useful in designing public policy to promote international expansion of firms (e.g., Cavusgil [1983]). For example, one can use the concept of "barriers to internationalization" for the purpose of formulating both firm and public policy measures to enhance company expansion into overseas markets. This is illustrated in Figure 2.

Managers encounter both perceived and real barriers in international expansion. A variety of tariff and non-tariff barriers translate into real barriers. Nevertheless, indifference toward international markets, fear of failure, reluctance to marshall proper resources, and similar inhibitions serve as perceptual barriers to interna-

Figure 2. Barriers as a Framework for Formulating Firm and Public Policy

		REAL BARRIERS	
		HIGH	LOW
PERCEIVED	HIGH	—Selective, cautious internationalization —Low priority for targeting assistance	—Follow examples of successful companies —Motivational/informational assistance —High priority for targeting
BARRIERS	LOW	—Seek alternative markets —Seek suitable partners —Target country for market access negotiations	—Seek aggressive expansion —Target if aiming at quick mobilization —Selective assistance

tionalization. An understanding of these barriers is essential to prescribing both management policy as well as measures to stimulate IB activity.

WHAT CONTEMPORARY FORCES ARE SHAPING THE EVOLUTION OF INTERNATIONAL MARKETING?

International marketing continues to be a very applied phenomenon. Managers develop IM strategies in response to a set of opportunities and threats in the environment. And the academic research seems to be driven by actual practice. All three authors recognize various environmental factors contributing to the globalization of markets. In particular, Sheth provides an exposition of "powerful macroeconomic forces" that are creating a "borderless world." Among them are: regional integration; technological advances; and a world that rids itself of ideologies in favor of market forces. These trends, according to Sheth, has led to demise of IM as we know it today. Emerging is the age of global marketing.

Global marketing features two kinds of shifts. First is the shift toward transnational similarities. Managers focus on "transnational similarities for target markets across national boundaries and less on international differences" [p. 565]. As a consequence, we are likely to see more global coverage, mass customization, emphasis on

relationship exchange (as opposed to transaction exchange), and market upstreaming (high-end applications). Second is the shift from functional adjustment to cross-functional integration and coordination. As a result, global accounts, consistency across all functional units, value creation and accounting, and networked organization will be paramount.

The idea to focus on transnational similarities and less on international differences is an appealing one. Indeed, practitioners rest many of their international moves on commonalities of customer requirements and preferences across markets. Searching for largest clusters of customers with common denominators enables firms to achieve scale economies. Differences, on the other hand, work to reduce the market potential. Therefore, managers attempt to understand international differences as a way of responding to them in creative ways.

Professor Sheth feels that such propositions can serve as the basis for a general theory of marketing. It is hoped that he and/or others will take up this challenge.

WHAT ARE SOME PROMISING RESEARCH DIRECTIONS IN INTERNATIONAL MARKETING?

Both Samiee and Mattsson provide assessments of the previous literature in IM. They also offer some directions for future research. Sheth, in discussing the ongoing shift from IM to global marketing, alludes also to some worthwhile research avenues.

Indeed, international marketing literature has seen rapid growth over the past two decades. In the process of preparing the most recent annotated bibliography in IM [Cavusgil and Li 1992], the authors have encountered more than 750 pertinent articles published between January 1982 and October 1991. These appeared in more than two dozen journals.

This growth in research output parallels the globalization of markets and the rise in the number of international marketing positions that have become available in North American and European institutions of higher education. Nevertheless, the rise in research output does not necessarily parallel an improvement in the quality of research efforts.

In evaluating past research, Samiee and Mattsson appear to be favorable about the nature of this research. Samiee recommends more research at a global scale and on the developing countries. They also propose greater comparative research including extension of buyer behavior research in the domestic context to international sphere.

These authors also suggest research on practical, managerial issues in IM.

I am of the opinion that we need to be more critical, while remaining constructive, in our assessments of research efforts in IM. In my own view, current research suffers from several limitations. We simply have too many examples of research which:

- does not have conceptual or theoretical foundations;
- does not integrate and build upon previous contributions;
- does not incorporate a critical number of predictors for a phenomenon we wish to investigate; and
- does not utilize sound methodology (e.g., data collection, reliability and validity issues, sampling).

Such neglect is due to both ignorance and sloppiness on the part of the researchers. To make maximum impact on the advancement of marketing knowledge, we cannot deviate from rigorous research standards, while remaining managerially relevant. This is, indeed, the fine balance we need to achieve.

In proposing future research avenues, Mattsson distinguishes issues between the

Figure 3. Potential Research Avenues in International Marketing

	Early Stages of Internationalization	Later Stages of Internationalization
Managerial Issues	—Entry and expansion strategy —Market selection —Export marketing strategy —Strategy-Performance relationship	—Standardization —Inter-market segmentation —Cross-functional integration and coordination —Interaction/Networking —Cooperative ventures —Countertrade —Multinational company organization
Public Policy Issues	—Promotion (programs, tools, infrastructure, incentives) —Training and HRD —Effectiveness of assistance programs —Overseas trade fairs —Overseas trade offices	—Climate and measures for competitiveness —Market access —Mega projects/contracting —Trade negotiations —Regional integration —Regional collaboration

early and the later stages of international-ization. Early stages would relate generally to exporting firms while the later stages would apply to more experienced multinationals. It is helpful to make another distinction—between issues of concern to management and those that are public-policy oriented. Therefore, a two-dimensional grid can be constructed as in Figure 3. Here, I have attempted to illustrate the types of research avenues which would be worthwhile to explore. Some of these are also proposed by Mattsson and Samiee.

I believe each of the four scenarios presents fruitful research efforts. Linkages between the four scenarios should also be explored. Researchers ought to consider making both empirical as well as conceptual and theoretical contributions in each area. Comparative perspectives (e.g., across several industries or countries) are also needed. Finally, my own bias would be to conduct more prescriptive rather than simply descriptive studies in the future.

CONCLUSION

In this brief commentary, I have attempted to react to ideas offered by Professors Mattsson, Samiee, and Sheth, and build upon these. I believe each author makes a unique contribution toward a more complete and contemporary understanding of IM phenomena. Hopefully, the suggestions made here will stimulate further discussion.

REFERENCES

Aaby, Nils-Erik and S. Slater. 1989. Management influences on export performance: A review of the empirical literature 1978–88. *International Marketing Review*, 6(4):7–26.

Adler, Nancy J., John L. Graham and Gehrke T. Scharz. 1987. Business negotiations in Canada, Mexico, and the United States. *Journal of Business Research*, 15 (5): 411–429.

Albaum, Gerald and Richard A. Peterson. 1984. Empirical research in international marketing, 1976–1982. *Journal of International Business Research*, 15(1): 161–173.

Albaum, Gerald, Joseph Strandskov, Edwin Duerr and Lawrence Dowd. 1989. *International Marketing and Export Management*. Wokingham, England: Addison-Wesley Publishing Company.

Alderson, W. 1957. *Marketing Behavior and Executive Action*. Homewood, IL: Richard D. Irwin.

Anderson, Erin and Anne T. Coughlan. 1987. International market entry and expansion via independent or integrated channel of distribution. *Journal of Marketing*, 51 (January): 71–82.

Anderson, E. and H. Gatignon. 1986. Modes of foreign entry: A transaction cost analysis and propositions. *Journal of International Business Studies*, XVII (3) Fall: 1–26.

Arndt, J. 1983. The political economy paradigm: Foundation for theory building in marketing. *Journal of Marketing*, 43(Fall): 44–45.

Axelsson, B. and G. Easton, editors. 1991. *Industrial Networks: A New View of Reality*. London: Routledge.

Axinn, Catherine N. 1988. Export performance: Do managerial perceptions make a difference? *International Marketing Review*, Summer: 61–71.

Bagozzi, R. P. 1975. Marketing as exchange. *Journal of Marketing*, 39(October): 32–39.

Banting, P. M., A. C. Gross and C. Holmes. 1985. Generalizations from a cross-national study of the industrial buying process. *International Marketing Review*, 2(4): 64–74.

Barksdale, H. C. 1982. A cross-national survey of consumer attitudes towards marketing practices, consumerism and government regulations. *Columbia Journal of World Business*, 17(2): 71–85.

Bartels, Robert. 1970. *Marketing Theory and Metatheory*. Homewood, IL: Richard D. Irwin.

Bartels, Robert. 1968. Are domestic and international marketing dissimilar? *Journal of Marketing*, 32(July): 56–61.

Bartels, Robert. 1962. *The Development of Marketing Thought*. Homewood, IL: Richard D. Irwin, Inc.

Bartlett, Christopher A., Yves Doz and Gunnar Hedlund, editors. 1990. *Managing the Global Firm*. London: Routledge.

Bartlett, Christopher A. and Sumantra Ghoshal.

1989. *Managing Across Borders: The Transnational Solution*. Boston, MA: Harvard Business School Press.

Bello, Daniel and N. C. Williamson. 1985. Contractual arrangement and marketing practices in the indirect export channel. *Journal of International Business Studies*, 16(2): 65–82.

Bilkey, Warren J. 1978. An attempted integration of the literature on the export behavior of firms. *Journal of International Business Studies*, 9(1): 33–46.

Bilkey, Warren J. and Erik Nes. 1982. Country-of-origin effects on product evaluations. *Journal of International Business Studies*, 13(1): 89–99.

Boddewyn, Jean. 1981. Comparative marketing: The first twenty-five years. *Journal of International Business Studies*, 12(1): 61–79.

Boddewyn, Jean. 1966. A construct for comparative marketing research. *Journal of Marketing Research*, May, 149–153.

Bradley, M. Frank. 1987. Nature and significance of international marketing: A review. *Journal of Business Research*, 15(3):205–19.

Buckley, Peter J. 1990. Problems and developments in the core theory of international business. *Journal of International Business Studies*, 21(4): 657–665.

Burnstein, Daniel. 1991. *Euroquake*. New York: Simon and Schuster.

Buzzell, Robert D. 1968. Can you standardize multinational marketing? *Harvard Business Review*, 46(November-December):102–113.

Buzzell, Robert D., John A. Quelch and Christopher Bartlett. 1991. *Global Market Management*. Reading, MA: Addison-Wesley Publishing Company.

Campbell, Nigel C. G. 1985. Buyer/seller relationships in Japan and Germany: An interaction approach. *European Journal of Marketing*, 19(3): 57–66.

Campbell, Nigel C. G., L. L. Graham, Alain Jolibert and H. G. Meissner. 1988. Marketing negotiations in France, Germany, the United Kingdom, and the United States. *Journal of Marketing*, 52(April): 49–62.

Casson, Mark. 1990. *Enterprise and Competitiveness: A System View of International Business*. Oxford: Clarendon Press.

Cateora, Philip R. 1990. *International Marketing*. Homewood, IL: Richard D. Irwin, Inc.

Caves, Richard E. 1982. *Multinational Enterprise and Economic Analysis*. New York: Cambridge University Press.

Cavusgil, S. Tamer. 1991. Internationalization of business and economics programs: Issues and perspectives. *Business Horizons*, 34(6): 92–100.

Cavusgil, S. Tamer. 1983. Public policy implications of research on the export behavior of firms. *Akron Business and Economic Review*, 14(2): 16–22.

Cavusgil, S. Tamer and Ed Sikora. 1988. How multinationals can counter gray market imports. *Columbia Journal of World Business* 23(4): 75–86.

Cavusgil, S. Tamer and J. Naor. 1987. Firm and management characteristics as discriminators of export marketing activity. *Journal of Business Research*, 15: 221–235.

Cavusgil, S. Tamer and John R. Nevin. 1981. The state of the art in international marketing: An assessment. *Review of Marketing*, eds. Ben Enis and Ken Roering. Chicago: The American Marketing Association.

Cavusgil, S. Tamer, Michael Schechter and Attila Yaprak, editors. 1992. *Internationalizing Business Education*. East Lansing, MI: Center for International Business Education and Research, The Eli Broad Graduate School of Management, Michigan State University.

Cavusgil, S. Tamer and Tiger Li. 1992. *International Marketing: An Annotated Bibliography*. Chicago: American Marketing Association.

Cespedes, F. V., E. R. Corey and V. Kasturi Rangan. 1988. Gray markets: Causes and cures. *Harvard Business Review*, 66(July-August): 75–82.

Chandler, A. D. 1962. *Strategy and Structure*. Cambridge, MA: MIT Press.

Christensen, Carl H., Angela da Rocha and Rosane Kerbel Gertner. 1987. An empirical investigation of the factors influencing exporting success of Brazilian firms. *Journal of International Business Studies*, 18(3): 61–77.

Clark, Terry. 1990. International marketing and national character: A review and proposal for an integrative theory. *Journal of Marketing*, 54(4): 66–79.

Clemens, John. 1987. Television advertising in Europe: The emerging opportunities. *Columbia Journal of World Business*, Fall: 35–41.

Collins, V. D. 1935. *World Marketing*. Philadelphia: J. B. Lippincott.

Contractor, Farok J. and Peter Lorange, editors. 1988. *Cooperative Strategies in International Business*. Lexington, MA: Lexington Books.

Cook, K. and R. Emerson. 1978. Power, equity and commitment in exchange networks. *American Sociological Review*, 43:712–739.

Cooper, Robert G. and Eiko J. Kleinschmidt. 1985. The impact of export strategy on export sales performance. *Journal of International Business Studies*, 16(1): 27–55.

Cunningham, William and Robert Green. 1984. From the editor. *Journal of Marketing*, 48(Winter): 9–10.

Czinkota, Michael R. and Ilkka A. Ronkainen. 1995. *International Marketing*. Fourth edition. Hinsdale, IL: The Dryden Press.

Dahmén, E. 1988. Development blocks in industrial economics. *Scandinavian Economic Historic Review*, 1.

Dahmén, E. 1970. *Entrepreneurial Activity and the Development of Swedish Industry 1919–1939. American Economic Translation Series*. Homewood, IL: R. D. Irwin.

Dahringer, Lee D. and Hans Mühlbacher. 1991. *International Marketing: A Global Perspective*. Reading, MA: Addison-Wesley Publishing Company.

Daniels, John D. 1991. Relevance in international business research: A need for more linkages. *Journal of International Business Studies*, 22(2): 177–186.

Davis, Harry L., Gary D. Eppen and Lars-Gunnar Mattsson. 1974. Critical factors in world-wide purchasing. *Harvard Business Review*, Nov/Dec: 81–90.

Davis, Harry L., Susan P. Douglas and Alvin J. Silk. 1981. Measure unreliability: A hidden threat to cross-national marketing research. *Journal of Marketing*, 45(Spring): 98–109.

Davis, Stanley M. 1987. *Future Perfect*. Waltham, MA: Addison-Wesley.

Dichtl, Erwin, Hans-Georg Koeglmayr and Stefan Mueller. 1990. International orientation as a precondition for export success. *Journal of International Business Studies*, 21(1): 23–40.

Douglas, Susan P. 1976. Cross-national comparisons of consumer stereotypes: A case study of working and non-working wives in the U.S. and France. *Journal of Consumer Research*, June.

Douglas, Susan P. and C. Samuel Craig. 1995. *Global Marketing Strategy*. NY: McGraw-Hill, Inc.

Douglas, Susan P. and C. Samuel Craig. 1989. Evolution of global marketing strategy. *Columbia Journal of World Business*, Fall: 47–56.

Douglas, Susan P. and C. Samuel Craig. 1983. *International Marketing Research*. Englewood Cliffs: Prentice Hall.

Douglas, Susan P. and Yoram Wind. 1987. The myth of globalization. *Columbia Journal of World Business*, Winter: 19–29.

Douglas, Susan P. and Yoram Wind. 1973. Environmental factors and marketing practices. *European Journal of Marketing*, 7(3):155–65.

Doz, Yves. 1991. Partnerships in Europe: The "soft restructuring" option? In L. G. Mattsson and B. Stymne, editors, *Corporate and Industry Strategies for Europe*. Amsterdam: North-Holland.

Drucker, Peter. 1989. *The New Realities*. New York: Harper and Row.

Duhan, Dale F. and Mary Jane Sheffet. 1988. Gray markets and the legal status of parallel importation. *Journal of Marketing*, 52(1): 108–25.

Dunn, S. Watson. 1976. Effect of national identity on multinational promotional strategy in Europe. *Journal of Marketing*, 40(October): 50–7.

Dunning, John H. 1991. Governments, economic organization and international competitiveness. In L. G. Mattsson and B. Stymne, editors, *Corporate and Industry Strategies for Europe*. Amsterdam: North-Holland.

Dunning, John H. 1988. The eclectic paradigm of international production: A restatement and some possible extensions. *Journal of International Business Studies*, 19(1): 1–31.

Dunning, John H. 1980. Toward an eclectic theory of international production: Some empirical tests. *Journal of International Business Studies*, 11(1): 9–31.

Dunning, John H. 1977. Trade, location of economic activity, and the MNE: A search for an eclectic approach, in *The International Allocation of Economic Activity*, Bertil Ohlin (ed.), NY: Holmed and Meier.

Egers, John M. 1987. Global television: An executive overview. *Columbia Journal of World Business*, Fall: 5–10.

Engardio, P., A. Fins, B. Baudoin and L. J. Tell. 1988. There's nothing black-and-white about gray markets. *Business Week,* November 7, 1988, p. 72.

Erramilli, M. Krishna. 1991. The experience factor in foreign market entry behavior of service-firms. *Journal of International Business Studies*, 22(3): 479–501.

Ford, David. 1984. Buyer-seller relationships in international industrial markets. *Industrial Marketing*, 13(2): 101–113.

Ford, David, editor. 1990. *Understanding Business Markets: Interaction, Relationships, Networks*. London: Routledge.

Forsgren, M. 1989. *Managing the Internationalization Process: The Swedish Case*. London: Routledge.

French, W. A., H. C. Barksdale and W. D. Perreault, Jr. 1982. *European Journal of Marketing*, 16(6): 20–30.

Gatignon, Hubert and Erin Anderson. 1988. The multinational corporation's degree of control over foreign subsidiaries: An empirical test of a transaction cost explanation. *Journal of Law, Economics, and Organizations*, 4(2): 89–120.

Gatignon, Hubert, Jehoshua Eliashberg and Thomas S. Robertson. 1989. Modeling multinational diffusion patterns: An efficient methodology. *Marketing Science*, 8(3): 231–247.

Gerstein, M. S. 1987. *The Technology Connection*. Reading, MA: Addison-Wesley.

Ghauri, P. 1983. *Negotiating International Package Deals*. Uppsala: Acta Universitatis Upsaliensis.

Ghoshal, Sumantra and Christopher A. Bartlett. 1990. The multinational as an interorganizational network. *Academy of Management Review*, 14: 4.

Goldman, M. I. 1963. *Soviet Marketing*. New York: Macmillan.

Gomes-Casseres, Benjamin. 1990. Firm ownership preferences and host government restrictions: An integrated approach. *Journal of International Business Studies*, 21(1): 1–22.

Graham, John L. 1985. The influence of culture on the process of business negotiations: An exploratory study. *Journal of International Business Studies*, 16(1): 81–96.

Green, Robert T. and Isabella Cunningham. 1980. Family purchasing roles in two countries. *Journal of International Business Studies*, Spring-Summer, 92–7.

Green, Robert T. and Phillip D. White. 1976. Methodological considerations in cross-national consumer research. *Journal of International Business Studies,* 7(Fall-Winter): 81–7.

Green, Robert T., J. P. Leonardi, J. L. Chandon, I. C. M. Cunningham, B. Verhage and A. Strazzieri. 1983. Societal development and family purchasing roles: A cross-national study. *Journal of Consumer Research*, March 9: 436–442.

Gripsrud, Geir. 1990. The determinants of export decisions and attitudes to a distant market: Norwegian fishery exports to Japan. *Journal of International Business Studies*, 21(3): 469–485.

Grönhaug, K. and T. Lorentzen. 1983. Exploring the impact of government subsidies. *European Journal of Marketing*, 17(2): 5–12.

Guile, Bruce and Harvey Brooks, editors. 1987. *Technology and Global Industry*. Washington: National Academy Press.

Håkansson, H. 1989. *Corporate Technological Behavior. Cooperation and Networks*. London: Routledge.

Håkansson, H. 1987. *Industrial Technological Development. A Network Approach*. London: Croom Helm.

Håkansson, H., editor. 1982. *International Marketing and Purchasing of Industrial Goods. An Interaction Approach*. New York: John Wiley.

Håkansson, L. and Peter Lorange. 1991. R&D based cooperative joint ventures. In L.G. Mattsson and B. Stymne, editors, *Corporate and Industry Strategies for Europe*. Amsterdam: North-Holland.

Hägg, I. and Jan Johanson, editors. 1982. *Företag i Nätverk*. Stockholm: SNS.

Hallén, Lars. 1979. *Sverige på Europa-marknaden. Åsikter om inköp och marknadsföring*. Lund: Studentlitteratur.

Hallén, Lars and Jan Johanson, editors. 1989. *Networks of Relationships in International Industrial Marketing. Advances in International Marketing, 3*. Greenwich, CT: JAB Press.

Hamel, Gary and C. K. Prahalad. 1985. Do you really have a global strategy? *Harvard Business Review*, July-August: 139–148.

Hamel, Gary, Yves Doz and C. K. Prahalad. 1989. Collaborate with your competitors and win. *Harvard Business Review*, Jan-Feb: 133–139.

Hammarkvist, K-O, H. Håkansson and Lars-Gunnar Mattsson. 1982. *Marknadsföring for Konkurrenskraft*. Malmö: Liber.

Hampton, G. M. and A. Van Gent, editors. 1984. *Marketing Aspects of International Business*. Boston: Kluwer-Nijhoff.

Harrigan, Kathryn R. 1986. *Managing for Joint Venture Success*. Lexington, MA: D.C. Heath.

Haugland, S. and T. Reve. 1989. Relational contracting and distribution channel cohesion. Unpublished manuscript. Norwegian School of Economics and Business Administration, Bergen.

Hawkins, Robert G. 1984. International business in academia: The state of the field, *Journal of International Business Studies*, 15(Winter): 13–18.

Hedlund, Gunnar. 1986. The hypermodern MNC—A hetarchy? *Human Resource Management*, 25(1): 9–35.

Heeler, Roger M. and Thomas P. Hustad. 1980. Problems in predicting new product growth for consumer durables. *Management Science*, 10(October): 1007–1020.

Hennart, Jean-Francois. 1991. The transaction costs theory of joint ventures: An empirical study of Japanese subsidiaries in the United States. *Management Science*, 37(4): 483–497.

Hertz, S. 1993. The Internationalization process of freight transport companies. Towards a dynamic network model of internationalization. The Economic Research Institute, Stockholm School of Economics. Dissertation.

Horaguchi, Haruo and Brian Toyne. 1990. Setting the record straight: Hymer, international theory and transaction cost economics. *Journal of International Business Studies*, 21(3): 487–494.

Hörnell, Erik, Jan-Erik Vahlne and Finn Wiedersheim-Paul. 1973. *Export och Utlandsetableringar*. Uppsala: Almqvist and Wiksell.

Houston, F. S. and J. B. Gassenheimer. 1987. Marketing and exchange. *Journal of Marketing*, 51(October): 3–18.

Hughes, T. P. 1987. The evolution of large technical systems. In W. B. Bijker, T. P. Hughes and T. J. Pinch, editors, *The Social Construction of Techological Systems, 51–82*. Cambridge: MIT Press.

Hunt, Shelby D. 1990. Truth in marketing theory and research. *Journal of Marketing*, 54(3):1–15.

Hunt, Shelby D. 1976. The nature and scope of marketing. *Journal of Marketing*, 40(July): 17–28.

Huszagh, Sandra M. and A. Murphy. 1984. Third world markets demand household data for successful consumer goods marketing: Mexico as a case example. *International Marketing Review*, Spring/Summer: 66–72.

Imai, K. 1987–88. The corporate network in Japan. *Japanese Economic Studies*, 16(2): 3–37.

Itaki, Masahiko. 1991. A critical assessment of the eclectic theory of the multinational enterprise. *Journal of International Business Studies*, 22(3): 445–460.

Jain, Subhash C. 1989. Standardization of international marketing strategy: Some research hypotheses. *Journal of Marketing*, 53(1): 70–79.

Jansson, Hans. 1982. *Interfirm Linkages in a Developing Economy*. Uppsala: Acta Universitatis Upsaliensis.

Jarillo, J. Carlos and Jon Martinez. 1991. The international expansion of Spanish firms: towards an integrative framework for international strategy. In L. G. Mattsson and B. Stymne, editors, *Corporate and Industry Strategies for Europe*. Amsterdam: North-Holland.

Jeannet, Jean-Pierre and Hubert D. Hennessey. 1988. *International Marketing Management: Strategies and Cases*. Boston: Houghton Mifflin Company.

Johanson, Jan and Jan-Erik Vahlne. 1977. The internationalization process of the firm—A model of knowledge development and increasing foreign market commitments. *Journal of International Business Studies*, 8(1): 23–32.

Johanson, Jan and Finn Wiedersheim-Paul. 1975. The internationalization of the firm: Four Swedish case studies. *Journal of Management Studies*, 12: 13.

Johanson, Jan and Lars-Gunnar Mattsson. 1994. The markets-as-networks tradition in Sweden. In G. Laurent, G. L. Lilien and B. Pras, editors, *Research Traditions in Marketing*. Boston: Kluwer.

Johanson, Jan and Lars-Gunnar Mattsson. 1991. Network positions and strategic action—An analytical framework. In B. Axelsson and G. Easton, editors, *Industrial Networks—The New Reality*. London: Routledge.

Johanson, Jan and Lars-Gunnar Mattsson. 1988. Internationalization in industrial systems—A network approach. In N. Hood and Jan-Erik Vahlne, editors, 1988, *Strategies In Global Competition*, 287–314. Beckenham: Croom Helm.

Johanson, Jan and Lars-Gunnar Mattsson. 1987. Interorganizational relations in industrial systems: A network approach compared with the transaction cost approach. *International Journal of Management and Organization*, 18(1): 34–48.

Johanson, Jan and Lars-Gunnar Mattsson. 1985. Marketing and market investments in industrial networks. *International Journal of Research in Marketing*, 2: 185–195.

Johansson, Johny K. 1989. Determinants and effects of the use of made-in labels. *International Marketing Review*, 6(1): 47–56.

Johansson, Johny K., Susan P. Douglas and I. Nonaka. 1985. Assessing the impact of country-of-origin on product evaluations: A new methodological perspective. *Journal of Marketing Research*, 22(November): 388–396.

Johansson, Johny K., T. Sakano and N. Onzo. 1990. Behavioral relations in a cross-culture distribution system: Influence, control and conflict in U.S.-Japanese marketing channels. *Journal of International Business Studies*, 21(4): 639–655.

Kale, Sudhir H. and D. Sudharshan. 1987. A strategic approach to international segmentation. *International Marketing Review*, 4(Summer): 60–71.

Kashani, K. 1992. *Global Marketing Management*. Boston: PWS-Kent Publishing Company.

Kashani, Kamran. 1989. Beware of the pitfalls of global marketing. *Harvard Business Review*, 5(September-October): 91–98.

Keegan, Warren J. 1969. Multinational product planning: Strategic alternatives. *Journal of Marketing*, 33(January): 58–62.

Kennedy, Paul. 1987. *The Rise and Fall of the Great Powers*. New York: Random House.

Kirzner, Israel I. 1973. *Competition and Entrepreneurship*. Chicago: University of Chicago Press.

Knoke, David and James H. Kuklinski. 1982. *Network Analysis*. Newbury Park, CA: Sage Publications.

Kogut, Bruce and Harbir Singh. 1988. The effect of national culture on the choice of entry mode. *Journal of International Business Studies*, 19(3): 411–432.

Kotabe, Masaaki. 1990. Corporate product policy and innovative behavior of European and Japanese multinationals: An empirical investigation. *Journal of Marketing*, 54(2): 19–33.

Kotabe, Masaaki and Glenn S. Omura. 1989. Sourcing strategies of European and Japanese multinationals: A comparison. *Journal of International Business Studies*, 20(1): 113–129.

Kotler, Philip. 1991a. *Marketing Management*, Seventh Edition. Englewood Cliffs, NJ: Prentice Hall.

Kotler, Philip. 1991b. Speech at the Trustees meeting of the Marketing Science Institute in November 1990, Boston. In *Marketing Science Institute Review*, Spring.

Kotler, Philip. 1988. *Marketing Management.* Englewood Cliffs, NJ: Prentice Hall.

Kotler, Philip, Liam Fahey and Somkid Jatusripitak. 1985. *The New Competition. What Theory Z Didn't Tell You About Marketing.* Englewood Cliffs, NJ: Prentice-Hall.

Lawrence, Peter R. and Jay W. Lorsch. 1967. *Organization and Environment.* Cambridge: Harvard University Press.

Levitt, Theodore. 1983. The globalization of markets. *Harvard Business Review,* 61(May-June): 92–102.

Li, Tiger and S. Tamer Cavusgil. 1991. International marketing: A classification of research streams and assessment of their development since 1982. In Mary C. Gilly, et. al., editors, *Enhancing Knowledge Development in Marketing.* Chicago: American Marketing Association, 592–607.

Liljegren, Gören. 1988. Interdependens och dynamik i långsiktiga kundrelationer. Industriell försaljning i ett nätverksperspektiv. Stockholm: MTC och EFI, dissertation.

Lindqvist, Maria. 1991. Infant multinational. The internationalization of young, technology-based Swedish firms. Stockholm: Institute of International Business, dissertation.

Lundgren, Anders. 1991. Technological innovation and industrial evolution—The emergence of an image processing network in Sweden. Stockholm: The Economic Research Institute, Stockholm School of Economics, dissertation.

Macneil, Ian R. 1980. *The New Social Contract: An Inquiry into Modern Contractual Relations.* New Haven: Yale University Press.

Mårtensson, R. 1987. Is standardization of marketing feasible in culture-bound industries? A European case study. *International Marketing Review,* 4(3):7–17.

Mattsson, Lars-Gunnar. 1989. Development of firms in networks—Positions and investments. In *Advances in International Marketing,* vol. 3. Greenwich, CT: JAB Press.

Mattsson, Lars-Gunnar, A. Lundgren, D. Ioannidis and J. Ottosson. 1990. Strategic alliances in the telecommunications industry—A network approach. Proceedings of the Annual Conference of the European International Business Association, December. Madrid.

Mayer, Charles S. 1978. Multinational marketing research: The magnifying glass of methodological problems. *European Research,* 6(March): 77–83.

Mintzberg, Henry. 1978. Patterns in strategy formulation. *Management Science,* 24(9): 934–948.

Morrison, Allen J. and Andrew C. Inkpen. 1991. An analysis of significant contributions to the international business literature. *Journal of International Business Studies,* 22(1): 143–153.

Mueller, Barbara. 1991. An analysis of information content in standardized vs. specialized multinational advertisements. *Journal of International Business Studies,* 22(1): 23–39.

Murray, J. A. and David L. Blenkhorn. 1985. Organizational buying process in North America and Japan. *International Marketing Review,* 2(4): 55–63.

Nordström, K. 1991. The internationalization process of the firm—Searching for new patterns and explanations. Stockholm School of Economics: IIB, dissertation.

Ohmae, Kenichi. 1990. *The Borderless World.* New York: Harper Business.

Ohmae, Kenichi. 1985. *Triad Power.* New York: Free Press.

Olson, Hans C. 1975. *Studies in Export Promotion: Attempts to Evaluate Export Stimulation Measures for the Swedish Textile and Clothing Industries.* Uppsala: Acta Universitatis Upsaliensis.

Onkvisit, Sak and John J. Shaw. 1989. *International Marketing: Analysis and Strategy.* Columbus, OH: Merrill Publishing Company.

Onkvisit, Sak and John J. Shaw. 1987. Standardized international advertising: A review and critical evaluation of the theoretical and empirical evidence. *Columbia Journal of World Business,* (Fall): 43–55.

Perlmutter, Howard D. 1969. The tortuous evolution of the multinational corporation. *Columbia Journal of World Business,* 4(January-February): 9–18.

Pettigrew, Andrew, editor. 1987. *The Management of Strategic Change.* London: Basil Blackwell.

Pfeffer, Jeffrey and Gerald R. Salancik. 1978. *The External Control of Organizations—A*

Resource Dependence Perspective. New York: Harper and Row.

Porter, Michael E. 1990. *The Competitive Advantage of Nations.* New York: The Free Press.

Porter, Michael E., editor. 1986. *Competition in Global Industries.* Boston: Harvard Business School.

Porter, Michael E. 1980. *Competitive Strategy.* New York: The Free Press.

Quelch, John A. and Edward J. Hoff. 1986. Customizing Global Marketing. *Harvard Business Review,* 64(May-June): 59–68.

Rasmussen, A. 1955. *Pristeori eller parameterteori? Studier omkring virksomhedens afsaetning.* Kobenhavn: Ehrvervsokonomisk Förlang.

Rau, Pradeep and J. F. Prebber. 1987. Standardization of marketing by multinationals. *International Marketing Review,* 4(3): 18–28.

Reich, Robert B. 1991. *The Work of Nations.* New York: Knopf.

Reid, Stanley. 1983. Firm internationalization, transaction costs and strategic choice. *International Marketing Review,* Winter: 44–56.

Ricks, David A., Marilyn Y. C. Fu and Jeffrey S. Arpan. 1974. *International Business Blunders.* Columbus, OH: Grid, Inc.

Robinson, Richard D. 1986. Some new competitive factors in international marketing. In S. Tamer Cavusgil, editor, *Advances in International Marketing,* 1: 1–20. Greenwich, CT: JAB Press.

Rogers, Kathryn S. 1986. *U.S. Coal Goes Abroad: A Social Action Perspective on Interorganizational Networks.* New York: Praeger.

Root, Franklin R. 1978. *International Trade and Investment,* Fourth Edition. Cincinnati: Southwestern Publishing Company.

Rosen, B. N., Jean J. Boddewyn and E. A. Louis. 1989. U.S. brands abroad: An empirical study of global branding. *International Marketing Review,* 6(1): 7–19.

Rosson, Peter J. and David Ford. 1982. The relationship between export manufacturers and overseas distributors. In M. R. Czinkota and G. Tesar, editors. *Export Management: An International Context.* New York: Praeger.

Ryans, A. B. 1988. Strategic market entry factors and market share achievement in Japan. *Journal of International Business Studies,* 19(3): 389–409.

Ryans, John K. Jr., Saeed Samiee and J. Wills. 1985. Consumerist movement and advertising regulation in the international environment; Today and in the future. *European Journal of Marketing,* 19(1): 5–11.

Samiee, Saeed. 1994. Customer evaluation of products in a global market. *Journal of International Business Studies,* 25(3):79–604.

Samiee, Saeed and Kendall Roth. 1992. The influence of global marketing standardization on performance. *Journal of Marketing,* 56(April).

Samiee, Saeed. 1990a. Strategic considerations of the EC 92 plan for small exporters. *Business Horizons,* (March-April): 48–52.

Saimee, Saeed. 1990b. Productivity planning and strategy in retailing. *California Management Review* (Winter): 54–76.

Schendel, Dan E. and Charles W. Hofer (eds.). 1979. *Strategic Management: A New View of Business Policy and Planning.* Boston, MA: Little, Brown and Company.

Scherer, Frederic M. and David Ross. 1990. *Industrial Market Structure and Economic Performance,* Third Edition. Boston: Houghton Mifflin Company.

Schollhammer, Hans. 1973. Strategies and methodologies in international business and comparative management research. *Management International Review,* 13(6): 7–32.

Seringhaus, F. H. Rolf and Guenther Botschen. 1991. Cross-national comparison of export promotion: The views of Canadian and Austrian companies. *Journal of International Business Studies,* 22(1): 115–133.

Sheth, Jagdish N. 1992. Emerging marketing strategies in a changing macroeconomic environment: A commentary. *International Marketing Review,* 9(1): 57–63.

Sheth, Jagdish N. 1986. Global markets or global competition? *Journal of Consumer Marketing,* 3(Spring): 8–9–11.

Sheth, Jagdish N. and Abdolrezza Eshghi, editors. 1989. *Global Marketing Perspectives.* Cincinnati: Southwestern Publishing Company.

Sheth, Jagdish N., David M. Gardner and Dennis E. Garrett. 1988. *Marketing Theory: Evolution and Evaluation*. New York: John Wiley and Sons.

Simmonds, Kenneth. 1985. Global strategy: Achieving the geocentric ideal. *International Marketing Review*, 2(Spring): 8–17.

Spekman, Robert E. and Kirti Sawhney. 1990. *Toward a Conceptual Understanding of the Antecedents of Strategic Alliances, Report no. 90–114*. Cambridge, MA: Marketing Science Institute.

Stern, Louis W. and T. Reve. 1980. Distribution channels as political economies: A framework for comparative analysis. *Journal of Marketing*, 44(Summer): 52–64.

Stopford, John and Louis T. Wells. 1972. *Managing the Multinational Enterprise*. London: Longmans.

Teece, David J., editor. 1987. *The Competitive Challenge. Strategies for Industrial Innovation and Renewal*. Cambridge, MA: Ballinger.

Terpstra, Vern. 1987. The evolution of international marketing. *International Marketing Review* (Summer): 47–59.

Terpstra, Vern and Ravi Sarathy. 1994. *International Marketing*. 6th edition. Hinsdale, IL: The Dryden Press.

Thorelli, Hans B. 1986. Networks: Between markets and hierarchies. *Strategic Management Journal*, 7(1):37–52.

Thorelli, Hans B., J. S. Lim and J. Ye. 1989. Relative importance of country of origin, warranty and retail store image on product evaluations. *International Marketing Review*, 6(1): 35–46.

Thorelli, Hans B., Helmut Becker and J. L. Engledow. 1975. *The Information Seekers—An International Study of Consumer Information and Advertising Image*. Cambridge, MA: Ballinger.

Toyne, Brian. 1989. International exchange: A foundation for theory building in international business. *Journal of International Business Studies*, 20(1): 1–17.

Toyne, Brian and Peter C. P. Walters. 1993. *Global Marketing Management: A Strategic Perspective*. 2nd edition. Boston: Allyn and Bacon.

Tse, D. K., Kwang Lee, I. Vertinsky and Donald A. Wehrun. 1988. Does culture matter? A cross-cultural study of executives' choice, decisiveness and risk adjustment in international marketing. *Journal of Marketing*, 52(October): 81–159.

Vernon, Raymond. 1964. Comments. *Education in International Business*. Stefan Robock and Lee Nehrt, editors. Bloomington: Graduate School of Business, Indiana University: 7–10.

Vernon, Raymond and Louis Wells, Jr. 1968. A product life cycle for international trade. *Journal of Marketing*, 32(July): 1–6.

Walters, Peter G. P. 1986. International marketing policy: A discussion of the standardization construct and its relevance for corporate policy. *Journal of International Business Studies*, 17(2): 55–69.

Waluszewski, Alexandra. 1989. Framväxten av en ny massateknik-en utvecklingshistoria. Department of Business Studies, Uppsala University, dissertation.

Wells, Louis T., Jr. 1968. A product life cycle for international trade. *Journal of Marketing*, 32(July): 1–6.

Wiedersheim-Paul, Finn, Hans C. Olson and Lawrence S. Welch. 1978. Pre-export activity: The first step in internationalization. *Journal of International Business Studies*, 9(1): 47–58.

Williamson, Oliver E. 1985. *The Economic Institutions of Capitalism*. New York: The Free Press.

Wind, Yoram, Susan P. Douglas and H. Perlmutter. 1973. Guidelines for developing international marketing strategies. *Journal of Marketing*, 37(April): 14–23.

Wind, Yoram and H. Perlmutter. 1977. On the identification of frontier issues in multinational marketing. *Columbia Journal of World Business* (Winter): 131–9.

Yip, George S. 1989. Global strategy. In a world of nations? *Sloan Management Review*, 31(Fall): 29–41.

Yoshino, Michael Y. 1976. *Japan's Multinational Enterprises*. Cambridge: Harvard University Press.

10

Financial Perspectives and International Business

EDITORS' COMMENTS

Finance is a basic business discipline and an important function in business. There's no doubt that in recent years the practice of finance has been internationalized in many important ways, but what about the internationalization of financial theory and research? What have been the contributions of finance and international finance to the systematic body of knowledge on international business? We asked our authors to review more recent theoretical advancements in international finance and international financial management. How does the state of theoretical development in such areas as international capital markets compare with that in international financial management? What roles do positive and normative theory play? As usual, we asked the authors to pay particular attention to the underlying paradigmatic assumptions of the theories and their influence on the development of international finance and its contributions to IB understanding.

In the lead paper, Lessard argues for a broad definition of finance. He sees a potentially vital role for finance in the development of IB understanding and, indeed, improved IB practice.

First Lessard argues that we need to understand the changed context in which IB takes place today versus that of the 1960–70s when original IB theorizing took place. Specifically he highlights the globalization of competition, the triadization of IB activity, the development of technological parity across the three regions of the Triad (i.e., Asia, Europe, and North America), and the more proactive role of governments in international business competition.

With this newly globalized competitive environment comes a new financial environment. "National financial markets have increasingly become linked into a single global market ... A significant deepening of financial technology has taken place, not only in terms of information, trading, and document processing, but also in terms of analytical technologies" [p. 592]. Lessard completes the picture by noting that a large periphery of developing countries are loosely linked to, yet dependent on, this increasingly integrated core.

With this background, Lessard plunges in to examine finance and the theory of the MNC. Following Kindleberger (1969), he uses the standard Net Present Value equation to operationalize his distinction between real (cash flows) and financial (tax rate and discount rate) determinants of foreign direct investment (FDI).[1] Lessard frames his inquiry largely by asking what advantages a multinational corporation has over a collection of independent uninational companies (or later on, an international market)—essentially a version of the question: why do MNCs exist.

His review of the influence of risk, cost of capital, and property rights on FDI shows the limited role that financial factors play directly. Rather, it's their influence on the internalization advantages, reflected in the distribution of cash flows, that seems to shed light on the motivations and determinants of FDI.

Introducing a cross-national comparative dimension, Lessard asks if cost of capital can serve as a competitive advantage for firms located (or domiciled) in one country vis-à-vis those in another country. Lessard concludes that the Japanese do have a 1 1/2 to 2 percent cost of capital advantage over the USA and raises the question of whether such advantages accrue to all firms located there or just those firms domiciled there. Again we see the importance of the societal context in which firms arise and develop, as well as the potential importance of the national identity of a firm and the "Who is Us?" debate addressed in chapter 5.

Turning to some prescriptions for firm behavior, Lessard first asserts that the separation of the finance function from strategic and operations management will lead to lost opportunities for building competitive advantage in the firm. To avoid this undesirable outcome, firms should integrate financial expertise with other aspects of international management, possibly through individuals whose expertise spans these areas or through processes that bring the diverse expertise of various individuals to bear on important decisions.

To illustrate this vision of financial management as a supportive, complementary function more tightly link with operating and strategic decisions, Lessard examines how a firm should cope with volatile exchange rates and how a firm should choose its participation mode in international activities. Here we will only comment on the latter illustration.

Lessard's first point is a good one: The choices are many for the international firm when it comes to deciding exactly how to structure its international involvement in a particular activity. More complex arrangements can now be fashioned due to the development of the financial and legal infrastructure worldwide.

"Creative" or "clever" structurings of international participation in a world of high economic and political uncertainty, however, don't necessarily contribute to the achievement of corporate objectives. Consider Lessard's Disney example: "Walt Disney participates in its European and Japanese fantasylands through creative vehicles for capturing revenues, maintaining its operating links but choosing more financially effective routes for profit extraction" [p. 599]. The $2 billion in losses of Euro Disney since its opening in 1992, the $625 million in write-offs by Disney so far, and the waiver of five years of royalties and management fees by Disney (Huey 1995), however, demonstrate the vulnerability of such creative vehicles to the underlying corporate projections concerning interest rates, exchange rates, general economic activity and a host of more micro considerations related to operations. The organizational challenge of integrating financial considerations into operating and strategic decisions effectively seem to be as great as that of developing one of Bartlett and Ghoshal's transnational corporations—an analogy Lessard himself introduces. [p. 596]

The charm of Lessard's paper lies in its optimistic view of the role of finance in international business and its expansion of the range of phenomena that finance and international finance scholars should be concerned with. The advantage of this point of view is that it provides a common arena where finance and non-finance oriented researchers can interact to understand such IB phenomena as the form of international business involvement, international management compensation, international corporate governance. There's no doubt that IB scholars with backgrounds in strategic management, organization behavior, business and society, or other areas have worked for some time to understand these areas of IB.

The challenge of Lessard's point of view, however, is to deliver some value-added to our understanding of these areas. What do finance-oriented approaches add to our existing understanding of such IB phenomena? The answer to this question awaits further work by Lessard and others who adopt this point of view. We are reminded of the transition of economics from the dismal science to the imperial science—with the application of economic theories and methods of analysis to arenas of human behavior usually considered outside its domain, e.g., marriage or the family.[2] Yes, it can be done, but what is the gain in understanding of the phenomena; to what extent do we get better explanations of human be-

havior? By redefining finance so much more broadly, Lessard opens himself to these same questions.

In the second paper, Errunza brings to center stage the periphery—the emerging markets (EMs) of the nonindustrialized world. Like Lessard, Errunza wants to expand finance's concerns. Although using the conventional phrase "emerging markets," Errunza is really interested in more than the financial markets emerging in the developing countries around the world. He is interested in all sorts of business forms and processes in the developing countries and their relationships with the rest of the world.

First Errunza takes the time to make sure we understand the diversity of institutional differences and market imperfections in the emerging markets. This environment is both changing and quite different from that of the industrialized world.

The implications of this different world of EMs for business and international business are explored. Errunza reviews the current state of our understanding and suggests topics for further research in a such areas as the organization and governance of firms in EMs, the emerging securities markets in EMs, external financing of EMs, and the role of EMs in global competition. Overall Errunza builds a case for EMs as a challenge and opportunity for IB theorizing and research.

For example, what should we expect of a theory of the firm that was developed in the industrialized world? Errunza argues that such a theory needs substantial modification when applied to firms in emerging markets. Due to the wide variety of market imperfections in EMs, group structure (a close-knit circle of friends, family, and business associates) has evolved as the dominant form of business organization in EMs. Here we find another example of the importance of recognizing the embeddedness of business processes and forms in the larger societal context.

Finally, Errunza suggests that studies of EMs call for a multidisciplinary approach. His concerns, like those of Lessard, go beyond traditional finance, with the accompanying benefits and challenges noted above.

The commentaries in this chapter take two different approaches. Walter presents a comprehensive model of global financial flows, which he relates to a few of the points made by Lessard and Errunza, while Dufey addresses the substantive points of each paper in a more systematic manner.

In his exploration of global financial markets, Walter too is expansionary: "We can broaden the definition of IB to include the nonfinancial firm (whether multinational or not) as well as governments and agencies as borrowers, individual and institutional investors, financial intermediaries of all kinds, and suppliers of financial infrastructure services—as well as the relevant regulatory bodies." [p. 612 in this volume] He thus echos several others who argue for both an expansion in the number and types of phenomena to be examined, and for the endogenization of these phenomena by adopting a multilevel framework.

After laying out the basics of his comprehensive, model of financial flows, Walter develops normative benchmarks for financial systems. Criteria include efficiency, creativity (product and process innovations), global competitiveness, and stability. He explains the rationale and importance of each criterion. He goes on to note that "retarded" financial systems (presumably found in EMs) have certain negative effects on the economy and tend to be disintermediated in global competition in which investors and borrowers who can do so go elsewhere. Walter concludes with a final review of the benefits of investing and borrowing globally and the importance of the development of the global financial market infrastructure.

In his commentary, Dufey begins with a very important point: the well developed framework of finance has advanced international finance (IF) inquiry in some ways, but its assumptions have also constrained international finance inquiry. Dufey finds that "one of the fundamental conditions of

IF management, i.e., operating under partially integrated, partially segmented markets, proves to be an intractable challenge for academics (and practitioners) seemingly to prevent substantive advances in the field" [p. 620]. Being caught in between perfect integration and perfect segmentation, which traditional finance frameworks can handle, is what distinguishes international finance and presents it with its major challenges. In commenting on Lessard's paper, Dufey applauds Lessard's overall approach of extending financial frameworks and methods to incorporate "nonfinancial" phenomena. He adds two areas for further investigation: (1) capital structure of multinationals and (2) the interaction of the firm with providers of financial services. In commenting on Errunza's paper, Dufey raises the interesting question of why the significance of EMs in real economic activity is so much greater than their financial market significance. He goes on to speculate on the role that access to the less regulated "off shore" segments of the industrialized financial markets has played in the economic development of these EMs.

As a group, the four papers in this chapter show us that scholars trying to understand international finance phenomena feel the need to expand beyond what has traditionally been considered the domain of finance. As IB scholars, we would be tremendously encouraged by increased interaction between international finance scholars and other IB scholars with different training and expertise. Too often in the past, these linkages have seemed to us to be the least well developed within the community of IB scholars.

What we miss in these papers is a more complete examination of the underlying assumptions of IF and their influence on theory, research, and IF's contribution to IB understanding. Finance and IF exhibit a continuing strong adherence to neoclassical economics. Some finance scholars call themselves financial economists. Finance tends to follow economics and as economics develops beyond the neoclassical paradigm, finance will follow, but probably with a significant lag.

Much of finance and international finance is normative in the sense of "given you want to maximize shareholder value (or economic efficiency), you should do the following: ..." Yet shareholder value at the firm level and economic efficiency at the societal level are only two of many possible values, as Behrman (chapter 11) points out.

Will international finance be able to make more significant contributions to IB understanding if it transcends certain core assumptions and concerns of finance? If the challenges of the future for IB revolve more around hierarchies and hybrids, rather than

markets, can international finance contribute significantly? If most of the world is quite different (as Errunza argues concerning emerging markets) from the Anglocentric (United States and United Kingdom) context in which much of finance theory developed, can international finance develop theories to help us better understand these phenomena too?

NOTES

1. Note here how easy it is for those with a financial background to slip from a theory of MNC to a theory of FDI, and vice versa.
2. Casson in Chapter 4 also discusses the imperialism of economics in the social sciences.

Finance and International Business
Donald R. Lessard

Finance plays a pervasive role in international business (IB). Much IB is finance, in the sense of the transfer of financial resources and the provision of financial services. The multinational corporation (MNC), the central actor in IB, internalizes numerous financial functions and in many cases finance is a critical motivation for its existence. Differences in financial systems and contexts are argued to have important consequences for the competitiveness of multinational firms domiciled in different countries. Finally, the fact that international firms span currency areas, tax jurisdictions, and property rights regimes creates numerous threats and opportunities that make financial management a critical factor in these firms' competitive success.

This review of the various roles of finance in IB is organized into four parts. Part I describes changes in the competitive and financial contexts of IB which provide important background for the discussion of finance and IB. Part II examines the extent to which finance, broadly defined, is important in explaining the existence of multinational firms. Part III addresses the extent to

which financial factors give rise to comparative advantage, affecting the competitiveness of firms (or clusters of core activities) domiciled in particular countries. Part IV examines dimensions of financial management which can give rise to competitive advantage among firms and the extent to which this requires that financial perspectives be integrated into general management versus remaining a separate function.

I. THE CHANGING COMPETITIVE AND FINANCIAL CONTEXT

The "modern theory" of foreign direct investment (FDI), emanating from the seminal work of Vernon [1966], Hymer [1960;1976], Kindleberger [1969] and others in the late 1960s and codified in the 1970s and early 1980s by Dunning [1973], Buckley and Casson [1976], Caves [1982], and others, was conceived in a very different competitive and financial context than the present one. Thus, while part of our changing understanding of IB simply reflects changing fashions in paradigms, it also reflects shifts in the phenomenon itself.

The Competitive Context

Current theories of FDI and IB in general came out of an era when IB primarily was in the form of FDI by U.S. firms—establishing downstream value-added functions in "strange places." A major shift in the nature of IB has taken place over the past 15 years and appears to be accelerating with the emergence of Europe as a single market and the increasing role of technology in the production of goods and services around the globe.

The first element of this shift is the globalization of competition—the increased international integration of markets for goods and services and geographic dispersion of firms' value-adding activities—that has resulted from a continuing decrease in barriers to trade, a convergence of customer preferences and requirements, an increase in the proportion of product costs represented by one-time investments in product and process technology, and the increased sophistication of business firms in simultaneously spreading their value-adding activities around the globe to gain favorable access to information, markets, and factors, while increasing the international coordination and shared know how of these geographically dispersed activities.

A second element is "triadization," involving among other things increasing competitive parity of firms based in North America, Europe, and the Far East, increasing concentration of world investment and trade within and among these three poles, and an increased density of intra- and interfirm interactions within each. This triadization is in part the result of the convergence in the scale of the three regions, but it also reflects the diffusion of the once dominant U.S. organizing principles and technologies among these sets of firms and the substantial innovations in organizing principles by non-U.S. players,[1] especially the Japanese, but also some European players such as the Swedes. With it has come much stronger and more symmetric cross-investment between the United States and Europe and a highly asymmetric pattern between these two regions, Japan and East Asia. An important aspect of this triadization at the firm level is the clustering of core activities within specific regions in each leg of the triad, reflecting the interactions of firms, universities as generators of science and educators, and governments as shapers of activities with important spillovers as noted by Piore and Sabel [1984], Porter [1990], and Krugman [1991]. Thus, those locational factors that shape the MNC include not only differential factor costs and market access, but also transaction costs and externalities that drive co-location.

The third element, both a cause and effect of the first two, is the increasing parity in basic and applied technological capability in the three key regions of the world economy and the corresponding dispersion of "lead users" of key technologies that represent an increasing source of producer firms' technological innovation. This technological parity and opening of corporate innovation implies that firms operating in only one region are likely to miss important external developments and stimuli to their own development. Even if the productivity of their own innovation processes remain world class, the payoffs they obtain from it will be limited relative to firms with a broader geographic scope.

A fourth element in this changing competitive context is a shift in the role of governments in international competition, from monitors of their internal economies and arbiters of cross-border transactions into competitive participants within industries and contenders for the direction of the emergent international regimes that govern international transfers of goods, technology, and finance.[2] This role of governments as active players is not totally new, but it differs fundamentally from earlier periods of mercantilism where states defined the commercial regime to one where they are only one set of players in it.

Financial Context

The emergence of global competition has coincided with and, to some extent, given rise to major changes in the financial environment. The world economy continues to display a high degree of turbulence that has plagued it since the early 1970s. Divergences in macroeconomic policies and massive structural pressures have led to violent shifts of interest rates, exchange rates, and relative prices of commodities. While such turbulence presents a challenge to any business organization, it is particularly salient for firms that face global competitors with differing geographic configurations and, hence, different exposures to these key market parameters.

National financial markets have increasingly become linked into a single global market, as a result of both deregulation and an increase in the market power and financial skills of corporate and institutional users of financial services vis-à-vis the traditional providers of these services. A significant deepening of financial technology has taken place, not only in terms of the information, trading, and document processing systems, but also in terms of analytical technologies reflected in new instruments, more precise pricing of assets, and more complex risk management.

A major feature of the new international financial environment, in North America and Europe in particular, is the emergence of an international market for corporate control.[3] Cross-border mergers and acquisitions are increasing rapidly, to the point where differences among nations in openness to foreign takeovers are likely to become the source of conflict among national and corporate interests. At a corporate level, firms based in different countries competing in a single European or global market must match their competitors in terms of the cost and access to capital, especially in periods of corporate reorganization and integration.

The trend toward greater integration of financial markets is not universal, though. Many less developed countries (which now include a large number of new countries in transition) remain cut off from the world system by debt overhang and incomplete internal contracting regimes. Thus the financial map of the world includes an increasingly integrated core, with pockets of local differences due to domestic interventions, and a large periphery that is dependent upon but only loosely linked to the core international market.

II. FINANCE AND THE THEORY OF THE MNC

Given the history of IB theory, it is ironic that there is no generally accepted link between financial factors and the theory of the MNC. After all, the point of departure (or perhaps the straw man to be dethroned) for the "modern theory" of the MNC was the theory of international capital flows. Capital, it was argued, flowed from regions where marginal returns were lowest toward those where they were highest. Of course it was recognized in some quarters that this flow was not determined solely by the underlying capital stocks and technological conditions, but also by factors influencing the private appropriability of economic returns; however, this was not a central theme.[4]

Early writing about the MNC typically began with a challenge to the capital flow theory, noting that observed FDI flowed to particular countries that were culturally close, that significant cross flows took place, or that although there were significant macro ebbs and flows, FDI patterns displayed too much differential behavior at an industry and firm level to be solely a macro phenomenon. Hymer convincingly argued that FDI was an industrial phenomenon, driven by "imperfections" in markets for intangibles rather than capital.

Earlier theory, however, was probably not so wrong in explaining FDI in that much pre-WWI FDI did seek to overcome imperfections in capital markets, especially in property rights regimes for appropriation of returns, but also in the mechanisms for aggregating and governing large capitals. U.S. expansion in Central America under the Monroe Doctrine reinforced by gunboat diplomacy, for example, was less a result of the superior technologies or organizing capabilities of U.S. firms than their ability to project the U.S. property rights regime into other jurisdictions. The same holds for the earlier expansions of the British and Dutch. It is interesting that Wilkins [1988] focuses on home country financial rather than operating competencies as a major factor in the pre-WWI surge in British FDI.

In order to distinguish "real" and "financial" determinants of FDI, I find it useful to refer to the standard discounted cash flow formula with an argument that differs only in small ways from that in Kindleberger [1969]:

$$NPV = \sum_{t=1}^{T} \frac{\overline{CF}_t^* (1 - \tau)}{(1 + p)^t}$$

Real factors are those that cause the distributions (over time and across states of nature) of operating cash flows, CF_t, for an MNC to dominate those of a similar collection of single country firms. Financial factors include differences in effective tax rates, or more generally in the proportion of the operating cash flows appropriable by investors for an MNC versus a collection of single country firms, captured here by the tax rate, and differences in the value placed on these flows, captured here by the discount rate. To the extent that the cash flows themselves are influenced by ownership for reasons other than scale or expertise, e.g., political influence, this also could be deemed a financial explanation of FDI.

Risk and Financial Motives for FDI

Many financial rationales for FDI in recent years have been based upon portfolio theory. Cohen [1972], Ragazzi [1973], and Rugman [1980], for example, argued that multinationals have an advantage vis-à-vis a collection of single-country firms as the result of their ability to diversify risk, given the relatively low correlations of earnings and stock prices across countries compared to those within countries. Others pointed out that this international diversification potential was a necessary but not sufficient

condition for risk reduction to serve as a motive for FDI. In addition, there has to be some reason why firms can pool risks more effectively than shareholders. Smoothing of cash flows or taxable earnings, however, may be relevant at the firm level to the extent that effective tax rates increase with earnings volatility or that financial distress is costly. It is unlikely that pure risk reduction is a primary motivation for FDI, however, since most firms do not fully hedge their exposures to macroeconomic exposures such as exchange rates and interest rates even though the transactions costs of such hedging are much smaller than the organizational costs of FDI.

There are, nevertheless, many reasons why volatility may give rise to internalization advantages, but most of these are more properly viewed as real advantages in that they affect the distributions of operating cash flows. Less than perfect correlation of demand across countries, for example, can allow firms to economize on capacity, something that could not be replicated by shareholders. Volatile real exchange rates can lead to valuable options to shift production among currency areas. In each of these cases involving risk pooling and/or the creation of options to respond to changing circumstances, internalization changes the distribution of operating cash flows in ways that cannot be replicated by investors.[5]

Uncertainty in tax obligations, because of variations in either tax rates or taxable profits of national subsidiaries, can also give rise to advantages of internalization. Muralhidar [1992], for example, shows that with the historical distribution of tax rates for Organization of Economic Cooperative Development (OECD) countries, the ability to shift profits in response to changing tax rates can have significant value, although much less than is typically possible by pooling capacity, shifting production, and so on.[6]

Cost of Capital and FDI

Aliber [1970] argues that due to "currency preference,"[7] firms domiciled in particular countries will have lower costs of capital and will, therefore, place higher value on foreign operations than will local firms. This argument requires two steps. First, there must be some reason why different investor groups apply different discount rates to the same set of cash flows. Second, there must be a reason why this advantage must be pursued via FDI rather than portfolio investment.

Froot [1990] makes a similar but subtler argument, suggesting that firms based in countries with currencies that have appreciated have greater liquidity than others and thus have an "inside" capital advantage enabling them to place higher values on foreign investments. Again, it is not clear why FDI should be the preferred channel. Such an argument might explain the surge in total Japanese foreign investment, but the FDI portion requires some industrial level explanation, especially given the ready availability of U.S. securities and "quasi-securities" such as Rockefeller Center.

Property Rights and FDI

In the case of less-developed countries, or in countries in transition, the MNC may have an ownership advantage over purely local firms since it can structure self-enforcing contracts that bridge jurisdictions given the cross-border co-specialization of its ongoing business activities. Much of the early literature on FDI in extractive industries, for example Vernon [1971] and Moran [1974], focused on mechanisms for extracting rents in a dynamic game with the host government; a concept that also has played a key role in the bargaining literature in technology-based FDI (e.g., Poynter [1986]). This particular internalization advantage depends upon the existence of limits on property rights within particular host countries which MNCs can better penetrate than local investors or international portfolio investors.[8]

III. FINANCE AND COMPARATIVE ADVANTAGE

Many of the financial factors that favor MNCs over single-country firms also favor MNCs domiciled in one country relative to those domiciled in others, particularly those factors associated with tax rates and costs of capital.

The Cost of Capital as a Competitive Variable

It has become commonplace for observers of competition between U.S. and Japanese industry to refer to differences in the cost of capital as a major factor favoring Japan. With its historically higher savings rates, Japan has been seen by many as having lower interest rates as well as greater advantages from financial leverage and other aspects of the corporate financial structure. This is reinforced by the observation that Japanese equities command much higher multiples than U.S. equities, although the "adjustment" of Japanese equity prices over the past two years has undercut many of these arguments.

The results of various studies vary widely, with some researchers contending that although differences in capital costs exist, they do not consistently favor one country or the other [Kester and Luehrman 1989]; some concluding that they favor Japan, but by a relatively small margin [French and Poterba 1989], others that they consistently favor Japan by a substantial margin [McCauley and Zimmer 1989], while Baldwin [1986] shows that Japanese investors have earned higher risk-adjusted returns than their U.S. counterparts.

While some of these conflicting findings can be traced to questionable assumptions or methodology, most result from different definitions of the phenomenon in question and to different time periods over which the rates are measured. Some studies focus on the pre-(personal) tax required returns to investors, or returns realized by investors as proxies for these *ex ante* required returns. Of these, some limit their comparisons to real (risk-free) interest rates, while others incorporate risk premium on equities and still others seek to determine the weighted average faced by industry at large. Others focus on the pre-(corporate) tax returns required on real investments, either in the aggregate or for particular projects, ultimately to meet the supply cost of capital. Still others focus on differences of the risk of doing business or coping with various forms of distress in the United States versus Japan which may affect both the rental and supply costs of capital, e.g., Hoshi, Kashyap, and Scharfstein [1991].

Focusing on the period after 1981 when virtually all formal capital controls were abolished, it appears that firms based in Japan may still have a cost of capital advantage but that this advantage is at most on the order of one to one-and-one half percent. However, even differences of one to one-and-one half percent can make a big difference in international competitiveness. Using a two percent difference in weighted average costs of capital, which is high given their own evidence, McCauley and Zimmer compute what they call costs of capital, but what in fact are implied "cash flow yields," that is, ratios of annual operating cash flows to the amount invested for specific projects. They show that while the United States, with its relatively low corporate tax rates, is favored for short-lived projects, Japanese firms, the required operating cash flows yield (annual operating cash flow divided by investment) required by a U.S. firm is much higher for R&D projects and long-lived projects involving tangible capital. For an R&D project with a 10-year payoff lag, for example, the required cash flow yield in the United States is 20.3% versus 8.7% in Japan. These figures overstate differences in costs of capital as the term is normally used, but they do show how large an impact of relatively small differences in costs of capital can be on the earning levels firms must achieve.

While more research is required to establish these differences, they do suggest that the fiscal and financial context of firms competing internationally differs sufficiently that Porter's [1990] diamond of location-specific sources of competitiveness—rivalry, demand conditions, factor conditions, and infrastructure—should be expanded to take these explicitly into ac-

count.[9] A related issue, discussed by Baldwin [1986], is whether they benefit from activities in those countries with low costs of capital and, hence, should be treated as a location advantage, or whether they benefit from only those firms domiciled in those countries.

Governance Arrangements

A number of observers argue that Japanese governance arrangements allow firms to have higher leverage than their Western counterparts and, hence, lower after-tax costs of capital. They may also have had an advantage in the earlier, less liberal Japanese financial system when credit was allocated at below market rates in line with government and business group preferences.[10]

Differences in ownership/governance factors may also have a direct impact on the operating cash flows. The U.S. system, with its relatively free market for corporate control as a potential discipline on management is viewed by some as being extremely effective in this regard, but as a major source of myopia by others including Porter [1992]. The Japanese system, with its dual external ordering of capital and labor interests, is seen by many observers as a key source of Japanese firms' competitive advantage.[11] Finally, many political scientists view systems such as the (old) Japanese system in which the state has substantial power over the allocation of resources as a key factor that can provide certain firms, industries, or even an entire country with a competitive advantage.

International Projection of Home Country Property Rights

In the previous section I argued that the ability of MNCs to project home country property rights into host countries via self-enforcing contracts could be a rationale for FDI. While this advantage does not depend strictly upon home country conditions, to the extent that firms based in a particular country have greater leverage over sovereign performance, the advantage will accrue to MNCs domiciled there.

IV. FINANCE AND COMPETITIVE ADVANTAGE

While much research on MNCs is properly focused on the positive questions of why they exist, how they affect home and host societies, and what gives rise to comparative advantage among firms domiciled in or activities located in different countries, there also are important positive and normative issues regarding what firms do and should do to gain competitive advantage. The financial dimension of the international firm is no exception.

Returning to the valuation formula presented in the first section, firms can gain advantage, or at least neutralize potential disadvantages, through finance by minimizing capital costs, minimizing taxes, and managing financial risks to the extent that these feed back to operating cash flows, taxes, and capital costs through financial distress. In these cases, finance is a relatively separate function, largely independent of strategic and operating management that determines the underlying operating cash flows. From the viewpoint of the practice of international management and IB teaching that attempts to prepare individuals for this practice, the inclusion of international finance in the tool kit of the international manager is an option, not a requirement. By the same logic, the inclusion of IB in the tool kit of the international finance specialist also is an option.

There are other aspects of finance in the pursuit of competitive advantage, however, that cannot be separated so easily from strategic and operational management. These include those aspects of coping with macroeconomic risks that involve the choice of operating strategies which maximize value across a divergent set of circumstances and operating tactics that make the best of the current circumstances given prior strategic choices, as opposed to the simpler and more separable activity of hedging of these risks. They also involve:

1. Imbedding of financial services in selling, sourcing or contracting, obvious in the case of turn-key construction projects where financing forms a visible part of the contractors value-added, but also increasingly critical in "normal" commercial dealings among firms given that their activities span currency areas, tax jurisdictions, and property rights regimes;

2. The selection of activities on the basis of fiscal/financial as well as operating advantages; and

3. The choice of modes of participation in particular activities that will maximize appropriable value for a given set of operating flows.

If finance is extended to include the shaping of incentives through contracts, ownership structures, etc., then it pervades virtually all international management.

In all of these cases, effective management calls for an integration of financial expertise with other aspects of international management, through individuals who span mind-sets or processes which bring together different mind-sets or both. This challenge is not unlike that of transnational management as outlined by Bartlett and Ghoshal [1989] and others, where effective management must be both locally imbedded and globally linked and leveraged. In this case, though, locality is defined in terms of perspective and expertise rather than geography. This challenge is made more difficult by the fact that financial technology itself is developing at an extremely rapid pace, requiring increased differentiation.[12]

I will illustrate the integrative domain of finance and international management with two activities: coping with volatile exchange rates and participation strategy.

Linking Finance and Global Operations: Coping with Volatile Exchange Rates

Corporations face many macroeconomic risks in the current volatile environment including those arising from shifts in interest rates, currency exchange rates, inflation, and relative prices of key commodities. The management of these risks often involves both hedging and responsiveness. Hedging involves pure risk reduction, while responsiveness involves the creation and exercise of operating options. This is particularly true in the case of exchange rate exposures, where the impact of exchange rate shifts on a firm's operating cash flow depends upon its competitive positioning and the speed and accuracy of its responses. This responsiveness in turn involves a complex set of strategic and organizational issues in addition to financial hedging. The hedging problem is also complicated by the fact that these are exposures to real shifts in exchange rates that follow different and more complex statistical processes than nominal rates and that they typically are of longer-term than most currently available hedges.

A major difference between multidomestic and global competition is the impact of exchange rates on the operations of a multinational firm. Under multidomestic competition, markets are national in scope and, typically, a substantial proportion of value added is local. Thus, exchange rate shifts do not significantly change the relative costs of firms operating in a particular market. As a result, firms' revenues and costs move together in response to shifts in exchange rates and profits from foreign operations, when converted into dollars (or other reference currency), move roughly proportionally with exchange rates. Further, operating decisions regarding pricing and output, for example, should be unaffected by these changes.

In contrast, under global competition, there will be a tendency toward world (or at least continental) prices and larger proportions of firms' value added are likely to be concentrated in particular countries. Thus, unless all firms have the same global patterns of value added, shifts in exchange rates will change their relative costs and profit margins. Even where prices remain localized through local regulation, product differentiation, or other factors that enable firms to maintain cross-border price dis-

crimination, the optimal competitive strategies of firms with different configurations are likely to shift.

It is useful to think of the responsiveness of operating profits to shifts in exchange rates as comprising two effects: a conversion effect and a competitive effect. The conversion effect, the proportional adjustment of foreign currency operating profits into the reference currency (dollars for U.S.-based firms), exists for all firms with foreign operations, but applies only to those foreign operations. The competitive effect, the response of local currency operating profits to exchange rate shifts resulting from the interaction of the various competitors' supply and price responses, applies only to firms facing some degree of cross-border competition. However, it applies to both domestic and overseas activities. While the conversion effect may create headaches for treasurers and controllers, the competitive effect, since it requires adjustments in operating decisions, also affects and increases the complexity of the operating managers' jobs.

Most treatments of exchange rate management stress hedging as the critical management response, despite the uneasy theoretical case for hedging.[13] However, hedging is only one of many potential management responses to exposure to exchange rate volatility, and in many cases it is unlikely to be an important one. The various impacts and responses to exchange rate volatility in the operating and financial domains at different levels within the firm is illustrated in Figure 1.

At the operating unit level, a shift in exchange rates may alter the relative costs of alternative sources of supply, requiring a tactical response, while the possibility of future shifts may require strategies that create options for such tactical shifts in the future. The same may apply on the marketing side, with different pricing and mix tactics for different circumstances and segmentation strategies that allow for such tactics in the longer run.

At a strategic level, large movements in

Figure 1. Coping with Volatile Exchange Rates: Operational and Financial Dimensions

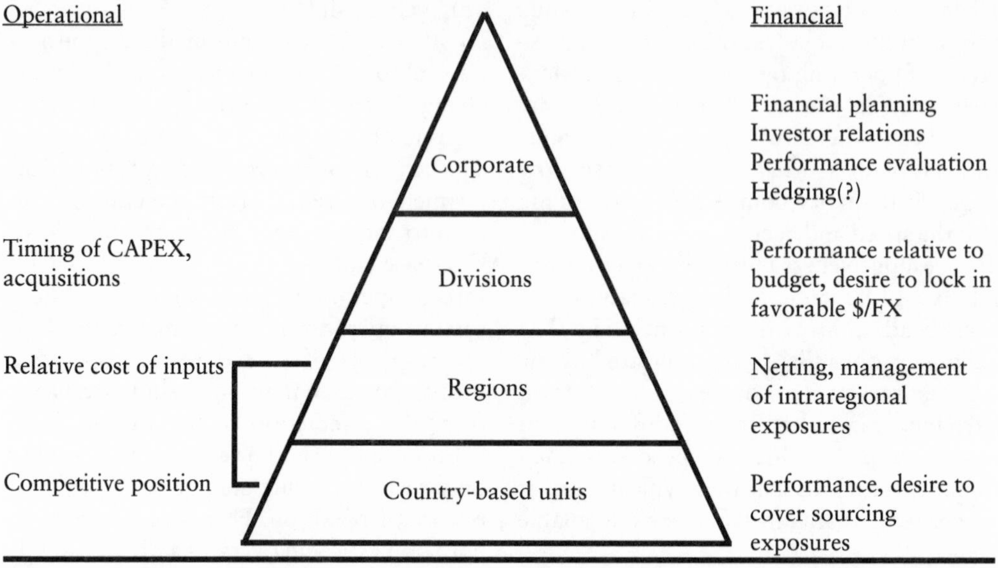

Operational   Financial

Corporate — Financial planning / Investor relations / Performance evaluation / Hedging(?)

Timing of CAPEX, acquisitions — Divisions — Performance relative to budget, desire to lock in favorable $/FX

Relative cost of inputs — Regions — Netting, management of intraregional exposures

Competitive position — Country-based units — Performance, desire to cover sourcing exposures

exchange rates may create windows of opportunity for asset acquisition, either in the case of capital expenditures or acquisitions. Kester and Luehrman [1988] and Froot [1989] underscore the impact of shifts in the real exchange rate not only on (flow) profitability of firms, but also on asset prices. The latter may be more important than former. The yen shock, for example, created a cost squeeze for Japanese firms, but it also created a window of opportunity for capital expenditures in the United States. As noted by Kester and Luehrman, these were not symmetrically shared by U.S. firms since they already had U.S. facilities, but little or no market franchise in Japan.

Risk exposure is typically larger at the business unit level than at the corporate level because of pooling across areas and businesses. Firms may find that they must address internal exposures in order to measure and motivate managers properly, even if their overall risk position is such that firms will self-insure.

Linking Finance and Global Strategy: Choice of Participation Mode

Global competition involves corporations that are diverse not only in the factor conditions, demand conditions, and degree of rivalry they face in their primary realms of activity, but also in terms of their financial structure and fiscal treatment. To the extent that capital markets are not perfectly integrated and that the taxes imposed on or the value placed on particular activities depend upon the domicile of the firm and/or its shareholders, finance comes into play not only by addressing issues that arise because of global competition in product markets, but also becomes a direct factor in that competition. The primary linkages between finance and strategy occur in three areas: funding, investment evaluation, and the selection of the way in which a firm structures its participation in a given activity. Here we focus only on the latter.[14]

With deregulation, financial innovation, and increasing investor sophistication, firms face a much broader range of modes for structuring their participation in particular commercial activities.[15] In many cases, the choice of alternatives to full equity ownership such as joint ventures, strategic alliances, or project finance are motivated primarily by the need to create compatible incentives for the various private participants and, in some cases, governments that significantly influence outcomes. Others, however, are largely motivated by financial considerations.

In resource-based industries, for example, firms with operating expertise may select among full ownership through a variety of ownership chains, joint ventures with other active partners, joint ventures with passive partners, and narrower forms of financial participation such as incentive management contracts or acting as general partner in a revenue trust. Further, they increasingly engage in sales and exchanges or assets that are driven as much by tax considerations as by operating synergies or differences in views regarding the prospects of particular properties. Technology-based firms similarly can choose ownership, joint ventures, or licensing. Union Carbide, for example, has largely retrenched to North America as an operating firm, but has increased its global reach as a licensor of technology. Even service firms face these options. Walt Disney participates in its European and

Japanese fantasylands through creative vehicles for capturing revenues, maintaining its operating links but choosing more financially effective routes for profit extraction.

The basic considerations in these structural choices are illustrated in Figure 2.

V. CONCLUSIONS

Global competition among corporations together with an increasingly integrated world financial system, continued macroeconomic volatility, and a rapid deepening of financial technology, increases not only the competitive impact of a corporate financing choices, but also the potential value added by financial inputs to strategic choices and operating decisions. Further, in many cases, the finance function can be expected to operate as a business in its own right, employing innovative instruments and risk management frameworks. This simultaneous broadening and deepening of financial management will require improved

Figure 2. Operating and Financial Considerations in Choice of Participation Mode

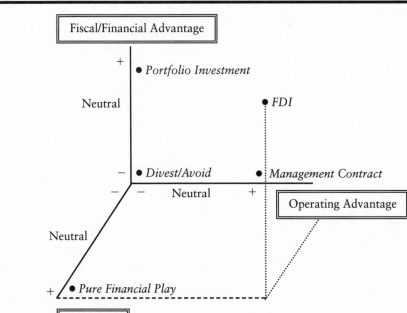

financial technology, but also greater sensitivity to the role of financial management as a supportive, complementary function in addition to its traditional control and oversight function. This means paying greater attention to the driving forces of strategy and to opportunities to improve management incentives and organizational structure.

The recognition that the financial environment is moving toward but has not yet become a fully integrated system means that multinationals can continue to gain from spanning systems to take advantage of "bargains" created by financial and fiscal distortions. Moreover, the existence of a less than perfectly integrated financial market also implies that valuation comparisons across countries will continue to be difficult—because value to a certain extent will continue to depend on the nationality (and tax position) of the beholding investor.

As global financial markets become increasingly integrated, corporate governance systems also appear to be converging, in large part spurred by the movement toward a single market in Europe. Japanese and continental European reliance on bank financing and concentrated institutional ownership seems to be lessening with the rise and expansion of relatively new capital markets, while institutions in the U.S. and the U.K. appear to be preparing for a larger role in corporate governance. One of the most interesting matters for speculation is whether a single homogeneous system will emerge— one which incorporates both aspects of the Japanese or German and American systems—or whether different countries will continue to preserve substantial differences in the role of capital markets in exercising corporate control. At present we lack a clear understanding of the competitive advantage of different systems and which elements of particular systems are most vulnerable as integration increases.

NOTES

1. The role of organizing principles in international competition is stressed by Kogut (1991).

2. See, for example, Thurow (1992).

3. See, for example, Walter and Smith (1990) and Kester (1991).

4. In particular Kindelberger and Vernon, whose articles in Herring (1985) aptly summarize their earlier contributions.

5. Kogut (1985b) describes a number of these internalization advantages. Muralhidar (1992), Kogut and Kulatilaka (1994), and Mello, Parsons, and Triantis (1993) develop explicit models of the value of such options.

6. There are many mechanisms for such tax shifting see, e.g., Giovannini (1989). One particularly interesting mechanism is to structure foreign operations as branches of domestic subsidiaries that can, at the parent firm's discretion, be consolidated or unconsolidated. This allows a continuous movement from deferral to nondeferral treatment and effectively creates an internal mechanism for shifting tax losses that can not be replicated by investors.

7. The term "currency preference" is ambiguous. It could mean currencies that have appreciated, are expected to appreciate, or currencies of investors who demand/expect lower real rates of return. In a world where pretax interest arbitrage holds, it cannot simply mean currencies with different nominal interest rates.

8. Eaton and Gersovitz (1981) introduce the concept of self-enforcing contracts in the case of intentional lending. Lessard (1989) discusses their application to FDI.

9. Porter (1992) explicitly addresses the financial and governance systems as competitive factors.

10. See for example, Yamamura (1986).

11. See for example, Aoki (1989).

12. For further discussion of the organizational aspects of this integration of finance and operating management in the context of foreign exchange risk management, see Lessard and Nohria (1989) and Lessard and Zaheer (1992).

13. Regarding motives for hedging, see Dufey and Srinivasulu (1984) and Froot, Scharfstein, and Stein (1993).

14. For a discussion of the other two areas, see Lessard (1986).

15. I use the term participation mode rather than entry mode since the context does not necessarily involve expansion into a new host country. Many of the determinants of participation mode, however, are similar to those of entry mode as outlined by Root and others.

■ ■ ■

Emerging Markets in Global Finance
Vihang R. Errunza

International competition and globalization of financial markets have revolutionized the finance function. In addition to the traditional tasks of raising and deploying funds, the finance professional is now expected to create relative advantage (rents) based on newly developed analytical technologies as well as participate in the firm's global strategic decisions.[1] In the years to come, the task will become more complicated. This is because of the imminent rise in the importance and role of Emerging Markets (EMs) in global business.[2] One need only be reminded that there were 138 nations (other than the industrialized world) at different stages of development that jointly constituted 23.8% of world output at the end of 1990.[3]

The diversity of institutional/structural differences and market imperfections that exist in EMs and the current efforts to reform their political, economic, and social environments provide a tremendous challenge and, hence, an unprecedented opportunity for both business and academics. Unfortunately, our understanding of these markets is rather limited. This is because many aspects of EMs have largely remained unexplored due to a lack of interest, difficulty in financial modeling under market imperfections, paucity of good reliable data, and aversion to a multidisciplinary approach. In particular, the last point affords comparative advantage to international business (IB) scholars who should seize the opportunity.[4]

To begin with, we should focus on the following issues:

1. Organization and governance of firms in EMs and their finances. Although these should be appropriately characterized as national studies, they are essential building blocks;
2. State of the emerging securities markets and their valuation in the global context;
3. External financial linkages—debt and equity financing of EMs; and
4. Role of EM firms and importance of MNC diversification into EMs in the context of global competition.

The organizational structure of this paper is, Section I begins with a discussion of institutional-structural differences and market imperfections that have traditionally afflicted emerging markets, followed by a brief discussion of the various reforms in progress. Section II describes the evolution of the "Group" Structure and related issues of diversification, governance, and financing. Section III examines issues related to investment and valuation. Section IV focuses on the problems and prospects related to foreign debt and equity financing of EMs. Section V narrates the implications of EMs in the context of global competition and the desirability of multinational corporation (MNC) diversification. Concluding remarks follow (Section VI).

I. THE STATE OF THE EM ENVIRONMENT

The environment has played a major role in the evolution of firms, their financing and competitiveness. In the case of EMs, the impact has been more pronounced given the severity of imperfections. Despite significant globalization and integration of real/financial markets and the relatively free flow of information among major nations, substantial imperfections/distinctiveness remain vis-à-vis the EMs. Hence, this section begins with a general discussion of the traditional environment followed by a brief overview of the reforms in progress.

In the parlance of Errunza and Losq [1989], the world market structure can be described as consisting of a largely integrated core of industrialized countries and "n" peripheral segments each representing an EM with its own distinct national characteristics and linkages with the core markets. For reasons of brevity and tractability I will treat all EMs as a single set and provide specific national examples where appropriate. The role of government across developed and emerging markets is also quite different. In EMs, the governments to a large extent continue being the regulators and monitors of the national economy. On the other hand, they have largely assumed the role of willing participants in the evolving global competition game within a number of developed countries. Although there are substantial interrelationships among various imperfections, for ease of exposition, I will classify them as relating to product markets, factor markets, financial markets and the international flow of goods, capital and services. Thus, for example, even though international barriers have enormous impact on product, factor and financial markets, we limit the discussion to the most direct interventions.

Product Market Imperfections

These include practices which regulate price, production, and entry/exit of firms. The most direct pricing distortion results from implementation of support prices (dairy and farm products), regulated delivery prices (utility services), and stipulated maximum sale prices (consumer goods). Input quotas, investment (dis)incentives, production licensing, and capacity limitations are some examples that inhibit development of a competitive productive sector at times under elaborate multiyear planning exercises. Large public sector firms are also quite common.

Entry barriers are implemented through production/input quotas, licensing requirements and government procurement policies whereas exit barriers involve government bailouts and subsidies. As mentioned earlier, although these barriers are commonplace in EMs, the developed countries are not completely devoid of them. Some examples are

farm support/subsidies in the European Community (EC), SandL bailouts in the United States, marketing boards in Canada and public sector firms in the United Kingdom.

Factor Market Imperfections

Labor market interventions are most prevalent. Restrictive labor legislation that stipulates rights to strike, hiring guidelines, lay-off procedures, remuneration packages, and working environment do not allow a competitive market to function. Although regulations pertaining to technology and innovation are not commonplace, the largely domestic orientation of EM firms lack global technological linkages or access to advanced technological innovations and low R&D at home imply significant barriers to the development of local firms in an increasingly competitive global market. Again, as in the case of product markets, many industrial countries with socialistic traditions have restrictive labor legislation, e.g., Canada, United Kingdom and Sweden.

Financial Market Imperfections

Many EM Financial Systems typically share the following characteristics: restrictions on interest rates for borrowing/lending, limited lending opportunities, binding domestic credit controls, high reserve requirements for commercial banks, segmented financial markets, and underdeveloped money and capital markets.[5] In addition, many EM financial institutions including commercial banks face severe "financial distress" due to large holdings of nonperforming loans, and are in danger of insolvency and failure. On average, commercial banks in EMs hold a higher percentage of financial assets (68%) than those in developed countries (40%). Finally, most EM countries have well established informal financial sectors typically servicing the household, small farmer and small business sectors that traditionally are unable to participate in the general banking system of the country. We now discuss some of the most important financial market imperfections.

Interest Rate Ceilings   Historically, EM governments have held local interest rates well below market to channel subsidized credit into sectors considered important. For example, governments frequently subsidize firms that provide products/services critical to economic development including firms that target the export market. Unfortunately, the actual results are quite the opposite: such subsidies inhibit economic development. Artificially low interest rates have been shown to repress the financial systems of EM countries, especially during inflationary periods.[6] In addition, according to the empirical findings of a recent study,[7] real interest rates are positively associated with economic development. Consequently, since low controlled nominal interest rates with high inflation imply lower levels of real interest rates, EM countries may not be realizing their maximum growth potential.

Interest rate ceilings also provide incentives for large firms to "over leverage" and (given subsidized borrowing costs) decrease lending to small risky firms that in many cases are the most dynamic, growth oriented firms in the local economy.

Directed Credit Programs   Many EM governments have channeled subsidized credit to public sector firms and other borrowers deemed to be in priority industrial sectors of the local economy. Many governments also have ownership stakes in local banks and financial institutions. Presumably, such ownership facilitates operationalization of policy objectives. However, such programs have inherent drawbacks. For instance, directed credit programs do not always lead to profitable investment decisions by recipient firms. Experience suggests that in general, such investments are not beneficial to the local economy. Furthermore, the high incidence of nonperforming loans made by EM banks, the higher levels of borrowers who knowingly default on outstanding loans, and the lower levels of financial intermediation, all increase the costs of directed credit programs. Finally, such programs also influence the level of competition for financial services in EMs. For instance, funds from banks under corporate control have been used to finance profitable but risky ventures in EMs that may not have been undertaken under prudent banking guidelines. If these risky investments pay off, EM firms become powerful industrial conglomerates.

Capital Markets   The linkage between (banks) finance and economic development has been extended to include capital markets.[8] In essence, the development of capital markets would reduce the proportion of self- or bank-financed investments and promote floatation of a range of financial instruments. An efficient capital market would allocate resources so that investors receive similar returns for a given risk, accumulate/disseminate vital information, facilitate comparisons of alternate investment opportunities, provide diversification opportunities, raise savings rates and capital accumulation of the economy.

Unfortunately, in most of the EMs, the prevailing conditions contributed a strong barrier to the development of securities markets and resulted in "Portfolio Suppression." These conditions include political and economic instability, religious and social practices, inadequate education and financial training, discriminatory taxation against income from financial assets and the interest ceilings discussed above. Factors specific to the securities markets include small size of the primary and secondary markets, preferential access to the primary market in favor of issuers and subscribers, inadequate market regulation and disclosure.

As a result, EM markets are small compared to major markets in terms of new issues, trading volume, market capitalization, and in relation to gross national product. It should be noted, however, that as a result of reform efforts, some of the larger EMs (Mexico, Brazil, India, Taiwan, S. Korea) are now quite comparable to the smaller (Sweden, Norway, Denmark) developed markets.

International Barriers

These include barriers that restrict free flow of goods, capital, and services across national boundaries. Tariff and nontariff barriers are the most common with respect to movement of goods and services. Although there have been a number of reductions under GATT, substantial barriers remain. For example, until March 1990, imports of 1,500 products were totally banned by the Brazilian government. On the capital side, there have been extensive controls on foreign direct investment (FDI) and portfolio investments in terms of entry/exit, repatriation of proceeds, percentage ownership, reinvestment, and foreign exchange.

Market Reforms

During the 1980s, many countries undertook political, social, and economic reforms. Despite their importance, we choose not to deal with political-social reforms as such but rather focus on economic reforms that deal with market imperfections of this section. The most important product market reform is the one dealing with price liberalization. The list of EMs that have adopted market-based pricing systems is very long—the most dramatic being the former USSR. The very difficult part of the reform effort has been the labor market due apparently to social and political implications. The most far reaching liberalization has been with respect to financial markets and international barriers.

During the 1980s, more than 25 EMs undertook extensive overhaul of their financial institutions. In perhaps a dozen EMs, interest rates are managed more flexibly than before, and directed credit programs have been curtailed, if not eliminated entirely. Furthermore, steps have been taken to foster competition among financial institutions by not only allowing the controlled creation of new banks, but also by opening

domestic markets to foreign banks. With respect to the securities markets, many EMs have undertaken numerous steps toward their development. These efforts began in the 1970s with Brazil, Chile, and S. Korea and extended to the major recent steps taken in India, China, Argentina, and Pakistan.

The reforms dealing with international barriers range from opening of domestic markets to foreign competition through trade liberalization to aggressive solicitation of direct and portfolio investments and dismantling of capital and foreign exchange controls (e.g., Mexico, Taiwan, S. Korea, Indonesia, Argentina, Brazil, and India).

Of course, the road to market reform is paved with numerous obstacles. Indeed, many EMs experimenting with financial market reform have been forced to curtail or reintroduce controls over credit. For example, a few Asian countries reintroduced direct credit controls to handle severe monetary disturbances to the economy. The experiences of a few Latin American countries (Argentina, Brazil, Chile, Venezuela, and Uruguay) that undertook extensive reform in the mid 1970s have also been similar. One important reason for limited success of these programs is that these policies were undertaken in isolation. As suggested by the 1991 issue of the World Development Report, a necessary precondition for success of liberalization policies is that such policies be carried out jointly with macroeconomic reforms. For instance, price distortions induced by protection and financial reform in a highly inflationary environment may not lead to the optimal allocation of resources. In addition, reform policies must be implemented against a backdrop of enforceable laws and regulations as well as a concerted effort to prepare the populace.[9]

Although successful implementation of reforms would move EMs toward the market systems of developed countries, it will certainly take many years for most EMs to be fully integrated in the world economy.[10] In the meantime, we have little choice but to understand the manner in which EM firms are organized, valued, and financed under constantly changing imperfections. It is also important to analyze their linkage with the world economy through debt/equity financing and multinational investments. It is only then that we can fully comprehend EM role in the global competition game.

II. CORPORATE GOVERNANCE AND ORGANIZATION

Based upon the discussion of the last section, it is apparent that the theory of the firm developed under a U.S. environment cannot be applied to EMs without substantial modifications. While some authors have tried to explain conceptually the structure and governance of organizations, a comprehensive treatment is not available.[11] Indeed, a general theory of the firm that would explain differential firm behavior across countries is called for with the United States as one polar case and EMs as the other polar case on a continuum of market (im)perfections. What follows is a description of the observed phenomena and some explanations as they relate to the theory of the firm.

Market imperfections give rise to substantial monopoly powers in EMs that persist over long time periods.[12] In response, the "Group Structure"—closely knit circle of friends, family, and business partners—as evolved in most countries.[13] They undertake activities that span many different areas including manufacturing, trade, services, and finance and invariably result in vertical/horizontal integration, diversification, coinsurance, partitioning of sectors among groups and captive markets.

The group structure results from a wide array of imperfections that are closely interlinked and reinforce each other.[14] Monopoly rents, availability of subsidized credit from (group) financial institutions, less developed nature of securities markets, desire to maintain control, and the need to perpetuate and expand rent opportunities through secretive business practices all lead to the closed form business organization. Even when publicly listed, they are closely controlled with limited float. There is little incentive to issue equity to the public and/or

share information which in turn inhibits the development of the financial sector or the modern organization with split control and ownership.

The groups generally are conglomerates of many small units specializing in different sectors of the economy. This has two effects. First, the risk diversification function is internalized within the firm. The small size of each unit reduces the lumpiness disadvantage of real sector diversification versus financial market diversification. Second, the creation of separate entities maximizes the value of limited liability. Thus, a portfolio of real projects with no cross default liability leads to maximization of the group wealth.

Although we have some understanding of the relationship between group structure and market imperfections, a number of questions remain. First, how would we expect groups to evolve as EMs develop and become more efficient? Note that groups are also quite prevalent in many developed economies and coexist with public corporations. Thus, we must attempt to develop a more general theory that goes beyond market imperfections as the motivation for group structure. From the perspective of smaller economies, groups may serve a very useful function in a globally competitive economy. Reforms are important and must be undertaken. There must be, however, viable business organizations capable of successfully competing with large multinationals. Second, we must inquire about the agency relationship between the controlling shareholders (who also manage the firm), minority holders and the debt holders (who may be a group controlled financial institution). Finally, how should we value the various parts of a group that trade on the market? The important issue is information and valuation asymmetry among private (group) and public holders.

III. EMERGING SECURITIES MARKETS AND VALUATION

In general, capital market imperfections have inhibited the growth and development of securities markets. However, the reforms of the 1970s and 1980s have led to about 20 EMs with reasonably well functioning securities markets in terms of capitalization, breadth, liquidity, and efficiency.[15] Although they have become active during the 1970s and 1980s, their historical development is quite varied. While some markets are very old (e.g., Greece, Chile, Brazil, India, Zimbabwe, Portugal, Mexico, and Argentina) and some new markets have developed as a result of government programs (e.g., S. Korea, Philippines, and Jordan), others have blossomed as a result of special circumstances (e.g., Singapore-Malaysia and Hong Kong). The following is a brief summary of our understanding of these markets.

1. Most of the primary and secondary markets have grown rapidly in absolute terms and in relation to their national economy and other financial assets. There is evidence that suggests their contribution to improvement in savings rates, capital accumulation and resource allocation. For example, during the initial stages of the Brazilian capital market development program, "The available evidence suggests that the increased domestic savings and their distribution through a competitive market characterized by improved information about investment opportunities seems to have resulted in a better allocation of resources, improvement in capital to output ratio and a sustained high economic growth rate." [Errunza 1979:365–366]

2. Most microefficiency tests of EMs suggest adequacy of random walk hypothesis (see for example, Niarchos [1972], Sharma and Kennedy [1977], and Errunza and Losq [1985a]).

3. In terms of performance, most EMs have yielded higher returns (in comparison to major markets) in local and U.S. dollar terms. In a number of EMs, the variability of return is also high.[16] The high domestic systematic risk is not surprising given less diverse economic activity, relatively few and less diverse firms that make up an EM index, and pervasive government (market) factor that impacts most firms on a given market. In a global context, most EMs display negligible systematic risk. Further, they are either uncorrelated or negatively correlated with the world market.

4. From the perspective of the foreign investor, the benefits of diversification into EMs are well documented (see, Levy and Sarnat [1970], Lessard [1973], and Errunza [1983]). From the perspective of the local economy, foreign portfolio investments would augment domestic resources, help capital market development, and increase domestic welfare through lowering of the cost of capital and increased resource mobilization.

5. In view of the various market imperfections, Stulz [1981], Errunza and Losq [1985b;1989], Eun and Jarakiramanan [1986], and Padmanabhan [1992] have developed international asset pricing models (IAPMs) under barriers to capital flows. The capital flow restrictions considered are appropriate for those imposed by most EMs. These models suggest that EM securities should command expected returns that reflect world systematic risk and nationalistic risk. The implication is that removal of barriers would integrate EMs in the world market and lower the cost of equity capital thereby improving efficiency and mobilization of capital. Another implication is that foreign investors should not be overly concerned about currency and political risks. Indeed, they would earn

returns more than commensurate for the risks borne under most conditions (see, Errunza and Losq [1987]).

6. Test of the above IAPM on a sample of EMs lends support to the hypothesis that EMs are neither fully integrated nor completely segmented from the world market. They are mildly segmented (see, Errunza, Losq, and Padmanabhan [1992]).

Further research on emerging securities markets should be aimed at increasing our understanding of how and why markets develop, the process of maturation and the link between market reform and development and economic growth. It would be useful to link various concepts of efficiency with the institutional and structural characteristics of the market under investigation. Finally, research on EMs potentially can resolve some of the outstanding anomalies, puzzles, and inconclusive evidence reported in the finance literature. Some prime candidates are size, P/E, calendar events (see, Agrawal and Tandon [1990]), the Initial Public Offering underpricing puzzle (see, Aggarwal [1991]), the closed-end fund discount puzzle (see, Errunza [1991]), and the inconclusive evidence on developed markets regarding world market integration/segmentation (see, Errunza, Losq, and Padmanabhan [1992]).

IV. EXTERNAL FINANCE

This section begins with a brief review of the history of external finance leading to the debt crisis.[17] This is followed by a discussion of the various alternative sources that would beneficially restructure less developed country (LDC) finance. The discussion focuses on modification of traditional sources and new market instruments.[18]

The structure of external finance changed dramatically during the decade leading to the LDC debt crisis. Private financial markets and banks assumed a major role in development finance, a large proportion of which was, with explicit/implicit government guarantees at floating interest rates.[19] This was at the expense of direct foreign investments, bonds, and suppliers' credits. The primary causes that led to the debt crisis include the structure of external finance (floating rate obligations denominated in U.S. dollars and not tied to repayment ability of the borrowers), an unprecedented and unanticipated rise in the real and nominal interest rates, appreciation of the U.S. dollar, adverse trade developments for non-oil LDCs including declining commodity export prices and real increases in the price of oil, borrowing for consumption and wasteful projects by some of the oil-exporting LDCs (e.g., Mexico and Venezuela) and economic mismanagement.

The general obligation borrowing (GOB) that seemed cheap at the time, left LDCs vulnerable to world economic shocks. The resulting crisis and its aftermath imposed heavy costs on LDCs and banks in the form of nonrepayments, reschedulings, markdowns, etc. It is now recognized that to be beneficial, external finance must be structured so as to satisfy all parties. In particular, different risks must be borne by the party most able to bear it. Further, financial obligations must be matched with ability to repay in terms of amounts and timing.[20] Thus, external finance must be restructured to be well diversified, able to deliver new resources, and provide for efficient risk sharing and cash flow matching.[21]

In terms of debt finance, LDCs should seek modifications and innovations that would serve their needs in terms of reduced default risk or improved cash flow matching. For example, they could seek to maintain real repayments constant over time, relate repayments to expected earnings, specify interest caps, issue bonds linked to commodity prices, export earnings or a basket of currencies.

The equity exposure and the link between repatriation and local profitability accord excellent risk sharing and cash flow matching attributes to the traditional FDI. Unfortunately, the divergence in goals of the multinational and host society as well as control/management issues have not allowed FDI to play a key role in providing external finance.[22] As a result, the different risks assumed by the foreign investor are being unbundled into quasi-equity forms of finance. These include production sharing agreements, management contracts, joint ventures, licensing arrangements, and so on. These innovative participations require foreign investors to provide services and assume risks where they have a comparative advantage. The contracts can be very specific, credible and tailor-made to suit the needs of the investor and the host country and hence can be very attractive to all parties.

Foreign portfolio investments (FPIs) provide a pure form of risk capital. Investors generally are not interested in management/control and possess the cash flow matching and risk sharing attributes. The FPI also provide other benefits related to the development of capital markets, investor welfare, and resource mobilization as discussed in Section I.[23] There are also substantial benefits to the foreign investor in terms of improving the risk profile and performance of their global portfolio to make this a mutually desirable alternative. Finally, contrary to widely held belief, the cost of FPIs has not been necessarily higher than GOB. For example, during 1971–1988, the U.S.-dollar cost of FPI was lower for Brazil and Mexico and higher for Argentina and Chile compared to floating rate GOB.[24]

There are many alternate avenues to mobilize FPIs. The most direct route is for foreign investors to trade on local exchanges. Given the current state of the market, further reforms and development of the market as well as relaxation of rules governing inflows/outflows are necessary for attracting substantial flows. In recent years, many EMs (e.g., Mexico, S. Korea, and Argentina) have listed their securities as American Depository Receipts (ADRs) or its international depository receipts (IDR) analog. This alternative is easier to implement since it involves lower monitoring costs and

foreign controls, and is less penetrating. It does require private institutional arrangements across exchanges and their related costs. Another obstacle is the need to meet the listing and disclosure requirements of the developed markets that can be satisfied only by the larger EM firms. A relatively newer innovation is the National Index Fund (NIF) that holds a well diversified portfolio of securities traded on a given national market and trades on NYSE or London exchange.[25] This is the easiest of the alternatives from the perspective of both the host government and foreign investor and is least threatening from a foreign control standpoint.

Finally, the successful management of external debt involves external and internal debt reduction (conversion), improvement in public sector finances and development of capital markets.[26] One of the avenues of debt reduction has been conversion of debt to equity or local currency assets. Debt-equity swaps also improve the structure of external obligations. However they have raised concern over potential inflationary impact and the eventual reconversion of local equity into convertible currency.[27] In recent years, privatizations have emerged as a means to improve public finance, foster capital market development, and encourage foreign portfolio investments in previously state owned firms.[28] For example, in Chile and Mexico, privatizations have aimed at widening company ownership in addition to improving public finance. As Luis [1992] states, "82% of privatization revenue in Latin America has been raised through placement of equity in domestic markets, including the distribution of shares to workers, retail sales and private placements." At times, the privatizations have been carried out in conjunction with debt conversion. Of course, a choice between privatization through domestic markets or debt exchange would depend upon the capacity of the domestic market (investors), debt discount and the discount rate applied to the debt transaction. On the other hand, the choice between domestic investors and foreign investors in a largely segmented EM would depend upon the differential valuation by the two classes of investors.

To summarize, EMs are moving away from the largely debt finance of 1970s and early 1980s and toward equity finance. Although a number of market innovations and instruments have been used and the urgency of the crisis has dissipated, the problem remains.[29] In the increasingly interlinked financial markets, the governments, institutions, and investors should work together toward a full resolution of this problem. After a slow start, academics have made substantial contributions but much remains to be done. We must better understand the linkages among macroeconomic policy, financial market development, and international flow of capital. Maximization of national welfare is called for through applied research aimed at developing action programs. Some examples are: how should the NIFs be structured (in terms of their size and composition); what should be the negotiating strategy vis-à-vis MNCs; how should we structure the external finance of an EM given its past record, market conditions, national objectives and country specific characteristics.

V. GLOBAL COMPETITION, EMS AND MNCS

The existing imperfections and the evolving new environment in the EMs must be reflected in the global competition game. Indeed, the role of EM firms and the importance of EMs from the perspective of the multinationals cannot be ignored.[30]

Role of EM Firms

The debate regarding U.S.-Japan competitiveness has often focused on relatively lower cost of debt and equity finance and financial leverage advantages enjoyed by Japanese firms.[31] Hence, the key question is, do financial market imperfections provide systematic advantages to EM firms?

Theoretically, under barriers to inflow of portfolio capital, investors would expect a return higher than what would be dicta-

ted in the absence of such barriers. Historically, the evidence on average is consistent with these expectations. For example, most EMs until recently, had very low P/E ratios. However, the situation has dramatically changed in recent years. Some of the markets (e.g., Taiwan, South Korea, India) command P/E ratios well in excess of twenty.[32] While more research is required to analyze this phenomenon, based upon our current understanding, we can attribute the current high multiples to recent opening and liberalization of financial markets, high growth prospects and speculative excesses. Whether these levels will be sustained to give EM firms a financial advantage or whether this phenomenon will be repeated in other EMs undergoing similar reforms is difficult to determine. It does, however, suggest that debate over Japanese P/E ratios may spill over to some of the successful EMs (NICs!). A related question is whether firms in these EMs can raise necessary equity funding. The answer is a qualified yes. These markets have become deeper and broader as a result of reforms. Large firms (that compete globally) can raise substantial equity. Thus, in terms of cost of equity, some EMs currently enjoy an advantage whereas many others are at a disadvantage. As EMs mature and become more integrated with the major markets, the field should become more level.

With respect to nonequity financing, most firms in EMs (despite reforms) continue to have access to subsidized short term and long term financing. The subsidy comes through development banks, government guarantees, industrial development corporations, group financial institutions, international organizations, foreign aid, and subsidies. Further, the restrictions on foreign borrowing have also been relaxed. The success of South Korean firms in tapping Euromarkets is well known. Similarly, many large Indian firms are poised to repeat the South Korean success. Thus, with respect to debt financing, EM firms are not at a disadvantage and maybe at an advantage.[33]

Nonfinancial factors such as fiscal distortions (subsidies), low input (labor) costs and natural resource endowments may also provide competitive advantage. Of course, as some of these advantages dissipate, countries (firms) have to create new advantages. Recent restructuring of NICs away from low tech products to high value added capital intensive products coupled with their investments in lower income/cost Asian countries (e.g., Thailand, Malaysia, Indonesia) is a case in point. Thus, as EMs evolve, there is restructuring of competitive advantage and reorganization of production.

Two other considerations must also be taken into account. First, some of the EMs have potentially very large domestic markets (e.g., India, Brazil, Indonesia) that would accord them a competitive advantage. Second, although R&D expenditures are very small, the similarities in social infrastructure, culture, and factor endowments (costs) have at times given an advantage to products and services developed in emerging markets. That is, products designed, developed and produced in one EM are generally (more) appropriate for use in other EMs. Low-tech engineering products and construction contracts are typical examples.

Multinational Diversification into EMs

Under market imperfections, the motive for multinational expansion is well established at the theoretical level with corroborating empirical evidence. Under barriers to free flow of capital, corporate international diversification is beneficial to preexisting shareholders and is value creating. In essence, multinationals act as an intermediary and provide (indirect) diversification services otherwise unavailable to investors.[34] As discussed earlier, the barriers to cross-border financial flows are most severe in emerging markets. They also provide the largest diversification gains in terms of risk reduction and portfolio performance. Thus, a pure diversification motive would suggest that multinationals should span the largely segmented markets of emerging economies.

The nonfinancial distortions continue to play a role in MNC investments. Some recent examples are investments by Ford and Volkswagen in Portugal (to take advantage of lower factor costs) and the Sun Microsystems Inc. laboratory in Moscow employing Russian scientists at Russian wages.

Further research should focus on cost of capital, movement of production facilities in response to shifts in competitive advantage, and the significance of EM specific R&D efforts that would affect competitive positioning of EMs. Improved understanding of the benefits of multinational expansion in EMs relative to developed markets could provide an additional edge to forward looking MNCs.

VI. CONCLUDING REMARKS

There are two potentially irreversible phenomena at work. The first relates to the globalization and forces of competition in the world at large. The second relates to the increasing emphasis on international and interdisciplinary research at leading business schools. In view of these developments and the increasing role of EMs, the importance of research in these markets is inescapable. We must understand how government and business function in EMs, how we should value and finance firms that operate under various market imperfections, what are the national concerns and aspirations, and how developed economies and emerging markets can complement each other in an environment of mutual understanding and competition. Indeed, the EMs must be brought into the new world order and accorded their rightful place. Academics have a major role to play.

NOTES

1. See Lessard (1991) for an excellent discussion of the related issues.
2. The World Bank defines emerging markets as those with per capita GDP of less than U.S. $6,000. We also include more affluent countries (e.g., Taiwan, S. Korea, Portugal) that are considered emerging by most investors.
3. World Economic Outlook, May 1991,

IMF, Washington, D.C., p. 125. Note that the United States accounted for 27.1% of world output.

4. Although this paper is written from a finance perspective, the multidisciplinary nature of various issues will be highlighted where appropriate.

5. See Tseung and Corker (1991) and the World Development Report, 1991.

6. From World Development Report, 1991, op. cit., pg. 54. For comprehensive treatment of the role of financial markets in economic development, see Goldsmith (1969), McKinnon (1973) and Shaw (1973).

7. See Greene and Villanueva (1991).

8. See Errunza (1977) for an in-depth discussion.

9. For example, the importance of judicial reform, education and management training in the case of former Soviet republics is well understood.

10. As pointed out by Stopford and Strange (1991), the success of S. Korea and Taiwan can be traced to pervasive and prolonged government intervention to remedy market failure. It was aimed at improving infrastructure, increasing human capital, protection of local R&D and industry, building financial institutions, and promoting exports.

11. See for example Leff (1976), Errunza and Rosenberg (1982), Senbet (1992), Thomadakis (1992), and Fischer and Palasvirta (1991).

12. See for example Bhagwati (1982) for a discussion of monopoly rents from government intervention.

13. Groups are also evident in industrialized economies (e.g., Canada, Italy, Scandinavia).

14. For a discussion of the relationship between corporate governance and government intervention, see Fischer and Palasvirta (1991).

15. Essentially they comprise the market coverage of International Finance Corporation's emerging markets databank. We do not include smaller European markets that are comparable to major EMs.

16. On the other hand, Errunza and Rosenberg (1982) report lower investment and business risk for their group of EMs in relation to major developed markets. They attribute it to a host of social, economic, and financial factors.

17. Since the debt crisis has been labeled as an LDC phenomenon, we use the terms EMs and LDCs interchangeably in this section.

18. Due to space limitations, country specificity and wide coverage in academic and popular press, we do not discuss debt reduction, IMF-IBRD intervention, government initiatives (Baker or Brady plan) or the process of negotiations. Note that many of the reforms discussed in Section I of this paper relate to the IMF-IBRD intervention.

19. Although there are substantial cross-country differences and hence generalizations based upon aggregate LDC experience must be interpreted with caution, the debt crisis did affect most of the major EMs.

20. Ex post, GOB turned out to be very risky since it did not provide for cash flow matching or efficient risk sharing.

21. See Lessard and Williamson (1985) for an excellent discussion.

22. Stopford and Strange (1991) note that despite the boom in worldwide FDI flows in recent years, the real value of FDI to LDCs was lower in 1980 compared to a decade ago. Further, the investments were concentrated in the relatively advanced countries of Asia.

23. For a detailed discussion of the role of FPI towards resolution of the debt crisis, see Errunza and Padmanabhan (1992).

24. In fact from the perspective of the United States and global investors, the expected return on most EM portfolios would be close to the risk free rate because of their closeness to the zero-beta asset.

25. Currently there are over 200 NIFs. They comprise public, private or venture capital funds. Some are multicountry funds.

26. In a similar vein, Dufey (1992) suggests that private sector solutions will provide only a minor improvement unless workable macroeconomic policy frameworks are also established.

27. See Dornbusch (1988), Krugman (1988), Errunza and Moreau (1989), and Froot (1989).

28. An excellent discussion is in Luis (1992).

29. For example, Brazil is currently negotiating rescheduling of previously rescheduled debt. Similarly, smaller countries are also laboring under excessive debt.

30. Note that our primary focus is on financial issues.

31. For a summary, see Lessard (1991).

32. Although there is also substantial divergence in terms of realized returns on equity portfolios, on average EMs have outperformed developed markets.

33. Note that bond markets are in general less developed. Given the availability of other alternate sources of debt financing including factoring, long term corporate IOUs, intergroup financing and equity that at times behaves like debt, there has not been much need for organized corporate bond markets.

34. See for example, Agmon and Lessard (1977), Jacquillat and Solnik (1978), and Errunza and Senbet (1981).

■ ■ ■

COMMENTARIES
Ingo Walter

Understanding the Structure and Dynamics of Global Financial Flows

The papers by Vihang Errunza and Donald Lessard present a challenge for any discussant due to their rather different characters.

Vihang Errunza's focus is on "emerging" markets; basically countries that in the past have relied upon distortions in markets for goods and services, factors of production, internal and external finance. Some now consider this reliance to have been misguided in terms of maximizing social welfare. These countries run from Eastern Europe and Africa to Latin America and parts of Asia. Many are undertaking serious market reforms for the first time in decades, sometimes at a breathless pace—hence the term "emerging."

Preemergence conditions in many of these countries guaranteed inefficiencies in virtually all dimensions of their respective national economies, as well as healthy profits for those able to avoid or evade the market distortions. As the transformation gets underway, significant market inefficiencies remain for various periods of time, and this makes emerging markets—particularly emerging financial markets—among the most attractive in the world for those institutions capable of accessing them effectively. There are wide spreads in all sorts of financial transactions, high market volatil-

ity (especially in equities), and large control premiums in the value of companies. Risks are high as well, which places a premium on exposure management tools. Financial infrastructure is often poorly developed, with broad scope for improvement.

Errunza's description provides an excellent starting point for an evolution toward normative financial system benchmarks, discussed below, and toward viable national linkages into the increasingly integrated global financial system. As they do so, of course, the process of "creative destruction" sets in and the "free lunches" begin to disappear, with vast potential benefits for the countries concerned.

Don Lessard's paper takes a broader view and provides an outstanding nontechnical overview of the financial context of IB and how it represents a core dimension of the management of multinational firms and their competitive performance in their respective industries.

I would like to take a somewhat different slant on this issue by focusing a bit more on the globalization of financial markets. Here we can broaden the definition of IB to include the nonfinancial firm (whether multinational or not) as well as governments and agencies as borrowers, individual and institutional investors, financial intermediaries of all kinds, and suppliers of financial market infrastructure services—as well as the relevant regulatory bodies.

STYLIZED PROCESS OF FINANCIAL INTERMEDIATION

A convenient model that can be used to guide thinking on international financial contracting and the role of financial institutions and markets is summarized in Figure 1.

The diagram depicts the financial process (flow-funds) among the different sectors of the global economy through:

1. Savings/commercial banking and other traditional forms of intermediated finance (Mode A). Depositors buy the "secondary" financial claims or liabilities issued by credit

Figure 1. Financial Flows

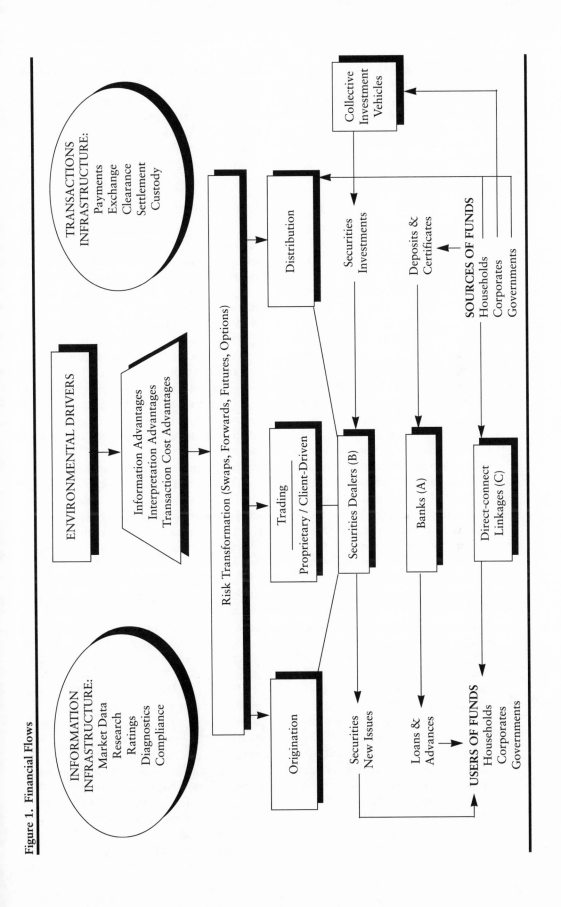

institutions, and benefit from liquidity, convenience, and safety through the ability of financial institutions to diversify risk and improve credit quality through professional asset management and monitoring of their holdings of primary financial claims (debt and equity). Savers can choose among a set of standardized contracts and receive payments services and interest that may or may nor be subject to varying degrees of government regulation.

2. Investment banking and secured intermediation (Mode B). Investors may select their own portfolios of financial assets directly from among the publicly issued debt and equity instruments on offer. This may provide a broader range of options than standardized bank contracts and permit the large investors to tailor portfolios more closely to their objectives while still achieving acceptable liquidity through rapid execution of trades— aided by linkages with banks and other financial institutions that are part of the domestic payments mechanism. Small investors may choose to have their portfolios professionally managed, for a fee, through various types of mutual funds.

3. Various financial direct-connect mechanisms between borrowers and lenders (Mode C). Investors buy large blocks of privately issued securities. In doing so, they often face a liquidity penalty—due to the absence or limited availability of a liquid secondary market—for which they are rewarded by a higher yield. Recent institutional and regulatory developments have added to the liquidity of some direct-placement markets.

Functional linkages across the three channels permit bank receivables, for exam-ple, to be repackaged and sold to nonbank securities investors, and privately placed securities (once seasoned) may be able to be sold in public markets. Geographic linkages make it possible for savers and borrowers to gain incremental benefits in foreign and off-shore markets, thereby enhancing liquidity and yield or reducing transaction costs.

Financial System Benchmarks

The structure of the financial intermediation process can be calibrated against a set of normative benchmarks that would appear to describe optimum, performance-oriented financial systems that are at once efficient, creative (in terms of generating innovative financial products and processes), globally competitive, and stable. The first three of these benchmarks can be discussed in terms of Figure 2.

Static efficiency is modeled in the diagram as the all-in, weighted average spread (differential) between rates of return provided to ultimate savers and the cost of funds to users. This "gap," or spread, depicts the overall cost of financial intermediation. In particular, it reflects the direct costs of producing financial services (operating and administrative costs, cost of capital, etc.). It also reflects losses incurred in the financial process, as well as any monopoly profits earned and liquidity premia. Financial processes that are considered "statically inefficient" are usually characterized by high "spreads" due to high overhead costs, high losses, barriers to entry, and the like.

Dynamic efficiency is characterized by high rates of financial product and process innovation through time.

Product innovations usually involve creation of new financial instruments (e.g., caps, futures, options, swaps) along with the ability to replicate certain instruments by bundling existing ones (synthetic securities) or to highlight a new financial attribute by rebundling existing instruments.

Process innovations include contract design (e.g., cash settlement futures contracts), methods of settlement and trading, techniques for efficient margin calculation,

Figure 2. Efficiency in Financial Intermediation

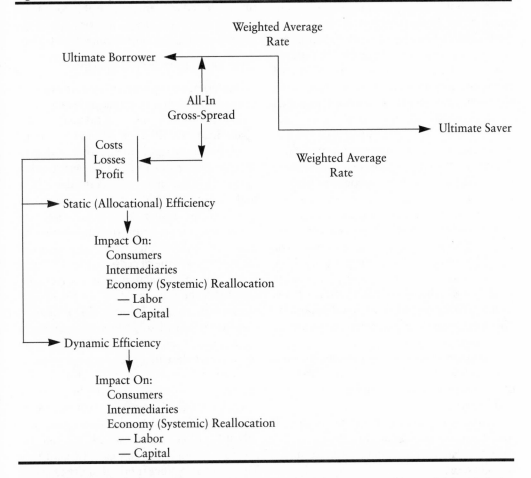

new approaches to contract pricing, passive or index-based portfolio investment techniques, and a range of others.

Successful product and process innovation broaden the menu of financial services available to ultimate borrowers and/or ultimate savers.

A final benchmark related to financial system stability, by which we mean the absence of negative externalities—costs imposed on society at large (the general public) that are attributable to either systemic failure or bailouts of individual institutions dictated by the political process. There are tradeoffs between stability (which is often addressed via regulation) and efficiency, so that the task is to find a socially optimum balance in a globally competitive environment.

Statically and dynamically efficient fi-nancial systems are those which minimize the "intermediation spread" depicted in Figure 2 and at the same time produce a constant stream of innovations which successfully address ever-hanging needs in the financial marketplace. Indeed, one can argue that the most advanced financial systems approach a theoretical, "complete" optimum where there are sufficient financial instruments and markets that, individually and in combination, span the entire state-space of risk and return outcomes. Financial systems that are deemed inefficient or incomplete are characterized by a limited range of financial services and obsolescent financial processes.

Both static and dynamic efficiency are of obvious importance from the standpoint of national and global resource allocation, not only within the financial services industry itself but also as it affects users of financial services. Since financial services can be viewed as "inputs" to the overall production process of a nation, the level of national output and income—as well as its rate of economic growth—are directly affected by the efficiency characteristics of the financial services sector.

A "retarded" financial services industry, in this sense, can represent a major impediment to a nation's overall real economic performance. Such retardation represents a burden on the final consumers of financial services and potentially reduces the level of private and social welfare. It also represents a burden on producers, by raising their cost structures and eroding their competitive performance in domestic and global markets. As such, they distort the patterns of resource allocation in the national economy. Financial system inefficiencies can be traced to a number of factors:

Regulations that prevent financial firms from complete access to alternative sources of funding or the full range of borrowers and issuers.

Taxation imposed at various stages of the financial intermediation process, including securities transfer taxes, transactions taxes, etc.

Lack of competition that reduces incentives to cut intermediation costs and promote innovation.

Lack of market discipline imposed on owners and managers of financial intermediaries, leading to poor risk management and significant losses.

National financial systems that are statically and/or dynamically inefficient tend themselves to be disintermediated. Borrowers or issuers in a position to do so seek foreign markets or offshore markets that offer lower costs or a more suitable range of products. Investors likewise seek markets abroad that offer higher rates of return or improved opportunities to construct more efficient portfolios. Such systems can be termed "uncompetitive" as venues for financial intermediation in the context of global markets—although individual institutions based in them may be able for a time to cross-subsidize foreign activities from abnormal profits earned at home.

The Global Investor's Perspective

International investors hope to benefit from higher after-tax risk-adjusted asset yields attributable to international portfolio diversification (IPD). It is clear from the available empirical evidence that IPD provides greater gains to equity investors than to fixed-income investors, yet the data show that both types of investors suboptimize in terms of the respective foreign shares of portfolios. Exploitation of IPD opportunities is of obvious importance as a determinant of the volume of cross-border financial flows. IPD-related activities themselves contribute to the creation of a unified capital market and to an erosion of IPD potential, even as they lead to greater efficiencies in the global allocation of capital in a process of "creative destruction."

Private individuals as a class of investors may from time to time buy foreign fixed income or equity securities, either abroad in national markets or in the Eurobond market, or domestically through depository receipts (in the case of equities). They may also place funds offshore to evade tax or for other secrecy-driven reasons. Or, they may place funds internationally through collective investment vehicles such as mutual funds and unit trusts.

Institutional investors' primary goal is to "hit the bogey" or "beat the index"—usually an index such as the Morgan Stanley EAFE equity index or the JP Morgan global bond index, but sometimes the performance of a specific competitor—with risk-related dimensions imbedded in constraints on "over allocation." Index-related success or failure often calls forth rapid (positive or negative) response from clients, so the pressure is intense.

For global investors transactions costs are quite important, especially in the light of the slim margins by which it is normally possible for portfolio managers to beat a particular index. In many cases, however, transaction costs are passed on to clients who seldom complain as long as the underlying investment performance is satisfactory. Liquidity is even more important, and institutional investors often do not trade securities in most domestic markets simply because they cannot absorb the large transaction volumes they require. Regulatory

and legal barriers—as well as securities clearance and settlement problems—remain major obstacles to investors, especially in emerging markets.

Derivatives represent an important area for growth on the part of institutional investor activity. This applies to exchange-traded futures for asset-allocation shifts between countries, foreign exchange for-

Figure 3. Financing Alternatives Available to Major Corporations

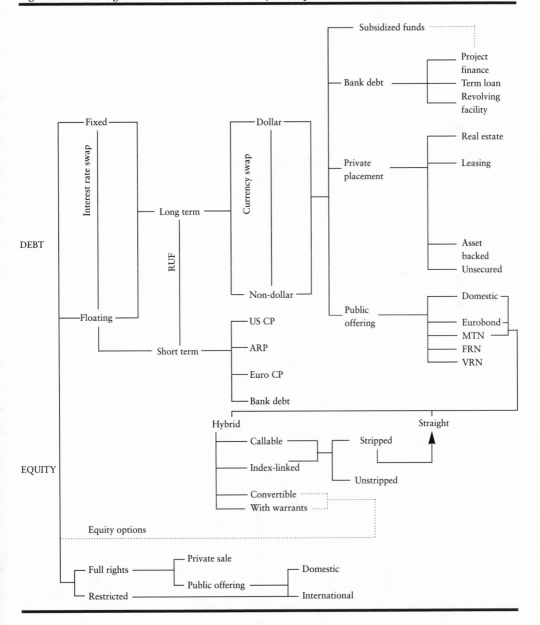

wards (used as "overlays" to the underlying investment portfolios), as well as some OTC options.

The Global Borrower's Perspective

Like the global investor, the modern international corporation has a broad range of options with respect to meeting its financial needs. These are depicted in Figure 3, which can be termed a "cafeteria" encompassing fixed-income securities, equities, equity-linked bonds and convertibles, and a variety of (especially OTC) derivatives. In their search for low cost debt and equity capital, firms will try to avail themselves as much as possible of the full range of financing alternatives, and bankers actively bring opportunities (including creative and competitive solutions) to them for consideration.

Governmental entities, whether national governments, supranational institutions, subnational entities, or parastatals, are equally concerned with globally competitive costs of funding. Many have access to the same broad palette of alternatives that face the international corporation.

Global Financial Market Infrastructure

International borrowers, no less than investors, have an interest in the "seamless" functioning of international debt and equity markets, as well as the markets for derivatives. They are vitally concerned with tapping global investor-tools that are as broad and deep as possible, characterized by sufficient liquidity to make their issues attractive to prospective buyers.

"Seamlessness" in large part depends upon the functioning of the value-chain of securities market services depicted in Figure 4. These comprise the global financial market infrastructure, and encompass:

"Information-gathering and dissemination.

Trading mechanisms, both on-exchange and over-the-counter.

Clearance and settlement, both for payments and for financial instruments and derivatives.

Post-trade custody, safekeeping and reporting on investment performance."

If the objective is to allocate global savings and investment efficiently to their most productive uses, the development of an efficient and resilient financial market infrastructure "utilities" arguably increases the availability, and lowers the cost, of risk capital. This is accomplished by allowing investors a high degree of portfolio diversification and asset-reallocation opportunities as well as significant liquidity. This means that investors will be much more willing to invest in assets that, on their

Figure 4. The Value-Chain of Securities Market Services

Competitors / Services	Euroclear and Cedel	Information Networks	Local Exchanges	Trade Confirmation Systems	Global Custodians
Quotation & Information		○	○		
Trading		○	○		
Trade Conformation	○	○	○	○	
Settlement	○		○		○
Custody	○		○		○

own, would seem risky and illiquid. Operation of the financial market infrastructure is clearly driven by process-related and information-related technologies, as well as characteristics of financial instruments themselves, such as dematerialization.

CONCLUSION

Finance and the macroeconomic forces that drive it are at the center of much that goes on in IB. Competitive viability of firms hinge in part upon the cost of capital and the ability to create and maintain shareholder value. This means tapping into global pools of funds using increasingly "seamless" financial market structures provided with the help of derivatives. It also means understanding how international financial firms, regulators, and markets operate and compete with each other, and what motivates the ultimate savers and their fund managers worldwide, whether banks or investment companies. It also means understanding how to manage the risks involved. Each these papers usefully attacks the issue from a different and interesting angle.

Gunter Dufey

Perspectives on International Business: Theory, Research, and Institutional Arrangements

Discussions of issues about International Finance (IF) always had the advantage of being able to rely on a fairly well ordered framework from the general finance area. There is corporate finance which, by its relatively narrow, but clearly defined objective of maximizing shareholder wealth, provides a clear focus. The issues arising in the management of the financial functions of the firm can then be ordered around the commitment of funds (i.e., **investment**), the acquisition of funds (i.e., **financing**), and the disbursement of funds (i.e., the **dividend** decision). Further, this perspective gave rise to two related areas: investments, i.e., managing the position of the providers of funds, with its core area of portfolio theory, and more recently the creation of "new" securities, usually referred to as derivatives, i.e., swaps, futures, and options, that would lead to the completion of markets for financial assets.

Obviously, the two areas had some overlaps and shared analytical tools, but they were distinct because they each had a clearly established focus.

International Finance benefited from this framework but, as we shall see, it also was constrained by its assumptions. Accordingly, and parallel to the main stream of IB, the issues and discussions in IF focused on the question "what is special when a firm becomes internationally active?" Internationally active was primarily defined as operating in, and therefore having significant exposure to, an environment that was characterized by different monetary and financial systems leading to two major issues: exchange risk, and a myriad of problems and opportunities that stem from operating in markets that are both segmented and integrated partially.

For the discussion at hand, I shall focus on the corporate aspects of IF, since issues in markets and investment can be grouped around that issue and are secondary to the primary focus of financial management and international operations. Note, we omit here deliberately the term "multinational corporation" because it requires a particular intensity of international involvement for the firm which, while it pertains to all issues of international corporate finance and markets, leaves open the relevance of IF for many firms that do confront these problems. Indeed, as has been shown in the literature, the concepts and theories of IF are relevant even for firms that have no direct involvement in international operations through exporting, importing, or investment; exposure to significant foreign competition may make them confront a number of significant IF issues, especially exchange risk and the need to compete with firms that have access to different sources of funds and/or markets that offer financial tools which allow better management of risks.

Reviewing the literature, especially the normative literature or the lack thereof, on corporate IF, it becomes obvious that one of the fundamental conditions of IF management, i.e., operating under partially integrated, partially segmented markets, proves to be an intractable challenge for academicians (and practitioners) seemingly to prevent substantive advances in the field. The reason is quite obvious: if international markets were perfectly integrated, there would be little requirement for a separate area of IF management as virtually most issues would simply converge with issues of financial management in general. Indeed, those who follow the discussion in corporate finance know that virtually all propositions in that field are based upon specific market imperfections and environmental conditions that abstract from perfect markets.[1]

Under such conditions, the foreign exchange rate problem itself becomes an exercise in stochastic analysis, if that much, even though it is difficult to imagine a world of different monies without some manifestations of market segmentation.

Finally, in markets that approach perfect segmentation, IF becomes irrelevant also: the firm simply conducts finance on the motto, "in Rome, do as the Romans do," as the high degree of segmentation prohibits the very fact that makes IF management interesting, namely, arbitraging different market conditions, including taxes, provided by segmented markets as the risk management issues that become possible at that stage.

Within this framework, the two papers presented in this chapter address important issues within the area of IF.

REVIEW OF PAPERS

Among the contributions, Don Lessard provides a most comprehensive overview of corporate IF. The paper starts quite properly with issues of global asset acquisition and deployment. It makes an important contri-

bution by starting to bridge a large gap in the literature between the fields of Finance and Business Strategy. A review of modern finance texts shows that the issue of how and where to look for projects is usually treated in a cursory fashion. Projects simply emerge and it is then up to financial management to choose properly among those that add value.

When businesses become global players, the cost of getting projects in a form where they can be analyzed with the rigorous techniques of modern finance makes it prohibitive to apply a random search. There has to be "method to the madness" and what little we have comes from strategy. Lessard nicely shows the transition from traditional foreign direct investment (FDI) theory to a systematic search for value adding opportunities in a global market. Most valuable here is the identification of the interaction of governments, scientific/technological institutions, and regional dynamics which become important factors in the search for projects that add shareholder value in a world of global competition. The paper also appropriately pays tribute to subtle shifts in the basic operating conditions of IF management: separate markets. Lessard refers to the seemingly contradictory phenomena of increasingly integrated markets among industrialized countries, usually referred to with the term "globalization," increasing turbulence of financial prices for equities, interest rates, and exchange rates that accompany growing market integration and the lack of coordination of macroeconomic policies pursued by individual governments.

Using the standard DCF formula, the reader's attention is focused on the crucial distinction between **real cash flows** vs. possible and tenuous differences in the **cost of capital**. Lessard does a particularly nice job of sorting out the argument of diversification and risk pooling via FDI. However, he deals with the currency preference theories of Aliber and Froot too gently. I believe both theories are fundamentally flawed in understanding of the real issue of acquiring operating assets vs. financial assets in an international context. They are examples of misperceptions that can trap even intelligent researchers.

Appropriately, he addresses the cost of capital controversy highlighting the methodological difficulties of this measure. However, Lessard's final observation deserves more attention. The question is, does the cost of capital advantage as a component of a set of locational factors benefit activities in those countries with a low cost of capital, or can it be used only by those firms domiciled in those countries and hence be used as an ownership advantage [p. 595]? What this means in terms of a truly multinational company with a distributed share ownership and multinational management is an issue that has not been fully explored.

Subsequently, the paper presents Lessard's earlier work on the role of finance in firm-level strategies to gain competitive advantage. Fortunately, the author followed the principle, "if it ain't broke, don't fix it," because the major message was as appropriate then as it is now: while the thesis that finance as a cost of capital advantage is properly subject to dispute, the increasing globalization of competition in markets for real assets as well as financial claims in combination with the lack of macroeconomic policy coordination gives IF a crucial role in managing financial risk.

The call for greater integration of financial management into overall strategic operating decisions at the firm level lays out a broad agenda for future research. This is particularly true for the central area of corporate exchange risk management. In this respect, the author's introduction of the *conversion* vs. *competitive* effects may be another contribution to weed out at least the most egregious sources of confusion, both in the popular as well as the academic discussion on the issue of corporate exchange risk.

One of the most interesting comments in the paper on the subject of corporate exchange rate management is the author's discussion of the fundamental argument for hedging at the corporate level. I also find a small point of disagreement. While the realization of growth options is clearly important, I think the dividend issue is overstated as well as a number of other issues based upon the argument that volatility of cash flows is costly due to the nonlinearity of tax payments, incentive schemes and other real operating variables.

Lessard delineates a number of crucial issues regarding the implementation of hedging transactions with respect to operating exposures of the firm. The presentation should be viewed as a research agenda.

His discussion of "benchmarking," to develop planning systems for multinational corporations (MNCs), systematically takes account of the impact of nominal exchange rate changes, differentiating them from the effect of real exchange rate changes. While not operationalized as yet, this presents an important aspect that the literature on account and control of multinational operations has barely addressed.[2]

Finally, Lessard has not only identified the organizational factors but contributes important insights in his joint work with Nohria that are not normally addressed in finance but which are crucial for the implementation of best practice consistent with policy prescriptions derived from theory.

Using finance as a tool to minimize tax burdens has long been recognized in practice and theory. He indicates a path where considerable work has been done during the past few years [Scholes and Wolfensohn 1991; Weisfelder 1991]. The author provides interesting insights into the firm, gleaned from the emerging literature of contracts and particularly addressing the issue of management incentives within the firm where the structuring of operations, to include financing, can add substantially to shareholder value maximization. The paper opens up rich avenues for further research.

The paper appropriately highlights the *supportive* and *complementary* function of financial management in addition to its traditional control and oversight functions. He ends on a necessarily vague but most interesting speculative note concerning the convergence of modes of corporate governance through financial market integration among Europe, the United States, and Japan.

Overall, Lessard's paper is a further extension of a comprehensive view with interesting insights which offer the profession an interesting agenda yet to be completed. In a broad sense, his work parallels that of corporate finance in general: the most interesting insights are to be gained by drawing on "nonfinancial" phenomena, including behavioral aspects of managers and investors, applying them to the rigor of the field to arrive at interesting and significant new insights that will enhance not only the literature but also the practice of IF management.

This also goes for a number of issues that the author did not address such as: the need for a systematic approach to *capital structure questions* in multinational companies, both at a consolidated level of the parent and of its entities; and *the interaction of the firm with providers of financial services* which range from questions about the listing and trading of equity in multiple markets to relations with providers of fixed income debt, short-term vs. long-term, and the full range of derivative products and global cash management services. Driven by the change in technology, substantial activity goes on that gives rise to research on issues that take the perspective of the firm as well as those that look at the market for financial services. Little has been done on tactical issues such as the choice of "straight" instruments, e.g., debt denomination, forwards and swaps, as compared to "kinky" instruments such as options and option-type instruments.

The second paper of the chapter is written by Vihang Errunza, a frequent and innovative contributor of scholarship on emerging markets. He puts his work into proper perspective by arguing that the importance of the emerging markets in global business adds a new dimension to IF, given the trilateralization of world financial mar-

kets. Consistent with Lessard, Errunza begins with a view of an integrated core of industrialized countries' markets and a number of peripheral segments with each representing an emerging market having its own distinct national characteristics and limited linkage to core markets.

Maybe this point can be refined in the sense that the characteristics of many, if not most, of the emerging markets is linked to the real economies which appear to be much closer than the linkages of the financial system that is typically stifled by government restrictions and institutional rigidities. Indeed, a large part of the significance of these Emerging Markets (EMs), particularly around the Pacific Rim, is that their significance in terms of *real economic activity* for the world economy far exceeds that of their *financial market significance*. In fact, in many of these countries real economic activity would be severely constrained were it not due to the fact that their institutions, both government and private, have access to the financial markets of the industrialized countries, particularly with respect to less regulated "offshore" segments of these markets. The analytical descriptions and characterizations of EMs he provides must be considered competent and complete.

The same can be said of the following section which organizes and reports major findings of the available research on these markets, much of which has been contributed by the author himself.

The discussion of the debt crisis seems to remain somewhat on the surface. In this reviewer's opinion, what is significant of this historic episode is that it has been constrained to a relative limited number of EMs. To wit, it has been almost completely a Latin phenomenon. The Far East has largely escaped that period, with the notable exception of the Philippines (another former colony of Spain). Furthermore, there is a significant number of countries that have virtually escaped the debt crisis because they never qualified for significant private sector debt; while they have difficulties both in terms of financial sector development and *real* sector development, they are truly marginal as far as the world economy is concerned. Unfortunately, most of Africa as well as Bangladesh belong to that group of countries.

The last section on multinational diversification into EMs has probably the most potential. Under what conditions and financial market constraints, "financial factors can supplant real factors" to such an extent that they show up in the empirical analysis of phenomena such as FDI? The relevant sections of Lessard's paper and this section of Errunza's paper provides a potentially fruitful avenue, benefiting not only conceptual clarification but ultimately improving empirical work.

CONCLUSIONS

The papers are very representative of financial perspectives within IB: they point out clearly the difficulties and challenges, also, the potential of this area. The great benefit of the multidisciplinary approach that is particularly representative in Lessard's paper shows the richness of the issues that can be addressed and the interesting insights that can be gained from combining this multi-seasoned approach. However, this will only be possible if we find more people with the rare skill of solid competency in several functional areas.

In the meantime, considerable knowledge will be gained by applying the rigor of traditional financial analysis to companies operating in an international environment.

Errunza tells us that this is a complex world. There are a number of phenomena that warrant study in and by themselves which will provide important insight into both finance and IB generally.

NOTES

1. The famous Miller-Modigliani proposition is only one, although a seminal manifestation of the irrelevancy of corporate finance.

2. For an exception to this see Laurent L. Jacque's, *Control in Hyperinflationary Environments*.

REFERENCES

Agarwal, Amer and K. Tandon. 1990. Stock market anomalies: The international evidence. Mimeo.

Aggarwal, R. 1991. The IPO puzzle: Evidence from Brazil. Mimeo.

Agmon, Tamir and Donald Lessard. 1977. Investor recognition of corporate international diversification. *Journal of Finance*, September:1049–1055.

Aliber, Robert Z. 1970. A theory of direct foreign investment. In C. P. Kindleberger, editor, *The International Corporation: A Symposium*. Cambridge, MA: MIT Press.

Arthur Andersen and Co. 1989. European capital markets: A strategic forecast. London: Economist Publications.

Baldwin, Carliss. 1986. The capital factor: The impact of home and host countries on the global corporation's cost of capital. In M. E. Porter, editor, *Competition in Global Industries*. Boston, MA: Harvard Business School Press.

Baldwin, Carliss and Kim Clark. 1992. Capabilities and capital investment: New perspectives on capital budgeting. *Journal of Applied Corporate Finance*, 52 (Summer):67–82.

Bartlett, Christopher and Sumantra Ghoshal. 1989. *Managing across borders: The transnational solution*. Boston, MA: Harvard Business School Press.

Bernstein, Peter L. 1992. Are financial markets the problem or the solution? A reply to Michael Porter. *Journal of Applied Corporate Finance*, 5(Summer):17–22.

Bhagwati, Jagdish N. 1982. Directly unproductive profit-seeking activities. *Journal of Political Economy*, 90(October):988–1002.

Buckley, Peter and Mark Casson. 1976. *The future of the multinational enterprise*. New York: Holmes and Meier.

Caves, Richard E. 1982. *Multinational enterprise and economic analysis. Cambridge Surveys of Economic Literature*. Cambridge: Cambridge University Press.

Cody, B. 1990. Reducing the costs and risks of trading foreign exchange. Federal Reserve Bank of Philadelphia. *Business Review*, November/December:13–23.

Cohen, Benjamin I. 1972. Foreign investment by U.S. firms as a way of reducing risk. Discussion paper no. 151. Economic Growth Center, Yale University.

Dornbusch, Rudiger. 1988. Our LDC debts. Martin Feldstein, editor. Chicago: University of Chicago Press.

Dufey, Gunter. 1992. Company debt vs. corporate debt: distinguishing between liquidity and solvency problems. In R. Grosse, editor, *Private Sector Solutions to the Latin American Debt Problem*. Miami: North-South Center, University of Miami.

Dufey, Gunter and S. Srinivasulu. 1984. The case for corporate management exchange risk. *Financial Management*, (Winter):54–62.

Dunning, John H. 1973. The determinants of international production. *Oxford Economic Papers*, 25(November):289–336.

Eaker, M., D. Grant and N. Woodard. 1991. International diversification and hedging: A Japanese and U.S. perspective. *Journal of Economics and Business*, November:363–574.

Eaton, Jonathan and Mark Gersovitz. 1981. Debt with potential repudiation: Theoretical and empirical analysis. *Review of Economic Studies*, 48(April): 289309.

Errunza, Vihang R. 1991. Pricing of national index funds. *Review of Quantitative Finance and Accounting*, 1(1):91–100.

Errunza, Vihang R. 1983. Emerging markets—a new opportunity for improving global portfolio performance. *Financial Analysts Journal*, September/October:51–58.

Errunza, Vihang R. 1979. Efficiency and the programs to develop capital markets—a Brazilian experience. *Journal of Banking and Finance*, December:355–382.

Errunza, Vihang R. and E. Losq. 1989. Capital flow controls, international asset pricing and investors' welfare: A multi country framework. *Journal of Finance*, September:1025–1037.

Errunza, Vihang R. and E. Losq. 1987. How risky are emerging markets?—Myths and perceptions vs. theory and evidence. *Journal of Portfolio Management*, Fall:62–67.

Errunza, Vihang R. and E. Losq. 1985a. The behavior of stock prices on LDC markets *Journal of Banking and Finance*, 5:561–575.

Errunza, Vihang R. and E. Losq. 1985b. International asset pricing under mild segmentation: theory and test. *Journal of Finance*, March:105–124.

Errunza, Vihang R., E. Losq and P. Padmanabhan. 1992. Tests of integration, mild segmentation and segmentation hypotheses. *Journal of Banking and Finance*, 16:949–972.

Errunza, Vihang R. and A. Moreau. 1989. Debt for equity swaps under a rational expectations equilibrium. *Journal of Finance*, July:663–680.

Errunza, Vihang R. and P. Padmanabhan. 1992. Role of foreign portfolio investments: toward resolution of the Latin American debt problem. In R. Grosse, editor, *Private Sector Solutions to the Latin American Debt Problem*. Miami: North-South Center, University of Miami.

Errunza, Vihang R. and B. Rosenberg. 1982. Investment risk in developed and less-developed countries. *Journal of Financial and Quantitative Analysis*, December:741–762.

Errunza, Vihang R. and L. Senbet. 1981. The effects of international operations on the market value of the firm: Theory and evidence. *Journal of Finance*, May:401–417.

Eun, C. and S. Janakiramanan. 1986. A model of international asset pricing with a constraint on foreign equity ownership. *Journal of Finance*, 41:897–914.

Eun, C. and B. G. Resnick. 1991. International diversification of investment portfolios: U.S. and Japanese perspectives. Working paper. University of Maryland, July.

Fischer, Klaus and A. Palasvirta. 1991. Corporate governance and market structure. Working Paper No. 91–54. Laval University, Quebec, Canada.

French, Kenneth and James Poterba. 1989. Are Japanese stock prices too high? Cambridge, MA: NBER.

Froot, Kenneth A. 1990. Multinational corporations, exchange rates and direct investment. In W. Branson, J. Frenkel and M. Goldstein, editors, *International Policy Coordination and Exchange Rate Determination*. Chicago: University of Chicago Press.

Froot, Kenneth A. 1989. Buybacks, exit bonds, and the optimality of debt and liquidity relief. *International Economic Review*, 30 (January): 49–70.

Froot, Kenneth A., David S. Scharfstein and Jeremy Stein. 1993. Risk management: coordinating corporate investment and financing policies. *Journal of Finance,* 48(December): 1629–58.

Giovannini, Alberto. 1989. Capital taxation. *Journal of Economic Policy,* (October): 345386.

Goldsmith, Raymond W. 1969. Financial structure and development. New Haven, CT: Yale University Press.

Greene, Jeffrey and D. Villanueva. 1991. Private investment in developing countries: An empirical analysis. International Monetary Fund Staff Papers, March, 38(1): 33–58.

Group of Thirty. 1989. Clearance and settlement systems in the world's securities markets. New York: Group of Thirty.

Herring, Richard. 1985. Managing international risk. Cambridge, England: Cambridge University Press.

Hoshi, Takeo, Anil Kashyap and David Scharfstein. 1989. Corporate structure, liquidity and investment: Evidence from Japanese industrial groups. *Quarterly Journal of Economics,* 56(February):33–60.

Huey, John, "Eisner Explains Everything," *Fortune,* April 17, 1995, 45–68.

Hymer, Stephen. 1960,1976. The international operations of national firms. Cambridge, MA: MIT Press.

Jacquillat, Bertrand and B. Solnik. 1978. Multinationals are poor tools for diversification. *Journal of Portfolio Management,* Winter:8–12.

Jorion, P. 1987. Why buy international bonds. *International Management Review,* Sept./Oct:19–28.

Kaplanis, E. and S. M. Schaefer. 1991. Exchange risk and international diversification in bond and equity portfolios. *Journal of Economics and Business,* November:287–307.

Kester, W. Carl. 1992. Governance, contracting, and investment horizons: A look at Germany and Japan. *Journal of Applied Corporate Finance,* 5(2):83–98.

Kester, W. Carl. 1991. Japanese takeovers: The global contest for corporate control. Boston, MA: Harvard Business School Press.

Kester, W. Carl and Timothy Luehrman. 1989.

Are we feeling competitive yet? The exchange rate gambit. *Sloan Management Review,* 30(2): 19–28.

Kester, W. Carl and Timothy Luehrman. 1989. Real interest rates and the cost of capital: A comparison of the United States and Japan. *Japan and the World Economy,* 1.

Kindleberger, Charles P. 1969. American business abroad. New Haven: Yale University Press.

Kogut, Bruce. 1991. Country capabilities and the permeability of borders. *Strategic Management Journal,* 12(Summer):33–47.

Kogut, Bruce. 1985a. Designing global strategies: Comparative and competitive value-added chains. *Sloan Management Review,* 26(Summer):15–28.

Kogut, Bruce. 1985b. Designing global strategies: Profiting from operational flexibility. *Sloan Management Review,* 27(Fall): 27–38.

Kogut, Bruce and Nalin Kulatilaka. 1994. Operational flexibility, global manufacturing, and the option value of a multinational network. *Management Science,* 40(1): 123–139.

Krugman, Paul. 1991. Geography and trade. Cambridge: MIT Press.

Krugman, Paul. 1988. Market-based debt reduction schemes. Working Paper 2587, Cambridge, MA: National Bureau of Economic Research.

Leff, N. 1976. Capital markets in the less developed countries: The group principle. In R. McKinnon, editor, *Money and Finance in Economic Growth and Development.* NY: Marcel Dekker Inc., 97–122.

Lessard, Donald. 1991. Corporate finance in the 1990s: Implications of a changing competitive and financial context.

Lessard, Donald. 1989. Country risk and the structure of international financial intermediation. In C. C. Stone, editor, *Financial Risk: Theory, Evidence, and Implications.* Norwell, MA: Kluwer Academic Publishers.

Lessard, Donald. 1986. Finance and global competition: Exploiting financial scope and coping with volatile exchange rates. In Michael Porter, editor, *Competition in Global Industries,* Boston: Harvard Business School Press.

Lessard, Donald. 1979. Transfer prices, taxes, and financial markets: implications of international financial transfers within the multi-national corporation. In Robert. G. Hawkins, editor, *The Economic Effects of Multinational Corporations*. Greenwich, CT: JAB Press.

Lessard, Donald. 1973. International portfolio diversification: A multivariate analysis for a group of Latin American countries. *Journal of Finance*, 28(June):619–633.

Lessard, Donald and John Williamson. 1985. Financial intermediation beyond the debt crisis. Washington, DC: Institute for International Economics.

Lessard, Donald and Nitin Nohria. 1989. Rediscovering functions in the MNC: The role of expertise in firms' responses to shifting exchange rates. In C. Bartlett, Y. Doz and G. Hedlund, editors, *Managing the Global Firm*. London: Routledge.

Lessard, Donald and Srilata Zaheer. 1992. Distributed knowledge and strategic responsiveness—study of corporate responses to volatile exchange rates. Unpublished working paper, MIT International Financial Services Research Center, December.

Levich, Richard M. 1988. Financial innovation in international financial markets. In M. Feldstein, editor, *The United States in the World Economy*. Chicago: University of Chicago Press.

Levich, Richard M. and Ingo Walter. 1988. The regulation of global financial markets. In T. Noyelle, editor, *New York's Financial Markets*. Boulder, Colorado: Westview Press.

Levy, Haim and Z. Lerman. 1988. The benefits of international diversification in bonds. *Financial Analysts Journal*, 44(5):56–64.

Levy, Haim and Marshall Sarnat. 1970. International diversification of investment portfolios. *American Economic Review*, 60:4 668–675.

Luis, R. 1992. Privatization, the foreign debt and capital market development in Latin America. In R. Grosse, editor, *Private Sector Solutions to the Latin American Debt Problem*. Miami: North-South Center, University of Miami.

McCauley, Robert N. and Steven A. Zimmer. 1989. Explaining international cost of capital differences. *Federal Reserve Board of New York Quarterly Review*, Summer:7–28.

McKinnon, Ronald. 1973. Money and capital in economic development. Washington, DC: The Brookings Institution.

Mello, Antonio, John Parsons and Alexander Triantis. 1993. An integrated model of multinational flexibility and financial hedging. Unpublished working paper, Baruch College, CUNY (January).

Moran, Theodore. 1974. Multinational corporations and the politics of dependence: Copper in Chile. Princeton, NJ: Princeton University Press.

Muralhidar, Arun. 1992. Essays in international finance. Unpublished Ph.D. dissertation, MIT.

Niarchos, N. 1972. The stock market in Greece. In G. Szegö and K. Shell, editors, *Symposium on Mathematical Methods in Investment and Finance*. Amsterdam: North-Holland Publishing Co.

Office of Technology Assessment. 1990. Trading Around the Clock: Global Securities Markets and Information Technology. Washington: OTA.

Padmanabhan, P. 1992. Investment barriers and international asset pricing. *Review of Quantitative Finance and Accounting*, 2:299–319.

Piore, Michael and Charles Sabel. 1984. The second industrial divide: Possibilities for prosperity. New York: Basic Books.

Porter, Michael E. 1992. Capital choices: Changing the way America invests in industry. Washington: Harvard Business School and Council on Competitiveness.(summarized in article of same title in *Journal of Applied Corporate Finance* 5 2 (Summer): 4–17.)

Porter, Michael E. 1990. The competitive advantage of nations. New York: The Free Press.

Porter, Michael E. 1986. Competition in global industries. Boston, MA: Harvard Business School Press.

Poynter, Thomas A. 1986. Managing government intervention: A strategy for defending the subsidiary. *Columbia Journal of World Business,* Winter: 55–65.

Ragazzi, Giorgio. 1973. Theories of direct foreign investment. *IMF Staff Papers*, 20(July): 471–498.

Robinson, Richard D. 1969. Ownership across

national frontiers. *Industrial Management Review.* Fall: 41–62.

Rugman, Alan. 1979. *International diversification and the multinational firm.* Lexington, MA: Lexington.

Sagari, Silvia B. 1986. The financial services industry: An international perspective. Doctoral dissertation completed at the Graduate School of Business Administration, New York University.

Saunders, A. and Ingo Walter. 1988. Competitive performance regulation and trade in banking services. In H.J. Vosgerau, editor, *New Institutional Arrangements for the World Economy.* Berlin: Springer-Verlag.

Senbet, L. 1992. Enterprise governance and growth: Notes on the theory of the firm in less developed capital markets. In K.P. Fischer and G.J. Papaioannou, editors, *Business Finance in Less Developed Capital Markets.* New York: Greenwood Press.

Sharma, J. and R. Kennedy. 1977. A comparative analysis of stock price behavior on the Bombay, London and New York Stock Exchanges. *Journal of Financial and Quantitative Analysis,* September:391–414.

Shaw, Edward. 1973. *Financial deepening in economic development.* New York: Oxford University Press.

Smith, Roy C. and Ingo Walter. 1991. Reconfiguration of global securities markets in the 1990s. In Richard O'Brien, editor, *Essays in Honor of Robert Marjolin: The 1990 Amex Bank Review Awards.* Cambridge: Cambridge University Press.

Smith, Roy C. and Ingo Walter. 1990. *Global financial services.* New York: Harper and Row.

Stopford, John and Susan Strange. 1991. *Rival states, rival firms.* Cambridge, U.K.: Cambridge University Press.

Stulz, R. M. 1981. On the effects of barriers to international investment. *Journal of Finance,* 36:923–934.

Stulz, R. M. and C. W. Smith. 1985. The determinants of firms' hedging policies. *Journal of Financial and Quantitative Analysis,* 20(4): 391–406.

Thomadakis, S. 1992. Enterprise governance and growth: Notes on the theory of the firm in less developed countries. In K. P. Fischer and G. J. Papaioannou, editors, *Business Finance in Less Developed Capital Markets.* Westport, Conn.: Greenwood Press.

Thurow, Lester C. 1992. *Head to head: The coming economic battle among Japan, Europe, and America.* New York: William Morrow.

Tseung, W. and R. Corker. 1991. Liberalization, money demand and monetary policy in Asian countries. *IMF Survey,* August 20:8.

Vernon, Raymond. 1971. *Sovereignty at Bay: The multinational spread of US enterprises.* New York: Basic Books.

Vernon, Raymond. 1966. International investment and international trade in the product cycle. *Quarterly Journal of Economics,* 80(May):190–207.

Walter, Ingo. 1991. European financial integration and its impact on the United States. In Claude Barfield, editor, *The European Community and the United States.* Washington, D.C.: American Enterprise Institute.

Walter, Ingo and R. C. Smith. 1990. *Investment banking in Europe: Restructuring for the 1990s.* Oxford and New York: Basil Blackwell.

Wilkins, Mira. 1988. The free-standing company, 1870–1914: An important type of British foreign direct investment. *The Economic History Review,* XLI(2):259–282.

Yamamura, Kozo. 1986. Caveat emptor: The industrial policy of Japan. In P. R. Krugman, editor, *Strategic Trade Policy and the New International Economics.* Cambridge: MIT Press.

11

Panel: Theory and Research Implications for International Business

CHAIR'S COMMENTS

As a community of scholars with a common interest in the conceptual domain known as international business, we have rarely sat down together to discuss what it is that we collectively seek to understand and explain. As noted in the opening chapter to this book, there have only been two formal conferences prior to the one held at the University of South Carolina in 1992. Both conferences were held at the Graduate School of Business, Indiana University, took place in 1957 and 1963, and focused almost exclusively on international business educational issues.

The primary impetus for the development of IB as a field of inquiry has come from the Academy of International Business (AIB). Initially launched as the Association for Education in International Business in 1958, its name made clear its widely accepted purpose. When renamed the Academy of International Business in 1972, its purpose became somewhat more complex as pointed out by Hawkins in his presidential address [1984]. He opined that the founders of the AIB shared three general objectives for the IB field. The first involved the teaching of international subject matter and the injection of international content into the business school curriculum. The second involved research that contributes to a widely-shared, common body of knowledge for those who consider IB their field.

The third, building on the first two, is to influence behavior and events through research, conceptualization, and teaching.

By most standards, the first objective has been met with singular success. An increasing number of schools of business are implementing plans aimed at internationalizing their curricula and their faculties. The second objective also has been met with success. However, as Hawkins noted, "international business [as inquiry] is a potpourri of functional fields, methodologies, descriptions, occasional theorizing and conceptualizing, which does not yet come together into a coherent package of 'received wisdom'" [1984, p. 15]. This, of course, has implications for the achievement of the third objective.

The lack of coherence, I believe, is partly attributable to the conspicuous absence of discourse over what constitutes the domain of IB inquiry, the ontological and epistemological assumptions that underpin IB inquiry, the direction(s) in which this inquiry is taking us, and what constitutes its generalized and certified body of knowledge. While most of us recognize and accept the fact that much of IB inquiry is based on the theory construction and research methodologies of the social sciences and the business disciplines, I am not so sure that we collectively understand and agree on the implications that their ontological and epistemological assumptions have for our inquiry.

This latter point is, perhaps, most evident in our apparent lack of discourse regarding the philosophy of science revolution occurring within these fields and that is whirling about us. Yet we should be concerned enough to contribute to this debate. Major challenges are emerging in the social sciences, and these challenges are being echoed in the business disciplines (e.g., postmodernism, deconstructionism, the erosion of logical positivism, the growing acceptance of holism). As a result of such challenges, the carefully erected boundaries demarking the social sciences and the business disciplines into sub-fields are being questioned. But these challenges and the changes they are bringing about, such as the fundamental, undermining effect they are having on the social sciences and the business disciplines are to be welcomed. If not now, they will eventually force us to explore more fully what it is we seek to understand and explain, the assumptions we make about reality, and the methodologies we use to verify what we know. For example, Richard Swedberg [1990] has called for more interaction and communication between economists and sociologists, and the reformulation of the boundaries that separate them—a call that is reflected in several of the papers presented in this book.

Importantly, these changes are harbingers of changes that are bound to affect the IB field. However, without a clear, enunciated understanding of what it is we do as IB scholars, the assumptions we make about reality, the phenomena and relationships we set out to study, and the methods and techniques we use when seeking truth (knowledge), IB inquiry will remain not only subservient to the social sciences and the business disciplines, but also subject to their whimsy.

It is also evident in our lack of discourse concerning the domain of IB, and the phenomena and relationships we are interested in studying within this domain. For example, Root [1969] defined IB inquiry as the study of *cross-national interactions* that create dynamic linkages among the elements comprising the international enterprise (intra-enterprise interactions) and between the enterprise as a whole and its multinational environmental systems (extra-enterprise interactions). The following year, Nehrt, Truitt, and Wright [1970] defined IB research as the study of firm-level business activity that crosses national boundaries or is conducted in locations other than the firm's home country. While both firm-level definitions of the domain of IB inquiry continue to be conspicuously dominant in the IB extant literature, and support the notion that IB inquiry is tolerant of multiple definitions, neither definition has been challenged until recently (see Toyne [1989] and the papers by Boddewyn and Toyne presented in the section of this book dealing with the domain of IB inquiry). Acceptance without discourse does not necessarily imply understanding. To the contrary, acceptance without discourse implies blind tolerance, even ignorance. For instance, Root concluded that IB inquiry is *inclusive* (i.e., includes the various branches of the social sciences), does not fall within any traditional field of business study, and is *multidisciplinary*; a form of inquiry that is not supported within schools of business because of the emphasis placed on functional specialization. Nehrt, Truitt, and Wright, on the other hand, concluded that IB inquiry is *exclusive*, falls within the traditional fields of business study, and is *uni-disciplinary*; the form of inquiry emphasized and supported by functional specialization.

Thus the purpose of this panel was not simply to continue the dialogue started with a discussion of the domain of IB inquiry. More importantly, it was hoped that this panel would stimulate further dialogue regarding recent developments in the social sciences and the business disciplines, and to investigate the implications these developments have for IB inquiry. To the extent that we are dependent on the ontological and epistemological assumptions, paradigms, theories, and constructs of the social sciences and the business disciplines, we must be sensitive to the philosophy of science debate that is occurring in these fields, and to the implications that this debate has for our work. But our sensitivity and our ability to respond appropriately is predicated on, and shaped by, what we collectively and individually perceive as constituting IB inquiry and its contributions to the body of knowledge dealing with business in general.

In preparation for the panel discussion reported here, the four panel members were asked to prepare "position" papers in response to the following brief statement and question to be resolved:

> Unlike the business disciplines, such as marketing and business policy/strategic management, IB scholars have neither attempted to define the dimensions and

boundaries of their field, nor collectively authored a statement helpful in identifying and prioritizing the opportunities that exist for theory-building, theory-testing, and research in the field that would help both students and practitioners better understand the purpose of this approach to organizational understanding. *The question to be resolved follows*: Can, or should, IB develop into a viable and distinct field of inquiry given its lack of a unifying definition and its current and foreseeable dependency on the paradigms, theories and constructs of economics, political science, sociology, and the business disciplines?

Although seeking to stimulate discourse, I hasten to note that I personally do not expect or seek consensus regarding a single view, a single paradigm for IB inquiry. To the contrary, the papers presented in this book unequivocally demonstrate that IB inquiry cannot be easily reduced to a single view, a single paradigm, a single theory. It involves multiple ontological and epistemological assumptions, is multi-level in terms of phenomena, and serves the knowledge needs of many audiences. However, I do believe that it is possible to identify what it is that is distinctive about what we seek to understand and explain.

The members of the panel were intentionally selected to elicit the greatest possible discussion, in terms of orientation and the fundamental assumptions underpinning our inquiry. The four panelists are well known and have made significant and important contributions to our better understanding of international business. Jack Behrman is perhaps best known for his contributions to our understanding of the interface between international business and governments, Jean Boddewyn for his many contributions to our understanding of international management and marketing, Rabi Bhagat for his contributions to our understanding of organization behavior within an international context, and Jean-François Hennart for his contributions to our understanding of the economic behavior of international business organizations.

Also, those members of the audience who chose to participate in the discussion brought to the discourse additional orientations and opinions.

The responses of the panelists to the statement and the question to be resolved are presented in the following papers. The first paper by Behrman examines the implications for IB inquiry of treating international business as a holistic phenomenon from a policy perspective. The second paper by Boddewyn deals with the dual issues of the distinctiveness of IB inquiry and our ability to develop a single, unifying theory of IB. The third paper by Hennart takes the position that IB inquiry is an established and distinct field, and has made original theoretical contributions. The fourth paper by Bhagat deals with the tension that exists between the various business disciplines and argues that while uni-disciplinary and multi-disciplinary IB research should not be neglected, an inter-disciplinary approach to the study of IB phenomena and their inter-relatedness is required.

As such, the four papers provide interesting, yet diverse responses to the question to be resolved. Collectively, they present an overarching summation of the issues that need to be addressed. Behrman's paper underscores the need for further discourse on the purpose of IB inquiry, and the value of the knowledge gained from such inquiry. Boddewyn's paper highlights the need for clarification concerning the levels of analysis, their interconnectedness, and the core constructs underpinning IB inquiry. Bhagat's paper underscores the need for a clearer understanding of the ontological and epistemological tensions, issues and problems inherent in interdisciplinary inquiry. Hennart's paper highlights the fact that IB inquiry is capable of developing theory that contributes uniquely to the body of knowledge concerned with business. Several of the issues raised in these papers were elaborated on during the one-hour panel discussion that appears immediately following the four papers.

Perspectives on International Business: Theory, Research, and Institutional Arrangements
Jack N. Behrman

Starting from the imperatives set forth by Brian Toynes's domain paper in this volume that any international business (IB) theory must reflect the *purpose* of the IB discipline and that this in turn must be seen as a *holistic, systemic* approach to business and its total environment, I wish to explore where this leads in terms of IB theory, research, and institutional structure.

I begin from the proposition that IB is a *policy* discipline and, therefore, that theory and research should enlighten policy—as formulated and implemented either by companies or by governments, labor, politicians, consumers, and other involved publics or stakeholders. Theory for the sake of refin-

ing methodologies is useful, but it is *not* a distinct part of IB. International business should obtain its methodologies from anywhere that appropriate processes of logic, investigation, measurement, validation, and presentation are being developed and refined. These can be borrowed and adapted from virtually *any* discipline, since IB is *holistic*.

Being holistic, the IB discipline should encompass *all* that is relevant to business operating in its various arenas—*other than purely in the home country and unrelated to international transactions*. The arena excluded is very small—being only that portion of GDP that is not even indirectly affected by imports, exports, technology transfers across borders, international financial transactions, acts of foreign governments, or whatever. It is hard to think of any such, but there must be some in the mountains of Appalachia and the Rockies or the backwaters of Charleston, Savannah, or New Orleans.

Given its *holistic* nature, IB will be involved in negotiations with all of the arenas affecting it through a decision-making role—formal or informal. The major arenas are depicted in Table 1, showing that the extent and nature of each involvement is similar—i.e., sometimes wholly within that arena, or across two or more such arenas, or within several simultaneously (which often affects the perception of roles in others, even if there is little cross-arena activity).

This matrix shows that IB is involved simultaneously in a wide variety of situations and environments. This condition itself is enough to force the question, what is the *purpose* of IB, and, therefore, of any theory. Being holistic, IB must take its purpose also from that of the whole system—it cannot have a purpose of its own. To the extent that its purpose is differentiated from that of the whole, it is merely a subset, and the subset must satisfy its *role* in advancing the purposes of the whole.

IB's purpose, therefore, is derived from the objectives of the world order, as presently being shaped or sought. If you observe carefully what governments are concerned with in their domestic and international affairs, the objectives are seen as multiple, complex, and requiring numerous trade-offs which, in turn, as Boddewyn insists in chapter 2, require negotiation. It is not only in a "free-market" or "at arm's length" that these negotiations take place and they certainly are *not* conducted under the restrictive assumptions of economists or of *any* of the IB theories supposedly widely accepted.

When IB theorists limit themselves to examining firm decisions in the absence of considerations of the various arenas in which they operate, they make themselves virtually irrelevant to policy problems. I have said enough about this situation elsewhere [Grosse and Behrman 1992], so I will not repeat it here, despite the fact that I know that the "investment of careers" in pursuit of the goal of (myopically conceived) efficiency will not be given up without a fierce battle. (Thomas Kuhn noted years ago this tunnel-vision tenacity in the struggle over shifting scientific paradigms.) But the world will not progress far in solutions to the "economic" goals of eliminating *poverty, disease, squalor, and ignorance* until these problems are brought to the fore as targets for all economic activity, including those of IB.

The *purpose* of IB relations and transactions are seen more clearly by examination of the "criteria of acceptability" voiced or inferred in the many negotiations among governments and corporations, and be-

Table 1. Arenas of Business

Global	Inter-governmental (UN, et al.)		
Regional	Inter-*,	Intra-#	Multi-@
Nation-State	Inter-,	Intra-,	Multi-,
Cultural	Inter-,	Intra-,	Multi-,
Provincial	Inter-,	Intra-,	Multi-,
Municipal	Inter-,	Intra-,	Multi-,
Sectoral	Inter-,	Intra-,	Multi-,
Corporate	Inter-,	Intra-,	Multi-,
Community	Inter-,	Intra-,	Multi-,
Markets	Global	Regional	National	Local

Note: * = across borders; # = within borders; @ = within several borders.

tween governments and business—internationally, multidomestically, and locally. I started studying these criteria many years ago and have continued to add to and refine them as the world moved from a few powerful states to participation in decision making by virtually all nations, and as the problems seemed to multiply *with* and *from* progress, rather than being more readily resolved by it. These criteria are noted in Table 2, with a brief explanation.

With the formation of nation-states and before, with the collection of families into tribes and tribal-nations, the primary concern of mankind has been with *security*—to permit perpetuation of the genetic materials which form other humans in their own image. This will remain the primary objective as long as there is a threat to existence of *any* given entity. This concern with security alters significantly what business is *permitted* and *asked* to do with any of the above arenas—you need not focus only on export and technology controls to understand this impact.

Progress has been taken over by the economists to such an extent that its characterization has been identified with GNP (now GDP—a wholly mercantilist concept), and its delineation made quantitative. This is such a travesty that it hardly merits comment were it not for the fact that IB academics seem to "buy into" this restrictive concept of the nature of man and his values. "Homo oeconomicus" was always an ab-

straction—explicitly so recognized by Marshall and clearly understood by Adam Smith in his prior *Theory of Moral Sentiments*. Further, it has been constrained by concepts of "efficiency"—so limited to "inputs and outputs" that can be measured as to make it virtually useless in guiding productivity efforts or in determining the *effectiveness* of an organization. The *coup de grace* is given by the fact that 200 years of effort at increasing efficiency has not solved any of the world's problems, though production has multiplied.

The neoclassical (capitalist) view of progress as merely greater production was accepted fully by the socialists, who corrupted it to the point of break-down. The Western corruption has been focused on the production organization and its profit-goal, rather than service to the consumer and alleviation of the problems of disease, squalor, ignorance, and poverty. Pursuit of the explanation of "firm behavior" assumes that the firm *knows how to behave* so that it is a socially acceptable institution. This is clearly not the case—reflected in our lack of understanding of the *purpose* of business itself in a society that is holistic.

A major objective of any social entity is to achieve the objectives of justice and *equity* —fairness within the system (once secure)— otherwise why not simply let the "chips fall where they may" and "the buyer beware?" Concepts of equality have been eliminated from economic analysis, since any adjust-

Table 2. Business Involvement in Nation-State Objectives

SECURITY	Independence; selective interdependence
PROGRESS	Production; efficiency; innovation
EQUITY	Justice; distribution of benefits in employment, technology, and balance of payments
PARTICIPATION	Cooperative decision-making; joint ventures; alliances
CREATIVITY	Invention; R&D; education
STABILITY	Order; guided change; business-government cooperation
AUTONOMY	Identity; inviolability
ENVIRONMENT	Future; ecological protection
HUMAN DIGNITY	Non-discrimination; compassion
RESPONSIBILITY	Ethical behavior: social and individual

ment toward it is considered detrimental to efficiency—an idea so ludicrous as to warrant scant comment were it not advanced by supposed experts. Some inquiring OB researchers using socio-psychological methods of observation have concluded that perceived equity in fact enhances efficiency. It behooves those interested in productivity to study the more "equitable" communitarian societies which are highly competitive today (see Lodge [1987]).

Participation is evident in the desire of virtually every group within and across the arenas noted to have a role in decision making. Business executives have been slow in recognizing the potential for productivity in participatory decision making, and it was little urged by academicians, though the evidence has been strong for decades. This change will seriously affect the behavior of corporations and should be the subject of intensive study.

Creativity is the current buzzword in the search for "executives of the future"; it has long been stated in the West that "a person is not really human unless they are creative"—otherwise, they are a sophisticated machine! How business and managers can become more creative—and not just in production or marketing—is a critical issue for the future and should not be left to those outside the discipline.

Stability is difficult to characterize in a dynamic setting, but it is better exemplified by a "balanced aquarium" in which there is movement and change that maintains vitality than by the mechanical clock which moves but atrophies. When one adds growth of the entire system, stability is even more difficult to characterize. It is essentially the condition of not being "blown away" by events—as in the break-up of the Soviet Union. Stability is a desired condition—not always permitted to mankind, or alternatively, not always generated by it.

Autonomy is criterion that will rise sharply to the fore in the coming years, for it is tied to the concept of "identity," and the global changes that are sweeping the continents are challenging people's concepts of

themselves—viz., China, Arabia, Yugoslavia, the Commonwealth of Independent Soviets, Japan, India, Africa, Latin America, Europe, and the United States. The effort to retain some identity is seen in the requirements for local ownership, joint ventures, use of local language, adherence to customs, etc.—all of which impinge on business behavior, especially cross-culturally.

The growing global concern for the *environment* is a recognition that mankind may not have a future without adequate attention being paid to its preservation. This is the most "holistic" of the "criteria of acceptability" for a new world order, requiring nation-state, intergovernmental, and transnational corporation (TNC) cooperation from global to local levels.

Human dignity has been observed more in declarations of intent than in behavior, but it is critical in any acceptable negotiation on the problems of the world. Corporate behavior has not always honored this objective, and much research could be directed toward it and still be within the IB domain.

Finally, the sleeper among the criteria of acceptability is the gradually emerging view that a return to concepts of "individual and social *responsibility*" are necessary to remove the heavy burdens on society of everexpanding "entitlements." Since business is being pressed to provide and pay for health maintenance and insurance (plus the cures for drug and alcohol abuse, mental disorders, and stress = disease), unemployment relief (= poverty), education and training (= ignorance), and often housing (= squalor)—it is evident that business is increasingly being asked to address the basic economic needs directly.

To achieve these goals requires that we do so under a system of *ethics and values* that is socially acceptable and enforced mainly by self-regulation, or self-discipline. IB cannot get away with the view that all relevant decisions are made in a market, when the entire environment of progress and change requires continuing trade-offs among multiple objectives and multiple players in nonmarket relationships.

These comments lead research into a wide range of topics—examples of which are given in Table 3. I have excluded the typical "firm-based" research since this is so widely engaged by IB academics; but even this must be seen and interpreted with a much wider lens than before if the discipline is to be *holistic*, *systemic*, and *relevant* to policy for all involved decision makers. Most of the subjects in Table 3 are seldom pursued in IB journals or other professional journals which permit an occasional IB article.

The lesson for *theory* from the above comments is that a theory encompassing IB as a *holistic* discipline is not presently feasible. The reason is that each of the "criteria of acceptability" of a world order—i.e., the *purposes* which business is to pursue—arise out of *different* academic disciplines. Not only is theory disputed in each of these, but there has been virtually no effort to develop cross-discipline (or integrative) theories so that one might begin to understand how to "put the world together" in the mutual pursuit of common problems. Academic disciplines typically are distinct in order to be seen as "professional." The difficulty of integration is seen in the number of academic disciplines related to each of the criteria in Table 2 and listed in Table 4.

What is most striking for the IB discipline is that economic theory is useful only in four of these criteria and is the principal source only in that of "efficiency," where it derives its paradigm from mechanical physics. Oddly, this is the one criterion *chosen* by neoclassicists to focus on *despite* a long tradition of philosophical, theological, psychological, and ethical roots to the discipline in Smith, Malthus, Mill, Marshall, Hayek, and Knight. These men and the "Philosophic Radicals" [Halevy 1934], who helped form the political and economic revolutions for the pursuit of freedom, know that the threat to the system they sought lay in the rapaciousness of mankind, i.e., in individual and collective drives to *power, greed,* and *licentiousness* [Hirschman 1977]. Unless these could be curbed by democracy, competitive private enterprise, and religiously-based self-constraint the system would be corrupted for mean purposes. Yet, liberty does not provide its own necessary virtue in the assumption of individual responsibility. This quandary was voiced by John Adams in a letter to Jefferson:

Have you ever found in history a single example of a nation thoroughly corrupted that was afterwards restored to virtue? And without virtue there can be no political liberty. Will you tell me how to prevent riches from becoming the effects of temperance and industry? Will you tell me how to prevent riches from producing

Table 3. Academic Disciplines Contributing to an Understanding of Nation-State Objectives

Nation-State Objectives	*Academic Disciplines*
SECURITY	Political theory, psychology, sociology, philosophy, theology, military strategy
PROGRESS	*Economics,* physics
EQUITY	theology, philosophy, psychology, sociology, law, political science
PARTICIPATION	political science, sociology, psychology, anthropology
CREATIVITY	art, music, literature, sciences, medicine, etc.
STABILITY	biology, physics, zoology, law, political science, psychology, sociology, *economics*
AUTONOMY	psychology, sociology, law, anthropology, *economics*
ENVIRONMENT	ecology, sciences, sociology, political science, *economics*
HUMAN DIGNITY	theology, philosophy, sociology, psychology
RESPONSIBILITY	religion, philosophy, psychology, sociology

Table 4. Research Topics for a Holistic IB Discipline

INTERNATIONAL = interventions by government and culture
    1.   Changes in the Political Economy
a)   Worldwide shift in role of women—labor and management
b)   Population shifts—aging, quantity, quality, location
c)   Migrations and immigration—labor force, education
d)   Agricultural protection and industrialization
e)   Religious fundamentalism—business attitudes
f)   Terrorism and security of persons—mobility
g)   New nationalism—problem of identity
h)   Regionalism and interdependence—alliances, etc.
i)   Industrial policies—sectoral competitiveness
j)   Mobile sectors—employment, technology, and BOP
k)   Factor mobility—foreign sourcing, job creation
l)   Emerging economic powers—receding stagnant poor
m)   Restructuring in Soviet republics—new arenas
n)   Re-linking of East and West Europe—competition
o)   Rising costs of health care—burden on companies
p)   Spread of organized and "spontaneous" crime
q)   Absence of a "Natural enemy"—policy dispersion
r)   Absence of a "Natural leader"—U.S. hegemony
s)   Mitigation of use of Force for Cohesion—reason
t)   Lack of worldwide "Ordering principle"—mercantilism
u)   Inability to achieve *worldwide* agreement—splits
v)   Necessity for "functional agreements"—partial steps
w)   Complex criteria of "Acceptability"—no theory
x)   Socially responsible Capitalism—China, Latin America
y)   Increasing role of intergovernmental institutions
z)   Shifting roles of national, state, and city governments

    2.   Technological Developments
a)   Telecommunications and cross-border regulations
b)   Transportation—air cargo
c)   Sophisticated materials
d)   Resulting resource shifts and foreign sourcing
e)   International financial transfers and linkages
f)   Biotechnology
g)   Artificial intelligence
h)   Location and promotion of R&D

    3.   Social Developments
a)   Cultural clashes—identity
b)   Cultural similarities—consumerism
c)   Language—communication
d)   Necessity for cultural change and adaptation
e)   Impacts on organization, modes of production, products, distribution, ownership and control, etc.
f)   Adjustments to "Rule of Law" vs. "Rule by Law"
g)   Individual vs. social vs. governmental responsibility

Table 4. *Continued*

DOMESTIC

    1. Role of Governments—guidance, support, prohibition, and punishment
a)   Lessening regulation with openings to world economy
b)   Increasing interdependence and mitigation of "national policy" objectives
c)   Intervention through support and incentives—not through prohibitions
d)   Concern for competitiveness—shifting bases
e)   Increasing role of states—attraction of business
f)   Role of cities—re-building, restructuring
g)   Role of communities—new bases
h)   Implications of privatization—liability and responsibility

    2. Changing Role of Cities—impacts of above changes
a)   Locus of production and living
b)   Need to attract *specific* economic activities
c)   Competition among cities—national and worldwide
d)   Competition with rural areas and smaller cities or towns
e)   Priorities in development—infrastructure and culture
f)   Cultural changes required
g)   Shifts in governance
h)   Business—city partnership

CORPORATIONS/TRANSNATIONALS

    1. Concept of Corporation—relation of business to society
a)   Provider of work and production organization
b)   Profit-making entity
c)   Means of creation and destruction—entrepreneurial opportunities; change agent; technology assessor
d)   Society
e)   Network of functions—alliances

    2. Socio/political Role—impact of business on society
a)   Corrector of Social ills—health, education, ethics
b)   Political activist—economic and foreign policies
c)   Community leader and hub
d)   International initiator, re-structuror, implementer of national/international policies
e)   Locus of creativity—attitude and orientation
f)   Generator of individual improvement

    3. Cross-cultural Aspects
a)   Corporations as change agent
b)   Adaptations—Expats—locals under foreigners
c)   Comparative management styles
d)   Value-bases and educational differences
e)   Authority structures
f)   Organizational patterns
g)   Relation to elites
h)   Political participation
i)   Impacts of different lifestyles.

luxury? Will you tell me how to prevent luxury from producing effeminacy, intoxication, extravagance, vice, and folly?

If IB is to be a *holistic* discipline, it must turn its attention to how we *conduct* business while *living* in a world which requires *virtue* on the part of individuals through the exercise of personal and social responsibility. Virtue is seen as the way we treat *others*, and this is not accomplished *solely* in a market and seldom even *within* markets, unless all parties are exercising the required virtue in acquiring the income or producing the products they bring to the market.

To understand such a *holistic* discipline, therefore, we must start by understanding the value-foundations of our system and those of others (in a comparative way), letting each inform the other of new approaches and accommodations. To understand our competitive position with Japan requires an assessment of its entire socio-political-economic-religious system, for "Japan is a Circle," an integrated whole. Though it is now being fractionated in some degree by importation of Western individualism and "rights," which diminishes the long-standing concepts of "obligation" to others in a complex web of dependent relationships.

There is too much for our "discipline" to do in furthering our understanding of the role of business in a rapidly changing environment to spend much time on disassociating ourselves from other disciplines. An effort to build a *unique* IB theory will move us diametrically away from the necessary *integrative* and *holistic* approach to the problems facing world business.

The "institutional arrangements"—which I presume refer to the nature and orientation of business schools themselves and their relationships to corporate and governmental entities—are not conducive to the systemic orientations required in the above argument. On the contrary, the imposed necessity to publish, the scarcity of viable outlets, and the myopic and structured orientation of the few professional journals ex-

tant reinforces the tunnel-vision nature of "expertise." Virtually every research piece in *JIBS* has the same structure of presentation and argument, the readability—to say nothing of the enjoyability—of which is not an encomium to the discipline. One yearns for the freshness and directness of John Stuart Mill or Frank P. Graham, the clarity of Alfred Marshall or Ray Mikesell (to come to our generation), the analytical precision of Jacob Viner or John Maynard Keynes, or the policy-orientation of John Bates Clark or Ray Vernon—none of whom went through the methodological contortions with (dubious) quantitative measurements that articles require of academics today. Most of the present articles have little purpose—other than that of getting published—as evidenced by the trite conclusions drawn.

Fortunately, there is an increasing questioning of the arrogant and myopic approach of business schools to the education of managers, who are supposedly "educated" (the word means "brought from darkness into the light") through a series of standard methodologies which reflect what I have termed elsewhere "The National Disease: Technique Over Purpose" (see, Behrman [1988 chapter 13]). This has made it easy for curriculum development, for when you do not know where you ought to be going almost any technique will do. And virtually anyone's definition of the goal is as acceptable as another's—with the winning definition being the one that is paid for by the Dean, sometimes with the advice of the faculty.

The faculty, of course, will decide in favor of not having to learn new approaches, new directions, or new relationships. Therefore, the continued urging to develop firmer relationships with business and the recommendations to business to form closer relationships with government do not come from academia. These would require new institutional orientations, and the academic faculty, which studies and even advises change, refuses to condone it for itself—much less encourage it.

Institutions are difficult to change—

even in traumatic situations such as the break-up of the USSR, one sees efforts to cling tenaciously to past power and perquisites through merely *formal* changes in institutions. This, of course, is the drive for security, coupled with the pursuit of power and pelf. For business schools not to recognize the same modes of behavior among CEOs of major U.S. corporations— looking after their personal security, income, perquisites, and power positions at the expense of other stakeholders in the company, to say nothing of the consumer and the society—is to have lost sight of the overriding purpose of business. The public and the Congress will see otherwise, and the schools will themselves begin to be seen as "kept mistresses," replicating managers who have not learned their role in pursuing the purposes of an emerging new world order.

The challenge of reforming ourselves is before us. It is not a matter of definition of domain but one of *purpose* and *will*.

■ ■ ■

Is International Business a Distinct Field of Inquiry? No and Yes, but Life Goes On
Jean J. Boddewyn

This is a crucial question because a positive answer, "Yes, International Business (IB) is a distinct field of inquiry," would provide a solid raison d'être for our occupation as IB scholars, for the role of the Academy of International Business (AIB), for specialized IB journals, and for separate IB departments—(Dunning [1989]). Yet, I find it difficult to come up with an unequivocal answer hence, the "No and Yes" subtitle—even though I detect various elements which will allow us to survive and even prosper under such ambiguity—hence, the "But Life Goes On" qualification.

IB IS NOT (CANNOT BE) A DISTINCT FIELD OF INQUIRY

The reason for answering in the negative is suggested in my first essay in this book namely, that there is no theory of "business." I do not know of courses in "business theory" or even in "business research," except in the more elementary forms of structuring research problems, tracing data sources, preparing reports, etc. If there is no theory of *business*,[1] there cannot be a theory of *international* business.

The absence of a theory of business is related to the latter being a complex and somewhat amorphous institution. "Business," the "market," or "bargaining" systems of exchange have been distinguished by anthropologists, economic sociologists, and political economists from other societal forms of organizing economic activity, like the command and traditional economies (Keezer [1930], Polanyi [1944], Smelser [1976]). However, this diversity of perspectives from anthropology, sociology, economics, and politics reveals that any attempt to theorize about business and, a fortiori, about IB will require a multi- and inter-disciplinary approach depending upon the paradigms, theories, and constructs of other disciplines. Therefore, IB does not derive any uniqueness or distinctiveness from such coupling with the market system.

But what about "business history"? Does not the existence of this discipline reveal that one can theorize about "business"? If my understanding is adequate, I would venture that business historians have *either* analyzed the emergence of firms linked to the "market system" as a complement to other ways of organizing economic activities (see Fernand Braudel and Jacques

Pirenne), in which case we are back to using a multi- and inter-disciplinary approach, *or* they have focused on particular "business institutions" such as the department store, the family enterprise, and the multinational enterprise (MNE) (Wilkins [1986]). However, a theory of the MNE, of the purely domestic enterprise or of the family enterprise, is still not "a theory of business" in the more comprehensive sense of the term.

Therefore, I can conclude that IB does not constitute a distinct field of inquiry because we have not sufficiently agreed upon what that "business" is that "crosses borders."

IB IS (CAN BE) A DISTINCT FIELD OF INQUIRY

I visualize four ways of developing IB into a distinct field of inquiry, although I am not sure that they will all meet Brian Toyne's criterion of being *"fundamentally* distinct"—whatever that means in terms of differences in nature or degree. After all, everything hangs together in real life and all theorizing efforts build upon previous ones.

The first approach sidesteps the previously mentioned problem connected with the absence of a theory of "business," simply by defining "international business" *autonomously.* In other words, IB is what we define IB to be (for an example, see my article in chapter 2), although alternative explicit definitions will achieve the same purpose. We can now apply to IB the traditional theoretical questions of why, how, who, when, and where, on the basis of appropriate methodologies and rules of interpretation (see Toyne, chapter 2, for a discussion of various research paradigms).

To be sure, this approach is a cop-out because it assumes that definitions of IB are totally arbitrary (hardly what it takes to map out a distinct field of inquiry). The next three approaches provide remedies to this problem.

The second way of developing a distinct IB field of inquiry is *to select business problems/topics/issues with a genuine "international" dimension*—that is, to select them

precisely because they are *not* uninational in nature. Our field is replete with such an approach: Why/how do firms internationalize? Why/how does foreign/international production take place? Why/how can firms from one country succeed in foreign ones? How does the organization structure of firms change when a geographic variable is added to the product and function variables that dominate in a uninational setting? Do international firms contribute to the welfare of home and host nations?

This approach depends upon a valid definition of "international." In practice, it is usually defined as anything other than domestic or uninational. It is "IB research" simply because more than one country is involved—whether one labels such situations as international, multinational, multidomestic, transnational, or global. The IB researcher claims a distinct field of inquiry because he/she knows about and can model a greater number and variety of physical, economic, political, social, and cultural variables, than a purely domestic business researcher can.

Such an approach may be essentially descriptive—that is, limit itself to providing categories, typologies, and metaphors—or be truly theoretical in terms of developing a system of constructs and variables (Bacharach [1989]). Its main shortcoming is that it does not discriminate among all the environmental factors found in foreign settings but simply assumes that they are all conceptually important in distinguishing between domestic and international business.

The third approach to developing a distinct field of IB inquiry is deliberately theoretical. It rests upon the notion that *various existing theories, by themselves or in combination, can provide a unique explanation (why, how, etc.) of IB*, thereby generating a distinct field of inquiry. International trade theory, location theory, industrial-organization theory, the theory of the firm, transaction-cost analysis, agency theory, and various strands of organization theory have been used for that purpose; while John Dunning's "eclectic paradigm" represents the best-known attempt to integrate several of these theories.

There are, at least, two problems with this approach. First, attempts to use existing theories are usually limited to some *particular* aspect of IB, rather than addressing its whole. Thus, the eclectic paradigm is restricted to explaining international *production*. Other theoretical attempts focus exclusively on the MNE (transnational, global), thereby leaving out other types of international firms but all such attempts are prisoners of the particular theoretical framework selected, which cannot do justice to all of the dimensions of IB.

Most IB researchers, I presume, will feel quite capable of living with such limitations because one can rarely study a total and complex phenomenon with all its ramifications, but must be content with adding and integrating building blocks toward that elusive goal. Still, such a partial if realistic approach does not amount to delimiting IB as a distinct field of inquiry.

A second objection to the extension of existing theories to IB has been forcefully articulated by Grosse and Behrman [1992]. Essentially, they argue that such attempts will *not* result in developing a genuine IB theory because the firm and market theories now applied to IB problems are *generic or universal in nature* —that is, they can be used to explain *both* intranational and international phenomena: how firms expand geographically, internalize markets, generate monopoly rents, match strategy and structure, etc. Therefore, they are not sufficient to differentiate a theory of IB from those explaining domestic business—at least, in the ways they have been used until now.

This brings up to the fourth and most demanding approach for developing a distinct field of IB inquiry, namely, to construct a theory that focuses on *unique variables not present in uninational settings*. Based upon my own research [Boddewyn 1986; 1988; Boddewyn and Brewer 1994], but in full sympathy with Grosse and Behrman's own endeavor (see their 1992 article based on a 1988 paper), I will argue that *this uniqueness lies in the existence of states* (sovereign governments)—as was already sketched out in my domain essay in chapter 2.

The concept "international" is related to the act of "crossing borders." These borders, however, assume several characteristics: physical, economic, social, cultural, and political. The first four characteristics coincide with the concept of "nation," while the political one is associated with the existence of "states."[2]

The theories now used to explain IB deal essentially with the "nation phenomenon" that is, with the fact that countries exhibit what Clark [1991] calls "differentials." They have different endowments (natural and human resources), market potentials, value systems, social structures, etc., which international firms attempt to bridge and ultimately homogenize. This is well expressed by Levitt's "globalizing markets" and Ohmae's "borderless world" metaphors.

These physical, economic, and sociocultural differentials, however, also exist *within* each country of the world (e.g., market segmentation), so that market theories based on such differentials (e.g., trade and location theories) apply to both domestic and IB situations. Similarly, theories related to the behavior of firms (e.g., transaction-cost and agency theory) were developed to explain domestic phenomena and were then applied to international ones, but without altering fundamentally their generic or universal nature. Therefore, the existence of "nations" provides a very weak reed on which to develop a unique field of inquiry for IB.

The existence of "states," however, is what creates the real borders crossed by international business actors and processes. What kept Albania out of world trade and investment during the cold-war period was not its climate, natural resources, purchasing power, languages, religions, or cultures, but that its government imposed an autarkic policy. Conversely, there will be more international trade and investment in the foreseeable future, simply because of the breakup of the old Soviet Union and of Yugoslavia creating new states which have now chosen to participate in such activities.

While "differentials" are associated with nations, the existence, volume, and form of IB depends primarily upon the "permeabilities" of states [Clark 1991], which decide to accept, reject, or modify IB activities *by fiat*. Unlike other political actors (including business firms) that exercise power, the state upholds a special claim to the exclusive regulation of the legitimate use of physical force in enforcing its rules within a given territorial area (to paraphrase Max Weber). This makes it the "sovereign" that cannot be bound by any domestic or international agreement. As the definer and enforcer of property rights, the state controls territorial access to its resources (including markets) in return for revenue and other benefits (cf. Boddewyn and Brewer [1994], for an elaboration of this argument).

Consequently, it is the existence of sovereignties (states, governments) which rule distinct "political economies," together with the concomitant assertion of governmental controls and of business devices to avoid or exploit them, that distinguishes "international" from "domestic" business [Supple 1989:3]. Hence, *"crossing borders" is primarily a political act that provides the unique basis for a theory of IB*. This is why Grosse and Behrman concluded that: "Any theory of *international* business must be a theory of policies and activities of business *and* governments, in conflict and cooperation" [1992 :92].

One could object that there is also a sovereign ruling over domestic business, as well as "business-government relations" within all market-based political economies, so that a political perspective is not proper to IB. However, in an international setting, there are several sovereigns, and this situation generates both negative and positive situations which are fundamentally distinct from those found in a uninational setting. Negatively put, an economic agent from one sovereignty cannot necessarily enforce its property rights in another sovereignty because there is no true international law, while it can do so under national law within its own borders (Schmidtchen and Schmidt-Trenz [1990]). Positively put, international firms have more political options, not only because of the variety of political economies that may allow abroad what is not possible at home, but because IB firms can enlist one government against another. Such options are not present to the same extent and quality within a uninational political setting. If states are not "permeable" but forbid or severely restrict IB, there will not be any of the latter; while the mere existence of nations invites IB, precisely because of their "differentials."

This emphasis on political variables for providing a unique focus to IB inquiry does not mean that a theory of IB has to be a purely political one. After all, IB firms are not only political actors but also economic ones, social-change agents, etc. (Fayerweather [1969;1982]). The challenge lies in incorporating (and sometimes privileging) political variables into other theories used in IB inquiry—as I attempted in my 1988 *JIBS* article on the "Political Aspects of MNE Theory," and in my 1994 article with Brewer on international business political-behavior research (Grosse and Behrman [1992] make related suggestions).

Even if a predominantly political theory of IB were to be developed, its contents and research paradigms are still inchoate—mainly because there are no unified theories of politics and political behaviors. Still, there are fruitful leads to be exploited from the political-economy, collective-action, international-relations, and bargaining literatures; while the business functional areas (management, marketing, finance, etc.) are more underdeveloped in this regard.

LIFE GOES ON

To paraphrase the Gospels, "there are many rooms in the IB mansion," and this plurality of interests, perspectives, and understandings makes us "theory-rich" rather than poor. Still, this optimistic evaluation begs the question of whether IB is a distinct field of inquiry. The task is crucial if daunting. I have outlined several answers, even propounding and privileging a political approach, but there are others.

Besides, life (including academic life) is full of surprises, and we have all been challenged by unanticipated theoretical developments that have recently shaken and recast our field of inquiry in fast succession, including monopolistic competition, transaction-cost analysis, agency theory, institutionalization theory, and the eclectic paradigm. Nobody commissioned such developments, and this most worthwhile conference, like most committees, is not going to result in a precise agenda, nor is it going to interfere with the spontaneous creativity of scholars from a variety of disciplines that have a bearing on the study of IB. Let us keep thinking afresh while remaining open to new surprises.

Having said this, I would like to add a few observations that are related to the development of IB as a distinct field of inquiry. First, I feel that most of our theories tend to be too *condition-based*, that is, they focus primarily if not exclusively on prerequisites and necessary antecedents.[3] The eclectic paradigm and strategic analysis provide good examples of this emphasis because they privilege the factors (ownership advantages and organizational resources/competencies) *without which* IB activity is not possible. A condition-based research approach is favored probably because it lends itself more readily to quantification: firm size, R&D and advertising intensities, industry concentration, and the like.

Motivations, on the other hand, are murkier and harder to trace and measure: are IB firms motivated by profitability, efficiency, power, legitimacy, emulation, or some combination thereof? *Precipitating circumstances* are even more ignored, possibly because of their evanescence and chancy nature: they are here now but then they are gone, compared to the longer-lasting conditions and motivations. Yet, many IB-related decisions represent close calls, quickly reversible commitments and even mistakes ruled by marginal and transient factors. I find business historians, such as Kindleberger [1988] and Wilkins [1986], much more curious about and sensitive to such "fleeting factors" than the typical IB researcher who wants to develop and test "solid" models.

Second, if the "firm" constitutes the proper focus of IB inquiry,[4] I think that we need to better differentiate and integrate its multiple dimensions. I would argue that it is simultaneously: (1) a "company" whose *worth* to its owners, the stock market and potential acquirers has to be maintained and preferably enhanced; (2) a "firm" (in a narrower sense) that creates (adds) economic *value*; (3) an "organization" that must *integrate* by inducing its member to participate and contribute, and (4) a "corporation" imbued with social *responsibility*, all dimensions, however conceptually imprecise and fluid, that are affected by the act of crossing borders.[5] (Jack Behrman's paper in this chapter addresses these various dimensions cogently, albeit in different terms.)

We tend to study these various facets in isolation: finance scholars are interested in how international expansion and diversification affect stock valuation; economists and strategists look at the arbitrage and leverage effects of internationalization on growth, efficiency, profitability, and innovation; organization theorists pay particular attention to the integrative and disintegrative impact of international operations; while social-performance scholars focus on IB interactions with society. A theory of IB that centers on the "firm" (Wilkins [1986]) has to integrate these dimensions, I believe.[6]

Finally, I will briefly return to "the limits of the IB firm." My second observation has already stressed that businesses engaging in IB activities have multiple dimensions (company, firm, organization, and corporation) that are not sufficiently identified and integrated in our field of inquiry. I will add that even when our research is limited to the economic aspects of the IB firm, it presents usually a flat or stunted characterization of the latter. Its true economic dimensions are typically restricted to readily measurable elements such as sales, profits, R&D expenditures, number of foreign subsidiaries and affiliates, etc., as found in annual reports and IB directories or uncovered through surveys. However, the IB firm's "economic reach" is much broader, including all sorts of contractual transactions and relationships (cross-licensing, distributorship, and alliance agreements, etc.) and associational participations (membership and leadership in cartels, lobbying groups, etc.).

In other words, IB studies frequently lack breadth and depth—a shortcoming that has to be remedied in order to develop IB as a distinct field of inquiry.

NOTES

1. Recent critical articles about business schools raise questions of whether the latter even teach "business." Instead, they are perceived as being discipline and methodology driven, and ignore or underplay some key dimensions of business such as entrepreneurship, communication, legal and ethical constraints.

2. The "states" I am discussing here, are at the national or federal level. There are subnational governments (states, provinces, cantons, etc.), but their sovereignty is more limited and subordinated to that of the capstone government. Only the latter are represented at the United Nations, have embassies, and are admitted to the WTO and World Bank, etc.

3. Aristotle argued that there are three types of explanation. *Condition* refers to something essential to the existence or occurrence of something else, a prerequisite—what Aristotle called a "necessary antecedent." *Motivation* refers to an inner drive, impulse, intention, incentive, goal, etc., that causes a person to do something or act in a certain way—Aristotle's "final cause" ("finis" means end or goal in Latin). A *precipitating circumstance* is a hastening element that causes something to happen before it is expected, needed or desired—Aristotle's "efficient cause" (see Boddewyn [1985] for an elaboration and application of these distinctions).

4. I do not fully subscribe to the view that the firm constitutes the only appropriate level for the study of IB, as I argue in my paper in chapter 2.

5. I am echoing here the older distinctions made by: (1) Burnham (1941:82–85) among "managers, finance-executives and finance-capitalists," and (2) Parsons (1960, chap. 2) among the technical, managerial, and institutional levels of analysis.

6. I could add that we should simultaneously apply alternative and/or complementary theories to the explanation of IB phenomena—as is done in John Dunning's eclectic paradigm. Bruce Kogut (1988:174–176) provided another example, when he used multiple approaches to explain joint ventures: transaction-cost economics, strategic analysis and organization theory.

■ ■ ■

International Business Research
Jean-François Hennart

Should IB develop into a viable and distinct field of inquiry given its lack of a unifying definition and its current and foreseeable dependency on the paradigms, theories, and constructs of economics, political science, sociology, and the business disciplines?

In his essay, Jean Boddewyn answers this question with an attempt to define what the field of IB is—*what we should research.* Jack Behrman sets forth in his essay what IB research should be—*how we should research.* My goal is more modest: I would like to describe a few cases where I feel IB research has made a clear contribution. In other words, I intend to describe *how we do research.* The goal of this exercise is to derive some tentative conclusions on what the field of enquiry of IB is, on what it is likely to become, and on the relationship between IB and the other disciplines.

The method used to derive those generalizations is to look at the process by which two IB theories, the transaction cost/internalization theory of the multinational enterprise (MNE) and the emerging theory of countertrade, were developed. These two theories were not chosen at random: there are research streams in which I have been involved. Hence the analysis is likely to be subjective. The sample size is also quite limited, and the extent to which one can generalize from such a small sample size is dubious. But because my goal is to stimulate discussion, I will ignore these methodological issues. The conclusions I draw from this exercise are as follows:

1. IB scholars have focused on issues which arise in both domestic and international contexts, but which are more salient internationally than domestically.
2. IB research has been policy-driven.
3. The concern of IB scholars with facts and data has often exposed the inadequacies of existing theories.
4. Lasting contributions have been made when research has moved from description to theory. Specifically, the need to develop theories to account for unexplained facts is providing the theoretical corpus of the emerging discipline of IB. This development seems also to be typical of new fields, such as finance and strategy.
5. Good IB theory does not deal exclusively with international phenomena. Instead "domestic" theories are a subset of IB theory.

WHAT IS IB RESEARCH?

It seems to be a feature of new fields to have soul-searching sessions about the boundaries of their discipline. This is the case of strategy, an emerging field like IB. Every Academy of Management meeting features a session, standing room only, in which senior researchers in the field discuss what strategy is and how it relates to other disciplines, especially industrial organization economics.[1] It is also typical of new fields to bemoan their dependence on the tools of other disciplines. This is often exaggerated. All new fields initially depend upon theories developed by established disciplines. In time, however, the theories developed in the emerging field take a life of their own. Finance, for example, borrowed initially much from economics, but now this field is seen as having a specific set of theories. These theories are, however, still very close to economics, as seen by the fact that there are many economist retreads in finance departments.[2]

What defines a field of inquiry such as IB is the type of questions asked. Locks differ in styles, so to open a particular lock one requires a particular type of key. Similarly, to solve a particular question one needs a particular bag of theoretical tools. If the tools do not exist, one must fashion new ones. IB has asked new questions, and in an attempt to answer them, has developed new tools. The best way to explore those issues is to look at two phenomena which have been tackled by IB scholars: the MNE and countertrade.

The Development of the Theory of the Multinational Enterprise

It is not my goal here to give a detailed historical account of the development of the theory of the MNE; my more limited purpose is to show how a separate and distinct theory was developed by IB researchers because they persistently asked questions which existing theories could not answer. As I will show, these efforts led to a line of questioning which constitutes one of the branches of IB theory.

The growth of firms outside their country of origin does not date from the 1960s. Yet until that date, the phenomenon was seen by economists as an export of capital.

In other words, when economists looked at the MNE, the only thing they saw was that parent firms sometimes invested funds from their home country into host countries. The international expansion of firms was considered an international movement of capital, and it was assumed that the magnitude of such flows depended upon relative returns in home vs. host countries (which themselves depended upon interest rates, tax rates, and the covariance of returns between countries). The phenomenon was called foreign direct investment (FDI), by analogy with foreign portfolio investment. Considerable effort in theory refinement and econometric sophistication were expended to test the hypothesis that the flow of FDI would be responsive to these variables, with very mixed results [Stevens 1969; Prachowny 1972; Mellors 1973]. A cursory look at the data on FDI shows, however, that this explanation is unconvincing, as the pattern of FDI does not match that predicted by the theory: most foreign investors seek control by taking large equity shares, invest overseas in their main industry, and invest in countries whose business cycle is highly correlated with the parent's home base [Hennart 1977;1982]. Hence while it is possible that increased stability of returns and reduction of risk are a consequence of the international expansion of firms, firms do not expand internationally as they would if they were behaving like international mutual funds.

Developing a satisfactory theory of the MNE took two major paradigm shifts. Stephen Hymer was responsible for the first. In his 1960 thesis [1960;1976] he showed that FDI should not be analyzed with the tools of international trade and finance but with those of industrial organization. Put in another way, Hymer showed that FDI was not principally the export of capital but was in essence a by-product of the international expansion of firms. Hence to explain FDI one had to explain why firms grew. In 1960, economics did not have a theory of why firms existed, but it had a theory of why they grew: they grew to gain monopoly power. They either acquired existing competitors, or they preempted the entry of new ones. Hymer therefore argued that FDI was caused by the desire of firms to increase their rents by taking over their licensees (or more generally their actual or potential competitors).[3]

Market power can perhaps explain why firms grow, and why they grow internationally, but it does not explain why firms exist. The second shift moved the FDI phenomenon from the field of industrial organization to that of transaction cost theory, or more precisely, to the new, emerging field of comparative institutional theory. The insight of the transaction cost theories of the MNE, simultaneously and independently developed in the 1970s by McManus [1972], Buckley and Casson [1976], Brown [1976], and Hennart [1977;1982], (and further developed by Rugman [1981], Caves [1982], and Teece [1986]) was that the MNE was one of many institutions devised to organize economic activities.[4] Hence to explain why there were MNEs one had to explain why the organization of international interdependencies within the firm was more efficient than the mediation of these interdependencies through the market or through contracts. This was a radical shift, because it moved the focus from how firms could maximize their rents by expanding overseas, to how organizing within the firm could be more efficient than organizing through the market. This new way of thinking about the nature and the growth of business firms has now spread from IB to strategy [Rumelt, Schendel, and Teece 1991] and to organization theory with the development of "organizational economics" [Barney and Ouchi 1986].

Two observations can be made on this second paradigm shift. First, and contrary to what is sometimes asserted, this shift was initiated by IB scholars in response to the challenge posed by the existence of MNEs [McManus 1972]. Transaction cost models of the MNE are not slavish applications of Williamson's [1975] framework to IB. They antedate it and have proceeded quite independently even though Williamson's influence has subsequently been significant. Second, the second paradigm shift is still incomplete. Many IB authors still write as if the presence of market failures was a necessary and sufficient condition for the existence of multinational firms. High transaction costs in international markets are not sufficient to explain multinational firms, since there may be cases where firms incur even higher costs than markets. Even if organization costs in firms are lower than those in markets, these organization costs must be lower than the potential gains that derive from organizing the transaction. If they are not, no economic interaction will take place, either in firms or markets. To understand why firms exist, one must consider simultaneously the costs of organizing interactions within firms and markets. Hence one needs not only a theory of why markets fail, but also a theory of why firms succeed [Hennart 1991a].

The impact of this paradigm shift on policy has been significant. The new theories showed that MNEs were institutions devised to reduce the cost of organizing interactions between agents located in different countries, and that this form of interaction was freely chosen by economic agents in home and host countries because it maximized their joint income. Organization within the firm had certain efficiency properties which could not be fully replaced by market or contractual arrangements. Hence, in contrast to what was argued at the time [Bergsten, Horst, and Moran 1978; Oman 1984], the mandated replacement of FDI by contracts (the forced replacement of traditional FDI by the so-called "new" forms of investment) was likely to have serious efficiency consequences, reducing the size of the rents to be shared between the multinational firm and the host country [Hennart 1989a]. The theory has also shed a new light on licensing contracts, showing that many of the stipulations of those contracts are not necessarily anticompetitive, but instead are a rational response to im-

perfect property rights [Caves, Crookell, and Killing 1982]. Although one cannot show that these theoretical developments are the main reason behind the startling policy change of less developed countries vis-à-vis multinational firms, I am sure that the new view of the MNE as an efficient economic institution played a part in legitimizing it.

The Emerging Theory of Countertrade

The same pattern of theory development is also visible in the case of countertrade. The term "countertrade" is used to describe a variety of trade practices which were developed in the 1960s by Soviet bloc countries to trade with Western firms which spread in the 1970s and 1980s to both developing and developed countries. These practices govern up to fifteen percent of world trade. Countertrade has been generally seen as barter and its use soundly condemned by the quasi-totality of economists working for national governments and international organizations.[5] Very little serious research on this topic has been undertaken by international trade theorists, in large part because, as in the case of the MNE, it is difficult to find many convincing explanations for this practice without relaxing some major assumptions of traditional trade and finance theory. Trade for goods is much inferior to trade for money, since the latter allows trade to be multilateral and spread over time, while the former requires it to be bilateral and instantaneous. Why then would anyone want to barter?

The conventional explanation of countertrade is that it is due to foreign exchange shortages, although the precise mechanism by which the latter leads to the former is not clearly described (e.g., Elderkin and Norquist [1987]; McVey [1980]). As Banks [1983] and Mirus and Yeung [1987] showed, this explanation is logically flawed. Furthermore, the fact that countertrade is used domestically, where trade can be transacted without foreign exchange, shows its limits [Hennart 1990]. As in the case of the MNE, looking at the facts is the first step toward an alternative theory. Contrary to what is often asserted, countertrade does not consist wholly, not even mostly, of exchanges of goods for goods (i.e., barters). Instead, the most common forms of countertrade (counter purchase, buy-backs, and offsets) feature two separate money for goods contracts, with imports made conditional on the exporter purchasing goods and services from the importer. Hence the essence of most countertrade contracts is not barter, but reciprocity [Kogut 1986; Parsons 1985; Hennart 1989b]. As Williamson has shown [1985], stipulating reciprocal obligations is a way to increase the enforceability of contracts when recourse to the courts is problematic. This puts countertrade in a totally different perspective: countertrade is a way to increase the enforceability of contracts when such contracts are difficult to enforce. Although much more research is needed, some of the implications of the theory seem consistent with empirical evidence [Hennart 1990;1993].

WHAT CAN WE LEARN FROM THESE TWO EXAMPLES?

These two examples were used because they are in my area of expertise. Other examples could probably be adduced from other subfields within IB, and their addition would no doubt make the discussion richer and more complete. Even though the preceding examples cover only a small part of the field, some useful generalizations can be made.

First, IB scholars have made a useful contribution in these topics because the weaknesses and inadequacies of conventional wisdom were more glaring—and the need of a good theory for policy purposes more crucial—in an international than in a domestic context. IB researchers played a crucial role in the development of the transaction cost theory of the firm because the lack of a theory of economic institutions was more apparent, and had more adverse consequences, internationally than domestically. Asking why firms set up manufacturing plants overseas is not conceptually different from asking why they set up mul-

tiplant operations within a country. But the international expansion of firms confronted decision makers with difficult policy decisions, such as whether to limit or ban incoming and/or outgoing FDI, while political decision makers were not faced with such dilemmas in the case of domestic multiplant operations. Likewise, the issue of why parties choose to practice barter and reciprocal trading, and whether these practices ought to be discouraged arises in both a domestic and an international context, yet the issue is much more salient, and the need for a workable theory higher internationally than domestically: governments and international organizations must take a position concerning countertrade, and this position must be defensible.

The second point worth noting here is that theory progressed when IB researchers confronted the conventional wisdom with empirical evidence. Hymer outlined the discrepancies between the stylized facts predicted by the then dominant theory and the actual pattern of FDI, using evidence from the surveys of the U.S. Department of Commerce and the data on FDI collected by Dunning [1958], Southard [1931], and others.[6] Without this concern and interest for the empirical evidence, the field would have probably evolved into the formulation of increasingly sophisticated but increasingly irrelevant formal models, of the type that seem to absorb most of the energies of today's economists. Likewise, little significant progress was made in understanding countertrade until a precise knowledge of the contractual clauses of the various types of contracts and some feel for the relative importance of various contract types was gained through interviews, questionnaires, perusal of the specialized literature, and systematic data collection [Lecraw 1987; Hennart 1990]. There is an interesting parallel here with strategy: many of today's theoretical developments in strategy were prompted by the empirical observation that firms in the same industry had widely different profit rates and that high profits tended to persist, two findings that could not be easily explained by traditional economic theory [Rumelt, Schendel, and Teece 1991].

A third generalization is that the weaknesses of existing explanations, and the tenacity with which these explanations were held as true in spite of the overwhelming evidence to the contrary, comes from the fact that they were based on assumptions widely held by the discipline. These assumptions, no doubt useful in other contexts, could not be readily abandoned by scholars fully immersed in their discipline. Trade theory is based on the assumption of zero transaction costs, and hence trade theorists have had great difficulty in explaining phenomena, such as multinational firms and countertrade, which owe their existence to transaction costs. Indeed, while the presence of MNEs has radically affected the workings of the international economy, few trade economists have taken up the challenge of reworking the theory to incorporate this institution. IB scholars were better able to devise new theories because they were less reluctant to break these assumptions.

A fourth point is that advances in IB did not take place apart from existing theories. New theories, like new architectural styles, result from the eclectic reconfiguration of existing elements. Hence the new comparative institutional theory of the MNE uses many of the traditional assumptions of economics (such as natural selection of efficient organizational forms) but transcends them. While neoclassical economics starts from the premise that the problem of organizing production is solved, comparative institutional theory studies how this problem gets solved [Alchian and Demsetz 1972]. Combined with location theory, the resulting eclectic paradigm [Dunning 1981] is highly successful in explaining why MNEs exist, the forms they take, the products they produce abroad, and which countries will be host and which will be home to them. Similarly, the transaction cost theory of countertrade is not a wholly new theory, but rather an extension of Williamson's theory of rec-

iprocal commitments [1985] to international transactions.

Lastly, the previous examples show that a new paradigm stimulates new questions, and attempts to answer them further to enrich the paradigm. Cumulative research tradition defines a field. This is the case for the transaction cost theory of the MNE, which is better described under the "comparative institutional" label, since it explains the form taken by international economic relations in terms of the relative level of organizing costs experienced by alternative institutions. A partial list of further developments of the theory include its operationalization and empirical testing (e.g., Swedenborg [1979]; Davidson and McFetridge [1985]; Yu and Ito [1988]), extensions to cover services (e.g., Casson [1989]; Terpstra and Yu [1988]), trading companies [Roehl 1983; Enderwick 1988], the role of entrepreneurs [Casson 1990], joint-ventures (e.g., Gatignon and Anderson [1988]; Hennart [1988;1991c]; Gomes-Casseres 1989]; Kogut [1989]; Blodgett [1991]), East-West trade [Kogut 1986], and relations with host governments [Murtha 1991].

In summary, successful IB research has the following characteristics:

1. The topic of interest has greater international than domestic salience.
2. The topic has important policy implications.
3. Existing theory is not consistent with the empirical evidence.
4. The topic at hand is one where the traditional assumptions of the discipline used to develop the theory do not apply.

WHAT ARE PROMISING AREAS FOR IB RESEARCH?

Can the criteria defined above help us identify promising areas for IB research? There are many such issues, but, because of space limitations, only one will be discussed here: control in MNEs. One pressing issue facing managers is how to organize a firm so as to obtain from employees both initiative and responsiveness to local needs, while at the same time achieving coordination and consistency.

This research topic seems to fulfill most of the criteria listed above. First, the control of subunits has greater international than domestic salience. While it applies to all subunits, it is especially relevant for subunits located abroad. The use of each of the three potential control modes, price control, hierarchy, and socialization incurs higher cost internationally than domestically [Hennart 1991b]. As a result, many MNEs experience great difficulty in controlling their subsidiaries. It is quite common to observe quasi-autonomous subsidiaries and there are even cases of rebellious ones.[7] The issue has also great policy implications, as there is general dissatisfaction with the solution to this problem—the matrix form of organization—which is being offered by management theorists [Doz and Prahalad 1991]. While what we know of control processes in MNEs does not seem consistent with some naive economic models (such as the firm as an "internal market" with internal prices set at marginal cost), it is harder to know whether they are consistent with the predictions of organization theories, given the difficulty of making these theories operational and the paucity of empirical tests. As Doz and Prahalad [1991:156] note, "much of the literature on multinational management ... while long on descriptive analysis, is short on theories, and even shorter on mid-range constructs." The results obtained by the few systematic, theoretically grounded studies like those of Egelhoff [1988] are mixed [Hennart 1991b]. Doz and Prahalad attribute the lack of empirical work by IB theorists to insufficient borrowing from organization theory. I would argue with Hesterly, Liebeskind, and Zenger [1990] that comparative institutional theory (or organizational economics, as it is known to organization theorists) provides a better base from which to develop a theory of control. Needless to say, this viewpoint is not shared by all.[8]

CONCLUSION

Compared to other disciplines, IB research exhibits a number of strengths. First, it is "problem-driven." It responds (even if sometimes belatedly) to empirical and policy challenges. As Boddewyn [1990] notes:

> a succession of problems have dominated the research agenda in international business and management; do MNEs generate a loss of domestic jobs? What factors account for the success or failure of joint ventures and alliances? How can headquarters control their foreign subsidiaries? What accommodations have to be made between global strategic goals and demands for responsiveness on the part of governments? And so on.

This responsiveness to changing circumstances has been beneficial. It has stimulated scholars to rethink many of their assumptions. For example, the success of Japanese firms on the world market has prompted many IB scholars to reconsider the efficiency of contracts and that of socialization as a mode of control of managers. One temptation has been to remain superficial. As Boddewyn [1990] notes, too much IB research has not advanced beyond descriptions, typologies (often created with a goal of product differentiation), or metaphors. The need to tackle real problems has also privileged relevance at the expense of elegance. This is in contrast with economics (and maybe other theory-based disciplines) which seem increasingly preoccupied by the further refinement of their theoretical structure and less and less concerned with describing real institutions [Rumelt, Schendel, and Teece 1991].

When IB comes up with theories, these theories are typically more than just applications to the IB field, no matter what people in other disciplines might say. The two examples used earlier show that IB researchers introduced a new conceptual lens with which to look at the phenomena studied. These new theories, though devised to answer a particular question, have general applicability. The transaction cost theory of the MNE is a general theory which explains, for example, why a firm will vertically integrate domestically as well as internationally. These theories were developed by IB researchers (as opposed to strategists or economists) because the phenomena at issue were more salient internationally than domestically.

Lastly, I believe that IB will continue to develop as a viable and distinct field of inquiry, and that the fears that it might get absorbed by more theoretical disciplines (such as economics or organization theory) are exaggerated. After all, if you were a population ecologist based in upper New York state, would you rather study the ecology of firms in the global semiconductor industry or that of grocery stores in Ithaca? Why would the average economist, who can get published manipulating equations of a principal-agent problem, devote years to collecting IB data? IB researchers need not be afraid of the potential competition of other disciplines, nor should they have any inferiority complex about the field's theoretical achievements.

NOTES

1. This seems to be a characteristic of emerging fields: I have never seen such a session offered at the American Economic Association meetings.

2. In the same vein, the distance between strategy and economics can be measured by the difficulty experienced by many newly minted economics Ph.D.s to pursue a successful career as strategy faculty in business schools.

3. He failed to realize that monopoly power can also be established by contracts and hence his theory was not complete, since he did not explain when and why international cartel agreements would be less efficient than the expansion abroad of domestic firms (Casson 1985).

4. This exaggerates somewhat the contrast between Hymer and transaction costs theorists. In his 1976 book, Hymer states that the multinational firm internalizes or supersedes the market (pp. 48–51). However, he chose to emphasize the internalization of pecuniary externalities to obtain market power, as opposed to that of nonpecuniary externalities to increase efficiency (see Dunning and Rugman [1985]; Hennart [1991a]).

5. See for example de Miramon (1985).

6. As is the case of much path breaking work, his contribution was not appreciated by his peers. His thesis was submitted for publication to the press of his alma mater, MIT, but was rejected because the argument was "too simple and too straightforward" (Kindleberger 1976:13). It was only published in 1976, two years after Hymer's death.

7. Ghoshal and Bartlett (1990) cite the case of the British and German subsidiaries of the Ruberoid corporation "that unilaterally severed all ties with their parent and, with the support of local financial institutions, secured complete legal independence."

8. For a review of some of the organization theory literature as applied to the MNE see Hennart (1991b). One bias of some of the organization theory work is the neglect of price as a control method in firms. See for example Martinez and Jarillo (1989).

■ ■ ■

The Yin and Yang of Progress in International Business: A Philosophy of Science Based Perspective
Rabi S. Bhagat

When I chose this title it seemed appropriate to discuss the issue raised by Brian Toyne for this chapter: Can (should) international business (IB) develop into a viable and distinct field of inquiry given its lack of a unifying definition and its current and foreseeable dependency on the paradigms, theories and constructs of economics, political science, sociology, and related business disciplines?

In choosing the title for this paper, I wish to say rather firmly what is wrong with the aspect of international business I am most familiar with and how its ills might be cured.

It was not long, however, before I felt misgivings about this process of developing IB into a viable and distinct field of inquiry and doubt if the challenge can be met (in theoretical terms) at the present time.

I believe that the current state of development in IB is best characterized by the dynamic interplay of *yin* and *yang*. These words, in Taoist philosophy, which originated in ancient China, denote the dark and sunny sides of a hill, depict how the *Tao* is underpinned by a flow of complementary yet opposite set of forces through which all trends eventually recycle. As the sage Lao-tzn put it, "reversion is the movement of *Tao*." Whenever a situation develops a strong tendency to move in one direction, it also sets in motion another set of tendencies which will eventually move in the reverse direction. Just as the bright light of the day passes into darkness of the night, extreme situations always keep reversing each other. The dynamic character of *yin* and *yang* is illustrated by the ancient Chinese symbol called *Tai-chi-Tu* or "Diagram of the Supreme Ultimate" (see Figure 1).

This diagram depicts the dark *yin* and the bright *yang* in a symmetric arrangement but the symmetry is in a dynamic state. It is a rotational symmetry suggesting a strong kinetic or continuous cyclic movement. The *yang* returns cyclically to its beginning, the *yin* reaches its maximum limits and gives its place to the *yang*. This diagram symbolizes the idea that each time one of the two forces attains its maximum limits, it immediately begins to create a force which is in sharp contrast, i.e., antithetical in nature to the earlier force.

Taoist philosophy in depicting this cyclical nature of the *yin* and *yang* emphasizes that the disposition of some situations could be best understood in terms of *yin* and *yang*.

Taoist notions have been developed and expressed in different ways by several social scientists in describing what is now known as a dialectical view of reality.

In adopting this notion to my arguments for this paper, I feel that the seemingly new emphasis on the interdisciplinary mode in the area of IB is best interpreted in the light of the *yin* and *yang* of discipline-based inquiries from the various social sciences. Progress will evolve as a result of the creative tensions among the disciplines. When such creative tensions among the disciplines are low, the progress will be uneven and when they are rather high rapid progress will result.

Figure 1. Yin and Yang: The Primordial Opposites Governing All Changes

Sometimes the progress will be slower than expected (i.e., *yin* will be at its maximum) as we take time to understand the complexity of a new phenomenon and at other times we will move faster (i.e., *yang* will be at its maximum) than usual because the creative tension among the disciplines would help us focus in the appropriate direction. In the next section, I provide an analytical framework for examining the status of IB theories. I should note that my examples are taken primarily from the international management (IM) literature even though the points are assumed to be valid for related fields of inquiries in the IB area.

AN ANALYTICAL FRAMEWORK

In figure 2, I show the utility of a two dimensional space characterized along one dimension by emphasis on a within-boarder operation versus cross-border operation of the multinational enterprise (MNE) and va-

lidity versus generalizability related concerns of the research design along the other dimension.

The four cells depict the developmental status of various IB theories. Cell 1 studies are concerned mainly with operations of the MNE in the domestic context. Researchers focus primarily on validity related issues and precision of measurement is generally achieved easily. There is not much reason for an interdisciplinary orientation since the phenomenon is interpreted without a lot of ambiguities by adopting unique paradigms of the disciplines. Examples include governmental influence over foreign direct investment (FDI) and the forms of involvement that multinational companies employ in a given national setting. Research on these topics can be conducted without a great deal of interdisciplinary orientation but the precision of measurement is of crucial importance.

In figure 2, cell 4, the focus is on cross-

Figure 2. An Analytical Framework for Examining the Status of International Business Theories

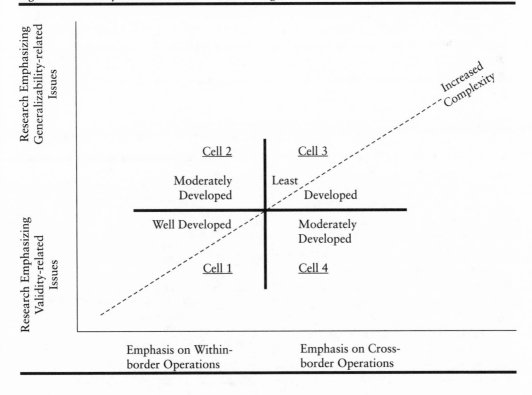

border operations with a concern for understanding some of the international aspects of the management of the multinational organization. The focus, however, on validity related issues and precision of measurement still takes precedence over generalizability related issues. Examples include research on structure and functioning of multinational organizations across national boundaries. Research on Stopford and Wells's [1972] contingency model and its validity across national settings is a good case in point. There are numerous examples of both good and poor research endeavors in this category.

In cell 2, the focus is to maximize understanding of IM processes emphasizing both within-border related operations of the firm along with generalizability related issues as posed by the respective disciplines. In cell 3, the concern is to maximize both the emphasis on cross-border operations along with generalizability related issues of the disciplines.

Examples of good research traditions in cell 2 are relatively difficult to find. In the area of business-government relations, we can find some research traditions that are concerned about within border related operations of the MNE by combining theoretical perspectives from economics and political science. Generalizability of the paradigms of these two disciplines and their relevance toward understanding the nature of complex interactions between business and government that evolve over time are important concerns of the studies in cell 2.

I suggest that cell 3 studies have the greatest potential for fostering interdisciplinary orientation in the domain of IB inquiry. However, they are the least developed at the present time. The network perspective of Bartlett and Ghoshal [1988] which suggests that management of MNEs can be viewed as the management of networks of foreign affiliates is a good example of the cell 3 type studies. By focusing on exchange between the various affiliates and the headquarters, the network perspective focuses on cross-border operations of a firm. And by adopt-

ing the network metaphor from the management literature [Aldrich and Whetten 1981; Benson 1975; Thorelli 1986] these studies extend the scope of the generalizability of this notion to the international context. The network perspective raises interesting questions concerning definition and permeability of organizational boundaries [Wilkins 1986] and the creation, maintenance, and destruction of international networks [Borys and Jemison 1989].

Even though there are some major methodological problems inherent in employing the network perspective, I believe that this line of inquiry can best enhance the interdisciplinary orientation in the domain of IM and IB. In Table 1, I provide a list of various research strategies that are appropriate for each of the cells.

Cell 3 studies demand the most rigorous combination of formal theory, field studies with interdisciplinary teams, and employ longitudinal methods. These studies also enhance the possibility of maximum creative tensions among the paradigms of various social science based disciplines.

These discipline based paradigms which comprise the domain of IB have two aspects, a *creative* and a *critical* component. Creative aspect is concerned with hypothesis generation, while the critical aspect involves the hypothesis-testing part of the

Table 1. Appropriate Research Strategies for the Four Cells

Cell 1:	Field Studies
	Archival Methods
Cell 2:	Formal Theory
	Computer Simulations
	Econometric Methods
Cell 3:	Field Studies with Formal Theory
	With Interdisciplinary Teams
	Longitudinal Methods
Cell 4:	Large Scale Field Studies
	With Interdisciplinary Teams
	Longitudinal Methods

paradigm. The creative aspect encourages us to derive our research hypotheses from current theoretical formulations in the respective disciplines. The critical, hypothesis-testing aspect of the paradigm calls for design of appropriate research strategies to test the validity and the generalizability of these derived hypotheses.

One of the two central messages I would like to convey in this paper is that now is the appropriate time for encouraging research strategies which emphasize generalizability related concerns a little more than validity related concerns. The second message is that now is the appropriate time for also encouraging the *creative* aspect of our research endeavor a little more at the expense of the *critical* aspect. In the next section, I provide some guidelines for fostering interdisciplinary orientation.

In developing these guidelines I have been influenced by the work of McGuire [1973] and by Mohr [1982] who advocated such strategies for developing more rigorous progress in social psychology and in organizational behavior (OB).

SOME GUIDELINES FOR FOSTERING INTERDISCIPLINARY ORIENTATIONS

Guide 1. *Perhaps the most powerful method of arriving at interdisciplinary hypotheses is to try to account for paradoxical incidents.* In our study of Japanese transplants in the United States [Bhagat and Kedia 1991], we found that existing conceptual frameworks that are typically employed to explain the success of these transplants were inadequate. We needed a combination of various theoretical approaches (i.e., transaction-cost models, theory of cultural variations, theory of work and authority) to explain the success of Japanese transplants in the United States. These transplant related incidents are typically regarded as paradoxical in the traditional context of organization theory [Florida and Kenney 1991]. By adopting these different theoretical perspectives we were able to conceptually grapple with the complexities of the transplant related phenomena in a more comprehensive fashion. Explanation provided by any one of these perspectives was only partially helpful. It was essential to consider the respective utility of all of these perspectives in understanding this paradoxical incident.

Guide 2. *A second method for generating interdisciplinary frameworks is by using analogy.* Even though this method is used frequently by researchers in this area, its rigorous use is still lacking in the field. In using analogy as a technique for formulating hypotheses, we also enhance the interdisciplinary character of our investigations. There are numerous documented examples of success in joint venture arrangements when they ought to fail—as well as examples of failures in such joint ventures when they ought to succeed. Using analogies to derive working hypotheses in these situations could enhance the interdisciplinary nature of our learning. What I am suggesting is that we make the use of analogies more explicit rather than implicit in our future endeavors. But at the same time we derive rigorous hypotheses based on these analogies.

Guide 3. *Another method of generating hypotheses is by trying to account for conflicting results.* For example, why is it that the meaning of working (MOW study [1987]) is declining in the Western Europe? Given the roots of the Protestant work ethic in Western Europe, such a decline is unexpected. In trying to account for this kind of conflicting result, the researcher almost has to adopt an interdisciplinary perspective. Contributions from various fields have to be creatively integrated in order to understand the nature of such conflicting results. Another example is drawn from the literature on technology transfer. Given the kind of effects absorption of technology produces in organizational contexts, it is indeed surprising that collectivist countries with high power distance norms are almost as effective as the individualistic countries with low power distance norms in absorbing new and innovative forms of technologies. Kedia and Bhagat [1988] provide some rationale for such conflicting findings based on other types of cultural norms found in these collectivistic countries. It is clear that this rationale could be improved by broadening the perspective to include insights from economics, sociology, political science, and other areas.

Guide 4. *Focus on multiple causes of an observed phenomenon.* As I review the literature on international management, I am often struck by the lack of explanations that focus on multiple causes of an observed phenomenon. In almost all IM related situations, effects are the outcome of multiple causes which are often in complex interactions. In addition, it is the rule rather than the exception that the effects act back on the causal variables. Hence, the investigators of IM processes should think big, or rather think complexly, with conceptual models that involve parallel processing, nets of causally interrelated factors, feedback loops, bidirectional causation, etc.

If investigators are to begin thinking in terms of more complex models, then explicit encouragement is necessary from editors of current established journals in fostering this line of work. Cell 3 types of studies which involve large scale field operations with interdisciplinary teams involving longitudinal methods are necessary. To this end we have to give greater play to techniques like computer simulation, parameter estimation, multivariate time series designs, and longitudinal analyses, etc. Currently such designs are somewhat infrequently employed by researchers in some of the functional disciplines comprising the domain of IB inquiry.

Guide 5. *Emphasize more process-theory based designs as opposed to only variance-theory based designs.* Most investigations in the domain of IM with which I am familiar, are cast in terms of the constructs of variance theories. In variance theory, the precursor (X) is regarded as a *necessary* and *sufficient* condition for the emergence of an outcome (Y). In other words, if X, then Y, and if X is absent, Y can not take place. In process theory X is a necessary condition for Y to emerge but condi-

tion of sufficiency which is so preeminent in variance theory framework is not regarded as a serious condition in the process-theory framework. Process theories deal with discrete states and events, and time ordering among these events is very important in ascertaining the nature of explanation.

Mohr [1982], in a fascinating book on explaining organizational behavior, advocates the use of process theories in designing investigations. He defines a process theory as "one that tells a little story about how something comes about, but in order to qualify as a theoretical explanation of recurrent behavior, the manner of story telling must conform to narrow specifications" [p. 45].

Even though process theories are rather important, the variance theory framework has dominated our thinking in much of social science. Such a development is unfortunate since some of our major conceptual dilemmas in the social sciences and indeed in the area of IB are best understood in terms of process theory-based frameworks. It is not my purpose to engage in an elaborate description of process theory in this paper. The reader is referred to Mohr's [1982] book for a detailed discussion. In reviewing the literature in the area of cross-cultural and cross-national management [Bhagat and McQuaid 1982; Bhagat et. al. 1990], we have encountered situations where process-theory based designs have much to offer. I believe that rigorous employment of process theory based designs will improve the quality of our interdisciplinary endeavors.

Guide 6. *To understand the nature of future trends in the present, find the present in the past.* One idea whose time has come in the field of IM is the accumulation of IB data archives. Such data archives should also include information on factors which might affect transactions across national and cultural boundaries. It could then enable us to permit analyses to tease out complex interrelations among important variables. The need for such archives is explicitly recognized in the area of IB strategy. But high quality data archives are still not readily available to researchers. I believe that these data archives will play important roles in fostering interdisciplinary orientation in the field. These data archives should allow us to see the future in the present as we attempt to understand the present in analyzing the past.

THE *YIN* AND *YANG* OF PROGRESS: SOME FINAL THOUGHTS

As I have noted earlier, the *yin* and *yang* of progress in IB will evolve out of creative tensions among the various disciplines. Some phenomenon are best investigated in terms of modal research strategies that are found in cells 1 and 4. However, for others we will need the research strategies found in cell 4. Research which involves both cross-border operations with focus on generalizability related issues are most likely to enhance the interdisciplinary character of the inquires in the field of IB. These are found in cell 3 type of designs.

However, this is not to say and we should abandon cell 1 and 4 types of studies altogether. As I mentioned earlier, we need more creative tension among all of the disciplines which comprises the domain of IB. It is in fostering this creative tension that we can make the field of IB more rigorous and focused in providing ourselves with the answers we need in an increasingly complex and borderless world. The guides developed in the earlier section should aid in this process.

The goal of IB research as in any other type of social science research is ultimately to draw causal inferences. Researchers wish to be able to conclude with reasonable internal validity that the variables studied in relation to the phenomenon are the origin of observed differences in our dependent variables of interest [Bhagat and McQuaid 1982; Bhagat et. al. 1990]. Thus it is crucial to design interdisciplinary investigations in which populations of respondents as well as populations of organizations across various national borders are adequately represented. Unless an interdisciplinary framework is adopted in the early stages of designing the investigation, it is unlikely that equivalence of concepts across national boundaries will be assured and plausible alternative explanations will be systematically ruled out. A related issue that needs some attention here is how the evolving discipline of IB would design and distribute its rewards. If scholars who pursue long-term research objectives with strong interdisciplinary orientations are rewarded, then we enhance the possibility of sustaining such orientations. On the other hand, if those who pursue only narrowly conceived research designs are rewarded, then we will know more and more about less and less and interdisciplinary orientation would suffer.

Individuals from different cultural and national settings may differ in many ways other than their specific cultural and national backgrounds. Specific attention to variables which might seem *exogenous* to the investigation in the initial stages might turn out to be of crucial importance and *endogenous* to the investigation in later stages. Within an interdisciplinary orientation, we might encounter more *Yang's* than *Yin's* in future theory building efforts in the domain of international business.

Panel Discussion

The panel discussion involved a lively debate of six questions prepared in advance and given the panelists the night before the discussion took place. The questions were based upon themes identified as common to at least two of the papers. Unfortunately, due to technical difficulties in the recording of the panel, not all of the discussion was available for printing. Thus, the reported discussion contains some usable, but edited portions of the tape as well as some summaries reported by the Ph.D. students assigned to this panel as rapporteurs: Ernie Csiszar, Tom Hench, and Jim Johnson. After the four panelists were given an opportunity to respond to a question, comments and questions were entertained from the floor.

I would like to conclude these remarks by personally thanking the panel members for their hard work in preparing their position statements and the additional insights they provided during the following discussion.

BRIAN TOYNE

In their papers, Professors Jack Behrman and Jean Boddewyn argue that a theory of IB is not presently feasible, but for seemingly different reasons. For example, Jean argued that it is impossible to develop a unifying theory of IB since we don't have a general theory of business. Jack's position is that it is not feasible if IB is viewed as holistic. My question to the panel is whether a comprehensive, all inclusive theory of IB is a prerequisite for establishing IB inquiry as a viable and distinct field.

JEAN BODDEWYN

An all-inclusive theory is not a prerequisite for IB, provided that IB is perceived, understood and accepted both by us and by significant others as having a genuine focus, and that there are real important problems and issues to be addressed. Let me use as an analogy our ideas about human sexuality: we have on the one hand Freud's complex but partial theories which took a long time to gain acceptance by the population at large. Then there is the primarily descriptive Kinsey Report on sexual practices. I think both contributed to the development of a field of investigation called sexual behavior which in the past was ignored or had been treated as a sin. So I don't think we need to have a single general theory of IB to establish it as a field, provided we and others agree that there are significant problems there. To finish on that point, we have to dispel the fallacy held by many Americans—not so much by Europeans—that business is business wherever you conduct it, or that going international is no different from spreading over the United States. That is, we still have to dispel the notion that there is no IB field.

JACK BEHRMAN

Brian, you say viable and distinct. I think Jean answered the first part of the question. It is clearly viable to have an IB discipline without a theory. However, in my view, IB *cannot* be a distinct field without a theory, but that is irrelevant to anybody but academics. What we in the Academy of International Business have thought for the last 10 to 20 years is that we are a profession. However, a profession, by its very nature, establishes barriers. Now that, in my view, is not what IB ought to do. I think we ought to accept the fact that we will wander through a variety of theories, adopting them from other places, and hopefully so. I would like to see others contribute to our field, participate in it, make contributions which we're perfectly willing to accept, and vice versa. After all, the highest freedom for an academic is to choose which problems to work on. I hope no one will tell us what to work on simply because the subject belongs in a particular field.

JEAN-FRANÇOIS HENNART

I don't think we have one theory of IB, we have theories of IB which contribute to our store of knowledge. The skill of the researcher is to know which theory to apply to what problem. A good way to convince ourselves that we have theories of IB is to look at the attempts of non-IB at addressing IB issues, and to see the errors that they commit when they do so—for example, mixing up parents and subsidiaries in their sample, and thus treating subsidiaries as if they were free-standing units. Non-IB scholars also often talk about a continuum from exporting to joint ventures to wholly-owned subsidiaries, ignoring the distinction between location and ownership dimensions of entry modes.

RABI BHAGAT

I don't think we really have a general theory of business. What we do have are mid-range theories constructed by different disciplines. In my opinion, it would be dangerous to try and build a general theory of international business if, in the process of doing so, we might lose some of the unique advantages that we get by pursuing inquiry in the distinct fields which comprise the domain of international business. So, I think, we should build *mid-range theories*, but not a general theory of international business. I think that would be a risky proposition and could throw roadblocks in the path of creative development of many mid-range theories.

BRIAN TOYNE

In your opinion, Rabi, what does establish a field or a sub-field of inquiry as distinct. It can be pointed out that this particular question has troubled our colleagues in other fields, such as economics and political science.

RABI BHAGAT

I think that fields develop their distinctive boundaries by pursuing different types of research paradigms and research methods. Take the field of experimental psychology which is often thought to be an extension of mainstream psychology. But, it is distinct from psychology because it employs a different type of research methodology in its pursuit for knowledge about the human mind. Different types of scientific inquiries employ different methodologies. It is primarily around distinctive methodologies that distinct boundaries tend to get established. So, to the extent that research methodologies are very similar in the various sub-fields within IB, then to that extent at

least, those distinctive boundaries slowly begin to converge.

JEAN-FRANÇOIS HENNART

Well, I think what establishes a field as distinct is that a field tries to address particular problems which are salient and have great policy relevance, but on which other disciplines are unable to throw much light because this would require abandoning some of the fundamental assumptions of the discipline. Then some researcher comes in and creates a new theory out of bits and pieces of other theories. In my paper, I make the point that the transaction cost theory is a distinct IB theory because it meets these criteria.

JACK BEHRMAN

It seems to me that the definition of a field occurs from continually narrowing its scope which is then recognized by colleagues in the discipline as valuable. Let's look, for example, at what economics did to itself in order to define itself as a distinct field. It removed the political aspects of economics because that was too fuzzy to handle. Secondly, it divorced itself from work (which was left in sociology), from population, from welfare, and from cultural issues. It then adopted a scientific paradigm in order to become a "science" which was highly mechanistic being based on mechanical physics, seeking an equilibrium; such an equilibrium is a very simplistic concept of the way in which social forces work. It made a culture-bound assumption about rationality in order to get rid of a whole set of decision-making criteria and it removed itself from philosophy and theology in order to achieve a clinical value-based discipline . . . all which makes it value-*less*.

JEAN BODDEWYN

I have very little to add here, except to say that the problems that Jack mentioned—and they are real—are at the level of the assumptions that underlie all theories. We do not have to fall into the trap of accepting assumptions which are too narrow. We can learn from economics. But beyond that, I think, the major problem in defining a field is to identify the problems, the issues which are relevant. For example, I think that John Fayerweather's 1969 book, *International Business Management*, is still an extremely powerful way of delineating the four issues in the IB field, and that's what we should focus on. So I think, taking Fayerweather as an example, we can define IB as a field of inquiry.

ALAN BAUERSCHMIDT

Do you see a difference between a theory and discourse? I hear a discourse, but I don't see a theory, and does that preclude research?

JEAN-FRANÇOIS HENNART

No, I think we have *theories*. A theory is a shortcut, a way to explain the maximum number of phenomena with a minimum number of ideas. We have such theories in IB. For example, John Dunning's eclectic theory—I think he has recently renamed it a paradigm—is such a theory. This paradigm, and transaction cost theory which is one part of this paradigm, can be used to throw light on a wide variety of topics. But no theory can answer all questions.

JACK BEHRMAN

You can have discourse without theory. You can have discourse *about* theories and the assumptions that surround them. You can have discourse about the application of a theory, whether it is a relevant theory or useful, and so on. So, yes, there is discourse and there are theories. The question is how applicable are the theories that we're dealing with, and that is a discourse about assumptions and logic as much as anything. Years ago, Joan Robinson said there are three ways of coming to an agreement: One is on the facts. Another is on the application of theoretical constructs and the use of the facts—which is logic. And the third is on

values, and that's where *most* of the disagreement really arises. When you throw out an examination of values, you are back into a rather mechanistic application of logic. You can have a lot of discourse about it, but it's not going to take you very far.

JEAN BODDEWYN

If I can return to the modernist-postmodernist distinction I made in my domain paper, the post-modernist basically say that anything you present and establish, such as a theory, is a form of discourse . . . meaning that you could come from a different direction . . . a feminist direction, a Marxist direction, or a religious direction, and you would recast the problem. I don't think we have done that much recasting in our field, but it's available and valuable. It can be done.

RABI BHAGAT

It seems to me that you need multiple discourses that are genuinely conflicting, and to the extent that you cannot reconcile these conflicts, you slowly develop midrange theories. You need discourse in the preparadigmatic stage, and as these discourses converge slowly, you build various theoretical foundations. These theoretical foundations can then be subject to empirical testing, and the validity of these frameworks are assessed by empirical procedures.

JOHN DUNNING

Since I think we are all agreed that IB addresses a set of rather different issues, it follows that we must have different theories to answer these particular questions, rather than an all embracing theory. My approach has been more pragmatic than theoretical. It makes a big difference as to whether you are trying to answer the question of why an American firm locates overseas, or how it is possible for an American firm to enter into the British market in relationship to an indigenous UK competitor, or why an American firm chooses to invest rather than to go into a foreign market by some other modality. Now these are very different sorts of questions and, if you mean by a theory a set of hypotheses which tend to explain in as rigorous a fashion as possible, what factors influence each of those decisions, then you are going to have different kinds of theories. There is a theory of economics, a theory of organization, a theory of psychology, and so on. There is no longer a single theory of international trade. There are a group of theories to explain different aspects of this phenomenon. I will go one step further and say that it is possible to have something like a paradigm which provides the framework for examining the relevance of different theories. Now I am not suggesting that the eclectic paradigm is all embracing—although some people think that I try to make it so—, but it does go one step up from a set of theories. I also think that internalization theory is in many ways a paradigm to the extent that there are many different forms of market failure. You can hypothesize in each particular kind of market failure whether it is likely to occur and what is likely to influence the extent to which different modalities are appropriate for overcoming these different sorts of failure. So, there are plenty of theories, and more often than not, they are not substitutable for, but complementary to one another. They do not seek to answer the same question and we do ourselves a disservice by saying, "A's talk is wrong because his theory is wrong when, in fact, he is trying to solve a slightly different problem than B." And that is why I believe that IB inquiry can encompass a whole set of theories, can encompass many paradigms, and that many of these theories and paradigms—although they may be put forth by economists using economic tools or by O.B. or management scholars—do embrace the output from other disciplines for a proper understanding.

STEPHEN KOBRIN

Following up on what John said, we have a contrast between theories and a theory. I wonder if we could have a field with-out a single unifying theory of IB. We can have a field in the sense of a body of knowledge about IB. It is interesting that Rabi is seated at one end and Jean-François is seated at the other end (referring to the seating arrangement of the panel members). Rabi does cross-cultural work and is interested in phenomena that are international. Jean-François is concerned with transaction cost economics as applied to international business. They are both using theories that have to be informed by what's specifically international, but they're poles apart. They explain different phenomena. We can have a field without a theory, and agree that it comprises expertise and knowledge, and not look for a single unifying theory for IB.

BRIAN TOYNE

Jean-François states that we should not be too concerned at either the lack of a unifying theory of IB, or the need to borrow theories and paradigms from other disciplines. This, it was suggested, is characteristic of all new fields. He then proceeds to demonstrate how IB researchers are making "clear contributions," and draws the following four conclusions concerning "successful" research: (1) the topic has greater international than domestic salience; (2) the topic has important policy implications; (3) existing theory is not consistent with empirical evidence; and (4) traditional assumptions underpinning the theory do not apply.

JEAN-FRANÇOIS HENNART

What I was trying to do was show how specific theories have been developed. I looked at the transaction costs theory of MNE and asked myself how this theory came about, and I came up with the four conditions you mentioned. The first one was that the problem of MNEs was not addressed by traditional international economics because traditional international economics assumes zero transaction costs. The traditional international economics answer to why a MNE exists was the theory of foreign direct investment, or FDI. Multinational enterprises were seen as investment flows, and the extent and direction of these flows were explained by differences in interest rates across countries. Hence, for traditional international economists, the expansion of firms across countries was seen only as the export of capital. Now this was not consistent with the facts. I am not going to go into details here because we do not have the time, but the actual pattern of these flows was not consistent with the theory, and the theory could not account for the fact that firms did not expand without any financial flows because they financed their expansion from local sources.

The MNE is basically a type of multiplant firm. The difference between the MNE and a multi-plant firm is that the salience of the phenomenon and the forces at work are very different. MNEs are very visible, while multi-plant firms are taken for granted. I think we are interested in developing theories for international problems which are salient and which have policy implications. The MNEs became salient in the 1960s because both home and host countries started to wonder what their impact was on taxation, on the balance of payments, and on national sovereignty. If the policy issues had not been so pressing, no one would have probably bothered to develop theory.

One more factor is important. That is the importance of data. Hymer's argument that the actual expansion of multinational firms is not consistent with traditional capital export theories was supported by data collected by John Dunning and by other researchers. Without such data, the argument would have lost a lot of its punch. Also, the transaction cost theory of the MNE is not just a slavish application of Williamson's work to the international area. The first development of the theory by John McManus dates from 1972, three years before Williamson published his book. We are talking here about a separate body of theory that is substantially different from

Williamson's argument, at least for those of us who are purists.

BRIAN TOYNE

Jean-François suggests that IB researchers are capable of contributing to our body of knowledge on business by transcending existing theories and creating specific theories that are starting to define the field of IB. My question to the panel members is whether you agree or disagree with this assessment of the IB researcher's role?

JACK BEHRMAN

The IB researcher is really not prepared to develop an integrated theory. Jean-François's paper suggests that there are multiple roles which business plays with nation states. Companies are involved in the issues of security, military sales, and so on. Now look at the various academic business disciplines and ask yourself which of them offers a theory to explain the importance of these varied relationships and how they work. And, you will find that it would come from virtually every other discipline of the university. Therefore, IB theorists are not versed in diversity and are not yet prepared to put all this together, nor maybe even to understand all of it. But, we do have to work with it and, therefore, the congeries of different theories.

JEAN BODDEWYN

Taking your question literally, namely creating specific theories, I'm very impressed with Jean-François's argument. But, I still think that essentially he says that transaction-cost analysis does apply to international phenomena, that it applies even better to international phenomena than to domestic phenomena, and that we have done a better job using it than people that limited themselves to domestic problems. But, I'm not sure that this amounts to a distinct theory of IB.

RABI BHAGAT

It seems to me that one of the more conceptually rigorous ways to develop multi-disciplinary theories of IB is accomplished by employing the framework involving the four cells I describe in my paper. Most theories in IB that you see right now, except for network theories, could be grouped in Cell 1. These theories emphasize within-border operations, primarily within the US context, and are focused on internal validity related issues. If you want to develop theories that are very complex and multi-disciplinary, then you need to emphasize cross-border operations and focus on generalizability related issues. To the extent that you can maximize the research process on these two dimensions, then you can develop theories which account for the complexity which is present in most IB situations. But so far, we have not done that. We have tried to develop theories which account for the complexity which is present in most IB situations. But so far, we have not done that. We have tried to develop theories primarily in Cell 1, and some in Cells 2 and 4. What I am trying to say is that the science of developing midrange theories in Cells 1, 4, and 2 is all right, but the theories which are developed primarily in the context of Cell 3 are the ones which will help us integrate contributions from the different disciplines. Here we are concerned with cross-border operations and, at the same time, we are concerned with developing theories which are basically applicable in different national and cultural contexts. By maximizing our output on both these dimensions we should end up developing interdisciplinary theories of international business.

JEAN-FRANÇOIS HENNART

Well, I think that Jean's point is whether the theory we develop in IB is only applicable to IB. I think we develop theories to solve IB problems. Yet, these theories have much wider application. I see that as a plus, not a minus.

MIRA WILKINS

I think we ought to re-examine the notion of IB enterprise versus IB activity. It seems to me if we are concerned about IB enterprise, we can talk about theory. We can talk about theoretical structure in relation to the IB enterprise. If we are talking about IB activity, then I feel there are different levels of analysis. I think we can have a good theory of enterprise, but I'm not confident that we can have a theory of IB activity.

Clearly, I feel that we can develop a theory of IB enterprise. If a theory is useless we should throw it out. By this, I mean if it is not consistent with the facts, then we have to search for a better explanation. The purpose of having theoretical structure is not for its own sake, it is for understanding. If theory is not useful to understanding, it's not appropriate. I think that a lot of the theoretical discussion that has emerged in the last thirty years has been useful. It has been useful in explaining IB and saying something in this discipline that hasn't been said by others. So I favor work in that direction.

ROBERT LOCKE

We need to remember that theory can be an obstacle to thought. For my part, I make it a point when staking out a new area to avoid the theoretical literature. I first go to the facts, then I start to build my theory. If I read what other people have to say in a theoretical sense, they may direct my thoughts in ways that might stop me from coming up with any useful results.

GUNNAR HEDLUND

Perhaps, we are attaching too much importance to devising a theoretical approach to the study of international business. I think there are some economists who say that the facts speak for themselves. We should also admit that IB scholars have done a very good job of trying to understand empirical reality, rather than justify the use of particular theories. I think that's why this type of economics has not become sterile. I mean, John Dunning has written a lot about the international investment that companies are actually making, and that's why the eclectic theory is interesting. It's not just throwing theoretical ideas in a can and blending them.

As a journal editor, I sometimes receive articles from people with certain theoretical prejudices, applying those to IB. For example, I received a population ecology article about the automobile industry and the authors didn't know about voluntary export restraints. They hadn't heard that imports to the United States were restricted. That's like talking about elements of the stomach without knowing about the appendix. I think we have a lot of applications to international business of that nature—starting with a bias really, and trying to convince people that they have something to say. We need to learn about empirical reality, I believe, with additional theoretical work. But today, I think that may be the problem—particularly among younger people—is that newer contributions are based on too little empirical knowledge rather than too little theoretical knowledge.

FRANKLIN (RUSS) ROOT

I just wanted to quote Goethe, who said, "All theory is grey, only real life is green."

BRIAN TOYNE

In his paper, Rabi echoes themes that are presented in the other papers, and that have been heard during the last three days; namely, that IB inquiry is multidisciplinary. He elaborated on this theme using the constructs of *yin* and *yang*, and suggested that progress in IB inquiry evolves out of creative tensions among the various disciplines.

RABI BHAGAT

It seems to me that IB research will never be either completely multi-disciplinary or completely uni-disciplinary. What will be happening in the future could be characterized by a series of creative tensions among disciplines comprising the domain of IB. Sometimes we will see the bright side of the yin-yang symbol, which could be interpreted in terms of the IB field emphasizing a multi-disciplinary approach. Then we will move away from this perspective and begin to focus on the same problems by adopting a series of uni-disciplinary perspectives. Basically, there is going to be continuous movement between the two perspectives and that's why I use the constructs of *yin and yang*. What we have is not a unified body of knowledge, but a series of creative tensions among the business disciplines, and from this tension creative theories about IB emerge.

BRIAN TOYNE

There are, however, paradigmatic and theoretical impediments to multi-disciplinary, more correctly, interdisciplinary discourse. Thus, my question to the panel is how can we begin to generate the creative tension that Rabi suggests is needed?

JEAN-FRANÇOIS HENNART

I think there are two problems with multi-disciplinary research. The major problem is conflicting assumptions. If you have two co-authors with very different paradigms, such as someone trained in economics and someone trained in organizational behavior, you have real problems with coming up with something which holds together. Now, one cannot generalize, because some organizational behavior researchers use paradigms which are consistent with economics. But, in general, those two paradigms are not compatible. That does not mean that as an economist you should not be informed by the insights and the theories of organization behavior or organization theory, but merging the two paradigms may be very frustrating. Each discipline has also its norms and its habits. Economists have no problems generalizing from small data sets. Historians need 2000 confirmations before they feel comfortable generalizing on anything, and then some historians will remark that the 1999th observation is really different. So there are differences in norms and habits which make it difficult to combine insights of different disciplines. One way by which one is forced to do so is to submit a paper to a journal outside one's main discipline. Last year I submitted a paper to *Organization Science* and the reviewers asked me to read a number of works in sociology. I had to do it because I wanted to get the paper published. I learned a lot through that process, and found out that this literature, which I did not know, was very much compatible with my own ideas.

JEAN BODDEWYN

I subscribe to what Jean-François said. I'll just add that we need to stretch ourselves. The creative tension has to be in ourselves. But we have to hire people from different disciplines. I think schools of business are still dominated by people trained in economics as the older tradition, then by scads of people trained in psychology after the 1960s, and then—echoing Gunnar Hedlund's comments, you sometimes see people with magnificent quantitative skills in search of problems but with no knowledge of any subject matter. So I think that we need, for example, to hire more sociologists. You'll hardly find sociologists in schools of business, or anthropologists and political scientists. One way to stretch ourselves and have creative tension is to complement what we have. Another way to have creative tension is to find collaborators from other disciplines for our research projects.

JACK BEHRMAN

Well, I think one of the first things each of us has to do, even in the functional areas of business, is to recognize the limitations of our theories and the assumptions that we have and to explain both to the students. That itself creates a little tension—to recognize that we are myopic in what we're asserting. Another way is to work at the

interfaces between the theories of the various disciplines. Clearly, having to deal with the interface between business practice and economic theory has created a great deal of tension in our discipline.

RABI BHAGAT

I agree, but in addition, we can do other things which will improve the creative tension among the disciplines. There are many phenomena that are inherently paradoxical, like the case of Japanese transplants in the American context. One cannot explain this phenomenon very well by using either an economics-based perspective or a transaction cost-based perspective. You need to bring in perspectives from psychology, sociology, and so on. So, if you move toward collaboration in IB in solving problems or understanding puzzles that are paradoxical, you might be able to improve your theories by using this creative tension. A second thing that can be done is to use analogies. If an idea has worked well in one discipline, maybe we should use this idea in an analogous manner in another discipline. A third thing is to try to account for conflicting results, not by using ideas and paradigms from our own discipline, but by borrowing paradigms and constructs from other disciplines as well. Again, let the empirical data dictate how we should modify our theories. And fourth, we should focus on *multiple* causes of an observed phenomenon. I don't see this done very much in the domain of IB. If a particular phenomenon can be observed from multiple perspectives, then we will develop a better theory. To some extent we should focus on multiple determinants which have their intellectual roots in different disciplines. By doing so we could enhance the creative tension and foster the nature of multi-disciplinary explanation. And fifth, a point which I would like to mention, is we need to create a rich data archives which would help us understand the nature of the present so we can understand how to predict the future. I think if we develop these data archives in different universities, and share these data, we can begin to understand come of the tensions that exist between the disciplines.

ALAN BAUERSCHMIDT

Based on what I have heard, how can there be differences in theories if such are based on fact. I've heard that mentioned a number of times today. How can there be differences in theories if they are based on fact?

JACK BEHRMAN

Because all theories are abstractions. We cannot know all the facts. We cannot know the truth. We cannot know reality. All of us operate on assumptions, and those assumptions lead to abstractions, and abstractions are theories. All of us think in terms of theories. Because we cannot think holistically, however much we would like to.

ALAN BAUERSCHMIDT

A science game?

JACK BEHRMAN

No, an art game.

JEAN-FRANCOIS HENNART

It is a creative process.

MARK CASSON

I think it might be useful to think of theory as a sequence of restrictions. So you start with Theory A, which is "Anything can happen." You say "That is very useful," so you develop Theory B which says that "People are rational." Then you say, "Yes, but, rational in pursuit of what?" So you have Theory C which says, "Self-interest is the dominant motive." As you progress with this sequence, different disciplines take different routes. One discipline may say "Selfishness is central"—that might be economics—and another discipline might say "Justice and a sense of fairness are just as important" and that might be political

science or sociology. So these disciplines branch off. As each branch develops it seizes on some particular problem that is easy to solve using its own restrictive and specialized assumptions. The legacy of this process is that we now have many narrow theories analyzing microscopic issues. The current challenge in IB is to move back up a middle range theory which avoids this kind of tunnel vision.

RABI BHAGAT

But when you do that, it seems to me that you get comprehensiveness at the expense of rigor. You lose rigor because you lose the distinctive perspectives of the different disciplines. It seems to me that you cannot maximize comprehensiveness and rigor at the same time.

MARK CASSON

Yes, that's the trade-off and that's part of the dialogue between the holistic person who doesn't want to make any assumptions and those who like to work in tightly defined fields. But there is a middle ground, and interaction between them.

FRANKLIN ROOT

An awful lot of discovery has occurred as a result of a kind of play rather than through a deterministic model of research. Playing with ideas. Oftentimes a discovery was made by a scientist outside of that particular area of science. It strikes me that we're all too serious in our research. I don't see much evidence of play here. Playing with ideas and developing insights leads discovery which becomes a deeper theory.

JACK BEHRMAN

Well, if you're not having fun, Russ, don't do it. Play is a good construct. Creativity, which we are all working on, is seeing things differently from the way that they have been seen before, or the way they are being seen by others. You have to be a little careful if you see too differently . . . you'll end up in a particular house. You should see just differently enough so that you spot the creative ideas. Such ideas come mostly from people who were playing around, just getting glimmers of things in a chosen field and then coming up with an "aha" insight, which then requires a theory and empirical testing.

ROBERT LOCKE

Are we not forced by the foundations to be serious. You cannot go to the National Science Foundation, for example, and say "Give me a billion dollars. I want to play."

JACK BEHRMAN

But that's what the MacArthur Foundation did. It selected people who were insightful and talented and said: "Take $50,000 and go play." That's an enlightened foundation.

BRIAN TOYNE

As a final area for discussion, I would like to return to Rabi's recommendation for the constructive and illuminating use of interdisciplinary tension, and briefly discuss the structural impediments to interdisciplinary research and theorizing. In your opinion Rabi, do I need to be concerned with the way schools of business have structured their research and educational activities? Am I, perhaps, being overly pessimistic about the future of IB inquiry by asserting that the departmentalization of business research and education along functionalized lines inhibits the interdisciplinary growth of IB inquiry?

RABI BHAGAT

In his paper, John Daniels makes some very good observations about what can be done to improve the creative tension. (Panel chair's comment: Daniels's paper is to appear in the second book of the conference.) I think new professors should be given at least seven to eight years before they are subject to the pressures of the tenure

process. Because, once in the traditional process, they try to do research in a rather narrow vein. They really cannot take advantage of a multi-disciplinary perspective. So, if you could lengthen the horizon that they have to produce empirical research before they come up for tenure, etc., then to that extent you have fostered interdisciplinary research involving creative tensions among the disciplines.

JACK BEHRMAN

I've talked to a good many Ph.D. candidates while they are going through their programs, and many of them are concerned about being shoved into boxes. Why don't we let them play with their dissertations? Instead, we try to get them to follow a very specific pattern which is duplicated in the *Journal of International Business Studies (JIBS)*. I must say, I do not enjoy *JIBS* anymore. Every article is cut out of a cookie pattern which is replicated in the dissertation. I don't see any joy in it. We need to get students to open their minds and be willing to take risks. The problem is that we are surrounded by colleagues in the business school who don't accept that, and by provosts and committees in the university who don't accept that. But, maybe it's time we start arguing that we remove the straitjackets of form and stimulate thinking. Creativity doesn't come from duplicating the same patterns of thinking over and over again with some data sets—in the same paradigm. We need to start now to push Ph.D. candidates to be a little creative, but this will take faculty who accept some risks.

JEAN BODDEWYN

In discussing what has been called multi-discipline, inter-discipline, supradiscipline, and so on, I think that pragmatically speaking there are really three routes. One route is uni-disciplinary, as most ground breaking research typically is. For example, John Dunning's eclectic paradigm is soundly grounded in economics, although borrowing from various parts of economics. The second route is what John Dunning has called "add-ons," whereby he has attempted to enrich his original purely economic paradigm, or Mark Casson investigating culture and entrepreneurship more recently. So that's what you might call the add-on—saying I'm still in economics, but I want to stretch it. Of course, there are problems in stretching because it's like an emulsion—like mayonnaise which is an emulsion of vinegar and oil. If you shake it, they mix, but when it's set down, they separate again. You have to be able to find a permanent binding agent like eggs, so to speak. The third approach is to develop research that simultaneously tests various paradigms. Here, one example that impressed me, but I'm sure there are others, is when Bruce Kogut analyzed joint-ventures simultaneously through transaction-cost analysis, resource-dependence theory, and inter-organizational theory. So, we don't have to be stuck on a single notion of what constitutes a multi-disciplinary approach. There is room for uni-disciplinary, uni-disciplinary with add-ons, and then—much more difficult, more mature, more senior stuff—where you simultaneously test different theories.

JEAN-FRANÇOIS HENNART

Actually, I was going to say very much the same thing. I want to add one footnote. Young-Ryeol Park and I did a paper on the choice of Japanese investors between greenfield entry and acquisitions, and submitted it for presentation at the Academy of Management meetings. In this paper we were testing the predictions of a number of theories, including Penrose's theory and finance theory. When the paper came back, the referees' comments were that we were looking at too many theories. Why didn't we stick instead with the most useful theory, transaction cost theory. So, you see, it is not always easy to be multi-disciplinary.

REFERENCES

Alchian, A. and H. Demsetz. 1972. Production, information costs, and economic organiza-tion. *American Economic Review*, 62: 777–795.

Aldrich, H. E. and D. A. Whetten. 1981. Organization-sets, action sets, and networks: Making the most of simplicity. In P. C. Nystrom and W. H. Starbuck, editors, *Handbook of Organizational Design*, 1:345–408. New York: Oxford University Press.

Bacharach, S. B. 1989. Organizational theories: Some criteria for evaluation. *Academy of Management Review*, 14(4):496–515.

Banks, G. 1983. The economics and politics of countertrade. *The World Economy*, 6:159–182.

Barney, Jay and William Ouchi. 1986. *Organizational Economics*. San Francisco: Jossey-Bass.

Bartlett, Christopher and Sumantra Ghoshal. 1988. Organizing for worldwide effectiveness: The transnational solution. *California Management Review*, 31(1):54.

Behrman, Jack N. 1988. *Essays on Ethics in Business and the Professions*. Englewood Cliffs: Prentice-Hall.

Bergsten, C., T. Horst, and T. Moran. 1978. *American Multinationals and American Interests*. Washington: Brookings Institute.

Bhagat, Rabi S. and Ben L. Kedia. 1991. Innocents abroad: A critical appraisal of the applicability of American organizational sciences in the Far Eastern context. Manuscript submitted for publication.

Bhagat, Rabi S., Ben L. Kedia, S. E. Crawford, and M. R. Kaplan. 1990. Cross-cultural issues in organization psychology: Emergent trends and directions for research in the 1990's. *International Review of Industrial and Organizational Psychology*.

Bhagat, Rabi S. and S. J. McQuaid. 1982. Role of subjective culture in organizations: A review and directions for future research. *Journal of Applied Psychology Monograph*, 67(5):653–685.

Blodgett, Linda. 1991. Partner contributions as predictors of equity share in joint ventures. *Journal of International Business Studies*, 22(1):63–78.

Boddewyn, Jean J. and Th. L. Brewer. 1994. International-business political behavior: New theoretical directions. *Academy of Management Review*, 19(1):119–143.

Boddewyn, Jean J. 1990. Key definitions, research issues and theories. Working document prepared for the workshop on theory development in international management research, Academy of Management Annual Meeting, San Francisco, 11–12 August.

Boddewyn, Jean J. 1988. Political aspects of MNE theory. *Journal of International Business Studies*, 19(3):341–363.

Boddewyn, Jean J. 1986. International political strategy: A fourth "generic" strategy? Working paper. New York: Baruch College (CUNY).

Boddewyn, Jean J. 1985. Theories of foreign direct investment and divestment: A classificatory note. *Management International Review*, 25(1):57–65.

Borys, B. and D. B. Jemison. 1989. Hybrid arrangements as strategic alliances: Theoretical issues in organizational combinations. *Academy of Management Review*, 14(2): 234–249.

Brown, W. B. 1976. Islands of conscious power: MNCs in the theory of the firm. *MSU Business Topics*, 24:37–45.

Buckley, Peter and Mark Casson. 1976. *The Future of Multinational Enterprise*. London: Macmillan.

Burnham, James. 1960. *The Managerial Revolution*. Bloomington: Indiana University Press.

Casson, Mark. 1990. *Enterprise and Competitiveness: A Systems View of International Business*. Oxford: Clarendon Press.

Casson, Mark. 1989. The economic theory of international banking. University of Reading Discussion Paper. In *International Investment and Business Studies*, September.

Casson, Mark. 1985. Multinational monopolies and international cartels. In P. J. Buckley and M. C. Casson, editors, *The Economic Theory of the Multinational Enterprise: Selected Papers*, 60–97. London: Macmillan.

Caves, Richard. 1982. *Multinational Enterprise and Economic Analysis*. New York: Cambridge University Press.

Caves, Richard, Harold Crookell, and Peter Killing. 1982. The imperfect market for technology licenses. *Oxford Bulletin of Economics and Statistics*.

Chandran, R., A. Phatak, and R. Sambharya.

1987. Transborder data flows: Implications for multinational corporations. *Business Horizons*, 30(6):74–82.

Child, J. 1981. Culture, contingency and capitalism in the cross-national study of organizations. In L.L. Cummings and B. M. Staw, editors, *Research in Organizational Behavior*, 3:303–356. Greenwich, CT: JAI Press.

Clark, Terry. 1991. International boundaries and international marketing: A survey of major concepts. Working paper. Notre Dame University, College of Business Administration.

Davidson, William H. and D. McFetridge. 1985. International technology transfer mode. *Journal of International Business Studies*, 16(2):5–21.

de Miramon, J. 1985. Countertrade: An illusory solution. *OECD Observer*, 134(May): 24–29.

Dunning, John N. 1989. The study of international business: A plea for a more interdisciplinary approach. *Journal of International Business Studies*, 20(3):411–436.

Dunning, John N. 1981. *International Production and the Multinational Enterprise*. London: George Allen and Unwin.

Dunning, John N. 1958. *American Investments in British Manufacturing Industry*. London: George Allen and Unwin.

Dunning, John N. and Alan Rugman. 1985. The influence of Hymer's dissertation on the theory of foreign direct investment. *American Economic Review*, (May):228–232.

Egelhoff, William. 1988. *Organizing the Multinational Enterprise*. Cambridge, MA: Ballinger.

Elderkin, K. and W. Norquist. 1987. *Creative Countertrade*. Cambridge, MA: Ballinger.

Enderwick, P. 1988. Between market and hierarchy: the multinational operations of Japanese general trading companies. *Managerial and Decision Economics*, 9:35–40.

Fayerweather, John. 1982. *International Business Strategy and Administration*. Cambridge: Ballinger.

Fayerweather, John. 1969. *International Business Management: A Conceptual Framework*. New York: McGraw-Hill.

Florida, R. and M. Kenney. 1991. Transplanted organizations: The transfer of Japanese organization to the U.S. *American Sociological Review*, 56:381–398.

Gatignon, Hubert and Erin Anderson. 1988. The multinational corporation degree of control over subsidiaries: An empirical test of a transaction cost explanation. *Journal of Law, Economics, and Organization*, 4(2): 305–336.

Ghoshal, Sumantra and Christopher Bartlett. 1990. The multinational corporation as an interorganizational network. *Academy of Management Review*, 15(4):603–625.

Gomes-Casseres, Benjamin. 1989. Ownership structures of foreign subsidiaries: Theory and evidence. *Journal of Economic Behavior and Organization*, 11:1–25.

Grosse, Robert and Jack N. Behrman. 1992. Theory in international business. *Transnational Corporations*, 1(1):91–102.

Halevy, Elie. 1934. *The Growth of Philosophic Radicalism*. London: Faber and Faber.

Hawkins, Robert G. 1984. International business in academia: The state of the field. *Journal of International Business*, 15(3): 13–18.

Hennart, J. F. and Anderson, E. 1993. Countertrade and the minimization of transaction costs: An empirical examination. *Journal of Law, Economics, and Organization*, 9(2): 290–313.

Hennart, Jean-François. 1991a. The transaction cost theory of the multinational enterprise. In C. Pitelis and R. Sugden, editors, *The Nature of the Transnational Firm*. London: Routledge.

Hennart, Jean-François. 1991b. Control in multinational firms: The role of price and hierarchy. *Management International Review*, 31(special issue):71–96.

Hennart, Jean-François. 1991c. The transaction cost theory of joint ventures: An empirical study of Japanese subsidiaries in the United States. *Management Science*, 37(4):483–497.

Hennart, Jean-François. 1990. Some empirical dimensions of countertrade. *Journal of International Business Studies*, 21(2):243–270.

Hennart, Jean-François. 1989a. Can the *new forms of investment* substitute for the *old forms*? A transaction costs perspective. *Journal of International Business Studies*, 20(2):211–233.

Hennart, Jean-François. 1989b. The transaction cost rationale for countertrade. *Journal of Law, Economics, and Organization*, 5:127–153.

Hennart, Jean-François. 1988. A transaction costs theory of equity joint ventures. *Strategic Management Journal*, 9(4):361–374.

Hennart, Jean-François. 1982. *A Theory of Multinational Enterprise*. Ann Arbor: University of Michigan Press.

Hennart, Jean-François. 1977. A theory of foreign direct investment. Ph.D dissertation, University of Maryland.

Hesterly, W., J. Liebeskind, and T. Zenger. 1990. Organizational economics: An impending revolution in organization theory? *Academy of Management Review*, 15:402–420.

Hirschman, Albert O. 1977. *The Passions and the Interests: Political Arguments for Capitalism Before its Triumph*. Princeton: Princeton University Press.

Hofstede, Geert. 1985. The interaction between national and organizational values systems. *Journal of Management Science*, 22(4): 347–357.

Hofstede, Geert. 1984. The cultural relativity of the quality of life concept. *Academy of Management*, 9(3):389–398.

Hymer, Stephen. 1960. The International Operations of National Firms. Ph.D. dissertation, MIT. Published in 1976 by MIT Press.

Kedia, Benjamin and Rabi Bhagat. 1988. Cultural constraints on the transfer of technology across nations: Implications for research in international and comparative management. *Academy of Management Review*, 13(October):559–571.

Keezer, D. M. 1930. Business. In E. R. A. Seligman, editor, *Encyclopedia of the Social Sciences*, 3: 80–87. New York: Macmillan.

Kindleberger, Charles P. 1988. The "new" multinationalization of business. *ASEAN Economic Bulletin*, 5(November):113–124.

Kindleberger, Charles P. 1976. Introduction to S. Hymer. *The International Operations of National Firms*. Cambridge: MIT Press.

Kogut, Bruce. 1989. The stability of joint ventures: Reciprocity and competitive rivalry. *Journal of Industrial Economics*, 38.

Kogut, Bruce. 1988. A study of the life cycle of

joint ventures. In F.J. Contractor and Peter Lorange, editors, *Cooperative Strategies in International Business*, 169–185. Lexington, MA: D.C. Heath.

Kogut, Bruce. 1986. On designing contracts to guarantee enforceability: Theory and evidence from East-West trade. *Journal of International Business Studies*, 17(1):47–62.

Kogut, Bruce. 1983. Selection of contracts in East-West trade. Working Paper, Stockholm School of Economics.

Lecraw, Donald. 1989. The management of countertrade: Factors influencing success. *Journal of International Business Studies*, 20(1):41–59.

Lodge, George C. and Ezra Vogel. 1987. *Ideology and National Competitiveness*. Boston: Harvard Business School Press.

Martinez, Jon and J. Carlos Jarillo. 1989. The evolution of research on coordination mechanisms in multinational corporations. *Journal of International Business Studies*, 20(3):489–514.

McManus, J. 1972. The theory of the multinational firm. In Gilles Paquet, editor, *The Multinational Firm and the Nation State*. Don Mills: Macmillan.

McGuire, W. J. 1973. The yin and yang of progress in social psychology. *Journal of Personality and Social Psychology*.

McVey, T. 1980. Countertrade and barter: Alternative trade financing by Third World nations. *International Trade Law Journal*, 6:197–220.

Mellors, J. 1973. International tax differentials and the location of overseas direct investment. Research Paper, University of Reading on International Investment and Business, no. 4.

Mirus, Rolf and Bernard Yeung. 1987. Countertrade and foreign exchange shortages. *Weltwirtschaftliches Archiv*, 123:535-544.

Mirus, Rolf and Bernard Yeung. 1986. Economic incentives for countertrade. *Journal of International Business Studies*, 17(3):27-39.

Mirus, Rolf and Bernard Yeung. 1984. Economic incentives for countertrade. Working paper, University of Alberta.

Mohr, L. B. 1982. *Explain Organizational Behavior*. San Francisco: Jossey-Bass.

Murrell, Peter. 1982. Product quality, market signaling, and the development of East-West trade. *Economic Inquiry*, 20: 589–603.

Murtha, Thomas. 1991. Credible enticements: Transaction cost analysis of MNC's supplier relationships in host-state-targeted industries. *Journal of Law, Economics, and Organization*.

Oman, C. 1984. *New Forms of International Investment in Developing Countries*. Paris: OECD.

Parsons, John. 1985. A theory of countertrade financing in international business. Working Paper 1632–85, Sloan School of Management, MIT.

Parsons, Talcott. 1960. *Structure and Process in Modern Societies*. New York: Free Press.

Polanyi, Karl. 1944. *The Great Transformation*. New York: Rinehart.

Prachowny, M. J. 1972. Direct investment and the balance of payments of the U.S.: A portfolio approach. In F. Machlup, W. Slant and L. Tarshis, editors, *International Mobility and Movement of Capital*. New York: National Bureau of Economic Research.

Roehl, Thomas. 1983. A transaction cost approach to international trading structures. *Hitotsubashi Journal of Economics*, 24: 119–135.

Root, Franklin R. 1969. A conceptual approach to international business. *Journal of Business Administration*, 1(1): 18–28.

Rugman, Alan M. 1981. *Inside the Multinationals*. New York: Columbia University Press.

Rumelt, R., D. Schendel, and David Teece. 1991. Strategic management and economics. *Strategic Management Journal*, 12(Special Winter Issue):5–29.

Schmidtchen, Dieter and H. J. Schmidt-Trenz. 1990. New institutional economics of international transactions: Constitutional uncertainty and the creation of institutions in foreign trade as exemplified by the multinational firm. In E. Boettcher et al., editors, *Jahrbuch für Neue Politische Oekonomie*, 9: 3–34. Tubingen, Germany: J. C. B. Mohr.

Shapiro, Alan. 1984. The evaluation and control of foreign affiliates. *Midland Corporate Finance Journal*, Spring:13–25.

Smelser, N. J. 1976. *The Sociology of Economic Life*. Englewood Cliffs, NJ: Prentice-Hall.

Southard, F. A. 1931. *American Industry in Europe*. Boston: Houghton Mifflin.

Stevens, G. V. G. 1969. Fixed investment expenditures of foreign manufacturing affiliates of U.S. firms: Theoretical models and empirical evidence. *Yale Economic Essays*, 9:137–198.

Stopford, John M. and Louis T. Wells. 1972. *Managing the Multinational Enterprise*. New York: Basic Books.

Supple, Barry. 1989. Introduction: Multinational enterprise. In A. Teichova et al., editors, *Historical Studies in International Corporate Business*, 1–6. New York: Cambridge University Press.

Swedberg, Richard. 1990. *Economics and Sociology*. Princeton, NJ: Princeton University Press.

Swedenborg, B. 1979. *The Multinational Operations of Swedish Firms*. Stockholm: Industrial Institute for Economic and Social Research.

Teece, David. 1981. The multinational enterprise: Market failure and market power considerations. *Sloan Management Review*, 22(3):3–17.

Terpstra, Vernon and Chwo-Ming Yu. 1988. Determinants of foreign investment of U.S. advertising agencies. *Journal of International Business Studies*, 19(1):33–46.

Thorell, Hans B. 1986. Networks: Between markets and hierarchies. *Strategic Management Journal*, 7(1):37–51.

Toyne, Brian. 1989. International exchange: A foundation for theory building in international business. *Journal of International Business*, 20(1): 1–17.

Wilkins, Mira. 1986. Defining a firm: History and theory. In Peter Hertner and Geoffrey Jones, editors, *Multinationals: Theory and History*, 80–95. Aldershot, England: Gower.

Williamson, Oliver E. 1985. *The Economic Institutions of Capitalism*. New York: Free Press.

Williamson, Oliver E. 1975. *Markets and Hierarchies: Analysis and Antitrust Implications*. New York: Free Press.

Yu, Chwo-Ming and Kiyohiko Ito. 1988. Oligopolistic reaction and foreign direct investment: The case of the U.S. tire and textile industries. *Journal of International Business Studies*, 19(3): 449–460.

12

The Future Development of
International Business Inquiry
Brian Toyne and Douglas Nigh

It's commonly thought that international business is a peripheral part of the scientific study of business—an added dimension of the functional disciplines, nice but not necessary. This view is wrong. In fact, international business is a core discipline of business. We make this assertion not to pump up the importance of the intellectual field in which we have chosen to work. Rather, it is based on factors both external and internal to scholarly inquiry. The increased incidence and importance of international business phenomena in the lives of people, as well as developments in the study of human beings and their social constructions have propelled international business toward a more central position in the study of business.

In this book, we have offered our view as to the nature of a new paradigm emerging in our field. Many of the contributing authors have provided analogous views on certain aspects of our vision; others have championed contrary positions. We conclude this book by addressing a number of questions. More specifically, in this chapter we focus on the future development of international business as an intellectual field of study. What do IB scholars need to understand about paradigmic conflict? What kind of intellectual field would international business become if some refined version of the emerging paradigm were adopted by a significant number of IB scholars? What would be IB's relationship with other fields? What would be the implications for IB research and theorizing?

NEW PERSPECTIVES, NEW CHALLENGES

Challenges to the way we see, think about, and study the world seldom come from those with whom we are in close, continuous contact. We generally agree with these people. More often, the challenges come from those with whom we have little contact and little opportunity to exchange ideas. Thus, the careful reader has probably been challenged by the many different viewpoints, the different bodies of knowledge used to support these positions, and the different interests evident in the preceding eleven chapters.

Stephen Jay Gould's and John Stuart Mill's quotes at the front of this book suggest that we are unique as a species because of our ability to transmit learned knowledge and behavior across generations, and that the progress we make is the result of the coming together with those who possess dissimilar bodies of learned knowledge and behavior. Excitingly, this twofold uniqueness is at the core of IB inquiry and poses two fundamental challenges for IB researchers. The first is to understand why and how learned knowledge and behavior vary, and thus to understand the essential reasons for the richness of our dissimilarities, our diversity. The second is to understand why and how people with dissimilar learned knowledge and behavior can purposefully and successfully interact, and, perhaps more important, what is likely to be the outcome of this interaction for the involved parties; how are people (and the organizations they create) changed as a consequence of such international interactions.

The history of science suggests that we gain new awareness and new understanding by enlarging on the number of paradigms, or conceptualizations, that underpin and guide our work. As a result of inductive, integrative reasoning, and convergence in findings we make conceptual progress, and as an outcome of deductive, specialized reasoning we verify and more fully describe this progress. The history of science also teaches us that our horizons remain unnecessarily narrow and our insights unnecessarily shallow when we refuse to consider and examine alternate conceptualizations of reality to those already acknowledged, accepted, and well entrenched. However, it is also in man's nature to eventually challenge and thus change the way things are perceived and done when new paradigms are suggested that appear to promise a more accurate representation of what we experience.

In light of such thoughts, we believe that a more emergent, a more inclusive view of international business practice should be central to our efforts as IB scholars. If one truth became abundantly clear at the conference at which the papers in this book were first presented, it was that we need to actively seek to enter into meaningful dialogue with our colleagues in the business disciplines, in other fields of human inquiry, and, importantly, in other parts of the world. In particular, it behooves us to open ourselves to what anthropologists, historians, political scientists, sociologists, psychologists, and many others have to say about why and how we interact as individuals, groups, and organizations, and how we may be changed by these interactions. We believe that in so doing, we will all benefit.

In chapter 1, we argue that international business is ultimately more than a set of firm-level "arms-length" or even "arms-linked" transactions that cross national borders (see Boddewyn's and Wilkin's domain pieces and Behrman's commentary in chapter 2). While IB inquiry has benefited from economic thinking, we do not believe that the economic explanations of firm-level international business practice is the alpha and omega of IB inquiry (see, for example, Casson's and Dunning's papers suggesting that other fields contribute to a better understanding of the economics of international business). Of equal importance is the study of the evolving consequences that such transactions have in changing national business processes and the organizations that these multi-level processes create, maintain, and eventually destroy. Thus, for us, IB inquiry is more than the economic study of the entities that a society creates in its efforts to satisfy the insatiable wants of its people. It is also the study of the consequences that arise because of the multi-level, multi-purpose interaction of two or more business processes. The consequences of these cultural, economic, social, and political interactions are important since they inevitably result in both the modification of the contextualizing, informing attributes of the societal fabrics in which business processes are embedded, and in the modification of the intrinsic attributes of the entities that are the outcome of these processes. As explained in chapter 1, it is not just firms and their people that learn from foreign involvement, and apply this learning at home and abroad. Higher-level societal organizations, such as industries and governments and their people, also learn from foreign involvement, and apply this learning in their dealings with lower-level societal organizations, such as firms.

Such a multi-level, multi-purpose interactive vision of international business, of course, strongly suggests that IB scholars are very fortunate. Their inquiry is at the frontiers of business process change, even societal transformation. It is not in the relatively quiet backwaters of national business processes that fundamental change is likely to occur, it is more likely to occur at the intersection of dissimilar business processes.[1] Thus, in light of this new vision, the field of IB has a research agenda that is ahead, if not truly independent, of the fragmented developments occurring in the business disciplines. As a distinct field of inquiry, IB need not, should not, and cannot be subservient to the business disciplines, since these business disciplines (or functions) collectively do not provide an exhaustive definition of business.

As we have seen in the preceding chapters, there are many paradigms underpinning and guiding the study of international business, and each paradigm raises different questions and requires different methodologies to answering them. However, the combined effects of the growing complexity of international interdependencies, environmental volatility, organizational change, and technological advancement, and the new ways of viewing human endeavor[2]—particularly in the areas of business conduct—are sufficient to raise serious questions concerning the adequacy and efficacy of the dominant, parochial paradigms underpinning and directing IB inquiry. This, of course, does not mean that the essentially static paradigms are without merit. They have successfully guided IB researchers for several decades in their quest for certifiable knowledge, and have also enabled them to contribute in significant ways to a broader, more global appreciation, if not understanding, of business behavior. Indeed, they are responsible for the advancement of IB as a field. What it does mean, however, is that IB researchers and theoreticians have advanced sufficiently to need to be alert to the possibility of new conceptualizations, and need to display a willingness to examine the value of the knowledge that these new perspectives, these new paradigms provide.

As Hench points out in chapter 2, we—like our colleagues in the "hard sciences"—are in the midst of paradigmic changes of Kuhnian proportions. For example, the functional, deterministic approach that dissects business into arbitrary groups of firm-level activities for the purpose of study is being challenged by calls on many fronts for the adoption of multi-disciplinary, inter-disciplinary, and holistic approaches. And, as can be expected of a field of inquiry at the leading edge of societal change, IB scholars are among some of the most vocal in their calls for both the retention of the "old," and its replacement with the "new."

GRAPPLING WITH AND BENEFITING FROM PARADIGMIC CONFLICT

Not too surprisingly, the arguments set forth in the papers and commentaries in this book, and in the IB literature in general, suggest that there is still considerable confusion regarding the precise meaning of such words as conceptualization, orientation, paradigm, and theory. There is also confusion over the meaning of other important words such as business, international business, marketing, management, and their relationship to one another. There are, we believe, at least three reasons for this confusion. The first is the reluctance of many IB scholars, possibly because of their strong pragmatic orientation, to enter into discussions with philosophers of science,[3] and among themselves, concerning the nature of their activities. Second, except possibly for marketing and strategic management scholars who have been quite open to self-examination (see, for example, Hunt 1991; Rumelt, Schendel, and Teece 1994), IB scholars have also been reluctant to enter into meaningful dialogs concerning what it is they actually do as theorizers and researchers, let alone with representatives from other business disciplines and the social sciences. Third, many IB scholars and business scholars have never seriously questioned the continuing impact that their vocational roots have on what they do as theorizers and researchers (e.g., they have never seriously attempted to define business in terms other than firm-level activities, and constantly challenge those who seek to advance the field beyond the constraints imposed by this truncated definition of business).

As IB scholars we need to enter into a more profound discussion concerning what it is we do, why we do it, and what assumptions underpin this activity. Merely as crude examples of this discussion we need to ask ourselves whether we are dealing with a single phenomenon, the firm, as Wilkins and others argue, or with a phenomenon that spans a number of different levels of society that some how interact and influence one another. Whether we are dealing with a set of narrowly defined economic-driven activities of the firm, such as finance, manufacturing, marketing, or with the ill-defined totality of what is loosely referred to as business? Whether we are dealing with higher levels of abstraction (i.e., non-observable phenomena) than the firm (e.g., transaction costs, economic motivation, political motivation)? The first three chapters raise many interesting questions concerned with questions such as these. Although the authors of the papers explore the scope, phenomena, and relationships of IB inquiry, they do not arrive at any mutually satisfactory conclusion.

For us, the conceptualization of international business involves more than the economic study of an adventurous set of entities that a particular society creates in its efforts to satisfy the insatiable wants of its people. It also includes the study of the consequences that arise because of the learning that takes place when two or more multi-level, multi-purpose business processes and their outcomes interact. The consequences of these economically, socially, and politically derived interactions are as important, if not more important, than the narrowly focused static study of firm-level activity within and across countries. The consequences of trans-societal interaction inevitably involve modification in the contextualizing, regulating, and informing attributes of the societal fabric in which business processes are embedded,[4] and in the intrinsic attributes[5] of the entities that are the outcome of these processes.

Although the primary focus of Dunning, Graham, and Ozawa in their papers presented in chapter 4 is on the firm, they clearly demonstrate the need to develop a more comprehensive, multi-level understanding of IB, as discussed in chapter 1, and by Boddewyn and Toyne in chapter 2, Hogner, Freeman, and Wartick in chapter 3, and Lessard, Walter, and Errunza in chapter 10. For example, the endogenous roles of government and society in contextualizing, informing, and selecting possible behaviors of the business process and the organizations this process create is increasingly clear. Yet, they remain difficult to include because of the paradigmic foundations on which much IB theorizing and research are based. It is also increasingly clear that many of the concepts examined can be studied at more than one societal level, yet many IB scholars would argue that the phenomena studied at higher societal levels are of only peripheral interest at best (e.g., Wilkins).

At the same time, it would appear from an examination of the papers that unwarranted restrictions should not be imposed by premature closure—the consequence of adopting one paradigm (not a meta-conceptualization). At the same time, however, it needs to be recognized that all paradigms are restrictive because they are based on a set of axiomatic assumptions concerning reality, and therefore require a high degree of self-discipline in their use. As noted by Hench in chapter 2, one of the problems faced by IB scholars partly because of their dislike for intellectual constraints, is the mixing of paradigms. Because we don't like to acknowledge the restraints imposed by paradigms, we don't take the time needed to fully explore their limiting assumptions.

Thus, as the contrasting arguments presented in these papers demonstrate so convincingly, the conduct of IB research demands that IB scholars must have a rich and deep understanding of the paradigmic roots and assumptions underpinning the theories and streams of research that are "part and parcel" of this field; an observation that has equal merit in any other area of inquiry. As Hench points out in chapter

2, we are in a period of paradigmic change and consequently tend to confuse our discussions and our research by shifting from one paradigm to another without fully addressing the theoretical and empirical implications of such shifts. There is, after all, merit in tight, disciplined research and theorizing.

ONE DEVELOPMENTAL PATH TOWARD (INTER)DISCIPLINARITY

International business is an intellectual field at a critical point in its development. In this book, we have reviewed its multi-paradigmic nature and even added to it by proposing a new paradigm we see emerging. If this emerging, multi-level, trans-societal paradigm became more central in international business inquiry, what would be its consequences?

First, the disciplinary nature of IB as an intellectual field would be better established. Part of disciplinarity involves accounting coherently for a particular set of phenomena.[6] The emerging interaction paradigm (chapter 1) sees IB as an evolving, hierarchical, social process that is the result of the interaction of national business processes and their outputs. In this view IB inquiry seeks to understand this interaction-reconciliation process and its outcomes (Toyne, chapter 2), and is fundamentally different from those of other fields. It addresses unique questions and has the potential to develop a unique body of knowledge. The emerging paradigm provides the field of IB with its distinct subject area—something that the earlier, somewhat parochial IB paradigms just didn't do.

While the emerging paradigm includes some phenomena and relationships that other fields of study do not, it also covers some phenomena and relationships that are the concern of other fields. This situation is quite common in the social sciences and, indeed, beneficial since it provides the possibility for cross-disciplinary validation of results.

To summarize, the emerging paradigm provides the field of IB with the uniqueness needed to distinguish its knowledge generation efforts from those of other fields. Interestingly, this paradigmic view of business and international business and their relationship provides both business scholars and IB scholars an opportunity to reverse the trend toward functional specialization and fragmentation—a trend that necessitates the elimination of broader perspectives. By linking societal levels, the emerging paradigm also has the potential to make the kinds of policy contributions called for so forcefully by Behrman in chapters 2 and 11.

For example, inherent in the adoption of the emerging paradigm would be a movement toward more agreement among IB scholars on what constitutes excellence in the field—on what questions are important, on what methods are useful, on what contributions to understanding are really significant. As a field, IB would give higher priority to the systematic integration of empirical work into a coherent theoretical structure. While the development of IB does not necessarily need "grand" theory, it does need an integrated set of middle range theories. The emerging paradigm can serve as one tool to advance the field of IB from its current fragmented, somewhat incoherent state in which research is "personal, idiosyncratic, and only weakly coordinated across research sites" (Whitley 1984, p.159).[7]

From its inception, the field of IB has been multidisciplinary in the sense of borrowing concepts, typologies, theories, methods, and even data from other intellectual fields. Also inherent in our emerging vision is a particular relationship between IB inquiry and other disciplines. First, borrowing from other fields would be an important part of the continued development of IB, but it would be thoughtful borrowing. Partly because of its overtly unique perspective, an IB scholar borrowing a concept, a typology, a theory, or a method from another discipline would recognize the need to have a basic understanding of its development and use in the original context (Klein 1990). At the present time, we believe that IB scholars borrow too much with little or no thought, resulting in the misapplication of the borrowed concept, theory, or method to IB inquiry.[8]

With the adoption of our vision of international business as an emerging, hierarchical social process that is the result of the interaction of national business processes and their outputs, we believe that IB inquiry would benefit most by stressing the need to look to the social sciences such as anthropology, psychology, sociology for judicious borrowing, rather than the functional business disciplines. The functional business disciplines get many of their concepts, theories, and methods from the behavioral sciences. Essentially, by borrowing from the business disciplines IB gets these concepts, theories, and methods second hand and filtered through the typically uni-national and narrowly focused lens of the functional business discipline. It's more fruitful to go back to the original and assume there the burden of comprehension inherent in good borrowing.

In addition, we see IB moving from a multidisciplinary relationship with other fields to an interdisciplinary one. In multidisciplinary research, although there is a drawing upon the concepts, theories, and methods of two or more disciplines, each remains basically as before. In interdisciplinary research, there's a sense of integration of aspects of the two disciplines, changing both in the process. Pursuing our emerging vision will entail an interaction with other disciplines that provides feedback to the other discipline of an enhanced and enlarged concept, theory, or method.

Finally on this point, in our vision, the field of IB will not wait around for other fields to develop the theories and methods it needs to pursue its most important questions. Rather the importance of questions will drive the search for potential interdisciplinary interaction. In the face of the lack of suitable borrowing from others to address important IB problems, IB researchers will need to create their own new concepts, typologies, theories, methods, and procedures, rather than look for something else

from the other disciplines that might be useful in pursuing other less important IB questions. In our vision, borrowing is used judiciously so as not to distract from the real issues of concern to the field.

We believe the emerging paradigm provides IB with an opportunity to develop into an intellectual field with its own distinct perspective and body of knowledge and with links to other fields that advance both IB's own knowledge generating objectives and a more general understanding of humans and their social constructions. It provides one viable path for IB inquiry to move away from its current fragmented state toward an (inter)disciplinarity that would accelerate our progress in understanding IB phenomena and relationships.

MORE IMPLICATIONS OF THE EMERGING PARADIGM

What else can we say about the nature of IB research if IB embraced the emerging paradigm with its more comprehensive, more inclusive framework that views international business as a dynamic, multi-level, multi-purpose, trans-societal phenomenon that cannot, and should not, be defined in strictly firm-level functional terms.

First IB research would involve multiple levels of analysis from the individual to the suprasocietal. Wrestling with multiple levels of analysis in both conceptual and empirical work is challenging. We believe that IB would benefit from an examination of fields that have dealt with the issues associated with multiple levels of analysis such as political science (Kuhlman, chapter 5) and biology. Also of potential help would be the "new" philosophy of social science that addresses questions concerning the relationship of the micro and macro levels (see Bohman 1991).

Since the emerging paradigm views business processes as inherently social (see also Hogner, chapter 3), IB research would place relatively less emphasis on economic conceptualizations that see business processes as separate from society. Rather, IB inquiry would seek a richer, more comprehensive understanding that involves judicious borrowings from the other social sciences.

Since the emerging paradigm places emphasis on national business process and their interaction/reconciliation, the contributions to IB by researchers from various countries around the world would take on an enhanced value. For one thing, these researchers have tacit knowledge of their home country societal processes, which would contribute to improved theorizing and research. Secondly, variation in societal processes extends also to knowledge generation, thus producing different ways of developing questions, theories, and methods. The emerging paradigm places great store in the benefits of the interaction of researchers from different societies.

Since the emerging paradigm gives us a field that is interdisciplinary, some of the most important IB research would be conducted by interdisciplinary individuals or interdisciplinary teams. At the conference, many, many individuals expressed high hopes for productive cross-disciplinary collaboration, yet the record of such efforts in many fields is pretty dismal (Klein 1990). Thus, a challenge for IB scholars would be to improve their understanding of the processes by which interdisciplinary research is successfully completed.[9]

Finally we look at the implications of the emerging paradigm for the purposes and beneficiaries of IB research. Consider the following question: "What knowledge do we seek, for what purpose, for whose benefit, and why?" The answer to this questions will vary depending on the conceptualization of IB that is used, and on the kind of IB inquiry undertaken. For example, as shown in Table 1, if international business is viewed simply as the extension of firm-level activities into or across a number of foreign countries, the answers will probably be considerably different than if international business is viewed as a trans-societal phenomenon. The answers will also differ if IB inquiry is viewed as discovery (or basic), integration, or application where discovery is

defined as original contributions to a particular body of knowledge, integration is viewed as the "drawing together" of several streams of discovery, and application is viewed as showing how knowledge can be applied to important problems and how important problems can define an agenda for research.[10] The emerging paradigm places value on all three: discovery, integration, and application.

As only one example, the meaning and value attached to basic IB inquiry will depend on the type of research undertaken.[11] For example, IB inquiry predicated on the extension paradigm contributes to the business disciplines by replicating national (parochial) findings in other settings. As a consequence of this "normal science" activity, IB scholars contribute by more clearly defining the international boundaries of national theories, but to do so they are obliged to use the methodologies and terminology agreed to by their nation-bound colleagues (see, for example, Feldman in chapter 7). At the same time, however, basic IB inquiry has the potential to make unique contributions to a better, more global understanding of business if international business is conceptualized as a trans-societal phenomenon. Moreover, Hennart in chapter 11, and Kogut, Doz, and Hitt in chapter 8 support the "unique contribution" argument by highlighting the leading edge contributions that IB inquiry has made to such disciplines as economics and strategic management. Interestingly, as disinterested outsiders, Rumelt, Schendel, and Teece [1994] acknowledge the significant contributions made by IB inquiry to the development of strategic management.

CLOSING REMARKS

One major purpose of the conference and this book was to define the field of international business, to develop the state-of-the-art in it, to expose to debate the assumptions and limitations imposed by, and the benefits derived from, the various paradigms that have guided and should guide

Table 1. Mode of IB Inquiry, IB Paradigms, and the Phenomena and Relationships Studied

Mode of Inquiry	Paradigms Employed in IB Inquiry		
	Extension	Cross-Border	Interaction
Discovery (basic research)	*Level of analysis*: the firm.	*Level of analysis*: the firm.	*Level of analysis*: the multi-level societal business process and its outcomes (individual-to-suprasocietal).
	Disciplinary emphasis: uni-disciplinary.	*Disciplinary emphasis*: uni-disciplinary.	*Disciplinary emphasis*: multi-disciplinary and inter-disciplinary.
	Focus of inquiry: replication of home-country inquiry.	*Focus of inquiry*: analysis of the implications for, and responses of, the firm to the unique differences found in the international business environment.	*Focus of inquiry*: analysis of the outcomes arising from the interaction of different societal business processes and their indigenous outcomes.
	Purpose of inquiry: test the explanatory power of home-country uni-disciplinary business knowledge in foreign settings.	*Purpose of inquiry*: develop explanations of how firms adjust/adapt/respond to unique differences.	*Purpose of inquiry*: develop explanations for the business-related outcomes of international interaction for particular societies, and the suprasocietal process.
Integration	*Level of analysis*: the firm.	*Level of analysis*: the firm.	*Level of analysis*: the multi-level societal business process and its outcomes (individual-to-suprasocietal).
	Disciplinary emphasis: uni-disciplinary.	*Disciplinary emphasis*: uni-disciplinary.	*Disciplinary emphasis*: multi-disciplinary and inter-disciplinary.
	Focus of inquiry: the synthesis of uni-disciplinary findings into a more cohesive body of firm-related knowledge.	*Focus of inquiry*: the synthesis of uni-disciplinary findings into a more cohesive body of firm-related knowledge.	*Focus of inquiry*: the synthesis of multi-disciplinary findings and inter-disciplinary findings with those of the social sciences and humanities.
	Purpose of inquiry: test the explanatory power of home-country business knowledge in foreign settings.	*Purpose of inquiry*: to arrive at a more cohesive understanding of how firms respond to environmental diversity and its opportunities.	*Purpose of inquiry*: to arrive at a more cohesive multi-disciplinary (social sciences and the humanities) understanding of the business process and its outcomes in particular societies, among societies, and the development of suprasocietal processes.

Table 1. *Continued*

Mode of Inquiry	Paradigms Employed in IB Inquiry		
	Extension	Cross-Border	Interaction
Application	*Level of analysis:* the firm. *Disciplinary emphasis:* uni-disciplinary. *Focus of inquiry:* demonstrate how uni-disciplinary knowledge can be applied to consequential problems, and how firm-specific problems define an agenda for inquiry. *Purpose of inquiry:* to provide possible solutions to uni-disciplinary firm-specific problems and to generalize these problems/solutions across categories of firms.	*Level of analysis:* the firm. *Disciplinary emphasis:* uni-disciplinary. *Focus of inquiry:* demonstrate how uni-disciplinary knowledge can be applied to consequential problems, and how firm-specific problems define an agenda for inquiry. *Purpose of inquiry:* to provide possible solutions to uni-disciplinary firm-specific problems and to generalize these problems/solutions across categories of firms.	*Level of analysis:* the multi-level societal business process and its outcomes. *Disciplinary emphasis:* multi-disciplinary and inter-disciplinary. *Focus of inquiry:* demonstrate how multi-disciplinary and inter-disciplinary knowledge can be applied to con-sequential problems, and how business process and business process outcome problems define an agenda for inquiry. *Purpose of inquiry:* to provide possible solutions to societal business-related problems and to generalize these problems/solutions across societal categories, and the suprasocietal context.

Source: Brian Toyne (1997). The Conceptual Frontiers of International Business Inquiry. In I. Islam and W. F. Shepherd (eds.) *Current Issues in International Business.* Sydney, Australia: Elgar Publications.

our investigations, and to suggest where theory building and theory testing is needed in the future. We believe that this book and the conference on which its is based were successful in satisfying this purpose. The book also, we feel, successfully overcame the challenges inherent in such an undertaking.

We can only hope that those who benefit from this work, whether IB functional specialists or IB generalists, will soon make this book obsolete. There is a terrific amount of challenging work to be done. This work will take the efforts of many IB scholars with different skills and knowledge. The development of IB as a significant and distinct area of inquiry will challenge our theoretical and methodological innovativeness. We therefore invite all interested parties to participate in taking this conversation to a higher level.

In this book we have focused on IB inquiry and research. We have left the consideration of IB teaching and institutional arrangements for the second book to come out of the conference. There we will address the challenges associated with disseminating the unique contributions that are being made by IB scholarship to business knowledge.

NOTES

1. The greatest challenge to the way we see reality and to the assumptions we make about this reality is more likely to occur from outside of the society in which we have been socialized.

2. It is, perhaps, more accurate to say that the changing paradigms underpinning the hard sciences (e.g., relativity, chaos theory) are introducing new thoughts concerning the separation of the hard sciences from the social sciences and human endeavor in general.

3. This is not an unusual phenomenon according to Casti [1989]. For example, most scientists appear to believe that ideologies plays no role in science—a belief that is obviously false if Kuhn's arguments are accepted.

4. The regulations governing business practice, and the array and purpose of industry, employee, consumer, and general public associations formed within particular societies, for ex-

ample, may change as a consequence of trans-societal interaction, and these changes in turn will impact on the viability of a firm's plans.

5. For examples, the attributes and traits of individuals and groups, the business practices supported, and so on, that collectively make up an organization may change as a consequence of trans-societal interaction.

6. Klein (1990: 104) writes: "The term discipline signifies the tools, methods, procedures, exempla, concepts, and theories that account coherently for a set of objects or subjects. Over time they are shaped and reshaped by external contingencies and internal intellectual demands. In this manner a discipline comes to organize and concentrate experience into a particular world view."

7. Whitley (1984) develops a typology of the intellectual and social organization of the sciences. International business as it is currently constituted would be categorized as a fragmented adhocracy. Also see Redding, chapter 7.

8. Awareness of such pitfalls would be enhanced if IB scholars were to enter into more discussions concerning the paradigms they borrow from the business disciplines and the social sciences.

9. See Klein (1990) for a recent bibliography on interdisciplinarity.

10. These research categories were suggested by Boyer [1990] in his book dealing with scholarship.

11. Implications for IB teaching and institutional arrangements are addressed in a second book to come out of the conference.

REFERENCES

Bohman, James. 1991. *New Philosophy of Social Science: Problems of Indeterminacy.* Cambridge, Mass.: MIT Press.

Boyacigiller, Nakiye A. and Nancy J. Adler. 1991. The parochial dinosaur: Organizational science in a global context. *Academy of Management Review,* 16(2): 262–290.

Boyer, Ernest L. 1990. Scholarship reconsidered: Priorities of the professorate. Princeton, N.J.: The Carnegie Foundation for the Advancement of Teaching.

Casti, John L. 1989. *Paradigms Lost: Tackling the Unanswered Mysteries of Modern Science.* New York, N.Y.: Avon Books.

Granovetter, Mark. 1985. Economic action and

social structure: A theory of embeddedness. *American Journal of Sociology,* 91: 481–510.

Hunt, Shelby D. 1991. *Modern Marketing Theory: Critical Issues in the Philosophy of Marketing Science.* Cincinnati: South-Western Publishing Co.

Klein, Julie Thompson. 1990. *Interdisciplinarity: History, Theory, and Practice.* Detroit: Wayne State University Press.

Rumelt, Richard P., Dan E. Schendel, and David J. Teece. 1994. *Fundamental Issues in Strategy: A Research Agenda.* Boston, MA.: Harvard Business School Press.

Whitley, Richard. 1984. *The Intellectual and Social Organization of the Sciences.* Oxford: Clarendon Press.

Contributing Authors

Nancy J. Adler is a Professor of Organizational Behavior and Cross-Cultural Management at the Faculty of Management, McGill University in Montreal, Canada. Dr. Adler's research focuses on strategic international human resource management, expatriation, women in international management, international negotiating, developing culturally synergistic approaches to problem solving, and international organization development. She has authored numerous articles, produced the film *A Portable Life,* and published the books, *International Dimensions of Organization Behavior,* Third Edition (1997), *Women in Management Worldwide* (1988), and *Competitive Frontiers: Women Managers in a Global Economy* (1994). Dr. Adler received McGill University's first Distinguished Teaching Award in Management (1986) and was again its recipient in 1990. She received ASTD's International Leadership Award, SIETAR's Outstanding Senior Interculturalist Award, and was named a 3M Teaching Fellow, a Fellow of the Academy of International Business, and a Fellow of the Academy of Management.

W. Graham Astley was an Associate Professor of Management at the Graduate School of Business Administration, University of Colorado at Denver. He did research on organizational design, intraorganizational power, organization-environment relationships, strategic decision making, the evolution of technical environments and industrial structure, and global competition. He served on the editorial boards of *Organization Science,* the *Academy of Management Review, Administrative Science Quarterly,* and the *Journal of High Technology Management.*

Jack N. Behrman is Luther Hodges Distinguished Professor Emeritus at the University of North Carolina's Kenan-Flagler Business School. His expertise lies in the areas of international business, international business/government relations, ethics, comparative management, and creativity and innovation. His extensive experience in governmental and international agencies includes serving as U.S. Assistant Secretary of Commerce for Domestic and International Business under Presidents Kennedy and Johnson (1961–1964), as a member of research panels for the National Research Council, the National Academy of Science, and the National Academy of Engineering, and as consultant to the U.N. Centre on Science and Technology for Development and to the U.N. Center on Transnational Corporations. He has published over 100 articles and some 40 books and monographs, among the most recent of which are *International Business/Government Relations* (1990) and *Direct Investment and Joint Ventures in China* (1991). Dr. Behrman is a co-founder, past President and Fellow of the Academy of International Business.

Rabi S. Bhagat is Professor of Organizational Behavior and International Management at the Fogelman College of Business and Economics of Memphis State University. Prior to this appointment, he was a professor at the University of Texas at Dallas (1976–1990), and a visiting professor at Louisiana State University (1986–1987). He has published extensively in the area of cross-national and cross-cultural studies of organizational behavior in academic journals and edited volumes. His publications have appeared in *Journal of Applied Psychology, Academy of Management Review, Academy of Management Journal,* and *Human Relations,* among others. His recent publications include two chapters dealing with the cross-cultural and cross-national aspects of organizational behavior and human resource management which appeared in *International Review of Industrial and Organizational Psychology* (1990), and *Research in Personnel and Human Resources Management* (1991). He currently serves on the editorial board of *International Review of Applied Psychology.*

Jean J. Boddewyn is Professor of International Business and Coordinator of the International Business Program at the Baruch College, City University of New York. He has held teaching positions at the University of Portland, New York University, and Columbia University. His teaching centers on international business, management and marketing; his research interests have successively centered on comparative marketing and management, international business/government relations and public affairs, foreign divestment, advertising regulation and self-regulation around the world, international business strategy, and international business political behavior. He has published widely in these and related areas. He has been the editor of *International Studies of Management and Organization* since 1971, and he serves on the editorial board of ten academic journals. Dr. Boddewyn is a Fellow of the Academy of International Business (AIB), the Academy of Management, and the International Academy of Management. He served as President of the AIBM from 1992 to 1994.

Nakiye Boyacigiller is Professor of International Management at San Jose State University. Her research on cross-cultural organizational science and international HRM has appeared in *Journal of International Business Studies, Academy of Management Review, Organization Studies, Research in Organizational Behavior, Advances in International Comparative Management,* and the *Handbook of International Management Research,* among others. She is currently Chair of the International Management Division of the Academy of Management.

Thomas L. Brewer is an Associate Professor of International Business at Georgetown University in Washington, D.C. Professor Brewer's research and teaching interests are interdisciplinary. His current research interests include changes in the international regime for foreign direct investment; country risk analysis in international business; and international trade and investment in the automotive industry. His publications have appeared in *Journal of International Business Studies, Columbia Journal of World Business, Journal of International Trade and Finance, Asia-Pacific Journal of Management, Journal of Money, Credit and Banking,* and *Journal of Comparative Economics.* He is editor of *Journal of International Business Studies.*

Mark Casson is Professor of Economics at the University of Reading, U.K. His research interests encompass entrepreneurship, international business, and the history of unemployment. His recent books include *Enterprise and Competitiveness* (1990) and *Economics of Business Culture* (1991). He has also edited *Global Research Strategy and International Business* (1991), *International Business and Global Integration* (1992), and *Multinational Enterprises in the World Economy: Essays in Honor of John Dunning,* co-edited with Peter Buckley (1992).

S. Tamer Cavusgil is Professor of Marketing and International Business at the Eli Broad Graduate School of Management, Michigan State University. He also serves as Executive Director of the Center for International Business Education and Research (CIBER) at Michigan State. His work has focused on the internationalization of the firm and export behavior. He is the editor of the recent book *Internationalizing Business Schools: Toward Meeting the Challenge,* East Lansing, Michigan: MSU Press. Recent work has concentrated on the research and development of expert systems for international business executives. Currently he serves as Vice President and member of the Board of Directors, American Marketing Association, and as Regional Chairperson of the Academy of International Business.

Philip L. Cochran is Associate Professor of Business Administration and Director of the Center for the Study of Business and Public Issues at the Pennsylvania State University. His research interests include business ethics, corporate governance, corporate crime, and issues management. He is Past Chair of the Social Issues in Management Division of the Academy of Management, and is Past President of the International Association for Business and Society. He has published articles in *Academy of Management Journal, Academy of Management Review, California Management Review, Management International Review, Quarterly Journal of Business and Ethics,* and *Research in Corporate Social Performance and Policy,* among others.

Yves Doz is the Timken Professor of Global Technology and Innovation at INSEAD, having held the John H. London Chair in International Management (term chair) from 1990 to 1994. He received his Doctoral degree from Harvard University and is a graduate of the Ecole des Hautes Etudes Commerciales (Jouy-en-Josas, France). His research on the strategy of multinational companies, examining specifically high-technology industries has led to numerous publications, including three books: *Government Control and Multinational Management* (1979), *Strategic Management in Multinational Companies* (1986) and *The Multinational Mission: Balancing Local Demands and Global Vision* (1987, with C. K. Prahalad). His research on the power systems and telecommunications equipment industries won the A. T. Kearney Academy of Management Award. Two further books are currently in the final stages of publication, *Winning Through Strategic Alliances* (co-authored with G. Hamel), and an edited volume *Managing Technology and Innovation for Corporate Renewal,* the culmination of a multi-disciplinary research effort at INSEAD involving about 20 faculty members. Yves Doz currently carries out research in large, complex firms on strategic partnerships and technological cooperation between companies and on the competitive revitalisation of companies.

Gunter Dufey is Professor of International Business and Finance at The University of Michigan's Business School. His research has focused on international financial markets, as well as on issues in the financial management of multinational corporations. He has contributed to the discussion of foreign exchange exposure measurement and management of corporations that are active in international markets. Recently his work has focused on the process of financial innovation, particularly with respect to the role of international markets, as well as strategic issues of financial institutions with respect to the EC 1992 Initiatives.

John H. Dunning holds a dual appointment as Emeritus Professor in International Business Studies at the University of Reading, U.K., and State of New Jersey Professor of International Business at Rutgers University, New Jersey. He is also Senior Economic Advisor to the Transnational Corporations and Investment Division of UNCTAD and Chair of the London-based Economics Advisory Group. He has authored, co-authored or edited 32 books on the economics of international direct investment and the multinational enterprise, and on industrial and regional economics, and he currently serves on a variety of editorial and advisory boards. Professor Dunning holds honorary doctorates from the University of Uppsala and the Autonomous University of Madrid.

William G. Egelhoff is an Associate Professor of Management at Fordham University's Graduate School of Business. His current research interests include emerging trends in the strategy and organizational design of U.S. multinationals and a study of foreign subsidiaries in Ireland. He has published articles in journals such as *Administrative Science Quarterly, Strategic Management Journal,* and the *Journal of International Business Studies.* He is the author of a book entitled *Organizing the Multinational Enterprise: An Information-Processing Perspective.*

Vihang Errunza is Professor of International Business and Finance at McGill University, Montreal, Canada. Following a two-year appointment at INCAE, a Harvard initiated business school in Latin America, he joined McGill University in 1976. He has published extensively on international investments and emerging markets. His publications include Efficiency and the programs to develop capital markets—a Brazilian experience," *Journal of Banking and Finance* (1979), "Emerging markets—a new opportunity for improving global portfolio performance," *Financial Analysts Journal* (1983), and "Capital flow controls, international asset pricing and investors' welfare: a multicountry framework," *Journal of Finance* (1989). He has served as an advisor to international organizations, national governments, and investment firms.

Daniel C. Feldman is Professor of Management and Distinguished Business Partnership Foundation Fellow at the University of South Carolina. He is the author of over seventy articles and five books on career development, including *Managing Careers in Organizations* (1988) and *Coping With Job Loss: How Individuals, Organizations, and Communities Respond to Layoffs* (1992). Professor Feldman is Past Chair of the Careers Division of the Academy of Management, and serves on the editorial boards of several academic journals. He has won numerous undergraduate and graduate teaching awards, and was recently named Eli Lilly Senior Teaching Fellow at USC.

R. Edward Freeman joined the Darden Graduate School of Business Administration in 1987 as Elis and Signe Olsson Professor of Business Administration and Director of the Olsson Center for Applied Ethics. Freeman is also Professor of Religious Studies. Prior to joining The Darden School Dr. Freeman taught at the University of Minnesota and at The Wharton School, University of Pennsylvania. Freeman's areas of interest are business ethics, business policy and strategy, and organizational behavior. His most recent books are *Ethics and Agency Theory* (with N. Bowie), *Business Ethics: The State of the Art, The Logic of Strategy* (with D. Gilbert, Jr., E. Hartman and J. Mauriel), *Management,* 5th Edition (with J. Stoner), and *Corporate Strategy and the Search for Ethics* (with D. Gilbert, Jr.) He published *Strategic Management: A Stakeholder Approach* with Pitman Publishing in 1984. He has published more than thirty articles in a wide variety of publications. He is on the editorial boards of *Business Ethics Quarterly Research in Corporate Social Performance and Policy,* and *Employee Rights and Responsibility,* and is the editor of the Ruffin Series in Business Ethics published by Oxford University Press. Professor Freeman has a Ph.D. in Philosophy from Washington University, and a B.A. in Mathematics and Philosophy from Duke University.

Hubert Gatignon is Professor of Marketing at the European Institute of Business Administration (INSEAD) in France. Prior to joining INSEAD, he was Professor of Marketing at the Wharton School, University of Pennsylvania. He holds a Ph.D. from the University of California, Los Angeles. His research interests include modeling the factors which influence the adoption and diffusion of innovations, and investigating the varying effects of marketing mix variables. His most recent research concerns strategies for establishing and defending a brand's position, as well as international marketing strategy. His publications have appeared in *Journal of Marketing, Journal of Marketing Research, Marketing Science, Journal of Consumer Research, Journal of Business Research, Journal of*

International Business Studies, Communications Research, and *Journal of Law, Economics, and Organization.* Dr. Gatignon also serves on the editorial board of several journals.

Sumantra Ghoshal joined the faculty of London Business School in 1994 and holds the Robert P. Bauman Chair in Strategic Leadership. Prior to this he was Professor of Business Policy at INSEAD and taught international business at the Sloan School, MIT. Professor Ghoshal's research, writing, and consulting focuses on the management of large worldwide firms. He has published a number of books, articles, and award-winning case studies including *Managing Across Borders: The Transnational Solution* (co-authored with Christopher A. Bartlett) and *Organisation Theory and the Multinational Corporation* (with Eleanor Westney). His latest book is *The Strategy Process: European Perspective,* written with Henry Mintzberg and J. B. Quinn.

Edward M. Graham is Senior Fellow at the Institute for International Economics in Washington, D.C. He previously served on the faculties of MIT and the University of North Carolina, and as an international economist at the U.S. Treasury in Washington, D.C. While at the Treasury Department, he was seconded for two years to the Organization for Economic Cooperation and Development (OECD) in Paris, France. While at the University of North Carolina, he spent two years as visiting professor at Duke University, and was a Fellow of the Japan Center of North Carolina. Dr. Graham has written extensively on international direct investment and multinational enterprises, including *Foreign Direct Investment in the United States,* co-authored with Paul Krugman of Stanford University and now in its third edition. Other recent works by Dr. Graham include over thirty scholarly articles published in 1990–1995. His latest book is *Foreign Direct Investment in Japan,* co-edited with Dr. Masaru Yoshitami.

Gunnar Hedlund is Professor of International Business at the Stockholm School of Economics. He has written extensively about the management of multinational corporations, entry strategies on foreign markets, and global innovation processes. He has been a visiting professor at the European Institute for Advanced Studies in Management (EIASM) in Brussels, and at the Stanford Graduate School of Business. He has been involved in consulting and speaking assignments with leading international companies, and is on the editorial board of several academic journals in the fields of international business, corporate strategy, and organization theory.

Thomas J. Hench is a Ph.D candidate in strategic management and international business at the University of South Carolina. He previously worked for sixteen years in private industry in numerous managerial capacities with high-growth domestic and international companies. Mr. Hench's research interests include managing complexity and creating new knowledge in international environments. These interests include managing complexity within international organizations; strategic and evolutionary change; self-organizing systems; entrepreneurship, product innovation, and strategic renewal.

Jean-François Hennart is Professor of International Business, Director of the Ph.D. program in International Business, and Research Director of the Center for International Business Education and Research at the University of Illinois at Urbana-Champaign. His main research interest is the transaction cost theory of international business institutions. He is the author of *A Theory of Multinational Enterprise* (University of Michigan Press, 1982). He has also published articles in a number of scholarly journals, including the *Journal of International Business Studies, Management International Review, Management Science, Organizational Science, the Strategic Management Journal, the Journal of Law, Economics, and Organization, the Journal of Economic Behavior and Organization,* and *Weltwirtschaftliches Archiv.* He serves on the editorial boards of the *Journal of International Business Studies,* the *Strategic Management Journal,* and *Management International Review.*

Michael A. Hitt holds the Paul M. and Rosalie Robertson Chair of Business Administration at Texas A & M University. He is the author or coauthor of several books and numerous articles. Examples of recent articles include "Effects of acquisitions on R&D inputs and outputs," *Academy of Management Journal* (1991); "Strategic decision models: integrating different perspectives," *Strategic Management Journal* (1991); "Managerial risk taking in diversified firms: an evolutionary perspective," *Organizational Science* (1991). His current research focuses on the cross-cultural examination of strategic decision models and the interactive effects of product and international diversification on firm innovation and performance. He is coauthor of *Downscoping: How to Tame the Diversified Firm* (Oxford University Press, 1994) and *Strategic Management: Competitiveness and Globalization* (West Publishing Co., 1995).

Robert Hogner is Associate Professor of Business Environment at Florida International University in Miami. His research interests span business environment studies and symbolic anthropology, and have focused on business ideology, institutional and social economics, and most currently on toxic chemical releases. He is on the Board and Past President of D.A.R.T., Inc., one of the nation's leading community organizing centers, and has served as state and local president of the United Faculty of Florida, Florida's higher education union. He is currently writing a book for Quorum Press on the development of international regimes for monitoring and publicly reporting the release and use of toxic chemicals.

W. Chan Kim is The Boston Consulting Group Bruce D. Henderson Chair Professor of Strategy and International Management at INSEAD. Prior to joining INSEAD, he was a professor at the Michigan Business School, where he also obtained his Ph.D. in International Management. He has published a number of articles on strategy and managing the multinational which can be found in *Academy of Management Journal, Management Science, Organization Science, Strategic Management Journal, Journal of International Business Studies, Sloan Management Review, Harvard Business Review,* and others. His recent research focuses on the effective conception and execution of multinationals' worldwide strategies. Over the past years, he has served as a board member for a number of multinational corporations in Europe, the U.S. and Pacific Asia.

Stephen J. Kobrin is William H. Wurster Professor of Multinational Management at the Wharton School of the University of Pennsylvania and Director of the Joseph H. Lauder Institute of Management and International Studies. His work focuses on the interaction between international business and international politics, the nature and the effects of trans-national integration, and the strategic implications of international human resource management. His publications include *Managing Political Risk Assessment* (University of California Press, 1982); "Testing the bargaining hypothesis in the manufacturing sector in developing countries," *International Organization* (1987); and "An empirical analysis of the determinants of global integration," *Strategic Management Journal* (1991).

Bruce Kogut is Professor of Management at the Wharton School, University of Pennsylvania. He received his Ph.D. from MIT in 1983 and has been a visiting scholar at the Humboldt Universitaet and the Wissenschaftszentrum in Berlin, the Stockholm School of Economics, and the École Polytechnique in Paris. His publications have been on direct investment, knowledge of the firm, multinational corporate strategy, economic history, and joint ventures, and have appeared in *Journal of International Business Studies, Management Science, Strategic Management Journal,* and *Review of Economics and Statistics,* among others. He has edited *Country Competition: Technology and the Organization of Work* and (with Ned Bowman) *Redesigning the Firm,* both with Oxford University Press.

James A. Kuhlman is the J. Willis Cantey Professor of International Business and Economics in the College of Business Administration at the University of South Carolina. He is Russian Track Advisor in the Masters in International Business Studies program. He has served as Executive Director of the International Studies Association (1979–85), Director of the International Business Division of South Carolina's State Development Board (1985–88), and is on the International Advisory Board of the Russian Science Foundation. His most recent publications are "Perestroika As A Western Marketplace" (1989) and "US-USSR Joint Ventures" (1990).

Donald R. Lessard is Professor of International Management at the Sloan School of Management, MIT. He has also taught at Dartmouth University and has held visiting appointments at the Institute for International Economics, the London Business School, and the Stockholm School of Economics. He was a Visiting Professor at IESE, Barcelona, Spain. Dr. Lessard's research interests are international aspects of corporate finance, competitive strategy for firms and countries, financing for developing countries with emphasis on privatization, and project and enterprise-level finance. He has authored or edited a number of books, including *Capital Flight and Third World Debt* (with J. Williamson) (1987), and *International Finance Management: Theory and Application* (2nd edition, 1985). He has also contributed chapters to books, and has published articles in journals such as the *Journal of International Financial Management and Accounting* and the *Continental Journal of Applied Corporate Finance*. He is editor of the *Journal of International Financial Management and Accounting,* and he is on the editorial board of the *Journal of International Business Studies* and the *Continental Journal of Applied Corporate Finance*. Dr. Lessard is a Fellow of the Academy of International Business.

Briance Mascarenhas is Professor of International Business and Strategy at Rutgers University. His Ph.D. is from the University of California, Berkeley. His current research, teaching, and consulting interest include international entry strategy, the international specialist strategy, and international competitiveness. His publications include "International strategies of non-dominant firms," *Journal of International Business Studies* (1986), and "Order of entry and performance in international markets," *Strategic Management Journal*. He has received the School of Business and University Awards for Teaching Excellence. Professor Mascarenhas has recently published studies in the *Academy of Management Journal, Administrative Science Quarterly, Journal of International Business Studies,* and *Strategic Management Journal*.

Lars-Gunnar Mattsson is a Professor of Business Administration at the Stockholm School of Economics. He has held chairs at Linköping University and at Uppsala University and has also been visiting professor at the University of California, Berkeley, and at the European Institute for Advanced Studies in Management in Brussels. His research interests are focused on distribution systems, industrial marketing, and internationalization of business using a "markets-as-networks" approach. His publications include *Integration and Efficiency in Marketing Systems* (EFI/Norstedts, 1969), *Marketing for Competitiveness* (co-authored, in Swedish, Liber, 1982), and *Corporate and Industry Strategies for Europe* (co-edited, North-Holland, 1991). Dr. Mattsson received his E.D. from the Stockholm School of Economics.

Mark E. Mendenhall holds the J. Burton Frierson Chair of Excellence in Business Leadership at the University of Tennessee, Chattanooga. He has authored a number of books and articles on expatriate adjustment and other international human resource management issues, including *Global Management* (1995; with B.J. Punnett and David Ricks); Global Assignments" (1992; with J.S. Black and Hal Gregersen); "Toward a comprehensive model of international adjustment: an integration of multiple theoretical perspectives,"(with J. Stewart Black and Gary Oddou); *Academy of Management Review* (1991); "The U-curve adjustment hypothesis revisited: a review and theoretical framework" (with J.S. Black), *Journal of International Business Studies* (1991); "Cross-cultural training effectiveness: a review and a theoretical framework for future research" (with J.S. Black), *Academy of Management Review* (1990); and "The dimensions of expatriate acculturation: a review" (with Gary Oddou), *Academy of Management Review* (1985).

Douglas Nigh is Associate Professor of International Business at the University of South Carolina and Research Director of USC's Center for International Business Education and Research. He received his PhD in international management from UCLA and his BA (economics) and MBA from Indiana University. Prior to joining USC, he served on the faculty of Penn State University. He has been a visiting professor at Wirtschaftsuniversität in Vienna. Honors received include the Best Dissertation Award from the Academy of International Business. His research interests include the multinational's management of relationships with political and social stakeholders, the management of inter-unit relations within multinationals, and top management teams in multinationals. His research has appeared in various journals including *Academy of Management Journal, Journal of International Business Studies, Journal of Business Research, Managerial and Decision Economics, Columbia Journal of World Business, International Trade Journal, Business and Society,* and *Management International Review.* Professor Nigh is Past President of the International Association for Business and Society and Program Chair-Elect of the International Management Division, Academy of Management. He has served as a consultant and advisor to business, government, and educational organizations, including the U.S. Department of Education and the United Nations Development Program's China Project. He currently serves as a member of the Advisory Board of the Center for the Study of Business and Public Issues, Penn State University.

Terutomo Ozawa received an MBA and a Ph.D. from Columbia University and is currently a professor of economics at Colorado State University. His major research areas are Japanese multinational corporations, technology transfers, and the structural dynamics of the Pacific Rim economies. His published books include *Japan's Technological Challenge to the West, 1950–1974: Motivation and Accomplishment* (1974), *Multinationalism, Japanese Style: The Political Economy of Outward Dependency* (1979, 1982), and *Recycling Japan's Surpluses for Developing Countries* (1989). He has served as a consultant to OECD, United Nations organizations (such as UNITAR, UNESCAP, UNCTC, and UNCTAD), the World Bank, Asian Development Bank, Asian Productivity Organization, and others.

Jean Pasquero is Professor of Corporate Societal Management at the University of Quebec at Montreal (UQAM). His research has focused on various dimensions of the business and society interface, at both the national and cross-national levels. Recent publications include "Bilateral protectionism: lessons from a cause celebre," *California Management Review* (1988); "Supraorganizational collaboration: the Canadian environmental experiment," *Journal of Applied Behavioral Science* (1991); and "An institutional approach to the reconstitution of Europe, *Business and Society* (1992).

Gordon Redding is Professor of Management Studies at the University of Hong Kong and Director of the University of Hong Kong Business School. A researcher on cross-cultural aspects of management and a specialist in the Asian region for the last 22 years, he has published extensively on Asian business, particularly that of the overseas Chinese. An earlier book on British managerial ideology, entitled *The Working Class Manager,* has now been followed by a book on Chinese managerial ideology entitled *The Spirit of Chinese Capitalism* and another on the region entitled *Managers for Pacific Asia.* Co-authored books are *The Enterprise and Management in East Asia* and *Capitalism in Contrasting Cultures.* Professor Redding is a visiting professor at the Euro-Asia Centre, INSEAD, and the University of Hawaii, and he has taught extensively on executive programs in many countries. He is an adviser on strategy and organization development to a number of international companies.

Jonas Ridderstråle is a teacher and research associate at the Institute of International Business, the Stockholm School of Economics. He teaches strategic management and international business, and conducts research on the management of cross-border innovation projects in multinational companies.

Saeed Samiee is Professor of Marketing and Director of the International Management Center at the University of Tulsa. He received his Ph.D. from the Ohio State University and previously taught at the University of South Carolina, the Graduate School of Management, Rutgers University, Kent State University, and University of Notre Dame. He has been a frequent participant in management development and executive MBA programs. The majority of Professor Samiee's research has been in the international marketing area. His publications have appeared in the *Journal of Marketing, California Management Review, Business Horizons, Journal of the Academy of Marketing Science, Journal of Business Research,* and *Journal of International Business Studies.* Current research interests include the consequences of the EC-1992 Plan, profit impact of international marketing strategies, retailing and distribution strategies in Europe, the U.S. and Japan, and the influence of country-of-origin on brand acceptance. Professor Samiee was a member of the Board of Directors and Vice President of the New Jersey Chapter of the American Marketing Association. He has also served as Vice President of Finance and a member of the Board of Governors of the Academy of Marketing Science, where he established the AMS Foundation and initiated a doctoral dissertation competition. He was voted Outstanding Professor by the USC's MIBS Class of 1991 and is a member of Beta Gamma Sigma. Professor Samiee is a member of several editorial review boards including those of *Journal of Marketing, Journal of International Business Studies, Journal of the International Marketing, Science, International Marketing Review,* and *Journal of Marketing Channels.*

Hans Schollhammer is Professor of Management and Chairman of the International Business and Comparative Management Program at the Anderson Graduate School of Management, University of California, Los Angeles. Besides UCLA he has held faculty positions at INSEAD, Fontainebleau (France); Columbia University, New York; Institute for International Studies and Training, Fujinomiya (Japan); and the Cranefield School of Management, Cranfield (England). He received a Dipl. Kfm. degree from the University of Munich (Germany) and MBA and DBA degrees from Indiana University. He is a member of the editorial boards of *Strategic Management Journal* and *Management International Review.* He is the author of books and articles on entrepreneurship as well as international management issues.

Jagdish N. Sheth is the Charles H. Kellstadt Professor of Marketing and Marketing Area Coordinator at Emory Business School. Prior to his present position, he taught at the University of Southern California, the University of Illinois, Columbia University, and the Massachusetts Institute of Technology. Dr. Sheth has published more than 200 books and research papers in different areas of marketing. His book *The Theory of Buyer Behavior* (1969) with John A. Howard is a classic in the field. He has recently published two scholarly books: *Marketing Theory: Evolution and Evaluation* (1988) and *Consumption Values and Market Choices* (1991). Dr. Sheth is an American Psychological Association Fellow and past President of APA's Consumer Psychology Division and Association for Consumer Research (ACR). He has been the recipient of a number of awards for his research and teaching. Dr. Sheth is on the editorial boards of at least a dozen scholarly journals in marketing, international business and quantitative methods, and is Series Editor of *Research in Marketing*. Professor Sheth's interests have shifted from consumer psychology, attitude research, and multivariate methods to marketing theory, global strategy, and relationship marketing.

Harvey Starr is the Dag Hammarskjold Professor in International Affairs in the Department of Government and International Studies at the University of South Carolina. He specializes in international relations theory, international conflict, alliances, and foreign policy analysis. His current research interests include geopolitics and the diffusion of international phenomena, and the relationship between war and revolution. His most recent books are *Inquiry, Logic and International Politics* (co-authored with Benjamin A. Most, 1989) and *The Diffusion of War: A Study of Opportunity and Willingness* (co-authored with Randolph M. Siverson, 1991) and the fifth edition of *World Politics: The Menu for Choice* (co-authored with Bruce Russett), 1995.

Jerry Sullivan is Professor of International Business at the University of Washington Graduate School of Business. He is a member of the Japan-America Society of Washington State and the Association of Japanese Business Studies, and specializes in research on Japanese management and investment. The author of many books and articles on Japan, Professor Sullivan's latest book is *Invasion of the Salarymen: The Japanese Business Presence in America*. He was also a visiting professor at New York University's Stern School of Business.

Brian Toyne the Emil C. E. Jurica Distinguished Professor of International Business at St. Mary's University, San Antonio, Texas. Prior to 1993, he was Professor of International Business and Business Partnership Fellow at the University of South Carolina. He served as the Acting Director of the International Business Program Area, the Coordinator for the Ph.D. International Business program, and the Series Editor for Critical Issues Facing Multinational Enterprises for the University of South Carolina Press. His research is multidisciplinary, and has recently focused on the interface between human resource management and corporate business strategy within the international context. He is the author or co-author of numerous books and articles dealing with international management and marketing issues. He has also served as the Associate Editor of the Journal of International Business Studies, and as Vice President of the Academy of International Business. He is Past Chair of the International Management Division, Academy of Management.

Ingo Walter is the Charles Simon Professor of Applied Financial Economics at the Stern School of Business, New York University, and also serves as Director of the New York University Salomon Center, an independent academic research institute founded in 1972 to focus on financial institutions, instruments, and markets. He holds a joint appointment as the Swiss Bank Corporation Professor of International Management, INSEAD. Dr. Walter's principal interests include international trade policy, international banking, environmental economics, and the economics of multinational corporations. He has published papers in various professional journals in these fields, and is the author or editor of 22 books, the most recent of which is *Universal Banking in the United States*. He has served as consultant to various government agencies, international institutions, banks and corporations, and has held a number of board memberships. Professor Walter's current interests focus on competitive structure, conduct and performance in the international banking and financial services industry, as well as international trade and investment issues.

Steven L. Wartick is Professor of Management and Policy at the University of Missouri-St. Louis. His research has focused on corporate social performance, issues management, and business-government relations. Currently, he is working with D. J. Wood) on an international dimensions of business and society book. His publications include "The evolution of the corporate social performance model," (with P. L. Cochran), *Academy of Management Review,* 1985, and "The relationship between intense media exposure and changes in corporate reputation," *Business and Society,* 1992.

D. Eleanor Westney is a Professor of Management in the Strategy and International Management group at the MIT Sloan School of Management. She is the author of *Imitation and Innovation: The Transfer of Western Organizational Forms in Meiji Japan* (1987).

She has written extensively on the organization of multinational corporations and is the co-editor (with Sumantra Ghoshal) of *Organization Theory and the Multinational Corporation* (Macmillan, 1993). Professor Westney's current research interests focus on the internationalization of R&D particularly on the growing number of U.S. and European firms setting up R&D centers in Japan. She is currently working on a project on the international management of R&D.

Mira Wilkins is Professor of Economics at Florida International University, Miami. Her specialty is the history of multinational enterprise. She is the author of *The History of Foreign Investment in the United States to 1914* (1989); *The Emergence of Multinational Enterprise: American Business Abroad from the Colonial Era to 1914* (1970), and *The Maturing of Multinational Enterprise: American Business Abroad from 1914 to 1970* (1974). All three books were published by Harvard University Press. A sequel to her history of foreign investment in the United States, which will cover 1914 to the present, is in process. She has also published "The History of French Multinationals in the United States" in *Entreprises et Histoire* (1993); "The Neglected Intangible Asset: The Influence of the Trade Mark on the Rise of the Modern Corporation," *Business History* (1992); an edited anthology, *The Growth of Multinationals* (1991) and "Japanese Multinationals in the United States: Continuity and Change, 1879–1990," *Business History Review* (1990). In addition, Dr. Wilkins is the author of numerous other scholarly articles and three other books. In connection with her research on the history of multinationals, she has visited some 60 countries in North and South America, Europe, Africa, the Middle East, and the Far East.

Donna J. Wood is Professor of Business Administration at the University of Pittsburgh. Her research interests include corporate social performance, international dimensions of business and society, and business and public policy. Publications include *Strategic Uses of Public Policy* (1986), *Business and Society* (1990, 1994), "Corporate social performance revisited," *Academy of Management Review* (1991), and *International Business and Society* (with S.L. Wartick, forthcoming). She is a former Chair of the Social Issues in Management Division of the Academy of Management, and is a founder of the International Association for Business and Society (IABS). She is currently the editor of *Business and Society*, IABS's scholarly journal.

List of Conference Participants and Affiliation at the Time of the Conference

Nancy J. Adler
McGill University, Canada

Sanjeev Agarwal
Iowa State University

Yair Aharoni
Duke University and
Tel Aviv University

Li Aimin
World University Service of Canada
Canada

Michele Akoorie
University of Waikato, New Zealand

Harvey Arbelaez
Penn State at Harrisburg

Jeffrey S. Arpan
University of South Carolina

W. Graham Astley
University of Colorado at Denver

Catherine N. Axinn
Ohio University

Alan D. Bauerschmidt
University of South Carolina

Paul W. Beamish
University of Western Ontario, Canada

M. D. Beckman
University of Victoria, Canada

Jack N. Behrman
The University of North Carolina

H. David Bess
University of Hawaii at Manoa

Rabi S. Bhagat
Memphis State University

David S. Bigelow
Rensselaer Polytechnic Institute

Linda Bleicken
Georgia Southern University

Mark S. Blodgett
Georgia Southern University

Jean J. Boddewyn
City University of New York

Nakiye Boyacigiller
San Jose State University

Thomas L. Brewer
Georgetown University

T. J. Byrnes
University College-Dublin
Ireland

Claudio Carpano
University of North Carolina at Charlotte

Mark C. Casson
Reading University, United Kingdom

S. Tamer Cavusgil
Michigan State University

Joseph Cheng
Virginia Polytechnical Institute

Kang R. Cho
University of Colorado at Denver

Philip L. Cochran
The Pennsylvania State University

J. Markham Collins
The University of Tulsa

Kerry Cooper
Texas A&M University

Charles T. Crespy
Miami University

John D. Daniels
Indiana University

Sayeste Daser
Wake Forest University

Candace Deans
Wake Forest University

Jose de la Torre
University of California at Los Angeles

Yves L. Doz
INSEAD, France

Gunter Dufey
University of Michigan

John H. Dunning
Rutgers University and
Reading University, U.K.

John Dutton
North Carolina State University

Carl L. Dyer
University of Tennessee at Knoxville

Richard Edelstein
AACSB

William G. Egelhoff
Fordham University

Kamal Elsheshai
Georgia State University

Peter Enderwick
University of Waikato, New Zealand

Vihang R. Errunza
McGill University, Canada

Leonid I. Evenko
Graduate School of International Business
Academy of National Economy, Russia

Daniel C. Feldman
University of South Carolina

Karin Fladmoe-Lindquist
University of Utah

William R. Folks, Jr.
University of South Carolina

Robert Edward Freeman
University of Virginia

J. Stanley Fryer
University of South Carolina

Paul Garner
University of Alabama

Hubert Gatignon
University of Pennsylvania

Sumantra Ghoshal
INSEAD, France

Edward M. Graham
Institute for International Economics

Robert Grosse
University of Miami

Robert G. Hawkins
Georgia Institute of Technology

Xiaohong He
Quinnipiac College

Gunnar Hedlund
Stockholm School of Economics, Sweden

Jean-François Hennart
University of Illinois
at Urbana-Champaign

Peter Herne
California State University
at Dominguez Hills

Michael A. Hitt
Texas A&M University

Robert H. Hogner
Florida International University

Hartmut H. Holzmuller
Wirtschaftsuniversität Wien, Austria

Giorgio Inzerilli
Erasmus University Rotterdam,
Netherlands

James F. Kane
University of South Carolina

Sara L. Keck
Texas A&M University

Ben L. Kedia
Memphis State University

Thomas I. Kindel
The Citadel

Stephen J. Kobrin
University of Pennsylvania

Bruce M. Kogut
University of Pennsylvania

Christopher M. Korth
University of South Carolina

Charles O. Kroncke
University of Texas at Dallas

James A. Kuhlman
University of South Carolina

Duane Kujawa
University of Miami

Chuck Chun-Yau Kwok
University of South Carolina

Michael Landeck
Laredo State University

Paul Latortue
University of Puerto Rico, Puerto Rico

Donald R. Lessard
M.I.T.

Peter Li
University of Dubuque

Neng Liang
Loyola College

Robert R. Locke
University of Hawaii at Manoa

Thomas J. Madden
University of South Carolina

Zaida L. Martinez
South Carolina State University

Briance Mascarenhas
Rutgers University

Ann B. Matasar
Roosevelt University

Lars-Gunnar Mattsson
Stockholm School of Economics
Sweden

Mike McCormick
Jacksonville State University

Mark Mendenhall
University of Tennessee at Chattanooga

Edwin L. Miller
University of Michigan

Joseph M. Moricz
Robert Morris College

Allen Morrison
Thunderbird

Ken Morse
State University of New York
at Geneseo

Richard W. Moxon
University of Washington

Motofusa Murayama
Chiba University, Japan

Douglas Nigh
University of South Carolina

Van N. Oliphant
Memphis State University

Lars Oxelheim
School of Economics, Sweden

Terutomo Ozawa
Colorado State University

Jong H. Park
Kennesaw State College

Young-Ryeol Park
University of Illinois at
Urbana-Champaign

Atul Parvatiyar
Emory University

Jean Pasquero
University of Quebec at Montreal,
Canada

Karen Paul
Florida International University

Clotilde Pérez
University of Puerto Rico, Puerto Rico

William H. Phillips
University of South Carolina

Zhou Ping
World University Service of Canada
Canada

Juan Antonio Poblete
Universidad Gabriela Mistral, Chile

Rebecca Porterfield
University of North Carolina
at Wilmington

Thomas A. Poynter
The Transitions Group, Inc.

Michael W. Pustay
Texas A&M University

Lee Radebaugh
Brigham Young University

Chandra Rajam
University of Colorado at Denver

Amitabh Raturi
University of Cincinnati

S. Gordon Redding
University of Hong Kong, Hong Kong

David A. Ricks
Thunderbird

Jonas Ridderstråle
Stockholm School of Economics,
Sweden

Franklin R. Root
University of Pennsylvania

Kendall J. Roth
University of South Carolina

Stephen Salter
Texas A&M University

Rakesh B. Sambharya
Rutgers University

Saeed Samiee
University of South Carolina

Ravi Sarathy
Northeastern University

Karl Sauvant
The United Nations

Hans Schollhammer
University of California

Robert Scott
University of Maryland

Manuel G. Serapio, Jr.
University of Colorado at Denver

Michael Sibley
Loyola University

Harvey Starr
University of South Carolina

Donald L. Stevens
University of Colorado at Denver

Arthur Stonehill
Oregon State University

Jeremiah Sullivan
University of Washington

Michael A. Taku
Tarleton State University

Jorge Talavera
ESAN/CLADEA, Peru

Stephen Tallman
University of Utah

Hans B. Thorelli
Indiana University

Paz Estrella Tolentino
United Nations

Richard Torrisi
University of Hartford

Brian Toyne
University of South Carolina

J. Frederick Truitt
Willamette University

Gerardo R. Ungson
University of Oregon

M. Reza Vaghefi
University of North Florida

Kanoknart Visudtibhan
George Washington University

Hans-Gerhard Wachsmuth
University of South Carolina

Ingo Walter
New York University

Steven Wartick
University of Missouri at St. Louis

Nikolai Wasilewski
Pace University

D. Eleanor Westney
M.I.T.

Mira Wilkins
Florida International University

Bernard M. Wolf
York University
Canada

John Wong
Iowa State University

Donna J. Wood
University of Pittsburgh

John Z. Yang
Fordham University

Ryh-song Yeh
Pennsylvania State University

Srilata Zaheer
University of Minnesota

University of South Carolina Ph.D. Students in Attendance:

Name	Department (Major)
Allen Amason	Management
Nicholas Athanassiou	International Business
Steven Barnett	International Business
Ernie Csiszar	Management
Dorothee Feils	Finance
Debbie Francis	Management
Tom Hench	Management
Insik Jeong	International Business
James Johnson	International Business
Frances Katrishen	Management
Tomasz Lenartowicz	International Business
David McArthur	International Business
Martin Meznar	International Business
Andrew Morris	Management
Carolyn Mueller	Management
James Ondracek	Management
Emmanuel Onifade	Accounting
Joy Pahl	International Business
Chul-whi Park	International Business
Randolph Piper	Management
Russell Teasley	Management
David Thomas	Management
Bijoy Sahoo	Finance
Cheryl van Deusen	Management
Alan Wallace	International Business
Carolyn White	International Business
Yangjin Yoo	International Business

ABOUT THE EDITORS:

BRIAN TOYNE is Emil C. E. Jurica Professor of International Business at St. Mary's University in San Antonio, Texas. He has served as a member of the editorial boards of several journals, including *Journal of Business Research* and *Journal of International Marketing*. The author or coauthor of many books, Toyne has also published more than 60 articles in such journals as *Academy of Management Review, Columbia Journal of World Business, Journal of International Marketing, Industrial Marketing Management,* and *Journal of International Business Studies*.

DOUGLAS NIGH is an associate professor of international business and the research director of the Center for International Business Education and Research at the University of South Carolina (USC). His articles have appeared in such publications as *Journal of International Business Studies, Columbia Journal of World Business*, and *Journal of Business Research*. Nigh teaches in USC's prestigious Masters of International Business Studies (MIBS) program.